THE ENDURING VISION

A History of the American People

Sixth Edition

Dolphin Edition

Paul S. Boyer
University of Wisconsin

Clifford E. Clark, Jr.
Carleton College

Joseph F. Kett
University of Virginia

Neal Salisbury
Smith College

Harvard Sitkoff
University of New Hampshire

Nancy Woloch
Barnard College

Houghton Mifflin Company

Boston   New York

Publisher: Suzanne Jeans
Senior Sponsoring Editor: Ann West
Senior Marketing Manager: Katherine Bates
Senior Development Editor: Jeffrey Greene
Senior Project Editor: Bob Greiner
Senior Art and Design Manager: Jill Haber
Cover Design Director: Anthony L. Saizon
Senior Photo Editor: Jennifer Meyer Dare
Senior Composition Buyer: Chuck Dutton
New Title Project Manager: Patricia O'Neill
Editorial Assistant: Evangeline Bermas
Marketing Associate: Lauren Bussard
Editorial Production Assistant: Laura Collins

Cover art: View of New Orleans, "Under My Wings Everything Prospers" 1803. Chicago Historical Society.

Printed in the U.S.A.

Library of Congress Catalog Number: 2007937003

ISBN-10: 0-547-05215-4
ISBN-13: 978-0-547-05215-1

2 3 4 5 6 7 8 9–VHO–11 10 09 08

Contents

4

THE BONDS OF EMPIRE, 1660–1750   88

5

ROADS TO REVOLUTION, 1750–1776   123

8

JEFFERSONIANISM AND THE ERA OF GOOD FEELINGS, 1801–1824 233

9

THE TRANSFORMATION OF AMERICAN SOCIETY, 1815–1840 261

10

DEMOCRATIC POLITICS, RELIGIOUS REVIVAL, AND REFORM, 1824–1840 290

32

GLOBAL DANGERS, GLOBAL CHALLENGES, 2001 TO THE PRESENT   1007

Preface

Much has changed in America and the world since we began planning *The Enduring Vision* more than two decades ago. Some of these developments have been welcome and positive, others deeply unsettling. This new Dolphin Edition, which is based on the sixth edition of *The Enduring Vision*, fully documents all these changes, as well as the continuities that offer reassurance for the future.

Although the United States of today differs in many ways from the nation of even a few decades ago, the will to live up to the values that give meaning to America—among them individual freedom, social justice, tolerance for diversity, and equality of opportunity—remains a guiding force in our life as a people. Our desire to convey the strength of this enduring vision in a world of change continues to guide our efforts in writing this book.

Since its inception, *The Enduring Vision* has been one of the most widely used American history textbooks. This edition builds on the underlying strategy that has guided us from the beginning. We want our history to be not only comprehensive and illuminating, but also lively, readable, and true to the lived experience of earlier generations of Americans. Within a clear political and chronological framework, we integrate the best recent scholarship in all areas of American history. Our interest in social and cultural history, which shapes our own teaching and scholarship, has suffused *The Enduring Vision* from the outset, and it remains central. We integrate the historical experience of women, African-Americans, Hispanic-Americans, Asian-Americans, and American Indians—in short, of men and women of all regions, ethnic groups, and social classes who make up the American mosaic.

We created this Dolphin Edition to provide instructors and students with an edition of *The Enduring Vision* that incorporates all of the narrative of the parent text, but in a format that is more concise.

New Interpretations, Expanded Coverage In each new edition of *The Enduring Vision* we carefully assess the coverage, interpretations, and analytic framework to incorporate the latest scholarship and emerging themes. In recent years, American historians have emphasized how deeply our history is embedded within a larger global context. In this edition we have underscored the wider context of American history throughout the narrative. From the origins of agriculture two millennia ago to the impact of globalization today, we have emphasized how the social, economic, and political developments central to our historical experience emerge with fresh new clarity when viewed within a broader world framework. The global theme is also the focus of an innovative new feature, "Beyond America: Global Interactions" (see "Special Features," on the following page).

As in earlier editions, coverage of environmental history, the land, and the West is fully integrated into the narrative, and is treated analytically, not simply "tacked on" to a traditional account. We also incorporate the best of the new political history, stressing the social, cultural, and economic issues at stake in political decisions and debates.

This edition of *The Enduring Vision* continues to emphasize science and technology. From the hunting implements of the Paleo-Indians to the inventions and manufacturing innovations of the industrial age and today's breakthroughs in information processing and genetic engineering, the applications of science and technology are central throughout. We have included new Technology and Culture boxed features (see "Revisions and Innovations in Each Chapter," below).

We again offer extensive coverage of medicine and disease, from the epidemics brought by European explorers and settlers to today's AIDS crisis, bioethics debates, and controversies over health-care financing. We also give careful attention to religious history, from the spiritual values of pre-Columbian communities to the political activism of contemporary conservative Christian groups.

Special Features   We are especially proud and excited to introduce a new feature, "Beyond America—Global Interactions," which highlights this edition's intensified global emphasis. The illustrated essays explore the wider context of key developments in American history. The essays examine such topics as "The American Revolution as an International War," "Slavery as a Global Institution," and "The Challenge of Globalization," underscoring how America's history takes on vivid new interest, and can be viewed in strikingly new ways, when seen in its global context. These new essays make clear that just as America has influenced the world, so has the world influenced America.

Revisions and Innovations in Each Chapter   A chapter-by-chapter glimpse of some of the changes in this edition highlights its new content and up-to-the-minute scholarship.

Chapter 1 launches the Beyond America feature with a comparative essay on the origins and spread of agriculture, enabling students to view the development of farming America in a global context. The chapter also explicitly links some additional pre-contact cultures with Native American peoples important in later periods of American history.

Chapter 2 incorporates further detail on Spanish colonization in the Caribbean and on Anglo-Indian relations in early Virginia, including a clarification of the roles of John Smith and Pocahontas. The material in the former "Mediterranean Crossroads" section has been distributed among other sections. In Chapter 3, the discussion of the Chesapeake colonies now precedes that of New England.

Chapter 4 offers an expanded definition of mercantilism and additional details on England's Navigation Acts. This chapter also draws a sharper contrast between the experiences of Europeans and Africans who arrived in the colonies in the first half of the eighteenth century. Chapter 5 includes a revised treatment of the Albany Congress and Plan of Union and of the Paxton Boys. This chapter also offers an expanded discussion of military maneuvering and fighting between the battles of Lexington and Concord and the Declaration of Independence.

The Beyond America essay in Chapter 6 presents a fresh perspective on the American Revolution as an international war, and deepens the explanation for Britain's defeat in North America. The chapter offers new material on ordinary soldiers' experiences in the Continental Army, white women's political activities during the Revolution, and the Articles of Confederation.

Chapter 7 considers more fully the implementation of the new national government, the emergence of political parties, Spanish relations with Native Americans in Texas and New Mexico, and Federalist policy toward Native Americans.

Chapter 8 extends the account of Lewis and Clark's negotiations with the Indians. Chapter 9 expands and restructures the discussion of equality and inequality in the early Republic and blacks' efforts to secure education. Chapter 10 offers expanded coverage of the Shakers.

Judicious cuts in Chapter 11 have resulted in an even more readable treatment of technology, culture, and everyday life in pre-Civil War America. An illuminating Beyond America essay in Chapter 12 examines slavery as a global phenomenon while noting how American slavery differed from that found elsewhere.

Chapter 16 includes a new Technology and Culture feature on the sewing machine, a key advance in domestic technology.

Chapter 17 includes a new table on legislation relating to Indians, new material on the Mormons, and a Beyond America feature placing American cowboys in a global context. Chapter 18 adds a new Technology and Culture essay on electricity, a discussion of the South's economy in world perspective, and expanded coverage of black workers in the South and the labor activist Mary Harris ("Mother") Jones.

Chapter 19 includes new material on African-Americans, baseball, and the painter Mary Cassatt. A unique new map illustrates both the Asian and European sources of immigration to the Western Hemisphere in the late nineteenth century. Chapter 20 expands coverage of Clara Barton, founder of the army nursing corps, and Ida B. Wells, the African-American crusader against lynching. A new table lists and explains Gilded Age currency legislation.

Chapter 21's Beyond America essay offers a comparative overview of the reform spirit that gripped many Western countries in the early twentieth century, while a new "Racism and Progressivism" section underscores the pervasiveness of racism in this era, from lynch mobs to the White House. Chapter 22 offers new material on American overseas missionaries, the Mexican leader Pancho Villa, local vigilante movements during World War I, and the growth of the NAACP.

Chapter 23 expands coverage of the 1929 Gastonia textile strike, Hollywood sex scandals, and Herbert Hoover's conservationist policies, and discusses the composer Ruth Crawford Seeger and the African-American filmmaker Oscar Micheaux. The chapter also expands coverage of movies and the National Youth Administration, and offers a concise assessment of New Deal agricultural policies.

The five chapters covering the four decades from 1933 to 1974 offers a new Beyond America essay on the intellectual migration from fascist regimes in Europe in the 1930s.

In addition, Chapter 25 includes more information on the causes and consequences of World War II and the impact of the war on American minorities and on U.S. society in general. Chapter 26 includes a greater emphasis on the Cold War as a global phenomenon and on the early stirrings of postwar conservatism.

Chapter 27 gives greater attention to the shift in the Cold War from Europe to what was then called the Third World, and discusses in more depth the consequences of the rise in TV ownership and viewing. Chapter 28 offers additional background on the American war in Vietnam, environmental issues, and the significance of the 1964 Goldwater campaign in the emergence of postwar conservatism. This chapter also explores more fully the civil rights struggles of African Americans, especially the roles of CORE and SNCC, as well as the activism of American Indians, Hispanic-Americans, and Asian-Americans.

Chapter 29 analyzes more fully the conservative resurgence of the 1970s as a reaction to the radicalism of the 1960s and the counterculture. This chapter also gives extensive attention to the rise of the Sunbelt, the Tet offensive as a turning point in the Vietnam War, and the importance of foreign affairs and energy issues in the Nixon administration.

The concluding three chapters, 30 to 32, incorporate new findings from recent scholarship. Chapter 30 expands coverage of popular culture; explores electronic-age privacy issues; and deepens the discussion of deindustrialization, labor activism, the Iran-Iraq War, violence associated with Islamic fundamentalism, and Soviet leader Mikhail Gorbachev's reasons for seeking better relations with the United States.

Chapter 31, extensively revised, now includes both terms of the Clinton Administration and an expanded discussion of the stock market boom, the influence of religious conservatives in the decade's culture wars, and bursts of domestic terrorism. This chapter also examines in more detail President George H. W. Bush's decision not to invade Iraq during the Persian Gulf War and updates the long-term effects of the Welfare Reform Act of 1996. A Beyond America essay weighs the cultural and economic impact of globalization.

Chapter 32 continues the story of American history to the 2006 elections. This chapter describes the Bush administration's response to the September 11, 2001, terrorist attacks, including the invasion of Iraq; new prisoner-detention policies; and domestic surveillance programs. The chapter also explores recent economic developments, social and demographic trends, and the ongoing debate over immigration policy. A new Technology and Culture essay examines the timely issue of global warming.

Paul S. Boyer
Clifford E. Clark, Jr.
Joseph F. Kett
Neal Salisbury
Harvard Sitkoff
Nancy Woloch

About the Authors

PAUL S. BOYER, Merle Curti Professor of History emeritus at the University of Wisconsin, Madison, earned his Ph.D. from Harvard University. An editor of *Notable American Women, 1607–1950* (1971), he also coauthored *Salem Possessed: The Social Origins of Witchcraft* (1974), for which, with Stephen Nissenbaum, he received the John H. Dunning Prize of the American Historical Association. His other works include *Urban Masses and Moral Order in America, 1820–1920* (1978), *By the Bomb's Early Light: American Thought and Culture at the Dawn of the Atomic Age* (1985), *When Time Shall Be No More: Prophecy Belief in Modern American Culture* (1992), and *Promises to Keep: The United States since World War II*, 3rd ed. (2003). He is also editor-in-chief of the *Oxford Companion to United States History* (2001). His articles and essays have appeared in the *American Quarterly, New Republic*, and other journals. He has been a visiting professor at the University of California, Los Angeles, Northwestern University, and the College of William and Mary.

CLIFFORD E. CLARK, JR., M.A. and A.D. Hulings Professor of American Studies and professor of history at Carleton College, earned his Ph.D. from Harvard University. He has served as both the chair of the History Department and director of the American Studies program at Carleton. Clark is the author of *Henry Ward Beecher: Spokesman for a Middle-Class America* (1978), *The American Family Home, 1800–1960* (1986), *The Intellectual and Cultural History of Anglo-America since 1789* in the *General History of the Americas*, and, with Carol Zellie, *Northfield: The History and Architecture of a Community* (1997). He also has edited and contributed to *Minnesota in a Century of Change: The State and Its People since 1900* (1989). A past member of the Council of the American Studies Association, Clark is active in the fields of material culture studies and historic preservation, and he serves on the Northfield, Minnesota, Historical Preservation Commission.

JOSEPH F. KETT, Commonwealth Professor of History at the University of Virginia, received his Ph.D. from Harvard University. His works include *The Formation of the American Medical Profession: The Role of Institutions, 1780–1860* (1968), *Rites of Passage: Adolescence in America, 1790–Present* (1977), *The Pursuit of Knowledge under Difficulties: From Self-Improvement to Adult Education in America, 1750–1990* (1994), and *The New Dictionary of Cultural Literacy* (2002), of which he is coauthor. A former History Department chair at Virginia, he also has participated on the Panel on Youth of the President's Science Advisory Committee, has served on the Board of Editors of the *History of Education Quarterly*, and is a past member of the Council of the American Studies Association.

NEAL SALISBURY, professor of history at Smith College, received his Ph.D. from the University of California, Los Angeles. He is the author of *Manitou and Providence:*

Indians, Europeans, and the Making of New England, 1500–1643 (1982), editor of *The Sovereignty and Goodness of God*, by Mary Rowlandson (1997), and coeditor, with Philip J. Deloria, of *The Companion to American Indian History* (2002). With R. David Edmunds and Frederick E. Hoxie, he has written *The People: A History of Native America* (2007), also published by Houghton Mifflin. He has contributed numerous articles to journals and edited collections, and coedits a book series, Cambridge Studies in North American Indian History. Formerly chair of the History Department at Smith, he has served as president of the American Society for Ethnohistory and is currently a member of the Council of the Omohundro Institute of Early American History and Culture.

HARVARD SITKOFF, professor of history at the University of New Hampshire, earned his Ph.D. from Columbia University. He is the author of *A New Deal for Blacks* (1978), *The Struggle for Black Equality, 1954–1992* (1992), and *Postwar America: A Student Companion* (2000); coauthor of the National Park Service's *Racial Desegregation in Public Education in the United States* (2000) and *The World War II Homefront* (2003); and editor of *Fifty Years Later: The New Deal Reevaluated* (1984), *A History of Our Time*, 6th ed. (2002), and *Perspectives on Modern America: Making Sense of the Twentieth Century* (2001). His articles have appeared in the *American Quarterly, Journal of American History,* and *Journal of Southern History,* among others. A frequent lecturer at universities abroad, he has been awarded the Fulbright Commission's John Adams Professorship of American Civilization in the Netherlands and the Mary Ball Washington Professorship of American History in Ireland.

NANCY WOLOCH received her Ph.D. from Indiana University. She is the author of *Women and the American Experience* (1984, 1994, 1996, 2000, 2002, 2006), editor of *Early American Women: A Documentary History, 1600–1900* (1992, 1997, 2002), and coauthor, with Walter LaFeber and Richard Polenberg, of *The American Century: A History of the United States since the 1890s* (1986, 1992, 1998). She is also the author of *Muller v. Oregon: A Brief History with Documents* (1996). She teaches American history and American Studies at Barnard College, Columbia University.

1

Native Peoples of America, to 1500

THE FIRST AMERICANS, C. 13,000–2500 B.C.

Precise details as to how and when the vast Western Hemisphere was first settled remains uncertain. Many Indians believe that their ancestors originated in the Americas, but most scientific findings point to the arrival of the first humans—ancestral Native Americans—from northeastern Asia sometime during the last Ice Age (c. 33,000–10,700 B.C.). These earliest Americans traveled by two different routes when land linked Siberia and Alaska. Thereafter, as the Ice Age waned and global temperatures rose, Native Americans dispersed throughout the hemisphere, adapting to environments ranging from tropical to frigid. Though divided into small, widely scattered groups, they interacted through trade and travel. Over several thousand years, Indians learned from one another and developed ways of life that had much in common despite their diverse backgrounds.

Peopling New Worlds — Most archaeologists agree that humans had begun to arrive in the Americas by 13,000 B.C. Traveling in small foraging bands in search of ample sources of food, the first Americans did not consciously move from one continent to another. Rather they apparently traveled by watercraft, following the then-continuous coastline from Siberia to Alaska and progressing southward along the Pacific coast. At various points along the way, groups stopped and either settled nearby or traveled inland to establish new homes. Coastal sites as far south as Monte Verde, in Chile, reveal evidence from about 12,000 B.C. of peoples who fed on marine life, birds, small mammals, and wild plants, as well as an occasional mastodon. (Archaeologists estimate dates by measuring the radioactive carbon 14 [radiocarbon] in organic materials such as food remains. They can extend their

1

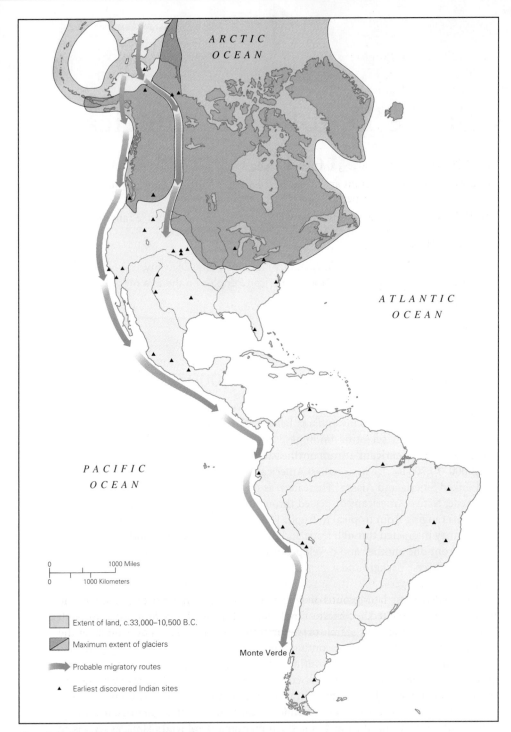

MAP 1.1 The Peopling of the Americas

Scientists postulate two probable routes by which the earliest peoples reached America. By 9500 B.C., they had settled throughout the Western Hemisphere.

CHRONOLOGY 13,000 B.C.–A.D. 1500

c. 13,000 B.C. • People present in Americas.

c. 9000 B.C. • Paleo-Indians established throughout Western Hemisphere. Extinction of big-game mammals.

c. 8000 B.C. • Earliest Archaic societies.

c. 7000 B.C. • Athapaskan-speaking peoples enter North America.

c. 5000 B.C. • First domesticated plants grown.

c. 3000 B.C. • First maize grown in Mesoamerica.

c. 3000–2000 B.C. • Inuit and Aleut peoples enter North America from Siberia.

c. 2500 B.C. • Archaic societies begin giving way to a more diverse range of cultures. First maize grown in North America.

c. 1200–900 B.C. • Poverty Point flourishes in Louisiana.

c. 400–100 B.C. • Adena culture flourishes in Ohio valley.

c. 250 B.C. • Hohokam culture begins in Southwest.

c. 100 B.C. • Anasazi culture begins in Southwest.

c. 100 B.C.–A.D. 600 • Hopewell culture thrives in Midwest.

c. A.D. 1 • Rise of chiefdoms on Northwest coast and in California.

c. 700 • Mississippian culture begins. Anasazi expansion begins.

c. 900 • Urban center arises at Cahokia.

c. 1000 • Norse attempt to colonize Vinland (Newfoundland).

c. 1200 • Anasazi and Hohokam peoples disperse in Southwest.

c. 1200–1400 • Cahokia declines and inhabitants disperse.

c. 1400 • Iroquois Confederacy formed.

1428 • Aztec empire expands.

1438 • Inca empire expands.

1492 • Christopher Columbus reaches Western Hemisphere.

estimates when organic remains are clearly associated with nonorganic materials such as stone tools.) Some later groups of migrants reached North America by land. As the glaciers gradually melted, a corridor developed east of the Rocky Mountains through which these nomadic travelers passed before dispersing themselves over much of the Western Hemisphere.

Linguists, biological anthropologists, and archaeologists have determined that most Native Americans are descended from these early migrants. However, the ancestors of some native peoples came later, also from northeastern Asia, after the land connecting Siberia with Alaska had submerged. Speakers of a language known as Athapaskan settled in Alaska and northwestern Canada in about 7000 B.C. Some of their descendants later migrated to the Southwest to form the Apaches and Navajos. After 3000 B.C., Inuits (Eskimos) and Aleuts crossed the Bering Sea from Siberia to Alaska.

Native American oral traditions offer conflicting support for scientists' theories, depending on how the traditions are interpreted. Pueblos and Navajos in the Southwest tell how their forebears experienced perilous journeys through other worlds before emerging from underground in their present homelands, while the Iroquois trace their ancestry to a pregnant woman who fell from the "sky world." Among the Iroquois and other peoples, the original humans could not settle the water-covered planet until a diving bird or animal brought soil from the ocean bottom, creating an island on which they could walk. Still other traditions recall large mammals, monsters, or "hairy people" with whom the first people shared Earth. Many Native Americans today insist that such accounts confirm that their ancestors originated in the Western Hemisphere. However, others note that the stories do not specify a place of origin and may well reflect the experiences of their ancestors as they journeyed from Asia, across water, ice, and unknown lands, and encountered large mammals before settling in their new homes. If not taken literally, they maintain, the traditions support rather than contradict scientists' theories.

Paleo-Indians, as archaeologists call the earliest Americans, established the foundations of **Native American** life. Paleo-Indians appear to have traveled within well-defined hunting territories in **bands** consisting of several families and totaling about fifteen to fifty people. Men hunted, while women prepared food and cared for the children. Bands left their territories when traveling to quarries to obtain favored materials for making tools and spear points. There they encountered other bands, with whose members they exchanged ideas and goods, intermarried, and participated in religious ceremonies. As in non-market economies and non-state societies throughout history, these exchanges followed the principle of **reciprocity**—the mutual bestowing of gifts and favors—rather than the notion that one party should accumulate profits or power at the expense of the other. These encounters enabled Paleo-Indians to develop a broad cultural life that transcended their small bands.

The earliest Paleo-Indians found a hunter's paradise in which large mammals—mammoths, mastodons, and giant species of horses, camels, bison, caribou, and moose—roamed America, innocent of the ways of human predators. Around 9000 B.C., the megafauna rather quickly became extinct. Although some scholars believe that Paleo-Indian hunters killed off all the large mammals, most maintain that the mammals were doomed not just by humans but by the warming climate, which disrupted the food chain on which they depended. In other words, the extinction of the mammals was symptomatic of environmental changes associated with the end of the Ice Age. Among the major beneficiaries of these changes were human beings.

Archaic Societies After about 8000 B.C., peoples throughout the Americas began modifying their Paleo-Indian ways of life. The warming of Earth's atmosphere continued until about 4000 B.C., with far-reaching global effects. Sea levels rose, flooding low-lying coastal areas, while glacial runoff filled interior waterways. As the glaciers receded northward, so did the arctic and subarctic environments that had previously extended into what are now the lower forty-eight states of the United States. Treeless plains and evergreen forests gave way to deciduous forests in the East, grassland prairies on the Plains, and desert in much of the West. The immense range of flora and fauna with which we are familiar today emerged during this period.

Archaic peoples, as archaeologists term Native Americans who flourished in these new environments, lived off the wider varieties of smaller mammals, fish, and wild plants that were now available. With more sources of food, communities required less land and could support larger populations. Some Indians in temperate regions began residing in year-round villages. From about 3900 to 2800 B.C., for example, the 100 to 150 residents of a community near Kampsville, Illinois, obtained ample supplies of fish, mussels, deer and other mammals, birds, nuts, and seeds without moving their homes.

Over time, Archaic Americans sharpened some distinctions between women's and men's roles. Men took responsibility for fishing as well as hunting, while women procured wild plant products. Gender roles are apparent in burials at Indian Knoll, in Kentucky, where tools relating to hunting, fishing, woodworking, and leatherworking were usually buried with men and those relating to cracking nuts and grinding seeds with women. Yet gender-specific distinctions did not apply to all activities, for objects used by religious healers were distributed equally between male and female graves.

Archaic Indians—women in most North American societies—honed their skills at harvesting wild plants. Through generations of close observation, they determined how to weed, prune, irrigate, transplant, burn, and otherwise manipulate their environments to favor plants that provided food and medicine. They also developed specialized tools for digging and grinding as well as more effective methods of drying and storing seeds. The most sophisticated early plant cultivators lived in **Mesoamerica** (central and southern Mexico and Central America), where maize agriculture was highly developed by 2500 B.C. (see Beyond America—Global Interactions: The Origins and Spread of Agriculture).

Cultural Diversity, c. 2500 b.c.–a.d. 1500

After about 2500 B.C., many Native Americans moved far beyond the ways of their Archaic forebears. The most far-reaching transformation occurred among peoples whose environments permitted them to produce food surpluses, by cultivating crops or other means. Some of these societies transformed trade networks into extensive religious and political systems linking several—sometimes dozens of—local communities. A few of these groupings evolved into formal confederacies and even states. In environments where food sources were few and widely scattered, mobile hunting-fishing-gathering bands persisted.

Mesoamerica and South America
As Mesoamerican farmers developed their methods, the quantity and quality of their crops increased. Farmers also planted beans alongside maize. The beans eaten released an amino acid, lysine, in the maize that further heightened its nutritional value. Higher yields and improved nutrition led some societies to center their lives around farming. Over the next eight centuries, maize-based farming societies spread throughout Mesoamerica.

After 2000 B.C., some Mesoamerican farming societies produced crop surpluses that they traded to less-populous, nonfarming neighbors. Expanding their trade contacts, a few of these societies established formal exchange networks that enabled them to enjoy more wealth and power than their partners. After 1200 B.C., a few communities, such as those of the Olmecs in Mesoamerica and Chavín de Huántar in the Andes, developed into large urban centers, subordinating smaller neighbors. Unlike in earlier societies, Indian cities were highly unequal, with a few wealthy elites dominating thousands of residents and with hereditary rulers claiming kinship with religious deities. Laborers built elaborate religious temples and palaces, including the earliest American pyramids, and artisans created statues of the rulers and the gods.

Although the earliest hereditary rulers exercised absolute power, their realms were limited to a few closely clustered communities. Anthropologists term such political societies **chiefdoms,** as opposed to **states** in which a ruler or government exercises direct authority over many communities. Chiefdoms eventually emerged in several parts of the Americas, from the Mississippi valley to the Amazon valley and the Andes Mountains. A few states arose in Mesoamerica after A.D. 1 and in South America after A.D. 500. Although men ruled most chiefdoms and states, women served as chiefs in some Andean societies until the Spanish arrived.

From capital cities with thousands of inhabitants, states centered at Monte Alban and Teotihuacán in Mesoamerica and at Wari in the Andes drafted soldiers and waged bloody wars of conquest. Bureaucrats administered state territories, collected taxes, and managed huge public works projects. Priests conducted ceremonies in enormous temples and presided over religious hierarchies extending throughout the states. The capital of the largest early state, Teotihuacán, was situated about fifty miles northeast of modern Mexico City and numbered about a hundred thousand people at the height of its power between the second and seventh centuries A.D. At its center was a complex of pyramids, the largest of which, the Sun Pyramid, was about 1 million cubic meters in volume. Teotihuacán dominated the peoples of the valley of Mexico, and its trade networks extended over much of modern-day Mexico. Although Teotihuacán declined in the eighth century, it exercised enormous influence on the religion, government, and culture of its neighbors.

Sun Pyramid, Teotihuacán   *Built over several centuries, this pyramid remained the largest structure in the Americas until after the Spanish arrived.*

Teotihuacán's greatest influence was on the Maya, whose kingdom-states flourished from southern Mexico to Honduras between the seventh and fifteenth centuries. The Maya moved far beyond their predecessors in developing a calendar, a numerical system (which included the concept of zero), and a system of phonetic, hieroglyphic writing. Maya scribes produced thousands of books on bark paper glued into long, folded strips. The books recorded religious ceremonies, historical traditions, and astronomical observations.

Other powerful states flourished in Mesoamerica and South America until the fifteenth century, when two mighty empires arose to challenge them. The first was the empire of the **Aztecs** (known at the time as the Mexica), who had migrated from the north during the thirteenth century and settled on the shore of Lake Texcoco as subjects of the local inhabitants. Overthrowing their rulers in 1428, the Aztecs went on to conquer other cities around the lake and extended their domain to the Gulf Coast. Aztec expansion took a bloody turn in the 1450s during a four-year drought, which the Aztecs interpreted as a sign that the gods, like themselves, were hungry. Aztec priests maintained that the only way to satisfy the gods was to serve them human blood and hearts. From then on, conquering Aztec warriors sought captives for sacrifice in order, as they believed, to nourish the gods.

A massive temple complex at the capital of Tenochtitlán formed the sacred center of the Aztec empire. The Great Temple consisted of two joined pyramids and was surrounded by several smaller pyramids and other buildings. Aztec culture reflected both Mesoamerican tradition and the multicultural character of the state. Most of the more than two hundred deities they honored originated with earlier and contemporary societies, including those they had subjugated. They based their system of writing on the one developed centuries before at Teotihuacán and their calendar on that of the Maya.

To support the nearly two hundred thousand people residing in and around Tenochtitlán, the Aztecs maximized their production of food. They drained swampy areas and added rich soil from the lake bottom to artificial islands that formed. The highly fertile islands enabled Aztec farmers to supply the urban population with food. Aztec engineers devised an elaborate irrigation system to provide fresh water for both people and crops.

The Aztecs collected taxes from subjects living within about a hundred miles of the capital. Conquered peoples farther away paid tribute, which replaced the free exchanges of goods they had formerly carried on with the Aztecs and other neighbors. Trade beyond the Aztec domain was conducted by *pochteca*, traders who traveled in armed caravans. The pochteca sought salt, cacao, jewelry, feathers, jaguar pelts, cotton, and precious stones and metals, including gold and turquoise, the latter obtained from Indians in the American Southwest.

The Aztecs were still expanding in the early sixteenth century, but rebellions constantly flared within their realm. They had surrounded and weakened, but not subjugated, one neighboring rival, while another blocked their westward expansion. Might the Aztecs have expanded still farther? We will never know because they were violently crushed in the sixteenth century by another, even more far-flung empire, the Spanish (see Chapter 2).

Meanwhile, a second empire, that of the **Incas,** had arisen in the Western Hemisphere. From their sumptuous capital at Cuzco, the Incas conquered and subordinated societies over much of the Andes and adjacent regions after 1438. One key to the

The Origins and Spread of Agriculture

For most of their two and a half million years on Earth, human beings lived as hunter-gatherers or foragers, subsisting on wild plants and animals. It was only between ten thousand and four thousand years ago that scattered groups of people transformed a few dozen wild plant species into domesticated crops. The grain, pulse (peas and beans), root, and melon/squash crops they produced remain the principal sources of plant food for humans and their domestic animals today.

The transformation of wild plants into crops was a gradual process. Through careful observation, gatherers selected varieties of plants that produced the highest yields. After planting the largest seeds of these varieties, they eliminated nearby, competing plants and harvested the favored plants when the food was ripe. As crop production intensified, farmer-gatherers developed specialized tools, such as digging sticks and hoes, to facilitate the planting of seeds and elimination of weeds. Over time, the new foods replaced many wild sources of food in farming peoples' diets.

Gatherers domesticated plants in just a few, widely separate parts of the world. People began cultivating wild species of wheat, barley, and peas in the Middle East in about 8000 B.C. Within 500 years, similar processes had begun with rice in southern China; bananas and taro, a root crop, in New Guinea; and sorghum, a grain, in the eastern Sahara region of Africa. (Climatic warming would later turn the Sahara into a desert, ending farming there.) The origins of farming in the Western Hemisphere date to about 5000 B.C., in Mesoamerica. By around 3500 B.C., Native Americans had domes-

ticated potatoes in the Andes Mountains and manioc—a starchy root crop—in the Amazon Basin. Within another one thousand years, women in the Mississippi and Ohio valleys of North America had begun cultivating favored varieties of squash, sunflowers, and grasses.

In domesticating wild plants, early farmers shaped the evolution of plant species. The most complex example of domestication occurred in the highland Mexican valley of Tehuacan, where Native Americans experimented with a lowland plant called teosinte. Through an intricate process of trial and error, they selected mutated seeds that flourished at higher elevations and yielded favorable characteristics such as larger cobs and kernels and better taste. By continuing to plant preferred seeds, the Indians eventually produced a new, much larger species—maize—with dozens of varieties. In so doing, geneticist Nina V. Federoff has written, they achieved "arguably man's first, and perhaps his greatest, feat of genetic engineering."

From its few points of origin, agriculture spread to other parts of the world. In some cases, nonfarming societies acquired seeds and agricultural know-how through trade or from immigrating farmers. Wheat and barley moved beyond the Middle East to Europe, reaching Greece by 6000 B.C., Central Europe by 5000 B.C., and parts of western Europe by 4000 B.C. Similarly, maize cultivation expanded in all directions from the Tehuacan Valley. By 2500 B.C., Indians were growing it elsewhere in Central America, in the Amazon River basin, and as far northward as what is now the American Southwest.

In other cases, whole societies of farmers invaded new lands, subordinating or expelling hunter-gatherers. For example, southern Chinese rice farmers took over favorable lands in northern China and Southeast Asia. In a few places, such as the British Isles in   c. 2500 B.C., arriving farmers were the first inhabitants.

As agriculture spread, farmers adapted plants to new environments. Maize arrived in eastern North America in about 300 B.C. but remained a minor crop for another thousand years, until women there developed a strain that produced high yields in climates with as few as one hundred frost-free days per year. Thereafter, it was a dietary mainstay for eastern North American Indians. Once they adopted crops originating elsewhere, some farmers then domesticated local plants, further diversifying their diets. For example, only after adopting wheat and barley from the Middle East did western Europeans discover how to cultivate indigenous oats and poppies.

Climate, topography, soil composition, and availability of water limited agricultural production to certain, mostly temperate areas. Within these areas, farming required that people have access to and knowledge of the select group of plants that could be effectively cultivated on a large scale. In the absence of these conditions, many people remained foragers and did not attempt to farm. Even where farming was a realistic option, its adoption was not inevitable. When members of a hunting-gathering band began to rely on crops, they had to remain in one place for longer periods of each year in order to tend the fields, thereby foregoing other food-gathering practices that had proven reliable. A decision to cultivate was often dictated by the shortage of a wild food source on which a group had depended, but in

other cases people took a risk that unfamiliar crops would flourish and not succumb to fluctuations in climate or to blight. While evidence is hard to come by, a group's cultural values and beliefs about their place in nature undoubtedly influenced their decisions.

In many parts of the world, as people began cultivating plants, they also domesticated animals. Although hunters had long used dogs to track prey, it was only after 8000 B.C. that people in the Middle East began to tame wild sheep, goats, and cattle. Soon people in the Eastern Hemisphere domesticated other species, including water buffalo, donkeys, pigs, chickens, and—much later—horses and camels. Various sorts of animals supplied their keepers not only with meat but also with milk, eggs, wool, labor (including in agricultural fields), and transportation. Animal domestication was severely limited in the Western Hemisphere. Ancestral species of horses and camels flourished in the Americas when humans first arrived but soon became extinct. By the time Native Americans began farming, the only species suitable for taming were dogs, llamas, turkeys, and guinea pigs.

Until A.D. 1492, domesticated plants (and animals) spread strictly within either the Eastern Hemisphere or the Western Hemisphere. Thereafter a "Columbian exchange" would transform many species into global crops (see Chapter 2).

Questions for Analysis

- By what processes were plants first domesticated?

- Why were domesticated crops a primary source of food in some parts of the world and not in others?

Incas' expansion was their ability to produce and distribute a wide range of surplus crops, including maize, beans, potatoes, and meats. They constructed terraced irrigation systems for watering crops on uneven terrain, perfected freeze-drying and other preservation techniques, built vast storehouses, and constructed a vast network of roads and bridges. The Incas were still expanding when they too were overcome by Spanish invaders in the sixteenth century.

The Southwest   The Southwest is a uniformly arid region with a variety of landscapes. Waters from rugged mountains and forested plateaus follow ancient channels through vast expanses of desert on their way to the gulfs of Mexico and California. The amount of water has fluctuated over time, depending on climatic conditions, but securing water has always been a challenge for southwestern peoples. Nevertheless, some of them augmented their supplies of water and became farmers.

Maize reached the Southwest via Mesoamerican trade links by about 2500 B.C. Yet full-time farming began only after 400 B.C., when the introduction of a more drought-resistant strain enabled some farmers to move from the highlands to drier lowlands. In the centuries that followed, southwestern populations rose, and Indian cultures were transformed. The two most influential new cultural traditions were the Hohokam and the Anasazi.

The **Hohokam culture** emerged during the third century B.C., when ancestors of the Akimel O'odham and Tohono O'odham Indians began farming in the Gila and Salt River valleys of southern Arizona. Hohokam peoples built irrigation canals that enabled them to harvest two crops a year, an unprecedented feat in the arid environment. To construct and maintain their canals, the Hohokam organized large, coordinated work forces. They built permanent towns, usually consisting of several hundred people. Although many towns remained independent, others joined confederations in which several towns were linked by canals. The central village in each confederation coordinated labor, trade, religion, and political life for all member communities.

Although a local creation, Hohokam culture drew extensively on Mesoamerican materials and ideas. From about the sixth century A.D., the large villages had ball courts and platform mounds similar to those in Mesoamerica at the time. Mesoamerican influence was also apparent in the creations of Hohokam artists, who worked in clay, stone, turquoise, and shell. Archaeologists have uncovered rubber balls, macaw feathers, cottonseeds, and copper bells from Mesoamerica at Hohokam sites.

The **Anasazi culture** originated during the first century B.C. in the Four Corners area where Arizona, New Mexico, Colorado, and Utah meet. By around A.D. 700, Anasazi people—ancestors of modern Pueblo Indians—were harvesting crops, living in permanent villages, and making pottery. Thereafter, they expanded over a wide area and became the most powerful people in the Southwest.

One distinguishing characteristic of Anasazi culture was its architecture. Anasazi villages consisted of extensive complexes of attached apartments and storage rooms, along with *kivas*—partly underground structures in which male religious leaders conducted ceremonies. To this day, Anasazi-style apartments and kivas are central features of Pueblo Indian architecture in the Southwest.

Anasazi culture reached its height between about 900 and 1150, during an unusually wet period in the Southwest. In Chaco Canyon, a cluster of twelve large towns forged a powerful confederation numbering about fifteen thousand people. A system of roads radiated from the canyon to satellite towns as far as sixty-five miles away. The roads were perfectly straight; their builders even carved out stairs or footholds on the sides of steep cliffs rather than go around them. By controlling rainwater runoff through small dams and terraces, the towns fed themselves as well as the satellites. The largest of the towns, Pueblo Bonito, had about twelve hundred inhabitants and was the home of two Great Kivas, each about fifty feet in diameter. People traveled over the roads from the satellites to Chaco Canyon's large kivas for religious ceremonies. The canyon was also a major trade center, importing and exporting a wide range of materials from and to Mesoamerica, the Great Plains, the Mississippi valley, and California.

The classic Anasazi culture, as manifested at Chaco Canyon, Mesa Verde in southwestern Colorado, and other sites, came to an end in the twelfth and thirteenth centuries. Although other factors contributed, the overriding cause of the Anasazi demise was drought. As has often happened in human history, an era of especially abundant rainfall, which the Anasazi thought would last forever, abruptly ended. Without enough water, the highly concentrated inhabitants abandoned the great Anasazi centers, dispersing to form new, smaller communities. Their Pueblo Indian descendants would encounter Spanish colonizers three centuries later (see Chapter 2). Hohokam communities also dispersed when drought came. With farming peoples now clustered in the few areas with enough water, the drier lands of the Southwest attracted the non-farming Apaches and Navajos, whose arrival at the end of the fourteenth century ended their long migration from the far north (mentioned above).

Pueblo Bonito, Chaco Canyon, New Mexico   *Pueblo Bonito illustrates the richness and grand scale of Anasazi architecture.*

The Eastern Woodlands

In contrast to the Southwest, the Eastern Woodlands—the vast expanse stretching from the Mississippi valley to the Atlantic Ocean—had abundant water. Water and deciduous forests provided Woodlands Indians with a rich variety of food sources, while the region's extensive river systems facilitated long-distance communication and travel. As a result, many eastern Indians established populous villages and complex confederations well before adopting full-time, maize-based farming.

By 1200 B.C., about five thousand people lived at **Poverty Point** on the lower Mississippi River. The town featured earthworks consisting of two large mounds and six concentric embankments, the outermost of which spanned more than half a mile in diameter. During the spring and autumn equinoxes, a person standing on the larger mound could watch the sun rise directly over the village center. As in some Mesoamerican societies at the time, solar observations were the basis for religious beliefs and a calendar.

Poverty Point was the center of a much larger political and economic unit. The settlement imported large quantities of quartz, copper, obsidian, crystal, and other materials from long distances for redistribution to nearby communities. These communities almost certainly supplied some of the labor for the earthworks. Poverty Point's general design and organization indicate Olmec influence from Mesoamerica (see above). Poverty Point flourished for about three centuries and then declined, for reasons unknown. Nevertheless, it foreshadowed later developments in the Eastern Woodlands.

A different kind of mound-building culture, called **Adena,** emerged in the Ohio valley around 400 B.C. Adena villages were smaller than Poverty Point, rarely exceeding four hundred inhabitants. But Adena people spread over a wide area and built hundreds of mounds, most of them containing graves. The treatment of Adena dead varied according to social or political status. Some corpses were cremated; others were placed in round clay basins; and still others were given elaborate tombs.

After 100 B.C., Adena culture evolved into a more complex and widespread culture known as **Hopewell,** which spread from the Ohio valley to the Illinois River valley. Some Hopewell centers contained two or three dozen mounds within enclosures of several square miles. The variety and quantity of goods buried with members of the elite were also greater. Hopewell elites were buried with thousands of freshwater pearls or copper ornaments or with sheets of mica, quartz, or other sacred substances. Hopewell artisans fashioned fine ornaments and jewelry, which their owners wore in life and took to their graves. The raw materials for these objects originated in locales throughout America east of the Rockies. Through far-flung trade networks, Hopewell religious and technological influence spread to communities as far away as Wisconsin, Missouri, Florida, and New York. Although the great Hopewell centers were abandoned by about 600 (for reasons that are unclear), they had an enormous influence on subsequent developments in eastern North America.

The peoples of Poverty Point and the Adena and Hopewell cultures did little farming. Indian women in Kentucky and Missouri had cultivated small amounts of squash as early as 2500 B.C., and maize first appeared east of the Mississippi by 300 B.C. But agriculture did not become the primary food source for Woodlands people until between the seventh and twelfth centuries A.D., as women moved beyond gathering and minor cultivating activities to become the major producers of food.

Cahokia Woman Grinding Food *This five-inch-tall figurine, carved from bauxite stone around 1200, depicted a woman using a mortar and pestle to prepare food, probably corn.*

The first full-time farmers in the East lived on the floodplains of the Mississippi River and its major tributaries. Beginning around A.D. 700, they developed a new culture, called **Mississippian.** The volume of Mississippian craft production and long-distance trade dwarfed that of the Adena and Hopewell peoples. As in Mesoamerica, Mississippian centers, numbering hundreds or even thousands of people, arose around open plazas. Large platform mounds adjoined the plazas, topped by sumptuous religious temples and the residences of chiefs and other elites. Religious ceremonies focused on the worship of the sun as the source of agricultural fertility. The people considered chiefs to be related to the sun. When a chief died, his wives and servants were killed so that they could accompany him in the afterlife. Largely in connection with their religious and funeral rituals, Mississippian artists produced highly sophisticated work in clay, stone, shell, copper, wood, and other materials.

After A.D. 900, Mississippian centers formed extensive networks based on river-borne trade and shared religious beliefs, each dominated by a single metropolis. The largest, most powerful such system centered on **Cahokia,** located near modern St. Louis, Missouri, where about twenty thousand people inhabited a 125-square-mile metropolitan area.

For about two and a half centuries, Cahokia reigned supreme in the Mississippi valley. After A.D. 1200, however, Cahokia and other valley centers experienced shortages of food and other resources. As in the Southwest, densely concentrated societies had taxed a fragile environment with a fluctuating climate. One result was competition for suddenly scarce resources, which led to debilitating warfare and the undermining of Cahokia and its allies. The survivors fled to the surrounding prairies and, in some cases, westward to the lower valleys of the Plains. By the fifteenth century, their descendants were living in villages linked by reciprocity rather than coercion. Mississippian chiefdoms and temple mound centers persisted in the Southeast, where

Spanish explorers would later encounter them as the forerunners of Cherokees, Creeks, and other southeastern Indian peoples (see Chapter 2).

Despite Cahokia's decline, Mississippian culture profoundly affected Native Americans in the Eastern Woodlands. Mississippians spread new strains of maize and beans, along with techniques and tools for cultivating these crops, enabling women to weave agriculture into the fabric of village life. Life for Indians as far north as the Great Lakes and southern New England revolved around village-based farming. Only in more northerly Woodlands areas was the growing season usually too short for maize (which required one hundred or more frost-free days) to be a reliable crop.

Woodland peoples' method of land management was environmentally sound and economically productive. Indian men systematically burned hardwood forests, eliminating the underbrush and forming open, parklike expanses. Although they occasionally lost control of a fire, so that it burned beyond their hunting territory, the damage was not lasting. Burned-over tracts favored the growth of grass and berry bushes that attracted a profusion of deer and other game. They then cleared fields so that women could plant corn, beans, and squash in soil enriched by ash. After several years of abundant harvests, yields declined, and the Indians moved to another site to repeat the process. Ground cover eventually reclaimed the abandoned clearing, restoring fertility naturally, and the Indians could return.

Nonfarming Societies
Outside the Southwest and the Eastern Woodlands, farming north of Mesoamerica was either impossible because of inhospitable environments or impractical because native peoples could obtain enough food from wild sources with less work. On the Northwest coast, from the Alaskan panhandle to northern California, and in the Columbia Plateau, Native Americans devoted brief periods of each year to catching salmon and other spawning fish. After drying the fish, they stored it in quantities sufficient to last the year. As a result, their seasonal movements gave way to a settled lifestyle in permanent villages. For example, the Makah Indians of Ozette, on Washington's Olympic Peninsula, pursued fish and sea mammals, including whales, while procuring shellfish, salmon and other river fish, land mammals, and wild plants.

By A.D. 1, most Northwest coast villages numbered several hundred people who lived in multifamily houses built of cedar planks. Trade and warfare with interior groups strengthened the wealth and power of chiefs and other elites. Leading families displayed their power in the potlatch—a feast at which they gave away to guests or destroyed their material wealth. From the time of the earliest contacts, Europeans were amazed by the artistic and architectural achievements of the Northwest coast Indians. "What must astonish most," wrote a French explorer in 1791, "is to see painting everywhere, everywhere sculpture, among a nation of hunters."

At about the same time, Native Americans on the coast and in the valleys of what is now California were clustering in villages of about a hundred people to coordinate the processing of acorns. After gathering millions of acorns from California's extensive oak groves each fall, tribal peoples such as the Chumash and Ohlones ground the acorns into meal, leached them of their bitter tannic acid, and then roasted, boiled, or baked the nuts prior to eating or storing them. Facing intense competition for acorns, California Indians combined their villages into chiefdoms and defended their territories. Chiefs conducted trade, diplomacy, war, and religious ceremonies.

Along with other wild species, acorns enabled the Indians of California to prosper. As a Spanish friar arriving in California from Mexico in 1770 wrote, "This land exceeds all the preceding territory in fertility and abundance of things necessary for sustenance."

Between the Eastern Woodlands and the Pacific coast, the Plains and deserts remained too dry to support large human settlements. Dividing the region are the Rocky Mountains, to the east of which lie the grasslands of the Great Plains, while to the west are several deserts of varying elevations that ecologists call the Great Basin. Except in the Southwest, Native Americans in this region remained in mobile hunting-gathering bands.

Plains Indian hunters pursued a variety of game animals, including antelope, deer, elk, and bear, but their favorite prey was buffalo, or bison, a smaller relative of the giant bison that had flourished before the arrival of humans. Buffalo provided Plains Indians with meat and with hides, from which they made clothing, bedding, portable houses (tipis), kettles, shields, and other items. They made tools from buffalo bones and containers and arrowheads from buffalo horns, and they used most other buffalo parts as well. Limited to travel by foot, Plains hunters stampeded herds of bison into small box canyons, easily killing the trapped animals, or over cliffs. Dozens, or occasionally hundreds, of buffalo would be killed. Since a single buffalo could provide two hundred to four hundred pounds of meat and a band had no means of preserving and storing most of it, the latter practice was especially wasteful. On the other hand, humans were so few in number that they had no significant impact on the bison population before the arrival of Europeans. There are no reliable estimates of the number of buffalo then roaming the Plains, but the earliest European observers were flabbergasted. One Spanish colonist, for example, witnessed a "multitude so great that it might be considered a falsehood by one who had not seen them."

During and after the Mississippian era, groups of Eastern Woodlands Indians migrated to the lower river valleys of the Plains, where over time the rainfall had increased enough to support cultivated plants. In contrast to Native Americans already living on the Plains, such as the Blackfeet and the Crow, farming newcomers like the Mandans and Pawnees built year-round villages and permanent earth lodges. But they also hunted buffalo and other animals. (Many of the Plains Indians familiar today, such as the Sioux and Comanches, moved to the region only after Europeans had begun colonizing North America [see Chapter 4].)

As Indians elsewhere increased their food production, the Great Basin grew warmer and drier, further limiting already scarce sources of foods. Ducks and other waterfowl on which Native Americans formerly feasted disappeared as marshlands dried up after 1200 B.C., and the number of buffalo and other game animals also dwindled. Great Basin Indians such as the Shoshones and the Utes countered these trends by relying more heavily on piñon nuts, which they harvested, stored, and ate in winter camps. Hunting improved after about A.D. 500, when Indians in the region adopted the bow and arrow.

In western Alaska, where the first Americans had appeared thousands of years earlier, Aleuts, carrying highly sophisticated tools and weapons from their Siberian homeland, arrived after 3000 B.C. Combining ivory, bone, and other materials, they fashioned harpoons and spears for the pursuit of sea mammals and—in the case of the Aleut—caribou. Through continued contacts with Siberia, the Aleut introduced the bow and arrow in North America. As they perfected their ways of living in the cold tundra environment, many Aleut spread westward across upper Canada and to Greenland.

The very earliest contacts between Native Americans and Europeans occurred in about A.D. 980, five centuries before the arrival of Columbus, when Norse expansionists from Scandinavia colonized parts of Greenland. The Greenland Norse hunted furs, obtained timber, and traded with Aleut people on the eastern Canadian mainland. They also made several attempts, beginning in about 1000, to colonize Vinland, as they called Newfoundland. The Vinland Norse initially exchanged metal goods for ivory with the local Beothuk Indians, but peaceful trade gave way to hostile encounters. Within a century, Beothuk resistance led the Norse to withdraw from Vinland. As a Norse leader, dying after losing a battle with some natives, put it, "There is fat around my belly! We have won a fine and fruitful country, but will hardly be allowed to enjoy it." Although some Norse remained in Greenland as late as the 1480s, it was later Europeans who would enjoy, at the expense of native peoples, the fruits of a "New World."

NORTH AMERICAN PEOPLES ON THE EVE OF EUROPEAN CONTACT

By A.D. 1500, native peoples had transformed the Americas into a dazzling array of cultures and societies. The Western Hemisphere numbered about 75 million people, most thickly clustered in urbanized areas of Mesoamerica and South America. But North America was no empty wasteland. Between 7 million and 10 million Indians lived north of Mesoamerica. They were unevenly distributed. As they had for thousands of years, small, mobile hunting bands peopled the Arctic, Subarctic, Great Basin, and much of the Plains. More sedentary societies based on fishing or gathering predominated along the Pacific coast, while village-based agriculture was typical in the Eastern Woodlands and the river valleys of the Southwest and Plains. Mississippian urban centers still prevailed in areas of the Southeast. All these peoples grouped themselves in several hundred nations and tribes, and spoke hundreds of languages and dialects.

Despite the vast differences among Native Americans, much bound them together. Rooted in common practices, Indian societies were based on kinship, the norms of reciprocity, and communal use and control of resources. Trade facilitated the exchange not only of goods but also of technologies and ideas. Thus, the bow and arrow, ceramic pottery, and certain religious values and practices characterized Indians everywhere.

Kinship and Gender Like their Archaic forebears, Indian peoples north of the Mesoamerican states were bound together primarily by kinship. Ties among biological relatives created complex patterns of social obligation and interdependence, even in societies that did not expect spouses to be married forever. Customs regulating marriage varied considerably, but strict rules always prevailed. In most cultures, young people married in their teens, generally after engaging in numerous sexual relationships, both casual and long-term. Some male leaders had more than one wife, but **nuclear families** (a husband, a wife, and their biological children) never stood alone. Instead, they lived with one of the parents' relatives in what social scientists call **extended families.**

In some Native American societies, such as the Iroquois, the extended families of women took precedence over those of men. Upon marriage, a new husband moved in with his wife's extended family. The primary male authority figure in a child's life was the mother's oldest brother, not the father. In many respects, a husband and father was simply a guest of his wife's family. Other Indian societies recognized men's extended families as primary, and still others did not distinguish sharply between the status of female and male family lines.

Kinship was also the basis for armed conflict. Indian societies typically considered homicide a matter to be resolved by the extended families of the victim and the perpetrator. If the perpetrator's family offered a gift that the victim's family considered appropriate, the question was settled; if not, political leaders attempted to resolve the dispute. Otherwise, the victim's family members and their supporters might seek to avenge the killing by armed retaliation. Such feuds could escalate into wars between communities. The potential for war rose when densely populated societies competed for scarce resources, as on the Northwest and California coasts, and when centralized Mississippian societies used coercion to dominate trade networks. Yet Native American warfare generally remained minimal, with rivals seeking to humiliate one another and seize captives rather than inflict massive casualties or conquer land. A New England officer, writing in the seventeenth century, described a battle between two Indian groups as "more for pastime than to conquer and subdue enemies." He concluded that "they might fight seven years and not kill seven men."

Women did most of the cultivating in farming societies except in the Southwest (where women and men shared the responsibility). With women producing the greater share of the food supply, some societies accorded them more power than did Europeans. Among the Iroquois, for example, women collectively owned the fields, distributed food, and played a decisive role in selecting chiefs. In New England, women often served as sachems, or political leaders.

Spiritual and Social Values   Native American religions revolved around the conviction that all nature was alive, pulsating with spiritual power— *manitou* in the Algonquian languages, *orenda* in the Iroquoian, and *wakan* in the Siouan. A mysterious, awe-inspiring force that could affect human life for both good and evil, such power united all nature in an unbroken web. *Manitou* encompassed "every thing which they cannot comprehend," reported Rhode Island's Roger Williams. Native Americans endeavored to conciliate the spiritual forces in their world—living things, rocks and water, sun and moon, even ghosts and witches. For example, Indian hunters prayed to the spirits of the animals they killed, thanking them for the gift of food.

Native Americans had several ways of gaining access to spiritual power. One was through dreams and visions, which most Native Americans interpreted as a form of spiritual instruction. Sometimes, as in Hiawatha's case, a dreamer received a message of importance for his or her people. Native people also sought power through difficult physical ordeals. Young men in many societies gained recognition as adults through a vision quest—a solitary venture that entailed fasting and awaiting the appearance of a spirit who would endow them with special powers. Some tribes initiated girls at the onset of menstruation into the spiritual world from which female reproductive power flowed. Entire communities often practiced collective power-seeking rituals such as the Sun Dance, performed by Indians of the Plains and Great Basin.

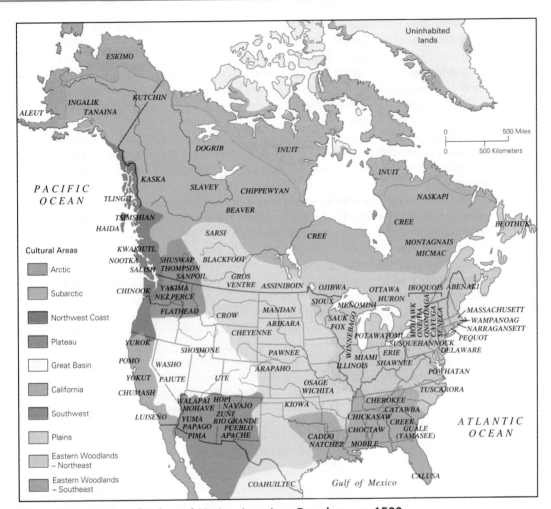

MAP 1.2 Locations of Selected Native American Peoples, A.D. 1500

Today's Indian nations were well established in homelands across the continent when Europeans first arrived. Many would combine with others or move in later centuries, either voluntarily or because they were forced.

Native Americans who had gained special religious powers assisted others in communicating with unseen spirits. These medicine men and women were healers who used both medicinal plants and magical chants to cure illnesses. They also served as spiritual advisers and leaders, interpreting dreams, guiding vision quests, and conducting ceremonies.

Native American societies demanded a strong degree of cooperation. From early childhood, Indians in most cultures learned to be accommodating and reserved—slow to reveal their own feelings until they could sense the feelings of others. Using physical punishment sparingly, if at all, Indians punished children psychologically, by public shaming. Communities sought unity through consensus rather than tolerating lasting divisions. Political leaders articulated slowly emerging agreements in dramatic oratory.

The English colonizer John Smith noted that the most effective Native American leaders spoke "with vehemency and so great passions that they sweat till they drop and are so out of breath they scarce can speak."

Native Americans reinforced cooperation with a strong sense of order. Custom, the demands of social conformity, and the rigors of nature strictly regulated life and people's everyday affairs. Exacting familial or community revenge was a ritualized way of restoring order that had broken down. On the other hand, the failure of measures to restore order could bring the fearful consequences experienced by Hiawatha's Iroquois—blind hatred, unending violence, and the most dreaded of evils, witchcraft. In fearing witchcraft, Native Americans resembled the Europeans and Africans they would encounter after 1492.

The principle of reciprocity remained strong among Native Americans. Reciprocity involved mutual give-and-take, but its aim was not to ensure equality. Instead, societies based on reciprocity tried to maintain equilibrium and interdependence between individuals of unequal power and prestige. Even in the most complex societies, chiefs coordinated families' uses of land and other resources, but never awarded these outright.

Most Indian leaders' authority depended on the obligations they bestowed rather than on coercion. By distributing gifts, they obligated members of the community to support them and to accept their authority, however limited. The same principle applied to relations between societies. Powerful communities distributed gifts to weaker neighbors who reciprocated with tribute in the form of material goods and submission. A French observer in early seventeenth-century Canada clearly understood: "For the savages have that noble quality, that they give liberally, casting at the feet of him whom they will honor the present that they give him. But it is with hope to receive some reciprocal kindness, which is a kind of contract, which we call . . . 'I give thee, to the end thou shouldst give me.'"

CONCLUSION

When Europeans "discovered" America in 1492, they did not, as they thought, enter an unchanging "wilderness" inhabited by "savages." American history had begun with the arrival of people in the Americas thousands of years earlier during an Ice Age, when Asia and North America were directly connected. As Earth's climate warmed, the earliest Paleo-Indians spread over the Americas, adapting to new, warmer environments by exploiting wider ranges of food sources that could support larger populations. They also learned from one another through inter-band exchanges. These developments eventually resulted in the emergence of new, regional cultures, termed Archaic. After 2500 B.C., Native Americans in several regions moved beyond Archaic cultures, clustering in seasonal or permanent villages where they produced food surpluses by growing crops, fishing for salmon, or processing acorns. Some built larger towns or cities. While people in the smallest bands were equal, political leaders in most societies came from prominent families. In a few, very large societies, hereditary chiefs, kings, and even emperors ruled far-flung peoples.

Underlying their diversity, North American Indians had much in common. First, they usually identified themselves as members of multigenerational families rather than as individuals or political subjects. Second, most emphasized reciprocity rather than domination and submission as the underlying principle for relations within and between communities. Third, they perceived the entire universe, including nature, as sacred. These core values arrived with the earliest Americans and persisted beyond the invasions of Europeans and their sharply contrasting ideas. Throughout their long history, Native Americans reinforced shared beliefs and customs through exchanges of material goods, new technologies, and religious ideas.

Although they had much in common with one another, Native Americans had never thought of themselves as a single people. Only after Europeans arrived and emphasized the differences between themselves and indigenous peoples did the term "Indian" come into usage. (The term originated with Columbus, who thought in 1492 that he had landed in the Indies [see Chapter 2].) The new America in which people were categorized according to continental ancestry was radically different from the one that had flourished for thousands of years before 1492.

2

The Rise of the Atlantic
World, 1400–1625

AFRICAN AND EUROPEAN BACKGROUNDS

When the Atlantic world emerged in the fifteenth and sixteenth centuries, all the continents facing the Atlantic Ocean were undergoing internal change. In the Americas, some societies rose, others fell, and still others adapted to new circumstances (see Chapter 1). West Africa and western Europe were also being transformed; a market society emerged on each continent alongside older systems of barter and local exchange. Wealthy merchants financed dynastic rulers seeking to extend their domains.

Western Europe's transformation was thoroughgoing. Its population nearly doubled in size, the distribution of wealth and power shifted radically, and new modes of thought and spirituality undermined established beliefs and knowledge. The result was social, political, and religious upheaval alongside remarkable expressions of creativity and innovation.

West Africa:
Tradition and
Change

Before the advent of Atlantic travel, the broad belt of grassland, or savanna, separating the Sahara Desert from the forests to the south played a major role in long-distance trade between the Mediterranean Sea and West Africa. The trans-Saharan caravan trade stimulated the rise of grassland kingdoms and empires, whose size and wealth rivaled any in Europe at the time. The richest grassland states were in West Africa, with its ample stores of gold. During the fourteenth and early fifteenth centuries, the empire of **Mali** was the leading power in the West African savanna. Through ties with wealthy Muslim rulers and merchants in North Africa and the Middle East, Mali's Muslim rulers imported brass, copper, cloth, spices, manufactured goods, and Arabian horses. Among their leading exports were gold and slaves. Mali's best-known city, Timbuktu, was widely recognized for its intellectual and academic vitality and for its beautiful mosque, designed and built by a Spanish Muslim architect.

During the fifteenth century, divisions within Mali's royal family severely weakened the empire, leading several territories to secede. A successor empire, Songhai, expanded from the south and forcibly united most of the seceded territory. But in 1591 Moroccan troops from North Africa defeated Songhai and established Morocco's domination of the western grassland.

Immediately south of the grassland empires lay a region of small states and chiefdoms. In Senegambia, at Africa's westernmost bulge, several Islamic states took root. Infestation by the tsetse fly, the carrier of sleeping sickness, kept livestock-herding peoples out of Guinea's coastal forests, but many small states arose here, too. Among these was Benin, where artisans had been fashioning magnificent metalwork for centuries.

Still farther south, along the coast and inland on the Congo River, a welter of chiefdoms consolidated into four major kingdoms by the fifteenth century. Their kings were chiefs who, after defeating neighboring chiefdoms, installed their own kin as local rulers of the newly conquered territories. Of these kingdoms, **Kongo** was the most powerful and highly centralized.

With gold having recently been made the standard for nearly all European currencies, demand for the precious metal rose. During the fifteenth century, this demand brought thousands of newcomers from the savanna and Central Africa to the region

Mali Horseman, c. 13th–14th century *This terra-cotta figure originated in Mali, one of several powerful empires in West Africa before the arrival of Europeans.*

CHRONOLOGY, 1400–1625

c. 1400–1600 • European Renaissance.

c. 1400–1500 • Coastal West African kingdoms rise and expand.

c. 1440 • Portuguese slave trade in West Africa begins.

c. 1450 • Songhai succeeds Mali as major power in West African grassland.

1492 • Christian "reconquest" of Spain. Columbus lands at Guanahaní.

1498 • Vasco da Gama rounds the Cape of Good Hope and reaches India.

1517 • Protestant Reformation begins in Germany.

1519–1521 • Cortés leads Spanish conquest of Aztec empire.

1519–1522 • Magellan's expedition circumnavigates the globe.

1532–1536 • Pizarro leads Spanish conquest of Inca empire.

1534 • Church of England breaks from Roman Catholic Church.

1541–1542 • Cartier attempts to colonize eastern Canada.

1539–1543 • De Soto attempts conquests in southeastern United States.

1540–1542 • Coronado attempts conquests in southwestern United States.

c. 1550 • Kongo declines in West Africa.

1558 • Elizabeth I becomes queen of England.

1565 • St. Augustine founded by Spanish.

1585–1590 • English colony of Roanoke established, then disappears.

1588 • England defeats the Spanish Armada.

1591 • Moroccan forces defeat Songhai in West Africa.

1598 • Oñate founds New Mexico.

1603 • James I becomes king of England.

1607 • English found colonies at Jamestown and Sagadahoc.

1608 • Champlain founds New France.

1609 • Henry Hudson explores the Hudson River.

1610–1614 • First Anglo-Powhatan War.

1614 • New Netherland founded.

1619 • Virginia begins exporting tobacco. First Africans arrive in Virginia.

1620 • Plymouth colony founded.

1622–1632 • Second Anglo-Powhatan War.

1624 • James I revokes Virginia Company's charter.

later known as Africa's Gold Coast. New states emerged to take advantage of the opportunities afforded by exporting gold, though none was as extensive or powerful as Mali at its height.

West African political leaders differed sharply in the amounts and kinds of political power they wielded. Some kings and emperors enjoyed semigodlike status, which they only thinly disguised if they adopted Islam. Rulers of smaller kingdoms depended largely on their ability to persuade, to conform to prevailing customs, and to satisfy their people when redistributing wealth.

As did Native Americans, West Africans lived within a network of interlocking mutual obligations to kinfolk (see Chapter 1). Not just parents but also aunts, uncles, distant cousins, and persons sharing clan ties formed an African's extended family and claimed his or her first loyalty. Africans held their grandparents in high esteem and accorded village or clan elders great deference. In centuries to come, the tradition of strong extended families would help enslaved Africans in the Americas endure the forced breakup of nuclear families by sale.

West Africans viewed marriage as a way for extended families to forge alliances for mutual benefit. A prospective husband made a payment to his bride's kin before marriage. He was not "buying" a wife; in effect, he was posting bond for good behavior and acknowledging the relative prestige of his own and his bride's extended families. West African wives generally maintained lifelong links with their own families. As among Native Americans, children in many societies traced descent through their mother's forebears, rather than their father's. These practices reinforced the status and power of women.

A driving force behind marriage in West Africa was the region's high mortality rate from frequent famines and tropical disease epidemics. The shortage of people placed a high premium on the production of children. Children contributed to a family's wealth by increasing its food production and the amount of land it could cultivate. Men of means frequently married more than one wife in order to produce children more frequently, and women generally married soon after reaching puberty.

West Africans depended on farming by both men and women for most of their food. The abundance of land relative to population enabled African farmers—like many Native Americans and unlike Europeans—to shift their fields periodically and thereby maintain high soil quality. Before planting new fields, men felled the trees and burned off the wild vegetation. After several years of intensive cultivation, largely by women, farmers shifted to a new location. After a few years, while the soil of the recently used fields was being replenished, they returned to repeat the cycle. In the coastal rain forests, West Africans grew such crops as yams, sugar cane, bananas, okra, and eggplant, among other foods, as well as cotton for weaving cloth. On the grasslands the staff of life was grain—millet, sorghum, and rice—supplemented by cattle raising and fishing.

By the fifteenth century, the market economy, stimulated by long-distance trade, extended to many small families. Farmers traded surplus crops at local marketplaces for other food or cloth. Artisans wove cotton or raffia palm leaves, made clothing and jewelry, and crafted tools and religious objects of iron and wood. While gold was the preferred currency among wealthy rulers and merchants, cowry shells served as the medium of exchange for most people.

Religion permeated African life. Like Native Americans and Europeans, Africans believed that another world lay beyond the one people perceived through their five senses. This other world was only rarely glimpsed by living persons besides priests, but the souls of most people passed there at death. Deities spoke to mortals through priests, dreams, religious "speaking shrines," and magical charms. Unlike Islam and Christianity, with their fixed dogmas, indigenous West African religions emphasized the importance of believers' continuous revelations as sources of spiritual truth. Like both Native Americans and Europeans, Africans explained misfortunes in terms of witchcraft. But African religion differed from other traditions by emphasizing ancestor worship, in which departed forebears were venerated as spiritual guardians.

Africa's magnificent artistic traditions were also steeped in religion. The ivory, cast iron, and wood sculptures of West Africa (whose bold designs would influence twentieth-century western art) were used in ceremonies reenacting creation myths and honoring spirits. A strong moralistic streak ran through African folk tales. Storytellers transmitted these tales in dramatic public presentations with ritual masks, dance, and music of a highly complex rhythmic structure, which is now appreciated as one of the foundations of jazz.

Among Africans, Islam appealed primarily to merchants trading with North Africa and the Middle East and to kings and emperors eager to consolidate their power. Some Muslim rulers modified Islam, retaining elements of traditional religion as a concession to popular opinion. By 1400, Islam was just beginning to affect the daily lives of some cultivators and artisans in the savanna.

European Culture and Society
When Columbus reached Guanahaní in 1492, western Europe was undergoing a cultural **Renaissance** (literally, rebirth). Intellectuals and poets celebrated Europe's descent from a classical tradition originating in ancient Greece and Rome but obscured for a thousand years during the "dark" or "middle" ages. Western European scholars discovered scores of forgotten ancient texts in philosophy, science, medicine, geography, and other subjects, and a rich tradition of commentary on them by Muslim, Eastern Orthodox, and Jewish scholars. Armed with the new learning, Renaissance scholars strove to reconcile ancient philosophy with Christian faith, to explore the mysteries of nature, to map the world, and to explain the motions of the heavens.

The Renaissance was also an era of intense artistic creativity. Wealthy Italian merchants and rulers—especially in the city-states of Florence and Venice, and in Rome (controlled by the papacy)—commissioned magnificent architecture, painting, and sculpture. Artists such as Leonardo da Vinci and Michelangelo created works that were rooted in classical tradition and were based on close observations of nature (including the human body) and attention to perspective. Europeans celebrated these artistic achievements, along with those of writers, philosophers, scientists, and explorers, as the height of "civilization" to which other cultures should aspire.

But European society was also quivering with tension. The era's artistic and intellectual creativity was partly inspired by intense social and spiritual stress as Renaissance Europeans groped for stability by glorifying order, hierarchy, and beauty. A concern for power and rank ("degree") dominated European life between the fifteenth and seventeenth centuries. Writing near the end of the Renaissance, William Shakespeare (1564–1616) expressed these values with eloquence:

> The heavens themselves, the planets and this center [earth]
> Observe degree, priority, and place . . .
> Take but degree away, untune that string,
> And hark, what discord follows!

Gender, wealth, inherited position, and political power affected every European's status, and few lived outside the reach of some political authority's taxes and laws. But this order was shaky. Conflicts between states, between religions, and between social classes constantly threatened the balance.

At the heart of these conflicts lay deep-seated forces of change. By the end of the fifteenth century, strong national monarchs in Spain, France, and England had consolidated royal authority at the expense of the Catholic Church and the nobility. The "new monarchs" cultivated powerful merchants by promoting their enterprises in exchange for financial support. On the Iberian Peninsula, King Ferdinand of Aragon had married Queen Isabella of Castile in 1479 to create the Spanish monarchy. France's boundaries expanded as a series of kings absorbed neighboring lands through interdynastic marriage and military conquest. England's Tudor dynasty gradually suppressed the aristocracy's ability to plunge the nation into deadly civil war.

Most Europeans—about 75 percent—were peasants, frequently driven to starvation by taxes, rents, and other dues owed to landlords and Catholic Church officials. Not surprisingly, peasant revolts were frequent, but the authorities mercilessly suppressed such uprisings.

Conditions among European peasants were made worse by a sharp rise in population, from about 55 million in 1450 to almost 100 million by 1600. Neighboring families often cooperated in plowing, sowing, and harvesting as well as in grazing their livestock on jointly owned "commons." But with new land at a premium, landlords, especially in England, wanted to "enclose" the commons—that is, convert the land to private property. Peasants who had no written title to their land were especially vulnerable to these pressures.

The environmental effects of land scarcity and population growth further exacerbated peasants' circumstances. Beginning in the fourteenth century, lower-than-average temperatures marked a "Little Ice Age" that lasted for more than four centuries. During this time, many European crops were less abundant or failed to grow. Hunger and malnutrition were widespread, and full-scale famine struck in some areas. Another consequence of population growth was deforestation resulting from increased human demand for wood to use as fuel and building materials. Deforestation also deprived peasants of wild foods and game (whose food sources disappeared with deforestation), accelerating the exodus of rural Europeans to towns and cities.

European towns were numerous but small, typically with several thousand inhabitants each. A great metropolis like London, whose population ballooned from fifty-five thousand in 1550 to two hundred thousand in 1600, was quite exceptional. But all towns were dirty and disease-ridden, and townspeople lived close-packed with their neighbors.

Unappealing as sixteenth-century towns might seem today, many men and women preferred them to the villages and tiny farms they left behind. Immigration from the countryside—rather than an excess of births over deaths—accounted for towns' expansion. Most people who flocked into towns remained at the bottom of the social order as servants or laborers and could not accumulate enough money to marry and live independently.

The consequences of rapid population growth were particularly acute in England, where the number of people doubled from about 2.5 million in 1500 to 5 million in 1620. As throughout western Europe, prices rose while wages fell during the sixteenth and early seventeenth centuries, widening the gap between rich and poor. Although English entrepreneurs expanded textile production by assembling spinners and weavers in household workshops, the workers were competing for fewer jobs in the face of growing competition that was diminishing European markets for English cloth. Enclosures of common lands severely aggravated unemployment, forcing large numbers of people to wander the country in search of work. To the upper and middle classes, these poor vagabonds seemed to threaten law and order. To control them, Parliament passed Poor Laws that ordered vagrants whipped and sent home, but most offenders only moved on to other towns. Some English writers, such as two men (cousins) named Richard Hakluyt, viewed overseas colonies as places where the unemployed, landless poor could find opportunity, thereby enriching their countries rather than draining resources.

As in America and Africa, traditional society in Europe rested on maintaining long-term, reciprocal relationships. European reciprocity required the upper classes to act with self-restraint and dignity, and the lower classes to show deference to their "betters." It also demanded strict economic regulation to ensure that no purchaser paid more than a "just price"—one that permitted a seller a "reasonable" profit but that barred him from taking advantage of buyers' and borrowers' misfortunes to make "excessive" profits.

Yet for several centuries Europeans had been compromising the ideals of traditional economic behavior. "In the Name of God and of Profit," thirteenth-century Italian merchants had written on their ledgers. By the sixteenth century, nothing could stop lenders' profiting from interest on borrowed money or sellers' raising prices in response to demand. New forms of business organization slowly spread in the commercial world—especially the **joint-stock company,** a business corporation that amassed capital through sales of stock to investors. Demand rose for capital investment, and so did the supply of accumulated wealth. A new economic outlook gradually took form that justified the unimpeded acquisition of wealth and insisted that individuals owed one another nothing but the money necessary to settle their transactions. This new outlook, the central value system of capitalism or the "market economy," rejected traditional demands that economic activity be regulated in order to ensure social reciprocity and maintain "just prices."

Sixteenth- and seventeenth-century Europeans therefore held conflicting attitudes toward economic enterprise and social change, and their ambivalence remained unresolved. A restless desire for fresh opportunity kept European life simmering with competitive tension. But those who prospered still sought the security and prestige provided by high social status, whereas the poor longed for the age-old values that would restrain irresponsible greed.

Perhaps the most sensitive barometer of social change was the family. Throughout Europe the typical household consisted of a small nuclear family—two parents and several children—in which the husband and father functioned as a head whose authority was not to be questioned. The role of the wife and mother was to bear and rear children as well as assist her husband in providing for the family's subsistence. Children were regarded as potential laborers who would assist in these tasks until they left home to start their own families. The household, then, was not only a family of intimately related people but also the principal economic unit in European society. Peasants on their tiny farms, artisans and merchants in their shops, and even nobles in their castles all lived and worked in households. People who did not live with their own families resided as dependents in the households of others as servants, apprentices, or relatives. Europeans regarded those who lived outside family-based households with extreme suspicion, often accusing them of crime or even witchcraft.

Europeans frequently characterized the nuclear family as a "little commonwealth." A father's authority over his family supposedly mirrored God's rule over Creation and the king's over his subjects. Even grown sons and daughters regularly knelt for their father's blessing. The ideal, according to a German writer, was that "wives should obey their husbands and not seek to dominate them; they must manage the home efficiently. Husbands . . . should treat their wives with consideration and occasionally close an eye to their faults." In practice, the father's sovereignty often had to make room for the wife's responsibility in managing family affairs and helping to run the farm or the workshop. Repeated male complaints, such as that of an English author in 1622 about wives "who think themselves every way as good as their husbands, and no way inferior to them," suggest that male domination had its limits.

| Religious Upheavals | Although Europe was predominantly Christian in 1400, it was also home to significant numbers of Muslims and Jews. Ad- |

herents to these three religious traditions worshiped a single supreme being, based on the God of the Hebrew Bible. While they often coexisted peacefully in lands bordering the Mediterranean, hatred and violence also marked their shared history. For more than three centuries, European Christians had conducted numerous Crusades against Muslims in Europe and the Middle East, and Muslims retaliated with "holy war." Each side labeled the other "infidels." Eventually, the participation of rulers transformed the religious conflicts into wars of conquest. While the Islamic Ottoman Empire seized Christian strongholds in the eastern Mediterranean, the Catholic monarchies of Portugal and Spain undertook a "reconquest" of the Iberian Peninsula by conquering Muslim states and expelling or forcibly converting non-Christians. Portugal was entirely Christian by 1250. As part of its national consolidation (discussed above), Spain in 1492 drove the last Muslim rulers from Iberia and expelled all Jews who refused to convert to Catholicism.

Following the Spanish Reconquest, the Roman Catholic Church dominated western and central Europe. Nevertheless, older, non-Christian beliefs persisted. Many Europeans feared witches and thought that individuals could manipulate nature by invoking unseen spiritual powers—that is, by magic. Others looked to astrology, insisting that a person's fate depended on the conjunction of various planets and stars. Such beliefs in spiritual forces not originating with a supreme deity resembled those of Native Americans and non-Muslim Africans.

Like Orthodox Christians in eastern Europe and the Middle East, Catholics believed that Jesus Christ, God's Son, had redeemed sinners by suffering crucifixion and rising from the dead. Equally vivid was Catholics' belief in the devil, Satan, whom God had hurled from heaven soon after the Creation and who ceaselessly lured people to damnation by tempting them to do evil.

The Catholic Church taught that Christ's sacrifice was repeated every time a priest said Mass, and that divine grace flowed to sinners through the sacraments that priests alone could administer—above all, baptism, confession, and the Eucharist (communion). The Church was a vast network of clergymen and religious orders, male and female, set apart from laypeople by the fact that its members did not marry. At the top was the pope, the "vicar [representative] of Christ" on earth.

Besides conducting services, priests heard the confessions of repentant sinners and assigned them penance, most often in the form of devotional exercises and good works that would demonstrate repentance. During the Middle Ages, the Church gradually assumed the authority to grant extra blessings, or "indulgences," to repentant sinners. Indulgences promised cancellation both of penance and of time in purgatory, where the dead atoned for sins they had already confessed and been forgiven. (Hell, from which there was no escape, awaited those who died unforgiven.) Given Catholics' anxieties about sinful behavior, indulgences were enormously popular. By the early sixteenth century, many religious authorities granted them in return for such "good works" as donating money to the Church. The jingle of one enterprising German friar promised that

> As soon as the coin in the cash box rings,
> The soul from purgatory's fire springs.

The sale of indulgences provoked charges that the materialism and corruption infecting economic life had spread to the Church. In 1517 a German monk, Martin Luther (1483–1546), openly attacked the practice. When the pope censured him, Luther broadened his criticism to encompass the Mass, purgatory, priests, and the papacy. After Luther refused to recant, the Roman Church excommunicated him. Luther's revolt initiated what became known as the **Protestant Reformation,** which changed Christianity forever. (The word *Protestant* comes from the *protest* of Luther's princely supporters against the anti-Lutheran policies of Holy Roman Emperor Charles V.)

To Luther, indulgence selling and similar examples of clerical corruption were evil not just because they bilked people. The Church, he charged, gave people false confidence that they could earn salvation simply by doing good works. His own agonizing search for salvation had convinced Luther that God bestowed salvation not on the basis of worldly deeds, but solely to reward a believer's faith. "I did not love a just and angry God," recalled Luther, ". . . until I saw the connection between the justice of God and the [New Testament] statement that 'the just shall live [be saved] by faith.' . . . Thereupon I felt myself to be reborn." Luther's spiritual struggle and experience of being "reborn" constituted a classic conversion experience—the heart of Protestant Christianity.

Other Protestant reformers followed Luther in breaking from Catholicism, most notably John Calvin (1509–1564), who fled his native France for Geneva, Switzerland. Whereas Luther stressed faith in Christ as the key to salvation, Calvin insisted on the stark doctrine of **predestination.** Calvin asserted that an omnipotent God predestined most sinful humans to hell, saving only a few in order to demonstrate his power and grace. It was only these few, called the "elect," "godly," or "saints," who would have a true conversion experience. At this moment, said Calvin, a person confronted the horrifying truth of his or her unworthiness and felt God's transcending power. A good Christian, in Calvin's view, would never be absolutely certain that he or she was saved and could do nothing to affect the outcome. But good Christians would be pious and avoid sin because they knew that godly behavior was a sign (not a cause and not a guarantee) of salvation.

Calvinists and Lutherans, as the followers of the two Reformation leaders came to be called, were equally horrified by more radical Protestants such as the Anabaptists, who appealed strongly to women and common people with their criticisms of the rich and powerful and sought to restrict baptism to "converted" adults. Judging the Anabaptists a threat to the social order, governments and mainstream churches persecuted them.

But Protestants also shared much common ground. For one thing, they denied that God had endowed priests with special powers. The church, Luther claimed, was a "priesthood of all believers." Protestant reformers insisted that laypeople take responsibility for their own spiritual and moral conditions. Accordingly, they placed a high value on reading. Protestants demanded that the Bible be translated from Latin into spoken languages so that believers could read it for themselves. The new faith was spread by the recently invented printing press. Wherever Protestantism became established, basic education and religious indoctrination followed. Finally, Protestantism represented a yearning in many people for the simplicity and purity of the ancient Christian church. More forcefully than Catholicism, it (initially) condemned the replacement of traditional reciprocity by marketplace values. Protestantism's greatest appeal was to all those—ordinary individuals, merchants, and aristocrats alike—who brooded over their chances for salvation and valued the steady performance of duty.

In the face of the Protestant challenge, Rome was far from idle. Reformers like Teresa of Ávila (1515–1582), a Spanish nun from a *converso* (converted Jewish) family, urged members of Catholic holy orders to repudiate corruption and to lead the Church's renewal by living piously and austerely. Another reformer, Ignatius Loyola (1491–1556), founded a militant religious order, the Society of Jesus, whose members (Jesuits) would distinguish themselves in coming centuries as royal advisers and missionaries. The high point of Catholic reform came during the Council of Trent (1545–1563), convened by the pope. The council defended Catholic teachings and denounced those of the Protestants. But it also reformed Church administration in order to combat corruption and broaden public participation in religious observances. This revival, the **Catholic** or **Counter-Reformation,** brought the modern Roman Catholic Church into existence.

The Protestant Reformation changed the religious map of Europe. Lutheranism became the state religion in the Scandinavian countries, while Calvinism made significant inroads in France, the Netherlands (which a royal marriage had brought under Spanish rule), England, and Scotland. The tiny states comprising the modern nations of Germany and Switzerland were divided among Catholics, Lutherans, and Calvinists.

| The Reformation in England, 1533–1625 | England's Reformation began not with the writings of a theologian or with cries of the people, but with the actions of a king and Parliament. King Henry VIII (ruled 1509–1547) |

wanted a male heir, but his queen, Catherine of Aragon, failed to bear a son. Henry asked the pope to annul his marriage, but the pope refused. Frustrated and determined, Henry persuaded Parliament to pass a series of acts in 1533–1534 dissolving his marriage and proclaiming him supreme head of the **Church of England** (or Anglican Church). The move justified Henry's seizure of income-producing Catholic Church properties, further consolidating royal power and financial independence.

Religion remained a source of conflict in England for more than a century after Henry's break with Rome. Under Edward VI (ruled 1547–1553), Henry's son by the third of his six wives, the church veered sharply toward Calvinism. Edward's sister and successor, Mary I (ruled 1553–1558), tried to restore Catholicism, in part by burning several hundred Protestants at the stake.

The reign of Elizabeth I (ruled 1558–1603), a half-sister of Edward and Mary, marked a crucial turning point. After the reign of "Bloody Mary," most English people were ready to become Protestant; *how* Protestant was the divisive question. Elizabeth took a middle road by affirming the monarch's role as head of the Anglican hierarchy of archbishops, bishops, and parish priests while endorsing the Calvinist belief in predestination. She also allowed individuals and parish churches wide latitude in deciding which customs and practices to follow.

Militant Calvinists, whose opponents derisively called them **"Puritans,"** demanded a more thorough purification of the Church of England from "popish [Catholic] abuses." Puritans insisted that membership in a congregation be limited to those who had had a conversion experience and that each congregation be independent of other congregations and of the Anglican hierarchy (body of ranked officials). Thus, they repudiated the Anglican (and Catholic) practices of extending membership to anyone who had been baptized and of subordinating congregations to the authority of priests, bishops, archbishops, and the head of the church (the monarch). Some "nonseparating" Puritans remained within the Church of England, hoping to reform it. Others, called Separatists, withdrew, insisting that a "pure" church had to be entirely free of Anglican "pollution."

The severe self-discipline and moral uprightness of Puritans appealed to few among the nobility and the poor. Puritanism appealed primarily to the small but growing number of people in the "middling" ranks of English society—landowning gentry, yeomen (small independent farmers), merchants, shopkeepers, artisans, and university-educated clergy and intellectuals. Self-discipline had become central to both the secular and spiritual dimensions of these people's lives. From their ranks, and particularly from among farmers, artisans, and clergy, would later come the settlers of New England (see Chapter 3).

Elizabeth distrusted Puritan militancy; but, after 1570 when the pope declared her a heretic and urged Catholics to overthrow her, she regarded English Catholics as even more dangerous. Thereafter, she courted influential Puritans and embraced militant anti-Catholicism.

Although opposed by Elizabeth, most Puritans still hoped to transform the Church of England into independent congregations of "saints." But her successor, James I (ruled 1603–1625), a distant cousin of Elizabeth who was king of Scotland, bitterly opposed Puritan calls to eliminate Anglican bishops. He made clear that he saw Puritan attacks on bishops as a threat to the throne when he snapped, "No bishop, no king." But while James insisted on outward conformity to Anglican practice, he tolerated Calvinists who did not publicly proclaim their dissent.

EUROPE AND THE ATLANTIC WORLD, 1400–1600

The forces transforming Europe quickly reverberated beyond that continent. During the fifteenth and sixteenth centuries, the alliances of merchants and dynastic monarchs organized imperial ventures to Africa, Asia, and the Americas. Besides seeking wealth and power, expanding Europeans proclaimed it their mission to introduce Christianity and "civilization" to the "savages" and "pagans" of alien lands. Two prominent outcomes of the new imperialism were a transatlantic slave trade and the colonization of the Americas. The multiple exchanges that resulted gave rise to a new Atlantic world.

Portugal and the Atlantic, 1400–1500

During the fifteenth century, some European merchants recognized that they could enhance their profits by circumventing costly Mediterranean-overland trade routes to and from Asia and Africa. Instead they hoped to establish direct contacts with sources of prized imports via the seas. Tiny Portugal led the way in overcoming impediments to long-distance oceanic travel.

Important changes in maritime technology occurred in the early fifteenth century. Shipbuilders and mariners along Europe's stormy Atlantic coast added the triangular Arab sail to their heavy cargo ships. They created a more maneuverable vessel, the caravel, which sailed more easily against the wind. Sailors also mastered the compass and astrolabe, by which they got their bearings on the open sea. Without this maritime revolution, European exploration would have been impossible.

Renaissance scholars' readings of ancient texts enabled fifteenth-century Europeans to look at their world with new eyes. The great ancient Greek authority on geography was Ptolemy, but Renaissance cartographers corrected his data when they tried to draw accurate maps based on recent European and Arabic observations. Thus, Renaissance "new learning" helped sharpen Europeans' geographic sense.

Led by Prince Henry "the Navigator" (1394–1460), Portugal was the first nation to capitalize on these developments. Henry gained the support of merchants seeking to circumvent Moroccan control of the African-European gold trade and of religious zealots eager to confront Muslim power. Henry encouraged Portuguese seamen to pilot the new caravels southward along the African coast, mastering the Atlantic's currents while searching for opportunities to trade or raid profitably. By the time of Henry's death, Portugal was exporting substantial quantities of gold and slaves from south of the Sahara. By then they were also in a position to expand their vision of a trading empire beyond Africa. In 1488 Bartolomeu Días reached the Cape of Good Hope at Africa's southern tip. A decade later Vasco da Gama led a Portuguese fleet around the Cape of Good Hope and on to India.

Although the Portuguese did not destroy older Euro-Asian commercial links, they showed western Europeans a way around Africa to Asia. In the process, they brought Europeans face-to-face with West Africans and an already flourishing slave trade.

The "New Slavery" and Racism

Slavery was well established in fifteenth-century Africa. The institution took two basic forms. Many Africans were enslaved because of indebtedness. Their debts were purchased by kings and emperors who made them servants or by families seeking additional laborers. They or their children were either absorbed into their new families over time or released from bondage when their debts were considered paid off through their work. But a long-distance commercial trade in slaves also flourished. For several centuries, Middle Eastern and North African traders had furnished local rulers with a range of fine, imported products in exchange for black laborers. Some of these slaves had been debtors, while others were captured in raids and wars.

One fifteenth-century Italian who witnessed Portuguese and Muslim slave trading noted that the Arabs "have many Berber horses, which they trade, and take to the Land of the Blacks, exchanging them with the rulers for slaves. Ten or fifteen slaves are given for one of these horses, according to their quality." Portuguese traders quickly realized how lucrative the trade in slaves could be for them, too. The same Italian observer continued, "Slaves are brought to the market town of Hoden; there they are divided. . . . [Some] are taken . . . and sold to the Portuguese leaseholders [in Arguin]. As a result every year the Portuguese carry away . . . a thousand slaves."

Although in 1482 the Portuguese built one outpost, Elmina, on West Africa's Gold Coast, they primarily traded through African-controlled commercial networks. Often Portuguese merchants traded slaves and local products to other Africans for gold. The local African kingdoms were too strong for the Portuguese to attack, and African rulers traded—or chose not to trade—according to their own self-interest.

Despite preventing the Portuguese from directly colonizing them, West African societies were profoundly affected by the new Atlantic slave trade. Portuguese traders enriched favored African rulers not only with luxury products but also with guns. As a result, they exacerbated conflicts among African communities and helped redraw the political map of West Africa. In Guinea and Senegambia, where most sixteenth-century slaves came from, small kingdoms expanded to "service" the trade. Some of their rulers became comparatively rich. Farther south, the kings of Kongo used the slave trade to expand their regional power and voluntarily adopted Christianity, just as rulers farther north had converted to Islam. Kongo flourished until the mid-sixteenth century, when a series of internal rebellions weakened it.

Although slavery had long been practiced in many parts of the Eastern Hemisphere, including in Europe, there were ominous differences between these older practices and the **"new slavery"** initiated by Portugal and later adopted by other western Europeans. First, the unprecedented magnitude of the trade resulted in a demographic catastrophe for West Africa and its peoples. Before the Atlantic slave trade finally ended in the nineteenth century, nearly 12 million Africans would be shipped in terrible conditions across the sea. Slavery on this scale had been unknown to Europeans since the collapse of the Roman Empire. Second, African slaves were subjected to new extremes of dehumanization. In medieval Europe and in West Africa itself, most slaves had lived in their masters' households and primarily performed domestic service. Africans shipped to Arab lands endured harsher conditions, but were nevertheless regarded as humans. But by 1450 the Portuguese and Spanish created large slave-labor plantations on their Atlantic and Mediterranean islands (see Technology and Culture: Sugar Production in the Americas). These plantations produced sugar for European markets, using capital supplied by Italian investors to buy African slaves who toiled until death. In short, Africans enslaved by Europeans were regarded as property rather than as persons of low status; as such, they were consigned to labor that was unending, exhausting, and mindless. By 1600 the "new slavery" had become a central, brutal component of the Atlantic world.

Finally, race became the ideological basis of the new slavery. Africans' blackness, along with their alien religions and customs, dehumanized them in European eyes. As their racial prejudice hardened, Europeans justified enslaving blacks as their Christian duty. From the fifteenth century onward, European Christianity made few attempts to soften slavery's rigors, and race defined a slave. Slavery became a lifelong, hereditary, and despised status.

To America and Beyond, 1492–1522

Europeans' varying motivations for expanding their horizons converged in the fascinating, contradictory figure of Christopher Columbus (1451–1506), the son of a weaver from the Italian port of Genoa. Columbus's maritime experience, self-taught geographical learning, and keen imagination led him to conclude that Europeans could reach Asia more directly by sailing westward across the Atlantic rather than around Africa and across the Indian Ocean. By the early 1480s, he was obsessed with this idea. Religious fervor led Columbus to dream of carrying Christianity around the globe and liberating Jerusalem from Muslim rule, but he also burned with ambition to win wealth and glory.

Columbus was not the first European to cross the Atlantic. Besides the early Norse (see Chapter 1), English fishermen in the North Atlantic may already have landed on the North American coast. But these efforts did not attract the attention of powerful rulers eager for wealth. Columbus was unique in the persistence with which he hawked his "enterprise of the Indies" around the royal courts of western Europe. John II of Portugal showed interest until Días's discovery of the Cape of Good Hope confirmed a sure way to the Indies. Finally, in 1492, hoping to break Portugal's threatened monopoly on direct trade with Asia, Queen Isabella and King Ferdinand of Spain accepted Columbus's offer. Picking up the westward-blowing trade winds at the Canary Islands, Columbus's three small ships reached Guanahaní within a month. After his meeting with the Tainos there, he sailed on in search of gold, making additional contacts with Tainos in Cuba (which he thought was Japan) and Hispaniola, the Caribbean island today occupied by Haiti and the Dominican Republic. Finding gold on Hispaniola, he returned to Spain to tell Isabella and Ferdinand about his discovery.

Returning to Hispaniola to found a colony, Columbus proved to be a poor administrator. Although he made two more voyages (1498–1502), he was shunted aside and died an embittered man, convinced that he had reached the threshold of Asia only to be cheated of his rightful rewards.

Meanwhile, word of Columbus's discovery caught Europeans' imaginations. To forestall competition between them as well as potential rivals, Isabella and Portugal's King John II in 1494 signed the Treaty of Tordesillas. The treaty drew a line in the mid-Atlantic dividing all future discoveries between Spain and Portugal.

Ignoring the Treaty of Tordesillas, England attempted to join the race for Asia in 1497 when Henry VII (ruled 1485–1509), sent an Italian navigator, John Cabot, to explore the North Atlantic. Sailing past Nova Scotia, Newfoundland, and the rich Grand Banks fisheries, Cabot claimed everything he saw and the lands beyond them for England. But England failed to follow up on Cabot's voyage for another sixty years.

The more Europeans explored, the more apparent it became that a vast landmass blocked the route to Asia. In 1500, a Portuguese voyage headed for India accidentally stumbled on Brazil (much of which lay, unexpectedly, east of the line established in the Treaty of Tordesillas). Other voyages soon revealed a continuous coastline from the Caribbean to Brazil. In 1507, this landmass got its name when a publisher brought out a collection of voyagers' tales. One of the chroniclers was an Italian named Amerigo Vespucci. With a shrewd marketing touch, the publisher devised a catchy name for the new continent: America.

Getting past America and reaching Asia remained the early explorers' primary aim. In 1513, the Spaniard Vasco Núñez de Balboa came upon the Pacific Ocean when he crossed the narrow isthmus of Panama. Then in 1519 the Portuguese Ferdinand

Magellan, sailing for Spain, began a voyage around the world by way of the stormy straits (later named for him) at South America's southern tip. In an incredible feat of endurance, he crossed the Pacific to the Philippines, only to die fighting with local natives. One of his five ships and fifteen emaciated sailors finally returned to Spain in 1522, the first people to have sailed around the world.

Spain's Conquistadors, 1492–1536

Columbus was America's first slave trader and the first Spanish conqueror, or conquistador. At his struggling colony on Hispaniola, he and the colonists who flocked there started the first American gold rush. Although fighting among themselves, they forced Native people to mine gold and supply the Spanish with food and other needs. After the crown took direct control of Hispaniola, Spain extended the search for gold to nearby islands, establishing new colonies at Puerto Rico (1508), Jamaica (1510), and Cuba (1511).

Tainos and other Native Americans in the Caribbean colonies died off in shockingly large numbers from smallpox, measles, and other imported diseases. To replace the perishing Indians, the colonists began importing enslaved Africans to perform labor. Spanish missionaries who came to Hispaniola to convert Native Americans had sent back grim reports of Spanish exploitation of Indians. But while the missionaries deemed Native Americans potential Christians, they joined most other colonizers in condemning Africans as less than fully human and thereby beyond hope of redemption. Blacks could therefore be exploited without limit. In Cuba, Puerto Rico, and other islands, they were forced to perform backbreaking work on Spanish sugar plantations (see Technology and Culture: Sugar Production in the Americas).

Meanwhile, Spanish colonists fanned out even farther in search of Indian slaves and gold. In 1519, a restless nobleman, Hernán Cortés (1485–1547), led six hundred troops to the Mexican coast. Destroying his boats, he enlisted the support of enemies and discontented subjects of the Aztecs (see Chapter 1) in a quest to conquer that empire. Besides military support, Cortés gained the services of Malintzin (or Malinche), later known as Doña Marina, an Aztec woman brought up among the Maya. Malintzin served as Cortés's interpreter, diplomatic broker, and mistress.

Upon reaching the Aztec capital of Tenochtitlán, the Spanish were stunned by its size and wealth. "We were amazed and said that it was like the enchantments they tell of [in stories], and some of our soldiers even asked whether the things that we saw were not a dream," recalled one soldier. Certainly, the golden gifts that the Aztec emperor, Moctezuma II (ruled 1502–1520), initially offered the invaders were no dream. "They picked up the gold and fingered it like monkeys," one Aztec recalled. "Their bodies swelled with greed, and their hunger was ravenous. They hungered like pigs for that gold."

The Spanish ignored Moctezuma's offer, raiding his palace and treasury, and melting down all the gold they could find. Despite their emperor's imprisonment, the Aztecs regrouped and drove the invaders from the city, killing three hundred Spanish and four thousand of their Indian allies before Spanish reinforcements arrived from Cuba. The Aztecs' defeat was ensured by a smallpox epidemic the Spanish brought with them, the same one that was killing large numbers of Indians on Hispaniola and the other islands. Lacking any previous contact with the disease, the Aztecs' and other Indians' immune systems were ill equipped to resist it. Just when the Aztecs took back Tenochtitlán, the epidemic struck. When the Spanish finally recaptured the city, wrote

Sugar Production in the Americas

Beginning with Christopher Columbus's first expedition, organisms ranging from bacteria to human beings crossed the Atlantic in both directions. This Columbian exchange had wide-ranging ecological, economic, political, and cultural consequences for the lands and peoples of the Americas, Africa, and Europe. One significant set of consequences arose from the transfer of Mediterranean sugar production to the Americas. Out of this transfer came the single-crop plantation system, based on enslaved African labor, and a new consumer product that revolutionized diets and, quite literally, taste in Europe and its colonies.

Domesticated in New Guinea before 8000 B.C., sugar cane was one of the earliest wild plants harvested by human beings. By 350 B.C., sugar was an ingredient in several dishes favored by elites in India, from where it spread to the Mediterranean world. It became a significant commodity in the Mediterranean in the eighth century A.D. when expanding Arabs carried it as far west as Spain and Morocco. The Mediterranean would remain the center of sugar production for Europe over the next seven centuries.

The basic process of making sugar from the sugar cane plant changed little over time. (Sugar made from sugar beets did not become widespread until the nineteenth century.) The earliest producers discovered that one of the six species of cane, Saccharum officinarum, produced the most sugar in the shortest span of time. The optimal time for harvesting was when the cane had grown twelve to fifteen feet in height, with stalks about two inches thick. At this point, it was necessary to extract the juice from the plant and then the sucrose (a carbohydrate) from the juice as quickly as possible or risk spoilage. Sugar makers crushed the cane fibers in order to extract the liquid, which they then heated so that it evaporated, leaving the sucrose—or sugar—in the form of crystals or molasses, depending on its temperature.

Sugar production was central to the emerging Atlantic world during the fifteenth century, after Spanish and Portuguese planters established large sugar plantations in the Madeira, Canary, and Cape Verde islands off Africa's Atlantic coast. Initially, the islands' labor force included some free Europeans, but enslaved Africans soon predominated. The islands were the birthplace of the European colonial plantation system. Planters focused entirely on the production of a single export crop and sought to maximize profits by minimizing labor costs. Although some planters used servants, the largest-scale, most profitable plantations imported slaves and worked them as hard as possible until they died. Utilizing such methods, the island planters soon outstripped the production of older sugar makers in the Mediterranean. By 1500 the Spanish and Portuguese had successfully tapped new markets across Europe, especially among the wealthy classes.

On his second voyage in 1493, Columbus took a cargo of sugar from the Canaries to Hispaniola. Early efforts by Spanish colonists to produce sugar failed because they lacked efficient milling technology, because the Taino Indians were dying so quickly from epidemic diseases, and because most colonists concentrated on mining gold. But as miners quickly exhausted Hispaniola's limited gold, the enslaved Africans brought to work in the mines became available for sugar production. In 1515 a planter named Gonzalo de Vellosa hired some experienced sugar masters from the Canaries who urged him to import a more efficient type of mill. The mill featured two vertical rollers that could be powered by either animals or water, through which laborers passed the cane in order to crush it. With generous subsidies from the Spanish crown, the combination of vertical-roller mills and slave labor led to a rapid proliferation of sugar plantations in Spain's island colonies, with some using as many as five hundred slaves. But when Spain discovered gold and silver in Mexico and the Andes, its interest in sugar declined almost as rapidly as it had arisen.

Originally discovered by accident (see above), Portugal's colony of Brazil emerged as the major source of sugar in the sixteenth century. Here, too, planters established the system of large plantations and enslaved Africans. By 1526, Brazil was exporting shiploads of sugar annually, and before the end of the century it supplied most of the sugar consumed in Europe. Shortly after 1600 Brazilian planters either invented or imported a three-roller mill that increased production still further and became the Caribbean standard for several more centuries. Portugal's sugar monopoly proved short-lived. Between 1588 and 1591, English privateers captured and diverted thirty-four sugar-laden vessels during their nation's war with Spain and Portugal. In 1630 the Netherlands seized Brazil's prime sugar-producing region and increased annual production to a century-high 30,000 tons. Ten years later some Dutch sugar and slave traders, seeking to expand their activity, shared

the technology of sugar production with English planters in Barbados, who were looking for a new crop following disappointing profits from tobacco and cotton. The combination of sugar and slaves took hold so quickly that, within three years, Barbados's annual output rose to 150 tons.

Sugar went on to become the economic heart of the Atlantic economy (see Chapter 3). Its price dropped so low that even many poor Europeans could afford it. As a result, sugar became central to European diets as they were revolutionized by the Columbian exchange. Like tobacco, coffee, and several other products of the exchange, sugar and such sugar products as rum, produced from molasses, proved habit-forming, making sugar even more attractive to profit-seeking planters and merchants.

More than any other single commodity, sugar sustained the early slave trade in the Americas, facilitating slavery's spread to tobacco, rice, indigo, and other plantation crops as well as to domestic service and other forms of labor. Competition between British and French sugar producers in the West Indies later fueled their nations' imperial rivalry (see Chapter 4) and eventually led New England's merchants to resist British imperial controls—a resistance that helped prepare the way for the American Revolution (see Chapter 5).

Questions for Analysis

- What role did Spain's and Portugal's island colonies play in revolutionizing sugar production?

- How did developments in mill technology interact with other factors to make sugar the most profitable crop in the Americas?

one Spanish chronicler, "the streets were so filled with dead and sick people that our men walked over nothing but bodies." In striking down other Indians, friends as well as foes, the epidemic enabled the Spanish to consolidate their control over much of central Mexico. By 1521, Cortés had overthrown the Aztecs and began to build a Spanish capital, Mexico City, on the ruins of Tenochtitlán.

Over the remainder of the sixteenth century, other conquistadors and officials established a great Spanish empire stretching from New Spain (Mexico) southward to Chile. The most important of these later conquests was that of the Inca empire (see Chapter 1) between 1532 and 1536 by a second reckless conquistador, Francisco Pizarro (c. 1478–1541). As with the Aztecs, smallpox and native unfamiliarity with European ways and weapons enabled a small army to overpower a mighty emperor and his realm. The human cost of the Spanish conquest was enormous.

> Broken spears lie in the roads;
> We have torn our hair in our grief.
> The houses are roofless now . . .
> And the walls are splattered with gore . . .
> We have pounded our hands in despair
> Against the adobe walls.

When Cortés landed in 1519, central Mexico's population had been between 13 and 25 million. By 1600, it had shrunk to about seven hundred thousand. Peru and other regions experienced similar devastation. America had witnessed the greatest demographic disaster in world history.

The Columbian Exchange   The emerging Atlantic world linked not only peoples but also animals, plants, and germs from Europe, Africa, and the Americas in a **Columbian exchange.** After 1492, vast numbers of Native Americans died because they lacked antibodies that could resist infectious diseases brought by Europeans and Africans—especially deadly, highly communicable smallpox. From the first years of contact, epidemics scourged defenseless Indian communities. A Spanish observer estimated that the indigenous population of the West Indies declined from about 1 million in 1492 to just five hundred a half century later. Whole villages perished at once, with no one left to bury the dead. Such devastation directly facilitated European colonization everywhere in the Americas, whether accompanied by a military effort or not.

The biological encounter of the Eastern and Western Hemispheres affected the everyday lives of peoples throughout the Atlantic world. Besides diseases, sixteenth-century Europeans introduced horses, cattle, sheep, swine, chickens, wheat and other grains, coffee, sugar, numerous fruits and garden vegetables, and many species of weeds, insects, and rodents to America. In the next century, enslaved Africans carried rice and yams with them across the Atlantic. The list of American gifts to Europe and Africa was equally impressive: corn, many varieties of beans, white and sweet potatoes, tomatoes, squash, pumpkins, peanuts, vanilla, cacao (for making chocolate and cocoa), avocados, pineapples, chilis, tobacco, and turkeys. Often, several centuries passed before new plants became widely accepted. For example, many Europeans initially suspected that potatoes were aphrodisiacs and that tomatoes were poisonous.

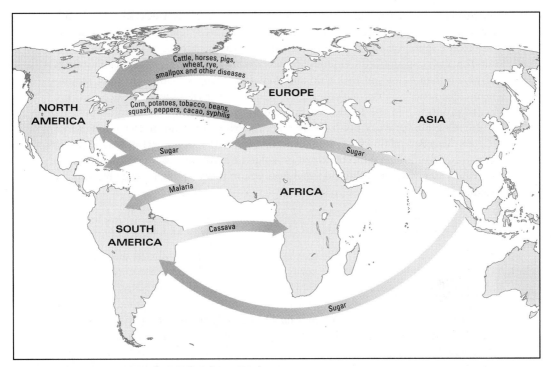

Map 2.1 Major Items in the Columbian Exchange

As European adventures traversed the world in the fifteenth and sixteenth centuries, they initiated the "Columbian Exchange" of plants, animals, and diseases. These events changed the lives of the people of the world forever, bringing new foods and new pestilence to both sides of the Atlantic.

European weeds and domestic animals drastically altered many American environments. Especially in temperate zones, livestock devoured indigenous plants, enabling hardier European weeds to take over. As a result, wild animals that had fed on the plants stayed away, depriving Indians of a critical source of food. Free-roaming livestock, especially hogs, also invaded Native Americans' cornfields. In this way, colonists' ways of life impinged directly on those of Native peoples. Settlers' crops, intensively cultivated on lands never replenished by lying fallow, often exhausted American soil. But the worldwide exchange of food products also enriched human diets and later made enormous population growth possible.

Another dimension of the Atlantic world was the mixing of peoples. During the sixteenth century, about three hundred thousand Spaniards immigrated, 90 percent of them male. Particularly in towns, a racially blended people emerged as these men married Indian women, giving rise to the large mestizo (mixed Spanish-Indian) population of Mexico and other Latin American countries. Lesser numbers of *métis*, as the French termed people of both Indian and European descent, would appear in the French and English colonies of North America. Throughout the Americas, particularly in plantation colonies, European men fathered mulatto children with enslaved African women, and African-Indian unions occurred in most regions. Colonial societies differed significantly in their official attitudes toward the different kinds of interracial unions and in their classifications of the children who resulted.

The Americas supplied seemingly limitless wealth for Spain. More important sources of wealth than Aztec and Inca gold and West Indian sugar plantations were the immense quantities of silver that crossed the Atlantic after rich mines in Mexico and Peru began producing in the 1540s. But Spanish kings squandered this wealth. Bent on dominating Europe, they needed ever more American silver to finance a long series of wars there. Several times they went bankrupt, and in the 1560s their efforts to squeeze more taxes from their subjects helped provoke the revolt of Spain's rich Netherlands provinces (see below). In the end, American wealth proved to be a mixed blessing for Spain.

FOOTHOLDS IN NORTH AMERICA, 1512–1625

Most European immigrants in the sixteenth century flocked to Mexico, the Caribbean, and points farther south. But a minority extended the Atlantic world to North America through exploratory voyages, fishing expeditions, trade with Native Americans, and piracy and smuggling. Except for a tiny Spanish base at St. Augustine, Florida, the earliest attempts to plant colonies failed, generally because they were predicated on unrealistic expectations of fabulous wealth and natives who would be easily conquered.

After 1600 the ravaging of Indian populations by disease and the rise of English, French, and Dutch power made colonization possible. By 1614, Spain, England, France, and the Netherlands had made often overlapping territorial claims and established North American footholds. Within another decade, each colony developed a distinct economic orientation and its own approach to Native Americans.

Spain's Northern Frontier The Spanish had built their American empire by subduing the Aztec, Inca, and other Indian states. The dream of more such finds drew would-be conquistadors northward to what would later be called Florida and New Mexico. "As it was his object to find another treasure like that . . . of Peru," a witness wrote of one such man, Hernando de Soto, he "would not be content with good lands nor pearls."

The earliest of these invaders was Juan Ponce de León, who had founded Puerto Rico. In 1513, he explored the coast of a peninsula he named "La Florida." Returning to Florida in 1521 to found a colony, Ponce de León's quest ended in death in a skirmish with Calusa Indians.

The most astonishing early expedition began in Florida in 1527. After provoking several attacks by Apalachee Indians, the three hundred explorers were separated into several parties. All were thought to have perished until eight years later, when four survivors, led by Alvar Nuñez Cabeza de Vaca and including an African slave, Esteban, arrived in northern Mexico. Cabeza de Vaca's account of their long journey, living in dozens of Native American communities, is the most compelling European literary work on North America before permanent colonization.

Cabeza de Vaca provided direct inspiration for two more formidable attempts at Spanish conquest. De Soto and his party in 1539–1543 blundered from Tampa Bay to the

Map 2.2 European Imperial Claims and Settlements in Eastern North America, 1565–1625

By 1625 four European nations contended for territory on North America's Atlantic coast. Except for St. Augustine, Florida, all settlements established before 1607 had been abandoned by 1625.

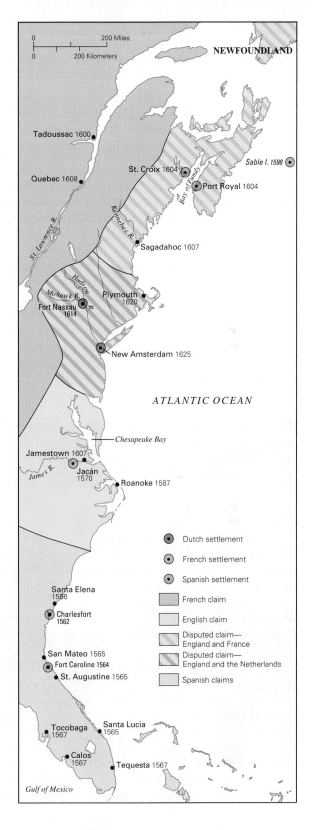

Appalachians to the southern Plains, scouring the land for gold and alienating Native people wherever they went. "Think, then," one Indian chief appealed to him vainly,

> what must be the effect on me and mine, of the sight of you and your people, whom we have at no time seen, astride the fierce brutes, your horses, entering with such speed and fury into my country, that we had no tidings of your coming—things so absolutely new, as to strike awe and terror into our hearts.

In 1540, a coalition of Native Americans gathered at the Mississippian city of Mábila to confront the invaders. Although victorious militarily, the expedition's own losses doomed the Spanish effort. Most of their horses died from arrow wounds while their livestock (their principal source of food aside from the corn they seized) scattered. Thereafter, the expedition floundered.

Although de Soto died without finding gold or extending Spanish rule, his and other expeditions spread epidemics that destroyed most of the remaining Mississippian societies (see Chapter 1). By the time Europeans returned to the southeastern interior late in the seventeenth century, only the Natchez on the lower Mississippi River still inhabited their sumptuous temple-mound center and remained under the rule of a Great Sun monarch. Depopulated groups like the Cherokees and Creeks had adopted the less-centralized village life of other eastern Indians.

Navajo View of Spanish Colonizers *This pictograph—a painting or drawing on rock—was sketched in the early colonial period in Cañón del Muerto, Arizona.*

Meanwhile Cabeza de Vaca had reported hearing of golden cities in the Southwest to Spanish officials in Mexico. In 1540–1542 Francisco Vásquez de Coronado led a massive expedition bent on finding and conquering these cities. Coronado plundered several pueblos on the Rio Grande and wandered from the Grand Canyon to present-day Kansas before returning to Mexico, finding no gold but embittering many Native Americans toward the Spanish. Other expeditions along the California coast and up the Colorado River likewise proved fruitless.

For several decades after these failed ventures, Spain's principal interest north of Mexico and the Caribbean lay in establishing strategic bases to keep out French and English intruders. In 1565, Spain established the first lasting European post in North America, a fortress at **St. Augustine, Florida.** Despite plans to strengthen Florida and to build a road with presidios (military forts) at key locations from there to Mexico, St. Augustine remained a lone military stronghold. It also served as a base for a chain of Catholic missions on the Florida peninsula and Atlantic coast as far northward as Chesapeake Bay. Rejecting missionary efforts to reorder their lives, the Guale, Powhatan, and other Indians rebelled and forced the closing of all the missions before 1600. Franciscan missionaries renewed their efforts in Florida in the early seventeenth century and secured the nominal allegiance of about sixteen thousand Guale and Timucua Indians. But epidemics in the 1610s killed about half the converts.

Meanwhile, in the 1580s, Spanish missionaries had returned to the Southwest, preaching Christianity and scouting the area's potential wealth. Encouraged by their reports, New Spain's viceroy in 1598 commissioned Juan de Oñate to lead five hundred Spaniards, mestizos, Mexican Indians, and African slaves into the upper Rio Grande Valley. They seized a pueblo of the Tewa Indians, renamed it San Juan, and proclaimed the royal colony of **New Mexico.**

The Spanish encountered swift resistance at the mesa-top pueblo of Ácoma in December 1598. When the Ácoma Indians refused Spanish demands for corn and other provisions, fifteen Spanish soldiers ascended the mesa to obtain the goods by force. But the natives resisted and killed most of the soldiers. Determined to make an example of Ácoma, Oñate ordered massive retaliation. In January, Spanish troops captured the pueblo, killing eight hundred inhabitants in the process. Oñate forced surviving men to have one foot cut off and, along with the women and children, to be servants of the soldiers and missionaries. Two prominent leaders also had their right hands amputated.

Despite having crushed Ácoma and imposed *encomiendas*—grants awarding Indian labor to wealthy colonists—on other Pueblo Indians, New Mexico barely survived. The Spanish government replaced Oñate in 1606 because of mismanagement and excessive brutality toward Native Americans, and seriously considered withdrawing from the Southwest altogether. Franciscan missionaries, aiming to save Pueblo Indian souls, persuaded the authorities to keep New Mexico alive. By 1630 Franciscans had been dispatched to more than fifty pueblos. Prompted by deadly epidemics and believing that Catholic rituals could be reconciled with traditional practices, a few thousand Indians accepted baptism. But resistance was common because, as the leading Franciscan summarized it, "the main and general answer given [by the Pueblos] for not becoming Christians is that when they do, . . . they are at once compelled to pay tribute and render personal service." New Mexico began, then, amidst uneasy tensions between colonists and natives.

France: Colonizing France entered the imperial competition in 1524 when King
Canada Francis I (ruled 1515–1547) dispatched an Italian navigator,
Giovanni da Verrazano, to find a more direct "northwest pas-
sage" to the Pacific. Verrazano explored the North American coast from the Carolinas
to Newfoundland. His several encounters with Native Americans ranged from violent
to friendly. In 1534 and 1535–1536, French explorer Jacques Cartier probed the coasts
of Newfoundland, Quebec, and Nova Scotia and sailed up the St. Lawrence River as far
as present-day Montreal. Although encountering large numbers of Native Americans
(some of whom called the land "kanata," or Canada), Cartier found neither gold nor a
northwest passage.

France made its first colonizing attempt in 1541 when Cartier returned to the St.
Lawrence Valley with ten ships carrying four hundred soldiers, three hundred sailors,
and a few women. Cartier had earned Native Americans' distrust during his previous
expeditions, and his construction of a fortified settlement on Stadacona Indian land
(near modern Quebec City) removed all possibility of friendly relations. Over the next
two years, the French suffered heavy losses from Stadacona attacks and harsh winters
before abandoning the colony.

The failed French expedition seemed to verify one Spaniard's opinion that "this
whole coast as far [south] as Florida is utterly unproductive." The next French effort at
colonization began in 1562 when French Huguenots (Calvinists) seeking religious freedom attempted to settle in Florida. In 1564, the Huguenots founded a settlement near
present-day Jacksonville. Sensing a Protestant threat to their control of the Caribbean,
Spanish forces destroyed the settlement a year later, executing all 132 male defenders.
These failures, along with a civil war in France itself between Catholics and Huguenots,
temporarily hindered France's colonizing efforts.

Meanwhile, French and other European fishermen were working the plenteous
Grand Banks fisheries off the coast of Newfoundland. Going ashore to dry their fish,
some sailors abused local Beothuk Indians, but others bartered with them for skins of
beaver. By the late sixteenth century, European demand for beaver hats was skyrocketing, and a French-dominated fur trade blossomed. Before the end of the century,
French traders were returning annually to sites from Newfoundland to New England
and along the lower St. Lawrence.

Unlike explorers such as de Soto and colonizers such as those at Roanoke (see below), most fur traders recognized the importance of reciprocity in dealing with Native
Americans. Consequently, they were generally more successful. In exchange for pelts,
they traded axes, knives, copper kettles, cloth, and glass beads. Usually dismissed by Europeans as "trinkets," glass beads were valued by northeastern Indians for possessing
spiritual power comparable to that of quartz, mica, and other sacred substances that
they had long obtained via trade networks (see Chapter 1). By the next century, specialized factories in Europe would be producing both cloth and glass for the "Indian trade."

Seeing the lucrative Canadian trade as a source of revenue, the French government
dispatched the explorer Samuel de Champlain to establish the colony of **New France**
at Quebec in 1608. The French concluded that a colony was the surest means of deter-
ring English, Dutch, and independent French competitors. Having previously explored
much of the Northeast and headed a small French settlement at Acadia (later Nova
Scotia), Champlain was familiar with Indian politics and diplomacy in the region.
Building on this understanding, he shrewdly allied with the Montagnais and Al-
gonquins of the St. Lawrence and the Hurons of the lower Great Lakes. He agreed to

help these allies defeat their enemies, the Mohawks of the Iroquois Confederacy, who sought direct access to European traders on the St. Lawrence. The Indians were equally shrewd in recognizing the advantage of having armed French allies when facing the dreaded Mohawks.

In July 1609 Champlain and two other Frenchmen accompanied sixty Montagnais and Huron warriors to Lake Champlain (which the explorer named for himself). Soon they encountered two hundred Mohawks at Point Ticonderoga near the lake's southern tip. After a night of mutual taunting, the two parties met on shore the following morning. As the main French-Indian column neared its opponents, Champlain stepped ahead and confronted the Mohawks' three spectacularly attired war leaders.

> When I saw them make a move to draw their bows upon us, I took aim with my arquebus [a kind of gun] and shot straight at one of the three chiefs, and with this same shot two fell to the ground, and one of their companions was wounded and died a little later. . . . As I was reloading my arquebus, one of my [French] companions fired a shot from within the woods, which astonished them again so much that, seeing their chiefs dead, they lost courage and took to flight.

The French and their allies pursued the fleeing Mohawks, killing about fifty and capturing a dozen prisoners. A few pro-French Indians suffered minor arrow wounds.

The battle at Lake Champlain marked the end of an era in Indian-European relations in the Northeast. Except in a few isolated places, casual encounters between small parties gave way to trade, diplomacy, and warfare coordinated by Indian and European governments. Through their alliance with the powerful Hurons and other Native American groups, the French gained access to the thick beaver pelts of the Canadian interior while providing their Indian allies with European goods and armed protection from Iroquois attacks. These economic and diplomatic arrangements, and Iroquois reactions (see below), defined the course of New France's history for the rest of the seventeenth century.

England and the Atlantic World, 1558–1603 When Elizabeth I became queen in 1558, Spain and France were grappling for supremacy in Europe, and England was a minor power. But largely Protestant England worried about Spain's suppression of Calvinists in the Netherlands and about the pope's call for Elizabeth's overthrow. Elizabeth adopted a militantly anti-Spanish foreign policy, with Anglicans and Puritans alike hailing England as an "elect nation" whose mission was to elevate "true" Christianity and to overthrow Catholicism, represented by Spain. Secretly, she stepped up her aid to Dutch Calvinists and encouraged English privateers (armed private ships), commanded by "sea dogs" like John Hawkins and Francis Drake, to attack Spanish ships.

The Anglo-Spanish rivalry in the Atlantic extended to Ireland after 1565, when Spain and the pope began directly aiding Irish Catholics' longtime resistance to English rule. In a war that ground on to the early seventeenth century, the English drove the Irish clans off their lands, especially in northern Ireland, or Ulster, and established their own settlements ("plantations") of English and Scottish Protestants. The English practiced "scorched earth" warfare to break the rebellious population's spirit, inflicting starvation and mass slaughter by destroying villages in the winter.

Elizabeth's generals justified these atrocities by claiming that the Irish were "savages" and that Irish customs, religion, and methods of fighting absolved the English

Roanoke Indian Town of Secota
Based on a water-color by John White, a member of the Roanoke expedition, this engraving celebrates the abundant crops and rich ceremonial life of the Roanoke Indians. Other English leaders took a dimmer view of the Native Americans.

from guilt in waging exceptionally cruel warfare. Ireland thus furnished precedents for later English tactics and rationales for crushing Native Americans.

England had two objectives in the Western Hemisphere in the 1570s. The first was to find the northwest passage to Asia and discover gold on the way; the second, in Drake's words, was to "singe the king of Spain's beard" by raiding Spanish fleets and ports. The search for the northwest passage led only to such embarrassments as explorer Martin Frobisher's voyages to the Canadian Arctic. Frobisher returned with several thousand tons of an ore that looked like gold but proved worthless. However, privateering raids proved spectacularly successful and profitable for their financial backers, including merchants, gentry, government leaders, and Elizabeth herself. The most breathtaking enterprise was Drake's voyage around the world (1577–1580) in quest of sites for colonies. During this voyage, he sailed up the California coast and entered Drake's Bay, north of San Francisco, where he traded with Miwok Indians.

Now deadly rivals, Spain and England sought to outmaneuver one another in North America. In 1572, the Spanish tried to fortify a Jesuit mission on Chesapeake Bay. They failed, largely because Powhatan Indians resisted. In 1583, an English attempt to colonize Newfoundland (where Europeans from several nations fished annually) also failed. Sir Walter Raleigh obtained a royal patent (charter) in 1584 to start an English colony farther south, closer to the Spanish—a region the English soon named

Virginia in honor of their virgin queen. Raleigh sent Arthur Barlowe to explore the region, and Barlowe returned singing the praises of Roanoke Island, its peaceable natives, and its ideal location as a base for anti-Spanish privateers. Raleigh then persuaded Elizabeth to dispatch an expedition to found Roanoke colony.

At first all went well, but by winter, the English had outlived the Roanoke Indians' welcome. Fearing that the natives were about to attack, English soldiers killed Wingina, the Roanoke leader, in June 1586. When Drake visited soon after on his way back to England, many colonists joined him.

Thereafter, the Anglo-Spanish conflict repeatedly prevented English ships from returning to Roanoke to supply those who remained. When a party finally arrived in 1590, it found only rusty armor, moldy books, and the word *CROATOAN* cut into a post. Although the stranded colonists were presumably living among the Croatoan Indians of Cape Hatteras, the exact fate of the "lost colony" remains a mystery to this day.

In 1588, while Roanoke struggled, England won a spectacular naval victory over the Armada, a huge invasion fleet sent into the English Channel by Spain's Philip II. This famous victory preserved England's independence and confirmed its status as a major power in the Atlantic.

Failure and Success in Virginia, 1603–1625 Anglo-Spanish relations took a new turn after 1603, when Elizabeth died and James I succeeded her. The cautious, peace-loving James signed a truce with Spain in 1604. Alarmed by Dutch naval victories (see below), the Spanish now considered England the lesser danger. Consequently, Spain's new king, Philip III (ruled 1598–1621), conceded what his predecessors had always refused: a free hand to another power in part of the Americas. Spain renounced its claims to Virginia, allowing England to colonize unmolested.

The question of how to finance English colonies remained. Neither the crown nor Parliament would agree to spend money on colonies, and Roanoke's failure had proved that private fortunes were inadequate to finance successful settlements. Political and financial leaders determined that joint-stock companies could raise enough funds for American settlement. Such stock offerings produced large sums with limited risk for each investor.

In 1606, James I granted a charter authorizing overlapping grants of land to two separate joint-stock companies. The Virginia Company of Plymouth received a grant extending south from modern Maine to the Potomac River, while the Virginia Company of London's lands ran north from Cape Fear, North Carolina, to the Hudson River. Both companies dispatched colonists in 1607.

The Virginia Company of Plymouth sent 120 men to Sagadahoc, on the Maine coast. After bickering among themselves, alienating nearby Abenaki Indians, and enduring a hard New England winter, the colonists returned to England and the company was disbanded.

The Virginia Company of London barely avoided a similar failure. Its first expedition included many gentlemen who, considering themselves above manual work, expected Native Americans to feed them and riches to fall into their laps. Choosing a site on the James River, they called it Jamestown and formally named their colony **Virginia.** Discipline quickly fell apart, and, as at Roanoke, the colonists neglected to plant crops. The local Powhatan Indians had sold them some corn but, with their own supplies running low, declined to offer more. By December, the English were running out of food. As with Roanoke and numerous Spanish ventures, Virginia's military leader, Captain John Smith, led some soldiers in an attempt to seize corn from the Powhatans. After capturing Smith, the Powhatan *weroance* (chief), also named Powhatan, released the captain but did share some of his people's remaining supplies with the English. (Many years later, Smith would claim that Powhatan's ten-year-old-daughter, Pocahontas, saved him at the last minute from execution. Because Smith claimed to have been rescued in similar fashion by females on two other occasions during his military adventures, the story's accuracy is doubtful.)

Powhatan's gesture was intended to remind the English that his people were the stronger force and that reciprocity was preferable to force in their dealings with one another. In releasing Smith and giving him more corn, he expected the English to support him in return. In particular he hoped the newcomers would ally with the Powhatans against local Indian enemies.

Powhatan recognized the early Virginians' weaknesses. When relief ships arrived in January 1608 with reinforcements, only 38 survivors remained out of 105 immigrants. Virginia also lacked effective leadership. The council's first president hoarded supplies, and its second was lazy and indecisive. By September 1608, three councilors had died, and three others had returned to England, leaving Smith in complete charge of the colony.

Twenty-eight years old and of yeoman origin, Smith had experience fighting Spaniards and Turks that prepared him for assuming control in Virginia. Organizing all but the sick in work gangs, he ensured sufficient food and housing for winter. Applying lessons learned in his soldiering days, he laid down rules for maintaining sanitation and hygiene to limit disease. Above all, he brought order through military discipline. During the next winter (1608–1609), Virginia lost just a dozen men out of two hundred.

Smith prevented Virginia from disintegrating as Sagadahoc had. But when he returned to England in 1609 after being wounded in a gunpowder explosion, discipline again crumbled. Expecting the Indians to provide them with corn, the colonists had not laid away sufficient food for the winter. A survivor wrote,

> So lamentable was our scarcity, that we were constrained to eat dogs, cats, rats, snakes, toadstools, horsehides, and what not; one man out of the misery endured, killing his wife powdered her up [with flour] to eat her, for which he was burned. Many besides fed on the corpses of dead men.

Of the 500 residents at Jamestown in September 1609, about 400 died by May 1610. But an influx of new recruits, coupled with renewed military rule, enabled Virginia to recover and to assert its supremacy to the Powhatans. When Powhatan refused to submit to the new governor's authority, the colony waged the First Anglo-Powhatan War (1610–1614). After the English captured Powhatan's daughter, Pocahontas, and she converted to Christianity, the war ended when the aging weroance agreed that she could marry a colonist named John Rolfe. The English population remained small—just 380 in 1616—and had yet to produce anything of value for Virginia Company stockholders.

Tobacco emerged as Virginia's salvation. Rolfe spent several years adapting a salable variety of Caribbean tobacco to conditions in Virginia. In 1616, he and Pocahontas traveled to England, where his tobacco was received enthusiastically. (While there, Pocahontas contracted a respiratory disease and died.) By 1619, tobacco commanded high prices, and Virginia exported large amounts to a newly emergent European market.

To attract labor and capital to its suddenly profitable venture, the Virginia Company awarded a fifty-acre "headright" for each person ("head") entering the colony, to whoever paid that person's passage. By paying the passage of prospective laborers, some enterprising planters accumulated sizable tracts of land. Thousands of young men and a few hundred women calculated that uncertainty in Virginia was preferable to continued unemployment and poverty in England. In return for their passage and such basic needs as food, shelter, and clothing, they agreed to work as **indentured servants** for fixed terms, usually four to seven years.

The Virginia Company abandoned military rule in 1619 and provided for an assembly to be elected by the "inhabitants" (apparently meaning only the planters). Although the assembly's actions were subject to the company's veto, it was the first representative legislature in North America.

By 1622 Virginia faced three serious problems. First, local officials systematically defrauded the shareholders by embezzling treasury funds, overcharging for supplies, and using company laborers to work their own tobacco fields. They profited, but the company sank deep into debt. Second, the colony's population suffered from an appallingly high death rate. Most of the 3,500 immigrants entering Virginia from 1618 to 1622 died within three years, primarily from malnutrition or from salt poisoning, typhus, or dysentery contracted from drinking polluted water from the James River. Finally, relations with Native Americans steadily worsened after Pocahontas and then Powhatan died. Leadership passed to Powhatan's younger brother, Opechancanough, who at first sought to accommodate the English. But relentless English expansion provoked Indian discontent and the rise of a powerful religious leader, Nemattenew, who urged the Powhatans to resist the English. After some settlers killed Nemattenew, the Indians launched a surprise attack in 1622 that killed 347 of the 1,240 colonists. With much of their livestock destroyed, spring planting prevented, and disease spreading through cramped fortresses, hundreds more colonists died in the ensuing months.

After the Virginia Company sent more men, Governor Francis Wyatt reorganized the settlers and took the offensive during the Second Anglo-Powhatan War (1622–1632). Using tactics developed during the Irish war, Wyatt inflicted widespread starvation by destroying food supplies, conducted winter campaigns to drive Indians from their homes when they would suffer most, and fought (in John Smith's words) as if he had "just cause to destroy them by all means possible." By 1625 the English had effectively won the war, and the Powhatans had lost their best chance of driving out the intruders.

The clash left the Virginia Company bankrupt. After receiving a report critical of the company's management, James I revoked its charter in 1624 and made Virginia a royal colony. Only about five hundred colonists now lived there, including a handful of Africans who had been brought in since 1619. With its combination of fabulous profits, unfree labor, and massive mortality, Virginia was truly a land of contradictions.

New England Begins, 1614–1625

The next English colony, after Virginia, that proved permanent arose in New England. In 1614, the ever-enterprising John Smith, exploring its coast, gave New England its name. "Who," he asked, "can but approve this most excellent place, both for health and fertility?" Smith hoped to establish a colony there, but in 1616–1618 a terrible epidemic spread by fishermen or traders devastated New England's coastal Native American communities by about 90 percent. Later visitors found the ground littered with the "bones and skulls" of the unburied dead and acres of overgrown cornfields.

Against this tragic backdrop, the Virginia Company of London gave a patent to some London merchants headed by Thomas Weston for a settlement. In 1620, Weston sent over twenty-four families (a total of 102 people) in a small, leaky ship called the *Mayflower*. The colonists promised to send lumber, furs, and fish back to Weston in England for seven years, after which they would own the tract.

The expedition's leaders, but only half its members, were Separatist Puritans (see above) who had withdrawn from the Church of England and fled to the Netherlands to practice their religion freely. Fearing that their children were assimilating into Dutch culture, they decided to emigrate to America.

In November 1620 the *Mayflower* landed at Plymouth Bay in present-day Massachusetts, north of Virginia's boundary. Knowing that they had no legal right to be there, the expedition's leaders insisted that all adult males in the group (including non-Puritans) sign the Mayflower Compact before they landed. By this document, they constituted themselves a "civil body politic," or government, and claimed the land for King James, establishing **Plymouth** colony.

Weakened by their journey and unprepared for winter, half the Pilgrims, as the colonists later came to be known, died within four months of landing. Those still alive in the spring of 1621 owed much to the aid of two English-speaking Native Americans. One was Squanto, a Wampanoag Indian who had been taken to Spain as a slave in 1614 but was freed and then traveled to England. Returning home with a colonizing expedition, he learned that most of the two thousand people of his village had perished in the recent epidemic. The other Indian, an Abenaki from Maine named Samoset, had experience trading with the English. To prevent the colonists from stealing the natives' food, Squanto showed them how to grow corn, using fish as fertilizer. Plymouth's first harvest was marked by a festival, "at which time . . . we exercised our arms, many of the Indians coming amongst us, . . . some 90 men, whom for three days we entertained and feasted." This festival became the basis for Thanksgiving, a holiday established in the nineteenth century.

Plymouth's relations with the Native Americans soon worsened. The alliance that Squanto and Samoset had arranged between Plymouth and the Wampanoags, headed by Massasoit, had united two weak parties. But news of the Powhatan attack in 1622 hastened the colony's militarization under Miles Standish, chosen as military commander over John Smith. Standish threatened Plymouth's "allies" with the colony's monopoly of firepower. For although Massasoit remained loyal, other Indians were offended by the colonists' conduct.

Plymouth soon became economically self-sufficient. After the colony turned from communal farming to individually owned plots, its more prosperous farmers produced corn surpluses, which they traded to nonfarming Abenaki Indians in Maine for furs. Within a decade, Plymouth's elite had bought out the colony's London backers and several hundred colonists had arrived.

Although a tiny colony, Plymouth was significant as an outpost for Puritans dissenting from the Church of England and for proving that a self-governing society consisting mostly of farm families could flourish in New England. In these respects, it proved to be the vanguard of a massive migration of Puritans to New England in the 1630s (see Chapter 3).

A "New Netherland" on the Hudson, 1609–1625

Among the most fervently Calvinist regions of Europe were the Dutch-speaking provinces of the Netherlands. The provinces had come under Spanish rule during the sixteenth century, but Spain's religious intolerance and high taxes drove the Dutch to revolt, beginning in 1566. Exhausting its resources trying to quell the revolt, Spain finally recognized Dutch independence in 1609. By then, the Netherlands was a wealthy commercial power. The Dutch built an empire stretching from Brazil to South Africa to Indonesia, and played a key role in colonizing North America.

Just as the French were routing the Mohawk Iroquois at Lake Champlain in 1609, Henry Hudson sailed up the river later named for him, traded with Native Americans, and claimed the land for the Netherlands. When Dutch traders returned the following year, some of their most eager customers were—not surprisingly—Mohawks. Having established lucrative ties with Indians on the lower Hudson River, Dutch traders in 1614 built Fort Nassau near what would become Albany, and established the colony of **New Netherland.** In 1626 local Munsee Indians allowed the Dutch to settle on an island at the mouth of the Hudson. The Dutch named the island Manhattan and the settlement, New Amsterdam.

The earliest New Netherlanders lived by the fur trade. Through the Mohawks, they relied on the Five Nations Iroquois, much as the French depended on the Hurons, as commercial clients and military allies. In the 1620s, to stimulate a flow of furs to New Netherland, Dutch traders obtained from coastal Indians large quantities of wampum—sacred shells—for trade with the Iroquois. The Dutch-Iroquois and French-Huron alliances became embroiled in an ever-deepening contest to control the movement of goods between Europeans and Indians (discussed in Chapter 3).

CONCLUSION

The sixteenth century marked the emergence of an Atlantic world linking Europe, Africa, and the Americas. Kings and emperors in West Africa were already competing ferociously for the wealth brought by long-distance trade, including trade in slaves. Western Europe entered a new era in which nation-states drew on Renaissance knowledge, merchants' capital, and religious zeal to advance national power and overseas expansion.

The Atlantic world brought few benefits to West Africans and Native Americans. Proclaiming that civilization and Christianity rendered them superior, Europeans denigrated Native Americans and Africans as savages whose land and labor Europeans could seize and exploit. Initial Portuguese incursions promised to expand West Africa's trade ties with Europe. But Europe's overwhelming demand for slave labor depleted the region's population and accelerated the reshaping of trade, politics, warfare, and societies. Africa's notorious underdevelopment, which persists in our own time, had begun.

After 1492, the Atlantic world spread to the Americas. Indigenous peoples in the Caribbean, Mexico, Peru, and elsewhere in Central and South America were the first to be ravaged by European epidemic diseases, leaving them vulnerable to violent conquest and exploitation. The forced and unforced movements of people, as well as of animals, plants, and disease-causing germs constituted a Columbian exchange that transformed environments throughout the Atlantic world.

Native peoples north of Mexico and the Caribbean held would-be conquerors and colonizers at bay until after 1600. Thereafter they too suffered the effects of European-borne diseases. Native North Americans cooperated with Europeans who practiced reciprocity while resisting those who tried to dominate them. By 1625, Spain had advanced only as far north as seemed worthwhile to protect its prized Mexican and Caribbean conquests. Meanwhile, French, English, and Dutch colonists focused on less spectacular resources. New France and New Netherland existed primarily to obtain furs from Indians, while the English in Virginia and Plymouth cultivated fields recently belonging to Native Americans. All these colonies depended for their success on maintaining stable relations with at least some Native Americans. The transplantation of Europeans into North America was hardly a story of inevitable triumph.

3

The Emergence of Colonial Societies, 1625–1700

CHAPTER OUTLINE

Chesapeake Society • Puritanism in New England • The Spread of Slavery: The Caribbean and Carolina • The Middle Colonies • Rivals for North America: France and Spain

CHESAPEAKE SOCIETY

Building on the tobacco boom of the 1620s, the English colonies on the Chesapeake Bay—Virginia and its neighbor Maryland—were the first to prosper in North America. Despite differences between their political and religious institutions, Virginia and Maryland had similar economies, populations, and patterns of growth that gave them a distinct regional identity.

Chesapeake society was highly unequal and unstable. Life for most colonists was short, good health was rare, and the familiar comforts of family and community were missing. After a civil conflict, Bacon's Rebellion, the English seized yet more Native American land for growing tobacco and shifted from white indentured servitude to black slavery as the principal source of labor. On this foundation, white Virginians finally achieved stability, harmony, and at least minimal prosperity within their own ranks.

State and Church in Virginia King James I had reorganized Virginia as a **royal colony,** to be administered by a crown-appointed governor, who would appoint and dismiss leading gentlemen in the colony to an advisory council. James did not reconvene Virginia's elected assembly. With civil war threatening, James's successor Charles I (ruled 1625–1649) in 1639 formally restored the assembly as a means of securing tobacco revenues and the support of Virginia's Anglican planters. The small number of elected representatives, or burgesses, initially met as a single body with the council to pass laws. During the 1650s, the legislature split into two chambers—the House of Burgesses and the Governor's Council, whose members held lifetime appointments.

Virginia adopted England's county-court system for local government. Justices of the peace served as judges but also set local tax rates, paid county officials, and oversaw the construction and maintenance of roads, bridges, and public buildings. Justices and sheriffs, who administered the counties during the courts' recesses, were chosen by the governor instead of by an electorate. Everywhere south of New England, unelected county courts became the basic unit of local government by 1710.

As in England, Virginia's established church was the Church of England. In each parish, six vestrymen managed church finances, determined who was deserving of poor relief, and prosecuted moral offenses such as fornication or drunkenness. Taxpayers, who were legally obliged to pay fixed rates to the Anglican Church, elected vestries until 1662, when the assembly made them self-perpetuating and independent of the voters.

Because the Anglican clergy could only be trained in England and could usually find pulpits there, few were attracted to Virginia. Consequently, Virginia experienced a chronic shortage of clergymen, and most ministers rotated among two or three parishes. But when a minister was conducting services in a parish, church attendance was required; violators were subject to fines payable in cash or labor on public works projects.

State and Church in Maryland   After 1632, the crown created new colonies by awarding portions of the Virginia Company's forfeited territory to wealthy, trusted English elites. One or more proprietors, as they were called, were responsible for peopling, governing, and defending each **proprietary colony.**

In 1632, Charles I awarded the first such grant to a Catholic nobleman, **Lord Baltimore,** for a large tract of land north of the Potomac River and east of Chesapeake Bay. The grant guaranteed Lord Baltimore freedom from royal taxation, the power to appoint all sheriffs and judges, and the privilege of creating a local nobility. The only checks on the proprietor's power were the crown's control of war and trade and the requirement that an elected assembly approve all laws.

Naming his colony Maryland, Lord Baltimore intended it as an overseas refuge for English Catholics, who constituted about 2 percent of England's population. Although many English Catholics were very wealthy and a few held political office, they could not worship in public and (like other dissenters) paid taxes to support the Anglican Church.

To avoid antagonizing English Protestants, Baltimore introduced the English institution of the manor—an estate on which a lord could maintain private law courts and employ a Catholic priest as his chaplain. Local Catholics could go to the manor to hear Mass and receive the sacraments privately. Baltimore adapted Virginia's headright system (see Chapter 2) by offering large land grants to English Catholic aristocrats on condition that they bring settlers at their own cost. Anyone transporting five adults (a requirement raised to twenty by 1640) received a two-thousand-acre manor. Baltimore hoped that this arrangement would allow Catholics to survive and prosper in Maryland while making it unnecessary to pass any special laws alarming to Protestants.

Maryland's colonization did not proceed as Baltimore envisioned. In 1634, the first two hundred immigrants landed. Maryland was the first colony spared a starving time, thanks to Baltimore's careful study of Virginia's early history. The new colony's success

CHRONOLOGY, 1625–1700

1629 • Massachusetts Bay colony founded.

1630–1642 • "Great Migration" to New England.

1633 • First English settlements in Connecticut.

1634 • Lord Baltimore establishes Maryland.

1636 • Roger Williams founds Providence. Harvard College established.

1636–1637 • Antinomian crisis in Massachusetts Bay.

1637 • Pequot War in Connecticut.

1638 • New Sweden established.

1642–1649 • English Civil War.

1643–1645 • Kieft's War in New Netherland.

1644–1646 • Third Anglo-Powhatan War in Virginia.

1647 • Rhode Island established.

1648–1657 • Iroquois "beaver wars."

1649 • Maryland's Act for Religious Toleration.
King Charles I executed in England.

1655 • New Netherland annexes New Sweden.

1660 • Restoration in England; Charles II crowned king.

1661 • Maryland defines slavery as a lifelong, inheritable racial status.

1662 • Halfway Covenant debated in New England.

1664 • English conquer New Netherland; establish New York and New Jersey.

1670 • Charles Town, Carolina, founded.
Virginia defines slavery as a lifelong, inheritable racial status.

1675–1676 • King Philip's War in New England.

1676 • Bacon's Rebellion in Virginia.

1680 • Pueblo Revolt begins in New Mexico.

1681 • William Penn founds Pennsylvania.

1682 • La Salle claims Louisiana for France.

1690s • End of Royal African Company's monopoly on English slave trade.

1691 • Spain establishes Texas.

1692–1700 • Spain "reconquers" New Mexico.

1692–1693 • Salem witchcraft trials.

1698 • First French settlements in Louisiana.

showed that English overseas expansion had come of age. Baltimore, however, stayed in England, governing as an absentee proprietor, and few Catholics went to Maryland. From the outset, Protestants formed the majority of the population. With land prices low, they purchased their own property, thereby avoiding becoming tenants on the manors. These conditions doomed Baltimore's dream of creating a manorial system of mostly Catholic lords collecting rents. By 1675, all of Maryland's sixty nonproprietary manors had evolved into plantations.

Religious tensions soon emerged. In 1642, Catholics and Protestants in the capital at St. Mary's argued over use of the city's chapel, which the two groups had shared until then. As antagonisms intensified, Baltimore drafted the **Act for Religious Toleration,** or Toleration Act, which the Protestant-dominated assembly passed in 1649. The act made Maryland the second colony (after Rhode Island) to affirm religious toleration. However, the act did not protect non-Christians, nor did it separate church and state, since it empowered the government to punish religious offenses such as blasphemy.

The Toleration Act also failed to secure religious peace. In 1654, the Protestant majority barred Catholics from voting, ousted Governor William Stone (a pro-tolerance Protestant), and repealed the Toleration Act. In 1655, Stone raised an army of both faiths to regain the government but was defeated at the Battle of the Severn River. The victors imprisoned Stone and hanged three Catholic leaders.

Lord Baltimore resumed control of Maryland in 1658, ironically by order of the Puritan authorities then ruling England. Even so, he and his descendants would encounter continued obstacles in governing Maryland because of Protestant resistance to Catholic rule.

Death, Gender, and Kinship Tobacco sustained a sharp demand for labor that lured about 110,000 English to the Chesapeake from 1630 to 1700. Ninety percent of these immigrants were indentured servants, and, because men were more valued as field hands than women, 80 percent of arriving servants were males. So few women initially immigrated to the Chesapeake that only a third of male colonists found brides before 1650. Male servants married late because their indentures forbade them to wed before completing their term of labor. Their scarcity gave women a great advantage in negotiating favorable marriages. Female indentured servants often found prosperous planters to be their suitors and to buy their remaining time of service.

The high death rates that characterized early Virginia persisted after tobacco production became routine. The greatest killers were typhoid fever and, after 1650, malaria. Malaria became endemic as sailors and slaves arriving from Africa brought a particularly virulent form and carried it into marshy lowlands, where mosquitoes spread it rapidly. Life expectancy in the 1600s was about forty-eight for men and forty-four for women—slightly lower than in England and nearly twenty years lower than in New England. Servants died at horrifying rates, with perhaps 40 percent going to their graves within six years of arrival, and 70 percent by age forty-nine. Such high death rates severely crippled family life. Half of all people married in Charles County, Maryland, during the late 1600s became widows or widowers within seven years. The typical Maryland family saw half of its four children die in childhood.

Chesapeake widows tended to enjoy greater economic power than widowed women elsewhere. Instead of leaving widows the one-third of an estate required by English law, Chesapeake husbands were usually more generous and often gave their wives perpetual and complete control of their estates. A widow in such circumstances gained economic independence yet still needed to marry a man who could produce income by farming her fields. But because there were so many more men than women, she had a wider choice of husbands than widows in most societies.

The prevalence of early death produced complex households in which stepparents might raise children with two or three different surnames. Mary Keeble of Middlesex County, Virginia, bore seven children before being widowed at age twenty-nine, whereupon she married Robert Beverley, a prominent planter. Mary died in 1678 at age forty-one after having five children by Beverley, who then married Katherine Hone, a widow with one child. Upon Beverley's death in 1687, Katherine quickly wed Christopher Robinson, who had just lost his wife and needed a mother for his four children. Christopher and Katherine's household included children named Keeble, Beverley, Hone, and Robinson. This tangled chain of six marriages among seven people eventually produced twenty-five children who lived at least part of their lives with one or more stepparents.

The combination of predominantly male immigration and devastating death rates sharply limited population growth. Although the Chesapeake had received perhaps one hundred thousand English immigrants by 1700, its white population stood at no more than seventy thousand that year. By contrast, a benign disease environment and a more balanced gender ratio among the twenty-eight thousand immigrants to New England during the 1600s allowed that region's white population to grow to ninety-one thousand by 1700.

The Chesapeake's dismal demographic history began improving in the late seventeenth century. By then, resistance acquired from childhood immunities allowed native-born residents to survive into their fifties, ten years longer than immigrants. As a result, more laborers now lived beyond their terms of indenture instead of dying without tasting freedom.

Tobacco Shapes a Region, 1630–1675 Compared to colonists in New England's compact towns, Chesapeake residents had few neighbors. A typical community contained about two dozen families in an area of twenty-five square miles, or about six persons per square mile. Friendship networks typically extended for a two- to three-mile walk from one's farm and included about fifteen other families.

The isolated folk in Virginia and Maryland shared a way of life shaped by one overriding fact—their future depended on the price of tobacco. Tobacco had dominated Chesapeake agriculture since 1618, when demand for the crop exploded and prices spiraled to dizzying levels. The boom ended in 1629 when prices sank a stunning 97 percent. After stabilizing, tobacco rarely again fetched more than 10 percent of its former price.

Despite the plunge, tobacco stayed profitable as long as it sold for more than two pence per pound and was cultivated on fertile soil near navigable water. The plant grew best on level ground with good internal drainage, so-called light soil, which was usually found beside rivers. Locating a farm along Chesapeake Bay or one of its tributary rivers also minimized transportation costs by permitting tobacco to be loaded on ships at wharves near one's home. Perhaps 80 percent of early Chesapeake homes lay within a half-mile of a riverbank, and most were within just six hundred feet of the shoreline.

From such waterfront bases, wealthy planters built wharves that served not only as depots for tobacco exports but also as distribution centers for imported goods.

Planters' control of commerce stunted the growth of towns and the emergence of a merchant class. Urbanization proceeded slowly in the Chesapeake, even in a capital like Maryland's St. Mary's, which as late as 1678 had just thirty scattered houses.

Taking advantage of the headright system, a few planters built up large landhold-ings and grew wealthy from their servants' labor. The servants' lot was harsh. Most were poorly fed, clothed, and housed. The exploitation of labor in the Chesapeake was un-equaled anywhere in the English-speaking world outside the West Indies, and the gap between rich and poor whites far exceeded that of New England.

Although servants after 1650 increasingly lived to complete their terms, their fu-tures remained bleak. Having received no pay, they entered into freedom impover-ished. Virginia obliged masters to provide a new suit of clothes and a year's supply of corn to a freed servant. Maryland required these items plus a hoe and an ax and gave the right to claim fifty acres—if an individual paid to have the land surveyed and deeded. Thus, Maryland's policy enabled many of its freedmen to become landowners. Two-thirds of all Chesapeake servants lived in Virginia, however, where no such enti-tlement existed. Moreover, large planters and absentee English speculators monopo-lized most land in Virginia that was suitable for cultivating tobacco.

After 1660, the possibility of upward mobility almost vanished from the Chesa-peake as the price of tobacco fell far below profitable levels, to a penny a pound. Large planters offset their tobacco losses through income from rents, trade, interest on loans to small planters, and fees earned as government officials. They also cut labor costs by extending servants' terms as penalties for even minor infractions. Lacking capital, many freedmen worked as tenants or wage laborers on large plantations at wages well below the level needed to accumulate savings.

Freedmen who managed to obtain land nevertheless remained poor. A typical fam-ily inhabited a shack barely twenty feet by sixteen feet and owned no more property than Adam Head of Maryland possessed when he died in 1698: three mattresses with-out bedsteads, a chest and barrel that served as table and chair, two pots, a kettle, "a par-cell of old pewter," a gun, and some books. Most tobacco farmers lacked furniture, lived on mush or stew because they had just one pot, and slept on the ground—often on a pile of rags. Having fled poverty in England for the promise of a better life, they found utter destitution in the Chesapeake.

Bacon's Rebellion, 1676   By the 1670s whites in Virginia seeking land turned their at-tention to nearby Native Americans. Virginia had been free of serious conflict with Indians since the **Third Anglo-Powhatan War** (1644–1646). Resentful of tobacco planters' continued encroachments on their land, a coalition of Native Americans led by Opechancanough, then nearly a century old but able to direct battles from a litter, killed five hundred of the colony's eight thousand whites before being defeated. By 1653, tribes encircled by English set-tlement began agreeing to remain within boundaries set by the government—in effect, on reservations. Thereafter white settlement expanded north to the Potomac River, and by 1675 Virginia's four thousand Indians were greatly outnumbered by forty thousand whites.

Tensions flared between Native Americans struggling to retain land and indepen-dence and expanding settlers, especially white freedmen who often squatted illegally on tribal lands. The conflict also divided white society because both Governor Berkeley and Lord Baltimore, along with a few wealthy cronies, held fur-trade monopolies that profited from friendly relations with some Indians. The monopolies alienated not only freedmen but also wealthier planters who were excluded from them and who wished to expand further their own landholdings. As a result, colonists' resentments against the governor and proprietor became fused with those against Native Americans. In June 1675, a dispute between some Doeg Indians and a Virginia farmer escalated until a force of Virginia and Maryland militia pursuing the Doegs instead murdered fourteen friendly Susquehannocks and then assassinated the Susquehannocks' leaders during a peace conference. The Susquehannocks retaliated by killing an equal number of settlers and then offered to make peace. But with most colonists refusing to trust any Indians, the violence was now unstoppable.

Tensions were especially acute in Virginia, reflecting the greater disparities among whites there. Governor Berkeley proposed defending the panic-stricken frontier with a chain of forts linked by patrols. Stung by low tobacco prices and taxes that took almost a quarter of their yearly incomes, small farmers preferred the less costly solution of waging a war of extermination. Nathaniel Bacon, a newly arrived, wealthy planter and Berkeley's distant relative, inspired them. Defying the governor's orders, three hundred colonists elected Bacon to lead them against nearby Indians in April 1676, thereby initiating **Bacon's Rebellion.** Bacon's expedition found only peaceful Indians but massacred them anyway.

When he returned in June 1676, Bacon demanded authority to wage war "against all Indians in generall," which an intimidated Berkeley granted. The assembly defined as enemies any Indians who left their villages without English permission (even if they did so out of fear of attack by Bacon), and declared their lands forfeited. Bacon's troops were free to plunder all "enemies" of their furs, guns, wampum, and corn harvests and also to keep Indian prisoners as slaves. The assembly's incentives for enlisting were directed at men eager to get rich quickly by seizing land and enslaving any Indians who fell into their clutches.

Berkeley soon had second thoughts about letting Bacon's thirteen hundred men continue their frontier slaughter and called them back. The rebels returned with their guns pointed toward Jamestown. Forcing Berkeley to flee across Chesapeake Bay, the rebels burned the capital, offered freedom to any Berkeley supporters' servants or slaves who joined the uprising, and looted their enemies' plantations. But at the very moment of triumph in late 1676, Bacon died of dysentery and his followers dispersed.

A royal commission dispatched from England in 1677 found that Berkeley had mismanaged the crisis but also that some of the Indian lands seized by Bacon's followers had been guaranteed to the tribes by previous treaties. Under the Treaty of Middle Plantation (1677), the tribes and the colony pledged peace toward one another, English-held captives were freed, and the tribes' lands were guaranteed in perpetuity. (Several more tribes joined the pact in 1680.) The leading tribe, the Pamunkeys, agreed to present the governor of Virginia with three arrowheads and twenty beaver pelts annually, a provision they honor to this day.

Most Indian-held land seized during Bacon's Rebellion was not protected by formal treaties. The colony retained most of this land and made it available to settlers.

The tortured course of Bacon's Rebellion revealed a society under stress. It was an outburst of long pent-up frustrations by marginal taxpayers and former servants seeking land, but also by wealthier planters. Although sheer economic opportunism was one motive for the uprising, the willingness of whites to murder, enslave, or expel all Native Americans, no matter how loyal, made clear that racial hostility also played a major role.

From Servitude to Slavery   Race was also fundamental in the reshaping of Chesapeake society that followed Bacon's Rebellion. Even before the uprising, planters had begun substituting black slaves for white servants.

Racial slavery had developed in three stages in the Chesapeake since 1619. Until about 1640, colonists carefully distinguished between blacks and whites in official documents, but did not assume that every African sold was a slave for life. The same was true for Native Americans captured in the colony's early wars. Some Africans gained their freedom during this period, and a few owned their own tobacco farms.

During the second phase, from 1640 to 1660, growing numbers of blacks and some Indians were treated as slaves for life, in contrast to white indentured servants who had fixed terms of service. Slaves' children inherited their parents' status. At the same time, evidence from this period shows that white and black laborers often ran away or rebelled against a master together, and occasionally married one another.

Apparently in reaction to such incidents, the colonies officially recognized and regulated slavery after 1660. Maryland first defined slavery as a lifelong, inheritable racial status in 1661. Virginia followed suit in 1670. This hardening of status lines did not prevent some black and white laborers from joining Bacon's Rebellion together. Indeed, the last contingent of rebels to lay down their arms consisted entirely of slaves and servants. By 1705, strict legal codes defined the place of slaves in society and set standards of racial etiquette. By then, free blacks had all but disappeared from the Chesapeake. Although this period saw racial slavery become fully legalized, many of the specific practices enacted into law had evolved into custom earlier.

Emerging gradually in the Chesapeake, slavery was formally codified by planter elites attempting to stabilize Chesapeake society and defuse the resentment of whites. In deeming nonwhites unfit for freedom, the elites created a common, exclusive identity for whites as free or potentially free persons.

Chesapeake planters began formulating this racial caste system before slavery itself became economically significant. As late as 1660, fewer than a thousand slaves lived in Virginia and Maryland. The number in bondage first became truly significant in the 1680s when the Chesapeake's slave population (by now almost entirely black, owing to Indian decline) almost tripled, rising from forty-five hundred to about twelve thousand. By 1700, slaves made up 22 percent of the inhabitants and over 80 percent of all unfree laborers.

Having developed as a labor system reserved for blacks, slavery replaced indentured servitude for economic reasons. First, it became more difficult for planters to import white laborers as the seventeenth century advanced. Between 1650 and 1700, wages rose in England by 50 percent, removing poor people's incentive to move to the Chesapeake. Second, before 1690 the Royal African Company, which held a monopoly on selling slaves to the English colonies, shipped most its cargoes to the West Indies. Some of these slaves were then transported to the Chesapeake and other mainland regions of English America. During the 1690s, this monopoly was broken, and rival companies began shipping large numbers of Africans directly to the Chesapeake.

Preparing a Slave Voyage *Africans weep as relatives or friends are taken to a slave vessel.*

The rise of a direct trade in slaves between the Chesapeake and West Africa exacerbated the growing gap between whites and blacks in another way. Until 1690, most blacks in the Chesapeake had either been born, or spent many years, in West African ports or in other American colonies. As a consequence, they were familiar with Europeans and European ways and, in many cases, spoke English. Such familiarity had enabled some blacks to carve out space for themselves as free landowners, and had facilitated marriages and acts of resistance across racial lines among laborers. But after 1690, far larger numbers of slaves poured into Virginia and Maryland, arriving directly from the West African interior. Language and culture now became barriers rather than bridges to mutual understanding among blacks as well as between blacks and whites, reinforcing the overt racism arising among whites.

The changing composition of the white population also contributed to the emergence of race as the foundation of Chesapeake society. As increasing numbers of immigrants lived long enough to marry and form their own families, the number of such families slowly rose, and the ratio of men to women became more equal, since half of all children were girls. By 1690, an almost even division existed between males and females. Thereafter, the white population grew primarily through an excess of births over deaths rather than through immigration, so that by 1720 most Chesapeake colonists were native-born. Whites' shared attachments to the colony heightened their sense of a common racial identity vis-à-vis an increasingly fragmented and seemingly alien black population.

From its beginnings as a region where profits were high but life expectancy was low, the Chesapeake had transformed by 1700. As nonwhites' conditions deteriorated, Virginia and Maryland expanded their territories, and their white colonists flourished.

Puritanism in New England

After the Chesapeake, New England was the next colonial region to prosper in North America. Separatist Puritans had established Plymouth in 1620 (see Chapter 2), which grew slowly but thrived over the next decade. Plymouth was dwarfed after 1630, when a massive Puritan-led "Great Migration" to New England began. By the time England's civil war halted the migration in 1642, about twenty-one thousand settlers had arrived. The newcomers established the colonies of Massachusetts Bay, Connecticut, New Haven (absorbed by Connecticut in 1662), and Rhode Island. New England's leaders endeavored to build colonies based on religious and social ideals. Although internal divisions and social-economic change undermined these ideals, Puritanism gave New England a distinctive regional identity.

New England offered a sharp contrast to the Chesapeake colonies. The religious foundations, economies, class structure, local communities, families, and living standards in the two regions could not have been more different. The Chesapeake and New England colonists did, however, share English nationality and a determination to expand at Native Americans' expense.

A City upon a Hill After becoming king in 1625, Charles I reversed James's policy of tolerating Puritans (see Chapter 2). Beginning a systematic campaign to eliminate Puritan influence within the Church of England, Anglican authorities insisted that services be conducted according to the Book of Common Prayer, which prescribed rituals similar to Catholic practices. Bishops dismissed Puritan ministers who refused to perform these "High Church" rites, and church courts fined or excommunicated Puritan laypersons who protested.

In the face of such harassment, a group of wealthy Puritans successfully petitioned the crown for a charter to colonize at Massachusetts Bay, north of Plymouth, in March 1629. Organizing as the Massachusetts Bay Company, they took advantage of a gap in their charter and later that year moved the seat of their colony's government, along with four hundred colonists, to Salem, Massachusetts. Like Plymouth, Massachusetts Bay would be a Puritan-dominated, self-governing colony rather than one controlled from England by stockholders, proprietors, or the crown. In 1630, the company sent out eleven ships and seven hundred passengers under Governor **John Winthrop.** Upon arriving at the new capital of Boston, Winthrop distributed an essay (perhaps already delivered as a shipboard address) titled **"A Model of Christian Charity,"** spelling out the new colony's social and political ideals. In it, he boldly declared that Massachusetts "shall be as a city upon a hill, the eyes of all people are upon us." The settlers would build a harmonious, godly community in which individuals would subordinate their personal interests to a higher purpose. The result would be an example for all the world and would particularly inspire England to live up to its role as God's "elect nation."

In outlining this ideal society, Winthrop denounced the economic jealousy that bred class hatred. God intended that "in all times some must be rich and some poor," he asserted. The rich had an obligation to show charity and mercy toward the poor, who should meekly accept rule by their social superiors as God's will. God expected the state to keep the greedy among the rich from exploiting the needy and to prevent the lazy among the poor from burdening their fellow citizens. In outlining a divine plan in which all people, rich and poor, served one another, Winthrop expressed a conservative

European's understanding of social hierarchy (see Chapter 2) and voiced Puritans' dismay at the forces of individualism and class warfare that were battering—and changing—English society.

By fall 1630, six towns had sprung up around Boston. During the unusually severe first winter, 30 percent of Winthrop's party died, and another 10 percent went home in the spring. By mid-1631, however, thirteen hundred new settlers had landed, and more were on the way. The worst was over. The colony would never suffer another starving time. Like Plymouth, Massachusetts Bay primarily attracted landowning farm families of modest means, most of them receptive if not actively committed to Calvinism. Compared to the Chesapeake in 1630, there were few indentured servants and almost no slaves. New Englanders quickly established a healthier, more stable colonial region than did their Chesapeake contemporaries. By 1642, more than fifteen thousand colonists had settled in New England.

Political participation was more broadly based in New England than elsewhere in Europe and its colonies. Instead of requiring voters or officeholders to own property, Massachusetts permitted voting by every adult male church member. By 1641, about 55 percent of the colony's twenty-three hundred men could vote. (The other Puritan colonies based male voting on property ownership.) But since most white men owned property, the suffrage was similarly broad. By contrast, English property requirements allowed fewer than 30 percent of adult males to vote.

In 1634, after protests that the governor (Winthrop) and council held too much power, the General Court (legislature) allowed each town to send two delegates. Initially resisting this effort, Winthrop was defeated for reelection and did not return to the governorship for three years. In 1644, the General Court became a bicameral (two-chamber) lawmaking body when the towns' deputies separated from the appointed Governor's Council.

New England Ways   Although most New Englanders nominally belonged to the Church of England, their self-governing congregations, like those in Separatist Plymouth, ignored Anglican bishops' authority. Control of each congregation lay squarely in the hands of its male "saints," as Puritans termed those who had been saved. By majority vote, these men chose their minister, elected a board of elders to handle finances, and decided who else deserved recognition as saints. Compared to Anglican parishes in England and Virginia, where a few powerful landowners selected priests (subject to a bishop's formal approval) and made other major decisions, control of New England churches was broadly based.

Although congregations were largely independent of one another and controlled by their male members, the clergy quickly asserted its power in New England's religious life. As members of a popular religious movement in England, Puritans had emphasized broad Calvinist principles and their common opposition to Anglican practices. But upon arriving in New England, many ministers feared that complete congregational independence would undermine Puritan unity and lead to religious disorder. Religious disharmony would as effectively undermine "the city upon a hill" as would the social disharmony feared by Winthrop. Accordingly, the ministers established a set of official practices—the **"New England Way"**—that strengthened their authority at the expense of that of laypersons (nonclergy) within their congregations.

In its church membership requirements, the New England Way diverged from other Puritans' practices. English Puritans accepted as saints any adult who correctly professed the Calvinist faith, repented his or her sins, and lived free of scandal. Massachusetts Puritans, however, insisted that candidates for membership stand before their congregation and provide a convincing, soul-baring "relation," or account, of their conversion experience (see Chapter 2). Many colonists shared the reluctance of Jonathan Fairbanks, who refused for several years to give a public profession of grace before the church in Dedham, Massachusetts, until the faithful persuaded him with many "loving conferences." The conversion relation would prove to be the New England Way's most vulnerable feature.

One means of ensuring orthodoxy was through education. Like most European Protestants, Puritans insisted that conversion required familiarity with the Bible and, therefore, literacy. Education, they believed, should begin in childhood and should be promoted by each colony. In 1647, Massachusetts Bay ordered every town of fifty or more households to appoint a teacher to whom all children could come for instruction, and every town of at least one hundred households to maintain a grammar school. This and similar laws in other Puritan colonies represented New England's first steps toward public education. But none of these laws required school attendance, and boys were more likely to be taught reading and especially writing than were girls.

To ensure a supply of ministers trained in the New England Way, Massachusetts founded Harvard College in 1636. From 1642 to 1671, the college produced 201 graduates, including 111 ministers. As a result, New England was the only part of English America to produce its own clergy and college-educated elite before 1700.

Puritans agreed that the church must be free of state control, and they opposed theocracy (government by clergy). But Winthrop and other Massachusetts Bay leaders insisted that a holy commonwealth required cooperation between church and state. The colony obliged all adults to attend services and levied taxes to support local churches. Thus Massachusetts, like England and Anglican Virginia, had an established church.

Driving the clergy's efforts to define orthodox practices was the arrival in New England of Puritans whose views threatened to divide Puritans along theological lines. Roger Williams and Anne Hutchinson led movements considered by political as well as religious authorities to be especially dangerous because they attracted popular followings.

Roger Williams, a Separatist minister who arrived in 1631, aroused elite anxieties by advocating the complete separation of church and state and religious toleration. He argued that civil government should play no role in regulating religious matters, whether blasphemy (cursing God), failure to pay tithes, refusal to attend worship, or swearing oaths on the Bible in court. Williams also opposed any kind of compulsory church service or government interference with religious practice, not because all religions deserved equal respect but because the state (a creation of sinful human beings) would corrupt the church.

As Williams's popularity grew, Winthrop and other authorities declared his opinions subversive and banished him in 1635. Williams moved south to a place that he called Providence, which he purchased from the Narragansett Indians. At Williams's invitation, a steady stream of dissenters drifted to the group of settlements near Providence, which in 1647 joined to form Rhode Island colony. (Other Puritans scorned the place as "Rogues Island.") True to Williams's ideals, Rhode Island was the only New

England colony to practice religious toleration. Growing slowly, the colony's four towns had eight hundred settlers by 1650.

A second major challenge to the New England Way began when **Anne Hutchinson,** a deeply religious member of the Boston congregation, publicly criticized the clergy for judging prospective church members on the basis of "good works"—the Catholic standard for salvation that Protestants had criticized since the Reformation (see Chapter 2). Supposedly, Puritans followed John Calvin in maintaining that God had "predestined" all persons for either salvation or damnation. But Hutchinson argued that ministers who scrutinized a person's outward behavior for "signs" of salvation, especially when that person was relating his or her conversion experience, were discarding God's judgment in favor of their own. Only by looking inward and ignoring such false prophets could individuals hope to find salvation. Hutchinson charged that only two of the colony's ministers had been saved; the rest lacked authority over the elect.

By casting doubt on the clergy's spiritual state, Hutchinson undermined its authority over laypersons. Critics charged that her beliefs would delude individuals into imagining that they were accountable to no one but themselves. Winthrop branded her followers Antinomians, meaning those opposed to the rule of law.

Hutchinson bore the additional liability of violating gender norms. As a woman steeped in Scripture, Hutchinson had led other women in discussions of ministers' sermons. But she went beyond that prescribed role by asserting her own opinions and by including men at the meetings. As one of her accusers put it, "You have stepped out of your place; you [would] have rather been a husband than a wife, a preacher than a hearer; and a magistrate than a subject."

By 1637, Massachusetts Bay had split into two camps. Hutchinson's supporters, primarily Bostonians, included merchants (like her husband) who disliked the government's economic restrictions on their businesses, young men chafing against the rigid control of church elders, and women impatient with their second-class status in church affairs. Even the colony's governor, Henry Vane, was an Antinomian. But most colonists outside Boston were alarmed by what they regarded as religious extremism. In the election of 1637 they rejected Vane and returned Winthrop to the governorship.

The victorious Winthrop brought Hutchinson to trial for heresy before the General Court, whose members peppered her with questions. Hutchinson's knowledge of Scripture was so superior to that of her interrogators, however, that she would have been acquitted had she not claimed to be converted through a direct revelation from God. Like most Christians, Puritans believed that God had ceased to make known matters of faith by personal revelation after New Testament times. Thus, Hutchinson's own words condemned her.

The General Court banished the leading Antinomians from the colony, and others voluntarily followed them to Rhode Island, New Hampshire, or back to England. The largest group, led by Hutchinson, settled in Rhode Island. Some Rhode Island Antinomians later converted to Quakerism (see below), returning to Massachusetts and again defying political and religious authorities.

Antinomianism's defeat was followed by new restrictions on women's independence and religious expression. Increasingly, women were prohibited from assuming the kind of public religious roles claimed by Hutchinson. To minimize their influence, they were required to relate their conversion experiences privately to ministers rather than publicly before their congregations.

Towns, Families, and Farm Life

To ensure that colonists would settle in communities with congregations, all New England colonies, including Rhode Island, provided for the establishment of towns, which would distribute land. Legislatures authorized a town by awarding a grant of land to several dozen landowning church members. These men then laid out the settlement, organized its church, distributed land among themselves, and established a town meeting—a distinctly New England institution. At the center of each town lay the meetinghouse, which served as both church and town hall.

Whereas justices of the peace in England and Virginia administered local government through county courts, New England's county courts served strictly as courts of law, and local administration was conducted by the town meeting. Town meetings decentralized authority over political and economic decisions to a degree unknown in England and its other colonies. Each town determined its own qualifications for voting and holding office in the town meeting, although most allowed all male taxpayers (including nonsaints) to participate. The meeting could exclude anyone from settling in town, and it could grant the right of sharing in any future land distributions to male newcomers, whose sons would inherit this privilege.

Few aspects of early New England life are more revealing than the first generation's attempt in many towns to promote communalism by keeping settlement tightly clustered. They did so by granting house lots near the town center and by granting families no more land than they needed to support themselves. Dedham's forty-six founders, for example, received 128,000 acres from Massachusetts Bay in 1636 yet gave themselves just 3,000 acres by 1656, or about 65 acres per family. The rest remained in trust for future generations.

With families clustered within a mile of one another, the physical settings of New England towns were conducive to traditional reciprocity. They also fostered an atmosphere of mutual watchfulness that Puritans hoped would promote godly order. For the enforcement of such order, they relied on the women of each town as well as male magistrates.

Although women's public roles had been sharply curtailed following the Antinomian crisis, women—especially female saints—remained a social force in their communities. With their husbands and older sons attending the family's fields and business, women remained at home in the tightly knit neighborhoods at the center of each town. Neighboring women exchanged not only goods—say, a pound of butter for a section of spun wool—but advice and news of other neighbors as well. They also gathered at the bedside when one of them gave birth, an occasion supervised by a midwife and entirely closed to men. In these settings, women confided in one another, creating a "community of women" within each town that helped enforce morals and protect the poor and vulnerable. In 1663, Mary Rolfe of Newbury, Massachusetts, was being sexually harassed by a high-ranking gentleman while her fisherman husband was at sea. Rolfe confided in her mother, who in turn consulted with a neighboring woman of influence before filing formal charges. Clearly influenced by the town's women, a male jury convicted the gentleman of attempted adultery. When a gentlewoman, Patience Dennison, charged her maidservant with repeatedly stealing food and clothing, a fourth woman testified that the maid had given the provisions to a poor young wife, whose family was thereby saved from perishing. The servant was cleared while her mistress gained a lifelong reputation for stinginess.

Puritans defined matrimony as a contract rather than a religious sacrament, and justices of the peace rather than ministers married New England couples. As a civil institution, a marriage could be dissolved by the courts in cases of desertion, bigamy, adultery, or physical cruelty. By permitting divorce, the colonies diverged radically from practices in England, where Anglican authorities rarely annulled marriages and civil divorces required a special act of Parliament. Still, New Englanders saw divorce as a remedy fit only for extremely wronged spouses, such as the Plymouth woman who discovered that her husband was also married to women in Boston, Barbados, and England. Massachusetts courts allowed just twenty-seven divorces before 1692.

New England wives enjoyed significant legal protections against spousal violence and nonsupport and also had more opportunity than other European women to escape failed marriages. But they also suffered the same legal disabilities as all English-women. An English wife had no property rights independent of her husband unless he consented to a prenuptial agreement leaving her in control of property she already owned. Only if a husband had no other heirs or so stipulated in a will could a widow claim more than the third of the estate reserved by law for her lifetime use.

In contrast to the Chesapeake, New England benefited from a remarkably benign disease environment. Most families owned farms and produced an ample amount and variety of foods to ensure an adequate diet, which improved resistance to disease and lowered death rates associated with childbirth. Malaria and other tropical diseases did not thrive in New England's frozen winters. And while settlements were compact, New Englanders rarely traveled outside their own towns. Thus while travelers brought communicable diseases to Boston and other ports, such diseases rarely spread inland.

Consequently, New Englanders lived longer and raised larger families than their contemporaries in England and other colonial regions. Life expectancy for men reached sixty-five, and women lived nearly that long. More than 80 percent of all infants survived long enough to get married. The 58 men and women who founded Andover, Massachusetts, for example, had 247 children; by the fourth generation, the families of their descendants numbered 2,000 (including spouses who married in from other families). Because most settlers came as members of family groups, the population was evenly divided between males and females from the beginning. This balance permitted rapid population growth without heavy immigration.

Most colonists had little or no cash, relying instead on the labor of their large, healthy families to sustain them and secure their futures. Male household heads managed the family's crops and livestock, conducted most of its business transactions, and represented it in town government. Their wives bore, nursed, and reared their children. Women were in charge of work in the house, barn, and garden, including the making of food and clothing. Women also did charitable work and played other roles in their communities (see above).

More than in England and the other colonies, the sons of New England's founding generation depended on their parents to provide them with acreage for farming. With eventual landownership guaranteed and few other opportunities available, sons delayed marriage and worked in their fathers' fields until finally receiving their own land, usually after age twenty-five. Because the average family raised three or four boys to adulthood, parents could depend on thirty to forty years of sons' labor.

While daughters performed equally vital labor, their future lay with another family— the one into which they would marry. Being young, with many childbearing years ahead of them, enhanced their value to that family. Thus first-generation women, on average, were only twenty-one when they married.

Economic and
Religious
Tensions

Saddled with the burdens of a short growing season, rocky soil salted with gravel, and (in most towns) a system of land distribution in which farmers cultivated widely scattered parcels, the colonists managed to feed large families and keep ahead of their debts, but few became wealthy from farming. Seeking greater fortunes than agriculture offered, some seventeenth-century New Englanders turned lumbering, fishing, fur trading, shipbuilding, and rum distilling into major industries. As its economy became more diversified, New England prospered. But the colonists grew more worldly and their values began to shift.

The most fundamental threat to Winthrop's city upon a hill was that colonists would abandon the ideal of a close-knit community to pursue self-interest. Other colonies—most pointedly, Virginia—displayed the acquisitive impulses transforming England, but in New England, as one minister put it, "religion and profit jump together." While hoping for prosperity, Puritans believed that there were limits to legitimate commercial behavior. Government leaders tried to regulate prices so that consumers would not suffer from the chronic shortage of manufactured goods that afflicted New England. In 1635, when the Massachusetts General Court forbade pricing any item more than 5 percent above its cost, Robert Keayne of Boston and other merchants objected. These men argued that they had to sell some goods at higher rates in order to offset their losses from other sales, shipwrecked cargoes, and inflation. In 1639, after selling nails at 25 percent to 33 percent above cost, Keayne was fined heavily in court and was forced to make a humiliating apology before his congregation.

Controversies between the Puritan clergy and farming elites on one hand, and merchants on the other, were part of a struggle for New England's soul. On various occasions, Elizabeth Clark Freake's father and each of her husbands (all wealthy merchants) clashed with colony leaders who sought to limit mercantile interests. Some merchants were attracted to less rigid variants of Calvinism. Merchants were prominent among the followers of both Roger Williams and Anne Hutchinson. William Pynchon of Springfield was banished from Massachusetts in 1652, after publishing a tract that authorities considered heretical. In all these conflicts, political and religious leaders sought to insulate their city upon a hill from the competitiveness and pursuit of self-interest basic to a market economy.

Other social and economic changes further undermined Winthrop's vision. After about 1660, farmers eager to expand their agricultural output and provide land for their sons voted themselves larger amounts of land after 1660 and insisted that their scattered parcels be consolidated. For example, Dedham, Massachusetts, which distributed only three thousand acres from 1636 to 1656, allocated five times as much in the next dozen years. Rather than continue living closely together, many farmers built homes on their outlying tracts. The dispersal of settlers away from town centers generated friction between townspeople settled near the meetinghouse and "outlivers," whose distance from the town center limited their influence over town affairs. Although groups of outlivers often formed new towns, John Winthrop's vision of a society sustained by reciprocity was slowly giving way to the materialistic, acquisitive society that the original immigrants had fled in England.

As New England slowly prospered, England fell into chaos. The efforts of Charles I to impose taxes without Parliament's consent sparked a civil war in 1642. Alienated by years of religious harassment, Puritans gained control of the successful revolt and beheaded Charles in 1649. Puritan Oliver Cromwell's consolidation of power raised orthodox New Englanders' hopes that England would finally heed their example and establish a truly reformed church. But Cromwell preferred Rhode Island's Roger Williams to other New Englanders and developed England's commercial empire. After Cromwell died, chaos returned to England until a provisional government "restored" the monarchy and crowned King Charles II (ruled 1660–1685). The **Restoration** left New England Puritans without a mission. Contrary to Winthrop's vision, "the eyes of all people" were no longer, if ever they had been, fixed on New England.

The erosion of Winthrop's social vision was accompanied by the decline of the religious vision embodied in the New England Way. This decline was reflected most vividly in a crisis over church membership. The crisis arose because many Puritans' children were not joining the elect. By 1650, for example, fewer than half the adults in the Boston congregation were saints. The principal reason was the children's reluctance to undergo public grilling on their conversion experience. Most children must have witnessed at least one ordeal like Sarah Fiske's. For more than a year, Fiske answered petty charges of speaking uncharitably about her relatives—especially her husband—and then was admitted to the Wenham, Massachusetts, congregation only after publicly denouncing herself as worse "than any toad."

Because Puritan ministers baptized only babies born to saints, the unwillingness of the second generation to provide a conversion relation meant that most third-generation children would remain unbaptized. Unless a solution were found, saints' numbers would dwindle and Puritan rule would end. In 1662 a synod of clergy proposed a compromise known as the Halfway Covenant, which would permit the children of baptized adults, including nonsaints, to receive baptism. Derisively termed the "halfway" covenant by its opponents, the proposal would allow the founders' descendants to transmit potential church membership to their grandchildren, leaving their adult children "halfway" members who could not take communion or vote in church affairs. Congregations divided bitterly over limiting membership to pure saints or compromising purity in order to maintain Puritan power in New England. In the end, they opted for worldly power over spiritual purity.

The crisis in church membership signaled a weakening of the old orthodoxy. Most second-generation adults remained in "halfway" status for life, and the saints became a shrinking minority as the third and fourth generations matured. Sainthood tended to flow in certain families, and soon there were more women than men among the elect. But because women could not vote in church affairs, religious authority stayed in male hands. Nevertheless, ministers publicly recognized women's role in upholding piety and the church itself.

Expansion and
Native Americans

New England's first colonists met with little sustained resistance from Native Americans, whose numbers were drastically reduced by the ravages of disease. After one epidemic killed about 90 percent of New England's coastal Indians (see Chapter 2), smallpox inflicted comparable casualties on Indians throughout the Northeast in 1633–1634. Having dwindled from twenty thousand in 1600 to a few dozen survivors by the mid-1630s, the coastal Massachusett and Pawtucket Indians were pressed to sell most of

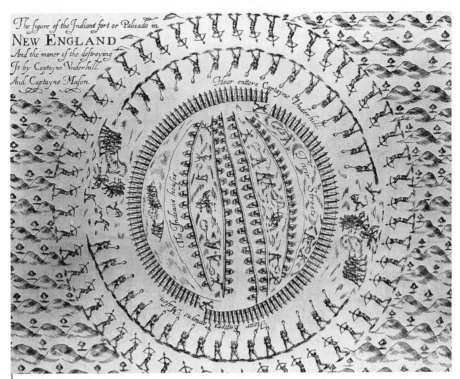

Attack on Mystic Fort, Pequot War   *This print, published in an English participant's account of the war, shows English troops, backed by allied Indians, surrounding the Pequot village while soldiers prepare to burn it.*

their land to the English. During the 1640s, Massachusetts Bay passed laws prohibiting them from practicing their own religion and encouraging missionaries to convert them to Christianity. Thereafter, they ceded more land to the colonists and moved into "praying towns" like Natick, a reservation established by the colony. In the praying towns, Puritan missionary John Eliot hoped to teach the Native Americans Christianity and English "civilization."

On the other hand, English expansion farther inland aroused Native American resistance. Beginning in 1633, settlers moved into the Connecticut River Valley and in 1635 organized the new colony of Connecticut. Friction quickly developed with the Pequot Indians, who controlled the trade in furs and wampum with New Netherland. After tensions escalated into violence, Massachusetts and Connecticut took coordinated military action in 1637, thereby beginning the **Pequot War.** Having gained the support of the Mohegan and Narragansett Indians, they waged a ruthless campaign, using tactics similar to those devised by the English to break Irish resistance during the 1570s (see Chapter 2). In a predawn attack, English troops surrounded and set fire to a Pequot village at Mystic, Connecticut, and then cut down all who tried to escape. Several hundred Pequots, mostly women and children, were killed. Although their Narragansett allies protested that "it is too furious, and slays too many men," the English found a cause for celebration in the grisly massacre. Wrote Plymouth's Governor William Bradford,

It was a fearful sight to see them [the Pequots] thus frying in the fire and the streams of blood quenching the same, and horrible was the stink and scent thereof; but the victory seemed a sweet sacrifice, and they [the English] gave the praise to God, who had wrought so wonderfully for them, thus to enclose their enemies in their hands and give them so speedy a victory over so proud and insulting an enemy.

By late 1637, Pequot resistance was crushed, with the survivors taken by pro-English Indians as captives or by the English as slaves. The Pequots' lands were awarded to the colonists of Connecticut and New Haven.

As settlements grew and colonists prospered, the numbers and conditions of Native Americans in New England declined. Although Indians began to recover from the initial epidemics by midcentury, the settlers brought new diseases such as diphtheria, measles, and tuberculosis as well as new outbreaks of smallpox, which took heavy tolls. New England's Indian population fell from 125,000 in 1600 to 10,000 in 1675.

Native Americans felt the English presence in other ways. The fur trade, which initially benefited interior Natives, became a liability after midcentury. Once Indians began hunting for trade instead of just for their own subsistence needs, they quickly depleted the region's beavers and other fur-bearing animals. Because English traders shrewdly advanced trade goods on credit to Indian hunters before the hunting season, the lack of pelts pushed many Natives into debt. Traders such as John Pynchon of Springfield, Massachusetts, began taking Indian land as collateral and selling it to settlers. The expansion of English settlement often separated Native villages from one another and from hunting, gathering, and fishing areas.

English expansion put new pressures on Native peoples and the land. As early as 1642, Miantonomi, a Narragansett sachem (chief), warned neighboring Indians,

These English having gotten our land, they with scythes cut down the grass, and with axes fell the trees; their cows and horses eat the grass, and their hogs spoil our clam banks, and we shall all be starved.

Within a generation, Miantonomi's fears were being borne out. By clearing away extensive stands of trees for fields and for use as fuel and building material, colonial farmers altered an entire ecosystem. Deer were no longer attracted, and the wild plants upon which Native Americans depended for food and medicine could not grow. The soil became drier and flooding more frequent in the face of this deforestation. The settlers also introduced domestic livestock, which, according to English custom, ranged freely. Pigs damaged Indian cornfields (until the Natives adopted the alien practice of fencing their fields) and shellfish-gathering sites. English cattle and horses quickly devoured native grasses, which the settlers then replaced with English varieties.

With their leaders powerless to halt the alarming decline of their population, land, and food sources, many Indians became demoralized. In their despair, some turned to alcohol, increasingly available during the 1660s despite colonial efforts to suppress its sale to Native Americans. Interpreting the crisis as one of belief, other Natives responded to an expanded initiative by John Eliot and other Puritan missionaries to convert them to Christianity. By 1675, about 2,300 Indians inhabited thirty praying towns in eastern Massachusetts, Plymouth, and offshore islands. Regularly visited by supervising missionaries, each praying town had its own Native American magistrate, usually a sachem, and many congregations had Indian preachers. Although the missionaries struggled to convert the Indians to "civilization" (meaning English culture and lifestyles) as well as Christianity, most praying Indians integrated the new faith with their native cultural identities.

Anglo-Indian conflict became acute during the 1670s because of pressures imposed on unwilling Indians to sell their land and to accept missionaries and the legal authority of colonial courts. Tension ran especially high in Plymouth colony where Metacom, or "King Philip," the son of the colony's onetime ally Massasoit (see Chapter 2), was now the leading Wampanoag sachem. The English had engulfed the Wampanoags, persuaded many of them to renounce their loyalty to Metacom, and forced several humiliating concessions on the sachem.

In 1675, Plymouth hanged three Wampanoags for killing a Christian Indian and threatened to arrest Metacom. A minor incident, in which several Wampanoags were shot while burglarizing a farmhouse, ignited the conflict known as **King Philip's War.**

Eventually, two-thirds of the colonies' Native Americans, including some Christians, rallied around Metacom. Unlike Indians in the Pequot War, they were familiar with guns and were as well armed as the colonists. Indian raiders attacked fifty-two of New England's ninety towns (entirely destroying twelve), burned twelve hundred houses, slaughtered eight thousand head of cattle, and killed twenty-five hundred colonists (5 percent).

The tide turned against Metacom in 1676 after the Mohawk Indians of New York and many Christian Indians joined the English against him. The colonists and their Native American allies scattered their enemies and destroyed their food supplies. About five thousand Indians starved or fell in battle, including Metacom himself, and others fled to New York and Canada. After crushing the uprising, the English sold hundreds of captives into slavery, including Metacom's wife and child.

King Philip's War reduced southern New England's Indian population by about 40 percent and eliminated overt resistance to white expansion. It also deepened English hostility toward all Native Americans, even the Christian and other Indians who had supported the colonies. In Massachusetts, ten praying towns were disbanded, and Native peoples restricted to the remaining four; all Indian courts were dismantled; and English "guardians" were appointed to supervise the reservations. "There is a cloud, a dark cloud upon the work of the Gospel among the poor Indians," mourned John Eliot. In the face of poverty and discrimination, remaining Indians struggled to survive and maintain their communities.

Salem Witchcraft, 1691–1693   Nowhere in New England did the conflicts dividing white New Englanders converge more forcefully than in Salem, Massachusetts, the region's second largest port. Trade made Salem prosperous but also destroyed the relatively equal society of first-generation fishermen and farmers. Salem's divisions were especially sharp in the precinct of Salem Village (now Danvers), an economically stagnant district located north of Salem Town. Residents of the village's eastern section farmed richer soils and benefited from Salem Town's commercial expansion, whereas those in the less fertile western half did not share in this prosperity and had lost the political influence that they once held in Salem.

In late 1691 several Salem Village girls encouraged an African slave woman, Tituba, to tell them their fortunes and talk about sorcery. When the girls later began behaving strangely, villagers assumed that they were victims of witchcraft. Pressed to identify their tormenters, the girls named two local white women and Tituba.

Images of Witchcraft   *Most seventeenth-century Europeans and colonists feared that, at any time, Satan and those in his grip (witches) could attack and harm them with the power of evil.*

So far, the incident was not unusual. Witchcraft beliefs remained strong in seventeenth-century Europe and its colonies. Witches were people (nearly always women) whose pride, envy, discontent, or greed supposedly led them to sign a pact with the devil. Thereafter, they allegedly used *maleficium* (the devil's supernatural power of evil) to torment neighbors and others by causing illness, destroying property, or—as with the girls in Salem Village—inhabiting or "possessing" their victims' bodies and minds. Witnesses usually also claimed that witches displayed aggressive, unfeminine behavior. In most earlier witchcraft accusations in New England, there was only one defendant and the case never went to trial. The few exceptions to this rule were tried with little fanfare. Events in Salem Village, on the other hand, led to a colony-wide panic.

By April 1692, the girls had denounced two locally prominent women and had identified the village's former minister as a wizard (male witch). Fears of witchcraft soon overrode doubts about the girls' credibility and led local judges to sweep aside normal procedural safeguards. Specifically, the judges ignored the law's ban on "spectral evidence"—testimony that a spirit resembling the accused had been seen tormenting a victim. Thereafter, accusations multiplied until the jails overflowed with 342 accused witches.

The pattern of hysteria in Salem Village reflected that community's internal divisions. Most accusations originated in the village's poorer western division, and were directed at wealthier families in the eastern village or in Salem Town.

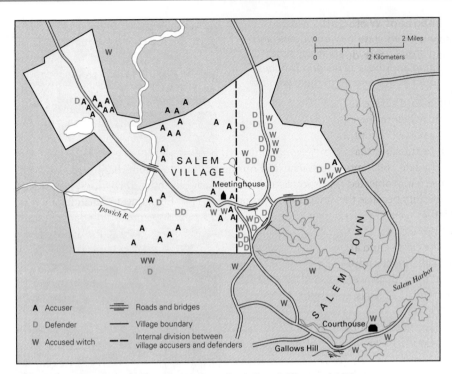

MAP 3.1 The Geography of Witchcraft: Salem Village, 1692

Geographic patterns of witchcraft testimony mirrored tensions within Salem Village. Accused witches and their defenders lived mostly in the village's eastern division or in Salem Town, whereas their accusers overwhelmingly resided in the village's western sector. (*Source:* Adapted from Paul Boyer and Stephen Nissenbaum. *Salem Possessed: The Social Origins of Witchcraft* [Cambridge, Mass.: Harvard University Press, 1974].)

Other patterns were also apparent. Two-thirds of all "possessed" accusers were females aged eleven to twenty, and more than half had lost one or both parents in Anglo-Indian conflicts in Maine. They and other survivors had fled to Massachusetts, where most were now servants in other families' households. These young women gained momentary power and prominence by voicing the anxieties and hostilities of others in their community and by virtually dictating the course of events in and around Salem for several months.

Accusers and witnesses most frequently named as witches middle-aged wives and widows—women who had avoided the poverty and uncertainty they themselves faced. A disproportionate number of accused women had inherited, or stood to inherit, property beyond the one-third of a husband's estate normally bequeathed to widows. In other words, the accused tended to be women who had or soon might have more economic power and independence than many men. For New Englanders who felt the need to limit both female independence and economic individualism, witches symbolized the dangers awaiting those who disregarded such limits.

The number of persons facing trial multiplied quickly. Those found guilty desperately tried to stave off death by implicating others. As the pandemonium spread beyond Salem, fear dissolved ties of friendship and family. A minister heard himself condemned by his own granddaughter. A seven-year-old girl helped send her mother to the gallows. Fifty persons saved themselves by confessing. Twenty others who refused to disgrace their own names or betray other innocents went to their graves. Shortly before she was hanged, a victim named Mary Easty begged the court to come to its senses: "I petition your honors not for my own life, for I know I must die . . . [but] if it be possible, that no more innocent blood be shed."

By late 1692, most Massachusetts ministers came to doubt that justice was being done. They objected that spectral evidence, crucial in most convictions, lacked legal credibility because the devil could manipulate it. New Englanders, concluded Increase Mather, a leading clergyman, had fallen victim to a deadly game of "blind man's bluff" set up by Satan and were "hotly and madly, mauling one another in the dark." Backed by the clergy (and alarmed by an accusation against his wife), Governor William Phips forbade further imprisonments for witchcraft in October—by which time over a hundred individuals were in jail and twice that many stood accused. Shortly thereafter, he suspended all trials, and in early 1693 he pardoned all those convicted or suspected of witchcraft.

The witchcraft hysteria marked the end of Puritan New England. Colonists reaching maturity after 1692 would reject the ideals of earlier generations and become "Yankees" who shrewdly pursued material gain. True to their Puritan roots, they would retain their forceful convictions and self-discipline, giving New England a distinctive regional identity that would endure.

THE SPREAD OF SLAVERY:
THE CARIBBEAN AND CAROLINA

As the Chesapeake and New England flourished, an even larger wave of settlement swept the West Indies. Between 1630 and 1642, almost 60 percent of the seventy thousand English who emigrated to the Americas went to the Caribbean. Beginning in the 1640s, some English planters began using slave labor to produce sugar on large plantations. After 1670, many English islanders moved to the new mainland colony of Carolina, thereby facilitating the spread of large-scale plantation slavery to the North American mainland.

Sugar and Slaves:
The West Indies

As on the North American mainland, the Netherlands, France, and England entered the colonial race in the West Indies during the early seventeenth century and expanded thereafter. Challenging Spain's monopoly in the region, each nation seized islands in the region. Most notably, the Dutch took over Curaçao, the French claimed St. Domingue, the western half of Hispaniola, and the English established Barbados and seized Jamaica from Spain.

The tobacco boom that powered Virginia's economy until 1630 led early English settlers to cultivate that plant in the Caribbean. But with most colonists arriving after 1630, few realized spectacular profits. Through the 1630s, the English West Indies remained a society with a large percentage of independent landowners, an overwhelmingly white population, and a relative equality of wealth.

During the early 1640s an alternative to tobacco rapidly revolutionized the islands' economy and society. Dutch merchants familiar with Portuguese methods of sugar production in Brazil began encouraging West Indian planters to raise and process sugar cane, which the Dutch would then market (see Technology and Culture, Chapter 2).

Because planters needed three times as many workers per acre to produce sugar as tobacco, rising production greatly multiplied the demand for labor. As in the Chesapeake, planters in the English West Indies initially imported white indentured servants. After 1640, however, sugar planters increasingly purchased enslaved Africans from Dutch traders to do common fieldwork and used their indentured servants as overseers or skilled artisans.

Sugar planters preferred black slaves to white servants because slaves could be driven harder and cost less to maintain. Whereas most servants ended their indentures after four years, slaves toiled until death. Although slaves initially cost two to four times more than servants, they proved a more economical long-term investment. In this way, the profit motive and the racism that emerged with the "new slavery" (see Chapter 2) reinforced one another.

By 1670, the sugar revolution had transformed the British West Indies into a predominantly slave society. Thereafter the number of blacks shot up from approximately 40,000 to 130,000 in 1713. Meanwhile, the white population remained stable at about 33,000 because the planters' preference for slave labor greatly reduced the importation of indentured servants after 1670.

Three victorious wars with the Dutch and enactment of the Navigation Acts (see Chapter 4) enabled English merchants and shippers to monopolize the trade in sugar and slaves (and other commodities) of England's colonies. The profits from its Caribbean colonies were a principal factor in England's becoming the wealthiest nation in the Atlantic world by 1700.

Declining demand for white labor in the West Indies diverted the flow of English immigration from the islands to mainland North America and so contributed to population growth there. Furthermore, because the expansion of West Indian sugar plantations priced land beyond the reach of most whites, perhaps thirty thousand people left the islands from 1655 to 1700. Most whites who quit the West Indies migrated to the mainland colonies, especially Carolina.

Rice and Slaves: Carolina
    In 1663, King Charles II bestowed the swampy coast between Virginia and Spanish Florida on several English supporters, making it the first of several Restoration colonies. The grateful proprietors named their colony Carolina in honor of Charles (*Carolus* in Latin).

One of the proprietors, Anthony Ashley Cooper, and his young secretary, John Locke—later acclaimed as one of the great philosophers of the age (see Chapter 4)—drew up a plan for Carolina's settlement and government. Their Fundamental Constitutions provided for a three-tiered nobility that would hold two-fifths of all land, make laws through a Council of Nobles, and dispense justice through manorial law courts. Ordinary Carolinians with smaller landholdings were expected to defer to this nobility, although they would enjoy religious toleration and English common law, and could elect an assembly. To induce settlement, the proprietors offered a headright of one hundred fifty acres to planters for each arriving family member or slave as well as one hundred acres to each servant who completed a term of indenture.

Uninterested in moving themselves, the proprietors arranged for settlers from the West Indian island of Barbados, where the largest sugar planters had bought up most of the land, to get their colony started. Accordingly, in 1670, two hundred white Barbadians and their slaves landed near modern-day Charleston, "in the very chops of the Spanish." The settlement called Charles Town formed the colony's nucleus.

Until the 1680s, most settlers were from Barbados, with smaller numbers from mainland colonies and some French Huguenots. Obtaining all the land they needed, the colonists saw little reason to obey absentee lords and ignored most of the plans drawn up for them across the Atlantic. Southern Carolinians raised livestock and exported Indian slaves (see below), while colonists in northern Carolina produced tobacco, lumber, and pitch, giving local people the name "tarheels." At first these activities did not produce enough profit to warrant maintaining many slaves, so self-sufficient white families predominated in the area.

But some southern Carolinians, particularly wealthier settlers from Barbados, sought a staple crop that could make them rich. By the early eighteenth century, they found it in rice. Because rice, like sugar, enormously enriched a few men with capital to invest in costly dams, dikes, and slaves, it remade southern Carolina into a society resembling the one from which they came. By earning annual profits of 25 percent, rice planters within a generation became the one mainland colonial elite whose wealth rivaled that of the Caribbean sugar planters.

Even when treated humanely, indentured English servants simply did not survive in humid rice paddies swarming with malaria-bearing mosquitoes. The planters' solution was to import an ever-growing force of enslaved Africans who, they calculated, possessed two major advantages. First, perhaps 15 percent of the Africans taken to Carolina had cultivated rice in their homelands in Senegambia, and their expertise was vital in teaching whites how to raise the unfamiliar crop. Second, many Africans had developed immunities to malaria and yellow fever, infectious and deadly diseases transmitted by mosquito bites, which were endemic to coastal regions of West Africa. Enslaved Africans, along with infected slave ships' crews, carried both diseases to North America. (Tragically, the antibody that helps ward off malaria also tends to produce the sickle-cell trait, a genetic condition often fatal to the children who inherit it.) These two advantages made commercial rice production possible in Carolina. Because a typical rice planter farming 130 acres needed sixty-five slaves, a great demand for black slave labor resulted. The proportion of slaves in southern Carolina's population rose from just 17 percent in 1680 to about half by 1700. Thereafter, Carolina would have a black majority.

Rice thrived only within a forty-mile-wide coastal strip extending from Cape Fear to present-day Georgia. Carolinians grimly joked that the malaria-infested rice belt was a paradise in spring, an inferno in summer, and a hospital in the wet, chilly fall. In the worst months, planters' families usually escaped to the relatively cool and more healthful climate of Charles Town and let overseers supervise their slaves during harvests.

Enslavement in Carolina was by no means confined to Africans. In the 1670s, traders in southern Carolina armed nearby Native Americans and encouraged them to raid rival tribes for slaves. After local supplies of Indian slaves were exhausted, the English-allied Indians captured unarmed Guale, Apalachee, and Timucua Indians at

Spanish missions in Florida and traded them to the Carolinians for guns and other European goods. The English in turn sold the enslaved Indians, mostly to planters in the West Indies but also in the mainland colonies as far north as New England. By the mid-1680s, the Carolinians had extended the trade through alliances with the Yamasees and the Creeks, a powerful confederacy centered in what is now western Georgia and northern Alabama. For three decades, these Indian allies of the English terrorized Catholic mission Indians in Spanish Florida with their slave raids. No statistical records of Carolina's Indian slave trade survive, but the most recent study estimates that thirty to fifty thousand Native Americans were enslaved between 1670 and 1715. Most of those shipped to the West Indies died quickly because they lacked immunities to both European and tropical diseases.

THE MIDDLE COLONIES

Between the Chesapeake and New England, two non-English nations established colonies. New Netherland and New Sweden were small commercial outposts, although the Dutch colony eventually flourished and took over New Sweden. But England seized New Netherland from the Dutch in 1664, and carved New York, New Jersey, and Pennsylvania out of the former Dutch territory. These actions together created a fourth English colonial region, the middle colonies.

Precursors: New Netherland and New Sweden   New Netherland was North America's first multiethnic colony. Barely half its colonists were Dutch; most of the rest were Germans, French, Scandinavians, and Africans, free as well as enslaved. In 1643, the population included Protestants, Catholics, Jews, and Muslims; and eighteen European and African languages were spoken. But religion counted for little (in 1642 the colony had seventeen taverns but not one place of worship), and the colonists' get-rich-quick attitude had fostered New Amsterdam's growth as a thriving port. The same attitude sapped company profits as private individuals persisted in illegally trading furs. In 1639, the company bowed to mounting pressure and legalized private fur trading.

Privatization led to a rapid rise in the number of guns reaching New Netherland's Iroquois allies, giving them a distinct advantage over rival Natives. As overhunting depleted local supplies of beaver skins and as smallpox epidemics took their toll, the Iroquois encroached on pro-French Indians in a quest for pelts and for captives who could be adopted into Iroquois families to replace the dead. Between 1648 and 1657, the Iroquois, in a series of bloody **"beaver wars,"** dispersed the Hurons and other French allies, incorporating many members of these nations into their own ranks. Then they attacked the French settlements along the St. Lawrence. "They come like foxes, they attack like lions, they disappear like birds," wrote a French Jesuit of the Iroquois.

Although the Dutch allied successfully with the inland Iroquois, their relations with nearby coastal Native Americans paralleled white-Indian relations in England's seaboard colonies. With its greedy settlers and military weakness, New Netherland had largely itself to blame. In 1643, all-out war erupted when the colony's governor ordered the massacre of previously friendly Indians who were protesting settler encroachments on Long Island. By 1645, the Dutch prevailed over these Indians and their allies only

MAP 3.2 European Colonization in the Middle and North Atlantic, c. 1650

North of Spanish Florida, four European powers competed for territory and trade with Native Americans in the early seventeenth century. Swedish and Dutch colonization was the foundation upon which England's middle colonies were built.

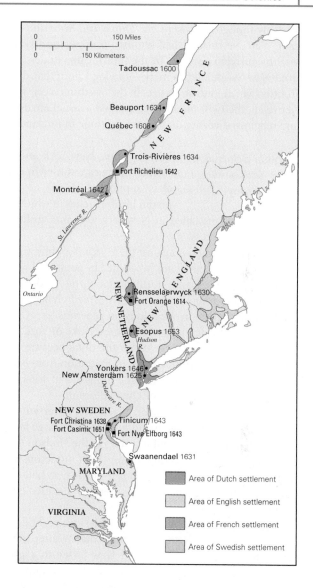

with English help and by inflicting additional atrocities. But the fighting, known as Kieft's War for the governor who ordered the massacre, helped reduce New Netherland's Indian population from sixteen hundred to seven hundred.

Another European challenger distracted the Dutch as they sought to suppress neighboring Native Americans. In 1638, Sweden had planted a small fur-trading colony in the lower Delaware Valley. Trading with the Delaware (or Lenni Lenape) and Susquehannock Indians, New Sweden diverted many furs from New Netherland. Annoyed, the Dutch colony's governor, Peter Stuyvesant, led seven warships and three hundred troops into New Sweden in 1655. The four hundred residents of the rival colony peacefully accepted Dutch annexation.

Tiny though they were, the Dutch and Swedish colonies were historically significant. New Netherland had attained a population of nine thousand and featured a wealthy, thriving port city by the time it came under English rule in 1664. Even short-lived New Sweden left a mark—the log cabin, that durable symbol of the American frontier, which Finnish settlers in the Swedish colony first introduced to the continent. Above all, the two colonies bequeathed a social environment characterized by ethnic and religious diversity that would continue in England's middle colonies.

English Conquests: New York and New Jersey Like Carolina, New York and New Jersey originated as proprietary colonies, awarded by King Charles II to favored upper-class supporters. Here, too, proprietors hoped to create hierarchical societies in which they would profit from settlers' rents. These plans failed in New Jersey, as in Carolina. Only in New York did they achieve some success.

In 1664, waging war against the Dutch Republic, Charles II dispatched a naval force to conquer New Netherland. Weakened by additional wars with Indians as New Netherland sought to expand northward on the Hudson River, Dutch governor Peter Stuyvesant and four hundred poorly armed civilians surrendered peacefully. Most of the Dutch remained in the colony on generous terms.

Charles II made his brother James, Duke of York, proprietor of the new province and renamed it New York. When the duke became King James II in 1685, he proclaimed New York a royal colony. Immigration from New England, Britain, and France boosted the population from nine thousand in 1664 to twenty thousand in 1700, of whom just 44 percent were of Dutch descent.

Following Dutch precedent, New York's governors rewarded their wealthiest political supporters, both Dutch and English, with large land grants. By 1703, five families held approximately 1.75 million acres in the Hudson River Valley, which they withheld from sale in hope of creating manors with numerous rent-paying tenants. Earning an enormous income from their rents over the next half-century, the New York **patroons** (the Dutch name for manor lords) formed a landed elite second in wealth only to the Carolina rice planters.

Ambitious plans collided with American realities in New Jersey, which also was carved out of New Netherland. Immediately after the Dutch province's conquest in 1664, the Duke of York awarded New Jersey to a group of proprietors headed by William Penn, John Lord Berkeley, and Sir Philip Carteret. About four thousand Delaware Indians and a few hundred Dutch and Swedes inhabited the area at the time. From the beginning New Jersey's proprietors had difficulty controlling their province. By 1672, several thousand New Englanders had settled along the Atlantic shore. After the quarrelsome Puritans renounced allegiance to them, Berkeley and Carteret sold the region to a group of even more contentious religious dissenters called Quakers, who split the territory into the two colonies of West Jersey (1676) and East Jersey (1682).

The Jerseys' Quakers, Anglicans, Puritans, Scottish Presbyterians, Dutch Calvinists, and Swedish Lutherans got along poorly with one another and even worse with the proprietors. Both governments collapsed between 1698 and 1701 as mobs disrupted the courts. In 1702, the disillusioned proprietors finally surrendered their political powers to the crown, which proclaimed New Jersey a royal province.

Quaker
Pennsylvania

In 1681 Charles II paid off a huge debt by making a supporter's son, **William Penn,** the proprietor of the last unallocated tract of American territory at the king's disposal. Perhaps the most distinctive of all English colonial founders, Penn (1644–1718) had two aims in developing Pennsylvania (Penn's Woods). First, he was a Quaker and wanted to launch a "holy experiment" based on the teachings of the radical English preacher George Fox. Second, "though I desire to extend religious freedom," he explained, "yet I want some recompense for my trouble."

Quakers in late-seventeenth-century England stood well beyond the fringe of respectability. Quakerism appealed strongly to men and women at the bottom of the economic ladder, and its adherents challenged the conventional foundation of the social order. George Fox, the movement's originator, had received his inspiration while wandering civil war–torn England's byways and searching for spiritual meaning among distressed common people. Tried on one occasion for blasphemy, he warned the judge to "tremble at the word of the Lord" and was ridiculed as a "quaker." Fox's followers called themselves the Society of Friends, but the name Quaker stuck. They were the most successful of the many radical religious sects born in England during the 1640s and 1650s.

The core of Fox's theology was his belief that the Holy Spirit or "Inner Light" could inspire every soul. Mainstream Christians, by contrast, found any such claim of direct, personal communication with God highly dangerous, as Anne Hutchinson's banishment from Massachusetts Bay in 1637 revealed. Although trusting direct inspiration and disavowing the need for a clergy, Friends also took great pains to ensure that individual opinions would not be mistaken for God's will. They felt confident that they understood the Inner Light only after having reached near-unanimous agreement through intensive and searching discussion led by "Public Friends"—ordinary laypeople. In their simple religious services ("meetings"), Quakers sat silently until the Inner Light prompted one of them to speak.

Some of the Friends' beliefs led them to behave in ways that aroused fierce hostility for being disrespectful to authorities and their social superiors. For example, insisting that individuals deserved recognition for their spiritual state rather than their wealth or status, Quakers refused to tip their hats to their social betters. They likewise flouted convention by not using the formal pronoun "you" when speaking to members of the gentry, instead addressing everyone with the informal "thee" and "thou" as a token of equality. By wearing their hats in court, moreover, Quakers appeared to mock the state's authority; and by taking literally Scripture's ban on swearing oaths, they seemed to place themselves above the law. The Friends' refusal to bear arms appeared unpatriotic and cowardly to many. Finally, Quakers accorded women unprecedented equality. The Inner Light, Fox insisted, could "speak in the female as well as the male." Acting on these beliefs, Quakers suffered persecution and occasionally death in England, Massachusetts, and Virginia.

Not all Quakers came from the bottom of society. The movement's emphasis on quiet introspection and its refusal to adopt a formal creed also attracted some well-educated and prosperous individuals disillusioned by the quarreling of rival faiths. The possessor of a great fortune, William Penn was hardly a typical Friend, but there were significant numbers of merchants among the estimated sixty thousand Quakers in the British Isles in the early 1680s. Moreover, the industriousness that the Society of Friends encouraged in its members ensured that many humble Quakers accumulated money and property.

Much care lay behind the Quaker migration to Pennsylvania that began in 1681, and it resulted in the most successful beginning of any European colony in North America. Penn sent an advance party to the Delaware Valley, where about five thousand Delaware Indians and one thousand Swedes and Dutch already lived. After an agonizing voyage in which one-third of the passengers died, Penn arrived in 1682. Choosing a site for the capital, he named it Philadelphia—the "City of Brotherly Love." By 1687, some eight thousand settlers had joined Penn across the Atlantic. Most were Quakers from the British Isles, but they also included Presbyterians, Baptists, Anglicans, and Catholics, as well as Lutherans and radical sectarians from Germany—most of them attracted by Pennsylvania's religious toleration as well as its economic promise. As in New England, most immigrants arrived in family groups rather than as single males, so that the population grew rapidly. In 1698, one Quaker reported that in Pennsylvania one seldom met "any young Married Woman but hath a Child in her belly, or one upon her lap."

After wavering between authoritarian and more democratic plans, Penn finally gave Pennsylvania a government with a strong executive branch (a governor and governor's council) and granted the lower legislative chamber (the assembly) only limited powers. Friends, forming the majority of the colony's population, dominated this elected assembly. Penn named Quakers and their supporters as governor, judges, and sheriffs. Like most elites of the time, he feared "the ambitions of the populace which shakes the Constitution," and he intended to check "the rabble" as much as possible. Because he also insisted on the orderly disposition of property and hoped to avoid unseemly wrangling, he carefully oversaw land sales in the colony. To prevent haphazard growth and social turmoil in Philadelphia, Penn designed the city with a grid plan, laying out the streets at right angles and reserving small areas for parks.

Unlike most seaboard colonies, Pennsylvania avoided early hostilities with Native Americans. This was partly a result of the reduced Native population in the Delaware Valley. But it was also a testament to Penn's Quaker tolerance. To the Delaware Indians Penn expressed a wish "to live together as Neighbours and Friends," and he made it the colony's policy to buy land it wanted for settlement from them.

Land was a key to Pennsylvania's early prosperity. Rich, level lands and a lengthy growing season enabled immigrants to produce bumper crops. West Indian demand for the colony's grain rose sharply and by 1700 made Philadelphia a major port.

Like other attempts to base new American societies on preconceived plans or lofty ideals, Penn's "peaceable kingdom" soon bogged down in human bickering. After the founder returned to England in 1684, the settlers quarreled incessantly. An opposition party attacked Penn's efforts to monopolize foreign trade and to make each landowner pay him a small annual fee. Bitter struggles between Penn's supporters in the governor's council and opponents in the assembly deadlocked the government. From 1686 to 1688, the legislature passed no laws, and the council once ordered the lower house's speaker arrested. Penn's brief return to Pennsylvania from 1699 to 1701 helped little. Just before he sailed home, he made the legislature a unicameral (one-chamber) assembly and allowed it to initiate measures.

Religious conflict shook Pennsylvania during the 1690s, when George Keith, a college-educated Public Friend, urged Quakers to adopt a formal creed and train ministers. This would have changed the democratically functioning Quaker movement—in which the humblest member had equal authority in interpreting the Inner Light—into a hierarchical church dominated by a clergy. The majority of Friends rejected Keith's views in 1692, whereupon he joined the Church of England, taking some Quakers with him. Keith's departure began a major decline in the Quaker share of Pennsylvania's population. The proportion fell further once Quakers ceased immigrating in large numbers after 1710.

William Penn met his strongest opposition in the counties on the lower Delaware River, where Swedes and Dutch had taken up the best lands. In 1704, these counties became the separate colony of Delaware, but Penn continued to name their governors.

The middle colonies demonstrated that British America could benefit by encouraging religious toleration and ethnic pluralism. New York and New Jersey successfully integrated New Netherland's Swedish and Dutch population; and neither Pennsylvania, New Jersey, nor Delaware required taxpayers to support an established church.

RIVALS FOR NORTH AMERICA: FRANCE AND SPAIN

In marked contrast to England's compact, densely populated settlements on the Atlantic, France and Spain established far-flung inland networks of fortified trading posts and missions. Unable to attract large numbers of colonists, they enlisted Native Americans as trading partners and military allies, and the two Catholic nations had far more success than English Protestants in converting Indians to Christianity. By 1700, French and Spanish missionaries, traders, and soldiers—and relatively few farmers and ranchers—were spreading European influence well beyond the range of England's colonies, to much of Canada and to what is now the American Midwest, Southeast, and Southwest.

France Claims a Continent

After briefly losing Canada to England (1629–1632), France resumed and extended its colonization there. Paralleling the early English and Dutch colonies, a privately held company initially assumed responsibility for settling New France. The Company of New France granted extensive tracts, called *seigneuries*, to large landlords (*seigneurs*), who could either import indentured servants or rent out small tracts within their holdings to prospective farmers. Although some farmers and other colonists spread along the St. Lawrence River as far inland as Montreal, Canada's harsh winters and short growing season sharply limited their numbers.

More successful in New France were commercial traders and missionaries who spread beyond the settlements and relied on stable relations with Indians to succeed. Despite the defeat of some of France's Native American allies in the beaver wars (see above), French-Indian trade prospered. Indeed, the more lucrative opportunities offered by trade diverted many French men who had initially arrived to take up farming.

The colony also benefited from the substantial efforts of Catholic religious workers, especially Jesuit missionaries and Ursuline nuns. Given a virtual monopoly on missions to Native Americans in 1633, the Jesuits followed the fur trade into the North American interior. Although the missionaries often feuded with the traders, whose morality they condemned, the two groups together spread French influence westward to the Great Lakes, securing the loyalty of the region's Indians in their struggles with the Iroquois. The Ursulines ministered particularly to Native American women and girls nearer Quebec, ensuring that Catholic piety and morality directly reached all members of Indian families.

The chief minister of France's King Louis XIV (reigned 1661–1715), Jean-Baptiste Colbert, was a forceful proponent of the doctrine of mercantilism (see Chapter 4), which held that colonies should provide their home country with raw materials for manufacturing and markets for manufactured goods. Ideally, the nation would not have to depend on rival countries for trade. Accordingly, Colbert hoped that New France could increase its output of furs, ship agricultural surpluses to France's new sugar-producing colonies in the West Indies, and export timber to those colonies and for the French navy. To begin realizing these goals, France revoked the charter of the Company of New France in 1663 and placed the colony under royal direction.

With the colony under its direct control, the French government sought to stifle the Iroquois threat to New France's economy. For more than half a century, and especially since the beaver wars, the Iroquois had limited New France's productivity by intercepting convoys of beaver pelts from the interior and taking them to Dutch merchants in New Netherland. (The Dutch maintained their ties to the Iroquois after the English takeover in 1664.) In 1666, France sent fifteen hundred soldiers to stop Iroquois interference with the fur trade. In that year, the troops sacked and burned four Mohawk villages that were well stocked with winter food. After the alarmed Iroquois made a peace that lasted until 1680, New France enormously expanded its North American fur exports.

Meanwhile, Colbert encouraged French immigration to Canada. Within a decade of the royal takeover, the number of whites rose from twenty-five hundred to eighty-five hundred. The vast majority consisted of indentured servants who were paid wages and given land after three years' work. Others were former soldiers and their officers who were given land grants and other incentives to remain in New France and farm while strengthening the colony's defenses. The officers were encouraged to marry among the "king's girls," female orphans shipped over with dowries.

The upsurge in French immigration petered out after 1673. Tales of disease and other hazards of the transatlantic voyage, of Canada's hard winters, and of wars with the "savage" Iroquois were spread by the two-thirds of French immigrants who returned to their native land. New France would grow slowly, relying on the natural increase of its small population rather than on newcomers from Europe.

Colbert had encouraged immigration in order to enhance New France's agricultural productivity. But as in earlier years, many French men who remained spurned farming in the St. Lawrence Valley, instead swarming westward in search of furs. By 1670, one-fifth of them were *voyageurs*, or *coureurs de bois*—independent traders unconstrained by government authority. Living in Indian villages and often marrying Native women, the *coureurs* built an empire for France. From Canadian and Great Lakes Indians they obtained furs in exchange for European goods, including guns to use against the Iroquois and other rivals. In their commercial interactions, the French and Indians observed Native American norms of reciprocity (see Chapter 1). Their exchanges of goods sealed bonds of friendship and alliance, which served their mutual interests in trade and in war against common enemies.

Alarmed by the rapid expansion of England's colonies and by Spanish plans to link Florida with New Mexico (see below), France boldly sought to dominate the North

American heartland. As early as 1672, fur trader Louis Jolliet and Jesuit missionary Jacques Marquette became the first Europeans known to have reached the upper Mississippi River (near modern Prairie du Chien, Wisconsin); they later paddled twelve hundred miles downstream to the Mississippi's junction with the Arkansas River. Ten years later, **Robert Cavelier de La Salle,** an ambitious upper-class adventurer, descended the entire Mississippi to the Gulf of Mexico. When he reached the delta, La Salle formally claimed the entire Mississippi basin—half the territory of the present-day continental United States—for Louis XIV, in whose honor he named the territory Louisiana.

Having asserted title to this vast empire, the French began settling the southern gateway into it. In 1698, the first colonizers arrived on the Gulf of Mexico coast. A year later the French erected a fort near present-day Biloxi, Mississippi. In 1702, they occupied the former Mississippian city of Mábila, where De Soto's expedition had faltered a century and a half earlier (see Chapter 2), founding a trading post, and calling it Mobile. But Louisiana's growth would stall for another decade.

New Mexico: The Pueblo Revolt

Spanish colonization in North America after 1625 expanded upon the two bases established earlier in New Mexico and Florida (see Chapter 2). Lying at the northerly margin of Spain's empire, both colonies remained small and weak through the seventeenth century. With few settlers, they needed ties with friendly Native Americans in order to obtain land, labor, and security. But Spanish policies made friendly relations hard to come by in both places.

From the beginning, the Spanish sought to rule New Mexico by subordinating the Pueblo Indians to their authority in several ways. First, Franciscan missionaries supervised the Indians' spiritual lives by establishing churches in most of the Indian communities (pueblos) and attempting to force the natives to attend mass and observe Catholic rituals and morality. Second, Spanish landowners were awarded *encomiendas* (see Chapter 2), which allowed them to exploit Indian labor and productivity for personal profits. Finally, the Spanish drove a wedge between the Pueblo Indians and their nonfarming neighbors, the Apaches and Navajos. Because the Spanish collected corn as tribute, the Pueblo Indians could no longer trade their surplus crops with the Apaches and Navajos. Having incorporated corn into their diets, the Apaches and Navajos raided the pueblos for the grain. They also raided the colonists to retaliate for Spanish slave traders having captured and sold some of their people to work in Mexican silver mines. A few outlying pueblos made common cause with the Apaches, but most Pueblo Indians relied on the Spanish for protection from the raids.

Although local rebellions erupted sporadically over the first six decades of Spanish rule, most Pueblo Indians initially accepted Spanish rule and tried to reconcile Catholicism with their own religious traditions. Beginning in the 1660s, however, many Natives grew disillusioned. For several consecutive years their crops withered under the effects of sustained drought. Drought-induced starvation plus deadly epidemic diseases sent the Pueblo population plummeting from about eighty thousand in 1598 to just seventeen thousand in the 1670s. In response, many Christian Indians openly resumed traditional Pueblo ceremonies, hoping to restore the spiritual balance that had brought ample rainfall, good health, and peace before the Spanish arrived. Seeking to suppress this religious revival as "witchcraft" and "idolatry," the Franciscan missionaries entered sacred kivas (underground ceremonial centers), destroyed religious objects, and publicly whipped Native religious leaders and their followers.

Matters came to a head in 1675 when Governor Juan Francisco Treviño ordered soldiers to sack the kivas and arrest Pueblo religious leaders. Three leaders were sentenced to the gallows; a fourth hanged himself; and forty-three others were jailed, whipped, and sold as slaves. In response, armed warriors from several pueblos converged on Santa Fe and demanded the prisoners' release. With most of his soldiers off fighting the Apaches, Governor Treviño complied.

Despite this concession, there was now no cooling of Pueblo resentment against the Spanish. Pueblo leaders began gathering secretly to plan the overthrow of Spanish rule. At the head of this effort was Popé, one of those who had been arrested in 1675. Besides Popé and one El Saca, the leaders included men such as Luis Tupatú, Antonio Malacate, and others whose Christian names signified that they had once been baptized. They and many of their followers had attempted to reconcile conversion to Christianity and subjection to Spanish rule with their identities as Indians. But deteriorating conditions and the cruel intolerance of the Spanish had turned them against Catholicism.

In August 1680 Popé and his cohorts were ready to act. On the morning of August 10, some Indians from the pueblo of Taos and their Apache allies attacked the homes of the seventy Spanish colonists residing near Taos and killed all but two. Then, with Indians from neighboring pueblos, they proceeded south and joined a massive siege of New Mexico's capital, Santa Fe. Thus began the **Pueblo Revolt** of 1680, the most successful Indian uprising in American history.

At each pueblo, rebels destroyed the churches and religious paraphernalia and killed those missionaries who did not escape. All told, about four hundred colonists were slain. Then they "plunge[d] into the rivers and wash[ed] themselves with amole," a native root, in order to undo their baptisms. As a follower later testified, Popé also called on the Indians "to break and enlarge their cultivated fields, saying now they were as they had been in ancient times, free from the labor they had performed for the religious and the Spaniards."

The siege of Santa Fe led to the expulsion of the Spanish from New Mexico for twelve years. Only in 1692 did a new governor, Diego de Vargas, arrive to "reconquer" New Mexico. Exploiting divisions that had emerged among the Pueblos in the colonists' absence, Vargas used violence and threats of violence to reestablish Spanish rule. Even then, Spain did not effectively quash Pueblo resistance until 1700, and thereafter its control of the province was more limited than before. To appease the Pueblos, on whom they depended for defense against the Apaches and other Indians, Spanish authorities abolished the hated *encomienda*. They also ordered the Franciscans not to disturb the Pueblos in their traditional religious practices and to cease inflicting corporal punishment on the Indians.

Pueblos' suspicions of the Spanish lingered after 1700, but they did not again attempt to overthrow them. With the missions and *encomienda* less intrusive, they sustained their cultural identities within, rather than outside, the bounds of colonial rule.

Florida and Texas   The Spanish fared no better in Florida, an even older colony than New Mexico. For most of the seventeenth century, Florida's colonial population numbered only in the hundreds, primarily Spanish soldiers and Franciscan missionaries. Before 1680, the colony faced periodic rebellions from Guale, Timucua, and Apalachee Indians protesting forced labor and Franciscan attempts to impose religious conformity. Thereafter Creek and other Indian slave raiders allied to the English in Carolina added to the Florida Indians' miseries. While the Spanish, with their small numbers of soldiers and arms looked on helplessly, the invading Indians killed and captured thousands of Florida's Natives and sold them to English slave traders in Carolina (see above). Even before a new round of warfare erupted in Europe at the turn of the century, Spain was ill prepared to defend its beleaguered North American colonies.

English expansion threatened Florida, while the French establishment of Louisiana defied Spain's hope of one day linking that colony with New Mexico. To counter the French, Spanish authorities in Mexico proclaimed the province of Texas (Tejas) in 1691. But no permanent Spanish settlements appeared there until 1716 (see Chapter 4).

CONCLUSION

In less than a century, from 1625 to 1700, the movements of peoples and goods, across the Atlantic and within the continent, transformed the map of North America. Immigrants and slaves spread far and wide among colonial regions in the Americas. Depending on their circumstances, Native Americans resisted or accommodated the newcomers.

The English colonies were by far the most populous. By 1700 the combined number of whites and blacks in England's mainland North American colonies was about 250,000, compared with 15,000 for those of France and 4,500 for those of Spain.

Within the English colonies, four distinct regions emerged. After beginning with a labor force consisting primarily of white indentured servants, the tobacco planters of the Chesapeake region replaced them with enslaved Africans. New England's Puritanism grew less utopian and more worldly as the inhabitants gradually reconciled their religious views with the realities of a commercial economy. Slavery had been instituted among the English by sugar planters in the West Indies, some of whom introduced it in the third North American region, Carolina. Between the Chesapeake and New England, a fourth region, the middle colonies, continued the ethnic pluralism and religious toleration of their Swedish and Dutch predecessors. Middle colonists, including the Quakers, embraced the market economy with far less hesitation than their Puritan neighbors in New England. While planters or merchants rose to prominence in each English region, most whites continued to live on family farms.

With far fewer colonists, French and Spanish colonists depended more on friendly relations with Native Americans for their livelihoods and security than did the English. Before 1700 most French North Americans lived in the St. Lawrence Valley, where a lively commercial-agrarian economy was emerging, though on a far smaller scale than in New England and the middle colonies. Most Spanish colonists not connected to the government, military, or a missionary order resided in the Rio Grande Valley in New Mexico. But smaller numbers and geographic isolation would prevent the Southwest from becoming a major center of colonization.

By 1700 there were clear differences between the societies and economies of the three colonial powers in North America. These differences would prove decisive in shaping American history during the century that followed.

4

The Bonds of Empire, 1660–1750

REBELLION AND WAR, 1660–1713

The Restoration (1660) of the monarchy in England did not resolve the nation's deep-seated political antagonisms. Charles II and James II (ruled 1685–1688) attempted to strengthen the crown at Parliament's expense and abolished locally elected offices and legislatures in several colonies. After England in 1689 overthrew James and replaced him with his daughter, Mary, and her husband, William, Massachusetts, New York, and Maryland carried out their own revolts. The outcome was a strengthening of both royal authority and representative legislatures in the colonies.

The overthrow of James, a pro-French Catholic, led directly to a period of warfare between England and France. By the time peace was restored in 1713, the colonists had become closely tied to a new, powerful British empire.

Royal Centralization, 1660–1688   The Restoration monarchs had little use for representative government. Charles II rarely called Parliament into session after 1674, and not at all after 1681. James II, Charles's younger brother, hoped to reign as an "absolute" monarch like France's Louis XIV, who never faced an elected legislature. Not surprisingly, the two English kings had little sympathy for American colonial assemblies.

Royal intentions of extending direct political control to North America first became evident in New York. The proprietor, the future James II, considered elected assemblies "of dangerous consequence" and forbade them to meet, except briefly between 1682 and 1686. Meanwhile, Charles II appointed former army officers to about 90 percent of all royal governorships, thereby compromising the time-honored English tradition of separating military from civilian authority. By 1680 such

CHRONOLOGY, 1660–1750

1651–1663 • England enacts first three Navigation Acts.

1660 • Restoration of the English monarchy.

1686–1689 • Dominion of New England.

1688–1689 • Glorious Revolution in England.

1689 • English Bill of Rights.

1689–1691 • Uprisings in Massachusetts, New York, and Maryland.

1689–1697 • King William's War (in Europe, War of the League of Augsburg).

1690 • John Locke, *Essay Concerning Human Understanding.*

1693 • Spain begins offering freedom to English-owned slaves escaping to Florida.

1701 • Iroquois Confederacy's Grand Settlement with England and France.

1702–1713 • Queen Anne's War (in Europe, War of the Spanish Succession).

1711–1713 • Tuscarora War in Carolina.

1715–1716 • Yamasee War in Carolina.

1716 • San Antonio de Béxar founded.

1718 • New Orleans founded.

1729–1730 • French war on Natchez Indians in Louisiana.

1733 • Georgia founded. Molasses Act.

1735 • John Peter Zenger acquitted of seditious libel in New York. Jonathan Edwards leads revival in Northampton, Massachusetts.

1737 • Walking Purchase of Delaware Indian lands in Pennsylvania.

1739 • Great Awakening begins with George Whitefield's arrival in British colonies. Stono Rebellion in South Carolina.

1739–1740 • Anglo-Spanish "War of Jenkins' Ear."

1740–1748 • King George's War (in Europe, the War of the Austrian Succession).

1743 • Benjamin Franklin founds American Philosophical Society.

1750 • Slavery legalized in Georgia.

"governors general" ruled 60 percent of all American colonists. James II continued this policy.

Established by Puritan dissenters, Massachusetts proved most stubborn in defending self-government and resisting English authority. The crown insisted that the colony base voting rights on property ownership rather than church membership, that it tolerate Anglicans and Quakers, and that it observe the Navigation Acts (see below). As early as 1661, the General Court defiantly declared Massachusetts colonists exempt from all parliamentary laws and royal decrees except declarations of war. Charles II moved to break the Puritan establishment's power. In 1679, he carved a new royal colony, New Hampshire, out of its territory. Then, in 1684, he declared Massachusetts a royal colony and revoked its charter, the very foundation of the Puritan city upon a hill. Puritan leaders repudiated the king's actions, calling on colonists to resist even to the point of martyrdom.

Royal centralization accelerated after James II ascended to the throne. In 1686, the new king consolidated Massachusetts, New Hampshire, Connecticut, Rhode Island, and Plymouth into a single administrative unit, the **Dominion of New England,** with its capital at Boston. He added New York and the Jerseys to the dominion in 1688. With these bold strokes, the legislatures in these colonies ceased to exist, and still another former army officer, Sir Edmund Andros, became governor of the new supercolony.

Massachusetts burned with hatred for the dominion and its governor. By "Exercise of an arbitrary Government," preached Salem's minister, "ye wicked walked on Every Side & ye Vilest of men ware [*sic*] exalted." Andros was indeed arbitrary. He limited towns to a single annual meeting, and strictly enforced religious toleration and the Navigation Acts. "You have no more privileges left you," Andros reportedly told a group of outraged colonists, "than not to be sold for slaves."

Tensions also ran high in New York, where Catholics held prominent political and military posts under James, himself a Catholic. By 1688, colonists feared that these Catholic officials would betray New York to France, England's chief imperial rival. When Andros's local deputy allowed the harbor's forts to deteriorate and downplayed rumors that Native Americans would attack, New Yorkers suspected the worst.

The Glorious Revolution, 1688–1689

Not only colonists but also most English people were alarmed by the religious, political, and diplomatic directions in which the monarchy was taking the nation. Charles II (who had secretly converted to Catholicism) and James II ignored Parliament and violated its laws, issuing decrees allowing Catholics to hold high office and worship openly. English Protestants' fears that they would have to accept Catholicism intensified after both kings expressed their friendship with France's King Louis XIV, just as the French monarch launched new persecutions of his country's Protestant Huguenots in 1685.

The English tolerated James's Catholicism only because the potential heirs to the throne, his daughters Mary and Anne, remained Anglican. But in 1688, James's wife bore a son who would be raised a Catholic and, as a male, precede his sisters in the line of succession to the throne. Aghast at the thought of another Catholic monarch, several leading political and religious figures invited Mary and her husband, William of Orange (head of state in the Protestant Netherlands), to intervene. When William led a small Dutch army to England in November 1688, most royal troops defected to them, and James II fled to France.

This revolution of 1688, called the **Glorious Revolution,** created a "limited monarchy" as defined by the **English Bill of Rights** (1689). The crown was required to summon Parliament annually, sign all its bills, and respect traditional civil liberties. This circumscribing of monarchial power and vindication of limited representative government burned deeply into the English political consciousness, and Anglo-Americans never forgot it.

News that England's Protestant leaders had overthrown James II electrified New Englanders. On April 18, 1689, well before confirmation of the English revolt's success, Boston's militia arrested Andros and his councilors. (The governor tried to flee in women's clothing but was caught after an alert guard spotted a "lady" in army boots.)

The Massachusetts political leaders acted in the name of William and Mary, risking their necks should James return to power in England.

Although William, now King William III, dismantled the Dominion of New England and restored the power to elect their own governors to Connecticut and Rhode Island, he used the opportunity to rein in Massachusetts's leanings toward independence of imperial authority. He issued a new charter for the colony in 1691, stipulating that the crown would continue to choose the governor. In addition, property ownership, not church membership, became the criterion for voting. Finally, the new charter required Massachusetts to tolerate all Protestants, especially the rising numbers of Anglicans, Baptists, and Quakers (although non-Puritans' taxes would continue to support the established Congregational church). While Plymouth and Maine remained within Massachusetts, New Hampshire became a separate royal colony. For Puritans already demoralized by the demise of the "New England Way" (see Chapter 3), this was indeed bitter medicine.

New York's counterpart of the anti-Stuart uprising was **Leisler's Rebellion.** Emboldened by news of Boston's coup, the city's militia—consisting mainly of Dutch and other non-English artisans and shopkeepers—seized the harbor's main fort on May 31, 1689. Captain Jacob Leisler of the militia took command of the colony, repaired its rundown defenses, and called elections for an assembly. When English troops arrived at New York in 1691, Leisler, fearing (wrongly) that their commander was loyal to James II, denied them entry to key forts. A skirmish resulted, and Leisler was arrested.

"Hott brain'd" Leisler unwittingly had set his own downfall in motion. He had jailed many elite New Yorkers for questioning his authority, only to find that his former enemies had persuaded the new governor to charge Leisler with treason for firing on royal troops. In the face of popular outrage, a packed jury found Leisler and his son-in-law, Jacob Milborne, guilty. Both men went to the gallows insisting that they were dying "for the king and queen and the Protestant religion."

News of England's Glorious Revolution heartened Maryland's Protestant majority, which had long chafed under Catholic rule. Hoping to prevent a repetition of religion-tinged uprisings that had flared in 1676 and 1681, Lord Baltimore sent a messenger from England in early 1689, ordering colonists to obey William and Mary. But the courier died en route, leaving Maryland's unknowing Protestants in fear that their Catholic proprietor still supported James II.

Acting on this fear, John Coode and three others organized the **Protestant Association** to secure Maryland for William and Mary. These conspirators may have been motivated more by their exclusion from high public office than by religious zeal, for three of them had Catholic wives. Coode's group seized the capital in July 1689, removed all Catholics from office, and requested a royal governor. They got their wish in 1691, and the Church of England became the established religion in 1692. Catholics, who composed less than one-fourth of the population, lost the right to vote and thereafter could worship only in private. Maryland stayed in royal hands until 1715, when the fourth Lord Baltimore joined the Church of England and regained his proprietorship.

The revolutionary events of 1688–1689 decisively changed the colonies' political climate by reestablishing representative government and ensuring religious freedom for Protestants. Dismantling the Dominion of New England and directing governors to call annual assemblies, William allowed colonial elites to reassert control over local affairs. By encouraging the assemblies to work with royal and proprietary governors, he expected colonial elites to identify their interests with those of England. A foundation was thus laid for an empire based on voluntary allegiance rather than submission to raw power imposed from faraway London. The crowning of William and Mary opened a new era in which Americans drew rising confidence from their relationship to the English throne. "As long as they reign," wrote a Bostonian who helped topple Andros, "New England is secure."

A Generation of War, 1689–1713   The Glorious Revolution ushered in a quarter-century of warfare, convulsing both Europe and North America. In 1689, England joined a general European coalition against France's Louis XIV, who supported James's claim to the English crown. The resulting War of the League of Augsburg, which Anglo-Americans called **King William's War,** would prove to be the first in a series of European wars that would be fought in part on North American soil.

With the outbreak of King William's War, New Yorkers and New Englanders launched a two-pronged invasion of New France in 1690, with one prong aimed at Montreal and the other at Quebec. After both invasions failed, the war took the form of cruel but inconclusive border raids against civilians carried out by both English and French troops, and their respective Indian allies.

Already weary from a new wave of wars with pro-French Indians, the Five Nations Iroquois Confederacy bore the bloodiest fighting. Standing almost alone against their foes, the Iroquois faced overwhelming odds. While their English allies failed to intercept most enemy war parties, they faced an alliance of the French and virtually all other Indians from Maine to the Great Lakes. In 1691, every Mohawk and Oneida war chief died in battle; by 1696 French armies had destroyed the villages and crops of every Iroquois nation, except the Cayugas.

Although King William's War ended in 1697, the Five Nations staggered until 1700 under invasions by pro-French Indians (including Iroquois who had become Catholic and moved to Canada). By then one-quarter of the Confederacy's two thousand warriors had been killed or taken prisoner or had fled to Canada. The total Iroquois population declined 20 percent over twelve years, from eighty-six hundred to fewer than seven thousand. (By comparison, the war cost about thirteen hundred English, Dutch, and French lives.)

By 1700, the Confederacy was divided into pro-English, pro-French, and neutralist factions. Under the impact of war, the neutralists set a new direction for Iroquois diplomacy. In two separate treaties, together called the **Grand Settlement of 1701,** the Five Nations made peace with France and its Indian allies in exchange for access to western furs, and redefined their alliance with Britain to exclude military cooperation. Skillful negotiations brought the exhausted Iroquois far more success than had war by allowing them to keep control of their lands, rebuild their decimated population, and avoid more losses in Europe's destructive wars.

In 1702 European war again erupted when England fought France and Spain in the War of the Spanish Succession, called **Queen Anne's War** by England's American colonists. This conflict reinforced Anglo-Americans' awareness of their military weakness. French and Indian raiders from Canada destroyed several towns in Massachusetts and Maine that expanding colonists had recently established on the Indians' homelands. In the Southeast, the Spanish invaded Carolina and nearly took Charles Town in 1706.

Enemy warships captured many English colonial vessels and landed looting parties along the Atlantic coast. Meanwhile, English colonists' sieges of Quebec and St. Augustine ended as expensive failures.

England's own forces had more success than those of the colonies, seizing Hudson Bay and Acadia (renamed Nova Scotia) and kept these gains in the Treaty of Utrecht (1713).

The most important consequence of the imperial wars for Anglo-Americans was political, not military. The conflicts with France reinforced colonists' identity with post-1689 England as a bastion of Protestantism and political liberty. Recognizing their own military weakness and the extent to which the Royal Navy had protected their shipping, colonists acknowledged their dependence on the newly formed United Kingdom of Great Britain (created by the formal union of England and Scotland in 1707). As a new generation of English colonists matured, war buttressed their loyalty to the crown and reinforced their identity as Britons.

COLONIAL ECONOMIES AND SOCIETIES, 1660–1750

The achievement of peace in 1713 enabled Britain, France, and Spain to concentrate on competing economically rather than militarily. Over several decades, England and France had developed maritime empires that successfully seized control of Atlantic commerce from the Dutch. Thereafter, all three powers hoped to expand their American colonies and integrate them into single imperial economies. Spain and France gained territory but realized few benefits from their mainland colonies north of Mexico. Meanwhile, British North America thrived.

Mercantilist
Empires in America

The imperial practices of Britain, France, and Spain were rooted in a set of political-economic assumptions known as **mercantilism.** Mercantilist theory held that each nation's power was measured by its wealth, especially in gold. To secure wealth, a country needed to maximize its sale of goods abroad in exchange for gold while minimizing foreign purchases paid for in gold. In pursuit of this goal, mercantilist nations—especially France and England—sought to produce everything they needed without relying on other nations, while obliging other nations to buy from them. Although the home country would do most manufacturing, colonies would supply vital raw materials. If needed, a country would go to war, financed by gold, in order to gain raw materials or markets, or to prevent a rival from doing the same.

Britain's mercantilist policies were articulated above all in a series of **Navigation Acts** governing commerce between England and its colonies. Parliament enacted the first Navigation Act in 1651, requiring that colonial trade be carried on in English, including colonial-owned, vessels in order to replace Dutch shippers with English. After the Restoration, Parliament enacted the Navigation Act of 1660, requiring that certain "enumerated" commodities (see below) be exported via England or Scotland, and barring imports from arriving in non-English ships. The Navigation Act of 1663 stipulated that imports to the colonies arrive via England rather than directly from another country. Later, the Molasses Act (1733) taxed all foreign molasses (produced from sugar cane and imported primarily for distilling rum) entering the mainland colonies at

Tobacco Production in Virginia
Slaves performed virtually every task in the production of tobacco on plantations as well as on many smaller farms in the Chesapeake colonies.

sixpence per gallon. This act was intended less to raise revenue than to serve as a tariff that would protect British West Indian sugar producers at the expense of French rivals on neighboring islands.

The Navigation Acts affected the British colonial economy in four major ways. First, they limited all imperial trade to British-owned ships whose crews were at least three-quarters British. The acts classified all colonists as British, including slaves (many of whom served as seamen). This restriction not only contributed to Britain's rise as Europe's foremost shipping nation but also laid the foundations of an American ship-building industry and merchant marine. By the 1750s, one-third of all "British" vessels were American-owned, mostly by merchants in New England and the middle colonies. The swift growth of this merchant marine diversified the northern colonial economy and made it more commercial. The expansion of colonial shipping also hastened urbanization by creating a need for centralized docks, warehouses, and repair shops in the colonies. By mid-century Philadelphia, New York City, Boston, and Charles Town had emerged as major transatlantic ports.

The second major way in which the Navigation Acts affected the colonies lay in their stipulating that "enumerated" exports pass through England or Scotland. The colonies' major "enumerated" exports were sugar (by far the most profitable commodity), tobacco, rice, furs, indigo (a Carolina plant that produced a blue dye), and naval stores (masts, hemp, tar, and turpentine). Parliament never restricted grain, livestock, fish, lumber, or rum, which together made up 60 percent of colonial exports. Parliament further reduced the burdens on exporters of tobacco and rice—the chief mainland commodities affected—with two significant concessions. First, it gave tobacco growers a monopoly over the British market by excluding foreign tobacco, even though this hurt British consumers. (Rice planters enjoyed a natural monopoly because they had no competitors.) Second, it minimized the added cost of landing tobacco and rice in Britain by refunding customs duties when those products were later shipped to other countries. With about 85 percent of all American tobacco and rice eventually being sold outside the British Empire, the acts reduced planters' profits by less than 3 percent.

The navigation system's third effect on the colonies was to encourage economic diversification. Parliament used British tax revenues to pay modest bounties to Americans producing such items as silk, iron, dyes, hemp, and lumber, which Britain would otherwise have had to import from other countries, and it raised the price of commercial rivals' imports by imposing protective tariffs on them. The trade laws did prohibit Anglo-Americans from competing with British manufacturing of certain products, most notably clothing. However, colonial tailors, hatters, and housewives could continue to make any item of dress in their households or small shops. Manufactured by low-paid labor, British clothing imports generally undersold whatever the colonists could have exported. The colonists were also free to produce iron, and by 1770 they had built 250 ironworks employing thirty thousand men, a work force larger than the entire population of Georgia or of any provincial city.

Finally, the Navigation Acts made the colonies a protected market for low-priced consumer goods and other exports from Britain. Steady overseas demand for colonial products spawned a prosperity that enabled white colonists to purchase ever larger amounts not only of clothing but also of dishware, furniture, tea, and a range of other imports from British and overseas sources. Shops sprang up in cities and rural crossroads throughout the colonies, and itinerant peddlers took imported wares into more remote areas of the countryside. One such peddler arrived in Berwick, Maine, in 1721 and sold several kinds of cloth, a "pair of garters," and various "small trifles" before local authorities confiscated his goods because he had failed to purchase a license. Other traders traveled to Native American communities where they exchanged cloth and other commodities for furs. As a result of colonial consumption, the share of British exports bound for North America spurted from just 5 percent in 1700 to almost 40 percent by 1760. Mercantilism had given rise to a "consumer revolution" in British America.

The economic development of the French and Spanish colonies in North America paled beside that of the British. Although France's most forceful proponent of mercantilism, Colbert (see Chapter 3), and his successors had great difficulty implementing mercantilist policies, New France became agriculturally self-sufficient and exported some wheat to the French West Indies. It also exported small amounts of fish and timber to the Caribbean and to France. Canada's chief imports were wine and brandy, its chief export, furs. Although European demand for furs had flattened, the French government expanded the fur trade, even losing money, in order to retain Native Americans as military allies against Britain. Moreover, France maintained a sizable army in its Canadian colony that, like the trade with Native Americans, was a drain on the royal treasury. Meanwhile, Canada attracted little private investment from France or from within the colony. French Canadians enjoyed a comfortable if modest standard of living but lacked the private investment, extensive commercial infrastructure, vast consumer market, and manufacturing capacity of their British neighbors.

France's wealthiest colonies were in the West Indies, where French planters, like their English neighbors, imported large numbers of enslaved Africans to produce sugar under appalling conditions. Ironically, French sugar planters' success was partly a result of their defying mercantilist policies. In St. Domingue, Martinique, and Guadeloupe, many planters built their own sugar refineries and made molasses instead of shipping their raw sugar to refineries in France, as French regulations prescribed. They then sold much of their molasses to merchants in Britain's mainland colonies, especially Massachusetts, which similarly ignored British mercantilist laws.

Although Spain had squandered the wealth from gold and silver extracted by the conquistadors and early colonists (see Chapter 2), its economy and that of Latin America revived during the eighteenth century. That revival did not extend to New Mexico, Texas, and Florida, where colonists conducted little overseas commerce.

At bottom, Britain's colonies differed from those of France and Spain in their respective economies and societies. While mercantilist principles governed all three nations, the monarchy, the nobility, and the Catholic Church controlled most wealth in France and Spain. Most private wealth was inherited and took the form of land. England, on the other hand, had become a mercantile-commercial economy, and a significant portion of the nation's wealth was in the form of capital held by merchants who reinvested it in commercial and shipping enterprises. For its part, the British government used much of its considerable income from duties, tariffs, and other taxes to enhance commerce. For example, the government strengthened Britain's powerful navy to protect the empire's trade and created the Bank of England in 1694 to ensure a stable money supply and lay the foundation for a network of lending institutions. These benefits extended not only to Britain but also to colonial entrepreneurs and consumers. Indeed the colonies' per capita income rose 0.6 percent annually from 1650 to 1770, a pace twice that of Britain.

Population Growth and Diversity   Britain's economic advantage over its rivals in North America was reinforced by its sharp demographic edge. In 1700, approximately 250,000 non-Indians resided in English America, compared to only 15,000 French colonists and 4,500 Spanish north of the Rio Grande. During the first half of the eighteenth century, all three colonial populations at least quadrupled in size—the British to 1,170,000, the French to 60,000, and the Spanish to 19,000—but this only magnified Britain's advantage.

Spanish emigrants could choose from among that nation's many Latin American colonies, most of which offered more opportunities than remote, poorly developed Florida, Texas, and New Mexico. Reports of Canada's harsh winters and Louisiana's poor economy deterred most potential French colonists. France and Spain made few attempts to attract immigrants to North America from outside their own empires. And both limited immigration to Roman Catholics, a restriction that diverted French Huguenots to the English colonies instead. The English colonies, for their part, boasted good farmlands, healthy economies, and a willingness to absorb Europeans of most Protestant denominations. While anti-Catholicism remained strong, small Jewish communities also formed in several Anglo-American cities.

Spain regarded its northernmost colonies less as centers of population than as buffers against French and English penetration of their more valued colonies to the south. While hoping to lure civilian settlers, the Spanish relied heavily on soldiers stationed in *presidios* (forts) for defense plus missionaries who would, they hoped, attract loyal Native Americans to strategically placed missions. Most colonists in Spanish North America came not from Spain itself but from Mexico and other Spanish colonies.

Although boasting more people than the Spanish colonies, New France and Louisiana were comparably limited. There too the military played a strong role, while missionaries and traders worked to enhance the colony's relations with Native Americans. New France's population growth in the eighteenth century resulted largely from natural increase rather than immigration. Some rural Canadians established new settlements along the Mississippi River in Upper Louisiana, in what are now Illinois and Missouri. On the lower Mississippi, Louisiana acquired a foul reputation, and few French went there willingly. To boost its population, the government sent paupers and criminals, recruited some German refugees, and encouraged large-scale slave imports. By 1732, two-thirds of lower Louisiana's 5,800 people were black and enslaved.

The British colonies outpaced the population growth of not only their French and Spanish rivals but of Britain itself. White women in the colonies had an average of eight children and forty-two grandchildren, compared to five children and fifteen grandchildren for women in Britain. The ratio of England's population to that of the mainland colonies plummeted from 20 to 1 in 1700 to 3 to 1 in 1775.

Although immigration contributed less to eighteenth-century population growth than did natural increase, it remained important. In the forty years after Queen Anne's War, the British colonies absorbed 350,000 newcomers, approximately 210,000 of them

Figure 4.1 Distribution of Non-Indian Nationalities Within the British Mainland Colonies, 1700–1755

The impact of heavy immigration from 1720 to 1755 can be seen in the reduction of the English and Welsh from four-fifths of the colonial population to a slight majority; in the doubling of the African population; and in the sudden influx of Germans and Irish, who together comprised a fifth of white colonists by 1755.

Source: Thomas L. Purvis, "The European Ancestry of the United States Population," *William & Mary Quarterly,* LXI (1984): 85–101.

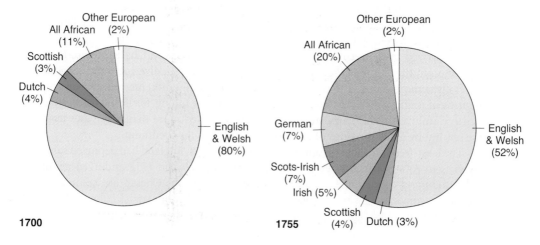

Other European (2%)
All African (11%)
Scottish (3%)
Dutch (4%)
English & Welsh (80%)

1700

Other European (2%)
All African (20%)
German (7%)
Scots-Irish (7%)
Irish (5%)
Scottish (4%)
Dutch (3%)
English & Welsh (52%)

1755

from Europe. A rising proportion of these white immigrants came from outside of England. Whereas between 1630 and 1700 an average of 2,000 English settlers landed annually, only about 500 English arrived each year after 1713. Rising employment and higher wages in England made voluntary immigration to America less attractive than before. But economic hardship elsewhere in the British Isles and northern Europe supplied a steady stream of immigrants, who contributed to greater ethnic diversity among white North Americans.

One of the largest contingents was made up of 100,000 newcomers from Ireland, two-thirds of them "Scots-Irish" descendants of Scottish Presbyterians who had previously sought economic opportunity in northern Ireland. After 1718, Scots-Irish fled to America to escape rack renting (frequent sharp increases in farm rents), usually moving as complete families. In contrast, most of the smaller number of Irish Catholics were unmarried males who arrived as indentured servants. Rarely able to find Catholic wives, they often abandoned their faith to marry Protestant women.

Meanwhile, from German-speaking regions in central Europe came 125,000 settlers, most of them fleeing terrible economic conditions in the Rhine Valley. Wartime devastation had compounded the misery of Rhineland peasants, many of whom were squeezed onto plots of land too small to feed a family. One-third of German immigrants financed their voyage by indenturing themselves or their children as servants. Most Germans were either Lutherans or Calvinists. But a significant minority belonged to small, pacifist religious sects that desired above all to be left alone.

Overwhelmingly, the eighteenth-century immigrants were poor. Those who were indentured servants worked from one to four years for an urban or rural master. Servants could be sold or rented out, beaten, granted minimal legal protection, kept from marrying, and sexually harassed. Attempted escape usually meant an extension of their service. But at the end of their terms, most managed to collect "freedom dues," which could help them marry and acquire land.

Few immigrants settled in New England, New Jersey, lower New York, and the southern tidewater, where land was most scarce and expensive. Philadelphia became immigrants' primary port of entry. So many foreigners went to Pennsylvania that by 1755 the English accounted for only one-third of that colony's population; the rest came mostly from elsewhere in the British Isles and from Germany.

Rising numbers of immigrants also traveled to the Piedmont region, stretching along the eastern slope of the Appalachians. A significant German community developed in upper New York, and thousands of other Germans as well as Scots-Irish fanned southward from Pennsylvania into western Maryland. Many more from Germany and Ireland arrived in the second-most popular American gateway, Charles Town. Most moved on to the Carolina Piedmont, where they raised grain, livestock, and tobacco, generally without slaves. After 1750, both streams of immigration merged with an outpouring of Anglo-Americans from the Chesapeake in the rolling, fertile hills of western North Carolina. In 1713, few Anglo-Americans had lived more than fifty miles from the sea, but by 1750 one-third of all colonists resided in the Piedmont.

The least-free white immigrants were convict laborers. England had deported some convicts to America in the seventeenth century, but between 1718 and 1783 about thirty thousand condemned prisoners arrived, mostly in the Chesapeake colonies. A few of the convicts were murderers; most were guilty of more trivial offenses, like a young Londoner who "got intoxicated with liquor, and in that condition attempted to

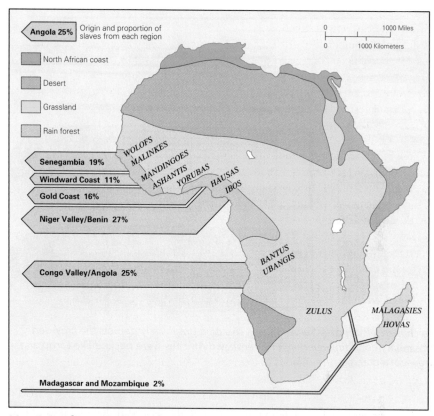

MAP 4.1 African Origins of North American Slaves, 1690–1807

Virtually all slaves brought to English North America came from West Africa, between Senegambia and Angola. Most were captured or bought inland and marched to the coast, where they were sold to African merchants who in turn sold them to European slave traders.

snatch a handkerchief from the body of a person in the street to him unknown." (English law authorized the death penalty for 160 offenses, including what today would be considered petty theft.) Convicts were sold as servants on arrival. Relatively few committed crimes in America, and some eventually managed to establish themselves as backcountry farmers.

Affluent English-descended colonists did not relish the influx of so many people different from themselves. "These confounded Irish will eat us all up," snorted one Bostonian. Benjamin Franklin spoke for many when he asked in a 1751 essay on population,

> Why should Pennsylvania, founded by the English, become a colony of aliens, who will shortly be so numerous as to Germanize us instead of us Anglicizing them, and will never adopt our language or customs any more than they can acquire our complexion?

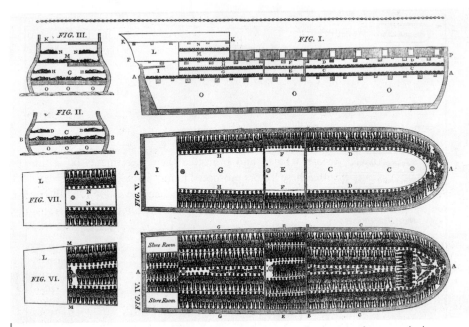

Architect's Plan of a Slave Ship *This plan graphically depicts the crowded, unsanitary conditions under which enslaved Africans were packed like cargo and transported across the Atlantic.*

In the same ungenerous spirit, Franklin objected to the slave trade because it would increase America's black population at the expense of industrious whites, and suggested that the colonists send rattlesnakes to Britain in return for its convict laborers.

About 40 percent (140,000) of newcomers to the British mainland colonies were African-born slaves who arrived not as passengers but as cargo. All but a few slave ships departed from West African ports with captives from dozens of West and Central African ethnic groups. Most North American planters deliberately mixed slaves who came from various regions and spoke different languages, in order to minimize the potential for collective rebellion. But some in Carolina and Georgia expressly sought slaves from Gambia and nearby regions for their rice-growing experience.

Conditions aboard slave ships during the **Middle Passage,** from Africa to America, were appalling by any standard. Africans were crammed into tight quarters with inadequate sanitary facilities, and many died from disease. A Guinea-born slave, later named Venture Smith, was one of 260 who were on a voyage out of a Gold Coast port in 1735. But "smallpox . . . broke out on board," Smith recalled, and "when we reached [Barbados], there were found . . . not more than two hundred alive."

Slaves who refused to eat or otherwise defied shipboard authority were flogged. Some hurled themselves overboard in a last, desperate act of defiance against those who would profit from their misery. When possible, others acted in groups. Rebellions on one scale or another erupted on about one in ten slave voyages. The rebellions forced shippers to hire full-time guards and install barricades to confine slaves. Shippers then passed the cost on to American buyers.

From 1713 to 1754, five times as many slaves poured onto mainland North America as in all the preceding years. The proportion of blacks in the colonies doubled, rising from 11 percent at the beginning of the century to 20 percent by midcentury. Slavery was primarily a southern institution, but 15 percent of its victims lived north of Maryland, mostly in New York and New Jersey. By 1750, every seventh New Yorker was a slave.

Because West Indian and Brazilian slave owners outbid those on the mainland, a mere 5 percent of enslaved Africans were transported to the present-day United States. Unable to buy as many male field hands as they wanted, rice and tobacco planters purchased African women and protected their investments by minimally maintaining slaves' health. These factors promoted family formation and increased life expectancy far beyond the Caribbean's low levels (see Chapter 3). By 1750 the rate of natural increase for mainland blacks almost equaled that for whites. Meanwhile, distinct cultural differences arose between African-born slaves and creoles born in America (see below).

Rural White Men and Women	Although most whites benefited from rising living standards in the British colonies, they enjoyed these advantages unevenly. Except for Benjamin Franklin (who was born neither rich nor

poor) and a few others, true affluence was reserved for those who inherited their wealth. For other whites, personal success was limited and came through hard work, if at all.

Because most farm families owned just enough acreage for a working farm, they could not provide all their children with land of their own when they married. A young male had to build savings to buy farm equipment by working (from about age sixteen to twenty-three) as a field hand for his father or neighbors. After marrying, he normally supported his growing family by renting a farm from a more prosperous landowner until his early or mid-thirties. In some areas, especially the oldest colonized areas of New England, the continued high birthrates of rural families combined with a shortage of productive land to close off farming opportunities altogether. As a result, many young men turned elsewhere to make their livings—the frontier, the port cities, or the high seas.

Families who did acquire land worked off mortgages slowly because the long-term cash income from a farm (6 percent) about equaled the interest on borrowed money (5 to 8 percent). After making a down payment of one-third, a husband and wife generally satisfied the next third upon inheriting shares of their deceased parents' estates. They paid off the final third when their children reached their teens and the family could expand farm output with two or three full-time workers. Only by their late fifties, just as their youngest offspring got ready to leave home, did most colonial parents free themselves of debt.

In general, the more isolated a community or the less productive its farmland, the more self-sufficiency and bartering its people practiced. Remote or poor rural families depended heavily on wives' and daughters' making items that the family would otherwise have had to purchase. Besides cooking, cleaning, and washing, wives preserved food, boiled soap, made clothing, and tended the garden, dairy, orchard, poultry house, and pigsty. They also sold dairy products to neighbors or merchants, spun yarn into cloth for tailors, knitted garments for sale, and even sold their own hair for wigs. A farm family's ability to feed itself and its animals was worth about half of its cash income (a luxury that few European peasants enjoyed), and women worked as much as men did in meeting this end.

Legally, however, white women in the British colonies were constrained (see Chapter 3). A woman's single most autonomous decision was her choice of a husband. Once married, she lost control of her dowry, unless she was a New Yorker subject to Dutch custom, which allowed her somewhat more authority. Women in the French and Spanish colonies retained ownership of, and often augmented, the property they brought to a marriage. Widows did control between 8 and 10 percent of all property in eighteenth-century Anglo-America, and a few—among them Eliza Pinckney of South Carolina, from a prominent planter family—owned and managed large estates.

Colonial Farmers and the Environment

The rapid expansion of Britain's colonies hastened environmental change east of the Appalachians. Whereas the earliest colonists farmed land already cleared and cultivated by Native Americans, eighteenth-century settlers usually removed trees before beginning their plots. Despite the labor involved, farmers and planters, especially those using slave labor, preferred heavily forested areas where the soil was most fertile. New England farmers had to clear innumerable heavy rocks—debris from the last Ice Age—with which they built walls around their fields. Colonists everywhere used timber to construct their houses, barns, and fences and to provide fuel for heating and cooking. Farmers and planters also sold firewood to the inhabitants of cities and towns. Only six years after Georgia's founding, a colonist noted, there was "no more firewood in Savannah; . . . it must be bought from the plantations for which reason firewood is already right expensive."

In removing the trees (deforestation), farmers drove away bears, panthers, wild turkeys, and other forest animals while attracting grass- and seed-eating rabbits, mice, and possums. By removing protection from winds and, in summer, from the sun, deforestation also brought warmer summers and colder winters, further increasing colonists' demand for firewood. By hastening the runoff of spring waters, it led both to heavier flooding and drier streambeds in most areas and, where water could not escape, to more extensive swamps. In turn, less stable temperatures and water levels, along with impediments created by mills and by the floating of timbers downstream, rapidly reduced the number of fish in colonial waters. Writing in 1766, naturalist John Bartram noted that fish "abounded formerly when the Indians lived much on them & was very numerous," but that "now there is not the 100th or perhaps the 1000th [portion of] fish to be found."

Deforestation dried and hardened the soil, but colonists' crops had even more drastic effects. Native Americans, recognizing the soil-depleting effects of intensive cultivation, rotated their crops regularly so that fields could lie fallow (unplanted) for several years and thereby be replenished with vital nutrients (see Chapter 1). But many colonial farmers either did not have enough land to leave some unplanted or were unwilling to sacrifice short-term profits for potential long-term benefits.

As early as 1637, one New England farmer discovered that his soil "after five or six years [of planting corn] grows barren beyond belief and puts on the face of winter in the time of summer." Chesapeake planters' tobacco yields declined after only three or four years in the same plot. Like farmers elsewhere, they used animal manure to fertilize their food crops but not their tobacco, fearing that manure would spoil the taste for consumers. As Chesapeake tobacco growers moved inland to hillier areas, away from rivers and streams, they also contributed to increased soil erosion.

Confronting a more serious shortage of land and resources, Europe's well-to-do farmers were already turning their attention to conservation and "scientific" farming. But most colonists ignored such techniques, either because they could not afford to implement them or because they believed that American land, including that still held by Indians, would sustain them and future generations indefinitely.

The Urban Paradox   The cities were British North America's economic paradox. As major ports of entry and exit, they were keys to the colonies' rising prosperity; yet they held only 4 percent of the colonies' population, and a growing percentage of city-dwellers were caught in a downward spiral of declining opportunity.

As colonial prosperity reached new heights after 1740, poverty spread among residents of the three major seaports—Philadelphia, New York, and, especially, Boston. The cities' poor rolls bulged as poor white men, women (often widowed), and children arrived from Europe and the colonial countryside. High population density and poor sanitation allowed contagious diseases to run rampant, so that half of all city children died before age twenty-one and urban adults lived ten years less on average than country folk.

Changing labor practices also contributed to poverty. Early-eighteenth-century urban artisans typically trained apprentices and employed them as journeymen for many years until they could open their own shops. By midcentury, however, more and more employers kept laborers only as long as business was brisk, releasing them when sales slowed. In 1751, a shrewd Benjamin Franklin recommended this practice to employers as a way to reduce labor costs. Recessions hit more frequently after 1720 and created longer spells of unemployment, making it increasingly difficult for many to afford rents, food, and firewood.

Insignificant before 1700, urban poverty became a major problem. By 1730, Boston ceased providing shelter for its growing number of homeless residents. The proportion of residents considered too poor to pay taxes climbed even as the total population leveled. Not until 1736 did New York build a poorhouse (for forty people), but by 1772, 4 percent of its residents (over eight hundred) required public assistance to survive. The number of Philadelphia families listed as poor on tax rolls jumped from 3 percent in 1720 to 11 percent by 1760.

Wealth, on the other hand, remained highly concentrated. For example, New York's wealthiest 10 percent (mostly merchants) owned about 45 percent of the property throughout the eighteenth century. Similar patterns existed in Boston and Philadelphia. Set alongside the growth of a poor underclass in these cities, such statistics underscored the polarization of status and wealth in urban America.

Most southern cities were little more than large towns. Charles Town, however, became North America's fourth-largest city. South Carolina's capital offered gracious living to the wealthy planters who flocked from their plantations to townhouses during the months of the worst heat and insect infestation. Shanties on the city's outskirts sheltered a growing crowd of destitute whites. The colony encouraged whites to immigrate in hopes of reducing blacks' numerical preponderance, but most European newcomers could not establish farms or find any work except as ill-paid temporary laborers. Like their counterparts in northern ports, Charles Town's poor whites competed for work with urban slaves whose masters rented out their labor.

Although middle-class women in cities and large towns performed somewhat less manual drudgery than farm women, they nonetheless managed complex households that often included servants, slaves, and apprentices. While raising poultry and vegetables as well as sewing and knitting, urban wives purchased their cloth and most of their food in daily trips to public markets. Many had one or more household servants, usually young single women or widows, to help with cooking, cleaning, and laundering—tasks that required more attention than in the country because of higher urban standards of cleanliness and appearance. Wives also worked in family businesses or their own shops, which were located in owners' homes.

Less affluent wives and widows had the fewest opportunities of all. They housed boarders rather than servants, and many spun and wove cloth in their homes for local merchants. Poor widows with children looked to the community for relief. Whereas John Winthrop and other Puritan forebears had deemed it a Christian's duty to care for poor dependents (see Chapter 3), affluent Bostonians in the eighteenth century scorned the needy. Preaching in 1752, the city's leading minister, Charles Chauncy, lamented "the swarms of children, of both sexes, that are continually strolling and playing about the streets of our metropolis, clothed in rags, and brought up in idleness and ignorance." Another clergyman warned that charity for widows and their children was money "worse than lost."

Slavery

For slaves, the economic progress achieved in colonial America meant only that most masters could afford to keep them healthy. Rarely did masters choose to make their human property comfortable. A visitor to a Virginia plantation from Poland (where peasants lived in dire poverty) recorded this impression of slaves' quality of life:

> We entered some Negroes huts—for their habitations cannot be called houses. They are far more miserable than the poorest of the cottages of our peasants. The husband and wife sleep on a miserable bed, the children on the floor . . . a little kitchen furniture amid this misery . . . a teakettle and cups . . . five or six hens, each with ten or fifteen chickens, walked there. That is the only pleasure allowed to the negroes.

To maintain slaves, masters normally spent just 40 percent of the amount paid for the upkeep of indentured servants. Whereas white servants ate two hundred pounds of meat yearly, black slaves consumed fifty pounds. The value of the beer and hard cider given to a typical servant alone equaled the expense of feeding and clothing the average slave. Masters usually provided adult slaves with eight quarts of corn and a pound of pork each week but expected them to grow their own vegetables, forage for wild fruits, and perhaps raise poultry.

Blacks worked for a far longer portion of their lives than whites. Slave children entered the fields as part-time helpers soon after reaching seven and began working full-time between eleven and fourteen. Whereas most white women worked in their homes, barns, and gardens, black females routinely tended tobacco or rice crops, even when pregnant, and often worked outdoors in the winter. Most slaves toiled until they died, although most who survived to their sixties were spared hard labor.

As the numbers of American-born creole slaves grew, sharp differences emerged between them and African-born blacks in the southern colonies. Unlike African-born slaves, creoles spoke a single language, English, and were familiar from birth with their environment and with the ways of their masters. These advantages occasionally translated into more autonomy for creoles. Until the 1770s, planters continued to import African-born slaves to labor in their fields, especially on more remote lands recently gained from Native Americans. But as wealthier, more long-established planters diversified economically and developed more elaborate lifestyles (see below), they diverted favored creoles toward such services as shoeing horses, repairing and driving carriages, preparing and serving meals, sewing and mending clothing, and caring for planters' children.

Africans and creoles proved resourceful at maximizing opportunities within this harsh, confining system. House slaves aggressively demanded that guests tip them for shining shoes and stabling horses. They also sought presents on holidays, as a startled New Jersey visitor to a Virginia plantation discovered early one Christmas morning when slaves demanding gifts of cash roused him from bed.

In the Carolina-Georgia rice country, slaves working under the task system gained control of about half their waking hours. Under tasking, each slave spent some hours caring for a quarter-acre, after which his or her duties ended for the day. This system permitted a few slaves to keep hogs and sell surplus vegetables on their own. In 1728, an exceptional slave, Sampson, earned enough money in his off-hours to buy another slave, whom he then sold to his master in exchange for his own freedom.

The gang system used on tobacco plantations afforded Chesapeake slaves less free time than those in Carolina. As one white observer noted, Chesapeake blacks labored "from daylight until the dusk of evening and some part of the night, by moon or candlelight, during the winter."

Despite Carolina slaves' greater autonomy, racial tensions ran high in the colony. As long as Europeans outnumbered Africans, race relations in Carolina remained relaxed. But as a black majority emerged, whites increasingly used force and fear to control "their" blacks. For example, a 1735 law, noting that many Africans wore "clothes much above the condition of slaves," imposed a dress code limiting slaves' apparel to fabrics worth less than ten shillings per yard and even prohibited their wearing their owners' cast-off clothes. Of even greater concern were large gatherings of blacks uncontrolled by whites. In 1721, Charles Town enacted a 9:00 P.M. curfew for blacks, while Carolina's assembly placed all local slave patrols under the colonial militia. Slaves responded to the colony's vigilance and harsher punishments with increased instances of arson, theft, flight, and violence.

Despite these measures, South Carolina (separated from North Carolina in 1729) was rocked in 1739 by a powerful slave uprising, the **Stono Rebellion.** It began when twenty Africans seized guns and ammunition from a store at the Stono River Bridge, outside Charles Town. Marching under a makeshift flag and crying "Liberty!" they collected eighty men and headed south toward Spanish Florida, a well-known refuge for escapees (see below). Along the way they burned seven plantations and killed twenty whites, but they spared a Scottish innkeeper known for being "a good Man and kind to his slaves." Within a day, mounted militia surrounded the slaves near a riverbank, cut them down mercilessly, and spiked a rebel head on every milepost between that spot and Charles Town. Uprisings elsewhere in the colony required more than a month to suppress, with insurgents generally "put to the most cruel Death." Thereafter, whites enacted a new slave code, essentially in force until the Civil War, which kept South Carolina slaves under constant surveillance. Furthermore, it threatened masters with fines for not disciplining slaves and required legislative approval for manumission (freeing of individual slaves). The Stono Rebellion and its cruel aftermath thus reinforced South Carolina's emergence as a rigid, racist, and fear-ridden society.

Slavery and racial tensions were by no means confined to plantations. By midcentury, slaves made up 20 percent of New York City's population and formed a majority in Charles Town and Savannah. Southern urban slave owners augmented their incomes by renting out the labor of their slaves, who were cheaper to employ than white workers. Slave artisans—usually creoles—worked as coopers, shipwrights, rope makers, and, in a few cases, goldsmiths and cabinetmakers. Some artisans supplemented their work as slaves by earning income of their own. Slaves in northern cities were more often unskilled. Urban slaves in both North and South typically lived apart from their masters in rented quarters alongside free blacks.

Although city life afforded slaves greater freedom of association than did plantations, urban blacks remained the property of others and chafed at racist restrictions. In 1712, rebellious slaves in New York City killed nine whites in a calculated attack. As a result, eighteen slaves were hanged or tortured to death, and six others committed suicide to avoid similar treatment. In 1741, a wave of thefts and fires was attributed on dubious testimony to conspiring New York slaves. Of the one hundred fifty-two blacks who were arrested, thirteen were burned at the stake, seventeen were hanged (along with four whites), and seventy were sent to the West Indies.

| The Rise of Colonial Elites | A few colonists benefited disproportionately from the growing wealth of Britain and its colonies. Most of these elite colonists inherited their advantages at birth and men augmented them by producing plantation crops, buying and selling commodities across the Atlantic or transporting them, or serving as attorneys for other elite colonists. They constituted British America's upper class, or gentry. |

A gentleman was expected by his contemporaries to behave with an appropriate degree of responsibility, to display dignity and generosity, and to be a community leader. His wife, a "lady," was to be a skillful household manager and, in the presence of men, a refined yet deferring hostess.

Before 1700, the colonies' class structure was less apparent because elites spent their limited resources buying land, servants, and slaves rather than luxuries. As late as 1715, a traveler noticed that one of Virginia's richest planters, Robert Beverley, owned "nothing in or about his house but just what is necessary, . . . [such as] good beds but no curtains and instead of cane chairs he hath stools made of wood."

As British mercantilist trade flourished, higher incomes enabled elite colonists to display their wealth more openly, particularly in their housing. The greater gentry— the richest 2 percent, owning about 15 percent of all property—constructed elaborate showcase mansions that broadcast their elite status. The lesser gentry, or second wealthiest 2 to 10 percent holding about 25 percent of all property, lived in more modest two-story dwellings. In contrast, middle-class farmers commonly inhabited one-story wooden buildings with four small rooms and a loft.

Colonial gentlemen and ladies also exhibited their status by imitating the "refinement" of upper-class Europeans. They wore costly English fashions, drove carriages instead of wagons, and bought expensive chinaware, books, furniture, and musical instruments. They pursued a gracious life by studying foreign languages, learning formal dances, and cultivating polite manners. Whereas ordinary men bet on cockfighting, considered a vulgar sport, gentlemen preferred horse races, a form of recreation which they alone could afford. A few young gentlemen even traveled abroad to get an English education. Thus, elites led colonists' growing taste for British fashions and consumer goods.

COMPETING FOR A CONTINENT, 1713–1750

After a generation of war, Europe's return to peace in 1713 only heightened British, French, and Spanish imperial ambitions in North America. Europeans expanded their territorial claims, intensifying both trade and warfare with Native Americans, and carving out new settlements. Native Americans welcomed some of these developments and resisted others, depending on how they expected their sovereignty and livelihoods to be affected.

France and the American Heartland France focused its imperial efforts on Louisiana. In 1718, Louisiana officials established New Orleans as the colony's capital and port. Louisiana's staunchest Indian allies were the Choctaws, through whom the French hoped to counter both the expanding influence of Carolina's traders and the Spanish presence in Florida. But by the 1730s inroads by the persistent Carolinians led the Choctaws to become bitterly divided into pro-English and pro-French factions.

Life was dismal in Louisiana for whites as well as blacks. A thoroughly corrupt government ran the colony. With Louisiana's sluggish export economy failing to sustain them, settlers and slaves found other means of survival. Like the Native Americans, they hunted, fished, gathered wild plants, and cultivated gardens. In 1727 a priest described how some whites eventually prospered: "A man with his wife or partner clears a little ground, builds himself a house on four piles, covers it with sheets of bark, and plants corn and rice for his provisions; the next year he raises a little more for food, and has also a field of tobacco; if at last he succeeds in having three or four Negroes, then he is out of difficulties."

But many red, white, and black Louisianans depended on exchanges with one another in order to stay "out of difficulties." Nearby Native Americans provided corn, bear oil, tallow (for candles), and above all deerskins to French merchants in return for blankets, kettles, axes, chickens, hogs, guns, and alcohol. Indian and Spanish traders from west of the Mississippi brought horses and cattle. Familiar with cattle from their homelands, enslaved Africans managed many of Louisiana's herds, and some became rustlers and illicit traders of beef.

French settlers in Upper Louisiana, or Illinois, were somewhat better off, but more than a third of the colony's twenty-six hundred inhabitants were enslaved in 1752. Illinois's principal export was wheat, a more reliably profitable crop than the plantation commodities grown farther south. In exporting wheat, the French colony resembled Pennsylvania to the east; but Illinois's remote location limited such exports and attracted

Huron (Wyandotte) Woman *Her cloth dress, glass beads, and iron hoe reflect the influence of French trade on this woman and other Indians of the Great Lakes–Ohio region in the eighteenth century.*

few whites, obliging it to depend on France's Native American allies to defend it from Indian enemies.

With Canada and the Mississippi Valley secure from European rivals, France sought to counter growing British influence in the Ohio Valley. The "Ohio country" was at peace after the Iroquois declared their neutrality in 1701 (see above), encouraging Indian refugees to settle there. Former inhabitants such as the Kickapoos and Shawnees returned from elsewhere to reoccupy homelands. Other arrivals were newcomers, such as Delawares escaping English encroachments in the East and Seneca Iroquois seeking improved hunting territories. Hoping to secure commercial and diplomatic ties with these Natives, the French expanded their trade activities. Several French posts ballooned into sizable villages housing Indians, French, and mixed-ancestry *métis*. But English traders were arriving with better goods at lower prices, and most Indians steered a more independent course.

Although generally more effective in Indian diplomacy than the English, the French were not always successful and could be equally oppressive. The Carolina-supported Chickasaws frequently attacked the French and their Native allies on the Mississippi River, while the French fought a long war against the Mesquakie (or Fox) Indians in the upper Midwest and brutally suppressed the Natchez in Louisiana. The French captured Native Americans in these wars and sold them as slaves in Louisiana, Illinois, Canada, and the West Indies.

By 1744, French traders were traveling as far west as North Dakota and Colorado, and were buying beaver pelts and Indian slaves on the Great Plains. These traders and their British competitors spread trade goods, including guns, to Native Americans throughout central Canada and the Plains. Meanwhile, Indians in the Great Basin and southern Plains were acquiring horses, thousands of which had been left behind by the Spanish when they fled New Mexico during the Pueblo Revolt of 1680. Adopting the horse and gun, Indians such as the Lakota Sioux and Comanches moved to the Plains and built a new, highly mobile way of life based on the pursuit of buffalo. By 1750, France had an immense domain, but one that depended on often-precarious relations with Native Americans.

Native Americans and British Expansion   As in the seventeenth century, British colonial expansion was made possible by the depopulation and dislocation of Native Americans. Epidemic diseases, environmental changes, war, and political pressures on Indians to cede land and to emigrate all combined to make new lands available to white immigrants.

Conflict came early to Carolina, where a trade in Indian slaves (see Chapter 3) and imperial war had already produced violence. The **Tuscarora War** (1711–1713) began when Iroquoian-speaking Tuscaroras, provoked by encroaching whites who enslaved some of their people, destroyed New Bern, a nearby settlement of seven hundred Swiss immigrants. To retaliate, northern Carolina enlisted the aid of southern Carolina and its well-armed Indian allies. By 1713, after about a thousand Tuscaroras (one-fifth of the total population) had been killed or enslaved, the nation surrendered. Most Tuscarora survivors migrated northward to what is now upstate New York and in 1722 became the sixth nation of the Iroquois Confederacy.

After helping defeat the Tuscaroras, Carolina's Indian allies experienced a growing number of abuses, including cheating, violence, and enslavement by English traders and encroachments on their land by settlers. The Yamasees were the most seriously affected. In the **Yamasee War** (1715–1716), they led a coordinated series of attacks by Catawbas, Creeks, and other allies on English trading houses and settlements. Only by enlisting the aid of the Cherokee Indians, and allowing four hundred slaves to bear arms, did the colony crush the uprising. Yamasees not killed or captured fled to Florida or to Creek towns in the interior.

The defeat of the Yamasees left their Catawba supporters vulnerable to pressures from English on one side and Iroquois on the other. As Carolina settlers moved uncomfortably close to some Catawba villages, the inhabitants abandoned these villages. Having escaped the settlers, however, the Catawbas faced rising conflict with the Iroquois. After making peace with the Indian allies of New France in 1701 (see above), the Iroquois looked south when launching raids for captives to adopt into their ranks. To counter the well-armed Iroquois, the Catawbas turned back to Carolina. By ceding land and helping defend Carolina against outside Indians, the Catawbas received guns, food, and clothing. Their relationship with the English allowed the Catawbas the security they needed to strengthen their traditional institutions. However, the growing gap in numbers between Catawbas and colonists greatly favored the English in the two peoples' competition for resources.

To the north, the Iroquois Confederacy accommodated English expansion while consolidating its own power among Native Americans. Late in the seventeenth century, the Iroquois and several colonies forged a series of treaties known as the **Covenant Chain.** Under these treaties the Confederacy helped the colonies subjugate Indians whose lands the English wanted. Under one such agreement, the Iroquois assisted Massachusetts in subjugating that colony's Natives following King Philip's War in New England (see Chapter 3). Under another, the Susquehannock Indians, after being crushed in Bacon's Rebellion, moved northward from Maryland to a new homeland adjacent to the Iroquois' own. By relocating non-Iroquois on their periphery as well as by inviting the Tuscaroras into their Confederacy, the Iroquois controlled a center of Native American power that was distinct from, but cooperative with, the British. At the same time, the Iroquois established buffers against, and deflected, potential English expansion to their own lands.

Although it did not formally belong to the Covenant Chain, Pennsylvania maintained a similar relationship with the Iroquois. With immigration and commercial success, William Penn's early idealism waned in Pennsylvania, along with his warm ties with the Delaware Indians. Between 1729 and 1734, Penn's sons, now the colony's proprietors, and his former secretary coerced the Delawares into selling more than fifty thousand acres. Then the Penn brothers produced a patently fraudulent "deed," which alleged that the Delawares had agreed in 1686 to sell their land as far westward as a man could walk in a day and a half. After selling much of the land to settlers and speculators in a lottery and hiring two men to rehearse the walk, the Penns in 1737 sent the two men on an "official" walk. The men covered sixty-four miles, meaning that the Delawares, in what became known as the **Walking Purchase,** had to hand over an additional twelve hundred square miles of land. Despite the protests of Delaware elders who had been alive in 1686 and remembered no such treaty, the Delawares were forced to move under Iroquois supervision. Settlers began pouring in and, within a generation, the Delawares' former lands were among the most productive in the British Empire.

British Expansion in the South: Georgia Britain moved to expand southward toward Spanish Florida in 1732 when Parliament authorized a new colony, Georgia. Charitable idealism and profits, as well as imperial strategizing, lay behind Georgia's founding. Although expecting Georgia to export such expensive commodities as wine and silk, the colony's sponsors intended that it be a refuge for bankrupt but honest debtors. A board of trustees was formed to oversee the colony for twenty-one years before turning it over to the crown. During that time, the trustees decreed, Georgia would do without slavery, alcohol, landholdings of more than five hundred acres, and representative government.

One of the trustees, **James Oglethorpe,** moved to Georgia and dominated it for a decade. Ignoring Spain's claims, Oglethorpe purchased the land for the colony from Creek Indians, with whom he cultivated close ties. Oglethorpe founded the port of Savannah in 1733, and by 1740 twenty-eight hundred colonists had arrived. Almost half the immigrants came from Germany, Switzerland, and Scotland, and most had their overseas passage paid by the government. A small number of Jews were among the early colonists. Along with Pennsylvania, early Georgia was the most inclusive of the British colonies.

Oglethorpe was determined to keep slavery out of Georgia. "They live like cattle," he wrote to the trustees after viewing Charles Town's slave market. "If we allow slaves, we act against the very principles by which we associated together, which was to relieve the distressed." Slavery, he thought, degraded blacks, made whites lazy, and presented a terrible risk. Oglethorpe worried that wherever whites relied on a slave labor force, they courted slave revolts, which the Spanish could then exploit. But most of all, he recognized that slavery undermined the economic position of poor whites like those he sought to settle in Georgia.

Oglethorpe's well-intentioned plans failed completely. Few debtors arrived because Parliament set impossibly stringent conditions for their release from prison. Limitations on settlers' rights to sell or enlarge their holdings, as well as the ban on slavery, also discouraged immigration. Raising exotic export crops proved impractical. Looking to neighboring South Carolina, some Georgians recognized that rice, which required large estates, substantial capital, and many cheap laborers, could flourish in Georgia's lowlands. Under pressure from colonists, the trustees lifted limits on the size of landholdings in 1744 and the ban on slavery in 1750. The trustees also authorized a representative assembly in 1750, just two years before turning the colony over to the crown. By 1760, 6,000 whites and 3,500 enslaved blacks were making Georgia profitable.

Spain's Borderlands While endeavoring to maintain its empire in the face of Native American, French, and British adversaries, Spain spread its language and culture over much of North America. Seeking to recolonize New Mexico after the Pueblo Revolt (see Chapter 3), Spain awarded grants of approximately twenty-six square miles wherever ten or more families founded a town. Soldiers erected strong fortifications to protect against Indian attacks, now coming primarily from mounted Apaches. As in early New England, settlers built homes on small lots around the church plaza, farmed separate fields nearby, grazed livestock at a distance, and shared a community wood lot and pasture.

The livestock-raising ranchos, radiating out for many miles from little clusters of houses, monopolized vast tracts along the Rio Grande and blocked further town settlement. On the ranchos, mounted cattle herders created the way of life later associated with the American cowboy, featuring lariat and roping skills, cattle drives, roundups (rodeos), and livestock branding.

By 1750 New Mexico numbered about 14,000, more than half of them Pueblo Indians. Most Pueblos now cooperated with the Spanish, and although many had converted to Catholicism, they also practiced their traditional religion. Like the colonists, the Pueblos were village-dwellers who grew crops and raised livestock, making them equally vulnerable to horse-mounted raiders. Apache raids were now augmented by those of armed and mounted Comanches from the north and east. The raiders sought livestock and European goods as well as captives, often to replace those of their own people who had been enslaved by Spanish raiders and sent to mine silver in Mexico.

Spain had established Texas in order to counter growing French influence among the Comanches and other Native Americans on the southern Plains. Colonization began after 1716, when Spaniards established several outposts on the San Antonio and Guadalupe Rivers. The most prominent center was at San Antonio de Béxar, where two towns, a presidio, and a mission (later known as the Alamo) were clustered. But most Indians in Texas preferred trading with the French to farming, Christianity, and the ineffective protection of the Spanish. Lack of security also deterred Hispanic settlement, so that by 1760 only twelve hundred Spaniards inhabited Texas.

Spain's position in Florida was only somewhat less precarious. As early as 1700, there were already thirty-eight hundred English in recently founded Carolina, compared to just fifteen hundred Spanish in Florida. This disparity widened thereafter.

Florida found ways to offset its small number of colonists. After the Yamasee War (see above), the Creeks broke off their alliance with Carolina in favor of a policy of neutrality. The Creeks' neutrality enabled some Spaniards to trade with them for deerskins, and to sponsor Creek raids into Carolina. But Florida's trade profits remained limited because it lacked ample supplies of cheap, desirable trade goods, compared to its British and French neighbors.

Florida gained more at English expense through its effective recruitment of escaped slaves from Carolina. From the time of Carolina's founding, some enslaved blacks had found their way to the Spanish colony. In 1693, Spain's King Charles II ruled that any English-owned slaves arriving in Florida would be freed upon converting to Catholicism. Word of the ruling spread back to Carolina, prompting more slaves to flee to Florida, especially while planters were distracted during the Yamasee War. In 1726, Spanish authorities created an all-black militia unit under the command of Francisco Menéndez, a former South Carolina slave, to help defend Florida. In 1738, the colony built a fortified village, Mose, for Menéndez's men and their families adjacent to the capital at St. Augustine. The unit would prove critical after England and Spain went to war the next year (see below).

By 1750, Spain controlled much of the Southeast and Southwest, while France exercised influence in the Mississippi, Ohio, and Missouri River valleys, as well as around the Great Lakes and in Canada. Both empires were spread thin and depended on the support or acquiescence of non-Europeans. In contrast, British North America was compact, wealthy, densely populated by whites, and aggressively expansionist.

The Return of War, 1739–1748

After a generation of war ended in 1713, the American colonies enjoyed a generation of peace as well as prosperity. But in 1739, British launched a war against Spain, using as a pretext Spain's cutting off the ear of a British smuggler named Jenkins. (Thus, the British termed the conflict the "War of Jenkins' Ear.") In 1740, James Oglethorpe led a massive British assault on Florida. The English captured Mose, but after Francisco Menéndez's black militia and other troops recaptured the town, Oglethorpe withdrew. Two years later, Oglethorpe led 650 men in repelling 3,000 Spanish troops who counterattacked Georgia.

The Anglo-Spanish War quickly merged with a larger one in Europe, the War of the Austrian Succession, called **King George's War** in British America (1740–1748). King George's War followed the pattern of earlier imperial conflicts. Few battles involved more than six hundred men, and most were attacks and counterattacks on civilians in the Northeast in which many noncombatants were killed and others captured. Most captives were New Englanders seized by French and Indians from isolated towns. Although prisoners were exchanged at the end of the war, some English captives, particularly women and children, elected to remain with the French or Indians.

King George's War produced just one major engagement in North America. In 1745, almost four thousand New Englanders under William Pepperell of Maine besieged and, after seven weeks of intense fighting, captured the French bastion of Louisbourg, which guarded the entrance to the St. Lawrence River. After three more years of

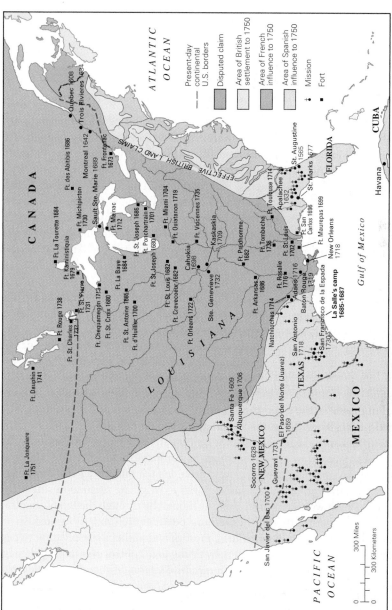

MAP 4.2 French and Spanish Occupation of North America, to 1750

While British colonists concentrated themselves on the Atlantic seaboard, the French and Spanish together established themselves thinly over two-thirds of the present-day United States.

inconclusive warfare, Britain signed the Treaty of Aix-la-Chapelle (1748), exchanging Louisbourg for a British outpost in India that the French had seized.

Public Life in British America, 1689–1750

During the early and middle eighteenth century, the ties linking Britain and its colonies consisted of much more than the movements of goods and peoples. England's new Bill of Rights was the foundation of government and politics in the colonies. The ideas of English thinkers initially inspired the intellectual movement known as the Enlightenment, while the English preacher George Whitefield sparked a generation of colonists to transform the practice of Protestantism in British America. While reinforcing the colonies' links with Britain, these developments were also significant because they involved many more colonists than before as active participants in politics, in intellectual discussions, and in new religious movements. Taken as a whole, this wider participation signaled the emergence of a broad Anglo-American "public."

Colonial Politics   The most significant political result of the Glorious Revolution was the rise of colonial legislatures, or assemblies, as a major political force. Except in Connecticut and Rhode Island, the crown or a proprietor in England chose each colony's governor. In most colonies the governor named a council, or upper house of the legislature. The assembly was therefore the only political body subject to control by colonists rather than by English officials. Before 1689, governors and councils took the initiative in drafting laws, and the assemblies followed their lead; but thereafter the assemblies assumed a more central role in politics.

Colonial leaders argued that their legislatures should exercise the same rights as those won by Parliament in its seventeenth-century struggle with royal authority. Indeed, Anglo-Americans saw their assemblies as comparable to England's House of Commons, which represented the people and defended their liberty against centralized authority, particularly through its exclusive power to originate revenue-raising measures. After Parliament won supremacy over the monarchy through the Bill of Rights in 1689, assemblymen insisted that their governors' powers were similarly limited.

The lower houses steadily asserted their prestige and authority by refusing to permit outside meddling in their proceedings, by taking firm control over taxes and budgets, and especially by keeping a tight rein on executive salaries. Although governors had considerable powers (including the right to veto acts, call and dismiss assembly sessions, and schedule elections), they were vulnerable to legislatures' financial pressure because they received no salary from British sources and relied on the assemblies for income. This "power of the purse" sometimes enabled assemblies to force governors to sign laws opposed by the crown.

The assemblies' growing importance was reinforced by British policy. The Board of Trade, established in 1696 to monitor American developments, could have weakened the assemblies by persuading the crown to disallow objectionable colonial laws signed by the governors. But it rarely exercised this power before midcentury. The resulting political vacuum allowed the colonies to become self-governing in most respects except for trade regulation, restrictions on printing money, and declaring war. Representative government in the colonies originated and was nurtured within the protective environment of the British Empire.

The elite planters, merchants, and attorneys who monopolized colonial wealth also dominated politics. Most assemblymen ranked among the wealthiest 2 percent of colonists. To placate them, governors invariably appointed other members of the greater gentry to sit on their councils and as judges on the highest courts. Although members of the lesser gentry sat less often in the legislature, they commonly served as justices of the peace.

Outside New England (where any voter was eligible for office), legal requirements barred 80 percent of white men from running for the assembly, most often by specifying that a candidate own a minimum of a thousand acres. (Farms then averaged 180 acres in the South and 120 acres in the middle colonies.) Even without such property qualifications, few ordinary colonists could have afforded to hold elective office. Assemblymen received only living expenses, which might not fully cover the cost of staying at their province's capital, much less compensate a farmer or an artisan for his absence from farm or shop for six to ten weeks a year. As a result, a few wealthy families in each colony dominated the highest political offices. Nine families, for example, provided one-third of Virginia's councilors after 1680. John Adams, a rising young Massachusetts politician, estimated that most towns in his colony chose their legislators from among just three or four families.

By eighteenth-century standards, the colonies set liberal qualifications for male voters, but all provinces barred women and nonwhites from voting. In seven colonies, voters had to own land (usually forty to fifty acres), and the rest demanded that an elector have enough property to furnish a house and work a farm with his own tools. About 40 percent of free white men—mostly indentured servants and young men still living with parents or just beginning family life—could not meet these requirements. Still, most white males in British North America could vote by age forty, whereas two-thirds of all men in England and nine-tenths in Ireland were never eligible.

In rural areas, voter participation was low unless a vital issue was at stake. The difficulties of voting limited the average rural turnout to about 45 percent (a rate of participation higher, however, than in typical U.S. elections today, apart from those for president). Most governors called elections when they saw fit, so that elections might lapse for years and suddenly be held on very short notice. Thus voters in isolated areas often had no knowledge of upcoming contests. The fact that polling took place at the county seat discouraged many electors from traveling long distances over poor roads to vote. In several colonies, voters stated their choices orally and publicly, often with the candidates present. This procedure inhibited the participation of humbler men whose views differed from those of elites, especially those who also depended on elites for credit, shipping privileges, or other favors. Finally, most rural elections before 1750 were uncontested. Local elites decided in advance which of them would "stand" for office. Regarding officeholding as a gentleman's public duty, they considered it demeaning to appear interested in being chosen, much less to compete or "run" for a position.

Given all these factors, many rural voters were indifferent about politics at the colony level. For example, to avoid paying legislators' expenses at the capital, many smaller Massachusetts towns refused to elect assemblymen. Thirty percent of men elected to South Carolina's assembly neglected to take their seats from 1731 to 1760, including a majority of those chosen in 1747 and 1749.

Despite these limitations, rural elections slowly emerged as community events in which many nonelite white men participated. In time, rural voters would follow urban colonists and express themselves more forcefully.

Competitive politics first developed in the northern seaports. Depending on their economic interests and family ties, wealthy colonists aligned themselves with or against royal and proprietary governors. To gain advantage over rivals, some factions courted artisans and small shopkeepers whose fortunes had stagnated or declined as the distribution of urban wealth tilted increasingly toward the rich. In actively courting nonelite voters, they scandalized rival elites who feared that an unleashing of popular passions could disturb the social order.

New York was the site of the bitterest factional conflicts. In one episode in 1733, Governor William Cosby suspended his principal rival, Chief Justice Lewis Morris, after Morris ruled against the governor. To mobilize popular support for Morris, his faction established the *New-York Weekly Journal,* which repeatedly accused Cosby and his associates of rampant corruption. In 1734, the governor's supporters engineered the arrest of the *Weekly Journal*'s printer, John Peter Zenger, on charges that he had seditiously libeled Cosby. Following a celebrated trial in August 1735, Zenger was acquitted.

Although it neither led to a change in New York's libel law nor significantly enhanced freedom of the press at the time, the Zenger verdict was significant for several reasons. In New York and elsewhere, it encouraged the broadening of political discussion and participation beyond a small circle of elites. Equally significant were its legal implications. Zenger's brilliant attorney, Andrew Hamilton, effectively employed the growing practice among colonial attorneys of speaking directly to a jury on behalf of a defendant. He persuaded the jury that it alone, without the judge's advice, could reject a charge of libel "if you should be of the opinion that there is no falsehood in [Zenger's] papers." Until then, truth alone was not a sufficient defense against a charge of libel in British and colonial courts of law. By empowering nonelites as voters, readers, and jurors, the Morris-Cosby rivalry and the Zenger trial encouraged broader participation in New York's public life.

The Enlightenment If property and wealth were keys to political participation and officeholding, literacy and education permitted Anglo-Americans to participate in the transatlantic world of ideas and beliefs. Perhaps 90 percent of New England's adult white men and 40 percent of white women could write well enough to sign documents, thanks to the region's traditional support for primary education. Among white males elsewhere in the colonies, the literacy rate varied from about 35 percent to more than 50 percent. (In England, by contrast, no more than one-third of all males could read and write.) How readily most of these people read a book or wrote a letter was another matter.

The best-educated colonists—members of the gentry, well-to-do merchants, educated ministers, and growing numbers of artisans and farmers—embraced a wider world of ideas and information. Though costly, books, newspapers, and writing paper could open up eighteenth-century European civilization to reading men and women. A rich, exciting world it was. Scientific advances seemed to explain the laws of nature; human intelligence appeared poised to triumph over ignorance, prejudice, superstition, and irrational tradition. For those who had the time to read and to ponder ideas, an age of optimism and boundless progress was dawning, an age known as the Enlightenment.

Enlightenment ideals combined confidence in human reason with skepticism toward beliefs not founded on science or strict logic. A major source of Enlightenment thought was English physicist Sir Isaac Newton (1642–1727), who in 1687 explained how gravitation ruled the universe. Newton's work appealed to educated Europeans by demonstrating the harmony of natural laws and stimulated others to search for rational principles in medicine, law, psychology, and government.

Before 1750, no American more fully embodied the Enlightenment spirit than **Benjamin Franklin.** Born in Boston in 1706, Franklin migrated to Philadelphia at age seventeen. He brought skill as a printer, considerable ambition, and insatiable intellectual curiosity. In moving to Philadelphia, Franklin put himself in the right place at the right time, for the city was growing much more rapidly than Boston and was attracting merchants and artisans who shared Franklin's zest for learning and new ideas. Franklin organized some of these men into a reading-discussion group called the Junto, and they helped him secure printing contracts. In 1732 he first published *Poor Richard's Almanack,* a collection of maxims and proverbs that made him famous. By age forty-two Franklin had earned enough money to retire and devote himself to science and public service.

These dual goals—science and public benefit—were intimately related in Franklin's mind, for he believed that all true science would be useful, in the sense of making everyone's life more comfortable. For example, experimenting with a kite, Franklin demonstrated in 1752 that lightning was electricity, a discovery that led to the lightning rod.

Although some southern planters, such as Thomas Jefferson, later championed progress through science, the Enlightenment's earliest and primary American centers were cities, where the latest European books and ideas circulated and where gentlemen and self-improving artisans met to investigate nature and conduct experiments. Franklin organized one such group, the American Philosophical Society, in 1743 to encourage "all philosophical experiments that let light into the nature of things, tend to increase the power of man over matter, and multiply the conveniences and pleasures of life." By 1769, this society had blossomed into an intercolonial network of amateur scientists. The societies emulated the Royal Society in London, the foremost learned society in the English-speaking world. In this respect, the Enlightenment initially strengthened the ties between colonial and British elites.

Just as Newton inspired the scientific bent of Enlightenment intellectuals, English philosopher John Locke, in his *Essay Concerning Human Understanding* (1690), led many to embrace "reasonable" or "rational" religion. Locke contended that ideas, including religion, are not inborn but are acquired by toilsome investigation of and reflection upon experience. To most Enlightenment intellectuals, the best argument for the existence of God was the harmony and order of nature, which pointed to a rational Creator. Some individuals, including Franklin and, later, Jefferson and Thomas Paine, carried this argument a step farther by insisting that where the Bible conflicted with reason, one should follow the dictates of reason. Called Deists, they concluded that God, having created a perfect universe, did not thereafter intervene in its workings but rather left it alone to operate according to natural laws.

Most colonists influenced by the Enlightenment described themselves as Christians and attended church. But they feared Christianity's excesses, particularly as indulged in by those who persecuted others in religion's name and by "enthusiasts" who emphasized emotion rather than reason in the practice of piety. Above all, they distrusted zealots and sectarians. Typically, Franklin contributed money to most of the churches in Philadelphia but thought that religion's value lay in its encouragement of virtue and morality rather than in theological hair splitting.

In 1750, the Enlightenment's greatest contributions to American life still lay in the future. A quarter-century later, Anglo-Americans drew on the Enlightenment's revolutionary ideas as they declared their independence from Britain and created the foundations of a new nation (see Chapters 5 and 6). Meanwhile, a series of religious revivals known as the Great Awakening challenged the Enlightenment's most basic assumptions.

The Great Awakening

Viewing the world as orderly and predictable, rationalists were inclined to a sense of smug self-satisfaction. Writing his will in 1750, Franklin thanked God for giving him "such a mind, with moderate passions" and "such a competency of this world's goods as might make a reasonable mind easy." But many Americans lacked such a comfortable competency of goods and lived neither orderly nor predictable lives. Earlier generations of young people coming of age had relied on established authority figures—parents, local leaders, clergy—for wisdom and guidance as they faced the future. But the world had changed by the middle decades of the eighteenth century. Older authorities were of little help when one's economic future was uncertain, when established elites seemed to act out of self-interest, and when one encountered more strangers than familiar faces on a daily basis. The result was a widespread spiritual hunger that neither traditional religion nor Enlightenment philosophy could satisfy.

Throughout the colonial period, religious fervor periodically surged within a denomination or region and then receded. But in 1739 an outpouring of European Protestant revivalism spread to British North America. This "Great Awakening," as colonial promoters termed it, cut across lines of class, gender, and even race. Above all, the revivals represented an unleashing of anxiety and longing among ordinary people—anxiety about sin, and longing for assurances of salvation. The answers they received were conveyed through the powerful preaching of charismatic ministers who appealed to their audiences' emotions rather than to their intellects. Some revivalists were themselves intellectuals, comfortable amid the books and ideas of the Enlightenment. But for all, religion was primarily a matter of emotional commitment.

In contrast to rationalists, who stressed the potential for human improvement, revivalist ministers aroused their audiences by depicting the emptiness of material comfort, the utter corruption of human nature, the fury of divine wrath, and the need for immediate repentance. Although well read in Enlightenment philosophy and science, the Congregationalist Jonathan Edwards, who led a revival at Northampton, Massachusetts, in 1735, drove home this message with breathtaking clarity. "The God that holds you over the pit of Hell, much as one holds a spider or other loathsome insect over the fire, abhors you," Edwards intoned in a famous sermon, "Sinners in the Hands of an Angry God." "His wrath toward you burns like fire; He looks upon you as worthy of nothing else but to be cast into the fire."

Even before Edwards's Northampton revival, two New Jersey ministers, Presbyterian William Tennent and Theodore Frelinghuysen of the Dutch Reformed Church, had stimulated conversions in prayer meetings called Refreshings. But the event that brought these threads of revival together was the arrival from Britain in 1739 of **George Whitefield** (see above). So overpowering was Whitefield that some joked that he could make crowds swoon simply by uttering "Mesopotamia." In an age without mi-

A Satirical View of George Whitefield, 1760

Whitefield's detractors portrayed him as a charlatan and demagogue who exploited simple-minded common people.

crophones, crowds exceeding twenty thousand could hear his booming voice clearly, and many wept at his eloquence.

Whitefield's American tour inspired thousands to seek salvation. Most converts were young adults in their late twenties. In Connecticut alone, church membership jumped from 630 in 1740 to 3,217 after Whitefield toured in 1741. Within two more years, every fifth Connecticut resident under forty-five had reportedly been saved by God's grace. Whitefield's allure was so mighty that he even awed potential critics. Hearing him preach in Philadelphia, Benjamin Franklin first vowed to contribute nothing to the collection. But so admirably did Whitefield conclude his sermon, Franklin recalled, "that I empty'd my Pocket wholly into the Collector's Dish, Gold and all." Divisions over the revivals quickly developed and were often exacerbated by social and economic tensions. For example, after leaving Boston in October 1740, Whitefield invited Gilbert Tennent (William's son) to follow "in order to blow up the divine flame lately kindled there." Denouncing Boston's established clergymen as "dead Drones" and lashing out at aristocratic fashion, Tennent built a following among the city's poor and downtrodden. So did another preacher, James Davenport, who spoke daily on the Boston Commons and then frightened polite Bostonians by leading processions of "idle or ignorant persons, and those of the lowest Rank" through the streets. Brought before a grand jury, Davenport was expelled for asserting "that Boston's ministers were leading the people blindfolded to hell."

Exposing colonial society's divisions, Tennent and Davenport sparked opposition to the revivals among established ministers and officials. As Whitefield's exchange with

Alexander Garden showed, the lines hardened between the revivalists, known as New Lights, and the rationalist clergy, or Old Lights, who dominated the Anglican, Presbyterian, and Congregational churches. In 1740, Gilbert Tennent published *The Danger of an Unconverted Ministry,* which hinted that most Presbyterian ministers lacked saving grace and hence were bound for hell, and urged parishioners to abandon them for the New Lights. By thus sowing the seeds of doubt about individual ministers, Tennent undermined one of the foundations of social order. For if the people could not trust their own ministers, whom would they trust?

Old Light rationalists fired back. In 1742, Charles Chauncy, Boston's leading Congregationalist minister, condemned the revival as an epidemic of the "enthusiasm" that enlightened intellectuals loathed. Chauncy particularly blasted those who mistook the ravings of their overheated imaginations for the experience of divine grace. He even provided a kind of checklist for spotting enthusiasts: look for "a certain wildness" in their eyes, the "quakings and tremblings" of their limbs, and foaming at the mouth. Put simply, the revival had unleashed "a sort of madness."

The Great Awakening opened unprecedented splits in American Protestantism. In 1741, New and Old Light Presbyterians formed rival branches that did not reunite until 1758, when the revivalists emerged victorious. The Anglicans lost many members to New Light congregations, especially Baptist and New Light Presbyterian. Congregationalists splintered so badly that by 1760, New Lights had seceded from one-third of New England's churches and formed New Light congregations or joined the Baptists.

The secession of New Lights was especially bitter in Massachusetts and Connecticut, where the Congregational church was established by law. Old Lights repeatedly denied new churches legal status, meaning that New Lights' taxes would go to their former churches. Connecticut passed repressive laws forbidding revivalists to preach or perform marriages, and the colony expelled New Lights from the legislature. In Connecticut's Windham County, an extra story was added to the jail to hold all the New Lights arrested for not paying church taxes (tithes). Elisha Paine, a revivalist imprisoned there for illegal preaching, gave sermons from his cell and drew such crowds that his followers built bleachers nearby to hear him. Paine and his fellow victims generated widespread sympathy for the New Lights, who finally won control of Connecticut's assembly in 1759.

Although New Lights made steady gains until the 1770s, the Great Awakening peaked in New England in 1742. The revival then crested everywhere but in Virginia, where its high point came after 1755 with an upsurge of conversions by Baptists, who also suffered legal harassment.

For all the commotion it raised at the time, the Great Awakening's long-term effects exceeded its immediate impact. First, the revival marked a decline in the influence of Quakers (who were not significantly affected by revivalism), Anglicans, and Congregationalists. In undermining Anglicans and Congregationalists, the Great Awakening contributed to the weakening of officially established denominations. As these churches' importance waned after 1740, the number of Presbyterians and Baptists increased.

The Great Awakening also stimulated the founding of new colleges as both Old and New Lights sought institutions free of one another's influence. In 1746, New Light Presbyterians established the College of New Jersey (Princeton). Then followed King's College (Columbia) for Anglicans in 1754, the College of Rhode Island (Brown) for

Baptists in 1764, Queen's College (Rutgers) for Dutch Reformed in 1766, and Dartmouth College for Congregationalists in 1769.

The revivals were also significant because they spread beyond the ranks of white society. The emphasis on piety over intellectual learning as the key to God's grace led some Africans and Native Americans to combine aspects of their traditional cultures with Christianity. The Great Awakening marked the beginnings of black Protestantism after New Lights reached out to slaves, some of whom joined white churches and even preached at revival meetings. Meanwhile, a few New Light preachers became missionaries to Native Americans residing within the colonies. A few Christian Indians trained in a special school to become missionaries to other Native Americans, and one, Samson Occom, a Mohegan born in Connecticut, became widely known among whites. Despite these breakthroughs, blacks and Indians still faced considerable religious discrimination, even among New Lights.

The Great Awakening also added to white women's religious prominence. For several decades non-Anglican ministers had singled out women—who constituted the majority of church members—as embodying the Christian ideal of piety. Now some New Light churches, mostly Baptist and Congregationalist, granted women the right to speak and vote in church meetings. Like Anne Hutchinson a century earlier (see Chapter 3), some women moved from leading women's prayer and discussion groups to presiding over meetings that included men. One such woman, Sarah Osborn of Newport, Rhode Island, conducted "private praying Societies Male and female" that included black slaves in her home. In 1770, Osborn and her followers won a bitter fight over their congregation's choice of a new minister. While most assertive women were prevented from exercising as much power as Osborn, none was persecuted as Hutchinson had been in Puritan New England.

Finally the revivals blurred denominational differences among Protestants. Although George Whitefield was an Anglican who defied his superior, Garden, and later helped found Methodism, he preached with Presbyterians such as Gilbert Tennent and Congregationalists like Jonathan Edwards. By emphasizing the need for salvation over details of doctrine and church governance, revivalism emphasized Protestants' common experiences and promoted the coexistence of denominations.

Historians have disagreed over whether the Great Awakening had political as well as religious effects. Although Tennent and Davenport called the poor "God's people" and flayed the wealthy, they never advocated revolution, and the Awakening did not produce a distinct political ideology. Yet by empowering ordinary people to assert and act openly on beliefs that countered those in authority, the revivals laid some of the groundwork for political revolutionaries a generation later.

CONCLUSION

By 1750, Britain's mainland colonies barely resembled those of a century earlier. Mercantilist policies bound an expanded number of colonies to the rising prosperity of the British Empire. A healthy environment for whites, along with encroachments on Native Americans' land, enabled the combined white and black population to grow by more than twenty times—from about fifty thousand to over one million. The political settlement that followed England's Glorious Revolution further bound the colonies to the empire and—at the same time—provided the foundation for representative government in the colonies. Educated Anglo-Americans joined the European intellectual ferment known as the Enlightenment. The Great Awakening, with its European origins and its intercolonial appeal, further signaled the colonies' emergence from provincial isolation. All these developments made British Americans more conscious of their ties to other colonies, to Great Britain, and to the broader Atlantic world.

The achievements of France and Spain on the North American mainland contrasted starkly with those of Britain. More lightly populated by Europeans, their colonies were more dependent on Native Americans for their survival. Despite their mercantilist orientations, neither France nor Spain profited significantly by colonizing mainland North America.

For all of its evident wealth and progress, British America was rife with tensions. In some areas, vast discrepancies in the distribution of wealth and opportunities fostered a rebellious spirit among whites who were less well off. The Enlightenment and the Great Awakening revealed deep-seated religious and ideological divisions. Slave resistance and Anglo-Indian warfare demonstrated the depths of racial antagonisms. The revived imperial warfare of 1739–1748 signaled that the peace that had nurtured prosperity was over and that an Anglo-French showdown was imminent.

5

Roads to Revolution, 1750–1776

TRIUMPH AND TENSIONS: THE BRITISH EMPIRE, 1750–1763

King George's War (see Chapter 4) ended in 1748 with Britain and France still intent on defeating one another. After a "diplomatic revolution" in which Austria shifted its allegiance from Britain to France, and Britain aligned with Prussia, the conflict resumed. Known as the Seven Years' War, it pitted British and French forces against one another in every continent except Australia. The war resulted in the expulsion of France from mainland North America, leaving the region to a triumphant British Empire. Yet even as war wound down, tensions developed within the victorious coalition of Britons, colonists, and Native Americans.

A Fragile Peace, 1750–1754
Soon after King George's War, Britain and France began preparations for another war, this time in the North American interior. The tinderbox for conflict was the Ohio valley, the subject of competing claims by Virginia, Pennsylvania, France, and the Six Nations Iroquois, as well as by the Native Americans who actually lived there.

Traders from Virginia and Pennsylvania were strengthening British influence among Indians in the Ohio valley. Seeking to drive out the traders, the French began building a chain of forts in the Ohio country in 1753. Virginia retaliated by sending a twenty-one-year-old surveyor and speculator, **George Washington,** to persuade or force the French to leave. Fearing that Washington had designs on their land, Native Americans refused to support him, and in 1754 French troops drove the Virginians back to their homes.

Chief Hendrick (Theyanoguin) of the Mohawk Iroquois
A longtime ally of the British, Hendrick led a Mohawk delegation to the Albany Congress (1754).

While Washington was still in Ohio, British officials called a meeting in mid-1754 of delegates from Virginia and colonies to the north to negotiate a treaty with the Six Nations Iroquois. Iroquois support would be vital in any effort to drive the French from the Ohio valley. Seven colonies (but neither Virginia nor New Jersey) sent delegates to the **Albany Congress** in Albany, New York. Long allied with Britain in the Covenant Chain, the Iroquois were also bound by the Grand Settlement of 1701 to remain neutral in any Anglo-French war (see Chapter 4). Moreover, the easternmost Mohawk Iroquois were angry because New York settlers were encroaching on their land. Despite these circumstances, the delegates obtained expressions of friendship from the Six Nations, but Iroquois suspicions of Britain persisted.

The delegates also endorsed a proposal for a colonial confederation, the Albany Plan of Union, largely based on the ideas of Pennsylvania's Franklin and Massachusetts's Thomas Hutchinson. The plan called for a Grand Council representing all the colonial assemblies, with a crown-appointed president general as its executive officer. The Grand Council would develop coordinated policies regarding military defense and Indian affairs, which the colonies would fund according to an agreed-upon formula. Although later regarded as a precedent for American unity, the Albany Plan in fact came to nothing, primarily because no colonial legislature approved it.

CHRONOLOGY, 1750–1776

1744–1748 • King George's War (in Europe, the War of Austrian Succession, 1740–1748).

1754 • Albany Congress.

1754–1761 • Seven Years' War (in Europe, 1756–1763).

1755 • British expel Acadians from Nova Scotia.

1760 • George III becomes king of Great Britain.
Writs of assistance.

1762 • Treaty of San Ildefonso.

1763 • Treaty of Paris.
Indian uprising in Ohio valley and Great Lakes.
Proclamation of 1763.

1763–1764 • Paxton Boys uprising in Pennsylvania.

1764 • Sugar Act.

1765 • Stamp Act.
African-Americans demand liberty in Charles Town.
First Quartering Act.

1766 • Stamp Act repealed.
Declaratory Act.

1767 • Revenue Act (Townshend duties).
American Board of Customs Commissioners created.

1768 • Massachusetts "circular letters."
John Hancock's ship *Liberty* seized by Boston customs commissioner.
First Treaty of Fort Stanwix.
St. George's Fields Massacre in London.

1770 • Townshend duties, except tea tax, repealed.
Boston Massacre.

1771 • Battle of Alamance Creek in North Carolina.

1772–1774 • Committees of correspondence formed.

1772 • Somerset decision in England.

1773 • Tea Act and Boston Tea Party.

1774 • Lord Dunmore's War.
Coercive Acts and Quebec Act.
First Continental Congress.

1775 • Battles of Lexington and Concord.
Lord Dunmore's Proclamation.
Olive Branch Petition.
Battles at Breed's Hill and Bunker Hill.
George III and Parliament declare colonies to be in rebellion.

1776 • Thomas Paine, *Common Sense*.
Declaration of Independence.

The Seven Years'
War in America,
1754–1760

Although France and Britain remained at peace in Europe until 1756, Washington's 1754 clash with French troops began the war in North America. In response, the British dispatched General Edward Braddock and a thousand regular troops to North America to seize Fort Duquesne at the headwaters of the Ohio.

Scornful of colonial soldiers and refusing Delaware Indians' offers of assistance, Braddock expected his disciplined British regulars to make short work of the enemy. On July 9, 1755, about 600 Native Americans and 250 French and Canadians ambushed Braddock's force of 2,200 Britons and Virginians nine miles east of Fort Duquesne. Riddled by three hours of steady fire from an unseen foe, Braddock's troops retreated. Nine hundred British and provincial soldiers died in Braddock's defeat, including the general himself, compared to just twenty-three French and Indians.

As British colonists absorbed the shock of Braddock's disastrous loss, French-armed Shawnees, Delawares, and Mingos from the upper Ohio valley struck hard at encroaching settlers in western Pennsylvania, Maryland, and Virginia. For three years, these attacks halted English expansion and prevented the three colonies from joining the British war against France.

Confronted by the numerically superior but disorganized Anglo-Americans, the French and their Native American allies—now including the Iroquois—captured Fort Oswego on Lake Ontario in 1756 and Fort William Henry on Lake George in 1757. The French now threatened central New York and western New England. In Europe, too, the war began badly for Britain, which by 1757 seemed to be facing defeat on all fronts.

In this dark hour, two developments turned the tide for the British. First, the Iroquois and most Ohio Indians, angered at French treatment of them and sensing that the French were gaining too decisive an advantage, agreed at a treaty conference at Easton, Pennsylvania, in 1758 to abandon the French. Their subsequent withdrawal from Fort Duquesne enabled the British to capture it and other French forts. Many Native Americans simply withdrew from the fighting, while others actively joined Britain's cause.

The second decisive development occurred when William Pitt took control of military affairs in the British cabinet and reversed the downward course. Pitt saw himself as the man of the hour. "I know," he declared, "that I can save this country and that no one else can." True to his word, Pitt reinvigorated British patriotism throughout the empire. By the war's end, he was the colonists' most popular hero, the symbol of what Americans and the English could accomplish when united.

Hard-pressed in Europe by France and its allies (which included Spain after 1761), Pitt chose not to send large numbers of additional troops to America. He believed that the key to crushing New France lay in the mobilization of colonial soldiers. To encourage the colonies to assume the military burden, he promised that if they raised the necessary men, Parliament would bear most of the cost of fighting the war.

Pitt's offer to free Anglo-Americans from the war's financial burdens generated unprecedented support. The colonies organized more than forty thousand troops in 1758–1759, far more soldiers than the crown sent to the mainland during the entire war.

The impact of Pitt's decision was immediate. Anglo-American troops under General Jeffery Amherst captured Fort Duquesne and Louisbourg in 1758 and drove the French from northern New York the next year. In September 1759, Quebec fell after General James Wolfe defeated the French commander-in-chief, Louis Joseph Montcalm, on the Plains of Abraham, where both commanders died in battle. French resistance ended in 1760 when Montreal surrendered.

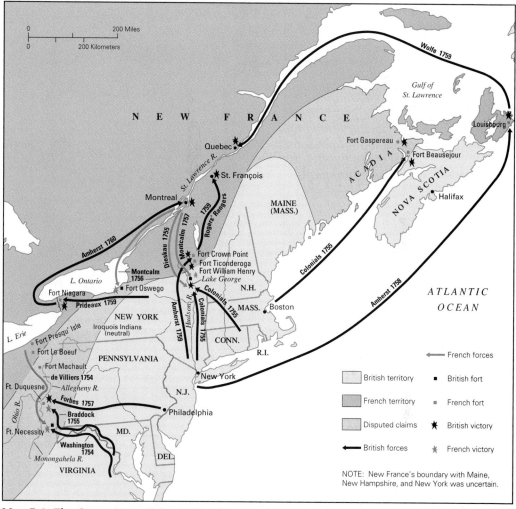

MAP 5.1 The Seven Years' War in North America, 1754–1760

After experiencing major defeats early in the war, Anglo-American forces turned the tide against the French in 1758 by taking Fort Duquesne and Louisbourg. After Canada fell in 1760, the fighting shifted to Spain's Caribbean colonies.

The End of French North America, 1760–1763

Although the fall of Montreal effectively dashed French hopes of victory in North America, the war continued in Europe and elsewhere, and France made one last desperate attempt to capture Newfoundland in June 1762. Thereafter, with defeat inevitable, France entered into negotiations with its enemies. The Seven Years' War officially ended in both America and Europe with the signing of the Treaty of Paris in 1763.

Under terms of the treaty, France gave up all its lands and claims east of the Mississippi (except New Orleans) to Britain. In return for Cuba, which a British expedition had seized in 1762, Spain ceded Florida to Britain. Neither France nor Britain wanted

MAP 5.2 European Territorial Claims, 1763

The treaties of San Ildefonso (1762) and Paris (1763) divided France's North American empire between Britain and Spain. Britain in 1763 established direct imperial authority west of the Proclamation Line.

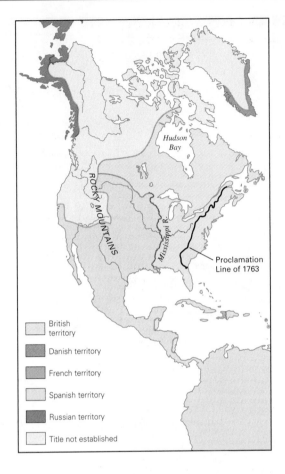

Hudson Bay

ROCKY MOUNTAINS

Mississippi R.

Proclamation Line of 1763

British territory

Danish territory

French territory

Spanish territory

Russian territory

Title not established

the other to control Louisiana, so in the Treaty of San Ildefonso (1762), France ceded the vast territory to Spain. Thus, France's once mighty North American empire was reduced to a few tiny fishing islands off Newfoundland and several prosperous sugar islands in the West Indies. Britain reigned supreme in eastern North America while Spain now claimed the west below Canada.

Several thousand French colonists in an area stretching from Quebec to Illinois to Louisiana were suddenly British and Spanish subjects. The most adversely affected Franco-Americans were the Acadians, who had been nominal British subjects since England took over Acadia in 1713 and renamed it Nova Scotia. In 1755, Nova Scotia's government ordered all Acadians to swear loyalty to Britain and not to bear arms for France. After most refused to take the oath, British soldiers drove them from their homes and attempted to disperse them among Britain's other colonies. About 7,000 of the 18,000 Acadians were forcibly deported in this way, while others were sent to France or French colonies. Facing poverty and intense anti-French, anti-Catholic prejudice in the British colonies and seeking to remain together, a majority of the exiles and refugees eventually moved to Louisiana, where their descendants became known as Cajuns.

King George's War and the Seven Years' War produced ironically mixed effects. On one hand, they fused the bonds between the British and the Anglo-Americans. Fighting side by side against the French Catholic enemy, the British and the American colonists came to rely on each other as rarely before and celebrated their common identity. But each war also planted seeds of mutual misunderstanding and suspicion.

Anglo-American Friction   During the Seven Years' War, British officers regularly complained about the quality of colonial troops, not only their inability to fight but also their tendency to return home—even in the midst of campaigns—when their terms were up or when they were not paid on time. For their part, colonial soldiers complained of British officers who, as one put it, treated their troops "but little better than slaves."

Tensions between British officers and colonial civilians also flared. Officers complained about colonists being unwilling to provide food and shelter while colonists resented the officers' arrogant manners. One general groused that South Carolina planters were "extremely pleased to have Soldiers to protect their Plantations but will feel no inconveniences for them." Quakers in the Pennsylvania assembly, acting from pacifist convictions, refused to vote funds to support the war effort, while assemblies in New York and Massachusetts opposed the quartering of British troops on their soil as an encroachment on their English liberties. English authorities regarded such actions as affronts to the king's prerogative and as undermining Britain's efforts to defend its territories.

Pitt's promise to reimburse the colonial assemblies for their military expenses angered many in Britain, who concluded that the colonists were escaping scot-free from the war's financial burden. The colonies had already profited enormously from the war, as military contracts and spending by British troops brought an influx of British currency into the hands of farmers, artisans, and merchants. Some merchants had even traded illicitly with the French enemy during wartime (see below). Meanwhile, Britain's national debt nearly doubled during the war, from £72 million to over £132 million. Whereas in 1763 the total debt of all the colonies collectively amounted to £2 million, the interest charges alone on the British debt came to more than £4 million a year. This debt was assumed by British landowners through a land tax and, increasingly, by ordinary consumers through excise duties on a wide variety of items, including beer, tea, salt, and bread.

Colonists felt equally burdened. Those who profited during the war spent their additional income on goods imported from Britain, the annual value of which doubled during the war's brief duration. Thus, the effect of the war was to accelerate the Anglo-American "consumer revolution" in which colonists' purchases of British goods fueled Britain's economy, particularly its manufacturing sector. But when peace returned in 1760, the wartime boom in the colonies ended as abruptly as it had begun. To maintain their lifestyles, many colonists went into debt. British creditors obliged their American merchant customers by extending the usual period for remitting payments from six months to a year. Nevertheless, many recently prosperous colonists suddenly found themselves overloaded with debts and, in some cases, bankrupt. As colonial indebtedness to Britain grew, some Americans began to suspect the British of deliberately plotting to "enslave" the colonies.

The ascension to the British throne of King **George III** (ruled 1760–1820) at age twenty-two reinforced Anglo-American tensions. The new king was determined to

Public Sanitation in Philadelphia

Even as the imperial crisis intruded on their lives, city-dwellers confronted long-standing problems occasioned by rapid growth. The fastest-growing city in eighteenth-century America was Philadelphia, whose population approached seventeen thousand in 1760. One key to Philadelphia's rise was its location as both a major Atlantic port and the gateway to Pennsylvania's farmlands and the Appalachian backcountry. Local geography also contributed to its success. Choosing a site where the Delaware and Schuylkill Rivers met, William Penn had built Philadelphia along a system of streams and the tidal cove on the Delaware into which they flowed. Philadelphians referred to the principal stream and cove together as "the Dock," for one of their principal functions. The Dock's shores were the setting for the early city's mansions and public gathering spaces. As some residents pointed out in 1700, the Dock was the city's heart and "the Inducing Reason . . . . to Settle the Town where it now is."

Over time, the growth that made Philadelphia so successful rendered its environment, especially its water, dangerous to inhabitants' health. Several leading industries used water for transforming animals and grains into consumer products. Tanneries made leather by soaking cowhides several times in mixtures of water and acidic liquids, including sour milk and fermented rye, and with an alkaline solution of buttermilk and dung. When cleaning their vats, tanners dumped residues from these processes into the streets or into underground pits from which they seeped into wells and streams. Breweries and distilleries also used water-based procedures and similarly discarded their waste, while slaughterhouses put dung, grease, fat, and other unwanted byproducts into streets and streams. Individual residents exacerbated the problems by tossing garbage into streets, using privies that polluted wells, and leaving animal carcasses to rot in the open air. Most of the city's sewers were open channels that frequently backed up, diverting the sewage to the streets. Buildings and other obstructions caused stagnant pools to form in streets, and when the polluted water did drain freely, it flowed into the Dock.

Almost from the city's founding, residents had complained about the stench arising from waste and stagnant water left by the tanneries and other large industries. Many attributed the city's frequent disease epidemics to these practices. In 1739, a residents' petition complained of "the great Annoyance arising from the Slaughter-Houses, Tan-yards, . . . etc. erected on the publick Dock, and Streets, adjacent." It called for prohibiting new tanneries and for eventually removing existing ones. Such efforts made little headway at first. Tanners, brewers, and other manufacturers were among the city's wealthiest residents and dissuaded their fellow elites from regulating their industries.

A turning point came in 1748 when, after another epidemic, the Pennsylvania Assembly appointed an ad hoc committee to recommend improvements in Philadelphia's sanitation. One member, Benjamin Franklin, was already known both for his innovative approaches to urban issues, as when he organized Philadelphia's first fire company in 1736, and for his interest in the practical applications of technology. Combining these interests, Franklin advocated applying new findings in hydrology (the study of water and its distribution) and water-pumping technology to public sanitation. Accordingly, the committee recommended building a wall to keep the high tides of the Delaware River out of the Dock, widening the stream's channel, and covering over a tributary that had become a "common sewer." The plan was innovative not only because it was based on hydrology but also because it acknowledged the need for a public approach to sanitation problems. But once again, neither the city, the colony, nor private entrepreneurs would pay for the proposal. Many elites declined to assume the sense of civic responsibility that Franklin and his fellow advocates of Enlightenment sought to inculcate.

Only in the 1760s, after both growth and pollution had accelerated, did Philadelphia begin to address the Dock's problems effectively. In 1762, the Pennsylvania Assembly appointed a board to oversee the "Pitching [sloping], Paving and Cleansing" of streets and walkways, and the design, construction, and maintenance of sewers and storm drains—all intended to prevent waste and stagnant water from accumulating on land. In the next year, residents petitioned that the Dock itself be "cleared out, planked at the bottom, and walled on each side" to maximize its flow and prevent it from flooding. The Pennsylvania Assembly responded by requiring adjoining property owners to build "a good, strong, substantial wall of good, flat stone from the bottom of the said Dock," and remove any "encroachments" that blocked drainage into or on the streams. Finally, legislators had implemented the kind of public, engineering-based solution that Franklin had advocated two decades earlier.

While some owners evaded their responsibility, others went even further by also building an arch over the principal stretch of the Dock. Then they installed market stalls on the newly available surface. Once an open waterway used for transport and valued as a central landmark, the Dock was now a completely enclosed, engineered sewer. A new generation of entrepreneurs dominated the neighborhood, catering to consumers who preferred a clean, attractive environment.

By 1763, however, Philadelphia's problem with sanitation had grown well beyond the Dock. Thereafter, the growing controversy over British imperial policies diverted official attention from public health problems. Yet by empowering poor and working people, that very controversy encouraged some to point out that improvements at the Dock had changed nothing in their own neighborhoods. Writing in a city newspaper in 1769, "Tom Trudge" lamented the lot of "such poor fellows as I, who sup on a cup of skim milk, etc., have a parcel of half naked children about our doors, . . . whose wives must, at many seasons of the Year, wade to the knees in carrying a loaf of bread to bake, and near whose penurious doors the dung-cart never comes, nor the sound of the paver will be heard for many ages." Both public and private solutions, Trudge and others asserted, favored the wealthy and ignored the less fortunate. Environmental controversy had once again shifted with the course of politics. But the Revolution would postpone the search for solutions. Philadelphia's problems with polluted water persisted until 1799, when the city undertook construction of the United States' first municipal water system.

Questions for Analysis

- How did early manufacturing contribute to pollution in Philadelphia?
- How did engineering provide a successful resolution of sanitary problems at the Dock?

have a strong influence on government policy, but neither his experience, his temperament, nor his philosophy suited him to the formidable task of building political coalitions and pursuing consistent policies. Until 1774, George III made frequent abrupt changes in government leadership that destabilized politics in Britain and exacerbated relations with the colonies.

Frontier Tensions   Victory over the French spurred new Anglo-Indian conflicts that drove the British debt even higher. With the French gone, Ohio and Great Lakes Indians recognized that they could no longer play the two imperial rivals off against each other. Their fears that the British would treat them as subjects rather than as allies were confirmed when General Jeffery Amherst, Britain's commander in North America, decided to cut expenses by refusing to distribute food, ammunition (needed for hunting), and other gifts. Moreover, squatters from the colonies were moving westward onto Indian lands and harassing the occupants, and many Native Americans feared that the British occupation was intended to support these incursions.

As tensions mounted, a Delaware Indian religious prophet named Neolin reported a vision in which the "Master of Life," or Great Spirit, instructed him to urge Native Americans of all tribes to unify and to repudiate European culture, material goods, and alliances. Meanwhile, other Native Americans hoped that the French would return so Indians could once again manipulate an imperial balance of power. Indian political leaders, including Pontiac, an Ottawa, drew on these sentiments to forge an explicitly anti-British movement, misleadingly called "Pontiac's Rebellion." During the spring and summer of 1763, they and their followers sacked eight British forts near the Great Lakes and besieged those at Pittsburgh and Detroit. But over the next three years, shortages of food and ammunition, a smallpox epidemic at Fort Pitt (triggered when British officers deliberately distributed infected blankets at a peace parley), and a recognition that the French would not return led the Indians to make peace with Britain. Although word of the uprising spread to Native Americans in the Southeast and Mississippi valley, British diplomacy prevented violence from erupting there.

Despite the uprising's failure, the Native Americans had not been decisively defeated. Hoping to conciliate the Indians and end the fighting, George III issued the **Proclamation of 1763,** asserting direct British control of land transactions, settlement, trade, and other activities of non-Indians west of a Proclamation Line along the Appalachian crest. The government's goal was to restore order to the process of colonial expansion by replacing the authority of the various (and often competing) colonies with that of the crown. The proclamation recognized existing Indian land titles everywhere west of the "proclamation line" until such time as tribal governments agreed to cede their land through treaties. Although calming Indian fears, the proclamation angered the colonies by subordinating their western claims to imperial authority and by slowing expansion.

The uprising was also a factor in the British government's decision to leave ten thousand soldiers in France's former forts on the Great Lakes and in the Ohio valley. The burden of maintaining control over the western territories would reach almost a half million pounds a year, fully 6 percent of Britain's peacetime budget. Britons considered it perfectly reasonable for the colonists to help offset this expense. Although the troops would help offset the colonies' unfavorable balance of payments with Britain, many Anglo-Americans regarded them as a peacetime "standing army" that threatened their liberty. With the French menace to their security removed, they saw westward expansion onto Indian lands as a way to prosperity, and they viewed British troops enforcing the Proclamation of 1763 as hindering rather than enhancing that expansion.

IMPERIAL AUTHORITY, COLONIAL OPPOSITION, 1760–1766

After the Seven Years' War, Anglo-American tensions centered on British efforts to finance its suddenly enlarged empire through a series of revenue measures and to enforce these and other measures directly rather than relying on local authorities. Following passage of the Stamp Act, opposition movements arose in the mainland colonies to protest not only the new measures' costs but also what many people considered a dangerous extension of Parliament's power. Their success revealed a widening gulf between British and colonial perceptions of the proper relationship between the empire and its colonies.

Writs of Assistance, 1760–1761 Even before the Seven Years' War ended, British authorities attempted to halt American merchants' trade with the French enemy in the West Indies. In 1760, the royal governor of Massachusetts authorized revenue officers to employ a document called a writ of assistance to seize illegally imported goods. The writ was a general search warrant that permitted customs officials to enter any ship or building where smuggled goods might be hidden. Because the document required no evidence of probable cause for suspicion, many critics considered it unconstitutional. The writ of assistance also threatened the traditional privacy of a family's home, since most merchants conducted business from home.

Writs of assistance proved effective against smuggling. In quick reaction to the writs, merchants in Boston, virtually the smuggling capital of the colonies, hired lawyer James Otis to challenge the constitutionality of these warrants. Arguing his case before the Massachusetts Supreme Court in 1761, Otis proclaimed that "an act against the Constitution is void"—even one passed by Parliament. But the court, influenced by Chief Justice Thomas Hutchinson, who noted the use of identical writs in England, ruled against the Boston merchants.

Despite losing the case, Otis expressed the fundamental conception of many, both in Britain and in the colonies, of Parliament's role under the British constitution. The British constitution was not a written document but instead a collection of customs and accepted principles that guaranteed certain rights to all citizens. Most British politicians assumed that Parliament's laws were themselves part of the constitution and hence that Parliament could alter the constitution at will. But Otis contended that Parliament possessed no authority to violate the "rights of Englishmen," and he asserted that there were limits "beyond which if Parliaments go, their Acts bind not." Such challenges to parliamentary authority would be renewed once peace was restored.

The Sugar Act, 1764 In 1764, just three years after Otis challenged the writs of assistance, Parliament passed the **Sugar Act.** The measure's goal was to raise revenues to help offset Britain's military expenses in North America, and thus end Britain's long-standing policy of exempting colonial trade from revenue-raising measures. The Navigation Acts had not been designed to bring money into the British treasury but rather to benefit the imperial economy indirectly by stimulating trade and protecting English manufacturers from foreign competition. English importers, not American producers, paid the taxes that Parliament levied on colonial products entering Britain, and then passed the cost on to consumers. So little revenue did the Navigation Acts bring in (just £1,800 in 1763) that they did not even pay the cost of their own enforcement.

The Sugar Act amended the Molasses Act of 1733 (see Chapter 4), the last of the Navigation Acts, which amounted to a tariff on French West Indian molasses entering British North America. But colonists had simply continued to import the cheaper French molasses after 1733, bribing customs officials into taking 11/2 pence per gallon to look the other way when it was unloaded. Aware of the widespread bribery, Parliament assumed that colonial rum drinkers would accept a three-pence per gallon duty.

New taxes were not the only feature of the Sugar Act that American merchants found objectionable. The act also stipulated that colonists could export lumber, iron, furs, and many other commodities to foreign countries only if the shipments first landed in Britain. Previously, American ships had taken these products directly to Dutch and German ports and returned with goods to sell to colonists. By channeling this trade through Britain, Parliament hoped that colonial shippers would purchase more British goods, buy fewer goods from foreign competitors, and provide jobs for Englishmen.

The Sugar Act also vastly complicated the requirements for shipping colonial goods. A captain now had to fill out a confusing series of documents to certify his trade as legal, and the absence of any of them left his entire cargo liable to seizure. The law's petty regulations made it virtually impossible for many colonial shippers to avoid committing technical violations.

Finally, the Sugar Act disregarded many traditional English protections for a fair trial. First, the law allowed customs officials to transfer smuggling cases from the colonial courts, in which juries decided the outcome, to vice-admiralty courts, where a British-appointed judge gave the verdict. Because the Sugar Act (until 1768) awarded vice-admiralty judges 5 percent of any confiscated cargo, judges had a financial incentive to find defendants guilty. Second, until 1767 the law did not permit defendants to be tried where their offense allegedly had taken place (usually their home province) but required all cases to be heard in the vice-admiralty court at Halifax, Nova Scotia. Third, the law reversed normal courtroom procedures, which presumed innocence until guilt was proved, by requiring the defendant to disprove the prosecution's charge.

The Sugar Act was no idle threat. British prime minister George Grenville ordered the navy to enforce the measure, and it did so vigorously. A Boston resident complained in 1764 that "no vessel hardly comes in or goes out but they find some pretense to seize and detain her." That same year, Pennsylvania's chief justice reported that customs officers were extorting fees from small boats carrying lumber across the Delaware River to Philadelphia from New Jersey and seemed likely "to destroy this little River-trade."

Rather than pay the three-pence tax, Americans continued smuggling molasses until 1766. Then, to discourage smuggling, Britain lowered the duty to a penny—less than the customary bribe American shippers paid to get their cargoes past inspectors. The law thereafter raised about £30,000 annually in revenue.

Opposition to the Sugar Act remained fragmented and ineffective. The law's burden fell overwhelmingly on Massachusetts, New York, and Pennsylvania; other provinces had little interest in resisting a measure that did not affect them directly. The Sugar Act's immediate effect was minor, but it heightened some colonists' awareness of the new direction of imperial policies and their implications.

The Stamp Act Crisis, 1765–1766 The revenue raised by the Sugar Act did little to ease Britain's financial crisis. The national debt continued to rise, and the British public groaned under the weight of the second-highest tax rates in Europe. Particularly irritating to Britons was the fact that by 1765 their rates averaged 26 shillings per person, whereas the colonial tax burden varied from 1/2 to 1 1/2 shillings per inhabitant, or barely 2 to 6 percent of the British rate. Well aware of how lightly the colonists were taxed, Grenville thought that they should make a larger contribution to the empire's American expenses.

To raise such revenues, Parliament passed the **Stamp Act** in March 1765. The law obliged colonists to purchase and use special stamped (watermarked) paper for newspapers, customs documents, various licenses, college diplomas, and legal forms used for recovering debts, buying land, and making wills. As with the Sugar Act, violators would face prosecution in vice-admiralty courts, without juries. The prime minister projected yearly revenues of £60,000 to £100,000, which would offset 12 to 20 percent of North American military expenses.

Unlike the Sugar Act, which was an external tax levied on imports as they entered the colonies, the Stamp Act was an internal tax, or a duty levied directly on property, goods, and government services in the colonies. Whereas external taxes were intended to regulate trade and fell mainly on merchants and ship captains, internal taxes were designed to raise revenue for the crown and affected many more people. In the case of the Stamp Act, anyone who made a will, transferred property, borrowed money, or bought playing cards or newspapers would pay the tax.

To Grenville and his supporters, the new tax seemed a small price for the benefits of the empire, especially since Britons had been paying a similar tax since 1695. Nevertheless, some in England, most notably William Pitt, objected in principle to Britain's levying an internal tax on the colonies. They emphasized that the colonists had never been subject to British revenue bills and noted that they already taxed themselves through their own elected assemblies.

Grenville and his followers agreed that Parliament could not tax any British subjects unless they enjoyed representation in that body. But they contended that Americans shared the same status as the majority of British adult males who either lacked sufficient property to vote or lived in large cities that had no seats in Parliament. Such people, they maintained, were "virtually" represented in Parliament. The principle of virtual representation held that every member of Parliament stood above the narrow interests of his constituents and considered the welfare of all subjects when deciding issues. By definition, then, British subjects, including colonists, were not represented by particular individuals but by all members of Parliament.

Grenville and his supporters also denied that the colonists were entitled to any exemption from British taxation because they elected their own assemblies. These legislative bodies, they alleged, were no different from British local governments, whose powers to pass laws and taxes did not nullify Parliament's authority over them. Accordingly, colonial assemblies were an adaptation to unique American circumstances and possessed no more power than Parliament allowed them to exercise. But Grenville's

New Hampshire Stamp Act Protest
In order to frighten stamp tax collectors into resigning their posts, crowds in colonial cities and towns would parade an agent's effigy through the streets.

position clashed directly with the stance of many colonists who had been arguing for several decades that their assemblies exercised legislative powers equivalent to those of the House of Commons in Great Britain (see Chapter 4).

Many colonists felt that the Stamp Act forced them either to confront the issue of parliamentary taxation head-on or to surrender any claim to meaningful rights of self-government. However much they might admire and respect Parliament, few colonists imagined that it represented them. They accepted the validity of virtual representation for England and Scotland but denied that it could be extended to the colonies. Instead, they argued, they enjoyed a substantial measure of self-governance similar to that of Ireland, whose Parliament alone could tax its people but could not interfere with laws, like the Navigation Acts, passed by the British Parliament. In a speech before the Boston town meeting opposing the Sugar Act, James Otis expressed Americans' basic argument: "that by [the British] Constitution, every man in the dominions is a free man: that no parts of His Majesty's dominions can be taxed without consent: that every part has a right to be represented in the supreme or some subordinate legislature." In essence, the colonists assumed that the empire was a loose federation in which their legislatures possessed considerable autonomy, rather than an extended nation governed directly from London.

To many colonists passage of the Stamp Act demonstrated both Parliament's indifference to their interests and the shallowness of the theory of virtual representation. Colonial agents in London had lobbied against passage of the law, and provincial legislatures had sent petitions warning against passage. But Parliament had dismissed the petitions without a hearing. Parliament "must have thought us Americans all a parcel of Apes and very tame Apes too," concluded Christopher Gadsden of South Carolina, "or they would have never ventured on such a hateful, baneful experiment."

In late May 1765, Patrick Henry, a twenty-nine-year-old Virginia lawyer and planter with a talent for fiery oratory, dramatically conveyed the rising spirit of resistance. Henry urged the Virginia House of Burgesses to adopt several strongly worded resolutions denying Parliament's power to tax the colonies. In the debate over the resolutions, Henry reportedly stated that "he did not doubt but some good American would stand up in favor of his country." Viewing such language as treasonous, the Assembly passed only the weakest four of Henry's seven resolutions. Garbled newspaper accounts of Henry's resolutions and the debates were published in other colonies, and by year's end seven other assemblies had passed resolutions against the act. As in Virginia, the resolutions were grounded in constitutional arguments and avoided Henry's inflammatory language.

Henry's words resonated more loudly outside elite political circles, particularly in Boston. There, in late summer, a group of mostly middle-class artisans and small business owners joined together as the Loyal Nine to fight the Stamp Act. They recognized that the stamp distributors, who alone could accept money for watermarked paper, were the law's weak link. If the public could pressure them into resigning before taxes became due on November 1, the Stamp Act would become inoperable.

It was no accident that Boston set the pace in opposing Parliament. A large proportion of Bostonians lived by shipbuilding, maritime trade, and distilling, and in 1765 they were not living well. In part, they could blame British policies for their misfortune. No other port suffered so much from the Sugar Act's trade restrictions. The law burdened rum producers with a heavy tax on molasses, dried up a flourishing import trade in Portuguese wines, and prohibited the direct export of many New England products to profitable overseas markets.

But Boston's misery was rooted in older problems. Even before the Seven Years' War, its shipbuilding industry had lost significant ground to New York and Philadelphia, and the output of its rum and sugar producers had fallen by half in just a decade. British impressment (forced recruitment) of Massachusetts fishermen for naval service had undermined the fishing industry. The resulting unemployment led to increased taxes for poor-relief. The taxes, along with a shrinking number of customers, drove many marginal artisans out of business and into the ranks of the poor. Other Bostonians, while remaining employed or in business, struggled in the face of rising prices for basic necessities as well as taxes. To compound its misery, the city still struggled to recover from a great fire in 1760 that had burned 176 warehouses and left every tenth family homeless.

Widespread economic distress produced an explosive situation in Boston. Already resentful of an elite whose fortunes had risen spectacularly while they suffered, many poor and working-class Bostonians blamed British officials and policies for the town's hard times. The crisis was sharpened because they were accustomed to gathering in large crowds that engaged in pointed political expression, both satirical and serious and usually directed against the "better sort."

In the aftermath of the Stamp Act, Boston's crowds aimed their traditional forms of protest more directly and forcefully at imperial officials. The morning of August 14 found a likeness of Boston's stamp distributor, Andrew Oliver, swinging from a tree guarded by a menacing crowd. Oliver apparently did not realize that the Loyal Nine were warning him to resign immediately, so at dusk several hundred Bostonians, led by a South End shoemaker named Ebenezer MacIntosh, demolished a new building of Oliver's at the dock. Thereafter, the Loyal Nine withdrew, and the crowd continued on its own. The men surged toward Oliver's house, where they beheaded his effigy and "stamped" it to pieces. The crowd then shattered the windows of his home, smashed his furniture, and even tore out the paneling. When Lieutenant Governor Hutchinson and the sheriff tried to disperse the crowd, they were driven off under a barrage of rocks. Surveying his devastated home the next morning, Oliver announced his resignation.

Bitterness against the Stamp Act unleashed spontaneous, contagious violence. Twelve days after the first Boston riot, Bostonians demolished the elegant home of Thomas Hutchinson. This attack occurred in part because smugglers held grudges against Hutchinson for certain of his decisions as chief justice and also because many financially pinched citizens saw him as a symbol of the royal policies crippling Boston's already troubled economy and their own livelihoods. In their view, wealthy officials "rioted in luxury," with homes and fancy furnishings that cost hundreds of times the annual incomes of most Boston workingmen. They were also reacting to Hutchinson's efforts to stop the destruction of his brother-in-law Andrew Oliver's house. Ironically, Hutchinson privately opposed the Stamp Act.

Meanwhile, groups similar to the Loyal Nine calling themselves Sons of Liberty were forming throughout the colonies. After the assault on Hutchinson's mansion and an even more violent incident in Newport, Rhode Island, the leaders of the **Sons of Liberty** sought to prevent more such outbreaks. They recognized that people in the crowds were casting aside their customary deference toward their social "superiors," a development that could broaden to include all elites if not carefully contained. Fearful of alienating wealthy opponents of the Stamp Act, the Sons of Liberty focused their actions strictly against property and invariably left avenues of escape for their victims. Especially fearful that a royal soldier or revenue officer might be shot or killed, they forbade their followers to carry weapons, even when facing armed adversaries. Realizing the value of martyrs, they resolved that the only lives lost over the issue of British taxation would come from their own ranks.

In October 1765, representatives of nine colonial assemblies met in New York City in the so-called Stamp Act Congress. The session was remarkable for the colonies' agreement on and bold articulation of the general principle that Parliament lacked authority to levy taxes outside Great Britain and to deny any person a jury trial. "The Ministry never imagined we could or would so generally unite in opposition to their measures," wrote a Connecticut delegate to the congress, "nor I confess till I saw the Experiment made did I."

By late 1765, most stamp distributors had resigned or fled, and without the watermarked paper required by law, most royal customs officials and court officers were refusing to perform their duties. In response, legislators compelled the reluctant officials to resume operation by threatening to withhold their pay. At the same time, merchants obtained sailing clearances by insisting that they would sue if cargoes spoiled while delayed in port. By late December, the courts and harbors of almost every colony were again functioning.

Thus colonial elites moved to keep an explosive situation from getting out of hand by taking over leadership of local Sons of Liberty groups, by coordinating protest through the Stamp Act Congress, and by having colonial legislatures restore normal business. Elite leaders feared that chaos could break out, particularly if British troops landed to enforce the Stamp Act. An influential Pennsylvanian, John Dickinson, summed up how respectable gentlemen envisioned the dire consequences of revolutionary turmoil: "a multitude of Commonwealths, Crimes, and Calamities, Centuries of mutual jealousies, Hatreds, Wars of Devastation, till at last the exhausted provinces shall sink into savagery under the yoke of some fortunate Conqueror."

To force the Stamp Act's repeal, New York's merchants agreed on October 31, 1765, to boycott all British goods, and businessmen in other cities soon followed their example. Because American colonists purchased about 40 percent of England's manufactures, this nonimportation strategy put the English economy in danger of recession. The colonial boycotts consequently triggered panic within England's business community, whose members descended on Parliament to warn that continuation of the Stamp Act would stimulate a wave of bankruptcies, massive unemployment, and political unrest.

The Marquis of Rockingham, who had succeeded Grenville as prime minister in mid-1765, hesitated to advocate repeal because the overwhelming majority within Parliament was outraged at colonial defiance of the law. Then in January 1766 William Pitt, a steadfast opponent of the Stamp Act, boldly denounced all efforts to tax the colonies, declaring, "I rejoice that America has resisted." Parliamentary support for repeal thereafter grew, though only as a matter of practicality, not as a surrender of principle. In March 1766, Parliament revoked the Stamp Act, but only in conjunction with passage of the **Declaratory Act,** which affirmed parliamentary power to legislate for the colonies "in all cases whatsoever."

Because the Declaratory Act was written in general language, Americans interpreted its meaning to their own advantage. Most colonial political leaders recognized that the law was modeled after an earlier statute of 1719 regarding Ireland, which was considered exempt from British taxation. The measure therefore seemed no more than a parliamentary exercise in saving face to compensate for the Stamp Act's repeal, and Americans ignored it. The House of Commons, however, intended that the colonists take the Declaratory Act literally to mean that they could not claim exemption from any parliamentary statute, including a tax law. The Stamp Act crisis thus ended in a fundamental disagreement between Britain and America over Parliament's authority in the colonies.

Although the Stamp Act crisis had not resolved the underlying philosophical differences between Britain and America, most colonists eagerly put the events of 1765 behind them, and they showered both king and Parliament with loyal statements of gratitude for the Stamp Act's repeal. The Sons of Liberty disbanded. Still possessing a deep emotional loyalty to "Old England," Anglo-Americans concluded with relief that their active resistance to the law had slapped Britain's leaders back to their senses. Nevertheless, the crisis led many to ponder British policies and actions more deeply than ever before.

Ideology, Religion, and Resistance
The Stamp Act and the conflicts that arose around it revealed a chasm between Britain and its colonies that startled Anglo-Americans. For the first time, some of them critically reconsidered the imperial relationship that they always thought of as beneficial to the colonies. In order to put their concerns into perspective, educated colonists turned to the works of philosophers, historians, and political writers. Many more, both educated and uneducated, looked to religion.

By the 1760s, the colonists were already widely familiar with the political writings of European Enlightenment thinkers, particularly John Locke (see Chapter 4). Locke argued that humans originated in a "state of nature" in which each man enjoyed the "natural rights" of life, liberty, and property. Thereafter, groups of men entered into a "social contract," under which they formed governments for the sole purpose of protecting those individual rights. A government that encroached on natural rights, then, broke its contract with the people. In such cases, people could resist their government, although Locke cautioned against outright rebellion except in the most extreme cases. To many colonial readers, Locke's concept of natural rights appeared to justify opposition to arbitrary legislation by Parliament.

Colonists also read European writers who emphasized excessive concentrations of executive power as threats to the liberty of the people. Some of them balanced Locke's emphasis on the rights of individuals with an emphasis on subordinating individual interests to the greater good of the people as a whole. Looking to the ancient Greeks and Romans as well as to more recent European theorists, these writers developed a set of ideas termed "republican." "Republicans" especially admired the sense of civic duty that motivated citizens of the Roman republic. Like the early Romans, they maintained that a free people had to avoid moral and political corruption, and practice a disinterested "public virtue." An elected leader of a republic, one author noted, would command obedience "more by the virtue of the people, than by the terror of his power."

Among those influenced by republican ideas were a widely read group of English political writers known as oppositionists. According to John Trenchard, Thomas Gordon, and others belonging to this group, Parliament—consisting of the freely elected representatives of the people—formed the foundation of England's unique political liberties and protected those liberties against the inherent corruption and tyranny of executive power. But since 1720, the oppositionists argued, prime ministers had exploited the treasury's vast resources to provide pensions, contracts, and profitable offices to politicians or had bought elections by bribing voters. Most members of Parliament, in their view, no longer represented the true interests of their constituents; rather, they had created self-interested "factions" and joined in a "conspiracy against liberty." Often referring to themselves as the "country party," these oppositionists feared that a power-hungry "court party" of unelected officials close to the king was using a corrupted Parliament to gain absolute power for themselves.

Influenced by such ideas, a number of colonists pointed to a diabolical conspiracy behind British policy during the Stamp Act crisis. James Otis characterized a group of pro-British Rhode Islanders as a "little, dirty, drinking, drabbing, contaminated knot of thieves, beggars, and transports . . . made up of Turks, Jews, and other infidels, with a few renegade Christians and Catholics." Joseph Warren of Massachusetts noted that the act "induced some to imagine that the minister designed by this to force the colonies into a rebellion, and from thence to take occasion to treat them with severity, and, by military power, to reduce them to servitude." Over the next decade, a proliferation of pamphlets denounced British efforts to "enslave" the colonies through excessive taxation and the imposition of officials, judges, and a standing army directed from London. In such assaults on liberty and natural rights, some Americans found principled reasons for opposing British policies and actions.

Beginning with the Stamp Act protest, many Protestant clergymen, both Old Lights and New Lights (see Chapter 4), wove resistance to British authority into their sermons, summoning their congregations to protect their God-given liberty. "A just regard to our liberties . . . is so far from being displeasing to God that it would be ingratitude to him who has given them to us to . . . tamely give them up," exhorted one New England minister. Most Anglican ministers, whose church was headed by the king, tried to stay neutral or opposed the protest; and pacifist Quakers kept out of the fray. But to large numbers of Congregationalist, Presbyterian, and Baptist clergymen, battling for the Lord and defending liberty were one and the same.

Voicing such a message, clergymen exerted an enormous influence on public opinion. Far more Americans heard sermons than had access to newspapers or pamphlets, and ministers always got a respectful hearing at town meetings. Community leaders' proclamations of days of "fasting and public humiliation"—a traditional means of focusing public attention on an issue and invoking divine aid—inspired sermons on the theme of God's sending the people woes only to strengthen and sustain them until victory. Even Virginia gentlemen (not usually known for their piety) felt moved by such proclamations. Moreover, protest leaders' calls for boycotting British luxuries meshed neatly with traditional pulpit warnings against self-indulgence and wastefulness. Few ordinary Americans escaped the unceasing public reminders that community solidarity against British tyranny and "corruption" meant rejecting sin and obeying God.

RESISTANCE RESUMES, 1766–1770

Although Parliament's repeal of the Stamp Act momentarily quieted colonial protests, its search for new sources of revenue soon revived them. While British leaders condemned the colonists for evading their financial responsibilities and for insubordination, growing numbers of Anglo-Americans became convinced that the Stamp Act had not been an isolated mistake but rather part of a deliberate design to undermine colonial self-governance. In this, they were joined by many in Britain who opposed policies that seemed to threaten Britons and colonists alike.

Opposing the
Quartering Act,
1766–1767

In August 1766, George III dismissed the Rockingham government and summoned William Pitt to form a cabinet. Opposed to taxing the colonies, Pitt might have repaired the Stamp Act's damage, for no man was more respected in America. But after Pitt's health collapsed in March 1767, effective leadership passed to his Chancellor of the Exchequer (treasurer) Charles Townshend.

Just as Townshend took office, a conflict arose with the New York legislature over the Quartering Act, enacted in 1765. This law ordered colonial legislatures to pay for certain goods needed by soldiers stationed within their respective borders. The necessary items were relatively inexpensive barracks supplies such as candles, windowpanes, mattress straw, polish, and a small liquor ration.

Despite its seemingly petty stipulations, the Quartering Act aroused resentment, for it constituted an indirect tax; that is, although it did not (like the Stamp Act) empower royal officials to collect money directly from the colonists, it obligated assemblies to raise a stated amount of revenue. Such obligations clashed with the assemblies' claimed power to initiate all revenue-raising measures. Likewise, by reinforcing the presence of a standing army, the Quartering Act further reinforced tyranny in the eyes of many colonists. The law fell lightly or not at all on most colonies; but New York, where more soldiers were stationed than in any other province, found compliance very burdensome and refused to grant any supplies.

New York's resistance to the Quartering Act produced a torrent of anti-American feeling in the House of Commons, whose members remained bitter at having had to withdraw the Stamp Act. Townshend responded by drafting the New York Suspending Act, which threatened to nullify all laws passed by the colony if the assembly refused to vote the supplies. By the time George III signed the measure, however, New York had appropriated the necessary funds.

Although New York's retreat averted further confrontation, the conflict over the Quartering Act demonstrated that British leaders would not hesitate to defend Parliament's authority through the most drastic of all steps: by interfering with American claims to self-governance.

Crisis over the Townshend Duties, 1767–1770

Parliamentary resentment toward the colonies expressed widespread British frustration over the government's failure to cut taxes from wartime levels. Dominating the House of Commons, members of the landed gentry slashed their own taxes by 25 percent in 1767. This move cost the government £500,000 and prompted Townshend to propose laws that would tax imports entering America from Britain and increase colonial customs revenue.

Townshend sought to tax the colonists by exploiting an oversight in their arguments against the Stamp Act. In confronting the Stamp Act, Americans had emphasized their opposition to internal taxes, but had said little about Parliament's right to tax imports as they entered the colonies. Townshend and other British leaders chose to interpret this silence as evidence that the colonists accepted Britain's right to tax their trade—to impose external taxes. Yet not all British politicians were so mistaken. "They will laugh at you," predicted a now wiser George Grenville, "for your distinctions about regulations of trade." Brushing aside Grenville's warnings, Parliament passed Townshend's **Revenue Act** (popularly called the Townshend duties) in June and July 1767. The new law taxed glass, paint, lead, paper, and tea imported to the colonies from England.

The Revenue Act differed significantly from what Americans had long seen as a legitimate way of regulating trade through taxation. To the colonists, charging a duty was a lawful way for British authorities to control trade only if that duty excluded foreign goods by making them prohibitively expensive to consumers. The Revenue Act, however, set moderate rates that did not price goods out of the colonial market; clearly, its purpose was to collect money for the treasury. Thus from the colonial standpoint, Townshend's duties were taxes just like the Stamp Act duties.

Although Townshend had introduced the Revenue Act in response to the government's budgetary problems, he had an ulterior motive for establishing an American source of revenue. Traditionally, royal governors had depended on colonial legislatures to vote their salaries; for their part, the legislatures had often refused to allocate these salaries until governors signed certain bills they themselves opposed. Through the Revenue Act, Townshend hoped to establish a fund that would pay the salaries of governors and other royal officials in America, thus freeing them from the assemblies' control. In effect, by stripping the assemblies of their most potent weapon, the power of the purse, the Revenue Act threatened to tip the balance of constitutional power away from elected colonial representatives and toward unelected royal officials.

In reality, the Revenue Act would never yield anything like the income that Townshend anticipated. Of the various items taxed, only tea produced any significant revenue—£20,000 of the £37,000 that the law was expected to yield. And because the measure would serve its purpose only if British tea were affordable to colonial consumers, Townshend eliminated £60,000 worth of import fees paid on tea entering Britain from India before transshipment to America. On balance, the Revenue Act worsened the British treasury's deficit by £23,000. By 1767, Britain's financial difficulties were more an excuse for, than the driving force behind, political demands to tax the colonies. From Parliament's standpoint, the conflict with America was becoming a test of national will over the principle of taxation.

Colonial resistance to the Revenue Act remained weak until December 1767, when John Dickinson published twelve essays entitled *Letters from a Farmer in Pennsylvania.* (Dickinson was actually a lawyer.) Appearing in nearly every colonial newspaper, the essays argued that although Parliament could regulate trade by imposing duties that produced small amounts of "incidental revenue," it had no right to tax commerce for the single purpose of raising revenue. In other words, the legality of any external tax depended on its intent. No tax designed to produce revenue could be considered constitutional unless a people's elected representatives voted for it. Dickinson said nothing that others had not stated or implied during the Stamp Act crisis. Rather, his contribution lay in persuading many Americans that the arguments they had marshaled against the Stamp Act also applied to the Revenue Act.

In early 1768, the Massachusetts assembly condemned the Townshend duties and called on Samuel Adams to draft a "circular letter" calling on other colonial legislatures to join it. Adams's letter forthrightly condemned both taxation without representation and the threat to self-governance posed by Parliament's making governors and other royal officials financially independent of the legislatures. But it acknowledged Parliament as the "supreme legislative Power over the whole Empire," and it advocated no illegal activities. Virginia's assembly warmly approved Adams's message and sent out a more strongly worded circular letter of its own, urging all colonies to oppose imperial policies that would "have an immediate tendency to enslave them." But most colonial legislatures reacted indifferently. In fact, resistance to the Revenue Act might have disintegrated had the British government not overreacted to the circular letters.

Parliamentary leaders regarded even the mild Massachusetts letter as "little better than an incentive to Rebellion." Disorganized by Townshend's sudden death in 1767, the king's Privy Council directed Lord Hillsborough, first appointee to the new post of secretary of state for the colonies, to express the government's displeasure. Hillsborough flatly told the Massachusetts assembly to disown its letter, forbade all colonial assemblies to endorse it, and commanded royal governors to dissolve any legislature that violated his instructions. George III later commented that he never met "a man of less judgment than Lord Hillsborough." A wiser man might have tried to divide the colonists by appealing to their sense of British patriotism, but Hillsborough had chosen to challenge their elected representatives directly, guaranteeing a unified, angry response.

To protest Hillsborough's crude bullying, many legislatures previously indifferent to the Massachusetts circular letter now adopted it enthusiastically. The Massachusetts House of Representatives voted 92 to 17 not to recall its letter. The number 92 immediately acquired symbolic significance for Americans; colonial politicians on more than one occasion drank 92 toasts in tipsy salutes to Massachusetts's action. In obedience to Hillsborough, royal governors responded by dismissing legislatures in Massachusetts and elsewhere. These moves played directly into the hands of Samuel Adams,

James Otis, and John Dickinson, who wanted nothing more than to ignite widespread public opposition to the Townshend duties.

Although increasingly outraged over the Revenue Act, the colonists still needed some effective means of pressuring Parliament for its repeal. One approach, nonimportation, seemed especially promising because it offered an alternative to violence and would distress Britain's economy. In August 1768, Boston's merchants therefore adopted a nonimportation agreement, and the tactic slowly spread southward. "Save your money, and you save your country!" became the watchword of the Sons of Liberty, who began reorganizing after two years of inactivity. Not all colonists supported nonimportation, however. Its effectiveness ultimately depended on the compliance of merchants whose livelihood relied on buying and selling imports. In several major communities, including Philadelphia, Baltimore, and Charles Town, South Carolina, merchants continued buying British goods until 1769. Nevertheless, the boycott was significant not only because it limited British imports but also because it mobilized colonists into more actively resisting British policies.

By 1770, a new British prime minister, Lord North, favored eliminating most of the Townshend duties to prevent the American commercial boycott from widening. But to underscore British authority, he insisted on retaining the tax on tea. Parliament agreed, and in April 1770, giving in for the second time in three years to colonial pressure, it repealed most of the Townshend duties.

Parliament's partial repeal produced a dilemma for American politicians. They considered it intolerable that taxes remained on tea, the most profitable item for the royal treasury. Colonial leaders were unsure whether they should press on with the nonimportation agreement until they achieved total victory, or whether it would suffice to maintain a selective boycott of tea. When the nonimportation movement collapsed in July 1770, colonists resisted external taxation by voluntary agreements not to drink British tea. Through nonconsumption, they succeeded in limiting revenue from tea to about one-sixth the level originally expected. This amount was far too little to pay the salaries of royal governors as Townshend had intended. Yet colonial resistance leaders took little satisfaction in having forced Parliament to compromise. The tea duty remained a galling reminder that Parliament refused to retreat from the broadest possible interpretation of the Declaratory Act.

| Women and Colonial Resistance | The boycotts of British goods provided a unique opportunity for white women to join the defense of Anglo-American liberties. White women's participation in public affairs had been widening slowly and unevenly in the colonies for several de- |

cades. By the 1760s, when colonial protests against British policies began, colonial women such as Sarah Osborn (see Chapter 4) had become well-known religious activists. Calling themselves the Daughters of Liberty, a contingent of upper-class female patriots had played a part in defeating the Stamp Act. Some had attended political rallies during the Stamp Act crisis, and many more had expressed their opposition in discussions and correspondence with family and friends.

Just two years later, women assumed an even more visible role during the Townshend crisis. To protest the Revenue Act's tax on tea, more than three hundred "mistresses of families" in Boston denounced consumption of the beverage in early 1770. In some ways, the threat of nonconsumption was even more effective than that of nonimportation, for women served and drank most of the tea consumed by colonists.

Nonconsumption agreements soon became popular and were extended to include English manufactures, especially clothing. Again women played a vital role, both because they made most decisions about consumption in colonial households and because it was they who could replace British imports with apparel of their own making. Responding to leaders' pleas that they expand domestic cloth production, women of all social ranks, even those who customarily did not weave their own fabric or sew their own clothing, organized spinning bees. These events attracted intense publicity as evidence of American determination to forgo luxury and idleness for the common defense of liberty. One historian calculates that more than sixteen hundred women participated in spinning bees in New England alone from 1768 to 1770. The colonial cause, noted a New York woman, had enlisted "a fighting army of amazons . . . armed with spinning wheels."

Spinning bees not only helped undermine the notion that women had no place in public life but also endowed spinning and weaving, previously considered routine household tasks, with special political virtue. "Women might recover to this country the full and free enjoyment of all our rights, properties and privileges," exclaimed the Reverend John Cleaveland of Ipswich, Massachusetts, in 1769, adding that this "is more than the men have been able to do." For many colonists, such logic enlarged the arena of supposed feminine virtues from strictly religious matters to include political issues.

Spinning bees, combined with female support for boycotting tea, dramatically demonstrated that American resistance ran far deeper than the protests of a few male merchants and the largely male crowds in American seaports. Women's participation showed that colonial protests extended into the heart of American households and congregations, and were leading to broader popular participation in politics.

Customs "Racketeering," 1767–1770   Besides taxing colonial imports, Townshend sought to increase revenues through stricter enforcement of the Navigation Acts. While submitting the Revenue Act of 1767, he also introduced legislation creating the American Board of Customs Commissioners. This law raised the number of port officials, funded the construction of a colonial coast guard, and provided money for secret informers. It also awarded an informer one-third of the value of all goods and ships appropriated through a conviction of smuggling. The fact that fines could be tripled under certain circumstances provided an even greater incentive to seize illegal cargoes. Smuggling cases were heard in vice-admiralty courts, moreover, where the probability of conviction was extremely high.

In the face of lax enforcement, including widespread bribery of customs officials by colonial shippers and merchants, Townshend wanted the board to bring honesty, efficiency, and more revenue to overseas customs operations. But the law quickly drew protests because of the way it was enforced and because it assumed those accused to be guilty until or unless they could prove otherwise.

Under the new provisions, revenue agents commonly filed charges for technical violations of the Sugar Act, even when no evidence existed of intent to conduct illegal trade. They most often exploited the provision that declared any cargo illegal unless it had been loaded or unloaded with a customs officer's written authorization. Customs commissioners also fanned angry passions by invading the traditional rights of sailors. Long-standing maritime custom allowed a ship's crew to supplement their incomes by making small sales between ports. Anything stored in a sailor's chest was considered private property that did not have to be listed as cargo on the captain's manifest. After 1767, however, revenue agents began treating such belongings as cargo, thus establishing an excuse to seize the entire ship. Under this new policy, crewmen saw their trunks ruthlessly broken open by arrogant inspectors who confiscated trading stock worth several months' wages because it was not listed on the captain's loading papers.

To merchants and seamen alike, the commissioners had embarked on a program of "customs racketeering" that constituted little more than a system of legalized piracy. The board's program fed an upsurge in popular violence. Above all, customs commissioners' use of informers provoked retaliation. In 1769, the *Pennsylvania Journal* scorned these agents as "dogs of prey, thirsting after the fortunes of worthy and wealthy men." By betraying the trust of employers, and sometimes of friends, informers aroused hatred in their victims and were roughly handled whenever found.

Nowhere were customs agents and informers more detested than in Boston, where in June 1768 citizens finally retaliated against their tormentors. The occasion was the seizure, on a technicality, of colonial merchant John Hancock's sloop *Liberty*. Hancock, reportedly North America's richest merchant and a leading opponent of British taxation, had become a chief target of the customs commissioners. Now they fined him £9,000, an amount almost thirteen times greater than the taxes he supposedly evaded on a shipment of Madeira wine. A crowd, "chiefly sturdy boys and Negroes," in Thomas Hutchinson's words, tried to prevent the towing of Hancock's ship and then began assaulting customs agents. Growing to several hundred as it surged through the streets, the mob drove all revenue inspectors from Boston.

Under Lord North, the British government, aware of officers' excesses, took steps to rein in the powers of the American Board of Customs Commissioners. The smuggling charges against Hancock were dropped because the prosecution feared that Hancock would appeal a conviction to England, where honest officials might take action against the commissioners responsible for violating his rights. But British officials were conceding nothing to the colonists. For at the same time, they dispatched four thousand troops to Boston, making clear that they would not tolerate further violent defiance of their authority.

"Wilkes and Liberty," 1768–1770   Although most Britons blamed the colonists for their own high taxes, a minority found common cause with the Americans. They formed a movement that arose during the 1760s to oppose the domestic and foreign policies of George III and a Parliament dominated by wealthy landowners. Their leader was John Wilkes, a fiery London editor and member of Parliament who first gained notoriety in 1763 when his newspaper regularly and irreverently denounced George III's policies. The government finally arrested Wilkes for seditious libel, but to great popular acclaim, he won his case in court. The government, however, succeeded in shutting down his newspaper and in persuading a majority in the House of Commons to deny Wilkes his seat. After again offending the government with a publication, Wilkes fled to Paris.

Wilkes returned to England in 1768, defying a warrant for his arrest, and again ran for Parliament. By this time, the Townshend acts and other government policies were stirring up widespread protests. Merchants and artisans in London, Bristol, and other cities demanded the dismissal of the "obnoxious" ministers who were "ruining our manufactories by invidiously imposing and establishing the most impolitic and unconstitutional taxations and regulations on your Majesty's colonies." They were joined by (nonvoting) weavers, coal heavers, seamen, and other workers who protested low wages and high prices that stemmed in part from government policies. All these people rallied around the cry "Wilkes and liberty!"

After he was again elected to Parliament, Wilkes was arrested. The next day, twenty to forty thousand angry "Wilkesites" massed on St. George's Fields, outside the prison where he was being held. When members of the crowd began throwing stones, soldiers and police responded with gunfire, killing eleven protesters. The "massacre of St. George's Fields" had given the movement some martyrs. Wilkes and an associate were elected twice more and were both times denied their seats by other legislators. Meanwhile, the imprisoned Wilkes was besieged by outpourings of popular support from the colonies as well as from Britain. Some Virginians sent him tobacco, and the South Carolina assembly voted to contribute £1,500 to help defray his debts. He maintained a regular correspondence with the Boston Sons of Liberty and, upon his release in April 1770, was hailed in a massive Boston celebration as "the illustrious martyr to Liberty."

Wilkes's cause sharpened the political thinking of government opponents in Britain and the colonies alike. Thousands of voters in English cities and towns signed petitions to Parliament protesting its refusal to seat Wilkes as an affront to the electorate's will. Like the colonists, they regarded the theory of "virtual representation" in Parliament as a sham. Fearing arbitrary government actions, some of them formed a Society of the Supporters of the Bill of Rights "to defend and maintain the legal, constitutional liberty of the subject." And while more "respectable" opponents of the government such as William Pitt and Edmund Burke disdained Wilkes for courting the "mob," his movement emboldened them to speak more forcefully against the government, especially on its policies toward the colonies. For the colonists themselves, Wilkes and his following made clear that Parliament and the government represented a small if powerful minority whose authority could be legitimately questioned.

THE DEEPENING CRISIS, 1770–1774

After 1770, the imperial crisis took on some ominous new dimensions. Colonists and British troops clashed on the streets of Boston. Resistance leaders in the colonies developed means of systematically coordinating their actions and policies. After Bostonians defied a new act of Parliament, the Tea Act, Britain was determined to subordinate the colonies once and for all. Adding to the general tensions of the period were several violent conflicts that erupted in the western backcountry.

The Boston Massacre, 1770 Responding to the violence provoked by Hancock's case, British authorities had dispatched four thousand British troops to Boston in the summer and fall of 1768 (see above). Regarding the redcoats as a standing army that threatened their liberty as well as a financial burden, Bostonians resented the military presence.

In the presence of so many soldiers, Boston took on the atmosphere of an occupied city and crackled with tension. Armed sentries and resentful civilians traded insults. The mainly Protestant townspeople found it especially galling that many soldiers were Irish Catholics. The poorly paid enlisted men, moreover, were free to seek employment following the morning muster. Often agreeing to work for less than local laborers, they generated fierce hostility in a community that was plagued by persistently high unemployment.

Poor Bostonians' deep-seated resentment against all who upheld British authority suddenly boiled over on February 22, 1770, when a customs informer shot into a crowd picketing the home of a customs-paying merchant, killing an eleven-year-old boy. While elite Bostonians had disdained the unruly exchanges between soldiers and crowds, the horror at a child's death momentarily united the community. "My Eyes never beheld such a funeral," wrote John Adams. "A vast Number of Boys walked before the Coffin, a vast Number of Women and Men after it. . . . This Shews there are many more Lives to spend if wanted in the Service of their country."

Although the army had played no part in the shooting, it became a natural target for popular frustration and rage. A week after the boy's funeral, tensions between troops and a crowd led by Crispus Attucks, a seaman of African and Native American descent, and including George Robert Twelves Hewes, erupted at the guard post protecting the customs office. When an officer tried to disperse the civilians, his men endured a steady barrage of flying objects and dares to shoot. A private finally did fire, after having been knocked down by a block of ice, and then shouted, "Fire! Fire!" to his fellow soldiers. The soldiers' volley hit eleven persons, five of whom, including Attucks, died.

The shock that followed the March 5 bloodshed marked the emotional high point of the Townshend crisis. Royal authorities in Massachusetts tried to defuse the situation by isolating all British soldiers on a fortified island in the harbor, and Governor Thomas Hutchinson promised that the soldiers who had fired would be tried. Patriot leader John Adams, an opponent of crowd actions, served as their attorney. Adams appealed to the Boston jury by claiming that the soldiers had been provoked by a "motley rabble of saucy boys, negroes and mulattoes, Irish teagues, and outlandish jack tarres," in other words, people not considered "respectable" by the city's elites and middle class. All but two of the soldiers were acquitted, and the ones found guilty suffered only a branding on their thumbs.

Burning hatreds produced by an intolerable situation underlay the Boston Massacre, as it came to be called in conscious recollection of the St. George's Fields Massacre in London two years earlier. The shooting of unarmed American civilians by British soldiers and the light punishment given the soldiers forced the colonists to confront the stark possibility that the British government was bent on coercing and suppressing them through naked force. In a play written by Mercy Otis Warren, a character predicted that soon "Murders, blood and carnage/Shall crimson all these streets" as patriots rose to defend their republican liberty against tyrannical authority.

The Committees of Correspondence, 1772–1773   In the fall of 1772, Lord North's ministry was preparing to implement Townshend's goal of paying the royal governors' salaries out of customs revenue. The colonists had always viewed efforts to free the governors from financial dependence on the legislatures as a threat to representative government. In response, Samuel Adams persuaded Boston's town meeting to request that every Massachusetts community appoint a committee whose members would be responsible for exchanging information and coordinating measures to defend colonial rights. Of approximately 260 towns, about half immediately established **"committees of correspondence,"** and most others did so within a year. The idea soon spread throughout New England.

The committees of correspondence were the colonists' first attempt to maintain close and continuing political cooperation over a wide area. By linking almost every interior community to Boston through a network of dedicated activists, the system enabled Adams to send out messages for each local committee to read at its own town meeting, which would then debate the issues and adopt a formal resolution. Involving tens of thousands of colonists to consider evidence that their rights were in danger, the system committed them to take a personal stand by voting.

Adams's most successful effort to mobilize popular sentiment came in June 1773, when he publicized certain letters of Massachusetts Governor Thomas Hutchinson that Benjamin Franklin had obtained. Massachusetts town meetings discovered through the letters that their own chief executive had advocated "an abridgement of what are called English liberties" and "a great restraint of natural liberty." The publication of the Hutchinson correspondence confirmed many colonists' suspicions of a plot to destroy basic freedoms.

In March 1773, Patrick Henry, Thomas Jefferson, and Richard Henry Lee proposed that Virginia establish colony-level committees of correspondence. Within a year, every province but Pennsylvania had followed its example. By early 1774, a communications web linked colonial leaders for the first time since 1766.

Conflicts in the Backcountry

Although most of the turbulence between 1763 and 1775 swirled in the eastern seaports, various combinations of protagonists also clashed in the West—Native Americans, various groups of colonists, colonial governments, and imperial authorities. These conflicts were rooted in the rapid population growth that had spurred the migration of whites to the Appalachian backcountry.

Backcountry tensions surfaced soon after the Seven Years' War in western Pennsylvania, where Scots-Irish Presbyterian settlers had fought repeatedly with Native Americans. Settlers in and around the town of Paxton resented Pennsylvania's Quaker-dominated assembly for failing to provide them with adequate military protection and for denying them equal representation in the legislature. They also concluded that all Native Americans, regardless of wartime conduct, were their racial enemies. In December 1763, armed settlers attacked two villages of peaceful Conestoga Indians, killing and scalping men, women, and children. In February 1764, about 200 "Paxton Boys," as they were called, set out for Philadelphia, with plans to kill Christian Indian refugees there. A government delegation headed by Benjamin Franklin met the armed, mounted mob on the outskirts of the city. After Franklin promised that the assembly would consider their grievances, the Paxton Boys returned home.

Land pressures and the lack of adequate revenue from the colonies left the British government utterly helpless in enforcing the Proclamation of 1763. Speculators such as George Washington sought western land because "any person who . . . neglects the present opportunity of hunting out good Lands will never regain it." Settlers, traders, hunters, and thieves also trespassed on Indian land, and a growing number of instances of violence by colonists toward Native Americans were going unpunished. In the meantime, the British government was unable to maintain garrisons at many of its forts, to enforce violations of laws and treaties, or to provide gifts to its Native allies. Under such pressure, Britain and its Six Nations Iroquois allies agreed in the Treaty of Fort Stanwix (1768) to grant land along the Ohio River that was occupied and claimed by the Shawnees, Delawares, and Cherokees to the governments of Pennsylvania and Virginia. The Shawnees now assumed leadership of the Ohio Indians who, along with the Cherokees, sensed that no policy of appeasement could stop colonial expansion.

The treaty served to heighten rather than ease western tensions, especially in the Ohio country, where settlers agitated to establish a new colony, Kentucky. Growing violence culminated in 1774 in the unprovoked slaughter by colonists of thirteen Shawnees and Mingos, including eight members of the family of Logan, until then a moderate Mingo leader. The outraged Logan led a force of Shawnees and Mingos who retaliated by killing an equal number of white Virginians. Virginia in turn opened a campaign against the Indians known as **Lord Dunmore's War** (1774), for the colony's governor. The two forces met at Point Pleasant on the Virginia side of the Ohio River, where the English soundly defeated Logan's people. During the peace conference that followed, Virginia gained uncontested rights to lands south of the Ohio in exchange for its claims on the northern side. But Anglo-Indian resentments remained strong, and fighting would resume once Britain and its colonies went to war.

The Treaty of Fort Stanwix resolved the conflicting claims of Pennsylvania and Virginia in Ohio at the Indians' expense. But other western disputes led to conflict among the colonists themselves. Settlers moving west in Massachusetts in the early 1760s found their titles challenged by some of New York's powerful landlords. When two landlords threatened to evict tenants in 1766, the New Englanders joined the tenants in an armed uprising, calling themselves Sons of Liberty after the Stamp Act protesters. In 1769, in what is now Vermont, settlers from New Hampshire also came into conflict with New York. After four years of guerrilla warfare, the New Hampshire settlers, calling themselves the Green Mountain Boys, established an independent government. Unrecognized at the time, it eventually became the government of Vermont. A third group of New England settlers from Connecticut settled in the Wyoming valley of Pennsylvania, where they clashed in 1774 with Pennsylvanians claiming title to the same land.

Expansion also provoked conflicts between backcountry settlers and their colonial governments. In North Carolina, a group known as the Regulators aimed to redress the grievances of westerners who, underrepresented in the colonial assembly, found themselves exploited by dishonest eastern officeholders. The Regulator movement climaxed on May 16, 1771, at the battle of Alamance Creek. Leading an army of perhaps thirteen hundred eastern militiamen, North Carolina's royal governor defeated about twenty-five hundred Regulators in a clash that produced almost three hundred casualties. Although the Regulator uprising then disintegrated, it crippled the colony's subsequent ability to resist British authority.

An armed Regulator movement also arose in South Carolina, in this case to counter the government's unwillingness to prosecute bandits who were terrorizing settlers. But the South Carolina government did not dispatch its militia to the backcountry for fear that the colony's restive slave population might use the occasion to revolt. Instead, it conceded to the principal demands of the Regulators by establishing four new judicial circuits and allowing jury trials in the newly settled areas.

Although not directly interrelated, these episodes all reflected the tensions generated by a increasing land-hungry white population and its willingness to resort to violence against Native Americans, other colonists, and British officials. As Anglo-American tensions mounted in older settled areas, the western settlers' anxious mood spread.

The Tea Act, 1773   Colonial smuggling and nonconsumption had taken a heavy toll on the British East India Company, which enjoyed a legal monopoly on the sale of tea within Britain's empire. By 1773, with tons of tea rotting in its warehouses, the company was teetering on the brink of bankruptcy. Lord North could not afford to let the company fail. Not only did it pay substantial duties on the tea it shipped to Britain, but it also provided huge indirect savings for the government by subsidizing British authority in India (see chapter 6, Beyond America—Global Interactions).

If the East India Company could only control the colonial market, North reasoned, its chances for returning to profitability would greatly increase. Americans supposedly consumed more than a million pounds of tea each year, but by 1773 they were purchasing just one-quarter of it from the company. In May 1773, to save the beleaguered company from financial ruin, Parliament passed the **Tea Act,** which eliminated all remaining import duties on tea entering England and thus lowered the selling price to consumers. (Ironically, the same saving could have been accomplished by repealing the Townshend tax, which would have ended colonial objections to the company's tea and produced enormous goodwill toward the British government.) To lower the price further, the Tea Act also permitted the East India Company to sell its tea directly to consumers rather than through wholesalers. These two concessions reduced the cost of company tea in the colonies well below the price of all smuggled competition. Parliament expected simple economic self-interest to overcome Anglo-American scruples about buying taxed tea.

But the Tea Act alarmed many Americans, above all because they saw in it a menace to liberty and virtue as well as to colonial representative government. By making taxed tea competitive in price with smuggled tea, the law would raise revenue, which the British government would use to pay royal governors. The law thus threatened to corrupt Americans into accepting the principle of parliamentary taxation by taking advantage of their weakness for a frivolous luxury. Quickly, therefore, the committees of correspondence decided to resist the importation of tea, though without violence and without destroying private property. Either by pressuring the company's agents to refuse acceptance or by intercepting the ships at sea and ordering them home, the committees would keep East India Company cargoes from being landed. In Philadelphia, an anonymous "Committee for Tarring and Feathering" warned harbor pilots not to guide any ships carrying tea into port.

In Boston, however, this strategy failed. On November 28, 1773, the first ship came under the jurisdiction of the customshouse, where duties would have to be paid on its cargo within twenty days. Otherwise, the cargo would be seized from the captain and the tea claimed by the company's agents and placed on sale. When Samuel Adams, John Hancock, and other popular leaders repeatedly asked the customs officers to issue a special clearance for the ship's departure, they were blocked by Thomas Hutchinson's refusal to compromise.

On the evening of December 16, five thousand Bostonians gathered at Old South Church. Samuel Adams informed the citizens of Hutchinson's insistence upon landing

Edenton Ladies' Tea Party *In October 1774, fifty-one women gathered at Edenton, North Carolina, and declared it their "duty" to boycott British imports. Nevertheless, the British man who drew this cartoon chose to satirize the event as an unruly "tea party."*

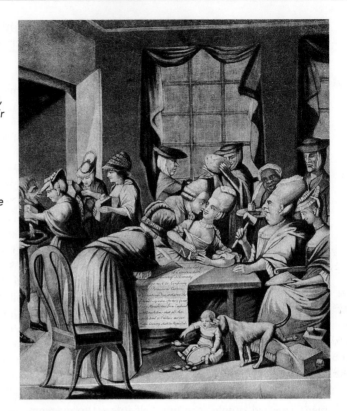

the tea and proclaimed that "this meeting can do no more to save the country." About fifty young men, including George Robert Twelves Hewes, stepped forward and disguised themselves as Mohawk Indians—symbolizing a virtuous, proud, and assertive American identity distinct from that of corrupt Britain. Armed with "tomahawks," they headed for the wharf, followed by most of the crowd.

The disciplined band assaulted no one and damaged nothing but the hated cargo. Thousands lined the waterfront to see them heave forty-five tons of tea overboard. For almost an hour, the onlookers stood silently transfixed, as if at a religious service, while they peered through the crisp, cold air of a moonlit night. The only sounds were the steady chop of hatchets breaking open wooden chests and the soft splash of tea on the water. When Boston's "Tea Party," as it was later called, was finished, the participants left quietly, and the town lapsed into a profound hush—"never more still and calm," according to one observer.

TOWARD INDEPENDENCE, 1774–1776

The calm that followed the Boston Tea Party proved to be a calm before the storm. The incident inflamed the British government and Parliament, which now determined once and for all to quash colonial insubordination. Colonial political leaders responded with equal determination to defend self-government and liberty. The empire and its American colonies were on a collision course, leading by spring 1775 to armed clashes. Yet even after blood was shed, colonists hesitated before declaring their complete independence from Britain. In the meantime, free and enslaved African-Americans pondered how best to realize their own freedom.

Liberty for
African-Americans

Throughout the imperial crisis, African-American slaves, as a deeply alienated group within society, quickly responded to calls for liberty and equality. In January 1766, when a group of blacks, inspired by the protests against the Stamp Act, had marched through Charles Town, South Carolina, shouting "Liberty!" they had faced arrest for inciting a rebellion. Thereafter, unrest among slaves—usually in the form of violence or escape—kept pace with that among white rebels. Then in 1772, a court decision in England electrified much of the black population. A Massachusetts slave, James Somerset, had accompanied his master to England, where he ran away but was recaptured. Imprisoned on a ship bound for Jamaica, Somerset sued for his freedom. Writing for the King's Court, Lord Chief Justice William Mansfield ruled that because Parliament had never explicitly established slavery in England, a master could not send a slave outside the country against his will.

Although the Somerset decision applied only to slaves being sent out of England, rumors spread that it abolished slavery there. In January 1773, some of Somerset's fellow Massachusetts blacks filed the first of three petitions to the legislature, arguing that the decision should be extended to the colony. In Virginia and Maryland, dozens of slaves ran away from their masters and sought passage aboard ships bound for England. As Anglo-American tensions mounted in 1774, many slaves, especially in the Chesapeake colonies, looked for war and the arrival of British troops as a means to their liberation. The young Virginia planter James Madison remarked that "if America and Britain come to a hostile rupture, I am afraid an insurrection among the slaves may and will be promoted" by England.

Madison's fears were borne out in November 1775 when Virginia's governor, Lord Dunmore, promised freedom to any able-bodied male slave who enlisted in the cause of restoring royal authority. Similarly to Florida when it provided a refuge for escaping South Carolina slaves (see Chapter 4), **Lord Dunmore's Proclamation** appealed to slaves' longings for freedom in order to undermine a planter-dominated society. Ignoring Dunmore's restrictions, about one thousand Virginia blacks joined Dunmore. Those who fought donned uniforms proclaiming "Liberty to Slaves." Dunmore's proclamation associated British forces with slave liberation in the minds of both blacks and whites in the southern colonies, an association that continued during the war that followed.

The "Intolerable
Acts"

Following the Boston Tea Party, Lord North fumed that only "New England fanatics" could imagine themselves oppressed by inexpensive tea. A Welsh member of Parliament drew wild applause by declaring that "the town of Boston ought to be knocked about by the ears, and destroy'd." In vain did the great parliamentary orator Edmund Burke plead for the one action that could end the crisis. "Leave America . . . to tax herself. . . . Leave the Americans as they anciently stood." The British government, however, swiftly asserted its authority by enacting four "Coercive Acts" that, together with the unrelated Quebec Act, became known to colonists as the "Intolerable Acts."

The first of the Coercive Acts, the Boston Port Bill, became law on April 1, 1774. It ordered the navy to close Boston harbor unless the Privy Council certified by June 1 that the town had arranged to pay for the ruined tea. Lord North's cabinet deliberately imposed this impossibly short deadline in order to ensure the harbor's closing, which would lead to serious economic distress.

The second Coercive Act, the Massachusetts Government Act, revoked the Massachusetts charter and restructured the government to make it less democratic. The colony's upper house would no longer be elected annually by the assembly but instead be appointed for life by the crown. The governor gained absolute control over the naming of all judges and sheriffs. Jurymen, previously elected, were now appointed by sheriffs. Finally, the new charter forbade communities to hold more than one town meeting a year without the governor's permission. These changes simply brought Massachusetts into line with other royal colonies, but the colonists interpreted them as evidence of hostility toward representative government and liberty.

The third of the new acts, the Administration of Justice Act, which some colonists cynically called the Murder Act, permitted any person charged with murder while enforcing royal authority in Massachusetts (such as the British soldiers indicted for the Boston Massacre) to be tried in England or in other colonies.

Finally, a new Quartering Act went beyond the earlier act of 1765 by allowing the governor to requisition empty private buildings for housing troops. These measures, along with the appointment of General Thomas Gage, Britain's military commander in North America, as the new governor of Massachusetts, struck New Englanders as proof of a plan to place them under a military tyranny.

Americans learned of the Quebec Act along with the previous four statutes and associated it with them. Intended to cement loyalty to Britain among conquered French-Canadian Catholics, the law established Roman Catholicism as Quebec's official religion. This provision alarmed Protestant Anglo-Americans who widely believed that Catholicism went hand in hand with despotism. Furthermore, the Quebec Act gave Canada's governors sweeping powers but established no legislature. It also permitted property disputes (but not criminal cases) to be decided by French law, which did not use juries. Additionally, the law extended Quebec's territorial claims south to the Ohio River and west to the Mississippi, a vast area populated by Native Americans and some French. Although designated off-limits by the Proclamation of 1763, several colonies continued to claim portions of the region.

The **"Intolerable Acts"** convinced Anglo-Americans that Britain was plotting to abolish traditional English liberties throughout North America. Rebel pamphlets fed fears that the governor of Massachusetts would starve Boston into submission and appoint corrupt sheriffs and judges to crush political dissent through rigged trials. By this reasoning, the new Quartering Act would repress any resistance by forcing troops on an unwilling population, and the "Murder Act" would encourage massacres by preventing local juries from convicting soldiers who killed civilians. Once resistance in Massachusetts had been smashed, the Quebec Act would serve as a blueprint for extinguishing representative government throughout the colonies. Parliament would revoke every colony's charter and introduce a government like Quebec's. Elected assemblies, freedom of religion for Protestants, and jury trials would all disappear.

Intended by Parliament simply to punish Massachusetts—and particularly that rotten apple in the barrel, Boston—the acts instead pushed most colonies to the brink of rebellion. Repeal of these laws became, in effect, the colonists' nonnegotiable demand. Of the twenty-seven reasons justifying the break with Britain that Americans later cited in the Declaration of Independence, six concerned these statutes.

The First
Continental
Congress
In response to the "Intolerable Acts," the extralegal committees of correspondence of every colony but Georgia sent delegates to a **Continental Congress** in Philadelphia. Among those in attendance when the Congress assembled on September 5, 1774, were many of the colonies' most prominent politicians: Samuel and John Adams of Massachusetts; John Jay of New York; Joseph Galloway and John Dickinson of Pennsylvania; and Patrick Henry, Richard Henry Lee, and George Washington of Virginia. The fifty-six delegates had come together to find a way of defending the colonies' rights in common, and in interminable dinner parties and cloakroom chatter, they took one another's measure.

The First Continental Congress opened by endorsing a set of statements of principle called the Suffolk Resolves that recently had placed Massachusetts in a state of passive rebellion. Adopted by delegates at a convention of Massachusetts towns just as the Continental Congress was getting under way, the resolves declared that the colonies owed no obedience to any of the Coercive Acts, that a provisional government should collect all taxes until the former Massachusetts charter was restored, and that defensive measures should be taken in the event of an attack by royal troops. The Continental Congress also voted to boycott all British goods after December 1 and to cease exporting almost all goods to Britain and its West Indian possessions after September 1775 unless a reconciliation had been accomplished. This agreement, the Continental Association, would be enforced by locally elected committees of "observation" or "safety," whose members in effect would be usurping control of American trade from the royal customs service.

Such bold defiance was not to the liking of all delegates. Jay, Dickinson, Galloway, and other moderates who dominated the middle-colony contingent most feared the internal turmoil that would surely accompany a head-on confrontation with Britain. These "trimmers" (John Adams's scornful phrase) vainly opposed nonimportation and tried unsuccessfully to win endorsement of Galloway's plan for a "Grand Council," an American legislature that would share the authority to tax and govern the colonies with Parliament.

Finally, however, the delegates summarized their principles and demands in a petition to the king. This document affirmed Parliament's power to regulate imperial commerce, but it argued that all previous parliamentary efforts to impose taxes, enforce laws through admiralty courts, suspend assemblies, and unilaterally revoke charters were unconstitutional. By addressing the king rather than Parliament, Congress was imploring George III to end the crisis by dismissing those ministers responsible for passing the Coercive Acts.

From Resistance
to Rebellion
Most Americans hoped that their resistance would jolt Parliament into renouncing all authority over the colonies except trade regulation. But tensions between moderates and radicals ran high, and bonds between men formerly united in outlook sometimes snapped. John Adams's onetime friend Jonathan Sewall, for example, charged that the Congress had made the "breach with the parent state a thousand times more irreparable than it was before." Fearing that Congress was enthroning "their High Mightinesses, the MOB," he and like-minded Americans refused to defy the king.

To solidify their defiance, colonial resistance leaders coerced those colonists who refused to support them. Thus the elected committees that Congress had created to enforce the Continental Association often turned themselves into vigilantes, compelling merchants who still traded with Britain to burn their imports and make public apologies, browbeating clergymen who preached pro-British sermons, and pressuring

Americans to adopt simpler diets and dress in order to relieve their dependence on British imports. Additionally, in colony after colony, the committees took on government functions by organizing volunteer military companies and extralegal legislatures. By the spring of 1775, colonial patriots had established provincial "congresses" that paralleled and rivaled the existing colonial assemblies headed by royal governors.

There as elsewhere, colonists had prepared for the worst by collecting arms and organizing extralegal militia units (locally known as minutemen) whose members could respond instantly to an emergency. The British government ordered Massachusetts's Governor Gage to quell the "rude rabble" by arresting the principal patriot leaders. On April 19, 1775, aware that most of these leaders had already fled Boston, Gage instead sent seven hundred British soldiers to seize military supplies that the colonists had stored at Concord. Two couriers, William Dawes and Paul Revere, rode out to warn nearby towns of the British troop movements and target. At Lexington, about seventy minutemen confronted the soldiers. After a confused skirmish in which eight minutemen died and a single redcoat was wounded, the British pushed on to Concord. There they found few munitions but encountered a growing swarm of armed Yankees. When some minutemen mistakenly became convinced that the town was being burned, they exchanged fire with the British regulars and touched off a running battle that continued for most of the sixteen miles back to Boston. By day's end, the redcoats had suffered 273 casualties, compared to only 92 for the colonists, and they had gained some respect for Yankee courage. These engagements awakened the countryside, and by the evening of April 20, some twenty thousand New Englanders were besieging the British garrison in Boston.

Three weeks later, the Second Continental Congress convened in Philadelphia. Most delegates still opposed independence and at Dickinson's urging agreed to send a "loyal message" to George III. Dickinson composed what became known as the **Olive Branch Petition.** Excessively polite, it nonetheless presented three demands: a cease-fire at Boston, repeal of the Coercive Acts, and negotiations to establish guarantees of American rights. Yet while pleading for peace, the delegates also passed measures that Britain could only construe as rebellious. In particular, they voted in May 1775 to establish an "American continental army" and appointed George Washington its commander.

The Olive Branch Petition reached London along with news of the Continental Army's formation and of a battle fought just outside Boston on June 17. In this engagement, British troops attacked colonists entrenched on Breed's Hill and Bunker Hill. Although successfully dislodging the Americans, the British suffered 1,154 casualties out of 2,200 men, compared to a loss of 311 patriots.

After Bunker Hill, many Britons wanted retaliation, not reconciliation. On August 23, George III proclaimed New England in a state of rebellion, and in October he extended that pronouncement to include all the colonies. In December, Parliament likewise declared all the colonies rebellious, outlawing all British trade with them and subjecting their ships to seizure.

Common Sense Despite the turn of events, many colonists clung to hopes of reconciliation. Even John Adams, who believed in the inevitability of separation, described himself as "fond of reconciliation, if we could reasonably entertain Hopes of it on a constitutional basis." Like many elites, Adams recognized that a war for independence would entail arming common people, many of whom reviled all men of wealth regardless of political allegiance. Such an outcome would threaten elite rule and social order as well as British rule.

Through 1775, many colonists, not only elites, clung to the notion that evil ministers rather than the king were forcing unconstitutional measures on them and that saner heads would rise to power in Britain. On both counts they were wrong. The Americans exaggerated the influence of Pitt, Burke, Wilkes (who finally took his seat in Parliament in 1774), and their other friends in Britain. And once George III himself declared the colonies to be in "open and avowed rebellion . . . for the purpose of establishing an independent empire," Anglo-Americans had no choice but either to submit or to acknowledge their goal of national independence.

Most colonists' sentimental attachment to the king, the last emotional barrier to their accepting independence, finally crumbled in January 1776 with the publication of Thomas Paine's **Common Sense.** A failed corset maker and schoolmaster, Paine immigrated to the colonies from England late in 1774 with a letter of introduction from Benjamin Franklin, a penchant for radical politics, and a gift for writing plain and pungent prose that anyone could understand.

Paine told Americans what they had been unable to bring themselves to say: monarchy was an institution rooted in superstition, dangerous to liberty, and inappropriate to Americans. The king was "the royal brute" and a "hardened, sullen-tempered Pharaoh." Whereas previous writers had maintained that certain corrupt politicians were directing an English conspiracy against American liberty, Paine argued that such a conspiracy was rooted in the very institutions of monarchy and empire. Moreover, he argued, America had no economic need for the British connection. As he put it, "The commerce by which she [America] hath enriched herself are the necessaries of life, and will always have a market while eating is the custom in Europe." In addition, he pointed out, the events of the preceding six months had made independence a reality. Finally, Paine linked America's awakening nationalism with the sense of religious mission felt by many in New England and elsewhere when he proclaimed, "We have it in our power to begin the world over again. A situation, similar to the present, hath not happened since the days of Noah until now." America, in Paine's view, would be not only a new nation but a new kind of nation, a model society founded on republican principles and unburdened by the oppressive beliefs and corrupt institutions of the European past.

Printed in both English and German, *Common Sense* sold more than one hundred thousand copies within three months, equal to one for every fourth or fifth adult male, making it a best seller. Readers passed copies from hand to hand and read passages aloud in public gatherings. The *Connecticut Gazette* described Paine's pamphlet as "a landflood that sweeps all before it." *Common Sense* had dissolved lingering allegiance to George III and Great Britain, removing the last psychological barrier to American independence.

Declaring Independence   As colonists absorbed Paine's views, the military conflict between Britain and the colonies escalated, making the possibility of reconciliation even less likely. In May 1775 irregular troops from Vermont and Massachusetts had captured Fort Ticonderoga and Crown Point on the key route connecting New York and Canada. Six months later Washington ordered Colonel Henry Knox, a Boston bookseller and the army's senior artillerist, to bring the British artillery seized at Ticonderoga to reinforce the siege of Boston. Knox and his men built crude sleds to haul their fifty-nine cannons through dense forest and rugged mountains covered by two feet of snow. Forty days and three hundred miles after leaving Ticonderoga, Knox and his exhausted New Yorkers reported to Washington in late January 1776. They had accomplished one of the Revolution's great feats of endurance. The

Thomas Paine *Having arrived in the colonies less than two years earlier, Paine became a best-selling author with the publication of Common Sense (1776).*

guns from Ticonderoga placed the outnumbered British in a hopeless position and forced them to evacuate Boston on March 17, 1776.

As Britain regrouped and added to its forces gathered at Halifax, Nova Scotia, it planned an assault on New York in order to drive a wedge between rebellious New England and the other colonies. Recognizing New York's strategic importance, Washington led most of his troops there in April 1776.

Other military moves reinforced the drift toward all-out war. In June Congress ordered a two-pronged assault on Canada in which forces under General Philip Schuyler would move northward via Fort Ticonderoga to Montreal while Benedict Arnold would lead a march through the Maine forest to Quebec. Schuyler succeeded but Arnold failed. As Britain poured troops into Canada, the Americans prudently withdrew. At the same time, a British offensive in the southern colonies failed after an unsuccessful attempt to seize Charles Town.

By spring 1776 Paine's pamphlet, reinforced by the growing reality of war, had stimulated dozens of local gatherings—artisan guilds, town meetings, county conventions, and militia musters—to pass resolutions favoring American independence. The groundswell quickly spread to the colonies' extralegal legislatures. New England was already in rebellion, and Rhode Island declared itself independent in May 1776. The middle colonies hesitated to support independence because they feared, correctly, that any war would largely be fought over control of Philadelphia and New York. Following the news in April that North Carolina's congressional delegates were authorized to vote for independence, several southern colonies pressed for separation. Virginia's legislature instructed its delegates at the Second Continental Congress to propose independence, which Richard Henry Lee did on June 7. Formally adopting Lee's resolution on July 2, Congress created the United States of America.

The task of drafting a statement to justify the colonies' separation from England fell to a committee of five, including John Adams, Benjamin Franklin, and Thomas Jefferson, with Jefferson as the principal author. Among Congress's revisions to Jefferson's first draft were its insertion of the phrase "pursuit of happiness" in place of "property" in the Declaration's most famous sentence, and its deletion of a statement blaming George III for foisting the slave trade on unwilling colonists. The **Declaration of Independence** (see Appendix) never mentioned Parliament by name, for Congress had moved beyond arguments over legislative representation and now wanted to separate America altogether from Britain and its head of state, the king. Jefferson listed twenty-seven "injuries and usurpations" committed by George III against the colonies. And he drew on a familiar line of radical thinking when he added that the king's actions had as their "direct object the establishment of an absolute tyranny over these states."

Like Paine, Jefferson elevated the colonists' grievances from a dispute over English freedoms to a struggle of universal dimensions. In the tradition of Locke and other Enlightenment figures, Jefferson argued that the English government had violated its contract with the colonists, thereby giving them the right to replace it with a government of their own design. And his eloquent emphasis on the equality of all individuals and their natural entitlement to justice, liberty, and self-fulfillment expressed republicans' deepest longing for a government that would rest on neither legal privilege nor exploitation of the majority by the few.

Jefferson addressed the Declaration of Independence as much to Americans uncertain about the wisdom of independence as to world opinion, for even at this late date a significant minority opposed independence or were uncertain whether to endorse it. Above all he wanted to convince his fellow citizens that social and political progress could no longer be accomplished within the British Empire. But he left unanswered just which Americans were and were not equal to one another and entitled to liberty. All the colonies endorsing the Declaration countenanced, on grounds of racial inequality, the enslavement of blacks and severe restrictions on the freedoms of those blacks who were not enslaved. Moreover, all had property qualifications that also prevented many white men from voting. The proclamation that "all men" were created equal accorded with the Anglo-American assumption that women could not and should not function politically or legally as autonomous individuals. And Jefferson's accusation that George III had unleashed "the merciless Indian savages" on innocent colonists seemed to place Native Americans outside the bounds of humanity.

Was the Declaration of Independence a statement that expressed the sentiments of all but a minority of colonists? In a very narrow sense it was, but by framing the Declaration in universal terms, Jefferson and the Continental Congress made it something much greater. The ideas motivating Jefferson and his fellow delegates had moved thousands of ordinary colonists to political action over the preceding eleven years, both on their own behalf and on behalf of the colonies in their quarrel with Britain. For better or worse, the struggle for national independence had hastened, and become intertwined with, a quest for equality and personal independence that, for many Americans, transcended boundaries of class, race, or gender. In their reading, the Declaration never claimed that perfect justice and equal opportunity existed in the United States; rather, it challenged the Revolutionary generation and all who later inherited the nation to bring this ideal closer to reality.

CONCLUSION

In 1763, Britain and its North American colonies concluded a stunning victory over France, entirely eliminating that nation's formidable mainland American empire. Colonists proudly joined in hailing Britain as the world's most powerful nation, and they fully expected to reap territorial and economic benefits from the victory. Yet by 1775, colonists and Britons were fighting with one another. The war had exhausted Britain's treasury and led the government to look to the colonies for help in defraying the costs of maintaining its enlarged empire. In attempting to collect more revenue and to centralize imperial authority, English officials confronted the ambitions and attitudes of Americans who felt themselves to be in every way equal to Britons.

The differences between British and American viewpoints sharpened slowly and unevenly between 1760 and 1776. One major turning point was the Stamp Act crisis (1765–1766), when many Americans began questioning Parliament's authority, as opposed to that of their own elected legislatures, to levy taxes in the colonies. Colonists also broadened their protests during the Stamp Act crisis, moving beyond carefully worded petitions to fiery resolutions, crowd actions, an intercolonial congress, and a nonimportation movement. Colonial resistance became even more effective during the crisis over the Townshend duties (1767–1770) because of increased intercolonial cooperation and support from Britain. Thereafter, growing numbers of colonists moved from simply denying Parliament's authority to tax them to rejecting virtually any British authority over them.

After 1774, independence was virtually inevitable. Yet Americans were the most reluctant of revolutionaries—even after their own state and national legislatures were functioning, their troops had clashed with Britain's, and George III had declared them to be in rebellion. Tom Paine's prose finally persuaded them that they could stand on their own, without the support of Britain's markets, manufactures, or monarch. Thereafter, a grass-roots independence movement began, leading Congress in July 1776 to proclaim American independence.

Americans by no means followed a single path to the point of advocating independence. Ambitious elites resented British efforts to curtail colonial autonomy as exercised almost exclusively by members of their own class in the assemblies. They and many more in the middle classes were angered by British policies that made commerce less profitable as an occupation and more costly to consumers. But others, including both western settlers and poor and working urban people like George Robert Twelves Hewes, defied conventions demanding that humble people defer to the authority of their social superiors. Sometimes resorting to violence, they directed their wrath toward British officials and colonial elites alike. Many African-Americans, on the other hand, considered Britain as more likely than white colonists, especially slaveholders, to liberate them. And Native Americans recognized that British authority, however limited, provided a measure of protection from land-hungry colonists.

6

Securing Independence,
Defining Nationhood,
1776–1788

THE PROSPECTS OF WAR

The Revolution was both a collective struggle that pitted the independent states against
Britain and a civil war between American peoples. Americans opposed to the colonies'
independence constituted one of several factors working in Britain's favor as war began. Others included Britain's larger population and its superior military resources and
preparation. America, on the other hand, was located far from Britain and enjoyed the
intense commitment to independence of patriots and the Continental Army, led by the
formidable George Washington.

**Loyalists and
Other British
Sympathizers**

As late as January 1776, most colonists still hoped that declaring independence from Britain would not be necessary. Not
surprisingly, when separation came six months later, some
Americans remained unconvinced that it was justified. About
20 percent of all whites either opposed the rebellion actively or refused to support the
Confederation until threatened with fines or imprisonment. Although these internal
enemies of the Revolution called themselves **loyalists**, they were "Tories" to their patriot, or Whig, opponents. Whigs remarked, only half in jest, that "a tory was a thing
with a head in England, a body in America, and a neck that needed stretching."

Loyalists shared many political beliefs with patriots. Like the rebels, they usually
opposed Parliament's claim to tax the colonies. Many loyalists thus found themselves
fighting for a cause with which they did not entirely agree, and as a result many would
change sides during the war. Most probably shared the worry expressed in 1775 by the

George Washington, by John Trumbull, 1780 *Washington posed for this portrait at the height of the Revolutionary War, accompanied by his personal servant, William Lee. Lee was a slave whom Washington had purchased in 1768.*

Reverend Jonathan Boucher, a well-known Maryland loyalist, who preached with two loaded pistols lying on his pulpit cushion: "For my part I equally dread a Victory by either side."

Loyalists disagreed, however, with the patriots' insistence that independence was the only way to preserve the colonists' constitutional rights. The loyalists denounced separation as an illegal act certain to ignite an unnecessary war. Above all, they retained a profound reverence for the crown and believed that if they failed to defend their king, they would sacrifice their personal honor.

The mutual hatred between Whigs and Tories exceeded that of patriots and the British. Each side saw its cause as so sacred that opposition by a fellow American was an unforgivable act of betrayal. Americans inflicted the worst atrocities committed during the war upon each other.

The most important factor in determining loyalist strength in any area was the degree to which local Whigs exerted political authority and successfully convinced their

CHRONOLOGY, 1776–1788

1776 • British force American troops from New York City.

1777 • Congress approves Articles of Confederation.
American victory at Saratoga.
British troops seize Philadelphia.

1778 • France formally recognizes the United States; declares war on Britain.
American victory in Battle of Monmouth Court House.

1779 • Spain declares war on Britain.
George Rogers Clark recaptures Vincennes.
John Sullivan leads American raids in Iroquois country.

1780 • British seize Charles Town.

1781 • Articles of Confederation become law.
Battle of Yorktown; British General Cornwallis surrenders.

1783 • Peace of Paris.

1784 • Spain closes New Orleans to American trade.
Economic depression begins in New England.
Second Treaty of Fort Stanwix.

1785 • Ordinance of 1785.
Treaty of Fort McIntosh.

1786 • Congress rejects Jay-Gardoqui Treaty.
Treaty of Fort Finney.
Joseph Brant organizes Indian resistance to U.S. expansion.

1786–1787 • Shays's Rebellion in Massachusetts.

1787 • Northwest Ordinance.
Philadelphia convention frames federal Constitution.

1787–1788 • Alexander Hamilton, James Madison, and John Jay, The Federalist.

1788 • Federal Constitution ratified.

neighbors that the king and Parliament threatened their liberty. New England town leaders, the Virginia gentry, and the rice planters of South Carolina's seacoast had vigorously pursued a program of political education and popular mobilization from 1772 to 1776. Repeatedly explaining the issues at public meetings, these elites persuaded the overwhelming majority to favor resistance. As a result, probably no more than 5 percent of whites in these areas were committed loyalists in 1776. Where leading families acted indecisively, however, their communities remained divided when the fighting began. The proportion of loyalists was highest in New York and New Jersey, where elites were especially reluctant to declare their allegiance to either side. Those two states eventually furnished about half of the twenty-one thousand Americans who fought as loyalists.

The next most significant factor influencing loyalist military strength was the geographic distribution of recent British immigrants, who remained closely identified with their homeland. Among these newcomers were thousands of British soldiers who had served in the Seven Years' War and stayed on in the colonies, usually in New York, where they could obtain land grants of two hundred acres. An additional 125,000 English, Scots, and Irish landed from 1763 to 1775—the greatest number of Britons to arrive during any dozen years of the colonial era. In New York, Georgia, and the backcountry of North and South Carolina, where native-born Britons were heavily concentrated, the proportion of loyalists among whites probably ranged from 25 percent to 40 percent in 1776. During the war, immigrants from the British Isles would form many Tory units, including the Loyal Highland Emigrants, the North Carolina Highlanders, and the Volunteers of Ireland. After the Revolution, foreign-born loyalists were a majority of those whom the British compensated for wartime property losses—including three-quarters of all such claimants from the Carolinas and Georgia.

Canada's religious and secular elites comprised another significant white minority to hold pro-British sympathies. After the British had conquered New France in the Seven Years' War, the Quebec Act of 1774 (see Chapter 5) retained Catholicism as the established religion in Quebec and continued partial use of French civil law, measures that reconciled Quebec's elites to British rule. When Continental forces invaded Quebec in 1775–1776, they found widespread support among non-elite French as well as English Canadians. Although British forces repulsed the invasion, many Canadians continued to hope for an American victory. But Britain's military kept a firm hold on the region throughout the war.

Other North Americans supported the British cause not out of loyalty to the crown but from a perception that an independent America would pose the greater threat to their own liberty and independence. For example, recent settlers in the Ohio valley disagreed among themselves about which course would guarantee the personal independence they valued above all. A few German, Dutch, and French religious congregations doubted that their rights would be as safe in an independent nation dominated by Anglo-Americans. Yet most non-British whites in the thirteen colonies supported the Revolution. The great majority of German colonists, for example, had embraced republicanism by 1776 and would overwhelmingly support the cause of American independence.

The rebels never attempted to win over three other mainland colonies—Nova Scotia and East and West Florida—whose small British populations consisted of recent immigrants and British troops. Nor was independence seriously considered in Britain's thirteen West Indian colonies, which were dominated by absentee plantation owners who lived in England and depended on selling their sugar exports in the protected British market.

The British cause would draw significant wartime support from nonwhites. Prior to the outbreak of fighting, African-Americans made clear that they considered their own liberation from slavery a higher priority than the colonies' independence from Britain. While Virginia slaves flocked to Lord Dunmore's ranks (see Chapter 5), hundreds of South Carolina slaves had escaped and had taken refuge on British ships in Charles Town's harbor. During the war about twenty thousand enslaved African-Americans, mostly from the southern colonies, escaped their owners. Although many were recaptured or died, especially from epidemics, about nine thousand achieved freedom, often after serving as laborers or soldiers in the Royal Army. Among the slaveholders whose slaves escaped to British protection was Thomas Jefferson. On the other hand, most

African-Americans in the northern colonies calculated that supporting the rebels would hasten their own liberation.

Although Native Americans were deeply divided, most supported the British, either from the beginning or after being pressured by one side or the other to abandon neutrality. In the Ohio country, most Shawnees, Delawares, Mingos, and other Indians continued to bristle at settlers' incursions, but some sought to remain neutral and a few Delaware and Shawnee towns initially supported the Americans. After the uprising of 1763 (see Chapter 5), Native Americans in the Upper Great Lakes had developed good relations with British agents in the former French forts and were solidly in the British camp.

The most powerful Native American confederacies—the Six Nations Iroquois, the Creeks, and the Cherokees—were badly divided when the war broke out. Among the Six Nations, the central council fire at Onondaga, a symbol of unity since Hiawatha's time (see Chapter 1), died out. Most Iroquois followed the lead of the Mohawk chief **Joseph Brant** (Thayendagea) in supporting Britain. But the Oneidas and Tuscaroras, influenced by Congregationalist missionary Samuel Kirkland, actively sided with the rebels against other Iroquois. Creeks' allegiances reflected each village's earlier trade ties with either Britain or Spain (the latter leaned toward the colonists). Cherokee ranks were split between anti-American militants who saw an opportunity to drive back settlers and those who thought that Cherokees' best hope was to steer clear of the Anglo-American conflict.

The patriots also had other sources of Indian support. Native Americans in upper New England, easternmost Canada, and the Illinois and Wabash valleys initially took an anti-British stand because of earlier ties with the French, though many of them became alienated from the colonists during the war. In eastern areas long dominated by colonial governments, there were fewer Indians, most of whom actively and effectively supported the American war effort.

The Opposing Sides

Britain entered the war with two major advantages. First, in 1776 the 11 million inhabitants of the British Isles greatly outnumbered the 2.5 million colonists, one-third of whom were either slaves or loyalists. Second, Britain possessed the world's largest navy and one of its best professional armies. Even so, the royal military establishment grew during the war years to a degree that strained Britain's resources. The number of soldiers stationed in North America, the British Isles, and the West Indies more than doubled from 48,000 to 111,000 men, especially after the war became an international conflict (see Beyond America—Global Interactions). To meet its manpower needs, the British government hired 30,000 German mercenaries known as Hessians and enlisted 21,000 loyalists.

Britain's ability to crush the rebellion was further weakened by the decline in its sea power, a result of budget cuts after 1763. Midway through the war, half of the Royal Navy's ships sat in dry dock awaiting major repairs. Although the navy expanded rapidly from 18,000 to 111,000 sailors, it lost 42,000 men to desertion and 20,000 to disease or wounds. In addition, Britain's merchant marine suffered from raids by American privateers. During the war rebel privateers and the fledgling U.S. navy would capture over two thousand British merchant vessels and sixteen thousand crewmen.

Britain could ill afford these losses, for it faced a colossal task in trying to supply its troops in America. In fact, it had to import from Britain most of the food consumed by its army, a third of a ton per soldier per year. Seriously overextended, the navy barely kept the army supplied and never effectively blockaded American ports.

Mindful of the enormous strain that the war imposed, British leaders faced serious problems maintaining their people's support for the conflict. The war more than doubled the national debt, thereby adding to the burdens of a people already paying record taxes. The politically influential landed gentry could not be expected to vote against their pocketbooks forever.

The United States faced different but no less severe wartime problems. Besides the fact that many colonists and Native Americans favored the British, the patriots faced a formidable military challenge. Americans were accustomed to serving as citizen-soldiers incolonial (now state) militias. Although militias sometimes performed well in hit-and-run guerrilla skirmishes, they lacked the training to fight pitched battles against professional armies like Britain's. Congress recognized that independence would never be secured if the new nation relied on guerrilla tactics, avoided major battles, and allowed the British to occupy all major population centers. Moreover, European powers would recognize that dependence on guerrilla warfare meant that the rebels could not drive out the British army, thereby dooming American hopes of gaining foreign loans, diplomatic recognition, and military allies. Finally, citizen-soldiers were accustomed to serving for a few weeks or months alongside neighbors and relatives and then returning home.

For the United States to succeed, the Continental Army would have to supersede the state militias and would need to fight in the standard European fashion. Professional eighteenth-century armies relied on the precisely executed movements of mass formations. Victory often depended on rapid maneuvers to crush an enemy's undefended flank or rear. Attackers needed exceptional skill in close-order drill in order to fall on an enemy before the enemy could re-form and return fire. Because muskets had a range of less than one hundred yards, armies in battle were never far apart. The troops advanced within musket range of each other, stood upright without cover, and fired volleys at one another until one line weakened from its casualties. Discipline, training, and nerve were essential if soldiers were to stay in ranks while comrades fell beside them. The stronger side then attacked at a quick walk with bayonets drawn and drove off its opponents.

In 1775, Britain possessed a well-trained army with a strong tradition of discipline and bravery under fire. In contrast, the Continental Army lacked an inspirational heritage as well as a deep pool of experienced officers and sergeants who could turn raw recruits into crack units. European officers such as Lafayette, and von Steuben (see below) helped make up for the shortage of leaders. Although the United States mobilized about 220,000 troops, compared to the 162,000 who served in the British army, most served short terms. Even with bounties (signing bonuses), promises of land after service, and other incentives, the army had difficulty attracting men for the long term. Most whites and blacks who did sign up for multiyear or indefinite lengths of time were poor and landless. Such men joined not out of patriotism but because, as one of them, a jailed debtor named Ezekiel Brown, put it, they had "little or nothing to lose."

The Americans experienced a succession of heartbreaking defeats in the war's early years, and the new nation would have been hard-pressed had it not been for the military contributions of France and Spain in the war's later stages. Yet, to win the war, the Continentals did not have to destroy the British army but only prolong the rebellion until Britain's taxpayers lost patience with the struggle. Until then, American victory would depend on the ability of one man to keep his army fighting despite defeat. That man was George Washington.

The young Washington's mistakes and defeats in the Ohio valley (see Chapter 5) taught him lessons that he might not have learned from easy, glorious victories. He discovered the dangers of overconfidence and the need for determination in the face of defeat. He also learned much about American soldiers, especially that they performed best when led by example and treated with respect.

After resigning his commission in 1758, Washington had sat in the Virginia House of Burgesses, where his influence grew, not because he thrust himself into every issue but because others respected him and sought his opinion. Having emerged as an early, though not outspoken, opponent of parliamentary taxation, he also sat in the Continental Congress. In the eyes of the many who valued his advice and remembered his military experience, Washington was the logical choice to head the Continental Army.

WAR AND PEACE, 1776–1783

The Revolutionary War had begun more than a year before Congress declared American independence in July 1776 (see Chapter 5). Until mid-1778 it remained centered in the North, where each side won some important victories. Meanwhile, American forces prevailed over British troops and their Native American allies to gain control of the trans-Appalachian West. The war was finally decided in the South when American and French forces won a stunning victory at Yorktown, Virginia, in 1781. In the peace treaty that followed, Britain finally acknowledged American independence.

Shifting Fortunes in the North, 1776–1778 During the second half of 1776, the two sides focused on New York. Under two brothers—General William Howe and Admiral Richard, Lord Howe—130 British warships carrying thirty-two thousand royal troops landed near New York harbor in the summer of 1776. Defending New York, America's second-largest city, were eighteen thousand poorly trained soldiers under George Washington.

By the end of the year, William Howe's men had killed or captured one-quarter of Washington's troops and had forced the survivors to retreat from New York across New Jersey and the Delaware River into Pennsylvania. Thomas Paine aptly described these demoralizing days as "the times that try men's souls."

With the British within striking distance of Philadelphia, Washington decided to seize the offensive before the morale of his army and country collapsed completely. On Christmas night 1776 he led his troops back into New Jersey and attacked a Hessian garrison at Trenton, where he captured 918 Germans and lost only 4 Continentals. Washington then attacked 1,200 British at Princeton on January 3, 1777, and killed or captured one-third of them while sustaining only 40 casualties.

These American victories at Trenton and Princeton had several important consequences. At a moment when defeat seemed inevitable, they boosted civilian and military morale. In addition, they drove a wedge between New Jersey's five thousand loyalists and the British army. Washington's victories forced the British to remove virtually all their New Jersey garrisons to New York early in 1777, while Washington

British Defeat at Saratoga, 1777
A British cartoonist expresses his disgust for Britain's surrender by depicting General Burgoyne, surrendering on his knees, and a sleeping General Howe.

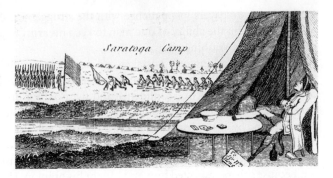

established winter quarters at Morristown, New Jersey, only twenty-five miles from New York City.

New Jersey loyalism never recovered after the British evacuated the state. Even before the Battle of Trenton, British troops had alienated the state's five thousand loyalists by indiscriminately looting loyalist and patriot civilians. Once the British were gone, New Jersey's militia disarmed known loyalists, jailed their leaders, and kept a constant watch on suspected Tories. Bowing to the inevitable, most loyalists who remained in the state swore allegiance to the Continental Congress. Some even enlisted in the rebel militia.

After the Battle of Princeton, the Marquis de Lafayette, a young French aristocrat, joined Washington's staff. The twenty-year-old Lafayette was brave, idealistic, and optimistic. Given Lafayette's close connections with the French court, his presence in America indicated that the French king, Louis XVI, might recognize American independence and declare war on Britain. Before recognizing the new nation, however, Louis wanted proof that the Americans could win a major battle, a feat they had not yet accomplished.

Louis did not have to wait long. In the summer of 1777, the British planned a two-pronged assault intended to crush American resistance in New York State and thereby isolate New England. Pushing off from Montreal, a force of regulars and their Iroquois allies under Lieutenant Colonel Barry St. Leger would march south along Lake Ontario and invade central New York from Fort Oswego in the west. At the same time General John Burgoyne would lead the main British force south from Quebec through eastern New York and link up with St. Leger near Albany.

Nothing went according to British plans. St. Leger's force of 1,900 British and Iroquois advanced one hundred miles and halted to besiege 750 New York Continentals at Fort Stanwix. Unable to take the post after three weeks, St. Leger retreated in late August 1777.

Burgoyne's campaign appeared more promising after his force of 8,300 British and Hessians recaptured Fort Ticonderoga. But Burgoyne ran short of supplies as General Horatio Gates gathered nearly 17,000 American troops for an attack. Gates fought two indecisive battles near Saratoga in the fall, inflicting another 1,200 casualties on Burgoyne. Surrounded and hopelessly outnumbered, Burgoyne's 5,800 troops honorably laid down their arms on October 17, 1777.

The diplomatic impact of the **Battle of Saratoga** equaled its military significance and would prove to be the war's turning point. The victory convinced France that the Americans could win the war. In February 1778 France formally recognized the United States. Four months later, it went to war with Britain. Spain declared war on Britain in 1779, but as an ally of France, not the United States, and the Dutch Republic joined them in the last days of 1780 (see Beyond America—Global Interactions). Britain faced a coalition of enemies, without allies of its own.

Meanwhile, as Gates and Burgoyne maneuvered in upstate New York, Britain's General Howe landed eighteen thousand troops near Philadelphia. With Washington at their head and Lafayette at his side, sixteen thousand Continentals occupied the imperiled city in late August 1777.

The two armies collided on September 11, 1777, at Brandywine Creek, Pennsylvania. In the face of superior British discipline, most Continental units crumbled, and Congress fled Philadelphia in panic, enabling Howe to occupy the city. Howe again defeated Washington at Germantown on October 4. In one month's bloody fighting, 20 percent of the Continentals were killed, wounded, or captured.

While the British army wintered comfortably eighteen miles away in Philadelphia, the Continentals huddled in the bleak hills of Valley Forge. Joseph Plumb Martin, a seventeen-year-old Massachusetts recruit, recorded the troops' condition in his diary: "The greatest part were not only shirtless and barefoot but destitute of all other clothing, especially blankets." However, he concluded, there was no alternative but desertion, and no one seriously entertained that idea. "We had engaged in the defense of our injured country and were willing nay, we were determined, to persevere as long as such hardships were not altogether intolerable." Shortages of provisions, especially food, would continue to undermine morale and, on some occasions, discipline among American forces.

The army also lacked training. At Saratoga, the Americans' overwhelming numbers more than their skill had forced Burgoyne to surrender. Indeed, when Washington's men had met Howe's forces on equal terms, they lost badly. The Continentals mainly lacked the ability to march as compact units and maneuver quickly. Regiments often straggled single-file into battle and then wasted precious time forming to attack, and few troops were expert in bayonet drill.

The Continental Army received a desperately needed boost in February 1778, when a German soldier of fortune, Friedrich von Steuben, arrived at Valley Forge. The short, squat Steuben did not look like a soldier, but this earthy German instinctively liked Americans and became immensely popular. He had a talent for motivating men (sometimes by staging humorous tantrums featuring a barrage of German, English, and French swearing); but more important, he possessed administrative genius. In a mere four months, General Steuben almost single-handedly turned the army into a formidable fighting force.

British officials decided to evacuate Philadelphia in June 1778 so as to free up several thousand troops for action in the West Indies. General Henry Clinton, the new commander-in-chief in North America, led the troops northward for New York. The Continental Army got its first opportunity to demonstrate Steuben's training when it caught up with Clinton's rear guard at Monmouth Court House, New Jersey, on June 28, 1778. The battle raged for six hours in one-hundred-degree heat until Clinton broke off contact. Expecting to renew the fight at daybreak, the Americans slept on

The American Revolution as an International War

Originating as a conflict between Britain and its colonies in mainland North America, the American Revolution turned into an international war that extended to Europe, the West Indies, South America, Africa, and Asia. The widening of the war contributed directly to America's struggle for independence from Britain.

Britain and France had emerged as rival maritime empires nearly a century earlier and had fought four major wars. Most recently, in the Seven Years' War (1754–1763), the balance of power between them shifted dramatically when France lost all its possessions in mainland North America and India.

The war left both nations facing enormous debts and populations that were heavily but inequitably taxed, especially in France. Britain also sought to finance and administer its suddenly enlarged empire. The East India Company, which functioned as both colonial government in India and monopolistic trade company throughout Asia, was financially troubled. Its local officials in India pursued personal profits, it had accumulated an enormous surplus of tea from China, and American colonists refused to buy its tea. To enhance Company revenues, Parliament passed the Tea Act (1773), which lowered the price of tea by lifting import duties and by allowing Company agents to sell directly to colonial consumers, bypassing American merchants. When, in the Boston Tea Party, radical protesters destroyed Company tea to prevent its unloading, British officials no longer doubted that Americans were disloyal to the empire (see Chapter 5).

The outbreak of Anglo-American conflict in 1775 provided France with an opportunity to avenge its defeat in the Seven Years' War. France borrowed even more money to supply funds and arms to the rebels and welcomed American ships at its ports. French military volunteers, most notably the Marquis de Lafayette, joined the American cause. France also sped up the rebuilding of its army and navy, achieving naval equality with Britain by 1778. Spain, an ally of France and rival of Britain for nearly a century, also contributed arms and other supplies to the rebels. Imported weapons and ammunition were a critical factor in the American victory at Saratoga in October 1777.

As a result of Saratoga, France in February 1778 formally recognized American independence, allied with the United States against Britain, and renounced all territorial claims in mainland North America. After declaring war on Britain in June, France dispatched warships and troops to the West Indies, forcing Britain to evacuate Philadelphia and divert 5,000 troops from North America to defend its wealthy colonies there. Over the next year, British troops seized France's military stronghold at St. Lucia while French forces captured the British colonies of St. Vincent, Grenada, and Dominica.

Spain, eager to reclaim Gibraltar from Britain, joined the war in 1779 as an ally of France but not of the Americans. (Spain feared that an independent United States would threaten Louisiana.) Spain and France then planned a massive invasion of England. Although they failed to launch the invasion, Britain as a precaution kept half its war fleet nearby and five thousand troops in Ireland, thereby spreading its forces even more thinly.

The Americans gained another ally when the Netherlands abandoned its alliance with Britain. Since the outbreak of the Revolution, Dutch merchants and Dutch West Indian planters had traded with the Americans. Many Dutch also linked their republican aspirations with those of the United States while resenting British domination of its trade and foreign policy. After the British in 1780 seized a Dutch convoy bound for France, the Netherlands declared war on Britain. British forces in 1781 captured most Dutch possessions in the West Indies and adjacent South American mainland.

Like the Netherlands, most European countries bristled under British naval domination and feared that the war would lead Britain to interfere with their trade. To prevent such an outcome, Empress Catherine II ("the Great") in 1780 declared Russia's "armed neutrality." She asserted Russia's right as a neutral country to trade commodities with any nation, threatened to retaliate against any belligerent attempting to search Russian ships, and called on other countries to join a League of Armed Neutrality. Sweden, Denmark, the Netherlands, Prussia, Portugal, Turkey, and several smaller nations joined the League. Recognizing its diplomatic isolation, Britain left League members alone (except the Netherlands) lest it find itself fighting even more enemies.

In 1781 a formidable French fleet commanded by Admiral François de Grasse sailed from France via the West Indies to Chesapeake Bay. Arriving in August, the fleet landed several thousand French troops. The French troops joined Continental forces under George Washington in besieging Lord Cornwallis's base at Yorktown while the fleet prevented any British from slipping out. The Franco-American trap forced Cornwallis to surrender in October.

Although the outcome at Yorktown ensured America's independence, it did not end the international war. In 1782 Spain attempted, unsuccessfully, to seize Gibraltar. Meanwhile, de Grasse had returned to the Caribbean. Although failing to recapture St. Lucia, he seized St. Kitts after five weeks of fierce British resistance. He was preparing a massive French-Spanish invasion of Jamaica when British forces cornered his fleet in an inter-island passage called the Saintes and captured four ships and de Grasse himself. Elsewhere France sought to regain territory that it had lost to Britain in the Seven Years' War. In 1779 its forces seized Senegal in West Africa. The most powerful state in India, Mysore, had long resisted the British East India Company and, before 1763, had favored France. In 1780, the ruler of Mysore, Hyder Ali, joined four other Indian rulers (usually political and religious rivals of one another) in calling for "the expulsion of the English nation from India." Although the alliance failed to act, Hyder Ali led Mysore's forces in a standoff with British troops for two years. In 1782, a French naval fleet arrived to aid Mysore, threatening Britain's presence in South India.

By then, however, the war's protagonists were discussing terms of peace. The result of their negotiations was the Treaty of Paris (1783), under which America became independent; Britain and France returned all territories seized from one another in the Caribbean (except for the French-held island of Tobago), India, and Senegal; and Britain returned an Indian Ocean port on Ceylon to the Netherlands.

The American Revolution left a volatile mix in the North Atlantic. In achieving independence, the United States accelerated the appeal of republican ideals that were fomenting popular discontent with monarchies across Europe. Ironically, by supporting the birth of a revolutionary republic, the French monarchy added to the nation's already crushing debts, thereby hastening its own downfall and the advent of an even more radical revolution in its own "country. Beginning in 1789, that" revolution would in turn generate a new cycle of global warfare lasting until 1815.

Questions for Analysis

- What impact did other countries have on the struggle between Britian and its American colonies?

- How did the results of the war in mainland North America compare with the outcome elsewhere?

their arms, but Clinton's army slipped away before then. The British would never again win easily, except when they faced more militiamen than Continentals.

The Battle of Monmouth Court House ended the contest for the North. Clinton occupied New York, which the Royal Navy made safe from attack. Washington kept his army nearby to watch Clinton, while the Whig militia hunted down the last few Tory guerrillas and extinguished loyalism.

The War in the West, 1776–1782   A different kind of war developed west of the Appalachians and along the western borders of New York and Pennsylvania, where the fighting consisted of small-scale skirmishes rather than major battles involving thousands of troops. Native Americans and Anglo-Americans had alternately traded, negotiated, and fought in this region for several decades. But long-standing tensions between Native peoples and land-hungry settlers continued to simmer. In one sense, then, the warfare between Indians and white Americans only continued an older frontier struggle. Despite its smaller scale, the war in the West was fierce, and the stakes—for the new nation, for the British, and for Indians in the region—could not have been higher.

The war in the West erupted in 1776 when Cherokees began attacking settlers from North Carolina and other southern colonies who had moved onto or near their homelands. After suffering heavy losses, the colonies recovered and organized retaliatory expeditions. Within a year these expeditions had burned most Cherokee towns, forcing the Cherokees to sign treaties that ceded most of their land in South Carolina and substantial tracts in North Carolina and Tennessee.

The intense fighting lasted longer in the Northwest. Largely independent of American and British coordination, Ohio Indians and white settlers fought for two years in Kentucky, with neither side gaining a clear advantage. But after British troops occupied French settlements in the area that is now Illinois and Indiana, Colonel George Rogers Clark led 175 Kentucky militiamen north of the Ohio River. After capturing and losing the French community of Vincennes on the Wabash River, Clark retook the settlement for good in February 1779. With the British unable to offer assistance, their Native American allies were vulnerable. In May, John Bowman led a second Kentucky unit in a campaign that destroyed most Shawnee villages, and in August a move northward from Pittsburgh by Daniel Brodhead inflicted similar damage on the Delawares and the Seneca Iroquois. Although these raids depleted their populations and food supplies, most Ohio Indians resisted the Americans until the war's end.

Meanwhile, pro-British Iroquois, led by the gifted Mohawk leader Joseph Brant, devastated the Pennsylvania and New York frontiers in 1778. They killed 340 Pennsylvania militiamen at Wyoming, Pennsylvania, and as many more in other raids. In 1779 American General John Sullivan retaliated by invading Iroquois country with 3,700 Continental troops, along with several hundred Tuscaroras and Oneidas who had broken with the other Iroquois nations. Sullivan fought just one battle, near present-day Elmira, New York, in which his artillery routed Brant's warriors. Then he burned two dozen Iroquois villages and destroyed a million bushels of corn, causing most Iroquois to flee without food into Canada. Untold hundreds starved during the next winter, when more than sixty inches of snow fell.

In 1780, Brant's thousand warriors fell upon their fellow Iroquois, the Tuscaroras and Oneidas, and then laid waste to Pennsylvania and New York for two years. But this final whirlwind masked reality: Sullivan's campaign had devastated the pro-British Iroquois.

Fighting continued in the West until 1782. Despite their intensity, the western campaigns did not determine the outcome of the war itself. Nevertheless, they had a significant impact on the future shape of the United States, as discussed later.

Victory in the South, 1778–1781   In 1778, the war's focus shifted to the South. By securing southern ports, Britain expected to acquire the flexibility needed to move its forces back and forth between the West Indies—where they faced French and Spanish opposition—and the mainland, as necessity dictated. In addition, the South looked like a relatively easy target. General Henry Clinton was certain that a renewed invasion there would tap a huge reservoir of loyalist support. In sum, the British plan was to seize key southern ports and, with the aid of loyalist militiamen, move back toward the North, pacifying one region after another.

The plan unfolded smoothly at first. In the spring of 1778, British troops from East Florida took control of Georgia. After a two-year delay caused by political bickering at home, Clinton sailed from New York with nine thousand troops and forced the surrender of Charles Town, South Carolina, and its thirty-four-hundred-man garrison on May 12, 1780. However, the British quickly found that there were fewer loyalists than they had expected.

Southern loyalism had suffered several serious blows since the war began. When the Cherokees had attacked the Carolina frontier in 1776, they killed whites indiscriminately. Numerous Tories had switched sides, joining the rebel militia to defend their homes. The arrival of British troops sparked a renewed exodus of enslaved Africans from their plantations. About one-third of Georgia's blacks and one-fourth of South Carolina's fled to British lines or to British-held Florida in quest of freedom. Although British officials attempted to return runaway slaves to loyalist masters, they met with limited success. Planters feared that loss of control over their human property would lead to a black uprising. Despite British efforts to placate them, many white loyalists

Joseph Brant, by Gilbert Stuart, 1786 *The youthful Mohawk leader was a staunch ally of the British during the Revolutionary War, and thereafter resisted U.S. expansion in the Northwest.*

abandoned the British and welcomed the rebels' return to power in 1782. Those who remained loyalists, embittered by countless instances of harsh treatment under patriot rule, took revenge. Patriots struck back whenever possible, perpetuating an ongoing cycle of revenge, retribution, and retaliation among whites.

The southern conflict was not all personal feuds and guerrilla warfare. After the capture of Charles Town, Horatio Gates took command of American forces in the South. With only a small force of Continentals at his disposal, Gates had to rely on poorly trained militiamen. In August 1780, Lord Charles Cornwallis inflicted a crushing defeat on Gates at Camden, South Carolina. Fleeing after firing a single volley, Gates's militia left his badly outnumbered Continentals to be overrun. Camden was the worst rebel defeat of the war.

Washington and Congress responded by relieving Gates of command and sending General Nathanael Greene to confront Cornwallis. Greene subsequently fought three major battles between March and September 1781, and he lost all of them. "We fight, get beat, rise, and fight again," he wrote back to Washington. Still, Greene won the campaign, for he gave the Whig militia the protection they needed to hunt down loyalists, stretched British supply lines until they began to snap, and sapped Cornwallis's strength by inflicting much heavier casualties than the British general could afford. Greene's dogged resistance forced Cornwallis to leave the Carolina backcountry in American hands and to lead his battered troops into Virginia.

Cornwallis established a base at Yorktown, Virginia. Britain's undoing began on August 30, 1781, when a French fleet dropped anchor off the Virginia coast and landed troops near Yorktown. Lafayette and a small force of Continentals from nearby joined the French while Washington arrived with his army from New York. In the **Battle of Yorktown,** six thousand trapped British troops stood off eighty-eight hundred Americans and seventy-eight hundred French for three weeks before surrendering with military honors on October 19, 1781.

Peace at Last, 1782–1783
"Oh God!" Lord North exclaimed upon hearing the news from Yorktown. "It's all over." Cornwallis's surrender drained the will of England's overtaxed people to continue fighting and forced Britain to negotiate for peace. John Adams, Benjamin Franklin, and John Jay were America's principal delegates to the peace talks in Paris, which began in June 1782.

Military realities largely influenced the terms of the **Treaty of Paris** (1783). Britain recognized American independence and agreed to withdraw all royal troops from the new nation's soil. The British had little choice but to award the Confederation all lands east of the Mississippi. Although the vast majority of Americans lived in the thirteen states clustered near the eastern seaboard, twenty thousand Anglo-Americans now lived west of the Appalachians. Moreover, Clark's victories had given Americans control of the Northwest, while Spain had kept Britain out of the Southwest. The treaty also gave the new nation important fishing rights off the Grand Banks of Canada.

On the whole, the settlement was highly favorable to the United States, but it left some disputes unresolved. Under a separate treaty, Britain returned East and West Florida to Spain, but the boundaries designated by this treaty were ambiguous. Spain interpreted the treaty to mean that it regained the same Florida territory that it had ceded to Britain in 1763 (see Chapter 5). But the Treaty of Paris named the thirty-first parallel as the Floridas' northern border, well south of the area claimed by Spain. Spain and the United States would dispute the northern boundary of Florida until 1795 (see below and Chapter 7).

The Treaty of Paris failed to prevent several future disputes between Britain and America. Not bound by the treaty, which extended only to national governments, state governments refused to compensate loyalists for their property losses and erected barriers against British creditors' attempts to collect prewar debts. In retaliation, Britain refused to honor treaty pledges to abandon forts in the Northwest and to return American-owned slaves under their control.

Notably missing in the Treaty of Paris was any reference to Native Americans, most of whom had supported the British in order to avert the alternative—an independent American nation that would be no friend to Indian interests. In effect, the treaty left the Native peoples to deal with the Confederation on their own, without any provision for their status or treatment. Joseph Brant and other Native American leaders were outraged. Not surprisingly, many Indians did not acknowledge the new nation's claims to sovereignty over their territory.

The Treaty of Paris ratified American independence, but winning independence had exacted a heavy price. At least 5 percent of all free males between the ages of sixteen and forty-five—white, black, and Native American—died fighting the British. Only the Civil War produced a higher ratio of casualties to the nation's population.

Furthermore, the war drove perhaps one of every six loyalists, several thousand slaves, and several thousand Native Americans into exile. Whites, blacks, and Indians moved to Canada, and whites moved to Britain and the West Indies. After finding that both the land and inhabitants in Nova Scotia were inhospitable, many blacks moved from there to the new British colony of Sierra Leone in West Africa. Perhaps as much as 20 percent of New York's white population fled. When the British evacuated Savannah in 1782, 15 percent of Georgia's whites accompanied them. Most whites who departed were recent British immigrants. Finally, although the war secured American independence, it did not address two important issues: what kind of society America was to become and what sort of government the new nation would possess. But the war had a profound effect on both questions.

THE REVOLUTION AND SOCIAL CHANGE

Two factors—the principles articulated in the Declaration of Independence and dislocations caused by the war itself—forced questions of class, gender, and race into public discussion during the Revolutionary era. As a result, popular attitudes regarding the rights of non-elite white men and of white women, and the future of slavery, shifted somewhat. Except for slaves in the northern states, however, there was little prospect of substantive change in status. Nevertheless, the discussions ensured that these issues would be debated again in the future. For Native Americans, however, the Revolution was a definite step backward.

Egalitarianism Among White Men   For much of the eighteenth century, social relations between elites and other white colonists became more formal, distant, and restrained (see Chapter 4). Members of the colonial gentry emphasized their social position by living far beyond the means of ordinary families. By the late 1760s, however, many elite politicians began wearing homespun rather than imported English clothes in order to win popular political approval during the colonial boycott of British goods. When Virginia planters organized minutemen companies in 1775, they put aside their expensive officers' uniforms and dressed in buckskin or homespun hunting shirts of a sort that even the poorest farmer could afford. By 1776, the anti-British movement had persuaded many elites to maintain the appearance, if not the substance, of equality with common people.

Then came war, which accelerated the trend by pressuring the gentry, who held officers' rank, to show respect to the ordinary men serving under them. Indeed, the soldiers demanded to be treated with consideration, especially in light of the ringing words of the Declaration of Independence, "All men are created equal." The soldiers would follow commands, but not if they were addressed as inferiors.

A few officers realized this fact immediately. Some, among them General Israel Putnam of Connecticut, went out of their way to show that they felt no superiority to their troops. While inspecting a regiment digging fortifications around Boston in 1776, Putnam saw a large stone nearby and told a soldier to throw it onto the outer wall. The individual protested, "Sir, I am a corporal." "Oh," replied Putnam, "I ask your pardon, sir." The general then dismounted his horse and hurled the rock himself, to the immense delight of the troops working there.

Unlike Putnam, many officers insisted that soldiers remain disciplined and subordinate under all circumstances. In May 1780—more than two years after the terrible winter at Valley Forge—Continental Army troops in New Jersey were again, in Joseph Plumb Martin's words, "starved and naked." "The men were now exasperated beyond endurance," Martin continued, "they could not stand it any longer." After a day of exercising with their arms, Martin's regiment defied orders to disarm and return to their quarters, instead urging two nearby regiments to join them in protesting their lack of provisions. A colonel, who "considered himself the soldier's friend," was wounded when trying to prevent his men from getting their weapons. After several officers seized one defiant soldier, his comrades pointed their rifles at the officers until they released the soldier. Other officers tried without success to order the men to disarm and finally gave up. The soldiers' willingness to defy their superiors paid off. Within a few days, more provisions arrived and, as Martin put it, "we had no great cause for complaint for some time."

After returning to civilian life, the soldiers retained their sense of self-esteem and insisted on respectful treatment by elites. As these feelings of personal pride gradually translated into political behavior and beliefs, many candidates took care not to scorn the common people. The war thus subtly but fundamentally democratized Americans' political assumptions.

The gentry's sense of superiority also diminished as elites met men who rose through ability rather than through advantages of wealth or family. The war produced numerous examples like James Purvis, the illiterate son of a nonslaveholding Virginia farmer, who joined the First Virginia Regiment as a private in 1775, soon rose to sergeant, and then taught himself to read and write so that he could perform an officer's duties. Captain Purvis fought through the entire war and impressed his well-born officers as "an uneducated man, but of sterling worth." As elites saw more and more men like Purvis performing responsibilities previously thought to be above their station in life, some came to recognize that a person's merit was not always related to his inherited wealth.

Many who considered themselves republicans did not welcome the apparent trend toward democracy. Especially among elites, they continued to insist that each social class had its own particular virtues and that a chief virtue of the lower classes was deference to those possessing the wealth and education necessary to govern. Writing to a friend in 1776, John Adams expressed alarm that "a jealousy or an Envy taking Place among the Multitude" would exclude "Men of Learning . . . from the public Councils and from Military Command." "A popular government is the worse Curse," he concluded, "despotism is better."

Nevertheless, most Revolutionary-generation Americans came to insist that virtue and sacrifice defined a citizen's worth independently of his wealth. Voters began to view members of the "natural aristocracy"—those who had demonstrated fitness for government service by personal accomplishments—as the ideal candidates for political office. This natural aristocracy had room for a few self-made men such as Benjamin Franklin, as well as for those, like Thomas Jefferson and John Hancock, who were born into wealth. Voters still elected the wealthy to office, but not if they flaunted their money or were condescending toward common people. The new emphasis on equality did not extend to propertyless males, women, and nonwhites, but it undermined the tendency to believe that wealth or distinguished family background conferred a special claim to public office.

Although many whites became more egalitarian in their attitudes, the Revolution left the actual distribution of wealth in the nation unchanged. The war had been directed at British imperial rule and not at the structure of American society. The exodus of loyalists did not affect the class structure because the 3 percent who fled the United States represented a cross-section of society and equally well-to-do Whig gentlemen usually bought up their confiscated estates. Overall, the American upper class seems to have owned about as much of the national wealth in 1783 as it did in 1776.

| White Women in Wartime | White women's support of colonial resistance before the Revolution (see Chapter 5) broadened into an even wider range of activities during the war. Female "camp followers," many of |

them soldiers' wives, served military units on both sides by cooking, laundering, and nursing the wounded. A few female patriots, such as Massachusetts's Deborah Sampson, even disguised themselves as men and joined in the fighting. But most women remained at home, where they managed families, households, farms, and businesses on their own.

Even the most traditional female roles took on new meaning in the absence of male household heads. After her civilian husband was seized by loyalists and turned over to the British on Long Island, Mary Silliman of Fairfield, Connecticut, tended to her four children (and bore a fifth), oversaw several servants and slaves, ran a commercial farm that had to be evacuated when the British attacked Fairfield, and launched repeated appeals for her husband's release. Despite often enormous struggles, such experiences boosted white women's confidence in their abilities to think and act on matters traditionally reserved for men. "I have the vanity," wrote another Connecticut woman, Mary Fish, to a female friend, "to think I have in some measure acted the *heroine* as well as my dear Husband the Hero."

As in all wars, women's public roles and visibility were heightened during the Revolution. Some women interpreted their public activities in militant terms. In 1779, as the Continental Army struggled to feed and clothe itself, Esther de Berdte Reed and Sally Franklin Bache (Benjamin Franklin's daughter) organized a campaign among Philadelphia women to raise money for the troops. Not content to see their movement's role as secondary, they compared it to those of Joan of Arc and other female heroes who had saved their people, and proclaimed that American women were "born for liberty" and would never "bear the irons of a tyrannic Government."

The most direct wartime challenge to established gender relations came from **Abigail Adams.** "In the new Code of Laws which I suppose it will be necessary for you to make," Adams wrote to her husband John in 1776, "I desire that you would Remember the Ladies." Otherwise, she continued, "we are determined to foment a Rebellion and will not hold ourselves bound by any Laws in which we have no voice, or Representation." Abigail made clear that, besides participating in boycotts and spinning bees, women recognized that colonists' arguments against arbitrary British rule also applied to gender relations. Despite his high regard for his wife's intellect, John dismissed her plea as yet another effort to extend rights and power to those who were unworthy. The assumption that women were naturally dependent—either as children subordinate to their parents or as wives to their husbands—continued to dominate discussions of the female role. For that reason, married women's property remained, in Abigail's bitter words, "subject to the control and disposal of our partners, to whom the law have given a sovereign authority."

Although the war ended in 1783, discussions of women's roles in the new republic would continue (see Chapter 7).

A Revolution for Black Americans

The wartime situation of African-Americans contradicted the ideals of equality and justice for which Americans were fighting. About five hundred thousand black persons—20 percent of the total population—inhabited the United States in 1776, all but about twenty-five thousand of whom were enslaved. Even those who were free could not vote, lived under curfews and other galling restrictions, and lacked the guarantees of equal justice held by the poorest white criminal. Free blacks could expect no more than grudging toleration, and few slaves ever gained their freedom.

Although the United States was a "white man's country" in 1776, the war opened some opportunities for African-Americans. Amid the confusion of war, some slaves, among them Jehu Grant of Rhode Island, ran off and posed as free persons. Grant later recalled his excitement "when I saw liberty poles and the people all engaged for the support of freedom, and I could not but like and be pleased with such a thing."

In contrast to the nine thousand who joined or supported British forces, approximately five thousand African-Americans, most of them from the North, served in the Continental forces. Even though the army forbade enlistment by African-Americans in 1775, black soldiers were already fighting in units during the siege of Boston, and the ban on black enlistments started to collapse in 1777. The majority were free blacks, but some were slaves serving with their masters' consent.

For the most part, these wartime opportunities for African-American men grew out of the army's need for personnel rather than a white commitment to equal justice. In fact, until the mid-eighteenth century, few Europeans and white Americans had criticized slavery at all. Like disease and sin, slavery was considered part of the natural order. But in the decade before the Revolution, American opposition to slavery had swelled, especially as resistance leaders increasingly compared the colonies' relationship with Britain to that between slaves and a master.

Recognizing that slavery violated Quaker views on human equality, the earliest American initiatives against slavery originated within the Quaker religion. The yearly meeting of the New England Quakers abolished slavery among its members in 1770, and the yearly meetings of New York and Philadelphia Quakers followed suit in 1776. By 1779, Quaker slave owners had freed 80 percent of their slaves.

Although the Quakers aimed mainly to abolish slaveholding within their own ranks, some of them, most notably Anthony Benezet and John Woolman, broadened their condemnations to include slavery everywhere. Discussions of liberty, equality, and natural rights, particularly in the Declaration of Independence, also spurred antislavery sentiments. Between 1777 and 1784 Vermont, Pennsylvania, Massachusetts, Rhode Island, and Connecticut began phasing out slavery. New York did not do so until 1799, and New Jersey until 1804. New Hampshire, unmoved by petitions like that written in 1779 by Portsmouth slaves demanding liberty "to dispose of our lives, freedom, and property," never freed its slaves; but by 1810 none remained in the state.

The Revolutionary generation, rather than immediately abolishing slavery, took steps that would weaken the institution and in this way bring about its eventual demise. Most state abolition laws provided for gradual emancipation, typically declaring all children born of a slave woman after a certain date—often July 4—free. (They still had to work, without pay, for their mother's master for up to twenty-eight years.) Furthermore, the Revolution's leaders did not press for decisive action against slavery in the South out of fear that widespread southern emancipation would either bankrupt or break up the Union. They argued that the Confederation, already deeply in debt as a result of the war, could not finance immediate abolition in the South, and any attempt to do so without compensation would drive that region into secession.

Yet even in the South, where it was most firmly entrenched, slavery troubled some whites. When one of his slaves ran off to join the British and later was recaptured, James Madison of Virginia concluded that it would be hypocritical to punish the runaway "merely for coveting that liberty for which we have paid the price of so much blood." Still, Madison did not free the slave, and no state south of Pennsylvania abolished slavery. Nevertheless, all states except South Carolina and Georgia ended slave imports and all but North Carolina passed laws making it easy for masters to manumit (set free) slaves. The number of free blacks in Virginia and Maryland had risen from about four thousand in 1775 to nearly twenty-one thousand, or about 5 percent of all African-Americans there, by 1790.

These "free persons of color" faced the future as destitute, second-class citizens. Most had purchased their freedom by spending small cash savings earned in off-hours and were past their physical prime. Once free, they found whites reluctant to hire them or to pay equal wages. Black ship carpenters in Charleston (formerly Charles Town), South Carolina, for example, earned one-third less than their white coworkers in 1783. Under such circumstances, most free blacks remained poor laborers, domestic servants, and tenant farmers.

One of the most prominent free blacks to emerge during the Revolutionary period was Boston's **Prince Hall.** Born a slave, Hall received his freedom in 1770 and immediately took a leading role among Boston blacks protesting slavery. During the war he formed a separate African-American Masonic lodge, beginning a movement that spread to other northern communities and became an important source of community support for black Americans. In 1786 Hall petitioned the Massachusetts legislature for support of a plan that would enable interested blacks "to return to Africa, our native country . . . where we shall live among our equals and be more comfortable and happy than we can be in our present situation." Hall's request was unsuccessful, but later activists would revive his call for blacks to "return to Africa."

An African-American who was more widely recognized among whites was the Boston poet and slave Phillis Wheatley. Wheatley drew on Revolutionary ideals in considering her people's status. Several of her poems explicitly linked the liberty sought by white Americans with a plea for the liberty of slaves, including one that was autobiographical:

I, young in life, by seeming cruel fate
Was snatch'd from Afric's fancy'ed happy seat:

. . . . .

Such, such my case. And can I then but pray
Others may never feel tyrannic sway?

Most states granted some civil rights to free blacks during and after the Revolution. Free blacks had not participated in colonial elections, but those who were male and met the property qualification gained this privilege in a few states during the 1780s. Most northern states repealed or stopped enforcing curfews and other colonial laws restricting free African-Americans' freedom of movement. These same states generally changed their laws to guarantee free blacks equal treatment in court hearings.

The Revolution neither ended slavery nor brought equality to free blacks, but it did begin a process by which slavery eventually might have been extinguished. In half the nation, the end of human bondage seemed to be in sight. White southerners increasingly viewed slavery as a necessary evil rather than as a positive good. Slavery had begun to crack, and free blacks had made some gains. But events in the 1790s would reverse the move toward egalitarianism (see Chapter 7).

Native Americans and the Revolution   Whereas Revolutionary ideology held out at least an abstract hope for white women, blacks, and others seeking liberty and equal rights within American society, it made no provision for Native Americans wishing to remain politically and culturally independent of Europeans and European-Americans. Regardless of which side they had fought on—or whether they had fought at all—Native Americans suffered worse than any group during the war. During the three decades encompassed by the Seven Years' War and the Revolution (1754–1783), the Native population east of the Mississippi had declined by about half, and many Indian communities had been uprooted. Moreover, in an overwhelmingly agrarian society like the United States, the Revolution's implicit promise of equal economic opportunity for all male citizens set the stage for territorial expansion onto Native American landholdings. Even where Indians remained on their land, the influx of settlers posed dangers in the form of deadly diseases, farming practices inimical to Indian subsistence (see Chapter 3), and alcohol.

In the face of these uncertainties, most Native Americans continued to incorporate useful aspects of European culture into their own. From the beginning of contact with Europeans, Indians had selectively adopted European-made goods of cloth, metal, glass, and other materials into their lives. But Native Americans did not give up their older ways altogether; rather, their clothing, tools, weapons, utensils, and other material goods combined elements of the old and the new. Many Indians, especially those no longer resisting American expansion, also participated in the American economy by working for wages or by selling food, crafts, or other products. This interweaving of the new with the traditional characterized Indian communities throughout eastern North America.

Native Americans, then, did not remain stubbornly rooted in traditional ways or resist participation in a larger world dominated by whites. But they did insist on retaining control of their homelands and their ways of life. In this spirit, the Chickasaws of the Mississippi valley addressed Congress in 1783. While asking "from whare and whome we are to be supplied with necessaries," they also requested that the Confederation "put a stop to any encroachments on our lands, without our consent, and silence those [white] People who . . . inflame and exasperate our Young Men."

In the Revolution's aftermath, it appeared doubtful that the new nation would concede even this much to Native Americans.

FORGING NEW GOVERNMENTS, 1776–1787

Even as they joined in resisting Britain's authority, white mainland colonists differed sharply among themselves over basic questions of social and political order. Many elite republicans welcomed hierarchical rule, so long as it was not based on heredity, and feared democracy as "mob rule." Working and poor people, especially in cities, worried that propertied elites profited at their expense. Rural colonists emphasized decentralizing power and authority as much as possible. These conflicts were reflected in the independent United States' first experiments in government at the state and national levels.

From Colonies to States Political conflicts within the new states during and after the Revolution magnified the prewar struggle between more radical democratic elements and elites who would minimize popular participation. While the new state constitutions retained colonial precedents that favored the wealthiest elites, they laid the foundations for republican government in America.

In keeping with colonial practice, eleven of the thirteen states maintained bicameral (two-chamber) legislatures. Colonial legislatures had consisted of an elected lower chamber (or assembly) and an upper chamber (or council) appointed by the governor or chosen by the assembly (see Chapter 4). These two-part legislatures mirrored Parliament's division into the House of Commons and House of Lords, symbolizing the assumption that a government should have separate representation by the upper class and the common people.

Despite participation by people from all classes in the struggle against Britain, few questioned the long-standing practice of setting property requirements for voters and elected officials. In the prevailing view, the ownership of property, especially land, gave voters a direct stake in the outcome of elections. Whereas poor, uneducated tenant farmers and hired laborers might vote to please their landlords or employers, sell their votes, or be fooled by a demagogue, property holders supposedly had the financial means and the education to express their political preferences freely and responsibly. The association between property and citizenship was so deeply ingrained that even radicals such as Samuel Adams opposed allowing all males—much less women—to vote and hold office.

Americans also retained the notion that "virtuous" elected representatives should exercise independent judgment in leading the people rather than simply carry out the popular will. Although Americans today take political parties for granted, the idea of parties as groups organized to mobilize public opinion in favor of a political agenda was alien to eighteenth-century Anglo-Americans. Following England's "country party" (see Chapter 5), Revolutionary Americans equated parties with "factions"—selfish groups that advanced their own interests at the expense of liberty or the public good. Most candidates for office did not present voters with a clear choice between policies calculated to benefit rival interest groups; instead, they campaigned on the basis of their personal reputations and fitness for office. As a result, voters often did not know where office seekers stood on specific issues and hence found it hard to influence government actions.

Another colonial practice that persisted into the 1770s and 1780s was the equal (or nearly equal) division of legislative seats among all counties or towns, regardless of differences in population. Inasmuch as representation had never before been apportioned according to population, a minority of voters normally elected a majority of assemblymen. Only the most radical constitution, Pennsylvania's, sought to avoid such outcomes by attempting to ensure that election districts would be roughly equal in population. Nine of the thirteen states slightly reduced property requirements for voting, but none abolished such qualifications entirely.

Despite the holdover of certain colonial-era practices, the state constitutions in other respects departed radically from the past. Above all, they were written documents that usually required popular ratification and could be changed only if voters chose to amend them. In short, Americans jettisoned the British conception of a constitution as a body of customary arrangements and practices, insisting instead that constitutions were written compacts that defined and limited the powers of rulers. Moreover, as a final check on government power, the Revolutionary constitutions spelled out citizens' fundamental rights. By 1784, all state constitutions included explicit bills of rights that outlined certain freedoms that lay beyond the control of any government.

Without intending to extend political participation, elites had found themselves pulled in a democratic direction by the logic of the imperial crisis of the 1760s and 1770s. Elite-dominated but popularly elected assemblies had led the fight against royal governors and their appointees—the executive branch of colonial governments—who had enforced laws and policies deemed dangerous to liberty. Colonists entered the Revolution dreading executive officeholders and convinced that even elected governors could no more be trusted with power than could monarchs. Recent history seemed to confirm British "country party" thinking that those in power tended to become either corrupt or dictatorial. Consequently, Revolutionary statesmen proclaimed the need to strengthen legislatures at the governors' expense.

Accordingly, the earliest state constitutions severely limited executive power. In most states, the governor became an elected official, and elections themselves occurred far more frequently. (Pennsylvania actually eliminated the office of governor altogether.) Whereas most colonial elections had been called at the governor's pleasure, after 1776 all states scheduled annual elections except South Carolina, which held them every two years. In most states, the power of appointments was transferred from the governor to the legislature. Legislatures usually appointed judges and could reduce their salaries or impeach them (try them for wrongdoing). By relieving governors of most appointive powers, denying them the right to veto laws, and making them subject to impeachment, the constitutions turned governors into figureheads who simply chaired executive councils that made militia appointments and supervised financial business.

As the new state constitutions weakened the executive branch and vested more power in the legislatures, they also made the legislatures more responsive to the will of the people. Nowhere could the governor appoint the upper chamber. Eight constitutions written before 1780 allowed voters to select both houses of the legislature; one (Maryland) used a popularly chosen "electoral college" for its upper house; and the remaining "senates" were filled by vote of their assemblies. Pennsylvania and Georgia abolished the upper house and substituted a unicameral (single-chamber) legislature. American assaults on the executive branch and enhancement of legislative authority reflected bitter memories of royal governors who had acted arbitrarily to dismiss assemblies and control government through their power of appointment, and fear that republics' undoing began with executive usurpation of authority.

Despite their high regard for popularly elected legislatures, Revolutionary leaders described themselves as republicans rather than democrats. Although used interchangeably today, these words had different connotations in the eighteenth century. To many elites, democracy suggested mob rule; at best, it implied the concentration of power in the hands of an uneducated multitude. In contrast, republicanism presumed that government would be entrusted to virtuous leaders elected for their superior talents and commitment to the public good. For most republicans, the ideal government would delicately balance the interests of different classes to prevent any one group from gaining absolute power. Some, including John Adams, thought that a republic could include a hereditary aristocracy or even a monarchy if needed to counterbalance democratic tendencies, but most thought otherwise. Having blasted one king in the Declaration of Independence, most elites had no desire to enthrone another.

In the first flush of revolutionary enthusiasm, elites had to content themselves with state governments dominated by popularly elected legislatures. Gradually, however, wealthier landowners, bankers, merchants, and lawyers reasserted their desires for centralized authority and the political prerogatives of wealth. In Massachusetts, an elite-dominated convention in 1780 pushed through a constitution stipulating stiff property qualifications for voting and holding office, state senate districts that were apportioned according to property values, and a governor with considerable powers in making appointments and vetoing legislative measures. The Massachusetts constitution signaled a general trend. Georgia and Pennsylvania substituted bicameral for unicameral legislatures by 1790. Other states raised property qualifications for members of the upper chamber in a bid to encourage the "senatorial element" and to make room for men of "Wisdom, remarkable integrity, or that Weight which arises from property."

Even many republican elites believed that social divisions, if deep-seated and permanent, could jeopardize liberty, and attempted to prevent such an outcome through legislation. In 1776 in Virginia, for example, Thomas Jefferson persuaded the legislature to abolish entails, legal requirements that prevented an heir and all his descendants from selling or dividing an estate. Although entails were easy to break through special laws—Jefferson himself had escaped the constraints of one—he hoped that their elimination would strip wealthy families of the opportunity to amass land continuously and become an overbearing aristocracy. Through Jefferson's efforts, Virginia also ended primogeniture, the legal requirement that the eldest son inherit all of a family's property in the absence of a will. Jefferson argued that these laws would ensure a continuous division of wealth. By 1791, no state provided for primogeniture, and only two still allowed entails.

The first years of independence also witnessed the end of established churches in most states. The exceptions were New Hampshire, Connecticut, and Massachusetts, where the Congregational church continued to collect tithes (church taxes) from citizens not belonging to recognized Christian denominations into the nineteenth century. Wherever colonial taxpayers had supported the Church of England, independent states abolished such support by 1786. Thomas Jefferson best expressed the ideal behind disestablishment in his Statute for Religious Freedom (1786), whose preamble resounded with a defense of religious freedom at all times and places. "Truth is great," proclaimed Jefferson, "and will prevail if left to itself."

The American Revolution, wrote Thomas Paine in 1782, was intended to ring in "a new era and give a new turn to human affairs." Paine was celebrating America's rejection of hereditary rule and adoption of republican principles. All political institutions, new and old alike, now were being judged by the standard of whether they served the public good rather than the interests of the powerful few. More than any single innovation of the era, it was this new way of thinking that made American politics revolutionary.

Formalizing a
Confederation,
1776–1781

As in their revolt against Britain and their early state constitutions, Americans' first national government reflected widespread fears of centralized authority and its potential for corruption. It also reflected their strong attachments to their states, most of which were about a century or more old, as opposed to the newly declared nation. In 1776, John Dickinson, who had stayed in Congress despite having refused to sign the Declaration of Independence, drafted a proposal for a national constitution. Congress adopted a weakened version of Dickinson's proposal, called the **Articles of Confederation,** and sent it to the states for ratification in 1777.

The Articles of Confederation explicitly reserved to each state—and not to the national government—"its sovereignty, freedom and independence." The "United States of America" was no more than "a firm league of friendship" among sovereign states, much like today's European Union. As John Adams later explained, the Whigs of 1776 never thought of "consolidating this vast Continent under one national Government" but instead erected "a Confederacy of States, each of which must have a separate government."

Under the Articles, the national government consisted of a single-chamber Congress, elected by the state legislatures, in which each state had one vote. Congress could request funds from the states but could not enact any tax without every state's approval, and could not regulate interstate or overseas commerce. The approval of seven states was required to pass minor legislation; nine states had to approve declarations of war, treaties, and the coining and borrowing of money. Besides for taxes, unanimous approval was required in order to ratify and amend the Articles. The Articles did not provide for an independent executive branch. Rather, congressional committees oversaw financial, diplomatic, military, and Indian affairs, and resolved interstate disputes. Nor was there a judicial system by which the national government could compel allegiance to its laws. The Articles did eliminate all interstate travel and trade barriers, and guaranteed that all states would recognize one another's judicial decisions.

Because of disputes among the states, especially over their claims to western lands, their contributions to Congress, and their representation in Congress, four years passed before all thirteen legislatures ratified the Articles. Only in February 1781—six months before the American victory at Yorktown—did the last state, Maryland, agree to ratification.

Finance, Trade, and
the Economy,
1781–1786

Aside from finishing the war on the battlefield, the greatest challenge facing the Confederation was putting the nation on a sound financial footing. The war cost the nation's six hundred thousand taxpayers a staggering $160 million, a sum that exceeded by 2,400 percent the taxes raised to pay for the Seven Years' War. Yet even this was not enough; to finance the war fully, the government borrowed funds from abroad and printed its own paper money, called Continentals. Lack of public faith in the government destroyed 98 percent of the value of the Continentals from 1776 to 1781, an inflationary disaster that gave rise to the expression "not worth a Continental."

Seeking to overcome the national government's financial weakness, Congress in 1781 appointed a wealthy Philadelphia merchant, Robert Morris, as Superintendent of Finance. Morris proposed that the states authorize the collection of a national import duty of 5 percent, which would finance the congressional budget and guarantee interest payments on the war debt. Because the Articles required that every state approve a national tax, the import duty failed because Rhode Island alone rejected it.

Meanwhile, seeing themselves as sovereign, most states had assumed some responsibility for the war debt and begun compensating veterans and creditors within their borders. But Morris and other nationally minded elites insisted that the United States needed sources of revenue independent of the states in order to establish its creditworthiness, enabling it to attract capital, and to establish a strong national government. Hoping to panic the country into seeing things their way, Morris and New York congressman Alexander Hamilton engineered a dangerous gamble known later as the Newburgh Conspiracy. In 1783, the two men secretly persuaded some army officers, then encamped at Newburgh, New York, to threaten a coup d'état unless the treasury obtained the taxation authority needed to raise their pay, which was months in arrears. But George Washington, learning of the conspiracy before it was carried out, ended the plot by delivering a speech that appealed to his officers' honor and left them unwilling to proceed. Although Morris may not have intended for a coup to actually occur, his willingness to take such a risk demonstrated the new nation's perilous financial straits and the vulnerability of its political institutions.

When peace came in 1783, Congress sent another tax measure to the states, but once again a single legislature, this time New York's, blocked it. From then on, the states steadily decreased their contributions to Congress. By the late 1780s, the states had fallen behind nearly 80 percent in providing the funds that Congress requested to operate the government and honor the national debt.

Nor did the Confederation succeed in prying trade concessions from Britain. After declaring the colonies in rebellion, Britain had virtually halted American trade with its Caribbean colonies and Great Britain itself (see Chapter 5). The continuation after the war of British trade prohibitions contributed to an economic depression that gripped New England beginning in 1784. A short growing season and poor soil kept yields so low, even in the best of times, that farmers barely produced enough grain for local consumption. New Englanders also faced both high taxes to repay the money borrowed to finance the Revolution and a tightening of credit that spawned countless lawsuits against debtors. Economic depression only aggravated the region's chronic overpopulation.

Resourceful New England captains took cargoes to the French West Indies, Scandinavia, and China. Some even smuggled foodstuffs to the British West Indies under the nose of the Royal Navy. Nevertheless, by 1791 discriminatory British treatment had reduced the number of fishers and whalers in Massachusetts by 42 percent compared to the 1770s.

The mid-Atlantic states, on the other hand, were less dependent on British-controlled markets for their exports. As famine stalked Europe, farmers in Pennsylvania and New York prospered from climbing export prices—much as Thomas Paine had predicted (see Chapter 5). By 1788, the region had largely recovered from the Revolution's ravages.

Southern planters faced frustration at the failure of their principal crops, tobacco and rice, to return to prewar export levels. Whereas nearly two-thirds of American exports originated in the South in 1770, less than half were produced by southern states in 1790. In an effort to stay afloat, many Chesapeake tobacco growers shifted to wheat, and others expanded their production of hemp. But these changes had little effect on the region's exports and, because wheat and hemp required fewer laborers than tobacco, left slave owners with a large amount of underemployed, restless "human property." These factors, along with Native American and Spanish resistance to westward expansion, reinforced nagging uncertainties about the South's future.

The Confederation
and the West,
1785–1787

After winning the war against Britain, one of the most formidable challenges confronting the Confederation was the postwar settlement and administration of American territory outside the boundaries of the states. White American settlers and speculators were determined to possess these lands, and Native Americans were just as determined to keep them out. At the same time, Britain and Spain supported the Indian nations in the hope of strengthening their own positions between the Appalachians and the Mississippi.

After the states surrendered claims to more than 160 million acres north of the Ohio River, forming the Northwest Territory, Congress established uniform procedures for surveying this land in the **Ordinance of 1785.** The law established a township six miles square as the basic unit of settlement. Every township would be subdivided into thirty-six sections of 640 acres each, one of which would be reserved as a source of income for schools. The Ordinance imposed an arbitrary grid of straight lines and right angles across the landscape that conformed to European-American notions of private property while utterly ignoring the land's natural features. Subsequently, in the **Northwest Ordinance** (1787), Congress defined the steps for the creation and admission of new states. This law designated the area north of the Ohio River as the Northwest Territory and provided for its later division into states. It forbade slavery while the region remained a territory, although the citizens could legalize the institution after statehood.

The Northwest Ordinance outlined three stages for admitting states into the Union. First, during the initial years of settlement, Congress would appoint a territorial governor and judges. Second, as soon as five thousand adult males lived in a territory, voters would approve a temporary constitution and elect a legislature that would pass the territory's laws. Third, when the total population reached sixty thousand, voters would ratify a state constitution, which Congress would have to approve before granting statehood.

The Ordinance of 1785 and the Northwest Ordinance had a lasting effect on later American history. Besides laying out procedures for settling and establishing governments in the Northwest, they later served as models for organizing territories farther west. The Northwest Ordinance also established a significant precedent for banning slavery from certain territories. But because Native Americans, who were determined to keep out settlers, controlled virtually the entire region north of the Ohio River, the ordinances could not be implemented immediately.

The Northwest Territory seemed to offer enough land to guarantee property to American citizens for centuries. This fact satisfied republicans like Thomas Jefferson who feared that the rapidly growing white population would quickly exhaust available land east of the Appalachians and so create a large class of tenants and poor laborers who could not vote. Such a development would undermine the equality among whites that expansionist republicans thought essential for a healthy nation.

The realization of these expansionist dreams was by no means inevitable. Most "available" territory from the Appalachians to the Mississippi River belonged to those

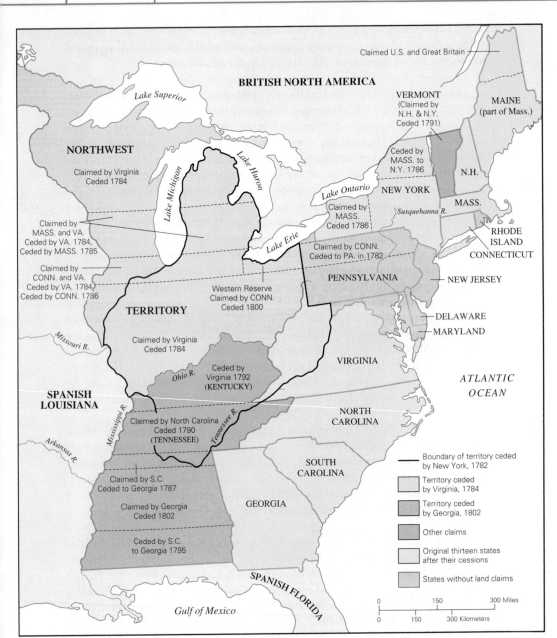

MAP 6.1 State Claims to Western Lands, and State Cessions to the Federal Government, 1782–1802

Eastern states' surrender of land claims paved the way for new state governments in the West.

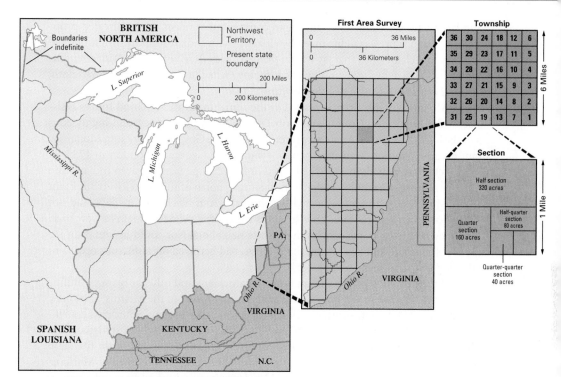

MAP 6.2 The Northwest Territory, 1785–1787

The Ordinance of 1785 provided for surveying land into townships of thirty-six sections, each supporting four families on 160-acre plots. In 1787 the Northwest Ordinance stipulated that states ultimately be created in the region.

peoples whom the Declaration of Independence had condemned as "merciless Indian savages." Divided into more than eighty tribes and numbering perhaps 150,000 people in 1789, these Native Americans were struggling to preserve their own independence. At postwar treaty negotiations, they repeatedly heard Confederation commissioners scornfully declare, "You are a subdued people . . . we claim the country by conquest."

Under threats of continued warfare with the United States, some northwestern Indian leaders gave in to American pressure. The Iroquois, who had suffered heavily during the war, lost about half their land in New York and Pennsylvania in the second Treaty of Fort Stanwix (1784). In the treaties of Fort McIntosh (1785) and Fort Finney (1786), Delaware and Shawnee leaders, respectively, were obliged to recognize American sovereignty over their lands. But upon hearing of the treaties, most Indians angrily repudiated them on the grounds that tribal members had never authorized their negotiators to give up territory.

Native Americans' resistance to Confederation encroachments also stemmed from their confidence that the British—still a presence in the West—would provide the arms and ammunition they needed to defy the United States. Contrary to the Treaty of Paris, Britain had refused to abandon seven northwestern forts within the new nation's boundaries, citing certain states' failure to compensate loyalists for confiscated property and to honor prewar debts owed by citizens. With Indian support, Britain hoped eventually to reclaim lands that lay within the Northwest Territory. The British strengthened their presence in the region by encouraging Canadian traders to exchange cloth, tools, and arms with Native peoples for furs.

The Mohawk Joseph Brant emerged as the initial inspiration behind Indian resistance in the Northwest. Courageous in battle, skillful in diplomacy, and highly educated (he had translated an Anglican prayer book and the Gospel of Mark into Mohawk), Brant became a minor celebrity when he visited King George in London in 1785. At British-held Fort Detroit in 1786, he helped organize some northwestern Indians into a military alliance to exclude Confederation citizens north of the Ohio River. But Brant and his Mohawks, who had relocated beyond American reach in Canada, could not win support from Senecas and other Iroquois who had chosen to remain in New York, where they now lived in peace with their white neighbors. Nor could he count on the support of the Ohio Indians, whom the Iroquois had betrayed on numerous occasions in the past (see Chapters 4 and 5).

Seizing on disunity within Indian ranks, Kentuckians and others organized militia raids into the Northwest Territory. These raids gradually forced the Miamis, Shawnees, and Delawares to evacuate southern Indiana and Ohio. The Indians' withdrawal northward, toward the Great Lakes, soon tempted whites to make their first settlements in what is now Ohio. In spring 1788, about fifty New Englanders sailed down the Ohio River in a bulletproof barge named the *Mayflower* and founded the town of Marietta. That same year some Pennsylvanians and New Jerseyites established a second community north of the Ohio on the site of modern-day Cincinnati. By then, another phase in the long-running contest for the Ohio valley was nearing a decisive stage.

The Confederation confronted similar challenges in the Southeast, where Spain and its Indian allies took steps to prevent American settlers from occupying their lands. The Spanish found a brilliant ally in the Creek leader **Alexander McGillivray.** In some fraudulent treaties, two Creeks had surrendered extensive territory to Georgia that McGillivray intended to regain. Patiently holding back his followers for three years, McGillivray negotiated a secret treaty in which Spain promised weapons so that the Creeks could protect themselves "from the Bears and other fierce Animals." When the Creeks finally attacked in 1786, they shrewdly expelled only those whites occupying disputed lands and then offered Georgia a cease-fire. Eager to avoid approving taxes for a costly war, Georgia politicians let the Creeks keep the land.

Spain also sought to prevent American infiltration by denying western settlers permission to ship their crops down the Mississippi River to New Orleans. Having negotiated a separate treaty with Britain (see above), Spain had not signed the Peace of Paris, by which Britain promised the United States export rights down the Mississippi, and in 1784 the Spanish closed New Orleans to Anglo-American commerce. Spain and the United States negotiated a treaty in 1786 that opened Spanish markets to American merchants and renounced Spanish claims to disputed southwestern lands—at the cost, however, of postponing American exporters' access to New Orleans for another twenty years. Westerners and southerners charged that this Jay-Gardoqui Treaty sacrificed their interests to benefit northern commerce, and Congress rejected it.

Unable to prevent American settlers from occupying territory it claimed in the Southeast, Spain sought to win the newcomers' allegiance by offering them citizenship. Noting that Congress seemed ready to accept the permanent closing of New Orleans in return for Spanish concessions elsewhere, many westerners began talking openly of secession. Most westerners who accepted Spanish favors and gold meant only to pocket badly needed cash in return for vague promises of goodwill. The episode showed, however, that leading citizens were susceptible to foreign manipulation. As young Andrew Jackson (the future U.S. general and president) concluded in 1789, making some arrangements with the Spanish seemed "the only immediate way to obtain peace with the Savage [Indians]."

TOWARD A NEW CONSTITUTION, 1786–1788

Under the Articles of Confederation, the United States made enormous strides in establishing itself as an independent nation. But impatience with the national government's limitations persisted among those seeking to establish the United States on a more solid financial and military footing. Impatience turned to anxiety in 1786 after Massachusetts farmers defied local authorities in protesting measures that would worsen their already severe economic circumstances. A national convention called to consider amendments to the Articles instead proposed a radical new frame of government, the Constitution. In 1788, the states ratified the Constitution, setting a new course for America.

Shays's Rebellion, 1786–1787
The Jay-Gardoqui Treaty revealed deep-seated tensions beneath the surface appearance of American national unity. The depression that had begun in 1784 persisted in New England, which had never recovered from the loss of its prime export market in the British West Indies. With farmers already squeezed financially, the state legislature, dominated by commercially minded elites, voted early in 1786 to pay off its Revolutionary debt in three years. This ill-considered policy necessitated a huge tax hike. Meanwhile, the state's unfavorable balance of payments with Britain had produced a shortage of specie (gold and silver coin) because British creditors refused any other currency. Fearing a flood of worthless paper notes, Massachusetts bankers and merchants insisted that they, too, be paid in specie, while the state mandated the same for payment of taxes. Lowest in this cycle of debt were thousands of small family farmers.

In contrast, the mid-Atlantic and southern states were emerging from the depression, thanks to rising tobacco and food exports to Europe. Taxpayers in these sections, moreover, were paying off war debts easily, and most were indifferent to national politics.

Despite the nation's prosperity outside New England, a growing minority was dissatisfied with the Confederation for various reasons. Merchants and shippers wanted a central government powerful enough to secure trading privileges for them abroad, and to ensure economic stability and America's standing in the Atlantic economy, still dominated by Britain. Land speculators and western settlers sought a government that would pursue a more activist policy against Spain, Britain, and Native Americans in the West. Meanwhile, urban artisans hoped for a stronger national government that would impose a uniformly high tariff and thereby protect them from foreign competition.

The spark that ignited this tinderbox originated in Massachusetts. The plight of that state's farmers was especially severe in the western part of the state, where agriculture was least profitable. Facing demands that they pay their debts and taxes in hard currency, which few of them had in abundance if at all, farmers held public meetings. As in similar meetings more than a decade earlier, the farmers—most of whom were Revolutionary War veterans—discussed "the Suppressing of tyrannical government," referring this time to the Massachusetts government rather than the British. In 1786, in a move reminiscent of pre-Revolutionary backcountry dissidents (see Chapter 5), farmer and former officer Daniel Shays led two thousand angry men in an attempt to shut down the courts in three western counties. The Shaysites hoped thereby to stop sheriffs' auctions for unpaid taxes and prevent foreclosures on farm mortgages. Although routed by state troops after several skirmishes, sympathizers of Shays won control of the Massachusetts legislature in 1787, cut taxes, and secured a pardon for their leader.

The Shaysites had limited objectives, were dispersed with relatively little bloodshed, and never seriously threatened anarchy. But their uprising, and similar but less militant movements in other states, became the rallying cry for advocates of a stronger central government. By threatening to seize weapons from a federal arsenal at Springfield, Massachusetts, the farmers' movement unintentionally enabled nationalists to argue that the United States had become vulnerable to "mobocracy." Writing to a fellow wartime general, Henry Knox, for news from Massachusetts, an anxious George Washington worried that "there are combustibles in every state, which a spark might set fire to," destroying the Republic. Meanwhile, rumors were flying that the Spanish had offered export rights at New Orleans to westerners if they would secede from the Union. Nationalists sowed fears that the United States was on the verge of coming apart.

Instead of igniting a popular uprising, as Washington feared, Shays's Rebellion sparked aggressive nationalists into pushing for a wholesale reform of the Republic's legal and institutional structure. Shortly before the outbreak of the rebellion, delegates from five states had assembled at Annapolis, Maryland. They had intended to discuss means of promoting interstate commerce but instead called for a general convention to propose amendments to the Articles of Confederation. Accepting their suggestion, Congress asked the states to appoint delegations to meet in Philadelphia.

The Philadelphia Convention, 1787   In May 1787, fifty-five delegates from every state but Rhode Island began gathering at the Pennsylvania State House in Philadelphia, later known as Independence Hall. Among them were established figures like George Washington and Benjamin Franklin, as well as talented newcomers such as Alexander Hamilton and James Madison. Most were wealthy and in their thirties or forties, and nineteen owned slaves. More than half had legal training.

The convention immediately closed its sessions to the press and the public, kept no official journal, and even appointed chaperones to accompany the aged and talkative Franklin to dinner parties lest he disclose details of what was happening. Although these measures opened the members of the convention to the charge of acting undemocratically and conspiratorially, the delegates thought secrecy essential to ensure freedom of debate without fear of criticism from home.

The delegates shared a "continental" or "nationalist" perspective, instilled through their extended involvement with the national government. Thirty-nine had sat in Congress, where they had seen the Confederation's limitations firsthand. In the postwar years, they had become convinced that unless the national government was freed from

James Madison
Although one of the Philadelphia convention's youngest delegates, Madison of Virginia was among its most articulate and politically astute. He played a central role in the Constitution's adoption.

the control of more popularly and locally oriented state legislatures, the country would fall victim to internal strife or foreign aggression.

The convention faced two basic issues. The first was whether to tinker with the Articles of Confederation, as the state legislatures had formally instructed the delegates to do, or to replace the Articles altogether with a new constitution that gave more power to the national government. The second fundamental question was how to balance the conflicting interests of large and small states. **James Madison** of Virginia, who had entered Congress in 1780 at twenty-nine, proposed an answer to each issue. Despite his youth and frail build, Madison commanded enormous respect for his profound knowledge of history and the passionate intensity he brought to debates.

Madison's **Virginia Plan,** introduced in late May, boldly called for the establishment of a strong central government rather than a federation of states. Madison's blueprint gave Congress virtually unrestricted rights of legislation and taxation, the power to veto any state law, and authority to use military force against the states. As one delegate immediately saw, the Virginia Plan was designed "to abolish the State Govern[men]ts altogether." The Virginia Plan specified a bicameral legislature and fixed representation in both houses of Congress proportionally to each state's population. The voters would elect the lower house, which would then choose delegates to the upper chamber from nominations submitted by the legislatures. Both houses would jointly name the country's president and judges.

Madison's scheme aroused immediate opposition, however, especially his call for state representation according to population—a provision highly favorable to his own Virginia. On June 15 William Paterson of New Jersey offered a counterproposal, the so-called **New Jersey Plan,** which recommended a single-chamber congress in which each state had an equal vote, just as under the Articles.

The two plans exposed the convention's great stumbling block: the question of representation. The Virginia Plan would have given the four largest states a majority in both houses. The New Jersey Plan would have allowed the seven smallest states, which included just 25 percent of all Americans, to control Congress. By July 2, the convention had arrived "at a full stop," as one delegate put it. To end the impasse, the delegates assigned a member from each state to a "grand committee" dedicated to compromise. The panel adopted a proposal offered earlier by the Connecticut delegation: an equal vote for each state in the upper house and proportional voting in the lower house. Although Madison and the Virginians doggedly opposed this compromise, it passed on July 17.

Despite their differences over representation, Paterson's and Madison's proposals alike would have strengthened the national government at the states' expense. No less than Madison, Paterson wished to empower Congress to raise taxes, regulate interstate commerce, and use military force against the states. The New Jersey Plan, in fact, defined congressional laws and treaties as the "supreme law of the land" and would also have established courts to force reluctant states to accept these measures. But other delegates were wary of undermining the sovereignty of the states altogether. Out of hard bargaining emerged the Constitution's delicate balance between the desire of nearly all delegates for a stronger national government and their fear that governments tended to grow despotic.

As finally approved on September 17, 1787, the **Constitution of the United States** (see Appendix) was an extraordinary document, and not merely because it reconciled the conflicting interests of the large and small states. The new frame of government augmented national authority in several ways. Although it did not incorporate Madison's proposal to give Congress a veto over state laws, it vested in Congress the authority to lay and collect taxes, to regulate interstate commerce, and to conduct diplomacy. States could no longer coin money, interfere with contracts and debts, or tax interstate commerce. Following the New Jersey Plan, all acts and treaties of the United States became "the supreme law of the land." All state officials had to swear to uphold the Constitution, even against acts of their own states. The national government could use military force against any state. These provisions added up to a complete abandonment of the principle on which the Articles of Confederation had rested: that the United States was a federation of sovereign states, with ultimate authority concentrated in their legislatures.

To allay the concerns of more moderate delegates, the Constitution's Framers devised two means of restraining the power of the new central government. First, in keeping with republican political theory, they established a **separation of powers** among the national government's three distinct branches—executive, legislative, and judicial; and second, they designed a system of **checks and balances** to prevent any one branch from dominating the other two. In the bicameral Congress, states' equal representation in the Senate was offset by the proportional representation, by population, in the House; and each chamber could block measures approved by the other. Furthermore, where the state constitutions had deliberately weakened the executive, the Constitution gave the president the power to veto acts of Congress; but to prevent abuse of the veto, Congress could override the president by a two-thirds majority in each house. The president could conduct diplomacy, but the Senate had to ratify treaties. The president appointed a cabinet, but only with Senate approval. The president and any presidential appointee could be removed from office by a joint vote of Congress, but only for "high crimes," not for political disagreements.

To further ensure the independence of each branch, the Constitution provided that the members of one branch would not choose those of another, except for judges, whose independence would be protected because they were appointed for life by the president with the "advice and consent" of the Senate. For example, the president was to be selected by an Electoral College, whose members the states would select as their legislatures saw fit. The number of electors in each state would equal the number of its senators and representatives. In the event of a deadlock in the Electoral College, the House of Representatives, with one vote per state, would choose the president. The state legislatures also elected the members of the Senate, whereas the election of delegates to the House of Representatives was achieved by direct popular vote.

In addition to checks and balances, the founders devised a system of shared power and dual lawmaking by the national and state governments—**"federalism"**—in order to place limits on central authority. Not only did the state legislatures have a key role in electing the president and senators, but the Constitution could be amended by the votes of three-fourths of the states. Thus, the convention departed sharply from Madison's plan to establish a "consolidated" national government entirely independent of, and superior to, the states.

A key assumption behind federalism was that the national government would limit its activities to foreign affairs, national defense, regulating interstate commerce, and coining money. Most other political matters were left to the states. Regarding slavery in particular, each state retained full authority.

The dilemma confronting the Philadelphia convention centered not on whether slavery should be allowed in the new Republic but only on the much narrower question of whether slaves could be counted as persons when it came to determining a state's representation at the national level. For most legal purposes, slaves were regarded not as persons but rather as the chattel property of their owners, meaning that they were on a par with other living property such as horses and cattle. But southern states saw their large numbers of slaves as a means of augmenting their numbers in the House of Representatives and in the electoral colleges that would elect the nation's presidents every four years. So strengthened, they could prevent northerners from ever abolishing slavery.

Representing states that had begun ending slavery, northern delegates opposed giving southern states a political advantage by allowing them to count people who had no civil or political rights. As Madison—himself a slave owner—observed, "it seemed now to be pretty well understood that the real difference of interests lay, not between the large & small [states] but between the N. & South." But after Georgia and South Carolina threatened to secede if their demands were not met, northerners agreed to the **"three-fifths clause,"** allowing three-fifths of all slaves to be counted for congressional representation and, thereby, in the Electoral College that selected the president.

The Constitution also reinforced slavery in other ways. Most notably, it forbade citizens of any state, even those that had abolished slavery, to prevent the return of escaped slaves to another state. The Constitution limited slavery only to the extent of prohibiting Congress from banning the importation of slaves before 1808, and by not repudiating Congress's earlier ban on slavery in the Northwest Territory.

Although leaving much authority to the states, the Constitution established a national government whose sovereignty, unlike under the Articles of Confederation, clearly superseded that of the states. Having thus strengthened national authority, the convention had to face the issue of ratification. For two reasons, it seemed unwise to submit the Constitution to state legislatures for ratification. First, the Framers realized that the state legislatures would reject the Constitution, which shrank their power relative to the national government. Second, most of the Framers repudiated the idea—implicit in ratification by state legislatures—that the states were the foundation of the new government. The opening words of the Constitution, "We the People of the United States," underlined the delegates' conviction that the government had to be based on the consent of the American people themselves, "the fountain of all power" in Madison's words, and not of the states.

In the end, the Philadelphia convention provided for the Constitution's ratification by special state conventions composed of delegates elected by the voters. Approval by nine such conventions would put the new government in operation. Because any state refusing to ratify the Constitution would legally remain under the Articles, the possibility existed that the country might divide into two nations.

Under the Constitution, the Framers expected the nation's elites to continue exercising political leadership, and took steps to rein in the democratic currents set in motion by the Revolution. Accordingly, they curtailed what they considered the excessive power of popularly elected state legislatures. And while they located sovereignty in the people rather than in the states, they provided for an Electoral College that would actually elect the president. The Framers did provide for one crucial democratic element in the new government, the House of Representatives. Moreover, by making the Constitution flexible and amendable (though not easily amendable), and by dividing political power among competing branches of government, the Framers made it possible for the national government to be slowly democratized, in ways unforeseen in 1787.

The Struggle over Ratification, 1787–1788

The Constitution's supporters began the campaign for ratification without significant popular support. Expecting the Philadelphia convention to offer some amendments to the Articles of Confederation, most Americans hesitated to restructure the entire system of government. Undaunted, the Constitution's friends moved decisively to marshal political support. In a clever stroke, they called themselves "Federalists," a term implying that the Constitution would more nearly balance the relationship between the national and state governments, and thereby undermined the arguments of those hostile to a centralization of national authority.

The Constitution's opponents became known as "Antifederalists." This negative-sounding title probably hurt them, for it did not convey the crux of their argument against the Constitution—that it was not "federalist" at all since it failed to balance the power of the national and state governments. By augmenting national authority, Antifederalists maintained, the Constitution would ultimately doom the states.

The Antifederalist arguments reflected Anglo-Americans' long-standing suspicion of concentrated power, reiterated by Americans from the time of the Stamp Act crisis, through the War of Independence, to the framing of the first state constitutions and the Articles of Confederation. Unquestionably, the Constitution gave the national government unprecedented authority in an age when most political thinkers argued that the best way to preserve liberty was to limit executive power. Compared to a distant national government, Antifederalists argued, state governments were far more responsive to the popular will. They acknowledged that the Framers had guarded against tyranny by preserving limited state powers and devising a system of checks and balances, but doubted that these devices would succeed. The proposed constitution, concluded one Antifederalist, "nullified and declared void" the constitutions and laws of the states except where they did not contradict federal mandates. Moreover, for all its checks and balances, opponents noted, the Constitution provided no guarantees that the new government would protect the liberties of individuals. The absence of a bill of rights made an Antifederalist of Madison's nationalist ally and fellow Virginian, George Mason, the author of the first such state bill in 1776.

Although the Antifederalists advanced some formidable arguments, they confronted a number of disadvantages in publicizing their cause. While Antifederalist ranks included some prominent figures, none had the stature of George Washington or Benjamin Franklin. As state and local leaders, the Antifederalists lacked their opponents' contacts and experience at the national level, acquired through service as Continental Army officers, diplomats, or members of Congress. Moreover, most American newspapers were pro-Constitution and did not hesitate to bias their reporting in favor of the Federalist cause.

The Federalists' advantages in funds and political organizing proved decisive. The Antifederalists failed to create a sense of urgency among their supporters, assuming incorrectly that a large majority would rally to them. Only one-quarter of the voters turned out to elect delegates to the state ratifying conventions, and most had been mobilized by Federalists.

The Constitution became the law of the land on June 21, 1788, when the ninth state, New Hampshire, ratified by the close vote of 57 to 47. Federalist delegates prevailed in seven of the first nine state conventions by margins of at least two-thirds. Such lopsided votes reflected the Federalists' organizational skills and aggressiveness rather than the degree of popular support for the Constitution. The Constitution's advocates rammed through approval in some states "before it can be digested or deliberately considered," in the words of a Pennsylvania Antifederalist.

But unless Virginia and New York—two of the largest states—ratified, the new government would be fatally weakened. In both states (and elsewhere) Antifederalist sentiment ran high among small farmers, who saw the Constitution as a scheme favoring city dwellers and moneyed interests. Prominent political leaders in these two states who called for refusing ratification included New York governor George Clinton and Virginia's Richard Henry Lee, George Mason, Patrick Henry, and future president James Monroe.

At Virginia's convention, Federalists won crucial support from the representatives of the Allegheny counties—modern West Virginia—who wanted a strong national government capable of ending Indian raids from north of the Ohio River. Western Virginians' votes, combined with James Madison's leadership among tidewater planters, proved too much for Henry's spellbinding oratory. On June 25, the Virginia delegates ratified by a narrow 53 percent majority.

The struggle was even closer and more hotly contested in New York. Antifederalists had solid control of the state convention and would probably have voted down the Constitution, but then news arrived that New Hampshire (the ninth state) and powerful Virginia had approved. Federalist forces, led by Alexander Hamilton and John Jay, spread rumors that if the convention voted to reject, pro-Federalist New York City and adjacent counties would secede from the state and join the Union alone, leaving upstate New York a landlocked enclave. When several Antifederalist delegates took alarm at this threat and switched sides, New York ratified on July 26 by a 30 to 27 vote.

So the Antifederalists went down in defeat, and they did not survive as a political movement. Yet they left an important legacy. At their insistence, the Virginia, New York, and Massachusetts conventions ratified the Constitution with the accompanying request that the new charter be amended to include a bill of rights protecting Americans' basic freedoms. So widespread was the public demand for a bill of rights that it became a high priority on the new government's agenda (see Chapter 7).

Antifederalists' objections in New York also stimulated a response in the form of one of the great classics of political thought, **The Federalist,** a series of eighty-five newspaper essays penned by Alexander Hamilton, James Madison, and John Jay. The Federalist Papers, as they are commonly termed, had little influence on voting in the New York State convention. Rather, their importance lay in articulating arguments for the Constitution that addressed Americans' wide-ranging concerns about the powers and limits of the new federal government, thereby shaping a new philosophy of government. The Constitution, insisted *The Federalist*'s authors, had a twofold purpose: first, to defend the rights of political minorities against majority tyranny; and second, to prevent a stubborn minority from blocking well-considered measures that the majority believed necessary for the national interest. Critics, argued *The Federalist,* had no reason to fear that the Constitution would allow a single economic or regional interest to dominate. In the most profound essay in the series, *Federalist* No. 10, Madison rejected the Antifederalist argument that establishing a republic for a nation as large as the United States would unleash a chaotic contest for power and ultimately leave the majority exploited by a minority. "Extend the sphere," Madison insisted, "and . . . you make it less probable that a majority of the whole will have a common motive to invade the rights of other citizens, . . . [or will be able to] act in unison with each other." The country's very size and diversity would neutralize the attempts of factions to push unwise laws through Congress.

Madison's analysis was far too optimistic, however. As the Antifederalists predicted, the Constitution afforded enormous scope for special interests to influence the government. The great challenge for Madison's generation would be how to maintain a government that would provide equal benefits to all and at the same time accord special privileges to none.

CONCLUSION

The entry of North Carolina into the Union in late 1789 and of Rhode Island in May 1790 marked the final triumph of an uncertain nationalism. Among whites, blacks, and Native Americans alike, the American Revolution was a civil war as well as a war of national independence. So long as the war involved only Britain and America, it cost both sides heavily in casualties and finances without producing a conclusive result. Once other nations joined the anti-British cause, making the Revolution an international war, the tide turned. Now fatally overextended, Britain was defeated by American-French forces at Yorktown and obliged to surrender.

Winning the war proved to be only the first step in establishing a new American nation. Forming new governments at the state and national levels was just as challenging, for most white Americans inherited older, Anglo-American suspicions of concentrated political power. As a result, they were deeply divided over how to strike proper balances between power and liberty and between national and state sovereignty. For a decade, conflicts between competing political visions were played out in the protracted debates over several state constitutions, the Articles of Confederation, and, most decisively, the new federal Constitution. The Constitution struck careful balances on these and many other questions and definitely limited democracy; but by locating sovereignty in the people it created a legal and institutional framework within which Americans could struggle to attain democracy. In that way its conception was a fundamental moment in the history of America's enduring vision.

7

Launching the New Republic, 1788–1800

CONSTITUTIONAL GOVERNMENT TAKES SHAPE, 1788–1796

Although the Constitution had replaced the Articles of Confederation as the law of the land, the first test of its effectiveness was yet to come. Given the social and political divisions among Americans, and particularly their persistent fears of centralized authority, the successful establishing of a government at the national level was by no means inevitable. Would the American people accept the results of a national election? Would the legislative, executive, and judicial branches of the new government be organized so as to function effectively? Would Congress and the states amend the Constitution with a Bill of Rights, which several states had made a condition when voting to ratify?

Implementing Government

The first step in implementing the new government was the election of a president and Congress. The first elections under the Constitution, in fall 1788, resulted in a Federalist sweep in Congress. Antifederalists won just two of twenty seats in the Senate and five of fifty-nine in the House of Representatives. An electoral college met in each state on February 9, 1789, with each elector voting for two presidential candidates. Although unaware of deliberations in other states, every elector in every state designated George Washington as one of their choices. Having gotten the second most votes, John Adams became the vice president. (The Twelfth Amendment would later supersede this Electoral College procedure for choosing the president and vice president; see Chapter 8).

CHRONOLOGY, 1788–1800

1788 • First election under the Constitution.

1789 • First Congress convenes in New York.
George Washington elected and inaugurated as first president.
Judiciary Act.
French Revolution begins.

1790 • Alexander Hamilton submits Reports on Public Credit and National Bank to Congress.
Treaty of New York.
Judith Sargent Murray, "On the Equality of the Sexes."
First Indian Trade and Intercourse Act.

1791 • Bank of the United States established with twenty-year charter.
Bill of Rights ratified.
National Gazette established.
Slave uprising begins in French colony of Saint Domingue.
Society for the Encouragement of Useful Manufactures founded.

1792 • Washington reelected president.

1793 • Fugitive Slave Law.
Chisholm v. Georgia.
France at war with Britain and Spain.
Washington's Neutrality Proclamation.
Citizen Genet arrives in United States.
First Democratic societies established.

1794 • Whiskey Rebellion.
Battle of Fallen Timbers.

1795 • Treaty of Greenville.
Jay's Treaty.

1796 • Treaty of San Lorenzo.
Washington's Farewell Address.
John Adams elected president.

1798 • XYZ Affair.
Alien and Sedition Acts.
Eleventh Amendment to the Constitution ratified.

1798–1799 • Virginia and Kentucky Resolutions.

1798–1800 • Quasi-War between United States and France.

1799 • Russia establishes colony in Alaska.
Fries Rebellion in Pennsylvania.
Handsome Lake begins reform movement among Senecas.

1800 • Gabriel's Rebellion in Virginia.
Thomas Jefferson elected president.

There was nothing surprising about the unanimity of Washington's victory. His leadership during the Revolutionary War and the Constitutional Convention earned him a reputation as a national hero whose abilities and integrity far surpassed those of his peers. Because of his exalted stature, Washington was able to calm Americans' fears of unlimited executive power.

Traveling slowly over the nation's miserable roads, the men entrusted with launching the federal experiment began assembling in New York, the new national capital, in March 1789. Because so few members were on hand, Congress opened its session a month late. George Washington did not arrive until April 23 and took his oath of office a week later.

The Constitution mentioned the executive departments only in passing, required the president to obtain the Senate's "advice and consent" to his nominees to head these bureaus, and made all executive personnel liable to impeachment. Otherwise, Congress was free to determine the organization and accountability of what became known as the cabinet. The first cabinet, established by Congress, consisted of five departments, headed by the secretaries of state, treasury, and war and by the attorney general and postmaster general. Vice President John Adams's tie-breaking vote defeated a proposal that would have forbidden the president from dismissing cabinet officers without Senate approval. This outcome reinforced the president's authority to make and carry out policy; it also separated the powers of the executive and legislative branches beyond what the Constitution required, and so made the president a more equal partner with Congress.

The Federal Judiciary and the Bill of Rights

The Constitution authorized Congress to establish federal courts below the level of the Supreme Court, but it offered no guidance in structuring a judicial system. Many citizens feared that the new federal courts would ride roughshod over local customs. Every state had gradually devised its own time-honored blend of judicial procedures. Any attempt to force states to abandon their legal heritages would have produced strong counterdemands that federal justice be narrowly restricted.

In passing the **Judiciary Act** of 1789, Congress managed to quiet popular apprehensions by establishing in each state a federal district court that operated according to local procedures. As the Constitution stipulated, the Supreme Court exercised final jurisdiction. Congress had struck a compromise between nationalists and states' rights advocates, one that respected state traditions while offering wide access to federal justice.

The Constitution offered some protection of citizens' individual rights. It barred Congress from passing ex post facto laws (criminalizing previously legal actions and then punishing those who had engaged in them) and bills of attainder (proclaiming a person's guilt and stipulating punishment without a trial). Nevertheless, the absence of a comprehensive bill of rights had led several delegates at Philadelphia to refuse to sign the Constitution and had been a condition of several states' ratification of the new frame of government. James Madison, who had been elected to the House of Representatives, played the leading role in drafting the ten amendments that became known as the **Bill of Rights** (see Appendix).

The First Amendment guaranteed the most fundamental freedoms of expression—religion, speech, press, and political activity—against federal interference. The Second Amendment ensured that "a well-regulated militia" would preserve the nation's security by guaranteeing "the right of the people to bear arms." Along with the Third

Amendment, it sought to protect citizens from what eighteenth-century Britons and Americans alike considered the most sinister embodiment of tyrannical power: standing armies. The Fourth through Eighth Amendments limited the police powers of the state by guaranteeing individuals' fair treatment in legal and judicial proceedings. The Ninth and Tenth Amendments reserved to the people or to the states powers not allocated to the federal government under the Constitution, but Madison headed off proposals to limit federal power more explicitly. In general, the Bill of Rights imposed no serious check on the Framers' nationalist objectives. The ten amendments were submitted to the states and ratified by December 1791.

HAMILTON'S DOMESTIC POLICIES, 1789–1794

President Washington left his secretary of the treasury, **Alexander Hamilton,** in charge of setting the administration's domestic priorities. Hamilton quickly emerged as an imaginative and dynamic statesman with a sweeping program for strengthening the federal government and promoting economic development. While Hamilton succeeded in pushing his program through Congress, the controversies surrounding his program undermined popular support for Federalist policies.

Hamilton and His Objectives   Even more than most Federalists, Hamilton was an extreme nationalist. Born on the British Caribbean island of Nevis in 1755, Hamilton arrived in New York in 1772. Serving on Washington's staff during the Revolutionary War, the brilliant Hamilton gained extraordinary influence over the future president. During the Annapolis and Philadelphia conventions, and while writing many of the Federalist Papers (see Chapter 6), he forcefully advocated creating a strong national government and an economic environment attractive to investment.

In Hamilton's mind, the most immediate danger facing the United States concerned the possibility of war with Britain, Spain, or both. The Republic could finance a major war only by borrowing heavily, but because Congress under the Confederation had not assumed responsibility for the Revolutionary debt, the nation's credit was weakened abroad and at home.

Hamilton also feared that the Union might disintegrate because Americans tended to think first of state and local loyalties and private interests. For him, the Constitution's adoption had been a close victory of national over state authority. Now he worried that the states might reassert power over the new government. If this happened, he doubted whether the nation could prevent ruinous trade discrimination between states, deter foreign aggression, and avoid civil war. Hamilton concluded that the federal government's survival depended not on building popular support but on cultivating politically influential citizens through a straightforward appeal to their financial interests. Private ambitions would then serve the national welfare.

Establishing the Nation's Credit   Finding the nation's Revolutionary war debts in disarray, the First Congress requested that Hamilton's Treasury Department investigate the war debt. Hamilton responded in January 1790 with the first of two **Reports on the Public Credit,** containing recommendations that would at once strengthen the country's credit, enable it to defer paying its

Alexander Hamilton, by John Trumbull, 1792 *Hamilton's self-confident pride clearly shines through in this portrait, painted at the height of his influence in the Washington administration.*

debt, and entice wealthy investors to place their capital at its service. The report listed $54 million in U.S. debt, $42 million of which was owed to Americans, and the rest to Europeans. Hamilton estimated that on top of the national debt, the states had debts of $25 million, some of which the United States had promised to reimburse.

Hamilton's first major recommendation was that the federal government support the national debt by "funding" it—that is, raise the $54 million needed to honor the debt by selling an equal sum in new government bonds. Purchasers of these securities would choose from several combinations of federal "stock" and western lands. Those who wished could retain their original bonds and earn 4 percent interest. All of the options would reduce interest payments on the debt from the full 6 percent set by the Confederation Congress. Hamilton knew that creditors would not object to this reduction because their investments would now be more valuable and more secure.

Second, the report proposed that the federal government pay off the $25 million in state debts remaining from the Revolution. This "assumption" of state debts would be funded along with the national debt in the manner described above.

Hamilton exhorted the government to use the money earned by selling federal lands in the West to pay off the $12 million owed to Europeans as quickly as possible. In a Second Report on the Public Credit, submitted to Congress in December 1790, he argued that the Treasury could easily accumulate the interest owed on the remaining $42 million by collecting customs duties on imports and an excise tax (a tax on domestic products transported within a nation's borders) on whiskey. In addition, Hamilton proposed that money owed to American citizens should be made a permanent debt. That is, he urged that the government not attempt to repay the $42 million principal but instead keep paying interest to bondholders. Under Hamilton's plan, the only burden on taxpayers would be the small annual cost of interest. The government could uphold the national credit at minimal expense, without ever paying off the debt itself.

Hamilton advocated a perpetual debt as a lasting means of uniting the economic fortunes of the nation's creditors to the United States. In an age when financial investments were notoriously risky, the federal government would protect the savings of wealthy bondholders through conservative policies while offering an interest rate competitive with the Bank of England's. The guarantee of future interest payments would unite the interests of the moneyed class with those of the government. Few other investments would entail so little risk.

Hamilton's recommendations provoked immediate controversy. Although no one in Congress doubted that they would greatly enhance the country's fiscal reputation, many objected that those least deserving of reward would gain the most. The original owners of more than three-fifths of the debt certificates issued by the Continental Congress were Revolutionary patriots of modest means who had long before sold their certificates for a fraction of their promised value, usually out of dire financial need. Foreseeing that the government would fund the debt, wealthy speculators had bought the certificates and now stood to reap huge gains at the expense of the original owners, even collecting interest that had accrued before they purchased the certificates. "That the case of those who parted with their securities from necessity is a hard one, cannot be denied," Hamilton admitted. But making exceptions would be even worse.

Hamilton's plan to fund the debt generated widespread resentment because it would reward rich profiteers while ignoring the wartime sacrifices of soldiers and other ordinary citizens. To Hamilton's surprise, Madison—his longtime colleague—emerged as one of the chief opponents of funding. Facing opposition to the plan in his home state of Virginia, Madison tried but failed to obtain compensation for original owners who had sold their certificates. Congress rejected his proposal primarily on the grounds that it would weaken the nation's credit.

Opposition to Hamilton's proposal that the federal government assume states' war debts also ran high. Only Massachusetts, Connecticut, and South Carolina had failed to make effective provisions for satisfying their creditors. Understandably, the issue stirred the fiercest indignation in the South, which except for South Carolina had paid off 83 percent of its debt. Madison and others maintained that to allow residents of the laggard states to escape heavy taxes while others had liquidated theirs at great expense was to reward irresponsibility.

Southern hostility almost defeated assumption. In the end, however, Hamilton managed to save his proposal by enlisting Secretary of State Thomas Jefferson's help. Jefferson and other Virginians expected that moving the capital to the Potomac River would make their state a national crossroads and thus help preserve its position as the largest, most influential state. In return for the northern votes necessary to transfer the capital, Hamilton secured enough Virginians' support to win the battle for assumption. The capital would move in the following year to Philadelphia and remain there until a new capital city was built. Despite this concession, the debate over state debts confirmed many white southerners' suspicions that northern financial and commercial interests would benefit from Hamilton's policies at their expense.

Congressional enactment in 1790 of Hamilton's recommendations dramatically reversed the nation's fiscal standing. Thereafter, European investors grew so enthusiastic about U.S. bonds that by 1792 some securities were selling at 10 percent above face value.

Creating a National Bank

Having significantly expanded the stock of capital available for investment, Hamilton intended to direct that money toward projects that would diversify the national economy through a federally chartered bank. Accordingly, in December 1790 he presented Congress with the **Report on a National Bank.**

The proposed bank would raise $10 million through a public stock offering. Private investors could purchase shares by paying for three-quarters of their value in government bonds. In this way, the bank would capture a significant portion of the recently funded debt and make it available for loans; it would also receive a substantial and steady flow of interest payments from the Treasury. Anyone buying shares under these circumstances had little chance of losing money and was positioned to profit handsomely.

Hamilton argued that the Bank of the United States would cost the taxpayers nothing and greatly benefit the nation. It would provide a safe place for the federal government to deposit tax revenues, make inexpensive loans to the government when taxes fell short, and help relieve the scarcity of hard cash by issuing paper notes that would circulate as money. Furthermore, it would possess authority to regulate the business practices of state banks. Above all, the bank would provide much needed credit to expand the economy.

Hamilton's critics denounced his proposal for a national bank, interpreting it as a dangerous scheme that would give a small, elite group special power to influence the government. These critics believed that the Bank of England had undermined the integrity of government in Britain. Shareholders of the new Bank of the United States could just as easily become the tools of unscrupulous politicians. If significant numbers in Congress owned bank stock, they would likely support the bank even at the cost of the national good. Jefferson openly opposed Hamilton, claiming that the bank would be "a machine for the corruption of the legislature [Congress]." Another Virginian, John Taylor, predicted that the bank would take over the country, which would thereafter, he quipped, be known as the United States of the Bank.

Madison led the opposition to the bank in Congress, arguing that it was unconstitutional. He pointed out that the Philadelphia convention had rejected a proposal giving Congress just such power. Unless Congress closely followed the Constitution, he and other critics argued, the central government might oppress the states and trample individual liberties, just as Parliament had done to the colonies. Strictly limiting federal power seemed the surest way of preventing the United States from degenerating into a corrupt despotism.

Congress approved the bank by only a thin margin. Uncertain of the bank's constitutionality, Washington turned to both Jefferson and Hamilton for advice before signing the measure into law. Like many southern planters whose investments in slaves left them short of capital and often in debt, Jefferson distrusted banking. Moreover, his fear of excessively concentrated economic and political power led him, like Madison, to favor a "strict interpretation" of the Constitution. "To take a single step beyond the boundaries thus specifically drawn around the powers of Congress is to take possession of a boundless field of power no longer susceptible of any definition," warned Jefferson.

Hamilton fought back, urging Washington to sign the bill. Because the Constitution authorized Congress to enact all measures "necessary and proper" (Article I, Section 8), Hamilton contended, it could execute such measures. The only unconstitutional activities of the national government, he concluded, were those expressly prohibited. In the end, the president accepted Hamilton's argument for a "loose interpretation" of the Constitution. In February 1791 the Bank of the United States obtained a charter guaranteeing its existence for twenty years. Washington's acceptance of the principle of loose interpretation was an important victory for those advocating an active, assertive national government. But the split between Jefferson and Hamilton, and Washington's siding with the latter, signaled a deepening political divide within the administration.

Emerging Partisanship
Hamilton's attempt to build political support for Federalist policies by appealing to economic self-interest proved highly successful but also divisive. His arrangements for rescuing the nation's credit provided enormous gains for the speculators, merchants, and other "monied men" of the port cities who by 1790 held most of the Revolutionary debt. As holders of bank stock, these same groups had yet another reason to favor centralized national authority. Assumption of the state debts liberated New England, New Jersey, and South Carolina taxpayers from a crushing burden. Hamilton's efforts to promote industry, commerce, and shipping also struck a responsive chord among entrepreneurs in the Northeast (see below). Federalists dominated politics in New England, New Jersey, and South Carolina, and had considerable strength in Pennsylvania and New York.

Opposition to Hamilton's program was strongest in sections of the country where it offered few benefits. Southern reaction to Hamilton's program, for example, was overwhelmingly negative. Outside of Charleston, South Carolina, few southerners retained Revolutionary certificates in 1790. The Bank of the United States attracted few southern stockholders, and it allocated very little capital for loans there.

Hamilton's plans offered little to the West, where agriculture remained unprofitable without the right to export through New Orleans. In Pennsylvania and New York, too, the uneven effect of Hamiltonian policies generated dissatisfaction. Resentment against a national economic program whose main beneficiaries seemed to be eastern "monied men" and New Englanders who refused to pay their debts gradually united westerners, southerners, and some mid-Atlantic citizens into a political coalition that challenged the Federalists and called for a return to the "true principles" of republicanism.

With Hamilton having presented his measures as "Federalist," Jefferson, Madison, and their supporters began referring to themselves as "republicans." In this way, they implied that Hamilton's schemes to centralize the national government would threaten liberty. Besides appealing to Federalist opponents of Hamilton's policies, Jefferson and Madison reached out to former Antifederalists whose ranks had been fatally weakened after the election of 1788. In 1791, they supported the establishment in Philadelphia of an opposition newspaper, *The National Gazette*, whose editor, Philip Freneau, had been an ardent Antifederalist. For the year preceding the election of 1792, Freneau attacked Hamilton relentlessly, accusing him of trying to create an aristocracy and a monarchy in America. Hamilton responded vigorously to the attacks through his own column in Philadelphia's Federalist newspaper, *The Gazette of the United States.* Using pseudonyms, he also wrote columns in which he attacked Jefferson as an enemy of President Washington and revealed that he had lured Freneau to the capital by hiring him as a translator in the State Department.

Although political partisanship intensified as the election approached, there was no organized political campaigning. For one thing, most voters believed that organized factions or parties were inherently corrupt and were threats to liberty. The Constitution's Framers had neither wanted nor planned for political parties. Indeed, in *Federalist* No. 10, James Madison had argued that the Constitution would prevent the rise of national political factions. For another thing, George Washington, by appearing to be above the partisan disputes, remained supremely popular.

Meeting in 1792, the electoral college was again unanimous in choosing Washington to be president. John Adams was reelected vice president but by a far closer vote than in 1788, receiving 77 votes compared to 50 for George Clinton, the Antifederalist governor of New York.

The Whiskey Rebellion   Hamilton's program not only sparked an angry debate in Congress but also helped ignite a civil insurrection in 1794 called the **Whiskey Rebellion.** Reflecting serious regional and class tensions, this popular uprising was the young republic's first serious crisis.

As part of his financial program, Hamilton had recommended an excise tax on domestically produced whiskey (see above). He insisted that such a tax would not only help in financing the national debt but would improve morals by inducing Americans to drink less liquor. Though Congress enacted the tax, many members doubted that Americans (who on average annually consumed six gallons of hard liquor per adult) would submit tamely to limitations on their drinking. James Jackson of Georgia, for example, warned the administration that his constituents "have long been in the habit of getting drunk and that they will get drunk in defiance of . . . all the excise duties which Congress might be weak or wicked enough to pass."

The validity of such doubts became apparent in September 1791 when a crowd tarred and feathered an excise agent near Pittsburgh. Western Pennsylvanians found the new tax especially burdensome. Unable to ship their crops to world markets through New Orleans, most farmers had grown accustomed to distilling their rye or corn into alcohol, which could be carried across the Appalachians at a fraction of the price charged for bulkier grain. Hamilton's excise equaled 25 percent of whiskey's retail value, enough to wipe out a farmer's profit.

The law also stipulated that trials for evading the tax be conducted in federal courts. Any western Pennsylvanian indicted for noncompliance thus had to travel three hundred miles to Philadelphia. Not only would the accused face a jury of unsympathetic easterners, but he would also have to bear the cost of the long journey and lost earnings while at court, in addition to fines and other court penalties if found guilty. Moreover, Treasury officials rarely enforced the law rigorously outside western Pennsylvania. For all these reasons, western Pennsylvanians complained that the whiskey excise was excessively burdensome.

In a scene reminiscent of pre- and post-Revolutionary popular protests, large-scale resistance erupted in July 1794. One hundred men attacked a U.S. marshal serving sixty delinquent taxpayers with summonses to appear in court at Philadelphia. A crowd of five hundred burned the chief revenue officer's house after a shootout with federal soldiers assigned to protect him. Roving bands torched buildings, assaulted tax collectors, chased government supporters from the region, and flew a flag symbolizing an independent country that they hoped to create from six western counties.

Echoing elites' denunciations of earlier protests, Hamilton condemned the rebellion as simple lawlessness. He pointed out that Congress had reduced the tax rate per gallon in 1792 and had recently voted to allow state judges in western Pennsylvania to hear trials. Showing the same anxiety he had expressed six years earlier during Shays's Rebellion (see Chapter 6), Washington concluded that failure to respond strongly to the uprising would encourage outbreaks in other western areas where distillers were avoiding the tax.

Washington accordingly mustered nearly thirteen thousand militiamen from Pennsylvania and neighboring states to march west under his command. Opposition evaporated once the troops reached the Appalachians, and the president left Hamilton in charge of making arrests. Of about 150 suspects seized, Hamilton sent twenty in irons to Philadelphia. Two men received death sentences, but Washington eventually pardoned them both, noting that one was a "simpleton" and the other "insane."

The Whiskey Rebellion set severe limits on public opposition to federal policies. In the early 1790s, many Americans—including the whiskey rebels—still assumed that it was legitimate to protest unpopular laws using the same tactics with which they had blocked parliamentary measures like the Stamp Act. Indeed, western Pennsylvanians had justified their resistance with exactly such reasoning. By firmly suppressing the first major challenge to national authority, Washington served notice that citizens who resorted to violent or other extralegal means of political action would feel the full force of federal authority. In this way, he gave voice and substance to elites' fears of "mobocracy," now resurfacing in reaction to the French Revolution (see below).

THE UNITED STATES IN A WIDER WORLD, 1789–1796

By 1793, disagreements over foreign affairs had emerged as the primary source of friction in American public life. The political divisions created by Hamilton's financial program hardened into ideologically oriented factions that argued vehemently over whether the country's foreign policy should favor industrial and overseas mercantile interests or those of farmers, planters, small businesses, and artisans. Moreover, having ratified its Constitution in the year that the French Revolution began (1789), the new government entered the international arena as European tensions were once again exploding. The rapid spread of pro-French revolutionary ideas and organizations alarmed Europe's monarchs and aristocrats. Perceiving a threat to their social orders as well as their territorial interests, most European nations declared war on France by early 1793. For most of the next twenty-two years—until Napoleon's final defeat in 1815—Europe and the Atlantic world remained in a state of war.

While most Americans hoped that their nation could avoid this latest European conflict, the fact was that the interests and ambitions of many citizens collided at critical points with those of Britain, France, and Spain. Thus, differences over foreign policy fused with differences over domestic affairs, further intensifying partisanship in American politics.

Spanish Power in Western North America

Stimulated by its winning Louisiana from France in 1762 (see Chapter 5), Spain enjoyed a limited revival of its North American fortunes in the late eighteenth century. In what is now northern Mexico, New Mexico, and Texas, Spain built new presidios, at which it stationed more troops, and coordinated the actions of military and civilian officials. North of the Rio Grande, Spain sought to force nomadic Apaches, Navajos, and Comanches to end their damaging raids on Spanish colonists and their Pueblo Indian allies and to submit to Spanish authority. This effort succeeded, but only up to a point. The Apaches and Navajos moved farther from Spanish settlements, but primarily to avoid Indian enemies rather than Spanish attacks. Ironically, Spanish colonists remained dependent on the Comanches as sources of European goods, which the Comanches obtained through trade networks extending to Louisiana and to American territory east of the Mississippi. By 1800, nomadic Indians had agreed to cease their raids in New Mexico and Texas although parties of warriors sometimes acted on their own. Whether the truce would become a permanent peace depended on whether Spain could strengthen and broaden its imperial position in North America.

Spain's efforts in New Mexico and Texas were part of its larger effort to counter European rivals for North American territory and influence. The first challenge arose in the northern Pacific Ocean, where Spain had enjoyed an unchallenged monopoly for more than two centuries. Russian traders in Siberia made inroads into North America during the 1740s by crossing the Bering Sea and brutally forcing the indigenous Aleut peoples to supply them with sea otter pelts, spreading deadly diseases in the process. As commercial overhunting exterminated the sea otter in the westernmost Aleutians, the traders moved eastward to mainland Alaska, where they would establish a colony in 1799.

Perceiving Russia's move into Alaska as a threat, Spain responded by expanding northward on the Pacific coast from Mexico. In 1769, it established the province of **Alta California** (the present American state of California). Efforts to encourage large-scale Mexican immigration to Alta California failed, leaving the colony to be sustained by a chain of religious missions, several presidios, and a few large ranchos (ranches). Seeking support against inland adversaries, coastal Indians welcomed the Spanish at first. But the Franciscan missionaries sought to convert them to Catholicism and "civilize" them by imposing harsh disciplinary measures and putting them to work in vineyards and in other enterprises. Meanwhile, Spanish colonists' spreading of epidemic and venereal diseases among natives precipitated a decline in the Native American population from about seventy-two thousand in 1770 to about eighteen thousand by 1830.

Having gained Louisiana and strengthened its positions in Texas, New Mexico, and California, Spain attempted to make alliances with Indians in the area later known as Arizona. In this way Spain hoped to dominate the colonization of North America between the Pacific and the Mississippi River. But resistance from the Hopi, Quechan (Yuma), and other Native Americans thwarted these hopes. Fortunately for Spain, Arizona had not yet attracted the interest of other imperial powers.

Challenging	Between the Appalachians and the Mississippi River, Spain,

Challenging American Expansion, 1789–1792

Between the Appalachians and the Mississippi River, Spain, Britain, the United States, and numerous Indian nations jockeyed for advantage in a region that all considered central to their interests and that Native Americans regarded as homelands.

Realizing that the United States was in no position to dictate developments immediately in the West, President Washington pursued a course of patient diplomacy that was intended "to preserve the country in peace if I can, and to be prepared for war if I cannot." The prospect of peace improved in 1789 when Spain unexpectedly opened New Orleans to American commerce, although exports remained subject to a 15 percent duty.

Thereafter, Spanish officials continued to bribe well-known political figures in Tennessee and Kentucky, among them a former general on Washington's staff, James Wilkinson. Thomas Scott, a congressman from western Pennsylvania, meanwhile schemed with the British. Between 1791 and 1796, the federal government anxiously admitted Vermont, Kentucky, and Tennessee to the Union, partly in the hope of strengthening their residents' flickering loyalty to the United States.

Washington also tried to weaken Spanish influence by neutralizing Spain's most important ally, the Creek Indians. The Creeks numbered more than twenty thousand, including perhaps five thousand warriors, and they bore a fierce hostility toward Georgian settlers, whom they called Ecunnaunuxulgee, or "the greedy people who want our lands." In 1790, the Creek leader Alexander McGillivray signed the Treaty of New York with the United States. The treaty permitted American settlers to remain on lands in the Georgia Piedmont fought over since 1786 (see Chapter 6), but in other respects preserved Creek territory against U.S. expansion. Washington insisted that Georgia restore to the Creeks' allies, the Chickasaws and Choctaws, the vast area along the Mississippi River known as the Yazoo Tract, which Georgia claimed and had begun selling off to white land speculators (see Chapter 8).

Washington and his secretary of war, Henry Knox, adopted a harsher policy toward Native Americans who resisted efforts by settlers and other whites to occupy the Ohio valley. In 1790, their first military effort collapsed when a coalition of tribes chased General Josiah Harmar and 1,500 troops from the Maumee River. A second campaign failed in November 1791, when one thousand Shawnee warriors surrounded an encampment of fourteen hundred soldiers led by General Arthur St. Clair. More than six hundred soldiers were killed and several hundred wounded before the survivors could flee for safety.

With Native Americans having twice humiliated U.S. forces in the Northwest Territory, Washington's western policy was in shambles. Matters worsened in 1792 when Spain persuaded the Creeks to renounce the Treaty of New York and resume hostilities. Ultimately, the damage done to U.S. prestige by these setbacks convinced many Americans that the combined strength of Britain, Spain, and the Native Americans could be counterbalanced only by an alliance with France.

France and Factional Politics, 1793

One of the most momentous events in world history, the French Revolution began in 1789. The French were inspired by America's Revolution, and Americans were initially sympathetic as France abolished nobles' privileges, wrote a constitution, bravely repelled invading armies from Austria and Prussia, and proclaimed itself a republic. But the Revolution took a radical turn in 1793 when France declared an

New Orleans   *The French and Spanish developed this port city during the eighteenth century. By century's end many in the United States saw New Orleans as a key to their nation's future expansion and prosperity.*

international revolutionary war of all peoples against all kings and began a "Reign of Terror," executing not only the king but dissenting revolutionaries.

Americans grew bitterly divided in their attitudes toward the French Revolution and over how the United States should respond to it. While republicans such as Jefferson supported it as an assault on monarchy and tyranny, Federalists like Hamilton denounced France as a "mobocracy" and supported Great Britain in resisting its efforts to sow revolution abroad.

White southern slave owners were among France's fiercest supporters. In 1793, a slave uprising in the Caribbean colony of Saint Domingue became a revolution against French rule. Thousands of terrified French planters fled to the United States, recounting how British invaders had supported the uprising. Inspired by the American and French Revolutions, blacks had fought with determination and inflicted heavy casualties on French colonists. Recalling British courting of their own slaves during the Revolution, southern whites concluded that the British had intentionally sparked the bloodbath and would do the same in the South. Anti-British hysteria even eroded South Carolina's loyalty to Federalist policies.

Many northerners, on the other hand, were more repelled by the blood being shed in revolutionary France. The revolution was an abomination—"an open hell," thundered Massachusetts's Fisher Ames, "still ringing with agonies and blasphemies, still smoking with sufferings and crimes." Middle-class and elite Protestants in New England detested the French for worshiping Reason instead of God. Middle Atlantic Federalists, while perhaps less religious than New Englanders, condemned French leaders as evil radicals who incited the poor against the rich.

Northern and southern reactions to the French Revolution also diverged for economic reasons. In the North, merchants' growing antagonism toward France reflected the facts that virtually all the nation's merchant marine operated from northern ports and that most of the country's foreign trade was with Great Britain. Merchants, shippers, and ordinary sailors in New England, Philadelphia, and New York feared that an alliance with France would provoke British retaliation against this valuable commerce, and they argued that the United States could win valuable concessions by demonstrating friendly intentions toward Britain. Indeed, some influential members of Parliament now seemed to favor liberalizing trade with the United States.

Southerners had no such reasons to favor Britain. Southern spokesmen viewed Americans' reliance on British commerce as a menace to national self-determination and wished to divert most U.S. trade to France. Jefferson and Madison repeatedly demanded that British imports be reduced through the imposition of steep discriminatory duties on cargoes shipped from England and Scotland in British vessels. Federalist opponents warned that Britain, which sold more manufactured goods to the United States than to any other country, would not stand by while a weak French ally pushed it into depression. If Congress adopted a discriminatory tariff, Hamilton predicted in 1792, "there would be, in less than six months, an open war between the United States and Great Britain."

Enthusiasm for a pro-French foreign policy intensified in the southern and western states after France went to war against Spain and Great Britain in 1793. Increasingly, western settlers and speculators hoped for a decisive French victory that, they reasoned, would induce Britain and Spain to cease blocking U.S. expansion. The United States could then insist on free navigation of the Mississippi, force the evacuation of British garrisons, and end both nations' support of Native American resistance.

After declaring war on Britain and Spain, France actively tried to embroil the United States in the conflict. The French dispatched Edmond Genet as minister to the United States with orders to mobilize republican sentiment in support of France, enlist American mercenaries to conquer Spanish territories and attack British shipping, and strengthen the French-American alliance. Much to the French government's dislike, however, President Washington issued a proclamation of American neutrality on April 22, 1793.

Undeterred by Washington's proclamation, **Citizen Genet** (as he was known in French Revolutionary style) found no shortage of southern volunteers for his American Foreign Legion. Making generals of George Rogers Clark of Kentucky and Elisha Clarke of Georgia, Genet directed them to seize Spanish garrisons at New Orleans and St. Augustine. Clark defied Washington's Neutrality Proclamation by advertising for recruits for his mission in Kentucky newspapers, and Clarke began drilling three hundred troops on the Florida border. But the French failed to provide adequate funds for either campaign. Although the American recruits were willing to fight for France, few were willing to fight for free, so both expeditions eventually dispersed.

However, Genet did not need funds to outfit privateers, who financed themselves with captured plunder. By the summer of 1793, almost a thousand Americans were at sea in a dozen ships flying the French flag. These privateers seized more than eighty British vessels and towed them to U.S. ports, where French consuls sold the ships and cargoes at auction.

Diplomacy and War, 1793–1796 Although the Washington administration swiftly closed U.S. harbors to Genet's buccaneers and requested that France recall him, Genet's exploits provoked an Anglo-American crisis. George III's ministers decided that only a massive show of force would deter American support for France. Accordingly, on November 6, 1793, the Privy Council issued secret orders confiscating any foreign ships trading with the French in the West Indies. The council purposely delayed publishing these instructions until after most American ships carrying winter provisions to the Caribbean left port, so that their captains would not know that they were sailing into a war zone. The Royal Navy then seized more than 250 American vessels.

Meanwhile, the Royal Navy inflicted a second galling indignity—the impressment (forced enlistment) of crewmen from U.S. ships. Thousands of British sailors had previously fled to the U.S. merchant marine, where they hoped to find an easier life than under the tough, poorly paying British system. In late 1793, British naval officers began routinely inspecting American crews for British subjects, whom they then impressed as the king's sailors. Overzealous commanders sometimes broke royal orders by taking U.S. citizens, and in any case the British did not recognize former subjects' right to adopt American citizenship. Impressment scratched a raw nerve in most Americans, who argued that their government's willingness to defend its citizens from such abuse was a critical test of national character.

Meanwhile, Britain, Spain, and many Native Americans continued to challenge the United States for control of territory west of the Appalachians. During a large intertribal council in February 1794, the Shawnees and other Ohio Indians welcomed an inflammatory speech by Canada's royal governor denying U.S. claims north of the Ohio River and urging destruction of every white settlement in the Northwest. Soon British troops were building an eighth garrison on U.S. soil, Fort Miami, near present-day Toledo. Meanwhile, the Spanish encroached on territory claimed by the United States by building Fort San Fernando in 1794 at what is now Memphis, Tennessee.

Hoping to halt the drift toward war, Washington launched three desperate initiatives in 1794. He authorized General Anthony Wayne to negotiate a treaty with the Shawnees and their Ohio valley allies, sent Chief Justice John Jay to Great Britain, and dispatched Thomas Pinckney to Spain.

Having twice defeated federal armies, the Shawnees and their allies scoffed at Washington's peace offer. "Mad Anthony" Wayne then led thirty-five hundred U.S. troops deep into Shawnee homelands, building forts and ruthlessly burning every village within his reach. On August 20, 1794, his troops routed four hundred Shawnees at the Battle of Fallen Timbers just two miles from British Fort Miami. (The British closed the fort's gates, denying entry to their fleeing allies.) Wayne's army then built an imposing stronghold to challenge British authority in the Northwest, appropriately named Fort Defiance. Indian morale plummeted, not only because of the American victory and their own losses but also because of Britain's betrayal.

In August 1795, Wayne compelled the Shawnees and eleven other tribes to sign the **Treaty of Greenville,** which opened most of modern-day Ohio and a portion of Indiana to white settlement and ended U.S.-Indian hostilities in the region for sixteen years. But aside from the older leaders who were pressured to sign the treaty, most Shawnees knew that American designs on Indian land in the Northwest had not been satisfied and would soon resurface. Among them was a rising young warrior named Tecumseh (see Chapter 8).

Wayne's victory at Fallen Timbers helped John Jay win a British promise to withdraw troops from American soil by June 1796. Jay also managed to gain access to West Indian markets for small American ships, but only by bargaining away other American complaints as well as U.S. rights to load cargoes of sugar, molasses, and coffee from

French colonies during wartime. Aside from fellow Federalists, few Americans interpreted **Jay's Treaty** as preserving peace with honor.

Jay's Treaty left Britain free not only to violate American neutrality but also to undermine profits by restricting U.S. trade with France. Opponents condemned the treaty's failure to end impressment and predicted that Great Britain would thereafter force even more Americans into the Royal Navy. Slave owners were resentful that Jay had not obtained compensation for slaves taken away by the British army during the Revolution. After the Senate ratified the treaty by just one vote in 1795, Jay nervously joked that he could find his way across the country at night by the fires of rallies burning him in effigy.

Despite its unpopularity, Jay's Treaty defused an explosive crisis with Great Britain before war became inevitable and finally ended Britain's post-Revolutionary occupation of U.S. territory. The treaty also helped stimulate an enormous expansion of American trade. Upon its ratification, British governors in the West Indies opened their harbors to U.S. ships. Other British officials permitted Americans to trade with India, even though such trade infringed on the East India Company's monopoly. Within a few years, American exports to the British Empire shot up 300 percent.

On the heels of Jay's controversial treaty came an unqualified diplomatic triumph engineered by Thomas Pinckney. Ratified in 1796, the **Treaty of San Lorenzo** with Spain (also called Pinckney's Treaty) won westerners the right of unrestricted, duty-free access to world markets via the Mississippi River. Spain also promised to recognize the thirty-first parallel as the United States' southern boundary, to dismantle its fortifications on American soil, and to discourage Native American attacks against western settlers.

By 1796, the Washington administration could claim to have successfully extended American authority throughout the trans-Appalachian West, opened the Mississippi for western exports, enabled northeastern shippers to regain British markets, and kept the nation out of a dangerous European war. As the popular outcry over Jay's Treaty demonstrated, however, the nation's foreign policy left Americans much more deeply divided in 1796 than they had been in 1789.

PARTIES AND POLITICS, 1793–1800

By the time Washington was reelected, the controversies over domestic and foreign policy had led to the formation of two distinct political factions. During the president's second term, these factions became formal political parties, Federalists and Republicans, which advanced their members' interests, ambitions, and ideals. Thereafter, the two parties waged a bitter battle, culminating in the election of 1800.

Ideological
Confrontation,
1793–1794

American attitudes about events in France accelerated the polarization of American politics. Linking the French Revolution and the Whiskey Rebellion, Federalists trembled at the thought of guillotines and "mob rule." They were also horrified by the sight of artisans in Philadelphia and New York bandying the French revolutionary slogan "Liberty, Equality, Fraternity" and rallying around pro-French politicians such as Jefferson. Citizen Genet had openly encouraged opposition to the Washington administration, and had found hundreds of Americans willing to fight for France. Federalists worried that all of this was just the tip of a revolutionary iceberg.

By the mid-1790s Federalists' worst fears of democracy seemed to have been confirmed. The people, they believed, were not evil-minded but simply undependable and vulnerable to rabble rousers such as Genet. As Senator George Cabot of Massachusetts put it, "the many do not think at all." For Federalists, democracy meant "government by the passions of the multitude." They argued that, as in colonial times, ordinary voters should not be presented with choices over policy, but should vote simply on the basis of the personal merits of elite candidates. Elected officials, they maintained, should rule in the people's name but be independent of direct popular influence.

Republicans offered a very different perspective on government and politics. They stressed the corruption inherent in a powerful government dominated by a highly visible few, and insisted that liberty would be safe only if power were widely diffused among white male property holders.

It might at first glance seem contradictory for southern slave owners to support a radical ideology like republicanism, with its emphasis on liberty and equality. Although a few southern republicans advocated abolishing slavery gradually, most did not trouble themselves over their ownership of human beings. Although expressed in universal terms, the liberty and equality they advocated were intended for white men only.

Political ambition drove men like Jefferson and Madison to rouse ordinary voters' concerns about civic affairs. The widespread awe in which Washington was held inhibited open criticism of him, his policies, and his fellow Federalists. If, however, the Federalists could be held accountable to the public, they would think twice before enacting measures opposed by the majority; or if they persisted in advocating misguided policies, they would ultimately be removed from office. Such reasoning led Jefferson, a wealthy landowner and large slaveholder, to say, "I am not among those who fear the people; they and not the rich, are our dependence for continued freedom."

Jefferson's frustration at being overruled at every turn by Hamilton and Washington finally prompted his resignation from the cabinet in 1793, and thereafter not even the president could halt the widening political split. Each side portrayed itself as the guardian of republican virtue and attacked the other as an illegitimate "cabal" or "faction."

In 1793–1794, opponents of Federalist policies began organizing Democratic (or Republican) societies. The societies formed primarily in seaboard cities but also in the rural South and West. Their members included planters, small farmers and merchants, artisans, distillers, and sailors; conspicuously absent were the clergy, the poor, nonwhites, and women.

The Republican Party, 1794–1796 Neither Jefferson nor Madison belonged to a Democratic society. However, these private clubs helped publicize their views, and they initiated into political activity numerous voters who would later support a new Republican Party.

In 1794, party development reached a decisive stage after Washington openly identified himself with Federalist policies. Republicans attacked the Federalists' pro-British leanings in many local elections and won a slight majority in the House of Representatives. The election signaled the Republicans' transformation from a coalition of officeholders and local societies to a broad-based party capable of coordinating local political campaigns throughout the nation.

Federalists and Republicans alike used the press to mold public opinion. In the 1790s, American journalism came of age as the number of newspapers rose from 92 to 242, mostly in New England and the mid-Atlantic states. By 1800, newspapers had about 140,000 paid subscribers (roughly one-fifth of the eligible voters), and their secondhand readership probably exceeded 300,000. Newspapers of both camps did not hesitate to engage in fear-mongering and character assassination. Federalists accused Republicans of plotting a reign of terror and of conspiring to turn the nation over to France. Republicans charged Federalists with favoring a hereditary aristocracy and even a royal dynasty that would form when John Adams's daughter married George III. Despite the extreme rhetoric, newspaper warfare stimulated many citizens to become politically active.

Washington grew impatient with the nation's growing polarization into openly hostile parties, and he deeply resented Republican charges that he secretly supported alleged Federalist plots to establish a monarchy. "By God," Jefferson reported him swearing, "he [Washington] would rather be in his grave than in his present situation . . . he had rather be on his farm than to be made emperor of the world." Lonely and surrounded by mediocre advisers after Hamilton returned to private life, Washington decided in the spring of 1796 to retire after two terms. Washington recalled Hamilton to give a sharp political twist to his Farewell Address.

The heart of Washington's message was a vigorous condemnation of political parties. Partisan alignments, he insisted, endangered the Republic's survival, especially if they became entangled in disputes over foreign policy. Washington warned that the country's safety depended on citizens' avoiding "excessive partiality for one nation and excessive dislike of another." Otherwise, "real patriots" would be overwhelmed by demagogues championing foreign causes and paid by foreign governments. Aside from scrupulously fulfilling its existing treaty obligations and maintaining its foreign commerce, the United States must avoid "political connection" with Europe and its wars. If the United States gathered its strength under "an efficient government," it could defy any foreign challenge; but if it became sucked into Europe's quarrels, violence, and corruption, the republican experiment was doomed. Washington and Hamilton had skillfully turned republicanism's fear of corruption against their Republican critics. They had also evoked a vision of an America virtuously isolated from foreign intrigue and power politics, which would remain a potent inspiration for long afterward.

Washington left the presidency in 1797 and died in 1799. Like many later presidents, he went out amid a barrage of partisan criticism.

| The Election of 1796 | With the **election of 1796** approaching, the Republicans cultivated a large, loyal body of voters. Their efforts to marshal popular support marked the first time since the Revolution |

that political elites had effectively mobilized non-elites to participate in public affairs. The Republicans' constituency included the Democratic societies, workingmen's clubs, and immigrant-aid associations.

Immigrants became prime targets for Republican recruiters. During the 1790s, the United States absorbed about twenty thousand French refugees from Saint Domingue and more than sixty thousand Irish, many of whom had been exiled for opposing British rule. Although potential immigrant voters were few—comprising less than 2 percent of the electorate—the Irish could make a difference in Pennsylvania and New

York, where public opinion was closely divided and a few hundred immigrant voters could tip the balance toward the Republicans.

In 1796, the presidential candidates were the Federalist vice president John Adams and the Republicans' Jefferson. Republicans expected to win as many southern electoral votes and congressional seats as the Federalists counted on in New England, New Jersey, and South Carolina. The crucial "swing" states were Pennsylvania and New York, where the Republicans fought hard to win the large immigrant vote with their pro-French and anti-British rhetoric. In the end, the Republicans took Pennsylvania but not New York, so that Jefferson lost the presidency by just three electoral votes. As the second-highest vote-getter in the electoral college, he became vice president. The Federalists narrowly regained control of the House and maintained their firm grip on the Senate.

Adams's intellect and devotion to principle have rarely been equaled among American presidents. But the new president was more comfortable with ideas than with people, more theoretical than practical. He inspired trust and often admiration but could not command personal loyalty or inspire the public. Adams's reserved and often stubborn personality likewise left him ill suited to govern, and he ultimately proved unable to unify the country.

The French Crisis, 1798–1799 Even before the election, the French had recognized that Jay's Treaty was a Federalist-sponsored attempt to assist Britain in its war against France. On learning of Jefferson's defeat, France began seizing American ships carrying goods to British ports, and within a year had plundered more than three hundred vessels. The French rubbed in their contempt for the United States by directing that every American captured on a British naval ship (even those involuntarily impressed) should be hanged.

Hoping to avoid war, Adams sent a peace commission to Paris. But the French foreign minister, Charles de Talleyrand, refused to meet the delegation, instead promising through three unnamed agents ("X, Y, and Z") that talks could begin after he received $250,000 and France obtained a loan of $12 million. This barefaced demand for a bribe became known as the XYZ Affair. Americans reacted to it with outrage. "Millions for defense, not one cent for tribute" became the nation's battle cry as the 1798 congressional elections began.

The XYZ Affair discredited the Republicans' foreign policy views, but the party's leaders compounded the damage by refusing to condemn French aggression and opposing Adams's call for military preparations. The Republicans tried to excuse French behavior, whereas the Federalists rode a wave of militant patriotism. In the 1798 elections, Jefferson's supporters were routed almost everywhere, even in the South.

Congress responded to the XYZ Affair by arming fifty-four ships to protect American commerce. During an undeclared Franco-American naval conflict in the Caribbean known as the **Quasi-War** (1798–1800), U.S. forces seized ninety-three French privateers while losing just one vessel. The British navy meanwhile extended the protection of its convoys to America's merchant marine. By early 1799, the French remained a nuisance but were no longer a serious threat at sea.

Meanwhile, the Federalist-dominated Congress tripled the size of the regular army to ten thousand men in 1798, with an automatic expansion to fifty thousand in case of war. Yet the risk of a land war with France was minimal. In reality, the Federalists wanted a military force ready in the event of a civil war, for the crisis had produced near-hysteria about conspiracies being hatched by French and Irish revolutionaries flooding into the United States.

The Alien and Sedition Acts, 1798

The most heated controversies of the late 1790s arose from the Federalists' insistence that the threat of war with France required strict laws to protect national security. In 1798, the Federalist-dominated Congress accordingly passed four measures known collectively as the **Alien and Sedition Acts.** Adams neither requested nor particularly wanted these laws, but he deferred to Federalist congressional leaders and signed them.

The least controversial of the laws, the Alien Enemies Act, outlined procedures for determining whether citizens of a hostile country posed a threat to the United States as spies or saboteurs. If so, they were to be deported or jailed. The law established fundamental principles for protecting national security and respecting the rights of enemy citizens. It was to operate only if Congress declared war and thus was not used until the War of 1812 (see Chapter 8).

Second, the Alien Friends Act, a temporary statute, authorized the president to expel any foreign residents whose activities he considered dangerous. The law did not require proof of guilt, on the assumption that spies would hide or destroy evidence of their crime. Republicans maintained that the law's real purpose was to deport immigrants critical of Federalist policies.

Republicans also denounced the third law, the Naturalization Act. This measure increased the residency requirement for U.S. citizenship from five to fourteen years (the last five continuously in one state), with the purpose of reducing Irish voting.

Finally came the Sedition Act, the only one of these measures enforceable against U.S. citizens. Its alleged purpose was to distinguish between free speech and attempts at encouraging others to violate federal laws or to overthrow the government. But the act defined criminal activity so broadly that it blurred any real distinction between sedition and legitimate political discussion. For example, it prohibited an individual or group from opposing "any measure or measures of the United States"—wording that could be interpreted to ban any criticism of the party in power. Another clause made it illegal to speak, write, or print any statement about the president that would bring him "into contempt or disrepute." Under such restrictions, for example, a newspaper editor might face imprisonment for criticizing an action by Adams or his cabinet members. The Federalist *Gazette of the United States* expressed the twisted logic of the Sedition Act perfectly: "It is patriotism to write in favor of our government—it is sedition to write against it." However one looked at it, the Sedition Act interfered with free speech. Ingeniously, the Federalists wrote the law to expire in 1801 (so that it could not be turned against them if they lost the next election) and to leave them free meanwhile to heap abuse on Vice President Jefferson (who did not participate in the making of government policy).

The principal target of Federalist repression was the opposition press. Four of the five largest Republican newspapers were charged with sedition just as the election campaign of 1800 was getting under way. The attorney general used the Alien Friends Act to threaten Irish journalist John Daly Burk with expulsion (Burk went underground instead). Scottish editor Thomas Callender was being deported when he suddenly qualified for citizenship. Unable to expel Callender, the government tried him for sedition before an all-Federalist jury, which sent him to prison for criticizing the president.

Federalist leaders never intended to fill the jails with Republican martyrs. Rather, they hoped to use a small number of highly visible prosecutions to silence Republican journalists and candidates during the election of 1800. The attorney general charged seventeen persons with sedition and won ten convictions. Among the victims was Republican congressman Matthew Lyon of Vermont ("Ragged Matt, the democrat," to the Federalists), who spent four months in prison for publishing a blast against Adams.

Vocal criticism of Federalist repression erupted during the summer of 1798 in Virginia and Kentucky. Militia commanders in these states mustered their regiments not to drill but to hear speeches demanding that the federal government respect the Bill of Rights. Entire units then signed petitions denouncing the Alien and Sedition Acts. The symbolic implications of these protests were sobering. Young men stepped forward to sign petitions on drumheads with a pen in one hand and a gun in the other, as older officers who had fought in the Continental Army looked on approvingly. It was not hard to imagine Kentucky rifles being substituted for quill pens as the men who had joined one revolution took up arms again.

Ten years earlier, opponents of the Constitution had warned that giving the national government extensive powers would eventually endanger freedom. By 1798, their prediction seemed to have come true. Shocked Republicans realized that because the Federalists controlled all three branches of the government, neither the Bill of Rights nor the system of checks and balances protected individual liberties. In this context, they advanced the doctrine of states' rights as a means of preventing the national government from violating basic freedoms.

Recognizing that opponents of federal power would never prevail in the Supreme Court, which was still dominated by Federalists, Madison and Jefferson anonymously wrote manifestos on states' rights known as the **Virginia and Kentucky Resolutions,** adopted respectively by the legislatures of those states in 1798. Madison's Virginia Resolutions declared that state legislatures had never surrendered their right to judge the constitutionality of federal actions and that they retained an authority called *interposition,* which enabled them to protect the liberties of their citizens. Jefferson's resolution for Kentucky went further by declaring that ultimate sovereignty rested with the states, which empowered them to "nullify" federal laws to which they objected. Although Kentucky's legislature deleted the term "nullify" before approving the resolution in 1799, the intention of both resolutions was to invalidate any federal law in a state that had deemed the law unconstitutional. Although the resolutions were intended as nonviolent protests, they challenged the jurisdiction of federal courts and could have enabled state militias to march into a federal courtroom to halt proceedings at bayonet point.

Although no other state endorsed these resolutions (ten expressed disapproval), their passage demonstrated the great potential for disunion in the late 1790s. So did a minor insurrection called the Fries Rebellion, which broke out in 1799 when crowds of Pennsylvania German farmers released prisoners jailed for refusing to pay taxes needed to fund the national army's expansion. But the disturbance collapsed when federal troops intervened.

The nation's leaders increasingly acted as if a crisis were imminent. Vice President Jefferson hinted that events might push the southern states into secession from the Union, while President Adams hid guns in his home. After passing through Richmond and learning that state officials were purchasing thousands of muskets for the militia, an alarmed Supreme Court justice wrote in January 1799 that "the General Assembly of Virginia are pursuing steps which will lead directly to civil war." A tense atmosphere hung over the Republic as the election of 1800 neared.

The Election of 1800

In the election campaign, the two parties once again rallied around the Federalist Adams and the Republican Jefferson. The leadership of moderates in both parties helped to ensure that the nation survived the **election of 1800** without a civil war. Thus Jefferson and Madison discouraged radical activity that might provoke intervention by the national army, while Adams rejected demands by extreme "High Federalists" that he ensure victory by deliberately sparking an insurrection or asking Congress to declare war on France.

"Nothing but an open war can save us," argued one High Federalist cabinet officer. But when Adams suddenly learned in 1799 that France wanted peace, he proposed a special diplomatic mission. "Surprise, indignation, grief & disgust followed each other in quick succession," said a Federalist senator on hearing the news. Adams obtained Senate approval for his envoys only by threatening to resign and so make Jefferson president. Outraged High Federalists tried unsuccessfully to dump Adams, but their ill-considered maneuver rallied most New Englanders around the stubborn, upright president.

Adams's negotiations with France did not achieve a settlement until 1801, but the expectation that normal—perhaps even friendly—relations with France would resume prevented the Federalists from exploiting charges of Republican sympathy for the enemy. Without the immediate threat of war, moreover, voters grew resentful that in merely two years, taxes had soared 33 percent to support an army that had done nothing except chase terrified Pennsylvania farmers. As the danger of war receded, voters gave the Federalists less credit for standing up to France and more blame for adding $10 million to the national debt.

While High Federalists spitefully withheld the backing that Adams needed to win, Republicans redoubled their efforts to elect Jefferson. They were especially successful in mobilizing voters in Philadelphia and New York, where artisans, farmers, and some entrepreneurs were ready to abandon the Federalists, whom they saw as defenders of privilege and wealth. As a result of Republican efforts, popular interest in politics rose sharply. Voter turnout in 1800 leaped to more than double that of 1788, rising from about 15 percent to almost 40 percent; in hotly contested Pennsylvania and New York, more than half the eligible voters participated.

Adams lost the presidency by just 8 electoral votes out of 138. He would have won if his party had not lost control of New York's state senate, which chose the electors, after a narrow defeat in New York City. Jefferson and his running mate, New York's Aaron Burr, also carried South Carolina after their backers made lavish promises of political favors to that state's legislators.

Although Adams lost, Jefferson's election was not assured. Because all 73 Republican electors voted for both of their party's nominees, the electoral college deadlocked in a Jefferson-Burr tie. Even more seriously than in 1796, the Constitution's failure to anticipate organized, rival parties affected the outcome of the electoral college's vote. The choice of president devolved upon the House of Representatives, where thirty-five ballots over six days produced no result. Aware that Republican voters and electors wanted Jefferson to be president, the wily Burr cast about for Federalist support. But after Hamilton—Burr's bitter rival in New York politics—declared his preference for Jefferson as "by far not so dangerous a man," a Federalist representative abandoned Burr and gave Jefferson the presidency by history's narrowest margin.

ECONOMIC AND SOCIAL CHANGE

During the nation's first twelve years under the Constitution, the spread of economic production for markets, even by households, transformed the lives of many Americans. For some people the changes were for the better and for others for the worse, but for most the ultimate outcome remained uncertain in 1800. At the same time, many Americans were rethinking questions of gender and race in American society.

The fierce political struggles that took place during the same period primarily involved white males, in other words those who had the right to vote and the guarantee of at least minimal civil rights. For those who were not both white and male, the struggle was to achieve those minimal rights or at the very least to survive.

Producing for Markets

For centuries the backbone of European societies and their colonial offshoots had been economies in which most production took place in household settings. At the core of each household was a patriarchal family—the male head, his wife, and their unmarried children. Beyond these family members, most households included other people. Some outsiders were relatives, but most were either boarders or workers—apprentices and journeymen in artisan shops, servants and slaves in well-off urban households, and slaves, "hired hands," and tenant farmers in rural settings. (Even slaves living in separate "quarters" on large plantations labored in an enterprise centered on their owners' households.) Unlike in our modern world, before the nineteenth century nearly everyone worked at what was temporarily or permanently "home." The notion of "going to work" would have struck them as odd.

Although households varied in size and economic orientation, in the late eighteenth century most were on small farms and consisted of only an owner and his family. By 1800, such farm families typically included seven children whose labor contributed to production. While husbands and older sons worked in fields away from the house, wives, daughters, and young sons maintained the barns and gardens near the house. Wives, of course, bore and reared the children as well. As in the colonial period, most farm families produced food and other products largely for their own consumption, adding small surpluses for bartering with neighbors or local merchants.

In the aftermath of the American Revolution, households in the most heavily populated regions of the Northeast began to change. Relatively prosperous farm families, particularly in the mid-Atlantic states, increasingly directed their surplus production to meet the growing demands of urban customers for produce, meat, and dairy products. These families often turned to agricultural experts, whose advice their parents and grandparents had usually, and proudly, spurned. Many farm men introduced clover into the pastures they tended, following the suggestion of one author who maintained that clover "flushes [a cow] to milk." Men also recognized that while milk production was lower during winter, when most cattle remained outdoors, protecting their herds then would improve milk production year-round. Accordingly, they expanded acreage devoted to hay and built barns to shelter the cows in cold weather and to store the hay. A federal census in 1798 revealed that about half the farms in eastern Pennsylvania had barns, usually of logs or framed but occasionally of stone. After the turn of the century, men would also begin to shop for particular breeds of cattle that produced more milk for more months of each year.

Farmwomen of the period—often referred to as "dairymaids"—likewise sought to improve cows' productivity. The milking process itself changed little. Mid-Atlantic women milked an average of six animals twice a day, with each "milch cow" producing about two gallons per day during the summer. Most of women's efforts to increase production had to do with making butter, the dairy product in greatest demand among urban consumers.

Poorer farm families, especially in New England, found less lucrative ways to produce for commercial markets. Small plots of land on New England's thin, rocky soil no longer supported large families, leading young people to look beyond their immediate locales for means of support. While many young men and young couples moved west, unmarried daughters more frequently remained at home, where they could help satisfy a growing demand for manufactured cloth. Before the Revolution, affluent colonists had imported cloth as well as finished clothing, but the boycott of British goods led many women to either spin their own or purchase it from other women (see Chapter 5). After the Revolution, enterprising merchants began catering to urban consumers as well as southern slave owners seeking to clothe their slaves as cheaply as possible. Making regular circuits through rural areas, the merchants supplied cloth to mothers and daughters in farm households. A few weeks later they would return and pay the women in cash for their handiwork.

A comparable transition began in some artisans' households. The shoemakers of Lynn, Massachusetts, had expanded their production during the Revolution when filling orders from the Continental Army. After the war, some more successful artisans began supplying leather to other shoemakers, paying them for the finished product. By 1800, these merchants were taking leather to farm families beyond Lynn in order to fill an annual demand that had risen from 189,000 pairs in 1789 to 400,000.

Numerous other enterprises likewise emerged, employing men as well as women to satisfy demands that self-contained households could never have met on their own. For example, a traveler passing through Middleborough, Massachusetts, observed,

> In the winter season, the inhabitants . . . are principally employed in making nails, of which they send large quantities to market. This business is a profitable addition to their husbandry; and fills up a part of the year, in which, otherwise, many of them would find little employment.

Behind the new industries was an ambitious, aggressive class of businessmen, most of whom had begun as merchants and now invested their profits in factories, ships, government bonds, and banks. Such entrepreneurs stimulated a flurry of innovative business ventures that pointed toward the future. The country's first private banks were founded in the 1780s in Philadelphia, Boston, and New York. Philadelphia merchants created the Pennsylvania Society for the Encouragement of Manufactures and the Useful Arts in 1787. This organization promoted the immigration of English artisans familiar with the latest industrial technology, including Samuel Slater, a pioneer of American industrialization who helped establish a cotton-spinning mill at Pawtucket, Rhode Island, in 1790 (see Chapter 9). In 1791 investors from New York and Philadelphia, with Hamilton's enthusiastic endorsement, started the Society for the Encouragement of Useful Manufactures, which attempted to demonstrate the potential of large-scale industrial enterprises by building a factory town at Paterson, New Jersey. That same year, New York merchants and insurance underwriters organized America's first formal association for trading government bonds, out of which the New York Stock Exchange evolved.

For many Americans, the choice between manufacturing and farming was moral as well as economic. Hamilton's aggressive support of entrepreneurship and industrialization was consistent with his larger vision for America and contradicted that of Jefferson. As outlined in his Report on the Subject of Manufactures (1791), Hamilton admired efficiently run factories in which a few managers supervised large numbers of workers. Manufacturing would provide employment opportunities, promote emigration, and expand the applications of technology. It would also offer "greater scope for the talents and dispositions [of] men," afford "a more ample and various field for enterprise," and create "a more certain and steady demand for the surplus produce of the soil." Jefferson, on the other hand, idealized white, landowning family farmers as bulwarks of republican liberty and virtue. "Those who labour in the earth are the chosen people," he wrote in 1784, whereas the dependency of European factory workers "begets subservience and venality, suffocates the germ of virtue, and prepares fit tools for the designs of ambition." For Hamilton, capital, technology, and managerial discipline were the surest roads to national order and wealth. Jefferson, putting more trust in white male citizens, envisioned land as the key to prosperity and liberty for all. The argument over the relative merits of these two ideals would remain a constant in American politics and culture for at least another two centuries.

White Women in the Republic

Alongside the growing importance of women's economic roles, whites' discussions of republicanism raised questions of women's rights and equality. The Revolution and the adoption of republican constitutions had not significantly affected the legal position of white women, although some states eased women's difficulties in obtaining divorces. Nor did women gain new political rights, except in New Jersey. That state's 1776 constitution, by not specifying gender and race, left a loophole that enabled white female and black property holders to vote, which many began to do. During the 1790s, New Jersey explicitly permitted otherwise qualified women to vote by adopting laws that stipulated "he or she" when referring to voters. In a hotly contested state election in 1797, seventy-five women voters nearly gave the victory to a Federalist candidate. His victorious Republican opponent, John Condict, would get his revenge in 1807 by successfully advocating a bill to disenfranchise women (along with free blacks).

In other areas of American life, social change and republican ideology together fostered more formidable challenges to traditional attitudes toward women's rights. American republicans increasingly recognized the right of a woman to choose her husband—a striking departure from the continued practice among some elites whereby fathers approved or even arranged marriages. Thus in 1790, on the occasion of his daughter Martha's marriage, Jefferson wrote to a friend that, following "the usage of my country, I scrupulously suppressed my wishes, [so] that my daughter might indulge her sentiments freely."

Advocating Women's Rights, 1792
In this illustration from an American magazine for women, the "Genius of the Ladies Magazine" and the "Genius of Emulation" present Liberty with a petition based on British feminist Mary Wollstonecraft's Vindication of the Rights of Woman.

FRONTISPIECE.

Outside elite circles, such independence was even more apparent. Especially in the Northeast, daughters increasingly got pregnant by preferred partners, thus forcing their fathers to consent to their marrying in order to avoid a public scandal. In Hallowell, Maine, in May 1792, for example, Mary Brown's father objected to her marrying John Chamberlain. In December, he finally consented and the couple wed—just two days before Mary Chamberlain gave birth. By becoming pregnant, northeastern women secured economic support in a region where an exodus of young, unmarried men was leaving a growing number of women single.

White women also had fewer children overall than had their mothers and grandmothers. In Sturbridge, Massachusetts, women in the mid-eighteenth century averaged nearly nine children per marriage, compared with six in the first decade of the nineteenth century. Whereas 40 percent of Quaker women had nine or more children before 1770, only 14 percent bore that many thereafter. Such statistics testify to declining farm sizes and urbanization, both of which were incentives for having fewer children. But they also indicate that some women were finding relief from the near-constant state of pregnancy and nursing that had consumed their grandmothers.

As white women's roles expanded, so too did republican notions of male-female relations. "I object to the word 'obey' in the marriage-service," wrote a female author calling herself Matrimonial Republican, "because it is a general word, without limitations or definition. . . . The obedience between man and wife is, or ought to be mutual." Lack of mutuality was one reason for a rising number of divorce petitions from women, from fewer than fourteen per year in Connecticut before the Revolution, to forty-five in 1795.

A few women also challenged the sexual double standard that allowed men to indulge in extramarital affairs while their female partners, single or married, were condemned. Writing in 1784, an author calling herself "Daphne" pointed out how a woman whose illicit affair was exposed was "forever deprive[d] . . . of all that renders life valuable," while "the base [male] betrayer is suffered to triumph in the success of his unmanly arts, and to pass unpunished even by a frown." Daphne called on her "sister Americans" to "stand by and support the dignity of our own sex" by publicly condemning seducers rather than their victims.

Gradually, the subordination of women, which once was taken for granted among most whites, became the subject of debate. In "On the Equality of the Sexes" (1790), essayist and poet Judith Sargent Murray contended that the genders had equal intellectual ability and deserved equal education. "We can only reason from what we know," she wrote, "and if an opportunity of acquiring knowledge hath been denied us, the inferiority of our sex cannot fairly be deduced from there." Murray hoped that "sensible and informed" women would improve their minds rather than rush into marriage (as she had at eighteen), enabling them to instill republican ideals in their children.

Like many of her contemporaries, Murray supported the idea of **"republican motherhood."** Advocates of republican motherhood emphasized the importance of educating white women in the values of liberty and independence in order to strengthen virtue in the new nation. It was the republican duty of mothers to inculcate these values in their sons—the nation's future leaders—as well as their daughters. John Adams reminded his daughter that she was part of "a young generation, coming up in America . . . [and] will be responsible for a great share of the duty and opportunity of educating a rising family, from whom much will be expected." Before the 1780s, only a few women had acquired an advanced education through private tutors. Thereafter, urban elites broadened such opportunities by founding numerous private schools, or academies, for girls. Massachusetts also established an important precedent in 1789 when it forbade any town to exclude girls from its elementary schools.

By itself, the expansion of educational opportunities for white women would have a limited effect. "I acknowledge we have an equal share of curiosity with the other sex," wrote Mercy Otis Warren to Abigail Adams, but men "have the opportunities of gratifying their inquisitive humour to the utmost, in the great school of the world, while we are confined to the narrow circle of domesticity." Although the great struggle for female political equality would not begin until the next century, republican assertions that women were intellectually and morally men's peers and played a vital public role provoked additional calls for political equality beyond those voiced by Abigail Adams and a few other women during the Revolution (see Chapter 6). In 1793, Priscilla Mason, a young woman graduating from a female academy, blamed "*Man*, despotic man" for shutting women out of the church, the courts, and government. In her salutatory oration, she urged that a women's senate be established by Congress to evoke "all that is human—all that is *divine* in the soul of woman." Warren and Mason had pointed out a fundamental limitation to republican egalitarianism in the America of the 1790s: while women could be virtuous wives and mothers, the world outside their homes still offered them few opportunities to apply their education.

Land and Culture: Native Americans   Perhaps the people in the most tenuous position in American society were Native Americans. By 1800, Indians east of the Mississippi had suffered severe losses of population, territory, and political and cultural self-determination. Thousands of deaths had resulted from battle, famine, and disease during the successive wars since the 1750s and from poverty, losses of land, and discrimination during peacetime as well. From 1775 to 1800, the Cherokee population declined from sixteen thousand to ten thousand, and Iroquois numbers fell from about nine thousand to four thousand. During the same period, Native Americans lost more land than the area inhabited by whites in 1775. Settlers, liquor dealers, and criminals trespassed on Indian lands, often stealing or inflicting violence on Native Americans and provoking them to retaliate. Indians who sold land or worked for whites were often paid in the unfamiliar medium of cash and then found little to spend it on in their isolated communities except alcohol.

While employing military force against Native Americans who resisted U.S. authority (see above), Washington and Secretary of War Knox recognized that actions by American citizens often contributed to Indians' resentment. Accordingly, they pursued a policy similar to Britain's under the Proclamation of 1763 (see Chapter 5) in which the government regulated relations between Indians and non-Indians. Congress enacted the new policy gradually in a series of **Indian Trade and Intercourse Acts** (1790–1796). (Thereafter, Congress periodically renewed and amended the legislation until making it permanent in 1834.) To halt fraudulent land cessions, the acts prohibited transfers of tribal lands to outsiders except as authorized in formal treaties or by Congress. Other provisions regulated the conduct of non-Indians on lands still under tribal control. To regulate intercultural trade and reduce abuses, the acts required that traders be licensed by the federal government. (But until 1802, the law did not prohibit the sale of liquor on Indian lands.) The law also defined murder and other abuses committed by non-Indians as federal offenses. Finally, the legislation authorized the federal government to establish programs that would "promote civilization" among Native Americans as a replacement for traditional culture. By "civilization," Knox and his supporters meant Anglo-American culture, particularly private property and a strictly agricultural way of life, with men replacing women in the fields. By abandoning communal landownership and seasonal migrations for hunting, gathering, and fishing, they argued, Indians would no longer need most of the land they were trying to protect, thereby making it available for whites.

Before 1800, the "civilization" program was offered to relatively few Native Americans. Although some Cherokees who were familiar with Anglo-American ways welcomed it, Nancy Ward was not one of them. She eventually discovered that "civilization" included male property ownership and political leadership and that Indian women were being urged to leave farming to men while taking up strictly domestic tasks like their white contemporaries. When she and twelve other War Women in 1817 protested a treaty that would give most Cherokee land in Georgia to the United States, they were ignored—not by the U.S. government but by their own male leaders. Women in general, and War Women in particular, no longer wielded power in Cherokee society.

Among the most devastated Native Americans in the 1790s were the Seneca Iroquois. A majority of surviving Iroquois had moved to Canada after the Revolution, and those who stayed behind were pressured to sell, or were simply defrauded of, most of their land, leaving them isolated from one another on tiny reservations. Unable to practice any of their traditional occupations, Seneca men frequently resorted to heavy

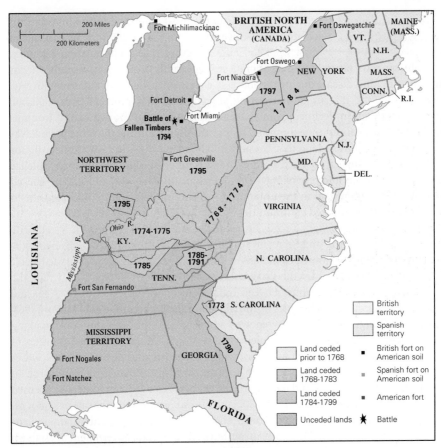

MAP 7.1 Indian Land Cessions, 1768–1799

During the last third of the eighteenth century, Native Americans were forced to give up extensive homelands throughout the eastern backcountry and farther west in the Ohio and Tennessee River valleys.

drinking, often becoming violent. All too typical were the tragedies that beset Mary Jemison, born a half-century earlier to white settlers but a Seneca since her wartime capture and adoption at age ten. Jemison saw one of her sons murder his two brothers in alcohol-related episodes before meeting a similar fate himself.

In 1799, a Seneca prophet, Handsome Lake, emerged and led his people in a remarkable spiritual revival. Severely ill, alcoholic, and near death, he experienced a series of visions, which Iroquois and many other Native American societies interpreted as prophetic messages. As in the visions of the Iroquois prophet Hiawatha in the fourteenth century (see Chapter 1), spiritual guides appeared to Handsome Lake and instructed him first in his own recovery and then in that of his people. Invoking Iroquois religious traditions, Handsome Lake preached against alcoholism and sought to revive unity and self-confidence among the Seneca. But whereas many Indian visionary prophets

Creek House, 1791   *By the end of the eighteenth century, most eastern Native Americans combined traditional and European ideas and materials in their everyday lives.*

rejected all white ways, Handsome Lake welcomed civilization, as introduced by Quaker missionaries (who did not attempt to convert Native Americans) supported by federal aid. In particular, he urged a radical shift in gender roles, with Seneca men displacing women not only in farming but also as heads of their families. At the same time, he insisted that men treat their wives respectfully and without violence.

The most traditional Senecas rejected the notion that Native men should work like white farmers. But many Seneca men welcomed the change. It was women who resisted most, because like Cherokee women they stood to lose their collective ownership of farmland, their control of the food supply, and their considerable political influence. Other Senecas accused women who rejected Handsome Lake's teachings of witchcraft, and even killed a few of them. The violence soon ceased and Handsome Lake's followers formed their own church, complete with traditional Iroquois religious ceremonies. The Seneca case would prove to be unique; after 1800, missionaries would usually introduce civilization to Native Americans and expect them to convert to Christianity as well as adopt the new ways of living.

African-American Struggles   The Republic's first years marked the high tide of African-Americans' Revolutionary era success in bettering their lot. Blacks and even many whites recognized that the ideals of liberty and equality were inconsistent with slavery. By 1790, 8 percent of all African-Americans had been freed from slavery, many having purchased their liberty or earned it through wartime service. Ten years later 11 percent were free. Various state reforms meanwhile attempted to improve the conditions of those who remained in slavery. In 1791, for example, the North Carolina legislature declared that the former

State	Total Number of Free Blacks	Free Blacks as a Percentage of Total Black Population
Massachusetts	7,378	100%
Vermont	557	100%
New Hampshire	855	99%
Rhode Island	3,304	90%
Pennsylvania	14,564	89%
Connecticut	5,300	85%
Delaware	8,268	57%
New York	10,374	33%
New Jersey	4,402	26%
Maryland	19,587	16%
Virginia	20,124	6%
North Carolina	7,043	5%
South Carolina	3,185	2%
Georgia	1,019	2%
Kentucky	741	2%
Tennessee	309	2%
UNITED STATES	108,395*	11%

* Total includes figures from the District of Columbia, Mississippi Territory, and Northwest Territory. These areas are not shown on the chart.

Figure 7.1 Number and Percentage of Free Blacks, by State, 1800

Within a generation of the Declaration of Independence, a large free black population emerged that included every ninth African-American. In the North, only in New Jersey and New York did most blacks remain slaves. Almost half of all free blacks lived in the South. Every sixth black in Maryland was free by 1800. *Source:* U.S. Bureau of the Census.

"distinction of criminality between the murder of a white person and one who is equally an human creature, but merely of a different complexion, is disgraceful to humanity" and authorized the execution of whites who murdered slaves. Although for economic as much as for humanitarian reasons, by 1794 most states had outlawed the Atlantic slave trade.

Hesitant measures to ensure free blacks' legal equality also appeared in the 1780s and early 1790s. Most states dropped restrictions on African-Americans' freedom of movement and protected their property. By 1796, all but three of the sixteen states either permitted free blacks to vote or did not specifically exclude them. But by then a countertrend was reversing many of the Revolutionary-era advances. Before the 1790s ended, abolitionist sentiment ebbed, slavery became more entrenched, and whites resisted accepting even free blacks as fellow citizens.

Federal law led the way in restricting the rights of blacks and other nonwhites. When Congress passed the Naturalization Act (1790), it limited eligibility for U.S. citizenship to "free white aliens." The federal militia law of 1792 required whites to enroll in local units but allowed states to exclude free blacks, an option that state governments increasingly chose. The navy and the marine corps forbade nonwhite enlistments in 1798. Delaware stripped free, property-owning black males of the vote in 1792, and by 1807 Maryland, Kentucky, and New Jersey had followed suit. Free black men continued to vote and to serve in some integrated militia organizations after 1800 (including in the slave states of North Carolina and Tennessee), but the number of settings in which they were treated as the equals of whites dropped sharply.

Even with these disadvantages, some free blacks became landowners or skilled artisans, and a few gained recognition among whites. One of the best known was Benjamin Banneker of Maryland, a self-taught mathematician and astronomer. In 1789, Banneker was one of three surveyors who laid out the new national capital in Washington, D.C., and after 1791 he published a series of widely read almanacs. Sending a copy of one to Thomas Jefferson, Banneker chided the future president for holding views of black inferiority that contradicted his own words in the Declaration of Independence.

In the face of growing constrictions on their freedom and opportunities, free African-Americans in the North turned to one another for support. Self-help among African-Americans flowed especially through religious channels. During the 1780s two free black Christians, Richard Allen and Absalom Jones, formed the Free African Society of Philadelphia, a community organization whose members pooled their scarce resources to assist one another and other blacks in need. After the white-dominated Methodist church they attended tried to restrict black worshipers to the gallery, Allen, Jones, and most of the black membership withdrew and formed a separate congregation. Comparable developments in other northern communities eventually resulted in the formation of a new denomination, the African Methodist Episcopal Church (see Chapter 9).

In 1793, Philadelphia experienced a yellow fever epidemic in which about four thousand residents eventually died. As most affluent whites fled, Allen and Jones organized a relief effort in which African-Americans, at great personal risk, tended to the sick and buried the dead of both races. But their only reward was a vicious publicity campaign wrongly accusing blacks from profiting at whites' expense. Allen and Jones vigorously defended the black community against these charges while condemning slavery and racism.

Another revealing indication of whites' changing racial attitudes also occurred in 1793, when Congress passed, and President Washington signed, the **Fugitive Slave Law.** This law required judges to award possession of an escaped slave upon any formal request by a master or his representative. Accused runaways not only were denied a jury trial but also were sometimes refused permission to present evidence of their freedom. Slaves' legal status as property disqualified them from claiming these constitutional privileges, but the Fugitive Slave Law denied free blacks the legal protections that the Bill of Rights guaranteed them as citizens. Congress nevertheless passed this measure without serious opposition. The law marked a striking departure from the atmosphere of the 1780s, when state governments had moved toward granting free blacks legal equality with whites.

The slave revolution on Saint Domingue (which victorious blacks would rename Haiti in 1802) heightened slave owners' fears of violent retaliation by blacks. In August 1800, such fears were kindled when a slave insurrection broke out near Richmond, Virginia's capital. Amid the election campaign that year, in which Federalists and Republicans accused one another of endangering liberty and hinted at violence, a slave named Gabriel calculated that the split among whites afforded blacks an opportunity to gain their freedom. Having secretly assembled weapons, he and several other blacks organized a march on Richmond by more than a thousand slaves. The plot of **Gabriel's Rebellion** was leaked on the eve of the march. Obtaining confessions from some participants, the authorities rounded up the rest and executed thirty-five of them, including Gabriel. "I have nothing more to offer than what General Washington would have had to offer, had he been taken by the British officers and put to trial by them," said one rebel before his execution. "I have ventured my life in endeavoring to obtain the liberty of my countrymen, and I am a willing sacrifice to their cause." In the end, Gabriel's Rebellion only confirmed whites' anxieties that Haiti's revolution could be replayed on American soil.

A technological development also strengthened slavery. During the 1790s, demand in the British textile industry stimulated the cultivation of cotton in coastal South Carolina and Georgia. The soil and climate were ideal for growing long-staple cotton, a variety whose fibers could be separated easily from its seed by squeezing it through rollers. In the South's upland and interior regions, however, the only cotton that would thrive was the short-staple variety, whose seed stuck so tenaciously to the fibers that rollers crushed the seeds and ruined the fibers. It was as if growers had discovered gold only to find that they could not mine it. But in 1793, a New Englander, Eli Whitney, invented a cotton gin that successfully separated the fibers of short-staple cotton from the seed. Quickly copied and improved upon by others, Whitney's invention removed a major obstacle to the spread of cotton cultivation. It gave a new lease on life to plantation slavery and undermined the doubts of those who considered slavery economically outmoded.

By 1800, free blacks had suffered noticeable erosion of their post-Revolutionary gains, and southern slaves were farther from freedom than a decade earlier. Two vignettes poignantly communicate the plight of African-Americans. By arrangement with her late husband, Martha Washington freed the family's slaves a year after George died. But many of the freed blacks remained impoverished and dependent on the Washington estate because Virginia law prohibited the education of blacks and otherwise denied them opportunities to realize their freedom. Meanwhile, across the Potomac at the site surveyed by Benjamin Banneker, enslaved blacks were performing most of the labor on the new national capital that would bear the first president's name. African-Americans were manifestly losing ground.

CONCLUSION

Although American voters were largely united when Washington took office in 1789, they soon became divided along lines of region, economic interest, and ideology. Hamilton pushed through a series of controversial measures that strengthened federal and executive authority as well as northeastern commercial interests. Jefferson, Madison, and many others opposed these measures, arguing that they favored a few Americans at the expense of the rest and that they threatened liberty. At the same time, Spain and Britain resisted U.S. expansion west of the Appalachians, and the French Revolution sharply polarized voters between those who favored and those who opposed it. During the mid-1790s, elites formed two rival political parties—the Federalists and the Republicans. Only with the peaceful transfer of power from Federalists to Republicans in 1800 could the nation's long-term political stability be taken for granted.

The election of 1800 ensured that white male property owners would enjoy basic legal and political rights. But other Americans remained without such rights, especially on the basis of their gender or race.

8

Jeffersonianism and the Era of Good Feelings, 1801–1824

CHAPTER OUTLINE

The Age of Jefferson • The Gathering Storm • The War of 1812
The Awakening of American Nationalism

THE AGE OF JEFFERSON

Narrowly elected in 1800, Jefferson saw his popularity rise during his first term, when he moved quickly to scale down government expenditures. Increasingly confident of popular support, he worked to loosen the Federalists' grip on appointive federal offices, especially in the judiciary. His purchase of Louisiana against Federalist opposition added to his popularity. In all of these moves, Jefferson was guided not merely by political calculation but also by his philosophy of government, eventually known as Jeffersonianism.

Jefferson and Jeffersonianism
A man of extraordinary attainments, Jefferson was fluent in French, read Latin and Greek, and studied several Native American languages. He served for more than twenty years as president of America's foremost scientific association, the American Philosophical Society. A student of architecture, he designed his own mansion in Virginia, Monticello. Gadgets fascinated him. He invented a device for duplicating his letters, of which he wrote over twenty thousand, and he improved the design for a revolving book stand, which enabled him to consult up to five books at once. His public career was luminous: principal author of the Declaration of Independence, governor of Virginia, ambassador to France, secretary of state under Washington, and vice president under John Adams.

Yet he was, and remains, a controversial figure. His critics, pointing to his doubts about some Christian doctrines and his early support for the French Revolution, portrayed him as an infidel and radical. During the election campaign of 1800, Federalists alleged that he kept a slave mistress. In 1802 James Callender, a former supporter furious about not receiving a government job he wanted, wrote a newspaper account naming Sally Hemings, a house slave at Monticello, as the mistress. Drawing on the DNA of Sally's male heirs and linking the timing of Jefferson's visits to Monticello with the start of Sally's pregnancies, most scholars now view it as very likely that Jefferson, a widower, was the father of at least one of her four surviving children.

Callender's story did Jefferson little damage in Virginia, because Jefferson had acted according to the rules of white Virginia gentlemen by never acknowledging any of Sally's children as his own. Although he freed two of her children (the other two ran away), he never freed Sally, the daughter of Jefferson's own father-in-law and so light-skinned that she could pass for white, nor did he ever mention her in his vast correspondence. Yet the story of Sally fed the charge that Jefferson was a hypocrite, for throughout his career he condemned the very "race-mixing" to which he appears to have contributed.

Jefferson did not believe that blacks and whites could live permanently side by side in American society. As the black population grew, he feared a race war so vicious that it could be suppressed only by a dictator. This view was consistent with his conviction that the real threat to republics rose less from hostile neighbors than from within. He believed that the French had turned to a dictator, Napoleon Bonaparte, to save them from the chaos of their own revolution. Only by colonizing blacks in Africa, an idea embodied in the American Colonization Society (1816), could America avert a similar fate, he believed.

Jefferson worried that high taxes, standing armies, and corruption could destroy American liberty by turning government into the master rather than servant of the people. To prevent tyranny, he advocated that state governments retain considerable authority. In a vast republic, he reasoned, state governments would be more responsive to the popular will than would the government in Washington.

He also believed that popular liberty required popular virtue. For republican theorists like Jefferson, virtue consisted of a decision to place the public good ahead of one's private interests and to exercise vigilance to keep governments from growing out of control. To Jefferson, the most vigilant and virtuous people were educated farmers, who were accustomed to act and think with sturdy independence. The least vigilant were the inhabitants of cities. Jefferson regarded cities as breeding grounds for mobs and as menaces to liberty. Men who relied on merchants or factory owners for their jobs could have their votes influenced, unlike farmers who worked their own land. When the people "get piled upon one another in large cities, as in Europe," he wrote, "they will become corrupt as in Europe."

Jefferson's "Revolution" Jefferson described his election as a revolution. But the revolution he sought was to restore the liberty and tranquillity that (he thought) the United States had enjoyed in its early years and to reverse what he saw as a drift into despotism. The $10 million growth in the national debt under the Federalists alarmed Jefferson and his secretary of the treasury, Albert Gallatin. They rejected Hamilton's idea that a national debt would strengthen the government by giving creditors a stake in its health. Just paying the interest on the debt would require taxes, which would suck money from industrious farmers, the backbone of the Republic. The money would then fall into the hands of

CHRONOLOGY, 1801–1824

1801 • Thomas Jefferson's inauguration.

1802 • Repeal of the Judiciary Act of 1801.
Yazoo land compromise.

1803 • *Marbury* v. *Madison.*
Conclusion of the Louisiana Purchase.

1804 • Impeachment of Justice Samuel Chase.
Aaron Burr kills Alexander Hamilton in a duel.
Jefferson elected to a second term.

1804–1806 • Lewis and Clark expedition.

1805 • British court declares the broken voyage illegal.

1807 • *Chesapeake* Affair.
Embargo Act passed.

1808 • James Madison elected president.

1809 • Non-Intercourse Act passed.
Embargo Act repealed.

1810 • Macon's Bill No. 2.

1811 • Battle of Tippecanoe.

1812 • United States declares war on Britain.
Madison reelected to a second term.
General William Hull surrenders at Detroit.
Battle of Queenston.

1813 • Battle of the Thames.

1814 • British burn Washington, D.C.
Hartford Convention.
Treaty of Ghent signed.

1815 • Battle of New Orleans.

1816 • James Monroe elected president.
Second Bank of the United States chartered.

1817 • Rush-Bagot Treaty.

1818 • British-American Convention of 1818 sets U.S.-Canada border in West.
Andrew Jackson invades East Florida.

1819 • Adams-Onís (Transcontinental) Treaty.
Dartmouth College v. *Woodward.*
McCulloch v. *Maryland.*

1820 • Monroe elected to a second term.

1820–1821 • Missouri Compromise.

1823 • Monroe Doctrine.

Man of the People   *Foreign diplomats in the United States were often shocked when Jefferson greeted them dressed in everyday working clothes and carpet slippers. But Jefferson thought of himself as a working politician and man of the people, not as an aristocratic figurehead.*

creditors—leeches who lived off interest payments. Increased tax revenues might also tempt the government to establish a standing army, always a threat to liberty.

Jefferson and Gallatin secured the repeal of many taxes, and they slashed expenditures by closing some embassies overseas and reducing the army, which declined from an authorized strength of over 14,000 in 1798 to 3,287 in 1802. They placed economy ahead of military preparedness. Gallatin calculated that the nation could be freed of debt in sixteen years if administrations held the line on expenditures. In Europe, the Peace of Amiens (1802) brought a temporary halt to the hostilities between Britain and France that had threatened American shipping, which buoyed Jefferson's confidence that minimal military preparedness was a sound policy. The Peace of Amiens, he wrote, "removes the only danger we have to fear. We can now proceed without risks in demolishing useless structures of expense, lightening the burdens of our constituents, and fortifying the principles of free government." This may have been wishful thinking, but it rested on a sound economic calculation, for the vast territory of the United States could not be secured from attack without astronomical expense.

While cutting back expenditures on the army, Jefferson was ready to use the navy to gain respect for the American flag. In 1801, he ordered a naval squadron into action in the Mediterranean against the so-called Tripolitan (or Barbary) pirates of North Africa. For centuries, the rulers of Tripoli, Morocco, Tunis, and Algiers had solved their budgetary problems by engaging in piracy and extorting tribute in exchange for protection; captured seamen were held for ransom or sold into slavery. Jefferson calculated that going to war would be cheaper than paying high tribute to maintain peace. Although suffering its share of reverses during the ensuing fighting, the United States did not come away empty-handed. In 1805, it was able to conclude a peace treaty with Tripoli. The war cost roughly half of what the United States had been paying annually for protection.

Jefferson and the Judiciary In his first inaugural address Jefferson reminded Americans that their agreements were more basic than their disagreements. "We are all republicans," he proclaimed, "we are all federalists." He hoped to conciliate the moderate Federalists, but conflicts over the judiciary derailed this objective. Washington and Adams had appointed only Federalists to the bench, including the new chief justice, **John Marshall.** Not a single Republican was sitting on the federal judiciary when Jefferson came to office. Still bitter about the zeal of federal courts in enforcing the Alien and Sedition Acts, Jefferson saw the Federalist-sponsored Judiciary Act of 1801 as the last straw. By reducing the number of Supreme Court justices from six to five, the act threatened to strip him of an early opportunity to appoint a justice. At the same time, the act created sixteen new federal judgeships, which outgoing president John Adams had filled by last-minute ("midnight") appointments of Federalists. To Jefferson, this was proof that the Federalists intended to use the judiciary as a stronghold from which "all the works of Republicanism are to be beaten down and erased." In 1802, he won congressional repeal of the Judiciary Act of 1801.

Jefferson's troubles with the judiciary were not over. On his last day in office, Adams had appointed a Federalist, William Marbury, as justice of the peace in the District of Columbia but failed to deliver Marbury's commission before midnight. When Jefferson's secretary of state, James Madison, refused to send him notice of the appointment, Marbury petitioned the Supreme Court to issue a writ compelling delivery. In ***Marbury* v. *Madison*** (1803), Chief Justice John Marshall wrote the unanimous opinion. Marshall ruled that, although Madison should have delivered Marbury's commission, he was under no legal obligation to do so because part of the Judiciary Act of 1789 that had granted the Court the authority to issue such a writ, was unconstitutional.

For the first time, the Supreme Court had asserted its authority to void an act of Congress on the grounds that it was "repugnant" to the Constitution. Jefferson did not reject this principle, known as the doctrine of judicial review and destined to become highly influential, but he was enraged that Marshall had used part of his decision to lecture Madison on his moral duty (as opposed to his legal obligation) to deliver Marbury's commission. This gratuitous lecture, which was really directed at Jefferson as Madison's superior, struck Jefferson as another example of Federalist partisanship.

While the *Marbury* decision was brewing, the Republicans took the offensive against the judiciary by moving to impeach (charge with wrongdoing) two Federalist judges. One, John Pickering, was an insane alcoholic; the other, Supreme Court justice Samuel Chase, was a partisan Federalist notorious for jailing several Republican editors under the Sedition Act of 1798. These cases raised the same issue: Was impeachment, which the Constitution restricted to cases of treason, bribery, and "high Crimes and Misdemeanors," an appropriate remedy for judges who were insane or excessively partisan? Pickering was removed from office, but the Senate narrowly failed to convict Chase, in part because moderate Republicans were coming to doubt whether impeachment was a solution to judicial partisanship.

Chase's acquittal ended Jefferson's skirmishes with the judiciary as Jefferson and the Federalist judges reached an uneasy truce. The Federalists did not attempt to use their control of the federal judiciary to undo Jefferson's "revolution" of 1800. The Marshall court, for example, upheld the constitutionality of the repeal of the Judiciary Act of 1801. For his part, Jefferson never proposed to impeach Marshall. No federal judge would be impeached for more than fifty years.

The Louisiana Purchase, 1803   When Jefferson was elected president, European powers had large landholdings in North America. Spain, a declining power, controlled East and West Florida as well as the vast Louisiana Territory. The latter was equal in size to the United States at that time. In 1800, Spain ceded the Louisiana Territory to France, which was fast emerging under Napoleon Bonaparte as the world's foremost military power. It took six months for news of the treaty to reach Jefferson and Madison but only a few minutes for them to grasp its significance.

Jefferson had long dreamed of an "empire of liberty" extending across North America and even into South America. He saw this empire being gained not by military conquest but by the inevitable expansion of the free and virtuous American people. An enfeebled Spain constituted no real obstacle to this expansion. But Bonaparte's capacity for mischief was boundless. If Bonaparte gave Britain a free hand in the Mediterranean in exchange for a license for French expansion in North America, the United States could be sandwiched between British Canada and French Louisiana. And if Britain refused to cooperate with France, the British might seize Louisiana, trapping the United States between two large British territories.

Although Americans feared these two possibilities, Bonaparte actually had a different goal. He dreamed of a new French empire bordering the Caribbean and the Gulf of Mexico, centering on the Caribbean colony of Saint Domingue (modern Haiti). He wanted to use Louisiana not as a base from which to threaten the United States but as a breadbasket for an essentially Caribbean empire. His immediate task was to subdue Saint Domingue, where by 1800 a bloody slave revolution had resulted in a takeover of the government by the former slave Toussaint L'Ouverture (see Chapter 7). Bonaparte dispatched an army to reassert French control and reestablish slavery, but the army was destroyed by a combination of an epidemic of yellow fever and fierce resistance by former slaves.

In the short run, Jefferson worried most about New Orleans. Because no rivers, roads, or canals connected the American territories of Ohio, Indiana, and Mississippi with the eastern ports, farmers in the interior had to ship their cash crops, worth $3 million annually, down the Ohio and Mississippi Rivers to New Orleans, a port that did not belong to the United States. The Spanish had temporarily granted Americans the right to park their produce there while awaiting transfer to seagoing vessels. But in 1802, the Spanish colonial administrator in New Orleans issued an order revoking this right. The order had originated in Spain, but most Americans assumed that it had come from Bonaparte, who, although he now owned Louisiana, had yet to take possession of it. An alarmed Jefferson described New Orleans as the "one single spot" on the globe whose possessor "is our natural and habitual enemy." "The day that France takes possession of N. Orleans," he added, "we must marry ourselves to the British fleet and nation."

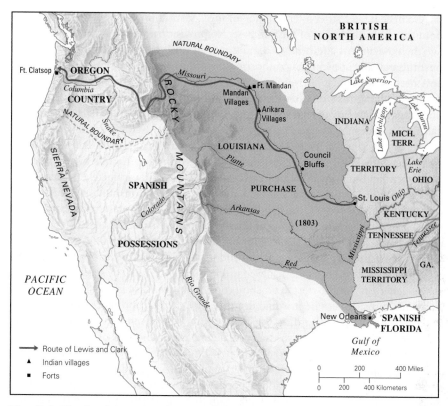

MAP 8.1 The Louisiana Purchase and the Exploration of the West

The explorations of Lewis and Clark demonstrated the vast extent of the area purchased from France.

The combination of France's failure to subdue Saint Domingue and the termination of American rights to deposit produce in New Orleans stimulated two crucial decisions—one by Jefferson and the other by Bonaparte—that ultimately resulted in the purchase of Louisiana by the United States. First, Jefferson nominated James Monroe and Robert R. Livingston to negotiate with France for the purchase of New Orleans and as much of the Floridas as possible. (Because West Florida had repeatedly changed hands among France, Britain, and Spain, no one was sure who owned it.) Meanwhile, Bonaparte, mindful of his military failure in Saint Domingue and of American opposition to French control of Louisiana, had concluded that his projected Caribbean empire was not worth the cost. In addition, he planned to resume war in Europe and needed cash. So he decided to sell all of Louisiana. After some haggling between the American commissioners and Bonaparte's minister, Talleyrand, a price of $15 million for the **Louisiana Purchase** was settled on. (One-fourth of the total represented an agreement by the United States to pay French debts owed to American citizens.) For this sum, the United States gained an immense, uncharted territory between the Mississippi River and the Rocky Mountains. No one knew its exact size; Talleyrand merely observed that the bargain was noble. But the purchase virtually doubled the area of the United States at a cost, omitting interest, of thirteen and one-half cents an acre.

As a believer in a strict interpretation of the Constitution, the president had doubts about the constitutionality of the purchase. No provision of the Constitution explicitly gave the government authority to acquire new territory. Jefferson therefore drafted a constitutional amendment that authorized the acquisition of territory and prohibited the American settlement of Louisiana for an indefinite period. Fearing that an immediate and headlong rush to settle the area would lead to the destruction of the Native Americans and an orgy of land speculation, Jefferson wanted to control development so that Americans could advance "compactly as we multiply." But few Republicans shared his reservations, and Jefferson soon began to worry that the long process of ratifying an amendment might give Napoleon time to change his mind. He quietly dropped the amendment and submitted the treaty to the Senate, where it was quickly ratified.

Believing in strict construction—the doctrine that the Constitution should be interpreted ("constructed") according to its letter—Jefferson was also committed to the principle of establishing an "empire of liberty." Doubling the size of the Republic would guarantee land for American farmers, the backbone of the nation and the true guardians of liberty. Strict construction was not an end in itself but a means to promote republican liberty. If that end could be achieved in some way other than by strict construction, so be it. Jefferson was also alert to practical considerations. Most Federalists opposed the Louisiana Purchase because it would decrease the relative importance of their strongholds on the eastern seaboard. As the leader of the Republican Party, Jefferson saw no reason to hand the Federalists an issue by dallying over ratification of the treaty.

The Election of 1804

Jefferson's acquisition of Louisiana left the Federalists dispirited and without a popular national issue. As the election of 1804 approached, the main threat to Jefferson was not the Federalist Party but his own vice president, Aaron Burr. In 1800, Burr had tried to take advantage of a tie in the Electoral College to gain the presidency, a betrayal in the eyes of most Republicans, who assumed that he had been nominated for the vice presidency. The adoption in 1804 of the Twelfth Amendment, which required separate and distinct ballots in the Electoral College for the presidential and the vice-presidential candidates, put an end to the possibility of an electoral tie for the chief executive. Burr continued to cause trouble. Between 1801 and 1804, he entered into enough intrigues with the Federalists to convince the Republicans that it would be unsafe to renominate him for the vice presidency. The Republicans in Congress rudely dumped Burr in favor of George Clinton.

Without a hope of success, the Federalists nominated Charles C. Pinckney and Rufus King, and then watched their candidates go down to an overwhelming defeat in the election. The Federalists carried only two states, failing to hold even Massachusetts. Jefferson's overwhelming victory brought his first term to a fitting close. Between 1801 and 1804, the United States had doubled its territory, taken steps to pay off its debt, and remained at peace.

The Lewis and Clark Expedition

Louisiana dazzled Jefferson. Here was an immense territory about which American citizens knew virtually nothing. No one was sure of its western boundary. A case could be made for the Pacific Ocean, but Spain claimed part of the Pacific coast. Jefferson was content to claim that Louisiana extended at least to the mountains west of the Mississippi, which few citizens of the United States had ever seen. Jefferson himself had never been more than fifty miles west of his home in Virginia. Thus the Louisiana Purchase was both a bargain and a surprise package.

Even before the acquisition of Louisiana, Jefferson had planned an exploratory expedition; picked its leader, his personal secretary and fellow Virginian Lieutenant Meriwether Lewis; and sent him to Philadelphia for a crash course in sciences such as zoology, astronomy, and botany that were relevant to exploration. Jefferson instructed Lewis to trace the Missouri River to its source, cross the western highlands, and follow the best water route to the Pacific. Jefferson was genuinely interested in the scientific information that could be collected on the expedition. His instructions to Lewis cited the need to learn about Indian languages and customs, climate, plants, birds, reptiles, and insects. But, above all, Jefferson hoped that the **Lewis and Clark expedition** would find a water route across the continent. The potential economic benefits from such a route included diverting the lucrative fur trade from Canadian to American hands and boosting trade with China.

Setting forth from St. Louis in May 1804, Lewis, his second-in-command William Clark, and about fifty others followed the Missouri River and then the Snake and Columbia Rivers. In the Dakota country, Lewis and Clark hired a French-Canadian fur trader, Toussaint Charbonneau, as a guide and interpreter. Slow-witted and inclined to panic in crises, Charbonneau proved to be a mixed blessing, but his wife, **Sacajawea,** who accompanied him on the trip, made up for his failings. A Shoshone and probably no more than sixteen years old in 1804, Sacajawea had been stolen by a rival tribe and then claimed by Charbonneau. When first encountered by Lewis and Clark, she had just given birth to a son; indeed, the infant's presence helped reassure Native American tribes of the expedition's peaceful intent.

Even with their peaceful intent established, Lewis and Clark faced obstacles. The expedition brought them in contact with numerous tribes, most importantly the powerful Sioux but also Mandans, Hidatsas, and Arikaras. Each tribe had a history of warring on other tribes and of carrying on its own internal clans and feuds. Reliant on Indians for guides, packers, and interpreters, Lewis and Clark had to become instant diplomats. Jefferson had told them to assert American sovereignty over the Purchase. This objective led them to distribute medals and uniforms to chiefs ready to support American authority and to stage periodic military parades and displays of their weapons, which included cannons. But no tribe had a single chief; rather, different tribal villages had different chiefs. At times, Lewis and Clark miscalculated, for example when they treated an Arikara chief as the "grand chief" to the outrage of his rivals. Yet their diplomacy was generally successful, less because they were sophisticated ethnographers than because they avoided violence.

The group finally reached the Pacific Ocean in November 1805 and then returned to St. Louis, but not before collecting a mass of scientific information, including the disturbing fact that more than three hundred miles of mountains separated the Missouri from the Columbia. The expedition also produced a sprinkling of tall tales, many of which Jefferson believed, about gigantic Indians, soil too rich to grow trees, and a mountain composed of salt. Jefferson's political opponents railed that he would soon be reporting the discovery of a molasses-filled lake. For all the ridicule, the expedition's drawings of the geography of the region led to more accurate maps and heightened interest in the West.

THE GATHERING STORM

In gaining control of Louisiana, the United States had benefited from the preoccupation of European powers with their own struggles. But between 1803 and 1814, the renewal of the Napoleonic Wars in Europe turned the United States into a pawn in a chess game played by others and helped make Jefferson's second term far less successful than his first.

Europe was not Jefferson's only problem. He had to deal with a conspiracy to dismantle the United States, the product of the inventive and perverse mind of Aaron Burr, and to face down challenges within his own party, led by John Randolph.

Challenges on the Home Front   Aaron Burr suffered a string of reverses in 1804. After being denied renomination as vice president, he entered into a series of intrigues with a faction of despairing and extreme (or "High") Federalists in New England. Led by Senator Timothy Pickering of Massachusetts, these High Federalists plotted to sever the Union by forming a pro-British Northern Confederacy composed of Nova Scotia (part of British-owned Canada), New England, New York, and even Pennsylvania. Although most Federalists disdained the plot, Pickering and others settled on Burr as their leader and helped him gain the Federalist nomination for the governorship of New York. Alexander Hamilton, who had thwarted Burr's grab for the presidency in 1800 by throwing his weight behind Jefferson, now foiled Burr a second time by allowing publication of his "despicable opinion" of Burr. Defeated in the election for New York's governor, Burr challenged Hamilton to a duel and mortally wounded him at Weehawken, New Jersey, on July 11, 1804.

Indicted in two states for his murder of Hamilton, Burr, still vice president, now hatched a scheme so bold that not even his political opponents could believe that he was capable of such treachery. He allied himself with the unsavory military governor of the Louisiana Territory, General James Wilkinson. Wilkinson had been on Spain's payroll intermittently as a secret agent since the 1780s. Together, Burr and Wilkinson conspired to separate the western states south of the Ohio River into an independent confederacy. In addition, Wilkinson had long entertained the idea of an American conquest of Mexico, and Burr now added West Florida as a possible target. They presented these ideas to westerners as having the covert support of the administration, to the British as a way to attack Spanish-owned Mexico and West Florida, and to the Spanish (not naming Mexico and West Florida as targets) as a way to divide up the United States.

By the fall of 1806, Burr and about sixty followers were making their way down the Ohio and Mississippi Rivers to join Wilkinson at Natchez. In October 1806, Jefferson, who described Burr as a crooked gun that never shot straight, denounced the conspiracy. Wilkinson abandoned the conspiracy and proclaimed himself the most loyal of Jefferson's followers. Burr tried to escape to West Florida but was intercepted. Brought back to Richmond, he was put on trial for treason. Chief Justice Marshall presided at the trial and instructed the jury that the prosecution had to prove not merely that Burr had treasonable intentions but also that he had committed treasonable acts, a virtually impossible task inasmuch as the conspiracy had never reached fruition. Jefferson was furious, but Marshall was merely following the clear wording of the Constitution, which deliberately made treason difficult to prove. The jury returned a verdict of not proved, which Marshall entered as "not guilty." Still under indictment for his murder of Hamilton, Burr fled to Europe, where he tried to interest Napoleon in making peace with Britain as a prelude to a proposed Anglo-French invasion of the United States and Mexico.

Besides the Burr conspiracy, Jefferson faced a challenge from a group of Republicans led by the president's fellow Virginian, John Randolph, a man of abounding eccentricities and acerbic wit. Like many propertied Americans of the 1770s, Randolph believed that governments always menaced popular liberty. Jefferson had originally shared this view, but he recognized it as an ideology of opposition, not power; once in office, he compromised. In contrast, Randolph remained frozen in the 1770s, denouncing every change as decline and proclaiming that he would throw all politicians to the dogs except that he had too much respect for dogs.

Not surprisingly, Randolph turned on Jefferson, most notably for backing a compromise in the Yazoo land scandal. In 1795, the Georgia legislature had sold the huge Yazoo tract (35 million acres comprising most of present-day Alabama and Mississippi) for a fraction of its value to land companies that had bribed virtually the entire legislature. The next legislature canceled the sale, but many investors, knowing nothing of the bribery, had already bought land in good faith. The scandal posed a moral challenge to Jefferson because of these good-faith purchases, and a political dilemma as well, for some purchasers were northerners whom Jefferson hoped to woo to the Republican Party. In 1803 a federal commission compromised with an award of 5 million acres to Yazoo investors. For Randolph, the compromise was itself a scandal—further evidence of the decay of republican virtue.

The Suppression of American Trade and Impressment Burr's acquittal and Randolph's taunts shattered the aura of invincibility that had surrounded Jefferson. Now foreign affairs posed an even sharper challenge. As Britain and France resumed their war in Europe, American commerce prospered. American ships carried sugar and coffee from the French and Spanish Caribbean to Europe. This trade not only provided Napoleon with supplies but also drove down the price of sugar and coffee from Britain's colonies by adding to the glut of these commodities on the world market.

Britain insisted that the American carrying trade violated its Rule of 1756, which stated that trade closed in peacetime could not be reopened during war. For example, France usually restricted its sugar trade to French ships during peace and thus could not reopen it to American ships in wartime, when French ships were likely to be seized by Britain's powerful navy. American shippers responded to this rule with the "broken voyage." American vessels would carry French sugar to an American port, pass it through customs, and then reexport it as American produce. Britain tolerated this dodge for nearly a decade but in 1805 initiated a policy of total war against France, including the strangulation of French trade. In 1805, a British court declared the broken voyage illegal.

Next came a series of British trade decrees, known as "Orders in Council," which established a blockade of French-controlled ports on the coast of Europe. Napoleon responded with his so-called Continental System, a series of counterproclamations that ships obeying British regulations would be subject to seizure by France. In effect, this Anglo-French war of decrees outlawed virtually all U.S. trade; if an American ship complied with British regulations, it became a French target, and vice versa.

Both Britain and France seized American ships, but British seizures were far more humiliating to Americans. France was a weaker naval power than Britain; much of the French fleet had been destroyed by the British at the Battle of Trafalgar in October 1805. Accordingly, most of France's seizures of American ships occurred in European ports where American ships had been lured by Napoleon's often inconsistent enforcement of his Continental System. In contrast, British warships hovered just beyond the American coast. The Royal Navy stopped and searched virtually every American vessel off New York, for example. At times, U.S. ships had to line up a few miles from the American coast to be searched by the Royal Navy.

To these provocations the British added **impressment.** For centuries, Royal Navy press gangs had scoured the docks and taverns of British ports and forced ("pressed") civilians into service. As war with France intensified Britain's need for sailors, Britain increasingly extended the practice to seizing alleged Royal Navy deserters on American merchant ships. British sailors had good reason to be discontented with their navy. Discipline on the Royal Navy's "floating hells" was often brutal and the pay low; sailors on American ships made up to five times more than those on British ships. Consequently, the Royal Navy suffered a high rate of desertion to American ships. In 1807, for example, 149 of the 419 sailors on the American warship *Constitution* were British subjects.

Impressment was galling to American pride, since the United States was unable to prevent the seizure even of U.S.-born seamen who could prove their American birth. Between 1803 and 1812, six thousand Americans were impressed. Although impressment did less damage to the American economy than the seizure of ships, it was more offensive.

Any doubts Americans had about British arrogance evaporated in June 1807. A British warship, HMS *Leopard,* patrolling off Hampton Roads, Virginia, attacked an unsuspecting American frigate, USS *Chesapeake,* and forced it to surrender. The British then boarded the vessel and seized four supposed deserters. One, a genuine deserter, was later hanged; the other three, former Britons, had "deserted" only from impressments and were now American citizens. Even the British had never before asserted their right to seize deserters off U.S. navy ships. The so-called *Chesapeake-Leopard* Affair enraged the country. Jefferson remarked that he had not seen so belligerent a spirit in America since 1775.

The Embargo Act of 1807   Yet while making some preparations for war, the president sought peace, first by conducting fruitless negotiations with Britain to gain redress for the *Chesapeake* outrage, and second by steering the Embargo Act through Congress in December 1807. By far the most controversial legislation of either of Jefferson's administrations, the **Embargo Act of 1807** prohibited vessels from leaving American ports for foreign ports. Technically, it prohibited only exports, but its practical effect was to stop imports as well, for few foreign ships would venture into American ports if they had to leave without cargo. Amazed by the boldness of the act, a British newspaper described the embargo as "little short of an absolute secession from the rest of the civilized world."

Jefferson advocated the embargo as a means of "peaceable coercion." By restricting French and especially British trade with the United States, he hoped to pressure both nations into respecting American neutrality. But the embargo did not have the intended effect. Although British sales to the United States dropped 50 percent between

1807 and 1808, the British quickly found new markets in South America, where rebellions against Spanish rule had flared up, and in Spain itself, where a revolt against Napoleon had opened trade to British shipping. Furthermore, the Embargo Act contained some loopholes. For example, it allowed American ships blown off course to put in at European ports if necessary; suddenly, many captains were reporting that adverse winds had forced them across the Atlantic. Treating the embargo as a joke, Napoleon seized any American ships he could lay hands on and then informed the United States that he was only helping to enforce the embargo. The British were less amused, but the embargo confirmed their view that Jefferson was an ineffectual philosopher, an impotent challenger compared with Napoleon.

The harshest effects of the embargo were felt not in Europe but in the United States. Some thirty thousand American seamen found themselves out of work. Hundreds of merchants went into bankruptcy, and jails swelled with debtors. A New York City newspaper noted that the only activity still flourishing in the city was prosecution for debt. Farmers were devastated. Unable to export their produce or sell it at a decent price to hard-pressed urban dwellers, many farmers could not pay their debts. In desperation, one farmer in Schoharie County, New York, sold his cattle, horses, and farm implements, worth eight hundred dollars before the embargo, for fifty-five dollars. Speculators who had purchased land, expecting to sell it later at a higher price, also took a beating because cash-starved farmers stopped buying land. "I live and that is all," wrote one New York speculator. "I am doing no business, cannot sell anybody property, nor collect any money."

The embargo fell hardest on New England and particularly on Massachusetts, which in 1807 had twice the ship tonnage per capita of any other state and more than a third of the entire nation's ship tonnage in foreign trade. For a state so dependent on foreign trade, the embargo was a calamity. Wits reversed the letters of embargo to form the phrase "O grab me."

The situation was not entirely bleak. The embargo forced a diversion of merchants' capital into manufacturing. In short, unable to export produce, Americans began to make products. Before 1808, the United States had only fifteen mills for fashioning cotton into textiles; by the end of 1809, an additional eighty-seven mills had been constructed (see Chapter 9). But none of this comforted merchants already ruined or mariners driven to soup kitchens. Nor could New Englanders forget that the source of their misery was a policy initiated by one of the "Virginia lordlings," "Mad Tom" Jefferson, who knew little about New England and who had a dogmatic loathing of cities, the very foundations of New England's prosperity. A Massachusetts poet wrote,

> Our ships all in motion once whitened the ocean,
> They sailed and returned with a cargo;
> Now doomed to decay they have fallen a prey
> To Jefferson, worms, and embargo.

James Madison and the Failure of Peaceable Coercion

Even before the Embargo Act, Jefferson had announced that he would not be a candidate for reelection. With his blessing, the Republican congressional caucus nominated **James Madison** and George Clinton for the presidency and vice presidency. The Federalists countered with Charles C. Pinckney and Rufus King, the same ticket that had made a negligible showing in 1804. In 1808, the Federalists staged a modest comeback, gaining twenty-four congressional seats. Still, Madison won 122 of 175 electoral votes for president, and the Republicans retained control of Congress.

The Federalist revival, modest as it was, rested on two factors. First, the Embargo Act gave the party the national issue it long had lacked. Second, younger Federalists had abandoned their elders' gentlemanly disdain for campaigning and deliberately imitated vote-winning techniques such as barbecues and mass meetings that had worked for the Republicans.

To some contemporaries, "Little Jemmy" Madison, five feet, four inches tall, seemed a weak and shadowy figure compared to the commanding presence of Jefferson. But in fact, Madison brought to the presidency an intelligence and a capacity for systematic thought that matched Jefferson's. He had the added advantage of being married to Dolley Madison. A striking figure in her turbans and colorful dresses, Dolley arranged Wednesday night receptions at the White House in which she charmed Republicans, and even some Federalists, into sympathy with her husband's policies.

Like Jefferson, Madison believed that American liberty had to rest on the virtue of the people, which he saw as being critically tied to the growth and prosperity of agriculture. More clearly than Jefferson, Madison also recognized that agricultural prosperity depended on trade—farmers needed markets. In particular, the British West Indies, dependent on the United States for much of their lumber and grain, struck Madison as a natural trading partner. Britain alone could not fully supply the West Indies. Therefore, if the United States embargoed its own trade with the West Indies, Madison reasoned, the British, who imported sugar from the West Indies, would be forced to their knees before Americans could suffer severe losses from the embargo. Britain, he wrote, was "more vulnerable in her commerce than in her armies."

The American embargo, however, was coercing no one. Increased trade between Canada and the West Indies made a shambles of Madison's plan to pressure Britain. On March 1, 1809, Congress replaced the Embargo Act with the weaker, face-saving Non-Intercourse Act. The act opened trade to all nations except Britain and France and then authorized Congress to restore trade with those nations if they stopped violating neutral rights. But neither complied. In May 1810, Congress substituted a new measure, Macon's Bill No. 2, for the Non-Intercourse Act. This legislation opened trade with Britain and France, and then offered each a clumsy bribe: if either nation repealed its restrictions on neutral shipping, the United States would halt trade with the other.

None of these steps had the desired effect. While Jefferson and Madison lashed out at France and Britain as moral demons ("The one is a den of robbers and the other of pirates," snapped Jefferson), the belligerents saw the world as composed of a few great powers and many weak ones. When great powers went to war, there were no neutrals. Weak nations like the United States should logically seek the protection of a great power and stop babbling about moral ideals and neutral rights. Despite occasional hints to the contrary, neither Napoleon nor the British intended to accommodate the Americans.

As peaceable coercion became a fiasco, Madison came under fire from militant Republicans, known as **war hawks,** who demanded more aggressive policies. Coming mainly from the South and West, regions where "honor" was a sacred word, the militants were infuriated by insults to the American flag. In addition, economic recession between 1808 and 1810 had convinced the firebrands that British policies were wrecking their regions' economies. The election of 1810 brought several war hawks to Congress. Led by thirty-four-year-old Henry Clay of Kentucky, who preferred war to the "putrescent pool of ignominious peace," the war hawks included John C. Calhoun of South Carolina, Richard M. Johnson of Kentucky, and William King of North Carolina, all future vice presidents. Clay was elected Speaker of the House.

Tecumseh and the Prophet   Voicing a more emotional and pugnacious nationalism than Jefferson and Madison, the war hawks called for the expulsion of the British from Canada and the Spanish from the Floridas. Their demands merged with western settlers' fears that the British in Canada were actively recruiting the Indians to halt the march of American settlement. In reality, American policy, not meddling by the British, was the source of bloodshed on the frontier.

In contrast to his views about blacks, Jefferson believed that Indians and whites could live peacefully together if the Indians abandoned their hunting and nomadic ways and took up farming. If they farmed, they would need less land. Jefferson and Madison insisted that the Indians be compensated fairly for ceded land and that only those Indians with a claim to the land they were ceding be allowed to conclude treaties with whites. Reality conflicted with Jefferson's ideals (see Chapter 7). The march of white settlement was steadily shrinking Indian hunting grounds, while some Indians themselves were becoming more willing to sign away land in payment to whites for

Tecumseh and William Henry Harrison at Vincennes, August 1810   *This portrait of a personal duel between Tecumseh and Indiana governor William Henry Harrison is fanciful. But the confrontation between the two at Vincennes nearly erupted into violence. Tecumseh told Harrison that Indians could never trust whites because "when Jesus Christ came upon the earth you kill'd him and nail'd him on a cross."*

blankets, guns, and the liquor that transported them into a daze even as their culture collapsed.

In 1809, no American was more eager to acquire Indian lands than William Henry Harrison, the governor of the Indiana Territory. The federal government had just divided Indiana, splitting off the present states of Illinois and Wisconsin into a separate Illinois Territory. Harrison recognized that, shorn of Illinois, Indiana would not achieve statehood unless it could attract more settlers and that the territory would not gain such settlers without offering them land currently owned by Indians. Disregarding instructions from Washington to negotiate only with Indians who claimed the land they were ceding, Harrison rounded up a delegation of half-starved Indians, none of whom lived on the rich lands along the Wabash River that he craved. By the Treaty of Fort Wayne in September 1809, these Indians ceded millions of acres along the Wabash at a price of two cents an acre.

This treaty outraged the numerous tribes that had not been party to it, and no one more than **Tecumseh,** the Shawnee chief, and his brother, Lalawéthica. Late in 1805 Lalawéthica had had a spiritual experience after a frightening dream in which he saw Indians who drank or beat their wives tormented for eternity. Until then, the Shawnees had looked down on Lalawéthica as a drunken misfit, a pale reflection of his handsome brother, Tecumseh. Overnight, Lalawéthica changed. He gave up liquor and began tearful preaching to surrounding tribes to return to their old ways and to avoid contact with whites. He quickly became known as the Prophet. Soon, he would take a new name, **Tenskwatawa,** styling himself the "Open Door" through which all Indians could revitalize their culture. Demoralized by the continuing loss of Native American lands to the whites and by the ravages of their society by alcoholism, Shawnees listened to his message. Meanwhile, Tecumseh sought to unite several tribes in Ohio and the Indiana Territory against American settlers.

The Treaty of Fort Wayne infuriated Tecumseh, who insisted that Indian lands belonged collectively to all the tribes and hence could not be sold by needy splinter groups. He held a conference with Harrison that nearly erupted into violence and that led Harrison to conclude that it was time to attack the Indians. His target was a Shawnee encampment called Prophetstown near the mouth of the Tippecanoe River. With Tecumseh away recruiting southern Indians to his cause, Tenskwatawa ordered an attack on Harrison's encampment, a mile from Prophetstown, in the predawn hours of November 7, 1811. Outnumbered two to one and short of ammunition, Tenskwatawa's force was beaten off after inflicting heavy casualties.

Although it was a small engagement, the Battle of Tippecanoe had several large effects. It made Harrison a national hero, and the memory of the battle would contribute to his election as president three decades later. It discredited Tenskwatawa, whose conduct during the battle drew criticism from his followers. It elevated Tecumseh into a position of recognized leadership among the western tribes. Finally, it persuaded Tecumseh, who long had distrusted the British as much as the Americans, that alliance with the British was the only hope to stop the spread of American settlement.

Congress Votes for War

By spring 1812, President Madison had reached the decision that war with Britain was inevitable. On June 1, he sent his war message to Congress. Meanwhile, an economic depression struck Britain, partly because the American policy of restricting trade with that country had finally started to work. Under pressure from its merchants, Britain suspended the Orders in Council on June 23. But Congress had already passed the declaration of war. Further, Britain's suspension was contingent on France's conduct toward neutrals and failed to meet Madison's demand that Britain unilaterally pledge to respect the rights of neutrals.

Neither war hawks nor westerners held the key to the vote in favor of war. The war hawks comprised a minority within the Republican Party; the West was still too sparsely settled to have many representatives in Congress. Rather, the votes of Republicans in populous states like Pennsylvania, Maryland, and Virginia were the main force propelling the war declaration through Congress. Opposition to war came mostly from Federalist strongholds in Massachusetts, Connecticut, and New York. Because Federalists were so much stronger in the Northeast than elsewhere, congressional opposition to war revealed a sectional as well as a party split. In general, however, southern Federalists opposed the war declaration, and northern Republicans supported it. In other words, the vote for war followed party lines more closely than sectional lines. Much like James Madison himself, the typical Republican advocate of war had not wanted war in 1810, or even in 1811, but had been led by the accumulation of grievances to demand it in 1812.

In his war message, Madison had listed impressment, the continued presence of British ships in American waters, and British violations of neutral rights as grievances that justified war. None of these complaints were new. Taken together, they do not fully explain why Americans went to war in 1812 rather than earlier—for example, in 1807 after the *Chesapeake-Leopard* Affair. Madison also listed British incitement of the Indians as a stimulus for war. This grievance of recent origin contributed to war feeling in the West. But the West had too few American inhabitants to drive the nation into war. A more important underlying cause was the economic recession that affected the South and West after 1808, as well as the conviction, held by John C. Calhoun and others, that British policy was damaging America's economy.

Finally, the fact that Madison rather than Jefferson was president in 1812 was of major importance. Jefferson had believed that the only motive behind British seizures of American ships was Britain's desire to block American trade with Napoleon. Hence Jefferson had concluded that time was on America's side; the seizures would stop as soon as the war in Europe ceased. In contrast, Madison had become persuaded that Britain's real motive was to strangle American trade once and for all and thereby eliminate the United States as a trading rival. War or no war in Europe, Madison saw Britain as a menace to America. In his war message, he stated flatly that Britain was meddling with American trade not because that trade interfered with Britain's "belligerent rights" but because it "frustrated the monopoly which she covets for her own commerce and navigation."

THE WAR OF 1812

Maritime issues had dominated Madison's war message, but the United States lacked a navy strong enough to challenge Britain at sea. American cruisers, notably the *Constitution,* would win a few sensational duels with British warships, but the Americans would prove unable to prevent the British from clamping a naval blockade on the American coast. Canada, which Madison viewed as a key prop of the British Empire, became the principal target. With their vastly larger population and resources, few Americans expected a long or difficult struggle. To Jefferson, the conquest of Canada seemed "a mere matter of marching."

Little justified this optimism. Although many Canadians were immigrants from the United States, to the Americans' surprise they fought to repel the invaders. Many of the best British troops were in Europe fighting Napoleon, but the British in Canada had an invaluable ally in the Indians, who struck fear by dangling scalps from their belts. The British played on this fear, in some cases forcing Americans to surrender by hinting that the Indians might be uncontrollable in battle. Too, the American state militias were filled with Sunday soldiers who "hollered for water half the time, and whiskey the other." Few militiamen understood the goals of the war. In fact, outside Congress there was not much blood lust in 1812. Opposition to the war ran strong in New England; and even in Kentucky, the home of war hawk Henry Clay, only four hundred answered the first call to arms. For many Americans, local attachments were still stronger than national ones.

On to Canada From the summer of 1812 to the spring of 1814, the Americans launched a series of unsuccessful attacks on Canada. In July 1812, General William Hull led an American army from Detroit into Canada, quickly returned when Tecumseh cut his supply line, and surrendered Detroit and two thousand men to thirteen hundred British and Indian troops. In the fall of 1812, a force of American regulars was crushed by the British at the Battle of Queenston, near Niagara Falls, while New York militiamen, contending that they had volunteered only to protect their homes and not to invade Canada, looked on from the New York side of the border. A third American offensive in 1812, a projected attack on Montreal from Plattsburgh, New York, via Lake Champlain, fell apart when the militia again refused to advance into Canada.

The Americans renewed their offensive in 1813 when General William Henry Harrison tried to retake Detroit. A succession of reverses convinced Harrison that offensive operations were futile as long as the British controlled Lake Erie. During the winter of 1812–1813, Captain Oliver H. Perry constructed a little fleet of vessels; on September 10, 1813, he destroyed a British squadron at Put-in-Bay on the western end of the lake. "We have met the enemy, and they are ours," Perry triumphantly reported. Losing control of Lake Erie, the British pulled back from Detroit, but Harrison overtook and defeated a combined British and Indian force at the Battle of the Thames on October 5. Tecumseh died in the battle; Colonel Richard Johnson's claim, never proved, to have killed Tecumseh later contributed to Johnson's election as vice president. These victories by Perry and Harrison cheered Americans, but efforts to invade Canada continued to falter. In June 1814, American troops crossed into Canada on the Niagara front but withdrew after fighting two bloody but inconclusive battles at Chippewa (July 5) and Lundy's Lane (July 25).

The British Offensive With fresh reinforcements from Europe, where Napoleon had abdicated as emperor after his disastrous invasion of Russia, the British took the offensive in the summer of 1814. General Sir George Prevost led a force of ten thousand British veterans in an offensive meant to split the New England states, where opposition to the war was strong, from the rest of the country. The British advanced down Lake Champlain until meeting the well-entrenched American forces at Plattsburgh. After his fleet met defeat on September 11, Prevost abandoned the campaign.

Washingtonians Fleeing the City as the British Invade on August 24, 1814
As the British approached Washington, Margaret Bayard Smith wrote, "a universal confidence reign'd among our citizens. Few doubted our conquering." When American resistance crumbled, she was stunned. After viewing the blackened ruins of the Capitol and the president's mansion, she concluded that Americans must "learn the dreadful[,] horrid trade of war."

Ironically, the British achieved a far more spectacular success in an operation originally designed as a diversion from their main thrust down Lake Champlain. In 1814, a British army sailed from Bermuda for Chesapeake Bay, landed near Washington, and met a larger American force, composed mainly of militia, at Bladensburg, Maryland, on August 24. The Battle of Bladensburg quickly became the "Bladensburg races" as the American militia fled, almost without firing a shot. The British then descended on Washington. Madison, who had witnessed the Bladensburg fiasco, escaped into the Virginia hills. His wife, Dolley, pausing only long enough to load her silver, a bed, and a portrait of George Washington onto her carriage, hastened to join her husband, while British troops ate the supper prepared for the Madisons at the presidential mansion. Then they burned the mansion and other public buildings in Washington. A few weeks later, the British attacked Baltimore, but after failing to crack its defenses, they broke off the operation.

The Treaty of Ghent, 1814

In August 1814, negotiations to end the war commenced between British and American commissioners at Ghent, Belgium. Initially, the British demanded territorial concessions from the United States. News of the American naval victory at Plattsburgh and Prevost's retreat to Canada, however, brought home to the British the fact that after two years of fighting, they controlled neither the Great Lakes nor Lake Champlain. Similarly, the spectacular raid on Washington had no strategic significance, so the British gave way on the issue of territorial concessions.

The final **Treaty of Ghent,** signed on Christmas Eve 1814, restored the *status quo ante bellum* (the state of things before the war); the United States neither gained nor lost territory. Several additional issues, including fixing a boundary between the United States and Canada, were referred to joint commissions for future settlement. Nothing was done about impressment, but the end of the war in Europe made neutral rights a dead issue.

Ironically, the most dramatic American victory of the war came after the conclusion of the peace negotiations. In December 1814, a British army, composed of veterans of the Napoleonic Wars and commanded by General Sir Edward Pakenham, descended on New Orleans. On January 8, 1815, two weeks after the signing of the Treaty of Ghent but before word reached America, Pakenham's force attacked an American army under General **Andrew** ("Old Hickory") **Jackson.** Although a legend for his ferocity as an Indian fighter, Jackson inspired little fear among the British, who advanced into the Battle of New Orleans far too confidently, but he did strike enough terror in his own men to prevent another American rout. In an hour of gruesome carnage, Jackson's troops shredded the line of advancing redcoats, killing Pakenham and inflicting more than two thousand casualties while losing only thirteen Americans.

The Hartford Convention

Because the Treaty of Ghent had already concluded the war, the Battle of New Orleans had little significance for diplomats. Indirectly, however, it had an effect on domestic politics by eroding Federalist strength.

The Federalist comeback in the election of 1808 had continued into the 1812 campaign. Buoyed by hostility to the war in the Northeast, the Federalists had thrown their support to DeWitt Clinton, an antiwar Republican. Although Madison won the electoral vote 128 to 89, Clinton carried all of New England except Vermont, as well as New York and New Jersey. American military setbacks in the war intensified Federalist disdain for the Madison administration. Federalists saw a nation misruled for over a decade by Republican bunglers. Jefferson's attack on the judiciary had seemed to threaten the rule of law. His purchase of Louisiana, a measure of doubtful constitutionality, had enhanced Republican strength and reduced the relative importance of Federalist New England in the Union. The Embargo Act had severely damaged New England's commerce. Now "Mr. Madison's War" was bringing fresh misery to New England in the form of the British blockade. A few Federalists began to talk of New England's secession from the Union. Most, however, rejected the idea, believing that they would soon benefit from popular exhaustion with the war and spring back into power.

In late 1814, a Federalist convention met in Hartford, Connecticut. Although some advocates of secession were present, moderates took control and passed a series of resolutions summarizing New England's grievances. At the root of these grievances lay the belief that New Englanders were becoming a permanent minority in a nation dominated by southern Republicans who failed to understand New England's commercial interests. The convention proposed to amend the Constitution to abolish the three-fifths clause (which gave the South a disproportionate share of votes in Congress by allowing it to count slaves as a basis of representation), to require a two-thirds vote of Congress to declare war and admit new states into the Union, to limit the president to a single term, to prohibit the election of two successive presidents from the same state, and to bar embargoes lasting more than sixty days.

The timing of these proposals was disastrous for the Federalists. News of the Treaty of Ghent and Jackson's victory at New Orleans dashed the Federalists' hopes of gaining broad popular support. The goal of the Hartford Convention had been to assert states' rights rather than disunion, but to many the proceedings smelled of a traitorous plot. The restoration of peace, moreover, stripped the Federalists of the primary grievance that had fueled the convention. In the election of 1816, Republican James Monroe, Madison's hand-picked successor and a fellow Virginian, swept the nation over negligible Federalist opposition. He would win reelection in 1820 with only a single dissenting electoral vote. As a force in national politics, the Federalists were finished.

THE AWAKENING OF AMERICAN NATIONALISM

The United States emerged from the War of 1812 bruised but intact. In its first major war since the Revolution, the Republic had demonstrated not only that it could fight on even terms against a major power but also that republics could fight wars without turning to despotism. The war produced more than its share of symbols of American nationalism. Whitewash cleared the smoke damage to the presidential mansion; thereafter, it became known as the White House. The British attack on Fort McHenry, guarding Baltimore, prompted a young observer, Francis Scott Key, to compose "The Star-Spangled Banner."

The Battle of New Orleans boosted Andrew Jackson onto the stage of national politics and became a source of legends about American military prowess. It appears to most contemporary scholars that the British lost because Pakenham's men, advancing within range of Jackson's riflemen and cannon, unaccountably paused and became sitting ducks. But in the wake of the battle, Americans spun a different tale. The legend arose that Jackson owed his victory not to Pakenham's blundering tactics but to hawk-eyed Kentucky frontiersmen whose rifles picked off the British with unerring accuracy. In fact, many frontiersmen in Jackson's army had not carried rifles; even if they had, gunpowder smoke would have obscured the enemy. But none of this mattered at the time. Just as Americans preferred militia to professional soldiers, they chose to believe that their greatest victory of the war had been the handiwork of amateurs.

Madison's Nationalism and the Era of Good Feelings, 1817–1824

The War of 1812 had three major political consequences. First, it eliminated the Federalists as a national political force. Second, it went a long way toward convincing the Republicans that the nation was strong and resilient, capable of fighting a war while maintaining the liberty of its people. Third, with the Federalists tainted by suspicion of disloyalty and no longer a force, and with fears about the fragility of republics fading, Republicans increasingly embraced doctrines long associated with the Federalists.

In a message to Congress in December 1815, Madison called for federal support for internal improvements such as roads and canals, tariff protection for the new industries that had sprung up during the embargo, and the creation of a new national bank. (The charter of the first Bank of the United States had expired in 1811.) In Congress, another Republican, Henry Clay of Kentucky, proposed similar measures, which he called the American System, with the aim of making the young nation economically self-sufficient and free from dependence on Europe. In 1816, Congress chartered the Second Bank of the United States and enacted a moderate tariff. Federal support for internal improvements proved to be a thornier problem. Madison favored federal aid in principle but believed that a constitutional amendment was necessary to authorize it. Accordingly, just before leaving office in 1817, he vetoed an internal-improvements bill.

As Republicans adopted positions that they had once disdained, an **"Era of Good Feelings"** dawned on American politics. A Boston newspaper, impressed by the warm reception accorded President James Monroe while touring New England, coined the phrase in 1817. It has stuck as a description of Monroe's two administrations from 1817 to 1825. Compared with Jefferson and Madison, Monroe was not brilliant, polished, or wealthy, but he keenly desired to heal the political divisions that a stronger intellect and personality might have inflamed. The phrase "Era of Good Feelings" reflects not only the war's elimination of some divisive issues but also Monroe's conscious effort to avoid political controversies.

But the good feelings were paper-thin. Madison's 1817 veto of the internal-improvements bill revealed the persistence of disagreements about the role of the federal government under the Constitution. Furthermore, the continuation of slavery was arousing sectional animosities that a journalist's phrase about good feelings could not dispel. Not surprisingly, the postwar consensus began to unravel almost as soon as Americans recognized its existence.

John Marshall and the Supreme Court   In 1819, Jefferson's old antagonist John Marshall, who was still chief justice, issued two opinions that stunned Republicans. The first case, *Dartmouth College* v. *Woodward,* centered on the question of whether New Hampshire could transform a private corporation, Dartmouth College, into a state university. Marshall concluded that the college's original charter, granted to its trustees by George III in 1769, was a contract. Since the Constitution specifically forbade states to interfere with contracts, New Hampshire's effort to turn Dartmouth into a state university was unconstitutional. The implications of Marshall's ruling were far-reaching. Charters or acts of incorporation provided their beneficiaries with various legal privileges and were sought by businesses as well as by colleges. In effect, Marshall said that once a state had chartered a college or a business, it surrendered both its power to alter the charter and, in large measure, its authority to regulate the beneficiary.

A few weeks later, the chief justice handed down an even more momentous decision in **McCulloch v. Maryland.** The issue here was whether the state of Maryland had the power to tax a national corporation, specifically the Baltimore branch of the Second Bank of the United States. Although the bank was a national corporation chartered by Congress, most of the stockholders were private citizens who reaped the profits the bank made. Speaking for a unanimous Court, Marshall ignored these private features of the bank and concentrated instead on two issues. First, did Congress

John Marshall   *In his first three decades as chief justice of the Supreme Court, Marshall greatly strengthened the power of the Court and the national government, each of which he thought vital to preserving the intrinsic rights of life, liberty, and property.*

have the power to charter a national bank? Nothing in the Constitution, Marshall conceded, explicitly granted this power. But the broad sweep of enumerated powers, he reasoned, implied the power to charter a bank. Marshall was clearly engaging in a broad, or "loose," rather than strict, construction (interpretation) of the Constitution. The second issue was whether a state could tax an agency of the federal government that lay within its borders. Marshall argued that any power of the national government, enumerated or implied, was supreme within its sphere. States could not interfere with the exercise of federal powers. A tax by Maryland on the Baltimore branch was such an interference. Since "the power to tax involves the power to destroy," Maryland's tax was plainly unconstitutional.

Marshall's decision in the *McCulloch* case dismayed many Republicans. Although Madison and Monroe had supported the establishment of the Second Bank of the United States, the bank had made itself unpopular by tightening its loan policies during the summer of 1818. This contraction of credit triggered the Panic of 1819, a severe depression that gave rise to considerable distress throughout the country, especially among western farmers. At a time when the bank was widely blamed for the panic, Marshall's ruling stirred controversy by placing the bank beyond the regulatory power of any state government. His decision, indeed, was as much an attack on state sovereignty as it was a defense of the bank. The Constitution, Marshall argued, was the creation not of state governments but of the people of all the states, and thus was more fundamental than state laws. His reasoning assailed the Republican theory, best expressed in the Virginia and Kentucky Resolutions of 1798–1799 (see Chapter 7), that the Union was essentially a compact among states. Republicans had continued to view state governments as more immediately responsive to the people's will than the federal government, and they regarded the compact theory of the Union as a guarantor of popular liberty. As Republicans saw it, Marshall's *McCulloch* decision, along with his decision in the *Dartmouth College* case, stripped state governments of the power to impose the will of their people on corporations.

The Missouri Compromise, 1820–1821

The fragility of the Era of Good Feelings became even more apparent in the two-year-long controversy over statehood for Missouri. Carved from the Louisiana Purchase, Missouri attracted slaveholders. In 1819, when the House of Representatives was considering a bill to admit Missouri as a state, 16 percent of the territory's inhabitants were slaves. Then a New York Republican offered an amendment that prohibited the further introduction of slaves and provided for the emancipation, at age twenty-five, of all slave offspring born after Missouri's admission as a state. Following rancorous debate, the House accepted the amendment, and the Senate rejected it. Both chambers voted along sectional lines.

Prior to 1819, slavery had not been the primary source of the nation's sectional divisions. For example, Federalists' opposition to the embargo and the War of 1812 had sprung from their fear that the dominant Republicans were sacrificing New England's commercial interests to those of the South and West—not from hostility to slavery. The Missouri question, which Jefferson compared to "a fire bell in the night, [which] awakened me and filled me with terror," now thrust slavery into the center of long-standing sectional divisions.

The slavery issue surfaced at this time for several reasons. In 1819, the Union had eleven free and eleven slave states. The admission of Missouri as a slave state would upset this balance to the advantage of the South. Equally important, northerners worried that admitting Missouri as a slave state would set a precedent for the extension of slavery into the northern part of the Purchase. The slave states of Alabama, Mississippi, and Louisiana, all carved from the Purchase before 1819 with little controversy, were south of Missouri, which was on the same latitude as the free states of Ohio, Indiana, and Illinois. Finally, the disintegration of the Federalists as a national force reduced the need for unity among Republicans, and they increasingly heeded sectional pressures more than calls for party loyalty.

Virtually every issue that was to wrack the Union during the next forty years was present in the controversy over Missouri: southern charges that the North was conspiring to destroy the Union and end slavery; accusations by northerners that southerners were conspiring to extend the institution. Southerners openly proclaimed that antislavery northerners were kindling fires that only "seas of blood" could extinguish. Such threats of civil war persuaded some northern congressmen who had originally supported the restriction of slavery in Missouri to back down. A series of congressional agreements known collectively as the **Missouri Compromise** resolved the crisis.

To balance the number of free and slave states, Congress in 1820 admitted Maine as a free state and Missouri as a slave state; to forestall a further crisis, it also prohibited slavery in the remainder of the Louisiana Purchase north of 36°30′ the southern boundary of Missouri. But compromise did not come easily. The individual components of the eventual compromise passed by close and ominously sectional votes.

No sooner had the compromise been forged than it nearly fell apart. As a prelude to statehood, Missourians drafted a constitution that prohibited free blacks, whom some eastern states viewed as citizens, from entering their territory. This provision clashed with the federal Constitution's provision that citizens of one state were entitled to the same rights as citizens of other states. Balking at Missourians' exclusion of free

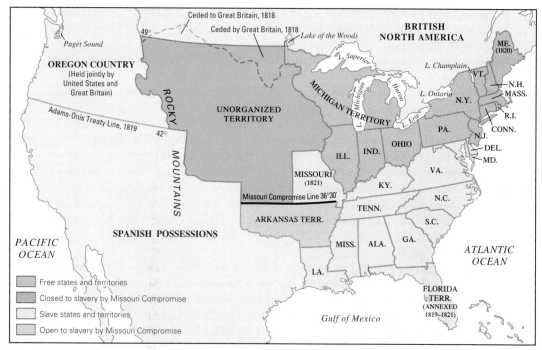

MAP 8.2 The Missouri Compromise, 1820–1821

The Missouri Compromise temporarily quelled controversy over slavery by admitting Maine as a free state and Missouri as a slave state, and by prohibiting slavery in the remainder of the Louisiana Purchase north of 36°30′.

blacks, antislavery northerners barred Missouri's admission into the Union until 1821, when Henry Clay engineered a new agreement. This second Missouri Compromise prohibited Missouri from discriminating against citizens of other states but left open the issue of whether free blacks were citizens.

The Missouri Compromise was widely viewed as a southern victory. The South had gained admission of Missouri, whose acceptance of slavery was controversial, while the North had merely gained Maine, whose rejection of slavery inspired no controversy. Yet the South had conceded to freedom a vast block of territory north of 36°30′. Although much of this territory was unorganized Indian country that some viewed as unfit for white habitation, the states of Iowa, Minnesota, Wisconsin, the Dakotas, Nebraska, and Kansas eventually would be formed out of it. Also, the Missouri Compromise reinforced the principle, originally set down by the Northwest Ordinance of 1787, that Congress had the right to prohibit slavery in some territories. Southerners had implicitly accepted the argument that slaves were not like other forms of property that could be moved from place to place at will.

Foreign Policy Under Monroe   American foreign policy between 1816 and 1824 reflected more consensus than conflict. The end of the Napoleonic Wars and the signing of the Treaty of Ghent had removed most of the foreign-policy disagreements between Federalists and Republicans. Moreover, Monroe was fortunate to have as his secretary of state an extraordinary diplomat, **John Quincy Adams.** The son of the last Federalist president, Adams had been the only Federalist in the Senate to support the Louisiana Purchase, and he later became an ardent Republican. An austere and scholarly man whose library equaled his house in monetary value, Adams was a tough negotiator and a fervent nationalist.

As secretary of state, Adams moved quickly to strengthen the peace with Great Britain. During his tenure, the United States and Britain signed the Rush-Bagot Treaty of 1817, which effectively demilitarized the Great Lakes by severely restricting the number of ships that the two powers could maintain there. Next the British-American Convention of 1818 restored to Americans the same fishing rights off Newfoundland that they had enjoyed before the War of 1812 and fixed the boundary between the United States and Canada from the Lake of the Woods west to the Rockies. Beyond the Rockies, the vast country known as Oregon was declared "free and open" to both American and British citizens. As a result of these two agreements, the United States had a secure border with British-controlled Canada for the first time since independence, and a claim to the Pacific.

The nation now turned its attention to dealing with Spain, which still owned East Florida and claimed West Florida. No one was certain whether the Louisiana Purchase included West Florida. Acting as if it did, the United States in 1812 had simply added a slice of West Florida to the state of Louisiana and another slice to the Mississippi Territory. Using the pretext that it was a base for Seminole Indian raids and a refuge for fugitive slaves, Andrew Jackson, now the military commander in the South, invaded East Florida in 1818. He hanged two British subjects and captured Spanish forts. Jackson had acted without explicit orders, but Adams supported the raid, guessing correctly that it would panic the Spanish into further concessions.

In 1819, Spain agreed to the **Adams-Onís (Transcontinental) Treaty.** By its terms, Spain ceded East Florida to the United States, renounced its claims to West Florida, and agreed to a southern border of the United States west of the Mississippi that ran north along the Sabine River (separating Texas from Louisiana) and then westward along the Red and Arkansas Rivers to the Rocky Mountains, finally following the forty-second parallel to the Pacific. In effect, the United States conceded that Texas was not part of the Louisiana Purchase, while Spain agreed to a northern limit to its claims to the West Coast. It thereby left the United States free to pursue its interests in Oregon.

The Monroe Doctrine, 1823

John Quincy Adams had long believed that God and nature had ordained that the United States would eventually span the entire continent of North America. Throughout his negotiations leading up to the Adams-Onís Treaty, he made it clear to Spain that, if the Spanish did not concede some of their territory in North America, the United States might seize all of it, including Texas and even Mexico. Americans were fast acquiring a reputation as an aggressive people. Yet Spain was concerned with larger issues than American encroachment. Its primary objective was to suppress the revolutions against Spanish rule that had broken out in South America. To accomplish this goal, Spain sought support from the European monarchs who had organized the Holy Alliance in 1815. The brainchild of the tsar of Russia, the Holy Alliance aimed to quash revolutions everywhere in the name of Christian and monarchist principles. By 1822, its members talked of helping Spain suppress the South American revolutions. But Britain, whose trading interests in South America were hampered by Spanish restrictions, refused to join the Holy Alliance. British foreign minister George Canning proposed that the United States and Britain issue a joint statement opposing any European interference in South America, while pledging that neither would annex any part of Spain's old empire in the New World.

While sharing Canning's opposition to European intervention in the New World, Adams preferred that the United States make a declaration of policy on its own rather than "come in as a cock-boat in the wake of the British man-of-war." Adams flatly rejected Canning's insistence on a joint Anglo-American pledge never to annex any part of Spain's former territories, for Adams wanted the freedom to annex Texas or Cuba, should their inhabitants one day "solicit a union with us."

This was the background of the **Monroe Doctrine,** as President Monroe's message to Congress on December 2, 1823, later came to be called. The message, written largely by Adams, announced three key principles: that unless American interests were involved, U.S. policy was to abstain from European wars; that the "American continents" were not "subjects for future colonization by any European power"; and that the United States would construe any attempt at European colonization in the New World as an "unfriendly act."

Europeans widely derided the Monroe Doctrine as an empty pronouncement. Fear of the British navy, not the Monroe Doctrine, prevented the Holy Alliance from intervening in South America. With hindsight, however, the Europeans might have taken the doctrine more seriously, for it had important implications. First, by pledging itself not to interfere in European wars, the United States was excluding the possibility that it would support revolutionary movements in Europe. For example, Adams opposed U.S. recognition of Greek patriots fighting for independence from the Ottoman Turks. Second, by keeping open its options to annex territory in the Americas, the United States was using the Monroe Doctrine to claim a preeminent position in the New World.

CONCLUSION

Jefferson's philosophy left a strong imprint on his age. Seeking to make the federal government more responsive to the people's will, Jefferson moved quickly to slash public expenditures and to contest Federalist control of the judiciary. His purchase of the Louisiana Territory in 1803 reflected his view that American liberty depended on the perpetuation of agriculture, and it would bring new states, dominated by Republicans, into the Union. As the Federalist Party waned, Jefferson had to face down challenges from within his own party, notably from the mischief of Aaron Burr and from die-hard old Republicans like John Randolph, who charged that Jefferson was abandoning pure Republican doctrines.

The outbreak of war between Napoleon's France and Britain, and the threat it posed to American neutrality, preoccupied Jefferson's second term and both terms of his successor, James Madison. The failure of the embargo and peaceable coercion to force Europeans to respect American neutrality led the United States into war with Britain in 1812. The war destroyed the Federalists, who committed political suicide at the Hartford Convention. It also led Madison to jettison part of Jefferson's legacy by calling for a new national bank, federal support for internal improvements, and protective tariffs. The Transcontinental Treaty of 1819 and the Monroe Doctrine's bold pronouncement that European powers must not meddle in the affairs of the Western Hemisphere expressed America's increasingly assertive nationalism.

Conflict was never far below the surface of the apparent consensus of the Era of Good Feelings. In the absence of Federalist opposition, Republicans began to fragment into sectional factions, most notably in the conflict over Missouri's admission to the Union as a slave state.

9

The Transformation of American Society, 1815–1840

WESTWARD EXPANSION

In 1790 the vast majority of the non-Indian population of the United States, nearly 4 million people, lived east of the Appalachian Mountains and within a few hundred miles of the Atlantic Ocean. But by 1840 one-third of the non-Indian population of just over 17 million were living between the Appalachians and the Mississippi River, the area that Americans of the time referred to as the West but that historians call the **Old Northwest** and **Old Southwest.** Migrants brought traditional values and customs with them, but in adapting to the West they gradually developed new values and customs. In short, they became westerners, men and women with a distinctive culture.

Only a few Americans moved west to seek adventure, and these few usually headed into the half-known region west of the Rocky Mountains, the present Far West. Most migrants desired and expected a better version of the life they had known in the East: more land and more bountiful crops. Several factors nurtured this expectation: the growing power of the federal government; its often ruthless removal of the Indians from the path of white settlement; and a boom in the prices of agricultural commodities after the War of 1812.

The Sweep West   Americans moved west in a series of bursts. Americans leap-frogged the Appalachians after 1791 to bring four new states into the Union by 1803: Vermont, Kentucky, Tennessee, and Ohio. The second burst occurred between 1816 and 1821, when six states entered the Union: Indiana, Mississippi, Illinois, Alabama, Maine, and Missouri. Even as Indiana and Illinois were gaining statehood, settlers were pouring farther west into Michigan. Ohio's population jumped from 45,000 in 1800 to 581,000 by 1820 and 1,519,000 by 1840; Michigan's from 5,000 in 1810 to 212,000 by 1840.

Seeking security, pioneers usually migrated as families rather than as individuals. To reach markets with their produce, most settlers clustered near the navigable rivers of the West, especially the magnificent water system created by the Ohio and Mississippi Rivers. Only with the spread of canals in the 1820s and 1830s, and later of railroads, did westerners feel free to venture far from rivers. In addition, westerners often clustered with people who hailed from the same region back east. For instance, in 1836 a group of farmers from nearby towns met at Castleton, Vermont, listened to a minister intone from the Bible, "And Moses sent them to spy out the land of Canaan," and soon established the town of Vermontville in Michigan. Other migrants to the West were less organized than these latter-day descendants of the Puritans, but most hoped to settle among familiar faces in the West. When they found that southerners already were well entrenched in Indiana, for example, New Englanders tended to prefer Michigan.

Western Society and Customs Most westerners craved sociability. Even before towns sprang up, rural families joined with their neighbors in group sports and festivities. Men met for games that, with a few exceptions like marbles (popular among all ages), were tests of strength or agility. These included wrestling, weightlifting, pole jumping (for distance rather than height), and a variant of the modern hammer toss. Some of these games were brutal. In gander pulling, horseback riders competed to pull the head off a male duck whose neck had been stripped of feathers and greased. Women usually combined work and play in quilting and sewing parties, carpet tackings, and even chicken and goose pluckings. Social activities brought the genders together. Group corn huskings usually ended with dances; and in a variety of "hoedowns" and "frolics," even westerners who in principle might disapprove of dancing promenaded to singing and a fiddler's tune.

Within western families, there was usually a clear division of labor between men and women. Men performed most of the heaviest labor such as cutting down trees and plowing fields. Women usually rose first in the morning because they were responsible for milking the cows and preparing breakfast. As they had always done, women fashioned the coverlets that warmed beds in unheated rooms, and spun yarn and wove the fabrics to make their family's shirts, coats, pants, and dresses. Farmwomen often helped butcher hogs. They knew that the best way to bleed a hog was to slit its throat while it was still alive, and after the bleeding, they were adept at scooping out the innards, washing the heart and liver, and hanging them to dry. There was nothing dainty about the work of pioneer women.

Most western sports and customs had been transplanted from the East, but the West developed a character of its own. Before 1840, few westerners could afford elegant living. Arriving on the Michigan frontier from New York City in 1835, the well-bred Caroline Kirkland quickly discovered that her neighbors thought that they had a right to borrow anything she owned with no more than a blunt declaration that "you've got plenty." "For my own part," Caroline related, "I have lent my broom, my thread, my tape, my spoons, my cat, my thimble, my scissors, my shawl, my shoes, and have been asked for my comb and brushes." Their relative lack of refinement made westerners easy targets for easterners' contemptuous jibes.

CHRONOLOGY, 1815–1840

1790 • Samuel Slater opens his first Rhode Island mill for the production of cotton yarn.

1793 • Eli Whitney invents the cotton gin.

1807 • Robert R. Livingston and Robert Fulton introduce the steamboat *Clermont* on the Hudson River.

1811 • Construction of the National Road begins at Cumberland, Maryland.

1813 • Incorporation of the Boston Manufacturing Company.

1816 • Second Bank of the United States chartered.

1817–1825 • Construction of the Erie Canal started.
Mississippi enters the Union.

1819 • Economic panic, ushering in four-year depression.
Alabama enters the Union.

1820–1850 • Growth of female moral-reform societies.

1820s • Expansion of New England textile mills.

1824 • *Gibbons* v. *Ogden*.

1828 • Baltimore and Ohio Railroad chartered.

1830 • Indian Removal Act passed by Congress.

1831 • *Cherokee Nation* v. *Georgia*.
Alexis de Tocqueville begins visit to the United States to study American penitentiaries.

1832 • *Worcester* v. *Georgia*.

1834 • First strike at the Lowell mills.

1835 • Treaty of New Echota.

1837 • Economic panic begins a depression that lasts until 1843.

1838 • The Trail of Tears.

1840 • System of production by interchangeable parts perfected.

Criticisms of westerners as yokels provoked westerners to assert that they lived in a land of honest democracy and that the East was soft and decadent. This exchange of insults fostered a regional identity among westerners that further shaped their behavior. Priding themselves on their simple manners, some westerners were intolerant of other westerners who had pretensions to gentility. On one occasion, a traveler who hung up a blanket in a tavern to shield his bed from public gaze had it promptly ripped down. On another, a woman who improvised a screen behind which to retire in a crowded room was dismissed as "stuck up." A politician who rode to a public meeting in a buggy instead of on horseback lost votes.

The Far West   The great majority of pioneers sought stability and prosperity in the area between the Appalachians and the Mississippi River, the region today known as the Midwest. By contrast, an adventuring spirit carried a few Americans far beyond the Mississippi. On an exploring expedition in the Southwest in

"Barroom Dancing" by John Lewis Krimmel, 1820 *We can only guess what George Washington, looking soberly down from the wall, would have thought of these tipsy celebrants at a country tavern.*

1806, Zebulon Pike sighted the Colorado peak that was later named after him. The Lewis and Clark expedition whetted interest in the Far West. In 1811, a New York merchant, John Jacob Astor, founded the fur-trading post of Astoria at the mouth of the Columbia River in the Oregon Country. In the 1820s and 1830s, fur traders also operated along the Missouri River from St. Louis to the Rocky Mountains and beyond. At first, whites relied on Native Americans to bring them furs, but during the 1820s white trappers or "mountain men"—among them, Kit Carson, Jedediah Smith, and the mulatto Jim Beckwourth—gathered furs on their own while performing astounding feats of survival in harsh surroundings.

Jedediah Smith was representative of these men. Born in the Susquehanna Valley of New York in 1799, Smith moved west with his family to Pennsylvania and Illinois and signed on with an expedition bound for the upper Missouri River in 1822. In the course of this and subsequent explorations, he was almost killed by a grizzly bear in the Black Hills of South Dakota, learned from the Native Americans to trap beaver and kill buffalo, crossed the Mojave Desert into California, explored California's San Joaquin Valley, and hiked back across the Sierras and the primeval Great Basin to the Great Salt Lake, a trip so forbidding that even Native Americans avoided it. The exploits of Smith and the other mountain men were popularized in biographies, and they became legends in their own day.

The Federal Government and the West

Of the various causes of expansion to the Mississippi from 1790 to 1840, the one that operated most generally and uniformly throughout the period was the growing strength of the federal government. Even before the Constitution's ratification, several states had ceded their western land claims to the national government, thereby creating the bountiful public domain. The Land Ordinance of 1785 had provided for the survey and sale of these lands, and the Northwest Ordinance of 1787 had established procedures for transforming them into states. The Louisiana Purchase of 1803 brought the entire Mississippi River under American control, and the Transcontinental Treaty of 1819 wiped out the last vestiges of Spanish power east of the Mississippi.

The federal government directly stimulated settlement of the West by promising land to men who enlisted during the War of 1812. With 6 million acres allotted to these so-called military bounties, many former soldiers and their families pulled up roots and settled in the West. To facilitate westward migration, Congress authorized funds in 1816 for the extension of the National Road, a highway begun in 1811 that reached Wheeling, Virginia, on the Ohio River in 1818 and Vandalia, Illinois, by 1838. Soon settlers thronged the road. "Old America seems to be breaking up," a traveler on the National Road wrote in 1817. "We are seldom out of sight, as we travel on this grand track towards the Ohio, of family groups before and behind us."

The same government strength that aided whites brought misery to the Indians. Virtually all the foreign-policy successes during the Jefferson, Madison, and Monroe administrations worked to Native Americans' disadvantage. The Louisiana Purchase and the Transcontinental Treaty stripped them of Spanish protection. In the wake of the Louisiana Purchase, Lewis and Clark bluntly told the Indians that they must "shut their ears to the counsels of bad birds" and listen henceforth only to the "Great Father" in Washington. The outcome of the War of 1812 also worked against the Native Americans; indeed, the Indians were the only real losers of the war. Early in the negotiations leading to the Treaty of Ghent, the British had insisted on the creation of an Indian buffer state between the United States and Canada in the Old Northwest. But after the American victory at the Battle of Plattsburgh, the British dropped the demand and essentially abandoned the Indians to the Americans.

The Removal of the Indians

Westward-moving white settlers found sizable numbers of Native Americans in their paths, particularly in the South, home to the so-called **Five Civilized Tribes**: the Cherokees, Choctaws, Creeks, Chickasaws, and Seminoles. Years of commercial dealings and intermarriage with whites had created in these tribes, especially the Cherokees, an influential minority of mixed-bloods who embraced Christianity, practiced agriculture, built gristmills, and even owned slaves. One of their chiefs, Sequoyah, devised a written form of their language; other Cherokees published a bilingual newspaper, the *Cherokee Phoenix*.

The "civilization" of the southern Indians impressed New England missionaries more than southern whites, who viewed the Civilized Tribes with contempt and their land with envy. Presidents James Monroe and John Quincy Adams had concluded several treaties with Indian tribes providing for their voluntary removal to public lands west of the Mississippi River. Although some assimilated mixed-bloods sold their tribal lands to the government, other mixed-bloods resisted because their prosperity depended on trade with close-by whites. In addition, full-bloods, the majority even in the "civilized" tribes, clung to their land and customs. They wanted to remain near the burial grounds of their ancestors and condemned mixed-bloods who bartered away tribal lands to whites. When the Creek mixed-blood chief William McIntosh sold all Creek lands in Georgia and two-thirds of Creek lands in Alabama to the government in the Treaty of Indian Springs (1825), a Creek tribal council executed him.

During the 1820s, whites in Alabama, Georgia, and Mississippi intensified pressure on the Indians by surveying tribal lands and squatting on them. Southern legislatures, loath to restrain white settlers, passed laws that threatened to expropriate Indian lands unless the Indians moved west. Other laws extended state jurisdiction over the tribes (which effectively outlawed tribal government) and declared that no Indian could be a witness in a court case involving whites (which made it difficult for Indians to collect debts owed them by whites).

These measures delighted President Andrew Jackson. Reared on the frontier and sharing its contempt for Indians, Jackson believed that it was ridiculous to treat the Indians as independent nations; rather, they should be subject to the laws of the states where they lived. This position spelled doom for the Indians, who could not vote or hold state office. In 1834, Cherokee chief John Ross got a taste of what state jurisdiction meant; Georgia, without consulting him, put his house up as a prize in the state lottery.

In 1830, Jackson secured passage of the **Indian Removal Act,** which authorized him to exchange public lands in the West for Indian territories in the East and appropriated $500,000 to cover the expenses of removal. But the real costs of removal, human and monetary, were vastly greater. During Jackson's eight years in office, the federal government forced Indians to exchange 100 million acres of their lands for 32 million acres of public lands. In the late 1820s and early 1830s the Choctaws (whom Tocqueville had observed near Memphis), Creeks, and Chickasaws started their "voluntary" removal to the West. In 1836, Creeks who clung to their homes were forcibly removed, many in chains. Most Seminoles were removed from Florida, but only after a bitter war between 1835 and 1842 that cost the federal government $20 million.

Ironically, the Cherokees, whose leaders were the most accommodating to American political institutions, suffered the worst fate. In 1827, the Cherokees proclaimed themselves an independent republic within Georgia. When the Georgia legislature subsequently extended the state's jurisdiction over this "nation," the Cherokees petitioned the U.S. Supreme Court for an injunction to halt Georgia's action. In the case of *Cherokee Nation* v. *Georgia* (1831), Chief Justice John Marshall denied the Cherokees' claim to status as a republic within Georgia; rather, they were a "domestic dependent nation," a kind of ward of the United States. Marshall added that prolonged occupancy had given the Cherokees a claim to their lands within Georgia. A year later, he clarified the Cherokees' legal position in *Worcester* v. *Georgia* by holding that they were a "distinct" political community entitled to federal protection from tampering by Georgia.

Reportedly sneering, "John Marshall has made his decision; now let him enforce it," President Jackson ignored it. Next, federal agents persuaded some minor Cherokee chiefs to sign the Treaty of New Echota (1835), which ceded all Cherokee lands in the United States for $5.6 million and free passage west. Congress ratified this treaty (by one vote), but the vast majority of Cherokees denounced it. In 1839, a Cherokee party took revenge by murdering its three principal signers, including a former editor of the *Cherokee Phoenix.*

The end of the story was simple and tragic. In 1838 the Cherokees were forcibly removed to the new Indian Territory in what is now Oklahoma. They traveled west along what became known as the **"Trail of Tears."** As a youth, a man who later became a colonel in the Confederate Army had participated in the forced removal of some sixteen thousand Cherokees from their lands east of the Mississippi River, where North Carolina, Georgia, Alabama, and Tennessee more or less converge. He recollected: "I fought through the civil war and have seen men shot to pieces and slaughtered by the thousands, but the Cherokees removal was the cruelest work I ever knew." Perhaps as many as eight thousand Cherokees, more than one-third of the entire nation, died during and just after the removal.

Indians living in the Northwest Territory fared no better. A series of treaties extinguished their land titles, and most moved west of the Mississippi. The removal of the northwestern Indians was notable for two uprisings. The first, led by Red Bird, a Winnebago chief, began in 1827 but was quickly crushed. The second, led by a Sac and Fox chief, Black Hawk, raged along the Illinois frontier until 1832, when federal troops and Illinois militia virtually annihilated Black Hawk's followers. Black Hawk's downfall persuaded the other Old Northwest tribes to cede their lands. Between 1832 and 1837, the United States acquired nearly 190 million acres of Indian land in the Northwest for $70 million in gifts and annual payments.

The Agricultural Boom

In pushing Indians from the paths of white settlers, the federal government was responding to whites' demands for more land. After the War of 1812, the rising prices of agricultural commodities such as wheat, corn, and cotton drew settlers westward in search of better farmland. Several factors accounted for the skyrocketing farm prices. During the Napoleonic Wars, the United States had quickly captured former British markets in the West Indies and former Spanish markets in South America. With the conclusion of the wars, American farmers found brisk demand for their wheat and corn in Britain and France, both exhausted by two decades of warfare. In addition, demand within the United States for western farm commodities intensified after 1815 as the quickening pace of industrialization and urbanization in the East spurred a shift of workers toward nonagricultural employment. Finally, the West's splendid river systems made it possible for farmers in Ohio to ship wheat and corn down the Ohio River to the Mississippi and down the Mississippi to New Orleans. There, wheat and corn were either sold or transshipped to the East, the West Indies, South America, or Europe. Just as government policies made farming in the West possible, high prices for foodstuffs made it attractive.

As the prospect of raising wheat and corn pulled farmers toward the Old Northwest, Eli Whitney's invention of the cotton gin in 1793 (see Chapter 7) cleared the path for settlement of the Old Southwest, particularly the states of Alabama and Mississippi. As cotton clothing came into fashion around 1815, the British textile industry provided seemingly bottomless demand for raw cotton. By 1820, Alabama and Mississippi were producing nearly half of the nation's cotton. With its warm climate, wet springs and summers, and relatively dry autumns, the Old Southwest was especially suited to cotton cultivation. The explosive thrust of small farmers and planters from the seaboard South into the Old Southwest resembled a gold rush. By 1817, "Alabama fever" gripped the South; settlers bid the price of good land up to thirty to fifty dollars an acre.

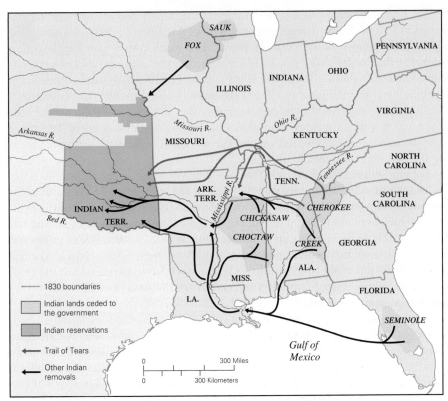

MAP 9.1 The Removal of the Native Americans to the West, 1820–1840

The so-called Trail of Tears, followed by the Cherokees, was one of several routes along which various tribes migrated on their forced removal to reservations west of the Mississippi.

Accounting for less than a quarter of all American exports between 1802 and 1807, cotton comprised just over half by 1830, and nearly two-thirds by 1836.

THE GROWTH OF THE MARKET ECONOMY

Many farmers traditionally had grown only enough food to feed their families (subsistence agriculture). With agricultural commodities like wheat and cotton commanding high prices, a growing number of farmers added a cash crop (called commercial agriculture, or the **market economy**). In the South, slaves increasingly became a valuable commodity; the sale of slaves from declining agricultural states in the Southeast to planters and farmers migrating to Alabama and Mississippi grew into a huge business after 1815. "Virginia," an observer stated in 1832, "is, in fact, a *negro* raising State for other States; she produces enough for her own supply and six thousand a year for sale."

The unprecedented scale of commercial agriculture after 1815 exposed farmers to new risks. Farmers had no control over prices in distant markets. Furthermore, the often long interval between harvesting a cash crop and selling it forced farmers to borrow money to sustain their families. Thus the market economy forced farmers into short-term debt in the hope of long-term profit.

The debt was frequently worse than most had expected. Many western farmers had to borrow money to buy their land. The roots of this indebtedness for land lay in the federal government's inability to devise an effective policy for transferring the public domain directly into the hands of small farmers.

Federal Land Policy   Partisan and sectional pressures buffeted federal land policy like a kite in a March wind. The result was a succession of land laws passed between 1796 and 1820, each of which sought to undo the damage caused by its predecessors.

At the root of early federal land policy lay a preference for the orderly settlement of the public domain. To this end, the Ordinance of 1785 divided public lands into sections of 640 acres (see Chapter 6). The architects of the ordinance did not expect that ordinary farmers could afford such large lots; rather, they assumed that farmers who shared ties based on religion or region of origin would band together to purchase sections. This outcome would ensure that compatible settlers would live on adjoining lots in what amounted to rural neighborhoods, and it would make the task of government much easier than if settlers were to live in isolation on widely scattered homesteads.

Political developments in the 1790s undermined the expectations of the ordinance's framers. Because their political bases lay in the East, the Federalists were reluctant to encourage headlong settlement of the West, but at the same time they were eager to raise revenue for the federal government from land sales. They reconciled the goals of retarding actual settlement while gaining revenue by encouraging the sale of huge tracts of land to wealthy speculators who had no intention of farming the land themselves. The speculators held onto the land until its value rose and then sold off parcels to farmers. For example, in the 1790s the Holland Land Company, composed mainly of Dutch investors, bought up much of western New York and western Pennsylvania. A federal land law passed in 1796 reflected Federalist aims by maintaining the minimum purchase at 640 acres at a minimum price of two dollars an acre, and by allowing only a year for complete payment. Few small farmers could afford to buy that much land at that price.

Believing that the small farmer was the backbone of the Republic and aware of Republican political strength in the West, Thomas Jefferson and the Republicans tried to ease the transfer of the public domain to farmers. The land law of 1800 dropped the minimum purchase to 320 acres and allowed up to four years for full payment but kept the minimum purchase price at $2 an acre. In 1804, the minimum purchase came down to 160 acres, in 1820 to 80 acres, and in 1832 to 40 acres. The minimum price also declined from $2 an acre in 1800 to $1.64 in 1804 and $1.25 in 1820.

Although Congress steadily liberalized land policy, speculators always remained one step ahead. Long before 1832, speculators were selling forty-acre lots to farmers. Farmers preferred small lots (and rarely bought more than 160 acres) because the farms they purchased typically were forested. A new landowner could clear no more than ten to twelve acres of trees a year. All land in the public domain was sold at auction, usually for much more than the two-dollar minimum. With agricultural prices soaring, speculators assumed that land would continue to rise in value and accordingly were willing to bid high on new land, which they resold to farmers at hefty prices.

After the War of 1812, speculators found it increasingly easy to borrow money. The chartering of the Second Bank of the United States in 1816 had the dual effect of increasing the amount of money in circulation and stimulating the chartering of private banks within individual states (state banks). The circulation of all banks grew from $45 million in bank notes in 1812 to $100 million in 1817. Many state banks were founded primarily to lend their directors money for land speculation. The result was an orgy of land speculation between 1815 and 1819. In 1819, the dollar value of sales of public land was over 1,000 percent greater than the average between 1800 and 1814.

The Speculator and the Squatter   Nevertheless, most of the public domain eventually found its way into the hands of small farmers. Because speculators gained nothing by holding land for prolonged periods, they were only too happy to sell it when the price was right. In addition, a familiar frontier type, the squatter, exerted a restraining influence on the speculator.

Even before the creation of the public domain, **squatters** had helped themselves to western land. George Washington himself had been unable to drive squatters off lands he owned in the West. Squatters were an independent and proud lot, scornful of their fellow citizens who were "softened by Ease, enervated by Affluence and Luxurious Plenty, & unaccustomed to Fatigues, Hardships, Difficulties or dangers." Disdaining land speculators above all, squatters formed claims associations to police land auctions and prevent speculators from bidding up the price of land. Squatters also pressured Congress to allow them preemption rights—that is, the right to purchase at the minimum price land that they had already settled on and improved. Seeking to undo the damaging effects of its own laws, Congress responded by passing special preemption laws for squatters in specific areas and finally, in 1841, acknowledged a general right of preemption.

Preemption laws were of no use to farmers who arrived after speculators had already bought up land. Having spent their small savings on livestock, seed, and tools, these settlers had to buy land from speculators on credit at interest rates that ranged as high as 40 percent. Many western farmers, drowning in debt, had to skimp on subsistence crops while expanding cash crops in the hope of paying off their creditors.

Countless farmers who had carried basically conservative expectations to the West quickly became economic adventurers. Forced to raise cash crops in a hurry, many worked their acreage to exhaustion and thus had to keep moving in search of new land. The phrase "the moving frontier" refers not only to the obvious fact that the line of settlement shifted farther west with each passing decade, but also to the fact that the same people kept moving. The experience of Abraham Lincoln's parents, who migrated from the East through several farms in Kentucky and then to Indiana, was representative of the westward trek.

The Panic of 1819   The land boom collapsed in the financial **Panic of 1819.** The state banks' loose practices contributed mightily to the panic. Like the Bank of the United States, these banks issued their own bank notes. A bank note was just a piece of paper with a printed promise from the bank's directors to pay the bearer ("redeem") a certain amount of specie (gold or silver coinage) on demand. State banks had long issued far more bank notes than they could redeem, and these notes had fueled the economic boom after 1815. With credit so readily available, farmers borrowed money to buy more land and to plant more crops, confident that they could repay their loans when they sold their crops. After 1817, however, the combination of bumper crops in Europe and a recession in Britain trimmed foreign demand for U.S. wheat, flour, and cotton at the very time when American farmers were becoming more dependent on exports to pay their debts.

In the summer of 1818, reacting to the flood of state bank notes, the Bank of the United States began to insist that state banks redeem in specie their notes that were held by the Bank of the United States. Because the Bank of the United States had more branches than any state bank, notes of state banks were often presented by their holders to branches of the Bank of the United States for redemption. Whenever the Bank of the United States redeemed a state bank note in specie, it became a creditor of the state bank. To pay their debts to the Bank of the United States, the state banks had no choice but to force farmers and land speculators to repay loans. The result was a general curtailment of credit throughout the nation, particularly in the West.

The biggest losers were the land speculators. Land that had once sold for as much as sixty-nine dollars an acre dropped to two dollars an acre. Land prices fell because the credit squeeze drove down the market prices of staples like wheat, corn, cotton, and tobacco. Cotton, which sold for thirty-two cents a pound in 1818, sank as low as seventeen cents a pound in 1820. Since farmers could not get much cash for their crops, they could not pay the debts that they had incurred to buy land. Since speculators could not collect money owed them by farmers, the value of land that they still held for sale collapsed.

The Panic left a bitter taste about banks, particularly the Bank of the United States, which was widely blamed for the hard times. Further, plummeting prices for cash crops demonstrated how much farmers were coming to depend on distant markets. In effect, it took a severe business reversal to show farmers the extent to which they had become entrepreneurs. The fall in the prices of cash crops accelerated the search for better forms of transportation to reach faraway markets. If the cost of transporting crops could be cut, farmers could keep a larger share of the value of their crops and thereby adjust to falling prices.

THE TRANSPORTATION REVOLUTION: STEAMBOATS, CANALS, AND RAILROADS

The transportation system linking Americans in 1820 had severe weaknesses. The great rivers west of the Appalachians flowed north to south and hence could not by themselves connect western farmers to eastern markets. Roads were expensive to maintain, and horse-drawn wagons could carry only limited produce. Consequently, after 1820 attention and investment shifted to improving transportation on waterways, thus initiating the **transportation revolution.**

In 1807, Robert R. Livingston and Robert Fulton introduced the steamboat *Clermont* on the Hudson River. They soon gained a monopoly from the New York legislature to run a New York–New Jersey ferry service. Spectacular profits lured competitors, who secured a license from Congress and then filed suit to break the Livingston-Fulton monopoly. After a long court battle, the Supreme Court decided against the monopoly in 1824 in the famous case of ***Gibbons v. Ogden.*** Speaking for a unanimous court,

Chief Justice John Marshall ruled that Congress's constitutional power to regulate interstate commerce applied to navigation and thus had to prevail over New York's power to license the Livingston-Fulton monopoly. In the aftermath of this decision, other state-granted monopolies collapsed, and steamboat traffic increased rapidly. The number of steamboats operating on western rivers jumped from 17 in 1817 to 727 by 1855.

Steamboats assumed a vital role along the Mississippi–Ohio River system. They were vastly superior to keelboats (covered flatboats pushed by oars or poles). It took a keelboat three or four months to complete the 1,350-mile voyage from New Orleans to Louisville; in 1817 a steamboat could make the trip in twenty-five days. The development of long, shallow hulls permitted the navigation of the Mississippi-Ohio system even when hot, dry summers lowered the river level. Steamboats became more ornate as well as practical. To compete for passengers, they began to offer luxurious cabins and lounges, called saloons. The saloon of the *Eclipse,* a Mississippi River steamboat, was the length of a football field and featured skylights, chandeliers, a ceiling crisscrossed with Gothic arches, and velvet-upholstered mahogany furniture.

Once steamboats had demonstrated the feasibility of upriver navigation, the interest of farmers, merchants, and their elected representatives shifted away from turnpikes and toward canals. Although the cost of canal construction was mind-boggling—Jefferson dismissed the idea as little short of madness—canals offered the prospect of connecting the Mississippi–Ohio River system with the Great Lakes, and the Great Lakes with eastern markets.

Constructed between 1817 and 1825, New York's **Erie Canal,** connecting the Hudson River with Lake Erie, enabled produce from Ohio to reach New York City by a continuous stretch of waterways. Completion of the Erie Canal started a canal boom during the late 1820s and 1830s. Ohio constructed a network of canals that allowed its farmers to send their wheat by water to Lake Erie. After transport across Lake Erie, the wheat would be milled into flour in Rochester, New York, then shipped on the Erie Canal to Albany and down the Hudson River to New York City. Throughout the nation, canals reduced shipping costs from twenty to thirty cents a ton per mile in 1815 to two to three cents a ton per mile by 1830.

When another economic depression hit in the late 1830s, states found themselves overcommitted to costly canal projects and ultimately scrapped many. As the canal boom was ending, the railroad, an entirely new form of transportation, was being introduced. In 1825, the world's first commercial railroad began operation in England, and by 1840 some three thousand miles of track had been laid in America, about the same as the total canal mileage in 1840. During the 1830s, investment in American railroads exceeded that in canals. Cities like Baltimore and Boston, which lacked major inland waterway connections, turned to railroads to enlarge their share of the western market. The Baltimore and Ohio Railroad, chartered in 1828, took business away from the Chesapeake and Ohio Canal farther south. Blocked by the Berkshire Mountains from building a canal to the Erie, Massachusetts chartered the Boston and Worcester Railroad in 1831 and the Western Railroad (from Worcester to Albany) in 1833.

Cheaper to build, faster, and able to reach more places, railroads had obvious advantages over canals. But railroads' potential was only slowly realized. Most early railroads ran between cities in the East, rather than from east to west, and carried more passengers than freight. Not until 1849 did freight revenues exceed passenger revenues, and not until 1850 was the East Coast connected by rail to the Great Lakes.

Two factors explain the relatively slow spread of interregional railroads. First, unlike canals, which were built by state governments, most railroads were constructed by private corporations seeking quick profits. To minimize their original investment, railroad companies commonly resorted to cost-cutting measures such as covering wooden rails with iron bars. As a result, although relatively cheap to build, American railroads needed constant repairs. In contrast, although expensive to construct, canals needed relatively little maintenance and were kept in operation for decades after railroads appeared. Second, it remained much cheaper to ship bulky commodities such as iron ore, coal, and nonperishable agricultural produce by canal.

The Growth of the Cities The transportation revolution speeded the growth of towns and cities. Canals and railroads vastly increased opportunities for city businesses: banks to lend money, insurers to cover risks of transport, warehouses and brokers to store and sell goods. In relative terms, the most rapid urbanization in American history occurred between 1820 and 1860. The Erie Canal turned New York City into the nation's largest city; its population rose from 124,000 in 1820 to 800,000 by 1860. An even more revealing change was the transformation of sleepy villages of a few hundred people into thriving towns of several thousand. For example, the Erie Canal turned Rochester, New York, from home to a few hundred villagers in 1817 into the Flour City with nine thousand residents by 1830.

City and town growth occurred with dramatic suddenness, especially in the West. Pittsburgh, Cincinnati, and St. Louis were little more than hamlets in 1800. The War of 1812 stimulated the growth of Pittsburgh, whose iron forges provided shot and weapons for American soldiers, and Cincinnati, which became a staging ground for attacks on the British in the Old Northwest. Meanwhile, St. Louis acquired some importance as a fur-trading center. Then, between 1815 and 1819, the agricultural boom and the introduction of the steamboat transformed all three places from outposts with transient populations of hunters, traders, and soldiers into bustling cities. Cincinnati's population nearly quadrupled between 1810 and 1820, then doubled in the 1820s.

With the exception of Lexington, Kentucky, whose lack of access to water forced it into relative stagnation after 1820, all the prominent western cities were river ports: Pittsburgh, Cincinnati, and Louisville on the Ohio; St. Louis and New Orleans on the Mississippi. Except for Pittsburgh, all were essentially commercial hubs rather than manufacturing centers and were flooded by individuals eager to make money. In 1819, land speculators in St. Louis were bidding as much as a thousand dollars an acre for lots that had sold for thirty dollars an acre in 1815. Waterfronts endowed with natural beauty were swiftly overrun by stores and docks.

The transportation revolution acted like a fickle god, selecting some cities for growth while sentencing others to relative decline. Just as the steamboat had elevated the river cities over landlocked Lexington, the completion of the Erie Canal shifted the center of western economic activity toward the Great Lakes. The result was a gradual decline in the importance of river cities such as Cincinnati and Louisville and a rise in the importance of lake cities such as Buffalo, Cleveland, Detroit, Chicago, and Milwaukee. In 1830, nearly 75 percent of all western city-dwellers lived in the river ports of New Orleans, Louisville, Cincinnati, and Pittsburgh; by 1840 the proportion had dropped to 20 percent.

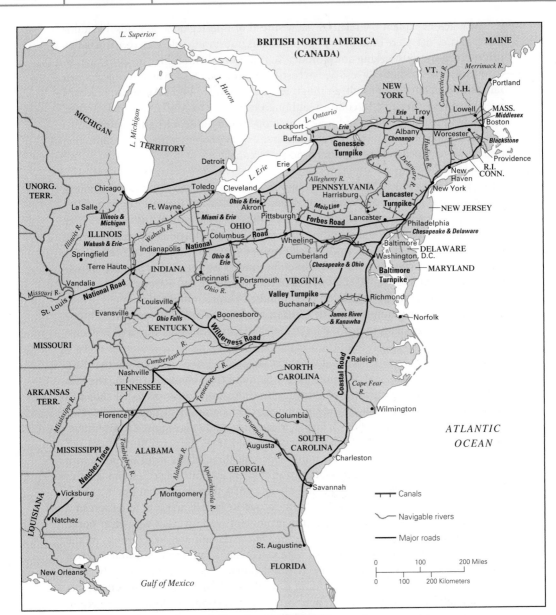

MAP 9.2 Major Rivers, Roads, and Canals, 1825–1860

Railroads and canals increasingly tied the economy of the Midwest to that of the Northeast.

INDUSTRIAL BEGINNINGS

Spurred initially by the transportation revolution and the development of interregional trade, the growth of cities and towns received an added boost from the development of industrialization. The United States lagged a generation behind Britain in building factories. Eager to keep the lead, Britain banned the emigration of its skilled mechanics. Passing himself off as a farm laborer, one of these mechanics, Samuel Slater, came to the United States in 1789 and helped design and build the first cotton mill in the United States at Pawtucket, Rhode Island, the following year. The mill spun yarn by using Slater's adaptation of the spinning frame invented by the Englishman Richard Arkwright. Slater's work force quickly grew from nine to one hundred, and his mills multiplied. From these beginnings, the pace of industrialization quickened in the 1810s and 1820s, especially in the production of cotton textiles and shoes.

Industrialization varied widely from region to region. There was very little in the South, whose economy was based on cash crops, especially cotton (see Chapter 12). Cold economic calculations led wealthy southerners to invest in land and slaves rather than machines. In contrast, New England's poor soil stimulated investment in factories instead of agriculture. Industrialization itself was a gradual process, with several distinct components. It always involved the subdivision of tasks, with each worker now fabricating only a part of the final product. Often, but not always, it led to the gathering of workers in large factories. Finally, high-speed machines replaced skilled handwork. In some industries, these elements arrived simultaneously, but more often their timing was spread out over several years.

Industrialization changed lives. Most workers in the early factories were recruited from farms. On farms, men and women had worked hard from sunrise to sunset, but they had set their own pace and taken breaks after completing tasks. Factory workers, operating machines that ran continuously, encountered the new discipline of industrial time, regulated by clocks rather than tasks and signaled by the ringing of bells. Industrialization also changed the lives of those outside of factories by encouraging specialization. During the colonial era, most farm families had made their own clothes and often their shoes. With industrialization, they concentrated on farming, while purchasing factory-made clothes and shoes.

Causes of Industrialization

A host of factors stimulated industrialization. Some were political. The Embargo Act of 1807 persuaded merchants who were barred from foreign trade to redirect their capital into factories. The Era of Good Feelings saw general agreement that the United States needed tariffs. Once protected from foreign competition, New England's output of cloth that was spun from cotton rose from 4 million yards in 1817 to 323 million yards by 1840. America also possessed an environmental advantage in the form of the many cascading rivers that flowed from the Appalachian Mountains to the Atlantic Ocean and that provided abundant waterpower for mills. The transportation revolution also played a key role by bringing eastern manufacturers closer to markets in the South and West.

Industrialization also sprang from tensions in the rural economy, especially in New England, where in the late eighteenth century population grew beyond the available land to support it. Farm families adopted new strategies to survive. For example, a farmer would decide to grow flax, which his wife and daughters would make into linen for sale; or he would choose to plant broomcorn (used for making broom whisks), and he and his sons would spend the winter months making brooms for local sale. In time, he would form a partnership with other broom makers to manufacture brooms on a larger scale and for more-distant markets. At some point, he would cease to be a farmer; instead, he would purchase his broomcorn from farmers and, with hired help, concentrate on manufacturing brooms. By now, his contacts with merchants, who would provide him with broom handles and twine and who would purchase and sell all the brooms he could make, had become extensive.

In contrast to broom making, some industries, like textiles, depended on new technologies. Although Britain had a head start in developing the technology relevant to industrialization, Americans had a strong incentive to close the gap. With a larger population and far less land, Britain contained a class of landless laborers who would work cheaply in factories. In contrast, the comparatively high wages paid unskilled laborers in the United States spurred the search for labor-saving machines. In some instances, Americans simply copied British designs. Ostensibly on vacation, a wealthy Boston merchant, Francis Cabot Lowell, used his visit to England in 1811 to charm information about British textile machinery out of his hosts; later he engaged an American mechanic to construct machines from drawings he had made each night in his hotel room. The United States also benefited from the fact that, unlike Britain, America had no craft organizations (called guilds) that tied artisans to a single trade. As a result, American artisans freely experimented with machines outside their crafts. In the 1790s, Oliver Evans, a wagon-maker from Delaware, built an automated flour mill that required only a single supervisor to watch as the grain poured in on one side and was discharged from the other as flour.

Even in the absence of new technology, Americans searched for new methods of production to cut costs. After inventing the cotton gin, **Eli Whitney** won a government contract in 1798 to produce ten thousand muskets by 1800. Whitney's idea was to meet this seemingly impossible deadline by using unskilled workers to make interchangeable parts that could be used in any of his factory's muskets. Whitney promised much more than he could deliver (see Chapter 11), and he missed his deadline by nearly a decade. But his idea captured the imagination of prominent Americans, including Thomas Jefferson.

Textile Towns in New England

New England became America's first industrial region. The trade wars leading up to the War of 1812 had devastated its commercial economy and persuaded its wealthy merchants to invest in manufacturing. The many swift rivers were ideal sources of waterpower for mills. The westward migration of many of New England's young men left a surplus of young women, who supplied cheap industrial labor.

Cotton textiles led the way. In 1813, a group of Boston merchants, known as the Boston Associates and including Francis Cabot Lowell, incorporated the Boston Manufacturing Company. With ten times the capital of any previous American cotton mill, this company quickly built textile mills in the Massachusetts towns of Waltham and Lowell. By 1836, the Boston Associates controlled eight companies employing more than six thousand workers.

The **Waltham and Lowell textile mills** differed in two ways from the earlier Rhode Island mills established by Samuel Slater. Slater's mills performed only two of the operations needed to turn raw cotton into clothing: carding (separating batches of cotton into fine strands) and spinning these strands into yarn. In what was essentially cottage manufacturing, he contracted the weaving to women working in their homes. Unlike Slater's mills, the Waltham and Lowell mills turned out finished fabrics that required only one additional step, stitching into clothes. In addition, the Waltham and Lowell

Mill Girl Around 1850
This girl mostly likely worked in a Massachusetts textile mill, at either Lowell or Waltham. Her swollen and rough hands suggest that she was a "warper," one of the jobs usually given to children. Warpers were responsible for constantly straightening out the strands of cotton or wool as they entered the loom.

mills upset the traditional order of New England society to a degree that Slater had never contemplated. Slater had sought to preserve tradition not only by contracting weaving to farm families but also by hiring entire families for carding and spinning in his mill complexes. Men raised crops on nearby company lands, while women and children tended the machines inside. In contrast, 80 percent of the workers in Waltham and Lowell, places that had not even existed in the eighteenth century, were young unmarried women who had been lured from farms by the promise of wages. Mary Paul, a Vermont teenager, settled her doubts about leaving home for Lowell by concluding that "I . . . must work where I can get more pay."

In place of traditional family discipline, the workers ("operatives") experienced new restraints. They had to live either in company boardinghouses or in licensed private dwellings, attend church on the Sabbath, observe a 10:00 P.M. curfew, and accept the company's "moral police." Regulations were designed to give the mills a good reputation so that New England farm daughters would continue to be attracted to factory work.

Mill conditions were far from attractive. To provide the humidity necessary to keep the threads from snapping, overseers nailed factory windows shut and sprayed the air with water. Operatives also had to contend with flying dust and the deafening roar of the machines. Keener competition and a worsening economy in the late 1830s led mill owners to reduce wages and speed up work schedules. The system's impersonality intensified the harshness of the work environment.

Each of the major groups that contributed to the system lived in a self-contained world. The Boston Associates raised capital but rarely visited the factories. Their agents, all men, gave orders to the operatives, mainly women. Some eight hundred Lowell mill women quit work in 1834 to protest a wage reduction. Two years later, there was another "turnout," this time involving fifteen hundred to two thousand women. These were the largest strikes in American history to that date, noteworthy as strikes not only of employees against employers but also of women against men.

The Waltham and Lowell mills were the most conspicuous examples of industrialization before 1840, but they were not typical of industrial development. Outside of textiles, many industries continued to depend on industrial **"outwork."** In contrast to the farmer who planted flax for fabrication into linen by his wife and daughters, the key movers behind outwork were merchants who provided households with raw materials and paid wages. For example, more than fifty thousand New England farmwomen, mainly daughters and widows, earned wages in their homes during the 1830s by making hats out of straw and palm leaves. Similarly, before the introduction of the sewing machine led to the concentration of all aspects of shoe manufacture in large factories in the 1850s, women often sewed parts of shoes at home and sent the piecework to factories for finishing.

Artisans and Workers in Mid-Atlantic Cities   Manufacturing in cities like New York and Philadelphia also depended on outwork. These cities lacked the fast-flowing rivers that powered machines in New England, and their high population densities made it unnecessary to gather workers into large factories. Nonetheless, they became industrial centers. Lured by the prospect of distant markets, some urban artisans and merchants started to scour the country for orders for consumer goods. They hired unskilled workers, often women, to work in small shops or homes fashioning parts of shoes or saddles or dresses. A New York reporter wrote,

> We have been in some fifty cellars in different parts of the city, each inhabited by a shoemaker and his family. The floor is made of rough plank laid loosely down, and the ceiling is not quite so high as a tall man. The walls are dark and damp and . . . the miserable room is lighted only by . . . the little light that struggles from the steep and rotting stairs. In this apartment often lives the man and his work-bench, the wife, and five or six children of all ages; and perhaps a palsied grandfather or grandmother and often both. . . . Here they work, here they cook, they eat, they sleep, they pray.

New York and Philadelphia were home to artisans with proud craft traditions and independence. Those with highly marketable skills like cutting leather or clothing patterns continued to earn good wages. Others grew rich by turning themselves into businessmen who spent less time making products than making trips to obtain orders. But artisans lacking the capital to become businessmen found themselves on the downslide in the face of competition from cheap, unskilled labor.

In the late 1820s, skilled male artisans in New York, Philadelphia, and other cities began to form trade unions and workingmen's political parties to protect their interests. Disdaining association with unskilled workers, most of these groups initially sought to restore privileges and working conditions that artisans had once enjoyed rather than to act as leaders of unskilled workers. But the steady deterioration of working conditions in the early 1830s tended to throw skilled and unskilled workers into the same boat. When coal haulers in Philadelphia struck for a ten-hour day in 1835, they were quickly joined by carpenters, cigar makers, shoemakers, leatherworkers, and other artisans in the United States' first general strike.

The emergence of organized worker protest underscored the mixed blessings of economic development. Although some benefited from the new commercial and industrial economy, others found their economic position worsening. By the 1830s, many white Americans wondered whether their nation was truly a land of equality.

EQUALITY AND INEQUALITY

That one (white) man was as good as another became the national creed in antebellum (pre–Civil War) America. For example, servants insisted on being called the "help" and on being viewed as neighbors invited to assist in running the household rather than as permanent subordinates. Merchants, held in disdain in Europe by the nobility, refused in America to bow to anyone. Politicians never lost an opportunity to celebrate artisans and farmers as every bit the equal of lawyers and bankers. Tocqueville observed that the wealthiest Americans pretended to respect equality by riding in public in ordinary rather than luxurious carriages.

The market and transportation revolutions, however, were placing new pressure on the ideal of equality between 1815 and 1840. Improved transportation enabled eastern farmers to migrate to the richer soils of the West, but also made it difficult for eastern farmers who lacked the means or the desire to move west to compete with the cheaper grains now carried east by canals and railroads. Unable to compete with western grains, many eastern farmers had to move to cities, where they took whatever work they could find, sometimes in factories but more often as casual day laborers on the docks or in small workshops where their willingness to work for low wages undercut the position of skilled artisans. Tocqueville thought that the wide distribution of land in America and the individual American's insistence on being treated as an equal created more equality in America than in France. But he worried that the lower classes in the major cities were becoming "a rabble more dangerous even than that of European towns."

Urban Inequality: The Rich and the Poor　A few large cities provided the most striking examples of growing inequality. In Boston, for example, the richest 10 percent of the population had owned a little over half of the city's real estate and personal property in 1771. By 1833, the richest 4 percent owned 59 percent of the wealth, and by 1848 nearly two-thirds. In New York City, the richest 4 percent owned nearly half the wealth in 1828 and more than two-thirds by 1845. Splendid residences and social clubs set the rich apart. In 1828, over half of the five hundred wealthiest families in New York City lived on just eight of its more than 250 streets. By the late 1820s the city had a club so exclusive that it was called simply The Club.

Although commentators celebrated the self-made American who rose from poverty to wealth, the vast majority of those who became extremely rich started out with considerable wealth. Fewer than five of every hundred wealthy individuals started poor, and close to ninety of every hundred started rich. The usual way to wealth was to inherit it, marry into more, and then invest wisely. There were just enough instances of fabulously successful poor boys like John Jacob Astor, who built a fur-trading empire, to sustain popular belief in the rags-to-riches myth, but not enough to turn that myth into a reality.

At the opposite end of the social ladder were the poor. By today's standards, most antebellum Americans were poor. They lived close to the edge of misery, depended heavily on their children's labor to meet expenses, and had little money to spend on medical care or recreation. But when antebellum Americans spoke of poverty, they were not thinking of the hardships that affected most people. Instead, they were referring to "pauperism," a state of dependency or inability to fend for oneself that affected some people. Epidemics of yellow fever and cholera could devastate families. A frozen canal, river, or harbor spelled unemployment for boatmen and dock workers, and for workers in factories that depended on waterpower. The absence of health insurance and old-age pensions condemned many infirm and aged people to pauperism.

Contemporaries usually classified all such people as the "deserving" poor and contrasted them with the "undeserving" poor, such as indolent loafers and drunkards whose poverty was seen as being self-willed. Most moralists assumed that since pauperism resulted either from circumstances beyond anyone's control, such as old age and disease, or from voluntary decisions to squander money on liquor, it could not afflict entire groups generation after generation.

This assumption was comforting but also misleading. A class of people who could not escape poverty was emerging in the major cities during the first half of the nineteenth century. One source was immigration. As early as 1801, a New York newspaper called attention to the arrival of boatloads of immigrants with large families, without money or health, and "expiring from the want of sustenance."

The poorest white immigrants were from Ireland, where English landlords had evicted peasants from the land and converted it to commercial use in the eighteenth century. Severed from the land, the Irish increasingly became a nation of wanderers, scrounging for wages wherever they could. "The poor Irishman," it was said, "the wheelbarrow is his country." By the early 1830s, the great majority of canal workers in the North were Irish immigrants. Without the backbreaking labor of the Irish, the Erie Canal would never have been built. Other Irish congregated in New York's infamous Five Points district. Starting with the conversion of a brewery into housing for hundreds of people in 1837, Five Points became the worst slum in America.

The Irish were not only poor but were also Catholics, a faith despised by the Protestant majority in the United States. In short, they were different and had little claim on the kindly impulses of most Protestants. But even the Protestant poor came in for rough treatment in the years between 1815 and 1840. The more that Americans convinced themselves that success was within everyone's grasp, the less they accepted the traditional doctrine that poverty was ordained by God, and the more they were inclined to hold the poor responsible for their own misery. Ironically, even as many Americans blamed the poor for being poor, they practiced discrimination that kept some groups mired in enduring poverty. Nowhere was this more true than in the case of northern free blacks.

Free Blacks in the North

Prejudice against blacks was deeply ingrained in white society throughout the nation. Although slavery had largely disappeared in the North by 1820, laws penalized blacks in many ways. One form of discrimination was to restrict their right to vote. In New York State, for example, a constitutional revision of 1821 eliminated property requirements

Richard Allen *First bishop of the African Methodist Episcopal Church, Richard Allen spent much of his time traveling, organizing societies of black Methodists, preaching on Sundays, and cutting wood on other days to earn his living.*

for white voters but kept them for blacks. Rhode Island banned blacks from voting in 1822; Pennsylvania did the same in 1837. Throughout the half-century after 1800, blacks could vote on equal terms with whites in only one of the nation's major cities, Boston.

Laws frequently barred free blacks from migrating to other states and cities. Missouri's original constitution authorized the state legislature to prevent blacks from entering the state "under any pretext whatsoever." Municipal ordinances often barred free blacks from public conveyances and facilities and either excluded them from public schools or forced them into segregated schools. Segregation was the rule in northern jails, almshouses, and hospitals.

Of all restrictions on free blacks, the most damaging was the social pressure that forced them into the least-skilled and lowest-paying occupations throughout the northern cities. Recollecting his youthful days in Providence, Rhode Island, in the early 1830s, the free black William J. Brown wrote: "To drive carriages, carry a market basket after the boss, and brush his boots, or saw wood and run errands was as high as a colored man could rise." Although a few free blacks became successful entrepreneurs and grew moderately wealthy, urban free blacks were only half as likely as city-dwellers in general to own real estate.

One important black response to discrimination was to establish their own churches. White churches confined blacks to separate benches or galleries. When black worshipers mistakenly sat in a gallery designated for whites at a Methodist church in Philadelphia, they were ejected from the church. Their leader, former slave and future bishop **Richard Allen,** related, "we all went out of the church in a body, and they were no longer plagued by us." Allen initiated a movement that resulted in the organization of the **African Methodist Episcopal Church,** the first black-run Protestant denomination, in 1816. By 1822, the A.M.E. Church had active congregations in Washington, D.C., Pittsburgh, New York City, and throughout the mid-Atlantic states. Its members campaigned against slavery, in part by refusing to purchase produce grown by slaves.

Just as northern African-Americans seceded from white churches to form their own, free blacks gradually acquired some control over the education of their children at a time when northern city governments made negligible provision for the education of free persons of color. Initially, northern blacks had to depend on the philanthropy of sympathetic whites to educate their children. For example, an antislavery society in New York launched the African Free School in 1787 with white teachers. But the 1820s and 1830s witnessed an explosion of black self-help societies like New York City's Phoenixonian Literary Society, devoted to encouraging black education and run by such black graduates of the African Free School as Samuel Cornish and Henry Garnett.

The "Middling Classes"	The majority of antebellum Americans lived neither in splendid wealth nor in grinding poverty. Most belonged to what men and women of the time called the middling classes. Even

though the wealthy owned an increasing proportion of all wealth, most people's standard of living rose between 1800 and 1860, particularly between 1840 and 1860 when per capita income grew at an annual rate of around 1.5 percent.

Americans applied the term *middling classes* to families headed by professionals, small merchants and manufacturers, landowning farmers, and self-employed artisans. Commentators portrayed these people as living stable and secure lives. In reality, life in the middle often was unpredictable. The increasingly commercial economy of antebellum America created greater opportunities for success and for failure. An enterprising import merchant, Alan Melville, the father of novelist Herman Melville, had an abounding faith in his nation, in "our national Eagle, 'with an eye that never winks and a wing that never tires,'" and in the inevitable triumph of honesty and prudence. The Melvilles lived comfortably in Albany and New York City, but Melville's business sagged in the late 1820s. In 1830, he begged his father for a loan of five hundred dollars, proclaiming, "I am destitute of resources and without a shilling—without immediate assistance I know not what will become of me." He got the five hundred dollars plus an additional three thousand dollars, but the downward spiral continued. In 1832 he died, broken in spirit and nearly insane.

In the emerging market economy, even such seemingly crisp occupational descriptions as farmer and artisan often proved misleading. Asa G. Sheldon, born in Massachusetts in 1788, described himself in his autobiography as a farmer, offered advice on growing corn and cranberries, and gave speeches about the glories of farming. Although Sheldon undoubtedly knew a great deal about farming, he actually spent very little time tilling the soil. In 1812, he began to transport hops from New England to brewers in New York City, and he soon extended this business to Philadelphia and Baltimore. He invested his profits in land, but rather than farm the land, he made money selling its timber. When a business setback forced him to sell his property, he was soon back in operation "through the disinterested kindness of friends" who lent him money with which he purchased carts and oxen. These he used to get contracts for filling in swamps in Boston and for clearing and grading land for railroads. From all this and from the backbreaking labor of the Irish immigrants he hired to do the shoveling, Sheldon the "farmer" grew prosperous.

The emerging market economy also transformed the lives of artisans. During the colonial period, artisans had formed a proud and cohesive group whose members often attained the goal of self-employment. They owned their own tools, made their own products on order from customers, boarded their apprentices and journeymen in their homes, and passed their skills on to their children. By 1840, in contrast, artisans had entered a new world of economic relationships. This was true even of a craft like carpentry that did not experience any industrial or technological change. Town and city growth in the wake of the transportation revolution created a demand for housing. Some carpenters, usually those with access to capital, became contractors. They took orders for more houses than they could build themselves and hired large numbers of journeymen to do the construction work. Likewise, as we have seen, in the early industrialization of shoe manufacturing during the 1820s, some shoemakers spent less time crafting shoes than making trips to obtain orders for their products, then hired workers to fashion parts of shoes. In effect, the old class of artisans was splitting into two new groupings. On one side were artisans who had become entrepreneurs; on the other, journeymen with little prospect of self-employment.

An additional characteristic of the middling classes, one they shared with the poor, was a high degree of transience, or spatial mobility. The transportation revolution made it easier for Americans to purchase services as well as goods and spurred many young men to abandon farming for the professions. For example, the number of medical schools rose from one in 1765 to twenty in 1830 and sixty-five in 1860. Frequently, the new men who crowded into medicine and into the ministry and law were forced into incessant motion. Physicians rode from town to town looking for patients. The itinerant clergyman mounted on an old nag and riding the countryside to visit the faithful or to conduct revivals became a familiar figure in newly settled areas. Even well-established lawyers and judges spent part of each year riding from one county courthouse to another, to plead and decide cases, bunking (usually two to a bed) in rough country inns.

Transience affected the lives of most Americans. Farmers who cultivated land intensively in order to raise a cash crop, and so pay their debts, exhausted the land quickly and had to move on. For skilled and unskilled workers alike, work was often seasonal; workers had to move from job to job to survive. Canal workers and boatmen had to secure new work when waterways froze. Even city-dwellers who shifted jobs often had to change residences, for the cities were spreading out at a much faster rate than was public transportation. Some idea of the degree of transience can be gained from a survey by the Boston police on Saturday, September 6, 1851. At a time when Boston's population was 145,000, the survey showed that from 6:30 A.M. to 7:30 P.M., 41,729 people entered the city and 42,313 left. At a time when there were few suburbs, it is safe to say that these people were not commuters. Most likely, they were moving in search of work, as much a necessity for many in the middling classes as for the poor.

THE REVOLUTION IN SOCIAL RELATIONSHIPS

Following the War of 1812, the growth of interregional trade, commercial agriculture, and manufacturing changed not only the lives of individuals but also the ways in which they related to each other. Two broad generalizations encompass these changes. First, many Americans questioned authority to an unprecedented degree. In 1775, they had rebelled against their king. Now, it seemed, they were rebelling as well against their lawyers, their physicians, their ministers, and even their parents. An attitude of individualism sprouted and took firm root in antebellum America. Once individualism had meant nothing more than selfishness, but now Americans used the word to signify positive qualities: self-reliance and the conviction that each person was the best judge of his or her own true interests. Ordinary Americans might still agree with the opinions of their leaders, but only after they had thought matters through on their own. Those with superior wealth, education, or social position could no longer expect the automatic deference of the common people.

Second, even as Americans widely proclaimed themselves a nation of self-reliant individualists and questioned the traditional basis of authority, they sought to construct new foundations for authority. For example, middle-class men and women came to embrace the idea that women possessed a "separate sphere" of authority in the home. In addition, individuals increasingly joined with others in these years to form voluntary associations through which they might influence the direction that their society would take.

The Attack on the Professions In the swiftly changing antebellum society, claims to social superiority were questioned as never before. As a writer put it in 1836, "Everywhere the disposition is found among those who live in the valleys to ask those who live on the hills, 'How came we here and you there?'"

Intense criticism of lawyers, physicians, and ministers exemplified this assault on authority. As far back as the 1780s, Benjamin Austin, a radical Boston artisan, had complained that lawyers needlessly prolonged and confused court cases so that they could charge high fees. Between 1800 and 1840, a wave of religious revivals known as the Second Great Awakening (see Chapter 10) sparked new attacks on the professions. Some revivalists blasted the clergy for creating complicated theologies that ordinary men and women could not comprehend, for drinking expensive wines, and for fleecing the people. One religious revivalist, Elias Smith, extended the criticism to physicians, whom he accused of inventing Latin and Greek names for diseases in order to disguise their own ignorance of how to cure them.

These jabs at the learned professions peaked between 1820 and 1850. In medicine, a movement arose under the leadership of Samuel Thomson, a farmer's son with little formal education, to eliminate all barriers to entry into the medical profession. Thomson believed that anyone could understand the principles of medicine and become a physician. His crusade was remarkably successful. By 1845, every state had repealed laws that required licenses and education to practice medicine. Meanwhile, attacks on lawyers sharpened, and relations between ministers and their parishioners grew tense and acrimonious. In colonial New England, ministers had usually served a single parish for life, but by the 1830s a rapid turnover of ministers was becoming the norm as finicky parishioners commonly dismissed clergymen whose theology displeased them.

Ministers themselves were becoming more ambitious—more inclined to leave small, poor congregations for large, wealthy ones.

The increasing commercialization of the economy contributed both to the growing number of professionals and to the attacks on them. Like so many other antebellum Americans, freshly minted lawyers and doctors often were transients without deep roots in the towns that they served and without convincing claims to social superiority. Describing lawyers and physicians, a contemporary observer wrote, "Men dropped down into their places as from clouds. Nobody knew who or what they were, except as they claimed, or as a surface view of their character indicated." A horse doctor one day would the next day hang up his sign as "Physician and Surgeon" and "fire at random a box of his pills into your bowels, with a vague chance of hitting some disease unknown to him, but with a better prospect of killing the patient, whom or whose administrator he charged some ten dollars a trial for his marksmanship."

The questioning of authority was particularly sharp on the frontier. Here, to eastern and foreign visitors, it seemed that every man they met was a "judge," "general," "colonel," or "squire." In a society in which everyone was new, such titles were easily adopted and just as easily challenged. Where neither law nor custom sanctioned claims of superiority, would-be gentlemen substituted an exaggerated sense of personal honor. Obsessed with their fragile status, many reacted testily to the slightest insult. Dueling became a widespread frontier practice. At a Kentucky militia parade in 1819, an officer's dog jogged onto the field and sat at his master's knee. Enraged by this breach of military decorum, another officer ran the dog through with his sword. A week later, both officers met with pistols at ten paces. One was killed; the other maimed for life.

The Challenge to Family Authority In contrast to adults' public philosophical attacks on the learned professions, children engaged in a quiet questioning of parental authority. Economic change created new opportunities that forced young people to choose between staying at home to help their parents and venturing out on their own. Writing to her parents in Vermont shortly before taking a job in a Lowell textile mill, eighteen-year-old Sally Rice quickly got to the point. "I must of course have something of my own before many more years have passed over my head and where is that something coming from if I go home and earn nothing. You may think me unkind but how can you blame me if I want to stay here. I have but one life to live and I want to enjoy myself as I can while I live."

A similar desire for independence tempted young men to leave home at earlier ages than in the past. Although the great migration to the West was primarily a movement of entire families, movement from farms to towns and cities within regions was frequently spearheaded by restless and single young people. Two young men in Virginia put it succinctly. "All the promise of life seemed to us to be at the other end of the rainbow—somewhere else—anywhere else but on the farm. . . . And so all our youthful plans had as their chief object the getting away from the farm."

Antebellum Americans also widely wished to be free of close parental supervision, and their changing attitudes influenced courtship and marriage. Many young people who no longer depended on their parents for land insisted on privacy in courting and wanted to decide for themselves when and whom to marry. Whereas seventeenth-century Puritans had advised young people to choose marriage partners whom they could learn to love, by the early 1800s young men and women viewed romantic love as indispensable to a successful marriage. "In affairs of love," a young lawyer in Maine wrote, "young people's hearts are generally much wiser than old people's heads."

One sign of young people's growing control over courtship and marriage was the declining likelihood that the young women of a family would marry in their exact birth order. Traditionally, fathers had wanted their daughters to marry in the order of their birth to avoid planting the suspicion that there was something wrong with one or more of them. Toward the end of the eighteenth century, however, daughters were making their own marital decisions, and the practice ceased to be customary. Another mark of the times was the growing number of long engagements. Having made the decision to marry, some young women were reluctant to tie the knot, fearing that marriage would snuff out their independence. For example, New Yorkers Caroline and William Kirkland were engaged for seven years before their marriage in 1828. Equally striking was the increasing number of young women who chose not to marry. **Catharine Beecher,** a leading author and the daughter of the prominent minister Lyman Beecher, broke off her engagement to a young man during the 1820s despite her father's pressure to marry him. She later renewed the engagement, but after her fiancé's death in a shipwreck, she remained single for the rest of her life.

Moralists reacted with alarm to signs that young people were living in a world of their own. They flooded the country with books of advice to youth, such as William Alcott's *The Young Man's Guide,* which went through thirty-one editions between 1833 and 1858. The vast number of such advice books sold in antebellum America all said the same thing. They did not advise young men and women to return to farms, and they assumed that parents had little control over them. Rather, the authors exhorted youths to develop habitual rectitude, self-control, and "character." It was an age not just of the self-made adult but also of the self-made youth.

| Wives and Husbands |

Another class of advice books pouring from the antebellum presses counseled wives and husbands on their rights and duties. These were a sign that relations between spouses, too, were changing. Young men and women who had grown accustomed to making decisions on their own as teenagers were more likely than their ancestors to approach wedlock as a compact between equals. Of course, wives remained unequal to their husbands in many ways. With few exceptions, the law did not allow married women to own property. But relations between wives and husbands were changing during the 1820s and 1830s toward a form of equality.

One source of the change, zealously advocated by Catharine Beecher, lay in the doctrine of **separate spheres.** Traditionally, women had been viewed as subordinate to men in all spheres of life. Now middle-class men and women developed a kind of separate-but-equal doctrine that portrayed men as superior in making money and governing the world, and women as superior for their moral influence on family members.

One of the most important duties assigned to the sphere of women was raising children. During the eighteenth century, church sermons reminded fathers of their duty to govern the family; by the 1830s child-rearing manuals were addressed to mothers rather than fathers. "How entire and perfect is this dominion over the unformed character of your infant," the popular writer Lydia Sigourney proclaimed in her *Letters to Mothers* (1838). Advice books instructed mothers to discipline their children by loving them and withdrawing affection when they misbehaved rather than by using corporal punishment. A whipped child might become more obedient but would remain sullen and bitter; gentler methods would penetrate the child's heart, making the child want to do the right thing.

The idea of a separate women's sphere blended with a related image of the family and home as refuges secluded from a society marked by commotion and disorder. The popular culture of the 1830s and 1840s painted an alluring portrait of the pleasures of home life through songs like "Home, Sweet Home" and poems such as Henry Wadsworth Longfellow's "The Children's Hour" and Clement Moore's "A Visit from St. Nicholas." The publication of Moore's poem coincided with the growing popularity of Christmas as a holiday season in which family members gathered to exchange warm affection. Even the physical appearance of houses changed. The prominent architect Andrew Jackson Downing published plans for peaceful single-family homes that he hoped would offset the "spirit of unrest" and the feverish pace of American life. He wrote of the ideal home, "There should be something to love. There must be nooks about it, where one would love to linger; windows, where one can enjoy the quiet landscape at his leisure; cozy rooms, where all fireside joys are invited to dwell."

Downing deserves high marks as a prophet, because one of the motives that impelled many Americans to flee cities for suburbs in the twentieth century was the desire to own their own homes. In the 1820s and 1830s, this ideal was beyond the reach of most people—not only blacks, immigrants, and sweatshop workers, but also most members of the middle class. In the countryside, although middle-class farmers still managed productive households, these were anything but tranquil; wives milked cows and bled hogs, and children fetched wood, drove cows to pasture, and chased blackbirds from cornfields. In the cities, middle-class families often had to sacrifice their privacy by taking in boarders to supplement family income.

Despite their distortions, the doctrine of separate spheres and the image of the home as a refuge from a harsh world intersected with reality at some points. The rising number of urban families headed by lawyers and merchants (who worked away from home) gave mothers time to spend on child rearing. Above all, even if they could not afford to live in a Downing-designed house, married women found that they could capitalize on these notions to gain new power within their families. A subtle implication of the doctrine of separate spheres was that women should have control not only over the discipline of children but also over the more fundamental issue of how many children they would bear.

In 1800, the United States had one of the highest birthrates ever recorded. The average American woman bore 7.04 children. It is safe to say that married women had become pregnant as often as possible. In the prevailing farm economy, children carried out essential tasks and, as time passed, took care of their aging parents. Most parents had assumed that the more children, the better. The spread of a commercial economy raised troublesome questions about children's economic value. Unlike a farmer, a merchant or lawyer could not send his children to work at the age of seven or eight. The average woman was bearing only 5.02 children by 1850, and 3.98 by 1900. The birthrate remained high among blacks and many immigrant groups, but it fell drastically among native-born whites, particularly in towns and cities. The birthrate also declined in rural areas, but more sharply in rural villages than on farms, and more sharply in the East, where land was scarce, than in the West, where abundant land created continued incentives for parents to have many children.

For the most part, the decline in the birthrate was accomplished by abstinence from sexual intercourse, by *coitus interruptus* (withdrawal before ejaculation), or by abortion. By the 1840s, abortionists advertised remedies for "female irregularities," a common euphemism for unwanted pregnancies. There were no foolproof birth-control devices, and as much misinformation as information circulated about techniques of birth control. Nonetheless, interest in birth-control devices was intensifying. In 1832, Charles Knowlton, a Massachusetts physician, described the procedure for vaginal douching in his book *Fruits of Philosophy*. Although Knowlton was frequently prosecuted and once jailed for obscenity, efforts to suppress his ideas publicized them even more. By 1865, popular tracts had familiarized Americans with a wide range of birth-control methods, including the condom and the diaphragm. The decision to limit family size was usually reached jointly by wives and husbands. Economic and ideological considerations blended together. Husbands could note that the economic value of children was declining; wives, that having fewer children would give them more time to nurture each one and thereby carry out domestic duties.

Supporters of the ideal of separate spheres did not advocate full legal equality for women. Indeed, the idea of separate spheres was an explicit alternative to legal equality. But the concept did enhance women's power within marriage by justifying their demands for influence over such vital issues as child rearing and the frequency of pregnancies. In addition, it allowed some women a measure of independence from the home. For example, it sanctioned the travels of Catharine Beecher, a leading advocate of separate spheres, to lecture women on better ways to raise children and manage their households.

Horizontal Allegiances and the Rise of Voluntary Associations

As some forms of authority, such as the authority of parents over their children and husbands over their wives, were weakening, Americans devised new ways for individuals to extend their influence over others. The pre–Civil War period witnessed the widespread substitution of **horizontal allegiances** for **vertical allegiances.** In vertical allegiances, authority flows from the top down. Subordinates identify their interests with those of their superiors rather than with others in the same subordinate role. The traditional patriarchal family was an example of a vertical allegiance: the wife and children looked up to the father for leadership. Another example occurred in the small eighteenth-century workshop, where apprentices and journeymen took direction from the master craftsman and even lived in the craftsman's house, subject to his authority.

Although vertical relationships did not disappear, they became less important in people's lives. Increasingly, relationships were more likely to be marked by horizontal allegiances that linked those in a similar position. For example, in large textile mills, operatives discovered that they had more in common with one another than with their managers and overseers. Similarly, married women formed maternal associations to exchange advice about child rearing. Young men formed debating societies to sharpen their wits and to bring themselves to the attention of influential older men. Maternal and debating societies exemplified the American zeal for **voluntary associations**— associations that arose apart from government and sought to accomplish some goal of value to their members. Tocqueville observed that the government stood at the head of every enterprise in France, but that in America "you will be sure to find an association."

Voluntary associations encouraged sociability. As transients and newcomers flocked into towns and cities, they tended to join others with similar characteristics, experiences, or interests. Gender was the basis of many voluntary societies. Of twenty-six religious and charitable associations in Utica, New York, in 1832, for instance, one-third were exclusively for women. Race was still another basis for voluntary associations. Although their names did not indicate it, Boston's Thompson Literary and Debating Society and its Philomathean Adelphic Union for the Promotion of Literature and Science were organizations for free blacks.

Voluntary associations also enhanced their members' public influence. At a time when state legislatures had little interest in regulating the sale of alcoholic beverages, men and women joined in temperance societies to promote voluntary abstinence. To combat prostitution, women formed moral-reform societies, which sought to shame men into chastity by publishing the names of brothel patrons in newspapers. Aiming to suppress an ancient vice, moral-reform societies also tended to enhance women's power over men. Moral reformers attributed the prevalence of prostitution to the lustfulness of men who, unable to control their passions, exploited poor and vulnerable girls. Just as strikes in Lowell in the 1830s were a form of collective action by working women, moral-reform societies represented collective action by middle-class women to increase their influence in society. Here, as elsewhere, the tendency of the times was to forge new forms of horizontal allegiance between like-minded Americans.

Conclusion

European demand for American cotton and other agricultural products, federal policies that eased the sale of public lands and encouraged the removal of Indians from the path of white settlement, and the availability of loose-lending banks and paper money all contributed to the flow of population into the area between the Appalachians and the Mississippi River after 1815. The collapse of the boom in 1819 reminded farmers of how dependent they had become on distant markets and prompted improvements in transportation during the 1820s and 1830s. The introduction of steamboats, the building of canals, and the gradual spread of railroads—the transportation revolution—encouraged a turn to commercial occupations and the growth of towns and cities. Now able to reach distant consumers, merchants plunged capital into manufacturing enterprises. Ranging from the great textile mills of Lowell and Waltham to rural cottages that performed outwork to urban sweatshops, early industrialization laid the foundations for America's emergence a half-century later as a major industrial power.

The changes associated with the market economy and early industrialization carved new avenues to prosperity for some—and to penury for others. They challenged traditional hierarchies and created new forms of social alignment based on voluntary associations. By joining voluntary associations based on shared interests or opinions, footloose Americans forged new identities that paralleled and often supplanted older allegiances to their parents or places of birth.

10

Democratic Politics, Religious Revival, and Reform, 1824–1840

THE RISE OF DEMOCRATIC POLITICS, 1824–1832

In 1824, Andrew Jackson and Martin Van Buren, who would guide the Democratic Party in the 1830s, and Henry Clay and John Quincy Adams, who would become that decade's leading Whigs, all belonged to the Republican Party of Thomas Jefferson. Yet by 1824 the Republican Party was coming apart under pressures generated by industrialization in New England, the spread of cotton cultivation in the South, and westward expansion. These forces sparked issues that would become the basis for the new political division between Democrats and Whigs. In general, Republicans who retained Jefferson's preference for states' rights became Democrats; Republicans who believed that the national government should actively encourage economic development, the so-called National Republicans, became Whigs.

Regardless of which path a politician chose, all leaders in the 1820s and 1830s had to adapt to the rising democratic idea of politics as a forum for the expression of the will of the common people rather than as an activity that gentlemen conducted for the people. Gentlemen could still be elected to office, but their success now depended less on their education and wealth than on their ability to identify and follow the will of the majority. Americans still looked up to their political leaders, but the leaders could no longer look down on the people.

CHRONOLOGY, 1824–1840

1824 • John Quincy Adams elected president by the House of Representatives.

1826 • American Temperance Society organized.

1828 • Andrew Jackson elected president.
"Tariff of Abominations."
John Calhoun anonymously writes *South Carolina Exposition* and Protest.

1830 • Jackson's Maysville Road Bill veto.
Indian Removal Act.

1830–1831 • Charles G. Finney's Rochester revival.

1831 • William Lloyd Garrison starts *The Liberator*.

1832 • Jackson vetoes recharter of the Bank of the United States.
Jackson reelected president.
South Carolina Nullification Proclamation.

1833 • Force Bill.
Compromise Tariff.
American Anti-Slavery Society founded.
South Carolina nullifies the Force Bill.

1834 • Whig Party organized.

1836 • Specie Circular.
Martin Van Buren elected president.

1837 • Horace Mann becomes secretary of the Massachusetts Board of Education.
Elijah Lovejoy murdered by proslavery mob.
Grimké sisters set out on lecture tour of New England.

1837–1843 • Economic depression.

1838 • Garrison's New England Non-Resistance Society founded.
Sarah Grimké's *Letters on the Condition of Women and the Equality of the Sexes* and Angelina Grimké's *Letters to Catharine E. Beecher*.

1840 • Independent Treasury Act passed.
William Henry Harrison elected president.
First Washington Temperance Society started.

1841 • Dorothea Dix begins exposé of prison conditions.
Brook Farm community founded.

1848 • Seneca Falls convention.

Democratic
Ferment

Political democratization took several forms. One of the most common was the abolition of the requirement that voters own property. None of the new western states required property ownership for voting, and eastern states gradually liberalized their laws. Moreover, written ballots replaced the custom of voting aloud, which had enabled superiors to influence their inferiors at the polls. Appointive office increasingly became elective. The Electoral College survived, but the choice of presidential electors by state legislatures gave way to their direct election by the voters. In 1800, rather than voting for Thomas Jefferson or John Adams, most Americans could do no more than vote for the men who would vote for the men who would vote for Jefferson or Adams. By 1824, however, legislatures chose electors in only six states, and by 1832 only in South Carolina.

The fierce tug of war between the Republicans and the Federalists in the 1790s and early 1800s had taught both parties to court voters. At grand party-run barbecues from Maine to Maryland, potential voters washed down free clams and oysters with free beer and whiskey. Republicans sought to expand suffrage in the North, and Federalists did likewise in the South, each in the hope of becoming the majority party in that section.

Political democratization developed at an uneven pace. In 1820, both the Federalists and Republicans were still organized from the top down. To nominate candidates, for example, both parties relied on the caucus (a conference of party members in the legislature) rather than on popularly elected nominating conventions. Nor was political democracy extended to all. Women continued to be excluded from voting. Free blacks in the North found that the same popular conventions that extended voting rights to nearly all whites effectively disfranchised African-Americans. Yet no one could mistake the tendency of the times: to oppose the people or democracy had become a formula for political suicide. The people, a Federalist moaned, "have become too saucy and are really beginning to fancy themselves equal to their betters."

The Election
of 1824

Sectional tensions brought the Era of Good Feelings to an end in 1824 when five candidates, all Republicans, vied for the presidency. John Quincy Adams emerged as New England's favorite. South Carolina's brilliant John C. Calhoun contended with Georgia's William Crawford, an old-school Jeffersonian, for southern support. Out of the West marched **Henry Clay** of Kentucky, ambitious, crafty, and confident that his American System of protective tariffs and federally supported internal improvements would endear him to manufacturing interests in the East as well as to the West.

Clay's belief that he was holding a solid block of western states was punctured by the rise of a fifth candidate, Andrew Jackson of Tennessee. At first, none of the other candidates took Jackson seriously. But he was popular on the frontier and in the South and stunned his rivals by gaining the support of opponents of the American System from Pennsylvania and other northern states.

Although the Republican congressional caucus chose Crawford as the party's official candidate early in 1824, the caucus could no longer unify the party. Three-fourths of the Republicans in Congress had refused to attend the caucus. Crawford's already diminished prospects evaporated when he suffered a paralyzing stroke. Impressed by Jackson's support, Calhoun withdrew from the race and ran unopposed for the vice presidency.

In the election, Jackson won more popular and electoral votes than any other candidate (Adams, Crawford, and Clay) but failed to gain the majority required by the Constitution. Thus the election was thrown into the House of Representatives, whose members had to choose from the three top candidates—Jackson, Adams, and Crawford. Hoping to forge an alliance between the West and Northeast in a future bid for the presidency, Clay gave his support to Adams. Clay's action secured the presidency for Adams, but when Adams promptly appointed Clay his secretary of state, Jackson's supporters raged that a "corrupt bargain" had cheated Jackson of the presidency. Although there is no evidence that Adams had traded Clay's support for an explicit agreement to appoint Clay his secretary of state (an office from which Jefferson, Madison, Monroe, and Adams himself had risen to the presidency), the allegation of a corrupt bargain was widely believed. It formed a cloud that hung over Adams's presidency.

John Quincy Adams as President Failing to understand the changing political climate, Adams made several other miscalculations that would cloak his presidency in controversy. For example, in 1825 he proposed a program of federal aid for internal improvements. Strict Jeffersonians had always opposed such aid as unconstitutional, but now they were joined by pragmatists like New York's governor and, later, U.S. senator Martin Van Buren. Aware that New York had just completed construction of the Erie Canal with its own funds, Van Buren opposed federal aid to improvements on the grounds that it would enable other states to build rival canals. Adams next proposed sending American delegates to a conference of newly independent Latin American nations, a proposal that infuriated southerners because it would imply U.S. recognition of Haiti, the black republic created by slave revolutionaries.

Instead of seeking new bases of support, Adams clung to the increasingly obsolete notion of the president as custodian of the public good, aloof from partisan politics. He alienated his supporters by appointing his opponents to high office and wrote loftily, "I have no wish to fortify myself by the support of any party whatever." Idealistic as his view was, it guaranteed him a single-term presidency.

The Rise of Andrew Jackson As Adams's popularity declined, Andrew Jackson's rose. Although Jackson's victory over the British in the Battle of New Orleans had made him a hero, veteran politicians distrusted his notoriously hot temper and his penchant for duels. (Jackson had once challenged an opposing lawyer to a duel for ridiculing his legal arguments in a court case.) But as the only presidential candidate in the election of 1824 not linked to the Monroe administration, Jackson benefited from discontent after the Panic of 1819, which, in Calhoun's words, left people with "a general mass of disaffection to the Government" and "looking out anywhere for a leader." To many Americans, Jackson, who as a boy had fought in the Revolution, seemed like a living link to a more virtuous past.

Jackson's supporters swiftly established committees throughout the country. Two years before the election of 1828, towns and villages across the United States buzzed with furious but unfocused political activity. With the exception of the few remaining Federalists, almost everyone called himself a Republican. Because supporters of Jackson, Adams, and Clay still styled themselves Republicans, few realized that a new political system was being born. The man most alert to the signs of the times was Martin Van

Buren, who was to become vice president during Jackson's second term and president upon Jackson's retirement.

Van Buren exemplified a new breed of politician. A tavernkeeper's son, he had started his political career in county politics. As governor, he built a powerful political machine, the Albany Regency, composed mainly of men like himself from the lower and middling ranks. His archrival in New York politics, DeWitt Clinton, was all that Van Buren was not—tall, handsome, and aristocratic. But Van Buren had a geniality that made ordinary people feel comfortable and an uncanny ability to sense the direction in which the political winds were about to blow. Van Buren loved politics, which he viewed as a wonderful game. He was one of the first prominent American politicians to make personal friends from among his political enemies.

The election of 1824 convinced Van Buren of the need for renewed two-party competition. Without the discipline imposed by a strong opposition party, the Republicans had splintered into sectional pieces. No candidate had secured an electoral majority, and the House of Representatives had decided the outcome amid charges of intrigue and corruption. It would be better, Van Buren concluded, to let all the shades of opinion in the nation be reduced to two. Then the parties would clash, and a clear popular winner would emerge. Jackson's strong showing in the election persuaded Van Buren that "Old Hickory" could lead a new political party. In the election of 1828, this party, which gradually became known as the **Democratic Party,** put up Jackson for president and Calhoun for vice president. Its opponents, calling themselves the National Republicans, rallied behind Adams and his running mate, treasury secretary Richard Rush. Slowly but surely, the second American party system was taking shape.

The Election of 1828	The 1828 campaign was a vicious, mudslinging affair. The National Republicans attacked Jackson as a gambler, an adulterer, and a murderer. He was directly responsible for several

men's deaths in duels and military executions; and in 1791 he had married Rachel Robards, erroneously believing that her divorce from her first husband had become final. "Ought a convicted adulteress and her paramour husband," the Adams men taunted, "be placed in the highest office of this free and Christian land?" Jackson's supporters replied in kind. They accused Adams of wearing silk underwear, being rich, being in debt, and having gained favor with the tsar of Russia by trying to provide him with a beautiful American prostitute.

Although both sides engaged in tossing barbs, Jackson's men had better aim. Charges by Adams's supporters that Jackson was an illiterate backwoodsman added to Jackson's popular appeal by making him seem like an ordinary citizen. Jackson's supporters portrayed the clash as one between "the democracy of the country, on the one hand, and a lordly purse-proud aristocracy on the other." Jackson, they said, was the common man incarnate, his mind unclouded by learning, his morals simple and true, his will fierce and resolute. In contrast, Jackson's men represented Adams as an aristocrat, a dry scholar whose learning obscured the truth, a man who could write but not fight. Much of this, of course, was wild exaggeration. Jackson was a wealthy planter, not a simple frontiersman. But it was what people wanted to hear. Jackson was presented as the common man's image of his better self as uncorrupt, natural, and plain.

The election swept Jackson into office with more than twice the electoral vote of Adams. Yet the popular vote, much closer, made it clear that the people were not simply responding to the personalities or images of the candidates. The vote also reflected

MAP 10.1 The Election of 1828

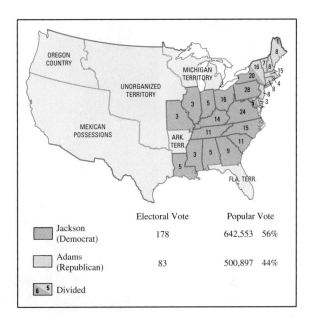

	Electoral Vote	Popular Vote
Jackson (Democrat)	178	642,553 56%
Adams (Republican)	83	500,897 44%
Divided		

the strongly sectional bases of the new parties. The popular vote was close only in the middle states and the Northwest. Adams gained double Jackson's vote in New England; Jackson received double Adams's vote in the South and nearly triple Adams's vote in the Southwest.

Jackson in Office   Riding to office on a wave of opposition to corruption and privilege, Jackson made the federal civil service his first target. Many officeholders, he thought, were treating their jobs as personal possessions to which their long service entitled them. Jackson disagreed. Believing that the duties of most officeholders were simple, he supported "rotation in office" so that as many plain people as possible would have a chance to work for the government. He did not invent rotation, but he applied it more harshly than his predecessors by firing nearly half of the higher civil service, especially postmasters and customs officers.

Although Jackson defended his removals on the democratically flavored grounds of rotation, he also had a partisan motive. His removals were concentrated in the Northeast, the stronghold of John Quincy Adams. In their place he appointed his supporters, including Samuel Swartwout. Appointed the chief customs officer for the port of New York, Swartwout caused Jackson embarrassment by running off with millions of dollars of customs receipts. Critics dubbed the practice of basing appointments on party loyalty the **"spoils system."**

At least to its victims, Jackson's application of rotation seemed arbitrary because he refused to offer any reasons to justify individual removals. His stand on internal improvements and tariffs sparked even more intense controversy. Although not opposed to all federal aid for internal improvements, Jackson was sure that public officials used such aid to woo supporters by handing out favors to special interests. To end this lavish and corrupt giveaway, he flatly rejected federal support for roads within states.

Andrew Jackson, by Ralph Earl *Jackson during the Nullification crisis, looking serene in the uniform of a major-general and determined to face down the greatest challenge to his presidency.*

Accordingly, in 1830 he vetoed a bill providing federal money for a road in Kentucky between Maysville and Lexington for its "purely local character."

Jackson's strongest support lay in the South. The Indian Removal Act of 1830 (see Chapter 9) enhanced his popularity there. The tariff issue, however, would test the South's loyalty to Jackson. In 1828, while Adams was still president, some of Jackson's supporters in Congress had contributed to the passage of a high protective tariff that was as favorable to western agriculture and New England manufacturing as it was unfavorable to southerners, who had few industries to protect and who now would have to pay more for manufactured goods. Taking for granted the South's support for Jackson in the coming election, Jackson's supporters had calculated that southerners would blame the Adams administration for this "Tariff of Abominations." In reality, Jackson, not Adams, bore the South's fury over the tariff.

Nullification   The tariff of 1828 laid the basis for a rift between Jackson and his vice president, John C. Calhoun, that was to shake the foundations of the Republic. Early in his career, Calhoun had been an ardent nationalist. He had entered Congress in 1811 as a war hawk, supported the protectionist tariff of 1816, and dismissed strict construction of the Constitution as refined philosophical nonsense. During the late 1820s, however, Calhoun the nationalist gradually became Calhoun the states' rights sectionalist. The reasons for his shift were complex. He had supported the tariff of 1816 as a measure conducive to national defense in the wake of the War of 1812. By encouraging fledgling industries, he had reasoned, the tariff would free the United States from dependence on Britain and provide revenue for military preparedness. By 1826, however, few Americans perceived national defense as a priority. Furthermore, the infant industries of 1816 had grown into troublesome adolescents that demanded higher and higher tariffs.

Calhoun also burned with ambition to be president. Jackson had stated that he would only serve one term, and Calhoun assumed that he would succeed Jackson. To do so, however, he had to maintain the support of the South, which was increasingly taking an antitariff stance. As the center of cotton production had shifted to Alabama and Mississippi in the Southwest, Calhoun's home state, South Carolina, had suffered an economic decline throughout the 1820s, which its voters blamed on high tariffs. Tariffs not only drove up the price of manufactured goods but also threatened to reduce the sale of British textile products in the United States. Such a reduction might eventually lower the British demand for southern cotton and cut cotton prices. The more New England industrialized, the clearer it became that tariff laws were pieces of sectional legislation. New Englanders like Massachusetts's eloquent Daniel Webster swung toward protectionism; southerners responded with militant hostility.

Calhoun followed the Virginia and Kentucky Resolutions of 1798–1799 in viewing the Union as a compact by which the states had conferred limited and specified powers on the federal government. Although the Constitution did empower Congress to levy tariffs, Calhoun insisted that only tariffs that raised revenue for such common purposes as defense were constitutional. Set so high that it deterred foreign exporters from shipping their products to the United States, the tariff of 1828 could raise little revenue, and hence it failed to meet Calhoun's criterion of constitutionality: that federal laws benefit everyone equally. In 1828, Calhoun anonymously wrote the widely circulated *South Carolina Exposition and Protest,* in which he spelled out his argument that the tariff of 1828 was unconstitutional and that aggrieved states therefore had the right to nullify, or override, the law within their borders.

Vehement opposition to tariffs in the South, and especially in South Carolina, rested on more than economic considerations, however. Southerners feared that a federal government that passed tariff laws favoring one section over another might also pass laws meddling with slavery. Because Jackson himself was a slaveholder, the fear of federal interference with slavery was perhaps far-fetched. But South Carolinians, long apprehensive of assaults on their crucial institution of slavery, had many reasons for concern. South Carolina was one of only two states in which blacks comprised a majority of the population in 1830. Moreover, in 1831 a bloody slave revolt led by Nat Turner boiled up in Virginia. That same year in Massachusetts, William Lloyd Garrison established *The Liberator,* an abolitionist newspaper. These developments were enough to convince many troubled South Carolinians that a line had to be drawn against tariffs and possible future interference with slavery.

Like Calhoun, Jackson was strong-willed and proud. Unlike Calhoun, he was already president and the leader of a national party that included supporters in protariff states like Pennsylvania (which had gone for Jackson in the election of 1828). Thus to retain key northern support while soothing the South, Jackson devised two policies.

The first was to distribute surplus federal revenue to the states. Tariff schedules kept some goods out of the United States but let many others in for a price. The price, in the form of duties on imports, became federal revenue. In the years before federal income taxes, tariffs were a major source of federal revenue. Jackson hoped that this revenue, fairly distributed among the states, would remove the taint of sectional injustice from the tariff and force the federal government to restrict its own expenditures. All of this was good Jeffersonianism. Second, Jackson hoped to ease tariffs down from the sky-high level of 1828.

Calhoun disliked the idea of distributing federal revenue to the states because he believed that such a policy could become an excuse to maintain tariffs forever. But he was loath to break openly with Jackson. Between 1828 and 1831, Calhoun muffled his protest, hoping that Jackson would lower the tariff and that he, Calhoun, would retain both Jackson's favor and his chances for the presidency. Congress did pass new, slightly reduced tariff rates in 1832, but these did not come close to satisfying South Carolinians.

Before passage of the tariff of 1832, however, two personal issues had ruptured relations between Calhoun and Jackson. In 1829, Jackson's secretary of war, John H. Eaton, married the widowed daughter of a Washington tavernkeeper. By her own account, Peggy O'Neale Timberlake was "frivolous, wayward, [and] passionate." While still married to a naval officer away on duty, Peggy had acquired the reputation of flirting with Eaton, who boarded at her father's tavern. After her husband's death and her marriage to Eaton, she and Eaton were snubbed socially by Calhoun's wife and by his friends in the cabinet. Jackson, still angry about how his own wife had been wounded by slander during the campaign of 1828, not only befriended the Eatons but concluded that Calhoun had initiated the snubbing to discredit him and to advance Calhoun's own presidential aspirations.

To make matters worse, in 1830 Jackson received convincing documentation of his suspicion that in 1818 Calhoun, as secretary of war under President Monroe, had urged that Jackson be punished for his unauthorized raid into Spanish Florida. The revelation that Calhoun had tried to stab him in the back in 1818, combined with the spurning of the Eatons, convinced Jackson that he had to "destroy [Calhoun] regardless of what injury it might do me or my administration." A symbolic confrontation occurred between Jackson and Calhoun at a Jefferson Day dinner in April 1830. Jackson proposed the toast, "Our Union: It must be preserved." Calhoun responded: "The Union next to Liberty the most dear. May we always remember that it can only be preserved by distributing equally the benefits and burdens of the Union."

The stage was now set for the **Nullification crisis,** a direct clash between the president and his vice president. In 1831, Calhoun acknowledged his authorship of the *South Carolina Exposition and Protest*. In November 1832, a South Carolina convention nullified the tariffs of 1828 and 1832 and forbade the collection of customs duties within the state. Jackson reacted quickly. He despised nullification, calling it an "abominable doctrine" that would reduce the government to anarchy, and he berated the South Carolina nullifiers as "unprincipled men who would rather rule in hell, than be subordinate in heaven." Jackson even began to send arms to loyal Unionists in South Carolina. In December 1832, he issued a proclamation that, while promising South Carolinians further tariff reductions, lambasted nullification as itself unconstitutional. The Constitution, he emphasized, had established "a single nation," not a league of states.

The crisis eased in March 1833 when Jackson signed into law two measures—"the olive branch and the sword," in one historian's words. The olive branch was the tariff of 1833 (also called the Compromise Tariff), which provided for a gradual but significant lowering of duties between 1833 and 1842. The sword was the Force Bill, authorizing the president to use arms to collect customs duties in South Carolina. Although South Carolina did not abandon nullification in principle—in fact, it nullified the Force Bill—it construed the Compromise Tariff as a concession and rescinded its nullification of the tariffs of 1828 and 1832.

Like most of the accommodations by which the Union lurched from one sectional crisis to the next before the Civil War, the Compromise of 1833 grew out of a mixture of partisanship and statesmanship. The moving spirit behind the Compromise Tariff was Kentucky's senator Henry Clay, who had long favored high tariffs. A combination of motives brought Clay and the nullifiers together in favor of tariff reduction. Clay feared that without concessions to South Carolina on tariffs, the Force Bill would produce civil war. Furthermore, he was apprehensive that without compromise, the principle of protective tariffs would disappear under the wave of Jackson's immense popularity. In short, Clay would rather take responsibility for lowering tariffs than allow the initiative on tariff questions to pass to the Jacksonians.

For their part, the nullifiers hated Jackson and defiantly toasted "Andrew Jackson: On the soil of South Carolina he received an humble birthplace. May he not find in it a traitor's grave!" Although recognizing that South Carolina had failed to gain support for nullification from other southern states and that they would have to bow to pressure, the nullifiers preferred that Clay, not Jackson, be the hero of the hour. So they supported Clay's Compromise Tariff. Everywhere Americans now hailed Clay as the Great Compromiser. Even Martin Van Buren frankly stated that Clay had "saved the country."

The Bank Veto and the Election of 1832

Jackson recognized that the gap between the rich and the poor was widening during the 1820s and 1830s (see Chapter 9). He did not object to the rich gaining wealth by hard work. But he believed that the wealthy often grew even richer by securing favors, "privileges," from corrupt legislatures. In addition, his disastrous financial speculations early in his career led him to suspect all banks, paper money, and monopolies. On each count, the Bank of the United States was guilty.

The **second Bank of the United States** had received a twenty-year charter from Congress in 1816. As a creditor of state banks, the Bank of the United States restrained their printing and lending of money by its ability to demand the redemption of state bank notes in specie (gold or silver coinage). The bank's power enabled it to check the excesses of state banks, but also provoked hostility. In fact, it was widely blamed for precipitating the Panic of 1819. Further, at a time of mounting attacks on privilege, the bank was undeniably privileged. As the official depository for federal revenue, its capacity to lend money vastly exceeded that of any state bank. Its capital of $35 million amounted to more than double the annual expenditures of the federal government. Yet this institution, more powerful than any bank today, was only remotely controlled by the government. Its stockholders were private citizens—a "few monied capitalists" in Jackson's words. Although chartered by Congress, the bank was located in Philadelphia, not Washington, and its directors enjoyed considerable independence. Its president, the aristocratic Nicholas Biddle, viewed himself as a public servant, duty-bound to keep the bank above politics.

Urged on by Henry Clay, who hoped to ride a probank bandwagon into the White House in 1832, Biddle secured congressional passage of a bill to recharter the bank. In vetoing the recharter bill, Jackson denounced the bank as a private and privileged monopoly that drained the West of specie, was immune to taxation by the states, and made "the rich richer and the potent more powerful." Failing to persuade Congress to override Jackson's veto, Clay now pinned his hopes on gaining the presidency himself.

By 1832, Jackson had made his views on major issues clear. He was simultaneously a staunch defender of states' rights and a staunch Unionist. Although he cherished the Union, he believed that the states were far too diverse to accept strong direction from Washington. The safest course was to allow the states considerable freedom so that they would remain content within the Union and reject dangerous doctrines like nullification.

Throwing aside earlier promises to retire, Jackson again ran for the presidency in 1832, with Martin Van Buren as his running mate. Henry Clay ran on the National Republican ticket, touting his American System of protective tariffs, national banking, and federal support for internal improvements. Jackson's overwhelming personal popularity swamped Clay. Secure in office for another four years, Jackson was ready to finish dismantling the Bank of the United States.

THE BANK CONTROVERSY AND THE SECOND PARTY SYSTEM, 1833–1840

Jackson's veto of the recharter of the Bank of the United States ignited a searing controversy. Following the veto, Jackson took steps to destroy the Bank of the United States so that it could never be revived. His banking policies spurred the rise of the opposition Whig Party, mightily stimulated popular interest in politics, and contributed to the severe economic downturn, known as the Panic of 1837, that greeted his successor, Martin Van Buren. By 1840, the Whig and Democratic parties divided crisply over a fundamental issue: banks or no banks.

In part, tempers flared over banking because the U.S. government did not issue paper currency of its own; there were no "official" dollar bills as we know them today. Paper currency consisted of notes (promises to redeem in specie) dispensed by banks. These IOUs fueled economic development by making it easier for businesses and farmers to acquire loans to build factories or buy land. But if a note depreciated after its issuance because of public doubts about a bank's solvency, wage earners who had been paid in paper rather than specie would suffer. Further, paper money encouraged a speculative economy, one that raised profits and risks. For example, paper money encouraged farmers to buy land on credit in the expectation that its price would rise, but a sudden drop in agricultural prices would leave them mired in debt. Would the United States embrace swift economic development at the price of allowing some to get rich quickly off investments while others languished? Or would it opt for more modest growth within traditional channels that were based on "honest" manual work and frugality? Between 1833 and 1840 these questions would dominate American politics.

The War on the Bank

Jackson could have allowed the bank to die a natural death when its charter ran out in 1836. But Jackson and several of his rabid followers viewed the bank as a kind of dragon that would grow new limbs as soon as old ones were cut off. When Biddle, anticipating further moves against the bank by Jackson, began to call in the bank's loans and contract credit during the winter of 1832–1833, Jacksonians saw their darkest fears confirmed. The bank, Jackson assured Van Buren, "is trying to kill me, but I will kill it." Accord-

GENERAL JACKSON SLAYING THE MANY HEADED MONSTER.

Jackson Versus the Bank   *Andrew Jackson, aided by Martin Van Buren (center), attacks the Bank of the United States, which, like the many-headed serpent Hydra of Greek mythology, keeps sprouting new heads. The largest head belongs to Nicholas Biddle, the bank's president.*

ingly, Jackson embarked on a controversial policy of removing federal deposits from the Bank of the United States and placing them in state banks, called "pet banks" by their critics because they were usually selected for their loyalty to the Democratic Party.

Jackson himself opposed paper money and easy credit for encouraging ordinary Americans to embark on get-rich-quick schemes. But as state banks became depositories for federal revenue, they were able to print more paper money and extend more loans to farmers who were eager to buy public lands in the West and to speculators who bought land in the expectation of reselling it at a profit. Government land sales rose from $6 million in 1834 to $25 million in 1836. The policy of removal seemed a formula for producing exactly the kind of economy that Jackson wanted to abolish.

Jackson recognized the danger and hoped to sharply limit the number of state banks that would become depositories for federal revenue. But as state banks increasingly clamored for federal revenue, the number of state-bank depositories soon multiplied beyond Jackson's expectations. There were twenty-three by the end of 1833. Jackson found himself caught between cross-winds. On the one hand, many Democrats resented the Bank of the United States because it periodically contracted credit and restricted lending by state banks. Western Democrats, in particular, had long viewed the Cincinnati branch of the Bank of the United States as inadequate to supply their need for credit and favored an expansion of banking activity. Advocating soft money (paper), these Democrats in 1836 pressured a reluctant Jackson to sign the Deposit Act, which increased the number of deposit banks and loosened federal control over them. On the other hand, Jackson believed that paper money sapped "public virtue," and "robbed honest labour of its earnings to make knaves rich, powerful and dangerous." Seeking to reverse the damaging effects of the Deposit Act, Jackson issued a proclamation in 1836 called the Specie Circular, which provided that only specie could be accepted in payment for public lands.

Prior to 1837, when a depression struck, most Democrats favored soft money. The rival hard-money (specie) view was warmly advocated within Jackson's inner circle of advisers and from a faction of the New York Democratic Party called the Locofocos. The Locofocos grew out of various "workingmen's" parties that had sprouted during the late 1820s in northern cities and that called for free public education, the abolition of imprisonment for debt, and a ten-hour workday. Most of these parties had collapsed within a few years, but in New York the "workies" had gradually been absorbed by the Democratic Party. Once in the party, they were hard to keep in line. A mixture of intellectuals and small artisans and journeymen threatened by economic change, they worried about inflation, preferred to be paid in specie, and distrusted banks and paper money. In 1835, a faction of workingmen had broken away from Tammany Hall, the main Democratic Party organization in New York City, and held a dissident meeting in a hall whose candles were illuminated by a newfangled invention, the "loco foco," or match. Thereafter, these radical workingmen were known as Locofocos.

The Rise of Whig Opposition

During Jackson's second term, the opposition National Republican Party gave way to the new **Whig Party,** which developed a broader base in both the South and the North than had the National Republicans. Jackson's magnetic personality had swept him to victory in 1828 and 1832. But as Jackson's vague Jeffersonianism was replaced by suspicion of federal aid for internal improvements and protective tariffs, and by hard-and-fast positions against the Bank of the United States and nullification, more of those alienated by Jackson's policies joined the opposition.

Jackson's crushing of nullification, for example, led some of its southern supporters into the Whig Party, not because the Whigs favored nullification but because they opposed Jackson. Jackson's war on the Bank of the United States produced the same result. His policy of removing deposits from the bank pleased some southerners but dismayed others who had been satisfied with the bank and who did not share westerners' mania for cheaper and easier credit. Jackson's suspicion of federal aid for internal improvements also alienated some southerners who feared that the South would languish behind the North unless it began to push ahead with improvements. Because so much southern capital was tied up in slavery, pro-improvement southerners looked to the federal government for aid, and when they were met with a cold shoulder, they drifted into the Whig Party. None of this added up to an overturning of the Democratic Party in the South; the South was still the Democrats' firmest base. But the Whigs were making significant inroads, particularly in southern market towns and among planters who had close ties to southern bankers and merchants.

Meanwhile, social reformers in the North were infusing new vitality into the opposition to Jackson. These reformers wanted to improve American society by ending slavery and the sale of liquor, improving public education, and elevating public morality. Most opponents of liquor (temperance reformers) and most public-school reformers gravitated to the Whigs. Whig philosophy was more compatible with their goals than were Democratic ideals. Where Democrats maintained that the government should not impose a uniform standard of conduct on a diverse society, the Whigs' commitment to Clay's American System implied an acceptance of active intervention by the government to change society. Reformers wanted the government to play a positive role by suppressing the liquor trade and by establishing centralized systems of public education. Thus a shared sympathy for active government programs tended to unite Whigs and reformers.

Reformers also indirectly stimulated new support for the Whigs from native-born Protestant workers. The reformers, themselves almost all Protestants, widely distrusted immigrants, especially the Irish, who viewed drinking as a normal recreation and who, as Catholics, suspected (correctly) that the public schools favored by reformers would teach Protestant doctrines. The rise of reform agitation and its frequent association with the Whigs drove the Irish into the arms of the Democrats but, by the same token, gained support for the Whigs from many native-born Protestant workers who were contemptuous of the Irish.

No source of Whig strength, however, was more remarkable than Anti-Masonry, a protest movement against the secrecy and exclusiveness of the Masonic lodges, which had long provided prominent men, including George Washington, with fraternal fellowship and exotic rituals. The spark that set off the Anti-Masonic crusade was the abduction and disappearance in 1826 of William Morgan, a New York stonemason, who had threatened to expose Masonic secrets. Every effort to solve the mystery of Morgan's disappearance ran into a stone wall because local officials were themselves Masons, seemingly bent on obstructing the investigation. Throughout the Northeast, the public became increasingly aroused against the Masonic order, and rumors spread that Masonry was a powerful, anti-Christian conspiracy of the rich to suppress popular liberty and an exclusive retreat for drunkards. Anti-Masonry brought intensely moralistic small farmers and artisans from the Northeast into the Whig Party.

By 1836, the Whigs had become a national party with widespread appeal. In both the North and South, they attracted those with close ties to the market economy— commercial farmers, planters, merchants, and bankers. In the North, they also gained support from reformers, evangelical clergymen (especially Presbyterians and Congregationalists), Anti-Masons, and manufacturers. In the South they appealed to some former nullificationists; Calhoun himself briefly became a Whig. Everywhere the Whigs assailed Jackson as an imperious dictator, "King Andrew I"; indeed, they had taken the name "Whigs" to associate their cause with that of the American patriots who had opposed King George III in 1776.

The Election of 1836	When it came to popularity, Jackson was a hard act to follow. In 1836, the Democrats ran Martin Van Buren for the presidency, a politician whose star had risen as Calhoun's had

fallen. Party rhetoric reminded everyone that Van Buren was Jackson's favorite, and then contended that the Democratic Party itself, with Van Buren as its mere agent, was the real heir to Jackson, the perfect embodiment of the popular will. Less cohesive than the Democrats, the Whigs could not unite on a single candidate. Rather, four anti–Van

Buren candidates emerged in different parts of the country. These included three Whigs—William Henry Harrison of Ohio, Daniel Webster of Massachusetts, and W. P. Mangum of North Carolina—and one Democrat, Hugh Lawson White of Tennessee, who distrusted Van Buren and who would defect to the Whigs after the election.

Democrats accused the Whigs of a plot to so divide the vote that no candidate would receive the required majority of votes in the Electoral College. That would throw the election into the House of Representatives, where, as in 1824, deals and bargains would be struck. In reality, the Whigs had no overall strategy, and Van Buren won a clear majority of the electoral votes. But there were signs of trouble ahead for the Democrats. The popular vote was close, notably in the South, where the Democrats had won two-thirds of the votes in 1832 but barely half in 1836.

The Panic of 1837 Jackson left office in a burst of glory and returned to his Nashville home in a triumphal procession. But the public's mood quickly became less festive, for no sooner was Van Buren in office than a severe depression, called the **Panic of 1837,** struck.

In the speculative boom of 1835 and 1836 that was born of Jackson's policy of removing federal deposits from the Bank of the United States and placing them in state banks, the total number of banks doubled, the value of bank notes in circulation nearly tripled, and both commodity and land prices soared. Encouraged by easy money and high commodity prices, states made new commitments to build canals. Then in May 1837, prices began to tumble, and bank after bank suspended specie payments. After a short rally, the economy crashed again in 1839. The Bank of the United States, which had continued to operate as a state bank with a Pennsylvania charter, failed. Nicholas Biddle was charged with fraud and theft. Banks throughout the nation once again suspended specie payments.

The ensuing depression was far more severe and prolonged than the economic downturn of 1819. Those lucky enough to find work saw their wage rates drop by roughly one-third between 1836 and 1842. In despair, many workers turned to the teachings of William Miller, a New England religious enthusiast whose reading of the Bible convinced him that the end of the world was imminent. Dressed in black coats and stovepipe hats, Miller's followers roamed urban sidewalks and rural villages in search of converts. Many Millerites sold their possessions and purchased white robes to ascend into heaven on October 22, 1843, the date on which Millerite leaders calculated the world would end. Ironically, by then the worst of the depression was over; but at its depths in the late 1830s and early 1840s, the economic slump fed the gloom that made despairing people receptive to Miller's predictions.

Called the "sly fox" and the "little magician" for his political craftiness, Van Buren would need these skills to confront the depression that was causing misery not only for ordinary citizens but also for the Democratic Party. Railing against "Martin Van Ruin," in 1838 the Whigs swept the governorship and most of the legislative seats in Van Buren's own New York.

To seize the initiative, Van Buren called for the creation of an independent Treasury. The idea was simple: instead of depositing its money in banks, which would then use federal funds as the basis for speculative loans, the government would hold its revenues and keep them from the grasp of corporations. When Van Buren finally signed the Independent Treasury Bill into law on July 4, 1840, his supporters hailed it as America's second Declaration of Independence.

The independent Treasury reflected the deep Jacksonian suspicion of an alliance between government and banking. But the Independent Treasury Act failed to address the banking issue on the state level, where newly chartered state banks—of which there were more than nine hundred by 1840—lent money to farmers and businessmen. Blaming the depression on Jackson's Specie Circular rather than on the banks, Whigs continued to encourage the chartering of banks as a way to spur economic development. In contrast, a growing number of Democrats blamed the depression on banks and on paper money and swung toward the hard-money stance long favored by Jackson and his inner circle. In Louisiana and Arkansas, Democrats successfully prohibited banks altogether, and elsewhere they imposed severe restrictions on banks—for example, by banning the issuing of paper money in small denominations. In sum, after 1837 the Democrats became an antibank, hard-money party.

The Election of 1840

Despite the depression, Van Buren gained his party's renomination. Avoiding their mistake of 1836, the Whigs settled on a single candidate, Ohio's William Henry Harrison, and ran former Virginia Senator John Tyler as vice president. Harrison, who was sixty-seven years old and barely eking out a living on a farm, was picked because he had few enemies. Early in the campaign, the Democrats made a fatal mistake by ridiculing Harrison as "Old Granny," a man who desired only to spend his declining years in a log cabin sipping cider. Without knowing it, the Democrats had handed the Whigs the most famous campaign symbol in American history. The Whigs immediately reminded the public that Harrison had been a rugged frontiersman, the hero of the Battle of Tippecanoe, and a defender of all frontier people who lived in log cabins.

Refusing to publish a platform, the Whigs ran a "hurrah" campaign. They used log cabins for headquarters, sang log-cabin songs, gave out log-cabin cider, and called their newspaper *Log Cabin*. For a slogan, they trumpeted "Tippecanoe and Tyler too." When not celebrating log cabins, they attacked Van Buren as a soft aristocrat who lived in "regal splendor." Whereas Harrison was content to drink hard cider from a plain mug, the Whigs observed, Van Buren had turned the White House into a palace fit for an oriental despot and drank fine wines from silver goblets while he watched people go hungry in the streets.

The election results gave Harrison a clear victory. Van Buren carried only seven states and even failed to hold his own state of New York. The depression would have made it difficult, if not impossible, for any Democrat to have triumphed in 1840, but Van Buren had other disabilities besides the economic collapse. Unlike Harrison and Jackson, he had no halo of military glory. Moreover, Van Buren ran a surprisingly sluggish campaign. Prior to 1840, the Whigs had been slower than the Democrats to mobilize voters by new techniques. But in 1840, it was Van Buren who directed his campaign the old-fashioned way by writing encouraging letters to key supporters, whereas Harrison broke with tradition and went around the country (often on railroads) campaigning. Ironically, Van Buren, the master politician, was beaten at his own game.

The Second Party System Matures

In losing the presidency in 1840, Van Buren actually received four hundred thousand more popular votes than any previous presidential candidate. The total number of votes cast in presidential elections had risen from 1.2 million in 1828 to 1.5 million in 1836 to 2.4 million in 1840. The 60 percent leap in the size of the popular vote between 1836 and 1840 is the greatest proportional jump between consecutive elections in American history. Neither lower suffrage requirements nor population growth was the main cause of this increase. Rather, it resulted from a jump in the percentage of eligible voters who chose to vote. In the three elections before 1840, the proportion of white males who voted had fluctuated between 55 percent and 58 percent; in 1840 it rose to 80 percent.

Both the depression and the frenzy of the log-cabin campaign had brought voters to the polls. Yet voter turnout stayed up even after prosperity returned in the 1840s. The second party system, which had been developing slowly since 1828, reached a high plateau in 1840 and remained there for more than a decade. Politicians increasingly presented clear alternatives to voters. The gradual hardening of the line between the two parties stimulated enduring popular interest in politics.

No less than the tariff and banking issues, reform also aroused partisan passions by 1840. Yet the seeds of many of the reform movements that burst upon the national scene in the 1830s were initially sown in the field of religion rather than politics.

THE RISE OF POPULAR RELIGION

In *Democracy in America*, Alexis de Tocqueville pointed out an important difference between France and the United States. "In France I had almost always seen the spirit of religion and the spirit of freedom pursuing courses diametrically opposed to each other; but in America I found that they were intimately united, and that they reigned in common over the same country." From this assertion Tocqueville drew a startling conclusion: religion was "the foremost of the political institutions" of the United States.

In calling religion a political institution, Tocqueville did not mean that Americans gave special political privileges to any particular denomination. Rather, he was referring to the way in which religious impulses reinforced American democracy and liberty. Just as Americans demanded that politics be made accessible to the average person, they insisted that ministers preach doctrines that appealed to ordinary people. The most successful ministers were those who used plain words to move the heart, not those who tried to dazzle their listeners with theological complexities. Increasingly, too, Americans demanded theological doctrines that put individuals in charge of their own religious destiny. They thrust aside the Calvinist creed that God had arbitrarily selected some people for salvation and others for damnation, and substituted the belief that anyone could attain heaven.

Thus heaven as well as politics became democratized in these years. The harmony between religious and democratic impulses owed much to a series of religious revivals known as the Second Great Awakening.

The Second Great Awakening   The **Second Great Awakening** had begun in Connecticut during the 1790s and set ablaze one section of the nation after another during the following half-century. At first, educated Congregationalists and Presbyterians such as Yale University's president Timothy Dwight had dominated the revivals. But as they spread from Connecticut to frontier states like Tennessee and Kentucky, revivals had undergone striking changes that were typified by the rise of camp meetings. These were gigantic revivals in which members of several denominations gathered together in sprawling open-air camps for up to a week to hear revivalists proclaim that the Second Coming of Jesus was near and that the time for repentance was now.

The most famous camp meeting occurred at Cane Ridge, Kentucky, in August 1801, when a huge crowd came together on a hillside to listen to thunderous sermons and to sing hymns and experience the influx of divine grace. One eyewitness described the meeting:

> At night, the whole scene was awfully sublime. The ranges of tents, the fires, reflecting light amidst the branches of the towering trees; the candles and lamps illuminating the encampment; hundreds moving to and fro, with lights or torches, like Gideon's army; the preaching, praying, singing, and shouting, all heard at once, rushing from different parts of the ground, like the sound of many waters, was enough to swallow up all the powers of contemplation.

The Cane Ridge revival was an episode of the larger Great Kentucky Revival of 1800–1801. Among the distinguishing features of these frontier revivals was the appearance of "exercises" in which men and women rolled around like logs, jerked their heads furiously (a phenomenon known simply as "the jerks"), and grunted like animals (the "barking exercise"). Observing the apparent pandemonium that had broken loose, critics had blasted the frontier frenzy for encouraging fleshly lust more than spirituality and complained that "more souls were begot than saved" in revivals. In fact, the early frontier revivals had challenged traditional religious customs. The most successful frontier revivalist preachers were not college graduates but ordinary farmers and artisans who had experienced powerful religious conversions and who had contempt for learned ministers with their dry expositions of orthodoxy.

No religious denomination had been more successful on the frontier than the Methodists. With fewer than seventy thousand members in 1800, the Methodists had become America's largest Protestant denomination by 1844, claiming a little over a million members. In contrast to New England Congregationalists and Presbyterians, Methodists emphasized that religion was primarily a matter of the heart rather than the head. The frontier Methodists disdained "settled" ministers tied to fixed parishes. Instead, they preferred itinerant circuit riders—young, unmarried men who moved on horseback from place to place and preached in houses, open fields, or wherever else listeners gathered.

Although the frontier revivals disrupted religious custom, they also promoted law, order, and morality on the frontier. Drunken rowdies who tried to invade camp meetings met their match in brawny itinerants like the Methodist Peter Cartwright. It was not only in camp meetings that Cartwright and his peers sought to raise the moral standard of the frontier. After Methodist circuit riders left, their converts formed weekly "classes" to provide mutual encouragement and to chastise one another for drunkenness, fighting, fornication, gossiping, and even sharp business practices.

Eastern Revivals   By the 1820s, the Second Great Awakening had begun to shift back to the East. The hottest revival fires blazed in an area of western New York known as the "Burned-Over District." No longer a frontier, western New York teemed with descendants of Puritans who hungered for religious experience and with people drawn by the hope of wealth after the completion of the Erie Canal. It was a fertile field of high expectations and bitter discontent.

The man who harnessed these anxieties to religion was **Charles G. Finney.** Finney began his career as a lawyer, but after a religious conversion in 1821, which he described as a "retainer from the Lord Jesus Christ to plead his cause," he became a Presbyterian minister and conducted revivals in towns like Rome and Utica along the canal. Although he also found time for trips to New York and Boston, his greatest "harvest" came in the thriving canal city of Rochester in 1830–1831.

The Rochester revival had several features that justify Finney's reputation as the "father of modern revivalism." First, it was a citywide revival in which all denominations participated. Finney was a pioneer of cooperation among Protestant denominations. In addition, in Rochester and elsewhere, Finney introduced devices for speeding conversions, such as the "anxious seat," a bench to which those ready for conversion were led so that they could be made objects of special prayer, and the "protracted meeting," which went on nightly for up to a week.

Finney's emphasis on special revival techniques sharply distinguished him from eighteenth-century revivalists, such as Jonathan Edwards. Whereas Edwards had portrayed revivals as the miraculous work of God, Finney made them out to be human creations. The divine spirit flowed in revivals, but humans made them happen. Although a Presbyterian, Finney flatly rejected the Calvinist belief that humans had a natural and nearly irresistible inclination to sin (the doctrine of "human depravity"). Rather, he affirmed, sin was purely a voluntary act; no one had to sin. Men and women could will themselves out of sin just as readily as they had willed themselves into it. Indeed, he declared, it was theoretically possible for men and women to will themselves free of all sin—to live perfectly. Those who heard Finney and similar revivalists came away convinced that they had experienced the washing away of all past guilt and the beginning of a new life. "I have been born again," a young convert wrote. "I am three days old when I write this letter."

Originally controversial, Finney's ideas came to dominate "evangelical" Protestantism—forms of Protestantism that focused on the need for an emotional religious conversion. He was successful because he told people what they wanted to hear: that their destinies were in their own hands. A society that celebrated the "self-made" individual embraced Finney's assertion that, even in religion, people could make of themselves what they chose. Moreover, compared to most frontier revivalists, Finney had an unusually dignified style. Taken together, these factors gave him a potent appeal to merchants, lawyers, and small manufacturers in the towns and cities of the North.

More than most revivalists, Finney recognized that few revivals would have gotten off the ground without the mass participation of women. During the Second Great Awakening, female converts outnumbered male converts by about two to one. Finney encouraged women to give public testimonies of their religious experiences in church, and he often converted husbands by first converting their wives and daughters. After a visit by Finney, Melania Smith, the wife of a Rochester physician who had little time for religion, greeted her husband with a reminder of "the woe which is denounced against the families which call not on the Name of the Lord." Soon Dr. Smith heeded his wife's pleading and joined one of Rochester's Presbyterian churches.

Critics of Revivals: The Unitarians   Whereas some praised revivals for saving souls, others doubted that they produced permanent changes in behavior and condemned them for encouraging "such extravagant and incoherent expressions, and such enthusiastic fervor, as puts common sense and modesty to the blush."

One small but influential group of revival critics was the Unitarians. The basic doctrine of Unitarianism—that Jesus Christ was less than fully divine—had gained quiet acceptance among religious liberals during the eighteenth century. However, it was not until the early nineteenth century that Unitarianism emerged as a formal denomination with its own churches, ministry, and national organization. In New England, hundreds of Congregational churches were torn apart by the withdrawal of socially prominent families who had embraced Unitarianism and by legal battles over which group—Congregationalists or Unitarians—could occupy church property. Although Unitarians won relatively few converts outside New England, their tendency to attract the wealthy and educated gave them influence beyond their numbers.

Unitarians criticized revivals as uncouth emotional exhibitions and argued that moral goodness should be cultivated by a gradual process of "character building" in which the individual learned to model his or her behavior on that of Jesus rather than by a sudden emotional conversion as in a revival. Yet Unitarians and revivalists shared the belief that human behavior could be changed for the better. Both rejected the Calvinist emphasis on innate human wickedness. William Ellery Channing, a Unitarian leader, claimed that Christianity had but one purpose: "the perfection of human nature, the elevation of men into nobler beings."

The Rise of Mormonism

The Unitarians' assertion that Jesus Christ was more human than divine challenged a basic doctrine of orthodox Christianity. Yet Unitarianism proved far less controversial than another of the new denominations of the 1820s and 1830s—the Church of Jesus Christ of Latter-day Saints, or **Mormons.** Its founder, Joseph Smith, grew to manhood in one of those families that seemed to be in constant motion to and fro, but never up. After moving his family nearly twenty times in ten years, Smith's ne'er-do-well father settled in Palmyra, New York, in the heart of the Burned-Over District. As a boy, Smith dreamed of finding buried treasure, while his religious views were convulsed by the conflicting claims of the denominations that thrived in the region. "Some were contending for the Methodist faith, some for the Presbyterian, and some for the Baptists," Smith later wrote. He wondered who was right and who wrong, or whether they were "all wrong together."

The sort of perplexity that Smith experienced was widespread in the Burned-Over District, but his resolution of the confusion was unique. Smith claimed that an angel led him to a buried book of revelation and to special seer stones for use in translating it. He completed his translation of this Book of Mormon in 1827. The Book of Mormon tells the story of an ancient Hebrew prophet, Lehi, whose descendants came to America and created a prosperous civilization that looked forward to the appearance of Jesus as its savior. Jesus had actually appeared and performed miracles in the New World, the book claimed, but the American descendants of Lehi had departed from the Lord's ways and quarreled among themselves. God had cursed some with dark skin; these were the American Indians, who, when later discovered by Columbus, had forgotten their history.

Despite his astonishing claims, Smith quickly gathered followers. The appeal of Mormonism lay partly in its positioning of America at the center of Christian history and partly in Smith's assertion that he had discovered a new revelation. The idea of an additional revelation beyond the Bible appeared to some to resolve the turmoil created by the Protestant denominations' inability to agree on what the Bible said or meant.

Smith and his followers steadily moved west from New York to Ohio and Missouri. Then they migrated to Illinois, where they built a model city, Nauvoo, and a magnificent temple supported by thirty huge pillars. By moving to these areas, the Mormons hoped to draw closer to the Indians, whose conversion was one of their goals, and to escape persecution. Smith's claim to have received a new revelation virtually guaranteed a hostile reception for the Mormons wherever they went because Smith had seemingly undermined the authority of the Bible, one of the two documents (the other being the Constitution) upon which the ideals of the American Republic rested.

Smith added fuel to the fire when he reported in 1843 that he had received still another revelation, this one sanctioning the Mormon practice of having multiple wives, or polygyny. Although Smith did not publicly proclaim polygyny as a doctrine, its practice among Mormons was a poorly kept secret. Smith's self-image also intensified the controversy that boiled around Mormonism. He refused to view himself merely as the founder of another denomination; instead, he saw himself as a prophet of the kingdom of God and was called a "Second Mohammed." Mormonism would be to Christianity what Christianity had been to Judaism: an all-encompassing, higher form of religion. In 1844, Smith announced his candidacy for the presidency of the United States. But the state of Illinois was already moving against him. Charged with treason, he was jailed in Carthage, Illinois, and along with his brother was murdered there by a mob in June 1844.

Mormonism is one of the few religions to have originated in the United States, and Smith initially had hoped that Americans would respond to his call. Some did, especially among the poor and downtrodden, but the hostility of the "Gentiles" (non-Mormons) gradually persuaded Smith that the future of Mormons lay in their separation from society. In this respect, Mormonism mirrored the efforts of several religious communal societies whose members resolutely set themselves apart from society. In general, these religious communitarians were less numerous, controversial, and long-lasting than the Mormons, but one group among them, the Shakers, has continued to fascinate Americans.

The Shakers

Mother Ann Lee, the illiterate daughter of an English blacksmith, founded the Shakers, a name that came from a convulsive religious dance that was part of their ceremony. Lee and her followers established several tightly knit agricultural-artisan communities after her arrival in America in 1774. Shaker furniture became renowned for its beauty and strength, and Shakers invented such conveniences as the clothespin and the circular saw.

For all their achievements as artisans, the Shakers were fundamentally otherworldly and hostile to materialism. Having watched four of her children die in infancy, Mother Lee claimed to have seen a vision in which God expelled Adam and Eve from the Garden of Eden for having engaged in sexual intercourse. Shaker communities banned marriage and rigidly separated the sleeping quarters and workshops of men and women to discourage casual contacts. To maintain their membership—at their peak in the 1830s and 1840s the Shakers numbered about six thousand in eight states—Shakers relied on converts and adopting orphans.

To avoid becoming dependent on the evil ways of the outside world, Shakers pooled their land and implements, and they created remarkably prosperous villages. A journalist exclaimed that the lawns of Shaker villages would arouse the envy of a monarch. Even their road dust seemed pure, said another, while a British visitor concluded that "the earth does not show more flourishing fields, gardens, and orchards than theirs."

Shakers chose to live apart from society. But the message of most evangelical Protestants, including Charles G. Finney, was that religion and economic individualism—a person's pursuit of wealth—were compatible. Most revivalists told people that getting ahead in the world was acceptable as long as they were honest, temperate, and bound by the dictates of their consciences. By encouraging assimilation into rather than retreat from society, evangelicalism provided a powerful stimulus to the numerous reform movements of the 1820s and 1830s.

THE AGE OF REFORM

Democratic ferment was not confined to politics and religion. During the 1820s and 1830s, unprecedented numbers of men and women joined organizations that aimed to improve society. The abolition of slavery, women's rights, temperance, better treatment of criminals and the insane, public education, and even the establishment of utopian communities were high on various reformers' agendas.

At a time when women were not allowed to vote, free people of color increasingly were excluded from politics, and the major parties usually avoided controversial issues like slavery and women's rights, participation in reform movements offered women and blacks an opportunity to influence public issues. The white males drawn to reform movements viewed politics as a sorry spectacle that allowed a man like Andrew Jackson, a duelist who had married a divorcee, to become president and that routinely rewarded persons who would sacrifice any principle for victory at the polls. Although they occasionally cooperated with political parties, especially the Whigs, reformers gave their loyalty to their causes, not to parties.

Inclined to view all social problems as clashes between good and evil, reformers believed that they were on God's side on every issue. Religious revivalism contributed to their intense moralism. Virtually all prominent temperance reformers of the 1820s and 1830s, for example, had initially been inspired by revivals. But revivalism and reform were not always intimately linked. Influential school reformers and women's rights advocates were frequently religious liberals—either hostile or indifferent to revivals. Abolitionists criticized the churches for condoning slavery. Yet abolitionists borrowed the evangelical preachers' language and psychology by portraying slaveholding as a sin that called for immediate repentance.

Although the reform movements appealed to those excluded from or repelled by politics, most lacked the political parties' national organizations. New England and those parts of the Midwest settled by New Englanders were hotbeds of reform. In contrast, southerners actively suppressed abolition, displayed only mild interest in temperance and education reform, ignored women's rights, and saw utopian communities as proof of the mental instability of northern reformers.

The War on Liquor   Agitation for temperance (either total abstinence from alcoholic beverages or moderation in their use) intensified during the second quarter of the nineteenth century. Temperance reformers addressed a growing problem. The spread of the population across the Appalachians stimulated the production and consumption of alcohol. Before the transportation revolution, western farmers, unable to get their grain to markets, commonly distilled it into spirits. Annual per capita consumption of rum, whiskey, gin, and brandy rose until it exceeded seven gallons by 1830, nearly triple today's rate. By the late 1820s, the average adult male drank a half-pint of liquor a day. With some justification, reformers saw alcoholic excess as a male indulgence whose bitter consequences (spending wages on liquor instead of food) fell on women and children.

There had been agitation against intemperance before 1825, but the Connecticut revivalist Lyman Beecher ushered in a new phase that year. In six widely acclaimed lectures, he thundered against all use of alcohol. A year later, evangelical Protestants created the **American Temperance Society,** the first national temperance organization. By 1834, some five thousand state and local temperance societies were loosely affiliated with the American Temperance Society. Although these societies were nearly always headed by men, from one-third to one-half of their members were women, who found in temperance agitation a public outlet for their moral energies. Whereas previous temperance supporters had advised moderation in the use of spirits, the American Temperance Society followed Beecher in demanding total abstinence. The society flooded the country with tracts denouncing the "amazing evil" of strong drink and urged churches to expel any members who condoned alcohol.

Among the main targets of the evangelical temperance reformers were moderate drinkers in the laboring classes. In the small shops where a handful of journeymen and apprentices worked informally, passing the jug every few hours was a time-honored way to relieve fatigue and monotony. But large factories demanded a more disciplined, sober work force, and evangelical temperance reformers quickly gained manufacturers' support. In East Dudley, Massachusetts, for example, three factory owners refused to sell liquor in factory stores, calculating that any profits from the sale would be more than offset by lost working time and "the scenes of riot and wickedness thus produced."

Workers showed little interest in temperance before the late 1830s. But after the Panic of 1837, a new stage of temperance agitation sprang up in the form of the Washington Temperance Societies. Starting in Baltimore in 1840, the Washingtonians were more likely to be mechanics (workingmen) and laborers than ministers and manufacturers. Many were reformed drunkards, and most had concluded that their survival in the harsh climate of depression depended on their commitment to sobriety and frugality. For example, Charles T. Woodman, a baker, had been forced by the collapse of his business to flee Boston for Philadelphia to escape his creditors. Like most Washingtonians, Woodman blamed his ruin on a relapse into his "old habit" of drink. The forces dislocating workers in the late 1830s were often far beyond their control. Part of the appeal of temperance was that it lay within their control. Take care of temperance, a Washingtonian assured a Baltimore audience, and the Lord would take care of the economy.

For all their differences from earlier temperance associations, the Washingtonians reflected the impact of revivals even more than did the American Temperance Society. Viewing drinking as sinful, they held "experience meetings" in which members described their "salvation" from liquor and their "regeneration" through abstinence or "teetotalism" (an emphatic form of the word *total*). Their wives joined "Martha Washington" societies in which they pledged to smell their husbands' breath each night and paraded with banners that read "Teetotal or No Husband." The Washingtonians spread farther and faster than any other antebellum temperance organization.

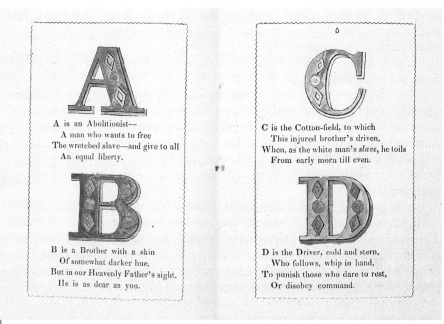

The Antislavery Alphabet   *Viewing children as morally pure and hence as natural opponents of slavery, abolitionists produced antislavery toys, games, and, as we see here, alphabet books.*

As temperance won new supporters, the crusaders gradually shifted from calls for individuals to abstain to demands that towns and even states ban all traffic in liquor. This shift from moral suasion to legal prohibition was controversial, even within the movement. But by the late 1830s, prohibition was scoring victories. In 1838, Massachusetts prohibited the sale of distilled spirits in amounts less than fifteen gallons, thereby restricting small purchases by individual drinkers; in 1851 Maine banned the manufacture and sale of all intoxicating beverages. Controversial though these laws were, the temperance movement won a measure of success. After rising steadily between 1800 and 1830, per capita consumption of distilled spirits began to fall during the 1830s. The rate of consumption during the 1840s was less than half that in the 1820s.

Public-School Reform   Like temperance reformers, school reformers encouraged orderliness and thrift in the common people. Rural America's "district" schools became a main target. Here students ranging in age from three to twenty or more crowded into a single room and learned to read and count, but little more. Students never forgot the primitive conditions and harsh discipline of these schools, especially the floggings until "the youngster vomited or wet his breeches."

Expecting little from education, rural parents were content with these schools. But reformers, who insisted that schools equip students for the emerging competitive and industrial economy, saw them in a different light. **Horace Mann,** who in 1837 became the first secretary of the newly created Massachusetts board of education, presided over sweeping reforms to transform schools into institutions that occupied most of a child's time and energy. Mann's goals included shifting financial support from parents to the state, extending the school term from two or three to as many as ten months, standardizing textbooks, classifying students into grades based on their age and attainment, and compelling attendance.

School reformers sought to spread uniform cultural values as well as to combat ignorance. Requiring students to arrive at a set time would teach punctuality, and matching students against their peers would stimulate the competitiveness required by an industrialized society. Children would read the same books and absorb such lessons as "Idleness is the nest in which mischief lays its eggs." The McGuffey readers, which sold 50 million copies between 1836 and 1870, preached industry, honesty, sobriety, and patriotism.

Although school reform made few gains in the South (see Chapter 12), much of the North remodeled its schools along the lines advocated by Mann, and in 1852 Massachusetts passed the nation's first compulsory school law. Success did not come easily. Educational reformers faced challenges from farmers, who were satisfied with the informality of the district schools, and from urban Catholics, led by New York City's Bishop John Hughes, who pointed out that the textbooks used in public schools dispensed anti-Catholic and anti-Irish barbs. And in both rural and urban areas, the laboring poor opposed compulsory education as a menace to parents who depended on their children's wages.

Yet school reformers prevailed, in part because their opponents, rural Protestants and urban Catholics, were incapable of cooperating with each other. In part, too, reformers succeeded by gaining influential allies. For example, their stress on free, tax-supported schools won the backing of the urban workingmen's parties that arose in the late 1820s; and their emphasis on punctuality appealed to manufacturers who needed a disciplined work force. The new ideas also attracted reform-minded women who recognized that the grading of schools would ease women's entry into teaching. Many people doubted that a woman could control a one-room school with pupils of widely variant ages, but managing a class of eight-year-olds was different. Catharine Beecher accurately predicted that school reform would render teaching a suitable profession for women. By 1900, about 70 percent of the nation's schoolteachers were women.

School reform also appealed to native-born Americans alarmed by the swelling tide of immigration. The public school emerged as the favorite device by which reformers forged a common American culture out of an increasingly diverse society. "We must decompose and cleanse the impurities which rush into our midst" through the "one infallible filter—the SCHOOL."

School reformers were eager to assimilate immigrants into the mainstream, but few stressed the integration of black and white children. When black children were fortunate enough to get any schooling, it was usually in segregated schools. Black children who entered integrated public schools met with such virulent prejudice that black leaders in northern cities frequently preferred segregated schools.

| Abolition | Antislavery sentiment among whites flourished in the Revolutionary era but declined in the early nineteenth century. The |

main antislavery organization founded between 1800 and 1830 was the American Colonization Society (1816), which displayed little moral outrage against slavery. The society proposed a plan for gradual emancipation, with compensation to the slave owner, and the shipment of freed blacks to what became the nation of Liberia in Africa. This proposal attracted support from some slaveholders in the Upper South who would never have dreamed of a general emancipation.

At its core, colonization was hard-hearted and soft-headed. Its proponents assumed that blacks were a degraded race that did not belong in American society, and they underestimated the growing dependence of the South's economy on slavery. Confronted by a soaring demand for cotton and other commodities, few southerners were willing to free their slaves, even if compensated. In any event, the American Colonization Society never had enough funds to buy freedom for more than a fraction of slaves. Between 1820 and 1830, only 1,400 blacks migrated to Liberia, and most were already free. In striking contrast, the American slave population, fed by natural increase (the excess of births over deaths), rose from 1,191,000 in 1810 to more than 2,000,000 in 1830.

During the 1820s, the main source of radical opposition to slavery was blacks themselves. Blacks had little enthusiasm for colonization. Most American blacks were native-born rather than African-born. How, they asked, could they be sent back to a continent that they had never left? "We are natives of this country," a black pastor in New York proclaimed. "We only ask that we be treated as well as foreigners." In opposition to colonization, blacks formed scores of abolition societies. David Walker, a Boston free black who opened a used clothing store in 1827, smuggled antislavery tracts into the South by stuffing them into the pockets of clothes he shipped to the South. In 1829, Walker published an *Appeal . . . to the Colored Citizens of the World,* which urged slaves to murder their masters if necessary to gain their freedom.

Not all whites acquiesced to the continuance of slavery. In 1821, the Quaker Benjamin Lundy began a newspaper, the *Genius of Universal Emancipation,* and put forth proposals that no new slave states be admitted to the Union, that the internal slave trade be outlawed, that the three-fifths clause of the Constitution be repealed, and that Congress abolish slavery wherever it had the authority to do so. In 1828, Lundy hired a young New Englander, **William Lloyd Garrison,** as an assistant editor. Prematurely bald, wearing steel-rimmed glasses, and typically donning a black suit and black cravat, Garrison looked more like a schoolmaster than a rebel. But in 1831, when he launched his own newspaper, *The Liberator,* he quickly established himself as the most famous and controversial white abolitionist. "I am in earnest," Garrison wrote. "I will not equivocate—I will not excuse—I will not retreat a single inch—AND I WILL BE HEARD."

Garrison's battle cry was "immediate emancipation." In place of exiling blacks to Africa, he substituted the truly radical notion that blacks should enjoy civil (or legal) equality with whites. He greeted slaves as "a Man and a Brother," "a Woman and a Sister." Even Garrison, however, did not think that all slaves could be freed overnight. "Immediate emancipation" meant that all people had to realize that slavery was sinful and its continued existence intolerable.

Garrison quickly gained support from the growing number of black abolitionists. A black barber in Pittsburgh sent Garrison sixty dollars to help with *The Liberator.* Black agents sold subscriptions, and three-fourths of *The Liberator*'s subscribers in the early years were black.

The escaped slave Frederick Douglass and a remarkable freed slave who named herself Sojourner Truth proved eloquent lecturers against slavery. Douglass could rivet an audience with an opening line. "I appear before the immense assembly this evening as a thief and a robber," he gibed. "I stole this head, these limbs, this body from my master, and ran off with them."

Relations between black and white abolitionists were not always harmonious. White abolitionists called for legal equality for blacks but not necessarily for social equality. Not without racial prejudice, they preferred light-skinned to dark-skinned Negroes and, with the exception of Garrison, were hesitant to admit blacks to antislavery societies. Yet the prejudices of white abolitionists were mild compared to those of most whites. A white man or woman could do few things less popular in the 1830s than become an abolitionist. Mobs, often including people in favor of colonization, repeatedly attacked abolitionists. For example, a Boston mob, searching for a British abolitionist in 1835, found Garrison instead and dragged him through town on the end of a rope. An abolitionist editor, Elijah Lovejoy, was murdered by a mob in Alton, Illinois, in 1837.

Abolitionists drew on the language of revivals and described slavery as sin, but the Protestant churches did not rally behind abolition as strongly as they rallied behind temperance. Lyman Beecher roared against the evils of strong drink but whimpered about those of slavery, and in 1834 he tried to suppress abolitionists at Cincinnati's Lane Theological Seminary. In response, Theodore Dwight Weld, an idealistic follower of Charles G. Finney, led a mass withdrawal of students. These "Lane rebels" formed the nucleus of abolitionist activity at antislavery Oberlin College.

As if external hostility were not enough, abolitionists argued continually with each other. The American Anti-Slavery Society, founded in 1833, was the scene of several battles between Garrison and prominent New York and midwestern abolitionists such as the Lewis brothers and Arthur Tappan, Theodore Dwight Weld, and James G. Birney. One of the issues between the two sides was whether abolitionists should enter politics as a distinct party. In 1840, Garrison's opponents ran Birney for president on the ticket of the newly formed Liberty Party. As for Garrison himself, he was increasingly rejecting all laws and governments, as well as political parties, as part of his doctrine of "nonresistance." In 1838, he and his followers had founded the New England Non-Resistance Society. Their starting point was the fact that slavery depended on force. Garrison then added that all governments ultimately rested on force; even laws passed by elected legislatures needed police enforcement. Because Garrison viewed force as the opposite of Christian love, he concluded that Christians should refuse to vote, hold office, or have anything to do with government. It is a small wonder that many abolitionists thought of Garrison as extreme, or "ultra."

The second issue that divided the American Anti-Slavery Society concerned the role of women in the abolitionist movement. In 1837 **Angelina and Sarah Grimké,** daughters of a South Carolina slaveholder, embarked on an antislavery lecture tour of New England. Women had become deeply involved in antislavery societies during the 1830s, but always in female auxiliaries affiliated with organizations run by men. What made the Grimké sisters so controversial was that they drew mixed audiences of men and women to their lectures at a time when it was thought indelicate for women to speak before male audiences. Clergymen chastised the Grimké sisters for lecturing men rather than obeying them.

Such criticism backfired, however, because the Grimkés increasingly took up the cause of women's rights. In 1838, each wrote a classic of American feminism. Sarah produced *Letters on the Condition of Women and the Equality of the Sexes,* and Angelina contributed *Letters to Catharine E. Beecher* (Lyman Beecher's daughter, a militant opponent of female equality). Some abolitionists tried to dampen the feminist flames. Abolitionist poet John Greenleaf Whittier dismissed women's grievances as "paltry" compared to the "great and dreadful wrongs of the slave." Even Theodore Dwight Weld, who had married Angelina Grimké, wanted to subordinate women's rights to antislavery. But the fiery passions would not be extinguished. Garrison, welcoming the controversy, promptly espoused women's rights and urged that women be given positions equal to men in the American Anti-Slavery Society. In 1840, the election of a woman, Abby Kelley, to a previously all-male committee split the American Anti-Slavery Society wide open. A substantial minority of profeminist delegates left—some to join the Liberty Party, others to follow Lewis Tappan into the new American and Foreign Anti-Slavery Society.

The disruption of the American Anti-Slavery Society did not greatly damage abolitionism. The national society had never had much control over the local societies that had grown swiftly during the mid-1830s. By 1840, there were more than fifteen hundred local societies, principally in Massachusetts, New York, and Ohio. By circulating abolitionist tracts, newspapers, and even chocolates with antislavery messages on their wrappers, these local societies kept the country ablaze with agitation.

One of the most disruptive abolitionist techniques was to flood Congress with petitions calling for an end to slavery in the District of Columbia. Congress had no time to consider all the petitions, but to refuse to address them meant depriving citizens of their right to have petitions heard. In 1836, southerners secured congressional adoption of the "gag rule," which automatically tabled abolitionist petitions and thus prevented discussion of them in Congress. Former president John Quincy Adams, then a representative from Massachusetts, led the struggle against the gag rule and finally secured its repeal in 1845.

The debate over the gag rule subtly shifted the issue from the abolition of slavery to the constitutional rights of free expression and petitioning Congress. Members of Congress with little sympathy for abolitionists found themselves attacking the South for suppressing the right of petition. In a way, the gag-rule episode vindicated Garrison's tactic of stirring up emotions on the slavery issue. By holding passions over slavery at the boiling point, Garrison kept the South on the defensive. The less secure southerners felt, the more they were tempted into clumsy overreactions like the gag rule.

Women's Rights

The position of American women in the 1830s contained many contradictions. Women could not vote. If married, they had no right to own property (even inherited property) or to retain their own earnings. Yet the spread of reform movements provided women with unprecedented opportunities for public activity without challenging the prevailing belief that their proper sphere was the home. By suppressing liquor, for example, women could claim that they were transforming wretched homes into nurseries of happiness.

The argument that women were natural guardians of the family was double-edged. It justified reform activities on behalf of the family, but it undercut women's demands for legal equality. Let women attend to their sphere, the counterargument ran, and leave politics and finance to men. So deeply ingrained was sexual inequality that most feminists did not start out intending to attack it. Instead, their experiences in other reform movements, notably abolition, led them to the issue of women's rights.

Elizabeth Cady Stanton with Sons, 1848
This daguerreotype shows Elizabeth Cady Stanton as she looked in 1848, the year of the Seneca Falls Convention. When she was eleven, her brother died, and her grieving father said to her, "Oh, my daughter, I wish you were a boy." The young Stanton resolved to prove to him that a daughter was as valuable as a son. Her career as a reformer, which carried her into temperance, antislavery, and women's rights, did not deter her from raising seven children.

Among the early women's rights advocates who started their reform careers as abolitionists were the Grimké sisters, the Philadelphia Quaker **Lucretia Mott,** Lucy Stone, and Abby Kelley. Like abolition, the cause of women's rights revolved around the conviction that differences of race and gender were unimportant and incidental. "Men and women," Sarah Grimké wrote, "are CREATED EQUAL! They are both moral and accountable beings, and whatever is right for man to do, is right for woman." The most articulate and aggressive advocates of women's rights, moreover, tended to gravitate to William Lloyd Garrison rather than to more moderate abolitionists. Garrison, himself a vigorous feminist, repeatedly stressed the special degradation of women under slavery. The early issues of *The Liberator* contained a "Ladies' Department" headed by a picture of a kneeling slave woman imploring, "Am I Not a Woman and a Sister?" It was common knowledge that slave women were vulnerable to the sexual demands of white masters. Garrison denounced the South as a vast brothel and described slave women as "treated with more indelicacy and cruelty than cattle."

Although their involvement in abolition aroused advocates of women's rights, the discrimination they encountered within the abolition movement infuriated them and impelled them to make women's rights a separate cause. In the 1840s, Lucy Stone became the first abolitionist to lecture solely on women's rights. When Lucretia Mott and other American women tried to be seated at the World's Anti-Slavery Convention in London in 1840, they were relegated to a screened-off section. The incident made a sharp impression not only on Mott but also on **Elizabeth Cady Stanton,** who had chosen to accompany her abolitionist husband to the meeting as a honeymoon trip. In

1848, Mott and Stanton organized a women's rights convention at Seneca Falls, New York. The **Seneca Falls convention**'s Declaration of Sentiments, modeled on the Declaration of Independence, began with the assertion that "all men and women are created equal." The convention passed twelve resolutions, and only one, a call for the right of women to vote, failed to pass unanimously; but it did pass. Ironically, after the Civil War, the call for woman suffrage became the main demand of women's rights advocates for the rest of the century.

Women's rights advocates won a few notable victories. For example, in 1860 Stanton's lobbying helped secure passage of a New York law allowing married women to own property. This was not the first such law, but it was the most comprehensive to date, and it helped meet the demand of the early feminists for greater equality within marriage. But women's rights had less impact than most other reforms. Temperance and school reform were far more popular, and abolitionism created more commotion. Women would not secure the right to vote throughout the nation until 1920, fifty-five years after the Thirteenth Amendment abolished slavery. One reason for the relatively slow advance of women's rights was that piecemeal gains—such as married women's securing the right to own property in several states by the time of the Civil War—satisfied many women. The cause of women's rights also suffered from a close association with abolitionism, which was unpopular. In addition, the advance of feminism was slowed by the competition that it faced from the alternative ideal of separate spheres (see Chapter 9). By sanctioning activities in reforms such as temperance and education, the doctrine of separate spheres provided many women with worthwhile pursuits beyond the family. In this way, it blunted the edge of female demands for full equality.

Penitentiaries and Asylums

Beginning in the 1820s, reformers tried to combat poverty, crime, and insanity by establishing highly regimented institutions, which were products of striking new assumptions about the causes of deviancy. As poverty and crime had increased and grown more visible in early-nineteenth-century cities, alarmed investigators concluded that indigence and deviant behavior resulted not from defects in human nature, as colonial Americans had thought, but from drunken fathers and broken homes. The failure of parental discipline, not the will of God or the wickedness of human nature, lay at the root of evil. Both religious revivalists and secular reformers increasingly concluded that human nature could be altered by the right combination of moral influences. Most grasped the optimistic logic voiced by William Ellery Channing: "The study of the causes of crime may lead us to its cure."

To cure crime, reformers created substitutes for parental discipline, most notably the penitentiary. Penitentiaries were prisons marked by an unprecedented degree of order and discipline. Of course, colonial Americans had incarcerated criminal offenders, but jails had been used mainly to hold prisoners awaiting trial or to lock up debtors. For much of the eighteenth century, the threat of the gallows rather than of imprisonment had deterred wrongdoers. In contrast, nineteenth-century reformers believed that, rightly managed, penitentiaries would bring about the sincere reformation of offenders.

To purge offenders' violent habits, reformers usually insisted on solitary confinement. Between 1819 and 1825, New York built penitentiaries at Auburn and Ossining ("Sing Sing") in which prisoners were confined in small, windowless cells at night. By day, they could work together but never speak and rarely even look at each other. Some reformers criticized this "Auburn system" for allowing too much contact and preferred the rival "Pennsylvania system," in which each prisoner spent all of his or her time in a single cell with a walled courtyard for exercise and received no news or visits from the outside.

Antebellum America also witnessed a remarkable transformation in the treatment of poor people. The prevailing colonial practice of offering relief to the poor by supporting them in a household ("outdoor relief") gradually gave way to the construction of almshouses for the infirm poor and workhouses for the able-bodied poor ("indoor relief"). The argument for indoor relief was much the same as the rationale for penitentiaries: plucking the poor from their demoralizing surroundings and exposing them to a highly regimented institution could change them into virtuous, productive citizens. However lofty the motives behind workhouses and almshouses, the results were often abysmal. In 1833, a legislative committee found that the inmates of the Boston House of Industry were packed seven to a room and included unwed mothers, the sick, and the insane as well as the poor.

As for insane people, those living in a workhouse such as the Boston House of Industry were relatively well off, for many experienced even worse treatment by confinement in prisons. In 1841, **Dorothea Dix,** an idealistic Unitarian schoolteacher, was teaching a Sunday school class in a jail in East Cambridge, Massachusetts, and discovered insane people kept in an unheated room. Dix then investigated jails and almshouses across the state. In 1843, she presented a memorial to the state legislature that described the insane confined "in cages, closets, cellars, stalls, pens! Chained, naked, beaten with rods, and lashed into obedience." With the support of Horace Mann and Boston reformer Samuel G. Howe, she encouraged legislatures to build insane asylums. By the time of the Civil War, twenty-eight states, four cities, and the federal government had constructed public mental institutions.

Penitentiaries, workhouses, and insane asylums all reflected the same optimistic belief that deviancy could be erased by resettling deviants in the right environment. But what was the "right" environment? Part of the answer was clear-cut. Heated rooms were better than frigid ones, and sober parents preferable to drunkards. But reformers demanded much more than warm rooms and responsible parents. They were convinced that the unfettered freedom and individualism of American society were themselves defects in the environment and that the poor, criminal, and insane needed extraordinary regimentation if they were to change. Prison inmates were to march around in lockstep; in workhouses the poor, treated much like prisoners, were often forbidden to leave or receive visitors without permission. The idealism behind such institutions was genuine, but later generations would question reformers' underlying assumptions.

Utopian
Communities

The belief that individuals could live perfectly took its most extreme form in the **utopian communities** that flourished during the reform years. Most of them, founded by intellectuals, were intended as alternatives to the prevailing competitive economy and as models whose success would inspire others.

American interest in utopian communities first surfaced during the 1820s. In 1825, the British industrialist and philanthropist Robert Owen founded the New Harmony community in Indiana. Owen had already acquired a formidable reputation (and a fortune) from his management of cotton mills at New Lanark, Scotland. His innovations at New Lanark had substantially improved his workers' educational opportunities and living conditions, and had left him convinced that similar changes could transform the lives of working people everywhere. He saw the problem of the early industrial age as social rather than political. If social arrangements could be perfected, all vice and misery would disappear; human character was formed, "without exception," by people's surroundings or environment. The key to perfecting social arrangements lay, in turn, in the creation of small, planned communities— "Villages of Unity and Mutual Cooperation" containing a perfect balance of occupational, religious, and political groups.

Lured to the United States by cheap land and by Americans' receptivity to experiments, Owen confidently predicted that by 1827 the northern states would embrace the principles embodied in New Harmony. By 1827, there was little left to embrace, for the community, a magnet for idlers and fanatics, had quickly fallen apart. Owen had clashed with clergymen, who still believed that original sin, not environment, shaped human character. Yet Owenism survived the wreckage of New Harmony. The notions that human character was formed by environment and that cooperation was superior to competition had a potent impact on urban workers for the next half-century. Owen's ideas, for example, impelled workingmen's leaders to support educational reform during the late 1820s.

Experimental communities with names like Hopedale, Fruitlands, and Brook Farm proliferated amid the economic chaos of the late 1830s and 1840s. Brook Farm, near Boston, was the creation of a group of religious philosophers called transcendentalists. Most transcendentalists, including Ralph Waldo Emerson, had started as Unitarians but then sought to revitalize Christianity by proclaiming the infinite spiritual capacities of ordinary men and women. Like other utopias, Brook Farm was both a retreat and a model. Certain that the competitive commercial life of the cities was unnatural, philosophers spent their evenings in lofty musings after a day perspiring in the cabbage patch. Brook Farm attracted several renowned writers, including Emerson and Nathaniel Hawthorne, and its literary magazine, *The Dial,* became a forum for transcendentalist ideas about philosophy, art, and literature (also see Chapter 11).

The most controversial of the antebellum utopian communities, the Oneida community established in 1848 in New York state by John Humphrey Noyes, challenged conventional notions of religion, property, gender roles, sex, dress, and motherhood. Renouncing private property, Oneidans practiced communism. Noyes insisted that men perform kitchen duties, and allowed women to work in the community's stores and factories. But what most upset outsiders was Noyes's application of communism to marriage. After exchanging wives with one of his followers, Noyes proclaimed that at Oneida all women would be married to all men and all men to all women. A committee of elders headed by "Father" Noyes decided on sexual pairings for procreation.

Contemporaries dismissed Noyes, who was also an abolitionist, as a licentious crackpot. Southerners cited him to prove that antislavery ideals threatened civilization itself. Yet Oneida achieved considerable economic prosperity and attracted new members long after less-radical utopias like Brook Farm had collapsed. By embracing communism in marriage, Oneidans had burned their bridges to society and had little choice but to stay together.

Widely derided as fit only for eccentrics, antebellum utopias nevertheless exemplified in extreme form the idealism and hopefulness that permeated nearly all reform in the Age of Jackson.

CONCLUSION

The voice of the common people resounded through politics during the 1820s and 1830s. As barriers to the direct expression of the popular will such as property requirements for voting and the indirect election of presidential electors collapsed, the gentlemanly leadership and surface harmony of the Era of Good Feelings gave way to the raucous huzzahs of mass political parties. A similar development transformed American religion. Mass revivals swelled the numbers of Methodists and Baptists—denominations that de-emphasized an educated ministry—while Presbyterians and Congregationalists who insisted on an educated clergy declined in relative numbers. Calvinist clergymen found their doctrine of human depravity hammered by popular revivalists' stress on Americans' capacity to remake themselves.

The louder the people spoke, the less unified they became. The cries of "foul" that had enveloped the election of 1824 later catapulted Andrew Jackson into office as the embodiment of the popular will. But Jackson's seemingly dictatorial manner and his stands on internal improvements, tariffs, nullification, and banking divided the electorate and contributed to the emergence of the Whig Party. The Panic of 1837 deepened party divisions by shoving wavering Democrats toward a hard-money, antibank position. Similarly, revivals, which aimed to unite Americans in a religion of the heart, spawned critics of religious excess (Unitarians) and indirectly gave rise to hotly controversial religious groups (Mormons).

Seeded in part by religious revivals, a variety of reform movements also sprouted in the 1820s and 1830s. Such causes as women's rights and the abolition of slavery promised legal equality for groups excluded from participation in politics. Other reforms, such as temperance, public-school reform, prison reform, and the establishment of utopian communities, rested on the view that human nature could be improved and even perfected by a combination of individual effort and the right environment. Yet for all of their optimism about improving human nature, reformers were gripped by profound anxieties about the direction of American society. Reformers did not hesitate to coerce people into change by calling for the legal prohibition of liquor and for compulsory education. For criminals they devised highly repressive institutions designed to bring out the basic goodness of human nature. Both reformers and politicians sought to slay the demons that threatened the Republic. Often disdaining politics as corrupt, reformers blasted liquor, ignorance, and slavery with the same fervor that Jacksonians directed at banks and monopolies. Yet reformers who called for the legal prohibition of liquor and the reform of public education or who organized an abolitionist political party were reluctantly acknowledging that in a mass democracy everything sooner or later became political.

11

Technology, Culture, and Everyday Life, 1840–1860

TECHNOLOGY AND ECONOMIC GROWTH

Widely hailed as democratic, the benefits of technology drew praise from all sides. Conservatives like Daniel Webster praised machines for doing the work of ten people without consuming food or clothing, while Sarah Bagley, a Lowell mill operative and labor organizer, traced the improvement of society to the development of technology.

The technology that transformed life in antebellum America included the steam engine, the cotton gin, the reaper, the sewing machine, and the telegraph. Some of these originated in Europe, but Americans had a flair for investing in others' inventions and perfecting their own. Improvements in Eli Whitney's cotton gin between 1793 and 1860, for example, led to an eightfold increase in the amount of cotton that could be ginned in a day. Of course, technology did not benefit everyone. For example, the cotton gin riveted slavery more firmly in place by intensifying southern dependence on cotton. Technology also rendered many traditional skills obsolete and so undercut the position of artisans. But technology contributed to improvements in transportation and increases in productivity, which in turn lowered commodity prices and raised the living standards of a sizable body of free Americans between 1840 and 1860.

Agricultural Advancement   Although few settlers ventured onto the treeless, semiarid Great Plains before the Civil War, settlements edged westward after 1830 from the woodlands of Ohio and Kentucky into parts of Indiana, Michigan, Illinois, and Missouri, where flat grasslands (prairies) alternated with forests. The prairie's matted soil was difficult to break for planting, but in 1837 John Deere invented a steel-tipped plow that halved the labor to clear acres to till. Timber for housing and fencing was available in nearby woods, and settlements spread rapidly.

Wheat became to midwestern farmers what cotton was to their southern counterparts. "The wheat crop is the great crop of the North-west, for exchange purposes," an agricultural journal noted in 1850. "It pays debts, buys groceries, clothing and lands, and answers more emphatically the purposes of trade among farmers than any other crop." Technological advances sped the harvesting as well as the planting of wheat on the midwestern prairies. Using the traditional hand sickle consumed huge amounts of time and labor, all the more so because cut wheat had to be picked up and bound. Experiments with horse-drawn machines to replace sickles had failed until Cyrus McCormick of Virginia developed the mechanical reaper. In 1834, he patented his machine; in 1847 he opened a factory in Chicago, and by 1860 he had sold 80,000 reapers. During the Civil War, McCormick made immense profits by selling more than 250,000 reapers. The mechanical reaper, which harvested grain seven times faster than traditional methods with half the work force, guaranteed that wheat would dominate the midwestern prairies.

Ironically, just as a Connecticut Yankee, Eli Whitney, had stimulated the foundation of the Old South's economy by inventing the cotton gin, Cyrus McCormick, a proslavery southern Democrat, would help the North win the Civil War. The North provided the main market for the **McCormick reaper** and for the models of his many competitors; the South, with its reliance on unpaid slave labor, had little incentive to invest in labor-saving agricultural machinery. The reaper would keep northern agricultural production high at a time when labor shortages caused by troop mobilization might otherwise have slashed production.

Although Americans proved resourceful at inventing and marketing machines to speed planting and harvesting, they farmed wastefully. With land abundant, farmers were more inclined to look for virgin soil than to improve "worn out" soil. But a movement for agricultural improvement in the form of more efficient use of the soil did develop before 1860, mainly in the East.

Confronted by the superior fertility of western soil, easterners who did not move west or take jobs in factories increasingly experimented with new agricultural techniques. In Orange County, New York, for example, farmers fed their cows the best clover and bluegrass and emphasized cleanliness in the processing of dairy products. Through these practices, they produced a superior butter that commanded more than double the price of ordinary butter. Still other eastern farmers turned to fertilizers to keep their wheat production competitive with that of the bountiful midwestern prairies. By fertilizing their fields with plaster left over from the construction of the James River Canal, Virginia wheat growers raised their average yield per acre to fifteen bushels by the 1850s, up from only six bushels in 1800. Similarly, during the 1840s American cotton planters began to import guano, left by the droppings of sea birds on islands off Peru, for use as fertilizer. Fertilizer helped eastern cotton farmers close the gap created by the superior fertility of soil in the Old Southwest.

Technology and Industrial Progress   Industrial advances between 1840 and 1860 owed an immense debt to the nearly simultaneous development of effective machine tools, power-driven machines that cut and shaped metal. In the early 1800s, Eli Whitney's plan to manufacture muskets by using interchangeable parts made by unskilled workers was stalled by the absence of machine tools. (See Technology and Culture: Guns and Gun Culture). Such tools were being de-

CHRONOLOGY, 1840–1860

1820 • Washington Irving, *The Sketch Book.*

1823 • Philadelphia completes the first urban water-supply system.
James Fenimore Cooper, *The Pioneers.*

1826 • Cooper, *The Last of the Mohicans.*

1831 • Mount Auburn Cemetery opens.

1832 • A cholera epidemic strikes the United States.

1833 • The *New York Sun,* the first penny newspaper, is established.

1834 • Cyrus McCormick patents the mechanical reaper.

1835 • James Gordon Bennett establishes the *New York Herald.*

1837 • Ralph Waldo Emerson, "The American Scholar."

1841 • P. T. Barnum opens the American Museum.
Edgar Allan Poe, "The Murders in the Rue Morgue."

1844 • First telegraph message transmitted.

1846 • W. T. G. Morton successfully uses anesthesia.
Elias Howe, Jr., patents the sewing machine.

1849 • Second major cholera epidemic.
Astor Place theater riot leaves twenty dead.

1850 • Nathaniel Hawthorne, *The Scarlet Letter.*

1851 • Hawthorne, *The House of the Seven Gables.*
Herman Melville, *Moby-Dick.*
Erie Railroad completes its line to the West.

1853 • Ten small railroads are consolidated into the New York Central Railroad.

1854 • Henry David Thoreau, *Walden.*

1855 • Walt Whitman, *Leaves of Grass.*

1856 • Pennsylvania Railroad completes Chicago link.

1857 • Baltimore–St. Louis rail service completed.

1858 • Frederick Law Olmsted is appointed architect in chief for Central Park.

veloped in Britain in Whitney's day, but Americans were near strangers to them until the 1830s. By the 1840s, precise machine tools had greatly reduced the need to hand-file parts to make them fit, and they were applied to the manufacture of firearms, clocks, and sewing machines. By 1851, Europeans had started to refer to manufacture by interchangeable parts as the **"American System of Manufacturing."** In 1853, a small-arms factory in England re-equipped itself with machine tools manufactured by two firms in the backwoods of Vermont. After touring American factories in 1854, a British engineer concluded that Americans "universally and willingly" resorted to machines as a substitute for manual labor.

The American manufacturing system had several distinctive advantages. Traditionally, damage to any part of a mechanical contrivance had rendered the whole useless,

The Climax Mower   *With its vast agricultural resources, the United States became the leading manufacturer of agricultural implements in the nineteenth century. The Pennsylvania company that manufactured this mowing device modestly called it "the most complete and perfect mower in the world."*

for no new part would fit. With the perfection of manufacturing by interchangeable parts, however, replacement parts could be obtained. In addition, the improved machine tools upon which the American System depended enabled entrepreneurs to push inventions swiftly into mass production. The likelihood that inventions would quickly enter production attracted investors. By the 1850s, Connecticut firms like Smith and Wesson were mass-producing the revolving pistol, which Samuel Colt had invented in 1836. Sophisticated machine tools made it possible, a manufacturer wrote, to increase production "by confining a worker to one particular limb of a pistol until he had made two thousand."

After the transmission of the first telegraph message in 1844, Americans also seized enthusiastically on the telegraph's promise to eliminate the constraints of time and space. The speed with which Americans formed telegraph companies and strung lines stunned a British engineer, who noted in 1854 that "no private interests can oppose the passage of a line through any property." Although telegraph lines usually transmitted political and commercial messages, some cities adapted them for reporting fires. By the early 1850s, Boston had an elaborate system of telegraph stations that could alert fire companies throughout the city to a blaze in any neighborhood. By 1852, more than fifteen thousand miles of lines connected cities as distant as Quebec, New Orleans, and St. Louis.

The Railroad Boom Even more than the telegraph, railroad expansion dramatized technology's democratic promise. In 1790, even European royalty could travel no faster than fourteen miles an hour and that only with frequent changes of horses. By 1850, an ordinary American could travel three times as fast on a train, and in considerable comfort. American railroads offered only one class of travel, in contrast to the several classes on European railroads. With the introduction of adjustable upholstered seats that could serve as couches at night, Americans in effect traveled first class except for African-Americans, who often were forced to sit separately.

Americans loved railroads "as a lover loves his mistress," one Frenchman wrote, but there was little to love about the earliest railroads. Sparks from locomotives showered passengers riding in open cars, which were common. In the absence of brakes, passengers often had to get out and pull trains to stop them. Lacking lights, trains rarely ran at night. Before the introduction of standard time zones in 1883, scheduling was a nightmare; at noon in Boston it was twelve minutes before noon in New York City. Delays were frequent, for trains on single-track lines had to wait on sidings for oncoming trains to pass. Because a train's location was a mystery once it left the station, these waits could seem endless. Between 1840 and 1860, the size of the rail network and the power and convenience of trains underwent a stunning transformation. Railroads extended track from three thousand to thirty thousand miles; flat-roofed coaches

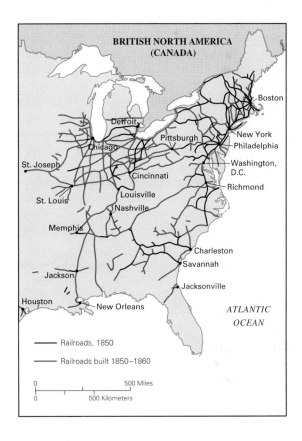

Map 11.1 Railroad Growth, 1850–1860

Rail ties between the East and the Midwest greatly increased during the railroad "boom" of the 1850s.

Guns and Gun Culture

Even in the early 1800s, some Americans painted an image of their countrymen as expert marksmen. A popular song attributed the American victory at the Battle of New Orleans in 1815 to the sharpshooting skills of the Kentucky militia. Yet Andrew Jackson, who commanded American forces in the battle, thought otherwise, and historians have agreed with him. Accurate guns were the exception in 1815 and for decades afterward. Balls exited smooth-bore muskets at unpredictable angles and started to tumble after fifty or sixty yards. In 1835, Jackson himself, now president, became a beneficiary of another feature of guns: their unreliability. A would-be assassin fired two single-shot pistols at Jackson at point-blank range. Both misfired.

Guns were not only inaccurate and unreliable; they were also expensive. A gunsmith would count himself fortunate if he could turn out twenty a year; at the Battle of New Orleans, less than one-third of the Kentucky militiamen had any guns, let alone guns that worked.

Believing that the safety of the Republic depended on a well-armed militia, Thomas Jefferson was keenly interested in finding ways to manufacture guns more rapidly. As president-elect in 1801, he witnessed a demonstration by Eli Whitney, the inventor of the cotton gin, of guns manufactured on the new principle of interchangeable parts. If each part of a gun could be machine-made and then fitted smoothly into the final product, there would be no need for the laborious methods of the skilled gunsmith. In Jefferson's presence, Whitney successfully fitted ten different gunlocks, one after another, to one musket, using only a screwdriver.

Eager to stave off the impending bankruptcy of his cotton-gin business, Whitney had already accepted a federal contract to manufacture ten thousand muskets by 1800. His demonstration persuaded Jefferson that, although Whitney had yet to deliver any muskets, he could do the job. What Jefferson did not know was that Whitney cheated on the test: he already had hand-filed each lock so that it would fit. It would be another eight years before Whitney finally delivered the muskets.

Whitney's problem was that as late as 1820 no machines existed that could make gun parts with sufficient precision to be interchangeable. During the 1820s and 1830s, however, John Hall, a Maine gunsmith, began to construct such machines at the federal arsenal at Harpers Ferry, Virginia. Hall devised new machines for drilling cast-steel gun barrels, a variety of large and small drop hammers for pounding pieces of metal into shape, and new tools for cutting metal (called milling machines). With improvements by others during the 1840s and 1850s, these machine tools made it possible to achieve near uniformity, and hence interchangeability, in the parts of guns.

At first, Hall's innovations had little effect, since the army was scaling back its demand for guns in the 1830s. The outbreak of war with Mexico in 1846 marked a turning point. Ten years earlier, a Connecticut inventor, Samuel Colt, had secured a patent for a repeating pistol with a rotating-chambered breech, usually called a revolver. At the start of the Mexican-American War, Colt won a federal contract to provide the army with one thousand revolvers. These proved to be of negligible value during the war, but Colt, a masterful publicist, was soon traveling the globe and telling all that his revolvers had won the war.

Eager to heighten the revolver's appeal to Americans, Colt made use of a recent invention, called a grammagraph, that engraved the same design repeatedly on steel. On the cylinders of his revolvers he impressed images of frontiersmen using their Colt pistols to heroically protect their wives and children from savage Indians.

In contrast to Hall, a man more interested in making than selling guns, Colt had a genius for popularizing gun ownership, not just on the frontier but also among respectable citizens in the East. He gave away scores of specially engraved revolvers to politicians and War Department officials, and he invited western heroes to dine at his Hartford, Connecticut, mansion. New England quickly became the center of a flourishing American gun industry. By 1860, nearly 85 percent of all American guns were manufactured there. By 1859, Colt had cut the price of a new revolver from fifty dollars to nineteen.

As guns became less expensive, they became the weapon of choice for both the military and street toughs. At the Astor Place Riot in 1849 (discussed later), soldiers from New York's Seventh Regiment fired a volley that killed twenty-two people, the first time that militia fired on unarmed citizens. Murderers, who traditionally had gone about their business with knives and clubs, increasingly turned to guns. In the 1850s a surge in urban homicides, usually caused by gun, led to calls for gun control. In 1857, Baltimore became the first city to allow its police to use firearms. Confronted with an outbreak of gang warfare the same year, some New York police captains authorized their men to carry guns. No

longer a luxury, guns could be purchased by ordinary citizens in new stores that sold only guns and accessories, forerunners of the modern gun supermarket.

Most states had laws barring blacks from owning guns. Women rarely purchased them. But for white American men, owning guns and knowing how to use them increasingly became a mark of manly self-reliance. Samuel Colt did all he could to encourage this attitude. When the home of a Hartford clergyman was burglarized in 1861, Colt promptly sent the clergyman "a copy of my latest work on 'Moral Reform,'" a Colt revolver. Two years earlier Dan Sickles, a New York congressman, had created a sensation by waylaying his wife's lover, Philip Barton Key (the son of the author of the "Star-Spangled Banner"), across the street from the White House. Armed with two pistols and shouting that Key was a "scoundrel" who had dishonored Sickles's marriage bed, Sickles shot the unarmed Key four times in front of several witnesses, killing him with the final shot. A notorious womanizer, Sickles had repeatedly cheated on his wife, but his behavior struck many men as justifiable. President James Buchanan, a political ally, paid one witness to disappear. Eventually, Sickles was acquitted of murder on the grounds of "temporary insanity." He continued to climb the ladder of politics, and in 1863 he led a regiment at the Battle of Gettysburg.

Question for Analysis

- Historians of technology remind us that innovations have often been linked, that an invention in one sphere gives rise to inventions in related spheres. How did this principle operate in the history of gun manufacture?

replaced open cars; kerosene lamps made night travel possible; and increasingly powerful engines let trains climb steep hills. Fifty thousand miles of telegraph wire enabled dispatchers to communicate with trains en route and thus to reduce delays.

Nonetheless, problems lingered. Sleeping accommodations remained crude, and schedules erratic. Because individual railroads used different gauge track, frequent changes of train were necessary; eight changes interrupted a journey from Charleston to Philadelphia in the 1850s. Yet nothing slowed the advance of railroads or cured Americans' mania for them. By 1860, the United States had more track than all the rest of the world.

Railroads spearheaded the second phase of the transportation revolution. Canals remained in use; the Erie Canal, for example, did not reach its peak volume until 1880. But railroads, faster and less vulnerable to winter freezes, gradually overtook them, first in passengers and then in freight. By 1860, the value of goods transported by railroads greatly surpassed that carried by canals.

As late as 1860, few rail lines extended west of the Mississippi, but railroads had spread like spider webs east of the great river. The railroads turned southern cities like Atlanta and Chattanooga into thriving commercial hubs. Most important, the railroads linked the East and the Midwest. The New York Central and the Erie Railroads joined New York City to Buffalo; the Pennsylvania Railroad connected Philadelphia to Pittsburgh; and the Baltimore and Ohio linked Baltimore to Wheeling, Virginia (now West Virginia). Simultaneously, intense construction in Ohio, Indiana, and Illinois created trunk lines that tied these routes to cities farther west. By 1860 rail lines ran from Buffalo to Cleveland, Toledo, and Chicago; from Pittsburgh to Fort Wayne; and from Wheeling to Cincinnati and St. Louis.

Chicago's growth illustrates the impact of these rail links. In 1849, it was a village of a few hundred people with virtually no rail service. By 1860, it had become a city of one hundred thousand served by eleven railroads. Farmers in the Upper Midwest no longer had to ship their grain, livestock, and dairy products down the Mississippi to New Orleans; they could now send products directly east. Chicago supplanted New Orleans as the interior's main commercial hub.

The east-west rail lines stimulated the settlement and agricultural development of the Midwest. By 1860, Illinois, Indiana, and Wisconsin had replaced Ohio, Pennsylvania, and New York as the leading wheat-growing states. Enabling farmers to speed their products to the East, railroads increased the value of farmland and promoted additional settlement. In turn, population growth triggered industrial development in cities such as Chicago; Davenport, Iowa; and Minneapolis, for the new settlers needed lumber for fences and houses and mills to grind wheat into flour.

Railroads also propelled the growth of small towns along their routes. The Illinois Central Railroad, which had more track than any other railroad in 1855, made money not only from its traffic but also from real estate speculation. Purchasing land for stations along its path, the Illinois Central then laid out towns around the stations. The selection of Manteno, Illinois, as a stop on the Illinois Central, for example, transformed the site from a crossroads without a single house in 1854 into a bustling town of nearly a thousand in 1860, replete with hotels, lumberyards, grain elevators, and gristmills. (The Illinois Central even dictated the naming of streets. Those running east and west were always named after trees, and those running north and south were numbered. Soon one rail town looked much like the next.) By the Civil War, few thought of the railroad-linked Midwest as a frontier region or viewed its inhabitants as pioneers.

As the nation's first big business, the railroads transformed the conduct of business. During the early 1830s, railroads, like canals, depended on financial aid from state governments. With the onset of depression in the late 1830s, however, state governments scrapped overly ambitious railroad projects. Convinced that railroads burdened them with high taxes and blasted hopes, voters turned against state aid, and in the early 1840s, several states amended their constitutions to bar state funding for railroads and canals. Federal aid would not become widely available until the Civil War. Although local and county governments tried to fill the void, the dramatic expansion of the railroad network in the 1850s encouraged a shift toward private investment. Well aware of the economic benefits of railroads, individuals living near them had long purchased railroad securities issued by governments and had directly bought stock in railroads, often paying by contributing their labor to building the railroads. But the large railroads of the 1850s needed more capital than such small investors could generate.

Gradually, the center of railroad financing shifted to New York City. In fact, it was the railroad boom of the 1850s that helped make Wall Street the nation's greatest capital market. The securities of all the leading railroads were traded on the floor of the **New York Stock Exchange** during the 1850s. In addition, the growth of railroads turned New York City into the center of modern investment firms. The investment firms evaluated the securities of railroads in Toledo or Davenport or Chattanooga and then found purchasers for these securities in New York, Philadelphia, Paris, London, Amsterdam, and Hamburg. Controlling the flow of funds to railroads, investment bankers began to exert influence over the railroads' internal affairs by supervising administrative reorganizations in times of trouble. A Wall Street analyst noted in 1851 that railroad men seeking financing "must remember that money is power, and that the [financier] can dictate to a great extent his own terms."

Rising Prosperity   Technological advances also improved the lives of consumers by bringing down the prices of many commodities. For example, clocks that cost $50 to fabricate by hand in 1800 could be produced by machine for fifty cents by 1850. In addition, the widening use of steam power contributed to a 25 percent rise in the average worker's real income (actual purchasing power) between 1840 and 1860. Early-nineteenth-century factories, which had depended on water wheels to propel their machines, had to shut down when the rivers or streams froze. With the spread of steam engines, however, factories could stay open longer, and workers could increase their annual wages by working more hours. Cotton textile workers were among those who benefited: although their hourly wages showed little gain, their average annual wages rose from $163 in 1830 to $176 in 1849 to $201 by 1859.

The growth of towns and cities also contributed to an increase in average annual wages. Farmers experienced the same seasonal fluctuations as laborers in the early factories. In sparsely settled rural areas, the onset of winter traditionally brought hard times. As demand for agricultural labor slumped, few alternatives existed to take up the slack. "A year in some farming states such as Pennsylvania," a traveler commented in 1823, "is only of eight months duration, four months being lost to the laborer, who is turned away as a useless animal." In contrast, densely populated towns and cities offered more opportunities for year-round work. The urban dockworker thrown out of his job as a result of frozen waterways might find work as a hotel porter or an unskilled indoor laborer.

Towns and cities also provided women and children with new opportunities for paid work. (Women and children had long performed many vital tasks on farms, but rarely for pay.) The wages of children between the ages of ten and eighteen came to play an integral role in the nineteenth-century family economy. Family heads who earned more than six hundred dollars a year might have been able to afford the luxury of keeping their children in school, but most breadwinners were fortunate if they made three hundred dollars a year. Although the cost of many basic commodities fell between 1815 and 1860 (another consequence of the transportation revolution), most families lived close to the margin. Budgets of working-class families in New York City and Philadelphia during the early 1850s reveal annual expenditures of five hundred to six hundred dollars, with more than 40 percent spent on food, 25 to 30 percent on rent, and most of the remainder on clothing and fuel. Such a family could not survive on the annual wages of the average male head of the household. It needed the wages of the children and, at times, those of the wife as well.

Life in urban wage-earning families was not necessarily superior to life in farming communities. A farmer who owned land, livestock, and a house did not have to worry about paying rent or buying fuel for cooking and heating, and rarely ran short of food. Many Americans continued to aspire to farming as the best of all occupations. But to purchase, clear, and stock a farm involved a considerable capital outlay that could easily amount to five hundred dollars, and the effort promised no rewards for a few years. The majority of workers in agricultural areas did not own farms and were exposed to seasonal fluctuations in demand for agricultural labor. In many respects, they were worse off than urban wage earners.

The economic advantages that attended living in cities help explain why so many Americans moved to urban areas during the first half of the nineteenth century. During the 1840s and 1850s cities also provided their residents with an unprecedented range of comforts and conveniences.

THE QUALITY OF LIFE

"Think of the numberless contrivances and inventions for our comfort and luxury," the poet Walt Whitman exclaimed, "and you will bless your star that Fate has cast your lot in the year of Our Lord 1857." Changes in the quality of daily life occurred within the home and affected such daily activities as eating, drinking, and washing. The patent office in Washington was flooded with sketches of reclining seats, beds convertible into chairs, street-sweeping machines, and fly traps. Machine-made furniture began to transform the interiors of houses. Stoves revolutionized heating and cooking. Railroads brought fresh vegetables to city-dwellers.

Yet change occurred unevenly. Technology enabled the middle class to enjoy luxuries formerly reserved for the rich, but it widened the distance between the middle class and the poor. As middle-class homes became increasingly lavish, the urban poor congregated in cramped tenements. Some critical elements such as medicine lagged far behind the changes wrought by the railroad and the telegraph. Still, the benefits of progress impressed Americans more than its limitations. Lacking medical advances, Americans turned to popular health movements that stressed diet and regimen over doctors.

Dwellings   During the early 1800s, the unattached wood-frame houses, all pointing in different directions, that dotted colonial cities yielded to uniform-looking brick row houses. Typically narrow and long, row houses were practical responses to rising urban land values (as much as 750 percent in Man-

Family Group   *This daguerreotype, taken about 1852, reveals the little things so important to etching a middle-class family's social status: curtains; a wall hanging; a piano with scrolled legs; a small desk with elegantly curved legs; a pet; ladies posed in nonproductive but "improving" activities (music, reading); and a young man seemingly staring into space—and perhaps pondering how to pay for it all.*

hattan between 1785 and 1815), and they drew criticism for their "extreme uniformity." But they were not all alike. Middle-class row houses, with cast-iron balconies, elegant doors, curved staircases, and rooms with odd shapes that emphasized their occupants' individuality and taste, were larger and more elaborate than working-class row houses, and less likely to be subdivided for occupancy by several families. The worst of these subdivided row houses were called tenements and became the usual habitats of Irish immigrants and free blacks.

Furniture also revealed the widening gap between the prosperous and the poor. Families in the middle and upper classes increasingly preferred an ornate furniture style known as rococo. The heavily upholstered backs of sofas were often trimmed with floral designs topped with carved medallions; vines, leaves, and flowers covered both wooden and upholstered surfaces. Mirrors with intricate gilded moldings weighed so much that they threatened to tumble from the walls. The rise of mass production in such furniture centers as Grand Rapids, Michigan, and Cincinnati between 1840 and 1860 reduced the cost of rococo furniture and tended to level taste between the middle and upper classes, while setting those classes off from everyone else.

In rural areas, the quality of housing depended as much on the date of settlement as on social class. In recently settled areas, the standard dwelling was a rude one-room log cabin with planked floors, crude clay chimneys, and windows covered by oiled paper or cloth. As rural communities matured, log cabins gave way to frame houses of two or more rooms and better insulation. Most of these were balloon-frame houses. In place of foot-thick posts and beams laboriously fitted together, a balloon-frame house had a skeleton of thin-sawn timbers nailed together in such a way that every strain ran against the grain of the wood. The simplicity and cheapness of such houses endeared them to western builders who had neither the time nor the skill to cut and fit heavy beams.

Conveniences and Inconveniences   By today's standards, everyday life in the 1840s and 1850s was primitive, but contemporaries were struck by how much better it was becoming. The transportation and industrial revolutions were affecting heating, cooking, and diet. In urban areas where wood was expensive, coal-burning stoves were rapidly displacing open hearths for heating and cooking. Stoves made it possible to cook several dishes at once and thus contributed to the growing variety of the American diet, while railroads brought in fresh vegetables, which in the eighteenth century had been absent from even lavish banquet tables.

Too, contemporaries were struck by the construction of urban waterworks—systems of pipes and aqueducts that brought fresh water from rivers or reservoirs to street hydrants. In the 1840s New York City completed the Croton aqueduct, which carried water into the city from reservoirs to the north, and by 1860 sixty-eight public water systems operated in the United States.

Despite these improvements, newly acquired elegance still bumped shoulders with squalor. Coal burned longer and hotter than wood, but it left a dirty residue that polluted the air and blackened the snow, and a faulty coal stove could fill the air with poisonous carbon monoxide. Seasonal fluctuations continued to affect diets. Only the rich could afford fruit out of season, since they alone could afford to use sugar to preserve it. Indeed, preserving almost any kind of food presented problems. Home iceboxes were rare before 1860, so salt remained the most widely used preservative. One reason antebellum Americans ate more pork than beef was that salt pork didn't taste quite as bad as salt beef.

Although public waterworks were among the most impressive engineering feats of the age, their impact is easily exaggerated. Since the incoming water usually ended its trip at a street hydrant, and only a fraction of the urban population lived near hydrants, houses rarely had running water. Taking a bath required first heating the water, pot by pot, on a stove. A New England physician claimed that not one in five of his patients took one bath a year.

Infrequent baths meant pungent body odors, which mingled with a multitude of strong scents. In the absence of municipal sanitation departments, street cleaning was let to private contractors who gained a reputation for slack performance, so people in cities relied on hogs, which they allowed to roam freely and scavenge. (Hogs that turned down the wrong street often made tasty dinners for the poor.) Stables backed by mounds of manure and outdoor privies added to the stench. Flush toilets were rare outside cities, and within cities sewer systems lagged behind water systems. Boston had only five thousand flush toilets in 1860 for a population of 178,000, a far higher ratio of toilets to people than most cities. Expensive conveniences like running water and flush toilets became another of the ways in which progress set the upper and middle classes apart from the poor. Conveniences also sharpened gender differences. In her widely popular *Treatise on Domestic Economy* (1841), Catharine Beecher told women that technological advances made it their duty to make every house a "glorious temple" by utilizing space more efficiently. Women who no longer made articles for home consumption were now expected to achieve fulfillment by obsessively sweeping floors and polishing furniture. Home, a writer proclaimed, had become woman's "royal court," where she "sways her queenly authority." Skeptical of this trend toward fastidiousness, another writer cautioned women in 1857 against "ultra-housewifery."

Disease and Health   Despite their improving standard of living, Americans remained vulnerable to disease. **Epidemics** swept through antebellum cities and felled thousands. Yellow fever and cholera killed one-fifth of New Orleans's population in 1832–1833, and cholera alone carried off 10 percent of St. Louis's population in 1849. Life expectancy for newborns in New York and Philadelphia during the 1830s and 1840s averaged only twenty-four years.

Ironically, the transportation revolution increased the peril from epidemics. The cholera epidemic of 1832, the first truly national epidemic, followed shipping routes: one branch of the epidemic ran from New York City up the Hudson River, across the Erie Canal to Ohio, and then down the Ohio River to the Mississippi and south to New Orleans; the other branch followed shipping up and down the East Coast from New York City.

The inability of physicians to explain epidemic diseases reinforced hostility toward the profession and made public health a low priority. No one understood that bacteria cause cholera and yellow fever. Physicians clashed over whether epidemic diseases were contagious, spread by touch, or resulted from "miasmas," air-carried gases from rotten vegetation or dead animals. But neither theory worked. Quarantines failed to prevent the spread of epidemics (an argument against the contagionist theory), and many residents of swampy areas contracted neither yellow fever nor cholera (a refutation of the miasma theory). Understandably, municipal leaders declined to delegate more than advisory powers to boards of health, which were dominated by physicians. Although most epidemic diseases baffled antebellum physicians, a basis for forward strides in surgery was laid during the 1840s by the discovery of anesthetics. Prior to 1840, young people often entertained themselves at parties by inhaling nitrous oxide, or "laughing gas," which produced sensations of giddiness and painlessness; and semicomical demonstrations of laughing gas became a form of popular entertainment. (Samuel Colt, the inventor of the revolver, had begun his career as a traveling exhibitor of laughing gas.) But nitrous oxide had to be carried around in bladders, which were difficult to handle, and in any case, few recognized its surgical possibilities. Then in 1842 Crawford Long, a Georgia physician who had attended laughing-gas frolics in his youth, employed sulfuric ether (an easily transportable liquid with the same properties as nitrous oxide) during a surgical operation. Long failed to follow up on his discovery, but four years later William T. G. Morton, a dentist, successfully employed sulfuric ether during an operation at Massachusetts General Hospital in Boston. Within a few years, ether came into wide use in American surgery.

The discovery of anesthesia improved the public image of surgeons, long viewed as brutes who hacked away at agonized patients. It also permitted longer and hence more careful operations. Nevertheless, the failure of most surgeons to recognize the importance of clean hands and sterilized instruments partially offset the benefits of anesthesia before 1860. In 1843, Boston physician and poet Oliver Wendell Holmes, Sr., published an influential paper on how the failure of obstetricians to disinfect their hands often spread a disease called puerperal fever among mothers giving birth in hospitals. Still, the medical profession only gradually accepted the importance of disinfection. Operations remained as dangerous as the diseases or wounds they tried to heal. The mortality rate for amputations hovered around 40 percent. During the Civil War, 87 percent of soldiers who suffered abdominal wounds died from them.

Popular Health Movements
Doubtful of orthodox medicine, antebellum Americans turned to a variety of therapies and regimens that promised longer and healthier lives. One popular response to disease was hydropathy, or the "water cure," which filtered into the United States from Europe during the 1840s. By the mid-1850s the United States had twenty-seven hydropathic sanatoriums, which used cold baths and wet packs to provide "an abundance of water of dewy softness and crystal transparency, to cleanse, renovate, and rejuvenate the disease-worn and dilapidated system." The water cure held a special attraction for well-off women, partly because hydropathics professed to relieve the pain associated with childbirth and menstruation, and partly because hydropathic sanatoriums were congenial gathering places in which middle-class women could relax and exercise in private.

In contrast to the water cure, which required the time and expense of a trip to a sanatorium, Sylvester Graham propounded a health system that anyone could adopt. Alarmed by the 1832 cholera epidemic, Graham counseled changes in diet and regimen as well as total abstinence from alcohol. He urged Americans to substitute vegetables, fruits, and coarse, whole-grain bread (called Graham bread) for meat and to abstain from spices, coffee, and tea as well as from alcohol. Soon Graham added sexual "excess" (by which he meant most sex) to his list of forbidden indulgences. Many of Graham's disciples were reformers. Grahamites had a special table at the Brook Farm community. Until forced out by indignant parents and hungry students, one of Graham's followers ran the student dining room at Oberlin College. Much like Graham, reformers traced the evils of American society to the unnatural cravings of its people. Abolitionists, for example, contended that slavery intensified white men's lust and contributed to the violent behavior of white southerners. Similarly, Graham believed that eating meat stimulated lust and other aggressive impulses.

Graham's doctrines attracted a broad audience. Many towns and cities had boarding houses whose tables were set according to his principles. His books sold well, and his public lectures were thronged. Grahamism addressed the popular desire for better health at a time when orthodox medicine seemed to do more damage than good.

Phrenology
The belief that each person was master of his or her own destiny underlay not only evangelical religion and popular health movements but also the most popular of the antebellum scientific fads: **phrenology**. Imported from Europe, phrenology rested on the idea that the human mind comprised thirty-seven distinct faculties, or "organs," each located in a different part of the brain. Phrenologists thought that the degree of each organ's development determined skull

shape, so that they could analyze a person's character by examining the bumps and depressions of the skull.

In the United States two brothers, Orson and Lorenzo Fowler, became the chief promoters of phrenology in the 1840s. Originally intending to become a Protestant missionary, Orson Fowler became instead a missionary for phrenology and opened a publishing house in New York City (Fowler and Wells) that mass-marketed books on the subject. The Fowlers replied to criticism that phrenology was godless by pointing to a huge organ called "Veneration" to prove that people were naturally religious, and they answered charges that phrenology was pessimistic by claiming that exercise could improve every desirable mental organ. Lorenzo Fowler reported that several of his skull bumps had actually grown. Orson Fowler wrapped it all into a tidy slogan: "Self-Made, or Never-Made."

Phrenology appealed to Americans as a "practical" science. In a mobile, individualistic society, it promised practitioners a quick way to assess other people. Some merchants used phrenological charts to pick suitable clerks, and some women even induced their fiancés to undergo phrenological analysis before tying the knot.

Unlike hydropathy, phrenology required no money; unlike Grahamism, it required no abstinence. Easily understood and practiced, and filled with the promise of universal improvement, phrenology was ideal for antebellum America. Just as Americans had invented machines to better their lives, so did they invent "sciences" that promised human betterment.

Democratic Pastimes

Between 1830 and 1860, technology increasingly transformed leisure by making free Americans more dependent on recreation that could be manufactured and sold. People purchased this commodity in the form of cheap newspapers and novels as well as affordable tickets to plays, museums, and lectures.

Just as the Boston Associates had daringly capitalized on new technology to produce textiles at Lowell and Waltham, imaginative entrepreneurs utilized technology to make and sell entertainment. Men like James Gordon Bennett, one of the founders of the penny press in America, and P. T. Barnum, the greatest showman of the nineteenth century, amassed fortunes by making the public want what they had to sell.

Technology also ignited the process by which individuals became spectators rather than creators of their own amusements. Americans had long found ways to enjoy themselves. Even the gloomiest Puritans had indulged in games and sports. After 1830, however, the burden of providing entertainment began to shift from individuals to entrepreneurs who supplied ways to entertain the public.

Newspapers In 1830, the typical American newspaper was a mere four pages long, with the front and back pages devoted almost wholly to advertisements. The second and third pages contained editorials, details of ship arrivals and cargoes, reprints of political speeches, and notices of political events. Few papers depended on their circulation for profit; even the most prominent papers had a daily circulation of only one or two thousand. Rather, papers often relied on subsidies from political parties or factions. When a party gained power, it inserted paid political notices only in papers loyal to it. "Journalists," a contemporary wrote, "were usually little more than secretaries dependent upon cliques of politicians, merchants, brokers, and office seekers for their prosperity and bread."

As a result, newspapers could be profitable without being popular. Because of their potential for profit, new papers were constantly being established. But most had limited appeal. The typical paper sold for six cents at a time when the average daily wage was less than a dollar. Papers often seemed little more than published bulletin boards. They typically lacked the exciting news stories and eye-catching illustrations that later generations would take for granted.

The 1830s witnessed the beginnings of a stunning transformation. Technological changes, most of which originated in Europe, vastly increased both the supply of paper (still made from rags) and the speed of printing presses. The substitution of steam-driven cylindrical presses for flatbed hand presses led to a tenfold increase in the number of printed pages that could be produced in an hour. Enterprising journalists, among them the Scottish-born James Gordon Bennett, applied the new technology to introduce the **penny press.** Newspapers could now rely on vast circulation rather than on political subsidies to turn a profit. In 1833, the *New York Sun* became America's first penny newspaper, and Bennett's *New York Herald* followed in 1835. By June 1835, the combined daily circulation of New York's three penny papers reached 44,000; in contrast, the city's eleven dailies had a combined daily circulation of only 26,500 before the dawn of the penny press in 1833. Spearheaded by the penny papers, the combined daily circulation of newspapers throughout the nation rose from roughly 78,000 in 1830 to 300,000 by 1840. The number of weekly newspapers spurted from 65 in 1830 to 138 in 1840.

The penny press also revolutionized the marketing and format of papers. Where single copies of the six-cent papers were usually available only at the printer's office, newsboys hawked the penny papers on busy street corners. Moreover, the penny papers subordinated the recording of political and commercial events to human-interest stories of robberies, murders, rapes, and abandoned children. They dispatched reporters to police courts and printed transcripts of trials. As sociologist Michael Schudson observes, "The penny press invented the modern concept of 'news.'" Rather than merely recording events, the penny papers wove events into gripping stories. They invented not only news but also news reporting. Relying on party stalwarts to dispatch copies of speeches and platforms, and reprinting news items from other papers, the older six-cent papers did little, if any, reporting. In contrast, the penny papers employed their own correspondents and were the first papers to use the telegraph to speed news into print.

Some penny papers were little more than scandal sheets, but the best, like Bennett's *New York Herald* and Horace Greeley's *New York Tribune* (1841), pioneered modern financial and political reporting. From its inception, the *Herald* contained a daily "money article" that analyzed and interpreted financial events. "The spirit, pith, and philosophy of commercial affairs is what men of business want," Bennett wrote. The relentless snooping of the *Tribune's* Washington reporters outraged politicians. In 1848, *Tribune* correspondents were temporarily barred from the House floor for reporting that Representative Sawyer of Ohio ate his lunch (sausage and bread) each day in the House chamber, picked his teeth with a jackknife, and wiped his greasy hands on his pants and coat.

The Theater

Like newspapers, theaters increasingly appealed to a mass audience. Antebellum theaters were large (twenty-five hundred to four thousand seats in some cities) and crowded by all classes. With seats as cheap as twelve cents and rarely more than fifty cents, the typical theater audience included lawyers and merchants and their wives, artisans and clerks, sailors and noisy boys, and a sizable body of prostitutes. Prostitutes usually sat in the top gallery, called the third tier, "that dark, horrible, guilty" place. The presence of prostitutes in theaters was taken for granted; the only annoyance came when they left the third tier to solicit customers in the more expensive seats.

The prostitutes in attendance were not the only factor that made the antebellum theater vaguely disreputable. Theater audiences were notoriously rowdy. They stamped their feet, hooted at villains, and threw potatoes and garbage at the stage when they disliked the characters or the acting. Individual actors developed huge followings, and the public displayed at least as much interest in the actors as in the plays. In 1849, a long-running feud between the leading American actor, Edwin Forrest, and popular British actor William Macready ended with the Astor Place riot in New York City, which left twenty-two people dead.

The Astor Place riot demonstrated the broad popularity of the theater. Forrest's supporters included Irish workers who loathed the British and appealed to the "working men" to rally against the "aristocrat" Macready. Macready, who projected a more polished and intellectual image than Forrest, attracted the better-educated classes. Had not all classes patronized the theater, the deadly riot would probably never have occurred.

The plays themselves were as diverse as the audiences. Most often performed were melodramas in which virtue was rewarded, vice punished, and the heroine married the hero. Yet the single most popular dramatist was William Shakespeare. In 1835, audiences in Philadelphia witnessed sixty-five performances of Shakespeare's plays. Americans who may never have read a line of Shakespeare grew familiar with Othello, King Lear, Desdemona, and Shylock. Theatrical managers adapted Shakespeare to a popular audience. They highlighted the sword fights and assassinations, cut some speeches, omitted minor characters, and pruned words or references that might have offended the audience's sense of propriety. For example, they substituted *pottels* for *urinals* and quietly advanced Juliet's age at the time that she falls in love with Romeo from fourteen to eighteen. They occasionally changed sad endings to happy ones.

The producers even arranged for short performances between acts. During such an interlude, the audience might have observed a brief impersonation of Tecumseh or Aaron Burr, jugglers and acrobats, a drummer beating twelve drums at once, or a three-year-old who weighed a hundred pounds.

Minstrel Shows

The Yankee or "Brother Jonathan" figure who served as a stock character in many antebellum plays helped audiences form an image of the ideal American as rustic, clever, patriotic, and more than a match for city slickers and decadent European blue bloods. In a different way, the minstrel shows that Americans thronged to see in the 1840s and 1850s forged enduring stereotypes that buttressed white Americans' sense of superiority by diminishing black people.

Minstrel shows arose in northern cities in the 1840s when white men in blackface took to the stage to present an evening of songs, dances, and humorous sketches. Minstrelsy borrowed some authentic elements of African-American culture, especially dances characterized by the sliding, shuffling step of southern blacks, but most of the songs had origins in white culture. Such familiar American songs as Stephen Foster's "Camptown Races" and "Massa's in the Cold Ground," which first aired in minstrel shows, reflected white Americans' notions of how blacks sang more than it represented authentic black music.

In addition, the images of blacks projected by minstrelsy both catered to and reinforced the prejudices of the working-class whites who dominated the audience. Minstrel troupes usually depicted blacks as stupid, clumsy, and obsessively musical, and emphasized the Africanness of blacks by giving their characters names like the Ethiopian Serenaders and their acts titles like the "Nubian Jungle Dance" and the "African Fling." At a time of intensifying political conflict over slavery, minstrel shows planted images and expectations about blacks' behavior through stock characters. These included Uncle Ned, the tattered, humble, and docile slave, and Zip Coon, the arrogant urban free black who paraded around in a high hat, long-tailed coat, and green vest and who lived off his girlfriends' money. Minstrels lampooned blacks who assumed public roles by portraying them as incompetent stump speakers who called Patrick Henry "Henry Patrick," referred to John Hancock as "Boobcock," and confused the word *statute* with *statue*.

By the 1850s, major cities from New York to San Francisco had several minstrel theaters. Touring professional troupes and local amateur talent even brought minstrelsy to small towns and villages. Mark Twain recalled how minstrelsy had burst upon Hannibal, Missouri, in the early 1840s as "a glad and stunning surprise." So popular was the craze that minstrels appeared at the White House and entertained presidents.

P. T. Barnum

P. T. Barnum understood how to turn the antebellum public's craving for entertainment into a profitable business. As a young man in Bethel, Connecticut, he started a newspaper, the *Herald of Freedom,* that assailed wrongdoing in high places. Throughout his life, he thought of himself as a public benefactor and pointed to his profits as proof that he gave people what they wanted. Yet honesty was never his strong suit. As a small-town grocer in Connecticut, he regularly cheated his customers on the principle that they were trying to cheat him. Barnum, in short, was a hustler raised in the land of the Puritans, a cynic and an idealist rolled into one.

After moving to New York City in 1834, Barnum started a new career as an entrepreneur of popular entertainment. His first venture exhibited a black woman, Joice Heth, whom Barnum billed as the 169-year-old former slave nurse of George Washington. Barnum neither knew nor cared how old Joice was (in fact, she was probably around 80); it was enough that people would pay to see her. Strictly speaking, he cheated the public, but he knew that many of his customers shared his doubts about Joice's age. Determined to expose Barnum's gimmick, some poked her to see whether she was really a machine rather than a person. He was playing a game with the public, and the public with him.

In 1841, Barnum purchased a run-down museum in New York City, rechristened it the American Museum, and opened a new chapter in the history of popular entertainment. The founders of most earlier museums had educational purposes. They exhibited stuffed birds and animals, specimens of rock, and portraits. Most of these museums had languished for want of public interest. Barnum, in contrast, made pricking public curiosity the main goal. To attract people, he added collections of curiosities and faked exhibits. Visitors to the American Museum could see ventriloquists, magicians, albinos, a five-year-old person of short stature whom Barnum named General Tom Thumb and later took on a tour of Europe, and the "Feejee Mermaid," a shrunken oddity that Barnum billed as "positively asserted by its owner to have been taken alive in the Feejee Islands." By 1850, the American Museum had become the best-known museum in the nation and a model for popular museums in other cities.

Blessed with a genius for publicity, Barnum recognized that newspapers could invent as well as report news. One of his favorite tactics was to puff his exhibits by writing letters (under various names) to newspapers in which he would hint that the scientific world was agog over some astonishing curiosity of nature that the public could soon see for itself at the American Museum. But Barnum's success rested on more than publicity. A staunch temperance advocate, he provided regular lectures at the American Museum on the evils of alcohol and soon gave the place a reputation as a center for safe family amusement. By marketing his museum as family entertainment, Barnum helped break down barriers that had long divided the pastimes of husbands from those of their wives.

Finally, Barnum tapped the public's insatiable curiosity about natural wonders. In 1835, the editor of the *New York Sun* had boosted his circulation by claiming that a famous astronomer had discovered pelicans and winged men on the moon. At a time when each passing year brought new technological wonders, the public was ready to believe in anything, even the Feejee Mermaid.

THE QUEST FOR NATIONALITY IN LITERATURE AND ART

Europeans took little notice of American poetry or fiction before the 1820s. "Who ever reads an American book?" a British literary critic taunted in 1820. Americans responded by pointing to Washington Irving, whose *Sketch Book* (1820) contained two famous stories, "Rip Van Winkle" and "The Legend of Sleepy Hollow." Naming hotels and steamboats after Irving, Americans soaked him in applause, but they had to concede that Irving had done much of his best writing, including the *Sketch Book,* while living in England.

After 1820, the United States experienced a flowering of literature called the **American Renaissance.** The leading figures of this Renaissance included James Fenimore Cooper, Ralph Waldo Emerson, Henry David Thoreau, Margaret Fuller, Walt Whitman, Nathaniel Hawthorne, Herman Melville, and Edgar Allan Poe. In 1800, American authors accounted for a negligible proportion of the output of American publishers. By 1830, 40 percent of the books published in the United States were written by Americans; by 1850 this had increased to 75 percent.

Not only were Americans writing more books; increasingly, they sought to depict the features of their nation in literature and art. The quest for a distinctively American literature especially shaped the writings of Cooper, Emerson, and Whitman. It also revealed itself in the majestic paintings of the so-called Hudson River school, the first home-grown American movement in painting, and in the landscape architecture of Frederick Law Olmsted.

Roots of the American Renaissance

Two broad developments, one economic and the other philosophical, contributed to this development. First, the transportation revolution created a national market for books, especially fiction. Initially, this worked to the advantage of British authors, especially Sir Walter Scott. With the publication of *Waverley* (1814), a historical novel set in Britain of the 1740s, Scott's star began its spectacular ascent on the American horizon. Americans named more than a dozen towns Waverley;

advertisements for Scott's subsequent novels bore the simple caption, "By the author of *Waverley*." Scott's success demonstrated that the public wanted to read fiction. Although American publishers continued to pirate British novels (reprinting them without paying copyright fees), Scott's success prompted Americans like James Fenimore Cooper to write fiction for sale.

Second, the American Renaissance reflected the rise of a philosophical movement known as romanticism. By insisting that literature reveal the longings of an individual author's soul, romanticism challenged the eighteenth-century view, known as classicism, that standards of beauty were universal. For the classicist, the ideal author was an educated gentleman who wrote elegant poetry and essays that displayed learning and refinement and that conformed to timeless standards of taste and excellence. In contrast, romantics expected a literary work to be emotionally charged, a unique reflection of its creator's inner feelings.

The emergence of a national market for books and the influence of romanticism combined to democratize literature. The conventions of classicism led writers to view literature as a pastime of gentlemen. They were to write only for one another (and never for profit) and use literature as a vehicle for displaying their learning, especially their knowledge of ancient Greek and Roman civilization. In contrast, the emerging national market for books tended to elevate the importance of fiction—a comparatively democratic form of literature—more than poetry and essays. Writing (and reading) fiction did not require knowledge of Latin and Greek or a familiarity with ancient history and mythology. Significantly, many of the best-selling novels of the antebellum period—for example, Harriet Beecher Stowe's *Uncle Tom's Cabin*—were written by women, who were still barred from higher education. In addition, fiction had a subversive quality that contributed to its popularity. Authors could create unconventional characters, situations, and outcomes. The essay usually had an unmistakable conclusion. In contrast, the novel left more room for interpretation by the reader. A novel might well have a lesson to teach, but the reader's interest was likely to be aroused less by the moral than by the development of characters and plot.

Cooper, Emerson, Thoreau, Fuller, and Whitman
James Fenimore Cooper was the first important figure in this literary upsurge. His most significant innovation was to introduce a distinctively American fictional character, the frontiersman Natty Bumppo ("Leatherstocking"). In *The Pioneers* (1823), Natty appears as an old man settled on the shores of Lake Otsego in upstate New York. A hunter, Natty blames farmers for the wanton destruction of game and for turning the majestic forests into deserts of tree stumps. As a spokesman for nature against the march of civilization, Natty immediately became a popular figure, and in subsequent novels such as *The Last of the Mohicans* (1826), *The Pathfinder* (1840), and *The Deerslayer* (1841), Cooper unfolded Natty's earlier life for an appreciative reading public.

Although he disliked fiction, **Ralph Waldo Emerson** emerged in the late 1830s as the most influential spokesman for American literary nationalism. As the leading light of the movement known as transcendentalism, an American offshoot of romanticism, Emerson contended that our ideas of God and freedom are inborn; knowledge resembles sight—an instantaneous and direct perception of truth. That being so, Emerson concluded, learned people enjoy no special advantage in pursuing truth. All persons can glimpse the truth if only they trust the promptings of their hearts.

Transcendentalist doctrine pointed to the exhilarating conclusion that the United States, a young and democratic society, could produce as noble a literature and art as the more traditional societies of Europe. "Our day of dependence, our long apprenticeship to the learning of other lands draws to a close," Emerson announced in his address "The American Scholar" (1837). The time had come for Americans to trust themselves. Let "the single man plant himself indomitably on his instincts and there abide," he proclaimed, and "the huge world will come around to him."

Emerson admired Cooper's fiction, but his own version of American literary nationalism was expressed mainly in his essays, which mixed broad themes—"Beauty," "Wealth," and "Representative Men"—with pungent and vivid language. For example, he wrote in praise of independent thinking that the scholar should not "quit his belief that a popgun is a popgun, though the ancient and honorable of the earth affirm it to be the crack of doom." Equally remarkable was Emerson's way of developing his subjects. A contemporary compared listening to Emerson to trying to see the sun in a fog; one could see light but never the sun itself. Believing that knowledge reflected God's voice within each person and that truth was intuitive and individual, he never amassed persuasive evidence or presented systematic arguments to prove his point. Rather, he relied on a sequence of vivid if unconnected assertions whose truth the reader would instantly see. (They did not always see it; one reader complained that she might have understood Emerson better if she had stood on her head.)

Emerson had a magnetic attraction for intellectually inclined young men and women who did not fit neatly into American society. In the 1830s, several of them gathered in Concord, Massachusetts, to share Emerson's intellectual pursuits. **Henry David Thoreau** was representative of the younger Emersonians. A crucial difference separated the two men. Adventurous in thought, Emerson was not adventurous in action. Thoreau was more of a doer. At one point he went to jail rather than pay his poll tax. This revenue, he knew, would support the war with Mexico, which he viewed as part of a southern conspiracy to extend slavery. The experience led Thoreau to write "Civil Disobedience" (1849), in which he defended a citizen's right to disobey unjust laws.

In the spring of 1845, Thoreau moved a few miles from Concord to the woods near Walden Pond. There he constructed a cabin on land owned by Emerson and spent parts of the next two years providing for his wants away from civilization. His stated purpose in retreating to Walden was to write a description (later published) of a canoe trip that he and his brother had taken in 1839. During his stay in the woods, however, he conceived and wrote a much more important book, *Walden* (1854). A contemporary described *Walden* as "the logbook of his woodland cruise," and indeed, Thoreau filled its pages with descriptions of hawks and wild pigeons, his invention of raisin bread, his trapping of the woodchucks that ate his vegetable garden, and his construction of a cabin for exactly $28.50. But true to transcendentalism, Thoreau had a larger message. His rustic retreat taught him that he (and by implication, others) could satisfy material wants with only a few weeks' work each year and thereby leave more time for reexamining life's purpose. The problem with Americans, he said, was that they turned themselves into "mere machines" to acquire wealth without asking why. Thoreau bore the uncomfortable truth that material and moral progress were not as intimately related as Americans liked to think.

Among the most remarkable figures in Emerson's circle was **Margaret Fuller,** whose status as an intellectual woman distanced her from conventional society.

Disappointed that his first child was not a boy, her Harvard-educated father, a prominent Massachusetts politician, determined to give Margaret the sort of education young men would have acquired at Harvard. Drilled by her father in Latin and Greek, her reading branched into modern German romantics and the English literary classics. Her exposure to Emerson's ideas during a sojourn in Concord in 1836 pushed her toward transcendentalism, with its vindication of the free life of the spirit over formal doctrines and of the need for each person to discover truth on his or her own.

Ingeniously, Fuller turned transcendentalism into an occupation of sorts. Between 1839 and 1844 she supported herself by presiding over "Conversations" for fee-paying participants drawn from Boston's elite men and women. Transcendentalism also influenced her classic of American feminism, *Woman in the Nineteenth Century* (1845). Breaking with the prevailing notion of separate spheres for men and women, Fuller contended that no woman could achieve the kind of personal fulfillment lauded by Emerson unless she developed her intellectual abilities and overcame her fear of being called masculine.

One of Emerson's qualities was an ability to sympathize with such dissimilar people as the reclusive and critical Thoreau, the scholarly and aloof Fuller, and the outgoing and earthy **Walt Whitman.** Self-taught and in love with virtually everything about America except slavery, Whitman left school at eleven and became a printer's apprentice and later a journalist and editor for various newspapers in Brooklyn, Manhattan, and New Orleans. A familiar figure at Democratic Party functions, he marched in party parades and put his pen to the service of its antislavery wing.

Journalism and politics gave Whitman an intimate knowledge of ordinary Americans; the more he knew them, the more he liked them. His reading of Emerson nurtured his belief that America was to be the cradle of a new citizen in whom natural virtue would flourish unimpeded by European corruption, a man like Andrew Jackson, that "massive, yet most sweet and plain character." The threads of Whitman's early career came together in his major work *Leaves of Grass,* a book of poems first published in 1855 and reissued with voluminous additions in subsequent years.

Leaves of Grass shattered most existing poetic conventions. Not only did Whitman write in free verse (that is, most of his poems had neither rhyme nor meter), but the poems were also lusty and blunt at a time when delicacy reigned in the literary world. Whitman wrote of "the scent of these armpits finer than prayer" and "winds whose soft-tickling genitals rub against me." No less remarkably, Whitman intruded himself into his poems, one of which he titled "Song of Walt Whitman" (later retitled "Song of Myself"). It was not egotism that moved him to sing of himself. Rather, he viewed himself—crude, plain, self-taught, and passionately democratic—as the personification of the American people. He was

> Comrade of raftsmen and coalmen, comrade of all who shake hands and welcome to drink and meat,
> A learner with the simplest, a teacher of the thoughtfullest.

By 1860, Whitman had acquired a considerable reputation as a poet. Nevertheless, the original edition of *Leaves* (a run of only about eight hundred copies) was ignored or derided as a "heterogeneous mass of bombast, egotism, vulgarity, and nonsense." One reviewer suggested that it was the work of an escaped lunatic. Only Emerson and a few others reacted enthusiastically. Within two weeks of publication, Emerson, never having met Whitman, wrote, "I find it the most extraordinary piece of wit and wisdom that America has yet contributed." Emerson had long called for the appearance of "the poet of America" and knew in a flash that Whitman was that poet.

Hawthorne, Melville, and Poe   Emerson, Fuller, Thoreau, and Whitman expressed themselves in essays and poetry. In contrast, two major writers of the 1840s and 1850s—**Nathaniel Hawthorne** and **Herman Melville**—primarily wrote fiction, and another, **Edgar Allan Poe,** wrote both fiction and poetry. Although they were major contributors to the American Renaissance, Hawthorne, Melville, and Poe paid little heed to Emerson's call for a literature that would comprehend the everyday experiences of ordinary Americans. Hawthorne, for example, set *The Scarlet Letter* (1850) in New England's Puritan past, *The House of the Seven Gables* (1851) in a mansion haunted not by ghosts but by memories of the past, and *The Marble Faun* (1859) in Rome. Poe set several of his short stories such as "The Murders in the Rue Morgue" (1841) and "The Cask of Amontillado" (1846) in Europe; as one critic has noted, "His art could have been produced as easily had he been born in Europe." Melville did draw materials and themes from his own experiences as a sailor and from the lore of the New England whaling industry, but for his novels *Typee* (1846), *Omoo* (1847), and *Mardi* (1849), he picked the exotic setting of islands in the South Seas; and for his masterpiece *Moby-Dick* (1851) the ill-fated whaler *Pequod*. If the only surviving documents from the 1840s and 1850s were its major novels, historians would face an impossible task in describing the appearance of antebellum American society.

The unusual settings favored by these three writers partly reflected their view that American life lacked the materials for great fiction. Hawthorne, for example, bemoaned the difficulty of writing about a country "where there is no shadow, no antiquity, no mystery, no picturesque and gloomy wrong, nor anything but a commonplace prosperity in broad and simple daylight, as is happily the case with my dear native land." In addition, psychology rather than society fascinated the three writers; each probed the depths of the human mind rather than the intricacies of social relationships. Their preoccupation with analyzing the mental states of their characters grew out of their underlying pessimism about the human condition. Emerson, Whitman, and (to a degree) Thoreau optimistically believed that human conflicts could be resolved if only individuals followed the promptings of their better selves. In contrast, Hawthorne, Melville, and Poe saw individuals as bundles of conflicting forces that, despite the best intentions, might never be reconciled.

Their pessimism led them to create characters obsessed by pride, guilt, a desire for revenge, or a quest for perfection, and then to set their stories along the byways of society, where they would be free to explore the complexities of human motivation without the jarring intrusion of everyday life. For example, in *The Scarlet Letter* Hawthorne turned to the Puritan past in order to examine the psychological and moral consequences of the adultery committed by Hester Prynne and the minister Arthur Dimmesdale. So completely did Hawthorne focus on the moral dilemmas of his central characters that he conveyed little sense of the social life of the Puritan village in which the novel is set. Melville, who dedicated *Moby-Dick* to Hawthorne, shared the latter's pessimism. In the novel's Captain Ahab, Melville created a frightening character whose relentless and futile pursuit of the white whale fails to fill the chasm in his soul and brings death to all of his mates save the narrator, Ishmael. Poe also channeled his pessimism into creative achievements. In perhaps his finest short story, "The Fall of the House of Usher" (1839), he demonstrated an uncanny ability to weave the symbol of a crumbling mansion with the mental agony of a crumbling family.

Hawthorne, Melville, and Poe ignored Emerson's call to write about the everyday experiences of their fellow Americans. Nor did they follow Cooper's lead by creating distinctively American heroes. Yet each contributed to an indisputably American literature. Ironically, their conviction that the lives of ordinary Americans provided inadequate materials for fiction led them to create a uniquely American fiction marked less by the description of the complex social relationships of ordinary life than by the analysis of moral dilemmas and psychological states. In this way, they unintentionally fulfilled a prediction made by Alexis de Tocqueville that writers in democratic nations, while rejecting many of the traditional sources of fiction, would explore the abstract and universal questions of human nature.

Literature in the Marketplace — Few eighteenth-century gentleman-authors imagined that they were writing for the public or that they would make money from their literary productions. That suspicion that commercialism corrupted art did not disappear during the American Renaissance. The shy and reclusive poet Emily Dickinson, who lived all of her fifty-six years on the same street in Amherst, Massachusetts ("I do not go from home," she wrote with characteristic pithiness) and who wrote exquisite poems that examined, in her words, every splinter in the groove of the brain, refused to publish her work. But in an age lacking university professorships or foundation fellowships for creative writers, authors were both tempted and often compelled to write for profit. For example, Poe, a heavy drinker always pressed for cash, scratched out a meager living writing short stories for popular magazines. Despite his reputation for aloof self-reliance, Thoreau craved recognition by the public and in 1843 tried, unsuccessfully, to market his poems in New York City. Only after meeting disappointment as a poet did he turn to detailed narratives of nature, and these did prove popular.

Emerson, too, wanted to reach a broader public, and after abandoning his first vocation as a Unitarian minister he virtually invented a new one, that of "lyceum" lecturer. Lyceums, local organizations for sponsoring lectures, spread throughout the northern tier of states between the late 1820s and 1860; by 1840 thirty-five hundred towns had lyceums. Most of Emerson's published essays originated as lectures before lyceums in the Northeast and Midwest. He delivered some sixty speeches in Ohio alone between 1850 and 1867, and lecture fees provided him with his main form of income. Thanks to newly built railroads and cheap newspapers that announced their comings and goings, others followed in his path. Thoreau presented a digest of *Walden* as a lyceum lecture before the book itself was published. One stalwart of the lyceum circuit said that he did it for "F-A-M-E—Fifty and My Expenses," and Herman Melville pledged, "If they will pay my expenses and give a reasonable fee, I am ready to lecture in Labrador or on the Isle of Desolation off Patagonia."

The age offered women few opportunities for public speaking, and most lyceum lecturers were men. But women discovered ways to tap into the growing market for literature. Writing fiction was the most lucrative occupation open to women before the Civil War. For example, the popular novelist Susan Warner had been brought up in luxury and then tossed into poverty by the financial ruin of her father in the Panic of 1837. Writing fiction supplied her with cash as well as pleasure.

Warner and others benefited from advances in the technology of printing that brought down the price of books. Before 1830, the novels of Sir Walter Scott had been issued in three-volume sets that retailed for as much as thirty dollars. As canals and railroads opened crossroads stores to the latest fiction, publishers in New York and Philadelphia vied to deliver inexpensive novels to the shelves. By the 1840s, cheap paperbacks that sold for as little as seven cents began to flood the market. Those who chose not to purchase books could read fiction in so-called story newspapers such as the *New York Ledger,* which was devoted mainly to serializing novels and which had an astonishing weekly circulation of four hundred thousand by 1860. In addition, the spread of (usually) coeducational public schools and academies contributed to higher literacy and a widening audience, especially among women, for fiction.

The most popular form of fiction in the 1840s and 1850s was the sentimental novel, a kind of women's fiction written by women about women and mainly for women. In the typical plot, a female orphan or spoiled rich girl thrown on hard times by a drunken father learned to master every situation. The moral of Warner's *The Wide, Wide World* (1850) was that women had what it took to clean up the messes left by men. Not all popular fiction was sentimental. More expressive of the rage felt by some women were novels like Ned Buntline's *The G'hals of New York* (1850), where a woman becomes the mistress of a criminal but, after years of maltreatment, plots his downfall and turns him over to the police. In George Thompson's *The Countess* (1849), wealthy New York women use their sexual charms to entrap and manipulate men, whom they deride as "self-styled Emperors."

Such authors as Emerson, Hawthorne, Poe, and Melville, who now are recognized as major figures, had to swim in the sea of popular culture represented by the story newspapers and sentimental novels. Emerson, the intellectual, competed on the lecture circuit with P. T. Barnum, the showman. Hawthorne complained about the popularity of the "female scribblers." Poe thought that the public's judgment of a writer's merits was nearly always wrong. Indeed, the public did fail to see Melville's genius; the qualities of *Moby-Dick* were not widely recognized until the twentieth century. By and large, however, the major writers were not ignored by their society. Emerson's lectures made him famous. Hawthorne's *The Scarlet Letter* enjoyed respectable sales. Poe's poem "The Raven" (1844) was so popular that some suggested substituting the raven for the eagle as the national bird. What these writers discovered, sometimes the hard way, was that to make a living as authors they had to meet certain popular expectations. For example, *The Scarlet Letter* had greater popular appeal than *Moby-Dick* in part because the former told a love story while the latter, with its all-male cast and high-seas exploits, was simply not what the public looked for in a novel.

American Landscape Painting American painters also sought to develop nationality in art between 1820 and 1860. Lacking the mythic past that European artists drew on—the legendary gods and goddesses of ancient Greece and Rome—Americans subordinated history and figure painting to landscape painting. Just as Hawthorne had complained about the flat, dull character of American society, so had the painters of the Hudson River school recognized that the American landscape lacked the European landscape's "poetry of decay" in the form of

Rainmaking Among the Mandan, 1837–1839 *George Catlin's paintings preserved the faces, customs, and habitats of the Indian tribes whose civilization was collapsing in the face of white advance.*

ruined castles and crumbling temples. Like everything else in the United States, the landscape was fresh, relatively untouched by the human imprint. This fact posed a challenge to the Hudson River school painters.

The **Hudson River school** flourished from the 1820s to the 1870s. Numbering more than fifty painters, it was best represented by Thomas Cole, Asher Durand, and Frederick Church. All three men painted scenes of the region around the Hudson River, a waterway that Americans compared in majesty to the Rhine. But none was exclusively a landscapist. Some of Cole's most popular paintings were allegories, including *The Course of Empire,* a sequence of five canvases depicting the rise and fall of an ancient city and clearly implying that luxury doomed republican virtue. Nor did these artists paint only the Hudson. Church, a student of Cole and internationally the best known of the three, painted the Andes Mountains during an extended trip to South America in 1853. After the Civil War, the German-born Albert Bierstadt applied many Hudson River school techniques in his monumental canvases of the Rocky Mountains.

The works of Washington Irving and the opening of the Erie Canal had sparked artistic interest in the Hudson during the 1820s. After 1830, the writings of Emerson and Thoreau popularized a new view of nature. Intent on cultivating land, the pioneers of Kentucky and Ohio had deforested a vast area. One traveler complained that Americans would rather view a wheat field or a cabbage patch than a virgin forest. But Emerson, Thoreau, and landscape architects like Frederick Law Olmsted glorified nature; "in wildness is the preservation of the world," Thoreau wrote. Their outlook blended with growing popular fears that, as one contemporary expressed it in 1847,

"The axe of civilization is busy with our old forests." As the "wild and picturesque haunts of the Red Man" became "the abodes of commerce and the seats of civilization," he concluded, "it behooves our artists to rescue from its grasp the little that is left before it is too late."

The Hudson River painters wanted to do more than preserve a passing wilderness. Their special contribution to American art was to emphasize emotional effect over accuracy. Cole's use of rich coloring, billowing clouds, massive gnarled trees, towering peaks, and deep chasms so heightened the dramatic impact of his paintings that the poet and editor William Cullen Bryant compared them to "acts of religion." Similar motifs marked Church's paintings of the Andes Mountains, which used erupting volcanoes and thunderstorms to evoke dread and a sense of majesty. Lacking the poignant antiquities that dotted European landscapes, the Americans strove to capture the natural grandeur of their own landscape.

Like Cole, the painter **George Catlin** also tried to preserve a vanishing America. Observing a delegation of Indians passing through Philadelphia in 1824, Catlin resolved on his life's work: to paint as many Native Americans as possible in their pure and "savage" state. Journeying up the Missouri River in 1832, he sketched at a feverish pace, and in 1837 he first exhibited his "Indian gallery" of 437 oil paintings and thousands of sketches of faces and customs from nearly fifty tribes.

Catlin's Indian paintings made him famous, but his romantic view of Indians as noble savages ("the Indian mind is a beautiful blank") was a double-edged sword. Catlin's admirers delighted in his portrayals of dignified Indians but shared his view that such noble creatures were "doomed" to oblivion by the march of progress.

By the 1830s, sprawling urban growth was prompting landscape architects to create little enclaves of nature that might serve as sources of spiritual refreshment to harried city-dwellers. Starting with the opening of Mount Auburn Cemetery near Boston in 1831, "rural" cemeteries with pastoral names such as "Harmony Grove" and "Greenwood" sprang up near major cities and quickly became tourist attractions, so much so that one orator described them as designed for the living rather than the dead. In 1858, New York City chose a plan drawn by **Frederick Law Olmsted** and Calvert Vaux for its proposed Central Park. Olmsted (who became the park's chief architect) and Vaux wanted the park to look as much like the countryside as possible, showing nothing of the surrounding city. A bordering line of trees screened out buildings, drainage pipes were dug to create lakes, and four sunken thoroughfares were cut across the park to carry traffic. The effect was to make Central Park an idealized version of nature, "picturesque" in that it would remind visitors of the landscapes that they had seen in pictures. Thus nature was made to mirror art.

CONCLUSION

Technological advances transformed the lives of millions of Americans between 1840 and 1860. The mechanical reaper increased wheat production and enabled agriculture to keep pace with the growing population. The development of machine tools, first in gun manufacture and next in the manufacturing of sewing machines, helped Americans achieve Eli Whitney's ideal of production by interchangeable parts and made a range of luxuries affordable for the middle class. Steam power reduced the vulnerability of factories to the vagaries of the weather, stretched out the employment season, and increased productivity and income. The spread of railroads and the invention of the telegraph shrunk the barriers of space and time.

Many of these developments unified Americans. Railroad tracks threaded the nation together. The telegraph speeded communication and made it possible for Americans in widely scattered areas to read about the same current events in their newspapers. The advances in printing that gave birth to the penny press and the inexpensive novel contributed to a widening of the reading public. Not only were Americans now more able to read the same news items; increasingly, they read the same best sellers, just as they flocked to the commercial amusements marketed by P. T. Barnum. Advocates of progress hailed these developments as instruments of ever-rising popular happiness. Even disease came to be seen less as a divine punishment for human depravity than as God's warning to those who ate or drank too much.

Progress carried a price. By bringing commodities once available only to the rich within the financial reach of the middle class, technology narrowed the social distance between these classes. At the same time, though, it set them off more sharply from the poor and intensified the division between the experiences of middle-class men and women. Progress also posed moral and spiritual challenges. The march of progress threatened to devour unspoiled nature. In different ways, writers like James Fenimore Cooper, Ralph Waldo Emerson, and Henry David Thoreau called attention to the conflict between nature and civilization as a distinctive feature of the American experience. Artists of the Hudson River school created majestic paintings of the natural wonders of the New World. For their part, Nathaniel Hawthorne and Herman Melville challenged the easy confidence that technology and democracy could liberate Americans from the dilemmas of the human condition.

12

The Old South and Slavery, 1830–1860

CHAPTER OUTLINE

King Cotton • The Social Groups of the White South • Social
Relations in the White South • Life Under Slavery • The Emergence
of African-American Culture

KING COTTON

In 1790, the South was essentially stagnant. Tobacco, its primary cash crop, had lost economic vitality even as it had depleted the once-rich southern soils. The growing of alternative cash crops, such as rice and cotton, was confined to coastal areas. Three out of four southerners still lived along the Atlantic seaboard, specifically in the Chesapeake and the Carolinas. One of three resided in Virginia alone.

The contrast between that South and the dynamic South of 1850 was stunning. By 1850, southerners had moved south and west. Now, only one of every seven southerners lived in Virginia, and cotton reigned as king, shaping this new South. The growth of the British textile industry had created a huge demand for cotton, while Indian removal (see Chapter 9) had made way for southern expansion into the **"Cotton Kingdom,"** a broad swath of territory that stretched from South Carolina, Georgia, and northern Florida in the east through Alabama, Mississippi, central and western Tennessee, and Louisiana, and from there on to Arkansas and Texas.

The Lure of Cotton   To a British traveler, it seemed that all southerners could talk about was cotton. "Every flow of wind from the shore wafted off the smell of that useful plant; at every dock or wharf we encountered it in huge piles or pyramids of bales, and our decks were soon choked with it. All day, and almost all night long, the captain, pilot, crew, and passengers were talking of nothing else."

A warm climate, wet springs and summers, and relatively dry autumns made the Lower South ideal for cultivating cotton. In contrast to the sugar industry, which thrived in southeastern Louisiana, cotton required neither expensive irrigation canals nor costly machinery. Sugar was a rich man's crop that demanded a considerable

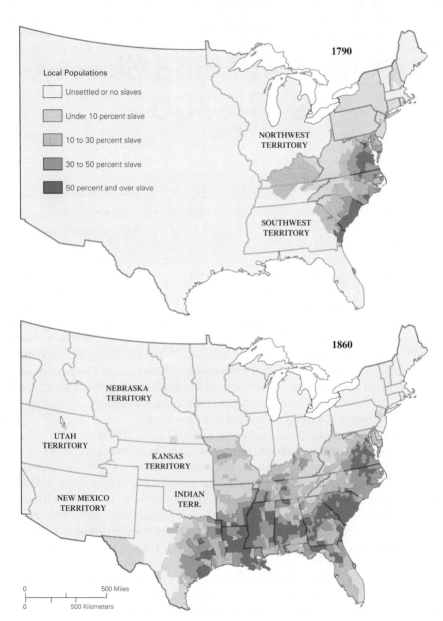

Map 12.1 Distribution of Slaves, 1790 and 1860

In 1790 the majority of slaves resided along the southeastern seaboard. By 1860, however, slavery had spread throughout the South, and slaves were most heavily concentrated in the Deep South states.

Source: Reprinted with permission of McGraw-Hill, Inc. from *Ordeal by Fire: The Civil War and Reconstruction* by James M. McPherson. Copyright 1982 by Alfred A. Knopf, Inc.

capital investment to grow and process. But cotton could be grown profitably on any scale. A cotton farmer did not even need to own a gin; commercial gins were available. Nor did a cotton farmer have to own slaves; in 1860, 35 to 50 percent of all farmers in the cotton belt owned no slaves. Cotton was profitable for anyone, even nonslaveholders, to grow; it promised to make poor men prosperous and rich men kings.

Although modest cotton cultivation did not require slaves, large-scale cotton growing and slavery grew together. As the southern slave population nearly doubled between 1810 and 1830, cotton employed three-fourths of all southern slaves. Owning slaves made it possible to harvest vast tracts of cotton speedily, a crucial advantage because a sudden rainstorm at harvest time could pelt cotton to the ground and soil it. Slaveholding planters could increase their cotton acreage and hence their profits.

An added advantage of cotton lay in its compatibility with the production of corn. Corn could be planted earlier or later than cotton and harvested before or after. Since the cost of owning a slave was the same whether or not he or she was working, corn production enabled slaveholders to shift slave labor between corn and cotton. By 1860, the acreage devoted to corn in the Old South actually exceeded that devoted to cotton. Economically, corn and cotton gave the South the best of two worlds. Fed by intense demand in Britain and New England, cotton prices remained high and money flowed into the South. Because of southern self-sufficiency in growing corn and raising livestock that thrived on corn (in 1860 the region had two-thirds of the nation's hogs), money did not drain away to pay for food. In 1860, the twelve wealthiest counties in the United States were all in the South.

Ties Between the Lower and Upper South

Two giant cash crops, sugar and cotton, dominated agriculture in the Lower South. The Upper South, a region of tobacco, vegetable, hemp, and wheat growers, depended far less on the great cash crops. Yet the Upper South identified with the Lower South rather than with the agricultural regions of the free states.

A range of social, political, and economic factors promoted this unity. First, many settlers in the Lower South had come from the Upper South. Second, all white southerners benefited from the three-fifths clause of the Constitution, which enabled them to count slaves as a basis for congressional representation. Third, all southerners were stung by abolitionist criticisms of slavery, which drew no distinction between the Upper and Lower South. Economic ties also linked the South. The profitability of cotton and sugar increased the value of slaves throughout the entire region and encouraged the **internal slave trade** from the Upper to the Lower South. Without the sale of its slaves to the Lower South, an observer wrote, "Virginia will be a desert."

The North and South Diverge

The changes responsible for the dynamic growth of the South widened the distance between it and the North. At a time when the North was rapidly urbanizing, the South remained predominantly rural. In 1860, the proportion of the South's population living in urban areas was only one-third that of New England and the mid-Atlantic states, down from one-half in 1820.

One reason for the rural character of the South was its lack of industries. Although one-third of the American population lived there in 1850, the South accounted for only 10 percent of the nation's manufacturing. The industrial output of the entire South in 1850 was less than that of New Hampshire and only one-third that of Massachusetts.

CHRONOLOGY, 1830–1860

1790s • Methodists and Baptists start to make major strides in converting slaves to Christianity.

1793 • Eli Whitney invents the cotton gin.

1800 • Gabriel Prosser leads a slave rebellion in Virginia.

1808 • Congress prohibits external slave trade.

1812 • Louisiana, the first state formed out of the Louisiana Purchase, is admitted to the Union.

1816–1819 • Boom in cotton prices stimulates settlement of the Old Southwest.

1819–1820 • Missouri Compromise.

1822 • Denmark Vesey's conspiracy uncovered in South Carolina.

1831 • William Lloyd Garrison starts *The Liberator*.
Nat Turner rebellion in Virginia.

1832 • Virginia legislature narrowly defeats a proposal for gradual emancipation.
Virginia's Thomas R. Dew writes an influential defense of slavery.

1835 • Arkansas admitted to the Union.

1837 • Economic panic begins, lowering cotton prices.

1844–1845 • Methodist Episcopal and Baptist Churches split into northern and southern wings over slavery.

1845 • Florida and Texas admitted to the Union.

1849 • Sugar production in Louisiana reaches its peak.

1849–1860 • Period of high cotton prices.

1857 • Hinton R. Helper, *The Impending Crisis of the South*.

1859 • John Brown's raid on Harpers Ferry.

1860 • South Carolina secedes from the Union.

Some southerners, including J. D. B. De Bow of New Orleans, advocated factories as a way to revive the economies of older states like Virginia and South Carolina, to reduce the South's dependency on northern manufactured products, and to show that the South was not a backwater. After touring northern textile mills, South Carolina's William Gregg established a company town for textiles at Graniteville in 1845. By 1860, Richmond boasted the nation's fourth-largest producer of iron products, the **Tredegar Iron Works,** which contributed greatly to the Confederate cause during the Civil War. But these were exceptions.

Compared to factories in the North, most southern factories were small, produced for nearby markets, and were closely tied to agriculture. The leading northern factories turned hides into tanned leather and leather into shoes, or cotton into threads and threads into suits. In contrast, southern factories, only a step removed from agriculture, turned grain into flour, corn into meal, and logs into lumber.

Slavery posed a major obstacle to southern industrialization, but not because slaves were unfit for factories. The Tredegar Iron Works employed slaves in skilled positions.

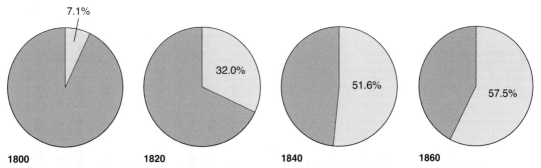

Figure 12.1 **Value of Cotton Exports as a Percentage of All U.S. Exports, 1800–1860**

By 1840 cotton accounted for more than half of all U.S. exports.

But industrial slavery troubled southerners. Slaves who were hired out to factory masters sometimes passed themselves off as free and acted as if they were free by negotiating better working conditions. A Virginia planter who rented slaves to an iron manufacturer complained that they "got the habit of roaming about and *taking care of themselves.*"

The chief brake on southern industrialization was money, not labor. To raise the capital needed to build factories, southerners would have to sell slaves. They had little incentive to do so. Cash crops like cotton and sugar were proven winners, whereas the benefits of industrialization were remote and doubtful. Successful industrialization, further, threatened to disrupt southern social relations by attracting antislavery white immigrants from the North. As long as southerners believed that an economy founded on cash crops would remain profitable, they had little reason to leap into the uncertainties of industrialization.

The South also lagged behind the North in provisions for public education. As was true of southern arguments for industrialization, pro-education arguments were bountiful, but these issued from a small segment of the South's leadership and made little impact. White southerners rejected compulsory education and were reluctant to tax property to support schools. They abhorred the thought of educating slaves, so much so that southern lawmakers made it a crime to teach slaves to read. Some public aid flowed to state universities, but for most whites the only available schools were private. As a result, white illiteracy, which had been declining in the North, remained high in the South. For example, nearly 60 percent of the North Carolinians who enlisted in the U.S. army before the Civil War were illiterate. The comparable proportion for northern enlistees was less than 30 percent.

Agricultural, self-sufficient, and independent, the middling and poor whites of the South remained unconvinced of the need for public education. They had little dependency on the printed word, few complex economic transactions, and infrequent dealings with urban people. Even the large planters, some of whom did support public education, had less commitment to it than did northern manufacturers. Whereas many northern businessmen accepted Horace Mann's argument that public schools would create a more orderly and alert work force, planters had no need for an educated white

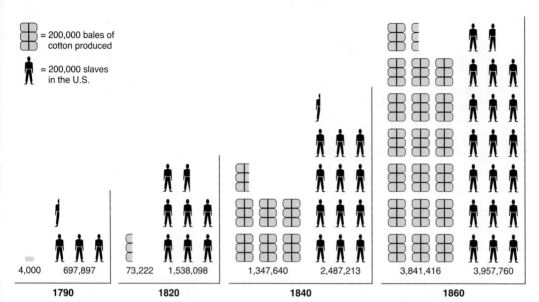

= 200,000 bales of cotton produced

= 200,000 slaves in the U.S.

4,000	697,897	73,222	1,538,098	1,347,640	2,487,213	3,841,416	3,957,760
1790		**1820**		**1840**		**1860**	

Figure 12.2 Growth of Cotton Production and the Slave Population, 1790–1860

Cotton and slavery rose together in the Old South.

work force. They already had a black one that they were determined to keep illiterate lest it acquire ideas of freedom.

Because the South diverged so sharply from the North, it is tempting to view the South as backward and lethargic, doomed to be bypassed by the more energetic northern states. Increasingly, northerners associated the spread of cities and factories with progress. Finding few cities and factories in the South, they concluded that the region was a stranger to progress as well. A northern journalist wrote of white southerners in the 1850s that "[t]hey work little, and that little, badly; they earn little, they sell little; they buy little, and they have little—very little—of the common comforts and consolations of civilized life." Visitors to the South sometimes thought that they were traveling backward in time. "It seems as if everything had stopped growing, and was growing backwards," novelist Harriet Beecher Stowe wrote of the region.

Yet the white South did not lack progressive features. In 1840, per capita income in the white South was only slightly below the national average, and by 1860 it exceeded the national average. Although it is true that southerners made few contributions to technology to rival those of northerners, many southerners had a progressive zeal for agricultural improvement. Virginian Edmund Ruffin, who fired the first cannon on Fort Sumter in 1861 and committed suicide in despair at the South's defeat in 1865, was an enthusiastic supporter of crop rotation and of the use of fertilizer, and was an important figure in the history of scientific agriculture. Like northerners, white southerners were restless, eager to make money, skillful at managing complex commercial enterprises, and, when they chose, capable of becoming successful industrialists.

The Social Groups of the White South

Although all agricultural regions of the South contained slaveholders and nonslave-holders, there was considerable diversity within each group. In every southern state, some slaveholders owned vast estates, magnificent homes, and hundreds of slaves, but most lived more modestly. In 1860, one-quarter of all white families in the South owned slaves. Of these, nearly half owned fewer than five slaves, and nearly three-quarters had fewer than ten slaves. Only 12 percent owned twenty or more slaves, and only 1 percent had a hundred or more. Large slaveholders clearly were a minority within a minority. Nonslaveholders also formed a diverse group. Most owned farms and drew on the labor of family members, but others squatted on land in the so-called pine barrens or piney woods and scratched out livelihoods by raising livestock, hunting and fishing, and planting a few acres of corn, oats, or sweet potatoes.

Planters (those owning twenty or more slaves), small slaveholders, yeomen (family farmers), and pine barrens folk composed the South's four main white groups. Lawyers, physicians, merchants, and artisans did not fall into any of these groups, but they tended to identify their interests with one or another of the agricultural groups. Rural artisans and merchants had extensive dealings with yeomen. Urban merchants and lawyers depended on the planters and adopted their viewpoint on most issues. Similarly, slave traders relied on the plantation economy for their livelihood. Nathan Bedford Forrest, the uneducated son of a humble Tennessee blacksmith, made a fortune as a slave trader in Natchez, Mississippi. When the Civil War broke out, Forrest enlisted in the Confederate army as a private and rose swiftly to become the South's greatest cavalry general. Plantation slavery directed Forrest's allegiances as surely as it did those of planters like Jefferson Davis, the Confederacy's president.

Planters and Plantation Mistresses

With porticoed mansion and fields teeming with slaves, the plantation still stands at the center of the popular image of the Old South. This romanticized view, reinforced by novels and motion pictures like *Gone with the Wind*, is not entirely misleading, for the South contained plantations that travelers found "superb beyond description." Whether devoted to cotton, tobacco, rice, or sugar, **plantation agriculture** was characterized by a high degree of division of labor. In the 1850s, Bellmead, a tobacco plantation on Virginia's James River, was virtually an agricultural equivalent of a factory village. Its more than one hundred slaves were classified into the domestic staff (butlers, waiters, seamstresses, laundresses, maids, and gardeners), the pasture staff (shepherds, cowherds, and hog drivers), outdoor artisans (stonemasons and carpenters), indoor artisans (blacksmiths, carpenters, shoemakers, spinners, and weavers), and field hands. Such a division of labor was inconceivable without abundant slaves and land. Wade Hampton's cotton plantation near Columbia, South Carolina, encompassed twenty-four hundred acres. With such resources, it is not surprising that large plantations could generate incomes that contemporaries viewed as immense (twenty to thirty thousand dollars a year).

During the first flush of settlement in the Piedmont and trans-Appalachian South in the eighteenth century, most well-off planters had been content to live in simple log cabins. In contrast, between 1810 and 1860, elite planters often vied with one another

H. E. Hayward and Slave Nurse Louisa, ca. 1858 *Slavery did not prevent white children and their slave nurses from forming attachments to each other.*

to build stately mansions. Some, like Lyman Hardy of Mississippi, hired architects. Hardy's Auburn, built in 1812 near Natchez, featured Ionic columns and a portico thirty-one feet long and twelve feet deep. Others copied designs from books like Andrew Jackson Downing's *Architecture of Country Houses* (1850), which sold sixteen thousand copies between 1850 and 1865.

However impressive, these were not typical planters. The wealth of most planters, especially in states like Alabama and Mississippi, consisted primarily in the value of their slaves rather than in expensive furniture or silver plate. In monetary terms, slaves were worth a great deal, as much as seventeen hundred dollars for a field hand in the 1850s. Planters could convert their wealth into cash for purchasing luxuries only by selling slaves. A planter who sold his slaves ceased to be a planter and relinquished the South's most prestigious social status. Not surprisingly, most planters clung to large-scale slaveholding, even if it meant scrimping on their lifestyles. A northern journalist observed that in the Southwest, men worth millions lived as if they were not worth hundreds.

In their constant worry about profit, planters enjoyed neither repose nor security. High fixed costs—housing and feeding slaves, maintaining cotton gins, hiring overseers—led them to search for more and better land, higher efficiency, and greater self-sufficiency. Because cotton prices fluctuated seasonally, planters often assigned their cotton to commercial agents in cities, who held the cotton until the price was right. The agents extended credit so that planters could pay their bills until the cotton was sold. Indebtedness became part of the plantation economy and intensified the planters' quest for profitability.

Plantation agriculture placed psychological strains as well as economic burdens on planters and their wives. Frequent moves disrupted circles of friends and relatives, all the more so because migration to the Old Southwest (Alabama, Mississippi, and eastern Texas) carried families into progressively less settled, more desolate areas. Until 1850, this area was still the frontier.

For plantation women, migration to the Southwest often amounted to a fall from grace, for many of them had grown up in seaboard elegance, only to find themselves in isolated regions, surrounded by slaves and bereft of the companionship of white social peers. "I am sad tonight, sickness preys on my frame," wrote a bride who moved to Mississippi in 1833. "I am alone and more than 150 miles from any near relative in the wild woods of an Indian nation." At times, wives lacked even their husbands' companionship. Plantation agriculture kept men on the road, scouting new land for purchase, supervising outlying holdings, and transacting business in New Orleans or Memphis.

Planters and their wives found various ways to cope with their isolation from civilized society. Hiring overseers to supervise their plantations, many spent long periods of time in cities. In 1850, fully one-half the planters in the Mississippi Delta were absentees living in or near Natchez or New Orleans rather than on their plantations. Most planters acted as their own overseers, however, and dealt with harsh living conditions by opening their homes to visitors. The responsibility for such hospitality fell heavily on wives, who might have to entertain as many as fifteen people for breakfast and attend to the needs of visitors who stayed for days. Plantation wives bore the burdens of raising their children, supervising house slaves, making clothes and carpets, looking after smokehouses and dairies, planting gardens, and keeping accounts. On the frequent occasions when their husbands were away on business or holding political office, their wives, along with their overseers, ran their plantations.

Among the greatest sorrows of some plantation mistresses was the presence of mulatto children, who stood as daily reminders of their husbands' infidelity. Mary Boykin Chesnut, an astute Charleston woman and famous diarist, commented, "Any lady is ready to tell you who is the father of all the mulatto children in everybody's household but her own. These, she seems to think, drop from clouds." Insisting on sexual purity for white women, southern men followed a looser standard for themselves. After the death of his wife, the brother of the abolitionist sisters Sarah and Angelina Grimké fathered three mulatto children. The gentlemanly code usually tolerated such transgressions as long as they were not paraded in public—and, at times, even if they were. Richard M. Johnson of Kentucky, the man who allegedly killed Tecumseh during the War of 1812, was elected vice president of the United States in 1836 despite having lived openly for years with his black mistress.

The isolation, drudgery, and humiliation that planters' wives experienced turned very few against the system. When the Civil War came, they supported the Confederacy as enthusiastically as any group. However much they might hate living as white islands in a sea of slaves, they recognized no less than their husbands that their wealth and position depended on slavery.

The Small Slaveholders

In 1860, 88 percent of all slaveholders owned fewer than twenty slaves, and most of these possessed fewer than ten. Some slave owners were not even farmers: one out of every five was employed outside of agriculture, usually as a lawyer, physician, merchant, or artisan.

As a large and extremely diverse group, small slaveholders experienced conflicting loyalties and ambitions. In the upland regions, they absorbed the outlook of yeomen (nonslaveholding family farmers), the numerically dominant group. Typically, small upland slaveholders owned only a few slaves and rarely aspired to become large planters. In contrast, in the low country and delta regions, where planters formed the dominant group, small slaveholders often aspired to planter status. In these planter-dominated areas, someone with ten slaves could realistically look forward to the day when he would own thirty. The deltas were thus filled with ambitious and acquisitive individuals who linked success to owning more slaves. Whether one owned ten slaves or fifty, the logic of slaveholding was much the same. The investment in slaves could be justified only by setting them to work on profitable crops. Profitable crops demanded, in turn, more and better land. Much like the planters, the small slaveholders of the low country and delta areas were restless and footloose.

The social structure of the deltas was fluid but not infinitely so. Small slaveholders were usually younger than large slaveholders, and many hoped to become planters in their own right. But as the antebellum period wore on, a clear tendency developed toward the geographical segregation of small slaveholders from planters in the cotton belt.

Small slaveholders led the initial push into the cotton belt in the 1810s and 1820s, whereas the large planters, reluctant to risk transporting their hundreds of slaves into the still turbulent new territory, remained in the seaboard South. Gradually, however, the large planters ventured into Alabama and Mississippi.

Colonel Thomas Dabney, a planter originally from tidewater Virginia, made several scouting tours of the Southwest before moving his family and slaves to the region of Vicksburg, Mississippi, where he started a four-thousand-acre plantation. The small slaveholders already on the scene at first resented Dabney's genteel manners and misguided efforts to win friends. He showed up at house raisings to lend a hand. However, the hands he lent were not his own, which remained gloved, but those of his slaves. The small slaveholders muttered about transplanted Virginia snobs. Dabney responded to complaints by buying up much of the best land in the region. In itself, this was no loss to the small slaveholders. They had been first on the scene, and it was their land that the Dabneys of the South purchased.

Dabney and men like him quickly turned the whole region from Vicksburg to Natchez into large plantations. The small farmers took the proceeds from the sale of their land, bought more slaves, and moved elsewhere to grow cotton. Small slaveholders gradually transformed the region from Vicksburg to Tuscaloosa, Alabama, into a belt of medium-size farms with a dozen or so slaves on each.

The Yeomen

Nonslaveholding family farmers, or yeomen, comprised the largest single group of southern whites. Most were landowners. Landholding yeomen, because they owned no slaves of their own, frequently hired slaves at harvest time to help in the fields. Where the land was poor, as in eastern Tennessee, the landowning yeomen were typically subsistence farmers, but most grew some crops for the market. Whether they engaged in subsistence or commercial agriculture, they controlled landholdings far more modest than those of the planters—more likely in the range of fifty to two hundred acres than five hundred or more acres.

Yeomen could be found anywhere in the South, but they tended to congregate in the upland regions. In the seaboard South, they populated the Piedmont region of

Georgia, South Carolina, North Carolina, and Virginia; in the Southwest, they usually lived in the hilly upcountry, far from the rich alluvial soil of the deltas. A minority of yeomen did not own land. Typically young, these men resided with and worked for landowners to whom they were related.

The leading characteristic of the yeomen was the value that they attached to self-sufficiency. As nonslaveholders, they were not carried along by the logic that impelled slaveholders to acquire more land and plant more cash crops. Although most yeomen raised cash crops, they devoted a higher proportion of their acreage to subsistence crops like corn, sweet potatoes, and oats than did planters. The ideal of the planters was profit with modest self-sufficiency; that of the yeomen, self-sufficiency with modest profit.

Yeomen dwelling in the low country and delta regions dominated by planters were often dismissed as "poor white trash." But in the upland areas, where they constituted the dominant group, yeomen were highly respectable. There they coexisted peacefully with the slaveholders, who typically owned only a few slaves (large planters were rare in the upland areas). Both the small slaveholders and the yeomen were essentially family farmers. With or without the aid of a few slaves, fathers and sons cleared the land and plowed, planted, and hoed the fields. Wives and daughters planted and tended vegetable gardens, helped at harvest, occasionally cared for livestock, cooked, and made clothes for the family.

In contrast to the far-flung commercial transactions of the planters, who depended on distant commercial agents to market their crops, the economic transactions of yeomen usually occurred within the neighborhood of their farms. Yeomen often exchanged their cotton, wheat, or tobacco for goods and services from local artisans and merchants. In some areas, they sold their surplus corn to the herdsmen and drovers who made a living in the South's upland regions by specializing in raising hogs. Along the French Broad River in eastern Tennessee, some twenty to thirty thousand hogs were fattened for market each year; at peak season a traveler would see a thousand hogs a mile. When driven to market, the hogs were quartered at night in huge stock stands, veritable hog "hotels," and fed with corn supplied by the local yeomen.

The People of the Pine Barrens

One of the most controversial groups in the Old South was the independent whites of the wooded pine barrens. Making up about 10 percent of southern whites, they usually squatted on the land, put up crude cabins, cleared some acreage on which they planted corn between tree stumps, and grazed hogs and cattle in the woods. They neither raised cash crops nor engaged in the daily routine of orderly work that characterized family farmers. With their ramshackle houses and handful of stump-strewn acres, they appeared lazy and shiftless.

Antislavery northerners cited the **pine barrens people** as proof that slavery degraded poor whites, but southerners shot back that while the pine barrens people were poor, they could at least feed themselves, unlike the paupers of northern cities. In general, the people of the pine barrens were self-reliant and fiercely independent. Pine barrens men were reluctant to hire themselves out as laborers to do "slave" tasks, and the women refused to become servants.

Neither victimized nor oppressed, these people generally lived in the pine barrens by choice. The grandson of a farmer who had migrated from Emanuel County, Georgia, to the Mississippi pine barrens explained his grandfather's decision: "The turpentine smell, the moan of the winds through the pine trees, and nobody within fifty miles of him, [were] too captivating . . . to be resisted, and he rested there."

SOCIAL RELATIONS IN THE WHITE SOUTH

Northerners often charged that slavery twisted the entire social structure of the South out of shape. The enslavement of blacks, they alleged, robbed lower-class whites of the incentive to work, reduced them to shiftless misery, and rendered the South a throwback in an otherwise progressive age. Stung by northern allegations that slavery turned the white South into a region of rich planters and poor common folk, southerners retorted that the real center of white inequality was the North, where merchants and financiers paraded in fine silks and never soiled their hands with manual labor.

In reality, a curious mix of aristocratic and democratic, premodern and modern features marked social relations in the white South. Although it contained considerable class inequality, property ownership was widespread. Rich planters occupied seats in state legislatures out of proportion to their numbers in the population, but they did not necessarily get their way, nor did their political agenda always differ from that of other whites.

Not just its social structure but also the behavior of individual white southerners struck northern observers as running to extremes. One minute southerners were hospitable and gracious; the next, savagely violent. "The Americans of the South," Alexis de Tocqueville asserted, "are brave, comparatively ignorant, hospitable, generous, easy to irritate, violent in their resentments, without industry or the spirit of enterprise." The practice of dueling intensified in the Old South at a time when it was dying in the North. Yet there were voices within the South, especially among the clergy, that urged white southerners to turn the other cheek when faced with insults.

Conflict and Consensus in the White South   Planters tangled with yeomen on several issues in the Old South. With their extensive economic dealings and need for credit, planters and their urban commercial allies inclined toward the Whig party, which was generally more sympathetic to banking and economic development. Cherishing their self-sufficiency and economically independent, the yeomen tended to be Democrats.

The occasions for conflict between these groups were minimal, however, and an underlying political unity reigned. Especially in the Lower South, each of the four main social groups—planters, small slaveholders, yeomen, and pine barrens people—tended to cluster in different regions. The delta areas that planters dominated contained relatively small numbers of yeomen. In other regions small slave-owning families with ten to fifteen slaves predominated. In the upland areas far from the deltas, the yeomen congregated. The people of the pine barrens lived in a world of their own. There was more geographical intermingling of groups in the Upper South than in the Lower, but throughout the South each group attained a degree of independence from the others. With widespread landownership and relatively few factories, the Old South was not a place where whites worked for other whites, and this tended to minimize friction.

In addition, the white South's political structure was sufficiently democratic to prevent any one social group from gaining exclusive control over politics. It is true that in both the Upper and the Lower South, the majority of state legislators were planters. Large planters with fifty or more slaves were represented in legislatures far out of proportion to their numbers in the population. Yet these same planters owed their election to the popular vote. The white South was affected by the same democratic currents that swept northern politics between 1815 and 1860, and the newer states of the South had usually entered the Union with democratic constitutions that included universal white manhood suffrage—the right of all adult white males to vote.

Although yeomen often voted for planters, the nonslaveholders did not issue their elected representatives a blank check to govern as they pleased. During the 1830s and 1840s, Whig planters who favored banks faced intense and often successful opposition from Democratic yeomen. These yeomen blamed banks for the Panic of 1837 and pressured southern legislatures to restrict bank operations. On banking issues, nonslaveholders got their way often enough to nurture their belief that they ultimately controlled politics and that slaveholders could not block their goals.

Conflict over Slavery   Nevertheless, there was considerable potential for conflict between the slaveholders and nonslaveholders. The white carpenter who complained in 1849 that "unjust, oppressive, and degrading" competition from slave labor depressed his wages surely had a point. Between 1830 and 1860, slaveholders gained an increasing proportion of the South's wealth while declining as a proportion of its white population. The size of the slaveholding class shrank from 36 percent of the white population in 1831 to 31 percent in 1850 and to 25 percent in 1860. A Louisiana editor warned in 1858 that "the present tendency of supply and demand is to concentrate all the slaves in the hands of the few, and thus excite the envy rather than cultivate the sympathy of the people." Some southerners began to support the idea of Congress's reopening the African slave trade to increase the supply of slaves, bring down their price, and give more whites a stake in the institution.

As the proposed **Virginia emancipation legislation** in 1831–1832 attests, slaveholders had good reasons for uncertainty over the allegiance of nonslaveholders to the "peculiar institution" of slavery. The publication in 1857 of Hinton R. Helper's *The Impending Crisis of the South,* which called upon nonslaveholders to abolish slavery in their own interest, revealed the persistence of a degree of white opposition to slavery. On balance, however, slavery did not create profound and lasting divisions between the South's slaveholders and nonslaveholders. Although antagonism to slavery flourished in parts of Virginia up to 1860, proposals for emancipation dropped from the state's political agenda after 1832. In Kentucky, calls for emancipation were revived in 1849 in a popular referendum. But the pro-emancipation forces went down to crushing defeat. Thereafter, the continuation of slavery ceased to be a political issue in Kentucky and elsewhere in the South.

The rise and fall of pro-emancipation sentiment in the South raises a key question. Since the majority of white southerners were not slaveholders, why did they not attack the institution more consistently? To look ahead, why did so many of them fight ferociously and die bravely during the Civil War in defense of an institution in which they appeared not to have had any real stake?

There are various answers to these questions. First, some nonslaveholders hoped to become slaveholders. Second, most simply accepted the racial assumptions upon which slavery rested. Whether slaveholders or nonslaveholders, white southerners dreaded the likelihood that emancipation might encourage "impudent" blacks to entertain ideas of social equality with whites. Blacks might demand the right to sit next to whites in railroad cars and even make advances to white women. "Now suppose they [the slaves] was free," a white southerner told a northern journalist in the 1850s; "you see they'd all think themselves just as good as we; of course they would if they was free. Now just suppose you had a family of children, how would you like to hev a niggar steppin' up to your darter?" Slavery, in short, appealed to whites as a legal, time-honored, and foolproof way to enforce the social subordination of blacks.

Finally, no one knew where the slaves, if freed, would go or what they would do. Colonizing freed blacks in Africa was unrealistic, southerners concluded, but they also believed that without colonization emancipation would lead to a race war. In 1860, Georgia's governor sent a blunt message to his constituents, many of them nonslaveholders: "So soon as the slaves were at liberty thousands of them would leave the cotton and rice fields . . . and make their way to the healthier climate of the mountain region [where] we should have them plundering and stealing, robbing and killing." There was no mistaking the conclusion. Emancipation would not merely deprive slaveholders of their property; it would also jeopardize the lives of nonslaveholders.

| The Proslavery Argument | Between 1830 and 1860, southern writers constructed a defense of slavery as a positive good rather than a necessary evil. |

Southerners answered northern attacks on slavery as a backward institution by pointing out that the slave society of ancient Athens had produced Plato and Aristotle and that Roman slaveholders had laid the basis of Western civilization. (See Beyond America—Global Interactions: Slavery as a Global Institution.) A Virginian, **George Fitzhugh,** launched another line of attack by contrasting the plight of northern factory workers, "wage slaves" who were callously discarded by their bosses when they were too old or too sick to work, with the southern slaves, who were fed and clothed even when old and ill because they were the property of conscientious masters.

Many proslavery treatises were aimed less at northerners than at skeptics among the South's nonslaveholding yeomanry. Southern clergymen, who wrote roughly half of all proslavery tracts, invoked the Bible, especially St. Paul's order that slaves obey their masters. Too, proslavery writers warned southerners that the real intention of abolitionists, many of whom advocated equal rights for women, was to destroy the family as much as slavery by undermining the "natural" submission of children to parents, wives to husbands, and slaves to masters.

As southerners closed ranks behind slavery, they increasingly suppressed open discussion of the institution within the South. In the 1830s, southerners seized and burned abolitionist literature mailed to the South. In Kentucky, abolitionist editor Cassius Marcellus Clay positioned two cannons and a powder keg to protect his press, but in 1845 a mob dismantled it anyway. By 1860, any southerner found with a copy of *The Impending Crisis* had reason to fear for his life.

The rise of the proslavery argument coincided with a shift in the position of the southern churches on slavery. During the 1790s and early 1800s, some Protestant ministers had assailed slavery as immoral. By the 1830s, however, most members of the southern clergy had convinced themselves that slavery was not only compatible with Christianity but also necessary for the proper exercise of the Christian religion. Slavery, they proclaimed, provided the opportunity to display Christian responsibility toward one's inferiors, and it helped blacks develop Christian virtues like humility and self-control. Southerners increasingly attacked antislavery evangelicals in the North for disrupting the "superior" social arrangement of the South. In 1837, southerners and conservative northerners had combined to drive the antislavery New School Presbyterians out of that denomination's main body. In 1844, the Methodist Episcopal Church split into northern and southern wings. In 1845, Baptists formed a separate Southern Convention. In effect, southern evangelicals seceded from national church denominations long before the South seceded from the Union.

Violence in the Old South

Throughout the colonial and antebellum periods, violence deeply colored the daily lives of white southerners. In the 1760s, a minister described backcountry Virginians "biting one anothers Lips and Noses off, and gowging one another—that is, thrusting out anothers Eyes, and kicking one another on the Cods [genitals], to the Great damage of many a Poor Woman." In the 1840s, a New York newspaper described a fight between two raftsmen on the Mississippi that started when one accidentally bumped the other into shallow water. When it was over, one raftsman was dead. The other gloated, "I can lick a steamboat. My fingernails is related to a sawmill on my mother's side, . . . and the brass buttons on my coat have all been boiled in poison."

Gouging out eyes became a specialty of sorts among poor whites. On one occasion, a South Carolina judge entered his court to find a plaintiff, a juror, and two witnesses all missing one eye. Stories of eye gouging and ear biting lost nothing in the telling and became part of the folklore of the Old South. Mike Fink, a legendary southern fighter and hunter, boasted that he was so mean that, in infancy, he refused his mother's milk and cried out for a bottle of whiskey. Yet beneath the folklore lay the reality of violence that gave the South a murder rate as much as ten times higher than that of the North.

The Code of Honor and Dueling

At the root of most violence in the white South lay intensified feelings of personal pride that themselves reflected the inescapable presence of slaves. Every day of their lives, white southerners saw slaves who were degraded, insulted, and powerless to resist. This experience had a searing impact on whites, for it encouraged them to react violently to even trivial insults in order to demonstrate that they had nothing in common with the slaves.

Among gentlemen, this exaggerated pride took the form of a distinctive **southern code of honor,** with honor defined as an extraordinary sensitivity to one's reputation, a belief that one's self-esteem depends on the judgment of others. In the antebellum North, moralists celebrated a rival ideal, character—the quality that enabled an individual to behave in a steady fashion regardless of how others acted toward him or her. A person possessed of character acted out of the prompting of conscience. In contrast, in the honor culture of the Old South, the slightest insult, as long as it was perceived as intentional, could become the basis for a duel.

Formalized by British and French officers during the Revolutionary War, dueling gained a secure niche in the Old South as a means by which gentlemen dealt with affronts to their honor. To outsiders, the incidents that sparked duels seemed trivial: a casual remark accidentally overheard, a harmless brushing against someone at a public

Slavery as a Global Institution

Defenders of slavery in the Old South, who often pointed to the antiquity and universality of slavery as justifications for keeping what northerners called the "peculiar institution," were right about one thing: slavery was ancient in origin and as late as 1800 it was a global institution, stretching from China and Japan to the Americas. Set within a broad historical context, slavery ranks among the most widespread institutions in history. Few groups today have ancestors who at one time or another were not slaves.

All of the great civilizations in history had sanctioned slavery, and so had the major religions. Slaves built the magnificent stone monuments of ancient Egypt, Greece, and Rome. According to the Hebrew Bible, the Lord told Moses on Mount Sinai that the Hebrews could hold slaves as long as they bought them from other nations. In the New Testament, St. Paul commanded slaves to obey their masters. The early Christians viewed enslavement as a just punishment for sin. Slavery persisted in Europe after the collapse of the Roman empire, though on a smaller scale. The bubonic plague that killed about one-third of the population of Europe in the 1340s intensified European demand for slaves. Because the popes of the Catholic church condemned taking Christians as slaves, slave traders increasingly sought slaves from the non-Christian people of Russia and eastern Europe.

No less than Judaism and Christianity, Islam sanctioned slavery. The prophet Muhammad described an idealized master-slave relationship as the basis of social order. Although Muslims were forbidden to enslave Christians and Jews (Christians thought nothing of enslaving Muslims), non-monotheists were fair game. In the centuries of Islamic expansion following Muhammad's death in 632, Muslim warriors surged across the Arabian peninsula, into the Persian and Byzantine empires, into east Africa, across North Africa and the Mediterranean, and into France, taking slaves from the peoples conquered. In the ninth century, Muslims transported African slaves to Basra in southern Iraq to prepare wetlands for agriculture. From the thirteenth through the fifteenth centuries, the Muslim rulers of Asia Minor and Egypt brought slaves from the Balkans and the Caucasus to serve them.

After Muslims captured Constantinople (now Istanbul) in 1453, they diverted the flow of slaves from east Europe exclusively to Muslim rulers. Christian rulers turned to sub-Saharan Africa for slaves. European traders did not have to conquer Africa to take slaves, for Africans routinely enslaved other Africans, usually captives taken in war, and sold them to the traders.

The maritime expansion of Portugal and Spain from 1450 to 1660 led to their settling African slaves first on islands in the Atlantic and then in the Caribbean, northeast Brazil, Mexico, and the Andes. The Portuguese also carried slaves to Asia during this period. In the century and a half after 1660, British, Dutch, French, and Brazilian merchants supplanted the Portuguese and the Spanish as the major players in the slave trade. The French carried slaves from Mozambique in Africa to islands in the Indian Ocean; the Dutch settled slaves in what is now Indonesia and in South Africa; and the British used slaves as labor in their valuable sugar colonies in the West Indies and began to ship a significant number of slaves to North America. (See Chapter 2, Technology and Culture: Sugar Production in the Americas.)

Slavery always involved the ownership of one person by another, and in all societies enslavement carried a taint. No one would make a free choice to become a slave. But slavery was not the same everywhere. Slavery in the Americas typically involved back-breaking labor on the sugar plantations of Barbados and Jamaica or in the cotton fields of the Lower South. In contrast, before the sixteenth and seventeenth centuries slaves had played only a limited role in agriculture. For example, the Romans employed slaves as domestic servants, gladiators, teachers, doctors, pharmacists, and administrators. Muslims turned captured boys and young men into slave soldiers, called Mamluks. Mamluks first appeared in Egypt in the ninth century; in the thirteenth century Mamluk officers assassinated the claimant to the Egyptian throne and became the effective rulers of Egypt until the sixteenth century. The crack infantry of the Muslim Ottoman empire, which was founded around 1300 in Asia Minor and which controlled most of southeast Europe by 1520, consisted of military slaves called "janissaries." Sub-Sahara African societies put slaves to work as domestics, soldiers, and officials. Africans also valued slaves as wives and children. By increasing the extent and influence of an African man's lineage, the offspring of slave mothers, although never fully escaping the taint of their slave origins, merged into local tribes and clans and added to the status of their father.

Gaining freedom was also a real possibility in most societies. In ancient Rome, the manumission of slaves was a frequent occurrence. A Roman who freed his slaves, who likely would then become loyal retainers of their former master, would earn the slaves' lasting gratitude without blemishing his own so-cial status. In addition, both Christianity and Islam encouraged the emancipation of converted slaves. Islam required slaveholders to make efforts to convert their slaves, and conversion very often led to freedom. Under Islam, concubinage also provided a route to freedom. Although a Muslim was allowed only four wives, there was no limit on the number of concubines (slave mistresses) he could acquire. A concubine who bore her master's children rose in status and had to be freed upon her master's death. By the mid-fourteenth century, Ottoman rulers had come to prefer concubinage over legal marriage, partly to avoid the political alliances that accompanied the latter. A sultan's concubine became a member of the royal family when she bore him a child. If her son ascended to the throne, she became the queen mother.

By these measures, slavery in the Americas, including the Old South, was extremely harsh, a fact which explains the greater frequency of slave rebellions in the New World than elsewhere. The vast majority of slaves in the Americas worked under disagreeable conditions as members of a despised race.

By 1700, it had become an established legal principle in the American South that conversion to Christianity was no basis for emancipation, and by 1860 manumissions had become rare. Southern defenders of slavery were correct in stating that slavery was an ancient institution and sanctioned by many world religions. But the form of slavery that they were defending differed from the type of slavery that had prevailed throughout much of history.

Question for Analysis

- In what basic ways did slavery in the New World differ from slavery in Europe, Africa, and the Islamic world?

event, even a hostile glance. Yet dueling did not necessarily terminate in violence. Dueling constituted part of a complex code of etiquette that governed relations among gentlemen in the Old South and, like all forms of etiquette, called for a curious sort of self-restraint. Gentlemen viewed dueling as a refined alternative to the random violence of lower-class life. The code of dueling did not dictate that the insulted party leap at his antagonist's throat or draw his pistol at the perceived moment of insult. Rather, he was to remain cool, bide his time, settle on a choice of weapons, and agree to a meeting place. In the interval, negotiations between friends of the parties sought to clear up the "misunderstanding" that had evoked the challenge. In this way, most confrontations ended peaceably rather than on the field of honor at dawn.

Although dueling was as much a way of settling disputes peaceably as of ending them violently, the ritual could easily terminate in a death or maiming. Dueling did not allow the resolution of grievances by the courts, a form of redress that would have guaranteed a peaceful outcome. As a way of settling personal disputes that involved honor, recourse to the law struck many southerners as cowardly and shameless. Andrew Jackson's mother told the future president, "The law affords no remedy that can satisfy the feelings of a true man."

In addition, dueling rested on the assumption that a gentleman could recognize another gentleman and hence would know when to respond to a challenge. Nothing in the code of dueling compelled a gentleman to duel someone beneath his status because such a person's opinion of a gentleman hardly mattered. An insolent porter who insulted a gentleman might get a whipping but did not merit a challenge to a duel. Yet it was often difficult to determine who was a gentleman. The Old South teemed with pretentious would-be gentlemen. A clerk in a country store in Arkansas in the 1850s found it remarkable that ordinary farmers who hung around the store talked of their honor and that the store's proprietor, a German Jew, kept a dueling pistol.

The Southern Evangelicals and White Values

With its emphasis on the personal redress of grievances and its inclination toward violence, the ideal of honor potentially conflicted with the values preached by the southern evangelical churches, notably the Baptists, Methodists, and Presbyterians. These evangelical denominations were on the rise even before the Great Kentucky Revival of 1800–1801 and continued to grow in the wake of the revival. For example, the Methodists grew from forty-eight thousand southern members in 1801 to eighty thousand by 1807. All of the evangelical denominations stressed humility and self-restraint, virtues in contrast to the entire culture of show and display that buttressed the extravagance and violence of the Old South.

Evangelicals continued to rail against dueling, but by the 1830s their values had changed in subtle ways. In the late eighteenth century, evangelical preachers had reached out to the South's subordinate groups: women, slaves, and the poor. They had frequently allowed women and slaves to exhort in churches open to both whites and blacks. By the 1830s, evangelical women were expected to remain silent in church. Pushed to the periphery of white churches, slaves increasingly conducted their own worship services. In addition, Methodists and Baptists increasingly attracted well-to-do converts, and they began to open colleges such as Randolph-Macon (Methodist, 1830) and Wake Forest (Baptist, 1838).

With these developments, the once antagonistic relationship between evangelicals and the gentry became one of cooperation. Evangelical clergymen absorbed some gentry values, including a regard for their honor and reputation that prompted them to throw taunts and threats back at their detractors. In turn, the gentry embraced evangelical virtues. By the 1860s, the South contained many Christian gentlemen like the Bible-quoting Presbyterian general Thomas J. "Stonewall" Jackson, fierce in a righteous war but a sworn opponent of strong drink, the gaming table, and the duel.

LIFE UNDER SLAVERY

As they fashioned the proslavery argument, southern clergymen emphasized the Christian responsibility of masters toward their slaves. "Give your servants that which is just and equal," a Baptist minister advised in 1854, "knowing that you also have a Master in heaven." Some masters were benevolent, and many more liked to think that they were benevolent. But masters bought slaves to make a profit on their labor, not to practice charity toward them. Kind masters might complain about cruel overseers, but the masters hired and paid the overseers to get as much work as possible out of blacks. When the master of one plantation chastised his overseer for "barbarity," the latter replied, "Do you not remember what you told me the time you employed me that [if] I failed to make you good crops I would have to leave?" Indeed, kindness was a double-edged sword, for the benevolent master came to expect grateful affection from his slaves and then interpreted that affection as loyalty to the institution of slavery. In fact, blacks felt little, if any, loyalty to slavery. When northern troops descended upon plantations during the Civil War, masters were dismayed to find many of their most trusted slaves deserting to Union lines.

Although the kindness or cruelty of masters made some difference to slaves, the most important determinants of their experiences under slavery depended on such impersonal factors as the kind of agriculture in which they were engaged, whether they resided in rural or urban areas, and whether they lived in the eighteenth or nineteenth century. The experiences of slaves working on cotton plantations in the 1830s differed drastically from those of slaves in 1700 for reasons unrelated to the kindness or brutality of masters.

The Maturing of the Plantation System

Slavery changed significantly between 1700 and 1830. In 1700, the typical slave was a young man in his twenties who had recently arrived aboard a slave ship from Africa or the Caribbean and worked in the company of other recent arrivals on isolated small farms. Drawn from different African regions and cultures, few such slaves spoke the same language. Because commercial slave ships contained twice as many men as women, and because slaves were widely scattered, blacks had difficulty finding sexual partners and creating a semblance of family life. Furthermore, as a result of severe malnutrition, black women who had been brought to North America on slave ships bore relatively few children. Thus the slave trade had a devastating effect on natural increase among blacks. Without importation, the number of slaves in North America would have declined between 1710 and 1730.

In contrast, by 1830 the typical North American slave was as likely to be female as male, had been born in America, spoke a form of English that made communication with other slaves possible, and worked in the company of numerous other slaves on a plantation. The key to the change lay in the rise of plantation agriculture in the Chesapeake and South Carolina during the eighteenth century. Plantation slaves had an

The Land of the Free and the Home of the Brave, by Henry Byam Martin, 1833 *White southerners could not escape the fact that much of the Western world loathed their "peculiar institution." In 1833, when a Canadian sketched this Charleston slave auction, Britain abolished slavery in the West Indies.*

easier time finding mates than those on the remote farms of the early 1700s. As the ratio between slave men and women fell into balance, marriages occurred with increasing frequency between slaves on the same or nearby plantations. The native-born slave population rose after 1730 and soared after 1750. Importation of African slaves gradually declined after 1760, and Congress banned it in 1808.

Work and Discipline of Plantation Slaves In 1850, the typical slave worked on a large farm or plantation with at least ten fellow bond servants. Almost three-quarters of all slaves that year were owned by masters with ten or more slaves, and slightly over one-half lived in units of twenty or more slaves. On smaller units, slaves usually worked under the **task system.** Each slave had a daily or weekly quota of tasks to complete. On the large cotton and sugar plantations, slaves would occasionally work under the task system, but more closely supervised and regimented **gang labor** prevailed.

The day of antebellum plantation slaves usually began an hour before sunrise with the sounding of a horn or bell. After a sparse breakfast, slaves marched to the fields. A traveler in Mississippi described a procession of slaves on their way to work. "First came, led by an old driver carrying a whip, forty of the largest and strongest women I ever saw together; they were all in a simple uniform dress of bluish check stuff, the skirts reaching little below the knee; their legs and feet were bare; they carried themselves loftily, each having a hoe over the shoulder, and walking with a free, powerful swing." Then came the plow hands, "thirty strong, mostly men, but few of them women. . . . A lean and vigilant white overseer, on a brisk pony, brought up the rear."

As this account indicates, slave men and women worked side by side in the fields. Female slaves who did not labor in the fields scarcely idled their hours away. A former slave, John Curry, described how his mother milked cows, cared for the children whose mothers worked in the fields, cooked for field hands, did the ironing and washing for her master's household, and took care of her own seven children. Plantations never lacked tasks for slaves of either gender. As former slave Solomon Northup noted, "ploughing, planting, picking cotton, gathering the corn, and pulling and burning stalks, occupies the whole of the four seasons of the year. Drawing and cutting wood, pressing cotton, fattening and killing hogs, are but incidental labors."

Regardless of the season, the slave's day stretched from dawn to dusk. Touring the South in the 1850s, Frederick Law Olmsted prided himself on rising early and riding late but added, "I always found the negroes in the field when I first looked out, and generally had to wait for the negroes to come from the field to have my horse fed when I stopped for the night." When darkness made fieldwork impossible, slaves transported cotton bales to the gin house, gathered up wood for supper fires, and fed the mules. Weary from their labors, they slept in log cabins on wooden planks. "The softest couches in the world," a former bondsman wryly observed, "are not to be found in the log mansions of a slave."

Although virtually all antebellum Americans worked long hours, no laboring group experienced the same combination of long hours and harsh discipline as did slave field hands. Northern factory workers did not have to put up with drivers who, like one described by Olmsted, walked among the slaves with a whip, "which he often cracked at them, sometimes allowing the lash to fall lightly upon their shoulders." The lash did not always fall lightly. The annals of American slavery contain stories of repulsive brutality. Pregnant slave women were sometimes forced to lie in depressions in the ground and endure whipping on their backs, a practice that supposedly protected the fetus while abusing the mother.

The disciplining and punishment of slaves were often left to white overseers and black drivers rather than to masters. "Dat was de meanest devil dat ever lived on the Lord's green earth," a former Mississippi slave said of his driver. The barbaric discipline meted out by others pricked the conscience of many a master. But even masters who professed Christianity viewed the disciplining of slaves as a priority—indeed, as a Christian duty to ensure the slaves' proper "submissiveness." The black abolitionist **Frederick Douglass,** once a slave, recalled that his worst master had been converted at a Methodist camp meeting. "If religion had any effect on his character at all," Douglass related, "it made him more cruel and hateful in all his ways."

Despite the relentless, often vicious discipline, plantation agriculture gave a minority of slaves opportunities for advancement, not from slavery to freedom but from unskilled and exhausting fieldwork to semiskilled or skilled indoor work. Some slaves developed skills like blacksmithing and carpentry, and learned to operate cotton gins. Others were trained as cooks, butlers, and dining-room attendants. These house slaves became legendary for their arrogant disdain of field hands and poor whites. The legend often distorted the reality, for house slaves were as subject to discipline as field slaves. "I liked the field work better than I did the house work," a female slave recalled. "We could talk and do anything we wanted to, just so we picked the cotton." Such sentiments were typical, but skilled slave artisans and house servants were greatly valued and treated accordingly; they occupied higher rungs than field hands on the social ladder of slavery.

The Slave Family   Masters had an incentive to encourage slave marriages in order to bring new slaves into the world and to discourage slaves from running away. Some masters baked wedding cakes for slaves and even arbitrated marital disputes. Still, the keenest challenge to the slave family came not from the slaves themselves but from slavery. The law did not recognize or protect slave families. Although some slaveholders were reluctant to break slave marriages by sale, economic hardships might force their hand. The reality, one historian has calculated, was that in a lifetime, on average, a slave would witness the sale of eleven family members.

Naturally, the commonplace buying and selling of slaves severely disrupted slaves' attempts to create a stable family life. Poignant testimony to the effects of sale on slave families, and to the desire of slaves to remain near their families, was provided by an advertisement for a runaway slave in North Carolina in 1851. The advertisement described the fugitive as presumed to be "lurking in the neighborhood of E. D. Walker's, at Moore's Creek, who owns most of his relatives, or Nathan Bonham's who owns his mother; or, perhaps, near Fletcher Bell's, at Long Creek, who owns his father." Small wonder that a slave preacher pronounced a slave couple married "until death or *distance* do you part."

Aside from disruption by sale, slave families experienced separations and degradations from other sources. The marriage of a slave woman gave her no protection against the sexual demands of a master nor, indeed, of any white. The slave children of white masters became targets of the wrath of white mistresses at times. Sarah Wilson, the daughter of a slave and her white master, remembered that as a child, she was "picked on" by her mistress until the master ordered his wife to let Sarah alone because she "got big, big blood in her." Slave women who worked in the fields were usually separated from their children by day; young sons and daughters often were cared for by the aged or by the mothers of other children. When slave women took husbands from nearby (rather than their own) plantations, the children usually stayed with the mother. Hannah Chapman remembered that her father tried to visit his family under cover of darkness "because he missed us and us longed for him." But if his master found him, "us would track him the nex' day by de blood stains."

Despite enormous obstacles, the relationships within slave families were often intimate and, where possible, long-lasting. In the absence of legal protection, slaves developed their own standards of family morality. A southern white woman observed that slaves "did not consider it wrong for a girl to have a child before she married, but afterwards were extremely severe upon anything like infidelity on her part." When given the opportunity, slaves sought to solemnize their marriages before clergymen. White clergymen who accompanied the Union army into Mississippi and Louisiana in the closing years of the Civil War conducted thousands of marriage rites for slaves who had long viewed themselves as married and desired a formal ceremony and registration.

On balance, slave families differed profoundly from white families. Even on large plantations where roughly equal numbers of black men and women made marriage a theoretical possibility, planters, including George Washington, often divided their holdings into several dispersed farms and distributed their slaves among them without regard to marriage ties. Conditions on small farms and new plantations discouraged the formation of families, and everywhere spouses were vulnerable to being sold as payment for the master's debts. Slave adults were more likely than whites never to marry or to marry late, and slave children were more likely to live with a single parent (usually the mother) or with neither parent.

In white families, the parent-child bond overrode all others; slaves, in contrast, emphasized ties between children and their grandparents, uncles, and aunts as well as their parents. Such broad kinship ties marked the West African cultures from which many slaves had originally been brought to America, and they were reinforced by the separations between children and one or both parents that routinely occurred under slavery. Frederick Douglass never knew his father and saw his mother infrequently, but he vividly remembered his grandmother, "a good nurse, and a capital hand at making nets for catching shad and herring."

In addition, slaves often created "fictive" kin networks; in the absence of uncles and aunts, they simply called friends their uncles, aunts, brothers, or sisters. In effect, slaves invested nonkin relations with symbolic kin functions. In this way, they helped protect themselves against the involuntary disruption of family ties by forced sale and established a broader community of obligation. When plantation slaves greeted each other as "brudder," they were not making a statement about actual kinship but about kindred obligations they felt for each other. Apologists for slavery liked to argue that a "community of interests" bound masters and slaves together. In truth, the real community of interests was the one that slaves developed among themselves in order to survive.

The Longevity, Diet, and Health of Slaves

In general, slaves in the United States reproduced faster and lived longer than slaves elsewhere in the Western Hemisphere. The evidence comes from a compelling statistic. In 1825, 36 percent of all slaves in the Western Hemisphere lived in the United States, whereas Brazil accounted for 31 percent. Yet of the 10 to 12 million African slaves who had been imported to the New World between the fifteenth and nineteenth centuries, only some 550,000 (about 5 percent) had come to North America, whereas 3.5 million (nearly 33 percent) had been taken to Brazil. Mortality had depleted the slave populations in Brazil and the Caribbean to a far greater extent than in North America.

Several factors account for the different rates. First, the gender ratio among slaves equalized more rapidly in North America, encouraging earlier and longer marriages and more children. Second, because growing corn and raising livestock were compatible with cotton cultivation, the Old South produced plenty of food. The normal ration for a slave was a peck of cornmeal and three to four pounds of fatty pork a week. Slaves often supplemented this nutritionally unbalanced diet with vegetables grown in small plots that masters allowed them to farm and with catfish and game. In the barren winter months, slaves ate less than in the summer; in this respect, however, they did not differ much from most whites.

As for disease, slaves had greater immunities to both malaria and yellow fever than did whites, but they suffered more from cholera, dysentery, and diarrhea. In the absence of privies, slaves usually relieved themselves behind bushes; urine and feces washed into the sources of drinking water and caused many diseases. Yet slaves developed some remedies that, though commonly ridiculed by whites, were effective against stomach ailments. For example, the slaves' belief that eating white clay would cure dysentery and diarrhea rested on a firm basis; we know now that kaolin, an ingredient of white clay, is a remedy for these ailments.

Although slave remedies were often more effective than those of white physicians, slaves experienced higher mortality rates than whites. At any age, a slave could expect a shorter life than a white, most strikingly in infancy. Rates of infant mortality for slaves were at least twice those of whites. Between 1850 and 1860, fewer than two out of three black children survived to the age of ten. Whereas the worst mortality occurred on plantations in disease-ridden, low-lying areas, pregnant, overworked field hands often miscarried or gave birth to weakened infants even in healthier regions. Masters allowed pregnant women to rest, but rarely enough. "Labor is conducive to health," a Mississippi planter told a northern journalist; "a healthy woman will rear most children."

Slaves off Plantations

Although plantation agriculture gave some slaves, especially men and boys, opportunities to acquire specialized skills, it imposed a good deal of supervision on them. The greatest opportunities for slaves were reserved for those who worked off plantations and farms, either as laborers in extractive industries like mining and lumbering or as artisans in towns and cities.

Because lucrative cotton growing attracted so many whites onto small farms, a perennial shortage of white labor plagued almost all the nonagricultural sectors of the southern economy. As a consequence, there was a steady demand for slaves to drive wagons, to work as stevedores (ship-cargo handlers) in port cities, to man river barges, and to perform various tasks in mining and lumbering. In 1860, lumbering employed sixteen thousand workers, most of them slaves who cut trees, hauled them to sawmills, and fashioned them into useful lumber. In sawmills, black engineers fired and fixed the steam engines that provided power. In iron-ore ranges and ironworks, slaves not only served as laborers but occasionally supervised less-skilled white workers. Just as mill girls comprised the labor force of the booming textile industry in New England, so did slave women and children work in the South's fledgling textile mills.

Slave or free, blacks found it easier to pursue skilled occupations in southern cities than in northern ones, partly because southern cities attracted few immigrants to compete for work, and partly because the profitability of southern cash crops long had pulled white laborers out of towns and cities, and left behind opportunities for blacks, slave or free, to acquire craft skills. Slaves who worked in factories, mining, or lumbering usually were hired rather than owned by their employers. If working conditions deteriorated to the point where slaves fell ill or died, masters would refuse to provide employers with more slaves. Consequently, working conditions for slaves off plantations usually stayed at a tolerable level. Watching workers load cotton onto a steamboat, Frederick Law Olmsted was amazed to see slaves sent to the top of the bank to roll the bales down to Irishmen who stowed them on the ship. Asking the reason for this arrangement, Olmsted was told, "The niggers are worth too much to be risked here; if the Paddies [Irish] are knocked overboard, or get their backs broke, nobody loses anything."

Life on the Margin: Free Blacks in the Old South

Free blacks were more likely than southern blacks in general to live in cities. In 1860, one-third of the free blacks in the Upper South and more than half in the Lower South were urban.

The relatively specialized economies of the cities provided free people of color with opportunities to become carpenters, coopers (barrel makers), barbers, and even small traders. A visitor to an antebellum southern market would find that most of the meat, fish, vegetables, and fruit had been prepared for sale by free blacks. Urban free blacks formed their own fraternal orders and churches; a church run by free blacks was often the largest house of worship in a southern city. In New Orleans, free blacks had their

A Barber's Shop at Richmond, Virginia, 1861   *Free blacks dominated the barber's trade in Richmond on the eve of the Civil War. As meeting places for men, barber shops supplied newspapers and political discussion. Black barbers were politically informed and prosperous. As was the custom at the time, barbers also performed medical procedures like drawing blood.*

own literary journals and opera. In Natchez, a free black barber, William Tiler Johnson, invested the profits of his shop in real estate, acquired stores that he rented out, purchased slaves and a plantation, and even hired a white overseer.

As Johnson's career suggests, some free blacks were highly successful. But free blacks were always vulnerable in southern society and became more so as the antebellum period wore on. Although free blacks continued to increase in absolute numbers (a little more than a quarter-million free people of color dwelled in the South in 1860), the rate of growth of the free-black population slowed after 1810. Between 1790 and 1810, this population had more than tripled, to 108,265. The reason for the slowdown after 1810 was that fewer southern whites were setting slaves free. Until 1820, masters with doubts about the rightness of slavery frequently manumitted (freed) their black mistresses and mulatto children, and some set free their entire work forces. In the wake of the Nat Turner rebellion in 1831, laws restricting the liberties of free blacks were tightened. During the mid-1830s, for example, most southern states made it a felony to teach blacks to read and write. Every southern state forbade free blacks to enter that state, and in 1859 Arkansas ordered all free blacks to leave.

So although a free-black culture flowered in cities like New Orleans and Natchez, that culture did not reflect the conditions under which most free blacks lived. Free blacks were tolerated in New Orleans, in part because there were not too many of them. A much higher percentage of blacks were free in the Upper South than in the Lower South. Furthermore, although a disproportionate number of free blacks lived in cities, the majority lived in rural areas, where whites lumped them together with slaves. Even a successful free black like William Tiler Johnson could never dine or drink with whites. When Johnson attended the theater, he sat in the colored gallery.

The position of free blacks in the Old South contained many contradictions. So did their minds. As the offspring, or the descendants of offspring, of mixed liaisons, a disproportionate number of free blacks had light brown skin. Some of them were as color-conscious as whites and looked down on "darky" field hands and coal-black laborers. Yet as whites' discrimination against free people of color intensified during the late antebellum period, many free blacks realized that whatever future they had was as blacks, not as whites. Feelings of racial solidarity grew stronger among free blacks in the 1850s, and after the Civil War, the leaders of the freed slaves were usually blacks who had been free before the war.

Slave Resistance   The Old South was a seedbed of organized slave insurrections. In the delta areas of the Lower South where blacks outnumbered whites, slaves experienced continuous forced labor on plantations and communicated their bitterness to each other in the slave quarters. Free blacks in the cities could have provided leadership for rebellions. Rumors of slave conspiracies flew around the southern white community, and all whites shuddered over the massive black insurrection that had destroyed French rule in Saint Domingue.

Yet Nat Turner's 1831 insurrection in Virginia was the only slave rebellion that resulted in the deaths of whites. A larger but more obscure uprising occurred in Louisiana in 1811 when some two hundred slaves sought to march on New Orleans. Other, better known, slave insurrections were merely conspiracies that never materialized. In 1800, Virginia slave Gabriel Prosser's planned uprising was betrayed by other slaves, and Gabriel and his followers were executed. That same year, a South Carolina slave, **Denmark Vesey,** won fifteen hundred dollars in a lottery and bought his freedom. Purchasing a carpentry shop in Charleston and becoming a preacher at that city's African Methodist Episcopal Church, Vesey built a cadre of black followers, including a slave of the governor of South Carolina and a black conjurer named Gullah Jack. In 1822, they devised a plan to attack Charleston and seize all the city's arms and ammunition, but other slaves informed authorities, and the conspirators were executed.

For several reasons, the Old South experienced far fewer rebellions than the Caribbean region or South America. Although slaves formed a majority in South Carolina and a few other states, they did not constitute a large majority in any state. In contrast to the Caribbean, an area of absentee landlords and sparse white population, the white presence in the Old South was formidable, and the whites had all the guns and soldiers. The rumors of slave conspiracies that periodically swept the white South demonstrated to blacks the promptness with which whites could muster forces and mount slave patrols. The development of family ties among slaves made them reluctant to risk death and leave their children parentless. Finally, blacks who ran away or plotted rebellions had no allies. Southern Indians routinely captured runaway slaves and exchanged them for rewards; some Indians even owned slaves.

Short of rebellion, slaves could try to escape to freedom in the North. Perhaps the most ingenious, Henry Brown, induced a friend to ship him from Richmond to Philadelphia in a box and won immediate fame as "Box" Brown. Some light mulattos passed as whites. More often, fugitive slaves borrowed, stole, or forged passes from plantations or obtained papers describing themselves as free. Frederick Douglass borrowed a sailor's papers in making his escape from Baltimore to New York City in 1838. Some former slaves, among them **Harriet Tubman** and Josiah Henson, made repeated trips back to the South to help other slaves escape. These sundry methods of escape fed the **"Underground Railroad,"** supposedly an organized network of safe houses owned by white abolitionists who spirited blacks to freedom in the North and Canada. In reality, fugitive slaves owed very little to abolitionists. Some white sympathizers in border states did provide safe houses for blacks, but these houses were better known to watchful slave catchers than to most blacks.

Escape to freedom was a dream rather than an alternative for most blacks. Out of millions of slaves, probably fewer than a thousand escaped to the North. Yet slaves often ran away from masters not to escape to freedom but to visit spouses or avoid punishment. Most runaways remained in the South; some returned to kinder former masters. During the eighteenth century, African slaves had often run away in groups to the interior and sought to create self-sufficient colonies or villages of the sort that they had known in Africa. But once the United States acquired Florida, long a haven for runaways, few uninhabited places remained in the South to which slaves could flee.

Despite poor prospects for permanent escape, slaves could disappear for prolonged periods into the free-black communities of southern cities. Because whites in the Old South depended so heavily on black labor, slaves enjoyed a fair degree of practical freedom to drive wagons to market and to come and go when they were off plantations. Slaves hired out or sent to a city might overstay their leave and even pass themselves off as free. The experience of slavery has sometimes been compared to the experience of prisoners in penitentiaries or on chain gangs, but the analogy is misleading. The supervision that slaves experienced was sometimes intense (for example, when working at harvest time under a driver), but often lax; it was irregular rather than consistent.

The fact that antebellum slaves frequently enjoyed some degree of practical freedom did not change the underlying oppressiveness of slavery. But it did give slaves a sense that they had certain rights on a day-to-day basis, and it helped deflect slave resistance into forms that were essentially furtive rather than open and violent. Theft was so common that planters learned to keep their tools, smokehouses, closets, and trunks under lock and key. Overworked field hands might leave valuable tools out to rust, or feign illness, or simply refuse to work. As an institution, slavery was vulnerable to such tactics; unlike free laborers, slaves could not be fired for negligence or malingering. Frederick Law Olmsted found slaveholders in the 1850s afraid to inflict punishment on slaves "lest the slave should abscond, or take a sulky fit and not work, or poison some of the family, or set fire to the dwelling, or have recourse to any other mode of avenging himself."

Olmsted's reference to arson and poisoning reminds us that not all furtive resistance was peaceful. Arson and poisoning, both common in African culture as forms of vengeance, were widespread in the Old South, and the fear of each was even more so. Masters afflicted by dysentery and similar ailments never knew for sure that they had not been poisoned.

Arson, poisoning, work stoppages, and negligence were alternatives to violent rebellion. Yet these furtive forms of resistance differed from rebellion. The goal of rebellion was freedom from slavery. The goal of furtive resistance was to make slavery bearable. The kind of resistance that slaves usually practiced sought to establish customs and rules that would govern the conduct of masters as well as that of slaves without challenging the institution of slavery as such. Most slaves would have preferred freedom but settled for less. "White folks do as they please," an ex-slave said, "and the darkies do as they can."

THE EMERGENCE OF AFRICAN-AMERICAN CULTURE

A distinctive culture emerged among blacks in the slave quarters of antebellum plantations. This culture drew on both African and American sources, but it was more than a mixture of the two. Enslaved blacks gave a distinctive twist to the American as well as African components of their culture.

The Language of Slaves — Before slaves could develop a common culture, they had to be able to communicate with one another. During the colonial period, verbal communication among slaves had often been difficult, for most slaves had been born in Africa, which contained an abundance of cultures and languages. The captain of a slave ship noted in 1744,

> As for the languages of Gambia [in West Africa], they are so many and so different that the Natives on either Side of the River cannot understand each other; which, if rightly consider'd, is no small happiness to the Europeans who go thither to trade for slaves.

In the pens into which they were herded before shipment and on the slave ships themselves, however, Africans developed a "pidgin"—a language that has no native speakers in which people with different native languages can communicate. Pidgin is not unique to black people. Nor is pidgin English the only form of pidgin; slaves who were sent to South America developed Spanish and Portuguese pidgin languages.

Many of the early African-born slaves learned pidgin English poorly or not at all, but as American-born slaves came to comprise an increasingly large proportion of all slaves, pidgin English took root. Indeed, it became the only language most slaves knew. Like all pidgins, it was a simplified language. Slaves usually dropped the verb *to be* (which had no equivalent in African tongues) and either ignored or confused genders. Instead of saying "Mary is in the cabin," they said, "Mary, he in cabin." To negate, they substituted *no* for *not,* saying, "He no wicked." Pidgin English contained several African words. Some, like *banjo,* became part of standard English; others, like *goober* (peanut), became part of southern white slang. Although they picked up pidgin terms, whites ridiculed field hands' speech. Some slaves, particularly house servants and skilled artisans, learned to speak standard English but had no trouble understanding the pidgin of field hands. However strange pidgin sounded to some, it was indispensable for communication among slaves.

African-American Religion — The development of a common language was the first step in forging African-American culture. No less important was the religion of the slaves.

Africa was home to rich and diverse religious customs and beliefs. Some of the early slaves were Muslims; a few had acquired Christian beliefs either in Africa or in the

New World. But the majority of the slaves transported from Africa were neither Muslims nor Christians but rather worshipers in one of many native African religions. Most of these religions, which whites lumped together as heathen, drew little distinction between the spiritual and material worlds. Any event or development, from a storm to an earthquake or an illness, was assumed to stem from supernatural forces. These forces were represented by God, by spirits that inhabited the woods and waters, and by the spirits of ancestors. In addition, the religions of West Africa, the region from which most American slaves originally came, attached special significance to water, which symbolized life and hope.

The majority of the slaves brought to America in the seventeenth and eighteenth centuries were young men who may not have absorbed much of this religious heritage before their enslavement. In any case, Africans differed from each other in their specific beliefs and practices. For these reasons, African religions could never have unified blacks in America. Yet some Africans probably clung to their beliefs during the seventeenth and eighteenth centuries, a tendency made easier by the fact that whites undertook few efforts before the 1790s to convert slaves to Christianity.

Dimly remembered African beliefs such as the reverence for water may have predisposed slaves to accept Christianity when they were finally urged to do so, because water has a symbolic significance for Christians, too, in the sacrament of baptism. The Christianity preached to slaves by Methodist and Baptist revivalists during the late eighteenth and nineteenth centuries, moreover, resembled African religions in that it also drew few distinctions between the sacred and the secular. Just as Africans believed that a crop-destroying drought or a plague resulted from supernatural forces, the early revivalists knew in their hearts that every drunkard who fell off his horse and every Sabbath-breaker struck by lightning had experienced a deliberate and direct punishment from God.

By the 1790s, blacks formed about a quarter of the membership of the Methodist and Baptist denominations. Masters continued to fear that a Christianized slave would be a rebellious slave. Converted slaves did in fact play a significant role in each of the three major slave rebellions in the Old South. The leaders of Prosser's rebellion in 1800 used the Bible to prove that slaves, like the ancient Israelites, could prevail against overwhelming numbers. Denmark Vesey read the Bible, and most of the slaves executed for joining his conspiracy belonged to Charleston's African Methodist Church. Nat Turner was both a preacher and a prophet.

Despite the "subversive" effect of Christianity on some slaves, however, these uprisings, particularly the Nat Turner rebellion, actually stimulated Protestant missionaries to intensify their efforts to convert slaves. Missionaries pointed to the self-taught Turner to prove that slaves would hear about Christianity in any event and that organized efforts to convert blacks were the only way to ensure that slaves learned correct versions of Christianity, which emphasized obedience rather than insurgence. Georgia missionary and slaveholder Charles Colcock Jones reassuringly told white planters of the venerable black preacher who, upon receiving some abolitionist tracts in the mail, promptly turned them over to the white authorities for destruction. A Christian slave, the argument ran, would be a better slave. For whites, the clincher was the split of the Methodists, Baptists, and Presbyterians into northern and southern wings by the mid-1840s. Now, they argued, it had finally become safe to convert slaves, for the churches had rid themselves of their antislavery wings. Between 1845 and 1860 the number of black Baptists doubled.

The experiences of Christianized blacks in the Old South illustrate many of the contradictions of life under slavery. Urban blacks often had their own churches, but in the rural South, where the great majority of blacks lived, slaves worshiped in the same churches as whites. Although the slaves sat in segregated sections, they heard the same sermons and sang the same hymns as whites. Some black preachers actually developed followings among whites, and Christian masters were sometimes rebuked by biracial churches for abusing Christian slaves in the same congregation. The churches were, in fact, the most interracial institutions in the Old South. Yet none of this meant that Christianity was an acceptable route to black liberation. Ministers went out of their way to remind slaves that spiritual equality was not the same as civil equality. The effort to convert slaves gained momentum only to the extent that it was certain that Christianity would not change the basic inequality of southern society.

Although they listened to the same sermons as whites, slaves did not necessarily draw the same conclusions. It was impossible to Christianize the slaves without telling them about the Chosen People, the ancient Jews whom Moses led from captivity in Pharaoh's Egypt into the Promised Land of Israel. Inevitably, slaves drew parallels between their own condition and the Jews' captivity. Like the Jews, blacks concluded, they themselves were "de people of de Lord." If they kept the faith, then, like the Jews, they too would reach the Promised Land. The themes of the Chosen People and the Promised Land ran through the sacred songs, or "spirituals," that blacks sang, to the point where Moses and Jesus almost merged:

> Gwine to write to Massa Jesus,
> To send some Valiant Soldier
> To turn back Pharaoh's army, Hallelu!

A listener could interpret a phrase like "the Promised Land" in several ways; it could refer to Israel, to heaven, or to freedom. From the perspective of whites, the only permissible interpretations were Israel and heaven, but some blacks, like Denmark Vesey, thought of freedom as well. The ease with which slaves constructed alternative interpretations of the Bible also reflected the fact that many plantations contained black preachers, slaves trained by white ministers to spread Christianity among blacks. When in the presence of masters or white ministers, these black preachers usually just repeated the familiar biblical command, "Obey your master." Often, however, slaves met for services apart from whites, usually on Sunday evenings but during the week as well. Then the message changed. A black preacher in Texas related how his master would say, "tell them niggers iffen they obeys the master they goes to Heaven." The minister quickly added, "I knowed there's something better for them, but I daren't tell them 'cept on the sly. That I done lots. I tells 'em iffen they keep praying, the Lord will set 'em free."

Some slaves privately interpreted Christianity as a religion of liberation from the oppression of slavery, but most recognized that their prospects for freedom were slight. On the whole, Christianity did not turn them into revolutionaries. Neither did it necessarily turn them into model slaves. It did, however, provide slaves with a view of slavery different from their masters' outlook. Where the masters argued that slavery was a benign and divinely ordained institution in blacks' best interests, Christianity told them that slavery was really an affliction, a terrible and unjust institution that God had allowed in order to test their faith. For having endured slavery, he would reward blacks. For having created it, he would punish masters.

Black Music and Dance

Compared to the prevailing cultural patterns among elite whites, the culture of blacks in the Old South was extremely expressive. In religious services, blacks shouted "Amen" and let their bodily movements reflect their feelings long after white religious observances, some of which had once been similarly expressive, had grown sober and sedate. Frederick Law Olmsted recorded how, during a slave service in New Orleans during the 1850s, parishioners "in indescribable expression of ecstasy" exclaimed every few moments: "Glory! oh yes! yes!—sweet Lord! sweet Lord!"

Slaves also expressed their feelings in music and dance. Drawing on their African musical heritage, which used hand clapping to mark rhythm, American slaves made rhythmical hand clapping—called patting juba—an indispensable accompaniment to dancing because southern law forbade them to own "drums, horns, or other loud instruments, which may call together or give sign or notice to one another of their wicked designs and intentions." Slaves also played an African instrument, the banjo, and beat tin buckets as a substitute for drums. Whatever instrument they played, their music was tied to bodily movement. Sometimes, slaves imitated white dances like the minuet, but in a way that ridiculed the high manners of their masters. More often, they expressed themselves in a dance African in origin, emphasizing shuffling steps and bodily contortions rather than the erect precision of whites' dances.

Whether at work or at prayer, slaves liked to sing. Work songs describing slave experiences usually consisted of a leader's chant and a choral response:

> I love old Virginny
> So ho! boys! so ho!
> I love to shuck corn
> So ho! boys! so ho!
> Now's picking cotton time
> So ho! boys! so ho!

Masters encouraged such songs, believing that singing induced the slaves to work harder and that the innocent content of most work songs proved that the slaves were happy. Recalling his own past, Frederick Douglass came closer to the truth when he observed that "slaves sing most when they are most unhappy. The songs of the slave represent the sorrows of his heart; and he is relieved by them, only as an aching heart is relieved by its tears."

Blacks also sang religious songs, later known as **spirituals.** The origin of spirituals is shrouded in obscurity, but it is clear that by 1820 blacks at camp meetings had improvised what one white described as "short scraps of disjointed affirmations, pledges, or prayers lengthened out with long repetition choruses." As this description suggests, whites usually took a dim view of spirituals and tried to make slaves sing "good psalms and hymns" instead of "the extravagant and nonsensical chants, and catches, and hallelujah songs of their own composing." Spirituals reflected the potent emphasis that the slaves' religion put on deliverance from earthly travails. To a degree, the same was true of white hymns, but spirituals were more direct and concrete. Slaves sang, for example,

> In that morning, true believers,
> In that morning,
> We will sit aside of Jesus
> In that morning,

If you should go fore I go,
In that morning,
You will sit aside of Jesus
In that morning,
True believers, where your tickets
In that morning,
Master Jesus got your tickets
In that morning.

Another spiritual proclaimed, "We will soon be free, when the Lord will call us home."

CONCLUSION

The cotton gin revitalized southern agriculture and spurred a redistribution of the South's population, slave and free, from Virginia and other southeastern states to southwestern states like Alabama and Mississippi. As the Old South became more dependent on cotton, it also became more reliant on slave labor.

Slavery left a deep imprint on social relations among the Old South's major white social groups: the planters, the small slaveholders, the yeomen, and the people of the pine barrens. The presence of slaves fed the exaggerated notions of personal honor that made white southerners so violent. Although there was always potential for conflict between slaveholders and nonslaveholders, slavery gave a distinctive unity to the Old South. Most whites did not own any slaves, but the vast majority concluded that their region's prosperity, their ascendancy over blacks, and perhaps even their safety depended on perpetuating slavery. Slavery also shaped the North's perception of the South. Whether northerners believed that the federal government should tamper with slavery or not, they grew convinced that slavery had cut the South off from progress and had turned it into a region of "sterile lands and bankrupt estates."

In contrast, to most white southerners the North, and especially the industrial Northeast, appeared to be the region that deviated from the march of progress. In their eyes, most Americans—indeed, most people throughout the world—practiced agriculture, and agriculture rendered the South a more comfortable place than factories rendered the North. In reaction to northern assaults on slavery, southerners portrayed the institution as a time-honored and benevolent response to the natural inequality of the black and white races. Southerners pointed to the slaves' adequate nutrition, their embrace of Christianity, the affection of some slaves for their masters, and even their work songs as evidence of their contentment.

These white perceptions of the culture that developed in the slave quarters with the maturing of plantation agriculture were misguided. In reality, few if any slaves accepted slavery. Although slaves rebelled infrequently and had little chance for permanent escape, they often engaged in covert resistance to their bondage. They embraced Christianity, but they understood it differently from whites. Whereas whites heard in the Christian gospel the need to make slaves submissive, slaves learned of the gross injustice of human bondage and the promise of eventual deliverance.

13

Immigration, Expansion, and Sectional Conflict, 1840–1848

NEWCOMERS AND NATIVES

Between 1815 and 1860, 5 million European immigrants landed in the United States. Of these, 4.2 million arrived between 1840 and 1860; 3 million of them came in the single decade from 1845 to 1854. This ten-year period witnessed the largest immigration proportionate to the total population (then around 20 million) in American history. The Irish led the way as the most numerous immigrants between 1840 and 1860, with the Germans running a close second. Smaller contingents continued to immigrate to the United States from England, Scotland, and Wales, and a growing number came from Norway, Sweden, Switzerland, and Holland. But by 1860 three-fourths of the 4.1 million foreign-born Americans were either Irish or German.

Expectations and Realities
A desire for religious freedom drew some immigrants to the United States. Mormon missionaries actively recruited converts in the slums of English factory towns. But a far larger number of Europeans sailed for America to better their economic condition. Travelers' accounts and letters from relatives described America as a utopia for poor people. German peasants learned that they could purchase a large farm in America for the price of renting a small one in Germany. Britons were told that enough good peaches and apples were left rotting in the orchards of Ohio to sink the British fleet.

Hoping for the best, emigrants often encountered the worst. Their problems began at ports of embarkation, where hucksters frequently sold them worthless tickets and where ships scheduled to leave in June might not sail until August. Countless emigrants

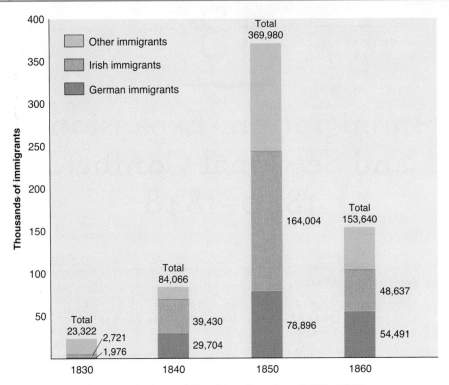

Figure 13.1 German, Irish, and Total Immigration, 1830–1860

Irish and German immigrants led the more than tenfold growth of immigration between 1830 and 1860. *Source:* U.S. Bureau of the Census, *Historical Statistics of the United States, Colonial Times to 1970, Bicentennial Edition* (Washington, D.C., 1975).

spent precious savings in waterfront slums while awaiting departure. The ocean voyage itself proved terrifying; many emigrants had never set foot on a ship. Most sailed on cargo ships as steerage passengers, where, for six weeks or more, they endured quarters almost as crowded as on slave ships.

For many emigrants, the greatest shock came when they landed. "The folks aboard ship formed great plans for their future, all of which vanished quickly after landing," wrote a young German from Frankfurt in 1840. Immigrants quickly discovered that farming in America bore little resemblance to farming in Europe. European farmers' lives revolved around villages that were fringed by the fields that they worked. In contrast, American farmers lived in relative isolation. Farmers on widely scattered plots of land met occasionally at revivals or militia musters. But they lacked the compact village life of European farmers, and they possessed an individualistic psychology that led them to speculate in land and to move frequently.

Clear patterns emerged amid the shocks and dislocations of immigration. Most of the Irish settlers before 1840 departed from Liverpool on sailing ships that carried English manufactures to eastern Canada and New England in return for timber. On arrival in America, few of these Irish had the capital to become farmers, so they crowded into

Chronology, 1840–1848

1822 • Stephen F. Austin founds the first American community in Texas.

1830 • Mexico closes Texas to further American immigration.

1835 • Santa Anna invades Texas.

1836 • Texas declares its independence from Mexico.
Fall of the Alamo.
Goliad massacre.
Battle of San Jacinto.

1840 • William Henry Harrison elected president.

1841 • Harrison dies; John Tyler becomes president.

1842 • Webster-Ashburton Treaty.

1844 • James K. Polk elected president.

1845 • Congress votes joint resolution to annex Texas.
Mexico rejects Slidell mission.

1846 • The United States declares war on Mexico.
John C. Frémont proclaims the Bear Flag Republic in California.
Congress votes to accept a settlement of the Oregon boundary issue
with Britain.
Tariff of 1846.
Colonel Stephen Kearny occupies Santa Fe.
Wilmot Proviso introduced.
Taylor takes Monterrey.

1847 • Taylor defeats Santa Anna at the Battle of Buena Vista.
Vera Cruz falls to Winfield Scott.
Mexico City falls to Scott.
Lewis Cass's principle of "squatter sovereignty."

1848 • Gold discovered in California.
Treaty of Guadalupe Hidalgo.
Taylor elected president.

the urban areas of New England, New York, Pennsylvania, and New Jersey, where they could more easily find jobs. In contrast, German emigrants usually left from continental ports on ships engaged in the cotton trade with New Orleans. Deterred from settling in the South by the presence of slavery, the oppressive climate, and the lack of economic opportunity, the Germans congregated in the upper Mississippi and Ohio valleys, especially in Illinois, Ohio, Wisconsin, and Missouri. Geographical concentration also characterized most of the smaller groups of immigrants. More than half of the Norwegian immigrants, for example, settled in Wisconsin, where they typically became farmers.

Cities, rather than farms, attracted most antebellum immigrants. By 1860, **German and Irish immigrants** formed more than 60 percent of the population of St. Louis;

nearly half the population of New York City, Chicago, Cincinnati, Milwaukee, Detroit, and San Francisco; and well over a third that of New Orleans, Baltimore, and Boston. These fast-growing cities created an intense demand for the labor of people with strong backs and a willingness to work for low wages. Irish construction gangs built the houses, new streets, and aqueducts that were changing the face of urban America and dug the canals and railroads that threaded together the rapidly developing cities. A popular song recounted the fate of the thousands of Irishmen who died of cholera contracted during the building of a canal in New Orleans:

> Ten thousand Micks, they swung their picks,
> To build the New Canal
> But the choleray was stronger 'n they.
> An' twice it killed them awl.

The cities provided the sort of community life that seemed lacking in farming settlements. Immigrant societies like the Friendly Sons of St. Patrick took root in cities and combined with associations like the Hibernian Society for the Relief of Emigrants from Ireland to welcome the newcomers.

The Germans

In the mid-nineteenth century, the Germans were an extremely diverse group. In 1860, Germany was not a unified state but a collection of principalities and small kingdoms. German immigrants thought of themselves as Bavarians, Westphalians, or Saxons rather than as Germans. Moreover, the German immigrants included Catholics, Protestants, and Jews as well as a sprinkling of freethinkers who denounced the ritual, clergy, and doctrines of all religions. Although few in number, these critics were vehement in their attacks on the established churches. A pious Milwaukee Lutheran complained in 1860 that he could not drink a glass of beer in a saloon "without being angered by anti-Christian remarks or raillery against preachers."

German immigrants came from a wide range of social classes and occupations. The majority had engaged in farming, but a sizable minority were professionals, artisans, and tradespeople. Heinrich Steinweg, an obscure piano maker from Lower Saxony, arrived in New York City in 1851, anglicized his name to Henry Steinway, and in 1853 opened the firm of Steinway and Sons, which quickly achieved international acclaim for the quality of its pianos. Levi Strauss, a Jewish tailor from Bavaria, migrated to the United States in 1847. On hearing of the discovery of gold in California in 1848, Strauss gathered rolls of cloth and sailed for San Francisco. When a miner told him of the need for durable work trousers, Strauss fashioned a pair of overalls from canvas. To meet a quickly skyrocketing demand, he opened a factory in San Francisco; his cheap overalls, later known as blue jeans or Levi's, made him rich and famous.

For all their differences, the Germans were bound together by their common language, which strongly induced recent immigrants to the United States to congregate in German neighborhoods. Even prosperous Germans bent on climbing the social ladder usually did so within their ethnic communities. Germans formed their own militia and fire companies, sponsored parochial schools in which German was the language of instruction, started German-language newspapers, and organized their own balls and singing groups. The range of voluntary associations among Germans was almost as broad as among native-born Americans.

Other factors beyond their common language brought unity to the German immigrants. Ironically, the Germans' diversity also promoted their solidarity. For example, because they were able to supply their own doctors, lawyers, teachers, journalists, merchants, artisans, and clergy, the Germans had little need to go outside their own neighborhoods. Moreover, economic self-sufficiency conspired with the strong bonds of their language to encourage a clannish psychology among the German immigrants. Although they admired the Germans' industriousness, native-born Americans resented their economic success and disdained their clannishness. German refugee Moritz Busch complained that "the great mass of Anglo-Americans" held the Germans in contempt. The Germans responded by becoming even more clannish. Their psychological separateness made it difficult for the Germans to be as politically influential as the Irish immigrants.

The Irish Between 1815 and the mid-1820s, most Irish immigrants were Protestants, small landowners and merchants in search of better economic opportunity. Many were drawn by enthusiastic veterans of the War of 1812, who had reported that America was a paradise filled with fertile land and abundant game, a place where "all a man wanted was a gun and sufficient ammunition to be able to live like a prince." Compared to Irish immigrants in the mid-1820s, those in the mid-1840s were poorer and more frequently Catholic, primarily comprising tenant farmers whom Protestant landowners had evicted as "superfluous."

Protestant or Catholic, rich or poor, eight hundred thousand to a million Irish immigrants entered the United States between 1815 and 1844. Then, between 1845 and the early 1850s, a blight destroyed every harvest of Ireland's potatoes, virtually the only food of the peasantry, and created one of the most devastating famines in history. The Great Famine inflicted indescribable suffering on the Irish peasantry and killed perhaps a million people. One landlord characterized the surviving tenants on his estate as no more than "famished and ghastly skeletons." To escape the ravages of famine, 1.8 million Irish migrated to the United States in the decade after 1845.

Overwhelmingly poor and Catholic, these newest Irish immigrants usually entered the work force at or near the bottom. The popular image of Paddy with his pickax and Bridget the maid contained a good deal of truth. Irish men in the cities dug cellars and often lived in them; outside the cities, they dug canals and railroad beds. Irish women often became domestic servants. Compared to other immigrant women, a high proportion of Irish women entered the work force, if not as maids then often as textile workers. By the 1840s, Irish women were displacing native-born women in the textile mills of Lowell and Waltham. Poverty drove Irish women to work at an early age, and the outdoor, all-season work performed by their husbands turned many of them into working widows. Winifred Rooney became a nursemaid at the age of seven and an errand girl at eleven. She then learned needlework, a skill that helped her support her family after her husband's early death. The high proportion of employed Irish women reflected more than simply their poverty. Compared to the predominantly male German immigrants, more than half of the Irish immigrants were women, most of whom were single adults. In both Ireland and America, the Irish usually married late, and many never married. For Irish women to become self-supporting was only natural.

The lot of most Irish people was harsh. One immigrant described the life of the average Irish laborer in America as "despicable, humiliating, [and] slavish"; there was "no love for him—no protection of life—[he] can be shot down, run through, kicked, cuffed, spat upon—and no redress, but a response of 'served the damn son of an Irish b____ right, damn him.'" Yet some Irish struggled up the social ladder. In Philadelphia, which had a more varied industrial base than Boston, Irish men made their way into iron foundries, where some became foremen and supervisors. Other Irish rose into the middle class by opening grocery and liquor stores.

The varied occupations pursued by Irish immigrants brought them into conflict with two quite different groups. The poorer Irish who dug canals and cellars, hauled cargo on the docks, washed laundry for others, and served white families competed directly with equally poor free blacks. This competition stirred up Irish animosity toward blacks and a hatred of abolitionists. At the same time, enough Irish men eventually secured skilled or semiskilled jobs that clashes with native-born white workers became unavoidable.

Anti-Catholicism, Nativism, and Labor Protest   The hostility of native-born whites toward the Irish often took the form of anti-Catholicism, a latent impulse among American Protestants since Puritan days. The surge of Irish immigration during the second quarter of the nineteenth century revived anti-Catholic fever. For example, in 1834 a mob, fueled by rumors that a Catholic convent in Charlestown, Massachusetts, contained dungeons and torture chambers, burned the building to the ground. In 1835, the combative evangelical Protestant Lyman Beecher issued *A Plea for the West*, a tract in which he warned faithful Protestants of an alleged Catholic conspiracy to send immigrants to the West in sufficient numbers to dominate the region. A year later, the publication of Maria Monk's best-selling *Awful Disclosures of the Hotel Dieu Nunnery in Montreal* rekindled anti-Catholic hysteria. Although Maria Monk was actually a prostitute who had never lived in a convent, she professed to be a former nun. In her book, she described how the mother superior forced nuns to submit to the lustful advances of priests who entered the convent by a subterranean passage.

As Catholic immigration swelled in the 1840s, Protestants mounted a political counterattack. It took the form of nativist (anti-immigrant) societies with names like the American Republican party and the United Order of Americans. Although usually started as secret or semisecret fraternal orders, most of these societies developed political offshoots. One, the Order of the Star-Spangled Banner, would evolve by 1854 into the "Know-Nothing," or American, party and would become a major political force in the 1850s.

During the 1840s, however, nativist parties enjoyed only brief moments in the sun. These occurred mainly during flare-ups over local issues, such as whether students in predominantly Catholic neighborhoods should be allowed to use the Catholic Douay rather than Protestant King James version of the Bible for the scriptural readings that began each school day. In 1844, for example, after the American Republican party won some offices in Philadelphia elections, fiery Protestant orators mounted soapboxes to denounce "popery," and Protestant mobs descended on Catholic neighborhoods. Before the militia quelled these "Bible Riots," thirty buildings lay in charred ruins, and at least sixteen people had been killed.

Nativism fed on an explosive mixture of fears and discontents. Protestants thought that their doctrine that each individual could interpret the Bible was more democratic than Catholicism, which made doctrine the province of the pope and bishops. In addition, at a time when the wages of native-born artisans and journeymen were depressed by the subdivision of tasks and by the aftermath of the Panic of 1837 (see Chapter 10), many Protestant workers concluded that Catholic immigrants, often desperately poor and willing to work for anything, were threats to their jobs.

Demand for land reform joined nativism as a proposed solution to workers' economic woes. Land reformers argued that workers' true interests could never be reconciled with an economic order in which factory workers sold their labor for wages and became "wage slaves." In 1844, the English-born radical George Henry Evans organized the National Reform Association and rallied supporters with the slogan "Vote Yourself a Farm." Evans advanced neo-Jeffersonian plans for the establishment of "rural republican townships" composed of 160-acre plots for workers. Land reform had some appeal to articulate and self-consciously radical workers, particularly artisans and small masters whose independence was being threatened by factories and who feared that American labor was "fast verging on the servile dependence" common in Europe. But the doctrine offered little to factory operatives and wage-earning journeymen who completely lacked economic independence. In an age when a horse cost the average worker three months' pay and most factory workers dreaded "the horrors of wilderness life," the idea of solving industrial problems by resettling workers on farms seemed a pipe dream.

Labor unions appealed to workers left cold by the promises of land reformers. For example, desperately poor Irish immigrants, refugees from an agricultural society, believed that they could gain more by unions and strikes than by plowing and planting. Even women workers organized unions in these years. The leader of a seamstresses' union proclaimed, "Too long have we been bound down by tyrant employers."

Probably the most important development for workers in the 1840s was a state court decision. In **Commonwealth v. Hunt** (1842), the Massachusetts Supreme Judicial Court ruled that labor unions were not illegal monopolies that restrained trade. But because less than 1 percent of the work force belonged to labor unions in the 1840s, this decision initially had little impact. Massachusetts employers brushed aside the *Commonwealth* decision, firing union agitators and replacing them with cheap immigrant labor. "Hundreds of honest laborers," a labor paper reported in 1848, "have been dismissed from employment in the manufactories of New England because they have been suspected of knowing their rights and daring to assert them." This repression effectively blunted demands for a ten-hour workday in an era when the twelve- or fourteen-hour day was typical.

Ethnic and religious tensions also split the working class during the 1830s and 1840s. Friction between native-born and immigrant workers inevitably became intertwined with the political divisions of the second party system.

Immigrant Politics   Few immigrants had ever cast a vote in an election prior to their arrival in America, and only a small fraction were refugees from political persecution. Political upheavals had erupted in Austria and several of the German states in the turbulent year of 1848 (the so-called Revolutions of 1848), but among the million German immigrants to the United States, only about ten thousand were political refugees, or "Forty-Eighters."

Once they had settled in the United States, however, many immigrants became politically active. They quickly found that urban political organizations, some of them dominated by earlier immigrants, would help them find lodging and employment, in return for votes. Both the Irish and the Germans identified overwhelmingly with the Democratic Party. An obituary of 1837 that described a New Yorker as a "warm-hearted Irishman and an unflinching Democrat" could have been written of millions of other Irish. Similarly, the Germans became stalwart supporters of the Democrats in cities like Milwaukee and St. Louis.

Immigrants' fears about jobs partly explain their widespread support of the Democrats. Former president Andrew Jackson had given the Democratic Party an anti-aristocratic coloration, making the Democrats seem more sympathetic than the Whigs to the common people. In addition, antislavery was linked to the Whig party, and the Irish loathed abolitionism because they feared that freed slaves would become their economic competitors. Moreover, the Whigs' moral and religious values seemed to threaten those of the Irish and Germans. Hearty-drinking Irish and German immigrants shunned temperance-crusading Whigs, many of whom were also rabid anti-Catholics. Even public-school reform, championed by the Whigs, was seen as a menace to the Catholicism of Irish children and as a threat to German language and culture.

Although liquor regulations and school laws were city or state concerns rather than federal responsibilities, the Democratic Party schooled immigrants in broad, national principles. It taught them to venerate George Washington, to revere Thomas Jefferson and Andrew Jackson, and to view "monied capitalists" as parasites who would tremble when the people spoke. It introduced immigrants to Democratic newspapers, Democratic picnics, and Democratic parades. The Democrats, by identifying their party with all that they thought best about the United States, helped give immigrants a sense of themselves as Americans. By the same token, the Democratic Party introduced immigrants to national issues. It redirected political loyalties that often had been forged on local issues into the arena of national politics. During the 1830s, the party had persuaded immigrants that national measures like the Bank of the United States and the tariff, seemingly remote from their daily lives, were vital to them. Now, in the 1840s, the Democrats would try to convince immigrants that national expansion likewise advanced their interests.

THE WEST AND BEYOND

As late as 1840, Americans who referred to the West still meant the area between the Appalachian Mountains and the Mississippi River or just beyond. West of that lay the inhospitable Great Plains, a semiarid plateau with few trees. Winds sucked the moisture from the soil. Bands of nomadic Indians—including the Pawnees, Kiowas, and Sioux—roamed this territory and gained sustenance mainly from the buffalo. They ate its meat, wore its fur, and covered their dwellings with its hide. Aside from some well-watered sections of northern Missouri and eastern Kansas and Nebraska, the Great Plains presented would-be farmers with massive obstacles.

The formidable barrier of the Great Plains did not stop settlement of the West in the long run. Temporarily, however, it shifted public interest toward the verdant region lying beyond the Rockies, the Far West.

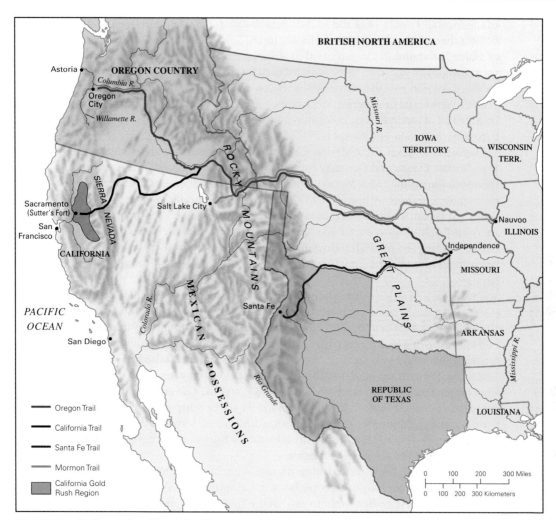

MAP 13.1 **Trails to the West, 1840**

By 1840 several trails carried pioneers from Missouri and Illinois to the West.

The Far West   By the Transcontinental (or Adams-Onís) Treaty of 1819, the United States had given up its claims to Texas west of the Sabine River. This had left Spain in undisputed possession not only of Texas but also of California and the vast territory of New Mexico. Combined, California and New Mexico included all of present-day California and New Mexico as well as modern Nevada, Utah, and Arizona, and parts of Wyoming and Colorado. Two years later, Mexico won its independence from Spain and took over all North American territory previously claimed by Spain.

The Adams-Onís Treaty also had provided for Spain to cede to the United States its claims to the **Oregon country** north of the forty-second parallel (the northern boundary of California). Then in 1824 and 1825, Russia abandoned its claims to Oregon south of 54°40′ (the southern boundary of Alaska). In 1827, the United States and Britain, each of which had claims to Oregon based on discovery and exploration, revived an agreement (originally signed in 1818) for joint occupation of the territory between 42° and 54°40′, a colossal area that contemporaries could describe no more precisely than the "North West Coast of America, Westward of the Stony [Rocky] Mountains" and that included all of modern Oregon, Washington, and Idaho as well as parts of present-day Wyoming, Montana, and Canada.

Collectively, Texas, New Mexico, California, and Oregon comprised an area larger than Britain, France, and Germany combined. Such a vast region should have tempted them, but during the 1820s Mexico, Britain, and the United States viewed the Far West as a remote and shadowy frontier. By 1820, the American line of settlement had reached only to Missouri, well over two thousand miles (counting detours for mountains) from the West Coast. El Paso on the Rio Grande and Taos in New Mexico lay, respectively, twelve hundred and fifteen hundred miles north of Mexico City. Britain, of course, was many thousands of miles from Oregon.

Far Western Trade   After sailing around South America and up the Pacific, early merchants had established American and British outposts on the West Coast. Between the late 1790s and the 1820s, for example, Boston merchants had built a thriving exchange of coffee, tea, spices, cutlery, clothes, and hardware—indeed, anything that could be bought or manufactured in the eastern United States—for furs (especially those of sea otters), cattle, hides, and tallow (rendered from cattle fat and used for making soap and candles). Between 1826 and 1828 alone, Boston traders took more than 6 million cattle hides out of California; in the otherwise undeveloped California economy, these hides, called "California bank-notes," served as the main medium of exchange. During the 1820s, the British Hudson's Bay Company developed a similar trade in Oregon and northern California.

The California trade created little friction with Mexico. Producing virtually no manufactured goods, Hispanic people born in California (called *Californios*) were as eager to buy as the traders were to sell. Many traders who did settle in California quickly learned to speak Spanish and became assimilated into Mexican culture.

Farther south, trading links developed during the 1820s between St. Louis and Santa Fe along the famed **Santa Fe Trail.** The Panic of 1819 left the American Midwest short of cash and its merchants burdened by unsold goods. Pulling themselves up from adversity, however, plucky midwesterners loaded wagon trains with tools, clothing, and household sundries each spring and rumbled westward to Santa Fe, where they traded their merchandise for mules and New Mexican silver. Mexico welcomed this trade. By the 1830s, more than half the goods entering New Mexico by the Santa Fe Trail trickled into the mineral-rich interior provinces of Mexico such as Chihuahua and Sonora, with the result that the Mexican silver peso, which midwestern traders brought back with them, quickly became the principal medium of exchange in Missouri.

The profitability of the beaver trade also prompted Americans to venture west from St. Louis to trap beaver in what is today western Colorado and eastern Utah. There they competed with agents of the Hudson's Bay Company. In 1825, on the Green River in Mexican territory, the St. Louis–based trader William Ashley inaugurated an annual encampment where traders exchanged beaver pelts for supplies, thereby saving themselves the trip to St. Louis. Although silk hats had become more fashionable than beaver hats by 1854, over a half-million beaver pelts were auctioned off in London alone that year.

For the most part, American traders and trappers operating on the northern Mexican frontier in the 1820s and 1830s posed more of a threat to the beaver than to Mexico's provinces. The Mexican people of California and New Mexico depended on the American trade for manufactured goods, and Mexican officials in both provinces relied on customs duties to support their governments. In New Mexico, the government often had to await the arrival of the annual caravan of traders from St. Louis before it could pay its officials and soldiers.

Although the relations between Mexicans and Americans were mutually beneficial during the 1820s, the potential for conflict was always present. Spanish-speaking, Roman Catholic, and accustomed to a more hierarchical society, the Mexicans formed a striking contrast to the largely Protestant, individualistic Americans. And although few American traders themselves became permanent residents of Mexico, many returned with glowing reports of the climate and fertility of Mexico's northern provinces. By the 1820s, American settlers were already moving into eastern Texas. At the same time, the ties that bound the central government of Mexico to its northern frontier provinces were starting to fray.

| The American
Settlement of
Texas to 1835 | During the 1820s, Americans began to settle the eastern part of the Mexican state known as Coahuila-Texas, which lacked the deserts and mountains that formed a natural barrier along the boundaries of New Mexico and California. Initially, Mex- |

ico encouraged this migration, partly to gain protection against Indian attacks that had intensified with the erosion of the Spanish-Mexican system of missions.

Spain, and later Mexico, recognized that the key to controlling the frontier provinces lay in promoting their settlement by civilized Hispanic people—Spaniards, Mexicans, and Indians who had embraced Catholicism and agriculture. The key instruments of Spain's expansion on the frontier had long been the Spanish missions. Paid by the government, the Franciscan priests who staffed the missions endeavored to convert Native Americans and settle them as farmers on mission lands. To protect the missions, the Spanish often had constructed forts, or presidios, near them. San Francisco was the site of a mission and a presidio founded in 1776, and did not develop as a town until the 1830s.

Dealt a blow by the successful struggle for Mexican independence, Spain's system of missions began to decline in the late 1820s. The Mexican government gradually "secularized" the missions by distributing their lands to ambitious government officials and private ranchers who turned the mission Indians into forced laborers. As many Native Americans fled the missions, returned to their nomadic ways, and joined with Indians who had always resisted the missions, lawlessness surged on the Mexican frontier, and few Mexicans ventured into the undeveloped territory.

In 1824, the Mexican government began to encourage American colonization of Texas by bestowing generous land grants on agents known as *empresarios* to recruit peaceful American settlers for Texas. Initially, most Americans, like the *empresario* Stephen F. Austin, were content to live in Texas as naturalized Mexican citizens. But trouble brewed quickly. Most of the American settlers were southern farmers, often

***Entirro de un Angel* (Funeral of an Angel), by Theodore Gentilz** *Protestant Americans who ventured into Texas came upon a Hispanic culture unlike anything they had seen. Here a San Antonio procession follows the coffin of a baptized infant who, in Catholic belief, will become an angel in heaven.*

slaveholders. Having emancipated its own slaves in 1829, Mexico closed Texas to further American immigration in 1830 and forbade the introduction of more slaves. But the Americans, white and black, kept coming, and in 1834 Austin secured repeal of the 1830 prohibition on American immigration. Two years later, Mexican general Manuel Mier y Téran ran a sword through his heart in despair over Mexico's inability to stem and control the American advance. By 1836, Texas contained some thirty thousand white Americans, five thousand black slaves, and four thousand Mexicans.

As American immigration swelled, Mexican politics (which Austin compared to the country's volcanic geology) grew increasingly unstable. In 1834, Mexican president Antonio López de Santa Anna instituted a policy of restricting the powers of the regimes in Coahuila-Texas and other Mexican states. His actions ignited a series of rebellions in those regions, the most important of which became known as the Texas Revolution.

The Texas Revolution, 1836 Santa Anna's brutality in crushing most of the rebellions alarmed Austin, who initially had hoped to secure greater autonomy for Texas within Mexico, not independence. When Santa Anna invaded Texas in the fall of 1835, however, Austin cast his lot with the more radical Americans who wanted independence.

At first, Santa Anna's army met with success. In late February 1836, his force of 4,000 men laid siege to San Antonio, whose 200 defenders retreated into an abandoned mission, the **Alamo.** After repelling repeated attacks, the remaining 187 Texans were overwhelmed on March 6. Most were killed in the final assault. A few, including the famed frontiersman Davy Crockett, surrendered. Crockett then was executed on Santa Anna's orders. A few weeks later, Mexican troops massacred some 350 prisoners taken from an American settlement at Goliad.

Even before these events, Texas delegates had met in a windswept shed in the village of Washington, Texas, and declared the Republic of Texas independent of Mexico. The rebels by then had settled on a military leader, **Sam Houston,** for their president. A giant man who wore leopard-skin vests, Houston retreated east to pick up recruits (mostly Americans who crossed the border to fight Santa Anna). Once reinforced, Houston turned and surprised Santa Anna on a prairie near the San Jacinto River in April. Shouting "Remember the Alamo," Houston's army of eight hundred tore through the Mexican lines, killing nearly half of Santa Anna's men in fifteen minutes and taking Santa Anna himself prisoner. Houston then forced Santa Anna to sign a treaty (which the Mexican government never ratified) recognizing the independence of Texas.

American
Settlements in
California,
New Mexico,
and Oregon

California and New Mexico, both less accessible than Texas, exerted no more than a mild attraction for American settlers during the 1820s and 1830s. Only a few hundred Americans resided in New Mexico in 1840 and perhaps four hundred in California. A contemporary observed that the Americans living in California and New Mexico "are scattered throughout the whole Mexican population, and most of them have Spanish wives. . . . They live in every respect like the Spanish."

Yet the beginnings of change were already evident. During the 1840s, Americans streamed into the Sacramento Valley, welcomed by California's Hispanic population as a way to encourage economic development and lured by favorable reports of the region. One tongue-in-cheek story told of a 250-year-old man who had to leave the idyllic region in order to die. For these land-hungry settlers, no sacrifice seemed too great if it led to California.

To the north, the Oregon country's abundant farmland beckoned settlers from the Mississippi valley. During the 1830s, missionaries like the Methodist Jason Lee moved into Oregon's Willamette valley, and by 1840 the area contained some five hundred Americans. Enthusiastic reports sent back by Lee piqued interest about Oregon. An orator in Missouri described Oregon as a "pioneer's paradise" where "the pigs are running around under the great acorn trees, round and fat and already cooked, with knives and forks sticking in them so that you can cut off a slice whenever you are hungry." To some, Oregon seemed even more attractive than California. Oregon was already jointly occupied by Britain and the United States, and its prospects for eventual U.S. annexation appeared better than California's.

The Overland Trails Whether bound for California or Oregon, the pioneers faced a four-month journey across terrain little known in reality but vividly depicted in fiction as an Indian killing ground. Assuming that they would have to fight their way across the Plains, settlers prepared for the trip by buying enough guns for an army from merchants in the rival jump-off towns of Independence and St. Joseph, Missouri. In reality, the pioneers were more likely to shoot themselves or each other by accident than to be shot by the usually cooperative Indians, and much more likely to be scalped by the inflated prices charged by merchants in Independence or "St. Joe."

Once embarked, the emigrants faced new hardships and hazards: kicks from mules, oxen that collapsed from thirst, overloaded wagons that broke down. Trails were difficult to follow—at least until they became littered by the debris of broken wagons and by the bleached bones of oxen. Guidebooks to help emigrants chart their course were more like guessbooks. The Donner party, which set out from Illinois in 1846, lost so much time following the advice of one such book that its members became snowbound in the High Sierras and reached California only after its survivors had turned to cannibalism.

Emigrants responded to the challenges of the overland trails by cooperating closely with one another. Most set out in huge wagon trains rather than as individuals. Reflecting firmly entrenched traditions, husbands depended on their wives to pack and unpack the wagon each day, to milk the cows brought along to stock the new farms in the West, to cook, and to assist with the childbirths that occurred on the trail at about the same frequency as in the nation as a whole. Men yoked and unyoked the oxen, drove the wagons and stock, and formed hunting parties.

Between 1840 and 1848, an estimated 11,500 emigrants followed an overland trail to Oregon, and some 2,700 reached California. These numbers were modest and concentrated in the years from 1844 to 1848. Yet even small numbers could make a huge difference in the Far West, for the British could not effectively settle Oregon at all, and the Mexican population in California was small and scattered. By 1845, California clung to Mexico by the thinnest of threads. The territory's Hispanic population, the *Californios,* felt little allegiance to Mexico, which they contemptuously referred to as the "other shore." Nor did they feel any allegiance to the United States. Some *Californios* wanted independence from Mexico; others looked to the day when California might become a protectorate of Britain or perhaps even France. But these *Californios,* with their shaky allegiances, now faced a growing number of American settlers with definite political allegiances.

THE POLITICS OF EXPANSION, 1840–1846

The major issue that arose as a byproduct of westward expansion was whether the United States should annex the independent Texas republic. In the mid-1840s, the Texas-annexation issue generated the kind of political passions that banking questions had ignited in the 1830s, and became entangled with equally unsettling issues relating to California, New Mexico, and Oregon. Between 1846 and 1848, a war with Mexico and a dramatic confrontation with Britain settled all these questions on terms favorable to the United States.

Yet at the start of the 1840s, western issues occupied no more than a tenuous position on the national political agenda. From 1840 to 1842, questions relating to economic recovery—notably, banking, the tariff, and internal improvements—dominated the attention of political leaders. Only after politicians failed to address the economic issues coherently did opportunistic leaders thrust issues relating to expansion to the top of the political agenda.

The Whig Ascendancy

The election of 1840 brought Whig candidate William Henry Harrison to the presidency and installed Whig majorities in both houses of Congress. The Whigs had raced to power with a program, based on Henry Clay's American System, to stimulate economic recovery, and they had excellent prospects of success. They quickly repealed Van Buren's darling, the Independent Treasury (see Chapter 10). They then planned to establish a national "fiscal agent," which, like the defunct Bank of the United States, would be a private corporation chartered by Congress and charged with regulating the currency. The Whigs also favored a revised tariff that would increase government revenues but remain low enough to permit the importation of foreign goods. According to the Whig plan, the states would then receive tariff-generated revenues for internal improvements, a measure as popular among southern and western Whigs as the tariff was among northeastern Whigs.

The Whig agenda might have breezed into law had it not been for the untimely death of Harrison after only one month in office. With Harrison's demise, Vice President **John Tyler,** an upper-crust Virginian who had been put on the ticket in 1840 to strengthen the Whigs' appeal in the South, assumed the presidency. From virtually every angle, the new president proved a disaster for the Whigs.

A former Democrat, Tyler had broken with Jackson over nullification, but he continued to favor the Democratic philosophy of states' rights. As president, he repeatedly used the veto to shred his new party's program. In August 1841, a Whig bill to create a new national bank fell victim to Tyler's veto, as did a subsequent modification.

Tyler also played havoc with Whig tariff policy. The Compromise Tariff of 1833 had provided for a gradual scaling down of tariff duties, until none was to exceed 20 percent by 1842. Amid the depression of the early 1840s, however, the provision for a 20 percent maximum tariff appeared too low to generate revenue. Without revenue, the Whigs would have no money to distribute among the states for internal improvements and no program with national appeal. In response, the Whig congressional majority passed two bills in the summer of 1842 that simultaneously postponed the final reduction of tariffs to 20 percent and ordered distribution to the states to proceed. Tyler promptly vetoed both bills. Tyler's mounting vetoes infuriated Whig leadership. "Again has the imbecile, into whose hands accident has placed the power, vetoed a bill passed by a majority of those legally authorized to pass it," screamed the *Daily Richmond Whig*. Some Whigs talked of impeaching Tyler. Finally, in August, needing revenue to run the government, Tyler signed a new bill that maintained some tariffs above 20 percent but abandoned distribution to the states.

Tyler's erratic course confounded and disrupted his party. By maintaining some tariffs above 20 percent, the tariff of 1842 satisfied northern manufacturers, but by abandoning distribution, it infuriated many southerners and westerners. Northern Whigs succeeded in passing the bill with the aid of many northern Democrats, particularly protariff Pennsylvanians, whereas large numbers of Whigs in the Upper South and West opposed the tariff of 1842.

In the congressional elections of 1842, the Whigs paid a heavy price for failing to enact their program. Although retaining a slim majority in the Senate, they lost control of the House to the Democrats. Now the nation had one party in control of the Senate, its rival in control of the House, and a president who appeared to belong to neither party.

Tyler and the Annexation of Texas

Although a political maverick disowned by his party, Tyler ardently desired a second term as president. Domestic issues offered him little hope of building a popular following, but foreign policy was another matter. In 1842, Tyler's secretary of state, Daniel Webster, concluded a treaty with Great Britain, represented by Lord Ashburton, that settled a long-festering dispute over the boundary between Maine and the Canadian province of New Brunswick. Awarding more than half of the disputed territory to the United States, the Webster-Ashburton Treaty was popular in the North. Tyler reasoned that if he could now arrange for the **annexation of Texas,** he would build a national following.

The issue of slavery, however, had long clouded every discussion of Texas. By the late 1830s, antislavery northerners viewed proposals to annex Texas as part of an elaborate southern conspiracy to extend American territory south into Mexico, Cuba, and Central America, thus allowing for an unlimited number of new slave states, while the British presence in Canada would limit the number of free states. In fact, some southerners talked openly of creating as many as four or five slave states out of the vast territory encompassed by Texas.

Nevertheless, in the summer of 1843, Tyler launched a propaganda campaign for Texas annexation. He justified his crusade by reporting that he had learned of certain British designs on Texas, which Americans, he argued, would be prudent to forestall. Tyler's campaign was fed by reports from his unofficial agent in London, Duff Green, a protégé of John C. Calhoun and a man whom John Quincy Adams contemptuously dismissed as an "ambassador of slavery." Green assured Tyler that, as a prelude to undermining slavery in the United States, the British would pressure Mexico to recognize the independence of Texas in return for the abolition of slavery there. Calhoun, who became Tyler's secretary of state early in 1844, embroidered these reports with fanciful theories about British plans to use abolition as a way to destroy rice, sugar, and cotton production in the United States and gain for itself a monopoly on all three staples.

In the spring of 1844, Calhoun and Tyler submitted to the Senate for ratification a treaty, secretly drawn up, annexing Texas to the United States. Among the supporting documents accompanying the treaty was a letter from Calhoun to Richard Pakenham, the British foreign minister in Washington, that defended slavery as beneficial to blacks, the only way to protect them from "vice and pauperism." Antislavery northerners now had evidence that the annexation of Texas was linked to a conspiracy to extend slavery. Both Martin Van Buren, the leading northern Democrat, and Henry Clay, the most powerful Whig, came out against immediate annexation on the grounds that annexation would provoke the kind of sectional conflict that each had sought to bury, and the treaty went down to crushing defeat in the Senate. Decisive as it appeared, however, this vote only postponed the final decision on annexation to the upcoming election of 1844.

The Election of 1844

Tyler's ineptitude turned the presidential campaign into a free-for-all. The president lacked a base in either party, and after testing the waters as an independent, he was forced to drop out of the race.

Henry Clay had a secure grip on the Whig nomination. Martin Van Buren appeared to have an equally firm grasp on the Democratic nomination, but the issue of Texas annexation split his party. Trying to appease all shades of opinion within his party, Van Buren stated that he would abide by whatever Congress might decide on the annexation issue. Van Buren's attempt to evade the issue succeeded only in alienating the modest number of northern annexationists, led by Michigan's former governor Lewis Cass, and the much larger group of southern annexationists. At the Democratic convention, Van Buren and Cass effectively blocked each other's nomination. The resulting deadlock was broken by the nomination of **James K. Polk** of Tennessee, the first "dark-horse" presidential nominee in American history and a supporter of immediate annexation.

Jeering "Who is James K. Polk?" the Whigs derided the nomination. Polk was little known outside the South, and he had lost successive elections for the governorship of Tennessee. Yet Polk was a wily campaigner, and he persuaded many northerners that annexation of Texas would benefit them. Conjuring an imaginative scenario, Polk and his supporters argued that if Britain succeeded in abolishing slavery in Texas, slavery would not be able to move westward; racial tensions in existing slave states would intensify; and the chances of a race war, which might spill over into the North, would increase. However far-fetched, this argument played effectively on northern racial phobias and helped Polk detach annexation from Calhoun's narrow, prosouthern defense of it.

In contrast to the Democrats, whose position was clear, Clay kept muddying the waters. First he told his followers that he had nothing against annexation as long as it would not disrupt sectional harmony. In September 1844, he came out against annexation. Clay's shifts on annexation alienated his southern supporters and prompted a small but influential body of northern antislavery Whigs to desert to the Liberty party, which had been organized in 1840. Devoted to the abolition of slavery by political action, the Liberty party nominated Ohio's James G. Birney for the presidency.

Annexation was not the sole issue of the campaign. The Whigs infuriated Catholic immigrant voters by nominating Theodore Frelinghuysen as Clay's running mate. A leading Presbyterian layman, Frelinghuysen gave "his head, his hand, and his heart" to temperance and other Protestant causes. His presence on their ticket fixed the image of the Whigs as the orthodox Protestant party and roused the largely Catholic foreign-born voters to turn out in large numbers for the Democrats.

On the eve of the election in New York City, so many Irish marched to the courthouse to be qualified for voting that the windows had to be left open for people to get in and out. "Ireland has reconquered the country which England lost," an embittered Whig moaned. Polk won the electoral vote 170 to 105, but his margin in the popular vote was only 38,000 out of 2.6 million votes cast, and he lost his own state of Tennessee by 113 votes. In most states the two main parties contended with each other on close terms, a sign of the maturity of the second party system. A shift of 6,000 votes in New York, where the immigrant vote and Whig defections to the Liberty party hurt Clay, would have given Clay both the state and the presidency.

Manifest Destiny, 1845   The election of 1844 demonstrated one incontestable fact: the annexation of Texas had more national support than Clay had realized. The surging popular sentiment for expansion that made the underdog Polk rather than Clay the man of the hour reflected a growing conviction among the people that America's natural destiny was to expand into Texas and all the way to the Pacific Ocean.

Expansionists emphasized extending the "area of freedom" and talked of "repelling the contaminating proximity of monarchies upon the soil that we have consecrated to the rights of man." For contemporary young Americans like Walt Whitman, such restless expansionism knew few limits. "The more we reflect upon annexation as involving a part of Mexico, the more do doubts and obstacles resolve themselves away," Whitman wrote. "Then there is California, on the way to which lovely tract lies Santa Fe; how long a time will elapse before they shine as two new stars in our mighty firmament?"

Americans awaited only a phrase to capture this ebullient spirit. In 1845, John L. O'Sullivan, a New York Democratic journalist, supplied that phrase when he wrote of "our **manifest destiny** to overspread and to possess the whole of the continent which Providence has given us for the development of the great experiment of liberty and federated self-government entrusted to us."

Advocates of Manifest Destiny used lofty language and invoked God and Nature to sanction expansion. Inasmuch as most proponents of Manifest Destiny were Democrats who favored annexing Texas, northern Whigs frequently dismissed Manifest Destiny as a smoke screen aimed at concealing the evil intent of expanding slavery. In reality, many expansionists were neither supporters of slavery nor zealous annexationists. Most had their eyes not on Texas but on Oregon and California. Despite their flowery phrases, these expansionists rested their case on hard material calculations. Most blamed the post-1837 depression on the failure of the United States to acquire markets for its agricultural surplus and saw the acquisition of Oregon and California as solutions. A Missouri Democrat observed that "the ports of Asia are as convenient to Oregon as the ports of Europe are to the eastern slope of our confederacy, with an infinitely better ocean for navigation." An Alabama Democrat praised California's "safe and capacious harbors," which, he assured, "invite to their bosoms the rich commerce of the East."

Expansionists desired more than profitable trade routes, however. At the heart of their thinking lay an impulse to preserve the predominantly agricultural character of the American people and thereby to safeguard democracy. Fundamentally, most expansionists were Jeffersonians. They equated urbanization and industrialization with social stratification and class strife. After a tour of New England mill towns in 1842, John L. O'Sullivan warned Americans that should they fail to encourage alternatives to factories, the United States would sink to the level of Britain, a nation that the ardent Democratic expansionist James Gordon Bennett described as a land of "bloated wealth" and "terrible misery."

Most Democratic expansionists came to see the acquisition of new territory as a logical complement to their party's policies of low tariffs and decentralized banking. Where tariffs and banks tended to "favor and foster the factory system," expansion would provide farmers with land and with access to foreign markets for their produce. As a consequence, Americans would continue to become farmers, and the foundations of the Republic would remain secure. The acquisition of California and Oregon would provide enough land and harbors to sustain not only the 20 million Americans of 1845 but the 100 million that some expansionists projected for 1900 and the 250 million that O'Sullivan predicted for 1945.

The expansionists' message, especially as delivered by the penny press, made sense to the laboring poor of America's antebellum cities. The *New York Herald*, the nation's largest-selling newspaper in the 1840s, played on the anxieties of its working-class readers by arguing relentlessly for the expulsion of the British from Oregon and for thwarting alleged British plans to abolish slavery in the United States. These readers, many of them fiercely antiblack, anti-British Irish immigrants, welcomed any efforts to open up economic opportunities for the common people. Most also favored the perpetuation of slavery, for the freeing of slaves would throw masses of blacks into the already intense competition for jobs.

The expansionists with whom these laboring-class readers sided drew ideas from Thomas Jefferson, John Quincy Adams, and other leaders of the early Republic who had proclaimed the American people's right to displace both "uncivilized" and European people from the path of their westward movement. Early expansionists, however, had feared that overexpansion might create an ungovernable empire. Jefferson, for example, had proposed an indefinite restriction on the settlement of Louisiana. In contrast, the expansionists of the 1840s, citing the virtues of the telegraph and the railroad, believed that the problem of distance had been "literally annihilated."

Polk and Oregon

The Oregon boundary dispute with Britain grew out of the rising spirit of Manifest Destiny. To soften northern criticism of the still-pending annexation of Texas, the Democrats had included in their 1844 platform the assertion that American title "to the whole of the Territory of Oregon is clear and unquestionable." Taken literally, the platform committed the party to acquire the entire area between California and 54°40′, the southern boundary of Alaska. Since Polk had not yet been elected, the British could safely ignore this extraordinary claim for the moment, and in fact the Oregon issue had aroused far less interest during the campaign than had the annexation of Texas. But in his inaugural address, Polk reasserted the "clear and unquestionable" claim to the "country of Oregon." If by this Polk meant all of Oregon, then the United States, which had never before claimed any part of Oregon north of the forty-ninth parallel, had executed an astounding and belligerent reversal of policy.

Polk's objectives in Oregon were more subtle than his language. He knew that the United States could never obtain all of Oregon without a war with Britain, and he wanted to avoid that. He proposed to use the threat of hostilities to persuade the British to accept what they had repeatedly rejected in the past—a division of Oregon at the forty-ninth parallel. Such a division, extending the existing boundary between the United States and Canada from the Rockies to the Pacific, would give the United States both the excellent deep-water harbors of Puget Sound and the southern tip of British-controlled Vancouver Island. For their part, the British had long held out for a division along the Columbia River, which entered the Pacific Ocean far south of the forty-ninth parallel.

Polk's comments in his inaugural speech roused among westerners a furious interest in acquiring the whole territory. Mass meetings adopted such resolutions as "We are all for Oregon, and *all* Oregon in the West" and "The Whole or None!" Furthermore, each passing year brought new American settlers into Oregon. Even John Quincy Adams, who advocated neither the annexation of Texas nor the 54°40′ boundary for Oregon, believed that the American settlements in Oregon gave the United States a far more reasonable claim to the territory than mere exploration and discovery gave the British. The United States, not Britain, Adams preached, was the nation bound "to make the wilderness blossom as the rose, to establish laws, to increase, multiply, and subdue the earth," all "at the first behest of God Almighty."

In April 1846, Polk secured from Congress the termination of joint British-American occupation of Oregon and promptly gave Britain the required one-year's notice. With joint occupation abrogated, the British could either go to war over American claims to 54°40′ or negotiate. They chose to negotiate. Although the British raged against "that ill-regulated, overbearing, and aggressive spirit of American democracy," they had too many domestic and foreign problems to welcome a war over what Lord Aberdeen, the British foreign secretary, dismissed as "a few miles of pine swamp." The ensuing treaty provided for a division at the forty-ninth parallel, with some modifications. Britain retained all of Vancouver Island as well as navigation rights on the Columbia River. On June 15, 1846, the Senate ratified the treaty, stipulating that Britain's navigation rights on the Columbia were merely temporary.

THE MEXICAN-AMERICAN WAR AND ITS AFTERMATH, 1846–1848

Between 1846 and 1848 the United States successfully fought a war with Mexico that led Mexico to renounce all claims to Texas and to cede its provinces of New Mexico and California to the United States. Many Americans rejoiced in the stunning victory. But some recognized that deep divisions over the status of slavery in New Mexico and California boded ill for their nation's future.

The Origins of the Mexican-American War
Even as Polk was challenging Britain over Oregon, the United States and Mexico moved steadily toward war. The impending conflict had both remote and immediate causes. One long-standing grievance lay in the failure of the Mexican government to pay some $2 million in debts owed to American citizens. In addition, bitter memories of the Alamo and the Goliad massacre reinforced American loathing of Mexico. Above all, the issue of Texas embroiled relations between the two nations. Mexico still hoped to regain Texas or at least to keep it independent of the United States.

Behind Mexican anxieties about Texas lay a deeper fear. Mexicans viewed the United States with a mixture of awe and aversion. The United States's political stability contrasted with political chaos in Mexico, where the presidency changed hands twenty times between 1829 and 1844. But Mexicans also saw this "Colossus of the North" as extremely aggressive, prone to trample on anyone in its path and to disguise its intentions with high-sounding phrases like Manifest Destiny. Once in control of Texas, the Mexicans feared, the United States might seize other provinces, perhaps even Mexico itself, and treat the citizens of Mexico much as it treated its slaves.

Unfortunately for Mexico, Polk's election increased the strength of the pro-annexationists, for his campaign had persuaded many northerners that enfolding Texas would bring national benefits. In February 1845, both houses of Congress responded to popular sentiment by passing a resolution annexing Texas. Texans, however, balked, in part because some feared that union with the United States would provoke a Mexican invasion and war on Texas soil.

Confronted by Texan timidity and Mexican belligerence, Polk moved on two fronts. To sweeten the pot for the Texans, he supported their claim to the Rio Grande as the southern boundary of Texas. This claim ran counter to Mexico's view that the Nueces River, a hundred miles northeast of the Rio Grande, bounded Texas. The area between the Nueces and the Rio Grande was largely uninhabited, but the stakes were high. Although only a hundred miles southwest of the Nueces at its mouth on the Gulf of Mexico, the Rio Grande meandered west and then north for nearly two thousand miles and encircled a huge slice of territory, including part of New Mexico. The Texas that Polk proposed to annex thus encompassed far more land than the Texas that had gained independence from Mexico in 1836. On July 4, 1845, reassured by Polk's largesse, a Texas convention overwhelmingly voted to accept annexation. In response to Mexican war preparations, Polk then made a second move, ordering American troops under General **Zachary Taylor** to the edge of the disputed territory. Taylor took up a position at Corpus Christi, a tiny Texas outpost situated just south of the Nueces and hence in territory still claimed by Mexico.

Never far from Polk's thoughts in his insistence on the Rio Grande boundary lay his desire for California and for its fine harbors of San Diego and San Francisco. In fact, Polk had entered the White House with the firm intention of extending American control over California. By the summer of 1845, his followers were openly proclaiming that, if Mexico went to war with the United States over Texas, "the road to California will be open to us." Then in October 1845, Polk received a dispatch from Thomas O. Larkin, the American consul at Monterey, California, that warned darkly of British designs on California but ended with the optimistic assurance that the Mexicans in California would prefer American to British rule. Larkin's message gave Polk the idea that California might be acquired by the same methods as Texas: revolution followed by annexation.

With Texans' acceptance of annexation and Taylor's troops at Corpus Christi, the next move belonged to Mexico. In early 1845, a new Mexican government agreed to negotiate with the United States, and Polk, locked into a war of words with Britain over Oregon, decided to give negotiations a chance. In November 1845, he dispatched John Slidell to Mexico City with instructions to gain Mexican recognition of the annexation of Texas with the Rio Grande border. In exchange, the United States government would assume the debt owed by Mexico to American citizens. Polk also authorized Slidell to offer up to $25 million for California and New Mexico. But by the time Slidell reached Mexico City, the government there had become too weak to make concessions to the United States, and its head, General José Herrera, refused to receive Slidell. Polk then ordered Taylor to move southward to the Rio Grande, hoping to provoke a Mexican attack and unite the American people behind war.

The Mexican government dawdled. Polk was about to send a war message to Congress when word finally arrived that Mexican forces had crossed the Rio Grande and ambushed two companies of Taylor's troops. Now the prowar press had its martyrs. *"American blood has been shed on American soil!"* one of Polk's followers proclaimed. On May 11, Polk informed Congress that war "exists by the act of Mexico herself" and called for a $10 million appropriation to fight the war.

Polk's disarming assertion that the United States was already at war provoked furious opposition in Congress, where antislavery Whigs protested the president's highhandedness. For one thing, the Mexican attack on Taylor's troops had occurred on land never before claimed by the United States. By announcing that war already existed, moreover, Polk seemed to be undercutting Congress's power to declare war and using a mere border incident as a pretext to acquire more slave territory. The pro-Whig *New York Tribune* warned its readers that Polk was "precipitating you into a fathomless abyss of crime and calamity." Antislavery poet James Russell Lowell of Massachusetts wrote of the Polk Democrats,

> They just want this Californy
> So's to lug new slave-states in
> To abuse ye, an' to scorn ye,
> An' to plunder ye like sin.

But Polk had maneuvered the Whigs into a corner. Few Whigs could forget that the Federalists' opposition to the War of 1812 had wrecked the Federalist Party, and few wanted to appear unpatriotic by refusing to support Taylor's beleaguered troops. Swallowing their outrage, most Whigs backed appropriations for war against Mexico.

Polk's single-minded pursuit of his goals had prevailed. A humorless, austere man who banned dancing and liquor at White House receptions, Polk inspired little personal warmth, even among his supporters. But he had clear objectives and pursued them unflinchingly. At every point, he had encountered opposition on the home front: from Whigs who saw him as a reckless adventurer; from northerners of both parties opposed to any expansion of slavery; and from John C. Calhoun, who despised Polk for his high-handedness and fretted that a war with Britain would strip the South of its market for cotton. Yet Polk triumphed over all opposition, in part because of his opponents' fragmentation, in part because of expansion's popular appeal, and in part because of the weakness of his foreign antagonists. Reluctant to fight over Oregon, Britain chose to negotiate. Too weak to negotiate, Mexico chose to fight over territory that it had already lost (Texas) and for territories over which its hold was feeble (California and New Mexico).

The Mexican-American War

Most European observers expected Mexico to win the war. Its regular army was four times the size of the American forces, and it was fighting on home ground. The United States, which had botched its one previous attempt to invade a foreign nation, Canada in 1812, now had to sustain offensive operations in an area remote from American settlements. American expansionists, however, hardly expected the Mexicans to fight at all. A leading Democrat confidently predicted that Mexico would offer only "a slight resistance to the North American race" because its mixed Spanish and Indian population had been degraded by "amalgamation." The newspaper publisher James Gordon Bennett proclaimed that the "imbecile" Mexicans were "as sure to melt away at the approach of [American] energy and enterprise as snow before a southern sun."

In fact, the Mexicans fought bravely and stubbornly, although unsuccessfully. In May 1846, Taylor, "Old Rough and Ready," routed the Mexican army in Texas and pursued it across the Rio Grande, eventually capturing the major city of Monterrey in September. War enthusiasm surged in the United States. Recruiting posters blared, "Here's to old Zach! Glorious Times! Roast Beef, Ice Cream, and Three Months' Advance." Taylor's conspicuously ordinary manner—he went into battle wearing a straw hat and a plain brown coat—endeared him to the public, which kicked up its heels in celebration to the "Rough and Ready Polka" and the "General Taylor Quick Step."

After taking Monterrey, Taylor, starved for supplies, halted and granted Mexico an eight-week armistice. Eager to undercut Taylor's popularity—the Whigs were already touting him as a presidential candidate—Polk stripped him of half his forces and reassigned them to General Winfield Scott. Scott was to mount an amphibious attack on Vera Cruz, far to the south, and proceed to Mexico City, following the path of Cortés and his conquistadors. Events outstripped Polk's scheme, however, when Taylor defeated a far larger Mexican army at the Battle of Buena Vista, on February 22–23, 1847.

Daguerreotype of Soldiers in the Mexican-American War   *This photograph shows General John F. Wool (in the center, wearing a heavy coat) and his staff at Saltillo, the capital of the Mexican state of Coahuila, in 1846 or 1847. Wool respected individual Mexicans as soldiers, but noted Mexico's lack of unity. "Had the nation [Mexico] been united," he wrote, "we could not have gained a single victory."*

While Taylor was winning fame in northern Mexico, and before Scott had launched his attack on Vera Cruz, American forces farther north were dealing decisive blows to the remnants of Mexican rule in New Mexico and California. In the spring of 1846, Colonel Stephen Kearny marched an army from Fort Leavenworth, Kansas, toward Santa Fe. Like the pioneers on the Oregon Trail, Kearny's men faced immense natural obstacles as they marched over barren ground. Finally reaching New Mexico, Kearny took the territory by a combination of bluff, bluster, and perhaps bribery, without firing a shot. The Mexican governor, following his own advice that "it is better to be thought brave than to be so," fled at Kearny's approach. After suppressing a brief rebellion by Mexicans and Indians, Kearny sent a detachment of his army south into Mexico. There, having marched fifteen hundred miles from Fort Leavenworth, these troops joined Taylor in time for the Battle of Buena Vista.

Like New Mexico, California fell easily into American hands. In 1845, Polk had ordered Commodore John D. Sloat and his Pacific Squadron to occupy California's ports in the event of war with Mexico. To ensure victory, Polk also dispatched a courier overland with secret orders for one of the most colorful and important actors in the conquest of California, John C. Frémont. A Georgia-born adventurer, Frémont had married Jesse Benton, the daughter of powerful Senator Thomas Hart Benton of Missouri. Benton used his influence to have accounts of Frémont's explorations in the Northwest (mainly written by Jesse Benton Frémont) published as government documents. All of this earned glory for Frémont as "the Great Pathfinder." Finally overtaken

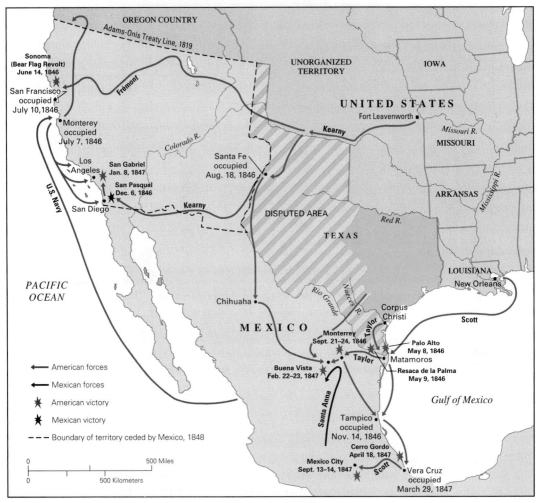

MAP 13.2 Major Battles of the Mexican-American War

The Mexican War's decisive campaign began with General Winfield Scott's capture of Vera Cruz and ended with his conquest of Mexico City.

by Polk's courier in Oregon, Frémont was dispatched to California to "watch over the interests of the United States." In June 1846, a small force of American settlers loyal to Frémont seized the village of Sonoma and proclaimed the independent "Bear Flag Republic." The combined efforts of Frémont, Sloat, his successor David Stockton, and Stephen Kearny (who arrived in California after capturing New Mexico) quickly established American control over California.

The final and most important campaign of the war saw the conquest of Mexico City itself. In March 1847, Winfield Scott landed near Vera Cruz at the head of twelve thousand men and quickly pounded the city into submission. Moving inland, Scott encountered Santa Anna at the seemingly impregnable pass of Cerro Gordo, but a young captain in Scott's command, Robert E. Lee, helped find a trail that led around the Mexican flank to a small peak overlooking the pass. There Scott planted howitzers and, on April 18, stormed the pass and routed the Mexicans. Scott now moved directly on Mexico City. Taking the key fortresses of Churubusco and Chapultepec (where another young captain, Ulysses S. Grant, was cited for bravery), Scott took the city on September 13, 1847.

In virtually all these encounters on Mexican soil, the Mexicans were numerically superior. In the final assault on Mexico City, Scott commanded eleven thousand troops against Santa Anna's twenty-five thousand. But doom stalked the Mexican army. Hampered by Santa Anna's nearly unbroken string of military miscalculations, the Mexicans fell victim to the vastly superior American artillery and to the ability of the Americans to organize massive military movements. The "barbarians of the North" (as Mexicans called the American soldiers) died like flies from yellow fever, and they carried into battle the agonies of venereal disease, which they picked up (and left) in many of the Mexican towns they took. But the Americans benefited from the unprecedented quality of their weapons, supplies, and organization.

By the **Treaty of Guadalupe Hidalgo** (February 2, 1848), Mexico ceded Texas with the Rio Grande boundary, New Mexico, and California to the United States. In return, the United States assumed the claims of American citizens against the Mexican government and paid Mexico $15 million. Although the United States gained the present states of California, Nevada, New Mexico, Utah, most of Arizona, and parts of Colorado and Wyoming, some rabid expansionists in the Senate denounced the treaty because it failed to include all of Mexico. But the acquisition of California, with its excellent Pacific ports of San Diego and San Francisco, satisfied Polk. Few senators, moreover, wanted to annex the mixed Spanish and Indian population of Mexico. A writer in the *Democratic Review* expressed the prevailing view that "the annexation of the country [Mexico] to the United States would be a calamity," for it would incorporate into the United States "ignorant and indolent half-civilized Indians," not to mention "free negroes and mulattoes" left over from the British slave trade. The virulent racism of American leaders allowed the Mexicans to retain part of their nation. On March 10, 1848, the Senate ratified the treaty by a vote of 38 to 10.

The War's Effects on Sectional Conflict	Wartime patriotic enthusiasm did not stop sectional conflict from sharpening between 1846 and 1848. Questions relating to territorial expansion intensified this conflict, but so too did President Polk's uncompromising and literal Jacksonianism.

Polk had restored the Independent Treasury, to the Whigs' dismay, and had eroded Democratic unity by pursuing Jacksonian policies on tariffs and internal improvements. Despite his campaign promise, applauded by many northern Democrats, to combine a revenue tariff with a measure of protection, his administration's Tariff of 1846 had slashed duties to the minimum necessary for revenue. Polk then disappointed western Democrats, thirsting for federal aid for internal improvements, by vetoing the Rivers and Harbors Bill of 1846.

Important as these issues were, territorial expansion sparked the Polk administration's major battles. To Polk, it mattered little whether new territories were slave or free. Expansion would serve the nation's interests by dispersing population and retaining its agricultural and democratic character. Focusing attention on slavery in the territories struck him as "not only unwise but wicked." The Missouri Compromise, prohibiting slavery north of 36°30′, impressed him as a simple and permanent solution to the problem of territorial slavery.

But many northerners were coming to see slavery in the territories as a profoundly disruptive issue that neither could nor should be solved simply by extending the 36°30′ line westward. Antislavery Whigs who opposed any extension of slavery on moral grounds were still a minority within their party. They posed a lesser threat to Polk than did northern Democrats who feared that expansion of slavery into California and New Mexico (parts of each lay south of 36°30′) would deter free laborers from settling those territories. These Democrats argued that competition with slaves degraded free labor, that the westward extension of slavery would check the westward migration of free labor, and that such a barrier would aggravate the social problems already beginning to plague the East: class strife, social stratification, and labor protest.

The Wilmot Proviso A young Democratic congressman from Pennsylvania, David Wilmot, became the spokesman for these disaffected northern Democrats. On a sizzling night in August 1846, he introduced an amendment to an appropriations bill for the upcoming negotiations with Mexico over Texas, New Mexico, and California. This amendment, known as the **Wilmot Proviso,** stipulated that slavery be prohibited in any territory acquired by the negotiations. Neither an abolitionist nor a critic of Polk on tariff policy, Wilmot spoke for those loyal Democrats who had supported the annexation of Texas on the assumption that Texas would be the last slave state. Wilmot's intention was not to split his party along sectional lines but instead to hold Polk to what Wilmot and other northern Democrats took as an implicit understanding: Texas for the slaveholders, California and New Mexico for free labor.

With strong northern support, the proviso passed in the House but stalled in the Senate. Polk refused to endorse it, and most southern Democrats opposed any barrier to the expansion of slavery south of the Missouri Compromise line. They believed that the westward extension of slavery would reduce the concentration of slaves in the older regions of the South and thus lessen the chances of a slave revolt.

The proviso raised unsettling constitutional issues. Calhoun and fellow southerners contended that since slaves were property, the Constitution protected slaveholders' right to carry their slaves wherever they chose. This position led to the conclusion (drawn explicitly by Calhoun) that the Missouri Compromise of 1820, prohibiting slavery in the territories north of 36°30′, was unconstitutional. On the other side were many northerners who cited the Northwest Ordinance of 1787, the Missouri Compromise, and the Constitution itself, which gave Congress the power to "make all needful rules and regulations respecting the territory or other property belonging to the United States," as justification for congressional legislation on slavery in the territories. With the election of 1848 approaching, politicians of both sides, eager to hold their parties together and avert civil war, frantically searched for a middle ground.

The Election of 1848 Having asserted that their policies of national banking and high tariffs alone could pull the nation out of the depression, the Whigs had watched in dismay as prosperity returned under Polk's program of an independent treasury and low tariffs. Never before had Clay's American System seemed so irrelevant. But the Wilmot Proviso gave the Whigs a political windfall; originating in the Democratic Party, it enabled the Whigs to portray themselves as the South's only dependable friends.

These considerations inclined the majority of Whigs toward Zachary Taylor. As a Louisiana slaveholder, he had obvious appeal to the South. As a political newcomer, he had no loyalty to the discredited American System. As a war hero, he had broad national appeal. Nominating Taylor as their presidential candidate in 1848, the Whigs presented him as an ideal man "without regard to creeds or principles" and ran him without any platform.

The Democrats faced a greater challenge because David Wilmot was one of their own. They could not ignore the issue of slavery in the territories, but if they embraced the position of either Wilmot or Calhoun, the party would split along sectional lines. When Polk declined to run for reelection, the Democrats nominated Lewis Cass of Michigan, who solved their dilemma by announcing the doctrine of "squatter sovereignty," or popular sovereignty as it was later called. Cass argued that Congress should let the question of slavery in the territories be decided by the people who settled there. Squatter sovereignty appealed to many because of its arresting simplicity and vagueness. It neatly dodged the divisive issue of whether Congress had the power to prohibit territorial slavery. In fact, few Democrats wanted a definitive answer to this question. As long as the doctrine remained ambiguous, northern and southern Democrats alike could interpret it to their respective benefit.

In the campaign, both parties tried to ignore the issue of territorial slavery, but neither succeeded. A faction of the Democratic Party in New York that favored the Wilmot Proviso, called the Barnburners, broke away from the party, linked up with former

"Union" Woodcut by Thomas W. Strong, 1848   *This 1848 campaign poster for Zachary Taylor reminded Americans of his military victories, unmilitary bearing (note the civilian dress and straw hat), and deliberately vague promises. As president, Taylor finally took a stand on the issue of slavery in the Mexican Cession, but his position angered the South.*

Liberty party abolitionists, and courted antislavery "Conscience" Whigs to create the **Free-Soil party.** Declaring their dedication to "Free Trade, Free Labor, Free Speech, and Free Men," the Free-Soilers nominated Martin Van Buren on a platform opposing any extension of slavery.

Zachary Taylor benefited from the Democrats' alienation of key northern states over the tariff issue, from Democratic disunity over the Wilmot Proviso, and from his war-hero stature. He captured a majority of electoral votes in both North and South. Although failing to carry any state, the Free-Soil party ran well enough in the North to demonstrate the grass-roots popularity of opposition to slavery extension. Defections to the Free-Soilers, for example, probably cost the Whigs Ohio. By showing that opposition to the spread of slavery had far greater appeal than the staunch abolitionism of the old Liberty party, the Free-Soilers sent the Whigs and Democrats a message that they would be unable to ignore in future elections.

The California Gold Rush

When Wilmot announced his proviso, the issue of slavery in the Far West was more abstract than practical because Mexico had yet to cede any territory and relatively few Americans resided in either California or New Mexico. Nine days before the signing of the Treaty of Guadalupe Hidalgo, however, an American carpenter discovered gold in the foothills of California's Sierra Nevada range. The **California gold rush** began within a few months. A San Francisco newspaper complained that "the whole country from San Francisco to Los Angeles, and from the shore to the base of the Sierra Nevada, resounds with the sordid cry to *gold*, GOLD, GOLD! while the field is left half-planted, the house half-built, and everything neglected but the manufacture of shovels and pickaxes."

Shovels and pickaxes to dig gold from crevices in and around streams were enough for most of the early gold prospectors. But as the most accessible deposits of gold were depleted, individual miners increasingly formed combinations to undertake such costly projects as diverting the course of streams and rivers to uncover gold-laden beds or excavating shafts in the earth. "Hydraulic mining," a development of the mid-1850s, involved channeling water from streams through narrow hoses to blast thousands of cubic yards of earth from hillsides and then sifting the earth through sluices to capture the precious particles of gold.

By December 1848, pamphlets with titles like *The Emigrant's Guide to the Gold Mines* had hit the streets of New York City. Arriving by sea and by land, gold-rushers drove up the population of California from around 15,000 in the summer of 1848 to nearly 250,000 by 1852. Miners came from every corner of the world. A female journalist reported walking through a mining camp in the Sierras and hearing English, Italian, French, Spanish, German, and Hawaiian. Conflicts over claims quickly led to violent clashes between Americans and Hispanics (mostly Mexicans, Chileans, and Peruvians). Americans especially resented the Chinese who flooded into California in the 1850s, most as contract laborers for wealthy Chinese merchants, and who struck Americans as slave laborers. Yet rampant prejudice against the Chinese did not stop some American businessmen from hiring them as contract workers for the American mining combinations that were forming in the 1850s.

Within a decade, the gold rush turned the sleepy Hispanic town of Yerba Buena, with 150 people in 1846, into "a pandemonium of a city" of 50,000 known as San Francisco. No other U.S. city contained people from more parts of the world. Many of the immigrants were Irish convicts who arrived by way of Australia, to which they had been exiled for their crimes. All the ethnic and racial tensions of the gold fields were evident in the city. A young clergyman confessed that he carried a harmless-looking cane, which "will be found to contain a sword two-and-a-half feet long." In 1851, San Francisco's merchants organized the first of several Committees of Vigilance, which patrolled the streets, deported undesirables, and tried and hanged alleged thieves and murderers.

With the gold rush, the issue of slavery in the Far West became practical as well as abstract, and immediate rather than remote. The newcomers attracted to California in 1849 included free blacks and slaves brought by planters from the South. White prospectors loathed the thought of competing with either of these groups and wanted to drive all blacks, along with California's Indians, out of the gold fields. Tensions also intensified between the gold-rushers and the *Californios,* whose extensive (if often vaguely worded) land holdings were protected by the terms of the Treaty of Guadalupe Hidalgo. Spawned by disputed claims and prejudice, violence mounted, and demands grew for a strong civilian government to replace the ineffective military government in place in California since the war. Polk began to fear that without a satisfactory congressional solution to the slavery issue, Californians might organize a government independent of the United States. The gold rush thus guaranteed that the question of slavery in the Mexican cession would be the first item on the agenda for Polk's successor and, indeed, for the nation.

CONCLUSION

The massive immigration of the 1840s changed the face of American politics. Angered by Whig nativism and anti-Catholicism, the new German and Irish immigrants swelled the ranks of the Democratic Party. Meanwhile, the Whigs were unraveling. The untimely death of President Harrison brought John Tyler, a Democrat in Whig's clothing, to the White House. Tyler's vetoes of key Whig measures left the Whig party in disarray. In combination, these developments led to the surprise election of James K. Polk, a Democrat and ardent expansionist, in 1844.

Wrapped in the language of Manifest Destiny, westward expansion appealed to Americans for many reasons. It fit their belief that settlers had more right to the American continent than did the Europeans (who based their claims on centuries-old explorations), the lethargic and Catholic Mexicans, and the nomadic Indians. Expansion promised trade routes to the Pacific, more land for farming, and, in the case of Texas, more slave states. Polk simultaneously rode the wave of national sentiment for Manifest Destiny and gave it direction by annexing Texas, provoking a crisis with Britain over Oregon, and leading the United States into a war with Mexico. Initially, Polk succeeded in uniting broad swaths of public opinion behind expansion. Polk and his followers ingeniously argued that national expansion was in the interests of northern working-class voters, many of them immigrants. By encouraging the spread of slavery to the Southwest, the argument went, the annexation of Texas would reduce the chances of a race war in the Southeast that might spill over into the North.

Yet even as war with Mexico was commencing, cracks in Polk's coalition were starting to show. The Wilmot Proviso exposed deep sectional divisions that had only been papered over by the ideal of Manifest Destiny and that would explode in the secession of Free-Soil Democrats in 1848. Victorious over Mexico and enriched by the discovery of gold in California, Americans counted the blessings of expansion but began to fear its costs.

14

From Compromise to Secession, 1850–1861

THE COMPROMISE OF 1850

Ralph Waldo Emerson's grim prediction that an American victory in the Mexican-American War would be like swallowing arsenic proved disturbingly accurate. When the war ended in 1848, the United States contained an equal number of free and slave states (fifteen each), but the vast territory acquired by the war threatened to upset this balance. Any solution to the question of slavery in the Mexican cession ensured controversy. The doctrine of **free soil,** which insisted that Congress prohibit slavery in the territories, horrified southerners. The idea of extending the Missouri Compromise line of 36°30′ to the Pacific angered free-soilers because it would allow slavery in New Mexico and southern California, while it angered southern proslavery extremists because it conceded that Congress could bar slavery in some territories. A third solution, **popular sovereignty,** which promised to ease the slavery extension issue out of national politics by allowing each territory to decide the question for itself, pleased neither free-soilers nor proslavery extremists.

As the rhetoric escalated, events plunged the nation into crisis. Utah and then California, both acquired from Mexico, sought admission to the Union as free states. Texas, admitted as a slave state in 1845, aggravated matters by claiming the eastern half of New Mexico, where the Mexican government had abolished slavery.

By 1850, these territorial issues had become intertwined with two other concerns. Northerners increasingly attacked slavery in the District of Columbia, within the shadow of the Capitol; southerners complained about lax enforcement of the Fugitive Slave Act of 1793. Any broad compromise would have to take both troublesome matters into account.

CHRONOLOGY, 1850–1861

1848 • Zachary Taylor elected president.

1849 • California seeks admission to the Union as a free state.

1850 • Nashville convention assembles to discuss the South's grievances.
Compromise of 1850.

1852 • Harriet Beecher Stowe, *Uncle Tom's Cabin.*
Franklin Pierce elected president.

1853 • Gadsden Purchase.

1854 • Ostend Manifesto.
Kansas-Nebraska Act.
William Walker leads filibustering expedition into Nicaragua.

1854–1855 • Know-Nothing and Republican parties emerge.

1855 • Proslavery forces steal the election for a territorial legislature in Kansas.
Proslavery Kansans establish a government in Lecompton.
Free-soil government established in Topeka, Kansas.

1856 • "The sack of Lawrence."
John Brown's Pottawatomie massacre.
James Buchanan elected president.

1857 • *Dred Scott* decision.
President Buchanan endorses the Lecompton constitution in Kansas.
Panic of 1857.

1858 • Congress refuses to admit Kansas to the Union under the Lecompton
constitution.
Lincoln-Douglas debates.

1859 • John Brown's raid on Harpers Ferry.

1860 • Abraham Lincoln elected president.
South Carolina secedes from the Union.

1861 • The remaining Lower South states secede.
Confederate States of America established.
Crittenden compromise plan collapses.
Lincoln takes office.
Firing on Fort Sumter; Civil War begins.
Upper South secedes.

Zachary Taylor at the Helm   Although elected president in 1848 without a platform, Zachary Taylor came to office with a clear position on the issue of slavery in the Mexican cession. A slaveholder himself, he took for granted the South's need to defend slavery. Taylor insisted that southerners would best protect slavery if they refrained from rekindling the issue of slavery in the territories. He rejected Calhoun's idea that the protection of slavery in the southern states ultimately depended on the expansion of slavery into the western territories. In Taylor's eyes, neither California nor New Mexico was suited to slavery; in 1849 he told a Pennsylvania audience that "the people of the North need have no apprehension of the further extension of slavery."

Although Taylor looked to the exclusion of slavery from California and New Mexico, his position differed from the one embodied in the Wilmot Proviso, the free-soil measure proposed in 1846 by a northern Democrat. The proviso had insisted that Congress bar slavery in any territories that might be ceded by Mexico. Taylor's plan, in contrast, left the decision to the states. Recognizing that most Californians opposed slavery in their state, Taylor had prompted California to bypass the territorial stage that normally preceded statehood, to draw up its constitution in 1849, and to apply directly for admission as a free state. The president strongly hinted that he expected New Mexico to do the same.

Taylor's strategy appeared to guarantee a quick, practical solution to the problem of slavery extension. It would give the North two new free states. At the same time, it would acknowledge a position upon which all southerners agreed: a state could bar or permit slavery as it chose. This conviction in fact served as the very foundation of the South's defense of slavery, its armor against all the onslaughts of the abolitionists. Nothing in the Constitution forbade a state to act one way or the other on slavery.

Despite its practical features, Taylor's plan dismayed southerners of both parties. Having gored the Democrats in 1848 as the party of the Wilmot Proviso, southern Whigs expected more from the president than a proposal that in effect yielded the proviso's goal—the banning of slavery in the Mexican cession. Many southerners, in addition, questioned Taylor's assumption that slavery could never take root in California or New Mexico. To one observer, who declared that the whole controversy over slavery in the Mexican cession "related to an imaginary negro in an impossible place," southerners pointed out that both areas already contained slaves and that slaves could be employed profitably in mining gold and silver. "California is by nature," a southerner proclaimed, "peculiarly a slaveholding State." Calhoun trembled at the thought of adding more free states. "If this scheme excluding slavery from California and New Mexico should be carried out—if we are to be reduced to a mere handful . . . wo, wo, I say to this Union." Disillusioned with Taylor, nine southern states agreed to send delegations to a southern convention that was scheduled to meet in Nashville in June 1850.

| Henry Clay Proposes a Compromise | Taylor might have been able to contain mounting southern opposition if he had held a secure position in the Whig party. But such leading Whigs as Daniel Webster of Massachusetts and Henry Clay of Kentucky, each of whom had presidential |

aspirations, never reconciled themselves to Taylor, a political novice. Early in 1850, Clay boldly challenged Taylor's leadership by forging a set of compromise proposals to resolve the range of contentious issues. Clay proposed (1) the admission of California as a free state; (2) the division of the remainder of the Mexican cession into two territories, New Mexico and Utah (formerly Deseret), without federal restrictions on slavery; (3) the settlement of the Texas–New Mexico boundary dispute on terms favorable to New Mexico; (4) as an incentive for Texas, an agreement that the federal government would assume the considerable public debt of Texas; (5) the continuance of slavery in the District of Columbia but the abolition of the slave trade; and (6) a more effective fugitive slave law.

Clay rolled all of these proposals into a single "omnibus" bill, which he hoped to steer through Congress. The debates over the omnibus during the late winter and early spring of 1850 witnessed the last major appearances on the public stage of Clay, Webster, and Calhoun—the trio of distinguished senators whose lives had mirrored every public event of note since the War of 1812. Clay played the role of the conciliator, as he had during the controversy over Missouri in 1820 and again during the nullification crisis in the early 1830s. Warning the South against secession, he assured the North that nature would check the spread of slavery more effectively than a thousand Wilmot Provisos. Gaunt and gloomy, a dying Calhoun listened as another senator read his address for him, a repetition of what he had been saying for years: the North's growing power, enhanced by protective tariffs and by the Missouri Compromise's exclusion of slaveholders from the northern part of the Louisiana Purchase, had created an imbalance between the sections. Only a decision by the North to treat the South as an equal could now save the Union. Three days later, Daniel Webster, who believed that slavery, "like the cotton-plant, is confined to certain parallels of climate," delivered his memorable "Seventh of March" speech. Speaking not "as a Massachusetts man, nor as a Northern man, but as an American," Webster chided the North for trying to "reenact the will of God" by legally excluding slavery from the Mexican cession and declared himself a forthright proponent of compromise.

However eloquent, the conciliatory voices of Clay and Webster made few converts. With every call for compromise, some northern or southern speaker would rise and inflame passions. The antislavery New York Whig William Seward, for example, enraged southerners by talking of a "**higher law** than the Constitution"—namely, the will of God against the extension of slavery. Clay's compromise became tied up in a congressional committee. To worsen matters, Clay, who at first had pretended that his proposals were in the spirit of Taylor's plan, broke openly with the president in May, and Taylor attacked Clay as a glory-hunter.

As the Union faced its worst crisis since 1789, a series of events in the summer of 1850 eased the way toward a resolution. When the Nashville convention assembled in June, extremists—called the fire-eaters because of their recklessness—boldly made their presence felt. But their talk of "southern rights" smelled suspiciously like a plot to disrupt the Union. "I would rather sit in council with the six thousand dead who have died of cholera in St. Louis," Senator Thomas Hart Benton of Missouri declared, "than go into convention with such a gang of scamps." Only nine of the fifteen slave states, most in the Lower South, sent delegates to the convention, where moderates took control and isolated the extremists. Then Zachary Taylor, after eating and drinking too much at an Independence Day celebration, fell ill with gastroenteritis and died on July 9.

His successor, Vice President Millard Fillmore, quickly proved to be more favorable than Taylor to the Senate's compromise measure by appointing Daniel Webster as his secretary of state. After the compromise suffered a devastating series of amendments in late July, Illinois Democrat **Stephen A. Douglas** took over the floor leadership from the exhausted Clay. Recognizing that Clay's "omnibus" lacked majority support in Congress, Douglas chopped it into a series of separate measures and sought to secure passage of each bill individually. To secure support from Democrats, he included the principle of popular sovereignty in the bills organizing New Mexico and Utah. By summer's end, Congress had passed each component of the **Compromise of 1850:** statehood for California; territorial status for Utah and New Mexico, allowing popular sovereignty; resolution of the Texas–New Mexico boundary disagreement; federal assumption of the Texas debt; abolition of the slave trade in the District of Columbia; and a new fugitive slave law.

Assessing the Compromise

President Fillmore hailed the compromise as a "final settlement" of sectional divisions, and Clay's reputation for conciliation reached new heights. Yet the compromise did not bridge the underlying differences between the two sections. Far from leaping forward to save the Union, Congress had backed into the Compromise of 1850; the majority of congressmen in one or another section opposed virtually all of the specific bills that made up the compromise. Most southerners, for example, voted against the admission of California and the abolition of the slave trade in the District of Columbia; the majority of northerners opposed the Fugitive Slave Act and the organization of New Mexico and Utah without a forthright congressional prohibition of slavery. These measures passed only because the minority of congressmen who genuinely desired compromise combined with the majority in either the North or the South who favored each specific bill.

Each section both gained and lost from the Compromise of 1850. The North won California as a free state, New Mexico and Utah as likely future free states, a favorable settlement of the Texas–New Mexico boundary (most of the disputed area was awarded to New Mexico, a probable free state), and the abolition of the slave trade in the District of Columbia. The South's benefits were cloudier. By stipulating popular sovereignty for New Mexico and Utah, the compromise, to most southerners' relief, had buried the Wilmot Proviso's insistence that Congress formally prohibit slavery in these territories. But to southerners' dismay, the position of the free-soilers remained

MAP 14.1 The Compromise of 1850

The Compromise of 1850 admitted California as a free state. Utah and New Mexico were left open to slavery or freedom on the principle of popular sovereignty.

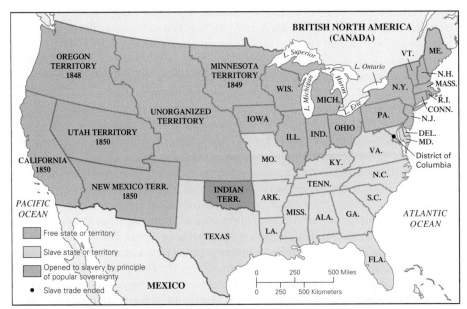

viable, for the compromise left open the question of whether Congress could prohibit slavery in territories outside of the Mexican cession.

Not surprisingly, southerners reacted ambivalently to the Compromise of 1850. In southern state elections during the fall of 1850 and in 1851, procompromise, or Unionist, candidates thrashed anticompromise candidates who talked of southern rights and secession. But even southern Unionists did not dismiss the possibility of secession. Unionists in Georgia, for example, forged the celebrated Georgia Platform, which threatened secession if Congress either prohibited slavery in New Mexico or Utah, or repealed the Fugitive Slave Act.

The one clear advantage gained by the South, a more stringent fugitive slave law, quickly proved a mixed blessing. Because few slaves had been taken into the Mexican cession, the question of slavery there had a hypothetical quality. However, the issues raised by the new fugitive slave law were far from hypothetical; the law authorized real southerners to pursue real fugitives on northern soil. Here was a concrete issue to which the average northerner, who may never have seen a slave and who cared little about slavery a thousand miles away, would respond with fury.

Enforcement of the Fugitive Slave Act   Northern moderates accepted the **Fugitive Slave Act** as the price of saving the Union. But the law contained a string of features distasteful to moderates and outrageous to staunchly antislavery northerners. It denied alleged fugitives the right of trial by jury, did not allow them to testify in their own behalf, permitted their return to slavery merely on the testimony of the claimant, and enabled court-appointed commissioners to collect ten dollars if they ruled for the slaveholder but only five dollars if they ruled for the fugitive. In authorizing federal marshals to raise posses to pursue fugitives on northern soil, the law threatened to turn the North into "one vast hunting ground." In addition, the law targeted not only recent runaways but also those who had fled the South decades earlier. For example, it allowed slave-catchers to wrench a former slave from his family in Indiana in 1851 and return him to the master from whom he had fled in 1832. Above all, the law brought home to northerners the uncomfortable truth that the continuation of slavery depended on their complicity. By legalizing the activities of slave-catchers on northern soil, the law reminded northerners that slavery was a national problem, not merely a peculiar southern institution.

Antislavery northerners assailed the law as the "vilest monument of infamy of the nineteenth century." "Let the President . . . drench our land of freedom in blood," proclaimed Ohio Whig congressman Joshua Giddings, "but he will never make us obey that law." His support for the law turned Senator Daniel Webster of Massachusetts into a villain in the eyes of the very people who for years had revered him as the "godlike Daniel." The abolitionist poet John Greenleaf Whittier wrote of his fallen idol,

> All else is gone; from those giant eyes
> The soul has fled:
> When faith is lost, when honor dies,
> The man is dead.

Efforts to catch and return fugitive slaves inflamed feelings in both the North and the South. In 1854, a Boston mob, aroused by antislavery speeches, broke into a courthouse and killed a guard in an abortive effort to rescue the fugitive slave Anthony Burns. Determined to prove that the law could be enforced "even in Boston," President Franklin

Pierce sent a detachment of federal troops to escort Burns to the harbor, where a ship carried him back to slavery. No witness would ever forget the scene. As five platoons of troops marched with Burns to the ship, some fifty thousand people lined the streets. As the procession passed, one Bostonian hung from his window a black coffin bearing the words "THE FUNERAL OF LIBERTY." Another draped an American flag upside down as a symbol that "my country is eternally disgraced by this day's proceedings." The Burns incident shattered the complacency of conservative supporters of the Compromise of 1850. "We went to bed one night old fashioned conservative Compromise Union Whigs," the textile manufacturer Amos A. Lawrence wrote, "and waked up stark mad Abolitionists." A Boston committee later successfully purchased Burns's freedom, but other fugitives had worse fates. Margaret Garner, about to be captured and sent back to Kentucky as a slave, slit her daughter's throat and tried to kill her other children rather than witness their return to slavery.

In response to the Fugitive Slave Act, "vigilance" committees spirited endangered blacks to Canada. Lawyers dragged out legal proceedings to raise slave-catchers' expenses, and nine northern states passed **personal-liberty laws.** By such techniques as forbidding the use of state jails to incarcerate alleged fugitives, these laws aimed to preclude state officials from enforcing the law.

The frequent cold stares, obstructive legal tactics, and occasional violence encountered by slaveholders who ventured north to capture runaway slaves helped demonstrate to southerners that opposition to slavery boiled just beneath the surface of northern opinion. In the eyes of most southerners, the South had gained little more from the Compromise of 1850 than the Fugitive Slave Act, and now even that northern concession seemed to be a phantom. After witnessing riots against the Fugitive Slave Act in Boston in 1854, a young Georgian studying law at Harvard wrote to his mother, "Do not be surprised if when I return home you find me a confirmed disunionist."

Uncle Tom's Cabin   The publication in 1852 of Harriet Beecher Stowe's novel ***Uncle Tom's Cabin*** aroused wide northern sympathy for fugitive slaves. Stowe, the daughter of the famed evangelical Lyman Beecher and the younger sister of Catharine Beecher, the stalwart advocate of domesticity for women, greeted the Fugitive Slave Act with horror and outrage. In a memorable scene from the novel, she depicted the slave Eliza, clutching her infant son, bounding across ice floes on the Ohio River to freedom.

Yet Stowe targeted slavery itself more than merely the slave-catchers who served the institution. Much of her novel's power derives from its view that even good intentions cannot prevail against so evil an institution. Torn from his wife and children by sale and shipped on a steamer for the Lower South, the black slave Uncle Tom rescues little Eva, the daughter of kindly Augustine St. Clare, from drowning. In gratitude, St. Clare purchases Tom from a slave trader and takes him into his home in New Orleans. But after St. Clare dies, his cruel widow sells Tom to the vicious (and northern-born) Simon Legree, who whips Tom to death. Stowe played effectively on the emotions of her audience by demonstrating to an age that revered family life how slavery tore the family apart.

Three hundred thousand copies of *Uncle Tom's Cabin* were sold in 1852, and 1.2 million by the summer of 1853. Stage dramatizations, which added dogs to chase Eliza across the ice, eventually reached perhaps fifty times the number of people as the novel itself. As a play, *Uncle Tom's Cabin* enthralled working-class audiences normally

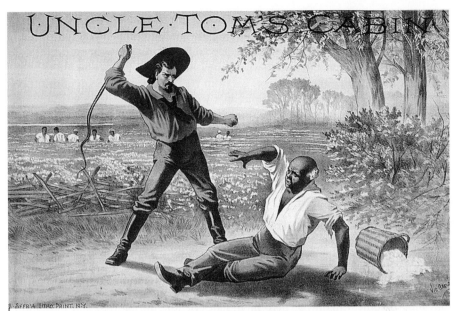

Uncle Tom's Cabin **Theater Poster**   *With its vivid word pictures of slavery, Harriet Beecher Stowe's* Uncle Tom's Cabin *translated well to the stage. Stowe herself was among the many who wrote dramatizations of the novel. Scenes of Eliza crossing the ice of the Ohio River with bloodhounds in pursuit and the evil Simon Legree whipping Uncle Tom outraged northern audiences and turned many against slavery. Southerners damned Mrs. Stowe as a "vile wretch in petticoats."*

indifferent, if not hostile, to abolitionism. During one stage performance, a reviewer for a New York newspaper observed that the gallery was filled with men "in red woollen shirts, with countenances as hardy and rugged as the implements of industry employed by them in the pursuit of their vocations." Astonished by the silence that fell over these men at the point when Eliza escapes across the river, the reviewer turned to discover that many of them were in tears.

The impact of *Uncle Tom's Cabin* cannot be precisely measured. Although the novel stirred deep feelings, it reflected the prevailing stereotypes of blacks far more than it overturned commonly held views. Stowe portrayed only light-skinned blacks as aggressive and intelligent; she depicted dark-skinned blacks such as Uncle Tom as docile and submissive. In addition, some of the stage dramatizations softened the novel's antislavery message. In one version, which P. T. Barnum produced, Tom was rescued from Legree and happily returned as a slave to his original plantation.

Surgery on the plot, however, could not fully excise the antislavery message of *Uncle Tom's Cabin*. Although the novel hardly lived up to the prediction of a proslavery lawyer that it would convert 2 million people to abolitionism, it did push many waverers toward a more aggressively antisouthern and antislavery stance. Indeed, fear of its effect inspired a host of southerners to pen anti–Uncle Tom novels. As historian David Potter concluded, the northern attitude toward slavery "was never quite the same after *Uncle Tom's Cabin.*"

<table>
<tr><td>

The Election
of 1852
</td><td>

The Fugitive Slave Act fragmented the Whig party. By master-
minding defiance of the law, northern Whigs put southern
Whigs, who long had come before the southern electorate as
</td></tr>
</table>

the party best able to defend slavery within the Union, on the spot.

In 1852, the Whigs' nomination of Mexican War hero Winfield Scott as their presidential candidate widened the sectional split within the party. Although a Virginian,
Scott owed his nomination to the northern free-soil Whigs. His single feeble statement
endorsing the Compromise of 1850 undercut southern Whigs trying to portray the
Democrats as the party of disunion and themselves as the party of both slavery and
the Union.

The Democrats bridged their own sectional division by nominating **Franklin
Pierce** of New Hampshire, a dark-horse candidate whose chief attraction was that no
faction of the party strongly opposed him. The "ultra men of the South," a friend of
Pierce noted, "say they can cheerfully go for him, and none, none, say they cannot."
North and South, the Democrats rallied behind both the Compromise and the idea of
applying popular sovereignty to all the territories. In the most one-sided election since
1820, Pierce swept to victory. Defeat was especially galling for southern Whigs. In 1848,
Zachary Taylor had won 49.8 percent of the South's popular vote; Scott, by comparison, limped home with only 35 percent. In state elections during 1852 and 1853, moreover, the Whigs were devastated in the South; one Whig stalwart lamented "the decisive
breaking-up of our party."

THE COLLAPSE OF THE SECOND PARTY SYSTEM, 1853–1856

Franklin Pierce had the dubious distinction of being the last presidential candidate for
eighty years to win the popular and electoral vote in both the North and the South. Not
until 1932 did another president, Franklin D. Roosevelt, repeat this accomplishment.
Pierce was also the last president to hold office under the second party system—Whigs
against Democrats. For two decades, the Whigs and the Democrats had battled, often
on even terms. Then, within the four years of Pierce's administration, the Whig party
disintegrated. In its place two new parties, first the American (Know-Nothing) Party,
then the Republican Party, arose.

Unlike the Whig party, the Republican Party was a purely sectional, northern party.
Its support came from former northern Whigs and discontented northern Democrats.
The Democrats survived as a national party, but with a base so shrunken in the North
that the Republican Party, although scarcely a year old, swept two-thirds of the free
states in 1856.

For decades, the second party system had kept the conflict over slavery in check
by giving Americans other issues—banking, internal improvements, tariffs, and
temperance—to argue about. By the 1850s the debate over slavery extension was
pushing such issues into the background and exposing raw divisions in each party. Of
the two parties, the Whigs had the larger, more aggressive free-soil wing, and hence
they were more vulnerable than the Democrats to disruption. When Stephen A. Douglas
put forth a proposal in 1854 to organize the vast Nebraska territory without restrictions on slavery, he ignited a firestorm that consumed the Whig party.

The Kansas-Nebraska Act   Signed by President Pierce at the end of May 1854, the **Kansas-Nebraska Act** shattered the already weakened second party system and triggered renewed sectional strife. The origins of the act lay in the seemingly uncontroversial desire of farm families to establish homesteads in the vast prairies west of Iowa and Missouri. Their congressional representatives had repeatedly introduced bills to organize this area so that Native American land titles could be extinguished and a basis for government provided. Also, since the mid-1840s, advocates of national expansion had looked to the day when a railroad would link the Midwest to the Pacific; and St. Louis, Milwaukee, and Chicago had vied to become the eastern end of the projected Pacific railroad.

In January 1854, Senator Stephen A. Douglas of Illinois proposed a bill to organize Nebraska as a territory. An ardent expansionist, Douglas had formed his political ideology in the heady atmosphere of Manifest Destiny during the 1840s. As early as the mid-1840s, he had embraced the ideas of a Pacific railroad and the organization of Nebraska as ways to promote a continuous line of settlement between the Midwest and the Pacific. Although he preferred a railroad from his hometown of Chicago to San Francisco, Douglas dwelled on the national benefits that would attend construction of a railroad from anywhere in the Midwest to the Pacific. Such a railroad would enhance the importance of the Midwest, which could then hold the balance of power between the older sections of the North and South, and guide the nation toward unity rather than disruption. In addition, westward expansion through Nebraska with the aid of a railroad struck Douglas as an issue, comparable to Manifest Destiny, around which the contending factions of the Democratic Party would unite.

Douglas recognized two sources of potential conflict over his Nebraska bill. First, some southerners advocated a rival route for the Pacific railroad that would start at either New Orleans or Memphis. Second, Nebraska lay within the Louisiana Purchase and north of the Missouri Compromise line of 36°30′, a region closed to slavery. Unless Douglas made some concessions, southerners would have little incentive to vote for his bill; after all, the organization of Nebraska would simultaneously create a potential free state and increase the chances for a northern, rather than a southern, railroad to the Pacific.

As the floor manager of the Compromise of 1850 in the Senate, Douglas thought that he had an ideal concession to offer to the South. The Compromise of 1850 had applied the principle of popular sovereignty to New Mexico and Utah, territories outside of the Louisiana Purchase and hence unaffected by the Missouri Compromise. Why not assume, Douglas reasoned, that the Compromise of 1850 had taken the place of the Missouri Compromise everywhere? Believing that expansion rather than slavery was uppermost in the public's mind, Douglas hoped to avoid controversy over slavery by ignoring the Missouri Compromise. But he quickly came under pressure from southern congressmen, who wanted an explicit repudiation of the Missouri Compromise. Soon they forced Douglas to state publicly that the Nebraska bill "superseded" the Missouri Compromise and rendered it "void." Still under pressure, Douglas next agreed to a division of Nebraska into two territories: Nebraska to the west of Iowa, and Kansas to the west of Missouri. Because Missouri was a slave state, most congressmen assumed that the division aimed to secure Kansas for slavery and Nebraska for free soil.

The modifications of Douglas's original bill set off a storm of protest. Congress quickly tabled the Pacific railroad (which, in the turn of events, would not be built until after the Civil War) and focused on the issue of slavery extension. Antislavery northerners assailed the bill as "an atrocious plot" to violate the "sacred pledge" of the Missouri Compromise and to turn Kansas into a "dreary region of despotism, inhabited by masters and slaves." Their rage electrified southerners, many of whom initially had reacted indifferently to the Nebraska bill. Some southerners had opposed an explicit repeal of the Missouri Compromise, from fear of stimulating sectional discord; others doubted that Kansas would attract many slaveholders. But the furious assault of antislavery northerners united the South behind the Kansas-Nebraska bill by turning the issue into one of sectional pride as much as slavery extension.

Despite the uproar, Douglas successfully guided the Kansas-Nebraska bill through the Senate, where it passed by a vote of 37 to 14. In the House of Representatives, where the bill passed by little more than a whisker, 113 to 100, the true dimensions of the conflict became apparent. Not a single northern Whig representative in the House voted for the bill, whereas the northern Democrats divided evenly, 44 to 44.

The Surge of Free Soil

Amid the clamor over his bill, Douglas ruefully observed that he could now travel to Chicago by the light of his own burning effigies. Neither a fool nor a political novice, he was the victim of a political bombshell—free soil—that exploded under his feet.

Support for free soil united northerners who agreed on little else. Some free-soilers opposed slavery on moral grounds and rejected racist legislation, but others were racists who opposed allowing any African-Americans, slave or free, into the West. An abolitionist traced the free-soil convictions of many westerners to a "perfect, if not supreme" hatred of blacks. Racist free-soilers in Iowa and Illinois secured laws prohibiting settlement by black people.

One opinion shared by free-soilers of all persuasions was that slavery impeded whites' progress. Because a slave worked for nothing, the argument ran, no free laborer could compete with a slave. A territory might contain only a handful of slaves or none at all, but as long as Congress refused to prohibit slavery in the territories, the institution would gain a foothold and free laborers would flee. Wherever slavery appeared, a free-soiler proclaimed, "labor loses its dignity; industry sickens; education finds no schools; religion finds no churches; and the whole land of slavery is impoverished." Free-soilers also blasted the idea that slavery had natural limits. One warned that "slavery is as certain to invade New Mexico and Utah as the sun is to rise"; others predicted that if slavery gained a toehold in Kansas, it would soon invade Minnesota.

To free-soilers, the Kansas-Nebraska Act, with its erasure of the Missouri Compromise, was the last straw, for it revealed, one wrote, "a continuous movement by slaveholders to spread slavery over the entire North." For a Whig congressman from Massachusetts who had voted for the Compromise of 1850 and opposed abolitionists, the Kansas-Nebraska Act, "that most wanton and wicked act, so obviously designed to promote the extension of slavery," was too much to bear. "I now advocate the freedom of Kansas under all circumstances, and the prohibition of slavery in all territories now free."

The Ebbing of Manifest Destiny

The uproar over the Kansas-Nebraska Act embarrassed the Pierce administration. It also doomed Manifest Destiny, the one issue that had held the Democrats together in the 1840s.

Franklin Pierce had come to office championing Manifest Destiny, but increasing sectional rivalries sidetracked his efforts. In 1853, his emissary James Gadsden negotiated the purchase from Mexico of a strip of land south of the Gila River (now southern Arizona and part of southern New Mexico), an acquisition favored by advocates of a southern railroad route to the Pacific. Fierce opposition to the Gadsden Purchase revealed mounting free-soilers' suspicion of expansion, and the Senate approved the treaty only after slashing nine thousand square miles from the parcel. The sectional rivalries beginning to engulf the Nebraska bill clearly threatened any proposal to gain new territory.

Cuba provided even more vivid proof of the change in public attitudes about expansion. In 1854, a former Mississippi governor, John A. Quitman, planned a filibuster (an unofficial military expedition) to seize Cuba from Spain. Eager to acquire Cuba, Pierce may have encouraged Quitman, but Pierce forced Quitman to scuttle the expedition when faced with intense opposition from antislavery northerners who saw filibusters as just another manifestation of the **Slave Power**—the conspiracy of slaveholders and their northern dupes to grab more territory for slavery.

Pierce still hoped to purchase Cuba, but events quickly slipped out of his control. In October 1854, the American ambassadors to Great Britain, France, and Spain, two of them southerners, met in Belgium and issued the unofficial Ostend Manifesto, calling on the United States to acquire Cuba by any means, including force. Beset by the storm over the Kansas-Nebraska Act and the furor over Quitman's proposed filibuster, Pierce rejected the mandate.

Despite Pierce's disavowal of the Ostend Manifesto, the idea of expansion into the Caribbean continued to attract southerners, including the Tennessee-born adventurer William Walker. Slightly built and so unassuming that he usually spoke with his hands in his pockets, Walker seemed an unlikely soldier of fortune. Yet between 1853 and 1860, the year a firing squad in Honduras executed him, Walker led a succession of filibustering expeditions into Central America. Taking advantage of civil chaos in Nicaragua, he made himself the chief political force there, reinstituted slavery, and talked of making Nicaragua a U.S. colony.

For all the proclamations and intrigues that surrounded the movement for southern expansion, its strength and goals remained open to question. With few exceptions, the adventurers were shady characters whom southern politicians might admire but on whom they could never depend. Some southerners were against expansion, among them Louisiana sugar planters who opposed acquiring Cuba because Cuban sugar would compete with their product. But expansionists stirred enough commotion to worry antislavery northerners that the South was conspiring to establish a Caribbean slave empire. Like a card in a poker game, the threat of expansion southward was all the more menacing for not being played. As long as the debate on the extension of slavery focused on the continental United States, prospects for expansion were limited. However, adding Caribbean territory to the pot changed all calculations.

The Whigs Disintegrate, 1854–1855

While straining Democratic unity, the Kansas-Nebraska Act wrecked the Whig party. In the law's immediate aftermath, most northern Whigs hoped to blame the Democrats for the act and to entice free-soil Democrats to their side. In the state and congressional elections of 1854, the Democrats were decisively defeated. But the Whig party failed to benefit from the backlash against the Democrats. However furious at Douglas for initiating the act, free-soil Democrats could not forget that the southern Whigs had supported Douglas. In addition, the northern Whigs themselves were deeply divided between antislavery "Conscience" Whigs, led by Senator William Seward of New York, and conservatives, led by former president Millard Fillmore. The conservatives believed that the Whig party had to adhere to the Compromise of 1850 to maintain itself as a national party.

Divisions within the Whig party repelled antislavery Democrats from affiliating with it and prompted many antislavery Whigs to look for an alternative party. By 1856, the new Republican Party would become the home for most of these northern refugees from the traditional parties; but in 1854 and 1855, when the Republican Party was only starting to organize, the American, or Know-Nothing, party emerged as the principal alternative.

The Rise and Fall of the Know-Nothings, 1853–1856
The **Know-Nothings** evolved out of a secret nativist organization, the Order of the Star-Spangled Banner, founded in 1850. (The party's popular name, Know-Nothing, derived from the standard response of its members to inquiries about its activities: "I know nothing.") This order was one of many such societies that mushroomed in response to the unprecedented immigration of the 1840s. It had sought to rid the United States of immigrant and Catholic political influence by pressuring the existing parties to nominate and appoint only native-born Protestants to office and by advocating an extension of the naturalization period before immigrants could vote.

Throughout the 1840s, nativists usually voted Whig, but their allegiance to the Whigs started to buckle during Winfield Scott's campaign for the presidency in 1852. In an attempt to revitalize his party, which was badly split over slavery, Scott had courted the traditionally Democratic Catholic vote. But Scott's tactic backfired. Most Catholics voted for Franklin Pierce. Nativists, meanwhile, felt betrayed by their party, and after Scott's defeat, many gravitated toward the Know-Nothings. The Kansas-Nebraska Act cemented their allegiance to the Know-Nothings, who in the North opposed both the extension of slavery and Catholicism. Indeed, an obsessive fear of conspiracies unified the Know-Nothings. They simultaneously denounced a papal conspiracy against the American republic and a Slave Power conspiracy spreading its tentacles throughout the United States.

The Know-Nothings' surge was truly stunning. In 1854, they captured the governorship, all the congressional seats, and almost all seats in the state legislature in Massachusetts. Know-Nothings were sufficiently strong in the West to retard the emergence of the Republican Party, and so strong in the East that they exploded any hopes that the Whigs had of capitalizing on hostility to the Kansas-Nebraska Act.

After rising spectacularly between 1853 and 1855, the star of Know-Nothingism nevertheless plummeted and gradually disappeared below the horizon after 1856. The Know-Nothings proved as vulnerable as the Whigs to sectional conflicts over slavery. Although primarily a force in the North, the Know-Nothings had a southern wing, comprised mainly of former Whigs who loathed both the antislavery northerners who were abandoning the Whig party and the southern Democrats, whom they viewed as disunionist firebrands. In 1855, these southern Know-Nothings combined with northern conservatives to make acceptance of the Kansas-Nebraska Act part of the Know-Nothing platform, and thus they blurred the attraction of Know-Nothingism to those northern voters who were more antislavery than anti-Catholic.

One such Whig refugee, Illinois congressman Abraham Lincoln, asked pointedly: "How can anyone who abhors the oppression of negroes be in favor of degrading classes of white people?" "We began by declaring," Lincoln continued, "that 'all men are created equal.' We now practically read it 'all men are created equal except negroes.' When the Know-Nothings get control, it will read 'all men are created equal, except Negroes and foreigners and Catholics.'" Finally, even most Know-Nothings eventually came to conclude that, as one observer put it, "neither the Pope nor the foreigners ever can govern the country or endanger its liberties, but the slavebreeders and slavetraders do govern it, and threaten to put an end to all government but theirs." Consequently, the Know-Nothings proved vulnerable to the challenge posed by the emerging Republican Party, which did not officially embrace nativism and which had no southern wing to blunt its antislavery message.

The Republican Party and the Crisis in Kansas, 1855–1856

Born in the chaotic aftermath of the Kansas-Nebraska Act, the **Republican Party** sprang up in several northern states in 1854 and 1855. With the Know-Nothings' demise after 1856, the Republicans would become the main opposition to the Democratic Party, and they would win each presidential election from 1860 until 1884; but in 1855 few would have predicted such a bright future. While united by opposition to the Kansas-Nebraska Act, the party held various shades of opinion in uneasy balance. At one extreme were conservatives who merely wanted to restore the Missouri Compromise; at the other was a small faction of former Liberty Party abolitionists; and the middle held a sizable body of free-soilers.

LIBERTY, THE FAIR MAID OF KANSAS_IN THE HANDS OF THE "BORDER RUFFIANS".

"Liberty, the Fair Maid of Kansas in the Hands of the 'Border Ruffians'"
This cartoon savagely attacks leading northern Democrats for their acquiescence in the murderous actions of proslavery mobs in Kansas. On the left, James Buchanan steals a watch from a corpse. In the center, a tipsy President Franklin Pierce and Lewis Cass leer at the fair maid of Kansas, while on the right Stephen Douglas scalps a victim.

In addition to bridging these divisions, the Republicans confronted the task of building organizations on the state level, where the Know-Nothings were already well established. Politicians of the day knew that the voters' allegiances were often shaped by state issues, including temperance. Maine's passage of the nation's first statewide prohibition law in 1851 spurred calls elsewhere for liquor regulation. Linking support for temperance with anti-Catholicism and antislavery, the Know-Nothings were well positioned to answer these calls.

Frequently, antislavery voters were also protemperance and anti-Catholic, believing that addiction to alcohol and submission to the pope were both forms of enslavement to be eradicated. Intensely moralistic, such voters viewed the traditional parties as controlled by unprincipled hacks, and they began to search for a new party. In competing with the Know-Nothings on the state level, the Republicans faced a dilemma, stemming from the fact that both parties were targeting many of the same voters. The Republicans had clearer antislavery credentials than did the Know-Nothings, but this fact alone did not guarantee that voters would respond more to antislavery than to anti-Catholicism or temperance. Thus, if the Republicans attacked the Know-Nothings for stressing anti-Catholicism over antislavery, they ran the risk of alienating the very voters whom they had to attract. If they conciliated the Know-Nothings, they might lose their own identity as a party.

Alternately attacking and conciliating, the Republicans had some successes in state elections in 1855; but as popular ire against the Kansas-Nebraska Act cooled, they also suffered setbacks. By the start of 1856, they were organized in only half the northern states and lacked any national organization. The Republicans desperately needed a development that would make voters worry more about the Slave Power than about rum or Catholicism. Salvation for the nascent party came in the form of violence in Kansas, which quickly became known as Bleeding Kansas. This violence united the party around its free-soil center, intensified antislavery feelings, and boosted Republican fortunes.

In the wake of the Kansas-Nebraska Act, Boston-based abolitionists had organized the New England Emigrant Aid Company to send antislavery settlers into Kansas. The abolitionists' aim was to stifle escalating efforts to turn Kansas into a slave state. But antislavery New Englanders arrived slowly in Kansas; the bulk of the territory's early settlers came from Missouri or elsewhere in the Midwest. Very few of these early settlers opposed slavery on moral grounds. Some, in fact, favored slavery; others wanted to keep all blacks, whether slave or free, out of Kansas.

Despite most settlers' racist leanings and utter hatred of abolitionists, Kansas became a battleground between proslavery and antislavery forces. In March 1855, thousands of proslavery Missourian "border ruffians," led by Senator David R. Atchison, crossed into Kansas to vote illegally in the first election for a territorial legislature. Drawing and cocking their revolvers, they quickly silenced any judges who questioned their right to vote in Kansas. These proslavery advocates probably would have won an honest election because they would have been supported by the votes both of slaveholders and of nonslaveholders horrified at rumors that abolitionists planned to use Kansas as a colony for fugitive slaves. But by stealing the election, the proslavery forces committed a grave tactical blunder. A cloud of fraudulence thereafter hung over the proslavery legislature subsequently established at Lecompton, Kansas. "There is not a proslavery man of my acquaintance in Kansas," wrote the wife of an antislavery farmer, "who does not acknowledge that the Bogus Legislature was the result of a gigantic and well planned fraud, that the elections were carried by an invading mob from Missouri." This legislature then further darkened its image by expelling several antislavery legislators and passing a succession of outrageous acts, limiting officeholding to individuals who would swear allegiance to slavery, punishing the harboring of fugitive slaves by ten years' imprisonment, and making the circulation of abolitionist literature a capital offense.

The territorial legislature's actions set off a chain reaction. Free-staters, including a small number of abolitionists and a much larger number of settlers enraged by the proceedings at Lecompton, organized a rival government at Topeka, Kansas, in the summer and fall of 1855. In response, the Lecompton government in May 1856 dispatched a posse to Lawrence, where free-staters, heeding the advice of antislavery minister Henry Ward Beecher that rifles would do more than Bibles to enforce morality in Kansas, had taken up arms and dubbed their guns "Beecher's Bibles." Riding under flags emblazoned "southern rights" and "let yankees tremble and abolitionists fall," the proslavery posse tore through the town like a hell-bent mob, burning several buildings and destroying two free-state presses. There were no deaths, but Republicans immediately dubbed the incident "the sack of Lawrence."

The next move was made by John Brown. The sack of Lawrence convinced Brown that God now beckoned him "to break the jaws of the wicked." In late May, Brown led seven men, including his four sons and his son-in-law, toward the Pottawatomie Creek near Lawrence. Setting upon five men associated with the Lecompton government, they shot one to death and hacked the others to pieces with broadswords. Brown's "Pottawatomie massacre" struck terror into the hearts of southerners and completed the transformation of Bleeding Kansas into a battleground between the South and the North. A month after the massacre, a South Carolinian living in Kansas wrote to his sister,

SOUTHERN CHIVALRY — ARGUMENT versus CLUB'S.

"Southern Chivalry"   *Cartoons like this one, showing the beating of antislavery Senator Charles Sumner by Preston "Bully" Brooks, confirmed northern images of white southerners as people who prided themselves on their genteel manners but who behaved like street toughs.*

I never lie down without taking the precaution to fasten my door and fix it in such a way that if it is forced open, it can be opened only wide enough for one person to come in at a time. I have my rifle, revolver, and old home-stocked pistol where I can lay my hand on them in an instant, besides a hatchet and an axe. I take this precaution to guard against the midnight attacks of the Abolitionists, who never make an attack in open daylight, and no Proslavery man knows when he is safe in this Ter[ritory.]

In Kansas, popular sovereignty flunked its major test. Instead of quickly resolving the issue of slavery extension, popular sovereignty merely institutionalized the division over slavery by creating rival governments in Lecompton and Topeka. The Pierce administration then shot itself in the foot by denouncing the Topeka government and recognizing only its Lecompton rival. Pierce had forced northern Democrats into the awkward position of appearing to ally with the South in support of the "Bogus Legislature" at Lecompton.

Nor did popular sovereignty keep the slavery issue out of national politics. On the day before the sack of Lawrence, Republican senator **Charles Sumner** of Massachusetts delivered a bombastic and wrathful speech, "The Crime Against Kansas," in which he verbally whipped most of the U.S. Senate for complicity in slavery. Sumner singled out Senator Andrew Butler of South Carolina for his choice of "the harlot, slavery" as his mistress and for the "loose expectoration" of his speech (a nasty reference to the aging Butler's tendency to drool). Sumner's oration stunned most senators. Douglas wondered aloud whether Sumner's real aim was "to provoke some of us to kick him as we would a dog in the street." Two days later, a relative of Butler, Democratic representative Preston Brooks of South Carolina, strode into the Senate chamber, found Sumner at his desk, and struck him repeatedly with a cane. The hollow cane broke after five or six blows, but Sumner required stitches, experienced shock, and did not return to the Senate for three years. Brooks became an instant hero in the South, and the fragments of his weapon were "begged as sacred relics." A new cane, presented to Brooks by the city of Charleston, bore the inscription "Hit him again."

Now Bleeding Kansas and Bleeding Sumner united the North. The sack of Lawrence, Pierce's recognition of the proslavery Lecompton government, and Brooks's actions seemed to clinch the Republican argument that an aggressive "slaveocracy" held white northerners in contempt. Abolitionists remained unpopular in northern opinion, but southerners were becoming even less popular. Northern migrants to Kansas coined a name reflecting their feelings about southerners: "the pukes." Other northerners attacked the slaveholding migrants to Kansas as the "Missouri savages." By denouncing Slave Power more than slavery itself, Republican propagandists sidestepped the issue of slavery's morality, which divided their followers, and focused on portraying southern planters as arrogant aristocrats and the natural enemies of the laboring people of the North.

The Election of 1856

The election of 1856 revealed the scope of the political realignments of the preceding few years. In this, its first presidential contest, the Republican Party nominated John C. Frémont, the famed "pathfinder" who had played a key role in the conquest of California during the Mexican War. The Republicans then maneuvered the northern Know-Nothings into endorsing Frémont. The southern Know-Nothings picked the last Whig president, Millard Fillmore, as their candidate, and the Democrats dumped Pierce for the seasoned James Buchanan of Pennsylvania. A four-term congressman and long an aspirant to the presidency, Buchanan finally secured his party's nomination because he had the good luck to be out of the country (as minister to Great Britain) during the furor over the Kansas-Nebraska Act. As a signer of the Ostend Manifesto, he was popular in the South: virtually all of his close friends in Washington were southerners.

The campaign quickly turned into two separate races—Frémont versus Buchanan in the free states and Fillmore versus Buchanan in the slave states. In the North, the candidates divided clearly over slavery extension; Frémont's platform called for congressional prohibition of slavery in the territories, whereas Buchanan pledged congressional "non-interference." In the South, Fillmore appealed to traditionally Whig voters and called for moderation in the face of secessionist threats. But by nominating a well-known moderate in Buchanan, the Democrats undercut some of Fillmore's appeal. Although Fillmore garnered more than 40 percent of the popular vote in ten of the slave states, he carried only Maryland. In the North, Frémont outpolled Buchanan in the popular vote and won eleven of the sixteen free states; if Frémont had carried Pennsylvania and either Illinois, Indiana, or New Jersey, he would have won the election. As it turned out, Buchanan, the only truly national candidate in the race, secured the presidency.

The election yielded three clear conclusions. First, the American party was finished as a major national force. Having worked for the Republican Frémont, most northern Know-Nothings now joined that party, and in the wake of Fillmore's dismal showing in the South, southern Know-Nothings gave up on their party and sought new political affiliations. Second, although in existence scarcely more than a year, lacking any base in the South, and running a political novice, the Republican Party did very well. A purely sectional party had come within reach of capturing the presidency. Finally, as long as the Democrats could unite behind a single national candidate, they would be hard to defeat. To achieve such unity, however, the Democrats would have to find more James Buchanans—"doughface" moderates who would be acceptable to southerners and who would not drive even more northerners into Republican arms.

THE CRISIS OF THE UNION, 1857–1860

No one ever accused James Buchanan of impulsiveness or fanaticism. Although he disapproved of slavery, he believed that his administration could neither restrict nor end the institution. In 1860, he would pronounce secession a grave wrong, but would affirm that his administration could not stop it. Understandably, contemporaries hailed his election as a victory for moderation. Yet his administration encountered a succession of controversies, first over the famed *Dred Scott* decision of the Supreme Court, then over the proslavery Lecompton constitution in Kansas, next following the raid by John Brown on Harpers Ferry, and finally concerning secession itself. Ironically, a man who sought to avoid controversy presided over one of the most controversy-ridden administrations in American history.

Buchanan's problems arose less from his own actions than from the fact that the forces driving the nation apart were already spinning out of control by 1856. By the time of Buchanan's inauguration, southerners who looked north saw creeping abolitionism in the guise of free soil, whereas northerners who looked south saw an insatiable Slave Power. Once these images had taken hold in the minds of the American people, politicians like James Buchanan had little room to maneuver.

The Dred Scott Case, 1857

Pledged to congressional "non-interference" with slavery in the territories, Buchanan had long looked to the courts for a nonpartisan resolution of the vexatious issue of slavery extension. A case that appeared to promise such a solution had been wending its way through the courts for years; and on March 6, 1857, two days after Buchanan's inauguration, the Supreme Court handed down its decision in ***Dred Scott* v. *Sandford.***

During the 1830s, Dred Scott, a slave, had been taken by his master from the slave state of Missouri into Illinois and the Wisconsin Territory, areas respectively closed to slavery by the Northwest Ordinance of 1787 and the Missouri Compromise. After his master's death, Scott sued for his freedom on the grounds of his residence in free territory. In 1856, the case finally reached the Supreme Court.

The Court faced two key questions. Did Scott's residence in free territory during the 1830s make him free? Regardless of the answer to this question, did Scott, again enslaved in Missouri, have a right to sue in the federal courts? The Court could have resolved the case on narrow grounds by answering the second question in the negative, but Buchanan wanted a far-reaching decision that would deal with the broad issue of slavery in the territories.

In the end, Buchanan got the broad ruling that he sought, but one so controversial that it settled little. In the most important of six separate majority opinions, Chief Justice Roger B. Taney, a seventy-nine-year-old Marylander whom Andrew Jackson had appointed to succeed John Marshall in 1835, began with the narrow conclusion that Scott, a slave, could not sue for his freedom. Then the thunder started. No black, whether a slave or a free person descended from a slave, could become a citizen of the United States, Taney continued. Next Taney whipped the thunderheads into a tornado. Even if Scott had been a legal plaintiff, Taney ruled, his residence in free territory years earlier did not make him free, because the Missouri Compromise, whose provisions prohibited slavery in the Wisconsin Territory, was itself unconstitutional. The compromise, declared Taney, violated the Fifth Amendment's protection of property (including slaves).

Contrary to Buchanan's hopes, the decision touched off a new blast of controversy over slavery in the territories. The antislavery press flayed it as a "willful perversion" filled with "gross historical falsehoods." Taney's ruling gave Republicans more evidence that a fiendish Slave Power conspiracy gripped the nation. Although the Kansas-Nebraska Act had effectively repealed the Missouri Compromise, the Court's majority now rejected even the principle behind the compromise, the idea that Congress could prohibit slavery in the territories. Five of the six justices who rejected this principle were from slave states. The Slave Power, a northern paper bellowed, "has marched over and annihilated the boundaries of the states. We are now one great homogenous slave-holding community."

Like Stephen Douglas after the Kansas-Nebraska Act, President Buchanan now appeared to be a northern dupe of the "slaveocracy." Republicans restrained themselves from open defiance of the decision only by insisting that it did not bind the nation; Taney's comments on the constitutionality of the Missouri Compromise, they contended, amounted merely to *obiter dicta*, opinions superfluous to settling the case.

Reactions to the decision underscored the fact that by 1857 no "judicious" or non-partisan solution to slavery extension was possible. Anyone who still doubted this needed only to read the fast-breaking news from Kansas.

The Lecompton Constitution, 1857 While the Supreme Court wrestled with the abstract issues raised by the expansion of slavery, Buchanan sought a concrete solution to the gnawing problem of Kansas, where the free-state government at Topeka and the officially recognized proslavery government at Lecompton viewed each other with profound distrust. Buchanan's plan for Kansas looked simple: an elected territorial convention would draw up a constitution that would either permit or prohibit slavery; Buchanan would submit the constitution to Congress; Congress would then admit Kansas as a state.

Unfortunately, the plan exploded in Buchanan's face. Popular sovereignty, the essence of Buchanan's plan, demanded fair play, a scarce quality in Kansas. The territory's history of fraudulent elections left both sides reluctant to commit their fortunes to the polls. An election for a constitutional convention took place in June 1857, but free-staters, by now a majority in Kansas, boycotted the election on the grounds that the proslavery side would rig it. Dominated by proslavery delegates, a constitutional convention then met and drew up a frame of government, the **Lecompton constitution,** that protected the rights of those slaveholders already living in Kansas to their slave property and provided for a referendum in which voters could decide whether to allow in more slaves.

The Lecompton constitution created a dilemma for Buchanan. A supporter of popular sovereignty, he had gone on record in favor of letting the voters in Kansas decide the slavery issue. Now he was confronted by a constitution drawn up by a convention that had been elected by less than 10 percent of the eligible voters, by plans for a referendum that would not allow voters to remove slaves already in Kansas, and by the prospect that the proslavery side would conduct the referendum no more honestly than it had other ballots. Yet Buchanan had compelling reasons to accept the Lecompton constitution as the basis for the admission of Kansas as a state. The South, which had provided him with 112 of his 174 electoral votes in 1856, supported the constitution. Buchanan knew, moreover, that only about two hundred slaves resided in Kansas, and he believed that the prospects for slavery in the remaining territories were slight. The contention over slavery in Kansas struck him as another example of how extremists could turn minor issues into major ones. To accept the constitution and speed the admission of Kansas as either a free state or a slave state seemed the best way to pull the rug from beneath the extremists and quiet the ruckus in Kansas. Accordingly, in December 1857 Buchanan endorsed the Lecompton constitution.

Stephen A. Douglas and other northern Democrats broke with Buchanan. To them, the Lecompton constitution, in allowing voters to decide only whether more slaves could enter Kansas, violated the spirit of popular sovereignty. "I care not whether [slavery] is voted down or voted up," Douglas declared. But to refuse to allow a vote on the constitution itself, with its protection of existing slave property, smacked of a "system of trickery and jugglery to defeat the fair expression of the will of the people."

Even as Douglas broke with Buchanan, events in Kansas took a new turn. A few months after electing delegates to the convention that drew up the Lecompton constitution, Kansans had gone to the polls to elect a territorial legislature. So flagrant was the fraud in this election—one village with thirty eligible voters returned more than sixteen hundred proslavery votes—that the governor disallowed enough proslavery returns to give free-staters a majority in the legislature. This territorial legislature then called for a referendum on the entire document. Whereas the Kansas constitutional convention had restricted the choice of voters to the narrow issue of the future introduction of slaves, the territorial legislature sought a referendum that would allow Kansans to vote against the protection of existing slave property as well.

In December 1857, the referendum called earlier by the constitutional convention was held. Boycotted by free-staters, the constitution with slavery passed overwhelmingly. Two weeks later, in the election called by the territorial legislature, the proslavery side abstained, and the constitution went down to crushing defeat. Buchanan tried to ignore this second election, but when he attempted to bring Kansas into the Union under the Lecompton constitution, Congress blocked him and forced yet another referendum. This time, Kansans were given the choice between accepting or rejecting the entire constitution, with the proviso that rejection would delay statehood. Despite the proviso, Kansans overwhelmingly voted down the constitution.

Buchanan simultaneously had failed to tranquilize Kansas and alienated northerners in his own party. His support for the Lecompton constitution confirmed the suspicion of northern Democrats that the southern Slave Power pulled all the important strings in their party. Douglas became the hero of the hour for northern Democrats. "The bone and sinew of the Northern Democracy are with you," a New Yorker wrote to Douglas. Yet Douglas himself could take little comfort from the Lecompton fiasco, as his cherished formula of popular sovereignty increasingly looked like a prescription for civil strife rather than harmony.

The Lincoln-Douglas Debates, 1858 Despite the acclaim he gained in the North for his stand against the Lecompton constitution, Douglas faced a stiff challenge in Illinois for reelection to the United States Senate. Of his Republican opponent, Abraham Lincoln, Douglas said: "I shall have my hands full. He is the strong man of his party—full of wit, facts, dates—and the best stump speaker with his droll ways and dry jokes, in the West."

Physically as well as ideologically, the two men formed a striking contrast. Tall (6'4") and gangling, **Abraham Lincoln** once described himself as "a piece of floating driftwood." Energy, ambition, and a passion for self-education had carried him from the Kentucky log cabin in which he was born in 1809 through a youth filled with various occupations (farm laborer, surveyor, rail-splitter, flatboatman, and storekeeper) into law and politics in his adopted Illinois. There he had capitalized on westerners' support for internal improvements to gain election to Congress in 1846 as a Whig. Having opposed the Mexican-American War and the Kansas-Nebraska Act, he joined the Republican Party in 1856.

Douglas was fully a foot shorter than the towering Lincoln. But his compact frame contained astonishing energy. Born in New England, Douglas appealed primarily to the small farmers of southern origin who populated the Illinois flatlands. To these and others, he was the "little giant," the personification of the Democratic Party in the West. The campaign quickly became more than just another Senate race, for it pitted the Republican Party's rising star against the Senate's leading Democrat and, thanks to the railroad and the telegraph, received unprecedented national attention.

Abraham Lincoln *Clean-shaven at the time of his famous debates with Douglas, Lincoln would soon grow a beard to give himself a more distinguished appearance.*

Although some Republicans extolled Douglas's stand against the Lecompton constitution, to Lincoln nothing had changed. Douglas was still Douglas, the author of the infamous Kansas-Nebraska Act and a man who cared not whether slavery was voted up or down as long as the vote was honest. Opening his campaign with the "House Divided" speech ("this nation cannot exist permanently half slave and half free"), Lincoln reminded his Republican followers of the gulf that still separated his doctrine of free soil from Douglas's popular sovereignty. Douglas dismissed the house-divided doctrine as an invitation to secession. What mattered to him was not slavery, which he viewed as merely an extreme way to subordinate a supposedly inferior race, but the continued expansion of white settlement. Like Lincoln, he wanted to keep slavery out of the path of white settlement. But unlike his rival, Douglas believed that popular sovereignty was the surest way to attain this goal without disrupting the Union.

The high point of the campaign came in a series of seven debates held from August to October 1858. The Lincoln-Douglas debates mixed political drama with the atmosphere of a festival. At the debate in Galesburg, for example, dozens of horse-drawn floats descended on the town from nearby farming communities. One bore thirty-two girls dressed in white, one for each state, and a thirty-third who dressed in black with the label "Kansas" and carried a banner proclaiming "they won't let me in."

Douglas used the debates to portray Lincoln as a virtual abolitionist and advocate of racial equality. Both charges were calculated to doom Lincoln in the eyes of the intensely racist Illinois voters. In response, Lincoln affirmed that Congress had no constitutional authority to abolish slavery in the South, and in one debate he asserted bluntly that "I am not, nor ever have been in favor of bringing about the social and political equality of the white, and black man." However, fending off charges of extremism was getting Lincoln nowhere; so in order to seize the initiative, he tried to maneuver Douglas into a corner.

In view of the *Dred Scott* decision, Lincoln asked in the debate at Freeport, could the people of a territory lawfully exclude slavery? In essence, Lincoln was asking Douglas to reconcile popular sovereignty with the *Dred Scott* decision. Lincoln had long contended that the Court's decision rendered popular sovereignty as thin as soup boiled from the shadow of a pigeon that had starved to death. If, as the Supreme Court's ruling affirmed, Congress had no authority to exclude slavery from a territory, then it seemingly followed that a territorial legislature created by Congress also lacked power to do so. To no one's surprise, Douglas replied that notwithstanding the *Dred Scott* decision, the voters of a territory could effectively exclude slavery simply by refusing to enact laws that gave legal protection to slave property.

Douglas's "Freeport doctrine" salvaged popular sovereignty but did nothing for his reputation among southerners, who preferred the guarantees of the *Dred Scott* ruling to the uncertainties of popular sovereignty. Whereas Douglas's stand against the Lecompton constitution had already tattered his reputation in the South ("he is already dead there," Lincoln affirmed), his Freeport doctrine stiffened southern opposition to his presidential ambitions.

Lincoln faced the problem throughout the debates that free soil and popular sovereignty, although distinguishable in theory, had much the same practical effect. Neither Lincoln nor Douglas doubted that popular sovereignty, if fairly applied, would keep slavery out of the territories. In the closing debates, in order to keep the initiative and sharpen their differences, Lincoln shifted toward attacks on slavery as "a moral, social, and political evil." He argued that Douglas's view of slavery as merely an eccentric and unsavory southern custom would dull the nation's conscience and facilitate the legalization of slavery everywhere. But Lincoln compromised his own position by rejecting both abolition and equality for blacks.

Neither man scored a clear victory in argument, and the senatorial election itself settled no major issues. Douglas's supporters captured a majority of the seats in the state legislature, which at the time was responsible for electing U.S. senators. But despite the racist leanings of most Illinois voters, Republican candidates for the state legislature won a slightly larger share of the popular vote than did their Democratic rivals. Moreover, in its larger significance, the contest solidified the sectional split in the national Democratic Party and made Lincoln famous in the North and infamous in the South.

The Legacy of Harpers Ferry   Although Lincoln rejected abolitionism, he called free soil a step toward the "ultimate extinction" of slavery. Similarly, New York Republican senator William H. Seward spoke of an "irrepressible conflict" between slavery and freedom. Predictably, many white southerners ignored the distinction between free soil and abolition, and concluded that Republicans and abolitionists were joined in an unholy alliance against slavery. To many in the

South, the North seemed to be controlled by demented leaders bent on civil war. One southern defender of slavery equated the doctrines of the abolitionists with those of "Socialists, of Free Love and Free Lands, Free Churches, Free Women and Free Negroes-of No-Marriage, No-Religion, No-Private Property, No-Law and No-Government."

Nothing did more to freeze this southern image of the North than the evidence of northern complicity in John Brown's raid on Harpers Ferry and northern sermons that turned Brown into a martyr. In Philadelphia, some 250 outraged southern students left the city's medical schools to enroll in southern schools. True, Lincoln and Seward condemned the raid, but white southerners suspected that they regretted the conspiracy's failure more than the attempt itself.

Brown's abortive raid also rekindled southern fears of a slave insurrection. Rumors flew around the South, and vigilantes turned out to battle conspiracies that existed only in their minds. Volunteers, for example, mobilized to defend northeastern Texas against thousands of abolitionists supposedly on their way to pillage Dallas and its environs. In other incidents, vigilantes rounded up thousands of slaves, tortured some into confessing to nonexistent plots, and then lynched them. The hysteria fed by such rumors played into the hands of the extremists known as fire-eaters, who encouraged the witch-hunt by spreading tales of slave conspiracies in the press so that southern voters would turn to them as alone able to "stem the current of Abolition."

More and more southerners concluded that the Republican Party itself directed abolitionism and deserved blame for Brown's raid. After all, had not influential Republicans assailed slavery, unconstitutionally tried to ban it, and spoken of an "irrepressible conflict" between slavery and freedom? The Tennessee legislature reflected southern views when it passed resolutions declaring that the Harpers Ferry raid was "the natural fruit of this treasonable 'irrepressible conflict' doctrine put forth by the great head of the Black Republican party and echoed by his subordinates."

The South Contemplates Secession	A pamphlet published in 1860 embodied in its title the growing conviction of southerners that *The South Alone Should Govern the South*. Southerners reached this conclusion gradually and often reluctantly. In 1850, few southerners could have

conceived of transferring their allegiance from the United States to some new nation. Relatively insulated from the main tide of immigration, southerners thought of themselves as the most American of Americans. But the events of the 1850s persuaded many southerners that the North had deserted the true principles of the Union. Southerners interpreted northern resistance to the Fugitive Slave Act and to slavery in Kansas as either illegal or unconstitutional, and they viewed headline-grabbing phrases such as "irrepressible conflict" and "a higher law" as virtual declarations of war on the South. To southerners, it was the North, not the South, that had grown peculiar. (See Beyond America—Global Interactions: Slave Emancipation in the Atlantic World.)

To white southerners, the North, not slavery, was the problem. A Mississippi planter, for example, could scarcely believe his eyes when he witnessed a group of northern free blacks refusing to surrender their seats to white women. When assured by northern friends of their support for the South, southerners could only wonder why northerners kept electing Republicans to office. Southerners increasingly described their visits to the North as forays into "enemy territory." More and more, they agreed with a South Carolinian's insistence that the South had to sever itself "from the rotten Northern element."

Viewed as a practical tactic to secure concrete goals, secession did not make a great deal of sense. Some southerners contended that secession would make it easier for the South to acquire more territory for slavery in the Caribbean; yet the South was scarcely united in desiring additional slave territory in Mexico, Cuba, or Central America. States like Alabama, Mississippi, and Texas contained vast tracts of unsettled land that could be converted to cotton cultivation far more easily than the Caribbean. Other southerners continued to complain that the North blocked the access of slaveholders to territories in the continental United States. But if the South were to secede, the remaining continental territories would belong exclusively to the North, which could then legislate for them as it chose. Nor would secession stop future John Browns from infiltrating the South to provoke slave insurrections.

Yet to dwell on the impracticality of secession as a choice for the South is to miss the point. Talk of secession was less a tactic with clear goals than an expression of the South's outrage at what southerners viewed as the irresponsible and unconstitutional course that the Republicans were taking in the North. It was not merely that Republican attacks on slavery sowed the seeds of slave uprisings. More fundamentally, southerners believed that the North was treating the South as its inferior—indeed, as no more than a slave. "Talk of Negro slavery," exclaimed southern proslavery philosopher George Fitzhugh, "is not half so humiliating and disgraceful as the slavery of the South to the North." Having persuaded themselves that slavery made it possible for them to enjoy unprecedented freedom and equality, white southerners took great pride in their homeland. They bitterly dismissed Republican portrayals of the South as a region of arrogant planters and degraded white common folk. Submission to the Republicans, declared Democratic senator Jefferson Davis of Mississippi, "would be intolerable to a proud people."

THE COLLAPSE OF THE UNION, 1860–1861

As long as the pliant James Buchanan occupied the White House, southerners did no more than talk about secession. Once aware that Buchanan had declined to seek reelection, however, they approached the election of 1860 with anxiety. Although not all voters realized it, when they cast their ballots in 1860 they were deciding not just the outcome of an election but the fate of the Union. Lincoln's election initiated the process by which the southern states abandoned the United States for a new nation, the Confederate States of America. Initially, the Confederacy consisted only of states in the Lower South. As the Upper South hesitated to embrace secession, moderates searched frantically for a compromise that would save the Union. But they searched in vain. The time for compromise had passed.

The Election of 1860   As a single-issue, free-soil party, the Republicans had done well in the election of 1856. To win in 1860, however, they would have to broaden their appeal in the North, particularly in states like Pennsylvania and Illinois, which they had lost in 1856. To do so, Republican leaders had concluded, they needed to forge an economic program to complement their advocacy of free soil.

A severe economic slump following the so-called Panic of 1857 furnished the Republicans with a fitting opening. The depression shattered more than a decade of American prosperity and thrust economic concerns to the fore. In response, in the late 1850s the Republicans developed an economic program based on support for a protective tariff (popular in Pennsylvania) and on two issues favored in the Midwest, federal aid for internal improvements and the granting to settlers of free 160-acre homesteads out of publicly owned land. By proposing to make these homesteads available to immigrants who were not yet citizens, the Republicans went far in shedding the nativist image that lingered from their early association with the Know-Nothings. Carl Schurz, an 1848 German political refugee who had campaigned for Lincoln against Douglas in 1858, now labored mightily to bring his antislavery countrymen over to the Republican Party.

The Republicans' desire to broaden their appeal also influenced their choice of a candidate. At their convention in Chicago, they nominated Abraham Lincoln over the early front-runner, William H. Seward of New York. Although better known than Lincoln, Seward failed to convince his party that he could carry the key states of Pennsylvania, Illinois, Indiana, and New Jersey. (Rueful Republicans remembered that their presidential candidate John C. Frémont would have won in 1856 if he had carried Pennsylvania and one of the other three states.) Lincoln held the advantage not only of hailing from Illinois but also of projecting a more moderate image than Seward on the slavery issue. Seward's penchant for controversial phrases like "irrepressible conflict" and "higher law" had given him a radical image. Lincoln, in contrast, had repeatedly affirmed that Congress had no constitutional right to interfere with slavery in the South and had explicitly rejected the "higher law" doctrine. The Republicans now needed only to widen their northern appeal.

The Democrats, still claiming to be a national party, had to bridge their own sectional differences. The *Dred Scott* decision and the conflict over the Lecompton constitution had weakened the northern Democrats and strengthened southern Democrats. While Douglas still desperately defended popular sovereignty, southern Democrats stretched *Dred Scott* to conclude that Congress now had to protect slavery in the territories.

The Democratic Party's internal turmoil boiled over at its Charleston convention in the spring of 1860. Failing to force acceptance of a platform guaranteeing federal protection of slavery in the territories, the delegates from the Lower South stalked out. The convention adjourned to Baltimore, where a new fight broke out over the question of seating hastily elected pro-Douglas slates of delegates from the Lower South states that had seceded from the Charleston convention. The decision to seat these pro-Douglas slates led to a walkout by delegates from Virginia and other states in the Upper South. The remaining delegates nominated Douglas; the seceders marched off to another hall in Baltimore and nominated Buchanan's vice president, John C. Breckinridge of Kentucky, on a platform calling for the congressional protection of slavery in the territories. Unable to rally behind a single nominee, the divided Democrats thus ran two candidates, Douglas and Breckinridge. The disruption of the Democratic Party was now complete.

The South still contained an appreciable number of moderates, often former Whigs who had joined with the Know-Nothings behind Fillmore in 1856. In 1860, these moderates, aided by former northern Whigs who opposed both Lincoln and Douglas, forged the new Constitutional Union Party and nominated John Bell, a Tennessee slaveholder who had opposed both the Kansas-Nebraska Act and the Lecompton constitution. Calling for the preservation of the Union, the new party took no stand on the divisive issue of slavery extension.

With four candidates in the field, voters faced a relatively clear choice. Lincoln conceded that the South had a constitutional right to preserve slavery but demanded that

Congress prohibit its extension. At the other extreme, Breckinridge insisted that Congress had to protect slavery in any territory that contained slaves. This left the middle ground to Bell and Douglas, the latter still committed to popular sovereignty but in search of a verbal formula that might reconcile it with the *Dred Scott* decision. Lincoln won a clear majority of the electoral vote, 180 to 123 for his three opponents combined. Although Lincoln gained only 39 percent of the popular vote, his popular votes were concentrated in the North, the majority section, and were sufficient to carry every free state. Douglas ran a respectable second to Lincoln in the popular vote but a dismal last in the electoral vote. As the only candidate to campaign in both sections, Douglas suffered from the scattered nature of his votes and carried only Missouri. Bell won Virginia, Kentucky, and Tennessee, and Breckinridge captured Maryland and the Lower South.

The Movement for Secession   The president-elect was so unpopular in the South that his name had not even appeared on the ballot in many southern states. Lincoln's election struck most of the white South as a calculated northern insult. The North, a South Carolina planter told a visitor from England, "has got so far toward being abolitionized as to elect a man avowedly hostile to our institutions."

Few southerners believed that Lincoln would fulfill his promise to protect slavery in the South, and most feared that he would act as a mere front man for more John Browns. "Now that the black radical Republicans have the power I suppose they will Brown us all," a South Carolinian lamented. An uneducated Mississippian residing in Illinois expressed his reaction to the election more bluntly:

MAP 14.2 The Election of 1860

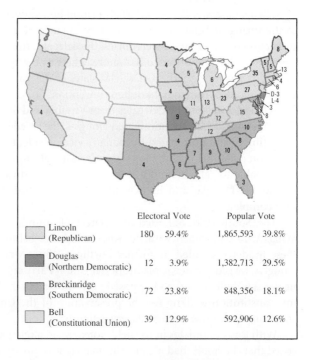

		Electoral Vote		Popular Vote	
Lincoln (Republican)		180	59.4%	1,865,593	39.8%
Douglas (Northern Democratic)		12	3.9%	1,382,713	29.5%
Breckinridge (Southern Democratic)		72	23.8%	848,356	18.1%
Bell (Constitutional Union)		39	12.9%	592,906	12.6%

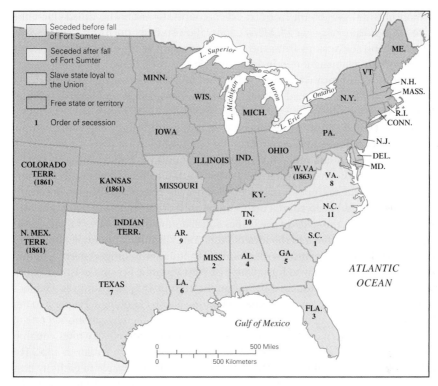

Seceded before fall of Fort Sumter

Seceded after fall of Fort Sumter

Slave state loyal to the Union

Free state or territory

1   Order of secession

L. Superior

MINN.

WIS.

L. Michigan

MICH.

L. Huron

L. Ontario

L. Erie

ME.

VT

N.H.

MASS.

N.Y.

R.I.

CONN.

PA.

N.J.

DEL.

MD.

IOWA

OHIO

ILLINOIS IND.

W.VA.
(1863)

VA.
8

COLORADO
TERR.
(1861)

KANSAS
(1861)

MISSOURI

KY.

TN.
10

N.C.
11

N. MEX.
TERR.
(1861)

INDIAN
TERR.

AR.
9

S.C.
1

ATLANTIC
OCEAN

MISS.
2

AL.
4

GA.
5

TEXAS
7

LA.
6

FLA.
3

Gulf of Mexico

0   500 Miles

0   500 Kilometers

MAP 14.3 Secession

Four key states—Virginia, Arkansas, Tennessee, and North Carolina—did not secede until after the fall of Fort Sumter. The border slave states of Maryland, Delaware, Kentucky, and Missouri stayed in the Union.

> It seems the north wants the south to raise cotton and sugar rice tobacco for the northern states, also to pay taxes and fight her battles and get territory for the purpose of the north to send her greasy Dutch and free niggers into the territory to get rid of them. At any rate that was what elected old Abe President. Some professed conservative Republicans Think and say that Lincoln will be conservative also but sir my opinion is that Lincoln will deceive them. [He] will undoubtedly please the abolitionists for at his election they nearly all went into fits with Joy.

Some southerners had threatened secession at the prospect of Lincoln's election. Now the moment of decision had arrived. On December 20, 1860, a South Carolina convention voted unanimously for secession; in short order Alabama, Mississippi, Florida, Georgia, Louisiana, and Texas followed. On February 4, delegates from these seven states met in Montgomery, Alabama, and established the **Confederate States of America.**

Despite the abruptness of southern withdrawal from the Union, the movement for secession was laced with uncertainty. Many southerners had resisted calls for immediate secession. Even after Lincoln's election, fire-eating secessionists had met fierce opposition in the Lower South from so-called cooperationists, who called upon the South to act in unison or not at all. Many cooperationists had hoped to delay secession in order to wring concessions from the North that might remove the need for secession. Jefferson Davis, inaugurated in February 1861 as president of the Confederacy, was a reluctant secessionist who remained in the United States Senate two weeks after his own state of Mississippi had seceded. Even zealous advocates of secession had a hard time reconciling themselves to secession and believing that they were no longer citizens of the United States. "How do you feel now, dear Mother," a Georgian wrote, "that *we* are in a foreign land?"

At first, the Upper South states of Virginia, North Carolina, Tennessee, and Arkansas flatly rejected secession. In contrast to the Lower South, which had a guaranteed export market for its cotton, the Upper South depended heavily on economic ties to the North that would be severed by secession. Furthermore, with proportionately far fewer slaves than the Lower South, the states of the Upper South doubted the loyalty of their sizable nonslaveholding populations to the idea of secession. Virginia, for example, had every reason to question the allegiance to secession of its nonslaveholding western counties, which would soon break away to form Unionist West Virginia. Few in the Upper South could forget the raw nerve touched by the publication in 1857 of Hinton R. Helper's *The Impending Crisis of the South*. A nonslaveholding North Carolinian, Helper had described slavery as a curse upon poor white southerners and thereby questioned one of the most sacred southern doctrines, the idea that slavery rendered all whites equal. If secession were to spark a war between the states, moreover, the Upper South appeared to be the likeliest battleground. Whatever the exact weight assignable to each of these factors, one point is clear: the secession movement that South Carolina so boldly started in December 1860 seemed to be falling apart by March 1861.

The Search for Compromise
The lack of southern unity confirmed the view of most Republicans that the secessionists were more bluster than substance. Seward described secession as the work of "a relatively few hotheads," and Lincoln believed that the loyal majority of southerners would soon wrest control from the fire-eating minority.

This perception stiffened Republican resolve to resist compromise. Moderate John J. Crittenden of Kentucky proposed compensation for owners of runaway slaves, repeal of northern personal-liberty laws, a constitutional amendment to prohibit the federal government from interfering with slavery in the southern states, and another amendment to restore the Missouri Compromise line for the remaining territories and protect slavery below it. But in the face of steadfast Republican opposition, the Crittenden plan collapsed.

Lincoln's faith in a "loyal majority" of southerners exaggerated both their numbers and their devotion to the Union. Many southern opponents of the fire-eating secessionists were sitting on the fence and hoping for major concessions from the North; their allegiance to the Union thus was conditional. Lincoln can be faulted for misreading southern opinion, but even if his assessment had been accurate, it is unlikely that he would have accepted the Crittenden plan. The sticking point was the proposed extension of the Missouri Compromise line. To Republicans this was a surrender, not a compromise, because it hinged on the abandonment of free soil, the founding principle of their party. In addition, Lincoln well knew that some southerners still talked of seizing more territory for slavery in the Caribbean. In proposing to extend the 36°30′ line, the Crittenden plan specifically referred to territories "hereafter acquired." Lincoln feared that it would be only a matter of time "till we shall have to take Cuba as a condition upon which they [the seceding states] will stay in the Union."

Beyond these considerations, the precipitous secession of the Lower South changed the question that Lincoln faced. The issue was no longer slavery extension but secession. The Lower South had left the Union in the face of losing a fair election. For Lincoln to have caved in to such pressure would have violated majority rule, the principle upon which the nation, not just his party, had been founded.

The Coming of War By the time Lincoln took office in March 1861, little more than a spark was needed to ignite a war. Lincoln pledged in his inaugural address to "hold, occupy, and possess" federal property in the seven states that had seceded, an assertion that committed him to the defense of Fort Pickens in Florida and **Fort Sumter** in the harbor of Charleston, South Carolina. William Seward, whom Lincoln had appointed secretary of state, now became obsessed with the idea of conciliating the Lower South in order to hold the Upper South in the Union. In addition to advising the evacuation of federal forces from Fort Sumter, Seward proposed a scheme to reunify the nation by provoking a war with France and Spain. But Lincoln brushed aside Seward's advice. Instead, the president informed the governor of South Carolina of his intention to supply Fort Sumter with much-needed provisions, but not with men and ammunition. To gain the dubious military advantage of attacking Fort Sumter before the arrival of relief ships, Confederate batteries began to bombard the fort shortly before dawn on April 12. The next day, the fort's garrison surrendered.

Proclaiming an insurrection in the Lower South, Lincoln now appealed for seventy-five thousand militiamen from the loyal states to suppress the rebellion. His proclamation pushed citizens of the Upper South off the fence upon which they had perched for three months. "I am a Union man," one southerner wrote, "but when they [the Lincoln administration] send men south it will change my notions. I can do nothing against my own people." In quick succession, Virginia, North Carolina, Arkansas, and Tennessee leagued with the Confederacy. After acknowledging that "I am one of those dull creatures that cannot see the good of secession," Robert E. Lee resigned from the army rather than lead federal troops against his native Virginia.

The North, too, was ready for a fight, less to abolish slavery than to punish secession. Worn out from his efforts to find a peaceable solution to the issue of slavery extension, and with only a short time to live, Stephen Douglas assaulted "the new system of resistance by the sword and bayonet to the results of the ballot-box" and affirmed: "I deprecate war, but if it must come I am with my country, under all circumstances, and in every contingency."

CONCLUSION

The expectation of most American political leaders that the Compromise of 1850 would finally resolve the vexing issue of slavery extension had a surface plausibility. In neither 1850 nor 1860 did the great majority of Americans favor the abolition of slavery in the southern states. Rather, they divided over slavery in the territories, an issue seemingly settled by the Compromise. Stephen A. Douglas, its leading architect and a man who assumed that he always had his finger on the popular pulse, was sure that slavery had reached its natural limits, that popular sovereignty would keep it out of the territories, and that the furor over slavery extension would die down.

Douglas believed that only a few hotheads had kept the slavery extension issue alive. He was wrong. The differences between northerners and southerners over slavery extension were grounded on different understandings of liberty, which to northerners meant their freedom to pursue self-interest without competition from slaves, and to southerners their freedom to dispose of their legally acquired property, slaves, as they chose. The Compromise, which had barely scraped through Congress, soon unraveled. Enforcement of the Fugitive Slave Act brought to the surface widespread northern resentment of slaveholders, people who seemingly lived off the work of others, and a determination to exclude the possibility of slavery in the territories. Southern support for Douglas's Kansas-Nebraska bill, with its repeal of the Missouri Compromise and its apparent invitation to southerners to bring slaves into Kansas, persuaded many northerners that the South harbored the design of extending slavery. For their part, southerners, already angered by northern defiance of the Fugitive Slave Act, interpreted northern outrage against Douglas's bill as further evidence of the North's disrespect for the rule of law.

By the mid-1850s, the sectional division was spinning out of the control of politicians. Deep divisions between the Whigs' free-soil northern wing and their proslavery southern wing led to the party's collapse in the wake of the Kansas-Nebraska Act. Divisions between northern and southern Democrats would be papered over as long as the Democratic Party could unite behind Douglas's formula of popular sovereignty. But popular sovereignty failed its test in Kansas. The outbreak of civil strife in Kansas pushed former northern Whigs and many northern Democrats toward the new, purely sectional, Republicans, a party whose very existence southerners interpreted as a mark of northern contempt for them.

The South was not yet ready for secession. Before it took that drastic step, it had to convince itself that the North's real design was not merely to restrict the extension of slavery but to destroy slavery and, with it, the South itself. Northern hostility to the *Dred Scott* decision and sympathy for John Brown struck southerners as proof of just such an intent.

As an expression of principled outrage, secession capped a decade in which each side had clothed itself in principles that were deeply embedded in the nation's political heritage. Both sides subscribed to the rule of law, which each accused the other of deserting. In the end, war broke out between siblings who, although they claimed the same heritage and inheritance, had become virtual strangers to each other.

15

Crucible of Freedom: Civil War, 1861–1865

MOBILIZING FOR WAR

North and South alike were unprepared for war. In April 1861, the Union had only a small army of sixteen thousand men scattered all over the country, mostly in the West. One-third of Union army officers had resigned to join the Confederacy. The nation's new president, Abraham Lincoln , struck many observers as a yokel. That such a government could marshal its people for war seemed a doubtful proposition. The federal government had levied no direct taxes for decades, and it had never imposed a draft. The Confederacy was even less prepared; it had no tax structure, no navy, only two tiny gunpowder factories, and poorly equipped, unconnected railroad lines.

During the first two years of the war, both sides would have to overcome these deficiencies, raise and supply large armies, and finance the heavy costs of war. In each region, mobilization for war expanded the powers of the central government to an extent that few had anticipated.

Recruitment and Conscription

The Civil War armies were the largest organizations ever created in America; by the end of the war, over 2 million men would serve in the Union army and 800,000 in the Confederate army. In the first flush of enthusiasm for war, volunteers rushed to the colors. "I go for wiping them out," a Virginian wrote to his governor. "War! and volunteers are the only topics of conversation or thought," a student at Oberlin College in Ohio told his brother in April 1861. "I cannot study. I cannot sleep. I cannot work, and I don't know as I can write."

At first, the raising of armies depended on local efforts rather than on national or even state direction. Citizens opened recruiting offices in their hometowns, held rallies, and signed up volunteers; regiments were usually composed of soldiers from the same locale. Southern cavalrymen provided their own horses, and uniforms everywhere were left mainly to local option. In both armies, officers up to the rank of colonel were elected by other officers and enlisted men.

This informal and democratic way of raising and organizing soldiers could not long withstand the stress of war. As early as July 1861, the Union began examinations for officers. Also, as casualties mounted, military demand soon exceeded the supply of volunteers. The Confederacy felt the pinch first and in April 1862 enacted the first **conscription** law in American history. It required all able-bodied white men aged eighteen to thirty-five to serve in the military for three years. Subsequent amendments raised the age limit to forty-five and then to fifty, and lowered it to seventeen.

The Confederacy's Conscription Act antagonized southerners. Opponents charged that the draft was an assault on state sovereignty by a despotic regime and that the law would "do away with all the patriotism we have." Exemptions that applied to many occupations, from religious ministry to shoemaking, angered the nonexempt. So did a loophole, closed in 1863, that allowed the well-off to hire substitutes. One amendment, the so-called 20-Negro law, exempted an owner or overseer of twenty or more slaves from service. Although southerners widely feared that the slave population could not be controlled if all able-bodied white men were away in the army, the 20-Negro law led to complaints about "a rich man's war but a poor man's fight."

Despite opposition, the Confederate draft became increasingly hard to evade, and this fact stimulated volunteering. Only one soldier in five was a draftee, but 70 to 80 percent of eligible white southerners served in the Confederate army. A new conscription law of 1864, which required all soldiers then in the army to stay in for the duration of the war, ensured that a high proportion of Confederate soldiers would be battle-hardened veterans.

Once the army was raised, the Confederacy had to supply it. At first, the South relied on arms and ammunition imported from Europe, weapons confiscated from federal arsenals, and guns captured on the battlefield. These stopgap measures bought time until an industrial base was established. By 1862, southerners had a competent head of ordnance (weaponry), Josiah Gorgas. The Confederacy assigned ordnance contracts to privately owned factories like the Tredegar Iron Works in Richmond, provided loans to establish new factories, and created government-owned industries like the giant Augusta Powder Works in Georgia. The South lost few, if any, battles for want of munitions.

Supplying troops with clothing and food proved more difficult. Southern soldiers frequently went without shoes; during the South's invasion of Maryland in 1862, thousands of Confederate soldiers had to be left behind because they could not march barefoot on Maryland's gravel-surfaced roads. Late in the war, Robert E. Lee's Army of Northern Virginia ran out of food but never out of ammunition. Southern supply problems had several sources: railroads that fell into disrepair or were captured, an economy that relied more heavily on producing tobacco and cotton than growing food, and Union invasions early in the war that overran the livestock and grain-raising districts of central Tennessee and Virginia. Close to desperation, the Confederate Congress in 1863 passed the Impressment Act, which authorized army officers to take food from reluctant farmers at prescribed prices. This unpopular law also empowered agents to impress slaves into labor for the army, a provision that provoked yet more resentment.

CHRONOLOGY, 1861–1865

1861 • President Abraham Lincoln calls for volunteers to suppress the rebellion (April).
Virginia, Arkansas, Tennessee, and North Carolina join the Confederacy (April–May).
Lincoln imposes a naval blockade on the South (April).
U.S. Sanitary Commission formed (June).
First Battle of Bull Run (July).
First Confiscation Act (August).

1862 • Legal Tender Act (February).
George B. McClellan's Peninsula Campaign (March–July).
Battle of Shiloh (April).
Confederate Congress passes the Conscription Act (April).
David G. Farragut captures New Orleans (April).
Homestead Act (May).
Seven Days' Battles (June–July).
Pacific Railroad Act (July).
Morrill Land Grant Act (July).
Second Confiscation Act (July).
Second Battle of Bull Run (August).
Battle of Antietam (September).
Preliminary Emancipation Proclamation (September).
Battle of Fredericksburg (December).

1863 • Emancipation Proclamation issued (January).
Lincoln suspends writ of *habeas corpus* nationwide (January).
National Bank Act (February).
Congress passes the Enrollment Act (March).
Battle of Chancellorsville (May).
Woman's National Loyal League formed (May).
Battle of Gettysburg (July).
Surrender of Vicksburg (July).
New York City draft riots (July).
Battle of Chickamauga (September).

1864 • Ulysses S. Grant given command of all Union armies (March).
Battle of the Wilderness (May).
Battle of Spotsylvania (May).
Battle of Cold Harbor (June).
Surrender of Atlanta (September).
Lincoln reelected (November).
William T. Sherman's march to the sea (November–December).

1865 • Congress passes the Thirteenth Amendment (January).
Sherman moves through South Carolina (January–March).
Grant takes Richmond (April).
Robert E. Lee surrenders at Appomattox (April).
Lincoln dies (April).
Joseph Johnston surrenders to Sherman (April).

The industrial North had fewer problems supplying its troops with arms, clothes, and food. However, recruiting troops was another matter. When the initial tide of enthusiasm for enlistment ebbed, Congress followed the Confederacy's example and turned to conscription with the Enrollment Act of March 1863; every able-bodied white male citizen aged twenty to forty-five now faced the draft.

Like the Confederate conscription law of 1862, the Enrollment Act granted exemptions, although only to high government officials, ministers, and men who were the sole support of widows, orphans, or indigent parents. It also offered two means of escaping the draft: substitution, or paying another man who would serve instead; and commutation, paying a $300 fee to the government. Enrollment districts often competed for volunteers by offering cash payments (bounties); dishonest "bounty jumpers" repeatedly registered and deserted after collecting their payment. Democrats denounced conscription as a violation of individual liberties and states' rights. Ordinary citizens of little means resented the commutation and substitution provision and leveled their own "poor man's fight" charges. Still, as in the Confederacy, the law stimulated volunteering. Only 8 percent of Union soldiers were draftees or substitutes.

Financing the War The recruitment and supply of huge armies lay far beyond the capacity of American public finance at the start of the war. In the 1840s and 1850s, annual federal spending had averaged only 2 percent of the gross national product. With such meager expenditures, the federal government met its revenue needs from tariff duties and income from the sale of public lands. During the war, however, annual federal expenditures gradually rose, and the need for new sources of revenue became urgent. Yet neither the Union nor the Confederacy initially wished to impose taxes, to which Americans were unaccustomed. In August 1861, the Confederacy enacted a small property tax and the Union an income tax, but neither raised much revenue.

Both sides therefore turned to war bonds; that is, to loans from citizens to be repaid by future generations. Patriotic southerners quickly bought up the Confederacy's first bond issue ($15 million) in 1861. That same year, a financial wizard, Philadelphia banker Jay Cooke, induced the northern public to subscribe to a much larger bond issue ($150 million). But bonds had to be paid for in gold or silver coin (specie), which was in short supply. Soaking up most of its available specie, the South's first bond issue threatened to be its last. In the North, many hoarded their gold rather than spend it on bonds.

Recognizing the limitations of taxation and of bond issues, both sides began to print paper money. Early in 1862, Lincoln signed into law the **Legal Tender Act,** which authorized the issue of $150 million of the so-called greenbacks. Christopher Memminger, the Confederacy's treasury secretary, and Salmon P. Chase, his Union counterpart, shared a distrust of paper money, but as funds dwindled each came around to the idea. The availability of paper money made it easier to pay soldiers, levy taxes, and sell war bonds. Yet doubts about paper money lingered. Unlike gold and silver, which had established market values, the value of paper money depended mainly on the public's confidence in the government that issued it. To bolster that confidence, Union officials made the greenbacks legal tender (that is, acceptable in payment of most public and private debts).

In contrast, the Confederacy never made its paper money legal tender, and suspicions arose that the southern government lacked confidence in its own paper issues. To compound the problem, the Confederacy raised less than 5 percent of its wartime revenue from taxes. (The comparable figure for the North was 21 percent.) The Confederacy did enact a comprehensive tax measure in 1863, but Union invasions and the South's relatively undeveloped system of internal transportation made tax collection a hit-or-miss proposition.

Confidence in the South's paper money quickly evaporated, and the value of Confederate paper in relation to gold plunged. The Confederacy responded by printing more paper money, a billion dollars by 1865, but this action merely accelerated southern inflation. Whereas prices in the North rose about 80 percent during the war, the Confederacy suffered an inflation rate of over 9,000 percent. What cost a southerner one dollar in 1861 cost forty-six dollars by 1864.

By raising taxes, floating bonds, and printing paper money, both the Union and the Confederacy broke with the hard-money, minimal-government traditions of American public finance. For the most part, these changes were unanticipated and often reluctant adaptations to wartime conditions. But in the North, the Republicans took advantage of the departure of the southern Democrats from Congress to push through one measure that they and their Whig predecessors had long advocated, a system of national banking. Passed in February 1863 over the opposition of northern Democrats, the **National Bank Act** established criteria by which a bank could obtain a federal charter and issue national bank notes (notes backed by the federal government). It also gave private bankers an incentive to purchase war bonds. The North's ability to revolutionize its system of public finance reflected both its long experience with complex financial transactions and its political cohesion in wartime.

Political Leadership in Wartime

The Civil War pitted rival political systems as well as armies and economies against each other. The South entered the war with several apparent political advantages. Lincoln's call for militiamen to suppress the rebellion had transformed hesitators in the South into tenacious secessionists. "Never was a people more united or more determined," a New Orleans woman wrote in the spring of 1861. Southerners also claimed a strong leader. A former secretary of war and U.S. senator from Mississippi, President **Jefferson Davis** of the Confederacy possessed experience, honesty, courage, and what one officer described as "a jaw sawed in *steel*."

In contrast, the Union's list of political liabilities appeared lengthy. Loyal but contentious, northern Democrats objected to conscription, the National Bank Act, and the abolition of slavery. Among Republicans, Lincoln had trouble commanding respect. Unlike Davis, he had served in neither the cabinet nor the Senate, and his informal western manners dismayed easterners. Northern setbacks early in the war convinced most Republicans in Congress that Lincoln was an ineffectual leader. Criticism of Lincoln sprang from a group of Republicans who became known as **Radical Republicans** and who included Secretary of the Treasury Salmon P. Chase, Senator Charles Sumner of Massachusetts, and Representative Thaddeus Stevens of Pennsylvania. The Radicals never formed a tightly knit unit; on some issues they cooperated with Lincoln. But they assailed him early in the war for failing to make emancipation a war goal and later for being too eager to readmit the conquered rebel states into the Union.

Lincoln's distinctive style of leadership at once encouraged and disarmed opposition within the Republican Party. Keeping his counsel to himself until ready to act, he met complaints with homespun anecdotes that caught his opponents off guard. The Radicals frequently concluded that Lincoln was a prisoner of the conservative wing of the party; conservatives complained that he was too close to the Radicals. But Lincoln's cautious reserve had the dual benefit of leaving open his lines of communication with both wings of the party and fragmenting his opposition. He also co-opted some of his critics, including Chase, by bringing them into his cabinet.

In contrast, Jefferson Davis had a knack for making enemies. A West Pointer, he would rather have led the army than the government. His cabinet suffered from frequent resignations; the Confederacy had five secretaries of war in four years, for example. Davis's relations with his vice president, Alexander Stephens of Georgia, bordered on disastrous. A wisp of a man, Stephens weighed less than a hundred pounds and looked like a boy with a withered face. But he compensated for his slight physique with a tongue as acidic as Davis's. Leaving Richmond, the Confederate capital, in 1862, Stephens spent most of the war in Georgia, where he sniped at Davis as "weak and vacillating, timid, petulant, peevish, obstinate."

The clash between Davis and Stephens involved not just personalities but also an ideological division, a rift, in fact, like that at the heart of the Confederacy. The Confederate Constitution, drafted in February 1861, explicitly guaranteed the sovereignty of the Confederate states and prohibited the Confederate Congress from enacting protective tariffs and from supporting internal improvements (measures long opposed by southern voters). For Stephens and other influential Confederate leaders—among them the governors of Georgia and North Carolina—the Confederacy existed not only to protect slavery but, equally important, to enshrine the doctrine of states' rights. In contrast, Davis's main objective was to secure the independence of the South from the North, if necessary at the expense of states' rights.

This difference between Davis and Stephens bore some resemblance to the discord between Lincoln and the northern Democrats. Like Davis, Lincoln believed that winning the war demanded a boost in the central government's power; like Stephens, northern Democrats resisted governmental centralization. But Lincoln could control his foes more skillfully than Davis because, by temperament, he was more suited to conciliation and also because the nature of party politics in the two sections differed.

In the South, the Democrats and the remaining Whigs agreed to suspend party rivalries for the duration of the war. Although intended to promote southern unity, this decision actually encouraged disunity. Without the institutionalization of conflict that party rivalry provided, southern politics disintegrated along personal and factional lines. Lacking a party organization to back him, Davis could not mobilize votes to pass measures that he favored, nor could he depend on the support of party loyalists.

In contrast, in the Union, northern Democrats' organized opposition to Lincoln tended to unify the Republicans. In the 1862 elections, which occurred at a low ebb of Union military fortunes, the Democrats won control of five large states, including Lincoln's own Illinois. Republican leaders learned a lesson: no matter how much they disdained Lincoln, they had to rally behind him or risk losing office. Ultimately, the Union would develop more political cohesion than the Confederacy, not because it had fewer divisions but because it managed its divisions more effectively.

<table>
<tr><td>Securing the
Union's Borders</td><td>Even before large-scale fighting began, Lincoln moved to safe-
guard Washington, which was bordered by two slave states
(Virginia and Maryland) and filled with Confederate sympa-</td></tr>
</table>

Securing the Union's Borders Even before large-scale fighting began, Lincoln moved to safeguard Washington, which was bordered by two slave states (Virginia and Maryland) and filled with Confederate sympathizers. A week after Fort Sumter, a Baltimore mob attacked a Massachusetts regiment bound for Washington, but enough troops slipped through to protect the capital. Lincoln then dispatched federal troops to Maryland, where he suspended the writ of *habeas corpus* (a court order requiring that the detainer of a prisoner bring that person to court and show cause for his or her detention); federal troops could now arrest pro-secession Marylanders without formally charging them with specific offenses. Cowed by Lincoln's bold moves, the legislatures of Maryland and Delaware (another border slave state) rejected secession.

Next Lincoln authorized the arming of Union sympathizers in Kentucky, a slave state with a Unionist legislature, a secessionist governor, and a thin chance of staying neutral. Lincoln also stationed troops under General Ulysses S. Grant just across the Ohio River from Kentucky, in Illinois. When a Confederate army invaded Kentucky early in 1862, the state's legislature turned to Grant to drive it out. Officially, at least, Kentucky became the third slave state to declare for the Union. The fourth, Missouri, was ravaged by four years of fighting between Union and Confederate troops, and between bands of guerrillas and bushwhackers, a name for Confederate guerrillas who lurked in the underbrush. These included William Quantrill, a rebel desperado, and his murderous apprentices, Frank and Jesse James. Despite savage fighting and the divided loyalties of its people, Missouri never left the Union. West Virginia, admitted to the Union in 1863, would become the last of five border states, or slave states that remained in the Union. (West Virginia was established in 1861, when thirty-five counties in the mainly nonslaveholding region of Virginia west of the Shenandoah Valley refused to follow the state's leaders into secession.)

By holding the first four border slave states—Maryland, Delaware, Kentucky, and Missouri—in the Union, Lincoln kept open his routes to the free states and gained access to the river systems in Kentucky and Missouri that led into the heart of the Confederacy. Lincoln's firmness, particularly in Maryland, scotched charges that he was weak-willed. The crisis also forced the president to exercise long-dormant powers. In the case *Ex parte* Merryman (1861), Chief Justice Roger B. Taney ruled that Lincoln had exceeded his authority in suspending the writ of *habeas corpus* in Maryland. The president, citing the Constitution's authorization of the writ's suspension in "Cases of Rebellion" (Article I, Section 9), insisted that he, rather than Congress, would determine whether a rebellion existed; and he ignored Taney's ruling.

IN BATTLE, 1861–1862

The Civil War was the first war to rely extensively on railroads, the telegraph, mass-produced weapons, joint army-navy tactics, iron-plated warships, rifled guns and artillery, and trench warfare. All of this lends some justification to its description as the first modern war. But to the participants, slogging through muddy swamps and weighed down with equipment, the war hardly seemed modern. In many ways, the soldiers had the more accurate perspective, for the new weapons did not always work, and both sides employed tactics that were more traditional than modern.

Armies, Weapons, and Strategies
Compared to the Confederacy's 9 million people, one-third of them slaves, the Union had 22 million people in 1861. The North also had 3.5 times as many white men of military age, 90 percent of all U.S. industrial capacity, and two-thirds of its railroad track. Yet the Union faced a daunting challenge. Its goal was to force the South back into the Union, whereas the South fought merely for its independence. To subdue the Confederacy, the North would have to sustain offensive operations over a vast area.

Measured against this challenge, the Union's advantages in population and technology shrank. The North had more men, but needing to defend long supply lines and occupy captured areas, it could commit a smaller proportion of them to frontline duty. The South, which relied on slaves for labor, could assign a higher proportion of its white male population to combat. The North required, and possessed, superior railroads, though it had to move troops and supplies huge distances. Fighting defensively on so-called interior lines, the South could shift its troops relatively short distances within its defensive arc without using railroads. Not only could guerrillas easily sabotage northern railroads, but once Union troops moved away from their railroad bases, their supply wagons often bogged down on wretched southern roads that became watery ditches in bad weather. Finally, southerners had an edge in soldiers' morale, for Confederate troops battled on home ground. "No people ever warred for independence," a southern general acknowledged, "with more relative advantages than the Confederates."

The Civil War witnessed experiments with a variety of newly developed weapons, including the submarine, the repeating rifle, and the multibarreled Gatling gun, the forerunner of the machine gun. Yet these innovations had less impact on the war than did the perfection in the 1850s of a bullet whose powder would not clog a rifle's spiraled internal grooves after a few shots. Like the smoothbore muskets that both armies had employed at the start of the war, most improved rifles had to be reloaded after each shot. But where the smoothbore musket had an effective range of only eighty yards, the Springfield or Enfield rifles widely employed by 1863 could hit targets accurately at up to four hundred yards.

The rifle's development challenged long-accepted military tactics, which identified the mass infantry charge against an opponent's weakest point as the key to victory. Military manuals of the 1840s and 1850s assumed that defenders armed with muskets would be able to fire only a round or two before being overwhelmed. Armed with rifles, however, a defending force could fire several rounds before closing with the enemy. Attackers would now have far greater difficulty getting close enough to thrust bayonets; fewer than 1 percent of the casualties in the Civil War resulted from bayonet wounds.

Thus the rifle produced some changes in tactics. Both sides came to understand the value of trenches, which provided defenders protection against withering rifle fire. By 1865, trenches pockmarked the landscape in Virginia and Georgia. In addition, growing use of the rifle forced generals to rely less on cavalry. Traditionally, the cavalry had ranked among the most prestigious components of an army, in part because cavalry charges were often devastatingly effective and in part because the cavalry helped maintain class distinctions within the army. More accurate rifles reduced the effectiveness of cavalry by increasing the firepower of foot soldiers. As cavalry charges against infantry became more difficult, both sides relegated cavalry to reconnaissance missions and raids on supply trains.

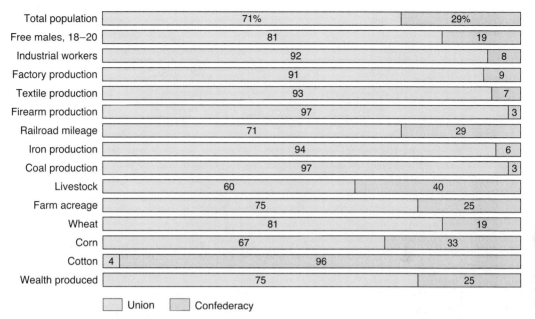

	Union	Confederacy
Total population	71%	29%
Free males, 18–20	81	19
Industrial workers	92	8
Factory production	91	9
Textile production	93	7
Firearm production	97	3
Railroad mileage	71	29
Iron production	94	6
Coal production	97	3
Livestock	60	40
Farm acreage	75	25
Wheat	81	19
Corn	67	33
Cotton	4	96
Wealth produced	75	25

Figure 15.1 Comparative Population and Economic Resources of the Union and the Confederacy, 1861

At the start of the war, the Union enjoyed huge advantages in population, industry, railroad mileage, and wealth, and, as it would soon prove, a superior ability to mobilize its vast resources. The Confederacy, however, enjoyed the many advantages of fighting a defensive war.

Although the rifle exposed traditional tactics to new hazards, it by no means invalidated those tactics. On the contrary, historians now contend, high casualties reflected the long duration of battles rather than the new efficacy of rifles. The attacking army still stood an excellent chance of success if it achieved surprise. The South's lush forests provided abundant opportunities for an army to sneak up on its opponent. For example, at the Battle of Shiloh in 1862, Confederate attackers surprised and almost defeated a larger Union army despite the rumpus created by green rebel troops en route to the battle, many of whom fired their rifles into the air to see if they would work.

In the absence of any element of surprise, an attacking army might invite disaster. At the Battle of Fredericksburg in December 1862, Confederate troops inflicted appalling casualties on Union forces attacking uphill over open terrain, and at Gettysburg in July 1863, Union riflemen and artillery shredded charging southerners. But generals might still achieve partial surprise by hitting an enemy before it had concentrated its troops; in fact, this is what the North tried to do at Fredericksburg. Because surprise often proved effective, most generals continued to believe that their best chance of success lay in striking an unwary or weakened enemy with all the troops they could muster rather than in relying on guerrilla or trench warfare.

Much like previous wars, the Civil War was fought basically in a succession of battles during which exposed infantry traded volleys, charged, and countercharged.

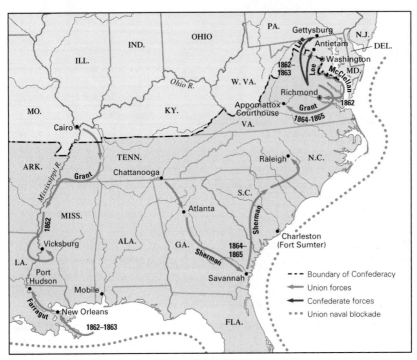

MAP 15.1 The War in the East, 1861–1862

Union advances on Richmond were turned back at Fredericksburg and the Seven Days' Battles, and the Confederacy's invasion of Union territory was stopped at Antietam.

Whichever side withdrew from the field usually was thought to have lost the battle, but the losing side frequently sustained lighter casualties than the supposed victor. Both sides had trouble exploiting their victories. As a rule, the beaten army moved back a few miles from the field to lick its wounds; the winners stayed in place to lick theirs. Politicians on both sides raged at generals for not pursuing a beaten foe, but it was difficult for a mangled victor to gather horses, mules, supply trains, and exhausted soldiers for a new attack. Not surprisingly, for much of the war, generals on both sides concluded that the best defense was a good offense.

To the extent that the North had a long-range strategy in 1861, it lay in the so-called **Anaconda plan.** Devised by a hero of the Mexican-American War, General Winfield Scott, the plan called for the Union to blockade the southern coastline and to thrust, like a snake, down the Mississippi River. Scott expected that sealing off and severing the Confederacy would make the South recognize the futility of secession and bring southern Unionists to power. But Scott, a southern Unionist, overestimated the strength of Unionist spirit in the South. Furthermore, although Lincoln quickly ordered a blockade of the southern coast, the North hardly had the troops and naval flotillas to seize the Mississippi in 1861. So while the Mississippi remained an objective, northern strategy did not unfold according to any blueprint like the Anaconda plan.

Early in the war, the pressing need to secure the border slave states, particularly Kentucky and Missouri, dictated Union strategy west of the Appalachian Mountains. Once in control of Kentucky, northern troops plunged southward into Tennessee. The Appalachians tended to seal this western theater off from the eastern theater, where major clashes of 1861 occurred.

Stalemate in the East

The Confederacy's decision in May 1861 to move its capital from Montgomery, Alabama, to Richmond, Virginia, shaped Union strategy. "Forward to Richmond" became the Union's first war cry. Before they could reach Richmond, one hundred miles southwest of Washington, Union troops had to dislodge a Confederate army brazenly encamped at Manassas Junction, Virginia, only twenty-five miles from the Union capital. Lincoln ordered General Irvin McDowell to attack his former West Point classmate, Confederate general P. G. T. Beauregard. "You are green, it is true," Lincoln told McDowell, "but they are green also; you are all green alike." In the resulting **First Battle of Bull Run** (or First Manassas), amateur armies clashed in bloody chaos under a blistering July sun. Well-dressed, picnicking Washington dignitaries gathered to view the action. Aided by last-minute reinforcements and by the disorganization of the attacking federals, Beauregard routed the larger Union army.

After Bull Run, Lincoln replaced McDowell with General George B. McClellan as commander of the Army of the Potomac, the Union's main fighting force in the East. Another West Pointer, McClellan had served with distinction in the Mexican-American War and mastered the art of administration by managing midwestern railroads in the 1850s. Few generals could match his ability to turn a ragtag mob into a disciplined fighting force. His soldiers adored him, but Lincoln quickly became disenchanted. Lincoln believed that the key to a Union victory lay in simultaneous, coordinated attacks on several fronts so that the North could exploit its advantage in manpower and resources. McClellan, a proslavery Democrat, hoped to maneuver the South into a relatively bloodless defeat and then negotiate a peace that would readmit the Confederate states with slavery intact.

In the spring of 1862, McClellan got a chance to implement his strategy. After Bull Run, the Confederates had pulled back to block the Union onslaught against Richmond. Rather than directly attack the Confederate army, McClellan decided to move the Army of the Potomac by water to the tip of the peninsula formed by the York and James Rivers and then move northwestward up the peninsula to Richmond. McClellan's plan had several advantages. Depending on water transport rather than on railroads (which Confederate cavalry could cut), the McClellan strategy reduced the vulnerability of northern supply lines. By dictating an approach to Richmond from the southeast, it threatened the South's supply lines. By aiming for the capital of the Confederacy rather than for the Confederate army stationed to its northeast, McClellan hoped to maneuver the southern troops into a futile attack on his army.

At first the massive Peninsula Campaign unfolded smoothly. Three hundred ships transported seventy thousand men and huge stores of supplies to the tip of the peninsula. Reinforcements swelled McClellan's army to one hundred thousand. By late May, McClellan was within five miles of Richmond. But then he hesitated. Overestimating the Confederates' strength, he refused to launch a final attack without further reinforcements, which were turned back by Confederate general Thomas "Stonewall" Jackson in the Shenandoah Valley.

While McClellan delayed, General **Robert E. Lee** took command of the Confederacy's Army of Northern Virginia. A foe of secession and so courteous that at times he seemed too gentle, Lee possessed the qualities that McClellan most lacked: boldness and a willingness to accept casualties. Seizing the initiative, Lee attacked McClellan in late June 1862. The ensuing Seven Days' Battles, fought in the forests east of Richmond, cost the South nearly twice as many men as the North and ended in a virtual slaughter of Confederates at Malvern Hill. Unnerved by mounting casualties, McClellan sent increasingly panicky reports to Washington. Lincoln, who cared little for McClellan's peninsula strategy, ordered McClellan to call off the campaign and return to Washington.

With McClellan out of the picture, Lee and his lieutenant, Stonewall Jackson, boldly struck north and, at the Second Battle of Bull Run (Second Manassas), routed a Union army under General John Pope. Lee's next stroke was even bolder. Crossing the Potomac River in early September 1862, he invaded western Maryland, where the forthcoming harvest could provide him with desperately needed supplies. By seizing western Maryland, moreover, Lee could threaten Washington, indirectly relieve pressure on Richmond, improve the prospects of peace candidates in the North's upcoming fall elections, and possibly induce Britain and France to recognize the Confederacy as an independent nation. But McClellan met Lee at the **Battle of Antietam** (or Sharpsburg) on September 17. Although a tactical draw, Antietam proved a strategic victory for the North, for Lee subsequently called off his invasion and retreated south of the Potomac.

Heartened by the apparent success of northern arms, Lincoln then issued the Emancipation Proclamation, a war measure that freed all slaves under rebel control. The toll of 24,000 casualties at Antietam, however, made it the bloodiest day of the entire war. A Union veteran recollected that one part of the battlefield contained so many bodies that a man could have walked through it without stepping on the ground.

Complaining that McClellan had "the slows," Lincoln faulted his commander for not pursuing Lee after the battle. McClellan's replacement, General Ambrose Burnside, thought himself and soon proved himself unfit for high command. In December 1862, Burnside led 122,000 federal troops against 78,500 Confederates at the Battle of Fredericksburg. Burnside captured the town of Fredericksburg, northeast of Richmond, but then sacrificed his army in futile charges up the heights west of the town. Even Lee was shaken by the northern casualties. "It is well that war is so terrible, or we should grow too fond of it," he told an aide during the battle. Richmond remained, in the words of a southern song, "a hard road to travel." The war in the East had become a stalemate.

| The War in the West | The Union fared better in the West. There, the war ranged over a vast and crucial terrain that provided access to rivers leading directly into the South. The West also spawned new |

leadership. During the first year of war, an obscure Union general, **Ulysses S. Grant,** proved his competence. A West Point graduate, Grant had fought in the Mexican-American War and retired from the army in 1854 with a reputation for heavy drinking. He then failed at ventures in farming and in business. When the Civil War began, he gained an army commission through political pressure.

In 1861–1862, Grant retained control of two border states, Missouri and Kentucky. Moving into Tennessee, he captured two strategic forts, Fort Henry on the Tennessee River and Fort Donelson on the Cumberland. Grant then headed south to attack Corinth, Mississippi, a major railroad junction.

In early April 1862, to defend Corinth, Mississippi, Confederate forces under generals Albert Sidney Johnston and P. G. T. Beauregard staged a surprise attack on Grant's army, encamped near a church named Shiloh twenty miles north of the town, in southern Tennessee. Hoping to whip Grant before Union reinforcements arrived, the Confederates exploded from the woods near Shiloh before breakfast and almost drove the federals into the Tennessee River. Beauregard cabled Richmond with news of a splendid Confederate victory. But Grant and his lieutenant, **William T. Sherman**—a West Point graduate and Mexican-American war veteran who had most recently run a southern military academy—steadied the Union line. Union reinforcements arrived in the night, and a federal counterattack drove the Confederates from the field the next day. Although Antietam would soon erase the distinction, the **Battle of Shiloh** was the bloodiest in American history to that date. Of the seventy-seven thousand men engaged, twenty-three thousand were killed or wounded, including Confederate general Albert Sidney Johnston, who bled to death from a leg wound. Defeated at Shiloh, the Confederates soon evacuated Corinth.

To attack Grant at Shiloh, the Confederacy had stripped the defenses of New Orleans, leaving only three thousand militia to guard its largest city. A combined Union land-sea force under General Benjamin Butler, a Massachusetts politician, and Admiral David G. Farragut, a Tennessean loyal to the Union, capitalized on the opportunity. Farragut took the city in late April and soon conquered Baton Rouge and Natchez as well. Meanwhile, another Union flotilla moved down the Mississippi and captured Memphis in June. Now the North controlled the entire river, except for a two-hundred-mile stretch between Port Hudson, Louisiana, and Vicksburg, Mississippi.

Union and Confederate forces also clashed in 1862 in the trans-Mississippi West. On the banks of the Rio Grande, Union volunteers, joined by Mexican-American

The Battle of Antietam *A painting of the Antietam battlefield by James Hope, a Union soldier of the Second Vermont Infantry, shows three brigades of Union troops advancing under Confederate fire.*

companies, drove a Confederate army from Texas out of New Mexico. A thousand miles to the east, in northern Arkansas and western Missouri, armies vied to secure the Missouri River, a crucial waterway that flowed into the Mississippi. In Pea Ridge, Arkansas, in March 1862, forewarned northern troops scattered a Confederate force of sixteen thousand that included three Cherokee regiments. (Indian units fought on both sides in Missouri, where guerrilla combat raged until the war's end.)

These Union victories changed the nature of the trans-Mississippi war. As the rebel threat faded, regiments of western volunteers that had mobilized to crush Confederates turned to fighting Indians. Conflict between Union forces and Native Americans erupted in Minnesota, Arizona, Nevada, Colorado, and New Mexico, where California volunteers and the New Mexico cavalry, led by Colonel Kit Carson, overwhelmed the Apaches and Navajos. After 1865, federal troops moved west to complete the rout of the Indians that had begun in the Civil War.

The Soldiers' War Civil War soldiers were typically volunteers who left farms and small towns to join companies of recruits from their locales. Many men who enrolled in 1861 and 1862—those who served at Shiloh and Antietam—reenlisted when their terms expired and became the backbones of their respective armies. Local loyalties spurred enrollment, especially in the South; so did ideals of honor and valor. Soldiers on both sides envisioned military life as a transforming experience in which citizens became warriors and boys became men. One New York father who sent two young sons to enlist marveled at how the war provided "so much manhood suddenly achieved." Exultant after a victory, an Alabama volunteer told his father, "With your first shot you become a new man." Thousands of underage volunteers, that is, boys under eighteen, also served in the war; so did at least 250 women disguised as men.

New soldiers moved from recruitment rallies to camps of rendezvous, where local companies were meshed into regiments, and then to camps of instruction. Military training proved notoriously weak, and much of army life was tedious and uncomfortable. Food was one complaint. Union troops ate beans, bacon, salt pork, pickled beef, and a staple called hardtack, square flour-and-water biscuits that were almost impossible to crack with a blow. Confederate diets featured bacon and cornmeal, and as a southern soldier summed it up, "Our rations is small." Rebel armies often ran out of food, blankets, clothes, socks, and shoes. On both sides, crowded military camps, plagued by poor sanitation and infested with lice, fleas, ticks, flies, and rodents, ensured soaring disease rates and widespread grievances. A sergeant from New York, only partly in jest, described his lot as "laying around in the dirt and mud, living on hardtack, facing death in bullets and shells, eat up by wood-ticks and body-lice."

Expectations of military glory swiftly faded. For most soldiers, Civil War battles meant inuring themselves to the stench of death. Soldiers rapidly grasped the value of caution in combat; you learned, a southerner wrote, "to become cool and deliberate." According to a northern volunteer, "The consuming passion is to get out of the way." Others described the zeal aroused by combat. "[I]t is a terrible sight to see a line of men, two deep, coming up within 300 or 400 yards of you, with bayonets flashing and waving their colors," a New Jersey artilleryman recalled. "[Y]ou know that every shot you fire into them sends some one to eternity, but still you are a prompted by a terrible desire to kill all you can." The deadly cost of battle fell most heavily on the infantry, in which at least three out of four soldiers served. Although repeating rifles were superior weapons, with three or four times the range of the old smoothbore muskets, a combination of inexperience, inadequate training, and barriers of terrain curbed their impact in practice. Instead, large masses of soldiers faced one another at close range for long periods of time, exchanging fire until one side or the other gave up and fell back. The high casualty figures at Shiloh and Antietam reflected not advanced technology but the armies' inability to use it effectively. "Our victories . . . seem to settle nothing; to bring us no nearer to the end of the war," a southern officer wrote in 1862. "It is only so many killed or wounded, leaving the war of blood to go on." Armies gained efficiency in battle through experience, and only late in the war.

In their voluminous letters home (Civil War armies were the most literate armies that had ever existed), volunteers often discussed their motives as soldiers. Some Confederates enlisted to defend slavery, which they paired with liberty. "I choose to fight for southern rights and southern liberty" against the "vandals of the North" who were "determined to destroy slavery," a Kentucky Confederate announced. "A stand must be made for African slavery or it is forever lost," wrote a South Carolinian. A small minority of northern soldiers voiced antislavery sentiments early in the war: "I have no heart in this war if the slaves cannot go free," a soldier from Wisconsin declared. Few Union recruits, however, initially shared this antipathy to slavery, and some voiced the opposite view. "I don't want to fire another shot for the negroes and I wish all the abolitionists were in hell," a New York soldier declared. But as the war went on, northern soldiers accepted the need to free the slaves, sometimes for humanitarian reasons. "Since I am down here I have learned and seen more of what the horrors of slavery was than I ever knew before," an Ohio officer wrote from Louisiana. Others had more practical goals. By the summer of 1862, Union soldiers in the South had become agents of liberation; they harbored fugitives who fled behind federal lines. Many who once had damned the "abolitionist war" now endorsed emancipation as part of the Union war effort. As a soldier from Indiana declared, "Every negro we get strengthens us and weakens the rebels."

Ironclads and Cruisers: The Naval War

By plunging its navy into the Confederacy like a dagger, the Union exploited one of its clearest advantages. The North began the war with over forty active warships against none for the South, and by 1865 the United States had the largest navy in the world. Steam-driven ships could penetrate the South's excellent river system from any direction.

Yet the Union navy faced an extraordinary challenge in its efforts to blockade the South's 3,500 miles of coast. Early in the war, small, sleek Confederate blockade-runners darted in and out of southern harbors and inlets with little chance of capture. The North gradually tightened the blockade by outfitting tugs, whalers, excursion steamers, and ferries as well as frigates to patrol southern coasts. The proportion of Confederate blockade-runners that made it through dropped from 90 percent early in the war to 50 percent by 1865. Northern seizure of rebel ports and coastal areas shrank the South's foreign trade even more. In daring amphibious assaults during 1861 and 1862, the Union captured the excellent harbor of Port Royal, South Carolina, the coastal islands off South Carolina, and most of North Carolina's river outlets. Naval patrols and amphibious operations shrank the South's ocean trade to one-third its prewar level.

Despite meager resources, the South strove to offset the North's naval advantage. Early in the war, the Confederacy raised the scuttled Union frigate *Merrimac,* sheathed its sides with an armor of iron plate, rechristened it *Virginia,* and dispatched it to attack wooden Union ships in Hampton Roads, Virginia. The *Merrimac* destroyed two northern warships but met its match in the hastily built Union ironclad the *Monitor.* In the first engagement of ironclads in history, the two ships fought an indecisive battle on March 9, 1862. The South constructed other ironclads and even the first submarine, which dragged a mine through the water to sink a Union ship off Charleston in 1864. Unfortunately, the "fish" failed to resurface and went down with its victim. But the South could never build enough ironclads to overcome the North's supremacy in home waters. The Confederacy had more success on the high seas, where wooden, steam-driven commerce raiders like the *Alabama* and the *Florida* (both built in England) wreaked havoc on the Union's merchant marine. Commerce raiding, however, would not tip the balance of the war in the South's favor because the North, unlike its foe, did not depend on imports for war materials. The South would lose the naval war.

The Diplomatic War While armies and navies clashed in 1861–1862, conflict developed on a third front, diplomacy. At the outbreak of the war, the Confederacy began a campaign to gain European recognition of its independence. Southern confidence ran high. Planning to establish a colonial empire in Mexico, Napoleon III of France had grounds to welcome the permanent division of the United States. Moreover, the upper classes in France and Britain seemed sympathetic to the aristocratic South and eager for the downfall of the brash Yankee republic. Furthermore, influential southerners had long contended that an embargo of cotton exports would bring Britain to its knees. These southerners reasoned that Britain, dependent on the South for four-fifths of its cotton, would break the Union blockade and provoke a war with the North rather than endure an embargo.

Leaving nothing to chance, the Confederacy in 1861 dispatched emissaries James Mason to Britain and John Slidell to France to lobby for recognition of an independent South. But their ship, the *Trent,* fell into Union hands, and when Mason and Slidell ended up in Boston as prisoners, British tempers exploded. Considering one war at a time enough, President Lincoln released Mason and Slidell. But settling the *Trent* affair did not eliminate friction between the United States and Britain. Union diplomats protested the construction in British shipyards of two Confederate commerce raiders, the *Florida* and the *Alabama.* In 1863, the U.S. minister to London, Charles Francis Adams (the son of former president John Quincy Adams), threatened war if two British-built ironclads commissioned by the Confederacy, the so-called Laird rams, were turned over to the South. Britain capitulated to Adams's protests and purchased the rams for its own navy.

On balance, the South fell far short of its diplomatic objectives. Although recognizing the Confederacy as a belligerent, neither Britain nor France ever recognized it as a nation. Basically, the Confederacy overestimated the power of its vaunted **"cotton diplomacy."** Southern notions of embargoing cotton exports in order to bring the British to their knees failed. Planters conducted business as usual by raising cotton and trying to slip it through the blockade. Still, the South's share of the British cotton market slumped from 77 percent in 1860 to only 10 percent in 1865. This loss reflected forces beyond southern control. Bumper cotton crops in the late 1850s had glutted the

British market by the start of the war and weakened British demand for cotton. In addition, Britain had found new suppliers in Egypt and India, thereby buffering itself from southern pressure. Gradually, too, the North's tightened blockade restricted southern exports.

The South also exaggerated Britain's stake in helping the Confederacy. As a naval power that had frequently blockaded its own enemies, Britain's diplomatic interest lay in supporting the Union blockade in principle; from Britain's standpoint, to help the South break the blockade would set a precedent that could easily boomerang. Finally, although France and Britain often considered recognizing the Confederacy, the timing never seemed quite right. The Union's success at Antietam in 1862 and Lincoln's subsequent issuance of the Emancipation Proclamation dampened Europe's enthusiasm for recognition at a crucial juncture. By transforming the war into a struggle to end slavery, the Emancipation Proclamation produced an upsurge of pro-Union feeling in antislavery Britain, particularly among liberals and the working class. Workingmen in Manchester, England, wrote Lincoln to praise his resolve to free the slaves. The proclamation, declared Henry Adams (diplomat Charles Francis Adams's son) from London, "has done more for us here than all of our former victories and all our diplomacy."

EMANCIPATION TRANSFORMS THE WAR, 1863

"I hear old John Brown knocking on the lid of his coffin and shouting 'Let me out! Let me out!'" abolitionist Henry Stanton wrote to his wife after the fall of Fort Sumter. "The Doom of Slavery is at hand." In 1861, this prediction seemed wildly premature. In his inaugural that year, Lincoln had stated bluntly, "I have no purpose, directly or indirectly, to interfere with the institution of slavery in the states where it exists." Yet in two years, the North's priorities shifted. A mix of practical necessity and ideological conviction thrust the emancipation of the slaves to the forefront of northern war goals.

The rise of emancipation as a war goal reflected the changing character of the war. As the struggle dragged on, demands intensified in the North for the prosecution of "total war"—a war that would shatter the social and economic foundations of the Confederacy. Even northerners who saw no moral value in abolishing slavery started to recognize the military value of emancipation as a tactic to cripple the South.

From Confiscation to Emancipation Union policy on emancipation developed in stages. As soon as northern troops began to invade the South, questions arose about the disposition of captured rebel property, including slaves. Slaves who fled behind the Union lines were sometimes considered "contraband"—enemy property liable to seizure—and were put to work for the Union army. Some northern commanders viewed this practice as a useful tool of war; others did not—especially when they faced the challenge of supervising contingents of former slaves; and the Lincoln administration was evasive. To establish an official policy, Congress in August 1861 passed the first Confiscation Act, which authorized the seizure of all property used in military aid of the rebellion, including slaves. Under this act, slaves who had been employed directly by the armed rebel forces and who later fled to freedom became "captives of war." But nothing in the act actually freed these individuals, nor did the law apply to fugitive slaves who had not worked for the Confederate military.

Several factors underlay the Union's cautious approach to the confiscation of rebel property. Officially maintaining that the South's rebellion lacked any legal basis, Lincoln argued that southerners were still entitled to the Constitution's protection of property. The president also had practical reasons to walk softly. The Union not only contained four slave states but also held a sizable body of proslavery Democrats who strongly opposed turning the war into a crusade against slavery. If the North in any way tampered with slavery, these Democrats feared, southern blacks might come north and compete with white workers. Aware of such fears, Lincoln assured Congress in December 1861 that the war would not become a "remorseless revolutionary struggle."

From the start of the war, however, Radical Republicans pushed Lincoln to adopt a policy of emancipation. Pennsylvanian Thaddeus Stevens urged the Union to "free every slave—slay every traitor—burn every Rebel mansion, if these things be necessary to preserve this temple of freedom." Radicals agreed with black abolitionist Frederick Douglass that "to fight against slaveholders without fighting against slavery, is but a half-hearted business." Each Union defeat, moreover, reminded northerners that the Confederacy, with a slave labor force in place, could commit a higher proportion of its white men to battle. The idea of emancipation as a military measure thus gained increasing favor in the North, and in July 1862 Congress passed the second Confiscation Act. This law authorized the seizure of the property of all persons in rebellion and stipulated that slaves who came within Union lines "shall be forever free." The law also authorized the president to employ blacks as soldiers.

Nevertheless, Lincoln continued to stall, even as pressure for emancipation rose. "My paramount object in this struggle is to save the Union, and is not either to save or destroy slavery," Lincoln told antislavery journalist Horace Greeley. "If I could save the Union without freeing *any* slave, I would do it; and if I could save it by freeing *all* the slaves, I would do it; and if I could do it by freeing some and leaving others alone, I would also do that." Yet Lincoln had always loathed slavery, and by the spring of 1862, he had come around to the Radical position that the war must lead to its abolition. He hesitated principally because he did not want to be stampeded by Congress into a measure that might disrupt northern unity; he was also reluctant to press the issue while Union armies reeled in defeat. After failing to persuade the Union slave states to emancipate slaves in return for federal compensation, Lincoln drafted a proclamation of emancipation, circulated it within his cabinet, and waited for a right moment to announce it. Finally, after the Union victory in September 1862 at Antietam, Lincoln issued the preliminary Emancipation Proclamation, which declared all slaves under rebel control free as of January 1, 1863. Announcing the plan in advance softened the surprise, tested public opinion, and gave the states still in rebellion an opportunity to preserve slavery by returning to the Union—an opportunity that none, however, took. The final **Emancipation Proclamation,** issued on January 1, 1863, declared "forever free" all slaves in areas in rebellion.

The proclamation had limited practical impact. Applying only to rebellious areas where the Union had no authority, it exempted the Union slave states and those parts of the Confederacy then under Union control (Tennessee, West Virginia, southern Louisiana, and sections of Virginia). Moreover, it mainly restated what the second Confiscation Act had already stipulated: if rebels' slaves fell into Union hands, those slaves would be free. Yet the proclamation was a brilliant political stroke. By issuing it as a military measure in his role as commander-in-chief, Lincoln pacified northern conservatives. Its aim, he stressed, was to injure the Confederacy, threaten its property, heighten its dread, sap its morale, and hasten its demise. By issuing the proclamation himself, Lincoln stole the initiative from the Radicals in Congress and mobilized support for the Union among European liberals far more dramatically than could any act of Congress. Furthermore, the declaration pushed the border states toward emancipation: by the end of the war, Maryland and Missouri would abolish slavery. Finally, it increased slaves' incentives to escape as northern troops approached. Fulfilling the worst of Confederate fears, it enabled blacks to join the Union army.

The Emancipation Proclamation did not end slavery everywhere or free "*all* the slaves." But it changed the war. From 1863 on, the war for the Union would also be a war against slavery.

| Crossing Union Lines | The attacks and counterattacks of the opposing armies turned many slaves into pawns of war. Some slaves became free when Union troops overran their areas. Others fled their planta- |

tions as federal troops approached to take refuge behind Union lines. A few were freed by northern assaults, only to be re-enslaved by Confederate counterthrusts. One North Carolina slave celebrated liberation on twelve occasions, as many times as Union soldiers marched through his area. By 1865, about half a million slaves were in Union hands.

In the first year of the war, when the Union had not yet established a policy toward "contrabands" (fugitive slaves), masters were able to retrieve them from the Union army. After 1862, however, the thousands of slaves who crossed Union lines were considered free. Many freedmen served in army camps as cooks, teamsters, and laborers. Some worked for pay on abandoned plantations or were leased out to planters who swore allegiance to the Union. In camps or outside them, freedmen had reason to question the value of their liberation. Deductions for clothing, rations, and medicine ate up most, if not all, of their earnings. Labor contracts frequently tied them to their employers for prolonged periods. Moreover, freedmen encountered fierce prejudice among Yankee soldiers, many of whom feared that emancipation would propel blacks north after the war. The best solution to the "question of what to do with the darkies," wrote one northern soldier, "would be to shoot them."

But this was not the whole story. Fugitive slaves who aided the Union army as spies and scouts helped to break down ingrained bigotry. "The sooner we get rid of our foolish prejudice the better for us," a Massachusetts soldier wrote home. Before the end of the war, northern missionary groups and freedmen's aid societies sent agents into the South to work among the freed slaves, distribute relief, and organize schools. In March 1865, just before the hostilities ceased, Congress created the **Freedmen's Bureau,** which had responsibility for the relief, education, and employment of former slaves. The Freedmen's Bureau law also stipulated that forty acres of abandoned or confiscated land could be leased to each freedman or southern Unionist, with an option to buy after three years. This was the first and only time that Congress provided for the redistribution of confiscated Confederate property.

| Black Soldiers in the Union Army | During the first year of war, the Union had rejected African-American soldiers. Northern recruiting offices sent black applicants home, and black companies that had been formed in |

the occupied South were disbanded. After the second Confiscation Act, Union generals formed black regiments in occupied New Orleans and on the Sea Islands off the coasts of South Carolina and Georgia. Only after the Emancipation Proclamation did large-scale enlistment begin. Prominent African-Americans such as Frederick Douglass and Harvard-educated physician Martin Delany worked as recruiting agents in northern cities. Douglass linked black military service to black claims as citizens. "Once let the black man get upon his person the brass letters, U.S.; let him get an eagle on his button, and a musket on his shoulder and bullets in his pocket, and there is no power on earth which can deny that he has earned the right to citizenship." Union drafts now included blacks, recruiting offices appeared in the loyal border states, and freedmen in refugee camps throughout the occupied South were enlisted. By the end of the war, 186,000 African-Americans had served in the Union army, one-tenth of all Union soldiers. Fully half came from the Confederate states.

White Union soldiers commonly objected to the new recruits on racial grounds. But some, including Colonel Thomas Wentworth Higginson, a liberal minister and former John Brown supporter who led a black regiment, welcomed the black soldiers. "Nobody knows anything about these men who has not seen them in battle," Higginson exulted after a successful raid in Florida in 1863. "There is a fierce energy about them beyond anything of which I have ever read, except it be the French Zouaves [French troops in North Africa]." Even Union soldiers who held blacks in contempt came to approve of "anything that will kill a rebel." Furthermore, black recruitment offered new opportunities for whites to secure commissions, for blacks served in separate regiments under white officers. Colonel Robert Gould Shaw of the 54th Massachusetts Infantry, an elite black regiment, died in combat—as did half his troops—in an attack on Fort Wagner in Charleston harbor in July 1863.

Black soldiers suffered a far higher mortality rate than white troops. Typically assigned to labor detachments or garrison duty, blacks were less likely than whites to be killed in action but more likely to die of illness in the disease-ridden garrisons. In addition, the Confederacy refused to treat captured black soldiers as prisoners of war, a policy that prevented their exchange for Confederate prisoners. Instead, Jefferson Davis ordered all blacks taken in battle to be sent back to the states from which they came, where they were re-enslaved or executed. In an especially gruesome incident, when Confederate troops under General Nathan Bedford Forrest captured Fort Pillow, Tennessee, in 1864, they massacred many blacks—an action that provoked outcries but no retaliation from the North.

Well into the war, African-American soldiers faced inequities in pay. White soldiers earned $13 a month plus a $3.50 clothing allowance; black privates received only $10 a month, with clothing deducted. "We have come out like men and we Expected to be Treated as men but we have bin Treated more Like Dogs then men," a black soldier complained to Secretary of War Edwin Stanton. In June 1864, Congress belatedly equalized the earnings of black and white soldiers.

Although fraught with hardships and inequities, military service became a symbol of citizenship for blacks. It proved that "black men can give blows as well as take them," Frederick Douglass declared. "Liberty won by white men would lose half its lustre." Above all, the use of black soldiers, especially former slaves, struck northern generals as a major blow against the Confederacy. "They will make good soldiers," General Grant wrote to Lincoln in 1863, "and taking them from the enemy weakens him in the same proportion they strengthen us."

COME AND JOIN US BROTHERS.

PUBLISHED BY THE SUPERVISORY COMMITTEE FOR RECRUITING COLORED REGIMENTS
1210 CHESTNUT ST. PHILADELPHIA.

Come and Join   *A recruitment poster urges black men to enlist in the Union army. African-American volunteers served in black regiments led by white officers.*

Slavery in Wartime   Anxious white southerners on the home front felt perched on a volcano. "We should be practically helpless should the negroes rise," declared a Louisiana planter's daughter, "since there are so few men left at home." When Mary Boykin Chesnut of South Carolina learned of her cousin's murder in bed by two trusted house slaves, she became almost frantic. "The murder," Chesnut wrote, "has clearly driven us all wild." To control 3 million slaves, white southerners tightened slave patrols, moved entire plantations to relative safety from Union troops in Texas or in the upland regions of the coastal South, and spread scare stories among the slaves. "The whites would tell the colored people not to go to the Yankees, for they would harness them to carts . . . in place of horses," reported Susie King Taylor, a black fugitive from Savannah.

Wartime developments affected slaves. Some remained faithful to their owners and helped hide family treasures from marauding Union soldiers. Others were torn between loyalty and lust for freedom: one slave accompanied his master to war, rescued him when he was wounded, and then escaped on his master's horse. Given a viable choice between freedom and bondage, slaves usually chose freedom. Few slaves helped the North as dramatically as Robert Smalls, a hired-out slave boatman who turned over a Confederate steamer to the Union navy, but most who had a chance to flee to Union lines did so. The idea of freedom held irresistible appeal. Upon learning from a Union soldier that he was free, a Virginia coachman dressed in his master's clothes, "put on his best watch and chain, took his stick, and . . . told him [the master] that he might for the future drive his own coach."

Most slaves, however, had no escape and remained under the nominal control of their owners. Despite the fears of southern whites, no general uprising of slaves occurred; and the Confederacy continued to impress thousands of slaves to toil in war plants, army camps, and field hospitals. But even slaves with no chance of flight were alert to the opportunity that war provided and swiftly tested the limits of enforced labor. As a Savannah mistress noted as early as 1861, the slaves "show a very different face from what they have had heretofore." Moreover, wartime conditions reduced the slaves' productivity. With most of the white men off at war, the master-slave relationship weakened. The women and boys who remained on plantations complained of their difficulty in controlling slaves, who commonly refused to work, performed their labors inefficiently, or even destroyed property. A Texas wife contended that her slaves were "trying all they can, it seems to me, to aggravate me" by neglecting the stock, breaking plows, and tearing down fences. "You may give your Negroes away," she finally wrote despairingly to her husband in 1864.

Whether southern slaves fled to freedom or merely stopped working, they acted effectively to defy slavery, to liberate themselves from its regulations, and to undermine the plantation system. Thus southern slavery disintegrated even as the Confederacy fought to preserve it. Hard-pressed by Union armies, short of manpower, and unsettled by the erosion of plantation slavery, the Confederate Congress in 1864 considered the drastic step of impressing slaves into its army as soldiers in exchange for their freedom at the war's end. Robert E. Lee favored the use of slaves as soldiers on the grounds that if the Confederacy did not arm its slaves, the Union would. Others were adamantly opposed. "If slaves will make good soldiers," a Georgia general argued, "our whole theory of slavery is wrong." Originally against arming slaves, Jefferson Davis changed his mind in 1865. In March 1865, the Confederate Congress narrowly passed a bill to arm three hundred thousand slave soldiers, although it omitted any mention of emancipation. Since the war ended a few weeks later, however, the plan was never put into effect.

Although the Confederacy's decision to arm the slaves came too late to affect the war, the debate over arming them damaged southern morale. By then, the South's military position had started to deteriorate.

The Turning Point of 1863

In the summer and fall of 1863, Union fortunes dramatically improved in every theater of the war. Yet the year began badly for the North. The slide, which had started with Burnside's defeat at Fredericksburg, Virginia, in December 1862, continued into the spring of 1863. Burnside's successor, General Joseph "Fighting Joe" Hooker, a windbag fond of issuing pompous proclamations to his troops, devised a plan to dislodge the Confederates from Fredericksburg by crossing the Rappahannock River north of the town and descending on the rebel rear. But Lee and Stonewall Jackson routed Hooker at Chancellorsville, Virginia, early in May 1863. The battle proved costly for the South because Jackson was accidentally shot by Confederate sentries and died a few days later. Still, Hooker had twice as many men as Lee, so the Union defeat at Chancellorsville humiliated the North. Reports from the West brought no better news. Although repulsed at Shiloh in western Tennessee, the Confederates still had a powerful army in central Tennessee under General Braxton Bragg. Furthermore, despite repeated efforts, Grant was unable to take Vicksburg; the two-hundred-mile stretch of the Mississippi between Vicksburg and Port Hudson remained in rebel hands.

The upswing in Union fortunes began with Lee's decision after Chancellorsville to invade the North. Lee needed supplies that war-wracked Virginia could no longer provide. He also hoped to push Lincoln into sending troops from besieged Vicksburg to the eastern theater. Lee envisioned a major Confederate victory on northern soil that would sway northern sentiment to the pro-peace Democrats and gain European recognition of the Confederacy. Moving his seventy-five thousand men down the Shenandoah Valley, Lee crossed the Potomac into Maryland and pressed forward into southern Pennsylvania. With Lee's army far to the west of Richmond, Hooker recommended a Union stab at the Confederate capital. "Lee's *army,* and not *Richmond,* is your true objective," Lincoln shot back, and he replaced Hooker with the more reliable George G. Meade.

Early in July 1863, Lee's offensive ground to a halt at a Pennsylvania road junction, Gettysburg. Confederates foraging for shoes in the town encountered some Union cavalry. Soon both sides called for reinforcements, and the war's greatest battle, the **Battle of Gettysburg,** began. On July 1, Meade's troops installed themselves in hills south of town along a line that resembled a fishhook: the shank ran along Cemetery Ridge and a northern hook encircled Culp's Hill. By the end of the first day of fighting, most of the troops on both sides had arrived: Meade's army outnumbered the Confederates ninety thousand to seventy-five thousand. On July 2, Lee rejected advice to plant the Confederate army in a defensive position between Meade's forces and Washington and instead attacked the Union flanks, with some success. But because the Confederate assaults were uncoordinated, and some southern generals disregarded orders and struck where they chose, the Union was able to move in reinforcements and regain its earlier losses.

By the afternoon of July 3, believing that the Union flanks had been weakened, Lee attacked Cemetery Ridge in the center of the North's defensive line. After southern cannon shelled the line, a massive infantry force of fifteen thousand Confederates, Pickett's charge, moved in. But as the Confederate cannon sank into the ground and fired a shade too high, and as Union fire wiped out the rebel charge, rifled weapons proved their deadly effectiveness. At the end of the day, Confederate bodies littered the field. "The dead and the dying were lying by the thousands between the two lines," a dazed Louisiana soldier wrote. A little more than half of Pickett's troops were dead, wounded, or captured in the horrible encounter. When Lee withdrew to Virginia on July 4, he had lost seventeen generals and over one-third of his army. Total Union and Confederate casualties numbered almost fifty thousand. Although Meade failed to pursue and destroy the retreating rebels, he had halted Lee's foray into the North, and the Union rejoiced.

Almost simultaneously, the North won a less bloody but more strategic victory in the West, at the **Battle of Vicksburg;** here Grant finally pierced Vicksburg's defenses. Situated on a bluff on the east bank of the Mississippi, Vicksburg was protected on the west by the river and on the north by hills, forests, and swamps. It could be attacked only over a thin strip of dry land to its east and south. Positioned to the north of Vicksburg, Grant had to find a way to get his army south of the city and onto the Mississippi's

MAP 15.2 Gettysburg, 1863

The failure of Pickett's charge against the Union center on July 3 was the decisive action in the war's greatest battle.

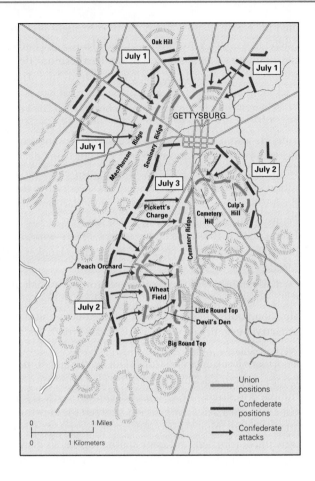

east bank. His solution lay in moving his troops far to the west of the city and down to a point on the river south of Vicksburg. Meanwhile, Union gunboats and supply ships ran past the Confederate batteries overlooking the river at Vicksburg (not without sustaining considerable damage) to rendezvous with Grant's army and transport it across to the east bank. Grant then swung in a large semicircle, first northeastward to capture Jackson, the capital of Mississippi, and then westward back to Vicksburg. After a six-week siege, during which famished soldiers and civilians in Vicksburg were reduced to eating mules and even rats, General John C. Pemberton surrendered his thirty-thousand-man garrison to Grant on July 4, the day after Pickett's charge at Gettysburg. Port Hudson, the last Confederate holdout on the Mississippi, soon surrendered to another Union army. "The Father of Waters flows unvexed to the sea," Lincoln declared.

Before the year was out, the Union won another crucial victory in the West. General William S. Rosecrans fought and maneuvered Braxton Bragg's Confederate army out of central Tennessee and into Chattanooga, in the southeastern tip of the state, and then forced Bragg to evacuate Chattanooga. Bragg defeated the pursuing Rosecrans at the Battle of Chickamauga (September 19–20, 1863), one of the bloodiest of the war, and drove him back into Chattanooga. But the arrival of Grant and reinforcements from the Army of the Potomac enabled the North to break Bragg's siege of Chattanooga in November. With Chattanooga secure, the way lay open for a Union strike into Georgia.

Union successes in the second half of 1863 stiffened the North's will to keep fighting and plunged some rebel leaders into despair. Hearing of the fall of Vicksburg, Confederate ordnance chief Josiah Gorgas wrote, "Yesterday we rode the pinnacle of success—today absolute ruin seems our portion. The Confederacy totters to its destruction."

Totter it might, but the South was far from beaten. Although the outcome at Gettysburg quashed southerners' hopes for victory on northern soil, it did not significantly impair Lee's ability to defend Virginia. The loss of Vicksburg and the Mississippi cut off the Confederate states west of the river—Arkansas, Louisiana, and Texas—from those to the east; but these western states could still provide soldiers. Even with the loss of Chattanooga, the Confederacy continued to hold most of the Carolinas, Georgia, Florida, and Mississippi. Few contemporaries thought that the fate of the Confederacy had been sealed.

WAR AND SOCIETY, NORTH AND SOUTH

Extending beyond the battlefields, the Civil War engulfed two economies and societies. By 1863, stark contrasts emerged: with its superior resources, the Union could meet wartime demand as the imperiled Confederacy could not. But both regions experienced labor shortages and inflation. As the conflict dragged on, both societies confronted problems of disunity and dissent, for war issues opened fissures between social classes. In both regions, war encroached on everyday life. Families were disrupted and dislocated, especially in the South. Women on both sides took on new roles at home, in the workplace, and in relief efforts.

The War's Economic Impact: The North The war affected the Union's economy unevenly. Some industries fared poorly: for instance, a shortage of raw cotton sent the cotton-textile industry into a tailspin. But industries directly related to the war effort, such as the manufacture of arms, shoes, and clothing, profited from huge government contracts; by 1865 the ready-made clothing industry received orders for more than a million uniforms a year. Railroads flourished in wartime. Some privately owned lines, which had overbuilt before the war, doubled their volume of traffic. In 1862, the federal government itself went into the railroad business by establishing the United States Military Railroads (USMRR) to carry troops and supplies to the front. By 1865, the USMRR was the largest railroad in the world.

The Republicans in Congress actively promoted business growth during the war. Holding 102 of 146 House seats and 29 of 36 Senate seats in 1861, they overrode Democratic foes and hiked the tariff in 1862 and again in 1864 to protect domestic industries. The Republican-sponsored Pacific Railroad Act of 1862 provided for the development of a transcontinental railroad, an idea that had foundered before the war on feuds over which route such a railroad should follow. With the South out of the picture and no longer able to demand a southern route from New Orleans across the Southwest, Congress chose a northern route from Omaha to San Francisco. Chartering the Union Pacific and Central Railroad corporations, Congress then gave to each large land grants and generous loans. These two corporations combined received more than 60 million acres in land grants and $20 million in government loans. The issuance of greenbacks and the creation of a national banking system, meanwhile, brought a measure of uniformity to the nation's financial system.

The Republicans designed these measures to benefit a variety of social classes, and partially succeeded. The **Homestead Act,** passed in 1862, embodied the party's ideal of "free soil, free labor, free men" by granting 160 acres of public land to settlers after five years of residence on the land. By 1865, twenty thousand homesteaders occupied new land in the West under the Homestead Act. The Republicans also secured passage in 1862 of the **Morrill Land Grant Act,** which gave to the states proceeds of public lands to fund the establishment of universities emphasizing "such branches of learning as are related to agriculture and mechanic arts." The Morrill Act spurred the growth of large state universities, mainly in the Midwest and West. Michigan State, Iowa State, and Purdue universities, among many others, profited from the law.

In general, however, the war benefited the wealthy more than the average citizen. Corrupt contractors grew rich by selling the government substandard merchandise such as the notorious "shoddy" clothing made from compressed rags, which quickly fell apart. Speculators made millions in the gold market. Because the price of gold in relation to greenbacks rose whenever public confidence in the government fell, those who bought gold in the hope that its price would rise gained from Union defeats, and even more from Union disasters. Businessmen with access to scarce commodities also reaped astounding profits. Manpower shortages stimulated wartime demand for the mechanical reaper that Cyrus McCormick had patented in 1834. When paid for reapers in greenbacks, which he distrusted, McCormick immediately reinvested them in pig iron and then watched in glee as wartime demand drove its price from twenty-three dollars to forty dollars a ton.

Ordinary Americans suffered. Higher protective tariffs, wartime excise taxes, and inflation hoisted the prices of finished goods, while wages lagged 20 percent or more behind cost increases for most of the war. Lagging wages became especially severe because boys and women poured into government offices and factories to replace adult male workers who had joined the army. For women employees, entry into government jobs—even at half the pay of male clerks—represented a major advance. Still, employers' threats of hiring more low-paid youths and females undercut the bargaining power of the men who remained in the work force.

Some workers decried their low wages. "We are unable to sustain life for the price offered by contractors who fatten on their contracts," Cincinnati seamstresses declared in a petition to President Lincoln. Cigar makers and locomotive engineers formed national unions, a process that would accelerate after the war. But employers often denounced worker complaints as unpatriotic hindrances to the war effort. In 1864, army troops were diverted from combat to put down protests in war industries from New York to the Midwest.

The War's Economic Impact: The South The war shattered the South's economy. Indeed, if both regions are considered together, the war retarded *American* economic growth. For example, the commodity output of the American economy, which had registered huge increases of 51 percent and 62 percent in the 1840s and 1850s respectively, rose only 22 percent during the 1860s. This modest gain depended wholly on the North, for in the 1860s commodity output in the South actually *declined* 39 percent.

Multiple factors offset the South's substantial wartime industrial growth. For example, the war wrecked the South's railroads; invading Union troops tore up tracks, twisted rails, and burned railroad cars. Cotton production, once the foundation of the South's prosperity, sank from more than 4 million bales in 1861 to three hundred thousand bales in 1865 as Union invasions took their toll on production, particularly in Tennessee and Louisiana.

Invading Union troops also occupied the South's food-growing regions. Moreover, in areas under Confederate control, the drain of manpower into the army decreased the yields per acre of crops like wheat and corn, and scarcities abounded. Agricultural shortages worsened the South's already severe inflation. By 1863, salt selling for $1.25 a sack in New York City cost $60 in the Confederacy. Food riots erupted in 1863 in Mobile, Atlanta, and Richmond; in Richmond the wives of ironworkers paraded to demand lower food prices.

Part of the blame for the South's food shortages rested with the planter class. Despite government pleas to grow more food, many planters continued to raise cotton, with far-reaching consequences. Slave labor, which could have been diverted to army camps, remained essential on cotton plantations. This increased the Confederacy's reliance on its unpopular conscription laws. Moreover, to feed its hungry armies, the Confederacy had to impress food from civilians, a policy that led to resentment and spurred military desertions. Food-impressment agents usually concentrated on the easiest targets—farms run by the wives of active soldiers. "I don't want you to stop fighting them Yankees," wrote the wife of an Alabama soldier, "but try and get off and come home and fix us all up some and then you can go back." By the end of 1864, half of the Confederacy's soldiers were absent from their units.

The manpower drain that hampered food production reshaped the lives of southern white women. With the enlistment of about three out of four men of military age over the course of the war, Confederate women found their locales "thinned out of men," as a South Carolina woman described her town in 1862. "There is a vacant chair in every house," mourned a Kentucky Confederate girl. Often left in charge of farms and plantations, women faced new challenges and chronic shortages. As factory-made goods became scarce, the southern press urged the revival of home production; one Arkansas woman, a newspaper reported with admiration, not only wove eight yards of cloth a day but had also built her own loom. More commonly, southern homemakers concocted replacements for goods no longer attainable, including inks, dyes, coffee, shoes, and wax candles. "I find myself, every day, doing something I never did before," a Virginia woman declared in 1863. The proximity of war forced many Confederate women into lives as refugees. Property destruction or even the threat of Union invasions drove women and families away from their homes; those with slave property to preserve, in particular, sought to flee before Union forces arrived. Areas remote from military action, especially Texas, were favored destinations. Disorienting and disheartening, the refugee experience sapped morale. "I will never feel like myself again," a Georgia woman who had escaped from the path of Union troops wrote to her husband in 1864.

In one respect, the persistence of cotton growing helped the South because cotton became the basis for the Confederacy's flourishing trade with the enemy. The U.S.

Congress virtually legalized this trade in July 1861 by allowing northern commerce with southerners loyal to the Union. In practice, of course, it proved impossible to tell loyalists from disloyalists, and northern traders happily swapped bacon, salt, blankets, and other necessaries for southern cotton. By 1864, traffic through the lines provided enough food to feed Lee's Army of Northern Virginia. To a northern congressman, it seemed that the Union's policy was "to feed an army and fight it at the same time."

Trading with the enemy alleviated the South's food shortages but intensified its morale problems. The prospect of traffic with the Yankees gave planters an incentive to keep growing cotton, and it fattened merchants and middlemen. "Oh! the extortioners," complained a Confederate war-office clerk in Richmond. "Our patriotism is mainly in the army and among the ladies of the South. The avarice and cupidity of men at home could only be exceeded by ravenous wolves."

Dealing with Dissent   Both wartime governments faced mounting dissent and disloyalty. Within the Confederacy, dissent took two basic forms. First, a vocal group of states' rights activists, notably Vice President Alexander Stephens and governors Zebulon Vance of North Carolina and Joseph Brown of Georgia, spent much of the war attacking Jefferson Davis's government as a despotism. Second, loyalty to the Union flourished among a segment of the Confederacy's common people, particularly those living in the Appalachian Mountain region that ran from western North Carolina through eastern Tennessee and into northern Georgia and Alabama. The nonslaveholding small farmers who predominated here saw the Confederate rebellion as a slave owners' conspiracy. Resentful of such measures as the 20-Negro exemption from conscription, they voiced reluctance to fight for what a North Carolinian called "an adored trinity," of cotton, slaves, and "chivalry." "All they want," an Alabama farmer complained of the planters, "is to get you pupt up and to fight for their infurnal negroes and after you do there fighting you may kiss there hine parts for o they care."

On the whole, the Confederate government responded mildly to popular disaffection. In 1862, the Confederate Congress gave Jefferson Davis the power to suspend the writ of *habeas corpus,* but Davis used his power only sparingly, by occasionally and briefly putting areas under martial law, mainly to aid tax collectors.

Lincoln faced similar challenges in the North, where the Democratic minority opposed both emancipation and the wartime growth of centralized power. Although "War Democrats" conceded that war was necessary to preserve the Union, "Peace Democrats" (called "Copperheads" by their opponents, to suggest a resemblance to a species of easily concealed poisonous snakes) demanded a truce and a peace conference. They charged that administration war policy was intended to "exterminate the South," make reconciliation impossible, and spark "terrible social change and revolution" nationwide.

Strongest in the border states, the Midwest, and the northeastern cities, the Democrats mobilized the support of farmers of southern background in the Ohio Valley and of members of the urban working class, especially recent immigrants, who feared losing their jobs to an influx of free blacks. In 1863, this volatile brew of political, ethnic, racial, and class antagonisms in northern society exploded into antidraft protests in several cities. By far the most violent eruptions were the **New York City draft riots** in July. Enraged by the first drawing of names under the Enrollment Act and by a longshoremen's strike in which blacks had been used as strikebreakers, mobs of Irish working-class men and women roamed the streets for four days until suppressed by federal troops. The city's Irish loathed the idea of being drafted to fight a war on behalf of the slaves who, once emancipated, might migrate north to compete with them for low-paying jobs. They also resented the provision of the draft law that allowed the rich to purchase substitutes. The rioters lynched at least a dozen blacks, injured hundreds more, and burned draft offices, the homes of wealthy Republicans, and the Colored Orphan Asylum.

President Lincoln's dispatch of federal troops to quash these riots typified his forceful response to dissent. Lincoln imposed martial law with far less hesitancy than Davis. After suspending the writ of *habeas corpus* in Maryland in 1861, he barred it nationwide in 1863 and authorized the arrest of rebels, draft resisters, and those engaged in "any disloyal practice." The contrasting responses of Davis and Lincoln to dissent underscored the differences between the two regions' wartime political systems. As we have seen, Davis lacked the institutionalization of dissent provided by party conflict and thus had to tread warily, lest his opponents brand him a despot. In contrast, Lincoln and other Republicans used dissent to rally patriotic fervor against the Democrats. After the New York City draft riots, the Republicans blamed the violence on New York's antidraft Democratic governor, Horatio Seymour.

Forceful as he was, Lincoln did not unleash a reign of terror against dissent. In general, the North preserved freedom of the press, speech, and assembly. Although some fifteen thousand civilians were arrested during the war, most were quickly released. A few cases, however, aroused widespread concern. In 1864, a military commission sentenced an Indiana man to be hanged for an alleged plot to free Confederate prisoners. The Supreme Court reversed his conviction two years later when it ruled that civilians could not be tried by military courts when the civil courts were open (*Ex parte* Milligan, 1866). Of more concern were the arrests of politicians, notably Clement L. Vallandigham, an Ohio Peace Democrat. Courting arrest, Vallandigham challenged the administration, denounced the suspension of *habeas corpus,* proposed an armistice, and in 1863 was sentenced to jail for the rest of the war by a military commission. When Ohio Democrats then nominated him for governor, Lincoln changed the sentence to banishment. Escorted to enemy lines in Tennessee, Vallandigham was left in the hands of bewildered Confederates and eventually escaped to Canada. The Supreme Court refused to review his case.

The Medical War Union and Confederacy alike witnessed remarkable wartime patriotism that impelled civilians, especially women, to work tirelessly to alleviate soldiers' suffering. The **United States Sanitary Commission,** formed early in the war by civilians to assist the Union's medical bureau, depended on women volunteers. Described by one woman as a "great artery that bears the people's love to the army," the commission raised funds at "sanitary fairs," bought and distributed supplies, ran special kitchens to supplement army rations, tracked down the missing, and inspected army camps. The volunteers' exploits became legendary. One poor widow, Mary Ann "Mother" Bickerdyke, served sick and wounded Union soldiers as both nurse and surrogate mother. When asked by a doctor by what authority she demanded supplies for the wounded, she shot back, "From the Lord God Almighty. Do you have anything that ranks higher than that?"

Andersonville Prison *Started in early 1864, the overcrowded Andersonville prison in south-west Georgia provided no shelter for its inmates, who built tentlike structures out of blankets, sticks, or whatever they could find. Exposure, disease, and poor sanitation contributed to a mortality rate almost double that in other Confederate prison camps and made Andersonville a scandal that outlived the war.*

Women also reached out to aid the battlefront through the nursing corps. Some 3,200 women served the Union and the Confederacy as nurses. Already famed for her tireless campaigns on behalf of the insane, Dorothea Dix became the head of the Union's nursing corps. Clara Barton, who began the war as a clerk in the U.S. Patent Office, found ingenious ways to channel medicine to the sick and wounded. Learning of Union movements before Antietam, Barton showed up at the battlefield on the eve of the clash with a wagonload of supplies. When army surgeons ran out of bandages and started to dress wounds with corn husks, she raced forward with lint and bandages. "With what joy," she wrote, "I laid my precious burden down among them." After the war, in 1881, she would found the American Red Cross.

The Confederacy, too, had extraordinary nurses. One, Sally Tompkins, was commissioned a captain for her hospital work; another, Belle Boyd, served the Confederacy as both a nurse and a spy and once dashed through a field, waving her bonnet, to give Stonewall Jackson information. Danger stalked nurses even in hospitals far from the front. Author Louisa May Alcott, a nurse at the Union Hotel Hospital in Washington, D.C., contracted typhoid. Wherever they worked, nurses witnessed haunting, unforgettable sights. "About the amputating table," one reported, "lay large piles of human flesh—legs, arms, feet, and hands . . . the stiffened membranes seemed to be clutching oftentimes at our clothing."

Pioneered by British reformer Florence Nightingale in the 1850s, nursing was a new vocation for women and, in the eyes of many, a brazen departure from women's proper sphere. Male doctors were unsure about how to react to women in the wards. Some saw the potential for mischief, but others viewed nursing and sanitary work as potentially useful. The miasma theory of disease (see Chapter 11) won wide respect among physicians and stimulated some valuable sanitary measures, particularly in hospitals behind the lines. In partial consequence, the ratio of disease to battle deaths was much lower in the Civil War than in the Mexican-American War. Still, for every soldier killed during the Civil War, two died of disease. "These Big Battles is not as Bad as the fever," a North Carolina soldier wrote. The scientific investigations that would lead to the germ theory of disease were only commencing in the 1860s. Arm and leg wounds frequently led to gangrene or tetanus, and typhoid, malaria, diarrhea, and dysentery raged through army camps.

Prison camps posed a special problem. Prisoner exchanges between the North and the South, common early in the war, collapsed by midwar, partly because the South refused to exchange black prisoners and partly because the North gradually concluded that exchanges benefited the manpower-short Confederacy more than the Union. As a result, the two sides had far more prisoners than either could handle, and prisoners on both sides suffered gravely. Miserable conditions plagued southern camps. Squalor and insufficient rations turned the Confederate prison camp at Andersonville, Georgia, into a virtual death camp; three thousand prisoners a month (out of a total of thirty-two thousand) were dying there by August 1864. After the war an outraged northern public secured the execution of Andersonville's commandant. Although the commandant was partly to blame, the deterioration of the southern economy had contributed massively to the wretched state of southern prison camps. Union camps were not much better, but had lower fatality rates.

The War and Women's Rights

Female nurses and Sanitary Commission workers were not the only women to serve society in wartime. In both northern and southern government offices and mills, thousands of women took over jobs vacated by men. Moreover, home industry revived at all levels of society. In rural areas, where manpower shortages were most acute, women often did the plowing, planting, and harvesting. "Women were in the field everywhere," an Illinois woman recalled. "No rebuffs could chill their zeal; no reverses repress their ardor."

Few women worked more effectively for their region's cause than Philadelphia-born Anna E. Dickinson. After losing her job in the federal mint (for denouncing General George McClellan as a traitor), Dickinson threw herself into hospital volunteer work and public lecturing. Her lecture "Hospital Life," recounting the soldiers' sufferings, won the attention of Republican politicians. In 1863, hard-pressed by the Democrats, these politicians invited Dickinson, then scarcely twenty-one, to campaign for Republicans in New Hampshire and Connecticut. This decision paid dividends. Articulate and poised, Dickinson captivated her listeners. Soon Republican candidates who had dismissed the offer of aid from a woman begged her to campaign for them.

Northern women's rights advocates hoped that the war would yield equality for women as well as freedom for slaves. Not only should a grateful North reward women for their wartime services, these women reasoned, but it should recognize the link between black rights and women's rights. In 1863, Elizabeth Cady Stanton and Susan B. Anthony organized the **Woman's National Loyal League.** The league's main activity was to gather four hundred thousand signatures on a petition calling for a constitutional amendment to abolish slavery, but Stanton and Anthony used the organization to promote woman suffrage as well.

Despite high expectations, the war did not bring women significantly closer to economic or political equality. Women in government offices and factories continued to be paid less than men. Sanitary Commission workers and most wartime nurses, as volunteers, earned nothing. Nor did the war alter the prevailing definition of woman's sphere. In 1860, that sphere already included charitable and benevolent activities; in wartime the scope of benevolence grew to embrace organized care for the wounded. Yet men continued to dominate the medical profession, and for the rest of the nineteenth century, nurses would be classified in the census as domestic help. The keenest disappointment of women's rights advocates lay in their failure to capitalize on rising sentiment for the abolition of slavery to secure the vote for women. Northern politicians could see little value in woman suffrage. The *New York Herald,* which supported the Loyal League's attack on slavery, dismissed its call for woman suffrage as "nonsense and tomfoolery." Stanton wrote bitterly, "So long as woman labors to second man's endeavors and exalt his sex above her own, her virtues pass unquestioned; but when she dares to demand rights and privileges for herself, her motives, manners, dress, personal appearance, and character are subjects for ridicule and detraction."

THE UNION VICTORIOUS, 1864–1865

Despite successes at Gettysburg and Vicksburg in 1863, the Union stood no closer to taking Richmond at the start of 1864 than in 1861, and most of the Lower South still remained under Confederate control. The Union invasion had taken its toll on the South's home front, but the North's inability to destroy the main Confederate armies had eroded the Union's will to keep attacking. Northern war weariness strengthened the Democrats and jeopardized Lincoln's prospects for reelection in 1864.

The year 1864 proved crucial for the North. While Grant dueled with Lee in the East, a Union army under William T. Sherman attacked from Tennessee into northwestern Georgia and took Atlanta in early September. Atlanta's fall boosted northern morale and helped to reelect Lincoln. Now the curtain rose on the last act of the war. After taking Atlanta, Sherman marched across Georgia to Savannah, devastated the state's resources, and cracked its morale. Pivoting north from Savannah, Sherman moved into South Carolina. Meanwhile, having backed Lee into trenches around Petersburg and Richmond, Grant forced the evacuation of both cities and brought on the Confederacy's collapse.

The Eastern Theater in 1864   Early in 1864, Lincoln made Grant commander of all Union armies and promoted him to lieutenant general. At first glance, the stony-faced Grant seemed an unlikely candidate for so exalted a rank, held previously only by George Washington. Grant's only distinguishing characteristics were his ever-present cigars and a penchant for whittling sticks into chips. "There is no glitter, no parade about him," a contemporary noted. But Grant's success in the West had made him the Union's most popular general. With his promotion, Grant moved his headquarters to the Army of the Potomac in the East and mapped a strategy for final victory.

Like Lincoln, Grant believed that the Union had to coordinate its attacks on all fronts in order to exploit its numerical advantage and prevent the South from shifting troops back and forth between the eastern and western theaters. Accordingly, Grant planned a sustained offensive against Lee in the East while ordering William T. Sherman to attack the rebel army in Georgia. Sherman's mission was to break up the Confederate army and "to get into the interior of the enemy's country . . . inflicting all the damage you can."

The pace of war quickened dramatically. In early May 1864, Grant led 118,000 men against Lee's 64,000 in a forested area near Fredericksburg, Virginia, called the Wilderness. Checked by Lee in a series of bloody engagements (the Battle of the Wilderness, May 5–7), Grant then tried to swing around Lee's right flank, only to suffer new reverses at Spotsylvania on May 12 and Cold Harbor on June 3. These engagements were among the war's fiercest; at Cold Harbor, Grant lost 7,000 men in a single hour. Oliver Wendell Holmes, Jr., a Union lieutenant and later a Supreme Court justice, wrote home how "immense the butcher's bill has been." But Grant refused to interpret repulses as defeats. Rather, he saw these violent engagements as less-than-complete victories. Pressing on, he forced Lee to pull back to the trenches guarding Petersburg and Richmond.

Once entrenched, Lee could no longer swing around to the Union rear, cut Yankee supply lines, or as at Chancellorsville, surprise the Union's main force. Lee did dispatch General Jubal A. Early on raids down the Shenandoah Valley, which the Confederacy had long used both as a granary and as an indirect way to menace Washington. But Grant countered by ordering General Philip Sheridan to march up the valley from the north and devastate it. The time had come, a Union chaplain wrote, "to peel this land." After defeating Early at Winchester, Virginia, in September 1864, Sheridan controlled the Shenandoah Valley.

While Grant and Lee grappled in the Wilderness, Sherman advanced into Georgia at the head of 98,000 men. Opposing him with 53,000 Confederate troops (soon reinforced to 65,000), General Joseph Johnston retreated toward Atlanta. Johnston's plan was to conserve strength for a final defense of Atlanta while forcing Sherman to extend his supply lines. But Jefferson Davis, dismayed by Johnston's defensive strategy, replaced him with the adventurous John B. Hood. Hood, who had lost the use of an arm at Gettysburg and a leg at Chickamauga, had to be strapped to his saddle; but for all his disabilities, he liked to take risks. In a prewar poker game, he had bet $2,500 with "nary a pair in his hand." Hood gave Davis what he wanted, a series of attacks on Sherman's army. The forays, however, failed to dislodge Sherman and severely depleted Hood's army. No longer able to defend Atlanta's supply lines, Hood evacuated the city, which Sherman took on September 2, 1864.

The Election of 1864   Atlanta's fall came at a timely moment for Lincoln, who faced a tough reelection campaign. Lincoln had secured the Republican renomination with difficulty. The Radicals, who had flayed Lincoln for delay in adopting emancipation as a war goal, now dismissed his plans to restore the occupied parts of Tennessee, Louisiana, and Arkansas to the Union. The Radicals insisted that only Congress, not the president, could set the requirements for readmission of conquered states and criticized Lincoln's reconstruction standards as too lenient. The Radicals endorsed Secretary of the Treasury Salmon P. Chase for the nomination. The Democrats, meanwhile, had never forgiven Lincoln for making emancipation a war goal. Now the Peace Democrats demanded an immediate armistice, followed by negotiations between the North and the South to settle outstanding issues.

Facing formidable challenges, Lincoln benefited from both his own resourcefulness and his foes' problems. Chase's challenge failed, and by the time of the Republican convention in July, Lincoln's managers were firmly in control. To isolate the Peace Democrats and attract prowar Democrats, the Republicans formed a temporary organization, the National Union party, and replaced Lincoln's vice president, Hannibal Hamlin, with a prowar southern Unionist, Democratic Senator Andrew Johnson of Tennessee. This tactic helped exploit the widening division among the Democrats, who nominated George B. McClellan, the former commander of the Army of the Potomac and an advocate of continuing the war until the Confederacy's collapse. But McClellan, saddled with a platform written by the Peace Democrats, spent much of his campaign distancing himself from his party's peace-without-victory plank.

Despite the Democrats' disarray, as late as August 1864, Lincoln seriously doubted that he would be reelected. Leaving little to chance, he arranged for furloughs so that Union soldiers, most of whom supported him, could vote in states lacking absentee ballots. But the timely fall of Atlanta aided him even more. The Confederate defeat punctured the northern antiwar movement and saved Lincoln's presidency. With 55 percent of the popular vote and 212 out of 233 electoral votes, Lincoln swept to victory.

The convention that nominated Lincoln had endorsed a constitutional amendment to abolish slavery, which Congress passed early in 1865. The **Thirteenth Amendment** would be ratified by the end of the year.

Sherman's March Through Georgia Meanwhile, Sherman gave the South a new lesson in total war. After evacuating Atlanta, Hood led his Confederate army north toward Tennessee in the hope of luring Sherman out of Georgia. But Sherman refused to chase Hood around Tennessee and stretch his own supply lines to the breaking point. Rather, Sherman proposed to abandon his supply lines altogether, march his army across Georgia to Savannah, and live off the countryside as he moved along. He would break the South's will to fight, terrify its people, and "make war so terrible . . . that generations would pass before they could appeal again to it."

Sherman began by burning much of Atlanta and forcing the evacuation of most of its civilian population. This harsh measure relieved him of the need to feed and garrison the city. Then, sending enough troops north to ensure the futility of Hood's campaign in Tennessee, he led the bulk of his army, sixty-two thousand men, on a 285-mile trek to Savannah. Soon thousands of slaves followed the army. "Dar's de man dat rules the world," a slave cried on seeing Sherman.

Sherman's four columns of infantry, augmented by cavalry screens, moved on a front sixty miles wide and at a pace of ten miles a day. They destroyed everything that could aid southern resistance—arsenals, railroads, munitions plants, cotton gins, cotton stores, crops, and livestock. Railroad destruction was especially thorough; ripping up tracks, Union soldiers heated rails in giant fires and twisted them into "Sherman neckties." Although Sherman's troops were told not to destroy civilian property, foragers carried out their own version of total war, ransacking and sometimes demolishing homes. Indeed, the havoc seemed a vital part of Sherman's strategy. By the time he occupied Savannah, he estimated that his army had destroyed about a hundred million dollars' worth of property.

After taking Savannah in December 1864, Sherman's army wheeled north toward South Carolina, the first state to secede and, in the general's view, one "that deserves all that seems in store for her." Sherman's columns advanced unimpeded to Columbia, South Carolina's capital. After fires set by looters, slaves, soldiers of both sides, and liberated Union prisoners gutted much of the city, Sherman headed for North Carolina. By the spring of 1865, his army had left in its wake over four hundred miles of ruin. Other Union armies moved into Alabama and Georgia and took thousands of prisoners. Northern forces had penetrated the entire Confederacy, except for Texas and Florida, and crushed its wealth. "War is cruelty and you cannot refine it," Sherman wrote. "Those who brought war into our country deserve all the curses and maledictions a people can pour out."

| Toward Appomattox | While Sherman headed north, Grant renewed his assault on the entrenched Army of Northern Virginia. His objective was Petersburg, a railroad hub south of Richmond. Although |

Grant had failed on several occasions to overwhelm the Confederate defenses in front of Petersburg, the devastation wrought by Sherman's army had taken its toll on Confederate morale. Rebel desertions reached epidemic proportions. Reinforced by Sheridan's army, triumphant from its campaign in the Shenandoah Valley, Grant late in March 1865 swung his forces around the western flank of Petersburg's defenders. Lee could not stop him. On April 2, Sheridan smashed the rebel flank at the Battle of Five Forks. A courier bore the grim news to Jefferson Davis, attending church in Richmond: "General Lee telegraphs that he can hold his position no longer."

Davis left his pew, gathered his government, and fled the city. In the morning of April 3, Union troops entered Richmond, pulled down the Confederate flag, and ran up the Stars and Stripes over the capitol. As white and black regiments entered in triumph, explosions set by retreating Confederates left the city "a sea of flames." "Over all," wrote a Union officer, "hung a canopy of dense smoke lighted up now and then by the bursting shells from the numerous arsenals throughout the city." Fires damaged the Tredegar Iron Works. Union troops liberated the town jail, which housed slaves awaiting sale, and its rejoicing inmates poured into the streets. On April 4, Lincoln toured the city and, for a few minutes, sat at Jefferson Davis's desk with a dreamy expression on his face.

Lee made a last-ditch effort to escape from Grant and reach Lynchburg, sixty miles west of Petersburg. He planned to use rail connections there to join General Joseph Johnston's army, which Sherman had pushed into North Carolina. But Grant and Sheridan swiftly choked off Lee's escape route, and on April 9 Lee bowed to the inevitable. He asked for terms of surrender and met Grant in a private home in the village of **Appomattox Courthouse,** Virginia, east of Lynchburg. While stunned troops gathered outside, Lee appeared in full dress uniform, with a sword. Grant entered in his customary disarray, smoking a cigar. When Union troops began to fire celebratory salutes, Grant put a stop to it. The final surrender of Lee's army occurred four days later. Lee's troops laid down their arms between federal ranks. "On our part," wrote a Union officer, "not a sound of trumpet . . . nor roll of drum; not a cheer . . . but an awed stillness rather." Grant paroled Lee's twenty-six thousand men and sent them home with their horses and mules "to work their little farms." The remnants of Confederate resistance collapsed within a month of Appomattox. Johnston surrendered to Sherman on April 18, and Davis was captured in Georgia on May 10.

Grant returned to a jubilant Washington, and on April 14 he turned down a theater date with the Lincolns. That night at Ford's Theater, an unemployed pro-Confederate actor, John Wilkes Booth, entered Lincoln's box and shot him in the head. Waving a knife, Booth leaped onstage shouting the Virginia state motto, *"Sic semper tyrannis"* ("Such is always the fate of tyrants") and then escaped, despite having broken his leg. That same night, a Booth accomplice stabbed Secretary of State Seward, who later recovered, while a third conspirator, assigned to Vice President Johnson, failed to attack. Union troops hunted down Booth in Virginia within two weeks and shot him to death. Of eight accused accomplices, including a woman boardinghouse keeper, four were hanged and the rest imprisoned. On April 15, when Lincoln died, Andrew Johnson became president. Six days later Lincoln's funeral train departed on a mournful journey from Washington to Springfield, Illinois, with crowds of thousands gathering at stations to weep as it passed.

The Impact of the War

The Civil War took a larger human toll than any other war in American history. The 620,000 soldiers who lost their lives nearly equaled the number of American soldiers killed in all the nation's earlier and later wars combined. The death count stood at 360,000 Union soldiers and 260,000 Confederates. Most families in the nation suffered losses. Vivid reminders of the price of Union remained beyond the end of the century. For many years, armless and legless veterans gathered at regimental reunions. Citizens erected monuments to the dead in front of town halls and on village greens. Soldiers' widows collected pensions well into the twentieth century.

The economic costs were staggering, but the war did not ruin the national economy, only the southern part of it. Vast Confederate losses, about 60 percent of southern wealth, were offset by northern advances. At the war's end, the North had almost all of the nation's wealth and capacity for production. Spurring economic modernization, the war provided a hospitable climate for industrial development and capital investment. No longer the largest slave-owning power in the world, the United States would now become a major industrial nation.

The war had political as well as economic ramifications. It created a "more perfect Union" in place of the prewar federation of states. The doctrine of states' rights did not disappear, but it was shorn of its extreme features. Talk of secession ended; states would never again exercise their antebellum range of powers. The national banking system, created in 1863, gradually supplanted state banks. The greenbacks provided a national currency. The federal government had exercised powers that many in 1860 doubted it possessed. By abolishing slavery and imposing an income tax, it asserted power over kinds of private property once thought untouchable. The war also promoted large-scale organization in both the business world and public life. The giant railroad corporation, with its thousands of employees, and the huge Sanitary Commission, with its thousands of auxiliaries and volunteers, pointed out the road that the nation would take.

Finally, the Civil War fulfilled abolitionist prophecies as well as Unionist goals. Freeing 3.5 million slaves and expediting efforts by slaves to liberate themselves, the war produced the very sort of radical upheaval within southern society that Lincoln had originally said that it would not induce.

MAP 15.3 The Final Virginia Campaign, 1864–1865

Refusing to abandon his campaign in the face of enormous casualties, Grant finally pushed Lee (below) into defensive fortifications around Petersburg, whose fall doomed Richmond. When Lee tried to escape to the west, Grant cut him off and forced his surrender.

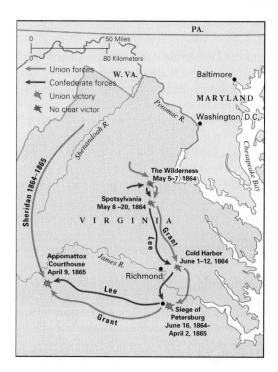

CONCLUSION

When war began in April 1861, both sides were unprepared, but each had distinct strengths. The Union held vast advantages of manpower and resources, including most of the nation's industrial strength and two-thirds of its railroads. The North, however, faced a stiff challenge. To achieve its goal of forcing the rebel states back into the Union, it had to conquer large pieces of southern territory, cripple the South's resources, and destroy its armies. The Union's challenge was the Confederacy's strength. To sustain Confederate independence, the South had to fight a defensive war, far less costly in men and materiel. It had to prevent Union conquest of its territory, preserve its armies from annihilation, and hold out long enough to convince the North that further effort would be pointless. Moreover, southerners expected to be fighting on home ground and to enjoy an advantage in morale. Thus, though its resources were fewer, the Confederacy's task was less daunting.

The start of war challenged governments, North and South, in similar ways: both sides had to raise armies and funds. Within two years, both the Union and the Confederacy had drafted troops, imposed taxes, and printed paper money. As war dragged on, both regions faced political and economic problems. Leaders on each side confronted disunity and dissent. Northern Democrats assailed President Lincoln; in the South, states' rights supporters defied the authority of the Confederate government. The North's two-party system and the skills of its political leaders proved to be assets that the Confederacy lacked. Economically, too, the North held an edge. Both regions endured labor shortages and inflation. But the Union with its far greater resources more handily met the demands of war. In the North, Republicans in Congress enacted innovative laws that enhanced federal might, such as the National Banking Act, the Pacific Railroad Act, and the Homestead Act. The beleaguered South, in contrast, had to cope with food shortages and economic dislocation. Loss of southern manpower to the army took a toll as well; slavery began to disintegrate as a labor system during the war. By 1864, even the Confederate Congress considered measures to free at least some slaves.

Significantly, war itself pressed the North to bring slavery to an end. To deprive the South of resources, the Union began to seize rebel property, including slaves, in 1861. Step by step, Union policy shifted toward emancipation. The second Confiscation Act in 1862 freed slaves who fled behind Union lines. Finally, seizing the initiative from Radical Republicans, Lincoln announced a crucial change in policy. A war measure, the Emancipation Proclamation of January 1, 1863, served many purposes. The edict freed only slaves behind Confederate lines, those beyond the reach of the Union army. But it won foreign support, outflanked the Radicals, and confounded the Confederates. It also gave Union soldiers the power to liberate slaves, enabled former slaves to serve in the Union army, and vastly strengthened the Union's hand. "Crippling the institution of slavery," as a Union officer declared, meant "striking a blow at the heart of the rebellion." Most important, the proclamation changed the nature of the war. After January 1, 1863, the war to save the Union was also a war to end slavery. Emancipation took effect mainly at the war's end and became permanent with the ratification of the Thirteenth Amendment in 1865. The proclamation of 1863 was a pivotal turning point in the war.

Historians have long debated the causes of the Union victory. They have weighed many factors, including the North's imposing strengths, or what Robert E. Lee called its "overwhelming numbers and resources." Recently, two competing interpretations have held sway. One focuses on southern shortcomings. Did the South, in the end, lose the will to win? Did the economic dislocations of war undercut southern morale? Were there defects of Confederate nationalism that could not be overcome? Some historians point to internal weaknesses in the Confederacy as a major cause of Union triumph. Other historians stress the utterly unpredictable nature of the conflict. In their view, the two sides were fairly equally matched, and the war was a cliffhanger; that is, the North might have crushed the South much earlier or, alternatively, not at all. The North won the war, these historians contend, because it won a series of crucial contests on the battlefield, including the battles of Antietam, Vicksburg, Gettysburg, and Atlanta, any one of which could have gone the other way. The factors that determined the military outcome of the war continue to be a source of contention.

The impact of the Civil War is more clear-cut than the precise cause of Union triumph. The war gave a massive boost to the northern economy. It left in its wake a stronger national government, with a national banking system, a national currency, and an enfeebled version of states' rights. It confirmed the triumph of the Republican Party, with its commitment to competition, free labor, and industry. Finally, it left a nation of free people, including the millions of African-Americans who had once been slaves. Emancipation and a new sense of nationalism were the war's major legacies. The nation now turned its attention to the restoration of the conquered South to the Union and to deciding the future of the former slaves.

16

The Crises of Reconstruction, 1865–1877

RECONSTRUCTION POLITICS, 1865–1868

At the end of the Civil War, President Johnson might have exiled, imprisoned, or executed Confederate leaders and imposed martial law indefinitely. Demobilized Confederate soldiers might have continued armed resistance to federal occupation forces. Freed slaves might have taken revenge on former owners and the rest of the white community. But none of these drastic possibilities occurred. Instead, intense *political* conflict dominated the immediate postwar years. In national politics, unparalleled disputes produced new constitutional amendments, a presidential impeachment, and some of the most ambitious domestic legislation ever enacted by Congress, the Reconstruction Acts of 1867–1868. The major outcome of Reconstruction politics was the enfranchisement of black men, a development that few—black or white—had expected when Lee surrendered.

In 1865, only a small group of politicians supported black suffrage. All were Radical Republicans, a minority faction that had emerged during the war. Led by Senator **Charles Sumner** of Massachusetts and Congressman **Thaddeus Stevens** of Pennsylvania, the Radicals had clamored for the abolition of slavery and a demanding reconstruction policy. Any plan to restore the Union, Stevens contended, must "revolutionize Southern institutions, habits, and manners." But the Radicals, outnumbered in Congress by other Republicans and opposed by the Democratic minority, faced long odds. Still, they managed to win broad Republican support for parts of their Reconstruction program, including black male enfranchisement. Just as civil war had led to emancipation, a goal once supported by only a minority of Americans, so Reconstruction policy became bound to black suffrage, a momentous change that originally had only narrow political backing.

The Devastated South *After the Civil War, parts of the devastated Confederacy resembled a wasteland. Homes, crops, and railroads had been destroyed; farming and business had come to a standstill; and uprooted southerners wandered about. Here, ruins of homes in Baton Rouge, Louisiana.*

Lincoln's Plan   Conflict over Reconstruction began even before the war ended. In December 1863, President Lincoln issued the Proclamation of Amnesty and Reconstruction, which enabled southern states to rejoin the Union if at least 10 percent of those who had cast ballots in the election of 1860 would take an oath of allegiance to the Union and accept emancipation. This minority could then create a loyal state government. Lincoln's plan excluded some southerners from taking the oath: Confederate government officials, army and naval officers, as well as those military or civil officers who had resigned from Congress or from U.S. commissions in 1861. All such persons would have to apply for presidential pardons. Also excluded, of course, were blacks, who had not been voters in 1860. Lincoln hoped to undermine the Confederacy by establishing pro-Union governments within it; to win the allegiance of southern Unionists (those who had opposed secession), especially former Whigs; and to build a southern Republican party.

Radical Republicans in Congress, however, envisioned a slower readmission process that would bar even more ex-Confederates from political life. The Wade-Davis bill, passed by Congress in July 1864, provided that a military governor would rule each former Confederate state and that after at least half the eligible voters took an oath of allegiance to the Union, delegates could be elected to a state convention that would re-

CHRONOLOGY, 1865–1877

1863 • President Abraham Lincoln issues Proclamation of Amnesty and Reconstruction.

1864 • Wade-Davis bill passed by Congress and pocket-vetoed by Lincoln.

1865 • Freedmen's Bureau established.
Civil War ends.
Lincoln assassinated.
Andrew Johnson becomes president.
Johnson issues Proclamation of Amnesty and Reconstruction.
Ex-Confederate states hold constitutional conventions (May–December).
Black conventions begin in the ex-Confederate states.
Thirteenth Amendment added to the Constitution.
Presidential Reconstruction completed.

1866 • Congress enacts the Civil Rights Act of 1866 and the Supplementary Freedmen's Bureau Act over Johnson's vetoes.
Ku Klux Klan founded in Tennessee.
Tennessee readmitted to the Union.
Race riots in southern cities.
Republicans win congressional elections.

1867 • Reconstruction Act of 1867.
William Seward negotiates the purchase of Alaska.
Constitutional conventions meet in the ex-Confederate states.
Howard University founded.

1868 • President Johnson is impeached, tried, and acquitted.
Omnibus Act.
Fourteenth Amendment added to the Constitution.
Ulysses S. Grant elected president.

1869 • Transcontinental railroad completed.

1870 • Congress readmits the four remaining southern states to the Union.
Fifteenth Amendment added to the Constitution.
Enforcement Act of 1870.

1871 • Second Enforcement Act.
Ku Klux Klan Act.

1872 • Liberal Republican party formed.
Amnesty Act.
Alabama claims settled.
Grant reelected president.

1873 • Panic of 1873 begins (September–October), setting off a five-year depression.

1874 • Democrats gain control of the House of Representatives.

1875 • Civil Rights Act of 1875.
Specie Resumption Act.

1876 • Disputed presidential election: Rutherford B. Hayes versus Samuel J. Tilden.

1877 • Electoral commission decides election in favor of Hayes.
The last Republican-controlled governments overthrown in Florida, Louisiana, and South Carolina.

1879 • "Exodus" movement spreads through several southern states.

peal secession and abolish slavery. To qualify as a voter or delegate, a southerner would have to take a second, "ironclad" oath, swearing that he had never voluntarily supported the Confederacy. Like the 10 percent plan, the congressional plan did not provide for black suffrage, a measure then supported by only some Radicals. Unlike Lincoln's plan, however, the Wade-Davis scheme would have delayed the readmission process almost indefinitely.

Claiming that he did not want to bind himself to any single restoration policy, Lincoln pocket-vetoed the Wade-Davis bill (that is, he failed to sign the bill within ten days of the adjournment of Congress). The bill's sponsors, Senator Benjamin Wade of Ohio and Congressman Henry Winter Davis of Maryland, blasted Lincoln's act as an outrage. By the war's end, the president and Congress had reached an impasse. Arkansas, Louisiana, Tennessee, and parts of Virginia under Union army control moved toward readmission under variants of Lincoln's plan. But Congress refused to seat their delegates, as it had a right to do. Lincoln, meanwhile, hinted that a more rigorous Reconstruction policy might be in store. What Lincoln's ultimate policy would have been remains unknown. But after his assassination, on April 14, 1865, Radical Republicans turned with hope toward his successor, **Andrew Johnson** of Tennessee, in whom they felt they had an ally.

Presidential Reconstruction Under Johnson	The only southern senator to remain in Congress when his state seceded, Andrew Johnson had served as military governor of Tennessee from 1862 to 1864. He had taken a strong

anti-Confederate stand, declaring that "treason is a crime and must be made odious." Above all, Johnson had long sought the destruction of the planter aristocracy. A self-educated man of humble North Carolina origins, Johnson had moved to Greenville, Tennessee, in 1826 and became a tailor. His wife, Eliza McCardle, had taught him how to write. He had entered politics in the 1830s as a spokesman for non-slave-owning whites and rose rapidly from local official to congressman to governor to senator. Once the owner of eight slaves, Johnson reversed his position on slavery during the war. When emancipation became Union policy, he supported it. But Johnson neither adopted abolitionist ideals nor challenged racist sentiments. He hoped mainly that the fall of slavery would injure southern aristocrats. Andrew Johnson, in short, had his own political agenda, which, as Republicans would soon learn, did not coincide with theirs. Moreover, he was a lifelong Democrat who had been added to the Republican, or National Union, ticket in 1864 to broaden its appeal and who had become president by accident.

In May 1865, with Congress out of session, Johnson shocked Republicans by announcing in two proclamations his own program to bring back into the Union the seven southern states still without reconstruction governments—Alabama, Florida, Georgia, Mississippi, North Carolina, South Carolina, and Texas. Almost all southerners who took an oath of allegiance would receive a pardon and amnesty, and all their property except slaves would be restored. Oath takers could elect delegates to state conventions, which would provide for regular elections. Each state convention, Johnson later added, would have to proclaim the illegality of secession, repudiate state debts incurred when the state belonged to the Confederacy, and ratify the Thirteenth Amendment, which abolished slavery. (Proposed by an enthusiastic wartime Congress early in 1865, the amendment would be ratified in December of that year.) As under Lincoln's plan, Confederate civil and military officers would still be disqualified, as would well-off ex-Confederates—those with taxable property worth $20,000 or more. This purge of the plantation aristocracy, Johnson said, would benefit "humble men, the peasantry and yeomen of the South, who have been decoyed . . . into rebellion." Poorer whites would now be in control.

Presidential Reconstruction took effect in the summer of 1865, but with unforeseen consequences. Southerners disqualified on the basis of wealth or high Confederate position applied for pardons in droves, and Johnson handed out pardons liberally—some thirteen thousand of them. He also dropped plans for the punishment of treason. By the end of 1865, all seven states had created new civil governments that in effect restored the status quo from before the war. Confederate army officers and large planters assumed state offices. Former Confederate congressmen, state officials, and generals were elected to Congress. Georgia sent Alexander Stephens, the former Confederate vice president, back to Washington as a senator. Some states refused to ratify the Thirteenth Amendment or to repudiate their Confederate debts.

Most infuriating to Radical Republicans, all seven states took steps to ensure a landless, dependent black labor force: they passed **"black codes"** to replace the slave codes, state laws that had regulated slavery. Because Johnson's plan assured the ratification of the Thirteenth Amendment, all states guaranteed the freedmen some basic rights—to marry, own property, make contracts, and testify in court against other blacks—but the codes harshly restricted freedmen's behavior. Some established racial segregation in public places; most prohibited racial intermarriage, jury service by blacks, and court testimony by blacks against whites. All codes included provisions that effectively barred former slaves from leaving the plantations. South Carolina required special licenses for blacks who wished to enter nonagricultural employment. Mississippi prohibited blacks from buying and selling farmland. Most states required annual contracts between landowners and black agricultural workers and provided that blacks without lawful employment would be arrested as vagrants and their labor auctioned off to employers who would pay their fines.

The black codes left freedmen no longer slaves but not really liberated either. Although "free" to sign labor contracts, for instance, those who failed to sign them would be considered in violation of the law and swept back into involuntary servitude. In practice, many clauses in the codes never took effect: the Union army and the Freedmen's Bureau (a federal agency that assisted former slaves) swiftly suspended the enforcement of racially discriminatory provisions of the new laws. But the black codes revealed white southern intentions. They showed what "home rule" would have been like without federal interference.

Many northerners denounced what they saw as southern defiance. "What can be hatched from such an egg but another rebellion?" asked a Boston newspaper. Republicans in Congress agreed. When Congress convened in December 1865, it refused to seat the delegates of the ex-Confederate states. Establishing the Joint (House-Senate) Committee on Reconstruction, Republicans prepared to dismantle the black codes and lock ex-Confederates out of power.

Congress Versus Johnson

Southern blacks' status now became the major issue in Congress. Radical Republicans like Congressman Thaddeus Stevens—who hoped to impose black suffrage on the former Confederacy and delay the readmission of the southern states into the Union—were still a minority in Congress. Conservative Republicans, who tended to favor the Johnson plan, formed a minority too, as did the Democrats, who also supported the president. Moderate Republicans, the largest congressional bloc, agreed with the Radicals that Johnson's plan was too feeble, but they wanted to avoid a dispute with the president. As none of the four congressional blocs could claim the two-thirds majority required to overturn a presidential veto, Johnson's program would prevail unless the moderates and the Radicals joined forces. Ineptly, Johnson alienated a majority of moderates and pushed them into the Radicals' arms.

Two proposals to invalidate the black codes, drafted by a moderate Republican, Senator Lyman Trumbull of Illinois, won wide Republican support. Congress first voted to continue the Freedmen's Bureau, established in 1865, whose term was ending. This federal agency, headed by former Union general O. O. Howard and staffed mainly by army officers, provided relief, rations, and medical care. It also built schools for the freed blacks, put them to work on abandoned or confiscated lands, and tried to protect their rights as laborers. Congress extended the bureau's life for three years and gave it new power: it could run special military courts to settle labor disputes and could invalidate labor contracts forced on freedmen by the black codes. In February 1866, Johnson vetoed the Freedmen's Bureau bill. The Constitution, he declared, did not sanction military trials of civilians in peacetime, nor did it support a system to care for "indigent persons."

In March 1866, Congress passed a second measure proposed by Trumbull, a bill that made blacks U.S. citizens with the same civil rights as other citizens and authorized federal intervention in the states to ensure black rights in court. Johnson vetoed the civil rights bill also. He argued that it would "operate in favor of the colored and against the white race." In April, Congress overrode his veto; the **Civil Rights Act of 1866** was the first major law ever passed over a presidential veto. In July, Congress enacted the Supplementary Freedmen's Bureau Act over Johnson's veto as well. Johnson's vetoes puzzled many Republicans because the new laws did not undercut presidential Reconstruction. The president insisted, however, that both bills were illegitimate because southerners had been shut out of the Congress that passed them. His stance won support in the South and from northern Democrats. But the president had alienated the moderate Republicans, who began to work with the Radicals against him. Johnson had lost "every friend he has," one moderate declared.

Some historians view Andrew Johnson as a political incompetent who, at this crucial turning point, bungled both his readmission scheme and his political future. Others contend that he was merely trying to forge a coalition of the center, made up of Democrats and non-Radical Republicans. In either case, Johnson underestimated the possibility of Republican unity. Once united, the Republicans took their next step: the passage of a constitutional amendment to prevent the Supreme Court from invalidating the new Civil Rights Act and block Democrats in Congress from repealing it.

The Fourteenth Amendment, 1866　　In April 1866, Congress adopted the **Fourteenth Amendment,** which had been proposed by the Joint Committee on Reconstruction. To protect blacks' rights, the amendment declared in its first clause that all persons born or naturalized in the United States were citizens of the nation and citizens of their states and that no state could abridge their rights without due process of law or deny them equal protection of the law. This section nullified the *Dred Scott* decision of 1857, which had declared that blacks were not citizens. Second, the amendment guaranteed that if a state denied suffrage to any of its male citizens, its representation in Congress would be proportionally reduced. This clause did not guarantee black suffrage, but it threatened to deprive southern states of some legislators if black men were denied the vote. This was the first time that the word *male* was written into the Constitution. To the dismay of women's rights advocates, woman suffrage seemed a yet more distant prospect. Third, the amendment disqualified from state and national office *all* prewar officeholders—civil and military, state and federal—who had supported the Confederacy, unless Congress removed their disqualifications by a two-thirds vote. In so providing, Congress intended to invalidate Johnson's wholesale distribution of amnesties and pardons. Finally, the amendment repudiated the Confederate debt and maintained the validity of the federal debt.

The most ambitious step that Congress had yet taken, the Fourteenth Amendment revealed Republican legislators' growing receptivity to Radical demands, including black male enfranchisement. The Fourteenth Amendment was the first national effort to limit state control of civil and political rights, and its passage created a firestorm. Abolitionists decried the second clause as a "swindle" because it did not explicitly ensure black suffrage. Southerners and northern Democrats condemned the third clause as vengeful. Southern legislatures, except for Tennessee's, refused to ratify the amendment, and President Johnson denounced it. His defiance solidified the new alliance between moderate and Radical Republicans, and turned the congressional elections of 1866 into a referendum on the Fourteenth Amendment.

Over the summer, Johnson set off on a whistle-stop train tour from Washington to St. Louis and Chicago and back. But this innovative campaign tactic—the "swing around the circle," as Johnson called it—failed. Humorless and defensive, the president made fresh enemies and doomed his hope of creating a new National Union party that would sink the Fourteenth Amendment. Moderate and Radical Republicans defended the amendment, condemned the president, and branded the Democratic Party "a common sewer . . . into which is emptied every element of treason, North and South."

Republicans carried the congressional elections of 1866 in a landslide, winning almost two-thirds of the House and almost four-fifths of the Senate. They had secured a mandate to overcome southern resistance to the Fourteenth Amendment and to enact their own Reconstruction program, even if the president vetoed every part of it.

Congressional Reconstruction, 1866–1867 The congressional debate over reconstructing the South began in December 1866 and lasted three months. Radical Republican leaders called for black suffrage, federal support for public schools, confiscation of Confederate estates, and an extended period of military occupation in the South. Moderate Republicans, who once would have found such a plan too extreme, now accepted parts of it. In February 1867, after complex legislative maneuvers and many late-night sessions, Congress passed the **Reconstruction Act of 1867.** Johnson vetoed the law, and on March 2 Congress passed it over his veto. Later that year and in 1868, Congress passed three further Reconstruction acts, all enacted over presidential vetoes, to refine and enforce the first.

The Reconstruction Act of 1867 invalidated the state governments formed under the Lincoln and Johnson plans. Only Tennessee, which had ratified the Fourteenth Amendment and had been readmitted to the Union, escaped further reconstruction. The new law divided the other ten former Confederate states into five temporary military districts, each run by a Union general. Voters—all black men, plus those white men who had not been disqualified by the Fourteenth Amendment—could elect delegates to a state convention that would write a new state constitution granting black suffrage. When eligible voters ratified the new constitution, elections could be held for state officers. Once Congress approved the state constitution, once the state legislature ratified the Fourteenth Amendment, and once the amendment became part of the federal Constitution, Congress would readmit the state into the Union—and Reconstruction, in a constitutional sense, would be complete.

The Reconstruction Act of 1867 was far more radical than the Johnson program because it enfranchised blacks and disfranchised many ex-Confederates. It fulfilled a central goal of the Radical Republicans: to delay the readmission of former Confederate states until Republican governments could be established and thereby prevent an immediate rebel resurgence. But the new law was not as harsh toward ex-Confederates as it might have been. It provided for only temporary military rule, did not prosecute Confederate leaders for treason or permanently bar them from politics, and made no provision for confiscation or redistribution of property.

During the congressional debates, Radical Republican congressman Thaddeus Stevens had argued for the confiscation of large Confederate estates to "humble the proud traitors" and to provide for the former slaves. He had proposed subdividing such confiscated property into forty-acre tracts to be distributed among the freedmen and selling the rest, some 90 percent of it, to pay off war debts. Stevens wanted to crush the planter aristocracy and create a new class of self-sufficient black yeoman farmers. His land-reform bill won the support of other Radicals but never made progress, for most Republicans held property rights sacred. Tampering with such rights in the South, they feared, would jeopardize those rights in the North. Moreover, Stevens's proposal would alienate southern ex-Whigs from the Republican cause, antagonize other white southerners, and thereby endanger the rest of Reconstruction. Thus land reform never came about. The "radical" Reconstruction acts were a compromise.

Congressional Reconstruction took effect in the spring of 1867, but it could not be enforced without military power. Johnson, as Commander in Chief, impeded its implementation by replacing military officers sympathetic to the Radical cause with conservative ones. Republicans seethed. More suspicious than ever of the president, congressional moderates and Radicals once again joined forces to block Johnson from obstructing Reconstruction.

The Impeachment Crisis, 1867–1868 In March 1867, Republicans in Congress passed two laws to limit presidential power. The **Tenure of Office Act** prohibited the president from removing civil officers without Senate consent. Cabinet members, the law stated, were to hold office "during the term of the president by whom they may have been appointed" and could be fired only with the Senate's approval. The goal was to bar Johnson from dismissing Secretary of War Henry Stanton, a Radical ally needed to enforce the Reconstruction acts. The other law, a rider to an army appropriations bill, barred the president from issuing military orders except through the commanding general, Ulysses S. Grant, who could not be removed without the Senate's consent.

The Radicals' enmity toward Johnson, however, would not die until he was out of office. They began to seek grounds on which to impeach him. The House Judiciary

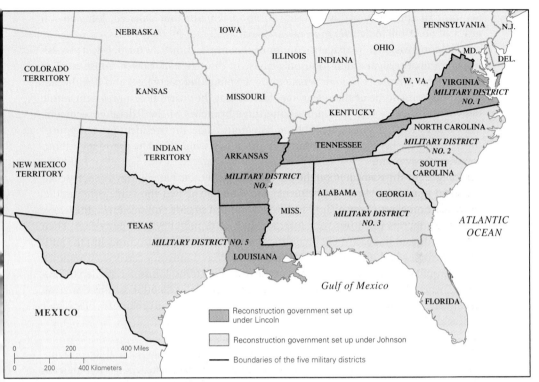

MAP 16.1 The Reconstruction of the South

The Reconstruction Act of 1867 divided the former Confederate states, except Tennessee, into five military districts and set forth the steps by which new state governments could be created.

Committee, aided by private detectives, could at first uncover no valid charges against Johnson. But Johnson again rescued his foes by providing the charges they needed.

In August 1867, with Congress out of session, Johnson suspended Secretary of War Stanton and replaced him with General Grant. In early 1868, the reconvened Senate refused to approve Stanton's suspension, and Grant, sensing the Republican mood, vacated the office. Johnson then removed Stanton and replaced him with an aged general, Lorenzo Thomas. Johnson's defiance forced Republican moderates, who had at first resisted impeachment, into yet another alliance with the Radicals: the president had "thrown down the gauntlet," a moderate charged. The House approved eleven charges of impeachment, nine of them based on violation of the Tenure of Office Act. The other charges accused Johnson of being "unmindful of the high duties of office," seeking to disgrace Congress, and not enforcing the Reconstruction acts.

Johnson's trial in the Senate, which began in March 1868, riveted public attention for eleven weeks. Seven congressmen, including leading Radical Republicans, served as prosecutors or "managers." Johnson's lawyers maintained that he was merely seeking a court test by violating the Tenure of Office Act, which he thought was unconstitutional. They also contended, somewhat inconsistently, that the law did not protect Secretary

Stanton, an appointee of Lincoln, not Johnson. Finally, they asserted, Johnson was guilty of no crime indictable in a regular court.

The congressional "managers" countered that impeachment was a political process, not a criminal trial, and that Johnson's "abuse of discretionary power" constituted an impeachable offense. Although Senate opinion split along party lines and Republicans held a majority, some of them wavered, fearful that the removal of a president would destroy the balance of power among the three branches of the federal government. They also distrusted Radical Republican Benjamin Wade, the president pro tempore of the Senate, who, because there was no vice president, would become president if Johnson were thrown out.

Intense pressure weighed on the wavering Republicans. Late in May 1868, the Senate voted against Johnson 35 to 19, one vote short of the two-thirds majority needed for conviction. Seven Republicans had risked political suicide and sided with the twelve Senate Democrats in voting against removal. In so doing, they set a precedent. Their vote discouraged impeachment on political grounds for decades to come. But the anti-Johnson forces had also achieved their goal: Andrew Johnson's career as a national leader would soon end. After serving out the rest of his term, Johnson returned to Tennessee, where he was reelected to the Senate five years later. Republicans in Congress, meanwhile, pursued their last major Reconstruction objective: to guarantee black male suffrage.

The Fifteenth Amendment and the Question of Woman Suffrage, 1869–1870

Black suffrage was the linchpin of congressional Reconstruction. Only with the support of black voters could Republicans secure control of the ex-Confederate states. The Reconstruction Act of 1867 had forced every southern state legislature to enfranchise black men as a prerequisite for readmission to the Union, but much of the North rejected black suffrage at home. Congressional Republicans therefore had two aims. The **Fifteenth Amendment**, drawn up by Republicans and proposed by Congress in 1869, sought to protect black suffrage in the South against future repeal by Congress or the states, and to enfranchise northern and border-state blacks, who would presumably vote Republican. The amendment prohibited the denial of suffrage by the states to any citizen on account of "race, color, or previous condition of servitude."

Democrats argued that the proposed amendment violated states' rights by denying each state the power to determine who would vote. But Democrats did not control enough states to defeat the amendment, and it was ratified in 1870. Four votes came from those ex-Confederate states—Mississippi, Virginia, Georgia, and Texas—that had delayed the Reconstruction process and were therefore forced to approve the Fifteenth Amendment, as well as the Fourteenth, in order to rejoin the Union. Some southerners contended that the new amendment's omissions made it acceptable, for it had, as a Richmond newspaper pointed out, "loopholes through which a coach and four horses can be driven." What were these loopholes? The Fifteenth Amendment neither guaranteed black officeholding nor prohibited voting restrictions such as property requirements and literacy tests. Such restrictions might be used to deny blacks the vote, and indeed, ultimately they were so used.

The debate over black suffrage drew new participants into the political fray. Since the end of the war, a small group of abolitionists, men and women, had sought to revive the cause of women's rights. In 1866, when Congress debated the Fourteenth Amendment, women's rights advocates tried to join forces with their old abolitionist allies to promote both black suffrage and woman suffrage. Most Radical Republicans, however, did not want to be saddled with the woman-suffrage plank; they feared it would impede their primary goal, black enfranchisement.

This defection provoked disputes among women's rights advocates. Some argued that black suffrage would pave the way for the women's vote and that black men deserved priority. "If the elective franchise is not extended to the Negro, he is dead," explained Frederick Douglass, a longtime women's rights supporter. "Woman has a thousand ways by which she can attach herself to the ruling power of the land that we have not." But women's rights leaders Elizabeth Cady Stanton and **Susan B. Anthony** disagreed. In their view, the Fourteenth Amendment had disabled women by including the word *male,* and the Fifteenth Amendment compounded the injury by failing to prohibit the denial of suffrage on account of sex. Instead, Stanton contended, the Fifteenth Amendment established an "aristocracy of sex" and increased women's disadvantages.

The battle over black suffrage and the Fifteenth Amendment split women's rights advocates into two rival suffrage associations, both formed in 1869. The Boston-based American Woman Suffrage Association, endorsed by reformers such as Julia Ward Howe and Lucy Stone, retained an alliance with male abolitionists and campaigned for woman suffrage in the states. The New York–based and more radical National Woman Suffrage Association, led by Stanton and Anthony, condemned its leaders' one-time male allies and promoted a federal woman suffrage amendment.

For the rest of the 1870s, the rival woman suffrage associations vied for constituents. In 1869 and 1870, independent of the suffrage movement, two territories, Wyoming and Utah, enfranchised women. But lacking support, suffragists failed to sway legislators elsewhere. In 1872, Susan B. Anthony mobilized about seventy women to vote nationwide and, as a result, was indicted, convicted, and fined. One of the women who tried to vote in 1872, Missouri suffragist Virginia Minor, brought suit with her husband against the registrar who had excluded her. The Minors based their case on the Fourteenth Amendment, which, they claimed, enfranchised women. In *Minor* v. *Happersett* (1875), however, the Supreme Court declared that a state could constitutionally deny women the vote. Divided and rebuffed, woman-suffrage advocates braced for a long struggle.

By the time the Fifteenth Amendment was ratified in 1870, Congress could look back on five years of momentous achievement. Since the start of 1865, three constitutional amendments had broadened the scope of American democracy by passing three constitutional amendments. The Thirteenth Amendment abolished slavery, the Fourteenth expanded civil rights, and the Fifteenth prohibited the denial of suffrage on the basis of race. Congress had also readmitted the former Confederate states into the Union. But after 1868 congressional momentum slowed, and in 1869, when Ulysses S. Grant became president, enmity between Congress and the chief executive ceased. The theater of action now shifted to the South, where tumultuous change was under way.

Stanton and Anthony, c. 1870
Women's rights advocates Susan B. Anthony and Elizabeth Cady Stanton began to promote woman suffrage in 1866 when the issue of black suffrage arose, and subsequently assailed the proposed Fifteenth Amendment for excluding women. By the end of the 1860s, activists had formed two competing suffragist organizations.

RECONSTRUCTION GOVERNMENTS

During the unstable years of presidential Reconstruction, 1865–1867, the southern states had to create new governments, revive the war-torn economy, and face the impact of emancipation. Social and economic crises abounded. War costs had cut into southern wealth, cities and factories lay in rubble, plantation-labor systems disintegrated, and racial tensions flared. Beginning in 1865, freedmen organized black conventions, political meetings at which they protested ill treatment and demanded equal rights. These meetings occurred in a climate of violence. Race riots erupted in major southern cities, such as Memphis in May 1866 and in New Orleans two months later. Even when Congress imposed military rule, ex-Confederates did not feel defeated. "Having reached bottom, there is hope now that we may rise again," a South Carolina planter wrote in his diary.

Congressional Reconstruction, supervised by federal troops, took effect in the spring of 1867. The Johnson regimes were dismantled, state constitutional conventions met, and voters elected new state governments, which Republicans dominated. In 1868, a majority of the former Confederate states rejoined the Union, and two years later, the last four states—Virginia, Mississippi, Georgia, and Texas—followed.

Readmission to the Union did not end the process of Reconstruction, for Republicans still held power in the South. But Republican rule was very brief, lasting less than a decade in all southern states, far less in most of them, and on average under five years. Opposition from southern Democrats, the landowning elite, thousands of vigilantes, and, indeed, most white voters proved insurmountable. Still, the governments formed under congressional Reconstruction were unique, because black men, including ex-slaves, participated in them. In no other society where slaves had been liberated—neither Haiti, where slaves had revolted in the 1790s, nor the British Caribbean islands, where Parliament had ended slavery in 1833—had freedmen gained democratic political rights.

A New Electorate The Reconstruction laws of 1867–1868 transformed the southern electorate by temporarily disfranchising 10 to 15 percent of potential white voters and by enfranchising more than seven hundred thousand freedmen. Outnumbering white voters in the South by one hundred thousand, blacks held voting majorities in five states.

The new electorate provided a base for the Republican Party, which had never existed in the South. To scornful Democrats, southern Republicans comprised three types of scoundrels: northern "carpetbaggers," who had allegedly come south seeking wealth and power (with so few possessions that they could be stuffed into traveling bags made of carpet material); southern "scalawags," predominantly poor and ignorant whites, who sought to profit from Republican rule; and hordes of uneducated freedmen, who were ready prey for Republican manipulators. Although the "carpetbag" and "scalawag" labels were derogatory and the stereotypes that they conveyed inaccurate, they remain in use as a form of shorthand. Crossing class and racial lines, the hastily established Republican Party was in fact a loose coalition of diverse factions with often contradictory goals.

To northerners who moved south after the Civil War, the former Confederacy was an undeveloped region, ripe with possibility. The carpetbaggers' ranks included many former Union soldiers who hoped to buy land, open factories, build railroads, or simply enjoy the warmer climate. Albion Tourgee, a young lawyer who had served with the New York and Ohio volunteers, for example, relocated in North Carolina after the war to improve his health; there he worked as a journalist, politician, and Republican judge. Perhaps no more than twenty thousand northern migrants like Tourgee—including veterans, missionaries, teachers, and Freedmen's Bureau agents—headed south immediately after the war, and many returned north by 1867. But those who remained held almost one out of three state offices and wielded disproportionate political power.

Scalawags, white southerners who supported the Republicans, included some entrepreneurs who applauded party policies such as the national banking system and high protective tariffs as well as some prosperous planters, former Whigs who had opposed secession. Their numbers included a few prominent politicians, among them James Orr of South Carolina and Mississippi's governor James Alcorn, who became Republicans in order to retain influence and limit Republican radicalism. Most scalawags, however, were small farmers from the mountain regions of North Carolina, Georgia, Alabama, and Arkansas. Former Unionists who had owned no slaves and felt no loyalty toward the landowning elite, they sought to improve their economic position. Unlike carpetbaggers, they were not committed to black rights or black suffrage; most came from regions with small black populations and cared little whether blacks voted or not. Scalawags held the most political offices during Reconstruction, but they proved the least stable element of the southern Republican coalition: eventually, many drifted back to the Democratic fold.

Freedmen, the backbone of southern Republicanism, provided eight out of ten Republican votes. Republican rule lasted longest in states with the largest black populations—South Carolina, Mississippi, Alabama, and Louisiana. Introduced to politics in the black conventions of 1865–1867, the freedmen sought land, education, civil

Republicans in the South Carolina Legislature, c. 1868 *Only in South Carolina did blacks comprise a majority in the legislature and dominate the legislative process during Reconstruction. This photographic collage of "Radical" legislators, black and white, suggests the extent of black representation. In 1874, blacks won the majority of seats in South Carolina's state senate as well.*

RADICAL MEMBERS
OF THE Sᵒ. Cᴬ. LEGISLATURE.

rights, and political equality, and remained loyal Republicans. As an elderly freedman announced at a Georgia political convention in 1867, "We know our friends." Although Reconstruction governments depended on African-American votes, freedmen held at most one in five political offices. Blacks served in all southern legislatures but constituted a majority only in the legislature of South Carolina, whose population was more than 60 percent black. In the House of Representatives, a mere 6 percent of southern members were black, and almost half of these came from South Carolina. No blacks became governor, and only two served in the U.S. Senate, Hiram Revels and Blanche K. Bruce, both of Mississippi. (Still, the same number of African-Americans served in the Senate during Reconstruction as throughout the entire twentieth century.)

Black officeholders on the state level formed a political elite. They often differed from black voters in background, education, wealth, and complexion. A disproportionate number were literate blacks who had been free before the Civil War. In the South Carolina legislature, for instance, most black members, unlike their constituents, came from large towns and cities; many had spent time in the North; and some were well-off property owners or even former slave owners. Color differences were evident, too: 43 percent of South Carolina's black state legislators were mulattos (mixed race), compared to only 7 percent of the state's black population.

Black officials and black voters often had different priorities. Most freedmen cared mainly about their economic future, especially about acquiring land, whereas black officeholders cared most about attaining equal rights. Still, both groups shared high expectations and prized enfranchisement. "We'd walk fifteen miles in wartime to find out about the battle," a Georgia freedman declared. "We can walk fifteen miles and more to find how to vote."

Republican Rule   Large numbers of blacks participated in American government for the first time in the state constitutional conventions of 1867–1868. The South Carolina convention had a black majority, and in Louisiana half the delegates were freedmen. The conventions forged democratic changes in their state constitutions. Delegates abolished property qualifications for officeholding, made many appointive offices elective, and redistricted state legislatures more equitably. All states established universal manhood suffrage, and Louisiana and South Carolina opened public schools to both races. These provisions integrated the New Orleans public schools as well as the University of South Carolina, from which whites withdrew.

But no state instituted land reform. When proposals for land confiscation and redistribution arose at the state conventions, they fell to defeat, as they had in Congress. Hoping to attract northern investment to the reconstructed South, southern Republicans hesitated to threaten property rights or to adopt land-reform measures that northern Republicans had rejected. South Carolina did set up a commission to buy land and make it available to freedmen, and several states changed their tax structures to force uncultivated land onto the market, but in no case was ex-Confederate land confiscated.

Once civil power shifted from the federal army to the new state governments, Republican administrations began ambitious programs of public works. They built roads, bridges, and public buildings; approved railroad bonds; and funded institutions to care for orphans, the insane, and the disabled. Republican regimes also expanded state bureaucracies, raised salaries for government employees, and formed state militia, in which blacks were often heavily represented. Finally, they created public-school systems, almost nonexistent in the South until then.

Because rebuilding the devastated South and expanding state government cost millions, taxes skyrocketed. State legislatures increased poll taxes or "head" taxes (levies on individuals); enacted luxury, sales, and occupation taxes; and imposed new property taxes. Before the war southern states had taxed property in slaves but had barely taxed landed property. Now state governments assessed even small farmers' holdings, and propertied planters paid what they considered an excessive burden. Although northern tax rates still exceeded southern rates, southern landowners resented the new levies. In their view, Reconstruction punished the propertied, already beset by labor problems and falling land values, in order to finance the vast expenditures of Republican legislators.

To Reconstruction's foes, Republican rule was wasteful and corrupt, the "most stupendous system of organized robbery in history." A state like Mississippi, which had an honest government, provided little basis for such charges. But critics could justifiably point to Louisiana, where the governor pocketed thousands of dollars of state funds and corruption permeated all government transactions (as indeed it had before the war). Or they could cite South Carolina, where bribery ran rampant. Besides government officials who took bribes, the main postwar profiteers were the railroad promoters who doled them out. Not all were Republicans. Nor did the Republican regimes in the South hold a monopoly on corruption. After the war, bribery pervaded government transactions North and South, and far more money changed hands in the North. But critics assailed Republican rule for additional reasons.

Counterattacks   Ex-Confederates chafed at black enfranchisement and spoke with dread about the "horror of Negro domination." As soon as congressional Reconstruction took effect, former Confederates campaigned to undermine it. Democratic newspapers assailed delegates to North Carolina's constitutional convention as an "Ethiopian minstrelsy . . . baboons, monkeys, mules . . . and other jackasses," and demeaned Louisiana's constitution as "the work of ignorant Negroes cooperating with a gang of white adventurers."

Democrats delayed mobilization until southern states were readmitted to the Union. Then they swung into action, calling themselves Conservatives in order to attract former Whigs. At first, they sought to win the votes of blacks; but when that effort failed, they tried other tactics. In 1868–1869, Georgia Democrats challenged the eligibility of black legislators and expelled them from office. In response, the federal government reestablished military rule in Georgia, but determined Democrats still undercut Republican power. In every southern state, they contested elections, backed dissident Republican factions, elected some Democratic legislators, and lured scalawags away from the Republican Party.

Vigilante efforts to reduce black votes bolstered the Democrats' campaigns to win white ones. Antagonism toward free blacks, long a motif in southern life, had resurged after the war. In 1865, Freedmen's Bureau agents itemized outrages against blacks, including shooting, murder, rape, arson, roasting, and "severe and inhuman beating." Vigilante groups sprang up spontaneously in all parts of the former Confederacy under names like moderators, regulators, and, in Louisiana, Knights of the White Camelia. One group rose to dominance. In the spring of 1866, when the Johnson governments were still in power, six young Confederate war veterans in Tennessee formed a social club, the **Ku Klux Klan,** distinguished by elaborate rituals, hooded costumes, and secret passwords. By the election of 1868, when black men could first vote, Klan dens had spread to all the southern states. Klansmen embarked on night raids to intimidate black voters. No longer a social club, the Ku Klux Klan was now a widespread terrorist movement and a violent arm of the Democratic Party.

The Klan sought to suppress black voting, reestablish white supremacy, and topple the Reconstruction governments. Its members attacked Freedmen's Bureau officials, white Republicans, black militia units, economically successful blacks, and black voters. Concentrated in areas where the black and white populations were most evenly balanced and racial tensions greatest, Klan dens adapted their tactics and timing to local conditions. In Mississippi the Klan targeted black schools; in Alabama it concentrated on Republican officeholders. In Arkansas terror reigned in 1868; in Georgia and Florida Klan strength surged in 1870. Some Democrats denounced Klan members as "cut-throats and riff-raff." But prominent ex-Confederates were also known to be active Klansmen, among them General Nathan Bedford Forrest, the leader of the 1864 Fort Pillow massacre, in which Confederate troops who captured a Union garrison in Tennessee murdered black soldiers after they had surrendered. Vigilantism united southern whites of different social classes and drew on the energy of many Confederate veterans. In areas where the Klan was inactive, other vigilante groups took its place.

Republican legislatures passed laws to outlaw vigilantism, but the state militia could not enforce them. State officials turned to the federal government for help. In response, between May 1870 and February 1871, Congress passed three **Enforcement Acts,** each progressively more stringent. The First Enforcement Act protected black voters, but witnesses to violations were afraid to testify against vigilantes, and local juries refused to convict them. The Second Enforcement Act provided for federal supervision of southern elections, and the Third Enforcement Act, or Ku Klux Klan Act, strengthened punishments for those who prevented blacks from voting. It also empowered the president to use federal troops to enforce the law and to suspend the writ of *habeas corpus* in areas that he declared in insurrection. (The writ of *habeas corpus* is a court order requiring that the detainer of a prisoner bring that person to court and show cause for his or her detention.) The Ku Klux Klan Act generated thousands of arrests; most terrorists, however, escaped conviction.

By 1872, the federal government had effectively suppressed the Klan, but vigilantism had served its purpose. Only a large military presence in the South could have protected black rights, and the government in Washington never provided it. Instead, federal power in the former Confederacy diminished. President Grant steadily reduced troop levels in the South; Congress allowed the Freedmen's Bureau to die in 1869; and the Enforcement acts became dead letters. White southerners, a Georgia politician told congressional investigators in 1871, could not discard "a feeling of bitterness, a feeling that the Negro is a sort of instinctual enemy of ours." The battle over Reconstruction was in essence a battle over the implications of emancipation, and it had begun as soon as the war ended.

THE IMPACT OF EMANCIPATION

"The master he says we are all free," a South Carolina slave declared in 1865. "But it don't mean we is white. And it don't mean we is equal." Emancipated slaves faced daunting handicaps. They had no property, tools, or capital and usually possessed meager skills. Only a minority had been trained as artisans, and more than 95 percent were illiterate. Still, the exhilaration of freedom was overwhelming, as slaves realized, "Now I am for myself" and "All that I make is my own." At emancipation, they gained the right to their own labor and a new sense of autonomy. Under Reconstruction the freed blacks struggled to cast off white control and shed the vestiges of slavery.

Confronting Freedom

For the former slaves, liberty meant they could move where they pleased. Some moved out of the slave quarters and set up dwellings elsewhere on their plantations; others left their plantations entirely. Landowners found that one freed slave after another vanished, with house servants and artisans leading the way. "I have never in my life met with such ingratitude," one South Carolina mistress exclaimed when a former slave ran off. Field workers, who had less contact with whites, were more likely to stay behind or more reluctant to leave. Still, flight remained tempting. "The moment they see an opportunity to improve themselves, they will move on," diarist Mary Chesnut observed.

Emancipation stirred waves of migration within the former Confederacy. Some freed slaves left the Upper South for the Deep South and the Southwest—Florida, Mississippi, Arkansas, and Texas—where planters desperately needed labor and paid higher wages. Even more left the countryside for towns and cities, traditional havens of independence for blacks. Urban black populations sometimes doubled or tripled after emancipation. Overall during the 1860s, the urban black population rose by 75 percent, and the number of blacks in small rural towns grew as well. Many migrants eventually returned to their old locales, but they tended to settle on neighboring plantations rather than with their former owners. Freedom was the major goal. "I's wants to be a free man, cum when I please, and nobody say nuffin to me, nor order me roun,'" an Alabama freedman told a northern journalist.

Freed blacks' yearnings to find lost family members prompted much movement. "They had a passion, not so much for wandering as for getting together," a Freedmen's Bureau official commented. Parents sought children who had been sold; husbands and wives who had been separated by sale, or who lived on different plantations, reunited; and families reclaimed youngsters from masters' homes. The Freedmen's Bureau helped former slaves get information about missing relatives and travel to find them. Bureau agents also tried to resolve conflicts that arose when spouses who had been separated under slavery married other people.

Reunification efforts often failed. Some fugitive slaves had died during the war or were untraceable. Other exslaves had formed new relationships and could not revive old ones. "I am married," one husband wrote to a former wife (probably in a dictated letter), "and my wife [and I] have two children, and if you and I meet it would make a very dissatisfied family." But there were success stories, too. "I's hunted an' hunted till I track you up here," one freedman told his wife, whom he found in a refugee camp twenty years after their separation by sale.

Once reunited, freed blacks quickly legalized unions formed under slavery, sometimes in mass ceremonies of up to seventy couples. Legal marriage affected family life. Men asserted themselves as household heads; wives of able-bodied men often withdrew from the labor force to care for homes and families. "When I married my wife, I married her to wait on me and she has got all she can do right here for me and the children," a Tennessee freedman explained.

Black women's desire to secure the privileges of domestic life caused planters severe labor shortages. Before the war at least half of field workers had been women; in 1866, a southern journal claimed, men performed almost all the field labor. Still, by the end of Reconstruction, many black women had returned to agricultural work as part of sharecropper families. Others took paid work in cities, as laundresses, cooks, and domestic servants. (White women often sought employment as well, for the war had incapacitated many white breadwinners, reduced the supply of future husbands, and left families destitute or in diminished circumstances.) However, former slaves continued to view stable, independent domestic life, especially the right to bring up their own children, as a major blessing of freedom. In 1870, eight out of ten black families in the cotton-producing South were two-parent families, about the same proportion as among whites.

African-American Institutions The freed blacks' desire for independence also led to the postwar growth of black churches. In the late 1860s, some freedmen congregated at churches operated by northern missionaries; others withdrew from white-run churches and formed their own. The African Methodist Episcopal church, founded by Philadelphia blacks in the 1790s, gained thousands of new southern members. Negro Baptist churches sprouted everywhere, often growing out o f plantation "praise meetings," religious gatherings organized by slaves.

The black churches offered a fervent, participatory experience. They also provided relief, raised funds for schools, and supported Republican policies. From the outset black ministers assumed leading political roles, first in the black conventions of 1865–1866 and later in the Reconstruction governments. After southern Democrats excluded most freedmen from political life at Reconstruction's end, ministers remained the main pillars of authority in black communities.

Black schools played a crucial role for freedmen as well; exslaves eagerly sought literacy for themselves and even more for their children. At emancipation, blacks organized their own schools, which the Freedmen's Bureau soon supervised. Northern philanthropic societies paid the wages of instructors, about half of them women. In 1869, the bureau reported more than four thousand black schools in the former Confederacy. Within three years, each southern state had a public-school system, at least in principle, generally with separate schools for blacks and whites. Advanced schools for blacks opened as well, to train tradespeople, teachers, and ministers. The Freedmen's Bureau and northern organizations like the American Missionary Association helped found Howard, Atlanta, and Fisk universities (all started in 1866–1867) and Hampton Institute (1868).

Despite these advances, black education remained limited. Few rural blacks could reach the freedmen's schools located in towns. Underfunded black public schools, similarly inaccessible to most rural black children, held classes only for very short seasons and were sometimes the targets of vigilante attacks. At the end of Reconstruction, more than 80 percent of the black population was still illiterate. Still, the proportion of youngsters who could not read and write had declined and would continue to fall.

School segregation and other forms of racial separation were taken for granted. Some black codes of 1865–1866 had segregated public-transit conveyances and public accommodations. Even after the invalidation of the codes, the custom of segregation continued on streetcars, steamboats, and trains as well as in churches, theaters, inns, and restaurants. On railroads, for example, whites could ride in the "ladies' car" or first-class car, whereas blacks had to stay in smoking cars or boxcars with benches. In 1870, Senator Charles Sumner of Massachusetts began promoting a bill to desegregate schools, transportation facilities, juries, and public accommodations. After Sumner's death in 1874, Congress honored him by enacting a new law, the **Civil Rights Act of 1875,** which encompassed many of his proposals, except for the controversial school-integration provision. But in 1883, in the *Civil Rights Cases,* the Supreme Court invalidated the law; the Fourteenth Amendment did not prohibit discrimination by individuals, the Court ruled, only that perpetrated by the state.

White southerners rejected the prospect of racial integration, which they insisted would lead to racial mixing. "If we have social equality, we shall have intermarriage," one white southerner contended, "and if we have intermarriage, we shall degenerate." Urban blacks sometimes challenged segregation practices, and black legislators promoted bills to desegregate public transit. Some black officeholders decried all forms of racial separatism. "The sooner we as a people forget our sable complexion," said a Mobile official, "the better it will be for us as a race." But most freed blacks were less interested in "social equality," in the sense of interracial mingling, than in black liberty and community. The newly formed postwar elite—teachers, ministers, and politicians—served black constituencies and therefore had a vested interest in separate black institutions. Rural blacks, too, widely preferred all-black institutions. They had little desire to mix with whites. On the contrary, they sought freedom from white control. Above all else, they wanted to secure personal independence by acquiring land.

Land, Labor, and Sharecropping
"The sole ambition of the freedman," a New Englander wrote from South Carolina in 1865, "appears to be to become the owner of a little piece of land, there to erect a humble home, and to dwell in peace and security, at his own free will and pleasure." Indeed, to freed blacks everywhere, "forty acres and a mule" (a phrase that originated in 1864 when Union general William T. Sherman set aside land on the South Carolina Sea Islands for black settlement) promised emancipation from plantation labor, from white domination, and from cotton, the "slave crop." Just as garden plots had provided a measure of autonomy under slavery, so did landownership signify economic independence afterward. "We want to be placed on land until we are able to buy it and make it our own," a black minister had told General Sherman in Georgia during the war.

But freedmen's visions of landownership failed to materialize, for, as we have seen, neither Congress nor the southern states imposed large-scale land reform. Some freedmen did obtain land with the help of the Union army or the Freedmen's Bureau, and black soldiers sometimes pooled resources to buy land, as on the Sea Islands of South Carolina and Georgia. The federal government also sought to provide exslaves with land. In 1866, Congress passed the Southern Homestead Act, which set aside 44 million acres of public land in five southern states for freedmen and loyal whites. This acreage contained poor soil, and few former slaves had the resources to survive even until their first harvest. About four thousand blacks resettled on homesteads under the law, but most were unable to establish farms. (White southern homesteaders fared little better.) By the end of Reconstruction, only a small minority of former slaves in each state owned working farms. In Georgia in 1876, for instance, blacks controlled a mere 1.3 percent of total acreage. Without large-scale land reform, the obstacles to black landownership remained overwhelming.

What were these obstacles? First, most freedmen lacked the capital to buy land and the equipment needed to work it. Furthermore, white southerners on the whole opposed selling land to blacks. Most important, planters sought to preserve a black labor force. Freedmen, they insisted, would work only under coercion, and not at all if the possibility of landownership arose. As soon as the war ended, the white South took steps to make sure that black labor would remain available on plantations.

During presidential Reconstruction, southern state legislatures tried to curb black mobility and to preserve a captive labor force through the black codes. Under labor contracts in effect in 1865–1866, freedmen received wages, housing, food, and clothing in exchange for field work. With cash scarce, wages usually took the form of a very small share of the crop, often one-eighth or less, divided among the entire plantation work force. Freedmen's Bureau agents promoted the new labor system; they urged freedmen to sign labor contracts and tried to ensure adequate wages. Imbued with the northern free-labor ideology, which held that wage workers could rise to the status of self-supporting tradesmen and property owners, bureau officials endorsed black wage labor as an interim arrangement that would lead to economic independence. "You must begin at the bottom of the ladder and climb up," Freedmen's Bureau head O. O. Howard exhorted a group of Louisiana freedmen in 1865.

But the freedmen disliked the new wage system, especially the use of gang labor, which resembled the work pattern under slavery. Planters had complaints, too. In some regions the black labor force had shrunk to half its prewar size or less, due to the migration of freedmen and to black women's withdrawal from fieldwork. Once united in defense of slavery, planters now competed for black workers. But the freedmen, whom planters often scorned as lazy or inefficient, did not intend to work as long or as hard as they had labored under slavery. One planter claimed that workers accomplished only "two-fifths of what they did under the old system." As productivity fell, so did land values. To top off the planters' woes, cotton prices plummeted, for during the war northern and foreign buyers had found new sources of cotton in Egypt and India, and the world supply had vastly increased. Finally, the harvests of 1866 and 1867 were extremely poor. By then, an agricultural impasse had been reached: landowners lacked labor, and freedmen lacked land. But free blacks, unlike slaves, had the right to enter into contracts—or to refuse to do so—and thereby gained some leverage.

Planters and freedmen began experimenting with new labor schemes, including the division of plantations into small tenancies. **Sharecropping,** the most widespread arrangement, evolved as a compromise. Under the sharecropping system, landowners subdivided large plantations into farms of thirty to fifty acres, which they rented to freedmen under annual leases for a share of the crop, usually half. Freedmen preferred sharecropping to wage labor because it represented a step toward independence. Heads of households could use the labor of family members. Moreover, a half-share of the crop far exceeded the fraction that freedmen had received as wages under the black codes. Planters often spoke of sharecropping as a concession, but they benefited, too. They retained power over tenants, because annual leases did not have to be renewed; they could expel undesirable tenants at the end of the year. Planters also shared the risk of planting with tenants: if a crop failed, both suffered the loss. Most important, planters retained control of their land and in some cases extended their holdings. The most productive land, therefore, remained in the hands of a small group of owners, as before the war. Sharecropping forced planters to relinquish daily control over the labor of freedmen but helped to preserve the planter elite.

Sharecropping arrangements varied widely. On sugar and rice plantations, the wage system continued; strong markets for sugar and rice meant that planters of those crops could pay their workers in cash—cash that cotton planters lacked. Some freedmen remained independent renters. Some landowners leased areas to white tenants, who then subcontracted with black labor. But by the end of the 1860s, sharecropping prevailed in the cotton South, and the new system continued to expand. A severe depression in 1873 drove many black renters into sharecropping. By then, thousands of independent white farmers had become sharecroppers as well. Stung by wartime losses and by the dismal postwar economy, they sank into debt and lost their land to creditors. Many backcountry residents, no longer able to get by on subsistence farming, shifted to cash crops like cotton and suffered the same fate. At the end of Reconstruction, one-third of the white farmers in Mississippi, for instance, were sharecroppers.

By 1880, 80 percent of the land in the cotton-producing states had been subdivided into tenancies, most of it farmed by sharecroppers, white and black. Indeed, white sharecroppers now outnumbered black ones, although a higher proportion of southern blacks, about 75 percent, were involved in the system. Changes in marketing and finance, meanwhile, made the sharecroppers' lot increasingly precarious.

Toward a Crop-Lien Economy Before the Civil War, planters had depended on factors, or middlemen, who sold them supplies, extended credit, and marketed their crops through urban merchants. These long-distance credit arrangements were backed by the high value and liquidity of slave property. When slavery ended, the factorage system collapsed. The postwar South, with hundreds of thousands of tenants and sharecroppers, needed a far more localized network of credit.

Into the gap stepped the rural merchants (often themselves planters), who advanced supplies to tenants and sharecroppers on credit and sold their crops to wholesalers or textile manufacturers. Because renters had no property to use as collateral, the merchants secured their loans with a lien, or claim, on each farmer's next crop. Exorbitant interest rates of 50 percent or more quickly forced many tenants and sharecroppers into a cycle of indebtedness. Owing part of the crop to a landowner for rent, a sharecropper also owed a rural merchant a large sum (perhaps amounting to the rest of his crop, or more) for supplies. Illiterate tenants who could not keep track of their financial arrangements often fell prey to unscrupulous merchants. "A man that didn't know how to count would always lose," an Arkansas freedman later explained. Once a tenant's debts or alleged debts exceeded the value of his crop, he was tied to the land, to cotton, and to sharecropping.

By the end of Reconstruction, sharecropping and crop liens had transformed southern agriculture. They bound the region to staple production and prevented crop

Sharecroppers during Reconstruction *By the end of the 1870s, about three out of four African-Americans in the cotton-producing states had become sharecroppers. Here, sharecroppers pick cotton in Aiken, South Carolina.*

diversification. Despite plunging cotton prices, creditors—landowners and merchants—insisted that tenants raise only easily marketable cash crops. Short of capital, planters could no longer invest in new equipment or improve their land by such techniques as crop rotation and contour plowing. Soil depletion, land erosion, and agricultural backwardness soon locked much of the South into a cycle of poverty.

Trapped in perpetual debt, tenant farmers became the chief victims of the new agricultural order. Raising cotton for distant markets, for prices over which they had no control, remained the only survival route open to poor farmers, regardless of race. But low income from cotton locked them into sharecropping and crop liens, from which escape was difficult. African-American tenants, who attained neither landownership nor economic independence, saw their political rights dwindle, too. As one southern regime after another returned to Democratic control, freedmen could no longer look to the state governments for protection. Nor could they turn to the federal government, for northern politicians were preoccupied with their own problems.

NEW CONCERNS IN THE NORTH, 1868–1876

The nomination of Ulysses S. Grant for president in 1868 launched an era of crises in national politics. Grant's two terms in office featured political scandals, a party revolt, a massive depression, and a steady retreat from Reconstruction policies. By the mid-1870s, northern voters cared more about the economic climate, unemployment, labor unrest, and currency problems than about the "southern question." Responsive to the shift in popular mood, Republicans became eager to end sectional conflict and turned their backs on the freedmen of the South.

Grantism   Republicans had good reason to bypass party leaders and nominate the popular Grant to succeed Andrew Johnson. A war hero, Grant was endorsed by Union veterans, widely admired in the North, and unscathed by the bitter feuds of Reconstruction politics. To oppose Grant in 1868, the Democrats nominated New York governor Horatio Seymour, arch-critic of the Lincoln administration during the war and now a foe of Reconstruction. Grant ran on his personal popularity more than on issues. Although he carried all but eight states, the popular vote was very close; in the South, newly enfranchised freedmen provided Grant's margin of victory.

A strong leader in war, Grant proved a passive president. Although he lacked Johnson's instinct for disaster, he had little political skill. Many of his cabinet appointees were mediocre if not unscrupulous; scandals plagued his administration. In 1869, financier Jay Gould and his partner Jim Fisk tried to corner the gold market with the help of Grant's brother-in-law, a New York speculator. When gold prices tumbled, Gould salvaged his own fortune, but investors were ruined, and Grant's reputation suffered. Then before the president's first term ended, his vice president, Schuyler Colfax, was found to be linked to the Crédit Mobilier, a fraudulent construction company created by the directors of the Union Pacific Railroad to skim off the railroad's profits. Discredited, Colfax was dropped from the Grant ticket in 1872.

More trouble lay ahead. Grant's private secretary, Orville Babcock, was unmasked in 1875 after taking money from the "whiskey ring," a group of distillers who bribed federal agents to avoid paying millions of dollars in whiskey taxes. In 1876, voters learned that Grant's secretary of war, William E. Belknap, had taken bribes to sell lucrative Indian trading posts in Oklahoma. Impeached and disgraced, Belknap resigned.

Although uninvolved in the scandals, Grant loyally defended his subordinates. To his critics, "Grantism" came to stand for fraud, bribery, and political corruption—evils that spread far beyond Washington. In Pennsylvania, for example, the Standard Oil Company and the Pennsylvania Railroad controlled the legislature. Urban politics also provided rich opportunities for graft and swindles. The New York City press revealed in 1872 that Democratic boss William M. Tweed, the leader of Tammany Hall, led a ring that had looted the city treasury and collected at least $30 million in kickbacks and payoffs. When Mark Twain and coauthor Charles Dudley Warner published their satiric novel *The Gilded Age* (1873), readers recognized the book's speculators, self-promoters, and opportunists as familiar types in public life. (The term "Gilded Age" was subsequently used to refer to the decades from the 1870s to the 1890s.)

Grant had some success in foreign policy. In 1872, his competent secretary of state, Hamilton Fish, engineered the settlement of the *Alabama* claims with Britain. To compensate for damage done by British-built ships sold to the Confederacy during the war, an international tribunal awarded the United States $15.5 million. But the Grant administration faltered when it tried to add nonadjacent territory to the United States, as the Johnson administration had done. In 1867, Johnson's secretary of state, William H. Seward, had negotiated a treaty in which the United States bought Alaska from Russia at the bargain price of $7.2 million. Although the press mocked "Seward's Ice Box," the purchase kindled expansionists' hopes. In 1870, Grant decided to annex the eastern half of the Caribbean island of Santo Domingo. Today called the Dominican Republic, the territory had been passed back and forth since the late eighteenth century among France, Spain, and Haiti. Annexation, Grant believed, would promote Caribbean trade and provide a haven for persecuted southern blacks. American speculators anticipated windfalls from land sales, commerce, and mining. But Congress disliked Grant's plan. Senator Charles Sumner denounced it as an imperialist "dance of blood." The Senate rejected the annexation treaty and further diminished Grant's reputation.

As the election of 1872 approached, dissident Republicans expressed fears that "Grantism" at home and abroad would ruin the party. Even Grant's new running mate, Henry Wilson, referred to the president privately as a burden on his fellow Republicans. The dissidents took action. Led by a combination of former Radicals and other Republicans left out of Grant's "Great Barbecue" (a disparaging reference to profiteers who feasted at the public trough), the president's critics formed their own party, the Liberal Republicans.

The Liberals' Revolt

The Liberal Republican revolt marked a turning point in Reconstruction history. By splitting the Republican Party, **Liberal Republicans** undermined support for Republican southern policy. (The label "liberal" at the time referred to those who endorsed economic doctrines such as free trade, the gold standard, and the law of supply and demand.) Liberals attacked the "regular" Republicans on several issues. Denouncing "Grantism" and "spoilsmen" (political hacks who gained party office), they demanded civil-service reform to bring the "best men" into government. Rejecting the usual Republican high-tariff policy, they espoused free trade. Most important, the Liberals condemned "bayonet rule" in the South. Even some Republicans once known for radicalism now claimed that Reconstruction had achieved its goal: blacks had been enfranchised and could manage for themselves from now on. Corruption in government, North and South, Liberals asserted, posed a greater danger than Confederate resurgence. In the South, indeed, corrupt Republican regimes were *kept* in power, Liberals said, because the "best men"—the most capable politicians—were ex-Confederates who had been barred from officeholding.

For president the new party nominated the editor of the *New York Tribune,* Horace Greeley, who had inconsistently supported both a stringent reconstruction policy and leniency toward former rebels. The Democrats endorsed Greeley as well; their campaign slogan explained their support: "Anything to Beat Grant." Horace Greeley proved so diligent a campaigner that he worked himself to death making speeches from the back of a campaign train. He died a few weeks after the election.

Grant, who won 56 percent of the popular vote, carried all the northern states and most of the sixteen southern and border states. But the division among Republicans affected Reconstruction. To deprive the Liberals of a campaign issue, Grant Republicans in Congress, the "regulars," passed the Amnesty Act, which allowed all but a few hundred ex-Confederate officials to hold office. The flood of private amnesty acts that followed convinced white southerners that any ex-Confederate save Jefferson Davis could rise to power. In Grant's second term, Republican desires to discard the "southern question" mounted as a depression of unprecedented scope gripped the nation.

The Panic of 1873   The postwar years brought accelerated industrialization and rapid economic growth; new businesses, factories, and technological advances transformed the nation's economy in the 1870s (see Technology and Culture: The Sewing Machine) Frantic speculation played a role, too. Investors rushed to profit from rising prices, new markets, high tariffs, and seemingly boundless opportunities. Railroads provided the biggest lure. In May 1869, railroad executives drove a golden spike into the ground at Promontory Point, Utah, joining the Union Pacific and Central Pacific lines. The first transcontinental railroad heralded a new era. By 1873, almost four hundred railroad corporations crisscrossed the Northeast, consuming tons of coal and miles of steel rail from the mines and mills of Pennsylvania and neighboring states. Transforming the economy, the railroad boom led entrepreneurs to overspeculate, with drastic results.

Philadelphia banker Jay Cooke, who had helped finance the Union effort with his wartime bond campaign, had taken over a new transcontinental line, the Northern Pacific, in 1869. Northern Pacific securities sold briskly for several years, but in 1873 the line's construction costs outran new investments. In September of that year, his vaults full of bonds he could no longer sell, Cooke failed to meet his obligations, and his bank, the largest in the nation, shut down. A financial panic began; other firms collapsed, as did the stock market. The Panic of 1873 triggered a five-year depression. Banks closed, farm prices plummeted, steel furnaces stood idle, and one out of four railroads failed. Within two years, eighteen thousand businesses went bankrupt, and 3 million employees were out of jobs by 1878. Those still at work suffered repeated wage cuts; labor protests mounted; and industrial violence spread. The depression of the 1870s revealed that conflicts born of industrialization had replaced sectional divisions.

The depression also fed a dispute over currency that had begun in 1865. During the Civil War, Americans had used both national bank notes, yellow in color, which would

The Sewing Machine

"You could scarcely believe . . . that such works were necessary for so small a machine," an observer wrote of the Singer Sewing Machine factory that arose in 1873 in Elizabethport, New Jersey. The massive brick building, which occupied a ten-acre plot near railroad lines and New York harbor, produced every part of the sewing machine except the wooden cabinet—made in South Bend, Indiana. Most parts were cast iron; a vast foundry, the size of a football field, had enough molds laid out on its floor to hold thirty tons of pig iron. The factory also housed the forging shop, rumbling room (to wear off the rough edges of metal pieces), drilling room (to put screw holes in product parts), Japanning room (to give machines a black glossy finish), ornamenting room, assembly room, and adjusting room, where inspectors and seamstresses tested machines. According to John Scott, the lawyer for a Singer executive, the new plant was "believed to be the largest establishment in the world devoted to the production of a single article."

The start of the 1873 factory crowned two decades of explosive growth in the sewing machine industry. In 1856, leading manufacturers set up a patent-sharing pool, the Sewing Machine Combination, as a way to avoid costly lawsuits. The patent pool reflected the complexity of sewing machine technology. The sewing machine did not replicate the movement of the human hand. Instead, inventors developed a process that involved a needle with the eye at the head, two threads, feeding devices, thread tension control, and new types of stitches. The lock-stitch machine, first patented in 1846 by its inventor, Elias Howe, was most effective; it used two spools of thread, one above the material and one below. Subsequent inventions refined this machine, and patents accumulated. Entrepreneur Isaac M. Singer, for instance, received patents in the 1850s for a device that sewed curved as well as straight seams and for a foot treadle (power to run the sewing machine came from the operator until the twentieth century).

Sewing machine production presented challenges. Until the late 1850s, skilled mechanics made each machine by hand; parts were not standardized, labor costs were high, and repairs were difficult. To achieve even a modicum of interchangeable parts required factories with special equipment and heavy investment of capital. By the 1870s, three manufacturers dominated the field: Wheeler and Wilson, Grover and Baker, and I. M. Singer. Each company strove for interchangeability of parts, though to varied degrees, and change was gradual, especially at the Singer company. When the New Jersey factory opened in 1873, Singer had fully adopted the "American" system of manufacturing; all parts were made by special machinery, thereby achieving uniformity though not true interchangeability. The company still relied on "fitters" to file parts so that they fit together. Singer's process remained a fusion of European custom-building and the "American" system until the early 1880s.

Heavy and costly, the earliest sewing machines sold only to factories. Ready-made clothing production had previously depended on seamstresses who worked at home; in the 1850s, sewing machines transformed the industry, first in men's clothing, then in cloaks, hats, and other items. Sewing machines also affected the making of shoes, sails, flags, trunks, valises, harnesses, mattresses, and umbrellas; producers eagerly adapted the machines to suit industrial demands. The impact of machines on garment production, though uneven, was momentous. In the late 1850s, each machine performed the work of six hand-sewers; seamstresses now competed with machine workers of both sexes and faced displacement. Manufacturers, however, gained a competitive edge. In 1860, a New Haven shirt factory that had once paid 2,000 hand-sewers each $3 a week could hire 400 machine workers at $4 each, cut costs, and hike profits, even while paying off the cost of the machines.

But factories were only part of the sewing machine's clientele: a huge home market beckoned. In 1856, Singer introduced the first machine intended solely for home use—its "family" machine—and other manufacturers followed. To appeal to individual purchasers, Edward Clark, a lawyer for the Singer company and later head of it, introduced the "hire-purchase" plan, or installment buying: by paying a percentage of the price, a buyer could "hire" a machine, make monthly payments (with interest), and eventually own it. Poor seamstresses could not afford the machines, but middle-class women flocked to buy them. Mass production of paper patterns, which began in the 1860s, enabled women at home to make up-to-date fashions; attachments and accessories simplified buttonholing, tucking, pleating, and other processes, both at the factory and at home. The zigzag stitch machine, for instance,

patented by inventor Helen Augusta Blanchard in 1873, sealed the edges of seams and made garments sturdier. In the 1870s, the home sewing machine proved a commercial triumph; profits soared. The machine that sold for $64 in 1870 cost only $12 to produce.

To reach the home market, major producers at first used independent agents who worked mainly on commission. Then they established company-owned-and-run centers in the business districts of major cities, such as New York's Union Square. Elegant stores with carpets, chandeliers, marble facades, and plate glass windows greeted customers, who could watch demonstrations by trained personnel. By the 1870s, manufacturers had developed many marketing tactics that included extensive advertising, door-to-door sales, discounts, and trade-in allowances for older models. The first mass-marketed appliance for home use, the sewing machine symbolized a family's middle-class status. Manufacturers promoted the machine as a labor-saving device that provided, in John Scott's words, "whatever saves the busy housewife's time and increases her opportunities for culture."

In the 1870s, the Singer company surged to preeminence. Its executives strove to improve the production process and reduce prices. Between 1874 and 1880, unscathed by the 1873 depression, Singer doubled its annual production of sewing machines to half a million and six years later doubled it again. In 1877, when the last patents in the patent pool of 1856 expired, Singer became an even more competitive marketer. The company reorganized its sales department, imposed a tight managerial scheme, built factories abroad, and found new markets worldwide. Edward Clark, who became Singer's president in 1876, sought to blanket the globe with regional branch offices; three years later, Singer produced three-quarters of the world's sewing machines. At the 1876 Centennial Exhibition in Philadelphia, thirty American firms exhibited sewing machines in "Machinery Hall," but Singer ruled. "Its system of agencies embraces the civilized world," John Scott boasted in 1880. "On every sea are floating the Singer machines."

Questions for Analysis

- Why were sewing machines a challenge to manufacture?

- How did manufacturers promote sales of sewing machines for home use?

- In what ways did the marketing of sewing machines set patterns for the marketing of consumer goods today?

eventually be converted into gold, and greenbacks, a paper currency not "backed" by a particular weight in gold. To stabilize the postwar currency, greenbacks would have to be withdrawn from circulation. This "sound-money" policy, favored by investors, won the backing of Congress. But those who depended on easy credit, both indebted farmers and manufacturers, wanted an expanding currency; that is, more greenbacks. Once the depression began, demands for such "easy money" rose. The issue divided both major parties and was compounded by another one: how to repay the federal debt.

In wartime, the Union government had borrowed what were then astronomical sums, on whatever terms it could get, mainly by selling war bonds—in effect, short-term federal IOUs—to private citizens. Bondholders wanted repayment in coin, gold or silver, even though many had paid for bonds in greenbacks. To pacify bondholders, Senator John Sherman of Ohio and other Republican leaders obtained passage of the Public Credit Act of 1869, which promised repayment in coin. With investors reassured by the Public Credit Act, Sherman guided legislation through Congress that swapped the old short-term bonds for new ones payable over the next generation. In 1872, another bill in effect defined "coin" as "gold coin" by dropping the traditional silver dollar from the official coinage. Through a feat of ingenious compromise, which placated investors and debtors, Sherman preserved the public credit, the currency, and Republican unity. In 1875, he engineered the Specie Resumption Act, which promised to put the nation on the gold standard in 1879, while tossing a few bones to Republican voters who wanted "easy money."

But when Democrats gained control of the House in 1875, with the depression in full force, a verbal storm broke out. Many Democrats and some Republicans demanded restoration of the silver dollar in order to expand the currency and relieve the depression. These "free-silver" advocates secured passage of the Bland-Allison Act of 1878, which partially restored silver coinage by requiring the Treasury to buy $2–4 million worth of silver each month and turn it into coin. In 1876, other expansionists formed the **Greenback Party,** which adopted the debtors' cause and fought to keep greenbacks in circulation, though with little success. As the nation emerged from depression in 1879, the clamor for "easy money" subsided, only to resurge in the 1890s. The controversial "money question" of the 1870s, never resolved, gave politicians and voters another reason to forget about the South.

Reconstruction and the Constitution The Supreme Court of the 1870s also played a role in weakening northern support for Reconstruction. In wartime, few cases of note had come before the Court. After the war, however, constitutional questions surged into prominence.

First, would the Court support congressional laws to protect freedmen's rights? The decision in *Ex parte* Milligan (1866) suggested not. In *Milligan,* the Court declared that a military commission established by the president or Congress could not try civilians in areas remote from war where the civil courts were functioning. Thus special military courts to enforce the Supplementary Freedmen's Bureau Act were doomed. Second, would the Court sabotage the congressional Reconstruction plan, as Republicans feared? Their qualms were valid, for if the Union was indissoluble, as the North had claimed during the war, then the concept of *restoring* states to the Union would be meaningless. In *Texas* v. *White* (1869), the Court ruled that although the Union was indissoluble and secession was legally impossible, the process of Reconstruction was still constitutional. It was grounded in Congress's power to ensure each state a republican form of government and to recognize the legitimate government in any state.

The 1869 decision protected the Republicans' Reconstruction plan. But in the 1870s, when cases arose involving the Fourteenth and Fifteenth amendments, the Court backed away from Reconstruction policy. In the **Slaughterhouse cases** of 1873, the Supreme Court began to chip away at the Fourteenth Amendment. The cases involved a business monopoly rather than freedmen's rights, but they provided an opportunity to interpret the amendment narrowly. In 1869, the Louisiana legislature had granted a monopoly over the New Orleans slaughterhouse business to one firm and closed down all other slaughterhouses in the interest of public health. The excluded butchers brought suit. The state had deprived them of their lawful occupation without due process of law, they claimed, and such action violated the Fourteenth Amendment, which guaranteed that no state could "abridge the privileges or immunities" of U.S. citizens. The Supreme Court upheld the Louisiana legislature by issuing a doctrine of "dual citizenship." The Fourteenth Amendment, declared the Court, protected only the rights of *national* citizenship, such as the right of interstate travel or the right to federal protection on the high seas. It did not protect those basic civil rights that fell to citizens by virtue of their *state* citizenship. Therefore, the federal government was not obliged to protect such rights against violation by the states. The *Slaughterhouse* decision came close to nullifying the intent of the Fourteenth Amendment—to secure freedmen's rights against state encroachment.

The Supreme Court again backed away from Reconstruction in two cases in 1876 involving the Enforcement Act of 1870, which had been enacted to protect black suffrage. In *United States* v. *Reese* and *United States* v. *Cruikshank,* the Supreme Court undercut the effectiveness of the act. Continuing its retreat from Reconstruction, the Supreme Court in 1883 invalidated both the Civil Rights Act of 1875 and the Ku Klux Klan Act of 1871. These decisions cumulatively dismantled the Reconstruction policies that Republicans had sponsored after the war and confirmed rising northern sentiment that Reconstruction's egalitarian goals could not be enforced.

Republicans in Retreat The Republicans did not reject Reconstruction suddenly but rather disengaged from it gradually, a process that began with Grant's election to the presidency in 1868. Although not an architect of Reconstruction policy, Grant defended it. But he shared with most Americans a belief in decentralized government and a reluctance to assert federal authority in local and state affairs.

In the 1870s, as the northern military presence shrank in the South, Republican idealism waned in the North. The Liberal Republican revolt of 1872 eroded what remained of radicalism. Although the "regular" Republicans, who backed Grant, continued to defend Reconstruction in the 1872 election, many held ambivalent views. Commercial and industrial interests now dominated both wings of the party, and few Republicans wished to rekindle sectional strife. After the Democrats won control of the House in the 1874 elections, support for Reconstruction became a political liability.

By 1875, the Radical Republicans, so prominent in the 1860s, had vanished from the political scene. Chase, Stevens, and Sumner were dead. Other Radicals had lost office or abandoned their former convictions. "Waving the Bloody Shirt"—defaming Democratic opponents by reviving wartime animosity—now struck many Republicans, including former Radicals, as counterproductive. Party leaders reported that voters were "sick of carpet-bag government" and tiring of both the "southern question" and the "Negro question." It seemed pointless to continue the unpopular and expensive policy of military intervention in the South to prop up Republican regimes that even President Grant found corrupt. Finally, few Republicans shared the egalitarian spirit that had animated Stevens and Sumner. Politics aside, Republican leaders and voters generally agreed with southern Democrats that blacks, although worthy of freedom, were inferior to whites. To insist on black equality would be a thankless, divisive, and politically suicidal undertaking. Moreover, it would quash any hope of reunion between the regions. The Republicans' retreat from Reconstruction set the stage for its demise in 1877.

RECONSTRUCTION ABANDONED, 1876–1877

"We are in a very hot political contest just now," a Mississippi planter wrote to his daughter in 1875, "with a good prospect of turning out the carpetbag thieves by whom we have been robbed for the past six to ten years." Similar contests raged through the South in the 1870s, as the resentment of white majorities grew and Democratic influence surged. By the end of 1872, the Democrats had regained power in Tennessee, Virginia, Georgia, and North Carolina. Within three years, they won control in Texas, Alabama, Arkansas, and Mississippi. As the 1876 elections approached, Republican rule survived in only three states—South Carolina, Florida, and Louisiana. Democratic victories in the state elections of 1876 and political bargaining in Washington in 1877 abruptly ended what little remained of Reconstruction.

"Redeeming" the South
Republican collapse in the South accelerated after 1872. Congressional amnesty enabled ex-Confederate officials to regain office; divisions among the Republicans weakened their party's grip on the southern electorate; and attrition diminished Republican ranks. Some carpetbaggers gave up and returned North; others became Democrats. Scalawags deserted in even larger numbers. Southerners who had joined the Republicans to moderate rampant radicalism tired of northern interference; once "home rule" by Democrats seemed possible, staying Republican meant going down with a sinking ship. Scalawag

defections ruined Republican prospects. Unable to win new white votes or retain the old ones, the always-precarious Republican coalition crumbled.

Meanwhile, the Democrats mobilized once-apathetic white voters. The resurrected southern Democratic Party was divided: businessmen who envisioned an industrialized "New South" opposed an agrarian faction called the Bourbons, the old planter elite. But all Democrats shared one goal: to oust Republicans from office. Their tactics varied from state to state. Alabama Democrats won by promising to cut taxes and by getting out the white vote. In Louisiana, the "White League," a vigilante organization formed in 1874, undermined the Republicans' hold. Intimidation also proved effective in Mississippi, where violent incidents—like the 1874 slaughter in Vicksburg of about three hundred blacks by rampaging whites—terrorized black voters. In 1875, the "Mississippi plan" took effect: local Democratic clubs armed their members, who dispersed Republican meetings, patrolled voter-registration places, and marched through black areas. "The Republicans are paralyzed through fear and will not act," the anguished carpetbag governor of Mississippi wrote to his wife. "Why should I fight a hopeless battle?" In 1876, South Carolina's "Rifle Clubs" and "Red Shirts," armed groups that threatened Republicans, continued the scare tactics that had worked so well in Mississippi.

New outbursts of intimidation did not completely squelch black voting, but Democrats deprived Republicans of enough black votes to win state elections. In some counties, they encouraged freedmen to vote Democratic at supervised polls where voters publicly placed a card with a party label in a box. In other instances, employers and landowners impeded black suffrage. Labor contracts included clauses barring attendance at political meetings; planters used the threat of eviction to keep sharecroppers in line. As the Enforcement acts could not be enforced, intimidation and economic pressure succeeded.

"Redemption," the word Democrats used to describe their return to power, introduced sweeping changes. Some states called constitutional conventions to reverse Republican policies. All cut back expenses, wiped out social programs, lowered taxes, and revised their tax systems to relieve landowners of large burdens. State courts limited the rights of tenants and sharecroppers. Most important, the Democrats, or "redeemers," used the law to ensure a stable black labor force. Legislatures restored vagrancy laws, revised crop-lien statutes to make landowners' claims superior to those of merchants, and rewrote criminal law. Local ordinances in heavily black counties often restricted hunting, fishing, gun carrying, and ownership of dogs and thereby curtailed the everyday activities of freedmen who lived off the land. States passed severe laws against trespassing and theft; stealing livestock or wrongly taking part of a crop became grand larceny with a penalty of up to five years at hard labor. By the end of Reconstruction, a large black convict work force had been leased out to private contractors at low rates.

For the freedmen, whose aspirations had been raised by Republican rule, redemption was devastating. The new laws, Tennessee blacks contended at an 1875 convention, would impose "a condition of servitude scarcely less degrading than that endured before the late civil war." In the late 1870s, as the political climate grew more oppressive, an "exodus" movement spread through Mississippi, Tennessee, Texas, and Louisiana. Some African-Americans decided to become homesteaders in Kansas. After a major outbreak of "Kansas fever" in 1879, four thousand **"exodusters"** from Mississippi and

Louisiana joined about ten thousand who had reached Kansas earlier in the decade. But the vast majority of freedmen, devoid of resources, had no migration options or escape route. Mass movement of southern blacks to the North and Midwest would not gain momentum until the twentieth century.

The Election of 1876

By the autumn of 1876, with redemption almost complete, both parties sought to discard the heritage of animosity left by the war and Reconstruction. Republicans nominated Rutherford B. Hayes, three times Ohio's governor, for president. Untainted by the scandals of the Grant years and popular with all factions in his party, Hayes presented himself as a "moderate" on southern policy. He favored "home rule" in the South and a guarantee of civil and political rights for all—two planks that were clearly contradictory. The Democrats nominated Governor Samuel J. Tilden of New York, a millionaire corporate lawyer and political reformer. Known for his assaults on the Tweed Ring that had plundered New York City's treasury, Tilden campaigned against fraud and waste. Both candidates favored sound money, endorsed civil-service reform, and decried corruption, an irony since the 1876 election would be extremely corrupt.

Tilden won the popular vote by a 3 percent margin and seemed destined to capture the 185 electoral votes needed for victory. But the Republicans challenged the pro-Tilden returns from South Carolina, Florida, and Louisiana. If they could deprive the Democrats of these nineteen electoral votes, Hayes would triumph. The Democrats, who needed only one of the disputed electoral votes for victory, challenged (on a technicality) the validity of Oregon's single electoral vote, which the Republicans had won. Twenty electoral votes, therefore, were in contention. But Republicans still controlled the electoral machinery in the three unredeemed southern states, where they threw out enough Democratic ballots to declare Hayes the winner.

The nation now faced an unprecedented dilemma. Each party claimed victory in the contested states, and each accused the other of fraud. In fact, both sets of southern results involved fraud: the Republicans had discarded legitimate Democratic ballots, and the Democrats had illegally prevented freedmen from voting. To resolve the conflict, Congress in January 1877 created a special electoral commission to decide which party would get the contested electoral votes. Made up of senators, representatives, and Supreme Court justices, the commission included seven Democrats, seven Republicans, and one independent, Justice David Davis of Illinois. When Davis resigned to run for the Senate, Congress replaced him with a Republican, and the commission gave Hayes the election by a vote of 8 to 7.

Congress now had to certify the new electoral vote. But since Democrats controlled the House, a new problem loomed. Some Democrats threatened to obstruct debate and delay approval of the electoral vote. Had they done so, the nation would have been without a president on inauguration day, March 4. Room for compromise remained, for many southern Democrats accepted Hayes's election: former scalawags with commercial interests to protect still favored Republican financial policies, and railroad investors hoped that a Republican administration would help them build a southern transcontinental line. Other southerners cared mainly about Democratic state victories and did not mind conceding the presidency as long as the new Republican administration would leave the South alone. Republican leaders, although sure of eventual triumph, were willing to bargain as well, for candidate Hayes desired not merely victory but southern approval.

MAP 16.2 The Disputed Election of 1876

Congress resolved the contested vote of 1876 in favor of Republican Rutherford B. Hayes.

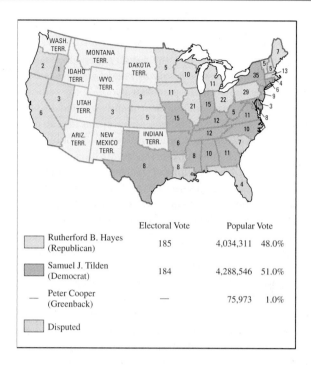

	Electoral Vote	Popular Vote	
Rutherford B. Hayes (Republican)	185	4,034,311	48.0%
Samuel J. Tilden (Democrat)	184	4,288,546	51.0%
Peter Cooper (Greenback)	—	75,973	1.0%
Disputed			

A series of informal negotiations ensued, at which politicians exchanged promises. Ohio Republicans and southern Democrats, who met at a Washington hotel, reached an agreement that if Hayes won the election, he would remove federal troops from South Carolina and Louisiana, and Democrats could gain control of those states. In other bargaining sessions, southern politicians asked for federal patronage, federal aid to railroads, and federal support for internal improvements. In return, they promised to drop the filibuster, to accept Hayes as president, and to treat freedmen fairly. With the threatened filibuster broken, Congress ratified Hayes's election. Once in office, Hayes fulfilled some of the promises his Republican colleagues had made. He appointed a former Confederate as postmaster general and ordered federal troops who guarded the South Carolina and Louisiana statehouses back to their barracks. Although federal soldiers remained in the South after 1877, they no longer served a political function. The Democrats, meanwhile, took control of state governments in Louisiana, South Carolina, and Florida. When Republican rule toppled in these states, the era of Reconstruction finally ended, though more with a whimper than with a resounding crash.

But some of the bargains struck in the **Compromise of 1877,** such as Democratic promises to treat southern blacks fairly, were forgotten, as were Hayes's pledges to ensure freedmen's rights. "When you turned us loose, you turned us loose to the sky, to the storm, to the whirlwind, and worst of all . . . to the wrath of our infuriated masters," Frederick Douglass had charged at the Republican convention in 1876. "The question now is, do you mean to make good to us the promises in your Constitution?" The answer provided by the 1876 election and the 1877 compromises was "No."

CONCLUSION

Between 1865 and 1877, the nation experienced a series of crises. In Washington, conflict between President Johnson and Congress led to a stringent Republican plan for restoring the South, a plan that included the radical provision of black male enfranchisement. President Johnson ineptly abetted the triumph of his foes by his defiant stance, which drove moderate Republicans into an alliance against him with Radical Republicans. In the ex-Confederate states, Republicans took over and reorganized state governments. A new electorate, in which recently freed African-Americans were prominent, supported Republican policies. Rebuilding the South cost millions, and state expenditures soared. Objections to taxes, resentment of black suffrage, and fear of "Negro domination" spurred counterattacks on African-Americans by former Confederates.

Emancipation reshaped black communities where former slaves sought new identities as free people. African-Americans reconstituted their families; created black institutions, such as churches and schools; and participated in government for the first time in American history. They also took part in the transformation of southern agriculture. By Reconstruction's end, a new labor system, sharecropping, replaced slavery. Begun as a compromise between freedmen and landowners, sharecropping soon trapped African-Americans and other tenant farmers in a cycle of debt; black political rights waned as well as Republicans lost control of the southern states.

The North, meanwhile, hurtled headlong into an era of industrial growth, labor unrest, and financial crises. The political scandals of the Grant administration and the impact of depression after the Panic of 1873 diverted northern attention from the South. By the mid-1870s, northern politicians were ready to discard the Reconstruction policies that Congress had imposed a decade before. Simultaneously, the southern states returned to Democratic rule, as Republican regimes toppled one by one. Reconstruction's final collapse in 1877 reflected not only a waning of northern resolve but a successful ex-Confederate campaign of violence, intimidation, and protest that had started in the 1860s.

The end of Reconstruction gratified both political parties. Although unable to retain a southern constituency, the Republican Party was no longer burdened by the unpopular "southern question." The Democrats, who had regained power in the former Confederacy, would remain entrenched there for over a century. To be sure, the South was tied to sharecropping and economic backwardness as securely as it had once been tied to slavery. But "home rule" was firmly in place. Reconstruction's end also signified a triumph for nationalism and the spirit of reunion. In the fall of 1877, President Hayes toured the South to champion reconciliation, and similar celebrations continued for decades.

As the nation applauded reunion, Reconstruction's reputation sank. Looking back on the 1860s and 1870s, most late-nineteenth-century Americans dismissed the congressional effort to reconstruct the South as a fiasco—a tragic interlude of "radical rule" or "black reconstruction" fashioned by carpetbaggers, scalawags, and Radical Republicans. With the hindsight of a century, historians continued to regard Reconstruction as a failure, though of a different kind.

No longer viewed as a misguided scheme that collapsed because of radical excess, Reconstruction is now widely seen as a democratic experiment that did not go far enough. Historians cite two main causes. First, Congress did not promote freedmen's independence through land reform; without property of their own, southern blacks lacked the economic power to defend their interests as free citizens. Property ownership, however, does not necessarily ensure political rights, nor does it invariably provide economic security. Considering the depressed state of southern agriculture in the postwar decades, the freedmen's fate as independent farmers would likely have been perilous. Thus the land-reform question, like much else about Reconstruction, remains a subject of debate. A second cause of Reconstruction's collapse is less open to dispute: the federal government neglected to back congressional Reconstruction with military force. Given the choice between protecting blacks' rights at whatever cost and promoting reunion, the government opted for reunion. Reconstruction's failure, therefore, was the federal government's failure to fulfill its own goals and create a biracial democracy in the South. As a result, the nation's adjustment to the consequences of emancipation would continue into the twentieth century.

The Reconstruction era left some significant legacies, including the Fourteenth and Fifteenth amendments. Although neither amendment would be used to protect minority rights for almost a century, they remain monuments to the democratic zeal that swept Congress in the 1860s. The Reconstruction years also hold a significant place in African-American history. The aspirations and achievements of the Reconstruction era left an indelible mark on black citizens. Consigning Reconstruction to history, other Americans turned to their economic futures—to railroads, factories, and mills, and to the exploitation of the country's bountiful natural resources.

17

The Transformation of the Trans-Mississippi West, 1860–1900

NATIVE AMERICANS AND THE TRANS-MISSISSIPPI WEST

No aspect of the transformation of the West was more visible and dramatic than the destruction of the traditional Indian ways of life. Even before settlers, ranchers, and miners poured onto the Great Plains at midcentury, Indian life in the trans-Mississippi West had changed considerably. In the Southwest, the Spanish had forcibly incorporated pueblo peoples such as the Hopis and Zuñis into their colonial economy. Other tribes, such as the Navajos, had gradually given up migratory life in favor of settled agriculture. To the north, the Cheyenne and the Lakota Sioux, already pushed out of the Great Lakes region by the expansion of the fur trade and later white settlement, had moved onto the grasslands of the Great Plains and had driven their enemies, the Pawnees and the Crows, farther west. These and other nomadic warrior tribes, dispersed in small bands and moving from place to place to follow the bison herds, had developed a resilient culture adapted to the High Plains.

When increasing numbers of whites invaded their territory at midcentury, these Indians protested and resisted. Caught between a stampede of miners and settlers who took their land and the federal government that sought to force them onto reservations, Native Americans fought back. By the 1890s confinement on inferior reservations had become the fate of almost every Indian nation. Undaunted, Native Americans struggled to preserve their customs and rebuild their numbers.

CHRONOLOGY, 1860–1900

1862 • Homestead Act.
Morrill Anti-Bigamy Act.
Pacific Railroad Act.

1864 • Nevada admitted to the Union.
Massacre of Cheyennes at Sand Creek, Colorado.
George Perkins Marsh, *Man and Nature.*

1867 • Joseph McCoy organizes cattle drives to Abilene, Kansas.
New Indian policy of smaller reservations adopted.
Medicine Lodge Treaty.
Purchase of Alaska.

1868 • Fort Laramie Treaty.

1869 • Board of Indian Commissioners established to reform Indian
reservation life.
Wyoming gives women the vote.

1872 • Yellowstone National Park established.

1873 • Panic allows speculators to purchase thousands of acres in the Red River
valley of North Dakota cheaply.
Timber Culture Act.
Biggest strike on Nevada's Comstock Lode.

1874 • Invention of barbed wire.
Gold discovered in the Black Hills of South Dakota.
Red River War.

1875 • John Wesley Powell, *The Exploration of the Colorado River.*

1876 • Colorado admitted to the Union, gives women the right to vote in
school elections.
Little Bighorn massacre.

1877 • Desert Land Act.

1878 • Timber and Stone Act.
John Wesley Powell, *Report on the Lands of the Arid Regions of the
United States.*

1879 • *United States* v. *Reynolds.*

1881 • Helen Hunt Jackson, *A Century of Dishonor.*

1883 • William ("Buffalo Bill") Cody organizes Wild West Show.
Women's National Indian Rights Association founded.

1884 • Helen Hunt Jackson, *Ramona.*

1886 • Severe drought on the Plains destroys cattle and grain.

1887 • Dawes Severalty Act.
Edmunds-Tucker Act.

1888 • White Caps raid ranches in northern New Mexico.

1889 • Oklahoma Territory opened for settlement.

1890 • Ghost Dance movement spreads to the Black Hills.
Massacre of Teton Sioux at Wounded Knee, South Dakota.

1892 • John Muir organizes Sierra Club.

1898 • Curtis Act.

The Plains Indians   The Indians of the Great Plains inhabited three major subregions. The northern Plains, from the Dakotas and Montana southward to Nebraska, were home to several large tribes, most notably the Lakota, as well as Flatheads, Blackfeet, Assiniboins, northern Cheyennes, Arapahos, Crows, Hidatsas, and Mandans. Some of these were allies, but others were bitter enemies frequently at war. In the Central Plains, the so-called Five Civilized Tribes, driven there from the Southeast in the 1830s, pursued an agricultural life in the Indian Territory (present-day Oklahoma). Farther west, the Pawnees of Nebraska maintained the older, more settled tradition characteristic of Plains river valley culture before the introduction of horses, spending at least half the year in villages of earthen lodges along watercourses. On the southern Plains of western Kansas, Colorado, eastern New Mexico, and Texas, the Comanches, Kiowas, Cheyennes, southern Arapahos, and Apaches still maintained a migratory life appropriate to the arid environment.

Considerable diversity flourished among the Plains peoples, and customs varied even within subdivisions of the same tribe. For example, the easternmost branch of the great Sioux Nation, the Dakota Sioux of Minnesota who inhabited the wooded edge of the prairie, led a semisedentary life based on small-scale agriculture, deer and bison hunting, wild-rice harvesting, and maple-sugar production. In contrast, many Plains tribes—not only the Lakota Sioux, but also the Blackfeet, Crows, and Cheyennes—using horses obtained from the Spanish and guns obtained from traders, roamed the High Plains to the west, and followed the bison migrations.

For all the **Plains Indians,** life revolved around extended family ties and tribal cooperation. Within the various Sioux-speaking tribes, for example, children were raised without physical punishment and were taught to treat each adult clan member with the respect accorded to relatives. Families and clans joined forces to hunt and farm, and reached decisions by consensus.

For the various Sioux bands, religious and harvest celebrations provided the cement for village and camp life. Sioux religion was complex. The Lakota Sioux thought of life as a series of circles. Living within the daily cycles of the sun and moon, Lakotas were born into a circle of relatives, which broadened to the band, the tribe, the Sioux Nation, and on to animals and plants. The Lakotas also believed in a hierarchy of spirits whose help could be invoked in ceremonies like the Sun Dance. To gain access to spiritual power, or to fulfill vows made on behalf of their relatives' well-being, young men would "sacrifice" themselves by forgoing food and water, dancing until exhausted, and suffering self-torture. For example, some suspended themselves from poles or cut pieces of their flesh and placed them at the foot of the Sun Dance pole. Painter George Catlin, who recorded Great Plains Indian life before the Civil War, described such a ceremony. "Several of them, seeing me making sketches, beckoned me to look at their faces, which I watched through all this horrid operation, without being able to detect anything but the pleasantest smiles as they looked me in the eye, while I could hear the knife rip through the flesh, and feel enough of it myself, to start involuntary and uncontrollable tears over my cheeks."

On the semiarid High Plains, where rainfall averaged less than twenty inches a year, both the bison and the Native peoples adapted to the environment. The huge bison herds, which at their peak contained an estimated 30 million animals, broke into small groups in the winter and dispersed into river valleys. In the summer, they returned to the High Plains in vast herds to mate and feed on the nutritious short grasses. Like the bison, the Indians dispersed across the landscape to minimize their impact on any one place, wintering in the river valleys and returning to the High Plains in summer. When their herds of horses consumed the grasses near their camps, they moved. Hunting the bison not only supplied the Native peoples with food, clothing, and tipi covers, but also created a valuable trading commodity, buffalo robes. To benefit from this trade, Indians themselves, as the nineteenth century progressed, increased their harvest of animals.

The movement of miners and settlers onto the eastern High Plains in the 1850s eroded the bison's habitat and threatened the Native American way of life. Pioneers who trekked westward occupied the river valley sites, where the buffalo had wintered, and exhausted the grasses. In the 1860s, the whites began systematically to hunt the animals, often with Indian help, to supply the eastern market with carriage robes and industrial belting. **William F. "Buffalo Bill" Cody,** a famous scout and Indian fighter, killed nearly forty-three hundred bison in 1867–1868 to feed construction crews building the Union Pacific Railroad. Army commanders also encouraged the slaughter of buffalo to undermine Indian resistance. The carnage that resulted was almost inconceivable in its scale. Between 1872 and 1875, hunters killed 9 million buffalo, taking only the skin and leaving the carcasses to rot. By the 1880s, the once-thundering herds had been reduced to a few thousand animals, and the Native American way of life dependent on the buffalo had been ruined.

The Assault on Nomadic Indian Life	In the 1850s, Indians who felt pressure from the declining bison herds and deteriorating grasslands faced the onslaught of thousands of pioneers lured by the discovery of gold and silver in the Rocky Mountains. The federal government's response

was to reexamine its Indian policies. Abandoning the previous position, which had treated much of the West as a vast Indian reserve, the federal government sought to introduce a system of smaller tribal reservations where the Indians were to be concentrated, by force if necessary. To achieve this goal, the army established outposts along well-traveled trails and stationed troops that could be mobilized at a moment's notice.

Some Native Americans, like the Pueblos of the Southwest (who had adapted to Spanish colonial life), the Crows of Montana, and the Hidatsas of North Dakota, peacefully adjusted to their new life. Others, among them the Navajos of Arizona and New Mexico and the eastern Dakota Sioux, opposed the new policy to no avail. By 1860, eight western reservations had been established.

Significant segments of the remaining tribes on the Great Plains, more than a hundred thousand people, fought against removal for decades. Between 1860 and 1890, the western Sioux, Cheyennes, Arapahos, Kiowas, and Comanches on the Great Plains; the Nez Percés and Bannocks in the northern Rockies; and the Apaches in the Southwest—faced the U.S. army, toughened by its experiences in the Civil War, in a series of final battles for the West.

Misunderstandings, unfulfilled promises, brutality, and butchery marked the conflict. Nowhere was this more evident than in the eroding relationship between the Cheyennes and Arapahos and the settlers near Sand Creek, Colorado, in 1864. During the gold rush six years earlier, more than a hundred thousand people (more than twice the number who went to California in 1849) had stampeded into the area. The Indians, facing starvation because of unfulfilled treaties that had promised food and support, slipped away from the reservations to hunt bison and steal livestock from settlers.

MAP 17.1 Indian Wars and Reservations in the West

Although they were never recognized as such in the popular press, the battles between Native Americans and the U.S. army on the Great Plains amounted to a major undeclared war.

In the spring of the year, soldiers from the local militia who had replaced regular army troops fighting in the Civil War, destroyed Cheyenne and Arapaho camps. The Indians retaliated with a flurry of attacks on travelers. The governor, in a panic, authorized Colorado's white citizenry to seek out and kill hostile Indians on sight. He then activated a regiment of troops under Colonel John M. Chivington, a Methodist minister. At dawn on November 29, under orders to "remember the murdered women and children on the Platte [River]," Chivington's troops massacred a peaceful band of Indians, including terrified women and children, camped at Sand Creek, who believed that they would be protected by federal troops.

This massacre and others that followed rekindled public debate over federal Indian policy. In response, in 1867 Congress sent a peace commission to end the fighting, and set aside two large land reserves, one north of Nebraska, the other south of Kansas. There, it was hoped, the tribes would take up farming and convert to Christianity. Behind the federal government's persuasion lay the threat of force. Any Native Americans who refused to "locate in [the] permanent abodes provided for them," warned Commissioner of Indian Affairs Ely S. Parker, himself a Seneca Indian, "would be subject wholly to the control and supervision of military authorities, [and] . . . treated as friendly or hostile as circumstances might justify."

At first the plan appeared to work. Representatives of sixty-eight thousand southern Kiowas, Comanches, Cheyennes, and Arapahos signed the Medicine Lodge Treaty of 1867 and pledged to live on land in present-day Oklahoma. The following year, scattered bands of Sioux, representing nearly fifty-four thousand northern Plains Indians, signed the **Fort Laramie Treaty** and agreed to move to reservations on the so-called Great Sioux Reserve in the western part of what is now South Dakota in return for money and provisions.

But Indian dissatisfaction with the treaties ran deep. As a Sioux chief, Spotted Tail, told the commissioners, "We do not want to live like the white man. . . . The Great Spirit gave us hunting grounds, gave us the buffalo, the elk, the deer, and the antelope. Our fathers have taught us to hunt and live on the Plains, and we are contented." Rejecting the new system, many bands of Indians refused to move to the reservations or to remain on them once there.

In August 1868, war parties of defiant Cheyennes, Arapahos, and Sioux raided settlements in Kansas and Colorado, burning homes and killing whites. In retaliation, army troops attacked Indians, even peaceful ones, who refused confinement. That autumn Lieutenant Colonel George Armstrong Custer's raiding party struck a sleeping Cheyenne village, killing more than a hundred warriors, shooting more than eight hundred horses, and taking fifty-three women and children prisoner. Other hostile Cheyennes and Arapahos were pursued, captured, and returned to the reservations.

In 1869, spurred on by Christian reformers, Congress established a Board of Indian Commissioners drawn from the major Protestant denominations to reform Indian agent abuses on the reservations. But the new and inexperienced church-appointed Indian agents, who distributed government rations and ran the reservations, quickly encountered problems. The pacifist Quaker agent Lawrie Tatum, a big-boned Iowa farmer, for example, failed to persuade the Comanches and Kiowas to stay on their reservations in Oklahoma rather than raid Texas settlements. Other agents were unable to restrain scheming whites who fraudulently purchased reservation lands from the Indians. Frustrated by the manipulation of Indian treaties and irritated by the ineptness of the Indian agents, Congress in 1871 abolished treaty making and replaced treaties with executive orders and acts of Congress. In the 1880s, the federal government ignored the churches' nominations for Indian agents and made its own appointments.

Caught in the sticky web of an ambiguous and deceptive federal policy, and enraged by continuing non-Indian settlement of the Plains, defiant Native Americans struck back in the 1870s. On the southern Plains, Kiowa, Comanche, and Cheyenne raids in the Texas Panhandle in 1874 set off the so-called Red River War. In a fierce winter campaign, regular army troops destroyed Indian supplies and slaughtered a hundred Cheyenne fugitives near the Sappa River in Kansas. With the exile of seventy-four "ringleaders" to reservations in Florida, Native American independence on the southern Plains came to an end. In the Southwest, in present-day Arizona and New Mexico, the Apaches fought an intermittent guerrilla war until their leader, Geronimo, surrendered in 1886.

Custer's Last Stand, 1876 Of all the acts of Indian resistance against the new reservation policy, none aroused more passion or caused more bloodshed than the battles waged by the western Sioux tribes in the Dakotas, Montana, and Wyoming. The 1868 Treaty of Fort Laramie had set aside the Great Sioux Reserve "in perpetuity." But not all the Sioux bands had fought in the war or signed the treaty.

In 1873, skillfully playing local officials against the federal government, Chief Red Cloud's Oglala band and Chief Spotted Tail's Brulé band won the concession of staying on their traditional lands. To protect their hunting grounds, they raided encroaching non-Indian settlements in Nebraska and Wyoming, intimidated federal agents, and harassed miners, railroad surveyors, and any others who ventured onto their lands.

Non-treaty Sioux found a powerful leader in the Lakota Sioux chief and holy man **Sitting Bull.** Broad-shouldered and powerfully built, Sitting Bull led by example and had considerable fighting experience. "You are fools," he told the reservation Indians, "to make yourselves slaves to a piece of fat bacon, some hard-tack, and a little sugar and coffee."

Pressured by would-be settlers and developers and distressed by the Indian agents' inability to prevent the Sioux from entering and leaving the reservations at will, the federal government took action. In 1874, General William Tecumseh Sherman sent a force under Colonel George Armstrong Custer into the Black Hills of South Dakota, near the western edge of the Great Sioux Reserve. Lean and mustachioed, with shoulder-length reddish-blond hair, the thirty-four-year-old Custer had been a celebrity since his days as an impetuous young Civil War officer.

Custer's mission was to extract concessions from the Sioux. In November 1875, negotiations to buy the Black Hills had broken down because the Indians' asking price was deemed too high. Custer now sought to drive the Indians out of the Black Hills. Indians still outside the reservations after January 31, 1876, the government announced, would be hunted down and taken in by force.

The army mobilized for an assault. In June 1876, leading 600 troops of the Seventh Cavalry, Custer proceeded to the Little Bighorn River area of present-day Montana, a hub of Indian resistance. On the morning of June 25, underestimating the Indian enemy and unwisely dividing his force, Custer, with 209 men, recklessly advanced against a large company of Cheyenne and Sioux warriors led by Chief Sitting Bull, who had encamped along the Little Bighorn. Custer and his outnumbered troops were wiped out.

Americans reeled from this unexpected Indian victory. Newspaper columnists groped to assess the meaning of "Custer's last stand." Some went beyond criticism of Custer's leadership to question the wisdom of current federal policy toward the Indians. Others worried that an outraged public would demand retaliation. Most, however, endorsed the federal government's determination to quash the Native American rebellion. "It is inconsistent with our civilization and with common sense," trumpeted a writer in the *New York Herald,* "to allow the Indian to roam over a country as fine as that around the Black Hills, preventing its development in order that he may shoot game and scalp his neighbors. That can never be. This region must be taken from the Indian."

Defeat at Little Bighorn made the army more determined. In Montana, troops harassed various Sioux bands for more than five years, attacking Indian camps in the

Indian Chiefs   *Early photographs of the Indian leaders Chief Joseph (left) and Sitting Bull (right) captured both their pride and the frustration they felt after years of alternately negotiating and battling with the U.S. army. "I don't want a white man over me," Sitting Bull insisted. "I want to have the white man with me, but not to be my chief. I ask this because I want to do right by my people. . . ."*

dead of winter and destroying all supplies. Even Sitting Bull, who had led his band to Canada to escape the army, surrendered in 1881 for lack of provisions. The slaughter of the buffalo had wiped out his tribe's major food source.

Similar measures were used elsewhere in the West against Chief Joseph and his Nez Percés of Oregon and against the northern Cheyennes, who had been forcibly transported to Oklahoma after the Battle of Little Bighorn. Chief Dull Knife led some 150 survivors, including men, women, and children, north in September 1878 to join the Sioux. But the army chased them down and imprisoned them in Fort Robinson, Nebraska. When the army denied their request to stay nearer to their traditional northern lands, tribal leaders refused to cooperate. The post commander then withheld all food, water, and fuel. On a frigid night in January 1879, a desperate Dull Knife and his followers, in a dramatic escape attempt, shot the guards and broke for freedom. Members of the startled garrison chased the Indians and gunned down half of them in the snow, including women and children as well as Dull Knife himself. The *Atlanta Constitution* condemned the incident as "a dastardly outrage upon humanity and a lasting disgrace to our boasted civilization." Although sporadic Indian resistance continued until the end of the century, these brutal tactics had sapped the Indians' will to resist.

"Saving" the
Indians

A growing number of Americans were outraged by the federal government's flagrant violation of its Indian treaties. The Women's National Indian Rights Association, founded in 1883, and other groups took up the cause. **Helen Hunt Jackson,** a Massachusetts writer who had recently moved to Colorado, published *A Century of Dishonor* in 1881 to rally public opinion against the government's record of broken treaty obligations. "It makes little difference . . . where one opens the record of the history of the Indians," she wrote; "every page and every year has its dark stain."

To help Indians abandon hunting and nomadic life, reformers like Jackson advocated the creation of Indian boarding schools, much like those established for emancipated slaves. Richard Henry Pratt, a retired military officer, opened such a school in Carlisle, Pennsylvania, in 1879. Pratt believed that the Indians' customs and languages had halted their progress toward white civilization. His motto therefore became "Kill the Indian and save the man." Modeled after Carlisle, other Indian boarding schools taught farming, carpentry, dress-making, and nursing.

Despite the reformers' best efforts, the attempt to stamp out Indian identity in the boarding schools often backfired. Forming friendships with Indians from many different tribes, boarding school students forged their own sense of Indian identity. As Mitch Walking Elk, a Cheyenne-Arapaho-Hopi student at the Phoenix Indian School, put it, "They put me in the boarding school and they cut off all my hair, gave me an education, but the Apache's still in there."

In addition to their advocacy of boarding schools, well-intentioned humanitarians concluded that the Indians' interests would be best served by breaking up the reservations, ending all recognition of tribal governments, and gradually incorporating individual Native Americans into mainstream society by giving them the rights of citizens. In short, they proposed to eliminate the "Indian problem" by eliminating the Indians as a culturally distinct entity. Inspired by this vision, they supported the **Dawes Severalty Act,** passed in 1887.

The Dawes Act was designed to turn Indians into landowners and farmers. The law emphasized severalty, or the treatment of Indians as individuals rather than as members of tribes, and called for the distribution of 160 acres of reservation land for farming, or 320 acres for grazing, to each head of an Indian family who accepted the law's provisions. The remaining reservation lands (often the richest) were to be sold to speculators and settlers, and the income thus obtained would go toward purchase of farm tools. To prevent unscrupulous people from gaining control of the lands granted to individual Indians, the government would hold the property of each tribal member in trust for twenty-five years. Those Indians who at that point had accepted allotments would also be declared citizens of the United States.

The Dawes Act did not specify a timetable for the breakup of the reservations. Few allotments were made to the Indians until the 1890s. The act proved to be a boon to speculators, who commonly evaded its safeguards and obtained the Indians' best land. By 1934, the act had slashed Indian acreage by 65 percent. Much of what remained in Indian hands was too dry and gravelly for farming. In the twentieth century, ironically, periodic droughts and the fragile, arid High Plains landscape would push many white farmers back off the land.

Although some Native Americans who received land under the Dawes Act prospered enough to expand their holdings and go into large-scale farming or ranching, countless others struggled just to survive. Hunting restrictions on the former reservation lands prevented many Indians from supplementing their limited farm yields. Alcoholism, a continuing problem exacerbated by the prevalence of whiskey as a trade item (and by the boredom that resulted from the disruption of hunting and other traditional pursuits), became more prevalent as Native Americans strove to adapt to the constraints of reservation life.

The Ghost Dance and the End of Indian Resistance on the Great Plains, 1890

Living conditions for the Sioux worsened in the late 1880s. The federal government reduced their meat rations and restricted hunting. When disease killed a third of their cattle, they became desperate. The Sioux, who still numbered almost twenty-five thousand, turned to Wovoka, a new visionary prophet popular among the Great Basin Indians in Nevada. Wovoka foresaw a catastrophic event that would bring the return of dead relatives, the restoration of the bison herds, and the renewal of traditional life. Some versions of his vision included the destruction of European-Americans and their removal from Indian lands. To bring on this new day, the prophet preached a return to traditional ethics, and taught his followers a cycle of ritual songs and dance steps known as the **Ghost Dance.** Wearing sacred Ghost Shirts—cotton or leather vestments decorated to ward off evil—the dancers moved in a circle, accelerating until they reached a trance-like state and experienced visions of the future. Many believed that the Ghost Shirts would protect them from harm.

In the fall of 1890, as the Ghost Dance movement spread among the Sioux in the Dakota Territory, Indian officials and military authorities grew alarmed. The local reservation agent decided that Chief Sitting Bull, whose cabin on the reservation had become a rallying point for the Ghost Dance movement, must be arrested. On a freezing, drizzly December morning, he dispatched a company of Indian policemen from the agency to take Sitting Bull into custody. When two policemen pulled the chief from his cabin, a scuffle ensued, shots rang out, and Sitting Bull was mortally wounded. As bullets whizzed by, Sitting Bull's horse began to perform the tricks it remembered from its days in the Wild West show. Some observers were terrified, convinced that the spirit of the dead chief had entered his horse.

Two weeks later, one of the bloodiest episodes of Indian-white strife on the Plains occurred. On December 29, the Seventh Cavalry was rounding up 340 starving and freezing Sioux at **Wounded Knee,** South Dakota, when someone fired a gun. The soldiers retaliated with cannon fire. Within minutes 300 Indians, including 7 infants, were slaughtered. Three days later, a baby who had miraculously survived was found wrapped in a blanket under the snow. She wore a buckskin cap on which a beadwork American flag had been embroidered. Brigadier General L. W. Colby, who adopted the baby, named her Marguerite, but the Indians called her Lost Bird.

As the frozen corpses at Wounded Knee were dumped into mass graves, a generation of Indian-white conflict on the Great Plains shuddered to a close. Lost Bird, with her poignantly patriotic beadwork cap, highlights the irony of the Plains Indians' response to white expansion. Many Natives did try to adapt to non-Indian ways, and some succeeded fully. Goodbird became a Congregational minister, a prosperous farmer, and a leader of the Hidatsa tribe. He carefully blended his traditional Indian religious beliefs with Christianity. Others did less well economically. Driven onto reservations, many Plains Indians became dependent on governmental support. By 1900, the Plains Indian population had shrunk from nearly a quarter-million to just over a hundred thousand. Nevertheless, the population began to increase slowly after 1900. Against overwhelming odds, the pride, religious traditions, and cultural identities of the Plains Indians survived all efforts at eradication.

Unlike the nomadic western Sioux, the more settled Navajos of the Southwest adjusted more successfully to the reservation system, preserving traditional ways while incorporating elements of the new order in a complex process of cultural adaptation. By 1900, the Navajos had tripled their reservation land, dramatically increased their numbers and their herds, and carved out for themselves a distinct place in Arizona and New Mexico.

These extraordinary changes were forced on the Indian population by the advance of non-Indian settlement. In the name of civilization and progress, non-Indians in the generation after the Civil War pursued a course that involved a mixture of sincere (if misguided) benevolence, coercion wrapped in an aura of legality, and outbursts of naked violence. Many white Americans felt toward the Indians only contempt, hatred, and greed for their land. Others viewed themselves as divinely chosen instruments for uplifting and Christianizing Native peoples. Both groups, however, were blind to the value of Native American life and traditions. And both were unsuccessful in their attempts to shatter proud peoples and their ancient cultures.

SETTLING THE WEST

The successive defeats of the Native Americans opened for settlement a vast territory that reached from the Great Plains to the Sierra Nevada and Cascade Mountains. In the 1840s, when nearly a quarter-million Americans had trudged overland to Oregon and California, they had typically endured a six- to eight-month trip in ox-drawn wagons. After 1870, railroad expansion made the trip faster and considerably easier. In the next three decades, more land was parceled out into farms than in the previous 250 years of American history combined, and agricultural production doubled.

The First Transcontinental Railroad

Passed in 1862, the Pacific Railroad Act authorized the construction of a new transcontinental link. The act provided grants of land and other subsidies to the railroads for each mile of track laid, which made them the largest landholders in the West. Over the next half-century, nine major routes, which ran from the South or Midwest to the West, were built. More than any other factor, the expansion of these railroads accelerated the transformation of everyday life west of the Mississippi.

Building the railroad took backbreaking work. Searching for inexpensive labor, the railroads turned to immigrants. The Central Pacific employed Chinese workers to chip and blast rail bed out of solid rock in the Sierra Nevada. The railroad preferred the Chinese laborers because they worked hard for low wages, did not drink, and furnished their own food and tents. Nearly twelve thousand Chinese graded the roadbed while Irish, Mexican-American, and black workers put down the track.

On May 10, 1869, Americans celebrated the completion of the first railroad spanning North America. As the two sets of tracks—the Union Pacific's, stretching westward from Omaha, Nebraska, and the Central Pacific's, reaching eastward from Sacramento,

Immigrants Looking for Homesteads, Kansas Garden City Square & Land Company, 1910 *Railroads often joined forces with land companies to settle foreign immigrants on their holdings. Posed in their Sunday clothes against a background of a productive farm, this picture was meant to suggest the endless acres of land available for those willing to move west.*

California—met at Promontory Point, Utah, beaming officials drove in a final ceremonial golden spike. The nation's vast midsection was now far more accessible than it had ever been.

The railroads quickly proved their usefulness. In the battles against Native Americans, the army shipped horses and men west in the dead of winter to attack the Indians when they were most vulnerable. From the same trains, hunters gained quick access to the bison ranges and increased their harvest of the animals. Once Indian resistance had been broken, the railroads not only expedited the shipment of new settlers and their supplies, but also provided fast access for the shipment of cattle and grain to eastern urban markets. In short, the railroads accelerated the development of the West.

Settlers and the Railroad During the decade after the passage of the Pacific Railroad Act, Congress awarded the railroads 170 million acres, worth over half a billion dollars. By 1893, Minnesota and Washington had also deeded to railroad companies a quarter of their state lands; Wisconsin, Iowa, Kansas, North Dakota, and Montana had turned over a fifth of their acreage. As mighty landowners, the railroads had a unique opportunity to shape settlement in the region—and to reap enormous profits.

The railroads set up land sales offices and sent agents to the East Coast and Europe to recruit settlers. While the agents glorified the West as a new Garden of Eden, the land bureaus offered prospective buyers long-term loans and free transportation. Acknowledging that life on the Great Plains could be lonely, the promoters advised young men to bring their wives (because "maidens are scarce") and to emigrate as entire families and with friends.

One unintended consequence of these land promotions was to make land available to single women, or "girl homesteaders" as they were known at the time. In Wyoming, single women made up more than 18 percent of the claimants. Women filed 10 to 20 percent of the claims in Colorado, sometimes as individuals and sometimes to add to family holdings.

In addition to the millions of Americans who migrated from nearby states, the railroads helped bring nearly 2.2 million foreign-born settlers to the trans-Mississippi West between 1870 and 1900. Some agents recruited whole villages of Germans and eastern Europeans to relocate to the North Dakota plains. Irish laborers hired to lay track could be found in every town along the rail lines. By 1905, the Santa Fe Railroad alone had transported sixty thousand Russian Mennonites to the fertile Kansas plains where black pioneers called exodusters had preceded them in the 1870s.

The railroads influenced agriculture as well. To ensure quick repayment of the money owed to them, the railroads urged new immigrants to specialize in cash crops—wheat on the northern Plains, corn in Iowa and Kansas, cotton and tobacco in Texas. Although these crops initially brought in high revenues, many farmers grew dependent on income from a single crop and became vulnerable to fluctuating market forces.

Homesteading on the Great Plains Liberalized land laws were another powerful magnet pulling settlers westward. The Homestead Act passed in 1862 reflected the Republican Party's belief that free land would enable the poor to achieve economic independence. It offered 160 acres of land to any individual who would pay a ten-dollar registration fee, live on the land for five years, and cultivate and improve it. Although nearly four hundred thousand families claimed land under the provisions of the Homestead Act between 1860 and 1900, the law did not function as Congress had envisioned. Advance agents representing unscrupulous speculators filed false claims for the choicest locations, and railroads acquired huge landholdings. The result was that only one acre in every nine went to the pioneers for whom it was intended.

A second problem resulted from the 160-acre limit specified by the Homestead Act. On the rich soils of Iowa or in the fertile lands in California, Oregon, and Washington, a 160-acre farm was ample, but in the drier areas west of the hundredth meridian, a farmer needed more land. In 1873, to rectify this problem, Congress passed the Timber Culture Act, which gave homesteaders an additional 160 acres if they planted trees on 40 acres. For states with little rainfall, Congress enacted the Desert Land Act in 1877, which made 640 acres available at $1.25 an acre on condition that the owner irrigate part of it within three years. However, this act, along with the Timber and Stone Act of 1878, which permitted the purchase of up to 160 acres of forest land for $2.50 an acre, was abused by grasping speculators, lumber-company representatives, and cattle ranchers seeking to expand their holdings. Yet, even though families did not receive as much land as Congress had intended, federal laws kept alive the dream of the West as a place for new beginnings.

In addition to problems faced by those who chose property in areas that lacked sufficient rainfall to grow crops, almost all settlers faced difficult psychological adjustments to frontier life. The first years of settlement were the most difficult. Toiling to build a house, plow the fields, plant the first crop, and dig a well, the pioneers put in an average of sixty-eight hours of tedious, backbreaking work a week in isolated surroundings. Howard Ruede, a Pennsylvania printer who migrated to Kansas to farm, wrote home in 1877 complaining about the mosquitoes and bedbugs infesting his house, which was cut out of thick grass sod and dug into the ground. He and countless others coping with the severe Plains conditions saw their shining vision of idyllic farm life quickly dim. For blacks who emigrated from the South to Kansas and other parts of the Plains after the Civil War, prejudice compounded the burdens of adjusting to a different life (see Chapter 16).

Many women found adaptation to Plains frontier life especially difficult. At least initially, some were enchanted by the landscape. But far more were struck by the "horrible tribes of Mosquitoes"; the violent weather-drenching summer thunderstorms with hailstones as "big as hen's eggs" and blinding winter blizzards; and the crude sod huts that served as their early homes because of the scarcity of timber. One woman burst into tears upon first seeing her new sod house. The young bride angrily informed her husband that her father had built a better house for his hogs.

The high transience rate on the frontier in these years reflected the difficulty that newcomers faced in adjusting to life on the Great Plains. Nearly half of those who staked homestead claims in Kansas between 1862 and 1890 relinquished their rights to the land and moved on. However, in places like Minnesota and the Pacific Northwest that were populated largely by Germans, Norwegians, and other immigrants with a tradition of family prosperity tied to continuous landownership, the persistence rate (or percentage of people staying for a decade or more) could be considerably higher.

Many who weathered the lean early years eventually came to identify deeply with the land. Within a decade, the typical Plains family that had "stuck it out" had moved into a new wood-framed house and had fixed up the front parlor. Women worked particularly hard on these farms and took pride in their accomplishments. "Just done the chores," wrote one woman to a friend. "I went fence mending and getting out cattle . . . and came in after sundown. I fed my White Leghorns [chickens] and then sat on the step to read over your letter. I forgot my wet feet and shoes full of gravel and giggled joyously."

New Farms,
New Markets

Farmers on the Plains took advantage of advances in farm mechanization and the development of improved strains of wheat and corn to boost production dramatically. Efficient steel plows; specially designed wheat planters; and improved grain binders, threshers, and windmills all allowed the typical Great Plains farmer of the late nineteenth century to increase the land's yield tenfold.

Barbed wire, patented in 1874, was another crucial invention that permitted farmers to keep roving livestock out of their crops. But fencing the land touched off violent clashes between farmers and cattle ranchers, who demanded the right to let their herds roam freely until the roundup. Generally the farmers won.

The invention of labor-saving machinery together with increased demand for wheat, milk, and other farm products created the impression that farming was entering a period of unparalleled prosperity. But few fully understood the perils of pursuing agriculture as a livelihood. The cost of the land, horses, machinery, and seed needed to start up a farm could exceed twelve hundred dollars, far more than the annual earnings of the average industrial worker. Faced with substantial mortgage payments, many farmers had to specialize in a crop such as wheat or corn that would fetch high prices. This specialization made them dependent on the railroads for shipping and put them at the mercy of the international grain market's shifting prices.

Far from being an independent producer, the western grain grower was a player in a complex world market economy. Railroad and steamship transport enabled the American farmer to compete in the international market. High demand could bring prosperity, but when world overproduction forced grain prices down, the heavily in-debted grower faced ruin. Confronted with these realities, many Plains farmers quickly abandoned the illusion of frontier independence and easy wealth.

Unpredictable rainfall and weather conditions further exacerbated homesteaders' difficulties west of the hundredth meridian, where rainfall averaged less than twenty inches a year. Farmers compensated through "dry farming"—plowing deeply to stim-ulate the capillary action of the soils and harrowing lightly to raise a covering of dirt that would retain precious moisture after a rainfall. They also built windmills and di-verted creeks for irrigation. But the onset of unusually dry years in the 1870s, together with grasshopper infestations and the major economic depression that struck the United States between 1873 and 1878 (see Chapter 16), made the plight of some mid-westerners desperate.

| Building a Society and Achieving Statehood | Despite the hardships, many remote farm settlements blos-somed into thriving communities. Among the first institutions to appear, churches and Sunday schools became humming centers of social activity as well as of worship. Farmers gath- |

ered for barn raisings and group threshings, and families pooled their energies in quilt-ing and husking bees. Neighbors readily lent a hand to the farmer whose barn had burned or whose family was sick. Cooperation was a practical necessity and a form of insurance in a rugged environment where everyone was vulnerable to instant misfor-tune or even disaster.

When the population increased, local boosters lobbied to turn the territory into a state. Achieving statehood required the residents of the territory to petition Congress to pass an enabling act establishing the territory's boundaries and authorizing an elec-tion to select delegates for a state constitutional convention. Once the state constitution had been drawn up and ratified by popular vote, the territory applied to Congress for admission as a state.

Under these procedures, Kansas entered the Union in 1861, followed by Nevada in 1864 and Nebraska in 1867. Colorado joined in 1876. Not until 1889 did North Dakota, South Dakota, Montana, and Washington gain statehood. Wyoming and Idaho came into the Union the following year. Utah finally entered in 1896. With Oklahoma's admission in 1907 and Arizona's and New Mexico's in 1912, the process of creating permanent political institutions in the trans-Mississippi West was complete.

Although generally socially conservative, the new state governments supported woman suffrage. As territories became states, pioneer women battled for the vote. Seven western states held referenda on this issue between 1870 and 1910. Success came first in the Wyoming Territory, where men outnumbered women 6 to 1. The tiny legis-lature enfranchised women in 1869 in the hope that it would attract women, families, and economic growth. The Utah Territory followed in 1870 and reaffirmed its support

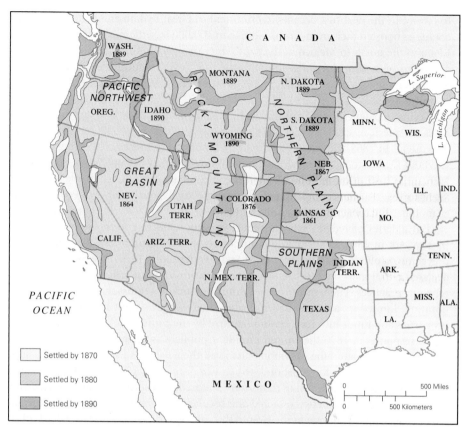

MAP 17.2 The Settlement of the Trans-Mississippi West, 1860–1890

The West was not settled by a movement of peoples gradually creeping westward from the East. Rather, settlers first occupied California and the Midwest and then filled up the nation's vast interior.

for woman suffrage when it became a state. Nebraska in 1867 and Colorado in 1876 permitted women to vote in school elections. Although these successes were significant, by 1910 only four states—Idaho, Wyoming, Utah, and Colorado—had granted women full voting rights. The very newness of their place in the Union may have sensitized legislators in these states to women's important contributions to settlements, and the intense competition among parties may have made them open to experimentation, but by and large, familiar practices persisted.

The Spread of Mormonism   Persecuted in Illinois, members of the Church of Jesus Christ of Latter-day Saints known as Mormons, had moved to the Great Salt Lake Valley in 1847. Led by Brigham Young, their prophet-president, and a Council of Twelve Apostles, they sought to create the independent country of Deseret. Their faith emphasized self-sufficiency and commitment to family. In the next two decades, recruitment in Great Britain and the Scandinavian countries boosted their numbers to more than 100,000 in settlements that ranged from Idaho in the north to Mexico in the south. Increasingly, these Mormon communities conflicted with non-Mormons and with the U.S. government, which disapproved of the church's involvement in politics, its communal business practices, and its support of polygamy.

Trying to balance their territorial claims for the Kingdom of God against the pressures of American secular society, the Mormons sought at first to be economically independent. In 1869, they developed their own railroad branches connecting Salt Lake City and Ogden to the Central Pacific Railroad, and they set up Zion's Cooperative Mercantile Institution to control wholesale and retail activities. They asked all Mormons to abstain from coffee, tea, and alcohol, and established their own People's Party to mobilize the Mormon vote.

But a series of federal acts and court decisions, starting with the Morrill Anti-Bigamy Act in 1862, challenged the authority of their church and their practice of polygamy or plural marriage. In *United States* v. *Reynolds* (1879), the Supreme Court declared plural marriages unlawful and held that freedom of religion did not protect religious practices. Then, in 1887, the **Edmunds-Tucker Act** dissolved the church corporation, limited its assets to $50,000, abolished women's right to vote, and put its properties and funds into receivership (control by the courts).

In response, in 1890 the church president publicly announced the official end of polygamy. A year later, the Mormons dissolved their People's Party. The church supported the application for statehood, which was granted in 1896. Confiscated church properties were returned, voting rights were restored, and jailed polygamists were pardoned, but the balance between sacred and secular had permanently shifted. Mormon settlements would continue in the twentieth century to draw new members and influence economic and social development in western communities.

SOUTHWESTERN BORDERLANDS

The annexation of Texas in 1845 and the Treaty of Guadalupe Hidalgo that had ended the Mexican-American War in 1848 ceded to the United States an immense territory, part of which became Texas, California, Arizona, and New Mexico. At the time, Mexicans had controlled vast expanses of the Southwest. They had built their own churches, maintained large ranching operations, and had traded with the Indians. Although the United States had pledged to protect the liberty and property of Mexicans who remained on American soil, over the next three decades American ranchers and settlers took control of the territorial governments. Like the displacement of the American Indians, much of the Spanish-speaking population was forced off the land. Mexicans who stayed in the region adapted to the new Anglo society with varying degrees of success.

In Texas, the struggle for independence from Mexico had left a legacy of bitterness and misunderstanding. After 1848, Texas cotton planters confiscated Mexican lands and began a racist campaign that labeled Mexicans as nonwhite. Only white people, the Texans asserted, deserved economic and legal rights. Angered by their loss of land and discriminatory treatment, Mexican bandits retaliated by raiding American communities. Tensions peaked in 1859 when Juan Cortina, a Mexican rancher, attacked the Anglo border community of Brownsville, Texas, and freed all the prisoners in jail. Cortina battled the U.S. army for years until the Mexican government, fearing a U.S. invasion, imprisoned him in 1875.

Mexican-Americans in California in the 1850s and 1860s faced similar pressures. A cycle of flood and drought, together with a slumping cattle industry, had ruined many of the large southern California ranches owned by the *californios,* Spanish-speaking descendants of the original Spanish settlers. The collapse of the ranch economy forced many of them to retreat into segregated urban neighborhoods called barrios. Spanish-surnamed citizens made up nearly half the 2,640 residents of Santa Barbara, California, in 1870; because of the influx of new settlers they comprised barely a quarter of the population ten years later. Maintaining a tenacious hold on their traditions, many Spanish-speaking people in Santa Barbara and other towns survived by working as day laborers.

In California, the pattern of racial discrimination, manipulation, and exclusion was similar for Mexicans, Native Americans, and Chinese. At first, the number of new "Anglos" was small. As the number of whites increased, they identified minority racial, cultural, and language differences as marks of inferiority. White state legislators passed laws that made ownership of property difficult for non-Anglos. Relegated to a migratory labor force, non-Anglos were tagged as shiftless and irresponsible. Yet their labor made possible increased prosperity for the farmers, railroads, and households that hired them.

The cultural adaptation of Spanish-speaking Americans to Anglo society initially unfolded more smoothly in Arizona and New Mexico, where Spanish settlement had been sparse and a small class of wealthy Mexican landowners had long dominated a poor, illiterate peasantry. Moreover, since the 1820s, well-to-do Mexicans in Tucson, Arizona, had educated their children in the United States and formed trading partnerships and business alliances with Americans. One of the most successful was Estevan Ochoa, who began a long-distance freight business in 1859 with a U.S. partner and then expanded it into a lucrative merchandising, mining, and sheep-raising operation.

The success of men such as Ochoa, who became mayor of Tucson, helped moderate American settlers' antagonistic attitudes. So, too, did the work of popular writers like Helen Hunt Jackson. By sentimentalizing the gracious colonial Spanish past, Jackson increased public sympathy for Spanish-speaking Americans. Jackson's 1884 romance *Ramona,* a tale of the doomed love of a Hispanicized mixed-blood (Irish-Indian) woman set on a California ranch overwhelmed by the onrushing tide of Anglo civilization, was enormously popular. Jackson's novel also appealed to upper-class Mexican-Americans known as *Nuevomexicanos* who traced their lineage back to the Spanish conquest.

Still, conflicts over property persisted in Arizona and New Mexico. In the 1880s, Mexican-American ranchers organized themselves into a self-protection vigilante group called Las Gorras Blancas (the **White Caps**). In 1888, they tore up railroad tracks and attacked both Anglo newcomers and those upper-class Hispanics who had fenced acreage in northern New Mexico previously considered public grazing land. But this vigilante action did not help, as Anglo-dominated corporate ranchers steadily increased their land holdings. Relations also changed in the urban centers, as discrimination forced Mexican-American businessmen to restrict their business dealings to their own people, and the Spanish-speaking population as a whole became more impoverished. Even in Tucson, where the Mexican-American elite enjoyed considerable economic and political success, 80 percent of the Mexican-Americans in the work force were laborers in 1880, taking jobs as butchers, barbers, cowboys, and railroad workers.

As increasing numbers of Mexican-American men were forced to search for seasonal migrant work, women took responsibility for holding families and communities together. Women managed the households when their husbands were away, and fostered group identification by maintaining traditional customs, kinship ties, and allegiance to the Catholic Church. They served as godmothers for one another's children; tended garden plots; and traded food, soap, and produce with other women. This economy, invisible to those outside the village, stabilized the community in times of drought or persecution by Anglos.

Violence and discrimination against Spanish-speaking citizens of the Southwest escalated in the 1890s, a time of rising racism in the United States. Rioters in Beeville and Laredo, Texas, in 1894 and 1899 attacked and beat up Mexican-Americans. Whites increasingly labeled Mexican-Americans as violent and lazy. For Spanish-speaking citizens, the battle for fair treatment and respect would continue into the twentieth century.

Exploiting the Western Landscape

The displacement of Mexican-American and Native peoples from their lands opened the way for the exploitation of the natural environment in the trans-Mississippi West. White publicists, developers, and boosters had long promoted the region as a land of boundless opportunity. Between 1860 and 1900, a generation of Americans sought to strike it rich by joining the ranks of miners, ranchers, and farmers intent on making a fortune. Although the mining, ranching, and farming "bonanzas" promised unheard-of wealth, they set in motion a boom-and-bust economy in which many people went bankrupt or barely survived and others were bought out by large-scale enterprises. Of all the groups that surged into the nation's midcontinent in the late nineteenth century, none had to revise their expectations more radically than the speculators and adventurers thirsting for quick fortunes.

The Mining Frontier In the half-century that began with the California gold rush in 1849, a series of mining booms swept from the Southwest northward into Canada and Alaska. Sensational discoveries in California's Sierra Nevada produced more than $81 million worth of gold bullion in 1852. The following year, Henry Comstock, an illiterate prospector, stumbled on the rich **Comstock Lode** along Nevada's Carson River. Later in the same decade, feverishly pursuing rumors of new strikes, prospectors swarmed into the Rocky Mountains and uncovered deep veins of gold and silver near present-day Denver. Over the next five decades, gold was discovered in Idaho, Montana, Wyoming, South Dakota, and, in 1896, in the Canadian Klondike. Although the popular press clearly exaggerated reports of miners scooping up gold by the panful, by 1900 more than a billion dollars' worth of gold had been mined in California alone.

The early discoveries of "placer" gold, panned from streams, attracted a young male population thirsting for wealth and reinforced the myth of mining country as "a poor man's paradise." In contrast to the Great Plains, where ethnic groups recreated their own ethnic enclaves, western mining camps became ethnic melting pots. In the Cali-

Juneau, Alaska, c. 1896   *Like other mining towns, Juneau grew rapidly and haphazardly after Kowee, a local Tlingit man, showed Joe Juneau and Richard Harris the location of gold nuggets in 1880. Between 1881 and 1944 Juneau's mines produced 6.7 million ounces of gold.*

fornia census of 1860, more than thirty-three thousand Irish and thirty-four thousand Chinese had staked out early claims.

Although a few prospectors became fabulously wealthy, the experience of Henry Comstock, who sold out one claim for eleven thousand dollars and another for two mules, was more typical. Because the larger gold and silver deposits lay embedded in veins of quartz deep within the earth, extracting them required huge investments in workers and expensive equipment. Deep shafts had to be blasted into the rock. Once lifted to the surface, the rock had to be crushed, flushed with mercury or cyanide to collect the silver, and smelted into ingots. No sooner had the major discoveries been made, therefore, than large mining companies backed by eastern or British capital bought them out and took them over.

Life in the new mining towns was vibrant but unpredictable. During the heyday of the Comstock Lode in the 1860s and 1870s, Virginia City, Nevada, erupted in an orgy of speculation and building. Started as a shantytown in 1859, it swelled by 1873 into a thriving metropolis of twenty thousand people complete with elaborate mansions, a six-story hotel, an opera house, 131 saloons, 4 banks, and uncounted brothels. Men outnumbered women three to one. Money quickly earned was even more rapidly lost.

The boom-and-bust cycle evident in Virginia City was repeated in towns across the West. Mark Twain captured the thrill of the mining "stampedes" in *Roughing It* (1872). "Every few days," wrote Twain, "news would come of the discovery of a brand-new mining region: immediately the papers would teem with accounts of its richness, and away the surplus population would scamper to take possession. By the time I was fairly inoculated with the disease, 'Esmeralda' had just had a run and 'Humboldt' was beginning to shriek for attention. 'Humboldt! Humboldt!' was the new cry, and straightway Humboldt, the newest of the new, the richest of the rich, the most marvelous of the marvelous discoveries in silver-land, was occupying two columns of the public prints to 'Esmeralda's' one."

One unintended consequence of the gold rush mania was the growth of settlement in Alaska. Small strikes were made there in 1869, two years after the United States had purchased the territory from Russia. More miners arrived in the 1880s after prospector Joe Juneau, for whom the town of Juneau was named, and others developed the Treadwell Mine. But it was the discovery of gold in the Canadian Klondike in 1897 that brought thousands of prospectors into the area and eventually enabled Alaska to establish its own territorial government in 1912.

Word of new ore deposits like the ones in Alaska lured transient populations salivating to get rich. Miners who worked deep within the earth for large corporations typically earned about $2,000 a year at a time when teachers made $450 to $650 and domestic help $250 to $350. But most prospectors at best earned only enough to go elsewhere, perhaps buy some land, and try again. Nevertheless, the production of millions of ounces of gold and silver stimulated the economy, lured new foreign investors, and helped usher the United States into the mainstream of the world economy.

Progress came at a price. The long-term cost to the environment to extract these metals was high. Hydraulic mining, which used water cannons to dislodge minerals, polluted rivers, turned creeks brown, and flushed millions of tons of silt into valleys. The scarred landscape that remained was littered with rock and gravel filled with traces of mercury and cyanide, and nothing would grow on it. Smelters spewed dense smoke containing lead, arsenic, and other carcinogenic chemicals on those who lived nearby and often made them sick. The destruction to the environment is still evident today.

Cowboys and the Cattle Frontier   Like the feverish expansion of the mining frontier during the 1860s and 1870s, open-range cattle ranching boomed in these same decades. In this case, astute businessmen and railroad entrepreneurs, eager to fund their new investments in miles of track, promoted cattle herding as the new route to fame and fortune. The cowboy, once scorned as a ne'er-do-well and drifter, was now glorified as a man of rough-hewn integrity and self-reliant strength.

In 1868, Joseph G. McCoy, a young cattle dealer from Springfield, Illinois, shrewdly combined organizational and promotional skills to turn the cattle industry into a new money-maker. With the forced relocation of the Plains Indians onto reservations and the extension of the railroads into Kansas in the post–Civil War period, McCoy realized that cattle dealers could now amass enormous fortunes by raising steers cheaply in Texas and bringing them north for shipment to eastern urban markets.

McCoy built a new stockyard in Abilene, Kansas. By guaranteeing to transport his steers in railcars to hungry eastern markets, he obtained a five-dollar kickback from the railroads on each cattle car shipped. To make the overland cattle drives from Texas to Abilene easier, McCoy also helped survey and shorten the Chisholm Trail in Kansas. Finally, in a clever feat of showmanship, he organized the first Wild West show, sending four Texas cowboys to St. Louis and Chicago, where they staged roping and riding exhibitions that attracted exuberant crowds. At the end of his first year in business, thirty-five thousand steers were sold in Abilene; the following year the number more than doubled.

The great **cattle drives** of the 1860s and 1870s turned into a bonanza for herd owners. Steers purchased in Texas at nine dollars a head could be sold in Abilene, after deducting four dollars in trail expenses, for twenty-eight dollars. A herd of two thousand head could thus bring a tidy thirty-thousand-dollar profit. But the cattlemen, like the grain growers farther north on the Great Plains, lived at the mercy of high interest rates and an unstable market. During the financial panic of 1873, cattle drovers, unable to get extensions on their loans, fell into bankruptcy by the hundreds.

Little of the money made by the large-scale cattle ranchers found its way into the pockets of the cowboys themselves. The typical cowpunchers who drove herds through the dirt and dust from southern Texas to Abilene earned a mere thirty dollars a month, about the same as common laborers. They also braved the gangs of cattle thieves that operated along the trails. The most notorious of the cattle rustlers, William H. Bonney, better known as Billy the Kid, may have murdered as many as eleven men before he was killed by a sheriff in 1881 at the age of twenty-one. The long hours, low pay, and hazardous work discouraged older ranch hands from applying. Most cowboys were men in their teens and twenties who worked for a year or two and then pursued different livelihoods.

Of the estimated 35,000 to 55,000 men who rode the trails in these years, nearly one-fifth were black or Mexican. Barred by discrimination from many other trades, blacks enjoyed the freedom of life on the trail. Although they were excluded from the position of trail boss, they distinguished themselves as resourceful and shrewd cowpunchers. **Nat Love,** the son of Tennessee slaves, left for Kansas after the Civil War to work for Texas cattle companies. As chief brander, he moved through Texas and Arizona "dancing, drinking, and shooting up the town." By his own account, he was "wild, reckless, free," and "afraid of nothing." On July 4, 1876, when the Black Hills gold rush was in full swing, Love delivered three thousand head of cattle to a point near the hills and rode into Deadwood to celebrate. Local miners and gamblers had raised prize money for roping and shooting contests, and Nat Love won both, as well as a new title, Deadwood Dick.

Close relationships sometimes developed between black and white cowboys. Shortly before Charles Goodnight, a white pioneer trailblazer, died in 1929, he recalled of the black cowboy Bose Ikard, a former slave, that "he was my detective, banker, and everything else in Colorado, New Mexico, and the other wild country I was in. The nearest and only bank was at Denver, and when we carried money I gave it to Bose." Goodnight revealed much about the economic situation of blacks on the Plains, however, when he added that "a thief would never think of robbing him [Ikard]—never think of looking in a Negro's bed for money."

The cattle bonanza, which peaked between 1880 and 1885, produced more than 4.5 million head of cattle for eastern markets. (See Beyond America—Global Interactions: Cattle-Raising in the Americas.) Prices began to sag as early as 1882, however, and many ranchers plunged heavily into debt. When President Grover Cleveland, trying to improve federal observance of Indian treaties, ordered cattlemen to remove their stock from the Cheyenne-Arapaho reservation in 1885, two hundred thousand more cattle were crowded onto already overgrazed ranges. That same year and the following, two of the coldest and snowiest winters on record combined with summer droughts and Texas fever to destroy nearly 90 percent of the cattle in some regions, pushing thousands of ranchers into bankruptcy. The cattle industry lived on, but railroad expansion brought the days of the open range and the great cattle drives to an end. As had the mining frontier, the cattle frontier left behind memories of individual daring, towering fortunes for some, and hard times for many.

Cattle Towns and Prostitutes

One legacy of the cattle boom was the growth of cities like Abilene, Kansas, which shipped steers to Chicago and eastern markets. Like other cattle towns, Abilene went through an early period of violence that saw cowboys pulling down the walls of the jail as it was being built. But the town quickly established a police force to maintain law and order. City ordinances forbade carrying firearms and regulated saloons, gambling, and prostitution. James B. "Wild Bill" Hickok served as town marshal in 1871, but his tenure was less eventful than legend had it. Dime novelists described him as "a veritable terror to bad men on the border," but during his term as Abilene's lawman, Hickok killed just two men, one of them by mistake. Transient, unruly types certainly gave a distinctive flavor to cattle towns like Abilene, Wichita, and Dodge City, but the overall homicide rates there were not unusually high.

If cattle towns were neither as violent nor as lawless as legend would have it, they did still experience a lively business in prostitution, as did most cities at this time. Given the large numbers of unattached young men and numerous saloons (Abilene, in the 1870s, with a permanent population of 500, had 32 drinking establishments), prostitution thrived. Prostitutes came from all social classes and from as far away as China, Ireland, Germany, and Mexico. Some became prostitutes as an escape from domestic violence or because of economic hardship. Others, like the Chinese, were forced into the trade. But whatever the reasons for entering the business, prostitutes risked venereal disease, physical abuse, and drug and alcohol addiction.

As western towns became more settled, the numbers of women in other occupations increased. Some found work as cooks or laundresses on ranches. Others married merchants, doctors, and businessmen. Although few of the first generation rode the range, their daughters became increasingly involved in the everyday work of the ranch and became proficient riders themselves.

Bonanza Farms

The enthusiasm that permeated mining and ranching in the 1870s and 1880s also percolated into agriculture. Like the gold rushes and cattle bonanzas, the wheat boom in the Dakota Territory started small but rapidly attracted large capital investments that produced the nation's first agribusinesses.

The boom began during the Panic of 1873, when the failure of numerous banks caused the price of Northern Pacific Railroad bonds to plummet. The railroad responded by exchanging land for its depreciated bonds. Speculators, including the railroad's own president, George W. Cass, jumped at the opportunity and purchased more than three hundred thousand acres in the fertile Red River valley of North Dakota for between fifty cents and a dollar an acre.

Operating singly or in groups, the speculators established factory-like ten-thousand-acre farms, each run by a hired manager, and invested heavily in labor and equipment. On the Cass-Cheney-Dalrymple farm near Fargo, North Dakota, which covered an area six miles long by four miles wide, fifty or sixty plows rumbled across the flat landscape on a typical spring day. The *New York Tribune* reported that Cass, who had invested fifty thousand dollars for land and equipment, paid all his expenses plus the cost of the ten thousand acres with his first harvest alone.

The publicity generated by the tremendous success of a few large investors like Cass and Oliver Dalrymple led to an unprecedented wheat boom in the Red River valley in 1880. Eastern banking syndicates and small farmers alike rushed to buy land. North Dakota's population tripled in the 1880s. Wheat production skyrocketed to almost 29 million bushels by the end of the decade. But the profits so loudly celebrated in the eastern press soon evaporated. By 1890, some Red River valley farmers were destitute.

The wheat boom collapsed for a variety of reasons. Overproduction, high investment costs, too little or too much rain, excessive reliance on one crop, and depressed grain prices on the international market all undercut farmers' earnings. Large-scale farmers who had invested in hopes of getting rich felt lucky just to survive. Oliver Dalrymple lamented in 1889 that "it seems as if the time has come when there is no money in wheat raising."

Large-scale farms proved most successful in California's Central Valley. Using canals and other irrigation systems to water their crops, farmers were growing higher-priced specialty crops and had created new cooperative marketing associations for cherries, apricots, grapes, and oranges by the mid-1880s. Led by the California Citrus Growers' Association, which used the "Sunkist" trademark for their oranges, large-scale agribusinesses in California were shipping a variety of fruits and vegetables in refrigerated train cars to midwestern and eastern markets by 1900.

The Oklahoma Land Rush, 1889   As farmers in the Dakotas and Minnesota were enduring poor harvests and falling prices, hard-pressed would-be homesteaders greedily eyed the Indian Territory, as present-day Oklahoma was then known. The federal government, considering much of this land virtually worthless, had reserved it for the Five Civilized Tribes since the 1830s. Because these tribes (except for some Cherokees) had sided with the Confederacy during the Civil War, Washington had punished them by settling thousands of Indians from other tribes on lands in the western part of the territory. By the 1880s, land-hungry non-Indians argued that the Civilized Tribes' betrayal of the Union justified further confiscation of their land.

In 1889, over the Native Americans' protests, Congress transferred to the federally owned public domain nearly 2 million acres in the central part of the Oklahoma Territory that had not been specifically assigned to any Indian tribe. At noon on April 22, 1889, thousands of men, women, and children in buggies and wagons stampeded into the new lands to stake out homesteads. (Other settlers, the so-called Sooners, had illegally arrived earlier and were already plowing the fields.) Before nightfall tent communities had risen at Oklahoma City and Guthrie near stations on the Santa Fe Railroad. Nine weeks later, six thousand homestead claims had been filed. In the next decade, the Dawes Severalty Act broke up the Indian reservations into individual allotments and opened the surplus to non-Indian settlement. The **Curtis Act** in 1898 dissolved the Indian Territory and abolished tribal governments.

Cattle-Raising in the Americas

Nineteenth-century dime novels and Wild West Shows celebrated cowboys as quintessentially American—independent, self-reliant, tough, and occasionally violent. Driving herds of cattle north from Texas to Kansas, the cowboys, who rode the open range from the end of the Civil War through the mid-1880s, appeared to be the unique product of the American West. From a more global perspective, however, North-American cowboys shared much in common with the Mexican *vaqueros* and Argentinian *gauchos*. Like their counterparts in Latin and South America, they drew on a long tradition of cattle herding that had begun centuries earlier in Africa, England, and Spain.

Spanish conquistadors and English colonists brought to the New World their practice of raising beef cattle on the open range rather than in fixed enclosures. In sixteenth-century Mexico, African slaves often joined mixed-bloods of Spanish and Indian ancestry to brand and tend cattle. On the rich grasslands of Argentina, horsemen first hunted wild cattle that had escaped earlier settlements. Later, after the Indians were driven off the open range, these horsemen, now called *gauchos,* tended cattle on large ranches.

Gauchos and cowboys were colorful characters, usually young men, often from lower-class backgrounds. The English naturalist, Charles Darwin, visiting Argentina in 1833, described them as being "generally tall and handsome, but with a proud and dissolute expression of countenance. They frequently wear their mustaches, and long black hair curling down their backs. With their brightly-colored garments, great spurs clanking about their heels, and knives stuck as daggers (and often so used) at their waists, they look a very different race of men from what might be expected from their name of Gauchos, or simple countrymen." Like cowboys, they busted broncos, taming the wild horses to accept riders, and rounded up strays. They also hunted wild ostriches, whose feathers fetched high prices in Europe. As in North America, some gauchos became bandits, which added to their romantic appeal.

Gauchos and cowboys, like other cattle herders around the world, whether Russian Cossacks, South African Dutch farmers, or Canadian cowhands, were often skilled horsemen. American cowboys drew on both Anglo and Hispanic traditions. Unlike the gauchos in Argentina who used *bolas,* an Indian invention of three balls connected by rawhide thongs, to entangle a steer's feet and immobilize it, American cowboys used the Hispanic *lariat* to rope the necks of their cattle and place them in a corral. Like British herders who used dogs, American cowboys taught their horses to maneuver quickly and sharply to keep the herd in line or to cut out a steer to be branded. Like their counterparts in Canada, they organized rodeos to show off their riding and lassoing skills.

Although horses were universally used to herd cattle throughout the Americas, each open-range cattle-raising region had its own distinctive features. In California, where the open-range cattle boom peaked in the decade after 1848, Hispanic cowhands used rawhide lassos, which they looped around the saddle horn to immobilize steers, and wore the Spanish great-rowel spurs over soft shoes. Since Anglo-Texans adapted British cattle-herding practices that used abrupt turns to cut a steer from the herd, they modified the traditional Spanish saddle by adding a second belt to hold it more securely on the horse, and adopted the pointed-toe, high-heeled riding boot, which would hold the boot, in the stirrup during these tight turns. Cattle-raisers on the Great Plains, while following many Texas cowboy practices, added river irrigation to grow hay fields to help tide their herds over the harsh winters. Canadian cattlemen, in contrast, employed acculturated Indians as cowhands and sometimes followed British practices and used collie dogs as well as horses to help herd cattle.

By the end of the nineteenth century, the cattle booms in both North and South America that depended on open-range grazing practices had passed. By maximizing herd size and fertility, cattlemen had inadvertently destroyed perennial grasses, damaged the landscape, and in some cases caused desertification. Farmers and sheep-raisers competed for grazing land and fenced off access to many ranges. At the same time, the extension of railroad lines made it possible to ship cattle directly from ranches to urban areas, a practice that fundamentally changed the livestock industry. In both North and South America, large-scale ranchers took control of cattle-raising and kept wages low. British investment syndicates, for example, purchased large ranches in Texas and Wyoming where they raised immense herds for eastern urban markets.

Not surprisingly, the idealization and romanticization of the cowboy that occurred after open-range grazing had disappeared in North America produced similar celebrations of gauchos and *vaqueros* in Argentina and Mexico. In all three areas, the reality was different. The colorful cowhands who had stirred the popular imagination as symbols of a freer, more independent way of life had been reduced to seasonal laborers with little chance of advancement.

Questions for Analysis

- What traditions shaped open-range ranching in the Americas?
- What was the popular mythic image of the cowboy, the *vaquero,* and the gaucho?
- What was the environmental impact of open-range grazing?

The Oklahoma land rush demonstrated the continuing power of the frontier myth, which tied "free" land to the ideal of economic opportunity. Despite early obstacles— the 1889 rush occurred too late in the season for most settlers to plant a full crop, and a drought parched the land the following year—Oklahoma farmers remained optimistic about their chances of making it on the last frontier. Most survived because they were fortunate enough to have obtained fertile land in an area where the normal rainfall was thirty inches, ten inches more than in the semiarid regions farther west. Still, within two generations a combination of exploitative farming, poor land management, and sporadic drought would place Oklahoma at the desolate center of what in the 1930s would be called the dust bowl (see Chapter 24).

The West of Life and Legend

In 1893, four years after the last major tract of western Indian land, the Oklahoma Territory, was opened to non-Indian settlement, a young Wisconsin historian, Frederick Jackson Turner, delivered a lecture entitled "The Significance of the Frontier in American History." "[T]he frontier has gone," declared Turner, "and with its going has closed the first period of American history." Although Turner's assertion that the frontier was closed was based on a Census Bureau announcement, it was inaccurate (more western land would be settled in the twentieth century than in the nineteenth). But his linking of economic opportunity with the transformation of the trans-Mississippi West caught the popular imagination and launched a new school of historical inquiry into the effects of the frontier on U.S. history.

Scholars now recognize that many parts of Turner's "frontier thesis," particularly its ethnocentric omission of Native Americans' claims to the land, were inaccurate. Yet his idealized view of the West did reflect ideas popular among his contemporaries in the 1890s. As farmers, miners, ranchers, Indian agents, and prostitutes had pursued their varied activities in the real West, a parallel legendary West had taken deep root in the American imagination. In the nineteenth century, this mythic West was a product of novels, songs, and paintings. In the twentieth century, it would be perpetuated by movies, radio programs, and television shows. The legend merits attention, for its evolution is fascinating and its influence has been far-reaching.

The American Adam and the Dime-Novel Hero In the early biographies of frontiersmen like Daniel Boone and in the wilderness novels of James Fenimore Cooper, the western hero's personal development sometimes parallels, but more often runs counter to, the interests of society. Mid-nineteenth-century writers, extending the theme of the western wilderness as an alternative to society, presented the frontiersman as a kind of mythic American Adam— simple, virtuous, and innocent—untainted by a corrupt social order. For example, an early biographer of Kit Carson, the Kentucky-born guide who made one of the first recorded crossings of California's Mojave Desert in 1830, depicted him as a perfect antidote to the evils of refined society, an individual of "genuine simplicity, . . . truthfulness . . . [and] bravery." At the end of Mark Twain's *Huckleberry Finn,* Huck rejects the constraints of settled society as represented by Aunt Sally and heads west with the declaration, "I reckon I got to light out for the territory ahead of the rest, because Aunt Sally she's going to adopt me and sivilize me, and I can't stand it. I been there before."

In this version of the legend, the West is a place of adventure, romance, or contemplation where one can escape from society and its pressures.

But even as this conception of the myth was being popularized, another powerful theme had emerged as well. The authors of the dime novels of the 1860s and 1870s offered the image of the western frontiersman as a new masculine ideal, the tough guy who fights for truth and honor. In *Buffalo Bill: King of the Border Men* (1869), a dime novel loosely based on real-life William F. "Buffalo Bill" Cody, Edward Judson (who published under the name Ned Buntline) created an idealized hero who is a powerful moral force as he drives off treacherous Indians and rounds up villainous cattle rustlers.

Cody himself, playing upon the public fascination with cowboys, organized his own **Wild West Show** in 1883. In the show, which toured the East Coast and Europe, cowboys engaged in mock battles with Indians, reinforcing the dime-novel image of the West as an arena of moral encounter where virtue always triumphed.

Revitalizing the Frontier Legend
Eastern writers and artists eagerly embraced both versions of the myth—the West as a place of escape from society and the West as a stage on which the moral conflicts confronting society were played out. Three young members of the eastern establishment, Theodore Roosevelt, Frederic Remington, and Owen Wister, spent much time in the West in the 1880s, and each was intensely affected by the adventure.

Each man found precisely what he was looking for. The frontier that Roosevelt glorified in such books as *The Winning of the West* (four volumes, 1889–1896), and that Remington portrayed in his statues and paintings, was a stark physical and moral environment that stripped away all social artifice and tested each individual's character. Drawing on a popular version of English scientist Charles Darwin's evolutionary theory, which characterized life as a struggle in which only the fittest survived, Roosevelt and Remington exalted the disappearing frontier as the proving ground for a new kind of virile manhood and the last outpost of an honest and true social order.

This version of the frontier myth reached its apogee in **Owen Wister**'s enormously popular novel *The Virginian* (1902), later reincarnated as a 1929 Gary Cooper movie and a 1960s television series. In Wister's tale, the elemental physical and social environment of the Great Plains produces individuals like his unnamed cowboy hero, "the Virginian," an honest, strong, and compassionate man, quick to help the weak and fight the wicked. The Virginian is one of nature's aristocrats—ill-educated and unsophisticated but tough, steady, and deeply moral. The Virginian sums up his own moral code in describing his view of God's justice: "He plays a square game with us." For Wister, as for Roosevelt and Remington, the cowboy was the Christian knight on the Plains, indifferent to material gain as he upheld virtue, pursued justice, and attacked evil.

Needless to say, the western myth was far removed from the reality of the West. Critics delighted in pointing out that not one scene in *The Virginian* showed the hard physical labor of the cattle range. The idealized version of the West also glossed over the darker underside of frontier expansion—the brutalities of Indian warfare, the forced removal of the Indians to reservations, the racist discrimination against Mexican-Americans and blacks, the risks and perils of commercial agriculture and cattle-raising, and the boom-and-bust mentality rooted in the selfish exploitation of natural resources.

Further, the myth obscured the complex links between the settlement of the frontier and the emergence of the United States as a major industrialized nation increasingly tied to a global economy. Eastern and foreign capitalists controlled large-scale mining, cattle, and agricultural operations in the West. The technical know-how of industrial America underlay the marvels of western agricultural productivity. Without the railroad, that quintessential symbol of the new industrial order, the transformation of the West would have been far slower.

Beginning a National Parks Movement

Despite its one-sided and idealized vision, Owen Wister's celebration of the western experience reinforced a growing recognition that many unique features of the western landscape were being threatened by overeager entrepreneurs. One important byproduct of the western legend was a surge of public support for creating national parks and the beginning of an organized conservation movement.

Those who went west in the 1860s and 1870s to map the rugged terrain of the High Plains and the Rocky Mountains were often awed by the natural beauty of the landscape. Major **John Wesley Powell,** the one-armed veteran of the Civil War who charted the Colorado River through the Grand Canyon in 1869, waxed euphoric about its towering rock formations and powerful cataracts. "A beautiful view is presented. The river turns sharply to the east, and seems enclosed by a wall, set with a million brilliant gems. . . . On coming nearer, we find fountains bursting from the rock, high overhead, and the spray in the sunshine forms the gems which bedeck the way."

In his important study, *Report on the Lands of the Arid Regions of the United States* (1878), Powell argued that settlers needed to change their pattern of settlement and readjust their expectations about the use of water in the dry terrain west of the hundredth meridian. Recognizing that incoming farmers had often mistakenly believed that rain would miraculously follow the plow, Powell called for public ownership and governmental control of watersheds, irrigation, and public lands, a request that went largely unheeded.

Around the time Powell was educating Congress about the arid nature of the far West, a group of adventurers led by General Henry D. Washburn visited the hot springs and geysers near the Yellowstone River in northwestern Wyoming and eastern Montana. They were stunned by what they saw. "You can stand in the valley of the Yosemite [the California park land protected by Congress in 1864]," wrote one of the party, "and look up its mile of vertical granite, and distinctly recall its minutest feature; but amid the canyon and falls, the boiling springs and sulphur mountain, and, above all, the mud volcano and the geysers of the Yellowstone, your memory becomes filled and clogged with objects new in experience, wonderful in extent, and possessing unlimited grandeur and beauty." Overwhelmed by the view, the Washburn explorers abandoned their plan to claim the area for the Northern Pacific Railroad and instead petitioned Congress to protect it from settlement, occupancy, and sale. Congress responded in 1872 by creating **Yellowstone National Park** to "provide for the preservation . . . for all time, [of] mineral deposits, natural curiosities, or wonders within said park . . . in their natural condition." In doing so, they excluded the Native Americans who had long considered the area a prime hunting range.

These first steps to conserve a few of the West's unique natural sites reflected the beginning of a changed awareness of the environment. In his influential study *Man and*

Nature in 1864, **George Perkins Marsh,** an architect and politician from Vermont, had attacked the view that nature existed to be tamed and conquered. Cautioning Americans to curb their destructive use of the landscape, he warned the public to change its ways. "Man," he wrote, "is everywhere a disturbing agent. Wherever he plants his foot, the harmonies of nature are turned to discords."

Marsh's plea for conservation found its most eloquent support in the work of **John Muir,** a Scottish immigrant who had grown up in Wisconsin. Temporarily blinded by an accident, Muir left for San Francisco in 1869 and quickly fell in love with the redwood forests. For the next forty years, he tramped the rugged mountains of the West and campaigned for their preservation. A romantic at heart, he struggled to experience the wilderness at its most elemental level. Once trekking high in the Rockies during a summer storm, he climbed the tallest pine he could find and swayed back and forth in the raging wind.

Muir became the late nineteenth century's most articulate publicist for wilderness protection. "Climb the mountains and get their good tidings," he advised city-dwellers. "Nature's peace will flow into you as the sunshine into the trees. The winds will blow their freshness into you, and the storms their energy, while cares will drop off like autumn leaves." Muir's spirited campaign to protect the wilderness contributed strongly to the establishment of Yosemite National Park in 1890. Two years later, the Sierra Club, an organization created to encourage the enjoyment and protection of the wilderness in the mountain regions of the Pacific coast, made Muir its first president.

The precedent established by the creation of Yellowstone National Park remained ambiguous well into the twentieth century. Other parks that preserved the high rugged landforms of the West were often chosen because Congress viewed the sites as worthless for other purposes. Awareness of the need for biological conservation would not emerge until later in the twentieth century (see Chapter 21).

Ironically, despite the crusades of Muir, Powell, and Marsh to educate the public about conservation, the campaign for wilderness preservation reaffirmed the image of the West as a unique region whose magnificent landscape produced tough individuals of superior ability. Overlooking the senseless violence and ruthless exploitation of the land, contemporary writers, historians, and publicists proclaimed that the settlement of the final frontier marked a new stage in the history of civilization, and they kept alive the legend of the western frontier as a seedbed of American virtues.

CONCLUSION

The image of the mythic West has long obscured the transformation of people and landscape that took place there in the second half of the nineteenth century. Precisely because industrialization, urbanization, and immigration were altering the rest of the nation in unsettling ways (see Chapters 18 and 19), many Americans embraced the legend of the West as a visionary, uncomplicated, untainted Eden of social simplicity and moral clarity. The mythic West represented what the entire society had once been like (or so Americans chose to believe), before the advent of cities, factories, and masses of immigrants.

But the reality of westward expansion was more complex than the mythmakers acknowledged. Under the banner of economic opportunity and individual achievement, nineteenth-century Americans used the army to subdue the Indians, undermine their traditional way of life, and drive them onto reservations. They also ruthlessly exploited the region's vast natural resources. In less than three decades, they killed off the enormous buffalo herds, tore up the prairie sod, and littered parts of the landscape with mining debris.

Thus the mythic view of the frontier West as the arena for society building and economic opportunity obscured the dark side of the expansion onto the Great Plains and beyond. Despite the promise of the Homestead Act, which offered 160 acres of free land to those who would settle on it for five years, much of the best land had been given to railroads to encourage their expansion. Speculators had grabbed other prime locations. Homesteaders were often forced to settle on poorer quality tracts in areas where rainfall was marginal. In many places, large business enterprises in mining, ranching, and agribusiness, financed by eastern and European bankers, shoved aside the small entrepreneur and took control of the choicest natural resources.

Nevertheless, the settlement of the vast internal continental land did reinforce the popular image of the United States as a land of unprecedented economic opportunity and as a seedbed for democracy. Although the exclusion of blacks, Indians, and Spanish-speaking Americans belied the voiced commitment to an open society, the founding of new towns, the creation of new territorial and state governments, and the interaction of peoples of different races and ethnicities tested these ideas and, with time, forced their rethinking. The increasing willingness to give women the vote in many of the new western states would spread within the next two decades.

Although the persistence of the mythic view of the West served to hide the more ruthless and destructive features of western expansionism, the experiences gained from settling the interior territories and the utilization of the region's extensive physical resources led to the beginnings of the conservation movement and a reassessment of traditional American views of the environment. By the turn of the century, the thriving farms, ranches, mines, and cities of that region would help make the United States into one of the world's most prosperous nations.

18

The Rise of Industrial America, 1865–1900

CHAPTER OUTLINE

The Rise of Corporate America   Stimulating Economic Growth
The New South   Factories and the Work Force   Labor Unions
and Industrial Conflict

THE RISE OF CORPORATE AMERICA

In the early nineteenth century, the corporate form of business organization had been used to raise large amounts of start-up capital for transportation enterprises such as turnpikes and canals. By selling stocks and bonds to raise money, the corporation separated the company's managers, who guided its day-to-day operation, from its owners. After the Civil War, American business leaders pioneered new forms of corporate organization that combined innovative technologies, creative management structures, and limited liability should the enterprise fail. The rise of the giant corporation is a story of risk-taking and innovation as well as of conspiracy and corruption.

The Character of Industrial Change   Six features dominated the world of large-scale manufacturing after the Civil War: first, the exploitation of immense coal deposits as a source of cheap energy; second, the rapid spread of technological innovation in transportation, communication, and factory systems; third, the need for enormous numbers of new workers who could be carefully controlled; fourth, the constant pressure on firms to compete tooth-and-nail by cutting costs and prices, as well as the impulse to eliminate rivals and create monopolies; fifth, the relentless drop in prices (a stark contrast to the inflation of other eras); and finally, the failure of the money supply to keep pace with productivity, a development that drove up interest rates and restricted the availability of credit.

All six factors were closely related. The great coal deposits in Pennsylvania, West Virginia, and Kentucky provided cheap energy to fuel railroad and factory growth. New technologies stimulated productivity and catalyzed breathtaking industrial expansion. Technology also enabled manufacturers to cut costs and hire cheap unskilled or semiskilled labor. Cost cutting enabled firms to undersell one another, destroy weaker competitors, and consolidate themselves into stronger, more efficient, and more ruthless firms. At least until the mid-1890s, cheap energy, cost reduction, new technology, and fierce competition forced down overall price levels.

But almost everyone struggled terribly during the depression years, when the government debated whether it should get involved but did nothing to relieve distress. "The sufferings of the working classes are daily increasing," wrote a Philadelphia worker in 1874. "Famine has broken into the home of many of us, and is at the door of all." Above all, business leaders' unflagging drive to maximize efficiency both created colossal fortunes at the top of the economic ladder and forced millions of wage earners to live near the subsistence level.

Out of the new industrial system poured clouds of haze and soot, as well as the first tantalizing trickle of what would become an avalanche of consumer goods. In turn, mounting demands for consumer goods stimulated heavy industry's production of capital goods—machines to boost farm and factory output even further. Together with the railroads, the corporations that manufactured capital goods, refined petroleum, and made steel became driving forces in the nation's economic growth.

| Railroad Innovations | Competition among the aggressive and innovative capitalists who headed American heavy industry was intense. As the post–Civil War era opened, nowhere was it more intense than among |

the nation's railroads. By 1900, 193,000 miles of railroad track crisscrossed the United States—more than in all of Europe including Russia. These rail lines connected every state in the Union and opened up an immense new internal market. Most important, railroad companies pioneered crucial aspects of large-scale corporate enterprise. These included the creation of national distribution and marketing systems, and the formation of new organizational and management structures.

Railroad entrepreneurs such as Collis P. Huntington of the Central Pacific Railroad, **Jay Gould** of the Union Pacific, and James J. Hill of the Northern Pacific faced enormous financial and organizational problems. To raise the staggering sums necessary for laying track, building engines, and buying out competitors, railroads obtained generous land and loan subsidies from federal, state, and local governments (see Chapter 17). Even so, the larger lines had to borrow heavily by selling stocks and bonds to the public. Bond holders earned a fixed rate of interest; stockholders received dividends only when the company earned a profit. By 1900, the yearly interest repayments required by the combined debt of all U.S. railroads (which stood at an astounding $5.1 billion—nearly five times that of the federal government) cut heavily into their earnings.

In addition to developing ways to raise large amounts of capital, the railroads created new systems for collecting and using information. To coordinate the complex flow of cars across the country, railroads relied heavily on the magnetic telegraph, invented in 1837. To improve efficiency, the railroads set up clearly defined, hierarchical organizational structures and divided their lines into separate geographic units, each with its own superintendent. Elaborate accounting systems documented the cost of every operation for each division, from coal consumption to the repair of engines and cars. Using these reports, railroad officials could set rates and accurately predict profits as early as the 1860s, a time when most businesses had no idea of their total profit until they closed their books at year's end. Railroad management innovations thus became a model for many other businesses seeking a national market.

CHRONOLOGY, 1865–1900

1859 • First oil well drilled in Titusville, Pennsylvania.

1866 • National Labor Union founded.

1869 • Transcontinental railroad completed.
Knights of Labor organized.

1870 • John D. Rockefeller establishes Standard Oil Company.

1873 • Panic of 1873 triggers a depression lasting until 1879.

1876 • Alexander Graham Bell patents the telephone.

1877 • Edison invents phonograph.
Railway workers stage first nationwide strike.

1879 • Henry George, *Progress and Poverty.*
Edison perfects incandescent lamp.

1882 • Standard Oil Trust established.
Edison opens first electric power station in New York City.
Chinese Exclusion Act.

1883 • William Graham Sumner, *What Social Classes Owe to Each Other.*
Lester Frank Ward, *Dynamic Sociology.*

1886 • American Federation of Labor (AFL) formed.
Haymarket riot in Chicago.

1887 • Interstate Commerce Act establishes Interstate Commerce Commission.

1888 • Edward Bellamy, *Looking Backward.*

1889 • Andrew Carnegie, "The Gospel of Wealth."

1890 • Sherman Anti-Trust Act.
United Mine Workers formed.

1892 • Standard Oil of New Jersey and General Electric formed.
Homestead Strike.
Columbian Exposition in Chicago.
Miners strike at Coeur d'Alene, Idaho.

1893 • Panic of 1893 triggers a depression lasting until 1897.

1894 • Pullman Palace Car workers strike.

1901 • J. Pierpont Morgan organizes United States Steel.

Consolidating the Railroad Industry   The expansion and consolidation of railroading reflected both the ingenuity and the dishonesty flourishing on the corporate management scene. Although by the 1870s railroads had replaced the patchwork of canal and stagecoach operations that dominated domestic transportation before the Civil War, the industry remained chaotic. Hundreds of small companies used different standards for car couplers, rails, track width, and engine size. Financed by large eastern and British banks, Huntington, Gould, and others devoured these smaller lines to create large, integrated track networks. In the Northeast

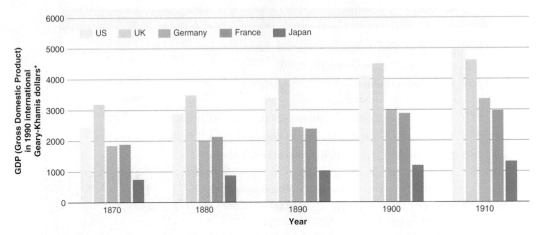

* 1990 international Geary-Khamis dollars represent the monetary values of the output of the final goods and services produced in a country in one year converted into 1990 dollars at the exchange rate which would pertain if the goods and services had the same prices in all countries (purchasing power parity). See the statistical definition at the UN site: http://unstats.un.org/unsd/methods/icp/ipc7_htm.htm

Figure 18.1 Late Nineteenth-Century Economic Growth in Global Perspective

four major trunk lines were completed. West of the Mississippi five great lines—the Union Pacific (1869); the Northern Pacific (1883); the Atchison, Topeka, and Santa Fe (1883); the Southern Pacific (1883); and the Great Northern (1893)—controlled most of the track by 1893.

Huntington, Gould, and the other larger-than-life figures who reorganized and expanded the railroad industry in the 1870s and 1880s were often depicted by their contemporaries as villains and robber barons who manipulated stock markets and company policies to line their own pockets. For example, newspaper publisher Joseph Pulitzer called Jay Gould, the short, secretive president of the Union Pacific, "one of the most sinister figures that have ever flitted batlike across the vision of the American people." Recent historians, however, have pointed out that the great industrialists were a diverse group. Although some were ironfisted pirates who engaged in fraudulent practices, others were upstanding businessmen who managed their companies with sophistication and innovation. Indeed, some of their ideas were startling in their originality and inventiveness.

The massive systems created by these entrepreneurs became the largest business enterprises in the world, towering over state and federal governments in the size and scale of their operations. As they consolidated small railroads into a few interlocking systems, these masterminds pioneered the most advanced methods of accounting and large-scale organization. They also standardized all basic equipment and facilities, from engines and cars to automatic couplers, air brakes, signal systems, and outhouses. In 1883, independently of the federal government, the railroads corrected scheduling problems by dividing the country into four time zones. In May 1886 all railroads shifted simultaneously to the new standard 4'8½" gauge track. Finally, cooperative billing arrangements enabled the railroads to ship cars from other roads, including dining and sleeping cars owned by the Pullman Palace Car Company, at uniform rates nationwide.

Abusive Monopoly Power

This Puck *cartoon depicts financiers Jay Gould (left) and Cornelius Vanderbilt (right) and suggests that their manipulation of markets and their ownership of railroads, telegraph companies, and newspapers is powerful enough to strangle Uncle Sam.*

But the systemization and consolidation of the railroads had its costs. Heavy indebtedness, overextended systems, and crooked business practices forced the railroads to compete recklessly with each other for traffic. They cut rates for large shippers, offered special arrangements for handling bulk goods, showered free passes on politicians, and granted substantial rebates and kickbacks to favored clients. None of these tactics, however, shored up the railroads' precarious financial position. And the continuous push to expand drove some overbuilt lines into bankruptcy.

Caught in the middle of the railroads' tug-of-war and stung by exorbitant rates and secret kickbacks, farmers and small business owners turned to state governments for help. In the 1870s many midwestern state legislatures responded by outlawing rate discrimination. Initially upheld by the Supreme Court, these and other decisions were negated in the 1880s when the Court ruled that states could not regulate interstate commerce. In response in 1887, Congress passed the **Interstate Commerce Act.** A five-member Interstate Commerce Commission (ICC) was established to oversee the practices of interstate railroads. The law banned monopolistic activity like pooling, rebates, and discriminatory short-distance rates.

The railroads challenged the commission's rulings in the federal courts. Of the sixteen cases brought to the Supreme Court before 1905, the justices found in favor of the railroads in all but one, essentially nullifying the ICC's regulatory clout. The Hepburn Act (see Chapter 21), passed in 1906, strengthened the ICC by finally empowering it to set rates.

The railroads' vicious competition weakened in 1893 when a national depression forced a number of roads into the hands of **J. Pierpont Morgan** and other investment bankers. Morgan, a massively built man with piercing eyes and a commanding presence, took over the weakened systems, reorganized their administration, refinanced their debts, and built intersystem alliances. By 1906, thanks to the bankers' centralized management, seven giant networks controlled two-thirds of the nation's rail mileage.

Applying the Lessons of the Railroads to Steel   The close connections between railroad expansion, which absorbed millions of tons of steel for tracks, and the growth of corporate organization and management are well illustrated in the career of **Andrew Carnegie.** Born in Scotland, Carnegie immigrated to America in 1848 at the age of twelve. His first job as a bobbin boy in a Pittsburgh textile mill paid only $1.20 a week. Although he worked a sixty-hour week, the aspiring youngster enrolled in a night course to learn bookkeeping. The following year, Carnegie became a Western Union messenger boy. Taking over when the telegraph operators wanted a break, he soon became the city's fastest telegraph operator. Because he had to decode the messages for every major business in Pittsburgh, Carnegie gained an insider's view of their operations.

Carnegie's big break came in 1852 when Tom Scott, superintendent of the Pennsylvania Railroad's western division, hired him as his secretary and personal telegrapher. When Scott became vice president of the Pennsylvania Railroad seven years later, the twenty-four-year-old Carnegie took over as head of the line's western division. A daring innovator, Carnegie, in his six years as division chief, used the complex cost-analysis techniques developed by Scott to more than double the road's mileage and quadruple its traffic. He slashed commuter fares to keep ridership at capacity and developed various cost-cutting techniques. Having invested his earnings in the railroads, by 1868 Carnegie was earning more than $56,000 a year from his investments, a substantial fortune in that era.

In the early 1870s Carnegie decided to build his own steel mill. His connections within the railroad industry, the country's largest purchaser of steel, ensured his success. Starting with his first mill, he introduced a production technology named after its English inventor, Henry Bessemer, which shot a blast of air through an enormous crucible of molten iron to burn off carbon and impurities. Adopting this new technology and combining it with the cost-analysis approach learned from his railroad experience, Carnegie became the first steelmaker to know the actual production cost of each ton of steel.

Carnegie's philosophy was deceptively simple: "Watch the costs, and the profits will take care of themselves." Using rigorous cost accounting and limiting wage increases to his workers, he lowered his production costs and prices below those of his competitors. When these tactics did not drive them out of business, he was not above asking for favors from his railroad-president friends or giving "commissions" to railroad purchasing agents to win business.

Figure 18.2 Iron and Steel Production, 1875–1915

New technologies, improved plant organization, economies of scale, and the vertical integration of production brought a dramatic spurt in iron and steel production. *Source:* Historical Statistics of the United States. *Note:* short ton = 2,000 pounds.

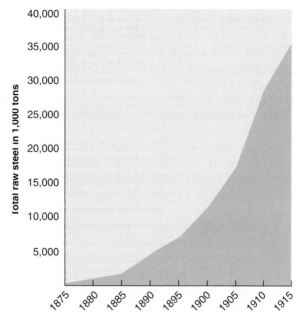

As output climbed, Carnegie discovered the benefits of **vertical integration**—that is, controlling all aspects of manufacturing, from extracting raw materials to selling the finished product. In Carnegie's case, this control embraced every stage from the mining and smelting of ore to the selling of steel rails. Carnegie Steel thus became the classic example of how sophisticated new technology could be combined with innovative management (and brutally low wages) to create a mass-production system that could slash consumer prices.

The management of daily operations by his close associates left Carnegie free to pursue philanthropic activities. While still in his early thirties, Carnegie resolved to donate his money to charitable projects. In his lifetime, he gave more than $300 million to libraries, universities, and international-peace causes.

By 1900, Carnegie Steel, employing twenty thousand people, had become the world's largest industrial corporation. Carnegie's competitors, worried about his domination of the market, decided to buy him out. In 1901, J. Pierpont Morgan, who controlled Federal Steel, asked Charles Schwab, Carnegie Steel's president, to inquire what Carnegie wanted for his share of Carnegie Steel. The next day Carnegie gave Schwab a penciled note asking for nearly half a billion dollars. Morgan's response was simple: "Tell Carnegie I accept his price." Combining Carnegie's companies with Federal Steel, Morgan set up the United States Steel Corporation, the first business capitalized at more than $1 billion. The corporation, made up of two hundred member companies employing 168,000 people, marked a new scale in industrial enterprise.

Throughout his chain of corporate-world triumphs, Carnegie consistently portrayed his success as the result of self-discipline and hard work. The full story was more complex. Carnegie did not mention his uncanny ability to see the larger picture, his cleverness in hiring talented associates who would drive themselves (and the company's factory workers) mercilessly, his ingenuity in transferring organizational systems and cost-accounting methods from railroads to steel, and his callousness in keeping wages as low as possible. To a public unaware of corporate management techniques, however, Carnegie's success reaffirmed the openness of the American economic system. For the new immigrants flooding the nation's shores, Carnegie's career gave credence to the idea that anyone might rise from rags to riches.

The Trust: Creating New Forms of Corporate Organization   Between 1870 and 1900, the same fierce competition that had stimulated consolidation in the railroad and steel industries also swept the oil, salt, sugar, tobacco, and meatpacking industries. Like steel, these highly competitive businesses required large capital investments. Entrepreneurs in each industry therefore raced to reduce costs, lower prices, and drive their rivals out of the market. Chicago meatpackers Philip Armour and Gustavus Swift, for example, used every part of the animal. Hides were tanned into leather, bones became fertilizer, and hooves were turned into gelatin. When lowering costs failed to drive out rivals, new organizational methods were pioneered to control competition and preserve market share.

The evolution of the oil industry illustrates the process by which new corporate structures evolved. After Edwin L. Drake drilled the first successful petroleum (or "crude-oil") well in 1859 near Titusville in northwestern Pennsylvania, competitors rushed into the business, sinking wells and erecting small refineries nearby. Petroleum was distilled into oil, which soon replaced animal tallow as the major lubricant, and into kerosene, which became the leading fuel for household and public lighting. By the 1870s the landscape near Pittsburgh and Cleveland, the sites of the first discoveries, was littered with rickety drilling rigs, assorted collection tanks, and ramshackle refineries. Oil spills were a constant problem. "So much oil is produced," reported one Pennsylvania newspaper in 1861, "that it is impossible to care for it, and thousands of barrels are running into the creek; the surface of the river is covered with oil for miles."

In this rush for riches, **John D. Rockefeller,** a young Cleveland merchant, gradually achieved dominance. Although he did not share Andrew Carnegie's outgoing personality, the solemn Rockefeller resembled the opportunistic steelmaker in other respects. Having gotten his start as a bookkeeper, Rockefeller opened his first refinery in 1863. Like Carnegie, Rockefeller had a passion for cost cutting and efficiency. When he became the head of the Standard Oil Company in 1873, he scrutinized every aspect of its operation. In one case, he insisted that a manager find 750 missing barrel stoppers. He realized that in a mass-production enterprise, small changes could save thousands of dollars.

Rockefeller resembled Carnegie, too, in his ability to understand the inner workings of an entire industry and the benefits of vertical integration. The firm that controlled the shipment of oil between the well and the refinery and between the refinery and the retailers, he realized, could dominate the industry. In 1872 he purchased his own tanker cars and obtained not only a 10 percent rebate from the railroads for hauling his oil shipments but also a kickback on his competitors' shipments. When new pipeline technology became available, Rockefeller set up his own massive interregional pipeline network.

Like Carnegie, Rockefeller aggressively forced out his competitors. When local refineries rejected his offers to buy them out, he priced his products below cost and strangled their businesses. When rival firms teamed up against him, Rockefeller set up a pool—an agreement among several companies—that established production quotas and fixed prices. By 1879 Rockefeller had seized control of 90 percent of the country's oil-refining capacity.

Worried about competition, Rockefeller in 1882 decided to eliminate it by establishing a new form of corporate organization, the **Standard Oil Trust.** In place of the "pool" or verbal agreement among companies to control prices and markets, which lacked legal status, the trust created an umbrella corporation that ran them all. To implement his trust, Rockefeller and his associates persuaded the stockholders of forty companies to exchange their stock for trust certificates. Under this arrangement, stockholders retained their share of the trust's profits while enabling the trust to control production. Within three years the Standard Oil Trust had consolidated crude-oil buying throughout its member firms and slashed the number of refineries in half. In this way Rockefeller integrated the petroleum industry both vertically, by controlling every function from production to local retailing, and horizontally, by merging the competing oil companies into one giant system.

Taking a leaf from Rockefeller's book, companies in the copper, sugar, whiskey, lead, and other industries established their own trust arrangements. By limiting the number of competitors, the trusts created an *oligopoly,* the market condition that exists when a small number of sellers can greatly influence prices. But their unscrupulous tactics, semimonopolistic control, and sky-high earnings provoked a public outcry. Both major political parties denounced them in the presidential election of 1888.

Fearful that the trusts would stamp out all competition, Congress, under the leadership of Senator John Sherman of Ohio, passed the **Sherman Anti-Trust Act** in 1890. The Sherman Act outlawed trusts and any other monopolies that fixed prices in restraint of trade and slapped violators with fines of up to five thousand dollars and a year in jail. But the act failed to define clearly either *trust* or *restraint of trade.* The government prosecuted only eighteen antitrust suits between 1890 and 1904. When Standard Oil's structure was challenged in 1892, its lawyers simply reorganized the trust as an enormous holding company. Unlike a trust, which literally owned other businesses, a holding company simply owned a controlling share of the stock of one or more firms. The new board of directors for Standard Oil (New Jersey), the new holding company, made more money than ever.

The Supreme Court further hamstrung congressional antitrust efforts by interpreting the Sherman Act in ways sympathetic to big business. In 1895, for example, the federal government brought suit against the sugar trust in *United States* v. *E. C. Knight Company.* It argued that the Knight firm, which controlled more than 90 percent of all U.S. sugar refining, operated in illegal restraint of trade. Asserting that manufacturing was not interstate commerce and ignoring the company's vast distribution network that enabled it to dominate the market, the Court threw out the suit. Thus vindicated, corporate mergers and consolidations surged ahead at the turn of the century. By 1900, these mammoth firms accounted for nearly two-fifths of the capital invested in the nation's manufacturing sector.

STIMULATING ECONOMIC GROWTH

Although large-scale corporate enterprise significantly increased the volume of manufactured goods in the late nineteenth century, it alone did not account for the colossal growth of the U.S. economy. Other factors proved equally important, including new

Electricity

Of all the technological achievements of the nineteenth century, none seemed more inspiring or mysterious than the ability to generate electricity. Using Alessandro Volta's discovery that chemical reactions in batteries produced a weak electric current, Samuel F. B. Morse had used batteries to power his telegraph in 1837. Alexander Graham Bell followed suit with his telephone in 1876. But higher voltages were needed to run lighting systems and motors. Michael Faraday in England and Joseph Henry in America discovered in 1831 that a rotating magnet surrounded by a conducting wire would produce a continuous flow of electric current. After the Civil War, American inventors used this discovery to develop powerful generators to run incandescent lights (1879), to power motors to run trolley cars (1888), and to drive machines in factories. For many Americans, the ability to harness electricity marked the subjugation of nature and indicated the progress of American civilization.

Nowhere did the knowledge of electricity seem more impressive than its promise to reveal the secrets of the human body. X-rays, discovered in 1895 by the German physicist Wilhelm Roentgen and developed into a practical hospital machine a year later by Thomas Edison, enabled doctors to see inside the body. Physicians discovered that the workings of the nervous system and the brain itself depended on electrical impulses. In short, electrical science, given the breadth of its applications and its power to provide insights into nature, seemed close to being the embodiment of super-natural power. It was no accident that Edison was known as the "wizard of Menlo Park," where his research laboratory was located.

The spread of electric lighting illustrates how technological advances pushed innovation. Thomas Edison's vision went far beyond the development of a practical light bulb. He conceived of an interrelated system of power plants, transmission lines, and light fixtures, all to be produced by companies that he had established. Edison's system of direct current lighting (DC—which flowed in only one direction in the wires) required that users be located near power plants. But in 1886 George Westinghouse set up a competing company that used the Italian inventor Nikola Tesla's discovery that alternating current (AC—which cycled back and forth within the wires) could send high-voltage electricity efficiently over long distances. Competition between the two systems was finally resolved in 1896 when Edison's successor company, General Electric, agreed to share its patents with the Westinghouse Company. With electric current now standardized as 110 volts AC at 60 Hertz (60 cycles per second), dozens of other inventors developed electric motors, spotlights, electric signs, water pumps, elevators, and household appliances—all drawing power from the same power grid. Only twenty years after the first power station had been built, electrification had started to transform everyday life.

By 1898, when the city of London had sixty-two different utilities that produced thirty-two different voltage levels, American companies had created a unified national electrical system with standardized voltages, and the United States had established itself as a world leader in electrical technology. The remarkable achievements of the American electrical industry resulted from a combination of factors. Skilled inventors such as Edison, Westinghouse, and Frank Sprague, who developed electric motors for trolley and subway cars, were critical. But the efforts might never have made it out of the laboratories without financiers, such as J. P. Morgan and Henry Villard, who funded the enormous investment in electric generators, power plants, and transmission lines. A third factor was the independence of large corporations like General Electric and Westinghouse, which were able to operate nationally and avoid conflicting state regulations. Operating as regional monopolies, these corporations standardized voltage, alternating current, and electrical fixtures nationwide. Finally, the pooling of patents was crucial. The American patent system, by granting inventors property rights in their inventions and by publicly identifying how the discoveries worked, stimulated technological innovation in general.

At first, electricity was very expensive, and the general public could not afford the cost of wiring homes. Still, even confined to the public sphere, the establishment of a national electrical system was one of the greatest technological innovations of the century. Electric streetcars and subways, public lighting systems, and electric elevators transformed urban America, allowing the construction of skyscrapers and the quick transportation of millions of people. The electrification of factories extended the workday into the night and made work safer. In the following decades, electrification made possible the invention of lighting systems, fans, washing machines, and a host of other devices to ease the drudgery of everyday life.

In the twentieth century, some shortcomings in Americans' love affair with electricity became obvious. In the early years, urban electrification accentuated the differences between city and country life. After World War II, massive power failures showed that the centralization of power distribution systems, first constructed as private monopolies between 1880 and 1932, made them vulnerable to failure when a subsystem problem cascaded throughout the network. The private ownership of power companies, now called utility companies, has enabled them at times to inflate energy prices for their own profit. Most electrical power in the United States today is produced from coal, a nonrenewable resource which also produces acid rain and air pollution. Nevertheless, the creation of a national system of electrical power generation paved the way for remarkable innovations, from lighting to televisions and computers, that remain today closely tied to America's sense of progress and material advancement.

Questions for Analysis

- Why did the early electrical inventions seem to mark the subjugation of nature?

- What technological breakthroughs paved the way for the widespread use of electricity for street lighting and transportation?

- Why did the standardization and consolidation of the electric industry take place more quickly in the United States than in England?

inventions, specialty production, and innovations in advertising and marketing. In fact, the resourcefulness of small enterprises, which combined innovative technology with new methods of advertising and merchandising, enabled many sectors of the economy to grow dramatically by adapting quickly to changing fashions and consumer preferences.

The Triumph of Technology

New inventions not only streamlined the manufacture of traditional products but also stimulated consumer demand by creating entirely new product lines. The development of a safe, practical way to generate electricity, for example, made possible a vast number of electrical motors, household appliances, and lighting systems.

Many of the major inventions that stimulated industrial output and underlay mass production in these years were largely hidden from public view. Few Americans had heard of the improved technologies that facilitated bottle making and glassmaking, canning, flour milling, match production, and petroleum refining. Fewer still knew much about the refrigerated railcars that enabled Gustavus Swift's company to slaughter beef in Chicago and ship it east or about the Bonsack cigarette-making machine that could roll 120,000 cigarettes a day, replacing sixty skilled handworkers.

The inventions that people did see were ones that changed the patterns of everyday life. Inventions like the sewing machine, mass-produced by the Singer Sewing Machine Company beginning in the 1860s (see Chapter 16); the telephone, developed by Alexander Graham Bell in 1876; and the light bulb, perfected by **Thomas A. Edison** in 1879, eased household drudgery and reshaped social interactions. With the advent of the sewing machine, many women were relieved of the tedium of sewing apparel by hand; inexpensive mass-produced clothing thus led to a considerable expansion in personal wardrobes. The spread of telephones—by 1900 the Bell Telephone Company had installed almost eight hundred thousand in the United States—not only transformed communication but also undermined social conventions for polite behavior that had been premised on face-to-face or written exchanges. The light bulb, by further freeing people from dependence on daylight, made it possible to shop after work.

In the eyes of many, Thomas A. Edison epitomized the inventive impulse and the capacity for creating new consumer products. Born in 1847 in Milan, Ohio, Edison, like Andrew Carnegie, had little formal education and got his start in the telegraphic industry. He also was a born salesman and self-promoter. When he modestly said that "genius is one percent inspiration and ninety-nine percent perspiration," he tacitly accepted the popular identification of himself as an inventing "wizard." Edison, moreover, shared Carnegie's vision of a large, interconnected industrial system resting on a foundation of technological innovation (see Technology and Culture: Electricity).

In his early work, Edison concentrated on the telegraph. His experimentation led to his first major invention, a stock-quotation printer, in 1868. The money earned from the patents on this machine enabled Edison to set up his first "invention factory" in Newark, New Jersey, a research facility that he moved to nearby Menlo Park in 1876. Assembling a staff that included university-trained scientists, Edison boastfully predicted "a minor invention every ten days, and a big one every six months."

Buoyed by the success and popularity of his invention in 1877 of a phonograph, or "sound writer" (*phono*: "sound"; *graph*: "writer"), Edison set out to develop a new filament for incandescent light bulbs. Characteristically, he announced his plans for an electricity-generation process before he perfected his inventions and then worked feverishly, testing hundreds of materials before he found a carbon filament that would glow dependably in a vacuum.

Edison realized that practical electrical lighting had to be part of a complete system containing generators, voltage regulators, electric meters, and insulated wiring and that the system needed to be easy to install and repair. It also had to be cheaper and more convenient than kerosene or natural gas lighting, its main competitors. In 1882, having built this system with the support of banker J. Pierpont Morgan, the Edison Illuminating Company opened a power plant in the heart of New York City's financial district, furnishing lighting for eighty-five buildings.

In the following years, Edison and his researchers pumped out invention after invention, including the mimeograph machine, the microphone, the motion-picture camera and film, and the storage battery. By the time of his death in 1931, he had patented 1,093 inventions and amassed an estate worth more than $6 million. Yet Edison's greatest achievement remained his laboratory at Menlo Park. A model for the industrial research labs later established by Kodak, General Electric, and Du Pont, Edison's laboratory demonstrated that the systematic use of science in support of industrial technology paid large dividends. Invention had become big business.

Specialized Production   Along with inventors, manufacturers of custom and specialized products such as machinery, jewelry, furniture, and women's clothes dramatically expanded economic output. Using skilled labor, these companies crafted one-of-a-kind or small batches of articles that ranged in size from large steam engines and machine tools to silverware, furniture, and custom-made dresses. Keenly attuned to innovations in technology and design, they constantly created new products tailored to the needs of individual buyers.

Although they were vastly different in terms of size and number of employees, Philadelphia's Baldwin Locomotive Works and small dressmaking shops were typical of flexible specialization displayed by small batch processors. Both faced sharp fluctuations in the demand for their products as well as the necessity of employing skilled workers to make small numbers of specialized items. Founded before the Civil War, by the 1890s the Baldwin Locomotive Works employed two thousand workers and produced about nine hundred engines a year. Each machine was custom-designed to meet the needs of its purchaser. Construction was systematized through precision plans for every part of an engine, but standardization was not possible since no single engine could meet the needs of every railroad.

Until the turn of the twentieth century, when ready-to-wear clothes came to dominate the market, most women's apparel was custom produced in small shops run by women proprietors. Unlike the tenement sweatshops that produced men's shirts and pants, dressmakers and milliners (a term derived from fancy goods vendors in sixteenth- and seventeenth-century Milan, Italy) paid good wages to highly skilled seamstresses. The small size of the shops together with the skill of the workers enabled them to shift styles quickly to follow the latest fashions.

Thus, alongside of the increasingly rationalized and bureaucratic big businesses like steel and oil in the late nineteenth century, American productivity was also stimulated by small producers who provided a variety of goods that supplemented the bulk-manufactured staples of everyday life.

Advertising and Marketing

As small and large factories alike spewed out an amazing array of new products, business leaders often discovered that their output exceeded what the market could absorb. This was particularly true in two kinds of businesses—those that manufactured devices for individual use such as sewing machines and farm implements, and those that mass-produced consumer goods such as matches, flour, soap, canned foods, and processed meats. Not surprisingly, these industries were trailblazers in developing advertising and marketing techniques. Strategies for whetting consumer demand and for differentiating one product from another represented a critical component of industrial expansion in the post–Civil War era.

The growth of the flour industry illustrates both the spread of mass production and the emergence of new marketing concepts. In the 1870s, the nation's flour mills adopted the most advanced European manufacturing technologies and installed continuous-process machines that graded, cleaned, hulled, ground, and packaged the product in one rapid operation. These companies, however, soon produced more flour than they could sell. To unload this excess, the mills thought up new product lines such as cake flours and breakfast cereals and sold them using easy-to-remember brand names like Quaker Oats.

Through the use of brand names, trademarks, guarantees, slogans, endorsements, and other gimmicks, manufacturers built demand for their products and won enduring consumer loyalty. Americans bought Ivory Soap, first made in 1879 by Procter and Gamble of Cincinnati, because of the absurdly overprecise but impressive pledge that it was "99 and 44/100ths percent pure." James B. "Buck" Duke's American Tobacco Company used trading cards, circulars, box-top premiums, prizes, testimonials, and scientific endorsements to convert Americans to cigarette smoking.

In the 1880s in the photographic field, George Eastman developed a paper-based photographic film as an alternative to the bulky, fragile glass plates then in use. Manufacturing a cheap camera for the masses, the Kodak, Eastman introduced a system whereby customers returned the one-hundred-exposure film and the camera to his Rochester factory. There, for a charge of ten dollars, the film was developed and printed, the camera reloaded, and everything shipped back. In marketing a new technology, Eastman had revolutionized an industry and democratized a visual medium previously confined to a few.

Economic Growth: Costs and Benefits

By 1900, the chaos of early industrial competition, when thousands of companies had struggled to enter a national market, had given way to the most productive economy in the world, supported by a legion of small, specialized companies and dominated by a few enormous ones. An industrial transformation that had originated in railroading and expanded to steel and petroleum had spread to every nook and cranny of American business and raised the United States to a position of world leadership.

For those who fell by the wayside in this era of spectacular economic growth, the cost could be measured in bankrupted companies and shattered dreams. John D. Rockefeller put things with characteristic bluntness when he said he wanted "only the big ones, only those who have already proved they can do a big business" in the Standard Oil Trust. "As for the others, unfortunately they will have to die."

The cost was high, too, for millions of American workers, immigrant and native-born alike. The vast expansion of new products was built on the backs of an army of laborers who were paid subsistence wages and who could be fired on a moment's no-tice when hard times or new technologies made them expendable.

Industrial growth often devastated the environment as well. Rivers fouled by oil or chemical waste, skies filled with clouds of soot, and a landscape littered with reek-ing garbage and toxic materials bore mute witness to the relentless drive for efficiency and profit.

The vast expansion of economic output brought social benefits as well, in the form of labor-saving products, lower prices, and advances in transportation and communi-cations. The benefits and liabilities sometimes seemed inextricably interconnected. The sewing machine, for example, created thousands of new factory jobs, made avail-able a wider variety of clothing, and eased the lives of millions of housewives. At the same time, it encouraged avaricious entrepreneurs to operate sweatshops in which the immigrant poor—often vulnerable young women—toiled long hours for pitifully low wages (see Chapter 21).

Whatever the final balance sheet of social gains and costs, one thing was clear: the United States had muscled its way onto the world stage as an industrial titan. The am-bition and drive of countless inventors, financiers, managerial innovators, and market-ing wizards had combined to lay the groundwork for a new social and economic order in the twentieth century.

THE NEW SOUTH

The South entered the industrial era far more slowly than the Northeast. As late as 1900, total southern cotton-mill output, for example, remained little more than half that of the mills within a thirty-mile radius of Providence, Rhode Island. Moreover, the South's $509 average per capita income was less than half that of northerners.

The reasons for the South's late economic blossoming are not hard to discern. The Civil War's physical devastation, racism, the scarcity of southern towns and cities, lack of capital, illiteracy, northern control of financial markets and patents, and a low rate of technological innovation crippled efforts by southern business leaders to promote industrialization. Economic progress was also impeded by the myth of the Lost Cause, which, through its nostalgic portrayal of pre–Civil War society, perpetuated an image of the South as traditional and unchanging. As a result, southern industrialization inched forward haltingly and was shaped in distinctive ways.

Obstacles to Economic Development   Much of the South's difficulty in industrializing arose from its lack of capital and the devastation of the Civil War. So many southern banks failed during the Civil War that by 1865 the South, with more than a quarter of the nation's population, possessed just 2 percent of its banks.

Federal government policies further restricted the expansion of the southern bank-ing system. The Republican-dominated wartime Congress, which had created a na-tional currency and banking structure, required anyone wishing to start a bank to have fifty thousand dollars in capital. Few southerners could meet this standard.

With banks in short supply, country merchants and storekeepers became bankers by default, lending supplies rather than cash to local farmers in return for a lien, or mortgage, on their crops (see Chapter 16). As farmers sank in debt, they increased their production of cotton and tobacco in an effort to stay afloat, and became trapped on the land. As a result, the labor needed for industrial expansion remained in short supply.

The shift from planting corn to specializing in either cotton or tobacco made small southern farmers particularly vulnerable to the fluctuations of commercial agriculture. When the price of cotton tumbled in national and international markets from eleven cents per pound in 1875 to less than five cents in 1894, well under the cost of production, many southern farmers grew desperate.

The South also continued to be the victim of federal policies designed to aid northern industry. High protective tariffs raised the price of machine technology imported from abroad; the demonetization of silver (see Chapter 20) further limited capital availability; and discriminatory railroad freight rates hiked the expense of shipping finished goods and raw materials.

The South's chronic shortage of funds affected the economy in indirect ways as well, by limiting the resources available for education. During Reconstruction northern philanthropists together with the Freedmen's Bureau, the American Missionary Association, and other relief agencies had begun a modest expansion of public schooling for both blacks and whites. But Georgia and many other southern states operated segregated schools and refused to tax property for school support until 1889. As a result, school attendance remained low, severely limiting the number of educated people able to staff technical and managerial positions in business and industry.

Southern states, like those in the North, often contributed the modest funds they had to war veterans' pensions. In this way, southern state governments built a white patronage system for Confederate veterans and helped reinforce southerners' idealization of the old Confederacy—the South's Lost Cause. As late as 1911, veterans' pensions in Georgia ate up 22 percent of the state's entire budget, leaving little for economic or educational development.

The New South Creed and Southern Industrialization   Despite the limited availability of private capital for investment in industrialization, energetic southern newspaper editors such as **Henry W. Grady** of the *Atlanta Constitution* and Henry Watterson of the *Louisville Courier Journal* championed the doctrine that became known as the New South creed. The South's rich coal and timber resources and cheap labor, they proclaimed in their papers, made it a natural site for industrial development.

The movement to industrialize the South gained momentum in the 1880s. To attract northern capital, southern states offered tax exemptions for new businesses, set up industrial and agricultural expositions, and leased prison convicts to serve as cheap labor. Florida, Texas, and other states gave huge tracts of lands to railroads, which expanded dramatically throughout the South and in turn stimulated the birth of new towns and villages. Other states sold forest and mineral rights on nearly 6 million acres of federal lands to speculators, mostly from the North, who significantly expanded the production of iron, sulfur, coal, and lumber.

Following the lead of their northern counterparts, the southern iron and steel industries expanded as well. Birmingham, Alabama, founded in 1871 in the heart of a region blessed with rich deposits of coal, limestone, and iron ore, grew in less than three decades to a bustling city with noisy railroad yards and roaring blast furnaces. By 1900 it was the nation's largest pig-iron shipper. In these same years, Chattanooga, Tennessee, housed nine furnaces, seventeen foundries, and numerous machine shops.

As large-scale recruiters of black workers, the southern iron and steel mills contributed to the migration of blacks to the cities. By 1900, 20 percent of the southern black population was urban. Many urban blacks toiled as domestics or in similar menial capacities, but others entered the industrial work force. Southern industry reflected the patterns of racial segregation in southern life. Tobacco companies used black workers, particularly women, to clean the tobacco leaves while white women, at a different location, ran the machines that made cigarettes. The burgeoning textile mills were lily-white. In the iron and steel industry, blacks, who comprised 60 percent of the unskilled work force by 1900, had practically no chance of advancement. Nevertheless, in a rare reversal of the usual pattern, southern blacks in the iron and steel industry had a higher skill level and on average earned more than did southern white textile workers.

Black miners were also recruited by the West Virginia coal industry that lured them with free transportation, high wages, and company housing. The coal boom at first forced companies to pay similar wages to blacks and whites, and they initially joined biracial labor unions. But, as a result of the depression of 1893, the unions were destroyed, and workers became increasingly confined to separate jobs.

Segregation, both in the coal industry and elsewhere in the South, while restricting black employment in many ways, opened up new opportunities for black barbers, doctors, and businessmen to work with black customers. Still, in many ways, economic opportunities for blacks remained severely limited. In lumbering, which was the South's largest industry, large numbers of blacks worked in the turpentine industry, collecting sap from trees. In good times, wages could be better than those offered to farm laborers, but during economic downturns workers were laid off or confined to work camps by vagrancy laws and armed guards.

The Southern Mill Economy

Unlike the urban-based southern iron and steel industry, the textile mills that mushroomed in the southern countryside in the 1880s often became catalysts for the formation of new towns and villages. (This same pattern had occurred in rural New England in the 1820s.) In those southern districts that underwent the gradual transition from an agricultural to a mill economy, country ways and values suffused the new industrial workplace.

The cotton-mill economy grew largely in the Piedmont, a beautiful highland country of rolling hills and rushing rivers stretching from central Virginia to northern Georgia and Alabama. The Piedmont had long been the South's backcountry, a land of subsistence farming and limited roads. But postwar railroad construction opened the region to outside markets and sparked a period of intense town building and textile-mill expansion. Between 1880 and 1900 track mileage in North Carolina grew dramatically; the number of towns and villages jumped, quickening the pulse of commerce; and the construction of textile mills accelerated. Between 1860 and 1900 cotton-mill capacity shot up 1,400 percent, and by 1920 the South was the nation's leading textile-mill center. Augusta, Georgia, with 2,800 mill workers, became known as the Lowell of the South, named after the mill town in Massachusetts where industrialization had flourished earlier. The expansion of the textile industry nurtured promoters' visions of a new, more prosperous, industrialized South.

Sharecroppers and tenant farmers at first hailed the new cotton mills as a way out of rural poverty. But appearances were deceptive. The chief cotton-mill promoters

Pig Iron Scene, Birmingham, Alabama, **by Charles Graham, 1886**   *Although Birmingham, Alabama's, extensive foundries turned out inexpensive iron ingots, the northern owners forced factory operators to price their products at the same rate as ingots produced in Pittsburgh.*

were drawn from the same ranks of merchants, lawyers, doctors, and bankers who had profited from the commercialization of southern agriculture (and from the misfortunes of poor black and white tenant farmers and sharecroppers trapped in the new system). R. R. Haynes, a planter and merchant from North Carolina, was typical of the new entrepreneurs. Starting out as a storekeeper, he formed a company in 1884 to finance construction of the Henrietta Mills. By 1913, Haynes owned not only one of the South's largest mills but also banks, railroads, lumber businesses, and general stores.

To run the mills, factory owners commonly hired poor whites from impoverished nearby farms. They promised that textile work would free these farming families from poverty and instill in them the virtues of punctuality and industrial discipline. The reality was different. Cotton-mill entrepreneurs shamelessly exploited their workers, paying just seven to eleven cents an hour, 30 percent to 50 percent less than what comparable mill workers in New England were paid.

The mills dominated most Piedmont textile communities. The mill operator not only built and owned the workers' housing and the company store but also supported the village church, financed the local elementary school, and pried into the morals and behavior of the mill hands. To prevent workers from moving from one mill to another, the mill owner usually paid them just once a month, often in scrip—a certificate redeemable only in goods from the company store. Since few families had enough money to get through a month, they often overspent and fell behind in their payments. The charges were deducted from workers' wages the following month. In this way, the mill drew workers and their families into a cycle of indebtedness very much like that faced by sharecroppers and tenant farmers.

Since farm families shared farm responsibilities together, southern mill superintendents accommodated themselves to local customs and hired whole families, including the children. Mothers commonly brought babies into the mills and kept them in baskets nearby while tending their machines. Little children sometimes learned to operate the machines themselves. Ties among the workers were strong. One employee put it simply: "The mill community was a close bunch of people . . . like one big family. We just loved one another."

To help make ends meet, mill workers kept their own garden patches and raised chickens, cows, and pigs. Southern mill hands thus brought communal farm values, long associated with large farm families and nurtured through cooperative planting and harvesting, into the mills themselves. Although they had to adapt to machine-paced work and received barely enough pay to live on, the working poor in the mill districts, like their prewar counterparts in the North, eased the shift from rural to village-industrial life by embracing a cooperative country ethic.

As northern cotton mills did before the Civil War, southern textile companies exploited the cheap rural labor around them, settling transplanted farm people in paternalistic company-run villages. Using these tactics, the industry underwent a period of steady growth.

The Southern Industrial Lag   Industrialization occurred on a smaller scale and at a slower rate in the South than in the North and also depended far more on outside financing, technology, and expertise. The late-nineteenth-century southern economy remained essentially in a colonial status, subject to domination by northern industries and financial syndicates. U.S. Steel, for example, controlled the foundries in Birmingham, and in 1900 its executives began to price Birmingham steel according to the "Pittsburgh plus" formula based on the price of Pittsburgh steel, plus the freight costs of shipping from Pittsburgh. As a result, southerners paid higher prices for steel than did northerners, despite the cheaper production costs.

An array of factors thus combined to retard industrialization in the South. Banking regulations requiring large reserves, scarce capital, absentee ownership, unfavorable railroad rates, cautious state governments, wartime debts, lack of industrial experience, a segregated labor force, discrimination against blacks, and control by profit-hungry northern enterprises all hampered the region's economic development. Dragged down by a poorly educated white population and by a largely unskilled black population, southern industry languished. While it did grow considerably, not until after the turn of the century did southern industry undergo the restructuring and consolidation that had occurred in northern business enterprise two decades earlier.

As in the North, industrialization brought significant environmental damage, including polluted rivers and streams, decimated forests, grimy coal-mining towns, and soot-infested steel-making cities. Although Henry Grady's vision of a New South may have inspired many southerners to work toward industrialization, economic growth in the South, limited as it was by outside forces, progressed in its own distinctly regional way.

FACTORIES AND THE WORK FORCE

Industrialization proceeded unevenly nationwide, and most late-nineteenth-century Americans still worked in small shops. But as the century unfolded, large factories with armies of workers sprang onto the industrial scene in more and more locales. The pattern of change was evident. Between 1860 and 1900, the number of industrial workers jumped from 885,000 to 3.2 million, and the trend toward large-scale production became unmistakable.

From Workshop to Factory   The transition to a factory economy came not as an earthquake but rather as a series of seismic jolts varying in strength and duration. Whether they occurred quickly or slowly, however, the changes in factory production had a profound impact on artisans and unskilled laborers alike, for they involved a fundamental restructuring of work habits and a new emphasis on workplace discipline. The impact of these changes can be seen by examining the boot and shoe industry. As late as the 1840s, almost every shoe was custom-made by a skilled artisan who worked in a small, independent shop. Shoemakers were aristocrats in the world of labor. Taught in an apprentice system, they took pride in their work and controlled the quality of their products. In some cases they hired and paid their own helpers.

A distinctive working-class culture subdivided along ethnic lines evolved among these shoemakers. Foreign-born English, German, and Irish workers set up ethnic trade organizations and joined affiliated benevolent associations. Bound together by religious and ethnic ties, they observed weddings and funerals according to old-country traditions and relaxed together at the local saloon after work. Living in neighborhood tenements and boardinghouses, they developed a strong community pride and helped one another weather accidents or sicknesses.

As early as the 1850s, even before the widespread use of machinery, changes in the ready-made shoe trade had eroded the status of skilled labor. The manufacturing process was broken down into a sequence of repetitive, easily mastered tasks. Thus instead of crafting a pair of shoes from start to finish, each team member specialized in only one part of the process, such as attaching the heel or polishing the leather.

In the 1880s, shoe factories became larger and more mechanized, and traditional skills largely vanished. Sophisticated sewing and buffing machines allowed shoe companies to replace skilled operatives with lower-paid, less-skilled women and children. By 1890 women made up more than 35 percent of the work force. In many other industries, skilled artisans found their responsibilities and relation to the production process changing. With the exception of some skilled construction crafts such as carpentry and bricklaying, artisans no longer participated in the production process as a whole. Like the laborer whose machine nailed heels on 4,800 shoes a day, even "skilled" workers in the new factories specializing in consumer goods found themselves performing numbingly repetitive tasks.

The Hardships of Industrial Labor   The expansion of the factory system spawned an unprecedented demand for unskilled labor. By the 1880s nearly one-third of the 750,000 workers employed in the railroad and steel industries, for example, were common laborers.

In the construction trades and the garment-making industries, the services of unskilled laborers were procured under the so-called contract system. To avoid the problems of hiring, managing, and firing their own workers, large companies negotiated an agreement with a subcontractor who took responsibility for employee relations. A foreman or boss employed by the subcontractor supervised gangs of unskilled day laborers. These common workers were seasonal help, hired in times of need and laid off in slack periods. The steel industry employed them to shovel ore in the yards and to move ingots inside the mills. The foremen drove the gangs hard; in the Pittsburgh area, the workers called the foremen "pushers."

Notoriously transient, unskilled laborers drifted from city to city and from industry to industry. In the late 1870s unskilled laborers earned $1.30 a day, while bricklayers and blacksmiths earned more than $3. Only unskilled southern mill workers, whose wages averaged a meager eighty-four cents a day, earned less.

Unskilled and skilled workers alike not only worked up to twelve-hour shifts but also faced grave hazards to their health and safety. The alarming incidence of industrial accidents stemmed from a variety of circumstances, including dangerous factory conditions, workers' inexperience, and the rapid pace of the production process. Author Hamlin Garland described the perilous environment of a steel-rail mill at Carnegie's Homestead Steel Works in Pittsburgh. One steelworker recalled that on his first day at the mill, "I looked up and a big train carrying a big vessel with fire was making towards me. I stood numb, afraid to move, until a man came to me and led me out of the mill." Under such conditions the accident rate in the steel mills was extremely high.

In the coal mines and cotton mills, child laborers typically entered the work force at age eight or nine. These youngsters not only faced the same environmental hazards as adults but were especially prone to injury. In the cotton mills, children could be injured by the unprotected pulley belts that powered the machines. They and the adults who toiled in the mills, constantly breathing in cotton dust, fell ill with brown lung, another crippling disease. In the coal industry, children were commonly employed as slate pickers. Sitting at a chute beneath the breakers that crushed the coal, they removed pieces of slate and other impurities. The cloud of coal dust that swirled around them gave them black lung disease—a disorder that leads to emphysema and heart failure.

For adult workers, the railroad industry was one of the most perilous. In 1889, the first year that the Interstate Commerce Commission compiled reliable statistics, almost two thousand rail workers were killed on the job and more than twenty thousand injured.

Disabled workers and widows received minimal financial aid from employers. Until the 1890s, the courts considered employer negligence to be one of the normal risks borne by employees. Railroad and factory owners fought the adoption of state safety and health standards on the grounds that the cost would be excessive. For sickness and accident benefits, workers joined fraternal organizations and ethnic clubs, part of whose monthly dues benefited those in need. But in most cases, the amounts set aside were too low to be of much help. When a worker was killed or maimed in an accident, the family had to rely on relatives or friends for support.

Immigrant Labor   As we shall see in more detail in Chapter 19, factory owners turned to unskilled immigrant workers for the muscle they needed. In Philadelphia, where native-born Americans and recent German immigrants dominated the highly skilled metalworking trades, Irish newcomers remained mired in unskilled horse-carting and construction occupations until the 1890s, when the "new immigrants" from southern and eastern Europe replaced them. Poverty-stricken French

Textile Workers *Young children like this one were often used in the textile mills because their small fingers could tie together broken threads more easily than those of adults.*

Canadians filled the most menial positions in northeastern textile mills. On the West Coast, Chinese immigrants performed the dirtiest and most physically demanding jobs in mining, canning, and railroad construction.

Writing home in the 1890s, eastern European immigrants described the hazardous and draining work in the steel mills. "Wherever the heat is most insupportable, the flames most scorching, the smoke and soot most choking, there we are certain to find compatriots bent and wasted in toil," reported one Hungarian. Yet those immigrants disposed to live frugally in a boardinghouse and to work an eighty-four-hour week could save fifteen dollars a month, far more than they could have earned in their homeland.

Although most immigrants worked hard, few adjusted easily to the fast pace of the factory. Peasants from southern and eastern Europe found it difficult to abandon their seasonal work habits for factory schedules. Factory operations were relentless, dictated by the unvarying speed of the machines. A brochure used by the International Harvester Corporation to teach English to its Polish workers promoted the "proper" values. Lesson 1 read:

> I hear the whistle. I must hurry.
> I hear the five minute whistle.
> It is time to go into the shop.

I take my check from the gate board and hang it
    on the department board.
I change my clothes and get ready to work.
The starting whistle blows.
I eat my lunch.
It is forbidden to eat until then.
The whistle blows at five minutes of starting time.
I get ready to go to work.
I work until the whistle blows to quit.
I leave my place nice and clean.
I put all my clothes in the locker.
I must go home.

As this "lesson" reveals, factory work tied the immigrants to a rigid timetable very different from the pace of farm life.

When immigrant workers resisted the tempo of factory work, drank on the job, or took unexcused absences, employers used a variety of tactics to enforce discipline. Some sponsored temperance societies and Sunday schools to teach punctuality and sobriety. Others cut wages and put workers on the piecework system, paying them only for the items produced. Employers sometimes also provided low-cost housing to gain leverage against work stoppages; if workers went on strike, the boss could simply evict them.

In the case of immigrants from southern Europe whose skin colors were often darker than northern Europeans', employers asserted that the workers were nonwhite and thus did not deserve the same compensation as native-born Americans. Because the concept of "whiteness" in the United States bestowed a sense of privilege and the automatic extension of the rights of citizenship, Irish, Greek, Italian, Jewish, and a host of other immigrants, although of the Caucasian race, were also considered nonwhite. Rather than being a fixed category based on biological differences, the concept of race was thus used to justify the harsh treatment of foreign-born labor.

Women and Work in Industrial America
Women's work experiences, like those of men, were shaped by marital status, social class, and race. Upper-class white married women widely accepted an ideology of "separate spheres" (see Chapter 19) and remained at home, raised children, and looked after the household. The well-to-do hired maids and cooks to ease their burdens.

Working-class married women, in contrast, not only lacked such assistance but also often had to contribute to the financial support of the family. In fact, working for wages at home by sewing, button-making, taking in boarders, or doing laundry had predated industrialization. In the late nineteenth century, unscrupulous urban entrepreneurs exploited this captive work force. Cigar manufacturers would buy or lease a tenement and require their twenty families to live and work there. In the clothing industry, manufacturers hired out finishing tasks to lower-class married women and their children, who labored long hours in crowded apartments.

Young, working-class single women often viewed factory work as an opportunity. In 1870, 13 percent of all women worked outside the home, the majority as cooks, maids, cleaning ladies, and laundresses. But most working women intensely disliked the long hours, low pay, and social stigma of being a "servant." When jobs in industry expanded in the last quarter of the century, growing numbers of single white women abandoned domestic employment for better-paying work in the textile, food-processing, and garment industries. Discrimination barred black working women from following this path. Between 1870 and 1900, the number of women of all races working outside the home nearly tripled. By the turn of the century, women made up 17 percent of the country's labor force.

A variety of factors propelled the rise in the employment of single women. Changes in agriculture prompted many young farmwomen to seek employment in the industrial sector (see Chapter 19), and immigrant parents often sent their daughters to the factories to supplement meager family incomes. Plant managers welcomed young immigrant women as a ready source of inexpensive unskilled labor. But factory owners assumed that many of these women would marry within a short time. They treated them as temporary help and kept their wages low. In 1890, young women operating sewing machines earned as little as four dollars for seventy hours of work while their male counterparts made eight.

Despite their paltry wages, long hours, and often unpleasant working conditions, many young women relished earning their own income and joined the work force in increasing numbers. Although the financial support that these working women contributed to their families was significant, few working women were paid enough to provide homes for themselves. Rather than fostering their independence, industrial work tied them more deeply to a family economy that depended on their earnings.

When the typewriter and the telephone came into general use in the 1890s, office work provided new employment opportunities, and women with high school educations moved into clerical and secretarial jobs earlier filled by men. They were attracted by the clean, safe working conditions and relatively good pay. First-rate typists could earn six to eight dollars a week, which compared favorably with factory wages. Even though women were excluded from managerial positions, office work carried higher prestige and was generally steadier than work in the factory or shop.

Despite the growing number of women workers, the late-nineteenth-century popular press portrayed women's work outside the home as temporary. Few people even considered the possibility that a woman could attain local or even national prominence in the emerging corporate order.

Hard Work and the Gospel of Success
Although women were generally excluded from the equation, influential opinion molders in these years preached that any man could achieve success in the new industrial era. In *Ragged Dick* (1867) and scores of later tales, **Horatio Alger,** a Unitarian minister turned dime novelist, recounted the adventures of poor but honest lads who rose through initiative and self-discipline. In his stories shoeshine boys stopped runaway horses and were rewarded by rich benefactors who gave them a start in business. The career of Andrew Carnegie was often offered as proof that the United States remained the land of opportunity and "rags to riches."

Some critics did not accept this belief. In an 1871 essay, Mark Twain chided the public for its naïveté and suggested that business success was more likely to come to those who lied and cheated. In testimony given in 1883 before a Senate committee investigating labor conditions, a New Yorker named Thomas B. McGuire dolefully recounted how he had been forced out of the horse-cart business by larger, better-financed concerns. Declared McGuire, "I live in a tenement house, three stories up, where the water comes in through the roof, and I cannot better myself. My children will have to go to work before they are able to work. Why? Simply because this present system . . . is all for the privileged classes, nothing for the man who produces the wealth." Only with starting capital of ten thousand dollars—then a large sum—said McGuire, could the independent entrepreneur hope to compete with the large companies.

What are the facts? Carnegie's rise from abject poverty to colossal wealth was the rare exception, as studies of nearly two hundred of the largest corporations reveal. Ninety-five percent of the industrial leaders came from middle- and upper-class backgrounds. However, even if skilled immigrants and native-born working-class Americans had little chance to move into management in the largest corporations, they did have a chance to rise to the top in small companies. Although only a few reaped immense fortunes, many attained substantial incomes.

The different fates of immigrant workers in San Francisco show the possibilities and perils of moving up within the working class. In the 1860s the Irish-born Donahue brothers grew wealthy from the Union Iron Works they had founded, where six hundred men built heavy equipment for the mining industry. In contrast, the nearly fifteen thousand Chinese workers who returned to the city after the Central Pacific's rail line was completed in 1869 were consigned by prejudice to work in cigar, textile, and other light-industry factories. Even successful Chinese entrepreneurs faced discrimination. When a Chinese merchant, Mr. Yung, refused to sell out to the wealthy Charles Crocker, a dry-goods merchant turned railroad entrepreneur who was building a mansion on Nob Hill, Crocker built a thirty-foot-high "spite fence" around Yung's house so that it would be completely sealed from view.

Thus, while some skilled workers became owners of their own companies, the opportunities for advancement for unskilled immigrant workers were considerably more limited. Some did move to semiskilled or skilled positions. Yet most immigrants, particularly the Irish, Italians, and Chinese, moved far more slowly than the sons of middle- and upper-class Americans who began with greater educational advantages and family financial backing. The upward mobility possible for such unskilled workers was generally mobility within the working class. Immigrants who got ahead in the late nineteenth century went from rags to respectability, not rags to riches.

One positive economic trend in these years was the rise in real wages, representing gains in actual buying power. Average real wages climbed 31 percent for unskilled workers and 74 percent for skilled workers between 1860 and 1900. Overall gains in purchasing power, however, were often undercut by injuries and unemployment during slack times or economic slumps. The position of unskilled immigrant laborers was particularly shaky. Even during a prosperous year like 1890, one out of every five nonagricultural workers was unemployed at least one month of the year. During the depressions of the 1870s and 1890s, wage cuts, extended layoffs, and irregular employment pushed those at the bottom of the industrial work force to the brink of starvation.

Thus the overall picture of late-nineteenth-century economic mobility is complex. At the top of the scale, a mere 10 percent of American families owned 73 percent of the nation's wealth in 1890, while less than half of industrial laborers earned more than the five-hundred-dollar poverty line annually. In between the very rich and the very poor, skilled immigrants and small shopkeepers improved their economic position significantly. So although the standard of living for millions of Americans rose, the gap between the poor and the well-off remained a yawning abyss.

LABOR UNIONS AND INDUSTRIAL CONFLICT

Aware that the growth of large corporations gave industrial leaders unprecedented power to control the workplace, labor leaders searched for ways to create broad-based, national organizations that could protect their members. But this drive to create a nationwide labor movement faced many problems. Employers deliberately accentuated ethnic and racial divisions within the work force, including competition between immigrant groups, to hamper unionizing efforts. Skilled craftsworkers, moreover, felt little kinship with low-paid common laborers. Divided into different trades, they often saw little reason to work together. Thus, unionization efforts moved forward slowly and experienced setbacks.

Two groups, the National Labor Union and the Knights of Labor, struggled to build a mass labor movement that would unite skilled and unskilled workers regardless of their specialties. After impressive initial growth, however, both efforts collapsed. Far more effective was the American Federation of Labor (AFL), which represented skilled workers in powerful independent craft unions. The AFL survived and grew, but it represented only a small portion of the total labor force.

With unions weak, labor unrest during economic downturns reached crisis proportions. When pay rates were cut or working conditions became intolerable, laborers walked off the job without union authorization. These actions, called **wildcat strikes,** which were born of desperation, often exploded into violence. The labor crisis of the 1890s, with its strikes and bloodshed, would reshape the legal environment, increase the demand for state regulation, and eventually contribute to a movement for progressive reform.

Organizing Workers

From the eighteenth century on, skilled workers had organized local trade unions to fight wage reductions and provide benefits for their members in times of illness or accident. In the 1850s some tradesmen had even organized national associations along craft lines. But the effectiveness of these organizations was limited. The challenge that labor leaders faced in the postwar period was how to boost the unions' clout. Some believed that this goal could be achieved by forming one big association that would transcend craft lines and pull in the mass of unskilled workers.

One person inspired by this vision was Philadelphian William H. Sylvis, who in 1863 was elected president of the Iron Molders' International Union, an organization of iron-foundry workers. Strongly built and bearded, Sylvis traveled the country exhorting iron molders to organize. Within a few years, Sylvis had built his union from "a mere pygmy" to a membership of eighty-five hundred.

In 1866, he acted on his dream of a nationwide association that represented all workers and called a convention in Baltimore to form a new organization, the **National Labor Union** (NLU). Reflecting the pre–Civil War idealism, the NLU endorsed the eight-hour-day movement, which insisted that labor deserved eight hours for work,

The Eight-Hour-Day Movement   *Striking artisans from more than three hundred companies filled New York streets for weeks in 1872 in a campaign to reduce the workday from ten hours to eight hours. As is evident in this illustration, the eight-hour movement gained additional support from local saloons catering to German immigrants.*

eight hours for sleep, and eight hours for personal affairs. Leaders also called for an end to convict labor, for the establishment of a federal department of labor, and for currency and banking reform. To push wage scales higher, they endorsed immigration restriction, especially of Chinese migrants, whom native-born workers blamed for undercutting prevailing wage levels. The NLU under Sylvis's leadership supported the cause of working women and elected a woman as one of its national officers. It urged black workers to organize as well, though in racially separate unions.

In the winter of 1866–1867, Sylvis's own union became locked in a harrowing strike against the nation's foundry owners. When the strike failed to improve wages, Sylvis turned to national political reform. He invited a number of reformers to the 1868 NLU convention, including woman suffrage advocates Susan B. Anthony and Elizabeth Cady Stanton, who, according to a reporter, made "no mean impression on the bearded delegates." But when Sylvis suddenly died in 1869, the NLU faded quickly. After a brief incarnation in 1872 as the National Labor Reform party, it vanished from the scene.

The dream of a labor movement that combined skilled and unskilled workers lived on in a new organization, the Noble and Holy Order of the **Knights of Labor,** founded in 1869. Led by Uriah H. Stephens, head of the Garment Cutters of Philadelphia, the Knights began as a secret society modeled on the Masonic Order. They welcomed all wage earners or former wage earners; they excluded only bankers, doctors, lawyers, stockbrokers, professional gamblers, and liquor dealers. The Knights demanded equal pay for women, an end to child labor and convict labor, and the cooperative employer-employee ownership of factories, mines, and other businesses. At a time when no federal income tax existed, they called for a progressive tax on all earnings, graduated so that higher-income earners would pay more.

The Knights grew slowly at first. But membership rocketed in the 1880s after Terence V. Powderly replaced Stephens as the organization's head. A young Pennsylvania machinist of Irish-Catholic immigrant origins, Powderly was an unlikely labor leader. He was short and slight, with a blond drooping mustache, elegant attire, and a fastidious, somewhat aloof manner. One journalist expressed surprise at finding such a fashionable man as the leader of "the horny-fisted sons of toil." But Powderly's eloquence, coupled with a series of successes in labor clashes, brought in thousands of new members.

During its growth years in the early 1880s, the Knights of Labor reflected both its idealistic origins and Powderly's collaborative vision. Powderly opposed strikes, which he considered "a relic of barbarism," and organized producer and consumer cooperatives. A teetotaler, he also urged temperance upon the membership. Powderly advocated the admission of blacks into local Knights of Labor assemblies, although he recognized the strength of racism and allowed southern local assemblies to be segregated. Under his leadership the Knights welcomed women members; by 1886 women organizers had recruited thousands of workers, and women made up an estimated 10 percent of the union's membership.

Powderly supported restrictions on immigration and a total ban on Chinese immigration. In the West, fears about competition from low-paid Chinese workers were heightened when California railroad magnate Leland Stanford declared, "[O]pen the door and let everybody come who wants to come . . . until you get enough [immigrants] here to reduce the price of labor to such a point that its cheapness will stop their coming." In 1877, San Francisco workers demonstrating for an eight-hour workday destroyed twenty-five Chinese-run laundries and terrorized the local Chinese population. In 1880 both major party platforms included anti-Chinese immigration plans. Two years later, Congress passed the Chinese Exclusion Act, placing a ten-year moratorium on Chinese immigration. The ban was extended in 1902 and not repealed until 1943.

Although inspired by Powderly's vision of a harmonious and cooperative future, most rank-and-file members of the Knights of Labor strongly disagreed with Powderly's antistrike position. In 1883–1884, local branches of the Knights led a series of spontaneous strikes that gained only reluctant support from the national leadership. In 1885, however, when Jay Gould tried to get rid of the Knights of Labor on his Wabash railroad by firing active union members, Powderly and his executive board instructed all Knights on the Wabash line to walk off the job and those on other lines to refuse to handle Wabash cars. This action crippled the Wabash's operations. To the nation's amazement, Gould met with Powderly and canceled his campaign against the Knights of Labor. "The Wabash victory is with the Knights," declared a St. Louis newspaper; "no such victory has ever before been secured in this or any other country."

With this apparent triumph, membership in the Knights of Labor soared. By 1886, more than seven hundred thousand workers were organized in nearly six thousand locals. Turning to political action that fall, the Knights mounted campaigns in nearly two hundred towns and cities nationwide, electing several mayors and judges (Powderly himself had served as mayor of Scranton since 1878). They secured passage of state laws banning convict labor, and federal laws against the importation of foreign contract labor. Business executives warned that the Knights could cripple the economy and take over the country if they chose.

But the organization's strength soon waned. Workers became disillusioned when a series of unauthorized strikes failed in 1886. By the late 1880s, the Knights of Labor was a shadow of its former self. Nevertheless, the organization had served as a major impetus to the labor movement and had awakened in thousands of workers a sense of group solidarity and potential strength. Powderly, who survived to 1924, always remained proud of his role "in forcing to the forefront the cause of misunderstood and downtrodden humanity."

As the Knights of Labor weakened, another national labor organization, pursuing more immediate and practical goals, was gaining strength. The skilled craft unions had long been uncomfortable with labor organizations like the Knights that welcomed skilled and unskilled alike. They were also concerned that the Knights' broad reform goals would undercut their own commitment to better wages and protecting the interests of their particular crafts. The break came in May 1886 when the craft unions left the Knights of Labor to form the **American Federation of Labor** (AFL).

The AFL replaced the Knights' grand visions with practical tactics aimed at bread-and-butter issues. This philosophy was vigorously pursued by **Samuel Gompers,** the immigrant cigar maker who became head of the AFL in 1886 and led it until his death in 1924. Gompers believed in "trade unionism, pure and simple." For Gompers, higher wages were not simply an end in themselves but were rather the necessary base to enable working-class families to exist decently, with respect and dignity. The stocky, mustachioed labor leader argued that labor, to stand up to the corporations, would have to harness the bargaining power of skilled workers, whom employers could not easily replace, and concentrate on the practical goals of raising wages and reducing hours.

A master tactician, Gompers believed that the trend toward large-scale industrial organization necessitated a comparable degree of organization by labor. He also recognized, however, that the skilled craft unions that made up the AFL retained a strong sense of independence. He knew that he had to persuade craftsworkers from the various trades to join forces without violating their sense of craft autonomy. Gompers's solution was to organize the AFL as a federation of trade unions, each retaining control of its own members but all linked by an executive council that coordinated strategy during boycotts and strike actions. "We want to make the trade union movement under the AFL as distinct as the billows, yet one as the sea," he told a national convention.

Focusing the federation's efforts on short-term improvements in wages and hours, Gompers at first sidestepped divisive political issues. The new organization's platform did, however, demand an eight-hour workday, employers' liability for workers' injuries, and mine-safety laws. Although women participated in many craft unions, the AFL did little to recruit women workers after 1894 because Gompers and others believed that women workers undercut men's wages. By 1904, under Gompers's careful tutelage, the AFL had grown to more than 1.6 million strong.

Although the unions held up an ideal toward which many might strive, labor organizations before 1900 remained weak. Less than 5 percent of the work force joined union ranks. Split between skilled artisans and common laborers, separated along ethnic and religious lines, and divided over tactics, the unions battled with only occasional effectiveness against the growing power of corporate enterprise. Lacking financial resources, they typically watched from the sidelines when unorganized workers launched wildcat strikes that sometimes turned violent.

Strikes and Labor Violence — Americans had lived with a high level of violence from the nation's beginnings, and the nineteenth century, with its international and civil wars, urban riots, and Indian-white conflict, was no exception. Terrible labor clashes toward the end of the century were part of this continuing pattern, but they nevertheless shocked and dismayed contemporaries. From 1881 to 1905, close to 37,000 strikes erupted, in which nearly 7 million workers participated.

The first major wave of strikes began in 1873 when a Wall Street crash triggered a stock-market panic and a major depression. Six thousand businesses closed the following year, and many more cut wages and laid off workers. Striking Pennsylvania coal miners were fired and evicted from their homes. Tramps roamed the streets in New York and Chicago. The tension turned deadly in 1877 during a wildcat railroad strike. Ignited by a wage reduction on the Baltimore and Ohio Railroad in July, the strike exploded up and down the railroad lines, spreading to New York, Pittsburgh, St. Louis, Kansas City, Chicago, and San Francisco. Rioters in Pittsburgh torched Union Depot and the Pennsylvania Railroad roundhouse. By the time newly installed president Rutherford B. Hayes had called out the troops and quelled the strike two weeks later, nearly one hundred people had died, and two-thirds of the nation's railroads stood idle.

The railroad strike stunned middle-class America. The religious press responded hysterically. "If the club of the policeman, knocking out the brains of the rioter, will answer, then well and good," declared one Congregationalist journal, "[but if not] then bullets and bayonets . . . constitute the one remedy." The same middle-class Americans who worried about Jay Gould and the corporate abuse of power grew terrified of mob violence from the bottom ranks of society.

Employers capitalized on the public hysteria to crack down on labor. Many required their workers to sign "yellow dog" contracts in which they promised not to strike or join a union. Some hired Pinkerton agents, a private police force, to defend their factories and, when necessary, turned to the federal government and the U.S. army to suppress labor unrest.

Although the economy recovered, more strikes and violence followed in the 1880s. On May 1, 1886, 340,000 workers walked off their jobs in support of the campaign for an eight-hour workday. Strikers in Cincinnati virtually shut down the city for nearly a month. Three days later, Chicago police shot and killed four strikers at the McCormick Harvester plant. At a protest rally the next evening in the city's Haymarket Square, someone threw a bomb from a nearby building, killing or fatally wounding seven policemen. In response, the police fired wildly into the crowd and killed four demonstrators.

Public reaction was immediate. Business leaders and middle-class citizens lashed out at labor activists and particularly at the sponsors of the Haymarket meeting, most of whom were associated with a German-language anarchist newspaper that advocated the violent overthrow of capitalism. Eight men were arrested. Although no evidence connected them directly to the bomb throwing, all were convicted of murder, and four were executed. One committed suicide in prison. In Haymarket's aftermath, still more Americans became convinced that the nation was in the grip of a deadly foreign conspiracy, and animosity toward labor unions intensified.

Confrontations between capital and labor became particularly violent in the West. When the Mine Owners' Protective Association cut wages at work sites along Idaho's Coeur d'Alene River in 1892, the miners, who were skilled in the use of dynamite, blew up a mill and captured the guards sent to defend it. Mine owners responded by mustering the Idaho National Guard to round up more than three hundred men and cripple their union.

Back east that same year, armed conflict broke out during the **Homestead Strike** at the Carnegie Steel Company plant in Homestead, Pennsylvania. To destroy the union, managers had cut wages and locked out the workers. When workers fired on the armed men from the Pinkerton Detective Agency who came to protect the plant, a battle broke out. Seven union members and three Pinkertons died. A week later the governor sent eight thousand National Guardsmen to restore order. The union crushed, the mills resumed full operation a month later.

The most systematic use of troops to smash union power came in 1894 during a strike against the Pullman Palace Car Company. In 1880 George Pullman, a manufacturer of elegant dining, parlor, and sleeping cars for the nation's railroads, had constructed a factory and town, called Pullman, ten miles south of Chicago. The carefully planned community provided solid brick houses for the workers, beautiful parks and playgrounds, and even its own sewage-treatment plant. Pullman also closely policed workers' activities, outlawed saloons, and insisted that his properties turn a profit.

When the depression of 1893 hit, Pullman slashed workers' wages without reducing their rents. In reaction thousands of workers joined the newly formed American Railway Union and went on strike. They were led by a fiery young organizer, **Eugene V. Debs,** who vowed "to strip the mask of hypocrisy from the pretended philanthropist and show him to the world as an oppressor of labor." Union members working for the nation's largest railroads refused to switch Pullman cars, paralyzing rail traffic in and out of Chicago, one of the nation's premier rail hubs.

In response, the General Managers' Association, an organization of top railroad executives, set out to break the union. The General Managers imported strikebreakers from among jobless easterners and asked U.S. attorney general Richard Olney, who sat on the board of directors of three major railroad networks, for a federal injunction (court order) against the strikers for allegedly refusing to move railroad cars carrying U.S. mail.

In fact, union members had volunteered to switch mail cars onto any trains that did not carry Pullman cars, and it was the railroads' managers who were delaying the mail by refusing to send their trains without the full complement of cars. Nevertheless, Olney, supported by President Grover Cleveland and citing the Sherman Anti-Trust Act, secured an injunction against the leaders of the American Railway Union for restraint of commerce. When the union refused to order its members back to work, Debs was arrested, and federal troops poured in. During the ensuing riot, workers burned seven hundred freight cars, thirteen people died, and fifty-three were wounded. By July 18 the strike had been crushed.

By playing upon a popular identification of strikers with anarchism and violence, crafty corporate leaders persuaded state and federal officials to cripple organized labor's ability to bargain with business. When the Supreme Court (in the 1895 case *In re Debs*) upheld Debs's prison sentence and legalized the use of injunctions against labor unions, the judicial system gave business a potent new weapon with which to restrain labor organizers.

Yet organizers persisted. In 1897, the feisty Irish-born Mary Harris Jones, known as Mother Jones, persuaded coal miners in Pennsylvania to join the United Mine Workers of America, a union founded seven years earlier. She staged parades of children, invited workers' wives to stockpile food, and dramatized the importance of militant mothers fighting for their families. Her efforts were successful. Wage reductions were restored because no large companies dominated the industry and the owners needed to restore production.

Despite the achievements of the United Mine Workers, whose members had climbed to 300,000 by 1900, the successive attempts by the National Labor Union, Knights of Labor, American Federation of Labor, and American Railway Union to build a national working-class labor movement achieved only limited success. Aggressive employer associations and conservative state and local officials hamstrung their efforts. In sharp contrast to Great Britain and Germany, where state officials often mediated disputes between labor and capital, federal and state officials in the United States increasingly sided with manufacturers. Ineffective in the political arena, blocked by state officials, divided by ethnic differences, harassed by employers, and frustrated by court decisions, American unions failed to expand their base of support. Post–Civil War labor turmoil had sapped the vitality of organized labor and given it a negative public image that it would not shed until the 1930s.

Social Thinkers Probe for Alternatives
Widespread industrial violence was particularly unsettling when examined in the context of working-class poverty. In 1879, after observing three men rummaging through garbage to find food, the poet and journalist Walt Whitman wrote, "If the United States, like the countries of the Old World, are also to grow vast crops of poor, desperate, dissatisfied, nomadic, miserably-waged populations, such as we see looming upon us of late years . . . , then our republican experiment, notwithstanding all its surface-successes, is at heart an unhealthy failure." Whitman's bleak speculation was part of a general public debate over the social meaning of the new industrial order. At stake was a larger issue: should government become the mechanism for helping the poor and regulating big business?

Defenders of capitalism preached the laissez-faire ("hands-off") argument, insisting that government should never attempt to control business. They buttressed their case by citing Scottish economist Adam Smith, who had argued in *The Wealth of Nations* (1776) that self-interest acted as an "invisible hand" in the marketplace, automatically regulating the supply of and demand for goods and services. In "The Gospel of Wealth," an influential essay published in 1889, Andrew Carnegie justified laissez-faire by applying the evolutionary theories of British social scientist Herbert Spencer to human society. "The law of competition," Carnegie argued, "may be sometimes hard for the individual, [but] it is best for the race, because it insures the survival of the fittest in every department."

Tough-minded Yale professor **William Graham Sumner** shared Carnegie's disapproval of government interference. His combative book *What Social Classes Owe to Each Other* (1883) applied the evolutionary theories of British naturalist Charles Darwin to human society. In an early statement of what became known as **Social Darwinism,** Sumner asserted that inexorable natural laws controlled the social order: "A drunkard in the gutter is just where he ought to be. . . . The law of survival of the fittest was not made by man, and it cannot be abrogated by man. We can only, by interfering with it, produce the survival of the unfittest." The state, declared Sumner, owed its citizens nothing but law, order, and basic political rights.

Sumner's argument did not go unchallenged. In *Dynamic Sociology* (1883), Lester Frank Ward, a geologist, argued that contrary to Sumner's claim, the supposed "laws" of nature could be circumvented by human will. Just as scientists had applied their knowledge to breeding superior livestock, government experts could use the power of the state to regulate big business, protect society's weaker members, and prevent the heedless exploitation of natural resources.

Other social theorists offered more utopian solutions to the problems of poverty and social unrest. Henry George, a self-taught San Francisco newspaper editor and economic theorist, proposed to solve the nation's uneven distribution of wealth through what he called the single tax. In *Progress and Poverty* (1879), he noted that speculators reaped huge profits from the rising price of land that they neither developed nor improved. By taxing this "unearned increment," the government could obtain the funds necessary to ameliorate the misery caused by industrialization. The result would bring the benefits of socialism—a state-controlled economic system that distributed resources according to need—without socialism's great disadvantage, the stifling of individual initiative. George's program was so popular that he lectured around the country and only narrowly missed being elected mayor of New York in 1886.

The vision of a harmonious industrialized society was vividly expressed in the utopian novel *Looking Backward* (1888) by Massachusetts newspaper editor Edward Bellamy. Cast as a glimpse into the future, Bellamy's novel tells of Julian West, who falls asleep in 1888 and awakens in the year 2000 to find a nation without poverty or strife. In this future world, West learns, a completely centralized, state-run economy and a new religion of solidarity have combined to create a society in which everyone works for the common welfare. Bellamy's vision of a conflict-free society where all share equally in industrialization's benefits so inspired middle-class Americans fearful of corporate power and working-class violence that nearly five hundred local Bellamyite organizations, called Nationalist clubs, sprang up to try to turn his dream into reality.

Ward, George, and Bellamy did not deny the benefits of the existing industrial order; they simply sought to humanize it. These utopian reformers envisioned a harmonious society whose members all worked together. Marxist socialists advanced a different view. Elaborated by German philosopher and radical agitator Karl Marx (1818–1883) in *Das Kapital* (1867) and other works, **Marxism** rested on the labor theory of value: a proposition (which Adam Smith had also accepted) that the labor required to produce a commodity was the only true measure of that commodity's value. Any profit made by the capitalist employer was "surplus value" appropriated from the exploited workers. As competition among capitalists increased, Marx predicted, wages would decline to starvation levels, and more and more capitalists would be driven out of business. Society would be divided between a shrinking bourgeoisie (capitalists, merchants, and middle-class professionals) and an impoverished proletariat (the workers). The proletariat would then revolt and seize control of the state and of the economy. Although Marx viewed class struggle as the essence of modern history, his eyes were also fixed on the shining vision of the communist millennium that the revolution would eventually usher in—a classless utopia in which the state would "wither away" and all exploitation would cease. To lead the working class in its showdown with capitalism, Marx and his collaborator Friedrich Engels helped found socialist parties in Europe, whose strength grew steadily, beginning in the 1870s.

Despite Marx's keen interest in the United States, Marxism proved to have little appeal in late-nineteenth-century America other than for a tiny group of primarily German-born immigrants. The Marxist-oriented Socialist Labor party (1877) had attracted only about fifteen hundred members by 1890. More alarming to the public at large was the handful of anarchists, again mostly immigrants, who rejected Marxist discipline and preached the destruction of capitalism, the violent overthrow of the state, and the immediate introduction of a stateless utopia. In 1892 Alexander Berkman, a Russian immigrant anarchist, attempted to assassinate Henry Clay Frick, the manager of Andrew Carnegie's Homestead Steel Works. Entering Frick's office with a pistol, Berkman shot him in the neck and then tried to stab him. A carpenter working in Frick's office overpowered the assailant. Rather than igniting a workers' insurrection that would usher in a new social order as he had hoped, Berkman came away with a long prison sentence. His act confirmed the business stereotype of "labor agitators" as lawless and violent.

Conclusion

By 1900 industrialization had propelled the United States into the forefront of the world's major powers, lowered the cost of goods through mass production, generated thousands of jobs, and produced a wide range of new consumer products. Using accounting systems first developed by the railroads and sophisticated new technologies, national corporations had pioneered innovative systems for distributing and marketing their goods. In the steel and oil industries, Andrew Carnegie and John D. Rockefeller had vertically integrated their companies, controlling production from the raw materials to the finished product. Through systematic cost-cutting and ruthless underselling of their competitors, they had gained control of most of their industry and lowered prices.

Despite these advantages, most Americans recognized that industrialization's cost was high. The rise of the giant corporations had been achieved through savage competition, exploited workers, shady business practices, polluted factory sites, and the collapse of an economic order built on craft skills. In the South in particular, the devastation of the Civil War and the control of banking and raw materials by northern capitalists encouraged industrialists to adopt a paternalistic, family-oriented approach in the cotton mills and to pay exceedingly low wages.

Outbursts of labor violence and the ominous phenomenon of urban slums and grinding poverty showed starkly that all was not well in industrial America. Although the Knights of Labor and the American Federation of Labor attempted to organize workers nationally, the labor movement could not control spontaneous wildcat strikes and violence. In response, company owners appealed to government authorities to arrest strikers, obtain court injunctions against union actions, and cripple the ability of labor leaders to expand their organizations.

As a result, Americans remained profoundly ambivalent about the new industrial order. Caught between their desire for the higher standard of living that industrialization made possible and their fears of capitalist power and social chaos, Americans of the 1880s and 1890s sought strategies that would preserve the benefits while alleviating the undesirable social byproducts. Efforts to regulate railroads at the state level and such national measures as the Interstate Commerce Act and the Sherman Anti-Trust Act, as well as the fervor with which the ideas of a utopian theorist like Edward Bellamy were embraced, represented early manifestations of this impulse. In the Progressive Era of the early twentieth century, Americans would redouble their efforts to formulate political and social responses to the nation's economic transformation after the Civil War.

19

Immigration, Urbanization, and Everyday Life, 1860–1900

THE NEW AMERICAN CITY

Nowhere were the changes in everyday life more visible than in cities. During the late nineteenth century, American cities grew spectacularly. Not only on the East Coast but also in the South, cities swelled at an astonishing pace. Between 1870 and 1900, New Orleans's population increased by nearly fifty percent, Buffalo's tripled, and Chicago's increased more than fivefold. By the start of the new century, Philadelphia, New York, and Chicago all had more than a million residents, and 40 percent of all Americans lived in cities. (In the census, cities were defined as having more than twenty-five hundred inhabitants.) In 1900, New York's 3.4 million inhabitants almost equaled the nation's entire 1850 urban population.

This spectacular urban growth, fueled by migration from the countryside and the arrival of nearly 11 million immigrants between 1870 and 1900, created a dynamic new environment for economic development. New urban jobs and markets in turn dramatically stimulated national economic expansion. Like the frontier, the city symbolized opportunity for all comers.

The city's unprecedented scale and diversity threatened traditional expectations about community life and social stability. Rural America had been a place of face-to-face personal relations where most people shared the same likes and dislikes. In contrast, the city was a seething caldron where immigrant groups contended with one another and with native-born Americans for jobs, power, and influence. Moreover, the same rapid growth that energized manufacturing and production strained city services, generated terrible housing and sanitation problems, and accentuated class differences.

Backyard Baseball, Boston, 1906, by Lewis Hyne *Often idealized as a rural pastime, baseball at the turn of the century became immensely popular in cities where professional teams turned the sport into entertainment for the masses.*

Native-born city-dwellers complained about the noise, stench, and congestion of this transformed cityscape. They fretted about the newcomers' squalid tenements, fondness for drink, and strange customs. When native-born reformers set about cleaning up the city, they sought not only to improve the physical environment but also to destroy the distinctive customs that made immigrant culture different from their own. The late nineteenth century thus witnessed an intense struggle to control the city and benefit from its economic and cultural potential. The stakes were high, for America was increasingly becoming an urban nation.

Migrants and Immigrants

The growing concentration of industries in urban settings produced demands for thousands of new workers. The promise of good wages and a broad range of jobs (labeled by historians as "pull factors") drew men and women from the countryside and small towns. So great was the migration from rural areas, especially New England, that some farm communities vanished from the map.

Young farmwomen led the exodus to the cities. With the growing mechanization of farming in the late nineteenth century, farming was increasingly male work. Rising sales of factory-produced goods through nationally distributed mail-order catalogs reduced the need for rural women's labor. So young farmwomen flocked to the cities, where they competed for jobs with immigrant, black, and city-born white women.

From 1860 to 1890, the prospect of a better life also attracted nearly 10 million northern European immigrants to East Coast and midwestern cities. Germans made up the largest group, numbering close to 3 million, followed by nearly 2 million Eng-

CHRONOLOGY, 1860–1900

1865 • Vassar College founded.

1869 • Boss William Marcy Tweed gains control of New York's Tammany Hall political machine.
First intercollegiate football game.

1872 • Anthony Comstock founds New York Society for the Suppression of Vice.

1873 • John Wanamaker opens his Philadelphia department store.

1875 • Smith and Wellesley colleges founded.

1876 • National League of baseball organized.

1880 • William Booth's followers establish an American branch of the Salvation Army.

1881 • Josephine Shaw Lowell founds New York Charity Organization Society (COS).

1884 • Mark Twain, *Huckleberry Finn*.

1885 • Stanford University founded.

1889 • Jane Addams and Ellen Gates Starr open Hull House.

1891 • University of Chicago founded.
Basketball invented at Springfield College, Massachusetts.

1892 • Ellis Island Immigration Center opened.
General Federation of Women's Clubs organized.

1895 • Coney Island amusement parks open in Brooklyn, New York.

1899 • Scott Joplin, "Maple Leaf Rag."
Kate Chopin, *The Awakening*.
Thorstein Veblen, *The Theory of the Leisure Class*.

1900 • Theodore Dreiser, *Sister Carrie*.
National Association of Colored Women's Clubs organized.

1910 • Angel Island Immigration Center opens in San Francisco.

lish, Scottish, and Welsh immigrants and almost 1.5 million Irish. Moreover, by 1900 more than eight hundred thousand French-Canadians had migrated south to work in the New England mills, and close to a million Scandinavian newcomers had put down roots in the rich farmlands of Wisconsin and Minnesota. On the West Coast, despite the Chinese Exclusion Act of 1882 (see Chapter 18), more than eighty-one thousand Chinese remained in California and nearby states in 1900.

In the 1890s, these earlier immigrants from northern and western Europe were joined by swelling numbers of **"new immigrants"**—Italians, Slavs, Greeks, and Jews from southern and eastern Europe, Armenians from the Middle East, and, in Hawaii, Japanese from Asia. In the next three decades, these new immigrants, many from peasant backgrounds, would boost America's foreign-born population by more than 18 million.

The overwhelming majority of immigrants settled in cities in the northeastern and north-central states, with the Irish predominating in New England and the Germans in the Midwest. The effect of their numbers was staggering. In 1890, New York City (including Brooklyn, still a legally separate municipality) contained twice as many Irish as Dublin, as many Germans as Hamburg, half as many Italians as Naples, and 2 1/2 times the Jewish population of Warsaw. That same year four out of five people living in New York had been born abroad or were children of foreign-born parents.

Some recent immigrants had been forced out of their home countries by overpopulation, crop failure, famine, religious persecution, violence, or industrial depression. (Historians call these reasons for immigration "push factors," since they drove immigrants out of their homelands.) Emigration from England, for example, spurted during economic downturns in 1873 and 1883. German peasants, squeezed by overpopulation and frustrated by church reorganizations that they opposed, left in large numbers in the 1880s. Others came voluntarily in search of better opportunities. More than one hundred thousand Japanese laborers, for example, were lured to Hawaii in the 1890s to work on sugar plantations by promises of high wages.

Figure 19.1 The Changing Face of U.S. Immigration, 1860–1930

Between 1865 and 1895, the majority of newcomers to America hailed from northern and western Europe. But the early twentieth century witnessed a surge of immigration from southern and eastern Europe.

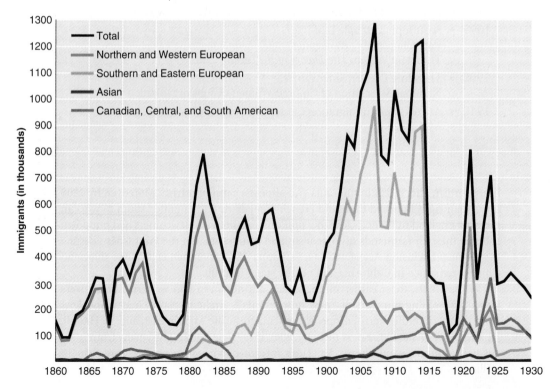

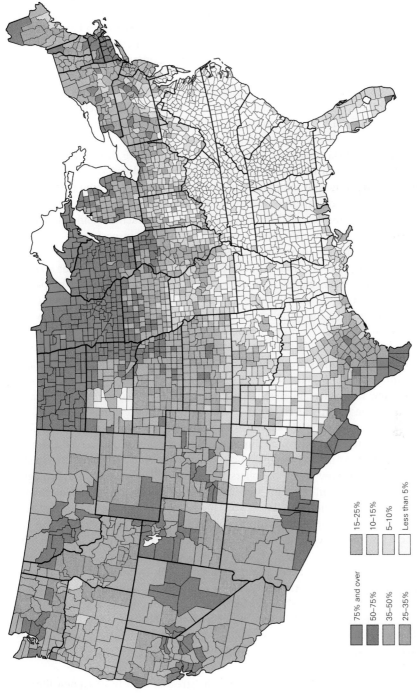

MAP 19.1 Percent of Foreign-born Whites and Native Whites of Foreign or Mixed Parentage in Total Population, by Counties, 1910

As this map indicates, new immigrants rarely settled in the South. *Source: D. W. Meinig, The Shaping of America—A Geographical Perspective of 500 Years of History. Yale University Press, Volume 3.*

Legend:
- 75% and over
- 50–75%
- 35–50%
- 25–35%
- 15–25%
- 10–15%
- 5–10%
- Less than 5%

A large number of immigrants were single young men. Birger Osland, an eighteen-year-old Norwegian, explained his reasons for leaving to a friend: "as I now probably have a foundation upon which I can build my own further education, I have come to feel that the most sensible thing I can do is to emigrate to America." Although significant numbers of young men remained in the United States after they had become successful, large numbers, especially Italians and Chinese, returned home as well.

Although single women were less likely to come on their own, Irish women often did so and sent their earnings back home. Most commonly, wives and children waited in the old country until the family breadwinner had secured a job and saved enough money to pay for their passage to America.

Would-be immigrants first had to travel to a port—Hamburg, Germany, was a major embarkation point—where they boarded a crowded steamship. The cramped ocean journey was noted for its poor food, lack of privacy, and rudimentary sanitary facilities. Immigrants arrived tired, fearful, and in some cases sick.

Further complications awaited the travelers when they reached their destination, most often New York City or San Francisco. Customs officials inspected the newcomers for physical handicaps and contagious diseases. After 1892, those with "loathsome" infections such as leprosy, trachoma (a contagious viral disease of the eye), or sexually transmitted diseases were refused admittance and deported. Immigrants who passed the physical examination then had their names recorded. If a customs inspector had difficulty pronouncing a foreign name, he often Anglicized it. One German Jew became flustered when asked for his name and mumbled, "Schon vergessen [already forgotten]," meaning that he could not recall it. The inspector, who did not understand German, wrote "Sean Ferguson" on the man's roster. In this manner, many immigrants ended up with Americanized names.

In 1855, New York State had established a special facility for admitting immigrants at Castle Garden on the tip of Manhattan Island. Later, when the numbers swelled, the federal government took control and built a new station on **Ellis Island** in New York harbor in 1892. Angel Island in San Francisco Bay on the West Coast served a similar purpose after 1910. At the immigrant processing centers, America's newest residents exchanged foreign currency for U.S. dollars, purchased railroad tickets, and arranged lodgings. In other cities immigrants were hounded by tavernkeepers, peddlers, and porters who tried to exploit them. "When you land in America," wrote one Swedish resident to friends back home, "you will find many who will offer their services, but beware of them because there are so many rascals who make it their business to cheat the immigrants."

Those who arrived with sufficient cash, including many German artisans and Scandinavian farmers, commonly traveled west to Chicago, Milwaukee, and the rolling prairies beyond. Most of the Irish, and later the Italians, who hailed largely from poor rural backgrounds, remained in eastern cities like Boston, New York, and Philadelphia. The Irish and Italians who did go west typically made the trip in stages, moving from job to job on the railroad and canal systems.

Adjusting to an Urban Society

For many immigrants the stress of adjusting to a new life was eased by settling among compatriots who had preceded them. (Historians call this tendency to relocate near friends or relatives from one's original town "chain migration.") If a map of New York City's streets and neighborhoods were colored in by nationality, Jacob Riis observed in 1890, it "would show more stripes than on the skin of a zebra, and more colors than any rainbow." The streets of Manhattan between the West Side Irish neighborhoods and the East Side German neighborhoods teemed with Poles, Hungarians, Russians, Italians, and Chinese.

Late-nineteenth-century social commentators often assumed that each nationality clumped together for reasons of national clannishness. But settlement patterns were far more complex. Most immigrants preferred to live near others not merely from their own country but also from their own village or region. On New York's Lower East Side, for example, Italians divided into many different subgroups: Neapolitans and Calabrians at Mulberry Bend, Genoese on Baxter Street, northern Italians west of Broadway, and Tyrolese Italians on Sixty-ninth Street near the Hudson River.

Some immigrant groups adjusted more easily than others. Skilled workers and those familiar with Anglo-American customs had relatively few problems. English-speaking immigrants from the British Isles, particularly those from mill, mining, and manufacturing districts, found comparable work and encountered relatively little discrimination. Ethnic groups that formed a substantial percentage of a city's population also had a major advantage. The Irish, for example, who by the 1880s made up nearly 16 percent of New York's population, 8 percent of Chicago's, and 17 percent of Boston's, facilitated Irish immigrants' entry into the American mainstream by dominating Democratic Party politics and controlling the hierarchy of the Catholic church in all three cities. Because of their success, upwardly mobile Irish became known as "lace curtain" Irish, a reference to their adoption of middle-class ideals.

Ironically, domination of urban institutions by members of larger immigrant groups often made adjustment to American society more difficult for members of smaller groups. Germans and other well-organized and skilled immigrants tended to exclude skilled newcomers from desirable jobs. English and German dominance of the building trades, for example, enabled those nationalities to limit the numbers of Italians hired.

The diversity of immigrants, even those from the same country, was remarkable. Nevertheless, the experience of being labeled a foreigner and of being discriminated against helped create a new common ethnic identity for many groups. Immigrants from the same home country forged a new sense of ethnic distinctiveness as Irish-American, German-American, or Jewish-American that helped them compete for political power and eventually assimilate into mainstream society.

Not all immigrants intended to remain in the United States. Young Chinese and Italian men often worked to save enough money to return home and buy a business. Expecting only a brief stay, they made little effort to learn English or understand American customs. Of the Italians who immigrated to New York before 1914, nearly 50 percent went back to Italy. Although the rate of return migration was greatest among Chinese and Italians, significant numbers of other nationalities eventually returned to their homelands as well.

Various factors thus influenced the ability of immigrants to adapt to urban society in America. Nevertheless, as the number of foreigners in U.S. cities ballooned toward the turn of the century, all immigrant groups faced increasing hostility from white native-born Americans who not only disliked the newcomers' social customs but also worried about their growing influence. Fearing the loss of the privileges and status that were associated with their white skin color, native-born whites often stigmatized immigrants as racially different and inferior. Only gradually, and with much effort, did Irish, Jews, Slavs, and Italians come to be considered "white."

Slums and Ghettos   Every major city had its share of rundown, overcrowded slum neighborhoods. Generally clustered within walking distance of manufacturing districts, slums developed when landlords subdivided long, narrow buildings with few windows, called tenements, and packed in too many residents. The poorer the renters, the worse the slum. Slums became ghettos when laws, prejudice, and community pressure prevented the tenement inhabitants from renting elsewhere. During the 1890s Italians in New York, blacks in Philadelphia and Chicago, Mexican-Americans in Los Angeles, and Chinese in San Francisco increasingly became locked in segregated ghettos.

Life in the slums was particularly difficult for children. Juvenile diseases such as whooping cough (pertussis), measles, and scarlet fever took a fearful toll, and infant mortality was high. In one immigrant ward in Chicago in 1900, 20 percent of infants died in their first year of life.

Since tenements often bordered industrial districts, residents had to put up with the noise, pollution, and foul odors of tanneries, foundries, factories, and packing houses. Because most factories used coal-fired steam engines as their energy source, and because coal was also the preferred fuel for heating apartment houses and businesses, vast quantities of soot and coal dust drifted skyward daily.

Most immigrants stayed in the shabbiest tenements only until they could afford better housing. Blacks, in contrast, were trapped in segregated districts. Driven out of the skilled trades and excluded from most factory work, blacks took menial jobs whose low pay left them little income for housing (see Chapter 18). Racist city-dwellers used high rents, real-estate covenants (agreements not to rent or sell to blacks), and neighborhood pressure to exclude them from areas inhabited by whites. Because the numbers of northern urban blacks in 1890 remained relatively small—for example, they composed only 1.2 percent of Cleveland's population and 1.3 percent of Chicago's—they could not overcome whites' concerted campaigns to shut them out. Instead, wealthy black entrepreneurs established their own churches and charitable organizations in the black neighborhoods where they lived.

Fashionable Avenues and Suburbs   As remains true today, the same cities that harbored slums, filth, suffering, and violence also boasted of neighborhoods of dazzling opulence with the latest lighting and plumbing technologies (see Technology and Culture: Flush Toilets and the Invention of the Nineteenth-Century Bathroom). John D. Rockefeller and Jay Gould lived near Fifth Avenue in New York; other wealthy Americans lived on Commonwealth Avenue in Boston, Euclid Avenue in Cleveland, and Summit Avenue in St. Paul. In the 1870s and 1880s, wealthy city-dwellers began moving to new suburbs. Promoters of the suburban ideal contrasted the rolling lawns and stately houses on the city's periphery with the teeming streets, noisy saloons, and mounds of garbage and horse excrement downtown. Soon, many major cities could boast of their own stylish suburbs: Haverford, Ardmore, and Bryn Mawr outside Philadelphia; Brookline near Boston; and Shaker Heights near Cleveland.

Flush Toilets and the Invention of the Nineteenth-Century Bathroom

The development of a system of indoor plumbing was typical of the technological breakthroughs that simplified everyday life in the late nineteenth century. In the 1860s, only about 5 percent of American houses had running water. Most Americans used chamber pots or outhouses that emptied into slimy, smelly cesspools. Two decades later, indoor plumbing standards had been established in most major U.S. cities, and wealthier urban Americans used flush toilets connected to municipal sewer systems.

The driving force for change came from outbreaks of cholera, typhoid, and yellow fever, diseases spread by polluted water, that periodically terrorized American cities. Building upon the discovery of germs by Louis Pasteur and Robert Koch, sanitary reformers established stringent metropolitan health laws, created state boards of health, and mandated the licensing of plumbers and the inspection of their work. By the turn of the century, George E. Waring, Jr., a prominent sanitary engineer, could confidently declare that "Plumbing, as we know it, is essentially and almost exclusively an American Institution."

The decision to adopt a water-based system for the removal of human wastes depended on a series of inventions. First, municipal water systems had to be built with reservoirs, pumps, and water towers to provide water to the pipes that supplied buildings. A sewage system of interconnected pipes was also necessary to remove and process wastes. Machines to manufacture lead, cast-iron, and glazed stoneware pipes had to be created,

as did a uniform system of pipe threads and melted lead joints to create a reliable standardized system for connecting them. Finally, a porcelain toilet with a built-in gas trap was needed because the bacteria in feces produce methane or sewer gas. (A trap is a U-shaped joint that uses the water at the low part of the U to prevent gas from seeping back into the bathroom. The gas is then vented through a pipe in the roof.)

Despite its usefulness, the new technology was not rapidly adopted. In 1890, only 24 percent of American dwellings had running water. As late as 1897, over 90 percent of the families in tenements had no baths and had to wash in hallway sinks or courtyard hydrants. By 1920, 80 percent of American houses, particularly those in rural areas, still lacked indoor flush toilets. The reason was simple: indoor plumbing was expensive and depended on the availability of water and sewer systems. Adding indoor plumbing increased the price of a new house by 20 percent.

Advertisers did their best to increase demand. They skillfully used the findings of science to advocate new standards of cleanliness or "hygiene," as it was called, which they associated with upper-class principles of respectability and decorum. Bathing and washing one's hands were touted as symbols of upper-class refinement.

Indoor plumbing not only reinforced higher standards for personal hygiene; it also enmeshed the homeowner in a web of local and state regulations. As sewage and water systems expanded to cover larger constituencies, political control moved from local to state and sometimes national arenas. Once largely independent, the homeowner now had to deal with water and power companies that often functioned regionally.

The adoption of strict sanitation systems and the use of indoor plumbing did achieve their intended result: they dramatically reduced the spread of disease. But the advances had unintended consequences. Indoor plumbing encouraged the phenomenal waste of water. A single faulty toilet could easily leak a hundred gallons of water a day. Not until the

1990s with the development of new low-water-usage toilets, which could save between 18,000 and 26,400 gallons of water a year, would new standards be established to reduce the use of water, an increasingly precious natural resource.

Question for Analysis

- Why does the successful introduction of new technologies often involve a system of inventions rather than a single invention?

Middle-class city-dwellers followed the precedents set by the wealthy. Skilled artisans, shopkeepers, clerks, accountants, and sales personnel moved either to new developments at the city's edge or to outlying suburban communities (although those at the lower fringe of the middle class typically rented apartments in neighborhoods closer to the city center). Lawyers, doctors, small businessmen, and other professionals moved farther out along the main thoroughfares served by the street railway, where they purchased homes on large lots. By the twentieth century, this process would result in suburban sprawl.

In time, a pattern of informal residential segregation by income took shape in the cities and suburbs. Built up for families of a particular income level, certain neighborhoods and suburbs developed remarkably similar standards for lot size and house design. (Two-story houses with front porches, set back thirty feet from the sidewalk, became the norm in many neighborhoods.) Commuters who rode the new street railways out from the city center could identify the social class of the suburban dwellers along the way as readily as a geologist might distinguish different strata on a washed-out riverbank.

By 1900, whirring trolley cars and hissing steam-powered trains had burst the boundaries of the compact midcentury city. As they expanded, cities often annexed contingent suburbs. Within this enlarged city, sharp dissimilarities in building height and neighborhood quality set off business sectors from fashionable residential avenues and differentiated squalid manufacturing districts from parklike suburban subdivisions. Musing about urban America in 1902, James F. Muirhead, a popular Scottish guidebook author, wrote that New York and other U.S. cities reminded him of "a lady in a ball costume, with diamonds in her ears, and her toes out at her boots." To Muirhead, urban America had become a "land of contrasts" in which the spatial separations of various social groups and the increasingly dissimilar living conditions for rich and poor had heightened ethnic, racial, and class divisions. Along with the physical change in American cities, in short, had come a new awareness of class and cultural disparities.

MIDDLE- AND UPPER-CLASS SOCIETY AND CULTURE

Spared the struggle for survival that confronted most Americans after the Civil War, society's middle and upper ranks faced a different challenge: how to rationalize their enjoyment of the products of the emerging consumer society. To justify the position of society's wealthier members, ministers such as Brooklyn preacher Henry Ward Beecher and advice-book writers appealed to **Victorian morality,** a set of social ideas embraced by the privileged classes of England and America during the long reign (1837–1901) of Britain's Queen Victoria.

E. L. Godkin, the editor of *The Nation,* Phillips Brooks, minister to Boston's Trinity Church, and other proponents of Victorian morality argued that the financial success of the middle and upper classes was linked to their superior talent, intelligence, morality, and self-control. They also extended the antebellum ideal of separate spheres by arguing that women were the driving force for moral improvement. While men were expected to engage in self-disciplined, "manly" dedication to the new industrial order, women would provide the gentle, elevating influence that would lead society in its upward march. While Beecher, Godkin, and others defended the superiority of America's middle and upper classes, a network of institutions, from elegant department stores and hotels to elite colleges and universities, reinforced the privileged position of these groups.

Manners and Morals The Victorian world view, which first emerged in the 1830s and 1840s, rested on a number of assumptions (see Chapter 8). One was that human nature was malleable: people could improve themselves. Hence, Victorian Americans were intensely moralistic and eager to reform practices they considered evil or undesirable. A second assumption was that work had social value: working hard not only developed self-discipline but also helped advance the progress of the nation. Finally, Victorian Americans stressed the importance of good manners and the cultivation of literature and art as marks of a truly civilized society. Although these genteel assumptions were sometimes ignored, they were held up as universal standards.

Before the Civil War, reformers such as Henry Ward Beecher had energized the crusades to abolish slavery and alcoholism by appealing to the ethical standards of Victorian morality. (Both slavery and intemperance threatened feminine virtue and family life.) After the war, Beecher and other preachers became less interested in social reform and more preoccupied with the importance of manners and social protocol. Following their advice, middle- and upper-class families in the 1870s and 1880s increasingly defined their own social standing in terms not only of income but also of behavior. Good manners, especially a knowledge of dining and entertaining etiquette, and good posture became important marks of status.

In her popular advice book *The American Woman's Home* (1869), Catharine Beecher (the sister of Henry Ward Beecher) displayed the typical Victorian self-consciousness about proper manners. The following dinner-table behaviors, she said, should be avoided by those of "good breeding":

> Reaching over another person's plate; standing up to reach distant articles, instead of asking to have them passed; . . . using the table-cloth instead of napkins; eating

fast, and in a noisy manner; putting large pieces in the mouth; . . . [and] picking the teeth at the table.

For Beecher and other molders of manners, meals became important rituals that differentiated the social classes. The elaborate china and silver that wealthy families exclusively possessed also provided telltale clues to a family's level of refinement and sophistication.

The Victorian code—with its emphasis on morals, manners, and proper behavior—thus served to heighten the sense of class differences for the post–Civil War generation. Prominent middle- and upper-class Americans made bold claims about their interest in helping others improve themselves. More often than not, however, their self-righteous, intensely moralistic outlook simply widened the gap that income disparities had already opened.

The Cult of Domesticity

Victorian views on morality and culture, coupled with the need to make decisions about a mountain of domestic products, had a subtle but important effect on middle-class expectations about women's role within the home. From the 1840s on, architects, clergymen, and other promoters of the so-called cult of domesticity had idealized the home as "the woman's sphere." They praised the home as a protected retreat where women could express their maternal gifts, including sensitivity toward children and an aptitude for religion. "The home is the wife's province," asserted one writer; "it is her natural field of labor . . . to govern and direct its interior management."

During the 1880s and 1890s, a new obligation was added: to foster an artistic environment that would nurture her family's cultural improvement. For many Victorian Americans of the comfortable classes, houses became statements of cultural aspiration. Excluded from the world of business and commerce, many middle- and upper-class women devoted considerable time and energy to decorating their homes, seeking to make the home, as one advice book suggested, "a place of repose, a refuge from the excitement and distractions of outside . . . , provided with every attainable means of rest and recreation."

Not all middle-class women pursued this domestic ideal. For some, housework and family responsibilities overwhelmed the concern for artistic accomplishment. For others the artistic ideal was not to their taste. Sixteen-year-old Mary Putnam complained privately to a friend that she played the piano because of "an abstract general idea . . . of a father coming home regularly tired at night (from the plow, I believe the usual legend runs), and being solaced by the brilliant yet touching performance of a sweet only daughter upon the piano." She then confessed that she detested the piano. In the 1880s and 1890s, as middle- and upper-class women sought other outlets for their creative energies in settlement-house work, social reform, and women's club activities, the older domestic ideal began to unravel.

Department Stores

Although Victorian social thought justified the privileged status of the well-to-do, many thrifty people who had grown up in the early nineteenth century found it difficult to accept the new preoccupation with accumulation and display. To lure these consumers, merchandisers in the 1880s stressed the high quality and low cost of the objects they sold, encouraging Americans to loosen their purse strings and enjoy prosperity without reservations. This argument particularly appealed to women who, in order to provide for their families, now had to shop for soap, canned foods, and other products formerly made at home.

A key agent in modifying attitudes about consumption was the **department store.** In the final quarter of the nineteenth century, innovative entrepreneurs led by Rowland H. Macy in New York, John Wanamaker in Philadelphia, and Marshall Field in Chicago built giant department stores that transformed the shopping experience for millions of women who became their most important consumers. The stores attracted these new customers by advertising "rock-bottom" prices and engaging in price wars. To avoid keeping their stock too long, they held giant end-of-the-season sales at drastically marked-down prices.

The major department stores tried to make shopping an exciting activity. Rapid turnover of merchandise created a sense of constant novelty. The mammoth stores themselves were imitation palaces, complete with stained-glass skylights, marble staircases, sparkling chandeliers, and plush carpets. The large urban department store functioned as a workplace for the lower classes and as a kind of social club for comfortably fixed women. For those who could afford it, shopping became an adventure, a form of entertainment, and a way to affirm their place in society.

The Transformation of Higher Education At a time when relatively few Americans had even a high school education, the upper classes dominated U.S. colleges and universities. In 1900, only 4 percent of the nation's eighteen- to twenty-one-year-olds were enrolled in institutions of higher learning.

Wealthy capitalists gained status and a measure of immortality by endowing colleges and universities. Leland Stanford and his wife, Jane Lathrop Stanford, launched Stanford University in 1885 with a bequest of $24 million in memory of their dead son; John D. Rockefeller donated $34 million to the University of Chicago in 1891. Industrialists and businessmen dominated the boards of trustees of most educational institutions.

Not only the classroom experience but also social contacts and athletic activities—especially football—prepared affluent young men for later responsibilities in business and the professions. Adapted by American college students in 1869 from English rugby, football was largely an elite sport. But the game, initially played without pads or helmets, was marred by violence. In 1905, eighteen students died of playing-field injuries. Many college presidents dismissed football as a dangerous waste of time and money. In 1873, when the University of Michigan challenged Cornell to a game in Ann Arbor, Cornell's president Andrew D. White huffily telegraphed back, "I will not permit thirty men to travel four hundred miles merely to agitate a bag of wind."

But eager alumni and coaches strongly defended the new sport. Some—among them Henry Lee Higginson, the Civil War veteran and Boston banker who gave Harvard "Soldiers' Field" stadium as a memorial to those who had died in battle—praised football as a character-building sport. Others, including famed Yale coach Walter Camp, insisted that football could function as a surrogate frontier experience in an increasingly urbanized society. By 1900, collegiate football had become a popular fall ritual, and team captains were campus heroes.

More than 150 new colleges and universities were founded between 1880 and 1900, and enrollments more than doubled. While wealthy capitalists endowed some institutions, others, such as the state universities in the South and Midwest, were financed largely

Chemistry Class, Smith College, 1889 *Thanks to their education in science at colleges and universities, increasing numbers of women in the 1890s became physicians. Nevertheless, most medical schools refused to appoint women doctors to their teaching staffs.*

through public funds generated from public land sales under the Morrill Land Grant Act (1862). Many colleges were also founded and funded by religious denominations.

Following the precedent set by Oberlin College in 1836, coeducational private colleges and public universities in the Midwest enrolled increasing numbers of women. In the East, Columbia, Brown, and Harvard universities admitted women to the affiliated but separate institutions of Barnard (1889), Pembroke (1891), and Radcliffe (1894), respectively. Some colleges—Mount Holyoke (1837), Vassar (1865), Wellesley and Smith (1875), and Bryn Mawr (1884)—were founded solely for women. At these institutions, participation in college organizations, athletics, and dramatics enabled female students to learn traditionally "masculine" strategies for gaining power. The generation of women educated at female institutions in the late nineteenth century developed the self-confidence to break with the Victorian ideal of passive womanhood and to compete with men by displaying strength, aggressiveness, and intelligence—popularly considered male attributes. Nationally, the percentage of colleges admitting women jumped from 30 percent to 71 percent between 1880 and 1900. By the turn of the century, women made up more than one-third of the total college-student population.

On the university level, innovative presidents such as Cornell's Andrew D. White and Harvard's Charles W. Eliot sought to change the focus of higher education. New discoveries in science and medicine sparked the reform. In the 1850s, most physicians had attended medical school for only two sixteen-week terms. They typically received their degrees without ever having visited a hospital or examined a patient. The Civil

War exposed the abysmal state of American medical knowledge. Twice as many soldiers died from infections as from wounds. Doctors were so poorly trained and ignorant about sanitation that they often infected soldiers' injuries when they probed wounds with hands wiped on pus-stained aprons. "The ignorance and general incompetency of the average graduate of American medical schools, at the time when he receives the degree which turns him loose upon the community," wrote Eliot in 1870, "is something horrible to contemplate."

In the 1880s and 1890s, leading medical professors, many of whom had studied in France and Germany, began restructuring American medical education. Using the experimental method developed by German scientists, they insisted that all medical students be trained in biology, chemistry, and physics, including working in a laboratory. Although medical school reform improved health care in some areas, it also effectively shut out African-American and poor women who could not afford the tuition. By 1900, graduate medical education had been placed on a firm professional foundation. New educational and professional standards, similarly, were established for architects, engineers, and lawyers.

These changes were part of a larger transformation in higher education, the rise of a new kind of institution, the **research university.** Unlike the best of the mid-nineteenth-century colleges, which focused on teaching Latin and Greek, theology, logic, and mathematics, the new research universities offered courses in a wide variety of subject areas, established professional schools, and encouraged faculty members to pursue basic research. At Cornell University, President Andrew D. White's objective was to create an environment "where any person can find instruction in any study." At Cornell, the University of Wisconsin at Madison, Johns Hopkins, Harvard, and other institutions, this new conception of higher education laid the groundwork for the central role that America's universities would play in the intellectual, cultural, and scientific life of the twentieth century.

WORKING-CLASS POLITICS AND REFORM

The contrast between the affluent world of the college-educated middle and upper classes and the gritty lives of the working class was most graphically on display in the nation's growing urban centers, where immigrant newcomers reshaped political and social institutions to meet their own needs. If fancy department stores and elegant hotels furnished new social spaces for the middle and upper classes, saloons became the poor man's club, and dance halls became single women's home away from home. While the rich and the wellborn looked suspiciously at lower-class recreational activities and sought to force the poor to change their ways, working-class Americans, the immigrant newcomers in particular, fought to preserve their own distinctive way of life. Indeed, the late nineteenth century witnessed an ongoing battle to eradicate social drinking, reform "boss" politics, and curb lower-class recreational activities.

Political Bosses and Machine Politics Earlier in the century the swelling numbers of urban poor had given rise to a new kind of politician, the "boss," who listened to his urban constituents and lobbied to improve their lot. The boss presided over the city's "machine"—an unofficial political organization designed to keep a particular party or faction in office. Whether officially serving as mayor or not, the boss, assisted by local ward or precinct captains, wielded enormous influence in city government. Often a former saloonkeeper or labor leader, the boss knew his constituents well.

For better or worse, the **political machine** was America's unique contribution to municipal government in an era of pell-mell urban growth. Typified by Tammany Hall, the Democratic organization that dominated New York City politics from the 1830s to the 1930s, machines emerged in Baltimore, Philadelphia, Atlanta, San Francisco, and a host of other cities during the Gilded Age.

By the turn of the century, many cities had experienced machine rule. Working through the local ward captains to turn out unusually high numbers of voters (see Chapter 20), the machine rode herd on the tangle of municipal bureaucracies, controlling who was hired for the police and fire departments. It rewarded its friends and punished its enemies through its control of taxes, licenses, and inspections. The machine gave tax breaks to favored contractors in return for large payoffs and slipped them insider information about upcoming street and sewer projects.

At the neighborhood level, the ward boss often acted as a welfare agent, helping the needy and protecting the troubled. To spend three dollars to pay a fine for a juvenile offense meant a lot to the poor, but it was small change to a boss who raked in millions from public-utility contracts and land deals. While the machine helped alleviate some suffering, it entangled urban social services with corrupt politics and often prevented city government from responding to the real problems of the city's neediest inhabitants.

Under New York City's boss **William "Magear" Tweed,** the Tammany Hall machine revealed the slimy depths to which extortion and contract padding could sink. Between 1869 and 1871, Tweed gave $50,000 to the poor and $2,250,000 to schools, orphanages, and hospitals. In these same years, his machine dispensed sixty thousand patronage positions and pumped up the city's debt by $70 million through graft and inflated contracts. The details of the Tweed ring's massive fraud and corruption were brilliantly satirized in *Harper's Weekly* by German immigrant cartoonist Thomas Nast. In one cartoon Nast portrayed Tweed and his cronies as vultures picking at the city's bones. Tweed bellowed in fury. "I don't care a straw for your newspaper articles—my constituents don't know how to read," he told *Harper's,* "but they can't help seeing them damned pictures." Convicted of fraud and extortion, Tweed was sentenced to jail in 1873, served two years, escaped to Spain, was reapprehended and reincarcerated, and died in jail in 1878.

By the turn of the century the bosses were facing well-organized assaults on their power, led by an urban elite whose members sought to restore "good government" (see Chapter 21). In this atmosphere, the bosses increasingly forged alliances with civic organizations and reform leagues. The results, although never entirely satisfactory to any of the parties involved, paved the way for new sewage and transportation systems, expanded parklands, and improved public services—a record of considerable accomplishment, given the magnitude of the problems created by urban growth.

Battling Poverty   Impatient with political bosses' piecemeal attempts to help the urban poor, middle-class city leaders sought comprehensive solutions for relieving poverty. Jacob Riis and the first generation of reformers believed that the basic cause of urban distress was the immigrants' lack of self-discipline and self-control. Consequently, Riis and his peers focused on moral improvement and exposing squalid tenement housing. Only later would Jane Addams, Florence Kelley, and other settlement-house workers examine the crippling impact of low wages and dangerous working conditions. Although many reformers genuinely sympathized with the suffering of the lower classes, the humanitarians often turned their campaigns to help the destitute into missions to Americanize the immigrants and eliminate customs that they perceived as offensive and self-destructive.

Poverty-relief workers first targeted their efforts at the young, who were thought to be most impressionable. Energized by the religious revivals of the 1830s and 1840s, Protestant reformers started charitable societies to help transient youths and abandoned street children. In 1843, Robert M. Hartley, a former employee of the New York Temperance Society, organized the New York Association for Improving the Condition of the Poor to urge poor families to change their ways.

Hartley's voluntaristic approach was supplemented by the more coercive tactics of Charles Loring Brace, who founded the New York Children's Aid Society in 1853. Brace admired "these little traders of the city . . . battling for a hard living in the snow and mud of the street" but worried that they might join the city's "dangerous classes." Brace established dormitories, reading rooms, and workshops where the boys could learn practical skills; he also swept orphaned children off the streets, shipped them to the country, and placed them with families to work as farm hands.

Where Brace's Children's Aid Society gave adolescents an alternative to living in the slums, the Young Men's Christian Association (YMCA), founded in England in 1841 and exported to America ten years later, provided housing and wholesome recreation for country boys who had migrated to the city. The Young Women's Christian Association (YWCA) similarly provided housing and a day nursery for young women and their children. In the Protestant tradition of moral improvement, both organizations subjected their members to curfews and expelled them for drinking and other forbidden behavior.

By 1900, more than fifteen hundred YMCAs and YWCAs served as havens for nearly a quarter-million young men and women. But YMCA and YWCA leaders reached only a small portion of the young adult population. Some whom they sought to help were put off by the organizations' close supervision and moralistic stance. Others, eager to assert their independence, preferred not to ask for help. Although charity workers made some progress in their efforts to aid youth, the strategy was too narrowly focused to stem the rising tide of urban problems.

New Approaches to Social Reform   The inability of the Children's Aid Society, YMCA, YWCA, and other relief organizations to cope with the explosive growth of the urban poor in the 1870s and 1880s convinced some reformers to search for other ways to fight poverty. One of the earliest and most effective agencies was the **Salvation Army.** A church established along pseudomilitary lines in England in 1865 by Methodist minister "General" William Booth, the Salvation Army sent uniformed volunteers to the United States in 1880 to provide food, shelter, and temporary employment for families. Its members ran soup kitchens and day nurseries and dispatched its "slum brigades" to carry the message of morality to the immigrant poor. The army's strategy was simple. Attract the poor with marching bands and lively preaching; follow up with offers of food, assistance, and employment; and then teach them the solid middle-class virtues of temperance, hard work, and self-discipline.

A similar approach to poor relief was implemented by the New York Charity Organization Society (COS), founded in 1882 by **Josephine Shaw Lowell.** Of a prominent

Boston family, the strong-willed Lowell had been widowed when her husband of a few months was killed during the Civil War, and she wore black for the rest of her life. Trying to make aid to the poor more efficient, Lowell and the COS leaders divided New York City into districts, compiled files on all aid recipients, and sent "friendly visitors," who were trained, salaried women, into the tenements to counsel families on how to improve their lives. Convinced that moral deficiencies lay at the root of poverty and that the "promiscuous charity" of overlapping church welfare agencies undermined the desire to work, the COS tried to foster self-sufficiency in its charges. In 1891, Lowell helped found the Consumers' League of New York, which encouraged women to buy only from manufacturers who paid fair wages and maintained decent working conditions.

Although the COS did serve as a useful coordinator for relief efforts and developed helpful statistics on the extent of poverty, critics justly accused the society of being more interested in controlling the poor than in alleviating their suffering. One of the manuals, for example, stressed the importance of introducing "messy housekeepers" to the "pleasures of a cheery, well-ordered home." Unable to see slum problems from the vantage point of the poor, they failed, for the most part, in their underlying objective: to convert the poor to their own standards of morality and decorum.

The Moral-Purity Campaign

While Josephine Shaw Lowell and other like-minded social disciplinarians worked to eradicate urban poverty, other reformers pushed for tougher measures against sin and immorality. In 1872, **Anthony Comstock,** a pious young dry-goods clerk, founded the New York Society for the Suppression of Vice. The organization demanded that municipal authorities close down gambling and lottery operations and censor obscene publications.

Nothing symbolized the contested terrain between middle- and lower-class culture better than the fight over prostitution. Considered socially degenerate by some and a source of recreation by others, prostitution both exploited women and offered them a steady income and a measure of personal freedom. After the Civil War, the number of brothels—specialized houses controlled by women known as madams where prostitutes plied their trade—expanded rapidly. In the 1880s, saloons, tenements, and cabarets, often controlled by political machines, hired prostitutes of their own. Even though immigrant women do not appear to have made up the majority of big-city prostitutes, reformers often labeled them as the major source of the problem.

In 1892, brothels, along with gambling dens and saloons, became targets for the reform efforts of New York Presbyterian minister Charles Parkhurst. Blaming the "slimy, oozy soil of Tammany Hall" and the New York City police—"the dirtiest, crookedest, and ugliest lot of men ever combined in semi-military array outside of Japan and Turkey"—for the city's rampant evils, he organized the City Vigilance League to clean up the city. Two years later a nonpartisan Committee of Seventy elected a new mayor who pressured city officials to enforce the laws against prostitution, gambling, and Sunday liquor sales.

The purity campaign lasted scarcely three years. The reform coalition quickly fell apart. New York City's population was too large, and its ethnic constituencies too diverse, for middle- and upper-class reformers to curb all the illegal activities flourishing within the sprawling metropolis.

The Social Gospel   In the 1870s and 1880s, a handful of Protestant ministers began to explore several radical alternatives for aiding the poor.
Instead of focusing on their alleged moral flaws and character defects, these ministers
argued that the rich and the wellborn deserved part of the blame for urban poverty and
thus had a responsibility to do something about it.

William S. Rainsford, the Irish-born minister of New York City's Saint George's
Episcopal Church, pioneered the development of the so-called institutional church
movement. Large downtown churches in once-elite districts that had been overrun by
immigrants would provide their new neighbors with social services as well as a place to
worship. With the financial help of J. Pierpont Morgan, a warden of his church, Rainsford organized a boys' club, built church recreational facilities for the destitute on the
Lower East Side, and established an industrial training program.

Another effort within Protestantism to right contemporary social wrongs was the
Social Gospel movement launched in the 1870s by Washington Gladden, a Congregational minister in Columbus, Ohio. Gladden insisted that true Christianity commits
men and women to fight social injustice wherever it exists. Thus, in response to the
wave of violent strikes in 1877, he urged church leaders to mediate the conflict between
business and labor. Their attempt to do so was unsuccessful.

If Gladden set the tone for the Social Gospel, Walter Rauschenbusch, a minister at
a German Baptist church in New York's notorious "Hell's Kitchen" neighborhood, articulated the movement's central philosophy. Educated in Germany, Rauschenbusch
argued that a truly Christian society would unite all churches, reorganize the industrial
system, and work for international peace. Rauschenbusch's appeal for Christian unity
led to the formation of the Federal Council of Churches in 1908, but his other goals
were never achieved. The Social Gospel's attack on what its leaders blasted as the complacent Christian support of the status quo attracted only a handful of Protestants.
Nevertheless, their earnest voices blended with a growing chorus of critics bemoaning
the nation's urban woes.

The Settlement-   By the late 1880s, many thoughtful Americans had become
House Movement   convinced that reform pressures applied from the top by the
Charity Organization Society and the purity crusaders, how-
ever well intentioned, were ineffective. A new approach to social work was needed. Relief workers would have to take up residence in poor neighborhoods, where, in the
words of **Jane Addams,** an early advocate of the movement, they could see firsthand
"the struggle for existence, which is so much harsher among people near the edge of
pauperism." A new institution—the settlement house—was born.

The youngest daughter of a successful Illinois businessman, Jane Addams purchased a dilapidated mansion on Chicago's South Halsted Street in 1889. After over-
seeing extensive repairs, she and her coworkers opened it as Hull House, the first
experiment in the settlement-house approach. Putting the middle-class ideal of true
womanhood into action, Addams turned Hull House into an immigrant social center.
She and her coworkers invited them to plays; sponsored art projects; held classes in
English, civics, cooking, and dressmaking; and encouraged them to preserve their traditional crafts. She set up a kindergarten, a laundry, an employment bureau, and a day
nursery for working mothers. Hull House also sponsored recreational and athletic programs and dispensed legal aid and health care.

In the hope of upgrading the filthy and overcrowded housing in its environs, Addams and her coworkers conducted surveys of city housing conditions and pressured politicians to enforce sanitation regulations. For a time, demonstrating her principle of direct engagement with the lives of the poor, Addams even served as garbage inspector for her local ward.

By 1895 at least fifty settlement houses had opened in cities around the nation. Settlement-house leaders trained a generation of young college students, mostly women, many of whom would later serve as state and local government officials. **Florence Kelley,** for example, who had worked at Hull House, became the chief factory inspector for Illinois in 1893. For Kelley as for other young female settlement workers, settlement houses functioned as a supportive sisterhood of reform that taught them how to work effectively with municipal governments. Many settlement-house veterans would later draw on their experience to play an influential role in the regulatory movements of the Progressive Era (see Chapter 21). Through their sympathetic attitudes toward the immigrants and their systematic publication of data about slum conditions, settlement-house workers gave turn-of-the-century Americans renewed hope for urban reform.

But in their attempt to promote class cooperation and social harmony, settlement houses had mixed success. Although many immigrants appreciated the settlement houses' resources and activities, they felt that the reformers were uninterested in increasing their political power. Settlement-house workers did tend to overlook immigrant organizations and their leaders. In 1894, Hull House attracted two thousand visitors per week, but this was only a fraction of the more than seventy thousand people who lived within six blocks of the building. "They're like the rest," complained one immigrant, "a bunch of people planning for us and deciding what is good for us without consulting us or taking us into their confidence."

WORKING-CLASS LEISURE IN THE IMMIGRANT CITY

In colonial America preachers had linked leisure time to "idleness," a dangerous step on the road to sin and wickedness. In the overwhelmingly rural culture of the early nineteenth century, the unremitting routines of farm labor left little time for relaxation. Family picnics, horse races, county fairs, revival meetings, and Fourth of July and Christmas celebrations had provided occasional permissible diversions. But most Americans continued to view leisure activities skeptically. Henry Clay Work's popular song "My Grandfather's Clock" (1876), which praised the ancient timepiece for "wasting no time" and working "ninety years, without slumbering," bore witness to the tenacity of this deep-seated reverence for work and suspicion of leisure.

After the Civil War, as immigration soared, urban populations shot up—and a new class of wealthy entrepreneurs arose—striking new patterns of leisure and amusement emerged, most notably among the urban working class. Although middle-class moralists questioned the wholesomeness of these new forms of recreation, they were little heeded by immigrants in the throbbing cities. After spending long hours in factories, in mills, behind department-store counters, or as domestic servants in the homes of the wealthy, working-class Americans sought relaxation and diversion. Scorning the museums and concert halls favored by the wealthy, they thronged the streets, patronized saloons and dance halls, cheered at boxing matches and baseball games, and organized group picnics and holiday celebrations. As amusement parks, vaudeville theaters, sporting clubs, and racetracks provided further outlets for workers' need for entertainment, leisure became a big business catering to a mass public rather than to a wealthy elite.

For millions of working-class Americans, leisure time took on increasing importance as factory work became routinized and impersonal. Although many recreational activities involved both men and women, others attracted one gender in particular. Saloons offered an intensely male environment where patrons could share good stories, discuss and bet on sporting events, and momentarily put aside pressures of job and family. Young working women preferred to share confidences with friends in informal social clubs, tried out new fashions in street promenading, and found excitement in neighborhood dance halls and amusement parks.

Streets, Saloons, and Boxing Matches No segment of the population had a greater need for amusement and recreation than the urban working class. Hours of tedious, highly disciplined, and physically exhausting labor left workers tired and thirsting for excitement and escape at the end of the day. A banner carried by the Worcester, Massachusetts, carpenters' union in an 1889 demonstration for the eight-hour workday summed up the importance of workers' leisure hours: "EIGHT HOURS FOR WORK, EIGHT HOURS FOR REST, AND EIGHT HOURS FOR WHAT WE WILL."

City streets provided recreation that anyone could afford. Relaxing after a day's work, shop girls and laborers clustered on busy corners, watching shouting pushcart peddlers and listening to organ grinders and street musicians play familiar melodies. For a penny or a nickel, they could buy bagels, baked potatoes, soda, and other foods and drinks. In the summer, when the heat and humidity in tenement apartments reached unbearable levels, the streets became a hive of neighborhood social life. One immigrant fondly recalled his boyhood on the streets of New York's Lower East Side: "Something was always happening, and our attention was continually being shifted from one excitement to another."

The streets were open to all, but other leisure institutions drew mainly a male clientele. For example, in cities with a strong German immigrant presence like Baltimore, Milwaukee, and Cincinnati, gymnastic clubs (called *Turnverein*) and singing societies (*Gesangverein*) provided both companionship and the opportunity to perpetuate old-world cultural traditions.

For workmen of all ethnic backgrounds, saloons offered companionship, conviviality, and five-cent beer, often with a free lunch thrown in. New York City had an estimated ten thousand saloons by 1900 and Denver nearly five hundred. As neighborhood gathering places, saloons reinforced group identity and became centers for immigrant politics. Saloonkeepers, who often doubled as local ward bosses and turned out the vote in their neighborhoods, performed small services for their patrons, including finding jobs and writing letters for illiterate immigrants. Sports memorabilia and pictures of prominent prizefighters adorned saloon walls. With their rich mahogany bars, etched glass, shiny brass rails, and elegant mirrors, saloons provided patrons with a taste of high-toned luxury. Although working-class women rarely joined their husbands at the saloon, they might send a son or daughter to the corner pub to fetch a "growler"—a large tin pail of beer.

The conventions of saloon culture thus stood in marked contrast to both the socially isolating routines of factory labor and the increasingly private and family-centered social life of the middle class. Nevertheless, it would be a mistake to view the old-time saloon through a haze of sentimental nostalgia. Prostitution and crime flourished in the rougher saloons. Moreover, drunken husbands sometimes beat their wives and children, squandered their limited income, and lost their jobs. The pervasiveness of alcoholism was devastating. Temperance reformers, in their attack on saloons, targeted a widespread social problem.

The Rise of Professional Sports

Contrary to the prevailing myth, schoolboy Abner Doubleday did not invent baseball in Cooperstown, New York, in 1839. As an English game called rounders, the pastime had existed in one form or another since the seventeenth century. But if Americans did not create baseball, they unquestionably took a children's game and turned it into a major professional sport. The first organized baseball team, the New York Knickerbockers, was formed in 1845. In the 1860s, the rules were codified, and the sport assumed its modern form. Overhand pitches replaced underhand tosses. Fielders, who now wore gloves, had to catch the ball on the fly to make an out instead of fielding it on one bounce. Games were standardized at nine innings, and bases were spaced ninety feet apart.

In that same decade, promoters organized professional clubs and began to charge admission and compete for players. The Cincinnati Red Stockings, the first team to put its players under contract for the whole season, gained fame in 1869 by touring the country and ending the season with fifty-seven wins and no losses. Team owners organized the National League in 1876, took control from the players by requiring them to sign contracts that barred them from playing for rival organizations, and limited each city to one professional team. Soon the owners were filling baseball parks with crowds of ten to twelve thousand fans and earning enormous profits. By the 1890s, baseball had become big business.

Although baseball attracted a national following from all social levels, the working class particularly took the sport to heart. The most profitable teams were those in major industrial cities with a large working-class population. Workers avidly followed their team's progress. Many saloons reported scores on blackboards and an estimated 50 percent of players worked in saloons in the off season or became saloon owners when they retired from the game.

If baseball helped build solidarity among some ethnic groups, it also fostered discrimination against blacks. Although at least fifty-five blacks played on integrated teams between 1883 and 1898, the refusal of the Chicago White Stockings in 1887 to play a team with George Stovey, a star black pitcher, marked a turning point. That same year, Colored baseball clubs opened in six cities. Increasingly thereafter, blacks were banned from playing on professional teams.

Newspapers thrived on baseball. Joseph Pulitzer introduced the first separate sports page when he bought the *New York World* in 1883, and much of the sporting news in the *World* and other papers was devoted to baseball. Fans who cheered the hometown team provided cities with a shared sports loyalty that reduced ethnic, class, and religious differences, but drinking and gambling continued to plague the game.

Although no organized sport attracted as large a following as baseball, horse racing and boxing contests drew big crowds of spectators and bettors. Louisville's Kentucky

FOR THE HEAVY-WEIGHT CHAMPIONSHIP OF THE WORLD.

John Lawrence Sullivan, the Champion, and James J. Corbett, the Adonis of the Fistic Arena, Who Are to Battle September 7th Next For a Purse and Stakes of $45,000 and the Big Fellow's Title.

World's Heavyweight Boxing Championship, 1892 *In dethroning ring champion John L. Sullivan, "Gentleman Jim" Corbett demonstrated that speed and finesse were more than a match for brute strength.*

Derby became an important social event for the rich, but professional boxing aroused more passionate devotion among laborers. For working-class men, bare-knuckled prizefighting became one of the most popular amusements. Drawing its heroes from the poorer ranks of society, the ring became an arena where lower-class men could assert their individuality and physical prowess.

By far the most popular sports hero of the nineteenth century was heavyweight fighter **John L. Sullivan,** "the Boston Strong Boy." Of Irish immigrant stock, Sullivan began boxing in 1877 at the age of nineteen. His first professional fight came in 1880 when he knocked out John Donaldson, "the Champion of the West," in a Cincinnati beer hall. With his massive physique, handlebar mustache, and arrogant swagger, Sullivan was enormously popular among immigrants. Barnstorming across the country, he vanquished a succession of local strongmen, invariably wearing his trademark green tights with an American flag wrapped around his middle. Cleverly, Sullivan also refused to fight blacks, in deference, he said, to the wishes of his fans. This policy conveniently allowed him to avoid facing the finest boxer of the 1880s, the Australian black, Peter Jackson.

Sullivan loved drink and high living, and by the end of the eighties he was sadly out of shape. But when the editor of the *Police Gazette*, a sensational tabloid, designed a new heavyweight championship belt—allegedly containing two hundred ounces of silver and encrusted with diamonds and pure gold—and awarded it to Sullivan's rival Jake Kilrain, the champion had to defend himself. The two met on a sweltering, hundred-degree day in New Orleans in July 1889 for the last bare-knuckles championship match. After seventy-five short but grueling rounds, Kilrain's managers threw in the towel. Newspapers around the nation banner-headlined the story. Contemptuously returning the championship belt to the *Police Gazette* after having had it appraised at $175, Sullivan went on the road to star in a melodrama written specifically for him. Playing the role of a blacksmith, he (in the words of a recent historian of bare-knuckles boxing) "pounded an anvil, beat a bully, and mutilated his lines." But his fans did not care; he was one of them, and they adored him. As one admirer wrote,

> His colors are the Stars and Stripes,
> He also wears the green,
> And he's the grandest slugger that
> The ring has ever seen.

Vaudeville, Amusement Parks, and Dance Halls   In contrast to the male preserve of saloons and prizefights, the world of vaudeville, amusement parks, and neighborhood dance pavilions welcomed all comers regardless of gender. Some of them proved particularly congenial to working-class women.

Vaudeville evolved out of the pre–Civil War blackface minstrel shows in which white comedians made up as blacks had sung and mocked African-American life. Vaudeville performances offered a succession of acts, all designed for mass appeal. The shows typically opened with a trained animal routine or a dance number. These were followed by a musical interlude featuring sentimental favorites such as "On the Banks of the Wabash, Far Away" or new hits such as "Meet Me in St. Louis, Louis," a jaunty spoof of a young wife's frustration with her stick-in-the-mud husband. Comic skits followed, ridiculing the trials of urban life, satirizing the ineptitude of the police and municipal officials, poking fun at the babel of accents in the immigrant city, and mining a rich vein of broad ethnic humor and stereotypes. Blackface skits were sometimes included. After a highbrow operatic aria and acts by ventriloquists, pantomimes, and magicians, the program ended with a "flash" finale such as flying-trapeze artists swinging against a black background.

By the 1880s, vaudeville was drawing larger crowds than any other form of theater. Not only did it provide an inexpensive evening of lighthearted entertainment, but in the comic sketches, immigrant audiences could also laugh at their own experience as they saw it translated into slapstick and caricature.

The white working class's fascination with vaudeville's blackface acts has been the subject of considerable recent scrutiny by historians. Some have interpreted it as a way for the white working class to mock middle-class ideals. By pretending to act like the popular stereotypes of blacks, white working-class youths could challenge traditional family structures, the virtue of sexual self-denial, and adult expectations about working hard. In this view popular culture was making fun of the ideals of thrift and propriety being promoted in marketplace and domestic ideology. Other historians have argued that blackface buffoonery, with its grotesque, demeaning caricatures of African-Americans, reinforced prejudice against blacks and restricted their escape from lower-class status. Paradoxically, therefore, the popularity of blackface vaudeville acts reinforced white racial solidarity and strengthened the expanding wall separating whites and African-Americans.

Where vaudeville offered psychological escape from the stresses of working-class life by exploiting its comic potential, amusement parks provided physical escape, at least for a day. The prototype of the sprawling urban amusement park was New York's Coney Island, a section of Brooklyn's oceanfront that evolved into a resort for the masses in the 1870s. At Coney Island, young couples went dancing, rode through the dark Tunnel of Love, sped down the dizzying roller coaster in Steeplechase Park, or watched belly dancers in the carnival sideshows. Customers were encouraged to surrender to the spirit of play, forget the demands of the industrial world, and lose themselves in fantasy.

By the end of the nineteenth century, New York City had well over three hundred thousand female wage earners, most of them young, unmarried women working as seamstresses, laundresses, typists, domestic servants, and department-store clerks. For this army of low-paid young working women and their counterparts in other cities, amusement parks exerted a powerful lure. Here they could meet friends, spend time with young men beyond the watchful eyes of their parents, show off their new dresses, and try out the latest dance steps. As a twenty-year-old German immigrant woman who worked as a servant in a wealthy household observed,

> I have heard some of the high people with whom I have been living say that Coney Island is not tony. The trouble is that these high people don't know how to dance. I have to laugh when I see them at their balls and parties. If only I could get out on the floor and show them how—they would be astonished.

For such women, the brightly decorated dance pavilion, the exciting music, and the spell of a warm summer night could seem a magical release from the drudgery of daily life.

Ragtime

Since the days of slavery, black Americans had developed a strong, creative musical culture, and thus it is not surprising that blacks made a major contribution to the popular music of the late nineteenth century in the form of ragtime. Nothing could illustrate more sharply the differences between middle- and working-class culture than the contrasting styles of popular music they favored. The middle class preferred hymns or songs that conveyed a moral lesson. The working class delighted in ragtime, which originated in the 1880s with black musicians in the saloons and brothels of the South and Midwest and was played strictly for entertainment.

Ragtime developed out of the rich tradition of sacred and secular songs through which African-Americans had long eased the burdens of their lives. Like spirituals, ragtime used syncopated rhythms and complex harmonies, but it blended these with marching-band musical structures to create a distinctive style. A favorite of "honky-tonk" piano players, ragtime was introduced to the broader public in the 1890s and became a national sensation.

The reasons for the sudden ragtime craze were complex. Inventive, playful, with catchy syncopations and an infectious rhythm in the bass clef, the music displayed an originality that had an appeal all its own. Part of ragtime's popularity also came from its origin in brothels and its association with blacks, who were widely stereotyped in the 1890s as sexual, sensual, and uninhibited by the rigid Victorian social conventions that restricted whites. The "wild" and complex rhythms of ragtime were widely interpreted to be a freer and more "natural" expression of elemental feelings about love and sex.

Ragtime's great popularity proved a mixed blessing for blacks. It testified to the achievements of brilliant composers like Scott Joplin, helped break down the barriers faced by blacks in the music industry, and contributed to a spreading rebellion against the repressiveness of Victorian standards. But ragtime simply confirmed some whites' stereotype of blacks as primitive and sensual, a bias that underlay the racism of the period and helped justify segregation and discrimination.

CULTURES IN CONFLICT

Even within the elite and middle classes, Victorian morality and genteel cultural standards were never totally accepted. As the century ended, increasing numbers of people questioned these beliefs. Women stood at the center of the era's cultural turbulence. Thwarted by a restrictive code of feminine propriety, middle-class women made their dissatisfactions heard. The rise of women's clubs, the growth of women's colleges, and even the 1890s bicycle fad testified to the emergence of what some began to call the "new woman."

Although Victorian culture was challenged from within the middle class, a widening chasm divided the well-to-do from urban working-class immigrants. In no period of American history have class conflicts—cultural as well as economic—been more open and raw. As middle-class leaders nervously eyed the sometimes disorderly culture of city streets, saloons, boxing clubs, dance halls, and amusement parks, they saw a challenge to their own cultural and social standing. Some middle-class reformers promoted the public school as a way to impose middle-class values on the urban masses. Others battled urban "vice" and "immorality." But ultimately it was the polite mores of the middle class, not urban working-class culture, that proved more vulnerable. By 1900, the Victorian social and moral ethos was crumbling on every front.

The Genteel Tradition and Its Critics

What was this genteel culture that aroused such opposition? In the 1870s and 1880s, a group of upper-class writers and magazine editors, led by Harvard art history professor Charles Eliot Norton and New York editors Richard Watson Gilder of *The Century* magazine and E. L. Godkin of *The Nation,* codified Victorian standards for literature and the arts. They campaigned to improve American taste in interior furnishings, textiles, ceramics, wallpaper, and books. By fashioning rigorous criteria for excellence in writing and design, they hoped to create a coherent national artistic culture.

In the 1880s Norton, Godkin, and Gilder, joined by the editors of other highbrow periodicals such as the *Atlantic Monthly* and *North American Review,* set up new guidelines for serious literature. They lectured the middle class about the value of high culture and the insights to be gained from painting and music. They censored their own publications to remove all sexual allusions, disrespectful treatments of Christianity, and unhappy endings. Expanding their combined circulation to nearly two hundred thousand copies, Godkin and the other editors of "quality" periodicals created an important forum for serious writing. Novelists Henry James, who published virtually all of his work in the *Atlantic,* and William Dean Howells, who served as editor of the same magazine, helped lead this elite literary establishment. James believed that "it is art that makes life. . . . [There is] no substitute whatever for [its] force and beauty. . . ."

This interest in art for art's sake paralleled a broader crusade called the "aesthetic movement," led in England by William Morris, Oscar Wilde, and other art critics, who sought to bring art into every facet of life. In America, Candace Wheeler and other reformers made its influence felt through the work of architects, jewelers, and interior decorators.

Although the magazines initially provided an important forum for new writers, their editors' elitism and desire to control the nation's literary standards soon aroused opposition. Samuel Langhorne Clemens, better known as **Mark Twain,** spoke for many young writers when he declared that he was through with "literature and all that bosh." Attacking aristocratic literary conventions, Twain and other authors who shared his concerns explored new forms of fiction and worked to broaden its appeal to the general public.

These efforts to chart new directions for American literature rested on fundamental changes taking place in the publishing industry. To compete with elite periodicals costing twenty-five to thirty-five cents, new magazines like *Ladies' Home Journal, Cosmopolitan,* and *McClure's* lowered their prices to a dime or fifteen cents and tripled or quadrupled their circulation. Supporting themselves through advertising, these magazines encouraged new trends in fiction while mass-marketing new products. Their editors sought writers who could provide accurate depictions of the "whirlpool of real life" and create a new civic consciousness to heal the class divisions of American society.

Some of these authors have been called regionalists because they captured the distinctive dialect and details of local life in their environs. In *The Country of the Pointed Firs* (1896), for example, Sarah Orne Jewett wrote of the New England village life that she knew in South Berwick, Maine. Others, most notably William Dean Howells, have been called realists because of their focus on the truthful depiction of the commonplace and the everyday, especially in urban areas. Still others have been categorized as naturalists because their novels and stories deny free will and stress the ways in which life's outcomes are determined by economic and psychological forces. Stephen Crane's *Maggie: A Girl of the Streets* (1892), a bleak story of an innocent girl's exploitation and ultimate suicide in an urban slum, is generally considered the first naturalistic American novel. Yet in practice, these categories are imprecise and often overlap. What many of these writers shared was a skepticism about literary conventions and an intense desire to understand the society around them and portray it in words.

The careers of Mark Twain and Theodore Dreiser highlight the changes in the publishing industry and the evolution of new forms of writing. Both authors grew up in the Midwest, outside the East Coast literary establishment. Twain was born near Hannibal, Missouri, in 1835, and Dreiser in Terre Haute, Indiana, in 1871. As young men both worked as newspaper reporters and traveled widely. Both learned from direct and sometimes bitter experience about the greed, speculation, and fraud that figured centrally in Gilded Age life.

Of the two, Twain more incessantly sought a mass-market audience. With his drooping mustache, white hair, and white suits, Twain turned himself into a media personality, lecturing from coast to coast, founding his own publishing house, and using door-to-door salesmen to sell his books. The name Mark Twain became his trademark, identifying him to readers as a literary celebrity much as the labels Coca-Cola and Ivory Soap won instant consumer recognition. Although Dreiser possessed neither

Twain's flamboyant personality nor his instinct for salesmanship, he, too, learned to crank out articles.

Drawing on their own experiences, Twain and Dreiser wrote about the human impact of the wrenching social changes taking place around them: the flow of people to the cities and the relentless scramble for power, wealth, and fame. In *The Adventures of Huckleberry Finn* (1884), Twain tells a story of two runaways, the rebellious Huck and the slave Jim, drifting down the Mississippi in search of freedom. Their physical journey, which contrasts idyllic life on the raft with the tawdry, fraudulent world of small riverfront towns, is a journey of identity that brings with it a deeper understanding of contemporary American society.

Dreiser's *Sister Carrie* (1900) also tells of a journey. In this case, the main character, Carrie Meeber, an innocent girl on her way from her Wisconsin farm home to Chicago, is seduced by a traveling salesman and then moves in with the married proprietor of a fancy saloon. Driven by her desire for expensive department-store clothes and lavish entertainment, Carrie is an opportunist incapable of feeling guilt. She follows her married lover to New York, knowing that he has stolen the receipts from his saloon, abandons him when his money runs out, and pursues her own career in the theater.

Twain and Dreiser broke decisively with the genteel tradition's emphasis on manners and decorum. *Century* magazine readers complained that *Huckleberry Finn* was coarse and "destitute of a single redeeming quality." The publisher of *Sister Carrie* was so repelled by Dreiser's novel that he printed only a thousand copies (to fulfill the legal terms of his contract) and then stored them in a warehouse, refusing to promote them.

Growing numbers of scholars and critics similarly challenged the self-serving certitudes of Victorian mores, including assumptions that moral worth and economic standing were closely linked and that the status quo of the 1870s and 1880s represented a social order decreed by God and nature alike. Whereas Henry George, Lester Ward, and Edward Bellamy elaborated their visions of a cooperative and harmonious society (see Chapter 18), economist Thorstein Veblen in *The Theory of the Leisure Class* (1899) offered a caustic critique of the lifestyles of the new capitalist elite. Raised in a Norwegian farm community in Minnesota, Veblen looked at the captains of industry and their families with a jaundiced eye, documenting their "conspicuous consumption" of expensive purchases and lamenting the widening gap between "those who worked without profit" and "those who profited without working."

Within the new discipline of sociology, Annie MacLean exposed the exploitation of department-store clerks, Walter Wyckoff uncovered the hand-to-mouth existence of unskilled laborers, and W. E. B. Du Bois documented the suffering and hardships faced by blacks in Philadelphia. The publication of these social scientists' writings, coupled with the economic depression and seething labor agitation of the 1890s, made it increasingly difficult for turn-of-the-century middle-class Americans to accept the smug, self-satisfied belief in progress and gentility that had been a hallmark of the Victorian outlook.

Modernism in Architecture and Painting   The challenge to the genteel tradition also found strong support among architects and painters. By the 1890s Chicago architects William Holabird, John Wellborn Root, and others had tired of copying European designs. Breaking with established architects such as Richard Morris Hunt, the designer of French châteaux for New York's Fifth Avenue, these Chicago architects followed the lead of Louis Sullivan, who argued that a building's form should follow its function. In their view, banks should look like the financial institutions they were, not like Greek temples. Striving to evolve functional American design standards, the Chicago architects looked for inspiration to the future—to **modernism**—not to the past.

The Chicago architect **Frank Lloyd Wright** designed "prairie-school" houses that represented a typical modernist break with past styles. Wright scorned the three-story Victorian house with its large attic and basement. His designs, which featured broad, sheltering roofs and horizontal silhouettes, used interconnecting rooms to create a sense of spaciousness.

The call of modernism, with its rejection of Victorian refinement, influenced late-nineteenth-century American painting as well. The watercolors of Winslow Homer, a magazine illustrator during the Civil War, revealed nature as brutally tough and unsentimental. In Homer's grim, elemental seascapes, lone men struggle against massive waves that constantly threaten to overwhelm them. Thomas Eakins's canvases of swimmers, boxers, and rowers (such as his well-known *Champion Single Sculls,* painted in 1871) similarly captured moments of vigorous physical exertion in everyday life. While Mary Cassatt shared Eakins's interest in everyday life, she often took as her subject the bond between mother and child, as in her painting *The Bath* (c. 1891). After studying at the Pennsylvania Academy of Fine Arts, she moved to Paris in 1874, where she worked closely with French Impressionist painters such as Monet and Degas.

The revolt by architects and painters against Victorian standards was symptomatic of a larger shift in middle-class thought. This shift resulted from fundamental economic changes that had spawned a far more complex social environment than that of the past. As Protestant minister Josiah Strong perceptively observed in 1898, the transition from muscle to mechanical power had "separated, as by an impassable gulf, the simple, homespun, individualistic world of the . . . past, from the complex, closely associated life of the present." The increasingly evident gap between rural or small-town life—a world of quiet parlors and flickering kerosene lamps—and life in the big, glittering, electrified cities of iron and glass made nineteenth-century Americans acutely aware of differences in upbringing and wealth. Given the disparities between rich and poor, between rural and urban, and between native-born Americans and recent immigrants, it is no wonder that pious Victorian platitudes about proper manners and graceful arts seemed out of touch with the new social realities.

Distrusting the idealistic Victorian assumptions about social progress, middle-class journalists, novelists, artists, and politicians nevertheless remained divided over how to replace them. Not until the Progressive Era would social reformers draw on a new expertise in social research and an enlarged conception of the federal government's regulatory power to break sharply with their Victorian predecessors' social outlook.

From Victorian Lady to New Woman Although middle-class women figured importantly in the revolt against Victorian refinement, their role was complex and ambiguous. Dissatisfaction with the cult of domesticity did not necessarily lead to open rebellion. Many women, although chafing against the constraints of deference and the assumption that they should limit their activities to the home, remained committed to playing a nurturing role within the family. In fact, early advocates of a "widened sphere" for women often fused the traditional Victorian ideal of womanhood with a firm commitment to political action.

The career of temperance leader **Frances Willard** illustrates how the cult of domesticity, with its celebration of special female virtues, could evolve into a broader view of women's social and political responsibilities. Like many of her contemporaries, Willard believed that women were compassionate and nurturing by nature. She was also convinced that drinking encouraged thriftlessness and profoundly threatened family life. Resigning as dean of women and professor of English at Northwestern University in 1874, Willard devoted her energies full-time to the temperance cause. Five years later she was elected president of the newly formed Woman's Christian Temperance Union (WCTU).

Willard took the traditional belief that women had unique moral virtues and transformed it into a rationale for political action. The domestication of politics, she asserted, would protect the family and improve public morality. Choosing as the union's badge a bow of white ribbon, symbolizing the purity of the home, she launched a crusade in 1880 to win the franchise for women so that they could vote to outlaw liquor. Willard soon expanded WCTU activities to include welfare work, prison reform, labor arbitration, and public health. Under her leadership the WCTU, with a membership of nearly 150,000 by 1890, became the nation's first mass organization of women. Through it, women gained experience as lobbyists, organizers, and lecturers, in the process undercutting the assumption of "separate spheres."

An expanding network of women's clubs offered another means by which middle- and upper-class women could hone their skills in civic affairs, public speaking, and intellectual analysis. In the 1870s, many well-to-do women met weekly to study topics of mutual interest. These clubwomen soon became involved in social-welfare projects, public library expansion, and tenement reform. By 1892, the General Federation of Women's Clubs, an umbrella organization established that year, boasted 495 affiliates and a hundred thousand members. Middle-class black women, excluded from many white clubs, formed their own National Association of Colored Women's Clubs in 1900.

While older women eroded the Victorian constraints placed on them by social conventions by joining women's clubs, younger women challenged social conventions by joining the bicycling craze that swept urban America at the turn of the century. The fascination with bicycle riding developed as part of a new interest in health and physical fitness. Middle- and upper-class Americans explored various ways to improve their vigor. Some used health products such as cod liver oil and sarsaparilla for "weak blood." Others played basketball, invented in 1891 by a physical education instructor at Springfield College in Massachusetts to keep students in shape during the winter months. But bicycling, which could be done individually or in groups, quickly became the most popular sport for those who wished to combine exercise with recreation.

Bicycles of various designs had been manufactured since the 1870s, but bicycling did not become a national craze until the invention in the 1880s of the so-called safety bicycle, with smaller wheels, ball-bearing axles, and air-filled tires. By the 1890s, over a million Americans owned bicycles.

Bicycling especially appealed to young women who had chafed under the restrictive Victorian attitudes about female exercise, which held that proper young ladies must never sweat and that the female body must be fully covered at all times. Pedaling along in a shirtwaist or "split" skirt, a woman bicyclist made an implicit feminist statement suggesting that she had broken with genteel conventions and wanted to explore new activities beyond the traditional sphere.

Changing attitudes about femininity and women's proper role also found expression in gradually shifting ideas about marriage. Charlotte Perkins Gilman, a suffrage advocate and speaker for women's rights, asserted that women would make an effective contribution to society only when they won economic independence from men through work outside the home (see Chapter 21). One very tangible indicator of women's changing relationship to men was the substantial rise in the divorce rate between 1880 and 1900. In 1880, one in every twenty-one marriages ended in divorce. By 1900, the rate had climbed to one in twelve. Women who brought suit for divorce increasingly cited their husbands' failure to act responsibly and to respect their autonomy. Accepting such arguments, courts frequently awarded the wife alimony, a monetary settlement payable by the ex-husband to support her and their children.

Women writers generally welcomed the new female commitment to independence and self-sufficiency. In the short stories of Mary Wilkins Freeman, for example, women's expanding role is implicitly compared to the frontier ideal of freedom. Feminist **Kate Chopin** pushed the debate to the extreme by having Edna Pontellier, the married heroine of her controversial 1899 novel *The Awakening,* violate social conventions. First Edna falls in love with another man; then she takes her own life when his ideas about women prove as narrow and traditional as those of her husband.

Despite the efforts of these and other champions of the new woman, attitudes changed slowly. The enlarged conception of women's role in society exerted its greatest influence on college-educated, middle-class women who had leisure time and could reasonably hope for success in journalism, social work, and nursing. For female immigrant factory workers and for shop girls who worked sixty hours a week to try to make ends meet, however, the ideal remained a more distant goal. Although many women were seeking more independence and control over their lives, most still viewed the home as their primary responsibility.

Public Education as an Arena of Class Conflict

While the debate over women's proper role remained largely confined to the middle class, a very different controversy, over the scope and function of public education, engaged Americans of all socioeconomic levels. This debate starkly highlighted the class and cultural divisions in late-nineteenth-century society. From the 1870s on, viewing the public schools as an instrument for indoctrinating and controlling the lower ranks of society, middle-class educators and civic leaders campaigned to expand public schooling and bring it under centralized control. Not surprisingly, the reformers' efforts aroused considerable opposition from ethnic and religious groups whose outlook and interests differed sharply from theirs.

Thanks to the crusade for universal public education started by Horace Mann and other antebellum educational reformers, most states had public school systems by the Civil War, and more than half the nation's children were receiving some formal education. But most attended school for only three or four years, and few went on to high school.

Concerned that many Americans lacked sufficient knowledge to participate wisely in public affairs or function effectively in the labor force, reformers such as William Torrey Harris worked to increase the number of years that children spent in school. First as superintendent of the St. Louis public schools in the 1870s and later as the federal commissioner of education, Harris urged teachers to instill in their students a sense of order,

Interior of an Urban School *Photographers were careful to picture public elementary schools, such as this one on New York's Lower East Side in 1886, as models of immigrant children's decorum and good behavior.*

decorum, self-discipline, and civic loyalty. Believing that modern industrial society depended on citizens' conforming to the timetables of the factory and the train, he envisioned the schools as models of punctuality and precise scheduling: "The pupil must have his lessons ready at the appointed time, must rise at the tap of the bell, move to the line, return; in short, go through all the evolutions with equal precision."

To achieve these goals and to wrest control of the schools from neighborhood leaders and ward politicians, reform-minded educators like Harris elaborated a philosophy of public education stressing punctuality, centralized administration, compulsory-attendance laws, and a tenure system to insulate teachers from political favoritism and parental pressure. By 1900, thirty-one states required school attendance of all children from eight to fourteen years of age.

The steamroller methods used by Harris and like-minded administrators to systematize public education quickly prompted protests. New York pediatrician Joseph Mayer Rice, who toured thirty-six cities and interviewed twelve hundred teachers in 1892, scornfully criticized an educational establishment that stressed singsong memorization and prisonlike discipline.

Rice's biting attack on public education overlooked the real advances in reading and mathematics made in the previous two decades. Nationally, despite the influx of immigrants, the illiteracy rate in English for individuals ten years and older dropped from 17 percent in 1880 to 13 percent in 1890, largely because of the expansion of urban educational facilities. American high schools were also coeducational, and girls made up the majority of the students by 1900. But Rice was on target in assailing many teachers' rigid emphasis on silence, docility, and unquestioning obedience to the rules. When a Chicago school inspector found a thirteen-year-old boy huddled in the basement of a stockyard building and ordered him back to school, the weeping boy blurted out, "[T]hey hits ye if yer don't learn, and they hits ye if ye whisper, and they hits ye if ye have string in yer pocket, and they hits ye if yer seat squeaks, and they hits ye if ye don't stan' up in time, and they hits ye if yer late, and they hits ye if ye ferget the page."

By the 1880s, several different groups found themselves in opposition to centralized urban public school bureaucracies. Although many working-class families valued education, those who depended on their children's meager wages for survival resisted the attempt to force their sons and daughters to attend school past the elementary grades. Although some immigrant families made great sacrifices to enable their children to get an education, many withdrew their offspring from school as soon as they had learned the rudiments of reading and writing, and sent them to work.

Furthermore, Catholic immigrants objected to the overwhelmingly Protestant orientation of the public schools. Distressed by the use of the King James translation of the Bible and by the schools' failure to observe saints' days, Catholics set up separate parochial school systems. In response, Republican politicians, resentful of Catholic immigrants' overwhelming preference for the Democratic Party, tried unsuccessfully to pass a constitutional amendment cutting off all public aid to church-related schools in 1875. Catholics in turn denounced federal aid to public schools as intended "to suppress Catholic education, gradually extinguish Catholicity in this country, and to form one homogeneous American people after the New England Evangelical type."

At the other end of the social scale, upper-class parents who did not wish to send their children to immigrant-thronged public schools enrolled their daughters in female seminaries such as Chatham Hall in Chatham, Virginia, and their sons in private academies and boarding schools like St. Paul's in Concord, New Hampshire. The proliferation of private and parochial schools, together with the controversies over compulsory education, school funding, and classroom decorum, reveals the extent to which public education had become mired in ethnic and class differences. Unlike Germany and Japan, which created national education systems in the late nineteenth century, the United States, reflecting its social heterogeneity, maintained a system of locally run public and private institutions that allowed each segment of society to retain some influence over the schools attended by its own children. Amid the disputes, school enrollments dramatically expanded. In 1870, fewer than seventy-two thousand students were attending the nation's 1,026 high schools. By 1900 the number of high schools had jumped to more than 5,000 and the number of students to more than half a million.

CONCLUSION

By the 1890s, class conflict was evident in practically every area of city life, from mealtime manners to popular entertainment and recreation. As new immigrants flooded the tenements and spilled out onto neighborhood streets, it became impossible for native-born Americans to ignore their strange religious and social customs. Ethnic differences were compounded by class differences. Often poor and from peasant or working-class backgrounds, the immigrants from southern and eastern Europe took unskilled jobs and worked for subsistence-level wages. The slums and tenements in which they lived had high rates of disease. Middle- and upper-class Americans often responded by moving to fashionable avenues or suburbs and by stigmatizing them as nonwhite and racially inferior.

To distinguish themselves from these newcomers, native-born Americans stressed their commitment to Victorian morality, with its emphasis on manners, decorum, and self-control. Although never fully accepted even among the well-to-do, these Victorian ideals were meant to apply new standards for society. Lavish department stores and artistically designed houses reflected the middle- and upper-class faith that the consumption of material goods indicated good taste.

To raise standards, the prosperous classes expanded the number of high schools and created a new research university system for training educators, lawyers, doctors, and other professionals. As defenders of the new Victorian morality, educated middle- and upper-class women were expected to become the protectors of the home.

In contrast to the upper classes, immigrant newcomers created their own political machines to gain access to work and address the problems of poverty and congestion in the inner city. Although political bosses, at times supported by graft and corruption, handed out jobs and helped many constituents face problems of sickness and misfortune, their efforts were overshadowed by native-born reformers who blamed the immigrants for part of their problems. While Jacob Riis, Jane Addams, and other reformers worked to improve overcrowded housing and dangerous working conditions, Anthony Comstock and less sympathetic reformers attacked immigrant values and cultures in an effort to uplift and Americanize them.

Nowhere was the conflict between the social classes more evident than in the controversy over leisure entertainment. Caught up in the material benefits of a prospering industrial society, middle- and upper-class Americans battled against what they deemed "indecent" lower-class behavior in all its forms, from dancing to ragtime, gambling, and prizefighting to playing baseball on Sunday and visiting bawdy boardwalk sideshows. Even public parks became arenas of class conflict. Whereas the elite favored large, impeccably groomed urban parks that would serve as models of orderliness and propriety, working people fought for parks where they could picnic, play ball, drink beer, and escape the stifling heat of tenement apartments.

Although the well-to-do classes often appeared to have the upper hand in these clashes, significant disagreements about moral standards surfaced early within their own ranks. Critics, among them Charlotte Perkins Gilman, faulted middle-class society for its obsession with polite manners, empty social rituals, and restrictions on the occupations open to women.

By 1900, the contest for power between the elite classes and the largely immigrant working class was heading toward a partial resolution. As Victorian morality eroded, undermined by dissension from within and opposition from without, new standards emerged that blended elements of earlier positions. For example, new rules regulated behavior in the boxing ring and on the baseball field. Still, it was immigrant heroes who captured the popular imagination. The elite vision of sport as a vehicle for instilling self-discipline and self-control was transformed into a new commitment to sports as spectacle and entertainment. Sports had become big business and an important part of the new consumerism.

Similar patterns of compromise and change took place in other arenas. Vaudeville houses, attacked by the affluent for their risqué performances, evolved into the nation's first movie theaters. Ragtime music, with its syncopated rhythms, gave rise to jazz. In short, the dashing, disreputable, and raucous working-class culture of the late-nineteenth-century city can be seen as the seedbed of twentieth-century mass culture. And everywhere popular culture became increasingly dominated by commercial interests that capitalized on the disposable income created by the nation's explosive urban growth.

20

Politics and Expansion in an Industrializing Age, 1877–1900

PARTY POLITICS IN AN ERA OF UPHEAVAL, 1877–1884

Between 1877 and 1894 four presidents squeezed into office by the narrowest of margins; control of the House of Representatives changed hands five times; and seven new western states were admitted into the Union. Competition between political parties was intense. No one party could muster a working majority.

To meet these challenges, Republicans, Democrats, and third-party leaders sought desperately to reshape their political organizations to win over and cement the loyalty of their followers. While the Democrats rebuilt their strength in the South and mounted new challenges, Republicans struggled to maintain the loyalties of the working class, to strengthen their support from business, and to fight off the threat of new third parties. Not until 1896, in the aftermath of a massive depression that hit when the Democrats and a new third party, the Populists, were in office, did the Republicans consolidate their power and build a coalition that would control Congress and the presidency for the next fifteen years.

Contested Political Visions   Between 1876 and 1896, the intense competition between parties produced an incredible turnout of voters. Although most women did not yet have the vote and blacks were increasingly being disenfranchised, more than 80 percent of eligible white males often voted, and in particularly hard-fought state and local elections, the percentage could rise to 95 percent. Voter participation a century later would equal scarcely half that level.

Higher voter turnout resulted in part from the attempts of the major parties to navigate the stormy economy created by postwar industrial and geographic expansion, the influx of millions of immigrants, and the explosive growth of cities (see Chapters 18 and 19). At the same time that voter turnout shot up, however, political parties sidestepped many of the issues created by industrialization, such as taxation of corporations, support for those injured in factory accidents, and poverty relief. Nor was the American labor movement, unlike its counterpart in Europe, able to organize itself effectively as a political force (see Chapter 18). Except for the Interstate Commerce Act of 1887 and the largely symbolic Sherman Anti-Trust Act of 1890, Washington generally ignored the social consequences of industrialization and focused instead on encouraging economic growth.

How can we explain this refusal to address economic concerns and, at the same time, account for the enormous popular support for parties? The answer lies in the political ideology of the period and the two major symbolic and economic issues that preoccupied lawmakers nationally. The first involved the economic issues of the tariff and the money supply. The second issue focused on civil-service reform, aimed at awarding government jobs on the basis of merit rather than political connections.

Political parties in the late nineteenth century energized voters not only by appealing to economic self-interest, as was evident in support for industrialization and pensions for Civil War veterans and their widows, but also by linking their programs to deeply held beliefs about the nature of the family and the proper role of government. In its prewar years, the Republican Party had enhanced economic opportunities for common people by using governmental authority to expand railroads, increase tariff protection for industry, and provide land subsidies to farmers. With encouragement from evangelical ministers, it had also espoused a belief in female moral superiority and a willingness to use government as an instrument to protect family life. Hostility to slavery was based in part on the assumption that slaveholding corroded family values. The Democrats, in contrast, had viewed emancipation as a threat to patriarchal order and racial control.

After the Civil War, these positions hardened into political ideologies. Republicans justified their support for the tariff and defended their commitment to Union widows' pensions as a protection for the family home and female wage earners. Men, in particular, associated loyalty to party with a sense of masculinity. Democrats countered, using metaphors of the seduction and rape of white women by external forces and labeling Republican programs as classic examples of the perils of using excessive government force. High tariffs imperiled the family and threatened economic disaster.

Despite their differences over the tariff and monetary policy, neither Republicans nor Democrats believed that the national government had any right to regulate corporations or to protect the social welfare of workers. Neither party therefore courted the labor union vote (see Chapter 18). Many members of the dominant parties, particularly among the middle and upper classes, embraced the doctrine of **laissez-faire**—the belief that unregulated competition represented the best path to progress. According to this view, the federal government should promote economic development but not regulate the industries that it subsidized.

Rather than looking to Washington, people turned to local or state authorities. On the Great Plains, angry farmers demanded that their state legislatures regulate railroad rates. In the cities, immigrant groups, organized by political bosses, battled for control

CHRONOLOGY, 1877–1902

1878 • Congress requires U.S. Treasury to purchase silver.

1880 • James Garfield elected president.

1881 • Assassination of Garfield; Chester A. Arthur becomes president.

1883 • Pendleton Civil Service Act.

1884 • Grover Cleveland elected president.

1886 • *Wabash v. Illinois.*

1887 • Interstate Commerce Act.

1888 • Benjamin Harrison elected president.

1889 • National Farmers' Alliance formed.

1890 • Sherman Silver Purchase Act.
Sherman Anti-Trust Act.
McKinley Tariff pushes tariffs to all-time high.

1893 • Panic of 1893; depression of 1893–1897 begins.
Repeal of the Sherman Silver Purchase Act.

1894 • Coxey's "army" marches on Washington.
Pullman strike.
Wilson-Gorman Tariff.

1895 • Supreme Court declares federal income tax unconstitutional.

1896 • Free-silver forces capture Democratic Party and nominate William
Jennings Bryan.
William McKinley elected president.

1898 • Acquisition of Hawaii.
Spanish-American War.

1898–1902 • Guerrilla uprising in Philippines.

1900 • Currency Act officially places United States on gold standard.

1901 • Platt Amendment retains U.S. role in Cuba.
Regular Army Nursing Corps founded.

1902 • Philippine Government Act.

of municipal governments and local contracts. In response, native-born reformers attempted to oust the political machines and clean up corruption (see Chapter 19).

Moreover, city and state governments vied with each other for control. Cities often could not change their system of government, alter their tax structure, or regulate municipal utilities without state approval. When Chicago wanted to issue permits to street popcorn vendors, for example, the Illinois legislature had to pass a special act.

Party loyalty for both Republicans and Democrats was reinforced by a sense of personal grievance that resulted from the belief, often true, that the other party had engaged in election fraud to steal elections. Although both parties, in both the North and the South, practiced fraud by rigging elections, throwing out opposition votes, and paying for "floaters" who moved from precinct to precinct to vote, each developed a sense of moral outrage at the other's behavior that invigorated party spirit.

By linking economic policy to family values, both parties reinforced the appeal of their platforms and, in the process, encouraged the participation of women in the political process. Although most women could not vote, they played an active role in politics in this period. Frances Willard and her followers in the Woman's Christian Temperance Union (WCTU), for example, helped create a Prohibition and Home Protection Party in the 1880s. A decade later, western women Populists won full suffrage in Colorado, Idaho, and Utah.

Patterns of Party Strength

In the 1870s and 1880s each party had its own ideological appeal and centers of regional strength. The Democrats ruled the South; southern sections of border states like Ohio; midwestern states like Wisconsin; and northern cities with large immigrant populations. In the South, the white Democratic party elite viewed Republicans as villains who had devastated their lands and set up fraudulent carpetbag governments in the defeated Confederacy. The Democrats campaigned for minimal government expenditures, opposed tariff increases, and generally attacked what they considered to be "governmental interference in the economy."

In addition to resisting government support for the economy, Democrats staunchly defended their immigrant followers. On the state and local levels, they fiercely opposed prohibition and other attempts to limit alcohol use and license saloons. They also advocated support for parochial schools and opposed attempts to require immigrant children to attend only those schools that taught in English.

The Republicans, who reigned in rural and small-town New England, Pennsylvania, and the upper Midwest and who drew support from the **Grand Army of the Republic (GAR)**, a social and political lobbying organization of northern Civil War veterans, often "waved the bloody shirt," reminding voters that their party had led the nation during the Civil War. "The Democratic Party," wrote one Republican, "may be described as a common sewer and loathsome receptacle, into which is emptied every element of treason North and South." To solidify their followers, the Republicans ran a series of former Union army generals for president and voted generous veterans' benefits.

State and local party leaders managed campaigns. They chose the candidates, raised money, organized rallies, and—if their candidate won—distributed public jobs to party workers. Bosses like the former saloonkeepers "Big Jim" Pendergast of Kansas City, a Democrat, and George B. Cox of Cincinnati, a Republican, turned out the vote by taking care of constituents, handing out municipal jobs, and financing campaigns with "contributions" extracted from city employees.

Although the struggle to define the legitimate use of governmental authority shaped the general debate between the two major parties on the federal level, family tradition, ethnic ties, religious affiliation, and local issues often determined an individual's vote. Outside the South, ethnicity and religion were the most reliable predictors of party affiliation. Catholics, especially Irish Catholics, and Americans of German ancestry tended to vote Democratic. Old-stock northerners, in contrast, including 75 percent of Methodists and Congregationalists, 65 percent of Baptists, and 60 percent of Presbyterians voted Republican. Among immigrant groups, most British-born Protestants and 80 percent of Swedish and Norwegian Lutherans voted Republican, as did African-Americans, North and South. Although intolerant of racial differences, the Democrats were generally more accepting of religious diversity than were the Republicans.

Political battles often centered on cultural differences, as native-born Protestants tried to force on immigrants their own views on gambling, temperance, and Sabbath observance. No issue on the local level aroused more conflict than prohibition. Irish whiskey drinkers, German beer drinkers, and Italian wine drinkers were equally outraged by antiliquor legislation. State and local prohibition proposals always aroused passionate voter interest.

Regulating the Money Supply
In the 1870s, politicians confronted a tough problem: how to create a money supply adequate for a growing economy without producing inflation. Americans' almost superstitious reverence for gold and silver added to the difficulty of establishing a coherent monetary policy. The only trustworthy money, many believed, was gold or silver, or certificates exchangeable for these precious metals. Reflecting this notion, all the federally issued currency in circulation in 1860 consisted of gold or silver coins or U.S. Treasury notes redeemable for gold or silver. (Currency from some sixteen hundred state banks was also in circulation, worsening a chaotic monetary situation.)

Opposing groups clashed over the money question. Bankers and creditors, most business leaders, economists, and politicians believed that economic stability required a strictly limited currency supply. Debtors, especially southern and western farmers, favored expanding the money supply to make it easier for them to pay off their debts. The monetary debate focused on a specific question: should the Civil War paper "greenbacks" currently in circulation be retained and even expanded, or phased out, leaving only a currency backed by gold (see Chapter 15)? The hard times associated with the Panic of 1873 sharpened this dispute.

The Greenback party (founded 1877) advocated an expanded money supply, health and safety regulations for the workplace, and other measures to benefit workers and farmers. In the 1878 midterm elections, with the support of labor organizations angered by the government's hostility in the labor unrest of 1877, Greenback candidates won fourteen seats in Congress.

As prosperity returned and the Greenback party faded, the debate became focused on the coinage of silver. In 1873, with little silver being mined, Congress instructed the U.S. mint to stop making silver coins. Silver had been "demonetized." But new discoveries in Nevada (see Chapter 17) vastly increased the silver supply, and debtor groups now demanded that the government resume the coinage of silver.

Enthusiastically backed by the silver-mine owners, silver forces won a partial victory in 1878, when Congress required the treasury to buy up to $4 million worth of silver each month and mint it into silver dollars. But the treasury, dominated by monetary conservatives, sabotaged the law's intent by refusing to circulate the silver dollars that it minted.

Frustrated silver advocates tried a new approach in the **Sherman Silver Purchase Act** of 1890. This measure instructed the treasury to buy, at current market prices, 4.5 million ounces of silver monthly—almost precisely the output of the nation's silver mines. The act further required the government to issue treasury notes, redeemable in gold or silver, equivalent to the cost of these purchases. This law did slightly increase the money supply; but as silver prices fell in 1893 and after, the government paid far less for its monthly purchases and therefore issued fewer treasury notes. The controversy over silver dragged on.

Civil-Service Reform For decades successful candidates in national, state, and local elections had rewarded supporters with jobs ranging from cabinet seats and ambassadorships to lowly municipal posts. To its defenders, this system, originally called rotation in office, seemed a democratic means of filling government positions. But unqualified and incompetent applicants often got jobs simply because of their party loyalty. Once in office, these appointees had to contribute to the reelection campaigns of their political patrons. Because of such abuses, this mode of filling public jobs came to be called the spoils system after the old expression, "To the victor belong the spoils."

For years, a small but influential group of upper-class reformers, including Missouri senator Carl Schurz and editor E. L. Godkin of the *Nation,* had campaigned for a professional civil service based on merit. Well bred, well educated, and wealthy, these reformers favored a civil service staffed by "gentlemen." Whatever their class biases, the reformers had a point. A professional civil service was needed as government grew more complex.

Elected through the compromise that ended Reconstruction (see Chapter 16), Republican president Rutherford B. Hayes cautiously embraced the civil-service cause. In 1877, he launched an investigation of the corruption-riddled New York City customs office and fired two high officials. One, Chester A. Arthur, had played a key role in passing out jobs. Hayes's willingness to confront factions within his own party won praise from civil-service reformers, but critics ridiculed "snivel service" and "Rutherfraud B. Hayes."

When Congressman James A. Garfield won the 1880 Republican presidential nomination, the delegates, to appease the opposing New York faction, chose Chester A. Arthur, the loyalist Hayes had recently fired, as Garfield's running mate. Since Garfield enjoyed excellent health, the choice of the totally unqualified Arthur seemed safe.

The Democrats nominated a career army officer from Pennsylvania, Winfield Scott Hancock, and the Greenbackers gave the nod to Congressman James B. Weaver of Iowa. Garfield's managers stressed his Civil War record and his log-cabin birth. By a razor-thin margin of under forty thousand votes (of 9.2 million cast), Garfield edged out Hancock; Weaver trailed far behind.

Garfield's assassination in 1881, which brought to the White House Vice President Arthur, the very symbol of patronage corruption, gave a powerful emotional thrust to the cause, as civil-service reformers portrayed the fallen president as a spoils-system martyr. In 1883 Congress enacted a civil-service law introduced by Senator George Pendleton of Ohio (Garfield's home state) and drafted by the Civil Service Reform League that had been created two years earlier. The **Pendleton Civil Service Act** set up a commission to prepare competitive examinations and establish standards of merit for a variety of federal jobs; it also forbade political candidates from soliciting contributions from government workers.

Although the Pendleton Act initially covered only about 12 percent of the more than 100,000 federal employees, the number of positions was gradually expanded by subsequent presidents. By the 1890s, the act had opened up new positions for women,

"Where Is the Difference?" 1894 *By equating criminal payoffs to the police to corporate contributions to senators, this cartoon suggests that corruption pervades society and needs to be stopped.*

who now held nearly a third of the jobs as federal clerks in government agencies. The creation of a professional civil service thus helped bring the federal government in step with the modernizing trends transforming society.

As for Chester A. Arthur, the fact that he proved to be a mediocre president pleasantly surprised those who had expected him to be an utter disaster. Arthur supported civil-service reform and proved quite independent. Fed up with the feuding Republicans, in 1882 the voters gave the Democrats a strong majority in the House of Representatives. In 1884, for the first time since 1856, they would put a Democrat in the White House: Grover Cleveland.

POLITICS OF PRIVILEGE, POLITICS OF EXCLUSION, 1884–1892

The stalemate between the two major parties in their battle to establish the standards for economic growth continued under President Cleveland. Although no radical, Cleveland challenged powerful interests by calling for cuts in the tariff and in veterans' pensions. In 1888, business groups and the veterans' lobby rallied to defeat Cleveland and elect Benjamin Harrison of Indiana, a former Civil War general, in one of the most corrupt campaigns in American history. Harrison further alienated voters by passing a high tariff and an expanded pension law that increased the number of pensioners by 43 percent.

Fed up with both the Democrats' and Republicans' fraud and inattention to the needs of rural Americans, farmers mounted protests and began to organize. While the Grange and Farmers' Alliance movements condemned the monopolistic practices of grain and cotton buyers in the post-Reconstruction South, the white majority consolidated their political power by denying the region's black citizens their most basic rights.

A Democrat in the White House: Grover Cleveland, 1885–1889 At a tumultuous Chicago convention in 1884, the Republicans nominated their best-known leader, James G. Blaine. A gifted orator with a keen memory for names and faces, Blaine spoke for the younger, more dynamic wing of the Republican Party eager to shed the taint of corruption, promote economic development, and reinvigorate foreign policy.

But Blaine's name had been stained by the revelation that he, as Speaker of the House, had offered political favors to a railroad company in exchange for stock. For reformers, Blaine epitomized the hated patronage system. To E. L. Godkin, he "wallowed in spoils like a rhinoceros in an African pool."

Sensing Blaine's vulnerability, the Democrats chose a sharply contrasting nominee, Grover Cleveland of New York. In a meteoric rise from reform mayor of Buffalo to governor, Cleveland had fought the bosses and spoilsmen. Short, rotund, and resembling a bulldog, Cleveland was his own man. The shrewdness of the Democrats' choice became apparent when Godkin, Carl Schurz, and other Republican reformers bolted to Cleveland. They were promptly nicknamed **Mugwumps,** an Algonquian term for a renegade chief.

But Cleveland had liabilities, including an illegitimate child he had fathered as a youth. Cleveland admitted the indiscretion, but Republicans still jeered at rallies: "Ma, Ma, where's my pa?" Cleveland also faced opposition from Tammany Hall, the New York City Democratic machine that he had fought as governor. If Tammany's immigrant voters stayed home on election day, Cleveland could lose his own state. But in October a New York City clergyman denounced the Democrats as the party of "Rum, Romanism, and Rebellion." Blaine failed to immediately repudiate the remark. The Cleveland campaign managers widely publicized this triple insult to Catholics, to patriotic Democrats tired of the "bloody shirt," and to drinkers. This blunder and the Mugwumps' defection allowed Cleveland to carry New York State by twelve hundred votes, and with it the election.

Cleveland embraced the belief that government must not meddle in the economy. In Andrew Jackson's day, laissez-faire had been a radical idea endorsed by small entrepreneurs who wanted business conditions favorable to competition; by the 1880s it had become the rallying cry of a corporate elite opposed to any public regulation. Sharing this outlook, Cleveland asserted the power of the presidency mostly through his vetoes and displayed a limited grasp of industrialization's impact. Vetoing a bill that would have provided seeds to drought-stricken farmers in Texas, he warned that people should not expect the government to solve their problems.

One public matter did arouse Cleveland's energies: the tariff, an issue involving a tangle of conflicting economic and political interests. Tariff duties were a major source of revenue in the era before a federal income tax, so the tariff was really a form of taxation. But which imported goods should be subject to duties, and how much? Opinions differed radically.

The producers of such commodities as coal, hides, timber, and wool demanded tariff protection against foreign competition, and industries that had prospered behind tariff walls—iron and steel, textiles, machine tools—wanted protection to continue. Many workers in these industries agreed, convinced that high tariffs meant higher wages. Other manufacturers, however, while seeking protection for their finished products, wanted low tariffs on the raw materials they required. Massachusetts shoe manufacturers, for example, urged high duties on imported shoes but low duties on imported hides. Most farmers, by contrast, hated the protective tariff, charging that it inflated farm-equipment prices and, by impeding trade, made it hard to sell American farm products abroad.

Cleveland's call for lower tariffs arose from a concern over the high tariffs' generation of millions of dollars in surplus federal revenue. This surplus tempted legislators to distribute the money in the form of veterans' pensions or expensive public-works programs in their home districts, commonly called pork-barrel projects. With his horror of paternalistic government, Cleveland viewed the budget surplus as a corrupting influence. In his annual message in 1887, Cleveland argued that lower tariffs not only would cut the federal surplus but would also reduce prices and slow the development of trusts. Although the Democratic campaign of 1888 gave little attention to the issue, Cleveland's talk of lowering the tariff angered many corporate leaders.

Cleveland created another problem when he took on the Grand Army of the Republic. Veterans' disability pensions cost the government millions of dollars annually. No one opposed pensions for the deserving, but by the 1880s fraudulent claims had become a public scandal. Unlike his predecessors, Cleveland investigated these claims and rejected many of them. In 1887 he vetoed a bill that would have pensioned all disabled veterans (even if their disability had nothing to do with military service) and their dependents. The pension list should be an honor roll, he declared, not a refuge for fraud.

Big Business Strikes Back; Benjamin Harrison, 1889–1893

By 1888, some influential interest groups had concluded that Cleveland must go. When Blaine decided not to challenge him, the Republicans turned to Benjamin Harrison of Indiana, the grandson of William Henry Harrison. A corporation lawyer and former senator, Harrison was so aloof that some ridiculed him as the human iceberg. His campaign managers learned to whisk him away after speeches before anyone could talk with him or experience his flabby handshake.

Harrison's managers also developed a new style of electioneering. They brought delegations to Indianapolis and hammered at the tariff issue. Falsely portraying Cleveland as an advocate of "free trade"—the elimination of all tariffs—they warned of the bad effects of such a step. The high protective tariff, they argued, ensured prosperity, decent wages for industrial workers, and a healthy home market for farmers.

The Republicans amassed a $4 million campaign fund from worried business leaders. (Because the Pendleton Civil Service Act had outlawed campaign contributions by government workers, political parties depended more than ever on corporate donors.) This war chest purchased not only posters and buttons but also votes.

Despite such fraud, Cleveland got almost a hundred thousand more votes than Harrison. But Harrison carried the key states of Indiana and New York and won in the Electoral College. The Republicans held the Senate and regained the House. When

Harrison piously observed that Providence had aided the Republican cause, his campaign chairman snorted, "Providence hadn't a damn thing to do with it.... [A] number of men ... approach[ed] the gates of the penitentiary to make him president."

Harrison swiftly rewarded his supporters. He appointed as commissioner of pensions a GAR official who, on taking office, declared "God help the surplus!" The pension rolls soon ballooned from 676,000 to nearly a million. This massive pension system (which was coupled with medical care in a network of veterans' hospitals) became America's first large-scale public-welfare program. In 1890, the triumphant Republicans also enacted the McKinley Tariff, which pushed rates to an all-time high.

Rarely has the federal government been so subservient to entrenched economic interests and so out of touch with the plight of the disadvantaged as during the 1880s. But discontent was rising. The midterm election of 1890, when the Democrats gained sixty-six congressional seats to win control of the House of Representatives, awakened the nation to a tide of political activism engulfing the agrarian South and West. This activism, spawned by chronic problems in rural America, had a long history.

Agrarian Protest and the Rise of the People's Party
As discussed in Chapter 17, Great Plains farming proved far riskier than many had anticipated. Terrible grasshopper infestations consumed nearly half the midwestern wheat crop between 1873 and 1877. Although overall production surged after 1870, the abundant harvests undercut prices. Wheat tumbled from $2.95 a bushel in 1866 to $1.06 in 1880. Countless farmers who had borrowed heavily to finance homesteads and expensive machinery went bankrupt or barely survived. One struggling Minnesota farmer wrote the governor in 1874, "[W]e can see nothing but starvation in the future if relief does not come."

When relief did not come, the farmers responded by setting up cooperative ventures. In 1867, under the leadership of Oliver H. Kelley, a Department of Agriculture clerk, midwestern farmers formed the **Grange**, or "Patrons of Husbandry," as it was officially called. Membership climbed to more than 1.5 million in the early 1870s. Patterned after the Masonic Order, the Grange offered information, emotional support, and fellowship. But the Grange's central concern was farmers' economic plight. An 1874 circular announced the organization's primary purpose: to help farmers "buy less and produce more, in order to make our farms more self-sustaining." Members sought to restore self-sufficiency to the family farm. They negotiated special discounts with farm-machinery dealers and set up "cash-only" cooperative stores and grain-storage elevators to cut out the "middlemen"—the bankers, grain brokers, and merchants who made money at their expense.

Grangers focused their wrath on railroads, which routinely gave discounts to large shippers, bribed state legislators, and charged higher rates for short runs than for long hauls. Stung by these practices, Grangers in Illinois, Wisconsin, Minnesota, and Iowa lobbied state legislatures in 1874 to pass laws fixing maximum rates for freight shipments.

The railroads appealed to the Supreme Court to declare these "Granger laws" unconstitutional. But in *Munn* v. *Illinois* (1877) the Court not only rejected the railroads' appeal but also upheld an Illinois law setting a maximum rate for the storage of grain. The regulation of grain elevators, declared the Court's majority, was legitimate under the federal Constitution's acknowledgment of the right of states to exercise police powers. When the Court in *Wabash* v. *Illinois* (1886) modified this position by prohibit-

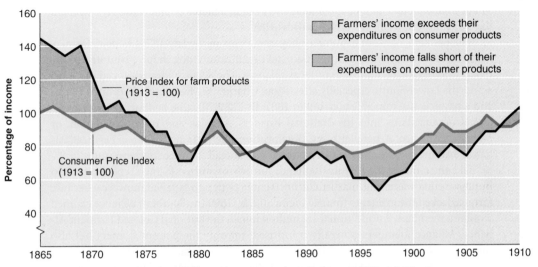

Figure 20.1 Consumer Prices and Farm-Product Prices, 1865–1913

From 1865 to 1895, the prices that farmers received for their crops gradually declined. Even when they increased after 1895, farmers had difficulty in making ends meet. As cycles of drought and debt battered Great Plains wheat growers, a Kansas farmer wrote, "At the age of 52, after a long life of toil, economy, and self-denial, I find myself and family virtually paupers."

ing states from regulating interstate railroad rates, Congress passed the Interstate Commerce Act (1887), reaffirming the federal government's power to investigate and oversee railroad activities and establishing a new agency, the Interstate Commerce Commission (ICC), to do just that. Although the commission failed to curb the railroads' monopolistic practices, it did establish the principle of federal regulation of interstate transportation.

Despite promising beginnings, the Grange movement soon faltered. The railroads, having lost their battle on the national level, lobbied state legislatures and won repeal of most of the rate-regulation laws by 1878. Moreover, the Grange system of cash-only cooperative stores failed because few farmers had sufficient cash. Ultimately, the Grange ideal of complete financial independence proved unrealistic. Under the conditions that prevailed on the Plains, it was impossible to farm without borrowing money.

When the prices of corn, wheat, and cotton briefly revived after 1878, many farmers deserted the Grange. Although the Grange lived on as a social and educational institution, it lost its economic clout because it was ultimately unable to improve its members' financial position. For all its weaknesses, the Grange laid the groundwork for an even more powerful wave of agrarian protest.

While the Grange was centered in the Midwest and the Great Plains, the **Farmers' Alliance** movement first arose in the South and West, where farmers grappled with many of the same problems. In the cotton South, small planters found themselves trapped by the crop-lien system, mortgaging future harvests to cover current expenses.

Mired in debt, many gave up their land and became tenants or sharecroppers. About a third of southern farmers were tenants by 1900.

The Farmers' Alliance movement began in Texas in the late 1870s as poor farmers gathered to discuss their hardships. Soon an organization took shape, promoted by activists who organized hundreds of local alliances. The alliance idea advanced eastward across the Lower South, especially after Texan Charles W. Macune, a self-trained lawyer and a physician, assumed leadership in 1887. By 1889, Macune had merged several regional organizations into the National Farmers' Alliance and Industrial Union, or Southern Alliance. A parallel black organization, the National Colored Farmers' Alliance, had meanwhile emerged in Arkansas and spread to other southern states.

Like the Grange, the Farmers' Alliance initially organized farmers' cooperatives to purchase equipment and market cotton. Many cooperatives failed, however, because farmers lacked the capital to finance them. Still, by 1890 the Southern Alliance claimed 3 million members. An additional 1.2 million joined the National Colored Farmers' Alliance. Alliance members generally comprised not only the poorest farmers but also those most dependent on a single crop and most geographically isolated. As they attended alliance rallies and picnics, read the alliance newspaper, and listened to alliance speakers, hard-hit farm families became increasingly aware of their political potential. An Arkansas member wrote in 1889, "Reform never begins with the leaders, it comes from the people."

Alliance fever soon spread to the Great Plains. In the drought-plagued years of 1880 and 1881, alliances sprang up in Kansas, Nebraska, Iowa, and Minnesota. Membership grew when drought returned, insects destroyed much of the wheat crop, and prices for agricultural produce fell as world production increased. Under these conditions, many settlers returned East. "In God we trusted, in Kansas we busted," some scrawled on their wagons. Western Kansas lost 50 percent of its population between 1888 and 1892. But others hung on, and the Northwestern Alliance grew rapidly. By 1890, the Kansas Alliance claimed 130,000 members, followed closely by alliances in Nebraska, the Dakotas, and Minnesota. What had begun as a desperate attempt to save their farms had now turned into a massive political campaign to change the American political and economic system.

Reformers at first tried to create a biracial movement. Southern Alliance leaders Tom Watson of Georgia and Leonidas Polk of North Carolina urged southern farmers, black and white, to act together. For a time, this message of racial cooperation in the interest of reform offered promise. In Kansas, meanwhile, Jerry Simpson, a rancher who lost his stock in the hard winter of 1886–1887, became a major alliance leader. Mary E. Lease, a Wichita lawyer, burst on the scene in 1890 as a fiery alliance orator.

Other women, veterans of the Granger or prohibition cause, rallied to the new cause, founding the National Women's Alliance (NWA) in 1891. Declared the NWA, "Put 1,000 women lecturers in the field and revolution is here." By no coincidence, a strong feminist strain pervades Ignatius Donnelly's *The Golden Bottle* (1892), a novel portraying the agrarian reformers' social vision.

As the movement swelled, the opposition turned nasty. When Jerry Simpson mentioned the silk stockings of a conservative politician in his district and noted that he had no such finery, a hostile newspaper editor labeled him "Sockless Jerry" Simpson, the nickname he carried to his grave. When Mary Lease advised Kansas to "raise less corn and more hell," another editor sneered: "[Kansas] has started to raise hell, as Mrs.

Lease advised, and [the state] seems to have an overproduction. But that doesn't matter. Kansas never did believe in diversified crops."

All this activity helped shape a new political agenda. In 1889, the Southern and Northwestern Alliances loosely merged and adopted a political litmus test for candidates in the 1890 midterm elections. They focused on increasing government action on behalf of farmers and workers, including tariff reduction, a graduated income tax, public ownership of the railroads, federal funding for irrigation research, a ban on landownership by aliens, and "the free and unlimited coinage of silver."

The 1890 elections revealed the strength of agrarian protest. Southern Democrats who endorsed alliance goals won four governorships and control of eight state legislatures. On the Great Plains, alliance-endorsed candidates secured control of the Nebraska legislature and gained the balance of power in Minnesota and South Dakota. In Kansas, the candidates of the alliance-sponsored People's Party demolished all opposition. Three alliance-backed senators, together with some fifty congressmen (including Watson and Simpson), went to Washington as angry winds from the hinterlands buffeted the political system.

Regional differences, which threatened to divide the movement, were soon overcome by shared economic grievance. Southern Alliance leaders who initially opposed endorsing a third party, fearing that it would weaken the southern Democratic Party, the bastion of white supremacy, eventually adopted the third-party idea, since many Democrats whom they had backed in 1890 had ignored the alliance agenda once in office. In February 1892, alliance leaders organized the People's Party of the United States, generally called the **Populist Party.** At the party convention in Omaha, Nebraska, that August, cheering delegates nominated for president the former Civil War general and Greenback nominee James B. Weaver of Iowa. Courting the South, they chose as Weaver's running mate the Virginian James Field, who had lost a leg fighting for the Confederacy.

The Populist platform restated the alliance goals while adding a call for the direct popular election of senators and other electoral reforms. It also endorsed a **subtreasury plan** devised by alliance leader Charles Macune by which farmers could store their nonperishable commodities in government warehouses, receive low-interest loans using the crops as collateral, and then sell the stored commodities when market prices rose. Ignatius Donnelly's ringing preamble pronounced the nation on "the verge of moral, political, and material ruin" and called for a return of the government "to the hands of 'the plain people' with which class it originated."

| African-Americans After Reconstruction | As the Populists geared up for the 1892 campaign, another group of citizens with profound grievances found themselves pushed even farther to the margins of American public life. |

The end of Reconstruction in 1877 and the restoration of power to the southern white elites, the so-called redeemers (see Chapter 16), was ominous for southern blacks. The redeemer coalition of large landowners, merchants, and "New South" industrialists had little interest in the former slaves except as a docile labor force or as political pawns. However, southern white opinion demanded an end to the hated "Negro rule," and local Democratic Party officials pursued this objective. Suppressing the black vote became a major goal. At first, black disfranchisement was achieved by intimidation, terror, and vote fraud, as blacks were either kept from the

The Knights of Labor
Black delegate Frank J. Farrell introduces Terence V. Powderly, head of the Knights of Labor, at the organization's 1886 convention. The Knights were unusual in accepting both black and female workers.

polls or forced to vote Democratic. Then in 1890 Mississippi amended its state constitution in ways that effectively excluded most black voters, and other southern states soon followed suit.

Because the Fifteenth Amendment (1870) (see Chapter 16) guaranteed all male citizens' right to vote, white southerners used indirect means such as literacy tests (a test of the ability to read), poll taxes (a tax paid to vote), and property requirements (which restricted the right to vote to those who owned property) to disfranchise blacks. The racist intent of these devices was obvious. One stratagem, the so-called grandfather clause, exempted from these electoral requirements anyone with an ancestor who had voted in 1860. Although black disfranchisement proceeded erratically over the South, by the early twentieth century it was essentially complete.

Disfranchisement was only one part of the system of white supremacy laboriously erected in the South. In a parallel development that culminated in the early twentieth century, state after state passed laws imposing strict racial segregation in many realms of life (see Chapter 21).

Black caterers, barbers, bricklayers, carpenters, and other artisans lost their white clientele. Blacks who went to prison—sometimes for minor offenses—faced the convict-lease system, by which cotton planters, railroad builders, coal-mine operators, and other employers "leased" prison gangs and forced them to work under slave-labor conditions.

The convict-lease system not only enforced the racial hierarchy but also played an important economic role as industrialization and agricultural change came to the South. The system brought income to hard-pressed state governments and provided factories, railroads, mines, and large-scale farms with a predictable, controllable, and cheap labor supply. The system also intimidated free laborers. One observer commented, "[O]n account of the convict employment, strikes are of rare occurrence." Recognizing this danger, free miners in Tennessee successfully agitated against the employment of convict labor in their state in the 1890s. Thousands died under the brutal convict-labor system. It survived into the early decades of the twentieth century, ultimately succumbing to humanitarian protest and to economic changes that made it unprofitable.

Lynching became the ultimate enforcer of southern white supremacy. Through the 1880s and 1890s, about a hundred blacks were lynched annually in the United States, mainly in the South. The stated reasons, often the rape of a white woman, frequently arose from rumor and unsubstantiated accusations. The charge of "attempted rape," as the black journalist Ida B. Wells pointed out to a national audience (see Chapter 21), could cover a wide range of behaviors unacceptable to whites, such as questioning authority or talking back.

The lynch mob demonstrated whites' absolute power. In the South, more than 80 percent of the lynchings involved black victims. Lynchings most commonly occurred in the Cotton Belt, and they tended to rise at times of economic distress when cotton prices were falling and job competition between poor whites and poor blacks was most intense. By no coincidence, lynching peaked in 1892 as many poor blacks embraced the Farmers' Alliance movement and rallied to the Populist Party banner. Fifteen black Populists were killed in Georgia alone, it has been estimated, during that year's bitter campaign.

The relationship between southern agrarian protest and white racism was complex. Some Populists, like Georgia's Tom Watson, sought to build an interracial movement. Watson denounced lynching and the convict-lease system. When a black Populist leader pursued by a lynch mob took refuge in his house during the 1892 campaign, Watson summoned two thousand armed white Populists to defend him. But most white Populists clung to racism. Watson complained that most poor whites "would joyously hug the chains of . . . wretchedness rather than do any experimenting on [the race] question."

The white elite, eager to drive a wedge in the protest movement, inflamed lower-class white racism. The agricultural crisis of the period, which included a precipitous decline in cotton prices, had driven poor white tenant farmers in the South to the brink of despair. Those who lost control of their farms felt that they not only faced economic ruin, but also risked loss of their manhood. Conscious of themselves as a racial group, they feared that if they fell further down the economic ladder they would lose the racial privileges that came from their "whiteness" and be treated like blacks, Mexicans, and the foreign born. Hence, they were swayed by conservative Atlanta editor Henry W. Grady when he warned against division among white southerners: the region's only hope, he said, was "the clear and unmistakable domination of the white race."

Even as they warned of the dangers of "Negro rule," the white elite manipulated the urban black vote as a weapon against agrarian radicalism, driving Tom Watson to despair. On balance, the rise of southern agrarian protest deepened racial hatred and ultimately worsened blacks' situation.

While southern blacks suffered racist oppression, the federal government stood aside. A generation of northern politicians paid lip service to egalitarian principles but failed to apply them to blacks.

The Supreme Court similarly abandoned blacks. The Fourteenth Amendment (1868) had granted blacks citizenship and the equal protection of the laws, and the Civil Rights Act of 1875 outlawed racial discrimination on juries, in public places such as hotels and theaters, and on railroads, streetcars, and other such conveyances. But the Supreme Court soon ripped gaping holes in these protective laws.

In the *Civil Rights Cases* (1883), the Court declared the Civil Rights Act of 1875 unconstitutional. The Fourteenth Amendment protected citizens only from governmental infringement of their civil rights, the justices ruled, not from acts by private citizens such as railroad conductors. In **Plessy v. Ferguson (1896),** the justices upheld a Louisiana law requiring segregated railroad cars. Racial segregation was constitutional, the Court held, if equal facilities were made available to each race. (In a prophetic dissent, Associate Justice John Marshall Harlan observed, "Our Constitution is color blind." Segregation, he added, violated the constitutional principle of equality before the law.) With the Supreme Court's blessing, the South segregated its public school system, ignoring the caveat that such separate facilities must be equal. White children studied in nicer buildings, used newer equipment, and were taught by better-paid teachers. Not until 1954 did the Court abandon the "separate but equal" doctrine. Rounding out their dismal record, in 1898 the justices upheld the poll tax and literacy tests by which southern states had disfranchised blacks.

Few northerners protested the South's white-supremacist society. Until the North condemned lynching outright, declared the aged abolitionist Frederick Douglass in 1892, "it will remain equally involved with the South in this common crime." The restoration of sectional harmony, in short, came at a high price: acquiescence by the North in the utter debasement of the South's African-American citizenry. Further, the separatist principle endorsed in *Plessy* had a pervasive impact, affecting blacks nationwide, Mexicans in Texas, Asians in California, and other groups.

Blacks responded to their plight in various ways. The nation's foremost black leader from the 1890s to his death in 1915 was **Booker T. Washington.** Born in slavery in Virginia in 1856, the son of a slave woman and her white master, Washington attended a freedman's school in Hampton, Virginia, and in 1881 organized a black state vocational school in Alabama that eventually became Tuskegee University. Although Washington secretly contributed to lawyers who challenged segregation, he publicly urged accommodation to a racist society. In a widely publicized address in Atlanta in 1895, he insisted that the first task of America's blacks must be to acquire useful skills such as farming and carpentry. Once blacks proved their economic value, he predicted, racism would fade; meanwhile, they must patiently accept their lot. This was a position later challenged by W. E. B. Du Bois (see Chapter 21). Washington lectured widely, and his autobiography, *Up from Slavery* (1901), recounted his rise from poverty thanks to honesty, hard work, and kindly patrons—themes familiar to a generation reared on Horatio Alger's self-help books.

Other blacks responded resourcefully to the racist society. Black churches provided emotional support, as did black fraternal lodges like the Knights of Pythias. Some African-Americans started businesses to serve their community. Two black-owned banks, in Richmond and Washington, D.C., were chartered in 1888. The North Carolina Mutual Insurance Company, organized in 1898 by John Merrick, a prosperous Durham barber, evolved into a major enterprise. Bishop Henry M. Turner of the African Methodist Episcopal church urged blacks to return to Africa and build a great Christian nation. Turner made several trips to Africa in pursuit of his proposal.

African-American protest never wholly died out. Frederick Douglass urged that blacks press for full equality. "Who would be free, themselves must strike the first blow," he proclaimed in 1883. Blacks should meet violence with violence, insisted militant New York black leader T. Thomas Fortune.

Other blacks answered southern racism by leaving the region. In 1879, several thousand moved to Kansas (see Chapter 16). Some ten thousand migrated to Chicago between 1870 and 1890. Blacks who moved north soon found that although white supremacy was not official policy, public opinion sanctioned many forms of de facto discrimination. Northern black laborers, for example, encountered widespread prejudice. The Knights of Labor did welcome blacks and by the mid-1880s had an estimated sixty thousand black members. Its successor, the American Federation of Labor, officially forbade racial discrimination, but in practice many of its member unions excluded blacks.

The rise of the so-called solid South, firmly established on racist foundations, had important political implications. For one thing, it made a mockery of the two-party system in the South. For years, the only meaningful election south of the Potomac was the Democratic primary. Only in the 1960s, in the wake of sweeping social and economic changes, would a genuine two-party system emerge there. The large bloc of southern Democrats elected to Congress each year, accumulating seniority and power, exerted a great and often reactionary influence on public policy. Above all, they mobilized instantly to quash any threat to southern white supremacy. Finally, southern Democrats wielded enormous clout in the national party. No Democratic contender for national office who was unacceptable to them stood a chance.

Above all, the caste system that evolved in the post-Reconstruction South shaped the consciousness of those caught up in it, white and black alike. White novelist Lillian Smith described her girlhood in turn-of-the-century Florida and Georgia: "From the day I was born, I began to learn my lessons. . . . I learned it is possible to be a Christian and a white southerner simultaneously; to be a gentlewoman and an arrogant callous creature at the same moment; to pray at night and ride a Jim Crow car the next morning; . . . to glow when the word democracy was used, and to practice slavery from morning to night."

THE 1890S: POLITICS IN A DEPRESSION DECADE

Discontent with the major parties and their commitment to supporting unrestricted business enterprise, which had smoldered during the 1870s and 1880s, burst into flames in the 1890s. As banks failed and railroads went bankrupt, the nation slid into a grinding depression. The crises of the 1890s laid bare the paralysis of the federal government—dominated by a business elite—when confronted by the new social realities of factories, urban slums, immigrant workers, and desperate farmers. In response, irate farmers, laborers, and their supporters joined a new party, the Populists, to change the system.

1892: Populists Challenge the Status Quo

The Populist Party platform adopted in July 1892 offered a broad vision of national reform. That same month, thirteen people died in a gun battle between strikers and strikebreakers at the Homestead steel plant near Pittsburgh, and President Harrison sent federal troops to Coeur d'Alene, Idaho, where a silver-mine strike had turned violent. Events seemed to justify the Populists' warnings of chaos ahead.

Faced with domestic turmoil and fearful that the powerful European socialist movement would spread to the United States, both major parties acted cautiously. The Republicans renominated Harrison and adopted a platform that ignored escalating unrest. The Democrats turned again to Grover Cleveland, who in four years out of office had made clear his growing conservatism and his opposition to the Populists. Cleveland won by more than 360,000 votes, a decisive margin in this era of close elections. A public reaction against labor violence and the McKinley Tariff hurt Harrison, while Cleveland's support for the gold standard won business support.

Although Populist strength proved spotty, their achievements sparked great hopes for the future. James B. Weaver got just over a million votes—8.5 percent of the total— and the Populists elected five senators, ten congressmen, and three governors. The new party carried Kansas and registered some appeal in the West and in Georgia, Alabama, and Texas, where the alliance movement had taken deep root. But it made no dent in New England, the urban East, or the traditionally Republican farm regions of the Midwest. It even failed to show broad strength in the upper Great Plains. "Beaten! Whipped! Smashed!" moaned Minnesota Populist Ignatius Donnelly in his diary.

Throughout most of the South, racism, ingrained Democratic loyalty, distaste for a ticket headed by a former Union general, widespread intimidation, and voter fraud kept the Populist vote under 25 percent. This failure killed the prospects for interracial agrarian reform in the region. After 1892, as Populism began to revive in the South and Midwest, many southern politicians seeking to appeal to poor whites—including a disillusioned Tom Watson—stayed within the Democratic fold and laced their populism with racism.

Capitalism in Crisis: The Depression of 1893–1897   Cleveland soon confronted a major crisis, an economic collapse in the railroad industry that quickly spread. In the economic boom of the 1880s, railroads had fed the speculative mania by issuing more stock (and enticing investors with higher dividends) than their business prospects warranted. Weakened by agricultural stagnation, railroad growth slowed in the early 1890s. The first hint of trouble flared up in February 1893 when the Philadelphia and Reading Railroad failed.

This bankruptcy came at a time of weakened confidence in the gold standard, the government's pledge to redeem paper money for gold on demand. This diminished confidence had several sources. First, when a leading London investment bank collapsed in 1890, hard-pressed British investors sold millions of dollars' worth of stock in American railroads and other corporations and converted their dollars to gold, draining U.S. gold reserves. Second, Congress's lavish veterans' benefits and pork-barrel appropriations during the Harrison administration drained government resources just as tariff revenues were dropping because of the high McKinley Tariff. Third, the 1890 Sherman Silver Purchase Act further strained the gold reserve. This measure required the government to pay for its monthly silver purchases with treasury certificates redeemable for either silver or gold, and many certificate holders chose to convert them to gold. Finally, the election of Grover Cleveland in 1892 further eroded confidence in the dollar. Although Cleveland endorsed the gold standard, his party harbored many advocates of inflationary policies.

Between January 1892 and March 1893, when Cleveland took office, the gold reserve had fallen sharply to around $100 million, the minimum considered necessary to support the dollar. This decline alarmed those who viewed the gold standard as the only sure evidence of the government's financial stability.

The collapse of a railroad triggered the **Panic of 1893.** Fear fed on itself as alarmed investors converted their stock holdings to gold. Stock prices fell in May and June; gold reserves sank; by the end of the year, seventy-four railroads and more than fifteen thousand commercial institutions, including six hundred banks, had failed. The Panic of 1893 set off four years of hard times.

By 1897, about a third of the nation's railroad mileage had plunged into bankruptcy. Just as the railroad boom had spurred the industrial prosperity of the 1880s, so had the railroad crisis of the early 1890s battered the entire economy as banks and other businesses failed. A full-scale depression gripped the nation.

The crisis took a heavy human toll. Industrial unemployment soared into the 20 to 25 percent range, leaving millions of factory workers with no money to feed their families and heat their homes. Recent immigrants faced disaster. Jobless men tramped the streets and rode freight trains from city to city seeking work.

The unusually harsh winters of 1893 and 1894 made matters worse. In New York City, where the crisis quickly swamped local relief agencies, a minister reported actual starvation. Amid the suffering, a rich New Yorker named Bradley Martin threw a lavish costume ball costing several hundred thousand dollars. Popular outrage over this flaunting of wealth in a prostrate city forced Martin and his family to move abroad.

Rural America, already hard-hit by declining agricultural prices, faced ruin. Farm prices dropped by more than 20 percent between 1890 and 1896. Corn plummeted from fifty cents to twenty-one cents a bushel; wheat, from eighty-four cents to fifty-one cents. Cotton sold for five cents a pound in 1894.

Some desperate Americans turned to protest. In Chicago, workers at the Pullman factory reacted to successive wage cuts by walking off the job in June 1894 (see Chapter 18). In Massillon, Ohio, self-taught monetary expert Jacob Coxey proposed as a solution to unemployment a $500 million public-works program funded with paper money not backed by gold but simply designated "legal tender" (just as it is today). A man of action as well as ideas, Coxey organized a march on Washington to lobby for his scheme. Thousands joined him en route, and several hundred actually reached Washington in late April 1894. Police arrested Coxey and other leaders when they attempted to enter the Capitol grounds, and his "army" broke up. Although some considered Coxey eccentric, his proposal closely resembled programs that the government would adopt during the depression of the 1930s.

As unrest intensified, fear clutched middle-class Americans. A church magazine demanded that troops put "a pitiless stop" to outbreaks of unrest. To some observers, a bloody upheaval seemed imminent.

Business Leaders Respond

In the face of suffering and turmoil, Cleveland refused to intervene. Boom-and-bust economic cycles were inevitable, he insisted, echoing the conventional wisdom of the day; the government could do nothing. Failing to grasp the larger picture, Cleveland focused on a single peripheral issue: defending the gold standard. As the gold reserve dwindled, he blamed the Sherman Silver Purchase Act, and in August 1893 he called on Congress to repeal it. Silver advocates protested, but Congress followed Cleveland's wishes.

Nevertheless, the gold drain continued. In early 1895, with the gold reserve down to $41 million, Cleveland turned to Wall Street. Bankers J. P. Morgan and August Belmont agreed to lend the government $62 million in exchange for U.S. bonds at a special discount. With this loan, the government purchased gold to replenish its reserve.

Meanwhile, Morgan and Belmont resold the bonds for a substantial profit. This complicated deal did help restore confidence in the government's economic stability. The gold drain stopped, and when the treasury offered $100 million in bonds early in 1896, they sold quickly.

Cleveland saved the gold standard, but at a high price. His dealings with Morgan and Belmont, and the bankers' handsome profits on the deal, confirmed radicals' suspicions of an unholy alliance between Washington and Wall Street. Cleveland's readiness to use force against the Pullman strikers and against Jacob Coxey's peaceful marchers deepened such suspicions.

In the ongoing maneuverings of competing interest groups, corporate interests held the whip hand, as a battle over the tariff made clear. Although Cleveland favored tariff reform, the Congress of 1893–1895—despite its Democratic majorities—generally yielded to high-tariff lobbyists. The Wilson-Gorman Tariff of 1894 lowered duties somewhat, but made so many concessions to protectionist interests that Cleveland disgustedly allowed it to become law without his signature.

Hinting at changes ahead, the Wilson-Gorman Tariff imposed a modest income tax of 2 percent on all income over $4,000 (about $40,000 in purchasing power today). But in *Pollock* v. *Farmers' Loan & Trust Co.* (1895), the Supreme Court narrowly held the law unconstitutional, ruling that the federal government could impose such a direct tax on personal property only if it were apportioned according to the population of each state. Whether one looked at the executive, the legislature, or the judiciary, Washington's subordination to financial interests seemed absolute.

Cleveland's policies split the Democratic Party. Farm leaders and silver Democrats condemned his opposition to the Sherman Silver Purchase Act. South Carolina's Ben Tillman, running for the Senate in 1894, proclaimed, "[T]his scoundrel Cleveland . . . is an old bag of beef and I am going to Washington with a pitchfork and prod him in his fat old ribs." This split in the Democratic ranks affected the elections of 1894 and 1896 and reshaped politics as the century ended.

The depression also helped reorient social thought. Middle-class charitable workers, long convinced that individual character flaws caused poverty, now realized—as socialists proclaimed and as the poor well knew—that even sober and hardworking people could succumb to economic forces beyond their control. As the social work profession took form in the early twentieth century, its members spent less time preaching to the poor and more time investigating the social sources of poverty.

Laissez-faire ideology weakened in the 1890s as many depression-worn Americans adopted a broadened view of the government's role in dealing with the social consequences of industrialization. In the early twentieth century, this new view would activate powerful political energies. The depression, in short, not only brought suffering; it also taught lessons.

1894: Protest Grows Louder   Republican gains in the 1894 midterm election revealed the depths of revulsion against Cleveland and the Democrats, who were blamed for the hard times. As 1896 approached, the monetary question became the overriding symbolic issue. Conservatives clung to the gold standard; agrarian radicals rallied to the banner of "free silver." At the 1896 Democratic convention, the nomination went to a young champion of the silver cause, **William Jennings Bryan.** Despite Bryan's eloquence, Republican William McKinley emerged victorious. His triumph laid the groundwork for a major political realignment that would influence American politics for a generation.

With the depression at its worst and President Grover Cleveland deeply unpopular, the midterm election of 1894 spelled Democratic disaster. The Republicans, gaining 5 seats in the Senate and 117 in the House, won both houses of Congress. They also secured control of several key states—including New York, Illinois, and Wisconsin—as immigrant workers, battered by the depression, abandoned their traditional Democratic allegiance.

Populist candidates garnered nearly 1.5 million votes in 1894, an increase of more than 40 percent over their 1892 total. Populism's most impressive gains occurred in the South. Although several western states that had voted Populist in 1892 returned to their traditional Republican allegiance in 1894, the overall results heartened Populist leaders.

The serious economic divisions that split Americans in the mid-1890s focused especially on a symbolic issue: free silver. Cleveland's rigid defense of the gold standard forced his opponents into an equally exaggerated obsession with silver, obscuring the genuine issues that divided rich and poor, creditor and debtor, and farmer and city-dweller. Although agrarian radicals preferred the subtreasury proposal that would have used their stored crops as collateral for loans, the tireless campaign by business leaders for the gold standard led them to counter by emphasizing silver. They were urged on and sometimes financed by western silver-mine owners who stood to profit if silver again became a monetary metal.

Each side had a point. Gold advocates recognized that a nation's paper money must be based on more than a government's ability to run printing presses and that uncontrolled inflation could be catastrophic. The silver advocates knew from experience how tight-money policies depressed prices and devastated farmers. Unfortunately, these underlying realities were rarely expressed clearly. The silverites' most influential propaganda, William H. Harvey's widely distributed *Coin's Financial School* (1894), explained the monetary issue in simplified partisan terms, denounced "the conspiracy of Goldbugs," and insisted that the free coinage of silver would banish debt and end the depression.

Silver Advocates Capture the Democratic Party

At the 1896 Democratic convention in Chicago, western and southern delegates adopted a platform—including a demand for the free and unlimited coinage of silver at the ratio to gold of sixteen to one—that in effect repudiated the Cleveland administration. The front-running candidate was Congressman Richard Bland of Missouri, a silverite. But behind the scenes, the groundwork was being laid for the nomination of a dark horse, William Jennings Bryan, a thirty-six-year-old Nebraska lawyer and politician. During two terms in Congress (1891–1895) he championed western agrarian interests.

Joining Christian imagery with economic analysis, Bryan delivered his major convention speech in the debate over the platform. In an era before electronic amplification, his booming voice easily reached the upper gallery of the cavernous hall. Bryan praised western farmers and scorned advocates of the gold standard. By the time he reached his rousing conclusion—"You shall not press down upon the brow of labor this crown of thorns, you shall not crucify mankind upon a cross of gold"—the wildly cheering delegates had identified their candidate.

MAP 20.1 The Election of 1896

Republicans won the election by carrying the urban vote.

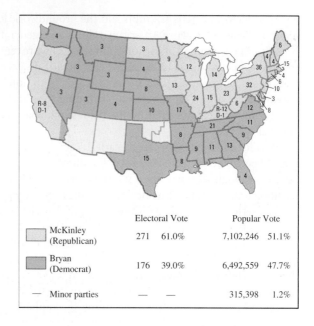

		Electoral Vote		Popular Vote	
■	McKinley (Republican)	271	61.0%	7,102,246	51.1%
■	Bryan (Democrat)	176	39.0%	6,492,559	47.7%
—	Minor parties	—	—	315,398	1.2%

The silverites' capture of the Democratic Party presented a dilemma to the Populists. They, too, advocated free silver, but only as one reform among many. To back Bryan would be to abandon the broad Populist program. Furthermore, fusion with the Democrats could destroy their influence as a third party. Yet the Populist leaders recognized that a separate Populist ticket would likely siphon votes from Bryan and ensure a Republican victory. Reluctantly, the Populists endorsed Bryan, while preserving a shred of independence (and confusing voters) by naming their own vice-presidential candidate, Tom Watson of Georgia. The Populists were learning the difficulty of organizing an independent political movement in a nation wedded to the two-party system.

The Republicans, meanwhile, had nominated former governor William McKinley, who as an Ohio congressman had given his name to the McKinley Tariff of 1890. The Republican platform embraced the high protective tariff and endorsed the gold standard.

1896: Republicans Triumphant Bryan tried to sustain the momentum of the Chicago convention. Crisscrossing the nation by train, he delivered his free-silver campaign speech to hundreds of audiences in twenty-nine states. One skeptical editor compared him to Nebraska's notoriously shallow Platte River: six inches deep and a mile wide at the mouth.

McKinley's campaign was shrewdly managed by Mark Hanna, a Cleveland industrialist. Dignified and aloof, McKinley could not match Bryan's popular touch. Accordingly, Hanna built the campaign not around the candidate but around posters, pamphlets, and newspaper editorials. These publications warned of the dangers of free silver, caricatured Bryan as a rabid radical, and portrayed McKinley and the gold standard as twin pillars of prosperity.

Women Bryan Supporters   *Although women could not vote in national elections in the 1890s, they actively participated in political campaigns. These women worked to turn out the vote for William Jennings Bryan.*

Drawing on a war chest possibly as large as $7 million, Hanna spent lavishly. J. P. Morgan and John D. Rockefeller together contributed half a million dollars, far more than Bryan's total campaign contributions. Like Benjamin Harrison in 1888, McKinley stayed home in Canton, Ohio, emerging from time to time to read speeches to visiting delegations. Carefully orchestrated by Hanna, McKinley's deceptively bucolic "front-porch" campaign involved elaborate organization. All told, some 750,000 people trekked to Canton that summer.

On election day, McKinley beat Bryan by over six hundred thousand votes. He swept the Northeast and the Midwest and even carried three farm states beyond the Mississippi—Iowa, Minnesota, and North Dakota—as well as California and Oregon. Bryan's strength was limited to the South and the sparsely settled Great Plains and mountain states. The Republicans retained control of Congress.

Why did Bryan lose despite the depression and the protest spirit abroad in the land? Certainly, Republican cash reserves, their influence on the East Coast press, and their scare tactics played a role. But Bryan's candidacy carried its own liabilities. His core constituency, while passionately loyal, was limited. Seduced by free silver and Bryan's oratory, the Democrats had upheld a platform and a candidate with little appeal for factory workers, the urban middle class, or the settled family farmers of the midwestern corn belt. Urban voters, realizing that higher farm prices, a major free-silver goal, also meant higher food prices, went heavily for McKinley. Bryan's weakness in urban America reflected cultural differences as well. To urban Catholics and Jews, this moralistic, teetotaling Nebraskan thundering like a Protestant revival preacher seemed utterly alien.

Finally, although parts of their critique of laissez-faire capitalism were endorsed by Bryan and the Democrats, the Populists' effort to define a humane and democratic alternative relied heavily on visions of a premodern economic order of independent farmers and entrepreneurs. Although appealing, this vision bore little relationship to the new corporate order taking shape in America.

The McKinley administration quickly translated its conservative platform into law. The Dingley Tariff (1897) pushed rates to all-time high levels, and the Currency Act of 1900 officially committed the United States to the gold standard. With returning prosperity, rising farm prices after 1897, and the discovery of gold in Alaska and elsewhere, these measures aroused little protest. Bryan won renomination in 1900, but the fervor of 1896 was missing. The Republican campaign theme of prosperity easily won McKinley a second term.

The elections of 1894 and 1896 produced a Republican majority that, except for Woodrow Wilson's two presidential terms (1913–1921), would dominate national politics until the election of Franklin D. Roosevelt in 1932. Bryan's defeat and the Republicans' emergence as the party of prosperity and the sound dollar killed the Populist Party and drove the Democrats back to their regional base in the South. But although populism collapsed, a new reform movement called progressivism was emerging. Many of the Populists' reform proposals would be enacted into law in the progressive years.

Expansionist Stirrings and War with Spain, 1878–1901

The same corporate elite that dominated late-nineteenth-century domestic politics influenced U.S. foreign policy as well, contributing to surging expansionist pressures. Not only business leaders but politicians, statesmen, and editorial writers insisted that national greatness required that America match Europe's imperial expansion. Fanned by sensationalistic newspaper coverage of a Cuban struggle for independence and by elite calls for greater American international assertiveness, war between the United States and Spain broke out in 1898.

Roots of Expansionist Sentiment

Ever since the first European settlers colonized North America's Atlantic coast, the newcomers had been an expansionist people. By the 1840s, the push westward had acquired a name: Manifest Destiny. Directed inward after 1865 toward the settlement of the trans-Mississippi West (see Chapter 17), this impulse turned outward in the 1880s as Americans followed the example set by Great Britain, France, Belgium, Italy, Germany, and Japan, which were busily collecting colonies from North Africa to the Pacific islands. National greatness, it appeared, demanded an empire.

Many business leaders believed that continued domestic prosperity required overseas markets. As American industrial capacity expanded, foreign markets offered a safety valve for potentially explosive pressures in the U.S. economy. Secretary of State James Blaine warned in 1890 that U.S. productivity was outrunning "the demands of the home market" and insisted that American business must look abroad.

Advocates of a stronger navy further fueled the expansionist mood. In *The Influence of Sea Power upon History* (1890), **Alfred Thayer Mahan** equated sea power with national greatness and urged a U.S. naval buildup. Since a strong navy required bases abroad, Mahan and other naval advocates supported the movement to acquire foreign territories, especially Pacific islands with good harbors. Military strategy, in this case and others, often masked the desire for access to new markets.

Religious leaders proclaimed America's mission to spread Christianity. This expansionist argument sometimes took on a racist tinge. As Josiah Strong put it in his 1885 work *Our Country*, "God is training the Anglo-Saxon race for its mission"—a mission of Christianizing and civilizing the world's "weaker races."

A group of Republican expansionists, led by Senator Henry Cabot Lodge of Massachusetts, diplomat John Hay, and Theodore Roosevelt of New York, preached imperial greatness and military might. "I should welcome almost any war," declared Roosevelt in 1897; ". . . this country needs one." Advocates of expansionism, like Roosevelt and Lodge, built upon the Social Darwinist rhetoric of the day and argued that war, as a vehicle for natural selection, would test and refurbish American manhood, restore chivalry and honor, and create a new generation of civic-minded Americans. This gendered appeal to renew American masculinity both counterbalanced concerns about women's political activism and helped forge the disparate arguments for expansionism into a simpler, more visceral plea for international engagement that had a broad appeal.

A series of diplomatic skirmishes between 1885 and 1895 revealed the newly assertive American mood and paved the way for the war that Roosevelt desired. In the mid-1880s, quarrels between the United States and Great Britain over fishing rights in the North Atlantic and in the Bering Sea off Alaska reawakened Americans' latent anti-British feelings as well as the old dream of acquiring Canada. A poem published in the *Detroit News* (adapted from an English music-hall song) supplied the nickname that critics would apply to the promoters of expansion—jingoists:

> We do not want to fight,
> But, by jingo, if we do,
> We'll scoop in all the fishing grounds
> And the whole dominion too!

The fishing-rights dispute was resolved in 1898, but by then attention had shifted to Latin America. In 1891, as civil war raged in Chile, U.S. officials seized a Chilean vessel that was attempting to buy guns in San Diego. Soon after, a mob in Valparaiso, Chile, killed two unarmed sailors on shore leave. President Harrison practically called for war. Only when Chile apologized and paid an indemnity was the incident closed.

Another Latin American conflict arose from a boundary dispute between Venezuela and British Guiana in 1895. The disagreement worsened after gold was discovered in the contested territory. When the British rejected a U.S. arbitration offer and condescendingly insisted that America's revered Monroe Doctrine had no standing in international law, a livid Grover Cleveland asked Congress to set up a commission to settle the disputed boundary even without Britain's approval. As patriotic fervor pulsed through the nation, the British in 1897 accepted the commission's findings.

Pacific Expansion Meanwhile, the U.S. navy focused on the Samoan Islands in the South Pacific, where it sought access to the port of Pago Pago as a refueling station. Britain and Germany had ambitions in Samoa as well, and in March 1889 the United States and Germany narrowly avoided a naval clash when a hurricane wrecked both fleets. Secretary of State Blaine's wife wrote to one of their children, "Your father is now looking up Samoa on the map." Once he found it, negotiations began, and the United States, Great Britain, and Germany established a three-way "protectorate" over the islands.

Attention had by that time shifted to the Hawaiian Islands, which had both strategic and economic significance for the United States. New England trading vessels had visited Hawaii as early as the 1790s, and Yankee missionaries had come in the 1820s. By the 1860s American-owned sugar plantations worked by Chinese and Japanese labor-

MAP 20.2 U.S. Territorial Expansion in the Late Nineteenth Century

The major U.S. territorial expansion abroad came in a short burst of activity in the late 1890s, when newspapers and some politicians urged Americans to acquire strategic ports and coaling stations abroad.

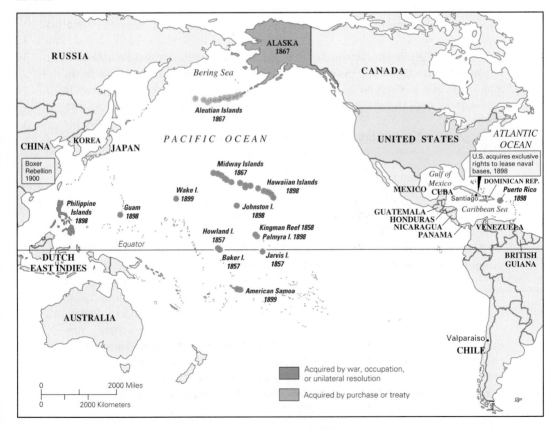

ers dotted the islands. Under an 1887 treaty (negotiated after the planters had forcibly imposed a new constitution on Hawaii's native ruler, Kala-kaua), the United States built a naval base at Pearl Harbor, near Honolulu. American economic dominance and the influx of foreigners angered Hawaiians. In 1891, they welcomed Liliuokalani, a strong-willed woman hostile to Americans, to the Hawaiian throne.

Meanwhile, in 1890, the framers of the McKinley Tariff, pressured by domestic sugar growers, eliminated the duty-free status enjoyed by Hawaiian sugar. In January 1893, facing ruin as Hawaii's wholesale sugar prices plunged 40 percent, the planters deposed Queen Liliuokalani, proclaimed the independent Republic of Hawaii, and requested U.S. annexation. The U.S. State Department's representative in Hawaii cabled Washington, "The Hawaiian pear is now fully ripe, and this is the golden hour for the United States to pluck it." But the grab for Hawaii troubled Grover Cleveland, who sent a representative to investigate the situation. This representative's report questioned whether the Hawaiian people actually desired annexation.

Cleveland's scruples infuriated expansionists. When William McKinley succeeded Cleveland in 1897, the acquisition of Hawaii was pushed forward by sugar companies that had similar investments in Cuba. In 1898 Congress proclaimed **Hawaii** an American territory. Sixty-one years later, it joined the Union as the fiftieth state.

Crisis over Cuba

Many of the same expansionists who had argued for the annexation of Hawaii turned their attention in 1898 to the Spanish colony of Cuba, ninety miles off Florida, where in 1895 an anti-Spanish rebellion had broken out. This revolt, organized by the Cuban writer José Martí and other Cuban exiles in New York City, won little support from U.S. business, which had $50 million invested in Cuba and annually imported $100 million worth of sugar and other products from the island. Nor did the rebels initially secure the backing of Washington, which urged Spain to grant Cuba a degree of autonomy.

But the rebels' cause aroused popular sympathy in the United States. This support increased with revelations that the Spanish commander in Cuba, Valeriano Weyler, was herding vast numbers of Cubans into squalid camps. Malnutrition and disease turned these camps into hellholes in which perhaps two hundred thousand Cubans died.

Fueling American anger was the sensationalized reporting of two competing New York City newspapers, William Randolph Hearst's *Journal* and Joseph Pulitzer's *World*. The *Journal*'s color comic strip, "The Yellow Kid," provided a name for Hearst's debased editorial approach: yellow journalism. The Hungarian immigrant Pulitzer normally had higher standards, but in the cutthroat battle for readers, Pulitzer's *World* matched the *Journal*'s sensationalism. Both editors exploited the Cuban crisis. Headlines turned rumor into fact, and feature stories detailed "Butcher" Weyler's atrocities. When a young Cuban woman was jailed for resisting a rape attempt by a Spanish officer, a Hearst reporter helped the woman escape and brought her triumphantly to New York.

In 1897, a new, more liberal Spanish government sought a peaceful resolution of the Cuban crisis. But Hearst and Pulitzer continued to inflame the public. On February 8, 1898, Hearst's *Journal* published a private letter by Spain's minister to the United States that described McKinley as "weak" and "a bidder for the admiration of the crowd." Irritation over this incident turned to outrage when on February 15 an explosion sank the U.S. battleship *Maine* in Havana harbor and killed 266 crewmen. Scholarly opinion about what caused the explosion is still divided, but a careful review of the evidence in 1998 concluded that a mine most likely set off the ammunition explosion that sank the ship. Newspaper headlines at the time blamed the same cause and war spirit flared high.

Despite further Spanish concessions, McKinley sent a war message to Congress on April 11, and legislators enacted a joint resolution recognizing Cuba's independence and authorizing force to expel the Spanish. The Teller Amendment, introduced by Senator Henry M. Teller of Colorado, renounced any U.S. interest in "sovereignty, jurisdiction, or control" in Cuba and pledged that America would leave the island alone once independence was assured.

The Spanish-American War, 1898 The war with Spain involved only a few days of actual combat. The first action came on May 1, 1898, when a U.S. fleet commanded by George Dewey steamed into Manila Bay in the Philippines and destroyed or captured all ten Spanish ships anchored there, at the cost of 1 American and 381 Spanish lives. In mid-August, U.S. troops occupied the capital, Manila.

In Cuba, the fighting centered on the military stronghold of Santiago on the southeastern coast. On May 19, a Spanish battle fleet of seven aging vessels sailed into the Santiago harbor, where five U.S. battleships and two cruisers blockaded them. On July 1, in the war's only significant land action, American troops seized three strongly defended Spanish garrisons on El Caney Hill, Kettleman's Hill, and San Juan Hill overlooking Santiago. Leading the volunteer "Rough Riders" unit in the capture of San Juan Hill was Theodore Roosevelt, who became a war hero. Emphasizing his toughness and sense of honor, Roosevelt would later use his war experience to reaffirm the aptitude of men like himself for political leadership.

On July 3, the Spanish attempted to break through the American blockade to the open sea. The U.S. navy fired and sank their archaic vessels. Spain lost 474 men in this gallant but doomed defense. Americans might have found a cautionary lesson in this sorry end to four hundred years of Spanish rule in the New World, but few had time for somber musings. The *Washington Post* observed, "A new consciousness seems to have come upon us—the consciousness of strength—and with it a new appetite, the yearning to show our strength. . . ." Secretary of State John Hay was more succinct. It had been, he wrote Roosevelt, "a splendid little war."

Many who served in Cuba found the war far from splendid. Ill-trained and poorly equipped, the troops went into summer combat wearing heavy woolen uniforms. The army also lacked adequate medical support. When **Clara Barton,** president of the American Association for Red Cross, visited Santiago, she found wounded soldiers lying in the rain, unable to eat the hardtack rations. Under her leadership, 1,000 trained nurses worked with the medical corps. Despite the efforts of these nurses and doctors, 379 American soldiers died in combat and more than 5,000 succumbed to food poisoning, yellow fever, malaria, and other diseases during and after the war.

Several thousand black troops fought in Cuba. Some, such as the Twenty-fourth Infantry and Tenth Cavalry, were seasoned regular-army "buffalo soldiers" transferred from bases in the West. Others were volunteers from various states. At assembly points in Georgia, and then at the embarkation port of Tampa, Florida, these troops encountered the racism of a Jim Crow society. Tampa restaurants and bars refused them service; Tampa whites disparaged them. On June 6, after weeks of racist treatment, some black troops exploded in riotous rage, storming into restaurants, bars, and other establishments that had barred them. White troops from Georgia restored order. Although white and black troops sailed to Cuba on the same transport ships (actually, hastily converted freighters), the ships themselves were segregated, with black troops often confined to the lowest quarters in the stifling heat, denied permission to mingle on deck with the other units, and in other ways discriminated against.

Despite the racism, African-Americans served with distinction once they reached Cuba. Black troops played key roles in the taking of both San Juan Hill and El Caney Hill. Of the total U.S. troops involved in the latter action, some 15 percent were black.

The Spanish sought an armistice on July 17. In the peace treaty signed that December in Paris, Spain recognized Cuba's independence and, after a U.S. payment of $20 million, ceded the Philippines, Puerto Rico, and the Pacific island of Guam to the United States. Americans now possessed an island empire stretching from the Caribbean to the Pacific.

From 1898 to 1902, the U.S. army governed Cuba under the command of General Leonard Wood. Wood's administration improved public health, education, and sanitation but nevertheless violated the spirit of the 1898 Teller Amendment. The troops eventually withdrew, though under conditions that limited Cuban sovereignty. The 1901 **Platt Amendment,** attached to an army appropriations bill offered by a Connecticut senator at the request of the War Department, authorized American withdrawal only after Cuba agreed not to make any treaty with a foreign power limiting its independence and not to borrow beyond its means. The United States also reserved the right to intervene in Cuba when it saw fit and to maintain a naval base there, an insistence resented by the Cubans. With U.S. troops still occupying the island, the Cuban constitutional convention of 1901 accepted the Platt Amendment, which remained in force until 1934. Under its terms the United States established a naval base at Guantánamo Bay, near Santiago de Cuba, which it still maintains. U.S. investments in Cuba, some $50 million in 1898, soared to half a billion dollars by 1920.

Critics of Empire   The victories of the expansionists in Cuba and the Philippines did not bring universal praise. Some Americans, who had opposed imperialism for more than a decade, were dismayed by the results. Although few in number, the critics, like the Mugwumps who had challenged the spoils system, were influential. Indeed, some of them, like Carl Schurz and E. L. Godkin, were former Mugwumps. Other anti-imperialists included William Jennings Bryan, settlement-house founder Jane Addams, novelist Mark Twain, and Harvard philosopher William James. Steel king Andrew Carnegie gave thousands of dollars to the cause. In 1898, these critics of empire had formed the **Anti-Imperialist League.**

For the United States to rule other peoples, the anti-imperialists believed, was to violate the principles of the Declaration of Independence and the Constitution. As one of them wrote, "Dewey took Manila with the loss of one man—and all our institutions." The military fever that accompanied expansionism also dismayed the anti-imperialists. Some labor leaders feared that imperial expansion would lead to competition from cheap foreign labor and products.

In February 1899, the anti-imperialists failed by one vote to prevent Senate ratification of the peace treaty with Spain. McKinley's overwhelming reelection victory in 1900 and the defeat of expansionist critic William Jennings Bryan eroded the anti-imperialists' cause. Nevertheless, at a time of jingoistic rhetoric and militaristic posturing, they had upheld an older and more traditional vision of America.

The Philippines Quagmire *Anticipating the Vietnam War, the U.S. suppression of the Philippines' independence struggle involved American troops in a long and nasty guerrilla campaign. One of the men in this 1900 photograph scrawled on the back: "27 hours on march, mud and rain, 24 hours without food."*

Guerrilla War in the Philippines, 1898–1902   The worst fears of the anti-imperialists were subsequently borne out by events in the Philippines. When the Spanish-American War ended, President McKinley was faced with the urgent problem of what to do about this group of Pacific islands that had a population of more than 5 million people. At the war's outset, few Americans knew that the Philippines belonged to Spain or even where they were. Without a map, McKinley later confessed, "I could not have told where those darn islands were within two thousand miles."

But the victory over Spain whetted the appetite for expansion. To the U.S. business community, the Philippines offered a steppingstone to the China market. McKinley, reflecting the prevailing mood as always, reasoned that the Filipinos were unready for self-government and would be gobbled up if set adrift in a world of imperial rivalries. McKinley further persuaded himself that American rule would enormously benefit the Filipinos, whom he called "our little brown brothers." A devout Methodist, he explained that America's mission was "to educate the Filipinos, and to uplift and civilize and Christianize them, and by God's grace do the very best we could by them." (In fact, most Filipinos were already Catholic, a legacy of centuries of Spanish rule.) Having prayerfully reached his decision, McKinley instructed the American peace negotiators in Paris to insist on U.S. acquisition of the Philippines.

"Uplifting" the Filipinos required a struggle. In 1896 young **Emilio Aguinaldo** had organized a Filipino independence movement to drive out Spain. In 1898, with arms supplied by George Dewey, Aguinaldo's forces had captured most of Luzon, the Philippines' main island. When the Spanish surrendered, Aguinaldo proclaimed Filipino independence and drafted a democratic constitution. Feeling betrayed when the peace treaty ceded his country to the United States, Aguinaldo ordered his rebel force to attack Manila, the American base of operations. Seventy thousand more U.S. troops were shipped to the Philippines, and by the end of 1899 the initial Filipino resistance had been crushed.

These hostilities became the opening phase of a long guerrilla conflict. Before it ended, over 125,000 American men had served in the Philippines, and 4,000 had been killed. As many as 20,000 Filipino independence fighters died. As in the later Vietnam and Iraq Wars, casualties and suffering ravaged the civilian population as well. Historians estimate that at least 200,000 civilians died in the conflict. Aguinaldo was captured in March 1901, but large-scale guerrilla fighting continued through the summer of 1902.

In 1902, a special Senate committee heard testimony from veterans of the Philippines war about the execution of prisoners, the torture of suspects, and the burning of villages. The humanitarian mood of 1898, when Americans had rushed to save Cuba from the cruel Spaniards, seemed remote indeed. In retrospect, the American troops' ambivalent attitudes about the peoples of the Philippines, while deplorable, are not hard to understand. Despite America's self-image as a beacon of liberty and a savior of the world's peoples, many Americans in the 1880s and 1890s had been deeply troubled by the new immigrants from southern and eastern Europe and had expressed concerns over "backward" and "useless" races. As American nationalism was reformulated in this cauldron of immigration, imperialism, and the "winning of the West," racist attitudes about Native peoples and foreigners intermixed with rhetorical pleas for supervision and stewardship. In the process, as was evident in the treatment of American Indians (see Chapter 17), well-meaning paternalism often degenerated into deadly domination.

The subjugation of the Philippines followed years of expansionism that proclaimed America's debut on the world stage and underscored the global reach of U.S. capitalism. Nevertheless, most Americans remained ambivalent about the acquisition of territory. While anti-imperialist Mark Twain could acidly condemn "the Blessings of Civilization Trust," labor leader Samuel Gompers warned that "an inundation of Mongolians" might steal jobs from white labor. From the debate over the annexation of Hawaii in 1898 to the end of the war against Philippine independence in 1902, white Americans recoiled from making these "barbarian peoples" a part of the United States. Not fit to manage their own affairs, Cuban, Puerto Rican, Hawaiian, and Filipino peoples were placed in a protective status that denied their independence and kept them under U.S. control.

To stabilize relations in the Philippines, Congress passed the Philippine Government Act in 1902, which vested authority in a governor general to be appointed by the president. The act also provided for an elected Filipino assembly and promised eventual self-government. Progress toward this goal inched forward, with intervals of semimilitary rule. In 1946, nearly half a century after Admiral Dewey's guns had boomed in Manila Bay, independence finally came to the Philippines.

CONCLUSION

By 1900 immigration, the settlement of the frontier West, and rapid industrial expansion had pushed America to the forefront of the world economy and had sparked a major realignment in American politics. After nearly two decades of hard-fought elections in which political control had seesawed back and forth between the major parties, the Republicans now held power.

It had been difficult to achieve political dominance. The dynamic growth of the American economy together with rapid urbanization and a massive influx of immigrants had initially strained the political process. As the parties struggled to define their vision of the proper role of government in stimulating economic development, they were forced to deal with ethnic, cultural, and racial issues that included prohibition, church schools, and segregation. All this was further complicated by the Democratic Party's attempt to throw off the limits imposed by Reconstruction and gain political control of the South.

On the national level, both parties built a loyal following by linking their positions to deeply held beliefs about the family and the proper role of government. Republicans justified their support for the tariff and soldiers' pensions in terms of patriotic protection of the family. Democrats countered that a high-tariff policy was indicative of precisely the kind of excessive governmental force that would destroy family life. On the local level, both parties secured loyal voters by stressing ethnic and cultural issues. Democrats courted the new immigrants, while Republicans catered to rural and small-town native-born Americans in the Northeast and Midwest.

In the competition for new voters, the needs of rural Americans were often overlooked. Caught between declining prices for grain and cotton, and high railroad and bank rates, farmers struggled to survive. Their precarious position was further strained by years of drought, insect infestation, and overspecialization in one crop. In desperation, farmers turned first to the Grange and Farmers' Alliance movements and then to the Populist Party for help. In the South, after first courting black farmers, members of the Farmers' Alliance and later the Populists joined with Democrats to disfranchise black voters. Using lynching and intimidation, Democrats seized control of southern politics.

In the face of these threats, the Republican Party in 1896 raised huge sums from big business to turn back the Populist challenge and take control of national politics. The fusion of the Populists and Democrats behind William Jennings Bryan and the silver issue created problems of its own. Although he carried the South and almost all the Midwest, the teetotaling Bryan had little appeal for urban workers and the middle class who believed that a monetary policy based on free silver promised only inflation and higher prices. McKinley won by playing down moral reforms such as prohibition and emphasizing patriotism and fiscal responsibility. Republicans won over the urban-industrial core of the nation—the Northeast and much of the Midwest. They would control the House of Representatives for twenty-eight out of the thirty-six years from 1894 to 1930.

McKinley's administration was drawn by events in Cuba and jingoistic advocates within his own party into the Spanish-American War and the subsequent acquisition of Hawaii, Samoa, Guam, the Philippines, and Cuba. Although the Republicans preferred the term "expansionism" to "imperialism," the move to acquire new bases for access to global markets fit the party's probusiness stance. But expansion into the Pacific created its own obstacles when the United States became involved in a guerrilla war with Philippine nationalists. Facing mounting criticism at home, the expansionists adopted the Teller and Platt Amendments, which foreshadowed eventual disengagement from the acquisition of foreign territory.

Notwithstanding these foreign interventions, the fundamental question of late-nineteenth-century American politics persisted: could a government designed for the needs of a small agrarian society serve an industrialized nation of factories and immigrant-crowded cities? The answer was by no means clear. Although issues such as patronage, the tariff, veterans' benefits, and monetary policy had enabled the industrial system to grow dramatically, the needs of farmers, workers, and immigrant Americans had largely been ignored. The Republicans successfully carried the field in 1896, but Populists and other critics who argued that government should play an assertive role in solving social and economic problems would help shape the political environment of the progressive movement.

21

The Progressive Era, 1900–1917

PROGRESSIVES AND THEIR IDEAS

As the twentieth century dawned, local groups across the nation grappled with the problems of the new urban-industrial order. Workers protested unsafe and exhausting jobs. Experts investigated social conditions. Women's clubs embraced reform. Intellectuals challenged the ideological foundations of a business-dominated social order, and journalists publicized municipal corruption and industrialism's human toll. Throughout America, activists worked to make government more democratic, eradicate dangerous conditions in cities and factories, and curb corporate power.

Surveying all these efforts, historians lumped them under a single label: "the progressive movement." In fact, "progressivism" was never a single movement. It is perhaps best understood as a spirit of discontent with the status quo and an exciting sense of new social possibilities. This mood found many outlets and focused on many issues. (See Beyond America—Global Interactions: Progressive Reformers Worldwide Share Ideas and Strategies.)

The Many Faces of Progressivism   Who were the progressives, and what reforms did they pursue? To answer these questions, we must examine the pattern of urban growth in the early twentieth century. Along with immigration, a growing middle class transformed U.S. cities. From the men and women of this class—most of them native-born, white, and Protestant—came many of the progressive movement's leaders and foot soldiers.

From 1900 to 1920, the number of white-collar workers jumped from 5.1 million to 10.5 million—more than double the growth rate of the labor force as a whole. As in-

CHRONOLOGY, 1900–1917

1900 • International Ladies' Garment Workers' Union (ILGWU) founded.
Socialist Party of America organized.
Theodore Dreiser, *Sister Carrie*.
Carrie Chapman Catt becomes president of the National American
Woman Suffrage Association (NAWSA).

1901 • Assassination of McKinley; Theodore Roosevelt becomes president.
J. P. Morgan forms United States Steel Company.

1902 • Jane Addams, *Democracy and Social Ethics*.

1903 • W. E. B. Du Bois, *The Souls of Black Folk*.
Wright brothers' flight.

1904 • Theodore Roosevelt elected president in his own right.
Lincoln Steffens, *The Shame of the Cities*.

1905 • Industrial Workers of the World (IWW) organized.

1906 • Upton Sinclair, *The Jungle*.

1907 • William James, *Pragmatism*.

1908 • William Howard Taft elected president.
Model T Ford introduced.

1909 • Ballinger-Pinchot controversy.
National Association for the Advancement of Colored People (NAACP)
founded.
Herbert Croly, *The Promise of American Life*.
Daniel Burnham, *Plan of Chicago*.

1910 • Insurgents curb power of House Speaker Joseph Cannon.

1911 • Triangle Shirtwaist Company fire.

1912 • Republican Party split; Progressive (Bull Moose) Party founded.
Woodrow Wilson elected president.
International Opium Treaty.

1913 • Sixteenth Amendment (Congress empowered to tax incomes).
Seventeenth Amendment (direct election of U.S. senators).

1914 • American Social Hygiene Association founded.
"Narcotics Act (Harrison Act)"

1915 • D. W. Griffith, *The Birth of a Nation*.

1916 • John Dewey, *Democracy and Education*.
Margaret Sanger opens nation's first birth-control clinic in Brooklyn,
New York.
National Park Service created.
Louis Brandeis appointed to Supreme Court.

1919 • Eighteenth Amendment (national prohibition).

1920 • Nineteenth Amendment (woman suffrage).

The Triangle Fire *The bodies of Triangle Shirtwaist factory workers lie on the sidewalk after they jumped from the burning building.*

dustry grew, so did the ranks of secretaries, civil engineers, and people in advertising. This white-collar class included corporate technicians and desk workers; the owners and managers of local businesses; and professionals such as lawyers, physicians, and teachers. Many new professional groups arose, from the American Association of University Professors (1915) to the American Association of Advertising Agencies (1917). The age of organization had dawned, bringing new professional allegiances and a more standardized, routinized society. For many middle-class Americans, membership in a national professional society provided a sense of identity that might earlier have come from neighborhood, church, or political party. Ambitious, well educated, and valuing social stability, the members of this new middle class were eager to make their influence felt.

For middle-class women, the city offered both opportunities and frustrations. Young unmarried women often became schoolteachers, secretaries, typists, clerks, and telephone operators. The number of women in such white-collar jobs surged from 949,000 in 1900 to 3.4 million in 1920. The ranks of college-educated women, although still small, more than tripled in this twenty-year period.

But for middle-class married women caring for homes and children, city life could mean isolation and frustration. The divorce rate rose from one in twelve marriages in 1900 to one in nine by 1916. As we shall see, many middle-class women joined female white-collar workers and college graduates in leading a revived women's movement. Cultural commentators wrote nervously of the "New Woman."

This urban middle class rallied to the banner of reform. The initial reform impetus came not from political parties but from women's clubs, settlement houses, and private groups with names like the Playground Association of America, the National Child Labor Committee, and the American League for Civic Improvement. In this era of organizations, the reform movement, too, drew strength from organized interest groups.

But the native-born middle class was not the only force behind progressivism. On issues affecting factory workers and slum dwellers, the urban-immigrant political machines—and workers themselves—often took the initiative. Some corporate leaders shaped regulatory measures in ways that served their interests.

What, then, was progressivism? Fundamentally, it was a broad-based response to industrialization and its byproducts: immigration, urban growth, growing corporate power, and widening class divisions. In contrast to populism, progressivism arose in the cities, and it enlisted many more journalists, academics, and social theorists. Finally, most progressives were *reformers,* not radicals. They wished to make the new urban-industrial order more humane, not overturn it entirely.

But which parts of this new order most needed attention, and what remedies were required? Reaching different answers to these key questions, progressive reformers spawned an array of activities that sometimes overlapped, sometimes diverged. Many reformers wanted stricter business regulation, from local transit companies to the almighty trusts. Others focused on protecting workers and the urban poor. Still others tried to reform the structure of government, especially at the municipal level. Some fought for immigration restriction or social-control strategies to regulate city-dwellers' behavior or address threats of urban disorder. All this contributed to the mosaic of progressive reform.

Progressives generally agreed that most social problems could be solved through study and organized effort. They respected science and expert knowledge. Since scientific and technological expertise had produced the new industrial order, such expertise could surely also solve the social problems spawned by industrialism. Progressives marshaled research data, expert opinion, and statistics to support their various causes.

Some historians have portrayed progressivism as an organizational stage that all modernizing societies pass through. This is a useful perspective, provided we remember that it was not an automatic process unfolding independently of human will. Eloquent leaders, gifted journalists, activist workers, and passionate reformers all played a role. Human emotion—whether indignation over child labor, intense moralism, fear of the alien, hatred of corporate power, or raw political ambition—drove the movement forward.

Intellectuals Offer New Social Views A group of early-twentieth-century thinkers provided progressivism's underlying ideas. As we have seen, some Gilded Age intellectuals had argued that Charles Darwin's theory of evolution justified unrestrained economic competition. In the 1880s and 1890s, sociologist Lester Ward, utopian novelist Edward Bellamy, and leaders of the settlement-house and Social Gospel movements had all attacked this harsh version of Social Darwinism (see Chapters 18 and 19). This attack intensified after 1900.

Economist Thorstein Veblen, a Norwegian-American reared on a Minnesota farm, sharply criticized the new business order. In *The Theory of the Leisure Class* (1899), Veblen satirized the lifestyle of newly rich capitalists. Dissecting their habits the way an anthropologist might study an exotic tribe, he argued that they built showy mansions, threw elaborate parties, and otherwise engaged in "conspicuous consumption" to flaunt their wealth and assert their claims to superiority.

The Harvard philosopher William James argued in *Pragmatism* (1907) that truth emerges not from abstract theorizing but from the experience of coping with life's realities through practical action. Truth is not an absolute; truth happens to ideas as they

Progressive Reformers Worldwide Share Ideas and Strategies

Progressive reform was not an American invention. U.S. progressives drew ideas from Continental Europe, the British Isles, Canada, and even faraway Australia and New Zealand. Sometimes, the exchange flowed in the other direction, as reformers abroad found inspiration in America.

Industrialization and urbanization had transformed other societies as well. The smoky factory cities of Manchester and Birmingham in England; Glasgow in Scotland; Liège in Belgium; and Düsseldorf and Essen in Germany's coal-rich Ruhr Valley all experienced the same social problems as did U.S. industrial cities like Pittsburgh, Chicago, and Cleveland. The grinding poverty of London's East End was as notorious as that of New York's Lower East Side.

The shocked response to these conditions crossed national boundaries as well. Jacob Riis's grim account of life in New York's immigrant wards, *How the Other Half Lives* (1890), echoed the Rev. Andrew Mearns's polemic *The Bitter Cry of Outcast London* (1883). William T. Stead's sensational 1885 exposé of prostitution in London, "The Maiden Tribute of Modern Babylon," helped inspire the American antiprostitution crusade. The sociological studies of poverty in Chicago, Pittsburgh, Philadelphia, and other cities undertaken by American investigators drew inspiration from Charles Booth's massive survey of London poverty. Beginning in 1886, Booth and his collaborators had painstakingly studied conditions in London's slums. Their handwritten data eventually filled 12,000 notebook pages. Booth published detailed maps showing the economic situation street by street,

first in the East End (1887) and eventually in the entire city (1902–1903).

Efforts to solve the problems of the new urban-industrial order crossed national boundaries, giving rise to a transnational reform movement. The breadth and diversity of this movement was showcased at the Paris Exposition of 1900 in a Musée Social (Social Museum) featuring exhibits of many nations' reform innovations.

As early as the 1880s, Germany's conservative Chancellor Otto von Bismarck, trying to keep the socialists from power, instituted a remarkable series of reforms, including a ban on child labor; maximum working hours; and illness, accident, and old-age insurance for workers. Britain's Liberal party, in power in 1906–1914, introduced minimum-wage laws, unemployment insurance, and a health-insurance program on the German model. In France, a coalition of reform parties established a maximum working day, a progressive income tax (one with higher rates for wealthier taxpayers), and a program of medical aid for the elderly poor. Denmark adopted an old-age pension system. Not all the reforms were state sponsored; some relied on voluntary philanthropy. For example, the first settlement house, Toynbee Hall, was started in London in 1884 by the Anglican clergyman Samuel Augustus Barnett and others. While Australia introduced an ambitious program of water-resource planning to promote agricultural development in its vast interior, New Zealand's trailblazing reforms included woman suffrage, arbitration courts to resolve labor disputes, and programs enabling small farmers to lease public lands.

American reformers followed these developments carefully. Jane Addams visited Toynbee Hall repeatedly in the 1880s. In 1900, the muckraking U.S. journalist Henry Demarest Lloyd praised New Zealand as "the political brain of the modern world." American students in German and Swiss universities and the London School of Economics (founded by socialists in 1895) encountered challenges to the laissez-faire doctrine that prevailed back home. The federal government's Bureau of Labor Statistics collected data on European social and labor conditions and labor-related issues, to give government officials and legislators a comparative perspective on issues of concern in America. For the same reason, reform-minded labor historian John R. Commons at the University of Wisconsin plastered his graduate-seminar room with charts showing labor laws around the world. American Social Gospel leaders kept in close touch with like-minded clergy in England and elsewhere. Experiments with publicly owned electric power companies in the Canadian province of Ontario offered a model for municipal reformers who were proposing this innovation in Cleveland and other U.S. cities.

Transatlantic conferences and delegations furthered the exchange of reform strategies. In 1910, ten Americans attended an International Congress on Unemployment in Paris while twenty-eight Americans came to Vienna for an International Housing Congress. The National Civic Federation sent fifteen experts to England and Scotland in 1906 to study new ideas in urban reform. A delegation from the Bureau of Municipal Research spent several months in Frankfurt in 1912 learning about administrative innovations in that city. In 1911, a sociology professor at the City College of New York offered social workers a package tour including visits to London settlement houses, planned cities elsewhere in England, workers' cooperatives in Belgium, and infant nurseries in Paris.

Reformers committed to causes such as world peace or women's rights often joined forces with kindred spirits abroad. The birth-control advocate Margaret Sanger, pacifist Jane Addams, and woman-suffrage leader Alice Paul all maintained close contact with activists elsewhere who shared their commitments. The introduction of woman suffrage in New Zealand (1893) and Australia (1902) energized the U.S. suffrage movement.

Housing reformers and city planners cultivated international ties as well. The New York State Tenement House Law of 1901, a key reform measure, owed much to the groundbreaking work of English housing reformers. Daniel Burnham's 1909 *Plan of Chicago* (see "Making Cities More Livable") drew inspiration from classical Athens and Rome; Renaissance Florence and Siena; Georges Haussmann's great Paris boulevards of the mid-nineteenth century; and Vienna's Ringstrasse, itself inspired by the Paris model.

Magazines contributed to the global flow of reform ideas. The muckraking journalist Ray Stannard Baker reported on reforms in Germany for *McClure's* magazine in 1900, providing a broader context for the magazine's articles on reform in the United States. Not to be outdone, *Everybody's* magazine sent Charles E. Russell around the world in 1905 to investigate reform initiatives in England, Switzerland, Germany, Australia, New Zealand, and elsewhere.

Reform-minded foreigners also visited the United States to report on the juvenile court system, the playground movement, innovative public schools, and other progressive developments. One English progressive visiting Madison, Wisconsin, in 1911 praised the university's role in promoting reform legislation. "The State has been practically governed by the University . . . ," he wrote. "[E]very question is threshed out in class before it is threshed out by the legislature." The Kansas editor William Allen White, recalling the Progressive Era in his 1946 autobiography, marveled at the movement's transnational character: "We were parts, one of another, . . . the United States and Europe. Something was welding us into one social and economic whole with local political variations, [but] . . . all fighting [for] a common cause."

American progressivism, in short, was simply one manifestation of a larger effort to cope with the social impact of rapid industrialization and urban growth. Through a dense network of publications, conferences, and personal ties, reformers of many nations kept in touch, shared strategies, and drew on a vast storehouse of ideas as they addressed the problems and circumstances of their societies.

Question for Analysis

- What early twentieth-century reforms transcended national boundaries, and how did reformers in different countries share ideas and strategies?

---

are tested in the real world. James's philosophy of pragmatism deepened the reformers' skepticism toward the older generation's entrenched ideas and strengthened their belief in the necessity of social change.

Herbert Croly shared this faith that new ideas could transform society. The son of reform-minded New York journalists, Croly grew up in a cosmopolitan world where social issues were hotly debated. In *The Promise of American Life* (1909), he called for an activist government of the kind advocated by Alexander Hamilton, the first secretary of the treasury. But rather than serving the interests of the business class, as Hamilton had proposed, Croly argued that this activist government should promote the welfare of all. In 1914, Croly founded the *New Republic* magazine to promote progressive ideas.

The settlement-house leader Jane Addams also played a key role in shaping the ideology of the Progressive Era. In *Democracy and Social Ethics* (1902) and *Twenty Years at Hull House* (1910), Addams rejected the claim that unrestrained competition offered the best path to social progress. Instead, she argued, in a complex industrial society, each individual's well-being depends on the well-being of all. Addams urged middle-class Americans to recognize their common interests with the laboring masses, and to demand better conditions in factories and immigrant slums. Teaching by example, Addams made her Chicago social settlement, Hull House, a center of social activism and legislative-reform initiatives.

With public-school enrollment growing from about 7 million in 1870 to more than 23 million in 1920, the educational reformer John Dewey saw schools as potent engines of social change. Banishing bolted-down chairs and desks from his model school at the University of Chicago, he encouraged pupils to interact with one another. The ideal school, he said in *Democracy and Education* (1916), would be an "embryonic community" where children would learn to live cooperatively as members of a social group.

Oliver Wendell Holmes, Jr., of Harvard Law School focused on changing judicial thinking. In these years, most judges interpreted the law in ways that protected corporate interests and struck down reform legislation. In *The Common Law* (1881), however, Holmes had insisted that law must evolve as society changes. In a phrase much quoted by progressives, he had declared, "The life of the law has not been logic; it has been experience." Appointed to the United States Supreme Court in 1902, Holmes often dissented from the conservative Court majority. As the new social thinking took hold, the courts slowly grew more open to reform legislation.

Novelists, Journalists, and Artists Spotlight Social Problems

While reform-minded intellectuals reoriented American social thought, novelists and journalists roused the reform spirit by chronicling corporate wrongdoing, municipal corruption, slum conditions, and industrial abuses. Advances in printing and photo reproduction ensured a mass audience and sharpened the emotional impact of their message.

In his novel *The Octopus* (1901), Frank Norris of San Francisco portrayed the epic struggle between California railroad barons and the state's wheat growers. Though writing fiction, Norris accurately described the bribery, intimidation, rate manipulation, and other means by which the railroad owners promoted their interests.

Theodore Dreiser's novel *The Financier* (1912) featured a hard-driving business tycoon utterly lacking a social conscience. Dreiser modeled his story on the scandal-ridden career of a railway financier named Charles Yerkes. Like Veblen's *Theory of the Leisure Class,* such works undermined the reputation of the industrial elite and stimulated pressures for tougher regulation of business.

Mass magazines such as *McClure's* and *Collier's* also fanned the flames of reform with articles exposing urban political corruption and corporate wrongdoing. President Theodore Roosevelt criticized the authors as **"muckrakers"** obsessed with dredging up the worst in American life, but the label became a badge of honor. Journalist Lincoln Steffens began the exposé vogue in October 1902 with a *McClure's* article documenting municipal corruption in St. Louis and the reform efforts of a crusading district attorney.

The muckrakers emphasized facts rather than abstractions. To gather material, some worked as factory laborers or lived in slum tenements. In a 1903 series, journalist Maria Van Vorst described her experiences working in a Massachusetts shoe factory where the caustic dyes rotted women's fingernails. The British immigrant John Spargo researched his 1906 book about child labor, *The Bitter Cry of the Children,* by visiting mines in Pennsylvania and West Virginia and attempting to do the work that young boys performed for ten hours a day, picking out slate and other refuse from coal in cramped, dangerous workspaces filled with choking coal dust.

The muckrakers awakened middle-class readers to conditions in industrial America. The circulation of *McClure's* and *Collier's* soared. Some magazine exposés later appeared in book form, including Lincoln Steffens's *The Shame of the Cities* (1904), Ida Tarbell's damning *History of the Standard Oil Company* (1904), and David Graham Phillips's *Treason of the Senate* (1906).

Artists and photographers played a role as well. A group of New York painters dubbed the Ashcan School portrayed the harshness as well as the vitality of slum life.

The Wisconsin-born photographer Lewis Hine captured images of immigrants and factory laborers. For the National Child Labor Committee Hine photographed child workers with stunted bodies and worn expressions. Such images built support for the campaign to outlaw child labor.

STATE AND LOCAL PROGRESSIVISM

Middle-class citizens did more than read about the problems of urban-industrial America. They observed these problems firsthand in their own communities. In fact, the progressive movement began with grass-roots campaigns from New York to San Francisco to end urban political corruption, regulate corporate behavior, and improve conditions in factories and city slums. Eventually, these state and local movements came together in a powerful national surge of reform.

Reforming the Political Process In a series of campaigns beginning in the 1890s, native-born elites and middle-class reformers battled corrupt city govern- ments. These city machines provided services and jobs to im- migrants, but often at the price of graft and rigged elections (see Chapter 19). In New York City, Protestant clergy rallied the forces of righteousness against Tammany Hall, the city's entrenched Democratic organization. In Detroit the reform mayor Hazen Pingree (served 1890–1897) brought honesty to city hall, lowered transit fares, adopted a fairer tax structure, and provided public baths and other services. Pingree once slapped a health quarantine on a brothel, holding hostage a well-known business leader until he promised to back Pingree's reforms.

In San Francisco, a courageous newspaper editor led a 1907 crusade against the city's corrupt boss, Abe Ruef. When the original prosecutor was gunned down in court, attorney Hiram Johnson took his place, winning convictions against Ruef and his cronies. Full of reform zeal—one observer called him "a volcano in perpetual eruption"— Johnson rode his newly won fame to the California governorship and the U.S. Senate.

In Toledo, Ohio, a colorful eccentric named Samuel M. ("Golden Rule") Jones led the reform crusade. A self-made businessman converted to the Social Gospel (see Chapter 19), Jones introduced profit sharing in his factory, and as mayor he established playgrounds, free kindergartens, and lodging houses for homeless transients.

The political reformers soon moved beyond simply "throwing the rascals out" to probing the roots of urban misgovernment, including the private monopolies that ran municipal water, gas, electricity, and transit systems. Reformers passed laws regulating the rates these utilities could charge and curbing their political influence. (Some even advocated public ownership of these companies.) This new regulatory structure would remain the rule for a century, until an equally strong deregulatory movement swept the nation in the 1990s.

Reflecting the Progressive Era vogue of expertise and efficiency, some municipal re- formers advocated substituting professional administrators and councils chosen in citywide elections for mayors and aldermen elected on a ward-by-ward basis. Disasters sometimes gave a boost to this reform. Dayton, Ohio, adopted a city-manager system after a ruinous flood in 1913. Supposedly above politics, these experts were expected to run the city like an efficient business.

Municipal reform attracted different groups depending on the issue. The native-born middle class, led by clergymen, editors, and other opinion molders, provided the initial impetus and core support. Business interests often pushed for citywide elections and the city-manager system, since these changes reduced immigrants' political clout and increased the influence of the corporate elite. Reforms that promised improved services or better conditions for ordinary city-dwellers won support from immigrants and even from political bosses who realized that explosive urban growth was swamping the old, informal system of meeting constituents' needs.

The electoral-reform movement soon expanded to the state level. By 1910, for example, all states had replaced the old system of voting, which involved preprinted ballots bearing the names of specific candidates, with the secret ballot, which made it harder to rig elections. The direct primary, introduced in Wisconsin in 1903, enabled rank-and-file voters rather than party bosses to select the candidates who would compete in the general election.

Hoping to trim the political power of corporate interests, some western states inaugurated the *initiative, referendum,* and *recall.* By an initiative, voters can instruct the legislature to consider a specific bill. In a referendum, they can actually enact a law or (in a nonbinding referendum) express their views on a proposed measure. By a recall petition, voters can remove a public official from office if they muster enough signatures.

While these reforms aimed to democratize voting, party leaders and interest groups soon learned to manipulate the new electoral machinery. Ironically, the new procedures may have weakened party loyalty and reduced voter interest. Voter-participation rates dropped steeply in these years, while political activity by organized interest groups increased.

Regulating Business, Protecting Workers

The late-nineteenth-century corporate consolidation that produced giants like Carnegie Steel and Standard Oil (see Chapter 18) continued after 1900. The United States Steel Company created by J. P. Morgan in 1901 controlled 80 percent of all U.S. steel production. A year later Morgan combined six competing companies into the International Harvester Company, which dominated the farm-implement business. The General Motors Company, formed in 1908 by William C. Durant with backing from the Du Pont Corporation, brought various independent automobile manufacturers, from the inexpensive Chevrolet to the luxury Cadillac, under one corporate umbrella.

Many workers benefited from this corporate growth. Industrial workers' average annual real wages (defined, that is, in terms of actual purchasing power) rose from $487 in 1900 to $687 by 1915. In railroading and other unionized industries, wages climbed still higher. But even though the cost of living was far lower than today, such wages could barely support a family and provided little cushion for emergencies.

To survive, entire families went to work. Two-thirds of young immigrant women entered the labor force in the early 1900s, working as factory help or domestics or in small establishments like laundries and bakeries. Even children worked. In 1910, the nonfarm labor force probably included at least 1.6 million children aged ten to fifteen employed in factories, mills, tenement sweatshops, and street trades such as shoe shining and newspaper vending. The total may have been higher, since many "women workers" listed in the census were in fact young girls. One investigator found a girl of five working at night in a South Carolina textile mill.

Most laborers faced long hours and great hazards. Despite the eight-hour movement of the 1880s, in 1900 the average worker still toiled 9 1/2 hours a day. Some southern textile mills required workdays of 12 or 13 hours. In one typical year (1907), 4,534 railroad workers and more than 3,000 miners were killed on the job. Few employers accepted responsibility for work-related accidents and illnesses. Vacations and retirement benefits were practically unheard of.

Factory workers accustomed to the rhythms of farm labor faced the discipline of the time clock and the machine. Efficiency experts used time-and-motion studies to increase production and make human labor as predictable as machines. In *Principles of Scientific Management* (1911), Frederick W. Taylor explained how to increase output by standardizing job routines and rewarding the fastest workers. "Efficiency" became a popular catchword, but most workers resented the pressures to speed up.

Many Americans concerned about the social implications of industrialization deplored the expansion of corporate power and the hazards facing the laboring masses. The drive to regulate big business, inherited from the populists, thus became an important component of progressivism. Since corporations had benefited from government policies such as high protective tariffs, reformers reasoned, they should also be subject to government supervision.

Wisconsin under Governor **Robert** ("Fighting Bob") **La Follette** took the lead in regulating railroads, mines, and other businesses. As a Republican congressman, La Follette had feuded with the state's conservative party leadership, and in 1900 he won the governorship as an independent. Challenging long-dominant business interests, La Follette and his administration adopted the direct-primary system, set up a railroad regulatory commission, increased corporate taxes, and limited campaign spending. Reflecting progressivism's faith in experts, La Follette met regularly with reform-minded professors at the University of Wisconsin. He also set up a legislative reference library so lawmakers would not be solely dependent on corporate lobbyists for factual information. La Follette's reforms gained national attention as the "Wisconsin Idea."

If electoral reform and corporate regulation represented the brain of progressivism, the impulse to improve conditions in factories and mills represented its heart. This movement, too, began at the local and state level. By 1907, for example, some thirty states had outlawed child labor. A 1903 Oregon law limited women in industry to a ten-hour workday.

Campaigns for industrial safety and better working conditions won support from political bosses in cities with large immigrant populations, such as New York, Cleveland, and Chicago. New York state senator Robert F. Wagner, a leader of Tammany Hall, headed the investigation of the 1911 Triangle fire. Thanks to his committee's efforts, New York passed fifty-six worker-protection laws, including required fire-safety inspections of factories. By 1914, spurred by the Triangle disaster, twenty-five states had made employers liable for job-related injuries or deaths.

Florence Kelley, a Hull House resident and the daughter of a conservative Republican congressman, helped launch the drive to remedy industrial abuses. In 1893, after investigating conditions in factories and sweatshops, Kelley persuaded the Illinois legislature to outlaw child labor and limit working hours for women. In 1899, she became general secretary of the National Consumers' League, which mobilized consumer pressure for improved factory conditions. Campaigning for a federal child-labor law, Kelley asked, "Why are seals, bears, reindeer, fish, wild game in the national parks, buffalo, [and] migratory birds all found suitable for federal protection, but not children?"

Like many progressive reforms, the crusade for workplace safety relied on expert research. Alice Hamilton, for example, a pioneer in the new field of "industrial hygiene," taught bacteriology at Northwestern University while also working with Jane Addams at Hull House. In 1910, fusing her scientific training and her reformist impulses, she studied lead poisoning among industrial workers. Later, as an investigator for the U.S. Bureau of Labor, Hamilton publicized work-related medical hazards.

Workers themselves, who well understood the hazards of their jobs, provided further pressure for reform. For example, when the granite industry introduced new power drills that created a fine dust that workers inhaled, the *Granite Cutters' Journal* warned of "stone cutters' consumption" and called the new drills "widow makers." Sure enough, investigators soon linked the dust to a deadly respiratory disease, silicosis.

| Making Cities More Livable | In the early twentieth century, America became an urban nation. By 1920 the urban population passed the 50 percent mark, and sixty-eight U.S. cities boasted more than a hundred |

thousand inhabitants. New York City grew by 2.2 million from 1900 to 1920, and Chicago by 1 million.

Political corruption was only one of many problems plaguing urban America. As manufacturing and businesses grew, a tide of immigrants and native-born newcomers engulfed the cities. Overwhelmed by this rapid growth, many cities became sprawling human warehouses. They lacked adequate parks, municipal services, public-health resources, recreational facilities, and other basic civic amenities. As the reform spirit gained momentum, this tangle of urban problems loomed large.

Building on the achievements of Frederick Law Olmsted and others (see Chapter 19), reformers campaigned for parks, boulevards, and street lights and proposed laws against billboards and overhead electrical wires. An influential voice for city planning and beautification was Daniel Burnham, chief architect of the 1893 Chicago world's fair. Burnham led a successful 1906 effort to revive a plan for Washington, D.C., first proposed by Charles L'Enfant in 1791. He also developed plans for Cleveland, San Francisco, and other cities.

Burnham's 1909 *Plan of Chicago* offered a seductive vision of a city both more efficient and more beautiful. He recommended lakefront parks and museums, wide boulevards to improve traffic flow, and a redesign of Chicago's congested major thoroughfare, Michigan Avenue. The focal point of Burnham's dream city was a majestic domed city hall and vast civic plaza. Chicago spent more than $300 million on projects reflecting his ideas. Many Progressive Era urban planners shared Burnham's faith that more beautiful cities and imposing public buildings would produce orderly, law-abiding citizens.

Beyond urban beautification, the municipal reform impulse also included such practical goals as decent housing and better garbage collection and street cleaning. Providing a model for other cities and states, the New York legislature imposed strict health and safety regulations on tenements in 1911.

Public health loomed large as well. With the discovery in the 1880s that germs cause cholera, typhoid fever, and other diseases, municipal hygiene became a high

A Poor Neighborhood in Philadelphia, c. 1915 *Scenes like this in the immigrant wards of America's great cities stirred middle-class reformers to action at the turn of the last century.*

priority. Reformers called for improved water and sewer systems, regulation of food and milk suppliers, school medical examinations and vaccination programs, and campaigns to spread public-health information.

All these efforts bore fruit. From 1900 to 1920, infant mortality (defined as death in the first year of life) dropped from 165 per 1,000 population to around 75, and the tuberculosis death rate fell by nearly half. The municipal health crusades had a social-class dimension. Middle-class reformers set the "sanitary agenda," and the campaigns often targeted immigrants and the poor as the sources of contagion. When Mary Mallon, an Irish-immigrant cook in New York, was found to be a healthy carrier of the typhoid bacillus in 1907, she was confined for years by the city health authorities and demonized in the press as "Typhoid Mary."

Urban reformers also shared the heightened environmental consciousness of these years (see Chapter 17). The battle against air pollution illustrates both the promise and the frustrations of municipal environmentalism. Coal-fueled steam boilers in factories produced massive amounts of soot and smoke. Factory chimneys belching smoke had once inspired pride, but by the early 1900s physicians had linked factory smoke to respiratory problems, and civic reformers were deploring the resulting air pollution.

Like other progressive reforms, the antismoke campaign combined expertise with activism. Civil engineers formed the Smoke Prevention Association in 1906, and researchers at the University of Pittsburgh—one of the nation's smokiest cities with its nearby steel mills—documented the hazards and costs of air pollution. Chicago merchant Marshall Field declared that the "soot tax" he paid to clean his stores was larger than his real-estate taxes. As women's clubs and other civic groups embraced the cause, many cities passed smoke-abatement laws.

Success proved elusive as railroads and corporations fought back in the courts. With coal still providing 70 percent of the nation's energy as late as 1920, cities remained smoky. Not until years later, with the shift to other energy sources, did municipal air pollution significantly diminish.

PROGRESSIVISM AND SOCIAL CONTROL

Progressives' belief that they could improve society through research, legislation, and aroused public opinion sprang from their confidence that they knew what was best for other people. While municipal corruption, unsafe factories, and corporate abuses captured their attention, so, too, did issues of personal behavior, particularly immigrant behavior. The problems they addressed deserved attention, but their moralistic rhetoric and often coercive remedies also betrayed an impulse to impose their own moral standards by force of law.

Moral Control in the Cities

Despite the overcrowded slums, exhausting labor, and other problems, early-twentieth-century cities also offered fun and diversion. Department stores, vaudeville, music halls, and amusement parks (see Chapter 19) continued to flourish. While some vaudeville owners strove for respectability, bawdy routines full of sexual innuendo, including those of the comedienne Mae West, were popular with working-class audiences. New York City's amusement park, Coney Island, drew more patrons than ever. A subway ride from the city, it attracted as many as a million visitors a day by 1914.

For families, amusement parks provided escape from tenements. For female workers, they provided an opportunity to spend time with friends, meet young men, and show off new outfits. With electrification, simply riding the streetcars or taking an evening stroll on well-lit downtown streets became leisure activities in themselves. Orville and Wilbur Wright's successful airplane flight in 1903, and the introduction of Henry Ford's Model T in 1908, transforming the automobile from a toy of the rich to a vehicle for the masses, foretold exciting changes ahead, with cities at the heart of the action.

Jaunty music-hall songs, produced in a district of Manhattan called Tin Pan Alley, added to the vibrancy of city life. The blues, rooted in the chants of southern black sharecroppers, reached a broader public with such songs as W. C. Handy's classic "St. Louis Blues" (1914). Ragtime, another import from the black South (see Chapter 19), enjoyed great popularity in early-twentieth-century urban America. Both the black composer Scott Joplin, with such works as "Maple Leaf Rag" (1899), and the white composer Irving Berlin, with his hit tune "Alexander's Rag-Time Band" (1911), contributed to this vogue.

These years also brought a new medium of mass entertainment—the movies. Initially a part of vaudeville shows, movies soon migrated to five-cent halls called "nickelodeons" in immigrant neighborhoods. At first featuring brief comic sequences like *The Sneeze* or *The Kiss,* the movies began to tell stories with *The Great Train Robbery*

(1903). *A Fool There Was* (1914), with its famous line, "Kiss me, my fool!," made Theda Bara (really Theodosia Goodman of Cincinnati) the first female movie star. The British music-hall performer Charlie Chaplin immigrated to America and appeared in some sixty short two-reel comedies between 1914 and 1917. Like amusement parks, the movies allowed immigrant youth briefly to escape parental supervision. As a New York garment worker recalled, "The one place I was allowed to go by myself was the movies. My parents wouldn't let me go anywhere else."

The diversions that eased city life for the poor struck some middle-class reformers as moral traps no less dangerous than the physical hazards of the factory or the slum. Fearful of immorality and social disorder, reformers campaigned to regulate amusement parks, dance halls, and the movies shown in darkened nickelodeons, which they saw as potential dens of vice. Several states and cities set up film censorship boards, and the Supreme Court upheld such measures in 1915.

Building on the moral-purity crusade of the Woman's Christian Temperance Union (WCTU) and other groups in the 1890s (see Chapter 19), reformers also targeted prostitution, a major urban problem. Male procurers lured young women into the business and then took a share of their income. The paltry wages paid women for factory work or domestic service attracted many to this more-lucrative occupation. One prostitute wrote that she was unwilling "to get up at 6:30 . . . and work in a close stuffy room . . . until dark for $6 or $7 a week" when an afternoon with a man could bring in more.

Adopting the usual progressive approach, investigators gathered statistics on what they called "the social evil." The American Social Hygiene Association (1914), financed by John D. Rockefeller, Jr., sponsored medical research on sexually transmitted diseases, paid for "vice investigations" in various cities, and drafted model municipal statutes against prostitution.

As prostitution came to symbolize the larger moral dangers of cities, a "white slave" hysteria gripped the nation. Novels, films, and magazine articles warned of kidnapped farm girls forced into urban brothels. The Mann Act (1910) made it illegal to transport a woman across a state line "for immoral purposes." Amid much fanfare, reformers shut down the red-light districts of New Orleans, Chicago, and other cities.

Racism, anti-immigrant prejudice, fear of the city, and anxieties about changing sexual mores all fueled the antiprostitution crusade. Authorities employed the new legislation to pry into private sexual behavior. Blackmailers entrapped men into Mann Act violations. In 1913, the African-American boxer Jack Johnson, the heavyweight champion, was convicted under the Mann Act for traveling with a (white) woman across state lines for "immoral purposes." Johnson went abroad to escape imprisonment.

Battling Alcohol and Drugs   Temperance had long been part of the American reform agenda, but reformers' objectives changed in the Progressive Era. Most earlier campaigns had urged individuals to give up drink. The powerful **Anti-Saloon League** (ASL), founded in 1895, shifted the emphasis to legislating a ban on the sale of alcoholic beverages. The ASL was a typical Progressive Era organization, run by full-time professionals, with Protestant ministers staffing a network of state committees. The ASL presses in Westerville, Ohio, produced propaganda documenting alcohol's role in many social problems and touting prohibition as the answer.

The Anti-Saloon League encouraged local churches and temperance groups to work for prohibition at the municipal, county, and state levels. As these campaigns built momentum, the ASL moved to its larger goal: national prohibition. Other Progressive Era campaigns followed this strategy of working locally while pursuing national reform as the long-range goal.

This was a heavy-drinking era, and alcohol abuse did indeed contribute to domestic abuse, health problems, and work injuries. But like the antiprostitution crusade, the prohibition campaign became a symbolic battleground pitting native-born citizens against the new immigrants. The ASL, while it raised legitimate issues, also embodied Protestant America's impulse to control the immigrant city.

These years also saw a campaign against drug abuse—and for good reason. Physicians, patent-medicine peddlers, and legitimate drug companies freely prescribed or sold opium (derived from poppies) and its derivatives morphine and heroin. Cocaine, extracted from coca leaves, was widely used as well. Coca-Cola contained cocaine until about 1900.

As reform pressure mounted, the federal government backed a 1912 treaty aimed at the international opium trade. The Narcotics Act of 1914, also known as the Harrison Act, banned the distribution of heroin, morphine, cocaine, and other addictive drugs except by licensed physicians or pharmacists. In this campaign, as in their environmental concerns, the progressives anticipated an issue that remains important today. But this reform, too, had racist undertones. Antidrug crusaders luridly described Chinese "opium dens" (places where this addictive narcotic was smoked) and warned that "drug-crazed Negroes" imperiled white womanhood.

Immigration Restriction and Eugenics

While many of the new city-dwellers came from farms and small towns, immigration remained the main source of urban growth. More than 17 million newcomers arrived from 1900 to 1917 (many passing through New York's immigration center, Ellis Island), and most settled in cities. As in the 1890s (see Chapter 19), the influx came mainly from southern and eastern Europe, but more than two hundred thousand Japanese arrived between 1900 and 1920. An estimated forty thousand Chinese entered in these years, despite the 1882 Chinese Exclusion Act (see Chapter 18), which was not repealed until 1943. Thousands of Mexicans came as well, seeking railroad work. Some immigrants prospered, but many sank into poverty or survived precariously.

The dismay that middle-class Americans felt about urban slum conditions stimulated support not only for protective legislation, but also for immigration restriction. If the immigrant city bred social problems, some concluded, then immigrants should be excluded. Prominent Bostonians formed the Immigration Restriction League in 1894. The American Federation of Labor, fearing job competition, also endorsed restriction.

Like most Progressive Era reformers, advocates of immigration restriction tried to document their case with statistical evidence. In 1911, a congressional commission produced a statistical study allegedly proving the new immigrants' innate degeneracy. Sociologist Edward A. Ross, a prominent progressive, described the recent immigrants as "low-browed, big-faced persons of obviously low mentality."

Led by Massachusetts senator Henry Cabot Lodge, Congress passed literacy-test bills in 1896, 1913, and 1915, only to see them vetoed. These measures would have excluded immigrants over sixteen years old who were unable to read either English or

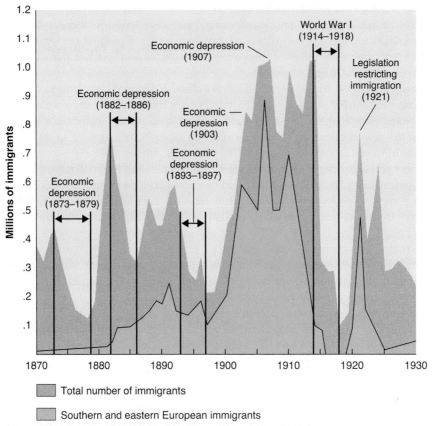

Figure 21.1 Immigration to the United States, 1870–1930

With the end of the depression of the 1890s, immigrants from southern and eastern Europe poured into American cities, spurring an immigration-restriction movement, urban moral-purity campaigns, and efforts to improve the physical and social conditions of immigrant life. *Sources: Statistical History of the United States from Colonial Times to the Present* (Stamford, Conn.: Fairfield Publishers, 1965); and report presented by Senator William P. Dillingham, Senate document 742, 61st Congress, 3rd session, December 5, 1910: Abstracts of Reports to the Immigration Commission.

their native language, thus discriminating against persons lacking formal education. In 1917, one such bill became law over President Woodrow Wilson's veto. Immigrants also faced physical examinations and tests in which legitimate public-health concerns became mixed up with stereotypes of entire ethnic groups as mental or physical defectives.

Anti-immigrant fears helped fuel the eugenics movement. Eugenics is the control of reproduction to alter a plant or animal species, and some U.S. eugenicists believed that human society could be improved by this means. A leading eugenicist, the zoologist Charles B. Davenport, urged immigration restriction to keep America from pollution by "inferior" genetic stock.

In *The Passing of the Great Race* (1916), Madison Grant, a prominent progressive and eugenics advocate, used bogus data to denounce immigrants from southern and eastern Europe, especially Jews. He also viewed African-Americans as inferior. Anticipating the program of Adolf Hitler in the 1930s (see Chapter 25), Grant called for racial segregation, immigration restriction, and the forced sterilization of the "unfit," including "worthless race types." The vogue of eugenics gave "scientific" respectability to anti-immigrant sentiment, as well as to the racism that pervaded white America in these years. Inspired by eugenics, many states legalized the sterilization of criminals, sex offenders, and persons adjudged mentally deficient. In the 1927 case *Buck* v. *Bell,* the Supreme Court upheld such laws.

Racism and Progressivism	Progressivism arose at a time of transition in African-American life, and also of intense racism in white America. These realities are crucial to a full understanding of the movement.

In 1900, most of the nation's 10 million blacks lived in the rural South as share-croppers and tenant farmers. As devastating floods and the cotton boll weevil, which spread from Mexico in the 1890s, worsened their lot, many southern blacks left the land. By 1910, over 20 percent of the black population lived in cities, mostly in the South, but many in the North as well. Black men in the cities took jobs in factories, docks, and railroads or became carpenters, plasterers, or bricklayers. Many black women became domestic servants, seamstresses, or workers in laundries and tobacco factories. By 1910, 54 percent of America's black women held jobs.

Across the South, legally enforced racism peaked in the early twentieth century. Local "Jim Crow" laws segregated streetcars, schools, parks, and even cemeteries. The facilities for blacks, including the schools, were invariably inferior. Many southern cities imposed residential segregation by law until the Supreme Court restricted it in 1917. Most labor unions excluded black workers. Disfranchised and trapped in a cycle of poverty, poor education, and discrimination, southern blacks faced bleak prospects.

Fleeing such conditions, two hundred thousand blacks migrated north between 1890 and 1910. Wartime job opportunities drew still more in 1917–1918 (see Chapter 22), and by 1920, 1.4 million African-Americans lived in the North. They found conditions only slightly better than in the South. In northern cities, too, racism worsened after 1890 as hard times and immigration heightened social tensions. (Immigrants, competing with blacks for jobs and housing, sometimes exhibited intense racial prejudice.) Segregation, though not imposed by law, was enforced by custom and sometimes by violence. Blacks lived in run-down "colored districts," attended dilapidated schools, and worked at the lowest-paying jobs.

Their ballots—usually cast for the party of Lincoln—brought little political influence. The only black politicians tolerated by Republican party leaders were those willing to distribute low-level patronage jobs and otherwise keep silent. African-Americans in the segregated army faced hostility from white soldiers and officers, as well as from nearby civilians. Even the movies preached racism. D. W. Griffith's *The Birth of a Nation* (1915) disparaged blacks and glorified the Ku Klux Klan.

Smoldering racism sometimes exploded in violence. Antiblack rioters in Atlanta in 1906 murdered twenty-five blacks and burned many black homes. From 1900 to 1920 an average of about seventy-five lynchings occurred yearly. Some lynch mobs used trumped-up charges to justify the murder of blacks whose assertive behavior or economic aspirations angered whites. Some lynchings involved incredible sadism, with large crowds on hand, victims' bodies mutilated, and graphic photo postcards sold later. Authorities rarely intervened. At a 1916 lynching in Texas, the mayor warned the mob to protect the hanging tree, since it was on city property.

In the face of such hostility, blacks developed strong social institutions and a vigorous culture. Black churches proved a bulwark of support. Working African-American mothers, drawing on strategies dating to slavery days, relied on relatives and neighbors for child care. A handful of black higher-education institutions such as Fisk in Nashville and Howard in Washington, D.C., carried on against heavy odds. John Hope, a classics scholar who became president of Atlanta's Morehouse College in 1906, assembled a distinguished faculty, championed African-American education, and fought racial segregation. His sister Jane (Hope) Lyons was dean of women at Spelman College, another black institution in Atlanta.

The urban black community included several black-owned insurance companies and banks, a small elite of entrepreneurs, teachers, ministers, and sports figures like Jack Johnson. Although major-league baseball excluded blacks, a thriving Negro League attracted many black fans.

In this racist age, progressives compiled a mixed record on racial issues. Lillian Wald, director of New York's Henry Street Settlement, protested racial injustice. Muckraker Ray Stannard Baker documented racism in his 1908 book, *Following the Color Line*. Settlement-house worker Mary White Ovington helped found the National Association for the Advancement of Colored People (see below) and wrote *Half a Man* (1911), about the psychological scars of racism.

But most progressives kept silent as blacks were lynched, disfranchised, and discriminated against. Many saw African-Americans, like immigrants, not as potential allies but as part of the problem. Viewing blacks as inferior and prone to immorality and social disorder, white progressives generally supported or tolerated segregated schools and housing, restrictions on black voting rights, the strict moral oversight of African-American communities, and, at best, paternalistic efforts to "uplift" this supposedly backward and childlike people. Viciously racist southern politicians like Governor James K. Vardaman of Mississippi and Senator Ben Tillman of South Carolina also supported progressive reforms. Southern woman-suffrage leaders argued that granting women the vote would strengthen white supremacy.

At the national level, President Theodore Roosevelt's record on race was marginally better than that of other politicians in this racist age. He appointed a black to head the Charleston customs house despite white opposition, and closed a Mississippi post office rather than yield to demands that he dismiss the black postmistress. In a symbolically important gesture, he dined with Booker T. Washington at the White House. In 1906, however, he approved the dishonorable discharge of an entire regiment of black soldiers, including Congressional Medal of Honor winners, in Brownsville, Texas, because some members of the unit, goaded by racist taunts, had killed a local civilian. The "Brownsville Incident" incensed black Americans. (In 1972, when most of the men were long dead, Congress reversed the dishonorable discharges.)

Under President Woodrow Wilson, racism became rampant in Washington. A Virginia native reared in Georgia, Wilson displayed at best a patronizing attitude toward blacks, praised the racist movie *The Birth of a Nation*, and allowed southerners in his cabinet and in Congress (some of them powerful committee chairmen) to impose rigid segregation on all levels of the government.

BLACKS, WOMEN, AND WORKERS ORGANIZE

The organizational strategy so central to progressivism generally also proved useful for groups facing discrimination or exploitation. African-Americans, middle-class women, and wage workers all organized to address their grievances and improve their situation.

African-American Leaders Organize Against Racism   With racism on the rise, Booker T. Washington's accommodationist message (see Chapter 20) seemed increasingly unrealistic, particularly to northern blacks. Washington's self-help theme would appeal to later generations of African-Americans, but in the early twentieth century, many blacks confronting lynching, blatant racism, and rising segregationist pressures tired of his cautious approach. In 1902, William Monroe Trotter, the editor of the *Boston Guardian,* a black newspaper, called Washington's go-slow policies "a fatal blow . . . to the Negro's political rights and liberty."

Another opponent was the black journalist and activist **Ida Wells-Barnett.** Moving to Chicago from Memphis in 1892 after a white mob destroyed her offices, Wells-Barnett mounted a national antilynching campaign, in contrast to Booker T. Washington's public silence on the subject. An eloquent speaker and writer, she toured the United States and Great Britain lecturing against lynching and other racial abuses, and documented the grim record in her 1895 book *A Red Record.*

Booker T. Washington's most potent challenger was **W. E. B. Du Bois** (1868–1963). After earning a Ph.D. in history from Harvard in 1895, Du Bois taught at Wilberforce College in Ohio, the University of Pennsylvania, and then Atlanta University. Openly criticizing Washington in *The Souls of Black Folk* (1903), he rejected Washington's call for patience and his exclusive emphasis on manual skills. Instead, Du Bois demanded full racial equality, including the same educational opportunities open to whites, and called on blacks to resist all forms of racism.

Du Bois's militancy signaled a new era of African-American activism. In 1905, under his leadership, blacks who favored vigorous resistance to racism held a conference at Niagara Falls. For the next few years, participants in the "Niagara Movement" met annually. Meanwhile, a group of white reformers led by newspaper publisher Oswald Garrison Villard, grandson of abolitionist William Lloyd Garrison, had also grown dissatisfied with Washington's cautiousness. In 1909, Villard and his allies joined with Du Bois and other blacks from the Niagara Movement to form the **National Association for the Advancement of Colored People** (NAACP). This new organization called for sustained activism, including legal challenges, to achieve political equality for blacks and full integration into American life. Attracting the urban black middle class, the NAACP by 1914 had six thousand members in fifty branches.

Revival of the Woman-Suffrage Movement   As late as 1910, women could vote in only four western states: Wyoming, Utah, Colorado, and Idaho. Woman suffrage failed in six state referenda after 1896. But the active role of women in the progressive reform movement revitalized the suffrage cause. Middle-class women found disfranchisement especially galling when recently arrived immigrant men could vote. A vigorous suffrage movement in Great Britain

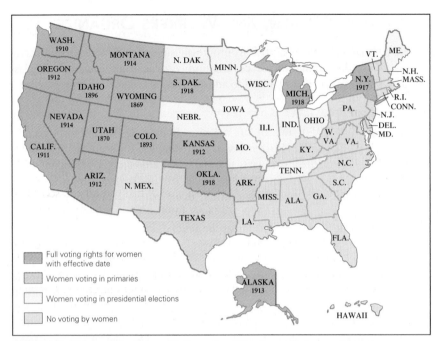

Map 21.1 Woman Suffrage Before the Nineteenth Amendment

Beginning with Wyoming in 1869, woman suffrage made steady gains in western states before 1920. Farther east, key victories came in New York (1917) and Michigan (1918). But much of the East remained an anti-woman-suffrage bastion throughout the period.

reverberated in America as well. Like progressivism itself, this revived campaign in America started at the grass roots. A suffrage campaign in New York State in 1915, though unsuccessful, underscored the new momentum.

So, too, did events in California. Indeed, the California campaign illustrates both the strengths and the limitations of the revived movement. In the 1880s, California's women's clubs focused on cultural and domestic themes. By the early 1900s, they had evolved into a potent statewide organization addressing municipal reforms and public-school issues. This evolution convinced many members that full citizenship meant the right to vote. A state woman-suffrage referendum lost in 1896, but the leaders bounced back to form alliances with labor leaders and male progressives, built on a shared commitment to "good government" and opposition to municipal corruption. But while joining forces with male reformers, the woman-suffrage strategists insisted on the unique role of "organized womanhood" in building a better society. Success came in 1911 when California voters approved woman suffrage.

"Organized womanhood" had its limits. Elite and middle-class women, mainly based in Los Angeles and San Francisco, led the California campaign. Working-class women and farmwomen played little role, while African-American, Mexican-American, and Asian-American women were almost totally excluded.

New leaders translated the momentum in California and other states into a revitalized national movement. When Susan B. Anthony retired from the presidency of the

National American Woman Suffrage Association (NAWSA) in 1900, **Carrie Chapman Catt** of Iowa succeeded her. Under Catt's shrewd direction, NAWSA adopted the so-called Winning Plan: grass-roots organization with tight central coordination.

Suffragists adopted techniques from the new urban consumer culture. They not only lobbied legislators, but also ran newspaper ads; put up posters; waved banners with catchy slogans; organized parades in open cars; arranged photo opportunities for the media; and distributed fans and other items emblazoned with the suffrage message. Gradually, state after state fell into the suffrage column. As in California (and like progressive organizations generally), NAWSA's membership remained largely white, native-born, and middle class. Few black, immigrant, or working-class women joined. Some upper-class women opposed the reform. The leader of the "Antis," the wealthy Josephine Dodge of New York, argued that women already had behind-the-scenes influence, and that to invade the male realm of electoral politics would tarnish their moral and spiritual role.

Not all suffragists accepted Catt's strategy. Alice Paul, who had observed the British suffragists' militant tactics while studying in England, grew impatient with NAWSA's state-by-state approach. In 1913, Paul founded the Congressional Union for Woman Suffrage, renamed the National Woman's Party in 1916, to pressure Congress to enact a woman-suffrage constitutional amendment. Targeting "the party in power"—in this case, the Democrats—Paul and her followers in the 1916 election opposed President Woodrow Wilson and congressional Democrats who had failed to endorse a suffrage amendment. In 1917–1918, with the United States at war, the suffrage cause won key victories in New York and Michigan and advanced toward final success (see Chapter 22).

Enlarging "Woman's Sphere" As the careers of such women as Florence Kelley, Alice Hamilton, and Ida Wells-Barnett make clear, the suffrage cause did not exhaust women's energies in the Progressive Era. Women's clubs, settlement-house residents, and individual female activists promoted a wide range of reforms. These included the campaigns to bring playgrounds and day nurseries to the slums, abolish child labor, and ban unsafe foods and quack remedies. As Jane Addams observed, the watchful care that women gave their own children could also draw them into broader political activism in an industrial age when hazards came from outside the home as well as inside.

Cultural assumptions about "woman's sphere" weakened as women became active on many fronts. Katherine Bement Davis served as New York City's commissioner of corrections. Emma Goldman crisscrossed the country lecturing on politics, feminism, and modern drama while coediting a radical monthly, *Mother Earth*. A vanguard of pioneering women in higher education included Marion Talbot, first dean of women at the University of Chicago.

In *Women and Economics* (1898) and other works, feminist intellectual Charlotte Perkins Gilman explored the cultural roots of gender roles and linked women's subordinate status to their economic dependence on men. Confining women to the domestic sphere, Gilman argued, was an evolutionary throwback that had become outdated and inefficient. She advocated gender equality in the workplace; the collectivization of cooking, cleaning, and other domestic tasks; and state-run day-care centers. In the utopian novel *Herland* (1915), Gilman wittily critiqued patriarchal assumptions by injecting three naïve young men into an exclusively female society.

Parading for Woman Suffrage *Suffrage leaders built support for the cause by using modern advertising and publicity techniques, including automobiles festooned with flags, bunting, banners, posters, and—in this case—smiling little girls.*

Some Progressive Era reformers challenged federal and state laws banning the distribution of contraceptives and birth-control information. Although countless women, particularly the poor, suffered exhaustion and ill health from frequent pregnancies, artificial contraception was widely denounced as immoral. In 1914, **Margaret Sanger** of New York, a practical nurse and socialist whose mother had died after bearing eleven children, began her crusade for birth control, a term she coined. When her journal *The Woman Rebel* faced prosecution on obscenity charges, Sanger fled to England. Returning in 1916, she opened the nation's first birth-control clinic in Brooklyn; launched a new journal, the *Birth Control Review;* and founded the American Birth Control League, the ancestor of today's Planned Parenthood Federation. Meanwhile, another New Yorker, Mary Ware Dennett, had also emerged as an advocate of birth control and sex education. (Her frank 1919 informational pamphlet for youth, *The Sex Side of Life,* was long banned as obscene.) While Sanger championed direct action to promote the cause, Dennett urged lobbying efforts to change the law. Sanger insisted that only physicians should supply contraceptives; Dennett argued for widespread distribution. These differences, coupled with Sanger's inability to tolerate rivals, soured relations between the two women and their respective organizations.

The birth-control movement stands as one of progressivism's most important legacies. At the time, however, it stirred bitter resistance among conservatives and many religious leaders. Indeed, not until 1965 did the Supreme Court fully legalize the dissemination of contraceptive materials and information.

Workers Organize;   In this age of organization, labor unions continued to expand.
Socialism Advances   The American Federation of Labor (AFL) grew from 625,000
members in 1900 to 4 million by 1920. This was still only
about 20 percent of the industrial work force. With recent immigrants hungry for jobs,
union activities could be risky. The boss could always fire an "agitator" and hire a docile
newcomer. Judicial hostility also plagued the movement. In the 1908 *Danbury Hatters*
case, for example, the Supreme Court forbade unions from organizing boycotts in support of strikes. Such boycotts were a "conspiracy in restraint of trade," said the high
court, and thus a violation of the Sherman Anti-Trust Act. The AFL's strength remained
in the skilled trades, not in the factories, mills, and sweatshops where most immigrants
and women worked.

A few unions did try to reach these laborers. The International Ladies' Garment
Workers' Union (ILGWU), founded in 1900 by immigrants working in New York City's
needle trades, conducted successful strikes in 1909 and after the 1911 Triangle fire. The
1909 strike began when young Clara Lemlich jumped up as speechmaking droned on
at a union meeting and passionately called for a strike. Thousands of women garment
workers stayed off the job the next day. Some of the picketers endured police beatings;
others lost their jobs. But the strikers did win higher wages and improved working
conditions.

Another union that targeted the most exploited workers was the **Industrial Workers of the World** (IWW), nicknamed the Wobblies, founded in Chicago in 1905. The
IWW's leader was William "Big Bill" Haywood, a compelling orator. Utah-born Haywood became a miner as a boy and joined the militant Western Federation of Miners
in 1896. In 1905 he was acquitted of complicity in the assassination of an antilabor former governor of Idaho. IWW membership peaked at around thirty thousand, mostly
western miners, lumbermen, fruit pickers, and itinerant laborers. But it captured the
imagination of young cultural rebels in New York City's Greenwich Village, where Haywood often visited.

The IWW led mass strikes of Nevada gold miners; Minnesota iron miners; and
timber workers in Louisiana, Texas, and the Northwest. In 1912 it won a bitter textile
strike in Massachusetts. This victory owed much to two women: the birth-control reformer Margaret Sanger, and Elizabeth Gurley Flynn, a fiery Irish-American orator
who publicized the cause by sending strikers' children to sympathizers in New York
City for temporary care. Although the IWW's reputation for violence was much exaggerated, it faced government harassment, especially during World War I, and by 1920
its strength was broken.

Other workers, as well as some middle-class Americans, turned to socialism. All socialists advocated an end to capitalism and public ownership of factories, utilities, railroads, and communications systems, but they differed on how to achieve these goals.
The revolutionary ideology of German social theorist Karl Marx won a few converts,
but the vision of democratic socialism achieved at the ballot box proved more appealing. In 1900 democratic socialists formed the Socialist Party of America (SPA). Members included Morris Hillquit, a New York City labor organizer; Victor Berger, the
leader of Milwaukee's German socialists; and **Eugene V. Debs,** the Indiana labor leader.
Debs, a popular orator, was the SPA's presidential candidate five times between 1900
and 1920. Many Greenwich Village cultural rebels embraced socialism as well and supported the radical magazine *The Masses,* founded in 1911.

Socialism's high-water mark came around 1912 when SPA membership stood at 118,000. Debs won more than 900,000 votes for president that year (about 6 percent of the total), and the Socialists elected a congressman (Berger) and hundreds of municipal officials. The Intercollegiate Socialist Society carried the message to college campuses. The party published over three hundred daily and weekly newspapers, many in foreign languages for immigrant members.

NATIONAL PROGRESSIVISM, PHASE I: ROOSEVELT AND TAFT, 1901–1913

By around 1905, local and state reform activities were coalescing into a national movement. Symbolically, in 1906 Wisconsin governor Robert La Follette went to Washington as a U.S. senator. Five years earlier, progressivism had found its first national leader, **Theodore Roosevelt,** nicknamed "TR."

Self-righteous, jingoistic, and fond of speechmaking—but also brilliant, politically savvy, and endlessly interesting—Roosevelt became president in 1901 and at once made the White House a cauldron of activism. Skillfully orchestrating public opinion, the popular young president pursued his goals—labor mediation, consumer protection, conservation, business virtue, and engagement abroad (see Chapter 20)—while embracing and publicizing progressives' ideas and objectives.

Roosevelt's activist approach permanently enlarged the powers of the presidency. TR's handpicked successor, William Howard Taft, proved politically inept, however, and controversy marked his administration. With the Republican Party split, the Democrat Woodrow Wilson, holding a somewhat different vision of progressive reform, won the presidency in 1912.

Roosevelt's Path to the White House On September 6, 1901, in Buffalo, anarchist Leon Czolgosz shot William McKinley. At first recovery seemed likely, and Vice President Theodore Roosevelt proceeded with a hiking trip in New York's Adirondack Mountains. But on September 14, McKinley died. At age forty-two, Theodore Roosevelt became president.

Many politicians shuddered at the thought of the impetuous Roosevelt as president. Republican kingmaker Mark Hanna exclaimed, "My God, that damned cowboy in the White House!" Roosevelt did, indeed, display many traits associated with the West. The son of an aristocratic New York family of Dutch origins, he was sickly as a child. But a bodybuilding program and summers in Wyoming transformed him into a model of physical fitness. When his young wife died in 1884, he stoically carried on. Two years on a Dakota ranch (1884–1886) further toughened him and deepened his enthusiasm for what he termed "the strenuous life."

Although his social peers considered politics unfit for gentlemen, Roosevelt served as a state assemblyman, New York City police commissioner, and a U.S. civil-service commissioner. In 1898, fresh from his Cuban exploits (see Chapter 20), he was elected New York's governor. Two years later, the state's Republican boss, eager to be rid of him, arranged for Roosevelt's nomination as vice president.

As was the case with everything he did, TR found the presidency energizing. "I have been President emphatically . . . ," he boasted; "I believe in a strong executive." He enjoyed public life and loved the limelight. "When Theodore attends a wedding he wants to be the bride," his daughter observed, "and when he attends a funeral he wants to be the corpse." With his toothy grin, machine-gun speech, and amazing energy, he dominated the political landscape. When he refused to shoot a bear cub on a hunting trip, a shrewd toy maker marketed a cuddly new product, the Teddy Bear.

Labor Disputes, Trustbusting, Railroad Regulation The new president's political skills were quickly tested. In May 1902, the United Mine Workers Union (UMW) called a strike to gain not only higher wages and shorter hours but also recognition as a union. The mine owners dug in their heels, and in October, with winter looming, TR acted. Summoning the two sides to the White House and threatening to seize the mines, he forced them to accept an arbitration commission to settle the dispute. The commission granted the miners a 10 percent wage increase and reduced their working day from ten to nine hours.

TR's approach to labor disputes differed from that of his predecessors, who typically sided with management, sometimes using troops as strikebreakers. Though not consistently prolabor, he defended workers' right to organize. When a mine owner insisted that the miners' welfare should be left to those "to whom God in his infinite wisdom has given control of the property interests of the country," Roosevelt derided such "arrogant stupidity."

With his elite background, TR neither feared nor much liked business tycoons. The prospect of spending time with "big-money men," he once wrote a friend, "fills me with frank horror." While he believed that corporations contributed to national greatness, he also embraced the progressive conviction that they must be regulated. A strict moralist, he held corporations, like individuals, to a high standard.

Yet as a political realist, Roosevelt also understood that many Washington politicians abhorred his views—among them Senator Nelson Aldrich of Rhode Island, a wily defender of business interests. Roosevelt's progressive impulses thus remained in tension with his grasp of power realities in capitalist America.

Roosevelt's political skills faced another test in 1901 when J. P. Morgan formed the United States Steel Company, the nation's first billion-dollar business. As public distrust of big corporations deepened, TR dashed to the head of the parade. His 1902 State of the Union message gave high priority to breaking up business monopolies, or "trustbusting." Roosevelt's attorney general soon filed suit against the Northern Securities Company, a giant holding company recently created to control railroading in the Northwest, for violating the Sherman Anti-Trust Act of 1890. On a speaking tour that summer, TR called for a "square deal" for all Americans and denounced special treatment for capitalists. "We don't wish to destroy corporations," he said, "but we do wish to make them . . . serve the public good." In 1904, a divided Supreme Court ordered the Northern Securities Company dissolved.

The Roosevelt administration filed forty-three other antitrust lawsuits. In two key cases decided in 1911, the Supreme Court ordered the breakup of the Standard Oil Company and the reorganization of the American Tobacco Company to make it less monopolistic.

As the 1904 election neared, Roosevelt made peace with J. P. Morgan and other business magnates. When the GOP convention that nominated Roosevelt in Chicago adopted a probusiness platform, $2 million in corporate contributions poured in. The

Democrats, meanwhile, eager to erase the taint of radicalism, embraced the gold standard and nominated a conservative New York judge, Alton B. Parker.

Winning easily, Roosevelt turned to one of his major goals: railroad regulation. He now saw corporate regulation as a more promising strategy than trustbusting. This shift underlay his central role in the passage of the **Hepburn Act** of 1906. This law empowered the Interstate Commerce Commission to set maximum railroad rates and to examine railroads' financial records. It also curtailed the railroads' practice of distributing free passes to ministers and other shapers of public opinion.

The Hepburn Act displayed TR's political talent, as he bargained with Senator Aldrich and other conservatives. In a key compromise, he agreed to delay tariff reform in return for railroad regulation. Although the Hepburn Act did not fully satisfy reformers, it did expand the government's regulatory powers.

Consumer Protection

Of all progressive reforms, the campaign against unsafe food, drugs, and medicine proved especially popular. Upton Sinclair's *The Jungle* (1906) graphically described the foul conditions in some meatpacking plants. Wrote Sinclair in one vivid passage, "[A] man could run his hand over these piles of meat and sweep off handfuls of dried dung of rats. These rats were nuisances, and the packers would put poisoned bread out for them, they would die, and then rats, bread, and meat would go into the hoppers together." (The socialist Sinclair also detailed the exploitation of immigrant workers, but this message proved less potent. "I aimed at the nation's heart, but hit it in the stomach," he later lamented.) Women's organizations and consumer groups rallied public opinion on this issue, and an Agriculture Department chemist, Harvey W. Wiley, helped shape the proposed legislation. Other muckrakers exposed useless or dangerous patent medicines, many laced with cocaine, opium, or alcohol. One tonic "for treatment of the alcohol habit" contained 26.5 percent alcohol. Peddlers of these nostrums freely claimed that they could cure cancer, grow hair, and restore sexual vigor.

Sensing the public mood, Roosevelt supported the **Pure Food and Drug Act** and the Meat Inspection Act, both passed in 1906. The former outlawed the sale of adulterated foods or drugs and required accurate ingredient labels; the latter imposed strict sanitary rules on meatpackers and set up a federal meat-inspection system. The more reputable food-processing, meatpacking, and medicinal companies, eager to regain public confidence, supported these regulatory measures.

Environmentalism Progressive-Style

Environmental concerns loomed large for Theodore Roosevelt. Singling out conservation in his first State of the Union message as America's "most vital internal question," he highlighted an issue that still reverberates.

By 1900 decades of urban-industrial growth and western expansion had taken a heavy toll on the land. In the West, land-use disputes raged as mining and timber interests, farmers, ranchers, sheep growers, and preservationists advanced competing claims.

While business interests and boosters preached exploitation of the West's resources and agricultural groups sought government aid for irrigation projects, organizations such as John Muir's Sierra Club (founded in San Francisco in 1892) battled to preserve wilderness areas. Socially prominent easterners also embraced the wilderness cause. Under an act passed by Congress in 1891, Presidents Harrison and Cleveland had set aside some 35 million acres of public lands as national forests.

In the early twentieth century, amid spreading cities and factories, a wilderness vogue swept America. Popular writers evoked the tang of the campfire and the lure of the primitive. Summer camps, which began in the 1890s, as well as the Boy Scouts (founded in 1910) and Girl Scouts (1912), gave city children a taste of wilderness living.

Between the wilderness enthusiasts and the developers stood government experts like Gifford Pinchot who saw the public domain as a resource to be managed wisely. Appointed by President Roosevelt in 1905 to head the new U.S. Forest Service, Pinchot stressed not preservation but conservation—the planned use of forest lands for public and commercial purposes.

Wilderness advocates viewed Pinchot's Forest Service warily. They welcomed his opposition to mindless exploitation but worried that the multiple-use approach would despoil wilderness areas. As a Sierra Club member wrote, "[T]rees are for human use. But there are . . . uses for the spiritual wealth of us all, as well as for the material wealth of some."

At heart Roosevelt was a preservationist. In 1903, he spent a blissful few days camping in Yosemite National Park with John Muir. He once compared "the destruction of a species" to the loss of "all the works of some great writer." But TR the politician backed the conservationists' call for planned development. He supported the **National Reclamation Act** of 1902, which designated the money from public-land sales for water management in arid western regions, and set up the Reclamation Service to construct dams and irrigation projects.

This measure (also known as the Newlands Act for its sponsor, a Nevada congressman) ranks in importance with the Northwest Ordinance of 1787 for promoting the development of a vast continental region. Reclamation projects increased settlement and productivity between the Rockies and the Pacific. The Roosevelt Dam in Arizona spurred the growth of Phoenix, and a complex of dams and waterways in Idaho's Snake River valley watered thousands of barren acres, stimulating the production of potatoes and other commodities. The law required farmers who benefited from these projects to repay the construction costs, creating a federal fund for further projects. The Newlands Act and other measures of these years helped transform the West from a series of isolated "island settlements" into a thriving, interconnected region.

The competition for scarce water resources in the West sparked bitter political battles. The Los Angeles basin, for example, with 40 percent of California's population in 1900, found itself with only 2 percent of the state's surface water. In 1907, the city derailed a Reclamation Service project intended for the farmers of California's Owens Valley, more than 230 miles to the north, and diverted the precious water to Los Angeles.

Meanwhile, President Roosevelt, embracing Pinchot's multiple-use land-management program, set aside 200 million acres of public land (85 million of them in Alaska) as national forests, mineral reserves, and waterpower sites. But this, too, provoked opposition in the West, and in 1907 Congress revoked the president's authority to create national forests in six timber-rich western states. Before signing the bill, Roosevelt designated 16 million more acres in the six states as national forests. TR also created fifty-three wildlife reserves, sixteen national monuments, and five new national parks. Congress established the National Park Service in 1916 to manage them. The Antiquities Act (1906) protected archaeological sites, especially in the Southwest, some of which later became national parks.

In 1908, Gifford Pinchot organized a White House conservation conference for the nation's governors. There, experts discussed the utilitarian benefits of resource management. John Muir and other wilderness preservationists were not invited. But the struggle between wilderness purists and multiple-use advocates went on. Rallying support through magazine articles, preservationists won key victories. For example, campaigns by private groups, including women's organizations, saved a large grove of California's giant redwoods and a lovely stretch of the Maine coastline from logging.

The Sierra Club lost a major battle to save the Hetch Hetchy Valley in Yosemite National Park when Congress in 1913 approved a dam on the Tuolumne River to provide water and hydroelectric power for San Francisco, 150 miles away. (Other opponents of the dam were less interested in preserving Hetch Hetchy as a pristine wilderness than in developing it for tourism.) While the preservationists lost this battle, the controversy did focus attention on the national-parks movement and publicized the environmentalist cause, as Americans for the first time weighed the aesthetic implications of a major public-works project.

Taft in the White House, 1909–1913 Roosevelt had pledged not to run for a third term, and as the 1908 election approached, the Republican Party's most conservative leaders regained party control. They nominated TR's choice, Secretary of War **William Howard Taft,** for president but selected a conservative vice-presidential nominee and adopted a deeply conservative party platform. The Democrats, meanwhile, nominated William Jennings Bryan for a third time. The Democratic platform called for a lower tariff, denounced the trusts, and embraced the cause of labor.

With Roosevelt's endorsement, Taft coasted to victory. But Bryan bested Alton B. Parker's 1904 vote total by 1.3 million, and progressive Republican state candidates outran the national ticket. Overall, the outcome suggested a lull in the reform movement, not its end.

Republican conservatives welcomed Roosevelt's departure to hunt big game in Africa. Quipped Senator Aldrich, "Let every lion do its duty." But even an ocean away, TR's presence remained vivid. "When I am addressed as 'Mr. President,'" Taft wrote him, "I turn to see whether you are not at my elbow."

Taft, from an old political family in Cincinnati, differed from TR in almost every respect. Whereas TR kept in fighting trim, Taft was obese. Roosevelt had set up a boxing ring in the White House; Taft preferred golf. TR loved speechmaking and battling evildoers; Taft disliked controversy. His happiest days would come later, as chief justice of the United States.

Pledged to support TR's program, Taft backed the Mann-Elkins Act (1910), which beefed up the Interstate Commerce Commission's regulatory authority and extended it to telephone and telegraph companies. The Taft administration actually prosecuted more antitrust cases than had Roosevelt, but without much publicity. To the public, TR remained the mighty trustbuster.

The reform spotlight, meanwhile, shifted from the White House to Congress. During the Roosevelt administration, a small group of reform-minded Republicans, nicknamed the Insurgents, including Senators La Follette and Albert Beveridge of Indiana and Congressman George Norris of Nebraska, had challenged their party's conservative congressional leadership. In 1909, the Insurgents and President Taft fought a bruising battle over the tariff. Taft at first backed the Insurgents' call for a lower tariff. But when high-tariff advocates in Congress pushed through the Payne-Aldrich Tariff raising duties on hundreds of items, Taft infuriated the Insurgents by not only signing the bill but praising it extravagantly.

The Insurgents next set their sights on Speaker of the House Joseph G. Cannon of Illinois, a powerful and reactionary Republican who kept most reform bills from even reaching a vote. In March 1910, the Insurgents joined with the Democrats to trim Cannon's power by removing him from the pivotal Rules Committee. This was a direct slap at Taft, who supported Cannon.

The so-called Ballinger-Pinchot controversy widened the rift. Taft's interior secretary, Richard Ballinger, was a Seattle lawyer who favored unregulated private development of natural resources. In one of several decisions galling to conservationists, Ballinger in 1909 approved the sale of several million acres of public lands in Alaska containing coal deposits to a group of Seattle businessmen. They in turn sold the land to J. P. Morgan and other New York financiers. When a Department of the Interior official protested, he was fired. In true muckraking style, he went public, blasting Ballinger's actions in a *Collier's* magazine article. When Gifford Pinchot of the Forest Service publicly criticized Ballinger, he too got the ax. TR's supporters seethed.

Upon Roosevelt's return to America in June 1910, Pinchot met the boat. Openly breaking with Taft, Roosevelt campaigned for Insurgent candidates in that year's midterm elections. In a speech that alarmed conservatives, he attacked judges who struck down progressive laws and even endorsed the radical idea of reversing judicial rulings by popular vote. Borrowing a term from Herbert Croly's *The Promise of American Life,* TR proposed a "New Nationalism" that would powerfully engage the federal government in reform.

The Democrats captured the House in 1910, and a coalition of Democrats and Insurgent Republicans controlled the Senate. As the reform tide rose, TR sounded more and more like a presidential candidate.

The Four-Way Election of 1912   In February 1912 Roosevelt announced his candidacy for the Republican nomination. But Taft wanted a second term, and a Republican battle loomed. In a series of Republican state primaries and conventions, Roosevelt generally walloped Taft. But Taft controlled the party machinery, and the Republican convention in Chicago disqualified many of Roosevelt's hard-won delegates. Outraged, TR's backers left the convention and formed the **Progressive Party.** What had been a general term for a broad reform movement now became the official name of a political party. Riding an emotional high, the cheering delegates nominated their hero, with California senator Hiram Johnson as his running mate.

"I feel fit as a bull moose," Roosevelt trumpeted, thereby giving his organization its nickname, the Bull Moose Party. The convention platform endorsed nearly every reform cause of the day, including lower tariffs, woman suffrage, business regulation, the abolition of child labor, the eight-hour workday, workers' compensation, the direct primary, and the popular election of senators. The new party attracted a diverse following, united mainly by affection for Roosevelt.

Meanwhile, the reform spirit had also infused the Democratic Party at the local and state levels. In New Jersey in 1910, voters had elected a political novice, **Woodrow Wilson,** as governor. A "Wilson for President" boom soon arose, and when the Democrats assembled in Baltimore in June 1912, Wilson won the nomination, defeating several established party leaders.

MAP 21.2 The Election of 1912

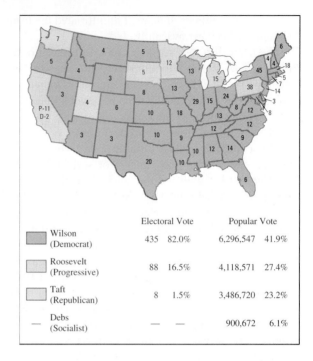

		Electoral Vote		Popular Vote	
Wilson (Democrat)		435	82.0%	6,296,547	41.9%
Roosevelt (Progressive)		88	16.5%	4,118,571	27.4%
Taft (Republican)		8	1.5%	3,486,720	23.2%
Debs (Socialist)		—	—	900,672	6.1%

In the campaign, Taft more or less gave up, happy to have kept his party safe for conservatism. The Socialist Party candidate Eugene Debs proposed an end to capitalism and a socialized economic order. TR preached his New Nationalism. The corporate order was here to stay, he conceded, but big business must be regulated in the public interest, the welfare of workers and consumers safeguarded, and the environment protected.

Woodrow Wilson and William Howard Taft *Having just squared off in the 1912 election campaign, the two politicians share a light moment before Wilson's inauguration on March 4, 1913.*

Wilson, by contrast, called his political vision the "New Freedom." Warning that big corporations were choking off opportunity for ordinary Americans, he nostalgically evoked an era of small government, small businesses, and free competition. "The history of liberty," he said, "is the history of the limitation of governmental power, not the increase of it."

Roosevelt outpolled Taft by 630,000 votes, but the Republican Party's split cost it dearly. Wilson easily won the presidency, and the Democrats took both houses of Congress. More than 900,000 voters opted for Debs and socialism.

The 1912 election linked the Democrats firmly with reform (except on the issue of race)—a link that Franklin D. Roosevelt would strengthen in the 1930s. TR's third-party campaign demonstrated the appeal of reform among grass-roots Republicans while leaving the national party itself in the grip of conservatives.

NATIONAL PROGRESSIVISM, PHASE II: WOODROW WILSON, 1913–1917

The son and grandson of Presbyterian ministers, Wilson grew up in southern towns in a churchly atmosphere that shaped his oratorical style and moral outlook. Although slow in school (probably because of the learning disorder dyslexia), Wilson graduated from Princeton and earned a Ph.D. in political science from Johns Hopkins University. He taught at Princeton and became its president in 1902. He lost support because of an unwillingness to compromise, and in 1910 left the academic world to enter politics. Three years later he was president of the United States.

Impressive in bearing, with piercing gray eyes, Wilson was an eloquent orator. But the idealism that inspired people could also alienate them. At his best, he excelled at political dealmaking. "He can walk on dead leaves and make no more noise than a tiger," declared one awed politician. But he could also retreat into a fortress of absolute certitude that tolerated no opposition. During his years as president, all these facets of his personality would come into play.

In his first term, Wilson exerted a key leadership role as Congress enacted an array of reform measures. Despite the nostalgia for simpler times he had evoked in the campaign, he proved ready to use government to address the problems of the new corporate order. Under Wilson, the progressive movement gained fresh momentum.

Tariff and Banking Reform Lowering tariff rates—long a goal of southern and agrarian Democrats—headed Wilson's agenda. Many progressives agreed that high protective tariffs increased corporate profits at the public's expense. Breaking a precedent dating from Thomas Jefferson's presidency, Wilson appeared personally before Congress on April 8, 1913, to read his tariff message. A low-tariff bill quickly passed the House but bogged down in the Senate. Showing his flair for drama, Wilson denounced the tariff lobbyists flooding into Washington. His censure led to a Senate investigation of lobbyists and of senators who profited from high tariffs. Stung by the publicity, the Senate slashed tariff rates even more than the House had done. The Underwood-Simmons Tariff reduced rates an average of 15 percent.

In June 1913 Wilson again addressed Congress, this time to call for banking and currency reform. The nation's banking system clearly needed overhauling. Totally decentralized, it lacked a strong central institution, a "lender of last resort" to help banks survive fiscal crises. The Panic of 1907, when many banks had failed, remained a vivid memory.

No consensus existed on specifics, however. Many reformers wanted a publicly controlled central banking system. But the nation's bankers, whose Senate spokesman was Nelson Aldrich, favored a privately controlled central bank similar to the Bank of England. The large banks of New York City advocated a strong central bank, preferably privately owned, so they could better compete with London banks in international finance. Others, including influential Virginia congressman Carter Glass, opposed any central banking authority, public or private.

No banking expert, Wilson did insist that the monetary system ultimately be publicly controlled. As the bargaining went on, Wilson played a crucial behind-the-scenes role. The result was the **Federal Reserve Act** of December 1913. This compromise measure created twelve regional Federal Reserve banks under mixed public/private control. Each regional bank could issue U.S. dollars, called Federal Reserve notes, to the banks in its district to make loans to corporations and individual borrowers. Overall control of the system was assigned to the heads of the twelve regional banks and a Washington-based Federal Reserve Board, whose members were appointed by the president for fourteen-year terms. (The secretary of the treasury and the comptroller of the currency were made ex officio members.)

The Federal Reserve Act stands as Wilson's greatest legislative achievement. Initially, the Federal Reserve's authority was diffuse, but eventually "the Fed" grew into the strong central monetary institution it remains today, setting interest rates and adopting fiscal policies to prevent financial panics, promote economic growth, and dampen inflationary pressures.

Regulating Business; Aiding Workers and Farmers	In 1914 Wilson and Congress turned to that perennial progressive cause, business regulation. Two key laws resulted: the Federal Trade Commission Act and the Clayton Antitrust Act. Though both sought a common goal, they embodied different approaches.

The first took an administrative approach. This law created a new "watchdog" agency, the **Federal Trade Commission** (FTC), with power to investigate violations of federal regulations, require regular reports from corporations, and issue cease-and-desist orders (subject to judicial review) when it found unfair methods of competition.

The Clayton Antitrust Act, by contrast, took a legal approach. It listed corporate activities that could lead to federal lawsuits. The Sherman Act of 1890, although outlawing business practices in restraint of trade, had been vague about details. The Clayton Act spelled out specific illegal practices, such as selling at a loss to undercut competitors.

Because some of Wilson's appointees to the FTC were conservatives with big-business links, this agency initially proved ineffective. But under the Clayton Act, the Wilson administration filed antitrust suits against nearly a hundred corporations.

Leading a party long identified with workers, Wilson supported the American Federation of Labor and defended workers' right to organize. He also endorsed a Clayton Act clause exempting strikes, boycotts, and picketing from the antitrust laws' prohibition of actions in restraint of trade.

In 1916 (an election year) Wilson and congressional Democrats enacted three important worker-protection laws. The Keating-Owen Act barred from interstate commerce products manufactured by child labor. (This law was declared unconstitutional in 1918, as was a similar law enacted in 1919.) The Adamson Act established an eight-hour day for interstate railway workers. The Workmen's Compensation Act provided accident and injury protection to federal workers. As we have seen, however, Wilson's sympathies for the underdog stopped at the color line.

Other 1916 laws helped farmers. The Federal Farm Loan Act and the Federal Warehouse Act enabled farmers, using land or crops as security, to get low-interest federal loans. The Federal Highway Act, providing matching funds for state highway programs, benefited not only the new automobile industry but also farmers plagued by bad roads.

Progressivism and the Constitution The probusiness bias of the courts softened a bit in the Progressive Era. Evidence of the changing judicial climate came in *Muller* v. *Oregon* (1908), in which the Supreme Court upheld an Oregon ten-hour law for women laundry workers. Defending the constitutionality of the Oregon law, Boston attorney **Louis Brandeis** offered economic, medical, and sociological evidence documenting how long hours harmed women workers. Rejecting a legal claim long made by business, the high court held that such worker-protection laws did not violate employers' rights under the due-process clause of the Fourteenth Amendment. *Muller* v. *Oregon* marked a breakthrough in making the legal system more responsive to new social realities.

In 1916, Woodrow Wilson nominated Brandeis to the Supreme Court. Disapproving of Brandeis's innovative approach to the law, the conservative American Bar Association protested, as did the *New York Times,* the president of Harvard, and Republican leaders in Congress. Anti-Semites opposed Brandeis because he was a Jew. But Wilson stood by his nominee, and after a fierce battle, the Senate confirmed him.

These years also produced four amendments to the Constitution, the first since 1870. The Sixteenth (ratified in 1913) granted Congress the authority to tax income, thus ending a long legal battle. A Civil War income tax had been phased out in 1872. Congress had authorized an income tax in an 1894 tariff act, but in 1895 the Supreme Court had declared this "communistic" measure unconstitutional. This ruling had spurred the campaign for a constitutional amendment. Exercising its new authority, Congress in 1913 imposed a graduated federal income tax with a maximum rate of 7 percent on incomes over five hundred thousand dollars. Income-tax revenues helped the government pay for the expanded regulatory activities assigned to it by various progressive reform measures.

The Seventeenth Amendment (1913) mandated the direct election of U.S. senators by the voters, rather than their selection by state legislatures as provided by Article I of the Constitution. This reform, earlier advocated by the Populists, sought to make the Senate less subject to corporate influence and more responsive to the popular will.

The Eighteenth Amendment (1919) prohibited the manufacture, sale, or importation of "intoxicating liquors." The Nineteenth (1920) granted women the vote. This remarkable wave of amendments underscored how profoundly the progressive impulse had transformed the political landscape.

1916: Wilson Edges Out Hughes Wilson easily won renomination in 1916. The Republicans turned to Charles Evans Hughes, a Supreme Court justice and former New York governor. The Progressive Party again courted Theodore Roosevelt, but TR was now obsessed with drawing the United States into the war that had broken out in Europe in 1914 (see Chapter 22). At his urging, the Progressive Party endorsed Hughes and effectively committed political suicide.

With the Republicans now more or less reunited, the election was extremely close. War-related issues loomed large. Wilson won the popular vote, but the Electoral College outcome remained in doubt for several weeks as the California tally seesawed back and forth. Ultimately, Wilson carried the state by fewer than four thousand votes and, with it, the election.

The progressive movement lost momentum as attention turned from reform to war. Final success for the prohibition and woman-suffrage campaigns came later, in 1919–1920, and Congress enacted a few reform measures in the 1920s. But, overall, the movement's zest and drive clearly waned as America went to war in 1917.

Conclusion

What we call the progressive movement began as preachers, novelists, journalists, photographers, and painters highlighted appalling conditions in America's cities and factories. Intellectuals offered ideas for reform through the creative use of government.

At the local and state level, reformers like Mayor Hazen Pingree of Detroit and Wisconsin governor Robert M. La Follette, together with a host of reform organizations, worked to combat political corruption, make cities safer and more beautiful, regulate corporations, and improve conditions for workers.

Progressivism had its coercive side. Some reformers concentrated on regulating urban amusements and banning alcohol consumption. Racism and hostility to immigrants comprise a part of the progressive legacy as well.

With the presidencies of Theodore Roosevelt and Woodrow Wilson, progressivism crested as a national movement. Although TR, Wilson, and other national progressive leaders differed in their political ideas, these years saw advances in corporate regulation, environmental conservation, banking reform, and consumer and worker protection. Constitutional amendments granted Congress the power to tax incomes and provided for the direct election of senators, woman suffrage, and national prohibition of alcohol—all aspects of the progressive impulse.

Progressivism's legacy included not only specific laws but also an enlarged view of government's social and economic role. Progressives expanded the meaning of democracy and challenged the cynical view of government as nothing but a tool of the rich and powerful. They did not seek "big government" for its own sake. Rather, they recognized that in an industrial age of great cities and concentrated corporate power, government, too, must grow to serve the public interest and protect society's more vulnerable members.

Unquestionably, this ideal sometimes faltered in practice. Reform laws and regulatory agencies often fell short of their purpose as bureaucratic routine set in. Reforms designed to promote the public good sometimes mainly benefited special interests. Corporations proved adept at manipulating the new regulatory state to their own advantage.

Still, the Progressive Era stands as a time when American politics seriously confronted the social upheavals caused by industrialization. It was also a time when Americans learned to think of government as an arena of possibility where public issues and social problems could be thrashed out. The next great reform movement, the New Deal of the 1930s, would draw on progressivism's legacy.

22

Global Involvements and
World War I, 1902–1920

DEFINING AMERICA'S WORLD ROLE, 1902–1914

As we saw in Chapter 20, the annexation of Hawaii, the Spanish-American War, the occupation of the Philippines, and other developments in the 1890s signaled America's growing involvement abroad, especially in Asia and Latin America. These foreign engagements reflected a desire to assert American power in an age of imperial expansion by European nations, to protect and extend U.S. business investments abroad, and to impose American standards of good government beyond the nation's borders. This process of foreign engagement continued under Presidents Theodore Roosevelt, William Howard Taft, and Woodrow Wilson.

America's dealings with Asian and Latin American nations in these years were shaped by both economic and ideological considerations. Certainly U.S. policy makers wanted to expand corporate America's access to foreign markets and raw materials. But they also believed that other societies would benefit by adopting the principles of democracy, individual freedom, and the rule of law. Sometimes the economic motive predominated, sometimes the ideological. Often, both motivations were in play as the United States exerted its power beyond its borders.

The "Open Door": Competing for the China Market   As the campaign to suppress the Philippines insurrection dragged on (see Chapter 20), American policy makers turned their attention farther west, to China. Their aim was not territorial but commercial. Proclaimed Indiana senator Albert J.

Beveridge in 1898, "American factories are making more than the American people can use; American soil is producing more than they can consume. . . . [T]he trade of the world must and shall be ours."

The China market beckoned. Textile producers dreamed of clothing China's millions; investors envisioned railroad construction. As China's 250-year-old Manchu Ch'ing empire grew weaker, U.S. businesspeople watched carefully. In 1896 a consortium of New York capitalists formed a company to promote trade and railroad investment in China.

But other nations were also eyeing the China market. Some pressured the weak Manchu rulers to designate certain regions as "spheres of influence" where they would enjoy exclusive trading and development rights. In 1896, Russia won both the right to build a railway across the Chinese province of Manchuria and a long-term lease on much of the region. In 1897, Germany forcibly secured a ninety-nine-year lease on a Chinese port as well as mining and railroad rights in the adjacent province. The British won concessions as well.

In 1899, U.S. Secretary of State John Hay asked the major European powers to assure American trading rights in China by opening the ports in their spheres of influence to all countries. The nations gave noncommittal answers, but Hay blithely announced that they had accepted the principle of an "Open Door" to American business in China.

Hay's Open Door note showed how commercial considerations were increasingly influencing American foreign policy. It reflected a form of economic expansionism that has been called "informal empire." The U.S. government did not seek Chinese territory, but it did want access to Chinese markets for American businesses.

As Hay pursued this effort, a more urgent threat emerged. For years, antiforeign feeling had simmered in China, fanned by the aged Ch'ing empress, who hated the West's growing influence. In 1899, a fanatical antiforeign secret society known as the Harmonious Righteous Fists (called "Boxers" by Western journalists) killed thousands of foreigners and Chinese Christians. In June 1900, the Boxers occupied Beijing (Peking), the Chinese capital, and besieged the foreign legations. The United States contributed twenty-five hundred soldiers to an international army that marched on Beijing, quashed the **Boxer Rebellion,** and rescued the occupants of the threatened legations.

The Boxers' defeat further weakened China's government. Fearing that the regime's collapse would allow European powers to carve up China, Hay issued a second, more important, series of **Open Door notes** in 1900. He reaffirmed the principle of open trade in China for all nations and announced America's determination to preserve China's territorial and administrative integrity. In general, China remained open to U.S. business interests and Christian missionaries. In the 1930s, when Japanese expansionism menaced China, Hay's policy helped shape the American response.

Along with U.S. economic expansion in China came missionary activity. American Protestant missionaries had come to Hawaii as early as the 1820s, and by the late nineteenth century they had reached China as well. Indeed, by 1900 some five thousand U.S. missionaries were active in China, Africa, India, and elsewhere. As they preached their religious message, the missionaries also spread American influence globally and blazed the way for U.S. economic expansion. As a U.S. diplomat in China wrote in 1895: "Missionaries are the pioneers for American trade and commerce. . . . The missionary, inspired by holy zeal, goes everywhere, and by degrees foreign trade and commerce follow."

CHRONOLOGY, 1902–1920

1899 • First U.S. Open Door note seeking access to China market.
Boxer Rebellion erupts in China.

1900 • Second U.S. Open Door note.

1904 • President Theodore Roosevelt proclaims "Roosevelt Corollary" to Monroe Doctrine.

1905 • Roosevelt mediates the end of the Russo-Japanese War.

1906 • At the request of Roosevelt, San Francisco ends segregation of Asian schoolchildren.
Panama Canal construction begins.

1911 • U.S.-backed revolution in Nicaragua.

1912 • U.S. Marines occupy Nicaragua.

1914 • U.S. troops occupy Veracruz, Mexico.
Panama Canal opens.
World War I begins.
President Wilson proclaims American neutrality.

1915 • U.S. Marines occupy Haiti and the Dominican Republic.
Woman's Peace Party organized.
British liner *Lusitania* sunk by German U-boat.
Wilson permits U.S. bank loans to Allies.

1916 • U.S. punitive expedition invades Mexico, seeking Pancho Villa.
Germany pledges not to attack merchant ships without warning.
Wilson reelected.

1917 • U.S. troops withdraw from Mexico.
Germany resumes unrestricted U-boat warfare; United States declares war.
Selective Service Act sets up national draft.
War Industries Board, Committee on Public Information, and Food Administration created.
Espionage Act passed.
War Risk Insurance Act authorizes payments to servicemen's dependents.
NAACP march in New York City protests upsurge in lynchings.
Bolsheviks seize power in Russia; Russia leaves the war.
New York State passes woman-suffrage referendum.
U.S. government operates the nation's railroads.
Striking miners forcibly expelled from Bisbee, Arizona.

1918 • Wilson outlines Fourteen Points.
Sedition Amendment passed.
Global influenza pandemic takes heavy toll in United States.
National War Labor Board created.

American forces see action at Château-Thierry,
Belleau Wood, St. Mihiel, and Meuse-Argonne campaign.
Republicans win control of both houses of Congress (November 5).
Armistice signed (November 11).

1919 • Eighteenth Amendment added to the Constitution (prohibition).
Peace treaty, including League of Nations covenant, signed at Versailles.
Supreme Court upholds silencing of war critics in *Schenck* v. *United States.*
Upsurge of lynchings; racial violence in Chicago.
Wilson suffers paralyzing stroke.
Versailles treaty, with League covenant, rejected by Senate.

1920 • "Red raids" organized by Justice Department.
Nineteenth Amendment added to the Constitution (woman suffrage).
Warren G. Harding elected president.

The Panama Canal: Hardball Diplomacy   Traders had long dreamed of a canal across the forty-mile-wide ribbon of land joining North and South America to eliminate the hazardous voyage around South America. In 1879 a French company secured permission from Colombia to build a canal across Panama, then part of Colombia. But mismanagement and yellow fever doomed the project, and ten years and $400 million later, it went bankrupt. Seeking to recoup its losses, the French company offered its assets, including the concession from Colombia, to the United States for $109 million.

America was in an expansionist mood. In 1902, after the French lowered their price to $40 million, Congress authorized President Theodore Roosevelt to accept the offer. The following year, Secretary of State Hay signed an agreement with a Colombian diplomat granting the United States a ninety-nine-year lease on the proposed canal for a down payment of $10 million and an annual fee of $250,000. But the Colombian senate, seeking a better deal, rejected the agreement. An outraged Roosevelt privately denounced the Colombians as "greedy little anthropoids."

Determined to have his canal, Roosevelt found a willing collaborator in Philippe Bunau-Varilla, an official of the bankrupt French company. Dismayed that his company might lose its $40 million, Bunau-Varilla organized a "revolution" in Panama from a New York hotel room. While his wife stitched a flag, he wrote a declaration of independence and a constitution for the new nation. When the "revolution" occurred as scheduled on November 3, 1903, a U.S. warship hovered offshore. Proclaiming Panama's independence, Bunau-Varilla appointed himself its first ambassador to the United States. John Hay quickly recognized the newly hatched nation and signed a treaty with Bunau-Varilla granting the United States a ten-mile-wide strip of land across Panama "in perpetuity" (that is, forever) on the terms earlier rejected by Colombia. Theodore Roosevelt later summed up the episode: "I took the Canal Zone, and let Congress debate, and while the debate goes on, the canal does also."

The U.S. canal builders' first challenge was the yellow fever that had haunted the French. Leading this effort was Dr. Walter Reed of the Army Medical Corps. Earlier, in a research project in Cuba, Reed and his team had used themselves and army volunteers as experimental subjects to prove that female mosquitoes that bred in stagnant water spread the yellow fever virus. In Panama, Reed organized a large-scale drainage project that eradicated the disease-bearing mosquito—a remarkable public-health achievement. Construction began in 1906, and in 1914 the first ship sailed through the **Panama Canal.** In 1921, implicitly conceding the dubious methods used to acquire the Canal Zone, the U.S. Senate voted a payment of $25 million to Colombia. But the ill feeling generated by Theodore Roosevelt's actions, combined with other instances of U.S. interventionism, would long shadow U.S.–Latin American relations.

Roosevelt and Taft Assert U.S. Power in Latin America and Asia   While the Panama Canal remains this era's best-known foreign-policy achievement, other U.S. actions underscored Washington's growing determination to assert U.S. power and protect U.S. business interests in Latin America and Asia. Two crises early in Theodore Roosevelt's presidency followed European intervention in Latin America. In 1902, German, British, and Italian warships blockaded and bombarded the ports of Venezuela, which had defaulted on its debts to European investors. The standoff ended when all sides agreed to Roosevelt's proposal of arbitration.

The second crisis flared in 1904 when several European nations threatened to invade the Dominican Republic, a Caribbean island nation that had also defaulted on its debts. Roosevelt reacted swiftly. If any nation intervened, he believed, it should be the United States. While denying any territorial ambitions in Latin America, Roosevelt in December 1904 declared that "chronic wrongdoing" by any Latin American nation would justify U.S. intervention.

This pronouncement has been called "the Roosevelt Corollary" to the 1823 Monroe Doctrine, which had warned European powers against meddling in Latin America. Now Roosevelt asserted that in cases of "wrongdoing" (a word he left undefined), the United States had the right to intervene. Suiting actions to words, the Roosevelt administration took over the Dominican Republic's customs service for two years and managed its foreign debt. Roosevelt summed up his foreign-policy approach in a 1901 speech quoting what he said was an old African proverb, "Speak softly and carry a big stick."

The foreign policy of the Taft administration (1909–1913) focused on advancing American commercial interests, a policy some called "dollar diplomacy." A U.S.-backed revolution in Nicaragua in 1911 brought to power Adolfo Díaz, an officer of an American-owned mine. Washington feared growing British influence in Nicaragua's affairs, and also worried that a foreign power might build a canal across Nicaragua to rival the Panama Canal. In exchange for control of Nicaragua's national bank, customs service, and railroad, American bankers lent Díaz's government $1.5 million. When a revolt against Díaz broke out in 1912, Taft sent in the marines to protect the bankers' investment. Except for one brief interval, they remained until 1933.

In Asia, too, both Roosevelt and Taft sought to project U.S. power and advance American business interests. In 1900, exploiting the turmoil caused by the Boxer uprising, Russian troops occupied Manchuria, and Russia promoted its commercial interests by building railroads. This alarmed the Japanese, who also had designs on

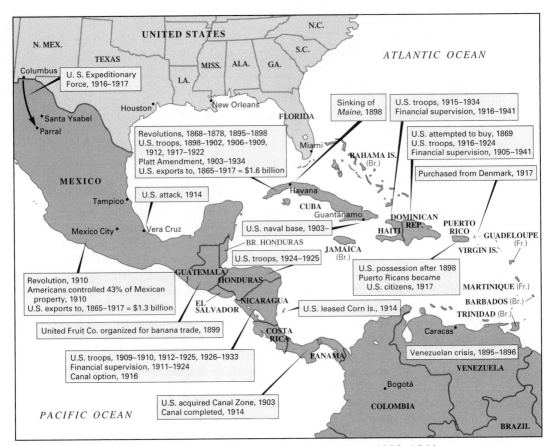

MAP 22.1 U.S. Hegemony in the Caribbean and Latin America, 1900–1941

Through many interventions, territorial acquisitions, and robust economic expansion, the United States became the predominant power in Latin America in the early twentieth century. Acting on Theodore Roosevelt's assertion of a U.S. right to combat "wrongdoing" in Latin America and the Caribbean, the United States dispatched troops to the region, where they met nationalist opposition.

Manchuria and nearby Korea. In February 1904 a surprise Japanese attack destroyed Russian ships anchored at Port Arthur, Manchuria. Japan completely dominated in the Russo-Japanese War that followed. For the first time, an Asian power had checked European imperialist expansion.

Roosevelt, while pleased to see Russian expansionism challenged, believed that a Japanese victory would disrupt the Asian balance of power and threaten America's position in the Philippines. Accordingly, he invited Japan and Russia to a peace conference at Portsmouth, New Hampshire. In September 1905 the two rivals signed a peace treaty. Russia recognized Japan's rule in Korea and made other territorial concessions. After this outcome, curbing Japanese expansionism—peacefully, if possible—became America's major objective in Asia. For his role in ending the war, Roosevelt received the Nobel Peace Prize.

In 1906, U.S.-Japanese relations soured when the San Francisco school board, reflecting West Coast hostility to Asian immigrants, assigned all Asian children to segregated schools. Japan angrily protested this insult. Summoning the school board to Washington, Roosevelt persuaded them to reverse this discriminatory policy. In return, in 1908 the administration negotiated a "gentlemen's agreement" with Japan by which Tokyo pledged to halt Japanese emigration to America. Racist attitudes continued to poison U.S.-Japanese relations, however. In 1913, California prohibited Japanese aliens from owning land.

While Californians warned of the "yellow peril," Japanese journalists, eyeing America's military strength and involvement in Asia, spoke of a "white peril." In 1907 Roosevelt ordered sixteen gleaming U.S. battleships on a "training operation" to Japan. Although officially treated as friendly, this "Great White Fleet" underscored America's growing naval might.

Under President Taft, U.S. foreign policy in Asia continued to focus on dollar diplomacy, which in this case meant promoting U.S. commercial interests in China—the same goal Secretary of State John Hay had sought with his Open Door notes. A plan for a U.S.-financed railroad in Manchuria did not work out, however. Not only did U.S. bankers find the project too risky, but Russia and Japan signed a treaty carving up Manchuria for commercial purposes, freezing out the Americans.

Wilson and Latin America

Taking office in 1913 as the first Democratic president in sixteen years, Woodrow Wilson criticized his Republican predecessors' expansionist policies. The United States, he pledged, would "never again seek one additional foot of territory by conquest." But he, too, soon intervened in Latin America. In 1915, after upheavals in Haiti and the Dominican Republic (two nations sharing the Caribbean island of Santo Domingo), Wilson sent in U.S. marines, who brutally suppressed Haitian resistance to U.S. rule. A Haitian constitution favorable to U.S. commercial interests was overwhelmingly ratified in a 1918 vote supervised by the marines. The marines occupied the Dominican Republic until 1924 and Haiti until 1934.

The most serious crisis Wilson faced in Latin America was the Mexican Revolution. Mexico had won independence from Spain in 1820, but the nation remained divided between a landowning elite and an impoverished peasantry. In 1911, rebels led by the democratic reformer Francisco Madero had ended the thirty-year rule of President Porfirio Díaz, who had defended the interests of the wealthy elite. Early in 1913, just as Wilson took office, Mexican troops loyal to General Victoriano Huerta, a full-blooded Indian, overthrew and murdered Madero.

Amid the chaos, Wilson tried to promote good government, protect U.S. investments, and safeguard U.S. citizens living in Mexico or along its border. Forty thousand Americans had settled in Mexico under Díaz's regime, and U.S. investors had poured some $2 billion into Mexican oil wells and other ventures. Reversing the long-standing U.S. policy of recognizing all governments, Wilson refused to recognize Huerta's regime, which he called "a government of butchers." Authorizing arms sales to General Venustiano Carranza, Huerta's rival, Wilson also ordered the port of Veracruz blockaded to prevent a shipment of German arms from reaching Huerta. Announced Wilson, "I am going to teach the South American republics to elect good men." In April 1914 seven thousand U.S. troops occupied Veracruz and engaged Huerta's forces.

Woodrow Wilson, Schoolteacher *This 1914 political cartoon captures the patronizing tone of Wilson's approach to Latin America, which planted the seeds of long-term resentments.*

Sixty-five Americans and approximately five hundred Mexicans were killed or wounded. Bowing to U.S. might, Huerta abdicated; Carranza took power; and the U.S. troops withdrew.

But the turmoil continued. In January 1916, a bandit chieftain in northern Mexico, Pancho Villa, murdered sixteen U.S. mining engineers. Soon after, Villa's gang burned the town of Columbus, New Mexico, and killed nineteen inhabitants. Enraged Americans demanded action. Wilson dispatched a punitive expedition under General **John J. Pershing.** When Pancho Villa not only eluded Pershing but brazenly staged another cross-border raid into Texas, Wilson ordered 150,000 National Guardsmen to the Mexican border—a massive response that stirred anti-American feelings among Mexico's poor, for whom Villa was a folk hero. (Villa ended his raids in 1920 in exchange for a large grant of land from the Mexican government, but he was assassinated in 1923.)

Although soon overshadowed by World War I, these involvements in Asia and Latin America illuminate the U.S. foreign-policy goal, which was, essentially, to achieve a global order that would welcome both American political values and American business. President Wilson summed up this view in a 1916 speech to the "World's Salesmanship Congress" meeting in Detroit: "[C]arry liberty and justice and the principles of humanity wherever you go. . . . [G]o out and sell goods that will make the world more comfortable and more happy, and convert them to the principles of America." Wilson's vision of an American-based world order shaped his response to a crisis unfolding in Europe.

These early-twentieth-century foreign involvements also illustrate the underlying world view of the old-stock, upper-class men who directed U.S. foreign policy. Convinced of their ethnic, gender, and social superiority, they confidently promoted America's global economic and political interests while viewing with patronizing condescension the "backward" societies they sought to manipulate.

WAR IN EUROPE, 1914–1917

When war engulfed Europe in 1914, most Americans wished only to remain aloof. For nearly three years, the United States officially stayed neutral. But by April 1917 cultural ties to England and France, economic considerations, visions of a world remade in America's image, and German violations of Wilson's definition of neutral rights all combined to draw the United States into the maelstrom.

The Coming of War With Europe at peace through much of the nineteenth century, some concluded that war was a thing of the past. However, a series of ominous developments, including a complex web of alliances, suggested otherwise. Germany, Austria-Hungary, and Italy signed a mutual-defense treaty in 1882, forming the Triple Alliance. In 1904 and 1907, Great Britain signed treaties with France and Russia, creating what came to be called the Triple Entente.

Beyond the treaties, imperial ambitions and nationalistic passions stirred. The once-powerful Ottoman Empire, centered in Turkey, weakened in the 1870s, leaving in its wake such newly independent nations as Romania, Bulgaria, and Serbia.

Serbian patriots dreamed of expanding their boundaries to include Serbs living in Bosnia-Herzegovina, Serbia's neighbor to the west. Russia, home to millions of Slavs, the same ethnic group as the Serbs, supported these ambitions. Meanwhile, the Austro-Hungarian Empire, with its capital in Vienna, also saw opportunities for expansion as Ottoman power faded. In 1908, Austria-Hungary annexed (took over) Bosnia-Herzegovina, alarming Russia and Serbia.

Germany, ruled by Kaiser Wilhelm II, also displayed expansionist impulses. Germany had achieved national unification only in 1871, and many Germans believed that their nation had lagged in the race for empire. Expansion, modernization, and military power became the goal in Berlin.

Such was the context when Archduke Franz Ferdinand of Austria made a state visit to Bosnia in June 1914. As he and his wife rode in an open car through Sarajevo, the Bosnian capital, a young Bosnian Serb gunned them down. In response, Austria declared war on Serbia. Russia, aligned with Serbia by a secret treaty, mobilized for war. Germany declared war on Russia and France. Great Britain, linked by treaty to France, declared war on Germany. An assassin's bullets had plunged Europe into war.

Thus began what contemporaries called the Great War, which we know as World War I. On one side were Great Britain, Russia, and France, called the Allies. On the other side were the Central Powers: Germany and Austria-Hungary. Italy, initially neutral despite its alliance with the Central Powers, joined the Allies in 1915.

The Perils of Neutrality Proclaiming U.S. neutrality, President Wilson urged the nation to be neutral "in thought as well as in action." Most Americans fervently agreed. A popular song summed up the mood: "I Didn't Raise My Boy to Be a Soldier." Fifteen hundred women marched down New York's Fifth Avenue protesting the war. Carrie Chapman Catt and other feminists joined Jane Addams in forming the Woman's Peace Party.

Neutrality proved difficult, however. Wilson privately dreaded a victory by militaristic Germany. Strong economic interests bound the United States and Britain. Many Americans, including Wilson himself, had ancestral ties to England. Well-to-do Americans routinely traveled to England. Schoolbooks stressed the English origins of American institutions. The English language itself—the language of Shakespeare, Dickens, and the King James Bible—deepened the bond. British propaganda subtly stressed the British-American link.

Many German-Americans, by contrast, sympathized with Germany's cause. Irish-Americans speculated that a German victory might free Ireland from British rule. Some Scandinavian immigrants identified more with Germany than with England. But these cultural and ethnic cross-currents did not at first override Wilson's commitment to neutrality. For most Americans, staying out of the conflict became the chief goal.

Neutral in 1914, America went to war in 1917. What caused this turnabout? Fundamentally, Wilson's vision of a world order in America's image conflicted with his neutrality. An international system based on democracy and capitalism would be impossible, he believed, in a world dominated by imperial Germany. Even an Allied victory would not ensure a transformed world order, Wilson gradually became convinced, without a U.S. role in the postwar settlement. To shape the peace, America would have to fight the war.

These underlying ideas influenced Wilson's handling of the immediate issue that dragged the United States into the conflict: neutral nations' rights on the high seas. When the war began, Britain intercepted U.S. merchant ships bound for Germany, insisting that their cargo might aid Germany's war effort. Wilson's protests intensified in late 1914 and early 1915 when Britain declared the North Sea a war zone; planted it with explosive mines; and blockaded all German ports, choking off Germany's imports, including food. Britain was determined to exploit its naval advantage, even if it meant alienating America.

But Germany, not England, ultimately pushed the United States into war. If Britannia ruled the waves, Germany controlled the ocean depths with its torpedo-equipped submarines, or U-boats. In February 1915 Berlin proclaimed the waters around Great Britain a war zone and warned off all ships. Wilson quickly responded: Germany would be held to "strict accountability" for any loss of U.S. ships or lives.

On May 1, 1915, in a small ad in U.S. newspapers, the German embassy cautioned Americans against travel on British or French vessels. Six days later, a U-boat sank the British liner *Lusitania* off the Irish coast, with the loss of 1,198 lives, including 128 Americans. (The *Lusitania*, historians later discovered, had carried munitions destined for England, a secret traffic in weapons known to British officials.)

In three stern notes to Germany, Wilson demanded that Berlin stop unrestricted submarine warfare and pay reparations for the U.S. deaths in the *Lusitania* sinking. Addressing the American public, however, he insisted that the United States could persuade the belligerents to recognize the principle of neutral rights without going to war. "There is such a thing as a man being too proud to fight," he said.

The *Lusitania* disaster exposed deep divisions in U.S. public opinion. Many Americans, now ready for war, ridiculed Wilson's "too proud to fight" speech. Theodore

Roosevelt denounced the president's "abject cowardice." The National Security League, a lobby of bankers and industrialists, promoted a U.S. arms buildup and universal military training and organized "preparedness" parades in major cities. By late 1915 Wilson himself called for a military buildup.

Other citizens, however, deplored the drift toward war. Some progressives warned that war fever was eroding support for reforms. Jane Addams lamented that the international movements to reduce infant mortality and improve care for the aged had been "scattered to the winds by the war." Late in 1915, automaker Henry Ford chartered a vessel to take a group of pacifists to Scandinavia to persuade the belligerents to accept neutral mediation and end the war by Christmas.

Divisions surfaced even within the Wilson administration. Secretary of State William Jennings Bryan, believing that Wilson's *Lusitania* notes were too hostile, resigned in June 1915. His successor, Robert Lansing, proved weak, and Wilson himself played the key role in shaping U.S. policy.

Some neutrality advocates concluded that incidents like the *Lusitania* crisis were inevitable if Americans persisted in sailing on belligerent ships. Early in 1916, Congress considered a bill to ban such travel, but President Wilson successfully opposed it, insisting that the principle of neutral rights must be upheld.

For a time, Wilson's approach seemed to work. Germany ordered U-boats to spare passenger ships, and offered compensation for the Americans lost in the *Lusitania* sinking. In March 1916, however, a German submarine sank a French passenger ship, the *Sussex*, in the English Channel, injuring several Americans. Wilson threatened to break diplomatic relations—a step toward war. In response, Berlin pledged not to attack merchant vessels without warning, provided that Great Britain, too, observed "the rules of international law." Ignoring this qualification, Wilson announced Germany's acceptance of American demands and the crisis eased.

Meanwhile, U.S. banks' support for the Allies eroded the principle of neutrality. Early in the war, Secretary of State Bryan had rejected banker J. P. Morgan's request to extend loans to France. Such loans, said Bryan, would violate "the true spirit of neutrality." But economic considerations, combined with outrage over the *Lusitania* sinking, undermined this policy. In August 1915, Treasury Secretary William G. McAdoo warned Wilson that Allied purchases of American munitions and farm products were essential "[t]o maintain our prosperity." Only substantial loans to England, agreed Secretary of State Lansing, could prevent serious financial problems in the United States, including "unrest . . . among the laboring classes." The neutrality principle must not "stand in the way of our national interests," warned Lansing.

Swayed by such arguments and personally sympathetic to the Allies, Wilson permitted Morgan's bank to lend $500 million to the British and French governments. By April 1917, U.S. banks had lent $2.3 billion to the Allies, in contrast to $27 million to Germany.

While Americans concentrated on neutral rights, the land war settled into a grim stalemate. A September 1914 German drive into France bogged down along the Marne River. The two sides then dug in, constructing trenches across France from the English Channel to the Swiss border. For more than three years, this line scarcely changed. Occasional offensives took a terrible toll. A German attack in February 1916 began with the capture of two forts near the town of Verdun and ended that June with the French recapture of the same two forts, now nothing but rubble, at a horrendous cost in human life. Trench warfare was a nightmare of mud, lice, rats, artillery bursts, poison gas, and random death.

British propaganda focused on the atrocities committed by "the Huns" (a derogatory term for Germans). After the war, much of this propaganda was exposed as false. Seized documents revealing German espionage in U.S. war plants, however, further discredited the German cause.

The war dominated the 1916 presidential election. Wilson faced Republican Charles Evans Hughes, a former New York governor (and future chief justice of the U.S. Supreme Court). The Democrats' campaign theme emerged when a convention speaker, praising Wilson's foreign policy, aroused wild applause as he ended each episode with the refrain "We didn't go to war."

Hughes criticized Wilson's lack of aggressiveness while rebuking him for policies that risked war. Theodore Roosevelt, still much admired, campaigned more for war than for the Republican ticket. The only difference between Wilson and the bearded Hughes, he jeered, was a shave. While Hughes did well among Irish-Americans and German-Americans who considered Wilson too pro-British, Wilson held the Democratic base and won support from women voters in western states that had adopted woman suffrage. Wilson's victory, although close, revealed the strength of the popular longing for peace as late as November 1916.

The United States Enters the War   In January 1917, facing stalemate on the ground, Germany resumed unrestricted submarine warfare. Germany's military leaders believed that even if the United States declared war as a result, full-scale U-boat warfare could bring victory before American troops reached the front.

Events now rushed forward. Wilson broke diplomatic relations on February 3. During February and March, U-boats sank five American ships. A coded telegram from the German foreign secretary, Arthur Zimmermann, to Germany's ambassador to Mexico promised that if Mexico would declare war on the United States, Germany would help restore Mexico's "lost territories" of Texas, Arizona, and New Mexico. Intercepted and decoded by the British, the "Zimmermann telegram" further inflamed the war spirit in America.

Events in distant Russia also helped create favorable conditions for America's entry into the war. In March 1917 Russian peasants, industrial workers, intellectuals inspired by Western liberal values, and revolutionaries who embraced the communist ideology of Karl Marx all joined in an uprising that overthrew the repressive government of Tsar Nicholas II. A provisional government under the liberal Alexander Kerensky briefly seemed to promise a democratic Russia, making it easier for President Wilson to portray the war as a battle for democracy. Many Americans, little understanding conditions in Russia, shared Wilson's hope that a liberal democratic state on the American model would eventually emerge.

On April 2, Wilson appeared before a joint session of Congress and called for a declaration of war. Applause rang out as Wilson described his vision of America's role in creating a postwar international order to make the world "safe for democracy." As the speech ended, Republican senator Henry Cabot Lodge of Massachusetts, one of Wilson's staunchest political foes, rushed forward to shake his hand.

After a short but bitter debate, the Senate voted 82 to 6 for war. The House agreed, 373 to 50. Three key factors—German attacks on American shipping, U.S. economic investment in the Allied cause, and American cultural links to the Allies, especially England—had propelled the United States into the war.

MOBILIZING AT HOME, FIGHTING IN FRANCE, 1917–1918

America's entry into World War I underscored a deepening international involvement that had been underway for several decades. Yet compared to its effects on Europe, the war only grazed the United States. Russia, ill-prepared for war and geographically isolated from its allies, suffered heavily. France, Great Britain, and Germany fought for more than four years; the United States, for nineteen months. Their armies suffered casualties of 70 percent or more; the U.S. casualty rate was 8 percent. The fighting left parts of France and Belgium brutally scarred; North America was physically untouched. Nevertheless, the war profoundly affected America. It changed not only those who participated in it directly, but also the home front and the nation's government and economy.

Raising, Training, and Testing an Army

April 1917 found America's military woefully unprepared. The regular army consisted of 120,000 men, few with combat experience, plus 80,000 National Guard members. An aging officer corps dozed away the years until retirement. Ammunition reserves were paltry. The War Department was a jungle of jealous bureaucrats, one of whom hoarded thousands of typewriters as the war approached.

While army chief-of-staff Peyton C. March brought order to the military bureaucracy, Wilson's secretary of war, Newton D. Baker, concentrated on raising an army. Formerly the reform mayor of Cleveland, Baker lacked administrative talent but was a public-relations genius. The **Selective Service Act** of May 1917 required all men between twenty-one and thirty (later expanded to eighteen through forty-five) to register with local draft boards. Mindful of the Civil War draft riots, Baker planned the draft-registration day, June 5, 1917, as a "festive and patriotic occasion."

By the war's end in November 1918, more than 24 million men had registered, of whom nearly 3 million were drafted. Volunteers and National Guardsmen swelled the total to 4.3 million. Recruits got their first taste of army life in home-front training camps. Along with military discipline and combat instruction, the camps built morale through shows, games, and recreation provided by volunteer organizations. The American Library Association contributed books. YMCA volunteers staffed base clubs and offered classes in literacy, French slang, and Bible study. In Plattsburgh, New York, local women opened a "Hostess House" to provide a touch of domesticity for homesick recruits. The idea soon spread to other communities near military camps.

The War Department monitored the off-duty behavior of young men cut off from family and community. The **Commission on Training Camp Activities** presented films, lectures, and posters on the dangers of alcohol and prostitution. Any soldier disabled by venereal (that is, sexually transmitted) disease, one poster warned, "is a Traitor!" Trainees were confined to camp until nearby towns closed brothels and saloons. The army's antiliquor, antiprostitution policies strengthened the moral-reform campaigns of the Progressive Era (see Chapter 21).

Beginning in December 1917, all recruits also underwent intelligence testing. Psychologists eager to demonstrate the usefulness of their new field claimed that tests measuring recruits' "intelligence quotient" (IQ) could help in assigning their duties and showing who had officer potential. Intelligence testing, declared the president of the American Psychological Association, would "help win the war."

When the psychologists announced that a high percentage of recruits were "morons," editorial writers reacted with alarm. In fact, the tests mostly revealed that many recruits lacked formal education and cultural sophistication. One question asked whether *mauve* was a drink, a color, a fabric, or a food. Another asked in which city a particular make of automobile was built. The testing also reinforced racial and ethnic stereotypes: native-born recruits of northern European origins scored highest; African-Americans and recent immigrants lowest.

In short, the World War I training camps not only turned civilians into soldiers, but also reinforced the prewar moral-control reforms, and signaled changes ahead, including a vogue for standardized testing.

Some twelve thousand Native Americans served in the **American Expeditionary Force** (AEF). While some reformers eager to preserve Indian culture argued for all-Indian units, military officials integrated Native Americans into the general army. Some observers predicted that the wartime experience would hasten the assimilation of Indians into mainstream American life, considered by many a desirable goal at the time.

In April 1917 the African-American leader W. E. B. Du Bois urged African-Americans to "close ranks" and support the war. Some blacks resisted the draft, especially in the South (see "Wartime Intolerance and Dissent"), but most followed Du Bois's advice. More than 260,000 blacks volunteered or were drafted, and 50,000 went to France. Racism pervaded the military, as it did American society. The navy assigned blacks only to menial positions, and the marines excluded them altogether.

Blacks in training camps endured crude racial abuse. One racist senator from Mississippi warned that the sight of "arrogant, strutting" black soldiers would trigger race riots. Tensions exploded in Houston in August 1917 when some black soldiers, endlessly goaded by local whites, seized weapons from the armory and killed seventeen white civilians. After a hasty trial with no appeal process, thirteen black soldiers were hanged and forty-one imprisoned for life. Not since the 1906 Brownsville Incident (see Chapter 21) had black confidence in military justice been so shaken.

Organizing the Economy for War   The war years of 1917–1918 helped shape modern America. The war's administrative innovations sped up longer-term processes of social reorganization. The war furthered many key developments of the 1920s and beyond—including the spread of mass production; the collaboration between government, business, and labor; and the growth of new professional and managerial elites.

The war led to unprecedented government oversight of the economy and the regulation of corporations, something Populists and progressives had long urged. In 1916, Congress had created an advisory body, the Council of National Defense, to oversee the government's preparedness program. After war was declared, this council set up the **War Industries Board** (WIB) to coordinate military purchasing; ensure production efficiency; and provide weapons, equipment, and supplies to the military. Wilson reorganized the WIB in March 1918 and put Bernard Baruch in charge. A South Carolinian of German-Jewish origin, Baruch had made a fortune on Wall Street. Under Baruch, the WIB controlled the industrial sector. It allocated raw materials, established production priorities, and induced competing companies to standardize and coordinate their products and processes to save scarce commodities. The standardization of bicycle manufacturing, for example, saved tons of steel.

Acting under legislation passed in August 1917, Wilson set up two more new agencies, the Fuel Administration and the Food Administration. The Fuel Administration controlled coal output, regulated fuel prices and consumption, and introduced daylight-saving time—an idea first proposed by Benjamin Franklin. The Food Administration, headed by Herbert Hoover, oversaw the production and allocation of wheat, meat, and sugar to ensure supplies for the army as well as for the desperately food-short Allies. Born in poverty in Iowa, Hoover had prospered as a mining engineer in Asia. He was organizing food relief in Belgium when Wilson brought him back to Washington.

These regulatory agencies relied on voluntary cooperation reinforced by government propaganda. Food Administration posters and magazine ads urged Americans to conserve food. Housewives signed pledges to observe "Meatless Monday" and "Wheatless Wednesday." Slogans such as "Serve Beans by All Means" promoted substitutes for scarce commodities.

Harriot Stanton Blatch, daughter of woman's-rights pioneer Elizabeth Cady Stanton, headed the Food Administration's Speakers' Bureau, which spread the administration's conservation message. Blatch also organized the Woman's Land Army, which recruited women to replace male farm workers.

These agencies were the tip of the regulatory iceberg. Nearly five thousand government boards supervised home-front activities. These included the National War Labor Board, which resolved labor-management disputes that jeopardized production, and the Railroad Administration, headed by Treasury Secretary William McAdoo. When a railroad tie-up during the winter of 1917–1918 threatened the flow of supplies to Europe, the Railroad Administration stepped in and soon transformed the thousands of miles of track operated by competing companies into an efficient national rail system.

American business, much criticized by progressive reformers, utilized the war emergency to improve its image. Corporate executives ran regulatory agencies. Factory owners distributed prowar propaganda to workers. Trade associations coordinated war production.

The war sped up the ongoing process of corporate consolidation and economic integration. In place of trustbusting, the government now encouraged cooperation among businesses. As corporate mergers jumped sharply, one magazine observed, "The war has accelerated . . . a tendency that was already irresistible. . . . Instead of punishing companies for acting in concert, the government is now in some cases forcing them to unite."

Overall, the war was good for business. Despite added taxes imposed by Congress, profits soared. After-tax profits in the copper industry, for example, jumped from 12 percent in 1913 to 24 percent in 1917.

The old laissez-faire suspicion of government, already weakened, eroded further in 1917–1918. The wartime regulatory agencies disappeared quickly after the war, but their influence lingered. In the 1930s, when the nation faced a different crisis, the government activism of World War I would be remembered (see Chapter 24).

With the American
Expeditionary
Force in France

When the United States entered the conflict, Allied prospects looked bleak. German U-boat attacks were taking a horrendous toll on Allied shipping. French troops mutinied after a failed French assault on the Marne. A British offensive along the French-Belgian border in November 1917 gained four miles at a cost of more than four hundred thousand killed and wounded. That same month, the Italian army suffered a disastrous defeat at Caporetto near the Austrian border.

Russia, ill-prepared for war, had suffered serious setbacks, contributing to the revolutionary upheaval. The communist faction of the revolution, the Bolsheviks (Russian for "majority"), gained strength when its top leaders, including Vladimir Lenin and Leon Trotsky, returned from exile abroad. On November 6, 1917 (October 24 by the Russian calendar), a Bolshevik coup overthrew Alexander Kerensky's provisional government and effectively removed Russia from the war. Early in 1918, the Bolsheviks signed an armistice with Germany, the Treaty of Brest-Litovsk, freeing thousands of German troops on the Russian front for fighting in France.

An important advance in military technology came in November 1917 when the British mobilized three hundred tanks along a six-mile section of the front near Cambrai, France, shattering the German defenses. Still the stalemate continued, punctuated by periodic battles.

Initially, U.S. aid to the Allies consisted of munitions and convoys to protect Allied ships crossing the dangerous Atlantic. The first U.S. troops reached France in October 1917. Eventually about 2 million American soldiers served in France as members of the AEF under General John J. Pershing. Ironically, Pershing was of German origin; his family name had been Pfoersching. A West Point graduate and commander of the 1916 expedition against Pancho Villa in Mexico, Pershing was an iron-willed officer with a ramrod bearing, steely eyes, and trim mustache. The death of his wife and three of their children in a fire in 1915 had further hardened him.

Most men of the AEF at first found the war a great adventure. Plucked from towns and farms, they sailed for Europe on crowded freighters; a lucky few traveled on captured German passenger liners. Once in France, railroad freight cars marked "HOMMES 40, CHEVAUX 8" (forty men, eight horses) took them to the front. Then began the routine of marching, training—and waiting.

The African-Americans with the AEF in France worked mainly as mess-boys (mealtime aides), laborers, and stevedores (ship-cargo handlers). Although discriminatory, the latter assignments vitally aided the war effort. Sometimes working twenty-four hours nonstop, black stevedores efficiently unloaded supply ships. Some whites of the AEF pressed the French to treat African-Americans as inferiors, but most ignored this advice and related to blacks without prejudice. This eye-opening experience would remain with black veterans after the war. Except for two segregated divisions, African-Americans did not engage in combat. Only in death was the AEF integrated: graves in military cemeteries were not segregated by race.

For the troops at the front, aerial dogfights between German and Allied reconnaissance planes offered spectacular sideshows. Germany's legendary "Red Baron," Manfred von Richthofen, shot down eighty British and French planes before his luck ran out in April 1918. In 1916, a group of American volunteers had joined the French air corps as the Lafayette Escadrille. Secretary of War Baker, grasping the importance of air power, pushed for plane construction. The program lagged, however—a rare U.S. war-production failure.

France offered other diversions as well, and the U.S. military warned recruits of the danger of venereal disease. One poster declared, "A German bullet is cleaner than a whore." When the French premier, Georges Clemenceau, offered to provide prostitutes for the American troops (as was the French practice), Secretary of War Baker exclaimed, "For God's sake, don't show this to the President, or he'll stop the war."

The YMCA, Red Cross, and Salvation Army, including many young American women volunteers, provided a touch of home. Some 16,500 U.S. women served directly in the AEF as nurses, telephone operators, canteen workers, and secretaries.

To underscore America's distinctive role in the war and to ensure a strong U.S. voice at the peace table, President Wilson insisted that the United States be called an "Associate Power" of the Allies. The Allied generals, facing desperate circumstances, wanted to absorb the Americans into existing units. But for both military and political reasons, Pershing and his superiors in Washington insisted that the AEF be "distinct and separate." Pershing, favoring aggressive combat, abhorred the defensive mentality ingrained by three years of trench warfare.

In March 1918, however, when Germany launched a major offensive along the Somme, the Allies created a unified command under Marshal Ferdinand Foch, chief of the French general staff. Some Americans participated in the fighting around Amiens and Armentières that stemmed the German advance.

The Germans' spring 1918 offensive resumed in May along the Aisne River, where they broke through to the Marne and faced a nearly open route to Paris, fifty miles away. On June 4, as the French government prepared for evacuation, American forces arrived in strength. Parts of three U.S. divisions and a marine brigade helped stop the Germans at the town of Château-Thierry and nearby Belleau Wood. (An AEF division at full strength consisted of twenty-seven thousand men and one thousand officers, plus twelve thousand support troops.)

These two German offensives had punched deep holes (or salients) in the Allied line. A German drive aimed at the cathedral city of Rheims between these two salients was stopped with the help of some eighty-five thousand American troops. This was the war's turning point. At enormous cost, the German offensive had been defeated. Contributing to this defeat was the fact that many German soldiers, already weakened by battle fatigue and poor diet, fell victim to influenza, an infectious disease that would soon emerge as a deadly worldwide epidemic (see "Public-Health Crisis: The 1918 Influenza Pandemic").

Turning the Tide The final Allied offensive began on July 18, 1918. Some 270,000 U.S. soldiers joined the Allied drive to push the Germans back from the Marne. Rain pelted down as the Americans moved into position. One wrote in his diary, "Trucks, artillery, infantry columns, cavalry, wagons, caissons, mud, MUD, utter confusion." Another 100,000 AEF troops joined a parallel British offensive to expel the Germans from the area north of the Somme.

Pershing's first fully independent command came in September, when Foch authorized an AEF campaign to close a German salient around the town of St. Mihiel on the Meuse River, 150 miles east of Paris. Eager to test his offensive strategy, Pershing assembled nearly five hundred thousand American and one hundred thousand French soldiers. Shelling of German positions began at 1:00 A.M. on September 11. Recorded an American in his diary, "[I]n one instant the entire front . . . was a sheet of flame, while the heavy artillery made the earth quake." Within four days, the salient was

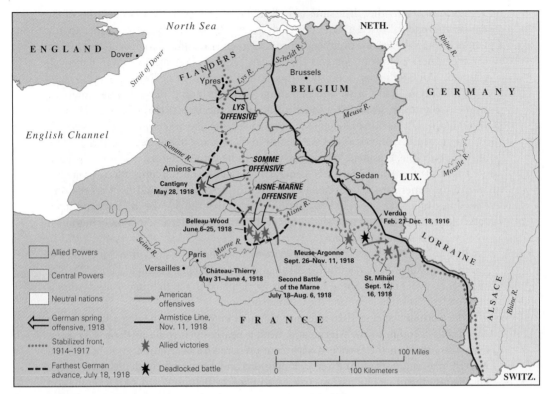

MAP 22.2 The United States on the Western Front, 1918

American troops first saw action in the campaign to throw back Germany's spring 1918 offensive in the Somme and Aisne-Marne sectors. The next heavy American engagement came that autumn as part of the Allies' Meuse-Argonne offensive, which ended the war.

closed. Although some German units had already withdrawn, St. Mihiel still cost seven thousand U.S. casualties.

The war's last battle began on September 26 as some 1.2 million Americans joined the struggle to drive the Germans from the Meuse River and the Argonne Forest north of Verdun. The stench of poison gas (first used by the Germans in 1915) hung in the air, and rats scurried in the mud, gorging on human remains. Americans now endured the filth, vermin, and dysentery familiar to veterans of the trenches. Frontline troops would never forget the terror of combat. As shells streaked overhead at night, one recalled, "We simply lay and trembled from sheer nervous tension." Some welcomed injuries as a ticket out of the battle zone. Others collapsed emotionally and were hospitalized for "shell shock."

The all-black Ninety-second Division saw combat in the Meuse-Argonne campaign. (The Germans showered them with leaflets describing U.S. racism and urging them to defect, but none did.) Four black infantry regiments served under French command. One entire regiment received the French Croix de Guerre, and several hundred black soldiers won French decorations for bravery.

African-Americans at the Front

Black troops of the 369th Infantry Regiment in the trenches near Maffrecourt, France, in 1918. Most African-American soldiers were assigned to noncombat duty, such as unloading supplies and equipment.

The AEF was assigned to cut the Sedan-Mezières Railroad, a major German supply route. In the way lay three long, heavily fortified German trenches, called *Stellungen.* "We are not men anymore, just savage beasts," wrote a young American. Death came in many forms, and without ceremony. Bodies, packs, rifles, photos of loved ones, and letters from home sank indiscriminately into the all-consuming mud. Influenza killed thousands of AEF troops at the front and in training camps back home. One day as General Pershing rode in his staff car, he buried his head in his hands and moaned his dead wife's name: "Frankie, Frankie, my God, sometimes I don't know how I can go on."

Religious and ethical principles faded as men struggled to survive. "Love of thy neighbor is forgotten," recalled one, with "all the falsities of a sheltered civilization." The war's brutality would shape the literature of the 1920s as writers such as Ernest Hemingway stripped away the illusions obscuring the reality of mass slaughter.

But the AEF at last overran the dreaded German trenches, and the survivors slogged northward. In early November the Sedan-Mezières Railroad was cut. The AEF had fulfilled its assignment, at a cost of 26,277 dead.

PROMOTING THE WAR AND SUPPRESSING DISSENT

In their own way, the war's domestic effects were as important as its battles. Spurred by government propaganda, patriotic fervor gripped America. The war fever, in turn, encouraged intellectual conformity and intolerance of dissent. Fueling the repressive spirit, government authorities and private vigilante groups hounded socialists, pacifists, and other dissidents, trampling citizens' constitutional rights.

Advertising the War To President Wilson, selling the war at home was crucial to success in France. "It is not an army we must shape and train for war, it is a nation," he declared. The administration drew on the new professions of advertising and public relations to pursue this goal. Treasury Secretary McAdoo orchestrated a series of government bond drives, called Liberty Loans, that financed about two-thirds of the $35.5 billion (including loans to the Allies) that the war cost the United States.

Posters exhorted citizens to "Fight or Buy Bonds." Liberty Loan parades featured flags, banners, and marching bands. Charlie Chaplin, Mary Pickford, and other movie stars promoted the cause. Schoolchildren purchased "thrift stamps" convertible into war bonds. Patriotic war songs reached a large public through phonograph recordings. Beneath the ballyhoo ran a note of coercion. Only "a friend of Germany," McAdoo warned, would refuse to buy bonds.

The balance of the government's war costs came from taxes. Using the power granted it by the Sixteenth Amendment, Congress imposed wartime income taxes that reached 70 percent at the top levels. War-profits taxes, excise taxes on liquor and luxuries, and increased estate taxes also helped finance the war.

Journalist George Creel headed the key wartime propaganda agency, the **Committee on Public Information** (CPI). While claiming merely to combat rumors with facts, the Creel committee in reality publicized the government's version of events and discredited all who questioned that version. One CPI division distributed posters drawn by leading illustrators. Another wrote propaganda releases that appeared in the press as "news" with no indication of their source. Popular magazines published CPI ads warning of spies, saboteurs, and anyone who "spreads pessimistic stories" or "cries for peace." Theaters screened CPI films bearing such titles as *The Kaiser: The Beast of Berlin*.

The CPI poured foreign-language pamphlets into immigrant neighborhoods and supplied prowar editorials to the foreign-language press. At a CPI media event at Mount Vernon on July 4, 1918, an Irish-born tenor sang "The Battle Hymn of the Republic" while immigrants from thirty-three nations filed reverently past George Washington's tomb. CPI posters in factories attacked the socialists' charge that this was a capitalists' war. Samuel Gompers of the American Federation of Labor headed a prowar "Alliance for Labor and Democracy" funded by the CPI. Seventy-five thousand CPI volunteers, called "Four-Minute Men," gave prowar pep talks to movie audiences and other gatherings. Teachers, writers, editors, and religious leaders overwhelmingly supported the war. These custodians of culture saw the conflict as a struggle to defend threatened values. Historians wrote essays contrasting German brutality with the Allies' lofty ideals. In *The Marne* (1918), expatriate American writer Edith Wharton expressed her love for France. The war poems of Alan Seeger, who volunteered to fight for France and died in action in 1916, enjoyed great popularity. Seeger portrayed the conflict as a noble crusade. An artillery barrage was for him "the magnificent orchestra of war."

Progressive reformers who had applauded Wilson's domestic program now cheered his war. Herbert Croly, Walter Lippmann, and other intellectuals associated with the *New Republic* magazine zealously backed the war. In gratitude, administration officials regularly briefed the editors on the government's policies.

The educator John Dewey endorsed the war and condemned its opponents in a series of *New Republic* essays. Socially engaged intellectuals must accept reality and shape it toward positive social goals, he wrote, not stand aside in self-righteous isolation. The war, he went on, presented exciting "social possibilities." The government's wartime activism could be channeled to reform purposes when peace returned, Dewey argued. Internationally, America's participation in the war would transform an imperialistic struggle into a global democratic crusade.

Wartime Intolerance and Dissent Responding to the propaganda, some Americans became almost hysterical in their strident patriotism and their hostility to radicals and dissenters. Isolated sabotage by German sympathizers, including an attack on a New Jersey munitions dump, fanned the flames. Persons suspected of pro-German sympathies were forced to kiss the flag or recite the Pledge of Allegiance. An Ohio woman accused of disloyalty was wrapped in a flag, marched to a bank, and compelled to buy a war bond. In Collinsville, Illinois, a mob lynched a German-American coal miner, Robert Prager, in April 1918. When a jury freed the mob leaders, a jury member shouted, "Nobody can say we aren't loyal now." The *Washington Post* condemned the lynching but saw it as evidence of "a healthful and wholesome awakening in the interior of the country."

Only when the German press made propaganda use of Prager's murder did President Wilson condemn it. "[N]o man who loves America . . . can justify mob action while the courts of justice are open," he declared in July 1918. But strident calls for patriotic "vigilance" against radicals and war critics created the climate that led to such actions. In a June 1917 speech urging home-front vigilance, Wilson declared ominously: "Woe be to the man or group of men that seeks to stand in our way." An Albany, New York, newspaper, advising direct action against war opponents, added: "You do not require any official authority to do this. . . . [T]he only badge you need is your patriotic fervor."

An Iowa politician charged that "90 percent of all the men and women who teach the German language are traitors." German books vanished from libraries, towns with German names changed them, and on some restaurant menus "liberty sandwich" and "liberty cabbage" replaced "hamburger" and "sauerkraut." The Boston Symphony Orchestra dismissed its German-born conductor for accepting a medal from Kaiser Wilhelm. The Philadelphia Orchestra banned all German music except for Bach, Beethoven, Mozart, and Brahms. A popular evangelist, Billy Sunday, proclaimed, "If you turn hell upside down you will find 'Made in Germany' stamped on the bottom." The zealots also targeted war critics and radicals. A Cincinnati mob horsewhipped a pacifist minister. Theodore Roosevelt branded antiwar Senator Robert La Follette "an unhung traitor." Columbia University fired two antiwar professors. The International Workers of the World faced fierce criticism for its opposition to the war. In Bisbee, Arizona, in July 1917, two thousand well-organized armed vigilantes calling themselves the Citizens Protective League forced twelve hundred striking copper miners, some of whom belonged to the IWW, onto a freight train that dumped them in the New Mexico desert without food, water, or shelter. Declared Theodore Roosevelt: "[N]o human being in his senses doubts that the men deported from Bisbee were bent on destruction and murder."

Despite the persecution, many Americans persisted in opposing the war. Some were immigrants with ancestral ties to Germany. Others were religious pacifists, including Quakers, Mennonites, and Jehovah's Witnesses. Congresswoman Jeannette Rankin of Montana, a pacifist and the first woman elected to Congress, voted against the declaration of war. "I want to stand by my country," she declared, "but I cannot vote for war."

Of some sixty-five thousand men who registered as conscientious objectors (COs), twenty-one thousand were drafted. Assigned to noncombat duty on military bases, such as cleaning latrines, these COs often experienced harsh treatment. Those who rejected this alternative were sent to military prisons. Woodrow Wilson heaped scorn on the pacifists. "[M]y heart is with them, but my mind has contempt for them," he declared in November 1917; "I want peace, but I know how to get it, and they do not."

Socialist leaders such as Eugene Debs and Victor Berger denounced the war as a capitalist struggle for markets, with the soldiers as cannon fodder. The U.S. declaration of war, they insisted, mainly reflected Wall Street's desire to protect its loans to England and France. But other socialists supported the war, dividing the party.

The war split the women's movement as well. While some leaders joined Jane Addams in opposition, others endorsed the war while keeping their own goals in view. In *Mobilizing Woman-Power* (1918), Harriot Stanton Blatch argued that women who wished to help shape the peace must support the war. Anna Howard Shaw, a former president of the National American Woman Suffrage Association (NAWSA), chaired the Woman's Committee of the Council of National Defense, a largely symbolic post.

Carrie Chapman Catt, Shaw's successor as president of NAWSA, had helped start the Woman's Peace Party in 1915. But she supported U.S. entry into the war in 1917, sharing to some extent Wilson's vision of a more liberal postwar world order. Catt continued to focus mainly on woman suffrage, however, insisting that this was NAWSA's "number one war job." For this, some superpatriots accused her of disloyalty.

Draft resistance extended beyond the ranks of conscientious objectors. An estimated 2.4 to 3.6 million young men failed to register, and of those who did, about 12 percent either did not appear when drafted or deserted from training camp. The rural South saw high levels of draft resistance. The urban elites who ran the draft boards were more inclined to defer young men of their own class than poor farmers, white or black, fueling class resentment. In June 1918, a truck carrying U.S. soldiers pursuing draft evaders in rural Georgia crashed when a bridge collapsed, killing three soldiers and injuring others. Investigators found that the bridge supports had been deliberately sabotaged.

Blacks had added reasons to oppose the draft. Of southern blacks who registered, one-third were drafted, in contrast to only one-quarter of whites. White draft boards justified this by arguing that low-income black families could more easily spare a male breadwinner. As an Alabama board observed: "[I]t is . . . common knowledge that it requires more for a white man and his wife to live than it does a negro man and his wife, due to their respective stations in life." But the dynamics of race worked in complex ways: some southern whites, fearful of arming black men even for military service, favored drafting only whites.

The war's most incisive critic was Randolph Bourne, a young journalist. Although Bourne admired John Dewey, he rejected Dewey's prowar argument in several penetrating essays. He dismissed Dewey's contention that reformers could direct the war to their own purposes. "If the war is too strong for you to prevent," he asked, "how is it going to be weak enough for you to . . . mould to your liberal purposes?"

Eventually, many prowar intellectuals came to agree. By 1919, Dewey conceded that the war, far from promoting reform, had encouraged reaction and intolerance. Bourne did not live to see his vindication, however. He died of influenza in 1918, at the age of thirty-two.

| **Suppressing Dissent by Law** | Wartime intolerance also surfaced in federal laws and official actions. The **Espionage Act** of June 1917 set fines and prison sentences for a variety of loosely defined antiwar activities. |

The **Sedition Amendment** (May 1918) imposed stiff penalties on anyone convicted of using "disloyal, profane . . . or abusive language" about the government, the Constitution, the flag, or the military.

Wilson's attorney general, Thomas W. Gregory, used these laws to stamp out dissent. Opponents of the war, proclaimed Gregory, should expect no mercy "from an outraged people and an avenging government." Under the federal legislation and similar state laws, some fifteen hundred pacifists, socialists, IWW leaders, and other war critics were arrested. One socialist, Rose Pastor Stokes, received a ten-year prison sentence (later commuted) for telling an audience, "I am for the people, and the government is for the profiteers." Kate Richards O'Hare, a midwestern socialist organizer, spent over a year in jail for declaring, "The women of the United States are nothing more than brood sows, to raise children to get into the army and be made into fertilizer." Eugene Debs was imprisoned for three years (1918–1921) for a speech discussing the economic causes of the war.

Under the Espionage Act, Postmaster General Albert S. Burleson, a reactionary superpatriot, suppressed socialist periodicals, including *The Masses,* published by radicals in New York City's Greenwich Village. Burleson "didn't know socialism from rheumatism," according to socialist Norman Thomas, but he pursued his repressive crusade. In January 1919 Congressman-elect Victor Berger was convicted under the Espionage Act for publishing antiwar articles in his socialist newspaper, the *Milwaukee Leader.* (The Supreme Court reversed Berger's conviction in 1921.) Upton Sinclair protested to President Wilson that no one of Burleson's "childish ignorance" should wield such power; but Wilson did little to restrain Burleson's excesses.

A patriotic group called the American Protective League and local "Councils of Defense" claiming vague governmental authority further enforced ideological conformity. Local and state volunteer organizations like the Connecticut Home Guard assisted the vigilance effort. A group called "Boy Spies of America" recruited young patriots. The 1917 Bolshevik takeover in Russia sharpened the attacks on domestic radicals. As communists, the Bolsheviks believed in a one-party state and anticipated the violent overthrow of the capitalist system. Some Americans feared that the United States could fall to communism as well.

In three 1919 decisions, the U.S. Supreme Court upheld the Espionage Act convictions of war critics. In *Schenck* v. *United States,* Justice Oliver Wendell Holmes, Jr., writing for a unanimous court, justified such repression in cases where a person's exercise of the First Amendment right of free speech posed a "clear and present danger" to the nation. When the war ended, Wilson vetoed a bill ending the Espionage Act, and it remained in force.

The early wartime mood of idealism had degenerated into persecution of all who failed to meet the zealots' notions of "100 percent Americanism." This climate of conformity and suspicion would linger long after the war's end.

ECONOMIC AND SOCIAL TRENDS
IN WARTIME AMERICA

While the war affected the lives of millions of Americans—including industrial workers, farmers, women, and blacks—another of the war's byproducts, a deadly influenza pandemic, took a grievous toll. Some Progressive Era reforms advanced in 1917–1918, but overall the war and its aftermath weakened the reform movement.

Boom Times in Industry and Agriculture

World War I benefited the U.S. economy. From 1914 to 1918, factory output grew by more than one-third. Even with several million men in the military, the civilian work force expanded by 1.3 million between 1916 and 1918, thanks largely to new jobs in war-related industries such as shipbuilding, munitions, steel, and textiles. Prices rose, but so did wages. Even unskilled workers enjoyed wartime wage increases averaging nearly 20 percent. Samuel Gompers urged workers not to strike during the war. Some IWW workers and maverick AFL locals went on strike anyway, but with the economy booming, most workers observed the no-strike request.

The war's social impact took many forms. Job seekers pouring into industrial centers strained housing, schools, and municipal services. The consumption of cigarettes, which soldiers and workers could carry in their shirt pockets with greater ease than pipes or cigars, more than tripled from 1914 to 1918. Reflecting wartime prosperity, automobile production jumped from 460,000 in 1914 to 1.8 million in 1917, then dipped briefly in 1918 as steel went for military production.

Farmers profited, too. With European farm production disrupted, U.S. agricultural prices more than doubled between 1913 and 1918, and farmers' real income rose significantly. Cotton prices soared from twelve cents a pound in 1913 to twenty-nine cents a pound by 1918, and corn prices surged as well.

This agricultural boom proved a mixed blessing. Farmers who borrowed heavily to expand production faced a credit squeeze when farm prices fell after the war. In the 1920s and 1930s, hard-pressed farmers would look back to the war years as a golden age of prosperity.

Blacks Migrate Northward

The war sped the exodus of southern blacks. An estimated half-million African-Americans moved north during the war, and most settled in cities. Each day, fresh arrivals crowded the railroad stations of Philadelphia, New York, Detroit, and Pittsburgh. Chicago's black population grew from 44,000 in 1910 to 110,000 in 1920, Cleveland's from 8,000 to 34,000.

With European immigration disrupted by the war, booming industries hired more black workers. Some companies sent labor agents south to recruit black workers. African-American newspapers like the *Chicago Defender* spread the word, as did letters and word-of-mouth reports. One southern black, newly settled near Chicago, wrote home, "Nothing here but money, and it is not hard to get." A Pittsburgh newcomer presented a more balanced picture: "They give you big money for what you do, but they charge you big things for what you get." As economic opportunity beckoned, impoverished southern blacks welcomed the prospect of earning three dollars a day or more in a region where racism seemed less intense. By 1920, 1.5 million African-Americans were working in northern factories and other urban-based jobs.

This vast population movement had social, political, and cultural ramifications. New city churches and storefront missions met the spiritual and social needs of deeply religious migrants from the South. The National Association for the Advancement of Colored People (NAACP) grew from 9,000 members before the war to nearly 100,000 by the early 1920s. Tireless NAACP organizers built a sturdy network of local branches throughout the nation. NAACP leaders pointed to African-American support for the war to buttress their demand for racial equality. The struggle against racism faced setbacks in the reactionary 1920s, but the heightened race consciousness and activism of the war years helped create the groundwork for the civil-rights movement that lay ahead. The concentration of blacks in New York City also prepared the way for the Harlem Renaissance, a cultural flowering of the 1920s (see Chapter 23).

Still, these African-American newcomers in northern cities faced severe challenges. White workers resented the labor competition, and white homeowners lashed out as jammed black neighborhoods spilled over into surrounding areas. A bloody outbreak erupted on July 2, 1917, in East St. Louis, Illinois, home to thousands of recently arrived southern blacks. In a coordinated attack, a white mob torched black homes and shot the residents as they fled. At least thirty-nine blacks died, including a two-year-old who was shot and then thrown into a burning house.

A few weeks later, a silent march down New York's Fifth Avenue organized by the NAACP protested racist violence. One banner echoed Wilson's phrase justifying U.S. involvement in the war: "Mr. President, Why Not Make AMERICA Safe for Democracy?"

Women in Wartime From one perspective, World War I seems a uniquely male experience. Male politicians led their nations into war. Male officers ordered other men into battle. Yet war touches all of society, not just half of it. The war affected women differently, but it affected them profoundly.

Feminist leaders like Carrie Chapman Catt hoped that the war would lead to full equality and greater opportunity for women. For a time, these goals seemed attainable. In addition to the women in the AEF and in wartime volunteer agencies, about 1 million women worked in industry. Thousands more held other jobs, from streetcar conductors to bricklayers. "Out of . . . repression into opportunity is the meaning of the war to thousands of women," wrote Florence Thorne of the American Federation of Labor in 1917.

As the woman-suffrage movement gained momentum, a key victory came in November 1917 when New York voters amended the state constitution to permit women to vote. In Washington, Alice Paul and members of her National Woman's Party (see Chapter 21) picketed the White House and posted banners criticizing President Wilson for opposing woman suffrage at home while championing democracy abroad. Several protesters were jailed and, when they went on a hunger strike, force-fed. Under growing pressure from all wings of the suffrage movement, Wilson declared that women's war service had earned them the right to vote. In 1919, barraged by prosuffrage petitions, the House and Senate overwhelmingly passed the **Nineteenth Amendment** granting women the vote. Ratification followed in 1920.

Beyond this victory, however, the war did little to better women's status permanently.

Relatively few women actually entered the work force for the first time in 1917–1918; most simply moved to better-paying jobs. Despite protests and War Labor Board rulings, even in these jobs most earned less than the men they replaced. As for the women in the AEF, the War Department refused their requests for military rank and benefits.

At the war's end, many women lost their jobs to returning veterans. The New York labor federation advised, "The same patriotism which induced women to enter industry during the war should induce them to vacate their positions after the war." Male streetcar workers in Cleveland went on strike to force women conductors off the job. In 1920, the percentage of U.S. women in the paid labor force was actually slightly lower than it had been in 1910.

Public-Health Crisis: The 1918 Influenza Pandemic   Amid battlefield casualties and home-front social changes, the nation in 1918 also coped with a global outbreak of influenza, a highly contagious viral infection. The **influenza pandemic,** spread by a particularly deadly strain of the virus, killed as many as 30 million people worldwide. Despite medical and public-health advances, doctors had few weapons against the flu in 1918.

Moving northward from its origins in southern Africa, the deadly flu spread from the war zone in France to U.S. military camps, striking Fort Riley, Kansas, in March and quickly advancing to other bases and the urban population. In September, an army health official visiting Camp Devens in Massachusetts wrote, "I saw hundreds of young stalwart men in uniform coming into . . . the hospital. . . . The faces wore a bluish cast, a cough brought up blood-stained sputum. In the morning, the dead bodies are stacked about the morgue like cordwood."

The flu hit the cities hard. In Philadelphia on September 19, 1918, the day after a massive Liberty Loan rally, doctors reported 635 new influenza cases. Many cities forbade all public gatherings. The worst came in October, when the flu killed 195,000 Americans. The total U.S. death toll was about 550,000, over six times the total of AEF battle deaths in France. More than 50,000 died in Canada.

In 1998 researchers with the U.S. Armed Forces Institute of Pathology recovered samples of the 1918 flu virus from the frozen corpse of a female victim buried in the Alaska tundra. Using this sample and tissue preserved from two U.S. soldiers who had died of influenza, scientists in 2004 announced that they had synthesized the 1918 virus for research purposes.

In 1997, a new avian (bird) virus similar to the 1918 flu virus killed six persons in Hong Kong. By 2005, the virus had spread to poultry in Asia, Turkey, and eastern Europe, and more than sixty people had died after direct contact with infected birds. Though the risk appeared low, public-health agencies worldwide took measures to prevent another global pandemic like that of 1918.

The War and Progressivism   As one weighs the war's effects on Progressive Era reform movements, a mixed picture emerges. As we have seen, the war strengthened the coercive, moral-control aspect of progressivism, including the drive for the prohibition of alcohol. Exploiting anti-German sentiment, prohibitionists pointed out that the nation's biggest breweries bore such German names as Pabst, Schlitz, and Anheuser-Busch. Beer, they hinted, was part of a

German plot to undermine American fitness. With food conservation a high priority, they stressed the wastefulness of using grain to make liquor. When the **Eighteenth Amendment** establishing national prohibition passed Congress in December 1917, it was widely seen as a war measure. Ratified in 1919, it went into effect on January 1, 1920.

Similarly, the war strengthened the Progressive Era antiprostitution campaign. The War Department closed red-light districts near military bases, including New Orleans's famed Storyville. (As Storyville's jazz musicians moved north, jazz reached a national audience.) Congress appropriated $4 million to combat venereal disease among soldiers and war workers. In San Antonio, a major military hub, an antiprostitution leader reflected the war mood when he declared, "We propose to fight vice . . . with the cold steel of the law, and to drive in the steel from the point to the hilt until the law's supremacy is acknowledged."

In the wartime climate of "vigilance," the antiprostitution drive expanded to a broader policing of morals. Female lecturers hired by the Commission on Training Camp Activities urged women to uphold standards of sexual morality. "Do Your Bit to Keep Him Fit" one pamphlet advised women. Urban "protective bureaus" set up with government authority monitored women's behavior. In Massachusetts, female social workers hid in the Boston Common after dark to apprehend young women dating soldiers from nearby bases.

All this moral-reform activity convinced some that traditional codes of sexual behavior, weakening before the war, had been restored. One antiprostitution crusader exulted, "Young men of today . . . are nearer perfection in conduct, morals, and ideals than any similar generation . . . in the history of the world. Their minds have been raised to ideals that would never have been attained save by the heroism of . . . the World War."

Along with woman suffrage, other reforms advanced as well. The **War Labor Board** (WLB), spurred by progressives interested in the cause of labor, encouraged workers to join unions and guaranteed unions' right to bargain with management. The WLB also pressured factory owners to introduce the eight-hour workday, end child labor, and open their plants to safety and sanitation inspectors. The Railroad Administration also recognized railway workers' right to unionize. Under these favorable conditions, union membership rose from 2.7 million in 1916 to more than 5 million by 1920.

Another wartime agency, the United States Housing Corporation, built housing projects for workers, including some that encompassed schools, playgrounds, and recreational centers. Several state legislatures, concluding that worker-protection laws would help the war effort, passed wage-and-hour laws and other measures benefiting factory laborers.

The **Bureau of War Risk Insurance** (BWRI), created in October 1917 to aid soldiers' families, established a precedent of government help for families at risk. As Julia Lathrop, head of the Federal Children's Bureau, observed, "The least a democratic nation can do, which sends men into war, is to . . . [care for] the families." By the war's end, the BWRI was sending regular checks to 2.1 million families.

Overall, however, at least in the short run, the war weakened the progressive social-justice impulse. While the war brought increased regulation of the economy—a key progressive goal—business interests often dominated the regulatory agencies, and they were quickly dismantled after the war.

The government's repression of radicals and antiwar dissenters fractured the fragile coalition of left-leaning progressives, women's groups, trade unionists, and some socialists that had provided the momentum for prewar worker-protection laws, and ushered in a decade of reaction. The 1918 midterm election signaled the shift: the Democrats lost both houses of Congress to a deeply conservative Republican Party.

Nevertheless, taking a longer view, reform energies, after diminishing in the 1920s, would reemerge in the depression decade of the 1930s. And as Franklin D. Roosevelt's New Deal took shape (see Chapter 24), the memory of such World War I agencies as the War Labor Board, the United States Housing Corporation, and the Bureau of War Risk Insurance provided ideas and inspiration.

JOYOUS ARMISTICE, BITTER AFTERMATH, 1918–1920

In November 1918, the war finally ended. The peace conference that followed stands as a high point of America's growing internationalist involvement, but it also triggered a sharp domestic reaction against that involvement. Woodrow Wilson dominated the peace conference but failed in his most cherished objective—American membership in the League of Nations. At home, as racism and intolerance worsened, the electorate repudiated Wilsonianism and in 1920 sent a conservative Republican to the White House.

Wilson's Fourteen Points; The Armistice

From the moment the United States entered the war, President Wilson planned to put his personal stamp on the peace. He and his reform-minded supporters believed that U.S. involvement could transform a sordid struggle for power and empire into a crusade for a democratic world order. Wilson recruited a group of advisers called The Inquiry to translate his vision into specific war aims. The need for a statement of U.S. war objectives grew urgent after the Bolsheviks, having seized power in Russia, published many of the self-serving secret treaties signed by European powers prior to 1914.

In a speech to Congress in January 1918, Wilson summed up U.S. war aims in fourteen points. Eight of these spelled out Wilson's belief that the subject peoples of the Austro-Hungarian and Ottoman empires should have the right of self-determination—that is, the freedom to choose their own political futures. A ninth point insisted that colonial disputes take into account the interests of the colonized peoples. The remaining five points offered Wilson's larger postwar vision: a world of free navigation, free trade, reduced armaments, openly negotiated treaties, and "a general association of nations" to resolve conflicts peacefully. The **Fourteen Points** helped solidify American support for the war, especially among liberals. They seemed proof that the United States had entered the war not for selfish reasons but out of noble motives.

In early October 1918, reeling from the Allies' advances, Germany proposed an armistice based on Wilson's Fourteen Points. The British and French hesitated, but when Wilson threatened to negotiate a separate peace, they agreed. Meanwhile, in Berlin, Kaiser Wilhelm II had abdicated and a German republic had been proclaimed.

In the early morning of November 11, 1918, the Allied commander Marshal Foch and his German counterparts signed an armistice ending hostilities at 11:00 A.M. Rockets burst over the front that night, not in anger but in relief and celebration. Back home, cheering throngs (some wearing protective masks against the influenza epidemic) filled the streets. "Everything for which America has fought has been accomplished," Wilson proclaimed.

Troop transports soon ferried the soldiers home. One returnee, artillery captain Harry Truman of Missouri, described his feelings in a letter to his fiancée, Bess Wallace:

> I've never seen anything that looks so good as the Liberty Lady in New York Harbor. . . . [T]he men . . . have been in so many hard places that it takes something real to give them a thrill, but when the band . . . played "Home Sweet Home" there were not many dry eyes. The hardest of hard-boiled cookies even had to blow his nose a time or two.

The Versailles Peace Conference, 1919 Eager to play a central role in the peace conference, Wilson decided to lead the U.S. delegation himself. This was probably a mistake. The strain of long bargaining sessions soon took its toll on his frail nerves. Wilson compounded his mistake by naming only one Republican to the delegation, an elderly diplomat with little influence in the party. Selecting some prominent Republicans might have spared Wilson future grief. The Democrats' loss of Congress in the 1918 midterm election was a further ill omen.

Nevertheless, spirits soared on December 4, 1918, as the *George Washington,* a converted German liner, left New York, bearing Wilson to Europe—the first president to cross the Atlantic while in office. Ships' whistles blared as Wilson waved to the crowd on shore. The giddy mood continued when Wilson reached France. In Paris, shouts of "Voodrow Veelson" rang out as he rode up the Champs-Élysées, the city's ceremonial boulevard. When he visited England, children at the dock in Dover spread flowers in his path. In Italy, a local official compared him to Jesus Christ.

The euphoria faded once the peace conference began at the palace of Versailles near Paris, where the treaty ending the Revolutionary War had been signed 136 years before. Joining Wilson were the other Allied heads of state: Italy's Vittorio Orlando; the aged and cynical Georges Clemenceau of France; and England's David Lloyd George, of whom Wilson said, "He is slippery as an eel, and I never know when to count on him." Japan participated as well.

The European statesmen at the **Versailles Peace Conference** were determined to avenge their nations' horrendous wartime losses, which they blamed directly on German aggression. Their goals bore little relation to Wilson's liberal vision. As Clemenceau remarked, "God gave us the Ten Commandments and we broke them. Mr. Wilson has given us the Fourteen Points. We shall see."

Differences surfaced quickly. Italy demanded a port on the eastern Adriatic Sea. Japan insisted on keeping the trading rights it had seized from Germany in the Chinese province of Shandong (Shantung). Clemenceau was obsessed with revenge. At one point, an appalled Wilson threatened to leave the conference.

Reflecting this toxic climate, the peace treaty signed by a sullen German delegation in June 1919 was harshly punitive. Though its industrial infrastructure remained intact, Germany was disarmed, stripped of its colonies, forced to admit sole blame for the war, and saddled with reparation payments of $56 billion. France regained the provinces of Alsace and Lorraine lost to Germany in 1871 and took control for fifteen years of Germany's coal-rich Saar Basin. The treaty demilitarized Germany's western border and transferred a slice of eastern Germany to Poland. All told, the treaty cost Germany one-tenth of its population and one-eighth of its territory. The treaty granted Japan's Shandong claims and gave Italy a slice of Austria that contained two hundred thousand German-speaking inhabitants. These harsh terms, bitterly resented in Germany, planted the seeds of an even more devastating future war.

Some treaty provisions did reflect Wilson's themes of democracy and self-determination. Germany's former colonies went to the various Allies under a "mandate" or trusteeship system that in theory would lead to eventual independence. The treaty also recognized the independence of Poland and the Baltic states of Estonia, Latvia, and Lithuania (territories seized by Germany in its 1918 peace treaty with Bolshevik Russia). Separate treaties provided for the independence of Czechoslovakia and Yugoslavia, new nations carved from the Austro-Hungarian and Ottoman empires.

Palestine, a part of Turkey's collapsed Ottoman Empire, went to Great Britain under a mandate arrangement. In 1917, after gaining military control of Palestine, the British had issued the Balfour Declaration supporting a Jewish "national home" in the region while also acknowledging the rights of the non-Jewish Palestinians.

But the treaty makers ignored the aspirations of colonized peoples in Asia and Africa. For example, Ho Chi Minh, a young Vietnamese nationalist who would later become head of his nation, tried unsuccessfully at Versailles to secure Vietnamese independence from France.

Nor did the peacemakers come to terms with revolutionary Russia. Indeed, in August 1918 a fourteen-nation Allied army, including some seven thousand U.S. troops, had landed at various Russian ports, ostensibly to secure them from German attack and to protect Allied war equipment. In fact, the aim was to overthrow the new Bolshevik regime, whose communist ideology stirred deep fear in the capitals of Europe and America. Wilson, having welcomed the liberal Russian revolution of March 1917, viewed the Bolshevik coup and Russia's withdrawal from the war as a betrayal of the Allies and of his hopes for a democratic Russia. The Versailles treaty reflected this hostility. Its territorial settlements in eastern Europe were designed to weaken Russia. Wilson and the other Allied leaders agreed to support a Russian military leader waging a last-ditch struggle against the Bolsheviks. Not until 1933 would the United States recognize the Soviet Union.

The Fight over the League of Nations Dismayed by the treaty's vindictive features, Wilson focused on his one shining achievement at Versailles—the creation of a new international organization, the **League of Nations.** The agreement or "covenant" to establish the League, written into the treaty, embodied Wilson's vision of a new world order of peace and justice.

But Wilson's League faced major hurdles. A warning sign had come in February 1919 when thirty-nine Republican senators and senators-elect, including Henry Cabot Lodge, signed a letter rejecting the League in its present form. Wilson had retorted defiantly, "You cannot dissect the Covenant from the treaty without destroying the whole vital structure."

When Wilson sent the treaty to the Senate for ratification in July 1919, Lodge bottled it up in the Foreign Relations Committee. Convinced that he could rally popular opinion to his cause, Wilson left Washington on September 3 for a speaking tour. Covering more than nine thousand miles by train, Wilson defended the League in thirty-seven speeches in twenty-two days. Crowds were large and friendly. People wept as Wilson described his visits to American war cemeteries in France and cheered his vision of a new world order.

But the trip exhausted Wilson, and on September 25 he collapsed in Colorado. His train sped back to Washington, where Wilson suffered a stroke on October 2 that for a time left him near death. He spent the rest of his term mostly in bed or in a wheelchair, a reclusive invalid, his mind clouded, his fragile emotions betraying him into vindictive actions and tearful outbursts. He broke with close advisers, refused to see the British ambassador, and dismissed Secretary of State Lansing, accusing him of disloyalty. In January 1920, his physician advised him to resign, but Wilson refused.

Wilson's first wife, Ellen, had died in 1914. His strong-willed second wife, Edith Galt, played a crucial role behind the scenes during this crisis. She hid Wilson's condition from the public, controlled his access to information, and decided who could see him. Cabinet members, diplomats, and congressional leaders were barred from the White House. When one leader seeking a meeting urged Mrs. Wilson to consider "the welfare of the country," she snapped, "I am not thinking of the country now, I am thinking of my husband." Since the Twenty-fifth Amendment, dealing with issues of presidential disability, was not adopted until 1967, the impasse continued.

The League drama unfolded against this grim backdrop. On September 10, 1919, the Foreign Relations Committee at last sent the treaty to the Senate, but with a series of amendments. The Senate split into three groups. First were Democrats who supported the League covenant without changes. Second were Republican "Irreconcilables," led by Hiram Johnson of California, Wisconsin's Robert La Follette, and Idaho's William Borah, who opposed the League absolutely. Progressive on domestic issues, but also intensely nationalistic, they feared that League membership would dangerously restrict U.S. freedom of action and entangle America with foreign powers they viewed as corrupt and reactionary. Finally, a group of Republican "Reservationists," led by Lodge, demanded amendments as a condition of their support. The Reservationists especially objected to Article 10 of the covenant, which pledged each member nation to preserve the political independence and territorial integrity of all other members. This provision, the Reservationists believed, limited America's sovereignty and infringed on Congress's constitutional power to declare war.

Had Wilson accepted compromise, the Senate would probably have ratified the Versailles treaty, including the League covenant. But Wilson's illness aggravated his tendency toward rigidity. Isolated in the White House, he instructed Senate Democrats to vote against the treaty, which now included Lodge's reservations. Although international-law specialists argued that these reservations would not significantly weaken U.S. participation in the League, Wilson rejected them as "a knife thrust at the heart of the treaty."

Despite Wilson's speaking tour, the public did not rally behind the League. The reactionary mood that Wilson's own administration had helped create was not conducive to bold gestures of political idealism. As the editor of *The Nation* magazine observed, "If [Wilson] loses his great fight for humanity, it will be because he was deliberately silent when freedom of speech and the right of conscience were struck down in America."

On November 19, 1919, pro-League Democrats obeying Wilson's instructions and anti-League Irreconcilables joined forces to defeat the version of the Versailles treaty that included Lodge's reservations. A second vote in March 1920 produced the same result. The United States would not join the League. A president elected amid high hopes in 1912, cheered when he called for war in 1917, and adulated in Europe in 1918 lay embittered and impotent. What might have been Wilson's crowning achievement had turned to ashes.

Racism and Red Scare, 1919–1920 The wartime spirit of "100 percent Americanism" left a bitter aftertaste. The years 1919–1920 saw new racial violence and antiradical hysteria. Seventy-six blacks were lynched in 1919, the worst toll in fifteen years. The victims included ten veterans, several still in uniform. In Omaha, Nebraska, a mob of 5,000 or more, inflamed by sensational newspaper stories, seized a black prisoner, Will Brown, from the county courthouse, in the process burning the building and assaulting the mayor. The mob hanged Brown from a lamppost, shot him multiple times, dragged his body through the streets, and burned it. Fourteen-year-old Henry Fonda, a future film actor, witnessed the lynching from his father's print shop. "It was the most horrendous sight I'd ever seen," he later recalled.

The worst violence exploded in Chicago, where simmering racial tension erupted on a hot afternoon in July 1919. When a black youth swimming at a Lake Michigan beach drowned after whites had pelted him with stones, black neighborhoods erupted in fury. A thirteen-day reign of terror followed as white and black marauders engaged in random attacks and arson. Black gangs stabbed an Italian peddler; white gangs pulled blacks from streetcars and shot or whipped them. Before an uneasy calm returned, the outbreak left fifteen whites and twenty-three blacks dead, over five hundred injured, and more than a thousand families, mostly black, homeless.

Wartime antiradicalism crested in a postwar Red Scare. (Communists were called "reds" because of the red flag favored by revolutionary organizations.) For some, the 1917 triumph of bolshevism in Russia offered a grim foretaste of what might happen in America. A rash of strikes in 1919 deepened such fears. When the IWW and other unions called a general strike in Seattle early that year, the mayor accused the strikers of seeking to "duplicate the anarchy of Russia" and called for federal troops to maintain order. Anxiety crackled again in April, when various public officials received packages containing bombs. One severely injured a senator's maid; another damaged the home of Attorney General A. Mitchell Palmer. When 350,000 steelworkers went on strike in September, mill owners ran newspaper ads describing the walkout as a plot by "Red agitators."

Antiradical paranoia also infected politics. In November 1919, the House of Representatives refused to seat Milwaukee socialist Victor Berger because of his indictment under the Espionage Act. Milwaukee voters promptly reelected him, but the House stood firm. The New York legislature expelled several socialist members. The Justice Department set up an antiradical division under young J. Edgar Hoover, future head of the Federal Bureau of Investigation, who ordered the arrest of hundreds of suspected communists and radicals. In December 1919, the government deported 249 Russian-born aliens, including Emma Goldman, a prominent radical and leader of the birth-control movement.

On January 2, 1920, in a Justice Department dragnet, federal marshals and local police raided the homes of suspected radicals and the headquarters of radical organizations in thirty-two cities. Without search warrants or arrest warrants, they arrested more than 4,000 persons (some 550 were eventually deported) and seized papers and records. In Lynn, Massachusetts, police arrested a group of people who were meeting to plan a cooperative bakery. In Boston, police paraded arrested persons through the streets in handcuffs and chains and then confined them in crowded and unsanitary cells without formal charges or the right to post bail.

Attorney General Palmer, ambitious for higher office, coordinated these "Red raids." A Quaker and one-time reform-minded congressman, Palmer had succumbed to the anticommunist hysteria. He later described the menace he believed the nation faced in 1919:

> The blaze of revolution was sweeping over every American institution of law and order . . . eating its way into the homes of the American workman, its sharp tongues of revolutionary heat . . . licking at the altars of the churches, leaping into the belfry of the school bell, crawling into the sacred corners of American homes, . . . burning up the foundations of society.

The Red Scare soon subsided. When a bomb exploded in New York City's financial district in September 1920, killing thirty-eight people, most Americans saw the deed as the work of an isolated fanatic, not evidence of approaching revolution.

The Election of 1920

In this unsettled climate, the election of 1920 approached. Wilson, out of touch with political reality, considered seeking a third term, but was persuaded otherwise. Few heeded his call to make the election a "solemn referendum" on the League. "The bitterness toward Wilson is everywhere . . . ," wrote a Democratic campaign worker; "he hasn't a friend."

Treasury Secretary McAdoo and Attorney General Palmer harbored presidential hopes. But when the Democrats convened in San Francisco, the delegates nominated James M. Cox, the mildly progressive governor of Ohio. As Cox's running mate they

"Convict No. 9653 for President" *Although socialist Eugene V. Debs was in prison in 1920 for his antiwar speeches in 1917–19, he still received over 900,000 votes for president.*

chose the young assistant secretary of the navy, Franklin D. Roosevelt, who possessed a potent political name.

The confident Republicans, meeting in Chicago, nominated Senator **Warren G. Harding** of Ohio, an amiable politician of little distinction. As one GOP leader observed, "There ain't any first raters this year. . . . We got a lot of second raters, and Harding is the best of the second raters." For vice president, they chose Massachusetts governor Calvin Coolidge, who had won attention in 1919 with his denunciation of a Boston policemen's strike.

Harding's vacuous campaign speeches reminded one critic of "an army of pompous phrases moving over the landscape in search of an idea." But his reassuring promise of a return to "normalcy" resonated with many voters, and he won by a landslide—16 million votes against 9 million for Cox. Nearly a million citizens defiantly voted for socialist Eugene Debs, who remained behind bars in an Atlanta penitentiary for his earlier antiwar speeches.

The election dashed all hope for American entry into the League of Nations. During the campaign, Harding vaguely endorsed some form of "international organization," but once elected he bluntly declared the League question "dead." Senator Lodge, who had praised Wilson's idealistic war message so highly, now expressed grim satisfaction that the voters had ripped "Wilsonism" up by the roots. The sense of high purpose that Wilson had evoked so eloquently in April 1917 seemed remote indeed as Americans turned to a new president and a new era.

CONCLUSION

The early twentieth century saw intensifying U.S. involvement abroad. Focused initially on Latin America and Asia, this new globalism arose from a desire to promote U.S. business interests internationally; export American values to other societies; and extend the power of a newly confident, industrialized United States as a counterweight to the expansive ambitions of Great Britain, Germany, and other imperial nations.

After 1914 this new internationalism focused on the European war. The nation's 1917 decision to enter the war on the Allied side reflected a combination of cultural ties, economic interests, concern for neutral rights, and President Wilson's vision of a transformed world order that would emerge from the struggle.

By a conservative estimate, World War I cost 10 million dead and 20 million wounded. Included in this toll were 112,000 deaths in the American military—49,000 in battle and 63,000 from diseases, mostly influenza. The conflict brought advances in the technology of slaughter, from U-boat torpedoes and primitive aerial bombs to tanks, poison gas, and deadlier machine guns.

The war also had far-reaching social, political, and economic effects. It advanced some reforms, notably woman suffrage and the campaigns against prostitution and alcohol. As a war measure, the government expanded its regulatory power over corporations and took steps to ensure workers' well-being and right to organize. Wartime regulatory agencies and social programs offered models that would prove influential in the future.

But the war undermined other aspects of progressivism—its openness to new ideas, its larger commitment to social justice, and its humanitarian concern for the underdog. As government propaganda encouraged ideological conformity and fear of radicalism, the reform impulse withered. The climate of reaction intensified in 1919–1920, as the nation repudiated Wilsonian idealism.

The war at least temporarily improved the economic prospects of many workers, farmers, blacks, and women, and enhanced the standing of the corporate executives, psychologists, public-relations specialists, and other professionals who contributed their expertise to the cause. Internationally, despite the wrangles that kept America out of the League of Nations, the conflict propelled the United States to the center of world politics and left the nation's businesses and financial institutions poised for global expansion.

Some of these changes endured; others proved fleeting. Cumulatively, however, their effect was profound. The nation that celebrated the armistice in November 1918 was very different from the one that Woodrow Wilson had solemnly taken into battle only nineteen months earlier.

23

The 1920s: Coping with
Change, 1920–1929

A NEW ECONOMIC ORDER

Fueled by new consumer products and new methods of producing and selling goods, the economy surged in the 1920s. Not everyone benefited, and farmers in particular suffered chronic economic woes. Still, the overall picture appeared rosy. As we shall see, these economic changes influenced the decade's political, social, and cultural climate, as Americans struggled to cope with a rapidly changing society.

Booming Business, Ailing Agriculture A recession struck in 1920 after the government canceled wartime defense contracts and returning veterans reentered the job market. Recovery came in 1922, however, and for the next few years the nonfarm economy hummed. Unemployment fell to as low as 3 percent, prices held steady, and the gross national product (GNP) grew by 43 percent from 1922 to 1929.

With the growth of cities, new consumer goods, including home electrical products, fed the prosperity. Many factories already ran on electricity, but now many urban households joined the grid as well. By the mid-1920s, with more than 60 percent of the nation's homes electrified, new appliances, from refrigerators and vacuum cleaners to fans and razors, filled the stores. The manufacture of such appliances, as well as of hydroelectric generating plants and equipment, provided a massive economic stimulus.

The automobile helped fuel the boom. Introduced before the war (see Chapter 21), the automobile came into its own in the 1920s. By 1930, some 60 percent of U.S. families owned cars. The Ford Motor Company led the market until mid-decade, when General Motors (GM) spurted ahead by touting greater comfort and a range of colors (Ford's Model T came only in black). GM's lowest-priced car, named for French auto-

CHRONOLOGY, 1920–1929

1920–1921 • Postwar recession.

1920 • Warren G. Harding elected president.
Radio station KDKA, Pittsburgh, broadcasts election returns.
Sinclair Lewis, *Main Street.*

1921 • Economic boom begins; agriculture remains depressed.
Sheppard-Towner Act.
Shuffle Along, all-black musical review.

1921–1922 • Washington Naval Arms Conference.

1922 • Supreme Court declares child-labor law unconstitutional.
Fordney-McCumber Tariff restores high rates.
Herbert Hoover, *American Individualism.*

1923 • Harding dies; Calvin Coolidge becomes president.

1924 • Teapot Dome scandals investigated.
National Origins Act (immigration restriction).
Calvin Coolidge elected president.

1925 • Scopes Trial.
Ku Klux Klan scandal in Indiana.
Alain Locke, *The New Negro.*
DuBose Heyward, *Porgy.*
F. Scott Fitzgerald, *The Great Gatsby.*

1926 • Book-of-the-Month Club founded.
National Broadcasting Company founded.
Langston Hughes, *The Weary Blues.*

1927 • *The Jazz Singer,* first sound movie.
Coolidge vetoes the McNary-Haugen farm bill.
Henry Ford introduces the Model A.
Ford apologizes for anti-Semitic publications.
Execution of Sacco and Vanzetti.
Charles A. Lindbergh's transatlantic flight.
Marcus Garvey deported.
Mississippi River flood.

1928 • Herbert Hoover elected president.

1929 • Federal Farm Board created.
Sheppard-Towner program terminated.
Textile strike in Gastonia, North Carolina.
Ernest Hemingway, *A Farewell to Arms.*
Claude McKay, *Home to Harlem.*

motive designer Louis Chevrolet, proved especially popular. Meeting the challenge, in 1927 **Henry Ford** introduced the stylish Model A in various colors. By the end of the decade, the automobile industry accounted for about 9 percent of all wages in manufacturing and had stimulated such industries as rubber, gasoline and motor oil, advertising, and highway construction.

The stock market at first reflected the prevailing prosperity, and then far outran it, as a speculative frenzy gripped Wall Street. By 1929, stock prices had reached stratospheric levels, creating conditions for a horrendous collapse (see Chapter 24).

The business boom had a global impact. To supply overseas markets, Ford, GM, and other corporations built production facilities abroad. Other U.S. firms acquired foreign factories or sources of raw materials. U.S. meatpackers built plants in Argentina; Anaconda Copper acquired Chile's biggest copper mine; the mammoth United Fruit Company established plants across Latin America. U.S. private investment abroad also increased as American investment firms loaned European nations money to repay war debts and modernize their economies. But the era of economic globalization still lay far in the future. Economic nationalism prevailed in the 1920s, as the industrialized nations, including the United States, erected high tariff barriers. The Fordney-McCumber Tariff (1922) and the Smoot-Hawley Tariff (1930) pushed U.S. import duties to all-time highs, benefiting domestic manufacturers but stifling foreign trade. The percentage of the GNP represented by exports actually fell between 1913 and 1929. Manufactured goods increasingly replaced agricultural commodities in U.S. exports, however, rising to 61 percent of the total by 1930.

While prosperity lifted overall wage rates, workers benefited unequally, reflecting regional variations and discriminatory practices by employers. The variation between North and South loomed largest. In 1928, unskilled laborers in New England earned an average of forty-seven cents an hour, in contrast to twenty-eight cents in the South. Textile corporations moved south in search of lower wage rates, devastating New England mill towns. Women workers, blacks, Mexican-Americans, and recent immigrants clustered at the bottom of the wage scale. African-Americans, including many recent migrants from the rural South, faced special difficulties. "Last hired and first fired," they generally held the most menial jobs.

For farmers, wartime prosperity gave way to hard times. Grain prices plummeted when government purchases for the army dwindled, European agriculture revived, and America's high tariffs depressed agricultural exports. Ironically, when tractors and other new machinery increased farm production, the resulting surpluses further weakened prices. Farmers who had bought land and equipment on credit during the war now felt the squeeze as payments came due.

New Modes of Producing, Managing, and Selling	The 1920s saw striking increases in productivity. New assembly-line techniques boosted the per capita output of industrial workers by some 40 percent. At the Ford plants near Detroit, workers stood in place and performed repetitive tasks as chains conveyed the partly assembled vehicles past them.

Assembly-line work influenced employees' behavior. Managers discouraged individual initiative. Even talking or laughter could distract workers from their task. Ford employees learned to speak without moving their lips and adopted an expressionless mask that some called "Fordization of the face." As work became more routine, job satisfaction diminished. Assembly-line labor did not foster the pride that came from farming or mastering a craft. Nor did it offer much prospect of advancement. In Muncie, Indiana, factories employing over four thousand workers announced only ten openings for foremen in 1924 and 1925.

Still, the new mass-production methods had a global impact. *Fordism* became a synonym worldwide for American industrial might and assembly-line methods. In Russia, which purchased twenty-five thousand Ford tractors in the 1920s, people "ascribed a magical quality to the name of Ford," a visitor reported.

Business consolidation, spurred by the war, continued. By the late 1920s, over a thousand companies a year vanished through merger. Corporate giants dominated the major industries: Ford, GM, and Chrysler in automobiles; General Electric and Westinghouse in electricity; and so forth. Samuel Insull, longtime president of Chicago's Commonwealth Edison Company, presided over a multi-billion-dollar empire of local and regional power companies and electric railroads. By 1930, one hundred corporations controlled nearly half the nation's business. Without actually merging, companies that made the same product often cooperated through trade associations on such matters as pricing, product specifications, and division of markets.

As U.S. capitalism matured, management structures evolved. Giant corporations set up separate divisions for product development, market research, economic forecasting, employee relations, and so on, each run by a professional manager.

The modernization of business affected wage policies. Rejecting the old view that employers should pay the lowest wages possible, business leaders now concluded that higher wages would improve productivity and increase consumer buying power. Henry Ford had led the way in 1914 by paying his workers five dollars a day, well above the average for factory workers. Other companies soon followed suit.

New systems for distributing goods emerged as well. Automobiles reached consumers through dealer networks. By 1926, nearly ten thousand Ford dealerships dotted the nation. The A&P grocery chain boasted 17,500 stores by 1928. Chain stores accounted for about a quarter of all retail sales by 1930. Department stores grew more inviting, with remodeled interiors and attractive display windows. Air conditioning, an early-twentieth-century invention, made department stores (as well as movie theaters and restaurants) welcome havens on summer days.

Advertising and credit sales further strengthened the new consumer economy. In 1929, corporations spent nearly $2 billion on radio, billboard, newspaper, and magazine ads, and advertising companies employed some six hundred thousand people. Chicago advertising baron Albert Lasker owned the Chicago Cubs baseball team and his own golf course. As they still do, 1920s' advertisers used celebrity endorsements, promises of social success, and threats of social embarrassment. Beneath a picture of a sad young woman, a Listerine mouthwash ad proclaimed: "She was a beautiful girl and talented too. . . . Yet in the one pursuit that stands foremost in the mind of every girl and woman—marriage—she was a failure." Her problem was "halitosis," or bad breath. The remedy, of course, was Listerine, and lots of it.

Advertisers offered a seductive vision of the new era of abundance. Portraying a fantasy world of elegance, grace, and pleasure, ads aroused desires that the new consumer-oriented capitalist system happily fulfilled. One critic in 1925 described the "dream world" created by advertising:

> [S]miling faces, shining teeth, schoolgirl complexions, cornless feet, perfect fitting [underwear], distinguished collars, wrinkleless pants, odorless breath, regularized

bowels, . . . charging motors, punctureless tires, perfect busts, shimmering shanks, self-washing dishes, backs behind which the moon was meant to rise.

The ballyhoo of advertising also stirred a skeptical reaction. *Your Money's Worth* (1927), by Stuart Chase and F. J. Schlink, cast a critical eye on advertisers' claims. One observer called the book "the *Uncle Tom's Cabin* of the consumer movement." The *Consumers' Research Bulletin,* launched by Chase and Schlink in 1929, tested products and reported the results to consumers.

Americans of the 1920s increasingly bought major purchases on credit. In earlier days, credit had typically involved pawnbrokers, personal loans, or informal arrangements between buyers and sellers. Now retailers routinely offered credit plans for big-ticket items such as automobiles, furniture, and refrigerators. By 1929 credit purchases accounted for 75 percent of automobile sales.

What some have called "the cult of business" saturated 1920s' U.S. culture. "America stands for one idea: Business . . . ," proclaimed the *Independent* magazine in 1921; "Thru business, . . . the human race is finally to be redeemed." Presidents Harding and Coolidge praised business values and hobnobbed with corporate leaders. Magazines profiled business tycoons. A 1923 opinion poll ranked Henry Ford as a leading presidential prospect. In *The Man Nobody Knows* (1925), ad man Bruce Barton described Jesus Christ as a managerial genius who "picked up twelve men from the bottom ranks of business and forged them into an organization that conquered the world."

Women in the New Economic Era   Although the ranks of women employed outside the home increased in the 1920s, their share as a proportion of the total female population hardly changed, hovering at about 24 percent. Male workers dominated the auto plants and other assembly-line factories.

Women who did enter the workplace faced wage discrimination. In 1929, for example, a male trimmer in the meatpacking industry received fifty-two cents an hour; a female trimmer, thirty-seven cents. The weakening of the union movement (see next section) hit women workers hard. By 1929, the proportion of women workers belonging to unions fell to a minuscule 3 percent.

Most women workers, especially recent immigrants and members of minority groups, held low-paying, unskilled positions. By 1930, however, some 2 million women were working in corporate offices as secretaries, typists, or filing clerks, although rarely at higher ranks. Indeed, office-space arrangements often segregated male managers and female clerks.

As for higher education, nearly fifty thousand women received college degrees in 1930, almost triple the 1920 figure. Of those who entered the workplace, most took clerical jobs or entered such traditional "women's professions" as nursing, librarianship, and school teaching. With medical schools imposing a 5 percent quota on female admissions, the number of women physicians actually declined from 1910 to 1930. A handful of women, however, following the lead of Progressive Era feminist trailblazers, pursued postgraduate education to become faculty members in colleges and universities.

While marginalized in the workplace, women were courted as consumers. In the decade's advertising, glamorous women smiled behind the steering wheel, swooned over new appliances, and smoked cigarettes in romantic settings. (One ad man promoted cigarettes for women as "torches of freedom.") In the advertisers' dream world, housework became an exciting challenge. As one ad put it, "Men are judged . . . according to their power to delegate work. Similarly the wise woman delegates to electricity all that electricity can do."

Struggling Labor Unions in a Business Age
Organized labor faced tough sledding in the 1920s. Union membership fell from 5 million in 1920 to 3.4 million in 1929. Several factors underlay this decline. For one thing, despite inequities and regional variations, overall wage rates rose in the decade, reducing the incentive to join a union. Further, the union movement's strength lay in older industries like printing, railroading, mining, and construction. These unions were ill suited to the new mass-production factories.

Management hostility further weakened organized labor. Henry Ford hired thugs to intimidate union organizers. In 1929, anti-union violence flared in North Carolina, where textile workers faced low wages, long hours, and appalling work conditions. In Marion, deputy sheriffs shot and killed six striking workers. In Gastonia, the communist-led National Textile Workers Union organized the strike. The mill's absentee owners refused to negotiate and evicted strikers from their company-owned homes. When armed thugs in league with the owners raided an encampment of strikers, the police chief was shot, possibly by one of his own deputies. Sixteen union leaders were indicted for murder, but released after a mistrial was declared. Later, a sniper shot and killed strike leader and balladeer Ella May Wiggins en route to a union rally. In the end, these strikes failed, and the textile industry remained nonunion.

Gastonia, North Carolina, 1929 *Two women textile workers confront an armed guard in a bitter strike that took several lives.*

As the wartime antiradical mood continued, opponents of labor unions often smeared them with the "communist" label, whether accurate or not. The anti-union campaign took subtler forms as well. Manufacturers' associations renamed the non-union shop the "open shop" and dubbed it the "American Plan" of labor relations. Some corporations provided cafeterias and recreational facilities for employees or sold them company stock at bargain prices. Corporate publicists praised "welfare capitalism" (the term for this anti-union strategy) as evidence of employers' benevolent concern for their workers.

Black membership in labor unions stood at only about eighty-two thousand by 1929, mostly miners, dockworkers, and railroad porters. The American Federation of Labor officially prohibited racial discrimination, but most AFL unions in fact barred African-Americans. Corporations often hired jobless blacks as strikebreakers, increasing organized labor's hostility toward them.

THE HARDING AND COOLIDGE ADMINISTRATIONS

With Republicans in control of Congress and the White House, politics reflected the decade's business orientation. Unsettled by rapid social change, many voters turned to conservative candidates who seemed to represent stability and traditional values. In this climate, former progressives, would-be reformers, and exploited groups had few political options.

Standpat Politics in a Decade of Change While the white South and the immigrant cities remained heavily Democratic, the Republican Party continued to attract northern farmers, businesspeople, native-born white-collar workers and professionals, and some skilled blue-collar workers. The GOP also benefited from the antiradical mood that had produced the early postwar Red Scare (see Chapter 22) and fed the decade's anti-union sentiment. Exploiting such fears, the Republican-led New York legislature set up a committee to investigate "seditious activities," expelled five socialist members, and required loyalty oaths of public-school teachers.

With Republican progressives having bolted to Theodore Roosevelt in 1912, GOP conservatives controlled the 1920 convention and nominated Senator **Warren G. Harding** of Marion, Ohio, for president. As a young newspaper editor, Harding had married the local banker's daughter, Florence Kling, who helped manage his election to the Senate in 1915. A genial backslapper, he enjoyed good liquor, a good poker game, and at least one long-term extramarital relationship. In the election, Harding swamped his Democratic opponent James M. Cox. After the stresses of war and Wilson's lofty moralizing, voters welcomed Harding's blandness and soothing oratory.

Harding made some notable cabinet selections: Henry C. Wallace, the editor of an Iowa farm periodical, as secretary of agriculture; **Charles Evans Hughes,** former New York governor and 1916 presidential candidate, secretary of state; and **Andrew Mellon,** a Pittsburgh financier, treasury secretary. **Herbert Hoover,** the wartime food czar, became secretary of commerce.

Harding also made some disastrous appointments: his political manager, Harry Daugherty, as attorney general; a Senate pal, Albert Fall of New Mexico, as secretary of the interior; a wartime draft dodger, Charles Forbes, as Veterans' Bureau head. Such men set the low ethical tone of Harding's presidency. By 1922, Washington rumor hinted at corruption in high places. "I have no trouble with my enemies . . . ," Harding told an associate; "[b]ut . . . my goddamn friends . . . keep me walking the floor nights." In July 1923, vacationing in the West, Harding suffered a heart attack; on August 2 he died in a San Francisco hotel.

A 1924 Senate investigation exposed the full scope of the scandals. Charles Forbes, convicted of stealing Veterans' Bureau funds, evaded prison by fleeing abroad. The bureau's general counsel committed suicide, as did an aide to Attorney General Daugherty accused of influence peddling. Daugherty himself narrowly escaped conviction in two criminal trials. Interior Secretary Fall went to jail for leasing government oil reserves, one in Teapot Dome, Wyoming, to two oilmen in return for a $400,000 bribe. Like "Watergate" in the 1970s, **"Teapot Dome"** became a shorthand label for a tangle of scandals.

With Harding's death, Vice President **Calvin Coolidge,** on a family visit in Vermont, took the presidential oath by lantern light from his father, a local magistrate. After graduating from Amherst College in Massachusetts, Coolidge had entered politics. Elected Massachusetts governor in 1918, he secured the Republican vice-presidential nomination in 1920.

Coolidge's image as "Silent Cal," a prim Yankee embodiment of old-fashioned virtues, was carefully crafted. The advertising executive Bruce Barton, an early master of political image-making, guided Coolidge's bid for national office in 1919–1920. Having persuaded the Boston publisher Houghton Mifflin to issue a book of Coolidge's speeches, Barton sent autographed copies to key GOP convention delegates. Barton planted pro-Coolidge articles in popular periodicals; organized "spontaneous" letter-writing campaigns to magazines urging more attention to Coolidge; and in general marketed his candidate as one would a soap or an automobile. The very name *Calvin Coolidge,* he wrote in a 1919 *Collier's* article building brand recognition, "seems cut from granite; one could almost strike sparks with such a name, like a flint." Targeting newly enfranchised women, Barton composed a "Message to Women" published under Coolidge's name in the March 1920 *Woman's Home Companion.*

Once Coolidge became president, Barton wrote speeches for him, arranged more book deals, and set up interviews with friendly reporters. Coolidge good-naturedly cooperated with Barton's image-making, donning cowboy hats and Indian war bonnets for photographers and reinforcing his "Silent Cal" reputation. When a journalist asked for a parting message to the people of California at the close of a presidential visit, Coolidge responded "Good-bye."

Long before Franklin D. Roosevelt's "fireside chats" of the 1930s (see Chapter 24), Barton understood the political potential of radio. He advised Coolidge to speak conversationally in his radio addresses, avoiding the spread-eagle oratory of earlier times. Wrote an admirer of Barton: "No man is his equal in [analyzing] the middle-class mind and directing an appeal to it."

Republican Policy Making in a Probusiness Era   While Coolidge raised the ethical tone of the White House, the probusiness policies, symbolized by high tariffs, continued. Prodded by Treasury Secretary Mellon, Congress lowered income-tax rates for the wealthy from their high wartime levels. Promoting what would later be called the "trickle-down theory" of prosperity, Mellon preached that tax cuts for the rich encouraged business investment and thus benefited everyone. In the same probusiness spirit, the Supreme Court under Chief Justice William Howard Taft (appointed by Harding in 1921) overturned a federal ban on child labor passed in 1919.

While promoting corporate interests, Coolidge opposed government assistance for other groups. This position faced a test in 1927 when torrential spring rains caused severe flooding on the Mississippi River. Soil erosion resulting from poor farming practices worsened the flood conditions, as did ill-considered engineering projects aimed at draining the river's natural floodplain for development purposes. One official described the river as "writh[ing] like an imprisoned snake" within its artificial confines. From Cairo, Illinois, to the Gulf of Mexico, water poured over towns and farms, flooding twenty-seven thousand square miles. Hundreds died, and the toll of the homeless, including many African-Americans, reached several hundred thousand. Disease spread in makeshift refugee camps. In an eerie preview of Hurricane Katrina in 2005, floodwaters swept over New Orleans's low-lying black neighborhoods.

Despite the flood's toll, Coolidge rejected calls for aid to the victims. The government had no duty to protect citizens "against the hazards of the elements," he declared. Coolidge did, however, sign the Flood Control Act of 1928 funding a ten-year program of levee construction along the Mississippi.

Another test of Coolidge's views came when hard-pressed farmers rallied behind the **McNary-Haugen Bill,** a price-support plan under which the government would annually purchase the surplus of six basic farm commodities—cotton, corn, rice, hogs, tobacco, and wheat—at their average price in 1909–1914 (when farm prices were high). The government would then sell these surpluses abroad at market prices and recover the difference, if any, through a tax on domestic sales of these commodities. Coolidge twice vetoed the McNary-Haugen bill, in 1927 and 1928, warning of "the tyranny of bureaucratic regulation and control." The government ought not favor a single interest group, he argued, even though corporations had long benefited from high tariffs and other measures. These vetoes led many angry farmers to vote Democratic in 1928. In the 1930s, New Deal planners would draw upon the McNary-Haugen approach in shaping farm policy (see Chapter 24).

Independent Internationalism Although U.S. officials participated informally in some League of Nations activities, the United States refused to join the League or its International Court of Justice (the World Court) in the Netherlands. Despite isolationist tendencies, however, the Republican administrations of the 1920s pursued global policies they saw as serving America's national interest—an approach historians have called independent internationalism.

President Harding's most notable achievement was the **Washington Naval Arms Conference.** After the war ended, the United States, Great Britain, and Japan edged toward a dangerous (and costly) naval-arms race. In 1921, Secretary of State Hughes called for a conference in Washington to address the problem. He startled the delegates by outlining a specific ratio of warships among the world's naval powers. He even proposed scrapping some vessels, which he mentioned by name. Great Britain and Japan, together with Italy and France, accepted Hughes's plan, and agreed to halt all battleship construction for ten years. The United States and Japan also pledged to respect each other's territorial holdings in the Pacific. Although this treaty ultimately failed to prevent war, it did represent an early arms-control effort.

Another U.S. peace initiative was mainly symbolic. In 1928, the United States and France, eventually joined by sixty other nations, signed the Kellogg-Briand Pact renouncing aggression and calling for the outlawing of war. Lacking enforcement mechanisms, this high-sounding document accomplished little.

The Republican administrations of these years used diplomacy to promote U.S. economic interests. For example, they vigorously sought repayment of $22 billion in Allied war debts and German reparation payments. A study commission in 1924 sharply reduced these claims, but high U.S. tariffs and Europe's economic problems, including runaway inflation in Germany, made repayment of even the reduced claims unrealistic. When Adolf Hitler rose to power in Germany in 1933 (see Chapter 25), he repudiated all reparations payments.

With U.S. foreign investments expanding, the Harding and Coolidge administrations promoted American business interests abroad. For example, they opposed Mexico's efforts to regain control of oilfields earlier granted to U.S. companies. Efforts to negotiate the issue collapsed in 1928 when Mexico's president was assassinated. Complicating U.S.-Mexican relations was Washington's fear that Mexico, gripped by revolutionary upheaval, might go communist. These fears deepened in 1924 when Mexico recognized the Soviet Union, nine years before the United States took the same step.

Progressive Stirrings, Democratic Party Divisions The reform spirit survived feebly in the legislative branch. Congress staved off Andrew Mellon's proposals for even deeper tax cuts for the rich. Senator George Norris of Nebraska prevented the Coolidge administration from selling a federal hydroelectric facility at Muscle Shoals, Alabama, to Henry Ford at bargain prices. And in 1927 Congress created the Federal Radio Commission, extending the regulatory principle to this new industry.

In the 1922 midterm election, an alliance of labor and farm groups helped defeat some conservative Republicans. In 1924, this alliance revived the Progressive Party and nominated Senator Robert La Follette for president. The Socialist Party and the American Federation of Labor endorsed La Follette.

The 1924 Democratic convention in New York City split evenly between urban and rural wings. By one vote, the delegates defeated a resolution condemning the **Ku Klux Klan** (see below). While the party's rural, Protestant, southern wing favored former Treasury Secretary William G. McAdoo, the big-city delegates rallied behind New York's Catholic governor **Alfred E. Smith,** of Irish, German, and Italian immigrant origins. The Democratic split mirrored deep divisions in the nation. After 102 ballots, the exhausted delegates nominated an obscure New York corporation lawyer, John W. Davis.

Calvin Coolidge, aided by his media adviser Bruce Barton, easily won the Republican nomination. The GOP platform praised the high protective tariff and urged tax cuts and reduced government spending. With the economy humming, Coolidge polled nearly 16 million votes, about twice Davis's total. La Follette's 4.8 million votes cut into the Democratic total, contributing to the Coolidge landslide.

Women and Politics in the 1920s: A Dream Deferred Suffragists' hope that votes for women would transform politics survived briefly after the war. Polling places shifted from saloons to schools and churches. The 1920 major-party platforms endorsed several measures proposed by the League of Women Voters. The Women's Joint Congressional Committee, a coalition of activist groups, lobbied for child-labor laws, protection of women workers, and federal support for education. It also backed the **Sheppard-Towner Act** (1921), which funded rural prenatal and baby-care centers staffed by public-health nurses.

Overall, however, the Nineteenth Amendment, though a historic achievement, had little short-term political effect. As former suffrage advocates scattered across the political spectrum, the women's movement lost focus. The League of Women Voters, drawing middle-class and professional women, abandoned feminist activism and instead conducted nonpartisan studies of civic issues. Alice Paul's National Woman's Party proposed a constitutional amendment guaranteeing women equal rights, but other reformers argued that such an amendment could jeopardize gender-based laws protecting women workers. Politically active African-American women battled racial discrimination rather than addressing feminist issues; Hispanic women in the Southwest put their energies into labor-union organizing.

The reactionary political climate intensified this retreat from feminism. Patriotic groups accused Jane Addams and other women's-rights leaders of communist sympathies. Younger women, bombarded by ads that defined liberation in terms of consumption, rejected the prewar feminists' civic idealism. One in 1927 criticized the prewar "fighting feminists" for their lack of "feminine charm" and their "constant clamor about equal rights."

The few reforms women's groups did achieve proved short-lived. The Supreme Court in 1922–1923 struck down child-labor and women's-protective laws. A 1924 constitutional amendment banning child labor passed Congress, but few states ratified it. The Sheppard-Towner Act, denounced by the American Medical Association as a threat to physicians' monopoly of health care, expired in 1929.

MASS SOCIETY, MASS CULTURE

As a conservative reaction dominated U.S. politics, major transformations were reshaping society. Assembly lines, new consumer products, advertising, the spread of mass entertainment, and innovations in corporate organization all signaled profound changes in American life. Some citizens found these changes exciting; others recoiled in fear and apprehension.

Cities, Cars, Consumer Goods   In the 1920 census, for the first time, the urban population (defined as persons living in communities of twenty-five hundred or more) surpassed the rural. The United States had become an urban nation.

Urbanization affected different groups of Americans in different ways. African-Americans, for example, migrated cityward in massive numbers, especially after the 1927 Mississippi River floods. By 1930, more than 40 percent of the nation's 12 million blacks lived in cities, 2 million of them in Chicago, Detroit, New York, and other urban centers of the North and West. The first black congressman since Reconstruction, Oscar De Priest of Chicago, won election in 1928.

For many women, city life meant eased housework thanks to laborsaving appliances: gas stoves, electric irons, refrigerators, washing machines, and vacuum cleaners. Store-bought clothes replaced hand-sewn apparel. Home baking and canning declined as commercial bakeries arose and supermarkets offered canned fruit and vegetables.

For social impact, however, nothing matched the automobile. In *Middletown* (1929), a study of Muncie, Indiana, Robert and Helen Lynd reported one resident's comment: "Why . . . do you need to study what's changing this country? I can tell you . . . in just four letters: A-U-T-O."

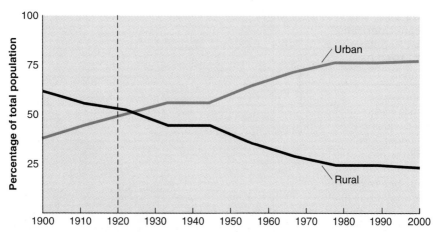

Figure 23.1 The Urban and Rural Population of the United States, 1900–2000

The urbanization of America in the twentieth century had profound political, economic, and social consequences. *Source:* Census Bureau, *Historical Statistics of the United States,* updated by relevant Statistical Abstracts of the United States.

The A-U-T-O's social impact was decidedly mixed, including traffic jams, parking problems, and highway fatalities (more than twenty-six thousand in 1924). In some ways, the automobile brought families together. Family vacations, rare a generation earlier, became more common. Tourist cabins and roadside restaurants served vacationing families. But the automobile also eroded family cohesion and parental authority. Young people could borrow the car to go to the movies, attend a distant dance, or simply park in a secluded lovers' lane.

Middle- and upper-class women welcomed the automobile. They could now drive to work, attend meetings, visit friends, and gain a sense of personal empowerment. Stereotypes of feminine delicacy faded as women mastered this new technology. As the editor of an automotive magazine wrote in 1927, "[E]very time a woman learns to drive, . . . it is a threat to yesterday's order of things."

For farm families, the automobile offered easier access to neighbors and to the city, lessening rural isolation. The automobile's country cousin, the tractor, proved instantly popular, with nearly a million in use in America by 1930, increasing productivity and reducing the physical demands of farm labor. Yet increased productivity did not always mean increased profits. And as farmers bought automobiles, tractors, and other mechanized equipment on credit, the rural debt crisis worsened.

Ads celebrated the freedom the automobile offered, in contrast to the fixed routes and schedules of trains and streetcars. Yet the automobile and other forms of motor transport in many ways further standardized American life. One-room schoolhouses stood empty as buses carried children to consolidated schools. Neighborhood grocery stores declined as people drove to supermarkets served by trucks bringing commercial foods from distant facilities. With the automobile came the first suburban shopping center (in Kansas City), and the first fast-food chain (A & W Root Beer).

Figure 23.2 The African-American Urban Population, 1880–1960 (in millions)

The increase in America's urban black population from under 1 million in 1880 to nearly 14 million by 1960 represents one of the great rural-urban migrations of modern history. *Source: Historical Statistics of the United States, Colonial Times to 1970* (Washington, D.C.: Bureau of the Census, 1975), vol. I, p. 12.

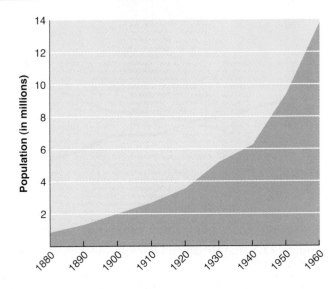

Even at $300 or $400, and despite a thriving used-car market, the automobile remained too expensive for many. The "automobile suburbs" that sprang up beyond the streetcar lines attracted mainly the well-to-do, widening class divisions in American society.

Soaring Energy Consumption and a Threatened Environment

Electrification and the spread of motorized vehicles placed heavy demands on the nation's natural resources and the environment. As electrical use soared, generating plants consumed growing quantities of coal. In 1929, with 20 million cars on the road, U.S. refineries used over a billion barrels of petroleum to meet the demand for gasoline and lubricating oil.

Rising gasoline consumption underlay Washington's efforts to ensure U.S. access to Mexican oil; played a role in the Teapot Dome scandal; and triggered fevered activity in the oilfields of Texas and Oklahoma as Texaco, Gulf, and many now-forgotten companies struggled for dominance. The natural gas found with petroleum seemed so abundant that it was simply burned off. In short, heavy fossil-fuel consumption, though small by later standards, already characterized America in the 1920s.

The wilderness that had inspired nineteenth-century artists and writers became more accessible as cars, improved roads, and tourist facilities gave vacationers easier access to the national parks and once-pristine regions. This development, too, had mixed effects. On one hand, it created a broader constituency for environmental protection and wilderness preservation. On the other, it subjected the nation's parks and wilderness areas to heavy pressures as visitors expected good highways, service stations, restaurants, and hotels.

Three Young Hispanic Women of Tucson, Arizona   *In this posed photograph featuring an open touring car, these confident and fashionably dressed young women make their social aspirations clear.*

These contradictions worried Secretary of Commerce Herbert Hoover. He believed that urban dwellers benefited from returning to nature, but he recognized the strains that tourism placed on parks and wilderness areas. Hoover called a National Conference on Outdoor Recreation to consider ways to balance the preservationist ethic and the vacation-minded leisure culture of the 1920s.

The Sierra Club and other groups worked to protect wilderness and wildlife. In 1923, the Izaak Walton League, devoted to recreational fishing, persuaded Congress to halt a private-development scheme to drain a vast stretch of wetlands on the upper Mississippi. Instead, Congress declared this beautiful waterway a wildlife preserve. Aldo Leopold of the U.S. Forest Service warned of technology run amok. For too long, Leopold wrote in 1925, "a stump was our symbol of progress." However, few Americans in the expansive 1920s worried about the environmental issues that would occupy future generations.

Mass-Produced Entertainment   Growing prosperity and routinized work stimulated interest in leisure activities in the 1920s. In their free hours, Americans sought the fulfillment many found missing in the workplace.

Mass-circulation magazines provided diversion. By 1922, ten U.S. magazines boasted circulation of more than 2.5 million. The venerable *Saturday Evening Post,* with its Norman Rockwell covers and fiction featuring small-town life, specialized in nostalgia. *Reader's Digest,* founded in 1921 by DeWitt and Lila Wallace, offered condensed versions of articles first published elsewhere. A journalistic equivalent of the Model T, the *Digest* offered standardized fare for mass consumption.

Book publishers broadened their market by selling through department stores or directly to the public via the Book-of-the-Month Club, launched in 1926. While critics accused such mass-market ventures of debasing literary taste, they did help sustain a common national culture in an increasingly diverse society.

In an age of standardized consumer goods, radio and the movies offered standardized cultural fare. The radio era began on November 2, 1920, when Pittsburgh station KDKA reported Warren Harding's election. In 1922, New York's WEAF began a regular news program, and a Newark station broadcast the World Series (the New York Giants beat the Yankees). In 1922, five hundred new stations began operations, as radio fever gripped America.

In 1926 three corporations—General Electric, Westinghouse, and the Radio Corporation of America—formed the first radio network, the National Broadcasting Company (NBC). The Columbia Broadcasting System (CBS) followed in 1927. Testing popular taste through market research, the networks soon ruled broadcasting. Americans everywhere laughed at the same jokes, heard the same news, and absorbed the same commercials.

WEAF broadcast the first sponsored program in 1922. Some public-policy commentators advocated preserving radio as a public educational and cultural medium, free of advertising, but commercial sponsorship soon won out. The first network comedy show, *Amos 'n' Andy* (1928), enriched its sponsor, Pepsodent toothpaste. White actors played the black characters on the program, which softened the realities of a racist society with stereotyped caricatures of African-American life.

Featuring stars like Valentino, the movies reached all social classes as they expanded from the nickelodeons of the immigrant wards into elegant uptown pleasure palaces with names like Majestic, Ritz, and Orpheum. In 1922, facing protests about sexually suggestive movies, and after a lurid sex scandal involving film star Roscoe "Fatty" Arbuckle, the movie industry named Will Hays, a member of President Harding's cabinet and former head of the Republican National Committee, to police movie morals. While enforcing a code of standards, Hays also served a public-relations role, promoting Hollywood films.

Despite charges that the movies undermined morality, they often reinforced traditional values. Charlie Chaplin, who had played anarchic, anti-authority figures in his prewar comedies, now softened his character in such feature-length films as *The Gold Rush* (1925). "America's sweetheart," Mary Pickford, with her golden curls and look of frail vulnerability, played innocent girls in need of protection, reinforcing traditional gender stereotypes at a time when many young women were challenging them. (Pickford sometimes played plucky young women facing danger courageously, and in real life was a shrewd businesswoman who became enormously wealthy.) *The Ten Commandments* (1923), directed by Cecil B. De Mille (the son of an Episcopal clergyman), warned of the consequences of breaking moral taboos.

Technical innovations kept moviegoers coming. Al Jolson's *The Jazz Singer* (1927) introduced sound. Walt Disney's cartoon *Steamboat Willy* (1928) not only marked the debut of Mickey Mouse but also showed the potential of animation. With technical advances came greater standardization. By 1930, with weekly attendance approaching 80 million, the corporate giants Metro-Goldwyn-Mayer, Warner Brothers, and Columbia, relying on formulaic plots and typecast stars, produced most films. As U.S. business expanded abroad, Hollywood, too, sought overseas markets for its product.

Like advertising, the movies created a dream world only loosely tethered to reality. One ad promised "all the adventure, . . . romance, . . . [and] excitement you lack in your daily life." These mass-produced fantasies shaped behavior and values, especially of the young. Hollywood, observed novelist John Dos Passos, offered a "great bargain sale of five-and-ten-cent lusts and dreams." The movies also stimulated consumption with alluring images of the good life. Along with department stores, mass magazines, and advertising, they opened new vistas of consumer abundance.

This spread of mass culture was a byproduct of urbanization. Even when advertisers, radio programmers, filmmakers, and magazine editors nostalgically evoked rural or small-town life, they did so from big-city offices and studios.

For all its influence, the new mass culture penetrated society unevenly. It had less impact in rural America, and met resistance among evangelical Christians suspicious of worldly amusements. Mexican-Americans preserved traditional festivals and leisure activities despite the "Americanization" efforts of non-Hispanic priests and well-intentioned outsiders. Working-class African-Americans flocked to concerts by performers outside the mass-culture mainstream like blues singers Bessie Smith and Gertrude "Ma" Rainey. Black-oriented "race records" catered to this specialized market.

Local radio stations broadcast not only network shows, but also farm reports, local news, religious programs, community announcements, and ethnic or regional music. Similarly, along with the downtown movie palaces, neighborhood theaters provided opportunities for socializing and for exuberant responses to the film. The *Chicago Defender,* the voice of the city's black middle class, deplored the raucousness of movie theaters in poor black neighborhoods, where "during a death scene . . . you are likely to hear the orchestra jazzing away." In short, despite the new mass culture, America still had room for diversity in the 1920s.

Celebrity Culture   Professional sports and media-promoted spectacles provided diversion as well. In 1921, Atlantic City promoters launched a bathing-beauty contest they grandly called the Miss America Pageant. Celebrities dominated professional sports: Babe Ruth of the New York Yankees, who hit sixty home runs in 1927; Ty Cobb, the Detroit Tigers' manager, whose earlier record of 4,191 hits still inspired awe; prizefighters Jack Dempsey and Gene Tunney, whose two heavyweight fights drew thousands of fans and massive radio audiences. Ruth was a coarse, heavy-drinking womanizer; Cobb, an exceedingly foul-tempered if not borderline psychotic racist. Yet the alchemy of publicity transformed them into heroes with contrived nicknames: "the Sultan of Swat" (Ruth) and "the Georgia Peach" (Cobb).

This celebrity culture illuminates the stresses facing ordinary Americans in these years of social change. For young women uncertain about society's shifting expectations, the beauty pageants offered one ideal to which they could aspire. For men grappling with unsettling developments from feminism to Fordism, the exploits of sports heroes like Dempsey or Ruth could help restore damaged self-esteem.

Celebrity worship reached a crescendo in the response to **Charles Lindbergh,** a daredevil stunt pilot who flew solo across the Atlantic in his small single-engine plane, *The Spirit of St. Louis,* on May 20–21, 1927. A Minnesotan of Swedish ancestry, Lindbergh had entered a $25,000 prize competition offered by a New York hotel for the first nonstop New York to Paris flight. His success gripped the public's imagination. In New York, thousands turned out for a ticker-tape parade. Radio, newspapers, magazines, and movie newsreels offered saturation coverage.

An instant celebrity, Lindbergh became a kind of blank screen onto which people projected their hopes, fears, and ideologies. President Coolidge praised the flight as a triumph of American business and corporate technology. Many editorial writers, by contrast, saw Lindbergh as proof that despite standardization and mechanization, the individual still counted. Others praised this native-born midwesterner of Scandinavian roots as more authentically American than the recent immigrants crowding the cities.

Overall, the new mass media had mixed social effects. Certainly, they promoted cultural standardization and uniformity of thought. But mass magazines, radio, and movies also helped forge a national culture and introduced new viewpoints and ways of behaving. Implicitly they conveyed a potent message: a person's immediate surroundings need not limit his or her horizons. If the larger world they opened for ordinary Americans was often superficial or tawdry, it could also be exciting and liberating.

CULTURAL FERMENT AND CREATIVITY

American life in the 1920s involved more than politics, assembly lines, and celebrity worship. Young people savored the postwar moment when familiar pieties and traditional ways came under challenge. As writers, artists, and musicians contributed to the modernist spirit of cultural innovation, African-Americans created a cultural flowering known as the Harlem Renaissance.

The Jazz Age and the Postwar Crisis of Values
The war and its disillusioned aftermath sharpened the cultural restlessness already evident before the war. The year 1918, wrote Randolph Bourne, marked "a sudden . . . stop at the end of an intellectual era." Poet Ezra Pound hammered the same point in 1920. America had gone to war, he wrote, to save "a botched civilization; . . . an old bitch gone in the teeth."

The postwar cultural ferment, summed up in the phrase "the Jazz Age," took many forms. Some young people—especially affluent college students—boisterously assailed conventional notions of proper behavior. Seizing the freedom offered by the automobile, they threw parties, drank bootleg liquor, flocked to jazz clubs, and danced the Charleston. Asked her favorite activity, a California college student replied, "I adore dancing; who doesn't?" Unaware of the risks, and urged by advertisers, many young women, especially college students and urban workers, defied prevailing taboos and took up cigarettes. For some, smoking became a feminist issue. As one woman college student put it, "[W]hy [should] men . . . be permitted to smoke while girls are expelled for doing it?"

Young people also discussed sex more freely than their elders had. Sigmund Freud, the Viennese physician who explored the sexual aspects of human psychology, enjoyed a popular vogue in a postwar climate that encouraged challenges to old taboos.

Despite much talk about sex and charges of rampant immorality, however, the 1920s' "sexual revolution" is hard to pin down. Premarital intercourse remained exceptional and widely disapproved. What *can* be documented are changing courtship patterns. "Courting" had once been a formal prelude to marriage. The 1920s brought the more casual practice of "dating," through which young people gained social confidence and a degree of sexual experience without necessarily contemplating marriage. Wrote novelist F. Scott Fitzgerald, "None of the Victorian mothers had any idea how casually their daughters were accustomed to be kissed." A Methodist bishop denounced new dances that brought "the bodies of men and women in unusual relation to each other."

The 1920s saw greater erotic freedom, but within bounds, as most young people drew a clear line between permissible and taboo behavior.

For women, these postwar changes in some ways proved liberating. Female sexuality was more openly acknowledged. Skirt lengths crept up; makeup became more acceptable; and the elaborate armor of petticoats and corsets fell away. The awesome matronly bosom mysteriously deflated as a more boyish figure became the fashion ideal.

The most enduring twenties stereotype is the flapper, the sophisticated, pleasure-mad young woman. The term originated with a magazine illustration of a fashionable young woman whose rubber rain boots were open and flapping. Although a journalistic creation, the flapper image played a significant cultural role. In the nineteenth century, the idealized woman on her moral pedestal had symbolized an elaborate complex of cultural ideals. The flapper, with her bobbed hair, defiant cigarette, lipstick, and short skirt, similarly epitomized youthful rejection of entrenched stereotypes.

But this image also objectified young women as decorative sexual objects. Many young women, while rejecting older taboos, now molded their appearance according to standards dictated by fashion magazines like *Vogue* and *Vanity Fair*. Advertisers and movies encouraged women to pursue a "glamorous" lifestyle by purchasing new fashions, cosmetics, silk stockings, and other consumer accessories. Further, the double standard, which held women to a stricter code of conduct, remained in force. Young men could boast of sexual exploits, but young women reputed to be "fast" risked damaged reputations. In some ways, in short, 1920s' popular culture worked against full gender equality nearly as effectively as had the older Victorian stereotypes.

Around 1922, according to F. Scott Fitzgerald, adults embraced the rebelliousness of the young. As middle-aged Americans "discovered that young liquor will take the place of young blood," he wrote, "the orgy began." But such sweeping cultural generalizations can mislead. During the years of Fitzgerald's alleged national orgy, the divorce rate remained constant, and many Americans adhered to traditional standards, rejecting alcohol and wild parties. Most farmers, industrial workers, blacks, Hispanics, and recent immigrants found economic survival more pressing than the latest fads and fashions.

The entire Jazz Age was partially a media and literary creation. Fitzgerald's romanticized novel about affluent postwar youth, *This Side of Paradise* (1920), spawned many imitators. With his movie-idol good looks, Fitzgerald not only wrote about the Jazz Age but lived it. But if the Jazz Age stereotype obscured the complexity of the 1920s, it did capture a part of the postwar scene, especially the brassy new mass culture and the hedonism and materialism of the well-to-do as they basked in the era's prosperity.

Alienated Writers   Like Fitzgerald, many young writers found the cultural turbulence of the 1920s energizing. Rejecting the moralistic pieties of the old order, they also disliked the business pieties of the new. In *Main Street* (1920), the novelist Sinclair Lewis satirized the smugness and cultural barrenness of Gopher Prairie, a fictional midwestern town based on his native Sauk Centre, Minnesota. In *Babbitt* (1922), Lewis skewered a mythic larger city, Zenith, and the title character George F. Babbitt, a real-estate agent trapped in middle-class conformity.

H. L. Mencken, a journalist, editor, and critic, in 1924 launched the iconoclastic *American Mercury* magazine, an instant success with the decade's alienated intellectuals and young people. Mencken championed writers like Lewis and Theodore Dreiser while ridiculing politicians, small-town America, Protestant fundamentalism, and the middle-class "Booboisie." His essays on Harding, Coolidge, and Bryan remain classics of political satire. Asked why he stayed in America, Mencken replied, "Why do people visit zoos?"

For the novelist Ernest Hemingway, seriously wounded in 1918 while serving as a Red Cross volunteer in northern Italy, World War I was a watershed experience. In 1926, now an expatriate in Paris, Hemingway published *The Sun Also Rises,* portraying a group of American and English young people, variously damaged by the war, as they drift around Spain. His *A Farewell to Arms* (1929), loosely based on his own experiences, depicts the war's futility and politicians' empty rhetoric. In one passage, the narrator says,

> I was always embarrassed by the words sacred, glorious, and sacrifice and the expression in vain. We . . . had read them, on proclamations that were slapped up . . . over other proclamations, now for a long time, and I had seen nothing sacred, and the things that were glorious had no glory and the sacrifices were like the stockyards at Chicago if nothing was done with the meat except to bury it.

Although writers like Lewis and Hemingway deplored the inflated rhetoric of the war and the vulgarity of postwar culture, they remained American at heart, striving to create a more authentic national culture. Even F. Scott Fitzgerald, himself caught up in Jazz Age excesses, was fundamentally a moralist. Fitzgerald's masterpiece, *The Great Gatsby* (1925), portrayed not only the party-filled lives of the decade's moneyed class, but also their decadence, selfishness, and heedless disregard for the less fortunate.

Architects, Painters, and Musicians Confront Modern America   A burst of architectural activity transformed the urban skyline in the 1920s. By 1930, America's cities boasted 377 buildings over seventy stories tall. The skyscraper, proclaimed one writer, "epitomizes . . . American civilization." The cultural critic Lewis Mumford, by contrast, in magazine essays and his 1924 book *Sticks and Bones,* deplored the modern city with its skyscrapers and automobile-clogged streets. Mumford preferred smaller communities and regional cultures to the congested cities and mass culture of 1920s' America.

The decade's leading painters took America as their subject—either the real nation around them or an imagined one. While Thomas Hart Benton evoked a past of cowboys, pioneers, and riverboat gamblers, Edward Hopper portrayed faded towns and lonely cities of the present. Hopper's painting *Sunday* (1926), picturing a man slumped on the curb of an empty street of abandoned stores, conveyed both the bleakness and potential beauty of urban America.

The painter and photographer Charles Sheeler found inspiration in factories, including Henry Ford's plant near Detroit. The Italian immigrant Joseph Stella captured New York's excitement and energy in such paintings as *The Bridge* (1926), an abstract representation of the Brooklyn Bridge. Wisconsin's Georgia O'Keeffe, who moved to New York City in 1918, evoked the allure of the metropolis in her paintings of the later 1920s.

The creative ferment of the 1920s inspired composers as well. Ruth Crawford Seeger arranged American folksongs for the poet Carl Sandburg's *American Songbag* (1927). Carl Ruggles set a Walt Whitman poem to music in 1923. And Frederick Converse's ambitious 1927 tone poem about the automobile, "Flivver Ten Million," featured such episodes as "May Night by the Roadside" and "The Collision."

Of all the musical innovations, jazz best captured the modernist spirit. The Original Dixieland Jass Band—white musicians imitating the black jazz bands of New Orleans—had debuted in New York City in 1917, launching a vogue that spread by live performances, radio, and phonograph records. The white bandleader Paul Whiteman offered watered-down "jazz" versions of standard tunes, and white composers embraced jazz as well. Aaron Copland's *Music for Theatre* (1925) and George Gershwin's *Rhapsody in Blue* (1924) and *An American in Paris* (1928) revealed strong jazz influences.

Meanwhile, black musicians preserved authentic jazz and explored its potential. The 1920s recordings of trumpeter Louis Armstrong and his "Hot Five" and "Hot Seven" groups decisively influenced the future of jazz. While the composer and bandleader Duke Ellington performed to sellout audiences at Harlem's Cotton Club, Fletcher Henderson's band, featuring singer Ethel Waters and saxophonist Coleman Hawkins, held forth at New York's Roseland Ballroom and recorded for the Black Swan and Columbia labels. Meanwhile, the piano's jazz potential was demonstrated by Fats Waller, Ferdinand "Jelly Roll" Morton, and Earl Hines, who joined Louis Armstrong's band in 1927. Although much of 1920s' popular culture faded quickly, jazz endured.

The Harlem Renaissance

Jazz was only one of many black contributions to 1920s' American culture. The social changes of these years energized African-American cultural life, especially in New York City's Harlem. An elite white suburb before World War I, Harlem attracted many African-Americans during and after the war, and by 1930 most of New York's 327,000 blacks lived within its boundaries. This concentration, plus the proximity of Broadway theaters, record companies, book publishers, and the NAACP's national headquarters, all contributed to the Harlem Renaissance.

This cultural flowering took varied forms. The Mississippi-born black composer William Grant Still, moving to Harlem in 1922, produced many works, including *Afro American Symphony* (1931). The painter Aaron Douglas and the sculptor Augusta Savage worked in the visual arts. In 1921 Savage, a Florida native, arrived in Harlem, where she opened a studio and later an art school. The 1921 Broadway hit *Shuffle Along* launched a series of popular all-black musicals. Oscar Micheaux made films featuring black actors and black story lines. The multitalented Paul Robeson gave vocal concerts; made films; and appeared on Broadway in Eugene O'Neill's *The Emperor Jones* and other plays.

Among a host of writers, poet Langston Hughes drew upon southern black oral traditions in *The Weary Blues* (1926), and the Jamaican-born poet and novelist Claude McKay evoked Harlem's vibrant, sometimes sinister nightlife in *Home to Harlem* (1928). In *Cane* (1923), Jean Toomer used poetry, drama, and fictional vignettes to convey the world of the rural black South. Nella Larsen, from the Danish West Indies, told of a mulatto woman's struggle with her mixed ethnicity in the 1928 novel *Quicksand*. In *The New Negro* (1925), Alain Locke, a philosophy professor at Howard University, assembled essays, poems, short stories, and reproductions of artworks to convey Harlem's rich cultural life.

Jazz Pioneer Ferdinand (Jelly Roll) Morton *Born to Creole parents in New Orleans in 1890, Morton came to Chicago, where in 1926 his group, Jelly Roll Morton and His Red Hot Peppers, made some of the earliest jazz recordings for the Victor phonograph company.*

The white cultural establishment took notice. Book publishers and magazine editors courted black writers. Broadway producers mounted black shows. Whites crowded Harlem's jazz clubs. The 1929 Hollywood film *Hallelujah,* featuring an all-black cast, romanticized plantation life and dramatized the city's dangers. DuBose Heyward's 1925 novel *Porgy* (adapted for the stage by Heyward and his wife Dorothy) offered a sympathetic picture of Charleston's African-American community. George Gershwin's musical version, *Porgy and Bess,* premiered in 1935.

The Harlem Renaissance reached beyond America's borders. Jazz won a following in Europe. Langston Hughes and Claude McKay were admired in Africa, Latin America, and Europe. The dancer and singer Josephine Baker, after debuting in Harlem, moved to Paris in 1925, where her highly erotic performances created a sensation.

Along with white support came misunderstanding and attempts at control. Rebellious young whites romanticized Harlem nightlife, ignoring the community's overcrowding, poverty, and social problems. Some whites idealized the spiritual or "primitive" qualities of black culture. When Langston Hughes's poems confronted the gritty realities of black life in America, his wealthy white patron angrily withdrew her support. Wrote Hughes: "Concerning Negroes, she felt that they were America's great link with the primitive.... But unfortunately I did not feel the rhythms of the primitive surging through me.... I was not Africa. I was Chicago and Kansas City and Broadway and Harlem."

The hard times of the 1930s ended the Harlem Renaissance. Nevertheless, this burst of creativity stands as a memorable achievement. Future black writers, artists, musicians, and performers would owe a great debt to their predecessors of the 1920s.

A Society in Conflict

The social changes of the 1920s produced a backlash, as a series of divisive episodes and social movements highlighted the era's tensions. While Congress restricted immigration, highly publicized court cases in Massachusetts and Tennessee underscored the nation's social and cultural divisions. Millions of whites embraced the racist bigotry and moralistic rhetoric of a revived Ku Klux Klan, and many newly urbanized African-Americans rallied to Marcus Garvey, a magnetic black leader with a riveting message of racial pride. Prohibition stirred further controversy in this conflict-ridden decade.

Immigration Restriction

Fed by wartime efforts to enforce patriotism, the old impulse to remake America into a nation of like-minded, culturally homogeneous people revived in the 1920s.

The **National Origins Act** of 1924, a revision of the immigration law, restricted annual immigration from any foreign country to 2 percent of the number of persons of that "national origin" in the United States in 1890. Since the great influx of southern and eastern Europeans had come after 1890, the intent of this provision was clear: to reduce the immigration of these nationalities. As Calvin Coolidge observed on signing the law, "America must be kept American."

In 1929, Congress changed the base year for determining "national origins" to 1920, but even under this formula, Poland's annual quota stood at a mere 6,524; Italy's at 5,802; and Hungary's, 869. This quota system, which survived to 1965, represented a strong counterattack by native-born Protestant America against the immigrant cities. Total immigration fell from 1.2 million in 1914 to 280,000 in 1929. The law excluded Asians and South Asians entirely.

Court rulings underscored the nativist message. In *Ozawa* v. *United States* (1922), the U.S. Supreme Court rejected a citizenship request by a Japanese-born student at the University of California. In 1923, the Supreme Court upheld a California law limiting the right of Japanese immigrants to own or lease farmland. That same year, the Supreme Court rejected an immigration application by a man from India who claimed that he was "Caucasian" and thus eligible for entry under the Nationality Act of 1790, which had limited naturalized citizenship to "free white persons." The 1790 law, the court ruled, referred only to "the type of man whom [the authors of the law] knew as white . . . [those] from the British Isles and northwestern Europe."

Needed Workers/ Unwelcome Aliens: Hispanic Newcomers

With all its restrictive provisions, the 1924 law placed no limits on immigration from the Western Hemisphere. Accordingly, immigration from Latin America (as well as from French Canada) soared. Poverty and political turmoil propelled thousands of Mexicans northward. By 1930, at least 2 million Mexican-born people lived in the United States, mostly in the Southwest. California's Mexican-American population surged from 90,000 to nearly 360,000 in the decade.

Many of these immigrants worked in low-paid migratory jobs in the region's large-scale agribusinesses. Mexican labor sustained California's citrus industry. Cooperatives such as the Southern California Fruit Growers Exchange (which marketed its fruit under the brand name "Sunkist") hired itinerant workers on a seasonal basis, provided substandard housing in isolated settlements the workers called *colonias,* and fought the migrants' attempts to form labor unions.

Not all Mexican immigrants were migratory workers; many settled into U.S. communities. Mexican-Americans in the Midwest worked not only in agriculture but also in the automobile, steel, and railroad industries. While still emotionally linked to "México Lindo" (Beautiful Mexico), they formed local support networks and cultural institutions. The Mexican-American community was divided, however, between recent arrivals and earlier immigrants who had become U.S. citizens. The strongest Mexican-American organization in the 1920s, the League of United Latin-American Citizens, ignored the migrant laborers of the Southwest.

Though deeply religious, Mexican-Americans found little support from the U.S. Catholic Church. Earlier, European Catholic immigrants had attended ethnic parishes and worshiped in their own languages, but church policy had changed by the 1920s. In parishes with non-Hispanic priests, Spanish-speaking Mexican newcomers encountered pressure to abandon their language and traditions.

In the larger society, Mexican immigrants faced ambivalent attitudes. Their labor was needed, but their presence disturbed nativists eager to preserve a "white" and Protestant nation. Would-be immigrants confronted strict literacy and means tests, and in 1929 Congress made illegal entry a criminal offense. The flow northward continued, however, as an estimated one hundred thousand Mexican newcomers arrived annually, legally and clandestinely, to fill the U.S. labor market's pressing demands.

Nativism, Antiradicalism, and the Sacco-Vanzetti Case The immigration-restriction movement reflected deep strains of ethnic, racial, and religious prejudice in 1920s' America. Anti-Semitic propaganda filled the *Dearborn Independent,* a weekly newspaper owned by Henry Ford. Distributed through Ford dealerships and mailed free to schools and libraries, the *Dearborn Independent* at its peak reached 600,000 readers. The anti-Semitic articles were reprinted in a series of pamphlets entitled *The International Jew.* Sued for defamation by a California Jewish attorney, Ford in 1927 issued an evasive apology (drafted by a prominent Jewish leader in New York) blaming subordinates.

Nativist, antiradical prejudices emerged starkly in the **Sacco-Vanzetti Case,** a Massachusetts murder case that began in April 1920, when robbers shot and killed the paymaster and guard of a shoe factory in South Braintree, Massachusetts, and stole two cash boxes. In 1921, a jury found two Italian immigrants, Nicola Sacco and Bartolomeo Vanzetti, guilty of the crime. After many appeals and a review by a commission of notable citizens, they were electrocuted on August 23, 1927.

These bare facts hardly convey the passions the case aroused. Sacco and Vanzetti were anarchists, and the prosecution harped on their radicalism. The judge barely concealed his hostility to the pair, whom he privately called "those anarchist bastards." While many conservatives supported the death sentence, liberals and socialists rallied to their cause. As the two went to the chair, John Dos Passos wrote a bitter poem that ended:

All right you have won you will kill the brave men our friends tonight . . . all right we are two nations.

Later research on Boston's anarchist community and ballistics tests on Sacco's gun pointed to their guilt. But the prejudices that tainted the trial remain indisputable, as does the case's symbolic importance in exposing the deep fault lines in 1920s' American society.

Fundamentalism and the Scopes Trial Meanwhile, an equally celebrated case in Tennessee highlighted another front in the cultural wars of the 1920s: the growing prestige of science. While scientists were "individually powerless," wrote the Harvard philosopher Alfred North Whitehead in *Science and the Modern World* (1925), they were "ultimately the rulers of the world." While many Americans welcomed the advance of science, some religious believers found it threatening. Their fears had deepened as scholars had subjected the Bible to critical scrutiny, psychologists and sociologists had studied supernatural belief systems as human social constructs and expressions of emotional needs, and biologists had embraced Charles Darwin's naturalistic explanation for the variety of life forms on Earth advanced in *Origin of Species* (1859).

While liberal Protestants had generally accepted the findings of science, evangelical believers had resisted. This gave rise to a movement called **Fundamentalism,** after *The Fundamentals,* a series of essays published in 1909–1914. Fundamentalists insisted on the Bible's literal truth, including the Genesis account of Creation.

In the early 1920s, fundamentalists targeted Darwin's theory of evolution as a threat to their faith. Many states considered legislation to bar public schools from teaching evolution, and several southern states enacted such laws. Texas governor Miriam "Ma" Ferguson personally censored textbooks that discussed evolution. "I am a Christian mother," she declared, "and I am not going to let that kind of rot go into Texas textbooks." The former Democratic presidential candidate and secretary of state William Jennings Bryan, still widely admired in the American heartland, endorsed the antievolution cause.

When Tennessee's legislature barred the teaching of evolution in the state's public schools in 1925, the American Civil Liberties Union (ACLU) offered to defend any teacher willing to challenge this law. A high-school teacher in Dayton, Tennessee, John T. Scopes, encouraged by local businessmen eager to promote their town, accepted the offer. Scopes summarized Darwin's theory to a science class and was arrested. Famed criminal lawyer Clarence Darrow headed the defense, while Bryan assisted the prosecution. Journalists poured into Dayton; a Chicago radio station broadcast the proceedings live; and the **Scopes Trial** became a media sensation.

Cross-examined by Darrow, Bryan embraced the fundamentalist view of the Bible and dismissed evolutionary theory. Although the jury found Scopes guilty (in a decision later reversed on a technicality), the trial exposed Fundamentalism to ridicule. When Bryan died of a heart attack soon after, H. L. Mencken wrote a column mercilessly deriding him and his fundamentalist admirers.

The Scopes Trial exposed broader tensions in a rapidly changing society. In his testimony, Bryan shrewdly appealed to citizens fearful of cultural forces outside their control, centered in distant cities. Let parents and local communities decide what children are taught, he pled, evoking memories of his earlier populist campaigns defending the common folk against the rich and powerful. Despite the setback in Dayton, Fundamentalism remained alive and well. Mainstream Protestant denominations grew more liberal, but many local congregations, radio preachers, Bible schools, and new conservative denominations upheld the traditional faith. So, too, did the flamboyant evangelist Billy Sunday, who remained popular in the 1920s. Southern and western states continued to pass antievolution laws, and textbook publishers deleted or modified their treatment of evolution to appease local school boards.

In Los Angeles, Aimee Semple McPherson, anticipating later TV evangelists, filled her cavernous Angelus Temple and reached thousands more by radio. The charismatic McPherson entranced audiences with theatrical sermons. She once used a gigantic electric scoreboard to illustrate the triumph of good over evil. Her followers, mainly transplanted midwesterners, embraced her fundamentalist theology while enjoying her mass-entertainment techniques. At her death in 1944, her International Church of the Foursquare Gospel had more than six hundred branches in the United States and abroad.

The Ku Klux Klan   The tensions gnawing at American society of the 1920s also emerged in a resurrected Ku Klux Klan (KKK). The original Klan of the post–Civil War South had faded by the 1870s (see Chapter 16), but in 1915 hooded men who had gathered at Stone Mountain, Georgia, revived it. D. W. Griffith's glorification of the Klan in his 1915 movie *The Birth of a Nation* provided further inspiration.

The movement remained obscure until 1920, when two Atlanta entrepreneurs organized a national membership drive to exploit the appeal of the Klan's ritual and its nativist, white-supremacist ideology. Their wildly successful scheme involved a ten-

The Ku Klux Klan in Washington, D.C.   *In a brazen display of power, the Ku Klux Klan organized a march in the nation's capital in 1926. By this time, the Klan was already in decline.*

dollar membership fee divided among the salesman (called the Kleagle), the local sales manager (King Kleagle), the district sales manager (Grand Goblin), the state leader (Grand Dragon), and the national leader (Imperial Wizard)—with a rake-off to themselves. The sale of Klan robes, masks, horse blankets, and the bottled Chattahoochee River water used in initiation rites added to the take.

Under the umbrella term "100 percent Americanism," the Klan demonized not only African-Americans but also Catholics, Jews, and aliens. Some Klan groups targeted whites suspected of sexual immorality or prohibition-law violations. Membership estimates for the KKK and its women's auxiliary in the early 1920s range as high as 5 million. From its southern base, the Klan spread through the Midwest and across the country from Long Island to the West Coast. The white working class and lower middle class in cities with native-born Protestant majorities proved especially receptive. In 1922 Imperial Wizard Hiram Wesley Evans admitted the Klan's image as a haven of "hicks" and "rubes" and urged college graduates to support the great cause.

Although corrupt at the top and basically a money-making scam, the Klan was not a haven for criminals or fanatics. Observers commented on members' ordinariness. (Evans, a Texas dentist, called himself "the most average man in America.") The Klan's promise to restore the nation's lost purity—racial, ethnic, religious, and moral—appealed to many economically marginal old-stock Protestants disoriented by social change. For some small businessmen threatened by the new corporate order, the Klan's litany of menace offered a vocabulary for articulating economic anxieties. Some citizens upset by changing sexual mores welcomed the Klan's defense of "the purity of white womanhood." Klan membership, in short, gave a sense of empowerment to people who felt adrift in a new social order of great corporations; a raucous mass culture; changing behavior; and immigrant-filled cities. The rituals, parades, and cross burnings added drama and a sense of camaraderie to lonely, unfulfilling lives.

But if individual Klan members seemed more needy than sinister, the Klan's menace as a mass movement was real. Some KKK groups employed threats, beatings, and lynching in their quest to purify America. In several states, the Klan won political power. Oklahoma's Klan-controlled legislature impeached and removed an anti-Klan governor. In Oregon, the Klan elected a governor and pushed through legislation requiring all children to attend public school, an attempt to destroy the state's Catholic schools.

The Klan collapsed with shocking suddenness. In March 1925, Indiana's Grand Dragon, David Stephenson, brutally raped his young secretary. When she swallowed poison, Stephenson panicked and refused to call a physician. The woman died several weeks later, and Stephenson went to prison, where he revealed sordid details of political corruption in Indiana. Its moral pretensions in shreds, the KKK faded. It did not disappear, however, and when African-Americans demanded equal rights in the 1950s, the Klan again reared its head.

The Garvey Movement

Among African-Americans who had fled southern rural poverty and racism only to experience discrimination and racism in the urban North, the decade's social strains produced a different kind of mass movement, led by the spellbinding **Marcus Garvey** and his Universal Negro Improvement Association (UNIA). Born in Jamaica in 1887, the son of a stonemason, Garvey founded UNIA in 1914 and two years later moved to Harlem, which became the movement's headquarters. In a white-dominated society, Garvey glorified all things black. Urging black economic solidarity and relying on capitalist enterprise as the lever of racial advance, he founded UNIA grocery stores and other businesses. He summoned blacks to return to "Motherland Africa" and established the Black Star Steamship Line to help them get there.

An estimated eighty thousand blacks joined UNIA, and thousands more felt the lure of Garvey's oratory, the excitement of UNIA parades and uniforms, and the appeal of the vision of economic self-sufficiency and a glorious future in Africa. Garvey's popularity unsettled black church leaders and the NAACP's middle-class leaders, who saw the African-American future in America, not in Africa, and advocated racial integration rather than separation. W. E. B. Du Bois was among Garvey's sharpest critics.

The movement also highlighted social tensions in Harlem, where two streams of the African diaspora, one from the Caribbean, the other from the American South, converged in the 1920s. The resulting economic and political rivalry shaped attitudes toward the UNIA, since Garvey was Jamaican, and Caribbean immigrants figured prominently in UNIA's leadership.

In 1923, a federal court convicted Garvey of fraud in the management of his Black Star Steamship Line. In 1927, after two years' imprisonment, he was deported to Jamaica, and the UNIA collapsed. But this first mass movement in black America had revealed both the social aspirations and the activist potential of African-Americans in the urban North. "In a world where black is despised," commented an African-American newspaper after Garvey's fall, "he taught his followers that black is beautiful."

The NAACP, meanwhile, remained active even in a reactionary decade with racism rampant. In some 300 branches nationwide, members kept the civil-rights cause alive and patiently laid the groundwork for legal challenges to segregation.

Prohibition: Cultures in Conflict A bitter controversy over alcohol further exposed the fissures in American society. As noted in Chapter 21, the Progressive Era **prohibition** campaign was both a legitimate effort to address social problems associated with alcohol abuse and a weapon in the struggle of native-born Americans to control the immigrant cities. These tensions persisted in the 1920s.

When the Eighteenth Amendment took effect in 1920, prohibitionists rejoiced. Billy Sunday proclaimed,

> The reign of tears is over. The slums will soon be only a memory. We will turn our prisons into factories and our jails into storehouses and corncribs. Men will walk upright now. Women will smile and children will laugh.

Sunday's dream seemed attainable as saloons closed, liquor advertising vanished, and arrests for drunkenness declined. In 1921, alcohol consumption stood at about one-third the prewar level. Yet prohibition gradually lost support, and in 1933 it ended.

What went wrong? Essentially, prohibition's failure illustrates the difficulty in an open society of enforcing a widely opposed law. The Volstead Act, the 1919 prohibition law, was underfunded and weakly enforced, especially in antiprohibition areas. New York, for example, repealed its prohibition-enforcement law as early as 1923. Would-be drinkers grew bolder as enforcement faltered. For rebellious youths, alcohol's illegality increased its appeal. Challenging the prohibition law, declared one college student, represented "the natural reaction of youth to rules and regulations."

Rum-runners smuggled liquor from Canada and the West Indies, and every city harbored speakeasies where customers could buy drinks. People concocted home brew, shady entrepreneurs sold flavored industrial-grade alcohol, and sacramental wine sales soared. By 1929, alcohol consumption reached about 70 percent of prewar levels.

Organized crime helped circumvent the law. Chicago, where rival gangs battled to control the liquor business, witnessed 550 gangland killings in the 1920s. Speakeasies controlled by Chicago gangster Al Capone generated annual profits of $60 million. Although not typical, Chicago's crime wave underscored prohibition's failure. A reform designed to improve the nation's morality was turning citizens into lawbreakers and mobsters into celebrities.

Thus prohibition, too, became a battleground in the decade's cultural wars. The "drys"—usually native-born Protestants—praised it. The "wets"—liberals, Jazz Age rebels, big-city immigrants—condemned it as moralistic meddling. One college student newspaper suggested a campus distillery as the senior class gift, "with the proceeds going to the college."

Prohibition influenced the 1928 presidential campaign. While Democratic candidate Al Smith advocated repeal of the Eighteenth Amendment, Republican Herbert Hoover praised it as "a great social and economic experiment, noble in motive and far-reaching in purpose." Once elected, Hoover characteristically appointed a study commission. In a confusing 1931 report, the commission admitted prohibition's failure, but urged its retention. A journalist parodied the findings:

> Prohibition is an awful flop.
>   We like it.
> It can't stop what it's meant to stop.
>   We like it.
> It's left a trail of graft and slime,
> It's filled our land with vice and crime,
> It don't prohibit worth a dime,
>   Nevertheless we're for it.

When the Eighteenth Amendment was finally repealed in 1933, prohibition seemed little more than a relic of another age.

HOOVER AT THE HELM

Herbert Hoover, elected president in 1928, appeared well fitted to sustain the nation's prosperity. No standpat conservative like Harding and Coolidge, his social and political philosophy reflected his engineering background. In some ways, he seemed the ideal president for the new technological age.

The Election of 1928

A Hollywood casting agent could not have chosen two individuals who better personified America's divisions than the 1928 presidential candidates. New York governor Al Smith easily won the Democratic nomination. The party's urban-immigrant wing had gained strength since the deadlocked 1924 convention. A Catholic and a wet, Smith exuded the flavor of immigrant New York. Originally a machine politician and basically conservative, he had impressed reformers by backing social-welfare measures. His inner circle

MAP 23.1 The Election of 1928

Although Hoover won every state but Massachusetts and six Deep South states, Smith's 1928 vote in the Midwestern farm belt and the nation's largest cities showed significant gains over 1924.

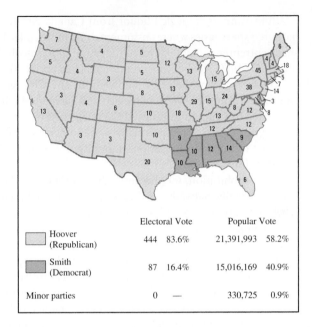

	Electoral Vote		Popular Vote	
Hoover (Republican)	444	83.6%	21,391,993	58.2%
Smith (Democrat)	87	16.4%	15,016,169	40.9%
Minor parties	0	—	330,725	0.9%

included several reform-minded women, notably Frances Perkins, the head of the state industrial board, and Belle Moskowitz, a key adviser.

Herbert Hoover won the Republican nomination after Calvin Coolidge chose not to run. Some conservative party leaders mistrusted the brilliant but aloof Hoover, who had never held elective office and had spent much of his adult life abroad. Born in Iowa and orphaned at an early age, Hoover had put himself through Stanford University and made a fortune as a mining engineer in China and Australia. His service as wartime food administrator had won him a place as secretary of commerce in the Harding and Coolidge cabinets.

Hoover disdained conventional campaigning. Instead, he issued "tons of reports on dull subjects" (in H. L. Mencken's jaundiced view) and read radio speeches in a droning monotone that obscured the originality of some of his ideas. Smith, by contrast, campaigned spiritedly across the nation. This may actually have hurt him, however, because his big-city wisecracking and New York accent put off many voters.

How Smith's Catholicism affected his candidacy remains debatable. Hoover urged tolerance, and Smith denied any conflict between his faith and the duties of the presidency, but anti-Catholic prejudice played a role. Rumors circulated that Smith would follow the Vatican's orders if he won. (A post-election joke had Smith sending the pope a one-word telegram, "Unpack.") But Smith's religion attracted Catholic voters, and in any event the decisive issue was probably not popery but prosperity. Republican orators pointed to the booming economy and warned of "soup kitchens instead of busy factories" if Smith won. In his nomination-acceptance speech, Hoover grandly predicted "the final triumph over poverty."

Hoover won in a landslide, grabbing 58 percent of the vote and even making deep inroads in the Democratic "solid South." Socialist Norman Thomas received only

Presidential Voting by Selected Ethnic Groups in Chicago, 1924, 1928, and 1932			
	Percent Democratic		
	1924	1928	1932
Blacks	10	23	21
Czechoslovaks	40	73	83
Germans	14	58	69
Italians	31	63	64
Jews	19	60	77
Lithuanians	48	77	84
Poles	35	71	80
Swedes	15	34	51
Yugoslavs	20	54	67

Source: John M. Allswang, *A House for All Peoples: Ethnic Politics in Chicago, 1890–1936* (Lexington: University Press of Kentucky, 1971).

267,000 votes. However, the outcome also hinted at an emerging political realignment. Smith did well in the rural Midwest, where hard-pressed farmers, angered by Coolidge's insensitivity to their plight, abandoned their normal Republican allegiance. In northern cities, Catholic and Jewish wards voted heavily Democratic. Smith carried the nation's twelve largest cities, all of which had gone Republican in 1924. Should prosperity falter, these portents suggested, the Republican Party faced trouble.

Herbert Hoover's Social Thought Americans looked hopefully to their new president, whom admirers dubbed "the Great Engineer." Although a self-made man himself, he did not uncritically praise big business. His Quakerism, humanitarian activities, engineering experience, and Republican loyalties combined to produce a unique social outlook, summed up in his 1922 book *American Individualism.*

Like Theodore Roosevelt (whom he had supported in 1912), Hoover opposed cutthroat capitalist competition. Rational economic development, he insisted, demanded corporate cooperation in marketing, wage policy, raw-material allocation, and product standardization. The economy, in short, should operate like an efficient machine. Believing that businesses must behave ethically, Hoover welcomed the growth of welfare capitalism. But above all, he advocated voluntarism. The smoothly functioning, socially responsible economic order he envisioned must arise from the voluntary action of capitalist leaders, not government coercion or labor-management power struggles.

Putting into practice his philosophy of corporate cooperation, Hoover as secretary of commerce had convened more than 250 conferences where business leaders discussed such issues as job creation and labor-management relations. He urged higher wages to increase consumer purchasing power, and in 1923 he persuaded the steel industry to adopt an eight-hour workday as an efficiency measure. During the 1927 Mississippi River floods, as President Coolidge remained in Washington, Hoover had rushed to the stricken area to mobilize private relief efforts.

A conservationist and environmentalist, Hoover as secretary of commerce had pushed for flood control, planned use of water resources, and protection of rivers and lakes. Pollution, he warned in 1924, "is destroying . . . our fisheries . . . [and] beaches and endangering our harbors." In 1922, he negotiated a compact among Western states for a division of Colorado River water. This agreement, implemented in 1929, opened the way for a dam on the Colorado to provide hydroelectric power and water for irrigation, and control spring flooding from the Rocky Mountain snowmelt. Construction began on Hoover Dam in 1930. (In an act of petty politics, Democrats changed the name to Boulder Dam in 1933, but Congress restored the original name in 1947.)

Hoover's ideology had limitations. He showed more enthusiasm for cooperation among capitalists than among consumers or workers. His belief that capitalists would behave ethically and voluntarily embrace enlightened labor policies overestimated the role of altruism in business decision making. And his opposition to government economic intervention brought him grief when such intervention became urgently necessary.

Hoover's presidency began promisingly. He set up a Council on Recent Social Trends and other commissions to gather data to guide policy makers. Responding to the farm problem, he persuaded Congress to create a Federal Farm Board to promote cooperative marketing. This, he hoped, would raise farm prices while preserving the voluntarist principle. But while Hoover applied his social philosophy to the business of government, a crisis was approaching that would overwhelm and ultimately destroy his presidency.

CONCLUSION

Reacting against Woodrow Wilson's exalted wartime idealism, America pursued a nationalistic foreign policy in the 1920s. But the myth of U.S. isolationism is belied by expanding foreign investment and corporate expansion in Europe and Latin America.

At home, the twenties brought new consumer products, new modes of mass production, new marketing and advertising strategies, and new entertainment media. As the economy exuded a glow of prosperity, Americans grappled with massive technological and social changes. Like jet-lagged world travelers, people struggled to adapt to the new order. Skyscrapers, radio, the automobile, the movies, and electrical appliances—all familiar today—were exciting novelties in 1920s America.

While the Harding and Coolidge administrations celebrated the new corporate, consumerist culture and pursued probusiness policies, society seethed in ferment. Ironically, the same stresses that sparked angry social conflict also stimulated cultural creativity. The young people adapting to Jazz Age fashions and behavior standards; the Mexican immigrants seeking a better life in the United States; the native-born advocates of immigration restriction, prohibition, and Fundamentalism; the whites who joined the Klan; the blacks who rallied to Marcus Garvey; the artists and writers of the Harlem Renaissance; the young musicians, painters, and novelists who revitalized American culture were all, in their different ways, responding to the promise and uncertainties of modernity.

24

The Great Depression and the New Deal, 1929–1939

CHAPTER OUTLINE

Crash and Depression, 1929–1932 • The New Deal Takes Shape, 1933–1935 • The New Deal Changes Course, 1935–1936 • The New Deal's End Stage, 1937–1939 • Social Change and Social Action in the 1930s • The American Cultural Scene in the 1930s

---

CRASH AND DEPRESSION, 1929–1932

The prosperity of the 1920s came to a jolting end in October 1929 with the collapse of the stock market. The Wall Street crash, and the economic problems that underlay it, launched a depression that hit every household. President Hoover struggled with the crisis, but his commitment to private initiative and his horror of government coercion limited his effectiveness. In November 1932 voters turned to the Democratic Party and its new leader, Franklin Roosevelt. This key election set the stage for a vast expansion in the federal government's role in addressing social and economic issues.

Black Thursday and the Onset of the Depression Stock prices had risen steadily through much of the 1920s, but 1928–1929 brought a frenzied upsurge as speculators plunged into the market. In 1925 the market value of all stocks had stood at about $27 billion; by October 1929, it hit $87 billion. With stockbrokers lending buyers up to 75 percent of a stock's cost, credit or "margin" buying spread. The income-tax cuts promoted by Treasury Secretary Andrew Mellon had increased the flow of money into the market. Upbeat statements also fed the speculative boom. In March 1929, former president Calvin Coolidge declared stocks "cheap at current prices." "Investment trusts," akin to today's mutual funds, but totally unregulated, lured novices into the market. The construction industry declined sharply in 1928–1929, signaling a glut in the housing market and a decline in business expansion.

In 1928, and again in September 1929, the Federal Reserve Board tried to dampen speculation by raising the interest rate on Federal Reserve notes. Early in 1929, the Fed warned member banks to tighten their lending policies. But with speculators paying up to 20 percent interest to buy more stock, lending institutions continued to loan money freely—an act akin to dumping gasoline on a raging fire.

The collapse came on October 24, 1929—"Black Thursday." As prices fell, some stocks found no buyers at all: they had become worthless. On Tuesday, October 29, a record 16 million stocks changed hands. In the ensuing weeks, feeble upswings alternated with further plunges.

President Hoover, in the first of many optimistic statements, pronounced the economy "sound and prosperous." Indeed, a weak upswing early in 1930 suggested that the worst might be over. Instead, the economy went into a long tailspin, producing a full-scale depression.

What were the underlying causes of this depression? Many economists focus on structural problems that made 1920s' prosperity so unstable. The agricultural sector remained depressed throughout the decade. In the industrial sector, wage increases did not keep pace with factory output, and this reduced consumer purchasing power. At the same time, assembly-line methods encouraged overproduction. By summer 1929, not only housing, but also the automobile, textile, tire, and other durable-goods industries were seriously overextended. Further, important sectors of industry—including railroads, steel, textiles, and mining—lagged technologically in the 1930s and could not attract the investment needed to stimulate recovery.

Some economists, called monetarists, also focus on the Federal Reserve System's tight-money policies in the early 1930s. This policy, they argue, strangled any hope of economic recovery by reducing the amount of money available to businesses for investment and growth.

All analysts link the U.S. depression to a global economic crisis. European economies, struggling with war-debt payments and a severe trade imbalance with the United States, collapsed in 1931, dealing a heavy blow to U.S. exports.

The worsening depression devastated the U.S. economy. From 1929 to 1932, the gross national product dropped from $104 billion to $59 billion. Farm prices, already low, fell by nearly 60 percent. By early 1933 more than fifty-five hundred banks had closed, and unemployment stood at 25 percent, or nearly 13 million workers. In some cities the jobless rate surged far higher. In Toledo in 1932, for example, it stood at 80 percent. Many who still had jobs faced cuts in pay and hours.

Hoover's Response Historically, Americans had viewed depressions as acts of nature: little could be done other than ride out the storm. President Hoover, with his activist impulses, disagreed. Drawing upon his experience as U.S. food administrator in World War I and as secretary of commerce, Hoover initially responded boldly. But his belief in localism and in private initiative limited his options.

Hoover urged business leaders to maintain wages and employment. Viewing unemployment as a local issue, he advised city and state officials to create public-works projects. In October 1930, he set up an Emergency Committee for Employment to coordinate voluntary relief efforts. In 1931, he persuaded the nation's largest banks to set up a private lending agency to help hard-pressed smaller banks make business loans.

Despite these initiatives, public opinion turned against Hoover as the crisis worsened. In the 1930 midterm election, the Republicans lost the House of Representatives and gave up eight Senate seats. In 1931, dreading a budget deficit, Hoover called for a tax increase, further angering hard-pressed Americans. That same year, despite their

CHRONOLOGY, 1929–1939

1929 • Stock market crash; onset of depression.

1932 • Reconstruction Finance Corporation.
Veterans' bonus march.
Franklin D. Roosevelt elected president.

1933 • Repeal of Eighteenth Amendment.
Civilian Conservation Corps (CCC).
Federal Emergency Relief Act (FERA).
Tennessee Valley Authority (TVA).
Agricultural Adjustment Administration (AAA).
National Recovery Administration (NRA).
Public Works Administration (PWA).

1934 • Securities and Exchange Commission (SEC).
Taylor Grazing Act.
Indian Reorganization Act.

1934–1936 • Strikes by Mexican-American agricultural workers in the West.

1935 • Supreme Court declares NIRA unconstitutional.
Works Progress Administration (WPA).
Resettlement Administration.
National Labor Relations Act (Wagner Act).
Social Security Act.
NAACP campaign for federal antilynching law.
Huey Long assassinated.
Revenue Act raises taxes on corporations and the wealthy.
Supreme Court reverses conviction of the "Scottsboro Boys."
Harlem riot.

1935–1939 • Era of the Popular Front.

1936 • Supreme Court declares AAA unconstitutional.
Roosevelt wins landslide reelection victory.
Autoworkers' sit-down strike against General Motors begins (December).

1937 • Roosevelt's "court-packing" plan defeated.
Farm Security Administration.
GM, U.S. Steel, and Chrysler sign union contracts.

1937–1938 • The "Roosevelt recession."

1938 • Fair Labor Standards Act.
Republicans gain heavily in midterm elections.
Congress of Industrial Organizations (CIO) formed.
Carnegie Hall concert by Benny Goodman Orchestra.

1939 • Hatch Act.
Marian Anderson concert at Lincoln Memorial.
John Steinbeck, *The Grapes of Wrath*.

1940 • Ernest Hemingway, *For Whom the Bell Tolls*.

pledges, U.S. Steel, General Motors, and other big corporations slashed wages. The crisis quickly swamped private charities and local welfare agencies. Philadelphia, with more than three hundred thousand jobless by 1932, cut weekly relief payments to $4.23 per family and then stopped them entirely.

In 1932, a presidential election year, Hoover swallowed his principles and took a bold step. In January, at Hoover's recommendation, Congress set up a new agency, the **Reconstruction Finance Corporation** (RFC), to make loans to banks and other lending institutions. By July, the RFC had pumped $1.2 billion into the economy. Congress also authorized the RFC to grant $2 billion to state and local governments for job-creating public-works programs, and allocated $750 million for loans to struggling businesses.

Hoover supported these measures reluctantly, warning that they could open the door to "socialism and collectivism." Blaming global forces for the depression, he argued that only international measures would help. His call for a moratorium on war-debt and reparations payments by European nations made sense, but seemed irrelevant to the plight of ordinary Americans.

As Hoover endlessly urged self-help and local initiative and saw recovery "just around the corner," his unpopularity deepened. When he appointed a new press secretary disliked by journalists, one reporter called it the first instance of a rat boarding a sinking ship. An administration launched so hopefully in 1929 was ending in bitterness and failure.

Mounting Discontent and Protest

An ominous mood spread as hordes of the jobless waited in breadlines, slept on park benches, trudged the streets, and rode freight trains seeking work. Americans reared on the ethic of hard work and self-reliance experienced chronic unemployment as a shattering emotional blow. The families of the jobless suffered as well.

Newspapers humanized the crisis. The *New York Times* described "Hoover Valley"— a section of Central Park where jobless men lived in boxes and packing crates. In winter they wrapped themselves in layers of newspapers they called Hoover blankets. The suicide rate soared. In Youngstown, Ohio, a jobless father of ten whose family faced eviction jumped to his death from a bridge. Violence threatened in some cities when landlords evicted people unable to pay their rent.

Hard times battered the nation's farms. Many underwent mortgage foreclosures or forced sales because of tax delinquency, with Iowa and the Dakotas especially hard hit. At some forced farm auctions, neighbors bought the foreclosed farm for a trivial sum, and returned it to the evicted family.

In 1931, midwestern farmers organized a boycott movement called the Farmers' Holiday Association to force prices up by withholding grain and livestock from the market. Dairy farmers angered by low prices dumped milk in Iowa and Wisconsin.

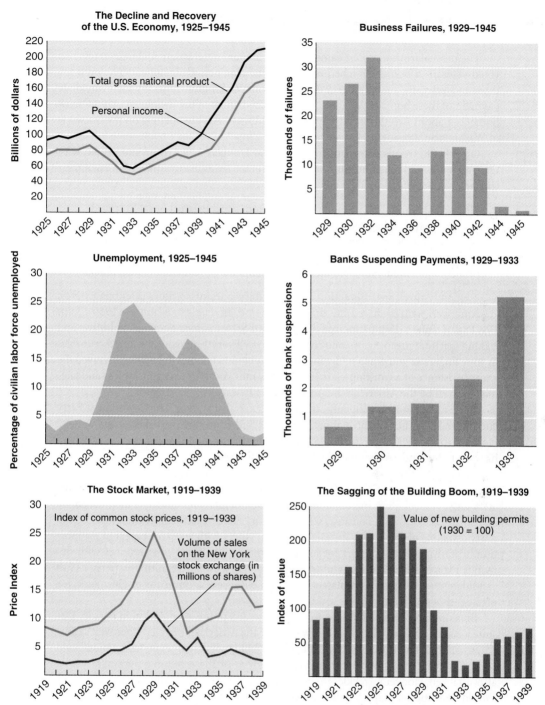

The Decline and Recovery of the U.S. Economy, 1925–1945

Billions of dollars

Total gross national product

Personal income

Business Failures, 1929–1945

Thousands of failures

Unemployment, 1925–1945

Percentage of civilian labor force unemployed

Banks Suspending Payments, 1929–1933

Thousands of bank suspensions

The Stock Market, 1919–1939

Price Index

Index of common stock prices, 1919–1939

Volume of sales on the New York stock exchange (in millions of shares)

The Sagging of the Building Boom, 1919–1939

Index of value

Value of new building permits (1930 = 100)

FIGURE 24.1 **The Statistics of Hard Times**

Figures on the gross national product, personal income, unemployment, the stock market, and business failures all show the Depression's shattering impact, with gradual and uneven improvement as the 1930s wore on. *Sources:* C. D. Bremmer, *American Bank Failures* (New York: Columbia University Press, 1935), 42; Thomas C. Cochran, *The Great Depression and World War II: 1929–1945* (Glenview, Ill. : Scott, Foresman, 1968); *Historical Statistics of the United States, Colonial Times to 1970* (Washington, D.C.: U.S. Government Printing Office, 1975).

The most alarming protest came from World War I veterans. In 1924, Congress had voted veterans a bonus stretched over a twenty-year period. In June 1932, some ten thousand veterans, many jobless, descended on Washington to lobby for immediate payment of these bonuses. When Congress refused, most of the "bonus marchers" went home, but about two thousand stayed on, building makeshift shelters on the outskirts of Washington. President Hoover called in the army.

On July 28, troops commanded by General Douglas MacArthur and armed with tear gas, tanks, and machine guns drove the veterans from their camp and burned their shelters. A journalist described the scene:

> [The veterans and their families] wandered from street to street or sat in ragged groups, the men exhausted, the women with wet handkerchiefs laid over their smarting eyes, the children waking from sleep to cough and whimper from the tear gas in their lungs. . . . Their shanties and tents had been burned, their personal property destroyed, except for the few belongings they could carry on their backs.

To many Americans, this action symbolized the administration's utter bankruptcy. American writers shared the despairing mood. In *The 42nd Parallel* (1930), John Dos Passos drew a dark panorama of the United States as money-mad, exploitive, and lacking spiritual meaning. As one character says, "Everything you've wanted crumbles in your fingers as you grasp it." In *Young Lonigan* (1932), James T. Farrell portrayed the empty existence of a working-class Irish-immigrant youth in Chicago. Jobless and feeling betrayed by the American dream, he aimlessly wanders the streets.

Some radical novelists openly attacked the capitalist system. The Communist Party encouraged such fiction through writers' clubs and contests for working-class writers. Jack Conroy's *The Disinherited* (1933) dealt with life in the Missouri coal fields, where his own father and brother had died in a mine disaster.

The Election of 1932

Gloom pervaded the 1932 Republican convention that renominated Hoover. The Democrats who gathered in Chicago, by contrast, scented victory. Their platform, crafted to erase the party divisions of the 1920s, appealed to urban voters with a call for repeal of prohibition, to farmers with support for aid programs, and to fiscal conservatives with demands for a balanced budget and spending cuts. Rejecting Al Smith, the party's 1928 candidate, the delegates nominated Franklin D. Roosevelt, governor of New York, for president.

Breaking precedent, FDR flew to Chicago to accept the nomination in person. Despite a rousing speech pledging "a new deal for the American people," Roosevelt's campaign offered few specifics. He called for "bold persistent experimentation" and compassion for "the forgotten man at the bottom of the economic pyramid," yet he also attacked Hoover's "reckless" spending and insisted that "only as a last resort" should Washington play a larger depression-fighting role.

But Roosevelt exuded confidence, and above all he was not Hoover. On November 8, FDR and his running mate, Texas congressman John Nance Garner, received nearly 23 million votes, compared with fewer than 16 million for Hoover. Roosevelt carried every state but Pennsylvania, Connecticut, Vermont, New Hampshire, and Maine. Both houses of Congress went heavily Democratic. How would Roosevelt use this impressive mandate? The nation waited.

THE NEW DEAL TAKES SHAPE, 1933–1935

The Roosevelt years began in a whirl of activity. An array of emergency measures proposed by Roosevelt and passed by Congress reflected three basic goals: industrial recovery through business-government cooperation and pump-priming federal spending; agricultural recovery through crop reduction; and short-term emergency relief distributed through state and local agencies when possible, but directly by the federal government if necessary. Taken together, these programs conveyed the sense of an activist government addressing urgent national problems. Hovering over the bustle loomed a confident Franklin Roosevelt, cigarette holder jauntily tilted upward, a symbol of hope. By 1935, however, the New Deal faced problems, and opposition was building.

Roosevelt and His Circle

FDR's inaugural address dedicated his administration to helping a people in crisis. "The only thing we have to fear," he intoned, "is fear itself." In an outpouring of support, half a million letters deluged the White House.

Roosevelt seemed an unlikely popular hero. Like his distant cousin Theodore, FDR was of the social elite, with merchants and landowners among his Dutch-immigrant ancestors. He attended Harvard College and Columbia Law School. But as a state senator and governor of New York, he had backed the Democratic Party's urban-immigrant wing. When the depression hit, he had introduced innovative measures in New York, including unemployment insurance and a public-works program. Intent on promoting recovery while preserving capitalism and democracy, Roosevelt encouraged competing proposals, compromised (or papered over) differences, and then backed the measures he sensed could be sold to Congress and the public.

Roosevelt brought to Washington a circle of advisers nicknamed the brain trust. It included Columbia University professor Rexford G. Tugwell and lawyer Adolph A. Berle. Shaped by the progressive reform tradition, Tugwell and Berle advocated federal economic planning and corporate regulation. But no single ideology or set of advisers controlled the New Deal, for FDR sought a broad range of opinions.

Eleanor Roosevelt played a key role. A niece of Theodore Roosevelt, she had been active in settlement-house work and in Florence Kelley's National Consumers' League. Through her, FDR met reformers, social workers, and advocates of minority rights. Recalled Rexford Tugwell: "No one who ever saw Eleanor Roosevelt sit down facing her husband, and holding his eyes firmly, say to him 'Franklin, I think you should . . . ,' or 'Franklin, surely you will not . . .' will ever forget the experience." Mrs. Roosevelt traveled ceaselessly and served as an astute observer for her wheelchair-bound husband. (A Washington newspaper once headlined "MRS. ROOSEVELT SPENDS NIGHT AT WHITE HOUSE.") In 1935, she began a newspaper column, "My Day."

Roosevelt's cabinet reflected the New Deal's diversity. Postmaster General James Farley, FDR's top political adviser, distributed patronage jobs, managed his campaigns, and dealt with state and local Democratic leaders. Secretary of Labor **Frances Perkins,** the first woman cabinet member, had served as industrial commissioner of New York. Interior Secretary **Harold Ickes** had organized liberal Republicans for Roosevelt in 1932. Secretary of Agriculture Henry A. Wallace of Iowa held the same post his father had occupied in the 1920s. Treasury Secretary Henry Morgenthau, Jr., FDR's neighbor and political ally, though a fiscal conservative, tolerated the spending necessary to finance New Deal anti-depression programs.

Eleanor Roosevelt Visits a West Virginia Coal Mine, 1933 *A New Yorker cartoon of 1933 portrayed one coal miner exclaiming to another: "Oh migosh, here comes Mrs. Roosevelt." But reality soon caught up with humor, as the First Lady immersed herself in the plight of the poor and the exploited.*

A host of newcomers poured into Washington in 1933—former progressives, liberal-minded professors, bright young lawyers. They drafted bills, staffed government agencies, and debated recovery strategies. From this pressure-cooker environment emerged the laws, programs, and agencies gathered under a catch-all label: the New Deal.

The Hundred Days Between March and June 1933, a period labeled the "Hundred Days," Congress enacted more than a dozen key measures. Rooted in the experience of the Progressive Era, World War I, and the Hoover presidency, these measures expanded Washington's involvement in the nation's economic life.

FDR first addressed the banking crisis. As borrowers defaulted, depositors withdrew savings, and homeowners missed mortgage payments, thousands of banks had failed, undermining confidence in the entire system. On March 5 Roosevelt ordered all banks to close for four days. At the end of this so-called bank holiday, he proposed an Emergency Banking Act. This law and a later one permitted healthy banks to reopen, set up procedures for managing failed banks, increased government oversight of banking, and required banks to separate their savings deposits from their investment funds. Congress also created the Federal Deposit Insurance Corporation (FDIC) to insure bank deposits up to five thousand dollars. In the first of a series of radio talks dubbed "fireside chats," the president assured Americans that they could again trust their banks.

Other measures of the Hundred Days addressed the urgent problem of relief for Americans struggling to survive. Two new agencies assisted those who were losing their homes. The Home Owners Loan Corporation (HOLC) helped city-dwellers refinance their mortgages. The Farm Credit Administration provided loans to rural Americans.

Another early relief program, the **Civilian Conservation Corps** (CCC), employed jobless youths in such government projects as reforestation, park maintenance, and erosion control. The CCC thus combined work relief with environmental programs. By 1935 half a million young men were earning thirty-five dollars a month in CCC camps—a godsend to desperate families.

The principal relief measure of the Hundred Days, the **Federal Emergency Relief Act,** appropriated $500 million for state and local relief agencies that had exhausted their funds. To head this program, FDR chose **Harry Hopkins,** the relief administrator in New York State, who soon emerged as a powerful New Deal figure.

While supplying immediate relief, the early New Deal also faced the longer-term challenge of promoting agricultural and industrial recovery. In tackling the chronic problem of low farm prices, New Dealers held different opinions. Some favored the approach of the 1920s McNary-Haugen bill (see Chapter 23), by which the government would buy agricultural surpluses and sell them abroad. Others, however, advocated reduced production as a way to raise farm income, and this approach won the day.

As a first step to cutting production, the government paid southern cotton planters to plow under much of their crop and midwestern farmers to slaughter some 6 million piglets and pregnant sows. Destroying crops and killing pigs amid widespread hunger proved a public-relations nightmare. Pursuing the same goal more systematically, Congress passed the Agricultural Adjustment Act in May 1933. This law gave payments, called subsidies, to producers of the major agricultural commodities—including hogs, wheat, corn, cotton, and dairy products—in return for cutting production. A tax on grain mills and other food processors (a tax ultimately passed on to consumers) financed these subsidies. A new agency, the **Agricultural Adjustment Administration** (AAA), supervised the program.

The other key recovery measure of the Hundred Days, the National Industrial Recovery Act, appropriated $3.3 billion for large-scale public-works projects to provide jobs and stimulate the economy. The **Public Works Administration** (PWA), headed by Interior Secretary Harold Ickes, ran this program.

This law also created the **National Recovery Administration** (NRA). The NRA brought together business leaders to draft codes of "fair competition" for their industries. These codes set production limits, prescribed wages and working conditions, and forbade price cutting and unfair competitive practices. The aim was to promote recovery by breaking the cycle of wage cuts, falling prices, and layoffs. This approach revived the trade associations that Washington had encouraged during World War I (see Chapter 22). Indeed, the NRA's head, Hugh Johnson, had served with the War Industries Board of 1917–1918. The NRA also echoed the theme of business-government cooperation that Herbert Hoover had promoted as secretary of commerce in the 1920s.

The NRA depended on voluntary support by business and the public. The flamboyant Johnson used parades, billboards, magazine ads, and celebrity events to persuade people to buy only from companies that subscribed to an NRA code and that displayed the NRA symbol, a blue eagle, and its slogan, "We Do Our Part."

While the NRA's purpose was economic recovery, some New Dealers saw its reform potential as well. Under pressure from Labor Secretary Frances Perkins, the NRA's textile-industry code banned child labor. And thanks to Senator Robert Wagner of New York, Section 7a of the National Industrial Recovery Act affirmed workers' right to organize unions.

The Reconstruction Finance Corporation, dating from the Hoover years, remained active in the New Deal era. Under its chairman Jesse Jones, a Houston banker, the RFC lent large sums to banks, insurance companies, and even new business ventures, making it a potent financial resource for corporate America. The early New Deal thus had a strong probusiness tone. In his speeches of 1933–1935, FDR always included business in the "all-American team" working for recovery.

A few measures adopted during the Hundred Days, however, took a tougher approach to business. The stock-market crash had produced an antibusiness reaction. A Senate investigation of Wall Street revealed that none of the twenty partners of the Morgan Bank had paid any income tax in 1931 or 1932. People jeered when the head of the New York Stock Exchange told a Senate committee considering regulatory measures, "You gentlemen are making a big mistake. The Exchange is a perfect institution."

Reflecting the public mood, Congress in 1933 passed the Federal Securities Act requiring corporations to inform the government fully on all stock offerings. This law also made executives personally liable for any misrepresentation of securities their companies issued. (In 1934 Congress curbed the purchase of stock on credit—a practice that had contributed to the crash—and created the Securities and Exchange Commission [SEC] to enforce the new regulations.)

The most innovative program of the Hundred Days was the **Tennessee Valley Authority** (TVA). This program had its origins in a World War I hydroelectric station on the Tennessee River in Alabama built by the War Department to power a nearby munitions plant. In the 1920s, Senator George Norris of Nebraska had urged the use of this facility to supply electricity to nearby farmers.

Expanding Norris's idea, TVA advanced the economic and social development of the entire Tennessee River valley, a region mired in poverty. A European visitor in the 1930s described the region's farms: "[K]itchens with ovens burning wood . . . ; no icebox . . . ; dim, smoking, smelly oil lamps . . . ; clothes [washed] by hand in antiquated tubs . . . ; the water . . . brought into the house by women and children, from wells invariably situated at inconvenient and tiring distances."

Such conditions stunted children's lives. Wrote a Tennessee school administrator of the pupils in her district, "Due to insufficient clothing and food, many are unable to attend school. . . . It is not uncommon for a child to have but one dress or one shirt. They have to stay at home the day the mother launders them."

While creating construction jobs, TVA dams brought electricity to the region, provided recreational facilities, and reduced flooding and soil erosion. Under director David Lilienthal, TVA proved one of the New Deal's most popular and enduring achievements.

The mind-boggling burst of laws and the "alphabet-soup" of new agencies during the Hundred Days symbolized both the dynamism and the confusion of the New Deal. How these new programs and agencies would work in practice remained to be seen.

Problems and Controversies Plague the Early New Deal

As the depression persisted, several early New Deal programs, including the NRA and the AAA, faced difficulties. The NRA's problems related partly to the personality of the hard-driving, hard-drinking Hugh Johnson, who left in 1934. But the trouble went deeper. As the unity spirit of the Hundred Days faded, corporate America chafed under NRA regulation. Code violations increased. Small businesses complained that the codes favored big corporations. The agency itself, meanwhile, became bogged down in drafting trivial codes. The shoulder-pad industry, for example, had its own code. Corporate trade associations used the codes to stifle competition and fix prices.

In May 1935, the Supreme Court unanimously ruled the NRA unconstitutional. The Court cited two reasons: first, the law gave the president regulatory powers that constitutionally belonged to Congress; second, the NRA regulated commerce within states, violating the constitutional provision limiting federal regulation to interstate commerce. Few mourned. As a recovery measure, the NRA had failed.

The AAA fared better, but it too proved controversial. Farm prices did rise as production fell, and from 1933 to 1937 overall farm income increased by 50 percent. But the AAA did not help farm laborers or migrant workers; indeed, its crop-reduction payments actually hurt southern tenants and sharecroppers, who faced eviction as cotton planters removed acreage from production. One Georgia sharecropper wrote Harry Hopkins, "I have Bin farming all my life But the man I live with Has Turned me loose. . . . I can't get a Job."

Some victims of this process resisted. In 1934 the interracial Southern Tenant Farmers' Union, led by the Socialist Party, emerged in Arkansas. Declared one black sharecropper at the organizing meeting, "The same chain that holds my people holds

MAP 24.1 The Dust Bowl

From the Dakotas southward to the Mexican border, farmers in the Great Plains suffered from a lack of rainfall and severe soil erosion in the 1930s, worsening the hardships of the Great Depression.

your people too. . . . [We should] get together and stay together." The landowners struck back, harassing union organizers.

While some New Dealers focused on raising total agricultural income, others took a more class-based approach and urged attention to the poorest farmers. Their cause was strengthened as a parching drought centered in the Oklahoma panhandle region turned much of the Great Plains into a dust bowl. The rains failed in 1930, devastating wheat and livestock on the southern plains. In 1934, dust clouds spread across the nation, darkening the skies over Boston, Washington, D.C., and Savannah. As a particularly dense dust cloud passed over Washington, one legislator commented: "There goes Oklahoma." On "Black Sunday," April 14, 1935, racing winds created dunes fifty feet high. Through 1939, each summer brought a new scourge of dust.

Even night brought no relief. Recalled a Kansas woman, "A trip for water to rinse the grit from our lips, and then back to bed with washcloths over our noses. We try to lie still, because every turn stirs the dust on the blankets." Folk singer Woody Guthrie recalled the most vivid memory of his 1930s' boyhood in Oklahoma and Texas in a song called "The Great Dust Storm."

Battered by debt, drought, and dust, many families gave up. Nearly 3.5 million people left the Great Plains in the 1930s. Some migrated to nearby cities, further swamping relief rolls. Others packed their meager belongings into old cars and headed west. Though coming from various states, they all bore a derisive nickname, Okies. The plight of dust-bowl migrants further complicated New Deal agricultural planning.

Policy differences also plagued the New Deal relief program. As unemployment continued, Harry Hopkins convinced FDR to support direct federal relief programs, rather than channeling funds through state and local agencies. Late in 1933, FDR named Hopkins to head a temporary agency, the Civil Works Administration (CWA). Through the winter the CWA funded short-term work projects for the jobless, but when warm weather returned, FDR abolished it. Like his conservative critics, FDR feared creating a permanent underclass living on welfare. As local relief agencies ran out of money, however, further federal programs became inevitable.

Hopkins and Harold Ickes, head of the Public Works Administration, competed to control federal relief policy. Large-scale PWA projects such as bridges, dams, and government buildings did promote economic recovery, but as the cautious Ickes examined every proposal with a fine-tooth comb, billions in relief funds remained stalled in the pipeline. Hopkins, by contrast, wanted to put people to work and get money circulating. Even make-work projects like raking leaves and collecting litter, he argued, furthered these goals. Given the urgency of the crisis, Hopkins's approach proved more influential.

1934–1935: Challenges from Right and Left

Despite the New Deal's brave beginnings, the depression persisted. In 1934 national income rose about 25 percent above 1933 levels, but remained far below that of 1929. Millions had been jobless for three or four years. The rising frustration found expression in 1934 in nearly two thousand strikes, some of them communist-led. With the NRA under attack, conflict flaring over farm policy, and relief spending growing, criticism mounted. Conservatives attacked the New Deal as socialistic. In 1934 several business leaders, joined by an embittered Al Smith, formed the anti–New

Deal American Liberty League. Anti-Roosevelt jokes circulated among the rich, many of whom denounced him as a traitor to his class.

But the New Deal remained popular, reflecting both its promise and FDR's political skills. Assisted by speechwriters and publicists, Roosevelt commanded the political stage. Pursuing his "national unity" theme, he exhorted Americans to join the battle for economic recovery just as they had united in 1917 against a foreign foe. Although Republican newspaper publishers remained hostile, FDR enjoyed good relations with the working press, and journalists responded with favorable stories.

Unlike Hoover, Roosevelt loved public appearances and took naturally to radio. Frances Perkins described his radio talks: "His head would nod and his hands would move in simple, natural, comfortable gestures. His face would smile and light up as though he were actually sitting . . . with [his listeners]." The nickname of these radio talks, "fireside chats," underscored their informal nature. Roosevelt's mastery of radio would provide a model for politicians of the television era.

The 1934 midterm election ratified the New Deal's popularity. Reversing the usual pattern, the Democrats increased their congressional majorities. As for FDR, Kansas journalist William Allen White observed, "He's been all but crowned by the people." As the returns rolled in, Harry Hopkins exulted to a group of New Deal associates, "Boys, this is our hour!"

Despite this outcome, the political scene was highly unstable in 1934–1935. While conservatives criticized the New Deal for going too far, critics on the left attacked it for not going far enough. Socialists and communists ridiculed Roosevelt's efforts to include big business in his "all-American team." Clifford Odets's 1935 play *Waiting for Lefty* portrayed noble workers battling evil bosses.

Pushing the New Deal's experimental spirit still further, demagogues peddled more radical nostrums. The Detroit Catholic priest and radio spellbinder Charles Coughlin attacked FDR as a "great betrayer and liar," made anti-Semitic allusions, and called for nationalization of the banks. For a time, Coughlin's movement, the National Union of Social Justice, drawn mainly from the lower middle class, seemed a potent force.

Meanwhile, California physician Francis Townsend proposed that the government pay two hundred dollars a month to all retired citizens, requiring them to spend it within thirty days. This plan, Townsend insisted, would help the elderly, stimulate the economy, and create jobs by encouraging retirement. The scheme would have bankrupted the nation, but many older citizens rallied to Townsend's banner.

FDR's wiliest rival was Huey Long of Louisiana. A country lawyer elected governor in 1928, Long built highways, schools, and public housing while fostering a climate of graft and political corruption. He roared into Washington as a senator in 1933, preaching his "Share Our Wealth" program: a 100 percent tax on all incomes over $1 million and appropriation of all fortunes over $5 million. With this money, Long promised, every family could enjoy a comfortable income, a house, a car, old-age benefits, and free college education. "Every man a king," Long proclaimed. By 1935 he boasted 7.5 million supporters. The title of his 1935 book, *My First Days in the White House*, made clear his ultimate goal. An assassin's bullet killed Long that September, but his organization survived.

Battling back, Roosevelt regained the political high ground in 1935 with a series of bold initiatives. The result was a fresh surge of legislation that rivaled that of the Hundred Days.

THE NEW DEAL CHANGES COURSE, 1935–1936

As the 1936 election neared, Roosevelt shelved the unity theme and championed the poor and the working class. His 1935 State of the Union address outlined six initiatives: expanded public-works programs, assistance to the rural poor, support for organized labor, benefits for retired workers and other at-risk groups, tougher business regulation, and heavier taxes on the well-to-do. These priorities translated into a bundle of reform measures some called "the Second New Deal." FDR's landslide victory in 1936 solidified a new Democratic coalition. The New Deal also addressed environmental issues and launched public-works and power projects in the West that stimulated the region's economic development.

Expanding Federal Relief — With unemployment still high, Congress passed the $5 billion Emergency Relief Appropriation Act in April 1935. Roosevelt swiftly set up the **Works Progress Administration** (WPA), with Harry Hopkins in charge, to funnel assistance directly to the jobless. Roosevelt insisted that the WPA provide work, not handouts. Over its eight-year life, the WPA employed more than 8 million Americans and constructed or improved vast numbers of bridges, roads, schools, post offices, and other public facilities.

The WPA also assisted writers, performers, and artists. The Federal Writers' Project (FWP) employed some ten thousand jobless writers nationwide to produce state and city guides and histories of ethnic and immigrant groups. In the South, research teams recorded the oral-history reminiscences of former slaves. Responding to the rise of totalitarian regimes abroad (see Chapter 25), the FWP encouraged cultural nationalism while recognizing regional and ethnic differences. Sterling Brown, the FWP's "Negro Affairs editor," pushed for the inclusion of African-American history and voices in FWP publications.

Under the WPA's Federal Music Project, unemployed musicians gave free concerts, often featuring American composers. By 1938, more than 30 million Americans had attended these events. Artists working for the Federal Arts Project designed posters, offered courses, and painted murals on public buildings.

The Federal Theatre Project (FTP) employed actors. One FTP project, the Living Newspaper, which dramatized current social issues, was criticized as New Deal propaganda. Nervous WPA officials canceled one FTP-funded production, Marc Blitzstein's radical musical *The Cradle Will Rock* (1937), before the opening-night performance. The cast and audience defiantly walked to another theater, and the show went on. Touring FTP drama companies gave many citizens their first taste of theater.

Another 1935 agency, the National Youth Administration (NYA), provided job training for unemployed youth and part-time work to enable college students to remain in school. Eleanor Roosevelt, viewing young people as the hope of the future, took particular pride in the NYA.

Harold Ickes's Public Works Administration, after a slow start, eventually completed some thirty-four thousand major construction projects, employing thousands of workers. Among the PWA's undertakings were New York City's Triborough Bridge and Lincoln Tunnel, and the awesome Grand Coulee Dam on the Columbia River.

All this relief spending generated large federal budget deficits, cresting at $4.4 billion in 1936. According to British economist John Maynard Keynes, governments should deliberately use deficit spending during depressions to fund public-works programs, thereby increasing purchasing power and stimulating recovery. The New Deal approach, however, was not Keynesian. Because every dollar spent on relief programs was withdrawn from the economy through taxation or government borrowing, the stimulus effect was nil. FDR saw deficits as an unwelcome necessity, not a positive good.

Aiding Migrants, Supporting Unions, Regulating Business, Taxing the Wealthy   The New Deal's second phase more frankly targeted the needs of workers, the poor, and the disadvantaged. Social-justice advocates like Frances Perkins and Eleanor Roosevelt helped shape this program, but so did hard-headed politics. Looking to 1936, FDR's political advisers feared that the followers of Coughlin, Townsend, and Long could siphon off enough votes to cost him the election. This worry underlay FDR's 1935 political agenda.

The Second New Deal's agricultural policy addressed the plight of sharecroppers (a plight the AAA had helped create) and other poor farmers. The Resettlement Administration (1935), directed by Rexford Tugwell, made loans to help tenant farmers buy their own farms and to enable displaced sharecroppers, tenants, and dust-bowl migrants to move to more productive areas.

The Resettlement Administration also funded two brilliant documentary films directed by Pare Lorenz. *The Plow That Broke the Plains* (1936) explained the farming practices that led to the dust bowl. *The River* (1938) dealt with the devastating effects of flooding in the Mississippi River valley, and the promise of TVA and other New Deal flood-control projects. Lorenz's films today rank among the outstanding cultural productions of the 1930s.

The Rural Electrification Administration, also started in 1935, made low-interest loans to utility companies and farmers' cooperatives to extend electricity to the 90 percent of rural America that still lacked it. By 1941, 40 percent of U.S. farms enjoyed electric power.

The agricultural-recovery program suffered a setback in January 1936 when the Supreme Court declared the Agricultural Adjustment Act unconstitutional. The processing tax that funded the AAA's subsidies, the Court held, was an illegal use of the government's tax power. To replace the AAA, Congress passed a soil-conservation act that paid farmers to plant grasses and legumes instead of soil-depleting crops such as wheat and cotton (which also happened to be the major surplus commodities).

Organized labor won a key victory in 1935, again thanks to Senator Robert Wagner. During the New Deal's national-unity phase, FDR had criticized Wagner's campaign for a prolabor law as "special interest" legislation. But in 1935, when the Supreme Court outlawed the NIRA, including Section 7a protecting union members' rights, as unconstitutional, FDR called for a labor law that would survive court scrutiny. The **National Labor Relations Act** of July 1935 (the Wagner Act) guaranteed collective-bargaining rights, permitted closed shops (in which all employees must join a union), and outlawed such management tactics as blacklisting union organizers. The law created the National Labor Relations Board (NLRB) to enforce the law and supervise shop elections. A wave of unionization soon followed (see below).

The Second New Deal's more class-conscious thrust shaped other 1935 measures as well. The Banking Act strengthened the Federal Reserve Board's control over the nation's financial system. The Public Utilities Holding Company Act, targeting the sprawling public-utility empires of the 1920s such as that of Samuel Insull (see Chapter 23), restricted gas and electric companies to one geographic region.

In 1935, too, Roosevelt called for steeper taxes on the rich to combat the "unjust concentration of wealth and economic power." Congress responded with a revenue act, also called the Wealth Tax Act, that raised taxes on corporations and on the well-to-do. This law had many loopholes and was not quite the "soak the rich" measure some believed, but it did express the Second New Deal's more radical spirit.

The Social Security Act of 1935; End of the Second New Deal   The **Social Security Act** of 1935 stands out among New Deal laws for its long-range significance. Drafted by a committee chaired by Frances Perkins, this measure drew upon Progressive Era ideas and the social-welfare programs of England and Germany. It established a mixed federal-state system of workers' pensions; unemployment insurance; survivors' benefits for victims of industrial accidents; and aid for disabled persons and dependent mothers with children.

Taxes paid partly by employers and partly by workers (in the form of sums withheld from their paychecks) funded the pension and survivors' benefit features. This cut in take-home pay helped bring on a recession in 1937. But it made sense politically because workers would fight any effort to end a pension plan they had contributed to. As FDR put it, "With those taxes in there, no damned politician can ever scrap my social security program."

The initial Social Security Act paid low benefits and bypassed farmers, domestic workers, and the self-employed. But it established the principle of federal responsibility for social welfare and laid the foundation for a vastly expanded welfare system in the future.

By September 1935, when Congress adjourned, the Second New Deal was complete. Without embracing the panaceas of Coughlin, Townsend, or Long, FDR had addressed the grievances they had exploited. Although conservatives called this phase of the New Deal "antibusiness," FDR insisted that he had saved capitalism by addressing the social problems it spawned. During much of the post–Civil War era the business class had dominated government, marginalizing other groups. Business remained influential in the 1930s, but as the New Deal evolved, it acted as a broker for all organized interest groups, including labor, not just corporate America. And in 1935, with an election looming, New Deal strategists reached farther still, to address the situation of sharecroppers and migrant workers, the disabled, the elderly, and others whose plight had rarely concerned politicians of the past.

In the process, the New Deal enlarged the role of the federal government in American life, as well as the power of the presidency. Building on earlier precedents set by Theodore Roosevelt, FDR so dominated 1930s' politics that Americans began to expect presidents to offer "programs," address national issues, and shape the public debate. This decisively altered the power balance between the White House and Congress. The New Deal's importance thus lies not only in specific laws, but also in the way it redefined the scope of the presidency and, more broadly, the social role of the state.

The 1936 Roosevelt Landslide and the New Democratic Coalition With the Second New Deal in place, FDR confidently faced the 1936 campaign. "There's one issue . . . ," he told an aide; "it's myself, and people must be either for me or against me."

The Republican candidate, Kansas governor Alfred Landon, a fiscal conservative who nevertheless believed that government must address social issues, proved an inept campaigner. ("Wherever I have gone in this country, I have found Americans," he revealed in one speech.) FDR, by contrast, responded zestfully when Republicans lambasted his alleged dictatorial ambitions or charged that the social security law would require all workers to wear metal dog tags. The forces of "selfishness and greed . . . are united in their hatred for me," he declared at a tumultuous election-eve rally in New York City, "and I welcome their hatred."

In the greatest landslide since 1820, FDR carried every state but Maine and Vermont. Landon even lost Kansas. Pennsylvania went Democratic for the first time since 1856. The Democrats increased their already top-heavy majorities in Congress. Roosevelt buried his minor-party opponents as well. Socialist Norman Thomas received under 200,000 votes, the Communist Party's presidential candidate only about 80,000. The Union Party, a coalition of Coughlinites, Townsendites, and Huey Long supporters, seemingly so formidable in 1935, polled under 900,000 votes.

The 1936 election signaled the emergence of a new Democratic coalition. Since Reconstruction, the Democrats had counted on three bases of support: the white South, parts of the West, and urban white ethnic voters. FDR retained these centers of strength. He rarely challenged state or local party leaders who produced the votes, whether they supported the New Deal or not. In Virginia he even withdrew support from a pro–New Deal governor who clashed with the state's conservative but powerful Democratic senators. When the Democratic boss of Jersey City, Frank Hague, faced mail-tampering charges, FDR told Jim Farley, "Tell Frank to knock it off . . . , but keep this thing quiet because we need Hague's support if we want New Jersey."

Building on Al Smith's urban breakthrough in 1928, FDR carried the nation's twelve largest cities in 1936. Aided by New Deal relief programs, many city-dwellers idolized Roosevelt. When he visited New York, Boston, or other cities, cheering crowds lined the route. FDR also turned to the newer urban-immigrant groups, including Catholics and Jews, in filling New Deal positions.

Expanding the Democratic base, FDR also reached out to farmers, union members, northern blacks, and women. Midwestern farmers, long rock-ribbed Republicans, liked the New Deal's agricultural program and voted accordingly. In Iowa, a GOP bastion in the 1920s, FDR won decisively in 1936. Union members, too, joined the Roosevelt bandwagon in 1936, and the unions pumped money into Roosevelt's campaign chest (though far less than business gave the Republicans). Despite his early criticism of the Wagner bill, FDR's reputation as a "friend of labor" proved unassailable.

Although most southern blacks remained disfranchised, northern blacks could vote, and as late as 1932, two-thirds of them went for Hoover, leading one African-American editor to insist: "[T]urn Lincoln's picture to the wall. That debt has been paid in full." The New Deal caused a historic shift. In 1934, Chicago's black voters replaced Republican congressman Oscar DePriest with a Democrat. In 1936, 76 percent of black voters supported FDR.

In economic terms, this shift made sense. Owing mainly to workplace racism, blacks' jobless rates in the 1930s outran those of the work force as a whole. Thus, New Deal relief programs greatly aided blacks. On racial-justice issues, however, the New Deal's record was mixed at best. Some NRA codes included racially discriminatory clauses, causing black activists to deride the agency as "Negroes Ruined Again." TVA and other New Deal agencies tolerated racial bias. Lynchings increased in the 1930s as some whites translated economic worries into racial violence, but Roosevelt kept aloof from an NAACP campaign to make lynching a federal crime. An antilynching bill passed the House of Representatives in 1935, but southern Democratic senators killed it with a filibuster. To protect his legislative program and retain southern white voters, FDR did little. "[T]he Roosevelt administration [has] nothing for [blacks]," the NAACP concluded bitterly.

In limited ways, FDR did address racial issues. He cautiously tried to rid New Deal agencies of blatant racism. He appointed more than a hundred blacks to policy-level and judicial positions, including Eleanor Roosevelt's friend Mary McLeod Bethune as director of minority affairs in the National Youth Administration. Bethune, a Florida educator and founder of the National Council of Negro Women (1936), led the so-called black cabinet that linked the administration and black organizations. The "Roosevelt Supreme Court" that took shape after 1936 issued antidiscrimination rulings in cases involving housing, voting rights, wage inequity, and jury selection.

The New Deal also supported racial justice in symbolic ways. In 1938, when the participants in a welfare conference in Birmingham, Alabama, were segregated in compliance with local statutes, Mrs. Roosevelt pointedly placed her chair halfway between the white and black delegates. In 1939, when the Daughters of the American Revolution barred black contralto Marian Anderson from performing in Washington's Constitution Hall, Mrs. Roosevelt resigned from the organization, and Harold Ickes arranged an Easter concert by Anderson at the Lincoln Memorial. Even symbolic gestures outraged many southern whites. When a black minister delivered the invocation at the 1936 Democratic convention, a South Carolina senator noisily stalked out.

Molly Dewson, head of the Democratic Party's women's division and a friend of the Roosevelts, led the party's effort to court women voters. In the 1936 campaign Dewson mobilized fifteen thousand women to distribute flyers describing New Deal programs. "[W]e did not make the old-fashioned plea that our nominee was charming," she recalled; ". . . we appealed to [women's] intelligence."

Unlike earlier feminists, Dewson did not promote a specifically feminist agenda. The New Deal's recovery and social-welfare programs, she argued, served the interests of both sexes. She did, however, successfully push for more women in policy-level positions. FDR appointed the first woman cabinet member, the first woman ambassador, and a number of female federal judges. Through Dewson's efforts, the 1936 Democratic platform committee reflected a fifty-fifty gender balance.

Symbolic gestures and the appointment of a few blacks and women, while noteworthy, ought not be overemphasized. Racism and sexism pervaded U.S. society in the 1930s, and Roosevelt, grappling with the depression, did relatively little to change things. That challenge would await a later time.

The Environment and the West

Environmental issues loomed large in the 1930s, reflecting FDR's priorities. While still in the New York Senate, he had sought to regulate logging that threatened wildlife. As presi-

Power to the People   *The New Deal's massive hydroelectric power projects were celebrated in this 1937 "Living Newspaper" production by the WPA's Federal Theatre Project.*

dent, he strongly supported the Civilian Conservation Corps' program of planting trees, thinning forests, and building hiking trails.

Soil conservation emerged as a major priority. The 1930s' dust storms resulted not only from drought, but from years of overgrazing and poor farming practices. For decades, Great Plains' wheat farmers had used powerful tractors, combines, and heavy-duty plows called "sodbusters" to uproot the native prairie grasses that anchored the soil. When the rains failed, as they periodically do in this drought-prone region, little remained to hold the baked earth in place, and parching winds whipped up devastating dust storms. By the 1930s, 9 million acres of farmland had been lost to erosion in the Great Plains, the South, and elsewhere.

In response, the Department of Agriculture's Soil Conservation Service set up projects to show the value of contour plowing, crop rotation, and soil-strengthening grasses. The Taylor Grazing Act of 1934 restricted the grazing on public lands that had contributed to the problem. The TVA helped control the floods that worsened erosion in the Tennessee valley.

New Deal planners also promoted the national-park movement. Olympic National Park in Washington, Virginia's Shenandoah National Park, and Kings Canyon National Park in California all date from the 1930s. The administration also created some 160 new national wildlife refuges. Roosevelt even closed a Utah artillery range that threatened a nesting site of the endangered trumpeter swan.

The wilderness-preservation movement gained momentum in the 1930s, supported by such diverse groups as the Wilderness Society (1935), started by environmentalist

Aldo Leopold and others, and the National Wildlife Federation (1936), funded by firearms makers eager to preserve wilderness areas for hunters. Under pressure from such groups, Congress set aside a portion of Kings Canyon National Park as a wilderness area. Building on these beginnings, the United States by 2006 had 680 officially designated national wilderness areas, comprising 105 million acres.

By later standards, the New Deal's environmental record was spotty. The decade's massive hydroelectric projects, while necessary at a time when many rural families still lacked electricity, had ecological consequences little noted at the time. The Grand Coulee Dam, for example, destroyed salmon spawning on much of the Columbia River's tributary system. Other New Deal dams disrupted fragile ecosystems and adversely affected local residents, particularly Native American communities, who depended on these ecosystems for their livelihood.

Viewed in context, however, the New Deal's environmental record remains impressive. While coping with a grave economic crisis, the Roosevelt administration focused a level of attention on environmental issues that had not been seen since the Progressive Era, and would not be seen again for a generation.

The New Deal had a big impact on the West, especially because the federal government owned a third or more of the land in eleven western states, with the figure rising far higher in some states. New Deal agencies and laws such as the AAA, the Soil Conservation Service, the Taylor Grazing Act, and the Farm Security Administration (see below) set new rules for western agriculture from the grain and cattle of the Great Plains to the Pacific coast citrus groves and truck farms dependent on migrant labor.

Some of the largest PWA and WPA projects were built in the West, including thousands of public buildings (246 in Washington State alone), from courthouses and post offices to tourist facilities such as beautiful Timberline Lodge on Oregon's Mount Hood. The highways linking the West to the rest of America, such as the Lincoln Highway from Philadelphia to San Francisco and Route 66 from Chicago to Los Angeles, were upgraded in the 1930s with federal assistance.

Above all, the PWA in the West built dams—not only Grand Coulee, but also Shasta on the Sacramento River, Bonneville on the Columbia, Glen Canyon on the Colorado, and others. The PWA completed Hoover Dam on the Colorado, authorized by Congress in 1928 (see Chapter 23), well ahead of schedule. Despite their ecological downside, these great undertakings—among the largest engineering projects in human history—supplied electric power to vast regions while also contributing to flood control, irrigation, and soil conservation. (Las Vegas owed its post–World War II emergence as a gambling and entertainment mecca to power from nearby Hoover Dam.)

A New Deal initiative especially important for the West was Harold Ickes's National Planning Board of 1934, later renamed the National Resources Planning Board. This agency, which extended Herbert Hoover's promotion of cooperative, multistate planning of western water resources (see Chapter 23), facilitated state and regional management of water, soil, timber, and minerals.

THE NEW DEAL'S END STAGE, 1937–1939

Buoyed by his 1936 victory, Roosevelt launched an abortive attack on the Supreme Court. After this bruising fight, FDR confronted both a stubborn recession and newly energized conservative opposition. A few final measures in 1937–1938 brought the New Deal to a close.

FDR and the Supreme Court

In 1937, four of the Supreme Court's nine elderly justices were archconservatives who abhorred the New Deal. Joined by others of more moderate views, these conservatives had struck down the NRA, the AAA, and progressive state laws. Roosevelt feared that key measures of the Second New Deal, including the Social Security Act and the Wagner Act, would meet a similar fate. Indeed, some corporate lawyers were so sure that the Social Security Act would be found unconstitutional that they advised their clients to ignore it.

In February 1937, FDR proposed a bill that would have allowed him to appoint an additional Supreme Court member for each justice over age seventy, up to a total of six. Roosevelt blandly insisted that this would ease aging justices' heavy workload, but his political motivation was obvious.

FDR hoped that his popularity would assure support for his Court plan, but the press and public reacted with sharp hostility. The Supreme Court's size (unspecified in the Constitution) had fluctuated in the early Republic, but the membership of nine, dating to 1869, had become almost sacrosanct. Warning of a power grab by FDR, conservatives blasted the "court-packing" scheme and the devious way FDR had presented it. Even many Democrats disapproved. When the Senate voted down the scheme in July, FDR quietly dropped it.

But was this a defeat? One conservative justice retired in May 1937; others announced retirement plans. In April and May the Court upheld several New Deal measures, including the Wagner Act, as well as a state minimum-wage law. This outcome may have been Roosevelt's objective all along. His challenge to the Court, plus his 1936 victory, sent powerful political signals that the justices heeded. From 1937 to 1939 FDR appointed four new Supreme Court justices, creating a judicial legacy that would long outlive him.

The Roosevelt Recession

After showing signs of recovery, the economy dipped ominously in August 1937. Industrial production slumped. Soaring unemployment again dominated the headlines. This "Roosevelt recession" resulted in part from federal policies that reduced consumer income. Social-security payroll taxes withdrew some $2 billion from circulation. The Federal Reserve Board had raised interest rates to forestall inflation, further contracting the money supply. FDR, meanwhile, concerned about mounting deficits, had seized on the signs of recovery to cut back the New Deal relief programs.

Echoing Hoover, FDR assured his cabinet, "Everything will work out . . . if we just sit tight." Meanwhile, however, John Maynard Keynes's advocacy of deficit spending as the key to recovery had persuaded some New Dealers. Aware that political rather than economic arguments carried more weight with FDR, they warned him of a political backlash if breadlines and soup kitchens returned. Convinced, FDR in April 1938 authorized new spending on work-relief projects by the WPA, PWA, and other New Deal agencies. By late 1938, unemployment had declined and industrial output increased. As late as 1939, however, more than 17 percent of the labor force remained jobless.

A Camera's-Eye View of Depression-Era America *This 1937 image by Dorothea Lange, a photographer with the Farm Security Administration, pictures migrants from the Texas dust bowl gathered at a roadside camp near Calipatria in southern California.*

Final Measures; Growing Opposition

Preoccupied by the Supreme Court fight, the recession, and menacing events abroad (see Chapter 25), FDR offered few domestic initiatives after 1936. Congress, however, enacted several significant measures.

In 1937, Congress created the **Farm Security Administration** (FSA), replacing Rexford Tugwell's underfunded Resettlement Administration. The FSA made low-interest loans to help tenant farmers and sharecroppers buy their own farms. These loans, totaling more than $1 billion through 1941, did help some rural folk become more self-sufficient. Ironically, however, the FSA often rejected the poorest farmers' loan applications, considering them a bad credit risk.

The FSA operated camps offering shelter and medical services to migrant farm workers living in wretched conditions. FSA nurses and home economists provided health, hygiene, and housekeeping advice to poor farm families. The FSA also commissioned gifted photographers to record the lives of migrant workers, tenant farmers, and uprooted dust-bowl families. These FSA photographs, published in various periodicals, helped shape a realistic documentary style that pervaded 1930s' popular culture, including Hollywood movies and Henry Luce's photo magazine *Life*, launched in 1936. Today they comprise a haunting album of depression-era images.

Other measures set precedents for the future. The 1937 Housing Act appropriated $500 million for urban slum clearance and public housing—projects that would loom large in the 1950s. The **Fair Labor Standards Act** of 1938 banned child labor and set a national minimum wage (initially forty cents an hour) and a maximum workweek of forty hours. This measure reflected not only humanitarianism but also some northern legislators' desire to undermine the competitive edge of the South, with its low wages. Despite many loopholes, the law helped exploited workers, and underscored the government's role in regulating abuses by employers.

In a final stab at raising farm income, the Agricultural Adjustment Act of 1938 created a mechanism by which the government, in years of big harvests and low prices, would make loans to farmers and warehouse their surplus crops. When prices rose, farmers could repay their loans and sell their commodities. This complicated system set the framework of federal farm price support for decades.

Overall, New Deal farm policy produced mixed results. Large-scale growers benefited from subsidy payments, but the cumbersome price-support mechanisms involved problems that would worsen with time. The FSA provided short-term help to some tenants, sharecroppers, and small farmers (though often not the neediest), but did little to slow the long-term decline of family farms and the rise of agribusinesses. In reality, many small farmers themselves aspired to become large-scale commercial operators. Most did not succeed, however, and gradually left the land.

The New Deal's slower pace after 1935 also reflected the rise of an anti–New Deal congressional coalition of Republicans and conservative southern Democrats. In 1937, this coalition rejected FDR's proposal to reorganize the executive branch. The plan made administrative sense, but critics again warned darkly of a White House power grab.

The conservative coalition also slashed relief appropriations; cut corporate taxes in 1938; and in 1939 killed the WPA's Federal Theatre Project for its alleged radicalism. Under Texas congressman Martin Dies, the House Un-American Activities Committee (created in 1937) investigated New Deal agencies for communist infiltration. The 1939 Hatch Act, barring federal employees from electoral campaigning, reflected conservatives' suspicions that FDR was using WPA staff for campaign purposes.

Although FDR campaigned actively in the 1938 midterm elections, the Republicans gained heavily in the House and Senate and won a net of thirteen governorships. In the Democratic primaries Roosevelt tried to defeat several anti–New Deal Democratic senators, but most bested their primary challengers and went on to win in November. Focusing on foreign affairs in his January 1939 State of the Union message, FDR proposed no new domestic measures and merely noted the need to "preserve our reforms." The New Deal was over.

SOCIAL CHANGE AND SOCIAL ACTION IN THE 1930S

American life in the 1930s involved more than politics. The depression affected most Americans, including the jobless and their families; working women; and all age groups. For industrial workers, African-Americans, a growing Hispanic community, and Native Americans, the crisis brought hard times, but the activist climate of the era also encouraged organized resistance to exploitation and brought new legislative initiatives.

The Depression's Psychological and Social Impact

The depression caused untold human suffering and marked all who lived through it. Despite the New Deal, unemployment never fell below about 14 percent in the 1930s, and for much of the decade it was considerably higher. A quarter of all farm families had to accept public or private assistance during the 1930s. Even the employed often had to take jobs below their level of training: college alumni pumped gas; business-school graduates sold furniture; a retired navy captain became an usher in a movie theater.

Psychologists described "unemployment shock": jobless persons who walked the streets seeking work and then lay awake at night worrying. When shoe soles wore out, cardboard or folded newspapers had to serve. Tacks pierced worn shoe heels, cutting the skin. "You pass . . . shoe-shops where a tack might be bent down," one young man observed bitterly, "but you can't pull off a shoe and ask to have that done—for nothing."

Advertisements for mouthwashes, deodorants, and correspondence courses exploited feelings of shame and failure. Women's magazines described low-cost meals and other budget-trimming strategies. Habits of scrimping and saving acquired in the 1930s often survived into more affluent times. As Caroline Bird wrote in *The Invisible Scar* (1966), a social history of the 1930s, the depression for many boiled down to "a dull misery in the bones."

New York senator Robert Wagner called the working woman in the depression "the first orphan in the storm." Indeed, for the 25 percent of U.S. women employed in 1930, the depression brought difficult times. The female jobless rate exceeded 20 percent for much of the decade. Women desperate to continue working often took lower-paying jobs. Laid-off factory workers became waitresses. Young women new to the job market took temporary or part-time work. Jobless men competed with women even for such traditional "women's work" as library work and school teaching.

Married women workers endured harsh criticism. Although most worked because of economic necessity, they were accused of stealing jobs from men. Even Secretary of Labor Frances Perkins urged married women to stay out of the labor market so more men could work. Many cities refused to employ married women as teachers and even fired women teachers who married.

Women workers also faced wage discrimination. In 1939, women teachers earned on average nearly 20 percent less than male teachers with comparable experience. Some NRA codes authorized lower pay for women workers. Many women workers were not covered by the minimum-wage clause of the Fair Labor Standards Act, including the more than 2 million who worked for wages in private households.

The late 1930s' unionization drive (see below) had mixed effects on women workers. Those employed in some mass-production industries benefited, but the most heavily female sectors of the labor force—textiles, sales, and clerical and service work—resisted unionization. Male managers and even male union leaders opposed a 1937 campaign to unionize mostly female clerical workers.

Despite the criticism, the percentage of married women holding wage-earning jobs increased from under 12 percent in 1930 to nearly 16 percent in 1940. The depression may actually have hastened the long-term movement of women into the workplace as married women took jobs out of necessity. When her husband gave up trying to find work in 1932, one working wife explained, "[At] twenty-eight, with two little girls, . . . I took a job as a salesclerk . . . , and worked through the Depression."

As this story suggests, the depression profoundly affected family life. The birthrate fell in the early thirties as married couples postponed a family or limited its size. Birth control became easier as condoms and diaphragms became more accessible. A declining birthrate plus reduced immigration held population growth in the 1930s to a scant 7 percent, in contrast to an average of 20 percent per decade from 1900 to 1930.

Making ends meet and holding one's family together posed major challenges. Parents patched clothes, stretched food resources, and sought public assistance when necessary. In homes with a tradition of strong male authority, the husband's loss of a job could prove a devastating psychological blow. "I would rather turn on the gas and put an end to the whole family than let my wife support me," one man told a social investigator. Desertions increased, and the divorce rate, after a dip in the early and mid-1930s, edged upward, hitting a then all-time high by 1940.

The depression spared neither old nor young. Bank failures wiped out the savings of many older Americans. By 1935, a million citizens over sixty-five were on relief. As for young people, one observer compared them to runners waiting for a starting gun that never sounded. High-school enrollment increased as many youths, lacking job prospects, simply stayed in school. The marriage rate declined as young people facing bleak prospects postponed this step. Commented Eleanor Roosevelt in 1934, "I have moments of real terror when I think we might be losing this generation. We have got to bring these young people into the active life of the community and make them feel that they are necessary."

Children found vacation plans canceled, birthdays with few presents, and mealtimes tense with anxious discussions. Maria Tighe of Long Island, who was seven years old in 1929, recalled sneaking to 6 A.M. mass so her friends would not see her ugly shoes, provided by the welfare bureau. Depression-era children wrote sad letters to Eleanor Roosevelt. A Michigan high-school senior described her shame at not having a graduation dress. "I give all I earn for food for the family," she explained. A thirteen-year-old Arkansas girl wrote, "I have to stay out of school because I have no books or clothes to ware."

Depression-era families also rediscovered traditional skills. They baked bread, canned fruit and vegetables, painted their own houses, and repaired their own cars. Many would later recall the 1930s as a time of simple, inexpensive pleasures and neighborly sharing of scant resources.

For the neediest—among them blacks, Hispanics, and southern sharecroppers—the depression imposed added misery on poverty-blighted lives. In his novel *Native Son* (1940), Richard Wright vividly portrayed the desperate conditions in Chicago's black slums. Yet hope survived. Emotional resilience, ingrained patterns of mutual aid, and survival skills honed through years of oppression helped poor families cope. In New York's Harlem a charismatic black religious leader calling himself Father Divine institutionalized this cooperative spirit by organizing kitchens that distributed thousands of free meals daily.

Industrial Workers Unionize

Between 1900 and 1930, the ranks of factory workers had soared from 3.7 million to 7.7 million. Yet most of these workers remained unorganized. Major industries such as steel, au-

FIGURE 24.2 **The Growth of Labor Union Membership, 1933–1946**

The CIO's industrial unions grew rapidly with passage of the pro-union National Labor Relations Act in 1935. Union membership increased still more as war plants hired workers in the early 1940s. *Source: Historical Statistics of the United States, Colonial Times to 1970 (1975), 176–177.*

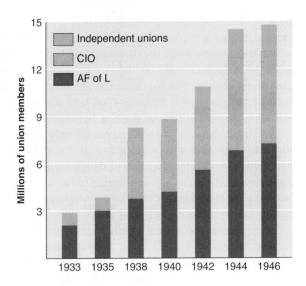

tomobiles, and textiles had resisted workers' attempts to unionize. The conservative mood of the 1920s had further weakened the labor movement.

But hard times and a favorable government climate bred a new labor militancy in the 1930s. Only through collective action, workers realized, could they pressure management to provide better wages and working conditions. The Wagner Act's guarantee of workers' right to organize energized some American Federation of Labor leaders. In November 1935, John L. Lewis of the United Mine Workers and Sidney Hillman of the Amalgamated Clothing Workers, frustrated by the AFL's slowness in organizing factory workers, started the Committee for Industrial Organization (CIO) within the AFL. Young CIO activists preached unionization in Pittsburgh steel mills, Detroit auto plants, Akron rubber factories, and southern textile mills. Unlike the craft-based and racially exclusive AFL unions, CIO unions welcomed all workers in a particular industry, regardless of race, gender, or degree of skill.

In 1936 a CIO-sponsored organizing committee geared up for a strike to unionize the steel industry. (In fact, John L. Lewis had already secretly worked out a settlement with the head of U.S. Steel.) In March 1937, U.S. Steel recognized the union, raised wages, and introduced a forty-hour workweek. Other big steel companies followed suit, and soon four hundred thousand steelworkers had signed union cards.

Other CIO organizers targeted General Motors, an anti-union stronghold. Their leader was a redheaded young autoworker and labor activist, Walter Reuther. Reuther's father, of German-immigrant stock, was a committed socialist, and when the depression hit, young Reuther rediscovered his radical roots. On December 30, 1936, employees at GM's two body plants in Flint, Michigan, stopped work and peacefully occupied the factories. This "sit-down" strategy (adopted so GM could not hire strikebreakers to keep the plants operating) paralyzed GM's production.

Although women workers did not participate in the plant occupation (to avoid gossip that might discredit the strike), they picketed on the outside. A Women's Auxiliary led by strikers' families provided meals, set up a speakers' bureau, and organized marches supporting the strike.

GM sent spies to union meetings, called in police to harass the strikers, and threatened to fire them. A showdown with the police led to the formation of the Women's Emergency Brigade, whose members remained on twenty-four-hour alert for picket duty or to surround the plants in case of further police raids.

GM asked President Roosevelt and the governor of Michigan to send troops to expel the strikers, as Herbert Hoover had done with the bonus marchers in 1932. Both officials declined, however. Although FDR disapproved of the sit-down tactic, he refused to intervene.

On February 11, 1937, GM signed a contract recognizing the United Automobile Workers (UAW). Bearded workers who had vowed not to shave until victory was won streamed out of the plants. As Chrysler fell into line also, the UAW soon boasted more than four hundred thousand members. Unionization of the electrical and rubber industries moved forward as well.

In 1938 the Committee for Industrial Organization broke with the AFL to become the **Congress of Industrial Organizations,** a 2-million-member association of industrial unions including the autoworkers. In response to the CIO challenge, the AFL began to adapt to the changed nature of the labor force. Overall, union membership in the United States shot from under 3 million in 1933 to over 8 million in 1941.

Some big corporations fought on. Henry Ford hated unions, and his tough lieutenant Harry Bennett organized a squad of union-busting thugs to fight the UAW. In 1937 Bennett's men viciously beat Walter Reuther and other UAW officials outside Ford's plant near Detroit. Not until 1941, faced with a wildcat (unauthorized) strike after Bennett fired several union sympathizers, did Ford yield to the union's pressure.

The Republic Steel Company, headed by a union hater named Tom Girdler, dug in as well. Even after the major steelmakers signed with the CIO, Republic and a group of smaller companies known collectively as "Little Steel" resisted. In May 1937 workers in twenty-seven Little Steel plants, including Republic's factory in South Chicago, walked off the job. Anticipating the strike, Girdler had assembled an arsenal of riot guns and tear gas. On May 30, Memorial Day, a group of strikers approached over 250 police guarding the factory. When someone threw a large stick at the police, they responded with gunfire that left four strikers dead and scores wounded. An investigative committee found that the police killings had been "clearly avoidable." In 1941, under growing pressure, the Little Steel companies, including Republic, finally accepted the CIO union.

Another holdout was the textile industry, with over six hundred thousand workers, mostly in the South and 40 percent female. Most textile workers earned little and had no recourse against autocratic bosses. The AFL's textile-workers union had made little headway in the 1920s owing to mill owners' hostility and the AFL's policy of admitting only skilled workers. In 1934, the CIO launched a new drive. Some four hundred thousand textile workers went on strike, but the mill owners fought back. Southern governors mobilized the National Guard to fight the strike. Several strikers were killed and thousands arrested. The strike failed, and most textile workers still did not belong to a union as the decade ended.

Indeed, despite the wave of unionization, more than three-quarters of the nonfarm labor force remained unorganized in 1940, including department-store and clerical workers and low-paid manual laborers, domestic workers, and restaurant and laundry employees—categories that included many women, blacks, and recent immigrants. Nevertheless, the unionization of key sectors of America's industrial work force ranks as one of the decade's memorable developments.

Why did powerful corporations yield to unionization after years of resistance? Certainly workers' militancy and the tactical skill of union organizers were crucial. But a changed government climate contributed as well. Historically, corporations had called on the government to help break strikes. Although this still happened in the 1930s, as in the textile-industry strike, in general the Roosevelt administration and key state officials refused to intervene on the side of management. A series of New Deal labor laws made clear that Washington would no longer automatically back management in labor disputes. Once corporate managers realized this, unionization often followed.

Organized labor's successes in the later 1930s concealed some complex tensions. A hard core of activists, some of them communists or socialists, led the unionizing drive. But most rank-and-file workers had no desire to overthrow the capitalist system. Indeed, many held back from striking, fearful for their jobs. But once the CIO's militant minority showed that picket lines and sit-down strikes could win union contracts and tangible gains, workers signed up by the thousands. As they did, the radical organizers lost influence, and the unions became more conservative.

Even Walter Reuther, despite his socialist roots, turned increasingly conservative. After World War II, in a different political climate, Reuther purged from the CIO some of the same radicals and leftists who had led the organizational battles of the 1930s.

Black and Hispanic Americans Resist Racism and Exploitation
The depression also stirred activism within the African-American and Hispanic communities. Although black migration northward slowed in the 1930s, four hundred thousand southern blacks moved to northern cities in the decade. By 1940, nearly one-quarter of the nation's 12 million blacks lived in the urban North.

Rural or urban, life was hard. Black tenant farmers and sharecroppers often faced eviction. Among black industrial workers, the depression-era jobless rate far outran the rate for whites, largely because of racism and discriminatory hiring. Although black workers in some industries benefited from the CIO's nondiscriminatory policy, workplace racism remained a fact of life.

Over one hundred blacks died by lynching in the 1930s, and other miscarriages of justice continued, especially in the South. In 1931 an all-white jury in Scottsboro, Alabama, sentenced eight black youths to death on highly suspect charges of rape. In 1935, after heavy publicity and an aggressive defense, the Supreme Court ordered a new trial for the "Scottsboro Boys" because they had been denied legal counsel and blacks had been excluded from the jury. Five of the group were again convicted, however, and served long prison terms.

But rising activism signaled changes ahead. The NAACP battled in courts and legislatures against lynching, segregation, and the denial of voting rights. Under the banner "Don't Shop Where You Can't Work," black protesters picketed and boycotted businesses that refused to hire blacks, particularly in black neighborhoods. In March 1935, hostility toward discriminatory white-owned businesses in Harlem, intensified

Young Mexican Cotton Picker in the 1930s
Whether in agricultural labor or urban barrios, Mexican-Americans endured harsh conditions during the depression.

by anger over racism and joblessness, ignited a riot that caused an estimated $200 million in damage and left three blacks dead.

The Communist Party publicized lynchings and racial discrimination, and supplied lawyers for the "Scottsboro Boys," as part of a depression-era recruitment effort in the black community. But despite a few notable recruits (including the novelist Richard Wright), few blacks joined the party.

Other minority groups also faced discrimination. California continued to restrict landownership by Japanese-Americans. In 1934, Congress set an annual limit of fifty on immigration from the Philippines, still a U.S. possession—lower than that for any other nation. Congress also offered free travel "home" for Filipinos long settled in the United States.

The more than 2 million Hispanic Americans faced trying times as well. Some were citizens with ancestral roots in the Southwest, but most were recent arrivals from Mexico or Caribbean islands such as Jamaica, Cuba, and Puerto Rico (a U.S. holding whose residents were and are American citizens). While the Caribbean immigrants settled in East Coast cities, most Mexican newcomers worked as migratory agricultural laborers in the Southwest and elsewhere, or in midwestern steel or meatpacking plants.

As the depression deepened, Mexican-born residents endured rising hostility. The western trek of thousands of "Okies" fleeing the dust bowl worsened the job crisis for Hispanic farm workers. By 1937 more than half of Arizona's cotton workers were out-of-staters who had supplanted Mexican-born laborers. With their patterns of migratory work disrupted, Mexican-Americans poured into the barrios (Hispanic neighborhoods) of southwestern cities. Lacking work, half a million Mexicans returned to their native land in the 1930s. While many did so voluntarily, others were repatriated by immigration officials and local authorities. Los Angeles welfare officials announced free one-way transportation to Mexico. The savings in relief payments, they calculated, would more than offset the cost of sending *repatriados* to Mexico. Though the plan was "voluntary," those who remained were denied relief payments or jobs with New Deal work programs. Under federal and local pressure, an estimated seventy thousand Mexicans left Los Angeles in 1931 alone.

Mexican-American farm workers who remained endured appalling conditions and near-starvation wages. A wave of protests and strikes (some led by Communist Party organizers) swept California. A labor organization called the Confederación de Uniones de Campesinos y Obreros Mexicanos (Confederation of Unions of Mexican Workers and Farm Laborers) emerged from a 1933 strike of grape workers in El Monte, California. More strikes erupted in 1935–1936 from the celery fields and citrus groves around Los Angeles to the lettuce fields of the Salinas Valley.

Organizations like the California Fruit Growers Exchange (which marketed its citrus under the brand name Sunkist) fought the unions, sometimes with violence. In October 1933, bullets ripped into a cotton pickers' union hall in Pixley, California, killing two men and wounding others. Resisting intimidation, the strikers won a 20 percent pay increase. Striking cotton pickers and other Mexican-American farm workers gained hard-fought victories as well. These strikes awakened at least some Americans to the plight of one of the nation's most exploited groups.

A New Deal for Native Americans

The 1930s also focused attention on the nation's 330,000 Native Americans, most of whom endured poverty, scant education, poor health care, and bleak prospects. The 1887 Dawes Act (see Chapter 17) had dissolved the tribes as legal entities, allocated some tribal lands to individual Indians, and offered the rest for sale. By the 1930s, whites held about two-thirds of the land that Indians had possessed in 1887, including much of the most valuable acreage. Indians had gained voting rights in 1924, but this did little to improve their lot.

In the 1920s a reform movement arose to reverse the Dawes Act approach. John Collier, who had lived among New Mexico's Pueblo Indians, founded the American Indian Defense Association in 1923 to preserve what he saw as the spiritual harmony of traditional Indian life. The National Council of American Indians, headed by Gertrude Bonnin, a Yankton Dakota Sioux, while not sharing all of Collier's goals, also pressed for reform.

Appointed commissioner of Indian affairs in 1933, Collier gathered funds from various New Deal agencies to construct schools, hospitals, and irrigation systems on reservations, and to preserve sites of cultural importance. The Civilian Conservation Corps employed twelve thousand Indian youths to work on projects on Indian lands.

Pursuing his vision of renewed tribal life, Collier drafted a bill to halt the sale of tribal land and restore the remaining unallocated lands to tribal control. Collier's bill also gave broad powers to tribal councils and required Indian schools to teach Native American history and handicrafts. Some Indian leaders criticized it as a plan to transform reservations into living museums and to treat Native Americans as an exotic people cut off from modern life. Indians who were thriving as individual property owners or entrepreneurs rejected the bill's tribalist assumptions. The bill did, indeed, reflect the idealism of well-meaning outsiders rather than the views of the nation's diverse Native American groups.

The **Indian Reorganization Act** of 1934, a compromise measure, halted the sale of tribal lands and enabled tribes to regain title to unallocated lands. But Congress scaled back Collier's proposals for tribal self-government and dropped his calls for renewal of traditional tribal culture.

A majority of tribes approved the law (a requirement for it to go into effect), but opinion differed. Of 258 tribes that voted, 181 favored the measure, while 77 did not. America's largest tribal group, the 40,000-strong Navajo, voted no, largely because the law, to promote soil conservation, restricted grazing rights.

Indian policy clearly remained contentious. But the law did recognize Indian interests and the value of cultural diversity. The restoration of tribes as legal entities laid the groundwork for later tribal business ventures as well as tribal lawsuits seeking to enforce long-violated treaty rights (see Chapter 30).

THE AMERICAN CULTURAL SCENE IN THE 1930S

Hard times and the New Deal shaped American cultural life in the 1930s. Radio and the movies offered mostly escapist fare, though some films addressed depression-era realities. The response of novelists, artists, playwrights, and photographers changed over time. When the depression first struck, as we have seen, their view of capitalist America tended to be highly critical. As the decade went on, however, a more positive view of America emerged, reflecting both optimism about the New Deal and apprehension about events abroad.

Avenues of Escape: Radio and the Movies

The standardization of mass culture continued in the 1930s. Each evening, Americans turned to their radios for network news, musical programs, and comedy shows. Radio humor flourished as hard times battered the real world. Comedians like Jack Benny and the husband-and-wife team George Burns and Gracie Allen attracted millions.

So, too, did the fifteen-minute afternoon domestic dramas known as soap operas (for the soap companies that sponsored them). Despite their assembly-line quality, these daily dollops of romance and melodrama won a devoted audience, consisting mostly of housewives. Identifying with the ordeals of the radio heroines, female listeners gained at least temporary escape from their own difficulties. As one put it, "I can get through the day better when I hear they have sorrows, too."

The movies, with their affordable ten or twenty-five cent admission, remained extremely popular. In 1939, 65 percent of Americans went to the movies at least once a week. Motion pictures, declared one Hollywood executive, had become "as necessary as any other daily commodity."

Films of the early 1930s like *Street Scene* (1931) and *I Am a Fugitive from a Chain Gang* (1932) captured the grimness of the early depression. The popular Marx Brothers movies reflected the confusion and uncertainty of the Hoover years, when the economy and the social order itself seemed on the verge of collapse. In zanily anarchic comedies like *Animal Crackers* (1930) and *Duck Soup* (1933), these vaudeville troupers of German-Jewish immigrant origins ridiculed authority and satirized the established order.

After Roosevelt took office, Warner Brothers studio (with close ties to the administration) made several topical films that presented the New Deal as the answer to the nation's problems. These included *Wild Boys of the Road* (1933), about unemployed youth; *Massacre* (1934), on the mistreatment of Indians; and *Black Fury* (1935), dealing with striking coal miners.

The gangster movies of the early thirties, inspired by real-life criminals like Al Capone and John Dillinger, served up a different style of film realism. Films like *Little Caesar* (1930) and *The Public Enemy* (1931) offered gritty images of depression America: menacing streets; forbidding industrial sites; gunfights between rival gangs. When civic groups protested the glorification of crime, Hollywood simply made the police and "G-men" (FBI agents) the heroes, while retaining the violence. The movie gangsters played by Edward G. Robinson and James Cagney, variants of the Horatio Alger hero battling adversity, appealed to depression-era moviegoers facing equally heavy odds.

Above all, Hollywood offered escape—the chance briefly to forget the depression. The publicist who claimed that the movies "literally laughed the big bad wolf of the depression out of the public mind" exaggerated, but cinema's escapist function in the 1930s is clear. Musicals such as *Gold Diggers of 1933* (with its theme song, "We're in the Money") offered dancing, music, and cheerful plots involving the triumph of pluck over all obstacles. In Frank Capra's *Mr. Deeds Goes to Town* (1936) and *Mr. Smith Goes to Washington* (1939), virtuous heroes representing "the people" triumph over entrenched interests. When color movies arrived in the late 1930s, they seemed an omen of better times ahead.

African-Americans appeared in 1930s' movies, if at all, only as stereotypes: the scatterbrained maid played by Butterfly McQueen in *Gone with the Wind* (1939); the indulgent house servant played by tap dancer Bill Robinson and patronized by child star Shirley Temple in *The Little Colonel* (1935). Under the denigrating screen name Stepin Fetchit, black actor Lincoln Perry played the slow-witted buffoon in many movies.

In representing women, Hollywood offered mixed messages. While some 1930s' movie heroines found fulfillment in marriage and domesticity, other films chipped away at the stereotype. Joan Bennett played a strong-willed professional in *The Wedding Present* (1936). Katharine Hepburn portrayed autonomous, independent-minded women in such films as *Spitfire* (1934) and *A Woman Rebels* (1936). Mae West, brassy, openly sexual, and fiercely independent, mocked conventional stereotypes in *I'm No Angel* (1933) and other 1930s' hits.

The Later 1930s: Opposing Fascism; Reaffirming Traditional Values
As the 1930s ended, many Americans viewed the nation more favorably. It had survived the depression. The social fabric remained whole; revolution had not come. As other societies collapsed into dictatorships, American democracy endured. Writers, composers, and other cultural creators reflected the changed mood, as despair gave way to a more upbeat and patriotic outlook.

International developments and a domestic political movement known as the **Popular Front** influenced this shift. In the early 1930s, the U.S. Communist Party attacked Roosevelt and the New Deal. But in 1935 Russian dictator Joseph Stalin, fearing attack by Nazi Germany, called for a worldwide alliance, or Popular Front, against Adolf

Hitler and his Italian fascist ally, Benito Mussolini. (Fascism is a form of government involving one-party rule, extreme nationalism, hostility to minority groups, and the forcible suppression of dissent.) Parroting the new Soviet line, U.S. communists now praised FDR and summoned writers and intellectuals to the antifascist cause. Many noncommunists, alarmed by developments in Europe, responded to the call.

The Popular Front's high-water mark came during the Spanish Civil War of 1936–1939. In July 1936 Spanish fascist general Francisco Franco began a military revolt against Spain's legally elected government, a coalition of left-wing parties. With aid from Hitler and Mussolini, Franco won backing from Spanish monarchists, landowners, industrialists, and the Catholic Church.

In America, the anti-Franco Spanish Loyalists (that is, those loyal to the elected government) won support from writers, artists, and intellectuals who backed the Popular Front. The novelist Ernest Hemingway, who visited Spain in 1936–1937, was among the writers who backed the Loyalists. In contrast to his antiwar novels of the 1920s (see Chapter 23), Hemingway's *For Whom the Bell Tolls* (1940) told of a young American volunteer who dies while fighting with the Loyalists. "The Spanish Civil War offered something which you could believe in wholly and completely," Hemingway later wrote, "and in which you felt an absolute brotherhood with the others who were engaged in it."

The Popular Front collapsed in August 1939 when the Soviet Union and Nazi Germany signed a nonaggression pact. Overnight, enthusiasm for joining with communists under the "antifascism" banner faded. But while it lasted, the Popular Front helped shape U.S. culture and alerted Americans to threatening events abroad.

The New Deal's programs for writers, artists, and musicians, as well as its turn leftward in 1935–1936, also contributed to the cultural shift of the later 1930s. The cynical tone of the 1920s and early 1930s now gave way to a more upbeat view. In John Steinbeck's best-selling novel *The Grapes of Wrath* (1939), an uprooted dust-bowl family, the Joads, make their difficult way from Oklahoma to California along Route 66. Steinbeck stressed the strength and endurance of ordinary Americans as well as their cooperation and mutual support. As Ma Joad tells her son Tom, "They ain't gonna wipe us out. Why, we're the people—we go on." Made into a movie by John Ford, and starring Henry Fonda, *The Grapes of Wrath* stands as a memorable cultural document of the later 1930s.

In 1936 journalist James Agee and photographer Walker Evans spent several weeks with Alabama sharecropper families while researching a magazine article. From this experience came Agee's masterpiece, *Let Us Now Praise Famous Men* (1941). Enhanced by Evans's powerful photographs, Agee's intensely personal work evoked the endurance and decency of Americans living on society's margins.

The new cultural mood also reached the stage. Thornton Wilder's play *Our Town* (1938) portrayed a New England town in which everyday events become, in memory, infinitely precious. William Saroyan's *The Time of Your Life* (1939) celebrated the foibles and virtues of a colorful collection of American "types" gathered in a San Francisco waterfront bar.

Composers, too, caught the spirit of cultural nationalism. In such works as *Billy the Kid* (1938), Aaron Copland drew upon American legends and folk melodies. George Gershwin's 1935 musical *Porgy and Bess*, based on the 1920s' novel and play by DuBose and Dorothy Heyward (see Chapter 23), brought this portrayal of black street life in Charleston, South Carolina, to a new and larger audience.

Jazz surged in popularity thanks to swing, a danceable style originated by the pianist Fletcher Henderson and popularized by the big bands of Count Basie, Benny Goodman, Duke Ellington, and others. The Basie band started at Kansas City's Reno Club, where, as Basie later recalled, "We played from nine o'clock in the evening to five or six the next morning. . . . [T]he boys in the band got eighteen dollars a week and I got twenty one." Moving to New York in 1936, Basie helped launch the swing era.

Benny Goodman, of a Chicago immigrant family, had played the clarinet as a boy at Jane Addams's Hull House. Challenging the color line in jazz, Goodman included black musicians like pianist Teddy Wilson and vibraphonist Lionel Hampton in his orchestra. A turning point in the acceptance of jazz came in 1938, when Goodman's band performed at New York's Carnegie Hall, a citadel of high culture.

The later 1930s also saw a heightened interest in regional literature, painting, and folk art. Zora Neale Hurston's novel *Their Eyes Were Watching God* (1937), exploring a black woman's search for fulfillment, was set in rural Florida. In *Absalom, Absalom!* (1936) William Faulkner continued the saga of his mythic Yoknapatawpha County in Mississippi. Painters Thomas Hart Benton of Missouri (a descendant of the nineteenth-century senator of the same name), John Steuart Curry of Kansas, and Grant Wood of Iowa struck strongly regional notes in their work.

Galleries displayed folk paintings, Amish quilts, and New England weather vanes. A 1938 show at New York's Museum of Modern Art introduced Horace Pippin, a black Philadelphia laborer partially disabled in World War I. In such paintings as *John Brown Going to His Hanging*, Pippin revealed a genuine, if untutored, talent. In 1939 the same museum featured seventy-nine-year-old Anna "Grandma" Moses of Hoosick Falls, New York, whose memory paintings of her farm girlhood enjoyed great popularity.

The surge of cultural nationalism heightened interest in the nation's past. Americans flocked to historical re-creations such as Henry Ford's Greenfield Village near Detroit and Colonial Williamsburg in Virginia, restored by John D. Rockefeller, Jr. Texans restored the Alamo in San Antonio, the "Cradle of Texas Liberty." Historical novels like Margaret Mitchell's Civil War epic *Gone with the Wind* (1936) became best sellers. These restorations and fictions often distorted history. Slavery was downplayed or sentimentalized at Colonial Williamsburg and in Mitchell's novel. "Texas Liberty" resonated differently for the state's Hispanic, African-American, and Indian peoples than it did for the patriotic organizations that turned the Alamo into a tourist shrine.

Streamlining and a World's Fair: Corporate America's Utopian Vision
A design style called streamlining also shaped the visual culture of the late 1930s. This style originated in the 1920s when industrial designers, inspired by the airplane, introduced smoothly flowing curves into the design of commercial products. Streamlining appealed to consumers—a vital business consideration during the depression. When Sears Roebuck streamlined its Coldspot refrigerators, sales surged. As products ranging from house trailers to pencil sharpeners and cigarette lighters emerged in sleek new forms, streamlining helped corporate America rebuild its image and present itself as the benevolent shaper of a better future.

Under the theme "The World of Tomorrow," the 1939 New York World's Fair represented the high point of the streamlining vogue and of corporate America's public-relations blitz. The fair's futuristic theme was symbolized by the Trylon and Perisphere: a seven-hundred-foot tapered tower and a globe that seemed to float on a pool of water. Inside the Perisphere, visitors found "Democracity," a revolving diorama portraying an idealized city of the future.

The hit of the fair was Futurama, the General Motors exhibit. Visitors entered a darkened circular auditorium where, amid piped-in music and a resonant recorded narration, a vision of America in the distant year 1960 slowly unfolded. A multilane highway network complete with cloverleaf exits and stacked interchanges dominated the imagined landscape. A brilliant public-relations investment by GM, Futurama built support for the interstate highway system that would soon become a reality. Forget the depression and even the bitter Flint strike of 1937, GM's exhibit seemed to whisper; behold the exciting future we are preparing for you.

Also featuring such wonders as television and automatic dishwashers, the World's Fair did, indeed, offer a glimpse of "The World of Tomorrow" as a harmonious technological utopia made possible by the nation's great corporations. A visit to the fair, a business magazine editorialized, "should convince [any doubters] that American business has been the vehicle which carried the discoveries of science and the benefits of machine production to . . . American consumers." The fair epitomized corporate America's version of the patriotism and hopefulness that pervaded U.S. culture as the 1930s ended.

But the hopefulness was tinged with fear. The nation had survived the depression, yet danger loomed beyond the seas. The anxiety triggered by the menacing world situation surfaced on October 31, 1938, when CBS radio aired an adaptation of H. G. Wells's science-fiction story *War of the Worlds* directed by Orson Welles. In realistic detail, the broadcast reported the landing of a spaceship in New Jersey, the emergence of aliens with ray guns, and their advance toward New York City. The show sparked a panic. Some terrified listeners jumped in their cars and sped off into the night. Others prayed. A few attempted suicide. Beneath the terror lay a more well-founded fear: of approaching war. For a decade, as America had battled the depression, the international situation had steadily worsened. By October 1938 another European war loomed on the horizon.

The panic triggered by Orson Welles's Halloween prank quickly faded, but the anxieties aroused by the all-too-real dangers abroad only escalated. By the time the New York World's Fair offered its vision of "The World of Tomorrow," the actual world of 1939 had become very scary indeed.

Conclusion

The 1929 stock-market crash and the ensuing Great Depression exposed major weaknesses in the U.S. and world economies. These ranged from chronically low farm prices and uneven income distribution to trade barriers, a glut of consumer goods, and a constricted money supply. As the crisis deepened, President Hoover struggled to respond. In 1932, with Hoover's reputation in tatters, Franklin D. Roosevelt and his promised "New Deal" brought a surge of hope.

Initially focusing on immediate economic relief and recovery, Roosevelt welcomed big business in his depression-fighting coalition. By 1935, however, the New Deal adopted a more class-based approach. FDR now addressed the plight of the poor, including sharecroppers and migrants; pursued tougher business regulation and higher taxes for the wealthy; and championed such fundamental reforms as the Social Security Act, centerpiece of the welfare state, and the Wagner Act, guaranteeing workers' right to unionize. FDR's smashing reelection victory in 1936 solidified the Democratic coalition he had forged, including the white South, farmers, urban ethnics, union members, and African-Americans. By 1938, facing rising conservative opposition and menaces abroad, the New Deal's reformist energies faded.

The depression and the New Deal affected different groups in different ways. For Tennessee valley residents and citizens across the West, public-works projects brought hydroelectric power and economic growth. Amid widespread joblessness, women were told to stay home so men could find work. Many resisted, however, and the female labor force expanded. For industrial workers, the decade's spirit of militance and favorable legislation brought a wave of strikes and unionization campaigns.

While African-Americans benefited from New Deal relief programs, the Roosevelt administration failed to address lynching and racial discrimination. Exploited Mexican-born farm laborers, facing deportation threats, organized strikes demanding better wages and working conditions. For Native Americans, New Deal legislation restored tribes' legal status, laying the groundwork for future enterprises and treaty claims.

American culture in the 1930s reflected the decade's economic and social realities. While the movies and radio offered diversion, writers, painters, and other cultural creators initially expressed despair and cynicism over capitalism's failure. But as New Deal programs assisted writers and artists, and as foreign threats loomed in the later 1930s, the cultural climate grew more patriotic and affirmative.

The New Deal has its downside. Some programs failed, and recovery proved elusive. Only in 1943, as war plants boomed, was full employment finally achieved. On racial issues, symbolic gestures substituted for genuine engagement. But the New Deal's achievements remain noteworthy, reflecting an unprecedented level of engagement with social and economic issues. The New Dealers radically reshaped the nature of the presidency, the nation's political agenda, and citizens' understanding of the role of government.

Looming over the decade is the larger-than-life image of Franklin D. Roosevelt. Neither saint nor superman, FDR could be devious, superficial, and cavalier about details. But for most Americans of the 1930s—and most historians since—his strengths outweighed his liabilities. His experimental approach served a suffering nation well. He once compared himself to a football quarterback, deciding which play to call after seeing how the last one worked out.

Above all, Roosevelt's optimism inspired a demoralized people. "We Americans of today . . . ," he told an audience of young people in 1939, "are characters in the living book of democracy. But we are also its author. It falls upon us now to say whether the chapters . . . to come will tell a story of retreat or a story of continued advance."

25

Americans and a World in
Crisis, 1933–1945

THE UNITED STATES IN A MENACING WORLD, 1933–1939

Apart from improving relations with Latin America, the early administration of President Franklin D. Roosevelt (FDR) remained largely aloof from the crises in the world. Americans reacted ambivalently as Italy, Germany, and Japan grew more aggressive. Millions of Americans, determined not to stumble into war again, supported neutrality. Only a minority wanted the United States to help embattled democracies abroad. All the while, the world slid toward the precipice.

Nationalism and the Good Neighbor During the Great Depression, Roosevelt put U.S. economic interests above all else. He showed little interest in free trade or international economic cooperation.

He did, however, adopt an internationalist approach in Latin America, where bitterness over decades of "Yankee imperialism" ran high. He declared a **"Good Neighbor" policy,** renouncing any nation's right to intervene in the affairs of another. To support this policy, FDR withdrew the last U.S. troops from Haiti and the Dominican Republic, and terminated the Platt Amendment, which had given the United States its right to intervene in Cuba since 1901. The key tests of the Good Neighbor policy came in Cuba and Mexico. In Cuba, an economic crisis in 1933 brought to power a leftist regime that the United States opposed. Instead of sending in the marines, as earlier administrations might have done, the United States provided indirect aid to a conservative revolt led by Fulgencio Batista in 1934 that overthrew the radical government. American economic assistance would then allow Batista to retain power until his overthrow by Fidel Castro in 1959.

In Mexico, a reform government came to power in 1936 and promptly nationalized several oil companies owned by U.S. and British corporations. While insisting on fair compensation, the United States refrained from military intervention and conceded Mexico's right to nationalize the companies. Subsequently, Mexico and the oil companies reached a compromise compensation agreement.

The Good Neighbor policy did not end U.S. interference in Latin American affairs. But it did substitute economic leverage for heavy-handed intervention and military occupation. The better relations fostered by FDR would help the United States pursue hemispheric solidarity in World War II, and later in the Cold War.

The Rise of Aggressive States in Europe and Asia	As early as 1922, economic and social unrest in Italy enabled **Benito Mussolini** to seize power. Dictator until 1943, Mussolini suppressed dissent and liberty, imposed one-party rule, strictly controlled business and labor, invaded Ethiopia in October 1935, and began to persecute Jews in 1938.

The rise of **Adolf Hitler** in Germany proved more menacing. Hitler's National Socialist (Nazi) Party had gained broad support as a result of the depression and German resentment of the harsh Versailles treaty, and Hitler became Germany's chancellor in January 1933. Crushing opponents and rivals, Hitler imposed a brutal dictatorship on Germany and began a program to purify it of Jews—whom he considered an "inferior race" responsible for Germany's defeat in World War I.

Violating the Versailles treaty, Hitler began rearming Germany in 1935. A year later, German troops reoccupied the Rhineland, a region between the Rhine River and France specifically demilitarized by the Versailles treaty. In 1938, as German tanks rolled into Vienna, Hitler proclaimed an *Anschluss* (union) between Austria and Germany. London, Paris, and Washington murmured their disapproval but took no action. An emboldened Hitler then claimed Germany's right to the Sudetenland, a part of neighboring Czechoslovakia containing 3 million ethnic Germans. British prime minister Neville Chamberlain and his French counterpart, insisting that their countries could not endure another war like that of 1914–1918, yielded to Hitler's demands in return for his assurance that Germany had no further territorial ambitions—a policy dubbed **appeasement**—at a conference in Munich in September 1938.

In Japan, meanwhile, militarists gained control of the government and launched a fateful course of expansion. In 1931, Japan sent troops into the northern Chinese province of Manchuria, and within two years took control of the province. In July 1937, it initiated a full-scale war against China itself, and soon controlled key parts of that nation. Weak protests by Washington did little to deter Japan's plans for further aggression.

The American Mood: No More War	The feeble American response reflected the people's belief that the decision to go to war in 1917 had been a mistake. This conviction was rooted in the nation's isolationist tradition— its wish to avoid military and political entanglements in Old

World quarrels—as well as in its desire to have the government focus on economic matters, not foreign affairs, in the midst of the Great Depression. Popular books stressing American disillusionment with World War I's failure to make the world safe for democracy strengthened isolationist sentiment. So did a 1934–1936 Senate investigation

CHRONOLOGY, 1933–1945

1931–1932 • Japan invades Manchuria and creates a puppet government.

1933 • Adolf Hitler becomes chancellor of Germany and assumes dictatorial powers.

1934–1936 • Nye Committee investigations.

1935–1937 • Neutrality Acts.

1937 • Japan invades China.

1938 • Germany annexes Austria; Munich Pact gives Sudetenland to Germany. *Kristallnacht*, night of Nazi terror against German and Austrian Jews.

1939 • Nazi-Soviet Pact.
Germany invades Poland; World War II begins.

1940 • Germany conquers the Netherlands, Belgium, France, Denmark, Norway, and Luxembourg.
Germany, Italy, and Japan sign the Tripartite Pact.
Selective Service Act.
Franklin Roosevelt elected to an unprecedented third term.

1941 • Lend-Lease Act.
Roosevelt establishes the Fair Employment Practices Commission (FEPC).
Germany invades the Soviet Union.
Japan attacks Pearl Harbor; the United States enters World War II.
War Powers Act.

1942 • Battles of Coral Sea and Midway halt Japanese offensive.
Internment of Japanese-Americans.
Revenue Act expands graduated income-tax system.
Allies invade North Africa (Operation TORCH).
First successful atomic chain reaction.
CORE founded.

1943 • Soviet victory in Battle of Stalingrad.
Coal miners strike; Smith-Connally War Labor Disputes Act.
Detroit and Los Angeles race riots.
Allied invasion of Italy.
Roosevelt, Churchill, and Stalin meet in Tehran.

1944 • Allied invasion of France (Operation Overlord).
U.S. forces invade the Philippines.
Roosevelt wins fourth term.
Battle of the Bulge.

1945 • Yalta Conference.
Battles of Iwo Jima and Okinawa.
Roosevelt dies; Harry S Truman becomes president.
Germany surrenders.
Truman, Churchill, and Stalin meet in Potsdam.
United States drops atomic bombs on Hiroshima and Nagasaki; Japan surrenders.

headed by Republican Gerald P. Nye of North Dakota, which concluded that banking and munitions interests, whom it called "merchants of death," had tricked the United States into war to protect their loans and weapon sales to England and France.

By the mid-1930s an overwhelming majority of Americans thought that the "mistake" of intervention should not be repeated. Congress responded by passing a series of Neutrality Acts in 1935–1937. To prevent a repetition of 1917, these measures outlawed arms sales and loans to nations at war and barred Americans from traveling on the ships of belligerent powers. The high point of antiwar sentiment came in 1938 when Indiana congressman Louis Ludlow proposed a constitutional amendment requiring a national referendum on any U.S. declaration of war except in cases of direct attack. Only a direct appeal from FDR steeled Congress to reject the Ludlow Amendment by the narrowest of margins.

With the public firmly isolationist and some American companies, like IBM, with large financial investments in German industry, confrontation with fascism came solely in sports. At the 1936 Olympics in Berlin, African-American track star Jesse Owens made a mockery of Nazi theories of racial superiority by winning four gold medals and breaking or tying three world records. In 1938, in a boxing match laden with symbolism, the black American Joe Louis knocked out German fighter Max Schmeling in the first round of their world heavyweight championship fight. Although Americans cheered Lewis, they still opposed any policies that might involve them in war.

The Gathering Storm: 1938–1939 The reduced tension that followed the Munich Pact proved tragically brief. Five and a half months later, on March 15, 1939, Nazi troops occupied what remained of Czechoslovakia, violating the Munich accords. Five months after that, Hitler reached an agreement with Soviet leader **Joseph Stalin** in the German-Soviet Nonaggression Pact that their nations would not fight one another and that they would divide Poland after Germany invaded it. No longer worried about a Soviet reaction, Hitler took aim on Poland despite claims by Britain and France that they would come to an invaded Poland's assistance.

Although isolationist sentiment remained strong in the United States, opinion began to shift rapidly. After the fall of Czechoslovakia, Roosevelt called for actions "short of war" to demonstrate America's will to check fascism, and he asked Hitler and Mussolini to pledge not to invade thirty-one listed nations. A jeering Hitler ridiculed FDR's message to the Reichstag (legislative assembly), while Mussolini mocked Roosevelt's physical disability, joking that the president's paralysis must have reached his brain.

Roosevelt, however, did more than send messages. In October 1938 he asked Congress for a $300 million military appropriation; in November he instructed the Army Air Corps to plan for an annual production of twenty thousand planes; and in January 1939 he submitted a $1.3 billion defense budget. Hitler and Mussolini, the now-aroused president proclaimed, were "two madmen" who "respect force and force alone."

America and the Jewish Refugees Hitler and the Nazis had used the power of the state and their own paramilitary organizations to assault German Jews, confiscate their property, and force them to emigrate. The Nuremberg Laws of 1935 stripped Jews of the rights of German citizenship, and increased restrictions on Jews in all spheres of German educational, social, and economic life. This campaign of hatred reached a violent crescendo on November 9–10, 1938, when the Nazis unleashed *Kristallnacht* (Night of the Broken Glass), a frenzy of arson, destruction, and looting against Jews throughout Germany.

No longer could anyone mistake the perilous situation of German Jews or misunderstand Hitler's evil intent. Some 300,000 Jews left Germany by 1939, and about 200,000 emigrated from Austria (see Beyond America—Global Interactions: Refugees from Fascism: The Intellectual Migration to the United States). But given the magnitude of the Great Depression and America's own anti-Semitism, Roosevelt did little other than deplore Hitler's persecution of the Jews, and Congress consistently rejected efforts to liberalize the immigration law or abolish its discriminatory quotas (see Chapter 23). When asked by pollsters in 1938 whether the immigration law should be changed to admit "a larger number of Jewish refugees from Germany," 75 percent said no.

The consequences of such attitudes became clear in June 1939 when the *St. Louis*, a vessel jammed with nine hundred Jewish refugees, asked permission to put its passengers ashore at Fort Lauderdale, Florida. Immigration officials refused the request, and a Coast Guard cutter stood by "to prevent possible attempts by refugees to jump off and swim ashore." The *St. Louis* turned slowly away from the lights of America and

Isolationism Versus Interventionism   *In front of the White House in 1941, an American soldier grabs a sign from an isolationist picketing against the United States entering the war in Europe. A diverse group, isolationists ran the gamut from pacifists who opposed all wars, to progressives who feared the growth of business and centralized power that a war would bring, to ultra-rightists who sympathized with fascism and/or shared Hitler's anti-Semitism.*

sailed back to Germany, where more than 700 of its passengers died at the hands of the Nazis.

INTO THE STORM, 1939–1941

After a decade of crises—worldwide depression and regional conflicts—war erupted in Europe in 1939. Following the lightning German victories in western Europe in the spring of 1940, President Roosevelt's policy of neutrality to keep America out of war gave way to a policy of economic intervention. He knew that extending increasing amounts of aid to those resisting aggression by the so-called Rome-Berlin-Tokyo Axis, as well as his toughening conduct toward Germany and Japan, could, as he said, "push" the U.S. into the crisis of worldwide war. Japan's attack on the U.S. fleet at Pearl Harbor would provide the push.

The European War Hitler began the war in Europe by demanding that Poland return the city of Danzig (Gdansk), taken from Germany after World War I. When Poland refused, Nazi troops poured into Poland on September 1, 1939. Two days later, Britain and France, honoring commitments to Poland, declared war on Germany. Although FDR invoked the Neutrality Acts, he would not ask Americans to be impartial in thought and deed (as had President Wilson in 1914).

Tailoring his actions to the public mood, which favored both preventing a Nazi victory and staying out of war, FDR persuaded Congress in November to amend the Neutrality Acts to allow the belligerents to purchase weapons from the United States if they paid cash and carried the arms away in their own ships. But "cash-and-carry" did not stop the Nazis. In the spring of 1940, Hitler's armies taught the world the meaning of *Blitzkrieg* (lightning war) as they quickly overwhelmed Denmark, Norway, Belgium, Holland, Luxembourg, and France and pinned the British army against the sea at Dunkirk. Narrowly escaping disaster, the British used every possible craft to evacuate their army and some French troops across the English Channel. By then, however, Hitler virtually controlled western Europe, and on June 22 he dictated France's surrender in the same railway car in which Germany surrendered in 1918.

Hitler now took aim at Great Britain. Round-the-clock aerial assaults by the *Luftwaffe* (air force) killed or wounded thousands of civilians, destroyed the city of Coventry, and reduced parts of London to rubble. Britain's new prime minister, **Winston Churchill,** who replaced Chamberlain in May 1940, pleaded for more U.S. aid. Most Americans, shocked at the use of German air power against British civilians, favored such aid. But a large and vocal minority opposed it as wasteful of materials needed for U.S. defenses or as a ruse to lure Americans into a war not vital to their interests.

From Isolation to Intervention In the United States in 1940, news of the "battle of Britain" competed with speculation about whether FDR would break with tradition and run for an unprecedented third term. Not until the eve of the Democrats' July convention did he reveal that, given the world crisis, he would consent to being drafted by his party. The Axis threat clinched his renomination and forced conservative Democrats to accept the very liberal Henry Wallace, FDR's former secretary of agriculture, as his running mate. Republicans bowed to the

Refugees from Fascism: The Intellectual Migration to the United States

In line with Adolf Hitler's obsessive and virulent anti-Semitism, the Nazi government undertook a systematic campaign to deprive German Jews of their legal rights. In 1933, they were dismissed from government service, and from the universities, where, although less than 1 percent of the German population, they constituted 12 percent of the professors. In 1935, the Nuremberg laws deprived Jews of the rights of citizenship, prohibited intermarriage with non-Jews, and excluded them from hospitals, theaters, museums, and athletic fields. In November 1938, Nazi gangs murdered scores of Jews, destroyed 267 synagogues, and vandalized thousands of Jewish businesses throughout Germany. In this pogrom known as the Night of the Broken Glass (Kristallnacht), for the many Jewish shop windows smashed by the brown shirts, the Nazis sent between twenty and thirty thousand Jews to concentration camps and ordered the rest to wear yellow Stars of David. Meanwhile, Hitler also stepped up his persecution of non-Jewish intellectuals, like Thomas Mann, who opposed his murderous regime.

Some Jews in central Europe (particularly Austria, Germany, and Hungary) saw the handwriting on the wall and sought to escape. Although most lacked the means to emigrate—being forbidden to bring their property out of the country with them—or found their way blocked by countries who refused to accept refugees, Nazi anti-Semitism and political repression led perhaps a half million immigrants, between 1933 and 1941, to seek safe haven in western Europe, Switzerland, or the United States—whose rigid numerical quotas on immigration blocked entry to most.

However, as the news of Nazi persecutions made its way out of Germany, various groups organized to find refuge for the many prominent artists, scholars, and scientists who were Jews or opponents of fascism. The British Academic Assistance Council and the American Emergency Committee in Aid of Displaced Foreign Scholars worked to obtain university positions in the United States for émigré scholars. To take a stand for academic freedom and add eminence to their faculty the presidents of some American colleges formed the Emergency Committee in Aid of German Displaced Scholars. The New School for Social Research, in New York, hired German émigrés to train American graduate students in its new University in Exile. Similarly, the Institute for Advanced Study at Princeton, North Carolina's Black Mountain College, and scores of other academic, artistic, and scientific institutions opened their doors to thousands of exiles.

Although the Nazis had sought to destroy what they sneered at as Jewish science and culture, they, as one refugee scholar wrote, "spread it all over the world. Only Germany would be the loser." The United States, given the extraordinary number and talents of the refugees it accepted, would be the big winner.

Because the Second World War was in no small part a struggle of opposing scientists, the intellectual migration weakened the Axis and strengthened the Allies. The most decisive impact of the émigré scientists came in the field of nuclear physics.

Fearing the possibility that Hitler might develop atomic weapons, two refugee physicists, Leo Szilard (from Hungary) and Enrico Fermi (from Italy) convinced fellow refugee Albert Einstein to sign a letter to President Roosevelt warning about recent German discoveries in uranium fission. The result would eventually be the Manhattan Project, an Anglo-American effort to produce atomic bombs. In it, scores of émigré scientists brought their different skills and intellectual traits to bear on the single objective of beating the Germans in building a super-bomb. The refugee scientists—Hans Bethe, James Franck, Edward Teller, Eugene Wigner, among others—succeeded, and changed the world.

Mainly due to the efforts of the American Psychoanalytic Association and the Menninger Clinic in Topeka, Kansas, a lion's share of Europe's psychoanalytic teachers, therapists, and thinkers, among whom Jews predominated, also came to the United States in the 1930s and had a huge impact. Bruno Bettelheim, Erich Fromm, and other psychologists influenced by Sigmund Freud changed America's approach to mental illness, stressing the value of therapy. They influenced Americans to have greater tolerance for adolescent rebellious behavior, and convinced parents to pay attention to the psychological needs of the young. They also shaped attitudes toward crime and criminals—from punishment to rehabilitation; made public relations and sales experts more savvy about what motivates buyers; and popularized the notion that everyone has a right to self-fulfillment and happiness.

Significant changes similarly came in the social sciences and humanities. The leading lights among Austrian intellectuals, known as the Vienna Circle, advanced the school of logical positivism in American philosophy. Joseph Schumpeter and Ludwig von Mises changed the teaching of economics in the United States, much as Hannah Arendt, Theodor Adorno, and Herbert Marcuse influenced political thought. Virtually en masse, the many political and social scientists at the Institute for Social Research in Frankfurt escaped to the United States with the assistance of sympathetic Columbia University faculty. They would go on to make fundamental changes in sociology, emphasizing both a quantitative approach to studying social issues and a psychological approach to social phenomena, especially prejudice and discrimination.

Some of the brightest stars in the new American firmament were émigré artists. From Germany's Bauhaus school of design, furniture-maker Marcel Breuer and architects Walter Gropius and Ludwig Mies van der Rohe became the giants of postwar American design. Great musicians—the conductors Otto Klemperer, Erich Leinsdorf, Pierre Monteux, George Szell, and Bruno Walter; the composers Paul Hindemith, Darius Milhaud, and Arnold Schoenberg; and the pianists Artur Rubinstein, Rudolf Serkin, and Vladimir Horowitz, among many others—added luster to the concert stage and, as master teachers, influenced an entire generation of American musicians.

No other immigrant group in history had ever brought such gifts as these émigré artists and scholars brought to the United States in the 1930s. They found in the United States the freedom of thought and freedom from fear that enabled them to pursue their talents and ideas. Despite the financial difficulties of the Great Depression, private American generosity provided the funds for many of the positions in colleges, laboratories, and music schools that enabled the refugees to earn a living. And most of the Americans they worked with welcomed them, and judged them on their abilities rather than their religion or place of birth. The government, moreover, displayed unprecedented trust in these foreign-born, hiring scores of them for positions of responsibility in the atomic bomb project and other war work.

In return, most of these refugees quickly learned English, sought and obtained American citizenship, and left an indelible mark on American life. Summing up her account of these "illustrious immigrants," Laura Fermi, the wife of atomic scientist Enrico Fermi, who had fled Italy's anti-Semitism and fascism with her husband in 1938, wrote: "In making room for countless Europeans

and saving many whose lives were threatened, America proved once more a land of opportunity and a haven to which the persecuted of the world might continue to look with confidence." In return, the United States would be more than repaid in full "in a currency compounded of prestige, knowledge, and a general enrichment of culture."

Questions for Analysis

- What were the major contributions to American life made by the refugees in the Intellectual Migration?

- What steps did Americans take to welcome émigré scholars and artists and facilitate their profound impact on American life and thought?

---

public mood by nominating Wendell Willkie of Indiana, an all-out internationalist who championed greater aid to Britain.

FDR adroitly played the role of the crisis leader too busy to engage in politics. He appointed Republicans Henry Stimson and Frank Knox as secretaries of war and the navy. He signed the Selective Service and Training Act, the first peacetime draft in U.S. history, and approved an enormous increase in spending for rearmament. With Willkie's support, FDR engineered a "destroyers-for-bases" swap with England, sending fifty vintage ships to Britain in exchange for leases on British naval and air bases in the Western Hemisphere. Although FDR pictured the agreement as a way to keep the country out of war, it infuriated isolationists.

In the 1930s the isolationist camp had included prominent figures from both major parties and both the Right and Left. But in 1940 the arch-conservative America First Committee was isolationism's dominant voice. Largely financed by Henry Ford, the committee featured pacifist Charles Lindbergh as its most popular speaker. It insisted that "Fortress America" could stand alone. But a majority of Americans supported Roosevelt's effort to assist Great Britain while staying out of war. Reassured by the president's promise never to "send an American boy to fight in a foreign war," 55 percent of the voters chose to give Roosevelt a third term.

Calling on the United States to be the "great arsenal of democracy," Roosevelt proposed a **"lend-lease"** program to supply war materiel to cash-strapped Britain. While Roosevelt likened the plan to loaning a garden hose to a neighbor whose house was on fire, isolationist senator Robert Taft compared it to chewing gum: after a neighbor uses it, "you don't want it back." A large majority of Americans supported lend-lease, however, and Congress approved the bill in March 1941, abolishing the "cash" provision of the Neutrality Acts and allowing the president to lend or lease supplies to any nation deemed "vital to the defense of the United States." Shipments to England began at once, and after Hitler invaded the USSR in June, U.S. war supplies flowed to the Soviet Union. To defeat Hitler, FDR confided, "I would hold hands with the Devil."

Moving toward war with Germany, Roosevelt in April 1941 authorized the U.S. navy to help the British track U-boats. In mid-summer he ordered the navy to begin convoying British ships carrying lend-lease supplies, with orders to destroy enemy vessels if necessary to protect the shipments. U.S. forces also occupied Greenland and Iceland to keep those strategic Danish islands out of Nazi hands.

In August, Roosevelt met with Churchill aboard a warship off the coast of Newfoundland to map strategy. They issued a document, the **Atlantic Charter,** that condemned international aggression, affirmed the right of national self-determination, and endorsed the principles of free trade, disarmament, and collective security. The Charter envisioned a postwar world in which the peoples of "all the lands may live out their lives in freedom from fear and want."

After a U-boat torpedoed and sank the *Reuben James,* killing 115 American sailors, Roosevelt persuaded Congress in November to permit the arming of merchant ships and their entry into belligerent ports in war zones. Virtually nothing remained of the Neutrality Acts. Unprepared for a major war, America was already fighting a limited one, and full-scale war seemed imminent.

Pearl Harbor and the Coming of War

Hitler's triumphs in western Europe encouraged Japan to expand farther into Asia. Seeing Germany as its primary danger, the Roosevelt administration tried to apply just enough pressure to frighten off the Japanese without provoking Tokyo to war before the United States had built the "two-ocean navy" authorized by Congress in 1940. "It is terribly important for the control of the Atlantic for us to keep peace in the Pacific," Roosevelt told Harold Ickes in mid-1941. "I simply have not got enough navy to go around—and every episode in the Pacific means fewer ships in the Atlantic."

Both Japan and the United States hoped to avoid war, but neither would compromise. Japan's desire to create a Greater East Asia Co-Prosperity Sphere (an empire embracing much of China, Southeast Asia, and the western Pacific) matched America's insistence on the Open Door in China and the status quo in the rest of Asia. Japan saw the U.S. stand as a ploy to block its rise to world power; and the United States viewed Japan's talk of legitimate national aspirations as a smoke screen to hide aggression.

The two nations became locked in a deadly dance. In 1940, believing that economic coercion would force the Japanese out of China, the United States ended a long-standing trade treaty with Japan and banned the sale of aviation fuel and scrap metal to it. Tokyo responded by occupying northern Indochina, a French colony, and signing the Tripartite Pact with Germany and Italy in September, creating a military alliance, the Berlin-Rome-Tokyo Axis, that required each government to help the others in the event of a U.S. attack.

With the French and Dutch defeated by Germany, and Britain with its back to the wall, Japan gambled on a war for hegemony in the western Pacific. It chose to conquer

Remember Pearl Harbor *At Minneapolis's Northern Pump Co., nightshift workers heralded the new year, 1942, with a demonstration of national unity and determination. Rather than resorting to drafting workers or compelling them to work in certain areas, the government relied primarily on what FDR called "voluntary cooperation" to fill the labor shortages in war-related jobs.*

new lands to obtain the resources it needed rather than retreat from China to gain a resumption of trade with the United States. Fatefully, Japan overran the rest of Indochina in July 1941. In turn, expecting that firmness would more likely deter Japan than provoke her to war, FDR froze all Japanese assets in the United States, imposed a new fuel embargo, and clamped a total ban on trade with Japan. But as Japan's fuel meters dropped toward empty, the expansionist General Hideki Tojo replaced a more conciliatory prime minister in October. Tojo set the first week in December as a deadline for a preemptive attack if the United States did not yield.

By late November U.S. intelligence's deciphering of Japan's top diplomatic code alerted the Roosevelt administration that war was imminent. Negotiators made no concessions, however, during the eleventh-hour talks under way in Washington. "I have washed my hands of it," Secretary of State Hull told Secretary of War Stimson on November 27, "and it is now in the hands of you and Knox—the Army and the Navy." War warnings went out to all commanders in the Pacific, advising that negotiations were deadlocked and that a Japanese attack was expected. But where? U.S. officials assumed that the Japanese offensive would continue southward, striking Malaya or the Philippines. The Japanese banked on a knockout punch; they believed that a surprise raid on

Pearl Harbor would destroy America's Pacific fleet and compel a Roosevelt preoccupied with Germany to seek accommodation with Japan.

On Sunday morning, December 7, 1941, Japanese dive-bombers and torpedo planes attacked the U.S. fleet at anchor in Pearl Harbor on the Hawaiian island of Oahu. Pounding the harbor and nearby airfields, the Japanese sank or crippled nearly a score of warships, destroyed or damaged some 350 aircraft, killed more than 2,400 Americans, and wounded another 1,200. American forces suffered their most devastating loss in history, and simultaneous attacks by Japan on the Philippines, Malaya, and Hong Kong opened the way for Japan's advance on Australia.

Critics later charged that Roosevelt knew the attack on Pearl Harbor was coming and deliberately left the fleet exposed in order to bring the United States into the war against Germany. There is no conclusive evidence to support this accusation. Roosevelt and his advisers knew that war was close but did not expect an assault on Pearl Harbor. Neither did the U.S. military officials at Pearl Harbor, who took precautions only against possible sabotage by the Japanese in Hawaii. Due to their own prejudices, Americans underestimated the resourcefulness, skill, and daring of the Japanese. They simply did not believe that Japan would attack an American stronghold five thousand miles from its home islands. At the same time, Japanese leaders erred in counting on a paralyzing blow to compel the soft, weak-willed Americans, unready for a two-ocean war, to compromise rather than fight. That miscalculation assured an aroused and united nation determined to avenge the attack.

On December 8 Congress declared war against Japan. (The only dissenter was Montana's Jeannette Rankin, who had also cast a nay vote against U.S. entry into World War I.) Three days later, honoring Germany's treaty obligation to Japan, Hitler declared war on the "half Judaized and the other half Negrified" American people; Mussolini followed suit. Congress immediately reciprocated without a dissenting vote. Confidently, Roosevelt cabled Churchill, "Today all of us are in the same boat with you and the people of the Empire, and it is a ship which will not and can not be sunk." Nevertheless, the United States faced a global war that it was not ready to fight.

After Pearl Harbor, U-boats wreaked havoc in the North Atlantic and prowled the Caribbean. Every twenty-four hours, five more Allied vessels went to the bottom. German submarines even bottled up the Chesapeake Bay for nearly six weeks. By the end of 1942, U-boat "wolf packs" had sunk more than a thousand Allied ships, offsetting the pace of American ship production. The United States was losing the Battle of the Atlantic.

The war news from Europe and Africa was, as Roosevelt admitted, "all bad." Hitler had painted the swastika across an enormous swath of territory, from the outskirts of Moscow and Leningrad—a thousand miles deep into Russia—to the Pyrenees on the Spanish-French border, and from northern Norway to the Libyan desert. In North Africa the German Afrika Korps swept toward Cairo and the Suez Canal, the British oil lifeline. It seemed as if the Mediterranean would become an Axis sea and that Hitler would be in India to greet Tojo marching across Asia before the United States was ready to fight.

Japan followed its attack on Pearl Harbor by seizing Guam, Wake Island, Singapore, Burma, and the Dutch East Indies. Having pushed the U.S. garrison on the Philippines first onto the Bataan peninsula and then onto the tiny island of Corregidor, Japan took more than eleven thousand American soldiers prisoner early in May 1942. Japan's Rising Sun flag blazed over hundreds of islands in the Pacific and over the entire eastern perimeter of the Asian mainland from the border of Siberia to the border of India.

AMERICA MOBILIZES FOR WAR

In December 1941, American armed forces numbered just 1.6 million, and war production accounted for only 15 percent of U.S. industrial output. Pearl Harbor changed everything. Congress passed a War Powers Act granting the president unprecedented authority over all aspects of the war. Volunteers and draftees swelled the armed forces; by war's end more than 15 million men and nearly 350,000 women would serve. More would work in defense industries. Mobilization required unprecedented coordination of the American government, economy, and military. In 1942 those responsible for managing America's growing war machine moved into the world's largest building, the newly constructed Pentagon. Like the Pentagon, which was intended to house civilian agencies after the war, American attitudes, behavior, and institutions would also be significantly altered by far-reaching wartime domestic changes.

Organizing for Victory To direct the military engine, Roosevelt formed the Joint Chiefs of Staff, made up of representatives of the army, navy, and army air force. (Only a minor "corps" within the army as late as June 1941, the air force would grow more dramatically than any other branch of the service, achieve virtual autonomy, and play a vital role in combat strategy.) The changing nature of modern warfare also led to the creation of the Office of Strategic Services (OSS), forerunner of the Central Intelligence Agency, to conduct the espionage required for strategic planning.

To organize the conversion of American industry to war production, Roosevelt established a host of new government agencies. The **War Production Board** (WPB) allocated materials, limited the production of civilian goods, and distributed contracts among manufacturers. The War Manpower Commission (WMC) supervised the mobilization of men and women for the military, agriculture, and industry, while the National War Labor Board (NWLB) mediated disputes between management and labor. Finally, the **Office of Price Administration** (OPA) rationed scarce products and imposed price and rent controls to check inflation. "The Americans can't build planes," a Nazi commander had jeered, "only electric iceboxes and razor blades." But soon after February 1942, when the last civilian car came off an assembly line, the United States achieved a miracle of war production. Automakers retooled to produce planes and tanks; a merry-go-round factory switched to fashioning gun mounts; a pinball-machine maker converted to armor-piercing shells. By late 1942 a third of the economy was committed to war production, equaling the military output of Germany, Italy, and Japan combined. Whole new industries appeared virtually overnight. With almost all of the nation's crude-rubber supply now in Japanese-controlled territory, the government built some fifty new synthetic-rubber plants. By the end of the war, the United States, once the world's largest importer of crude rubber, had become the world's largest exporter of synthetic rubber.

America also became the world's greatest weapons manufacturer, producing twice as much war material than all its Axis enemies by 1944. "To American production," Stalin would toast FDR and Churchill, "without which the war would have been lost." Indeed, the three hundred thousand military aircraft, 2.6 million machine guns, 6 million tons of bombs, and more than five thousand cargo ships and eighty-six thousand warships assembled by Americans did essentially win the war for the United States and its allies. Henry J. Kaiser, who had supervised the construction of Boulder Dam, introduced prefabrication to cut the time needed to produce a Liberty-class merchant ship from six months in 1941 to less than two weeks in 1943, and then just ten days. In 1945 Kaiser, dubbed "Sir Launchalot," and other shipbuilders were completing a cargo ship a day.

Such breakneck production had its costs. The size and powers of the government swelled as defense spending zoomed from 9 percent of the GNP in 1940 to 46 percent in 1945 and the budget soared from $9 billion to $98 billion. The number of federal civilian employees mushroomed from 1.1 million to 3.8 million. The executive branch, directing the war effort, grew the most; and an alliance formed between the defense industry and the military. (A generation later, Americans would call these concentrations of power the "imperial presidency" and the "military-industrial complex.") Because the government sought the greatest volume of war production in the shortest possible time, it encouraged corporate profits. "If you are going to try to go to war in a capitalist country," Secretary of War Stimson pointed out, "you have to let business make money out of the process or business won't work."

"Dr. New Deal," in FDR's words, gave way to "Dr. Win the War." To encourage business to convert to war production and expand its capacity, the government guaranteed profits, provided generous tax write-offs and subsidies, and suspended antitrust prosecutions. America's ten biggest corporations got a third of the war contracts, and two-thirds of all war-production spending went to the hundred largest firms, greatly accelerating trends toward economic concentration.

The War Economy   The United States spent more than $320 billion ($250 million a day) to defeat the Axis—ten times more than the cost of World War I in real dollars and nearly twice the amount that had been spent by the government since its founding. This massive expenditure ended the depression and stimulated an industrial boom that brought prosperity to most American workers. It doubled U.S. industrial output and the per capita GNP, created 17 million new jobs, increased corporate after-tax profits by 70 percent, and raised the real wages or purchasing power of industrial workers by 50 percent.

The government poured nearly $40 billion into the West, more than any other region, and four times as much as it had in the preceding decade, making the West an economic powerhouse. California alone secured more than 10 percent of all federal funds, and by 1945 nearly half the personal income in the state came from expenditures by the federal government.

A newly prospering South also contributed to the emergence of a dynamic Sunbelt. In an arc stretching from the Southeast to the Southwest, the billions spent by Uncle Sam meant millions of jobs in the textile, oil and natural gas, chemical, and aluminum industries, as well as in the shipyards of Norfolk, Mobile, and New Orleans, and the aircraft plants in Dallas–Fort Worth and Marietta, Georgia. The South's industrial capacity increased by 40 percent, and per capita income tripled. Boom times enabled hundreds of thousands of sharecroppers and farm tenants to leave the land for better-paying industrial jobs. While the South's farm population decreased by 20 percent in the 1940s, its urban population grew 36 percent.

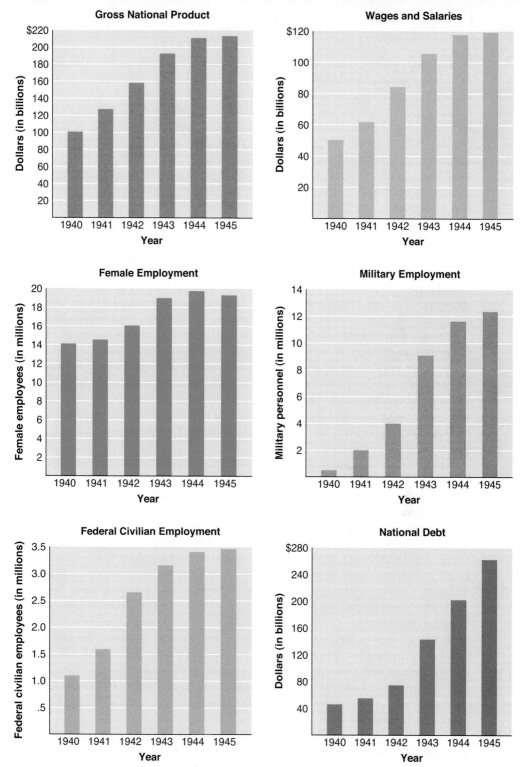

FIGURE 25.1 U.S. Wartime Production

Between 1941 and 1945, the economy grew at a remarkable pace.

Full employment, longer workweeks, larger paychecks, and the increased hiring of minorities, women, the elderly, and teenagers brought a middle-class standard of living to millions of families. In California, the demand for workers in the shipyards and aircraft factories opened opportunities for thousands of Chinese-Americans previously confined to menial jobs within their own communities. In San Diego, 40 percent of retirees returned to work. Deafening factories hired the hearing-impaired, and aircraft plants employed dwarfs as inspectors because of their ability to crawl inside small spaces. The war years produced the only significant shift toward greater equality in the distribution of income in the twentieth century. The earnings of the bottom fifth of all workers rose 68 percent, and those of the middle class doubled. The richest 5 percent, conversely, saw their share of total disposable income drop from 23 to 17 percent.

Large-scale commercial farmers prospered as a result of higher consumer prices and increased productivity thanks to improved fertilizers and more mechanization. As the consolidation of small farms into fewer large ones proceeded, corporations dominated commercial farming. Organized agriculture (later called agribusiness) took its seat in the council of power, alongside big government, big business, and organized labor.

Labor-union membership leaped from 9 million in 1940 to 14.8 million in 1945 (35 percent of nonagricultural employment). This growth resulted from the huge increase in the work force and the NWLB's "maintenance-of-membership" rule, which automatically enrolled new workers in unions and required workers to retain their union membership through the life of a contract. In return, unions agreed not to strike and to limit wage increases to 15 percent. In lieu of higher pay, they negotiated unprecedented fringe benefits for their members, including paid vacation time, health insurance, and pension plans.

Only a minority of unionists broke the no-strike pledge. Most occurred in "wildcat strikes," not authorized by union officials and of brief duration, which swept the country from 1943 to 1945. All told, however, strikes amounted to less than one-tenth of 1 percent of wartime working hours, barely affecting war production. In the most glaring exception, John L. Lewis, the iron-willed head of the United Mine Workers (UMW), led more than half a million coal-field workers out of the pits three times in 1943. Although the miners won wage concessions, their victory cost the union movement dearly. Many states passed laws to limit union power, and, over Roosevelt's veto, Congress passed the Smith-Connally War Labor Disputes Act of 1943, which empowered the president to take over any facility where strikes interrupted war production.

Far more than strikes, inflation threatened the wartime economy. Throughout 1942 prices climbed by 2 percent a month as a result of the combination of increased spending power and a scarcity of consumer goods. At the end of the year, Congress gave the president authority to control wages, prices, and rents, and as the OPA clamped down, inflation slowed dramatically. Consumer prices rose just 8 percent during the last two years of war.

The OPA also instituted rationing to combat inflation and conserve scarce materials. Under the slogan "Use it up, wear it out, make it do or do without," the OPA rationed gasoline, coffee, sugar, butter, cheese, and meat. Americans endured "meatless Tuesdays" and cuffless trousers, ate sherbet instead of ice cream, and put up with imitation chocolate that tasted like soap and imitation soap that did not lather. American men and women planted 20 million victory gardens, served as air-raid wardens, and organized collection drives to recycle cooking grease and used paper and tires, while their children, known as "Uncle Sam's Scrappers" and "Tin-Can Colonels," scoured their neighborhoods for scrap metal and other valuable trash.

Buying war bonds further curtailed inflation by decreasing consumer purchasing power, while giving civilians a sense of involvement in the distant war. The sale of bonds—"bullets in the bellies of Hitler's hordes!" claimed the Treasury Department— to schoolchildren, small investors, and corporations raised almost half the money needed to finance the war. Roosevelt sought to raise the rest by drastically increasing taxes. Congress refused the president much of what he sought. Still, the Revenue Act of 1942 raised the top income-tax rate from 60 percent to 94 percent and imposed income taxes on middle- and lower-income Americans for the first time, quadrupling the number of people who paid taxes. Beginning in 1943, the payroll-deduction system automatically withheld income taxes from wages and salaries. By 1945 the federal government was taking in nearly twenty times the tax revenue that it had in 1940.

"A Wizard War"   Winston Churchill labeled the conflict "a wizard war" in tribute to the importance of wartime scientific and technological developments. Mathematicians went to work deciphering enemy codes, psychologists devised propaganda, and, as never before, the major combatants mobilized scientists into virtual armies of invention. Their labors brought forth both miracles in healing and advances in the technology of killing. They became as indispensable to national defense as military officers, both as creators of new weapons technologies and as advisers on their use and their consequences for national security. In 1941, Roosevelt formed a committee to organize scientists for a weapons race against the Axis, and created the Office of Scientific Research and Development (OSRD) for the development of new ordnance and military medicine. OSRD spent more than $1 billion to generate radar and sonar devices, rocket weapons, and bomb fuses. It advanced the development of jet aircraft and high-altitude bombsights, and its employment of scientists to devise methods for utilizing new weapons resulted in a brand-new field called operational analysis. The need to improve military radar spurred the development of the laser, while research in quantum physics to build atomic bombs later became the basis for transistors and semiconductors. The need to supply rapidly advancing troops with unspoiled food resulted in the instant mashed potatoes on sale today.

The quest for greater accuracy in ordinance, moreover, required the kind of rapid, detailed calculations that only computing machines could supply. So a half-dozen teams of scientists went to work in 1942 to develop what would become the earliest computers. By mid-1944 navy personnel in the basement of Harvard's physics laboratory were operating IBM's Automatic Sequence Controlled Calculator, known as Mark I—a cumbersome device 51 feet long and 8 feet high that weighed five tons, used 530 miles of wire, and contained 760,000 parts. ENIAC (electronic numerical integrator and computer), developed to improve artillery accuracy for the army, reduced the time required to multiply two tenth-place numbers from Mark I's three seconds to less than three-thousandths of a second.

Nothing saved the lives of more wounded servicemen than blood plasma and improvements in blood-transfusion and blood-banking techniques. Military needs led to advances in heart and lung surgery, and to the use of synthetic antimalarial drugs to substitute for scarce quinine and toxoid vaccine to prevent tetanus. So-called miracle drugs, antibiotics to combat infections, a rarity on the eve of war, would be copiously produced. The military, which had only enough penicillin for about a hundred patients at the Battle of Midway in June 1942, had enough for all major casualties by D-Day in June 1944, and far more than it could use by V-J Day in August 1945, allowing the beginning of the sale of penicillin for civilian use.

Insecticides initially seemed as much a miracle. The use of DDT cleared many islands of malaria-carrying mosquitoes, like those at Guadalcanal that had caused five times as many casualties as combat in 1942. DDT also stopped an incipient typhus epidemic in Naples in January 1944. Along with innovations like the Mobile Auxiliary Surgical Hospital (MASH), science helped save tens of thousands of lives, halving the World War I death rate of wounded soldiers who reached medical installations. It improved the health of the nation as well. Life expectancy rose by three years during the war, and infant mortality fell by more than a third.

No scientific endeavor had a higher priority than the **Manhattan Project** to develop the atomic bomb. In August 1939 physicist Albert Einstein, a Jewish refugee, warned Roosevelt that German scientists were seeking to construct a weapon of extraordinary destructiveness, based on the discovery of nuclear fission—the splitting of the uranium atom and the release of nuclear energy. The president promptly established an advisory committee and in late 1941 launched an Anglo-American secret program—the Soviets were excluded—to produce atomic bombs. In 1942 the participating physicists, both Americans and Europeans, achieved a controlled atomic chain reaction under the University of Chicago football stadium, the first step toward developing the bomb. In 1943–1944 the Manhattan Engineer District—the code name for the atomic project—stockpiled uranium-235 at Oak Ridge, Tennessee, and plutonium at Hanford, Washington. In 1945, engineers and scientists headquartered on an isolated mesa in Los Alamos, New Mexico, assembled two bombs utilizing fissionable materials. By then the Manhattan Project employed more than 120,000 people and had spent nearly $2 billion.

Just before dawn on July 16, 1945, a blinding fireball with "the brightness of several suns at midday" rose over the Alamogordo, New Mexico, desert at a test site named Trinity. A huge, billowing mushroom cloud soon towered 40,000 feet above the ground. With a force of twenty thousand tons of TNT, the blast shattered windows more than 120 miles away. "A few people laughed, a few people cried," recalled J. Robert Oppenheimer, the Manhattan Project's scientific director. "Most people were silent. I remembered the line from the Hindu scripture, the Bhagavad-Gita: 'Now I am become Death, the destroyer of worlds.'" The atomic age had dawned.

Propaganda and Politics

People as well as science and machinery had to be mobilized for the global conflict. To sustain a spirit of unity and fan the fires of patriotism, the Roosevelt administration managed public opinion. The Office of Censorship examined letters going overseas and worked with publishers and broadcasters to suppress information that might hinder the war effort. A year passed before casualty and damage figures from Pearl Harbor were disclosed. Fearful of demoralizing the public, the government banned the publication of photographs of American war dead until 1943. Then, concerned that the public had become overconfident, the media were prompted to display pictures of American servicemen killed by the enemy and to emphasize accounts of Japan's atrocities against American prisoners.

To shape public opinion and sell the faraway war to the American people, Roosevelt created the Office of War Information (OWI) in June 1942. The OWI employed more than four thousand artists, writers, and advertising specialists to explain the war and counter enemy propaganda. The OWI depicted the war as a mortal struggle between good and evil and harped on the necessity of totally destroying, not merely defeating, the enemy.

Hollywood answered the OWI directive—"Will this help win the war?"—by highlighting the heroism and unity of the American forces, while inciting hatred of the enemy. Films about the war portrayed the Japanese, in particular, as treacherous and cruel, as beasts in the jungle, as "slant-eyed rats." Jukeboxes blared songs like "We're Gonna Have to Slap the Dirty Little Jap." U.S. propaganda also presented the war as a struggle to preserve the "American way of life," usually depicted in images of small-town, middle-class, white Americans enjoying a bountiful consumer society.

While the Roosevelt administration concentrated on the war, Republican critics seized the initiative in domestic politics. Full employment and higher wages undercut the appeal of the New Deal, and resentment over wartime shortages and dismay over Axis victories further weakened the Democrats. With voter turnout low because many soldiers and defense workers were far from the hometowns where they had registered and were thus unable to vote, the Republicans gained forty-four seats in the House and nine in the Senate in 1942.

Politics shifted to the Right. The conservative coalition of Republicans and southern Democrats abolished some New Deal agencies, such as the WPA and CCC, drastically curtailed others, and rebuffed the adoption of new liberal programs. But the dynamics of the war enormously expanded governmental power, especially the power of the executive branch. As never before, the federal government managed the economy, molded public opinion, funded scientific research, and influenced people's daily lives.

THE BATTLEFRONT, 1942–1944

Following the Japanese attack on Pearl Harbor, the outlook for the Allies appeared critical. Then America's industrial might and Soviet manpower turned the tides of war, and diplomacy followed in its wake. Allied unity dwindled as Germany and Japan weakened, and the United States, Soviet Union, and Great Britain each sought wartime strategies and postwar arrangements best suited to its own interests.

Liberating Europe   British and American officials agreed to concentrate on defeating Germany first and then smashing Japan. But they differed on where to attack. While German U-boats sank Allied ships at an appalling rate in early 1942, Hitler's forces advanced toward the Suez Canal in Egypt and penetrated deeper into the Soviet Union. Roosevelt sought to placate Stalin, who demanded a second front in western Europe to relieve the pressure on the Soviet Union, which faced the full fury of two hundred German divisions. But Churchill, fearing a repeat of the World War I slaughter in the trenches of France and wanting American assistance in maintaining British control of the vital Suez Canal, persuaded FDR to postpone the "second front" in Europe and invade North Africa instead. In Operation TORCH, begun in November 1942, American forces landed in Morocco and Algeria, and pressing eastward trapped the German and Italian armies being driven westward by the British, forcing some 260,000 German and Italian troops to surrender, despite Hitler's orders to fight to the death.

The Soviet Union proved to be the graveyard of the Wehrmacht (German army). In the main turning point of the European war, the Russians defeated the Germans in the protracted Battle of Stalingrad (August 1942–January 1943. As the Russian snow turned red with blood (costing each side more battle deaths in half a year than the United States suffered in the entire war), and its hills strewn with human bones became "white fields," Soviet forces defended Moscow, saved Stalingrad, and relieved besieged Leningrad.

Stalin pleaded again for a second front; Churchill objected again; and again Roosevelt gave in to Churchill, agreeing to invade Sicily. In summer 1943, after a month of fighting, the Allies seized Sicily and landed in southern Italy. Italian military officials deposed Mussolini and surrendered to the Allies in early September. But as Allied forces moved up the Italian peninsula, German troops poured into Italy. Facing elite

"Full Victory—Nothing Else!" *Commander-in-Chief of the Allied Expeditionary Force General Dwight D. ("Ike") Eisenhower gives the order of the day to U.S. paratroopers in England on the eve of D-Day.*

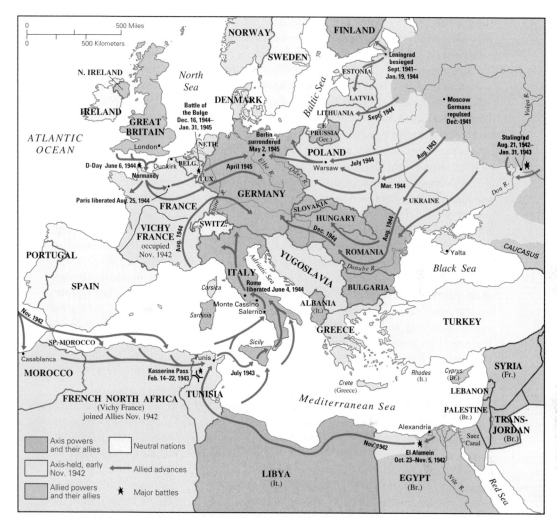

MAP 25.1 World War II in Europe and Africa

The momentous German defeats at Stalingrad and in Tunisia early in 1943 marked the turning point in the war against the Axis. By 1945 Allied conquest of Hitler's "thousand-year" Reich was imminent.

Nazi divisions in strong defensive positions, the Allies spent eight months inching their way 150 miles to Rome. They were still battling through the mud and snow of northern Italy when the war in Europe ended in 1945.

In 1943–1944 the Allies turned the tide in the Atlantic and instituted round-the-clock bombardment of Germany. American science and industry developed sophisticated radar and sonar systems and better torpedoes and depth charges, and produced ever-increasing quantities of destroyers and aircraft. Britain's Royal Air Force by night and the U.S. army air force by day rained thousands of tons of bombs on German cities. In raids on Hamburg in July 1943 Allied planes dropped incendiary bombs mixed with high explosives, killing at least 35,000 people and leveling the city, much as they had earlier done to Cologne and would do to Dresden in February 1945, where an estimated sixty thousand people died and another thirty-seven thousand were injured.

Meanwhile, in July 1943 German and Soviet divisions fought the largest tank battle in history near the city of Kursk in the Ukraine, and the victorious Red Army began an offensive that rid the Soviet Union of Germans by mid-1944. It then plunged into Poland and established a puppet government, took control of Romania and Bulgaria, and assisted communist guerrillas led by Josip Broz Tito in liberating Yugoslavia.

As the Soviets swept across eastern Europe, Allied forces finally opened the long-delayed second front. Early on the morning of June 6, 1944—D-Day—nearly two hundred thousand American, British, and Canadian troops, accompanied by six hundred warships and more than ten thousand planes, stormed a sixty-mile stretch of the Normandy coast in the largest amphibious invasion in history. Led by General Eisenhower, now Supreme Commander of the Allied Expeditionary Force in Western Europe, **Operation OVERLORD** gradually pushed inland, securing the Low Countries, liberating Paris, and approaching the border of Germany. There, in the face of supply problems and stiffened German resistance, the Allied offensive ground to a halt. In mid-December, as the Allies prepared for a full-scale assault on Germany, Hitler threw his last reserves against Americans in the forest of Ardennes. The **Battle of the Bulge**—named for the eighty-mile-long and fifty-mile-wide "bulge" that the German troops drove inside the American lines—raged for nearly a month, and ended with American forces on the banks of the Rhine, the German army depleted, and the end of the European war in sight.

War in the Pacific   The day after the Philippines fell to Japan in mid-May 1942, the U.S. and Japanese fleets clashed in the Coral Sea off northeastern Australia in the first battle in history fought entirely by planes from aircraft carriers. Each lost a carrier, but the battle stymied the Japanese advance on Australia.

Less than a month later, a Japanese armada headed toward Midway Island, a crucial American outpost between Hawaii and Japan. The U.S. Signal Corps, however, had broken the Japanese naval code. Knowing the plans and locations of Japan's ships, the U.S. carriers and planes won a decisive victory, sinking four Japanese carriers and destroying hundreds of planes. Suddenly on the defensive, the stunned Japanese could now only try to hold what they had already won.

On the offensive, U.S. marines waded ashore at Guadalcanal in the Solomon Islands in August 1942. Facing fierce resistance as well as tropical diseases like malaria, the Americans needed six months to take the island, a bitter preview of the battles to come. As the British moved from India to retake Burma, the United States began a two-pronged advance toward Japan in 1943. The army, under General Douglas MacArthur, advanced north on the islands between Australia and the Philippines, and the navy and marines, under Admiral Chester Nimitz, "island-hopped" across the central Pacific to seize strategic bases and put Tokyo in range of American bombers. In fall 1944 the navy annihilated what remained of the Japanese fleet at the battles of the Philippine Sea and Leyte Gulf, giving the United States control of Japan's air and shipping lanes and leaving the Japanese home islands open to invasion.

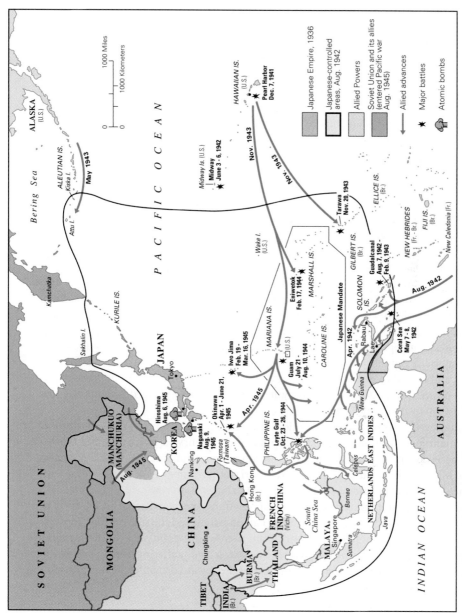

MAP 25.2 World War II in the Pacific

American ships and planes stemmed the Japanese offensive at the Battles of the Coral Sea and Midway Island. Thereafter, the Japanese were on the defensive against American amphibious assaults and air strikes.

The Grand Alliance   President Roosevelt had two main goals for the war: the total defeat of the Axis at the least possible cost in American lives, and the establishment of a world order strong enough to preserve peace, open trade, and ensure national self-determination in the postwar era. Aware that only a common enemy fused the Grand Alliance together, Roosevelt tried to promote harmony by concentrating on military victory and postponing divisive postwar matters.

Churchill and Stalin had other goals. Britain wanted neither the United States nor the Soviet Union to reshape and dominate the postwar world; it especially sought to retain its imperial possessions. As Churchill said, he had "not become the King's First Minister to preside over the liquidation of the British Empire." The Soviet Union wanted a permanently weakened Germany and a sphere of influence (a region whose governments can be counted on to do a great power's bidding) in eastern Europe. To hold together this fragile alliance, FDR relied on personal diplomacy to mediate conflicts.

The first president to travel by plane while in office, Roosevelt arrived in Casablanca, Morocco's main port, in January 1943 to confer with Churchill. They resolved to attack Italy before invading France and proclaimed that the war would continue until the "unconditional surrender" of the Axis. By so doing, they sought to reduce Soviet mistrust of the West, which had deepened because of the postponement of the second front. Ten months later, in Cairo, Roosevelt met with Churchill and Jiang Jieshi (Chiang Kai-shek), the anticommunist head of the Chinese government. To keep China in the war, FDR promised the return of Manchuria and Taiwan to China and a "free and independent Korea." From Cairo, FDR and Churchill continued on to Tehran, Iran's capital, to meet with Stalin. Here they set the invasion of France for June 1944, and agreed to divide Germany into zones of occupation and to impose reparations on the Reich. Most importantly to Roosevelt, Stalin pledged to enter the war against Japan after Hitler's defeat.

Roosevelt then turned his attention to domestic politics. Increasing conservative sentiment in the nation led him to drop the liberal Henry A. Wallace from the ticket and accept Harry S Truman as his vice-presidential candidate. A moderate senator from Missouri, now dubbed "the new Missouri Compromise," Truman restored a semblance of unity to the Democrats for the 1944 campaign. To compete, the Republicans nominated moderate and noncontroversial New York governor Thomas E. Dewey. The campaign focused more on personalities than on issues, and the still-popular FDR defeated his dull GOP opponent, but with the narrowest margin since 1916—winning 53 percent of the popular vote. A weary Roosevelt, secretly suffering from hypertension and heart disease, now directed his waning energies toward defeating the Axis and constructing an international peacekeeping system.

WAR AND AMERICAN SOCIETY

The crisis of war altered the most basic patterns of American life, powerfully affecting those on the home front as well as those who served in the armed forces. Few families were untouched: more than 15 million Americans went to the war, an equal number were on the move, and unprecedented numbers of women went to work outside the home. As well, the war opened some doors of opportunity for African-Americans and other minorities, although many remained closed. It heightened minority aspirations and widened cracks in the wall of white racist attitudes and policy, while maintaining much of America's racial caste system, thereby tilling the ground for future crises.

The GIs' War

Most Americans in the armed forces griped about regimentation and were more interested in dry socks than in ideology. They knew little of the big strategies, and cared less. They fought because they were told to and wanted to stay alive. Reluctant recruits rather than heroic warriors, most had few aims beyond returning to a safe, familiar United States.

But the GIs' war dragged on for almost four years, transforming them in the process. Millions who had never been far from home traveled to unfamiliar cities and remote lands, shedding their parochialism. Sharing tents and foxholes with Americans of different religions, ethnicities, and classes, their military service acted as a "melting pot" experience that freed them from some prewar prejudices.

In countless ways, the war modified how GIs saw themselves and others. Besides serving with people they had never previously encountered, over a million married overseas, broadening personal horizons and sowing the seeds of a more tolerant and diverse national culture that placed far less emphasis on divisions of class, national origin, region, and religion. At the same time many GIs became evermore distrustful of foreigners and outsiders, and returned home obsessed with the flag as a symbol of patriotism.

Physical misery, chronic exhaustion, and, especially, intense combat took a heavy toll, leaving lasting psychological as well as physical wounds. Both American and Japanese troops saw the other in racist images, as animals to be exterminated, and brutality became as much the rule as the exception in "a war without mercy." Both sides machine-gunned hostile flyers in parachutes; both tortured and killed prisoners in cold blood; both mutilated enemy dead for souvenirs. In the fight against Germany, cruelties and atrocities also occurred, although on a lesser scale. A battalion of the Second Armored Division calling itself "Roosevelt's Butchers" boasted that it shot all the German soldiers it captured. Some U.S. pilots laughed at the lifeboats they strafed and the bodies they exploded out of trucks. Some became cynical about human life; others, haunted by nightmares about the war, would long languish in veterans' hospitals.

The Home Front

Nothing transformed the social topography more than the vast internal migration of an already mobile people. About 15 million men moved because of military service, often accompanied by family members. Many other Americans moved to secure new economic opportunities, especially in the Pacific coast states. Nearly a quarter of a million found jobs in the shipyards of the Bay area and at least as many in the aircraft industry that arose in the orange groves of southern California. More than one hundred thousand worked in the Puget Sound shipyards of Washington State and half as many in the nearby Boeing airplane plants. Others flocked to the world's largest magnesium plant in Henderson, Nevada, to the huge Geneva Steel Works near Provo, Utah, and to the Rocky Mountain Arsenal and Remington Rand arms plant outside Denver.

At least 6 million people left farms to work in urban areas, including several million southern blacks and whites. They doubled Albuquerque's population and increased

San Diego's some 90 percent. This mass uprooting of people from familiar settings made Americans both more cosmopolitan and lonelier. Some who moved far from their hometowns left behind their traditional values. Housing shortages left millions living in converted garages and trailer camps, even in cars. Some workers in Seattle lived in chicken coops. The swarms of migrants to Mobile, Alabama, attracted by a new aluminum plant, two massive shipyards, an air base, and an army supply depot, transformed a sleepy fishing village into a symbol of urban disorder.

Overcrowding, and wartime separations, strained family and community life. High rates of divorce, mental illness, family violence, and juvenile delinquency reflected the disruptions caused in part by the lack of privacy, the sense of impermanence, the absence of familiar settings, and the competition for scarce facilities. Few boom communities had the resources to supply their swollen populations with transportation, recreation, and social services. Urban blight and conflicts between newcomers and oldtimers accelerated.

While military culture fostered a sexist mentality, emphasizing the differences between "femininity" and "masculinity," millions of American women donned pants, put their hair in bandannas, and went to work in defense plants. Reversing a decade of efforts to exclude women from the labor force, the federal government urged women into war production in 1942. Songs like "We're the Janes Who Make the Planes" encouraged women to take up war work. Propaganda called upon them to take jobs and "release able-bodied men for fighting." More than 6 million women entered the labor force during the war, increasing the number of employed women to 19 million. Less than a quarter of the labor force in 1940, women constituted well over a third of all workers in 1945.

Before the war most female wage earners had been young and single. By contrast, 75 percent of the new women workers were married, 60 percent were over thirty-five, and more than 33 percent had children under the age of fourteen. They tended blast furnaces, operated cranes, greased locomotives, drove taxis, welded hulls, loaded shells, and worked in coke plants and rolling mills. On the Pacific coast, more than one-third of all workers in aircraft and shipbuilding were women. **"Rosie the Riveter,"** holding a pneumatic gun in arms bulging with muscles, became the symbol of the woman war worker; she was, in the words of a popular song, "making history working for victory."

Yet traditional attitudes and gender discrimination existed throughout the war. Women earned only about 65 percent of what men earned for the same work, and were often denied equal seniority rights. Labor unions often stipulated that women had to give up their jobs to men on their return from military service, and government propaganda portrayed women's war work as a temporary response to an emergency. "A woman is a substitute," claimed a War Department brochure, "like plastic instead of metal." As a result, the public attitude about women's employment changed little in World War II. In 1945, only 18 percent of the respondents in a poll approved of married women working.

Traditional notions of a woman's place and the stigma attached to working mothers also shaped government resistance to establishing child-care centers for women employed in defense. "A mother's primary duty is to her home and children," the Labor Department's Children's Bureau stated. "This duty is one she cannot lay aside, no matter what the emergency." New York mayor Fiorello LaGuardia proclaimed that the worst mother was better than the best nursery. Funds for federal child-care centers covered fewer than 10 percent of defense workers' children, and the young suffered. Terms like "eight-hour orphans" and "latch-key children" described unsupervised children forced to take care of themselves. Fueling the fears of those who believed that the employment of women outside the home would cause the family to disintegrate, juvenile delinquency increased fivefold and the divorce rate zoomed from 16 per 100 marriages in 1940 to 27 per 100 in 1944.

The impact of war on women and the family proved multifaceted and even contradictory. As the divorce rate soared, so did marriage rates and birthrates. Although some women remained content to roll bandages for the Red Cross, more than three hundred thousand joined the armed forces and, for the first time in American history, were given regular military status and served in positions other than that of nurse. As members of the Women's Army Corps (WACs) and the Navy's Women Appointed for Volunteer Emergency Service (WAVES), they replaced men in such noncombat jobs as mechanics and radio operators, and served as mapmakers and ferry pilots. About a thousand women became civilian pilots with the WASPs (Women's Airforce Service Pilots). When they left the service, moreover, women had the same rights and privileges as male veterans.

Despite lingering notions of separate spheres, female workers gained unprecedented employment opportunities and public recognition. Although some eagerly gave up their jobs at the end of the war, others did not relish losing the income, independence, and self-esteem they had gained in contributing to the war effort. As Inez Sauer, who went to work for Boeing in Seattle, recalled,

> My mother warned me when I took the job that I would never be the same. She said, "You will never want to go back to being a housewife." She was right, it definitely did. At Boeing I found a freedom and an independence I had never known. After the war I could never go back to playing bridge again, being a clubwoman and listening to a lot of inanities when I knew there were things you could use your mind for. The war changed my life completely.

Overall, women gained a new sense of their potential. The war proved their capabilities and widened their world. Recalled one war wife whose returning husband did not like her independence, "He had left a shrinking violet and come home to a very strong oak tree." Wartime experiences markedly affected a generation of women and the sons and daughters they later raised.

Some of these women were among the 350,000 teachers who took better-paying war work or joined the armed services, leaving schools badly understaffed. Students, too, abandoned school in record numbers. High school enrollments sank as the full-time employment of teenagers rose from 900,000 in 1940 to 3 million in 1944.

The loss of students to war production and the armed services forced colleges to admit large numbers of women and to contract themselves out to the armed forces. Nearly a million servicemen took college classes in science, engineering, and foreign languages. The military presence was all-pervasive. Harvard University awarded four military-training certificates for every academic degree it conferred. The chancellor of one branch of the University of California announced that his school was "no longer an academic tent with military sideshows. It is a military tent with academic sideshows." Higher education became more dependent on the federal government, and most universities sought increased federal contracts and subsidies, despite their having to submit to greater government interference and regulation. The universities in the West received some $100 billion from the Office of Scientific Research and Development, more money than had been spent on scientific research by all the western universities since their founding.

The war profoundly affected American culture. Spending on books and theater entertainment doubled. More than 60 million people (in a population of 135 million) attended movies weekly, and the film industry reached its zenith in 1945–1946. But as the war dragged on, people tired of patriotic war films, and Hollywood reemphasized romance and nostalgia with such stars as Katharine Hepburn and Judy Garland.

Similarly, popular music early in the war featured patriotic themes. "Goodbye, Mama, I'm Off to Yokohama" became the first hit of 1942. As the war continued, themes of lost love and loneliness dominated lyrics. Numbers like "They're Either Too Young or Too Old" expressed the laments of women separated from the men they loved. So, too, did the dozens of "dream songs" in which love denied by the real world could be achieved only in a dream. By 1945 bitterness rather than melancholy pervaded the lyrics of best-selling records, and songs like "Saturday Night Is the Loneliest Night of the Week" revealed impatience for the war's end.

In bookstores, nonfiction ruled the roost and every newsmagazine increased its circulation. The Government Printing Office published Armed Services Editions, paperback reprints of classics and new releases; and the nearly 350 million copies distributed free to soldiers sped up the American acceptance of quality paperbacks, which were introduced in 1939 by the Pocket Book Company. Wendell Willkie's *One World* (1943) became the fastest-selling title in publishing history to that time, with 1 million copies snapped up in two months. A euphoric vision of a world without military alliances and spheres of influence, this brief volume expressed hope that an international organization would extend peace and democracy through the postwar world. Most startlingly, Willkie attacked "our imperialisms at home." Unless the United States ended its own racism, he concluded, nonwhites around the globe would rebuff its claim to world leadership. "If we want to talk about freedom, we must mean freedom for everyone inside our frontiers."

An avid interest in wartime news also spurred the major radio networks to increase their news programs from 4 percent to nearly 30 percent of broadcasting time, and enticed Americans to listen to the radio an average of 4½ hours a day. Daytime radio serials, like those featuring Dick Tracy tracking down Axis spies, reached the height of their popularity, as did juvenile comic books in which a platoon of new superheroes, including Captain America and Captain Marvel, saw action on the battlefield. Even Bugs Bunny donned a uniform to combat America's foes.

Racism and New Opportunities   Recognizing that the government needed the loyalty and labor of a united people, black leaders entered World War II determined to secure equal rights. In 1942 civil-rights spokesmen insisted that African-American support of the war hinged on America's commitment to racial justice. They demanded a *"Double V"* campaign to gain victory over racial discrimination at home as well as over the Axis abroad.

Membership in the NAACP multiplied nearly ten times, reaching half a million in 1945. The association pressed for legislation outlawing the poll tax and lynching, decried discrimination in defense industries and the armed services, and sought to end black disfranchisement. The campaign for voting rights gained momentum when the Supreme Court, in *Smith* v. *Allwright* (1944), ruled the Texas all-white primary unconstitutional. The decision eliminated a bar that had existed in eight southern states, although these states promptly resorted to other devices to minimize voting by blacks.

A new civil-rights organization, the Congress of Racial Equality (CORE), was founded in 1942. Employing the same forms of nonviolent direct action that Mohandas Gandhi used in his campaign for India's independence, CORE sought to desegregate public facilities in northern cities.

Also proposing nonviolent direct action, **A. Philip Randolph,** president of the Brotherhood of Sleeping Car Porters, in 1941 called for a "thundering march" of one hundred thousand blacks on Washington "to wake up and shock white America as it has never been shocked before." He warned Roosevelt that if the president did not end discrimination in the armed services and the defense industry, angry African-Americans would besiege Washington. FDR agreed to compromise.

In June 1941 Roosevelt issued Executive Order 8802, the first presidential directive on race since Reconstruction. It prohibited discriminatory employment practices by federal agencies and all unions and companies engaged in war-related work, and established the Fair Employment Practices Commission (FEPC) to monitor compliance. Although the FEPC lacked effective enforcement powers, booming war production and a labor supply depleted by military service resulted in the employment of some 2 million African-Americans in industry and two hundred thousand in the federal civil service. Between 1942 and 1945 the proportion of blacks in war-production work rose from 3 to 9 percent. Black membership in labor unions doubled to 1.25 million, and the number of skilled and semiskilled black workers tripled. Formerly mired in low-paying domestic and farm jobs, some three hundred thousand black women found work in factories and the civil service. "Hitler was the one that got us out of the white folks' kitchen," recalled one black woman who went to work for Boeing in Seattle, a city whose black population rose from four thousand to forty thousand during the war. Overall, the average wage for African-Americans increased from $457 to $1,976 a year, compared with a gain from $1,064 to $2,600 for whites.

About 1 million African-Americans served in the armed forces. Wartime needs forced the military to end policies of excluding blacks from the marines and coast guard, restricting them to jobs as mess boys in the navy, and confining them to noncombatant units in the army. From just five in 1940—three of them chaplains—the number of black officers grew to over seven thousand in 1945. The all-black 761st Tank Battalion gained distinction fighting in Germany, and the 99th Pursuit Squadron won eighty Distinguished Flying Crosses for its combat against the *Luftwaffe* in Europe. In 1944 both the army and navy began token integration in some training facilities, ships, and battlefield platoons.

The great majority of blacks, however, served throughout the war in segregated service units commanded by white officers. This indignity, made worse by the failure of military authorities to protect black servicemen off the post and by the use of white military police to keep blacks "in their place," sparked rioting on army bases. At least fifty black soldiers died in racial conflicts during the war. "I used to sing gospel songs until I joined the Army," recalled blues-guitar great B. B. King, "then I sang the blues."

Violence within the military mirrored growing racial tensions on the home front. As blacks protested against discrimination, many whites resisted all efforts by blacks to improve their economic and social status. Numerous clashes occurred. Scores of cities reported pitched battles between blacks and whites. Race riots erupted in 1943 in Harlem, Mobile, and Beaumont, Texas. The bloodiest melee exploded in Detroit that year when white mobs assaulted blacks caught riding on trolleys or sitting in movie theaters and blacks smashed and looted white-owned stores and shops. After thirty hours of racial beatings, shootings, and burning, twenty-five African-Americans and nine whites lay dead, more than seven hundred had been injured, and over $2 million of property had been destroyed. The fear of continued violence led to a greater emphasis on racial tolerance by liberal whites and to a reduction in the militancy of African-American leaders.

Yet the war brought significant changes that would eventually result in a successful drive for black civil rights. The migration of over seven hundred thousand blacks from the South turned a southern problem into a national concern. It created a new attitude of independence in African-Americans freed from the stifling constraints of caste. Despite the continuation of racial prejudice and discrimination, most who left the rural South found a more abundant and hopeful life than the one they had left behind. As the growing numbers of blacks in northern cities began to vote, moreover, African-Americans could hold a balance of power in close elections. This prompted politicians in both major parties to extend greater recognition to blacks and to pay more attention to civil-rights issues.

African-American expectations of greater government concern for their rights also resulted from the new prominence of the United States as a major power in a predominantly nonwhite world. As Japanese propaganda appeals to the peoples of Asia and Latin America emphasized lynchings and race riots in the United States, Americans had to confront the peril that white racism posed to their national security. In addition, the horrors of Nazi racism discredited America's own white-supremacist attitudes and practices. A former governor of Alabama complained, Nazism has "wrecked the theories of the master race with which we were so contented so long." And Roosevelt proclaimed, "There never has been, there isn't now, and there never will be, any race of people on earth fit to serve as masters over their fellow men." A pluralist vision of American society now became part of official rhetoric, and of the liberal-left agenda. The contradiction between American ideals of freedom and equality and the actual state of African-Americans became manifest. Swedish economist Gunnar Myrdal, in his massive study of race problems, *An American Dilemma* (1944), concluded that "not since Reconstruction had there been more reason to anticipate fundamental changes in American race relations. . . . [T]here is bound to be a redefinition of the Negro's status as a result of this War." Returning black veterans, and African-Americans who had served the nation on the home front, expected to soon gain all the rights enjoyed by whites.

War and Diversity   Wartime winds of change also brought new opportunities and difficulties to other minorities. More than twenty-five thousand Native Americans served in the armed forces, including 400 Navajo "code talkers" who confounded the Japanese by using their complex native language to relay messages between U.S. command centers. "Were it not for the Navajos, the Marines would never have taken Iwo Jima," one Signal Corps officer declared.

Another fifty thousand Indians left the reservation to work in defense industries, mainly on the West Coast. The Rosebud Reservation in South Dakota lost more than a quarter of its population to migration during the war. It was the first time most had lived in a non-Indian world, and the average income of Native American households tripled during the war. Such economic improvement encouraged many Indians to remain outside the reservation and to try to assimilate into mainstream life. But anti-Indian discrimination, particularly in smaller towns near reservations such as Gallup, New Mexico, and Billings, Montana, forced many Native Americans back to their reservations, which had suffered severely from budget cuts during the war. Prodded by those who coveted Indian lands, lawmakers demanded that Indians be taken off the backs of the taxpayers and "freed from the reservations" to fend for themselves. To mobilize against the campaign to end all reservations and trust protections, Native Americans organized the National Congress of American Indians in 1944.

To relieve labor shortages in agriculture, caused by conscription and the movement of rural workers to city factories, the U.S. government negotiated an agreement with Mexico in July 1942 to import **braceros**, or temporary workers. Classified as foreign laborers rather than as immigrants, an estimated two hundred thousand braceros, half of them in California, received short-term contracts promising adequate wages, medical care, and decent living conditions. But farm owners frequently violated the terms of these contracts and also encouraged an influx of illegal migrants from Mexico desperate for employment. Unable to complain about their working conditions without risking arrest and deportation, hundreds of thousands of Mexicans were exploited by agribusinesses in Arizona, California, and Texas. At the same time, tens of thousands of Chicanos left agricultural work for jobs in factories, shipbuilding yards, and steel mills. By 1943 about half a million Chicanos were living in Los Angeles County, 10 percent of the total population. In New Mexico nearly 20 percent of Mexican-American farm laborers escaped from rural poverty to urban jobs. Even as their occupational status and material conditions improved, most Mexican-Americans remained in communities called *colonias,* segregated from the larger society and frequently harassed by the police.

Much of the hostility toward Mexican-Americans focused on young gang members who wore "zoot suits"—a fashion that originated in Harlem and emphasized long, broad-shouldered jackets and pleated trousers tightly pegged at the ankles. Known as pachucos, zoot-suited Mexican-Americans aroused the ire of servicemen stationed or on leave in Los Angeles who saw them as delinquents and draft dodgers. After a luridly publicized trial arising from a Mexican-American gang fight at a swimming hole called Sleepy Lagoon, and newspaper headlines of a Chicano "crime wave," bands of sailors from nearby bases and soldiers on leave in Los Angeles rampaged through the city in early June 1943, stripping pachucos, cutting their long hair, and beating them. Military authorities looked the other way. City police intervened only to arrest Mexican-Americans. *Time* magazine described the violence as "the ugliest brand of mob action since the coolie race riots of the 1870s"; yet Los Angeles officials praised the servicemen's actions, and the city council made the wearing of a zoot suit a misdemeanor. Nothing was done about the substandard housing, disease, and racism Hispanics had to endure.

Unlike African-Americans, however, more than 350,000 Mexican-Americans served in the armed forces without segregation, and in all combat units. They volunteered in much higher numbers than warranted by their percentage of the population and earned a disproportionate number of citations for distinguished service as well as seventeen Medals of Honor. Air corps hero Jose Holguin from Los Angeles won the Distinguished Flying Cross, the Air Medal, and the Silver Star. Returning Mexican-American GIs joined established antidiscrimination groups, like the League of United Latin American Citizens (LULAC), and organized their own associations, like the American GI Forum, to press for equal rights.

Thousands of gay men and lesbians who served in the armed forces also found new wartime opportunities. Although the military officially barred those they defined as "sexual perverts," the urgency of building a massive armed forces led to just four to five thousand men out of 18 million examined for induction to be excluded because of homosexuality. For the vast majority of gays not excluded, being emancipated from traditional expectations and the close scrutiny of family and neighbors, and living in overwhelmingly all-male or all-female environments, brought freedom to meet like-minded gay men and women. Like other minorities, many gays saw the war as a chance to prove their worth under fire. Yet some suspected of being gay were dishonorably discharged, sent to psychiatric hospitals, or imprisoned in so-called queer stockades. In 1945, gay veterans established the Veteran's Benevolent Association, the first organization in the United States to combat discrimination against homosexuals.

The Internment of Japanese-Americans

Far more than any other minority in the United States, Japanese-Americans suffered grievously during the war. The internment of about thirty-seven thousand first-generation Japanese immigrants (Issei) and nearly seventy-five thousand native-born Japanese-American citizens of the United States (Nisei) in "relocation centers" guarded by military police was a tragic reminder of the fragility of civil liberties in wartime.

The **internment of Japanese-Americans** reflected forty years of anti-Japanese sentiment on the West Coast, rooted in racial prejudice and economic rivalry. Nativist politicians and farmers who wanted Japanese-American land had long decried the "yellow peril." Following the attack on Pearl Harbor, they whipped up the rage of white Californians, aided by a government report falsely blaming Japanese-Americans in Hawaii for aiding the Japanese naval force. Patriotic associations and many newspapers clamored for evacuating the Japanese-Americans, as did the army general in charge of the Western Defense Command, who proclaimed, "It makes no difference whether he is an American citizen or not. . . . I don't want any of them."

In February 1942, President Roosevelt gave in to the pressure and issued Executive Order 9066, authorizing the removal from military areas of anyone deemed a threat. Although not a single Japanese-American was apprehended for espionage or sedition and neither the FBI nor military intelligence uncovered any evidence of disloyal behavior by Japanese-Americans, the military ordered the eviction of all first-generation Japanese immigrants (Issei) and native-born Japanese-American citizens of the United States (Nisei) from the West Coast. Only Hawaii was excepted. Despite the far larger number of Hawaiians of Japanese ancestry, as well as of Japanese living in Hawaii, no internment policy was implemented there, and no sabotage occurred.

Forced to sell all they owned at whatever prices they could obtain, Japanese-Americans lost an estimated $2 billion in property and possessions. Tagged with numbers rather than names, they were herded into barbed-wire-encircled detention camps in the most desolate parts of the West and Great Plains—places, wrote one historian, "where nobody had lived before and no one has lived since." Few other Americans protested the incarceration. Stating that it would not question government claims of military necessity during time of war, the Supreme Court upheld the constitutionality of the evacuation in the *Korematsu* case (1944). By then the hysteria had subsided, and the government had begun a program of gradual release, allowing some Nisei to attend college or take factory jobs (but not on the West Coast); about eighteen thousand served in the military. The 442nd Regimental Combat Team, entirely Japanese-American, became the most decorated unit in the military.

In 1982 a special government commission concluded in its report, *Personal Justice Denied,* that internment "was not justified by military necessity." It blamed the Roosevelt administration's action on "race prejudice, war hysteria, and a failure of political leadership" and apologized to Japanese-Americans for "a grave injustice." In 1988 Congress voted to pay twenty thousand dollars in compensation to each of the nearly sixty-two thousand surviving internees; and in 1998 President Bill Clinton further apologized for the injustice by giving the nation's highest civilian honor, the Presidential Medal of Freedom, to Fred Korematsu, who had protested the evacuation decree all the way to the Supreme Court.

TRIUMPH AND TRAGEDY, 1945

Spring and summer 1945 brought stunning changes and new crises. In Europe a new balance of power emerged after the collapse of the Third Reich. In Asia continued Japanese reluctance to surrender led to the use of atomic bombs. And in the United States a new president, Harry Truman, presided over both the end of World War II and the beginning of the Cold War and the nuclear age.

The Yalta Conference By the time Roosevelt, Churchill, and Stalin met in the Soviet city of Yalta in February 1945, the military situation favored the Soviet Union. The Red Army had overrun Poland, Romania, and Bulgaria; driven the Nazis out of Yugoslavia; penetrated Austria, Hungary, and Czechoslovakia; and was massed just fifty miles from Berlin. American forces, in contrast, were still recovering from the Battle of the Bulge and facing stiff resistance on the route to Japan. The Joint Chiefs of Staff, contemplating the awesome cost in American casualties of an invasion of Japan, insisted that Stalin's help was worth almost any price. And Stalin was in a position to make demands. The Soviet Union had suffered most in the war against Germany, it already dominated eastern Europe, and, knowing that the United States did not want to fight a prolonged war against Japan, Stalin had the luxury of deciding whether and when to enter the Pacific war.

The **Yalta accords** reflected these realities. Stalin again vowed to declare war on Japan "two or three months" after Germany's surrender, and in return Churchill and Roosevelt reneged on their arrangement with Jiang Jieshi and promised the Soviet Union concessions in Manchuria and the territories it had lost in the Russo-Japanese War (1904). The Big Three delegated a final settlement of the German reparations issue to a postwar commission, and left vague the matter of partitioning Germany and its eventual reunification. The conference also vaguely called for interim governments in eastern Europe "broadly representative of all democratic elements" and for eventual freely elected permanent governments. On the matter dearest to FDR's heart, the negotiators accepted a plan for a new international organization and agreed to a founding conference of the new United Nations in San Francisco in April 1945.

Stalin proved adamant about the nature of the postwar Polish government. Twice in the twentieth century German troops had used Poland as a springboard for invading Russia. Stalin would not expose his land again, and after the Red Army had captured Warsaw in January 1945 he installed a procommunist regime and brutally

Yalta Conference, 1945 *The palaces where Roosevelt, Churchill, Stalin, and their advisers gathered were still standing, but the rest of Yalta had been reduced to ruin during the German occupation.*

subdued the anticommunist Poles. Conservative critics would later charge that FDR "gave away" eastern Europe. Actually, the Soviet Union gained little it did not already control, and short of going to war against the Soviet Union while still battling Germany and Japan, FDR could only hope that Stalin would keep his word.

Victory in Europe As the Soviets prepared for their assault on Berlin, American troops crossed the Rhine at Remagen in March 1945 and encircled the Ruhr Valley, Germany's industrial heartland. Churchill now proposed a rapid thrust to Berlin. But Eisenhower, with Roosevelt's backing, overruled Churchill. They saw no point in risking high casualties to rush to an area of Germany that had already been designated as the Soviet occupation zone. So Eisenhower advanced methodically along a broad front until the Americans met the Russians at the Elbe River on April 25. By then the Red Army had taken Vienna and reached the suburbs of Berlin. On April 30, as Soviet troops approached his headquarters, Hitler committed suicide. Berlin fell to the Soviets on May 2, and on May 8 a new German government surrendered unconditionally.

Jubilant Americans celebrated Victory in Europe (V-E) Day less than a month after they had mourned the death of their president. On April 12 an exhausted President Roosevelt had abruptly clutched his head, moaned that he had a "terrific headache," and fell unconscious. A cerebral hemorrhage ended his life. As the nation grieved, Roosevelt's unprepared successor assumed the burden of ending the war and dealing with the Soviet Union.

"I don't know whether you fellows ever had a load of hay or a bull fall on you," Harry S Truman told reporters on his first full day in office, "but last night the moon, the stars, and all the planets fell on me." An unpretentious politician awed by his new responsibilities, Truman struggled to continue FDR's policies. But Roosevelt had made no effort to familiarize his vice president with world affairs. Perhaps sensing his own inadequacies, Truman adopted a tough pose toward adversaries. In office less than two weeks, he lashed out at Soviet ambassador V. M. Molotov that the United States was tired of waiting for the Russians to allow free elections in Poland, and he threatened to cut off lend-lease aid if the Soviet Union did not cooperate. The Truman administration then reduced U.S. economic assistance to the Soviets and stalled on their request for a $1 billion reconstruction loan. Simultaneously, Stalin strengthened his grip on eastern Europe, ignoring the promises he had made at Yalta.

The United States neither conceded the Soviet sphere of influence in eastern Europe nor tried to end it. Although Truman still sought Stalin's cooperation in establishing the United Nations and in defeating Japan, Soviet-American relations deteriorated. By June 1945, when the Allied countries succeeded in framing the United Nations Charter, hopes for a new international order had dimmed, and the United Nations emerged as a diplomatic battleground. Truman, Churchill, and Stalin met at Potsdam, Germany, from July 16 to August 2 to complete the postwar arrangements begun at Yalta. But the Allied leaders could barely agree to demilitarize Germany and to punish Nazi war criminals. All the major divisive issues were postponed and left to the Council of Foreign Ministers to resolve later. Given the diplomatic impasse, only military power remained to determine the contours of the postwar world.

The Holocaust   When news of the **Holocaust**—the term later given to the Nazis' extermination of European Jewry—first leaked out in early 1942, many Americans discounted the reports. Not until November did the State Department admit knowledge of the massacres. A month later the American broadcaster Edward R. Murrow, listened to nationwide, reported on the systematic killing of millions of Jews: "It is a picture of mass murder and moral depravity unequalled in the history of the world. It is a horror beyond what imagination can grasp. . . . There are no longer 'concentration camps'—we must speak now only of 'extermination camps.'" Most Americans considered the annihilation of Europe's 6 million Jews beyond belief. There were no photographs to prove it, and, some argued, the atrocities attributed to the Germans in World War I had turned out to be false. So few took issue with the military's view that the way to liberate those enslaved by Hitler was by speedily winning the war. Pleas by American Jews for the Allies to bomb the death camps and the railroad tracks leading to them fell on deaf ears. In fall 1944 U.S. planes flying over Auschwitz in southern Poland bombed nearby factories but left the gas chambers and crematoria intact, in order, American officials explained, not to divert air power from more vital raids elsewhere. "How could it be," historian David Wyman has asked, "that Government officials knew that a place existed where 2,000 helpless human beings could be killed in less than an hour, knew that this occurred over and over again, and yet did not feel driven to search for some way to wipe such a scourge from the earth?"

How much could have been done remains uncertain. Still, the U.S. government never seriously considered rescue schemes or searched for a way to curtail the Nazis' "final solution" to the "Jewish question." Its feeble response was due to its overwhelming focus on winning the war as quickly as possible, congressional and public fears of an influx of destitute Jews into the United States, Britain's wish to placate the Arabs by keeping Jewish settlers out of Palestine, and the fear of some Jewish-American leaders that pressing the issue would increase anti-Semitism at home. The War Refugee Board managed to save the lives of just two hundred thousand Jews and twenty thousand non-Jews. Six million other Jews, about 75 percent of the European Jewish population, were gassed, shot, and incinerated, as were several million gypsies, communists, homosexuals, Polish Catholics, and others deemed unfit to live in the Third Reich.

"The things I saw beggar description," wrote General Eisenhower after visiting the first death camp liberated by the U.S. army. He sent immediately for a delegation of congressional leaders and newspaper editors to make sure Americans would never forget the gas chambers and human ovens. Only after viewing the photographs and newsreels of corpses stacked like cordwood, boxcars heaped with the bones of dead prisoners, bulldozers shoving emaciated bodies into hastily dug ditches, and liberated, barely alive living skeletons lying in their own filth, their vacant, sunken eyes staring through barbed wire, did most Americans see that the Holocaust was no myth.

The Atomic Bombs   Meanwhile, the war with Japan ground on. Early in 1945 an assault force of marines invaded Iwo Jima, 700 miles from Japan. In places termed the "Meat Grinder" and "Bloody Gorge," the marines savagely battled thousands of Japanese soldiers hidden in tunnels and behind concrete bunkers and pillboxes. Securing the five-square-mile island would cost the marines nearly twenty-seven thousand casualties, and one-third of all the marines killed in the Pacific. In June American troops waded ashore on Okinawa, 350 miles from Japan and a key staging area for the planned U.S. invasion of the Japanese home islands. Death and destruction engulfed Okinawa as waves of Americans attacked nearly impregnable Japanese defenses head-on, repeating the bloody strategy of World War I. After eighty-three days of fighting on land and sea, twelve thousand Americans lay dead and three times as many wounded, a 35 percent casualty rate, higher than at Normandy.

The appalling rate of loss on Iwo Jima and Okinawa weighed on the minds of American strategists as they thought about an invasion of the Japanese home islands. The Japanese Cabinet showed no willingness to give up the war despite Japan's being blockaded and bombed daily (on March 9–10 a fleet of B-29s dropped napalm-and-magnesium bombs on Tokyo, burning sixteen square miles of the city to the ground and killing some eighty-four thousand). Its military leaders insisted on fighting to the bitter end; surrender was unthinkable. Japan possessed an army of over 2 million, plus up to 4 million reservists and five thousand kamikaze aircraft, and the U.S. Joint Chiefs estimated that American casualties in invasions of Kyushu and Honshu (the main island of Japan) might exceed 1 million.

The successful detonation of history's first nuclear explosion at Alamogordo in mid-July gave Truman an alternative. On July 25, while meeting with Stalin and Churchill in Potsdam, Truman ordered the use of an atomic bomb if Japan did not surrender before August 3. The next day, in the **Potsdam Declaration,** he warned Japan to surrender unconditionally or face "prompt and utter destruction." Japan refused, and on August 6 a B-29 bomber named *Enola Gay* took off from the Marianas island of Tinian and dropped a uranium bomb on Hiroshima. It plunged the city into what Japanese novelist Masuji Ibuse termed "a hell of unspeakable torments." The 300,000 degree centigrade fireball incinerated houses and vaporized people. More than sixty thousand died immediately from the blast, and another seventy-five thousand died from burns and radiation poisoning by late 1945. On August 8 Stalin declared war on Japan, and U.S. planes dropped leaflets on Japan warning that another bomb would be dropped if it did not surrender. Japan refused. Its military leaders preferred death to surrender. The next day, at high noon, the *Bock's Car* flattened Nagasaki with a plutonium bomb, killing over thirty-five thousand, and injuring more than sixty thousand. On August 14, Japan accepted the American terms of surrender, which implicitly permitted the emperor to retain his throne but subordinated him to the U.S. commander of the occupation forces. General MacArthur received Japan's surrender on the battleship *Missouri* on September 2, 1945. The war was over.

While Americans at the time overwhelmingly backed the atomic bombings of Japan as the necessary way to end the war quickly and with the least cost in lives, many critics later contended that Japan would have soon surrendered without the horrendous bombing. Some believed that racist American attitudes toward the Japanese motivated the decision to drop the bombs. As war correspondent Ernie Pyle wrote, "The Japanese are looked upon as something inhuman and squirmy—like some people feel about cockroaches or mice." While racial hatred undoubtedly stirred exterminationist sentiment, those involved in the Manhattan Project had regarded Germany as the target; and, considering the ferocity of the Allied bombings of Hamburg and Dresden, there is little reason to assume that the Allies would not have dropped atomic bombs on Germany had they been available. By 1945 the Allies as well as the Axis had abandoned restraints on attacking civilians.

Other critics maintain that demonstrating the bomb's terrible destructiveness on an uninhabited island would have moved Japan to surrender. We will never know for sure. American scientists rejected a demonstration bombing because the United States had an atomic arsenal of only two bombs, and they did not know whether the mechanism for detonating them in the air would work. A large number of those critical of Truman's decision believe that the president, aware of worsening relations between the United States and the USSR, ordered the atomic attack primarily to end the Pacific war before Stalin could enter it and share in the postwar occupation of Japan. At the same time, its use might also intimidate Stalin into making concessions in eastern Europe. Referring to the Soviets, President Truman noted just before the atomic test at Alamogordo, "If it explodes, as I think it will, I'll certainly have a hammer on those boys." Truman's new secretary of state, James Byrnes, thought that the bomb would "make Russia more manageable" and would "put us in a position to dictate our own terms at the end of the war."

Although the president and his advisers believed that the atomic bombs would strengthen their hand against the Soviets, the foremost reason for Truman's decision was to shorten the war and save American lives. As throughout the war, American leaders in August 1945 relied on production and technology to win the war with the minimum loss of American life. Every new weapon was put to use; the concept of "total war" easily accommodated the bombing of civilians; and the atomic bomb was one more item in an arsenal that had already wreaked enormous destruction on the Axis. The rules of war that had once stayed the use of weapons of mass destruction against enemy civilians no longer prevailed. No responsible official counseled that the United States should sacrifice American servicemen to lessen death and destruction in Japan, or not use a weapon developed with 2 billion taxpayer dollars. To the vast majority of Americans, the atomic bomb was, in Churchill's words, "a miracle of deliverance" that saved Allied lives. So E. B. Sledge and his comrades in the First Marine Division, slated to take part in the first wave of the invasion of Japan's home islands, breathed "an indescribable sense of relief." Hearing the news of the atomic bombs and Japan's surrender, Sledge wrote, they sat in stunned silence:

> We remembered our dead. So many dead. So many maimed. So many bright futures consigned to the ashes of the past. So many dreams lost in the madness that engulfed us. Except for a few widely scattered shouts of joy, the survivors of the abyss sat hollow-eyed and silent, trying to comprehend a world without war.

The atomic bombs ended the deadliest war in history. A truly global conflict, involving over half the world's peoples, with armies ranging over continents and navies fighting on every ocean, the war affected women, men, and children as victims of civilian bombing campaigns, as war workers, as slave laborers, and comfort women. Neither side gave much quarter in seeking to destroy the other's will and resources. Some 50 million died—more than half of them noncombatants. The Soviet Union lost roughly 20 million people, China 15 million, Poland 6 million, Germany 4 million, and Japan 2 million. Much of Asia and Europe was rubble. Some four hundred thousand American servicemen had also perished, and, although physically unscathed, the United States had changed profoundly—for better and worse.

CONCLUSION

Most Americans, and their government, initially responded to the war clouds over Asia and Europe by intensifying their post–World War I isolationism. As one senator proclaimed, prior to the vote that defeated Roosevelt's effort to have the United States join the World Court, "To hell with Europe and the rest of those nations!" Not till the Japanese attack on the American fleet at Pearl Harbor, more than two years after the war in Europe had begun, did the United States enter the fray, and even then it waited until Hitler and Mussolini declared war on it before joining the armed struggle engulfing the world. Once engaged, the Americans rapidly went on a war footing. Mobilization transformed the scope and authority of the federal government, vastly expanding presidential powers. It ended the unemployment of the depression and made American industry more productive than it had ever been, and most Americans more prosperous than they had ever been. It tilted the national economic balance toward the South Atlantic, Gulf, and Pacific coasts. It accelerated trends toward bigness in business, agriculture, and labor. It involved the military in the economy and education as never before.

To achieve an unconditional victory, with the least possible cost in American lives, Roosevelt concentrated on defeating Germany first, yet delaying a second front in Europe until Soviet forces had routed the German army in eastern Europe. Meanwhile, half a world away, a two-pronged American offensive, across the central Pacific and north from Australia, brought Japan to the brink of defeat. On the home front, the war catalyzed vital changes in racial and social relations, sometimes intensifying prejudices against minorities and women, but also broadening educational and employment opportunities that widened public spheres and heightened expectations. Fighting and winning the greatest war in history, moreover, restored American faith in capitalism and democratic institutions. It was a vital coming-of-age experience for an entire generation that did much to give postwar American society a confident "can-do" spirit for the "American Century" that they knew lay ahead.

The awesome development and use of an atomic bomb bolstered that spirit and enabled the United States to defeat Japan promptly, to try to force the Soviets to be more manageable, and to avoid an invasion of the Japanese home islands that might have cost tens, possibly hundreds, of thousands of American casualties. The mass destruction of the war and total defeat of the Axis, however, brought new crises to cloud the bright dawn of peace. The world's two superpowers—the United States and USSR—soon squared off in a Cold War that would see the United States play a role in global affairs that would have seemed inconceivable to most Americans just five years before.

26

The Cold War Abroad and at Home, 1945–1952

THE POSTWAR POLITICAL SETTING, 1945–1946

The Cold War profoundly changed the United States for better and for worse. It spurred more than a quarter of a century of economic growth and prosperity, the longest such period in American history. It propelled research in medicine and science that, for the most part, made lives longer and better. And it contributed to a vast expansion of higher education that enabled many Americans to become middle class.

Demobilization and Reconversion — When the war ended, GIs and civilians alike wanted those who had served overseas "home alive in '45." Troops demanding transport ships barraged Congress with threats of "no boats, no votes." On a single day in December 1945, sixty thousand postcards arrived at the White House with the message "Bring the Boys Home by Christmas." Truman bowed to popular demand, and by 1948 American military strength had dropped from 12 million to just 1.5 million.

Returning veterans faced readjustment problems intensified by a soaring divorce rate and a drastic housing shortage. Others feared the return of mass unemployment and economic depression as war plants closed, and memories revived of the hard times immediately after World War I (see Chapter 22). Defense spending dropped from $76 billion in 1945 to under $20 billion in 1946, and more than a million defense jobs vanished.

By the end of the decade more women were working outside the home than during World War II. Most took jobs in traditional women's fields, especially office work and sales, to pay for family needs. Although the postwar economy created new openings for women in the labor market, many public figures urged women to seek fulfillment at

CHRONOLOGY, 1945–1952

1944 • Servicemen's Readjustment Act (GI Bill).

1945 • Postwar strike wave begins.

1946 • Employment Act.
George Kennan's "long telegram."
Winston Churchill's "iron curtain" speech.
Coal miners' strike.
Inflation soars to more than 18 percent.
Republicans win control of Congress.

1947 • Truman Doctrine.
Federal Employee Loyalty Program.
Jackie Robinson breaks major league baseball's color line.
Taft-Hartley Act.
National Security Act.
President's Committee on Civil Rights issues *To Secure These Rights.*
HUAC holds hearings on Hollywood.

1948 • Communist coup in Czechoslovakia.
State of Israel founded.
Berlin airlift.
Congress approves Marshall Plan to aid Europe.
Truman orders an end to segregation in the armed forces.
Communist leaders put on trial under the Smith Act.
Truman elected president.

1949 • North Atlantic Treaty Organization (NATO) established.
East and West Germany founded as separate nations.
Communist victory in China; People's Republic of China established.
Soviet Union detonates an atomic bomb.

1950 • Soviet spy ring at Los Alamos uncovered.
Joseph McCarthy launches anticommunist crusade.
Korean War begins.
McCarran Internal Security Act.
Truman accepts NSC-68.
China enters the Korean War.

1951 • Julius and Ethel Rosenberg convicted of espionage.

1952 • First hydrogen bomb exploded.
Dwight D. Eisenhower elected president.
Republicans win control of Congress.

home. Popular culture romanticized married bliss and demonized career women as a threat to social stability.

The GI Bill of Rights The Servicemen's Readjustment Act of 1944, commonly called the GI Bill of Rights or **GI Bill,** was designed to forestall the expected recession by easing veterans back into the work force, and to reward the "soldier boys" and reduce their fears of female competition. The GI Bill gave veterans priority for many jobs, occupational guidance, and, if need be, fifty-two weeks of unemployment benefits. It also established veterans' hospitals and provided low-interest loans to returning GIs who were starting businesses or buying homes or farms. Almost four million veterans bought homes with government loans, fueling a baby boom, suburbanization, and a record demand for new goods and services.

Most vitally, the government promised to pay up to four years of further education or job training for veterans. Not all Americans approved. Some opposed it as opening the door to socialism or to demands by minorities to special entitlements. Many university administrators, fearing that "riffraff" would sully their bastions of privilege,

Veterans Go to College *So many World War II veterans wanted to use their GI benefits for higher education that colleges were overwhelmed; many had to turn away students. In 1946, registration of new students was done at temporary desks set up in Wildermuth Field House at Indiana University.*

FIGURE 26.1 **Gross National Product, 1929–1990**

Following World War II, the United States achieved the highest living standard in world history. Between 1950 and 1970, the real GNP, which factors out inflation and reveals the actual amount of goods and services produced, steadily increased. However, in 1972, 1974–1975, 1980, and 1982 the real GNP declined. *Source: Economic Report of the President, 1991.* Note: Data shown in 1982 dollars.

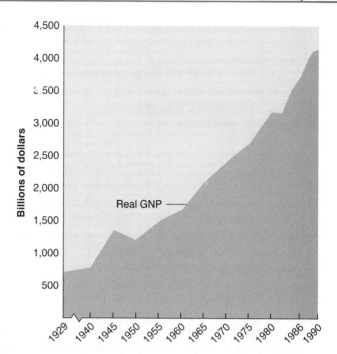

echoed the complaint of the University of Chicago president that their hallowed halls of learning would become "educational hobo jungles."

In 1946, flush with stipends of sixty-five dollars a month—ninety dollars for those with dependents—and up to five hundred dollars a year for tuition and books, 1.5 million veterans were attending college, spurring a huge increase in higher education and the creation of many new state and community colleges. California State University established additional campuses in Fullerton, Hayward, Long Beach, Los Angeles, Northridge, Sacramento, and San Bernardino. Various "normal schools" for the training of teachers were upgraded into full-fledged colleges to create the State University of New York in 1948. Veterans made up over half of all college students in 1947. Often married and the fathers of young children, they were less interested in knowledge ("what good will it do me?") than in a degree and a higher-paying job. To accommodate them, colleges converted old military barracks and Quonset huts into so-called Veterans' Village housing units and featured accelerated programs and more vocational or career-oriented courses.

To make room for the millions of GIs pursuing higher education after the war, many colleges limited the percentage of women admitted or barred students from out of state. The percentage of female college graduates dropped from 40 percent in 1949 to 25 percent in 1950. By then most women students were the working wives of the 8 million veterans who took advantage of the GI Bill to go college.

The GI Bill democratized higher education. By 1956 nearly 10 million veterans had used the GI Bill to enroll in colleges, universities, and vocational training programs (most the first in their families to do so). No longer a citadel of privilege, universities awarded twice as many degrees in 1950 as in 1940. Two decades later, these educated veterans expected their children to follow suit. Higher education became an accepted part of the American Dream.

The cost was huge, but well spent. The $15 billion that veterans received sent them to colleges and technical schools, helped them buy homes, and financed their new businesses. It propelled millions of veterans into the middle class, heightening the postwar demand for goods and services.

The Economic Boom Begins

In addition to the assistance given returning servicemen, a 1945 tax cut of $6 billion spurred corporate investment in new factories and equipment and helped produce an economic boom that began in late 1946. Further kindling postwar growth and prosperity, Americans spent much of the $135 billion they had saved from wartime work and service pay to satisfy their desire for consumer goods formerly beyond their means or not produced during the war. Advertisements promising "a Ford in your future" and an "all-electric kitchen of the future" also increased the desire to consume, and sales of homes, cars, and appliances skyrocketed. Scores of new products—televisions, high-fidelity phonographs, filter cigarettes, automatic transmissions, freezers, and air conditioners—became hallmarks of the middle-class lifestyle.

The Bretton Woods Agreement (1944) among the Allies had set the stage for the United States to become economic leader of the noncommunist world. It created the International Monetary Fund (IMF) to stabilize exchange rates by valuing ("pegging") other currencies in relation to the U.S. dollar; established the International Bank for Reconstruction and Development (World Bank) to help rebuild war-battered Asia and Europe; and laid the groundwork for the 1947 General Agreement on Tariffs and Trade (GATT) to break up closed trading blocs and expand international trade. Since the United States largely controlled and funded these powerful economic institutions, they gave the United States an especially favorable position in international trade and finance.

With many nations in ruins, American firms could import raw materials cheaply; with little competition from other industrial countries, they could increase exports to record levels. U.S. economic dominance also resulted from the 35 percent increase in the productivity of American workers in the decade following the war. Wartime advances in science and technology, which led to revolutionary developments in such industries as electronics and plastics, further bolstered visions of limitless growth and the dawn of "the American century."

Truman's Domestic Program

Americans' hunger for the fruits of affluence left them with little appetite for extending the New Deal. Truman agreed. "I don't want any experiments," he confided. "The American people have been through a lot of experiments and they want a rest." His only major domestic accomplishment in the Seventy-ninth Congress was the **Employment Act of 1946.** It committed the federal government to ensuring economic growth and established the Council of Economic Advisers to confer with the president and formulate policies for maintaining employment, production, and purchasing power. Congress, however, gutted both the goal of full employment and the enhanced executive powers to achieve that objective.

Congressional eagerness to dismantle wartime controls worsened the nation's chief economic problem: inflation. Consumer demand outran the supply of goods, intensifying the pressure on prices. The Office of Price Administration (OPA) sought to hold the line by enforcing price controls, but food producers, manufacturers, and retailers opposed continuing wartime controls. While some consumers favored the OPA, others deplored it as an irksome relic of wartime regulations. In June 1946, Truman vetoed a bill that would have extended the OPA's life, but deprived it of power, effectively ending all price controls. Within a week food costs rose 16 percent and the price of beef doubled. "PRICES SOAR, BUYERS SORE, STEERS JUMP OVER THE MOON," headlined the *New York Daily News*.

Congress then passed, and Truman signed, a second bill extending price controls in weakened form. Protesting any price controls, however, farmers and meat producers threatened to withhold food from the market. Knowing that "meatless voters are opposition voters," Truman lifted controls on food prices just before the 1946 midterm elections. When Democrats fared poorly anyway, Truman ended all price controls. By then the consumer price index had jumped nearly 25 percent since the end of the war.

Sharp price rises and shrinking paychecks shorn of overtime goaded organized labor to demand higher wages. More than 4.5 million workers went on strike in 1946. When a United Mine Workers walkout paralyzed the economy for forty days, Truman ordered the army to seize the mines. A week later, after Truman had pressured owners to grant most of the union's demands, the miners returned to work, only to walk out again six months later. Meanwhile, on the heels of the first mine workers settlement, railway engineers and trainmen announced that they would shut down the nation's railroad system for the first time in history. "If you think I'm going to sit here and let you tie up this whole country," Truman shouted at the heads of the two unions, "you're crazy as hell." In May he asked Congress for authority to draft workers who struck vital industries. Before he could finish his speech, the unions gave in. Still, Truman's threat alienated labor leaders.

By the fall of 1946, Truman had angered most major interest groups. Less than a third of the Americans polled approved of his performance. "To err is Truman," some gibed. Summing up the public discontent, Republicans asked, "Had enough?" In the 1946 elections, they captured twenty-five governorships and, for the first time since 1928, won control of both houses of Congress.

The public mood reflected more than just economic discontent. Under the surface laughter at stores advertising atomic sales or bartenders mixing atomic cocktails ran a new, deep current of fear, symbolized by the rash of "flying saucer" sightings that had begun after the war. An NBC radio program depicted a nuclear attack on Chicago in which most people died instantly. "Those few who escaped the blast, but not the gamma rays, died slowly after they had left the ruined city," intoned the narrator. "No attempt at identification of the bodies or burial ever took place. Chicago was simply closed." There was much talk of urban dispersal—resettling people in small communities in the country's vast open spaces—and of how to protect oneself in a nuclear attack. Schoolchildren wore dog tags in order to be identified after an atomic attack, and practiced crawling under their desks and putting their hands over their heads— "Duck and Cover"—to protect themselves from the bomb. The end of World War II had brought an uneasy peace.

ANTICOMMUNISM AND CONTAINMENT, 1946–1952

By late 1946 the simmering antagonisms between Moscow and Washington had come to a boil. With the Nazis defeated, the "shotgun wedding" between the United States and the USSR dissolved into a struggle to fill the power vacuums left by the defeat of Germany and Japan, the exhaustion of Western Europe, and the crumbling of colonial empires in Asia and Africa. Misperception and misunderstanding mounted as the two powers sought greater security, each feeding the other's fears. The Cold War resulted.

Polarization and Cold War   The destiny of Eastern Europe, especially Poland, stood at the heart of the strife between the United States and the USSR. Wanting to end the Soviet Union's vulnerability to invasions from the West, Stalin insisted on a demilitarized Germany and a buffer zone of nations friendly to Russia along its western flank. He considered a Soviet sphere of influence in Eastern Europe essential to Russian security, a just reward for bearing the brunt of the war against Germany, and no different than the American spheres of influence in Western Europe, Japan, and Latin America. Stalin also believed that Roosevelt and Churchill had implicitly accepted a Soviet zone in Eastern Europe at the Yalta Conference (see Chapter 25).

With the Red Army occupying half of Europe at war's end, Stalin installed pro-Soviet puppet governments in Bulgaria, Hungary, and Romania, and supported the establishment of communist regimes in nominally independent Albania and Yugoslavia. Ignoring the Yalta Declaration of Liberated Europe, Stalin barred free elections in Poland and brutally suppressed Polish democratic parties. Poland, he said, was "not only a question of honor for Russia, but one of life and death."

Stalin's insistence on dominance in Eastern Europe collided with Truman's unwillingness to concede Soviet supremacy beyond Russia's borders. What Stalin saw as critical to Russian security, Truman viewed as a violation of national self-determination, a betrayal of democracy, and a cover for communist aggression. Truman and his advisers believed that the appeasement of dictators only fed their appetites for expansion. They thought that traditional balance-of-power politics and spheres of influence had precipitated both world wars, and that only a new world order based on the self-determination of all nations working in good faith within the United Nations could guarantee peace.

Truman also thought that accepting the "enforced sovietization" of Eastern Europe would betray American war aims and condemn nations rescued from Hitler's tyranny to another totalitarian dictatorship. He worried, too, that a Soviet stranglehold on Eastern Europe would hurt American businesses dependent on exports and on access to raw materials. In addition, Truman understood that the Democratic Party would invite political disaster if he reneged on the Yalta agreements. The Democrats counted on winning most of the votes of the 6 million Polish-Americans and millions of other Americans of Eastern European origin, who remained keenly interested in the fates of their homelands. He resolved not to appear "soft on communism."

Combativeness fit the temperament of the feisty Truman. Eager to demonstrate his command, the president matched Stalin's intransigence on controlling Poland with his own demands for Polish free elections. Encouraged by America's monopoly of atomic weapons and its position as the world's economic superpower, the new president hoped that the United States could control the terms of the postwar settlement. His foreign policy sought, in the words of a November 1945 State Department document, to "establish the kind of world we want to live in."

The Iron Curtain Descends	As Truman's assertiveness deepened Stalin's mistrust of the West, the Soviet Union tightened its grip on Eastern Europe,

stepped up its confiscation of materials and factories from occupied territories, and forced its satellite nations (countries under Soviet control) to close their doors to American trade and influence. In a February 1946 speech that the White House considered a "declaration of World War III," Stalin asserted that there could be no lasting peace with capitalism and vowed to overcome the American lead in weaponry no matter what the cost.

Two weeks later, **George F. Kennan,** an American diplomat in Moscow, wired a long telegram to the State Department. A leading student of Russian affairs, Kennan described Soviet expansionism as moving "inexorably along a prescribed path, like a toy automobile wound up and headed in a given direction, stopping only when it meets some unanswerable force." Therefore, U.S. policy must be the "long-term, patient but firm and vigilant containment of Russian expansive tendencies," with the expectation that the Soviet state would eventually mellow or break up. Truman, who had already insisted that the time had come "to stop babying the Soviets" and "to get tough with Russia," accepted Kennan's advice. **Containment**—a policy uniting military, economic, and diplomatic strategies to "contain" any further Soviet communist expansion and to enhance America's security and influence abroad—became Washington gospel.

In early March 1946 Truman accompanied Winston Churchill to Westminister College in Missouri. In a speech, the former British prime minister warned of a new threat to Western democracies, this time from Moscow. Stalin, he said, had drawn an iron curtain across the eastern half of Europe. To meet the threat of further Soviet aggression, Churchill called for an alliance of the English-speaking peoples and the maintenance of an Anglo-American monopoly of atomic weapons: "There is nothing the Communists admire so much as strength and nothing for which they have less respect than for military weakness."

Truman agreed. In spring 1946, he threatened to send in American combat troops unless the Soviets withdrew from oil-rich Iran. In June he submitted an atomic-energy control plan to the United Nations requiring the Soviet Union to stop all work on nuclear weapons and to submit to UN inspections before the United States destroyed its own atomic arsenal. As expected, the Soviets rejected the proposal and offered an alternative plan equally unacceptable to the United States. As mutual hostility escalated, the Soviets and Americans rushed to develop their own doomsday weapons. In 1946 Congress established the Atomic Energy Commission (AEC) to develop nuclear energy and nuclear weaponry. The AEC devoted more than 90 percent of its effort to atomic weapon development. By 1950, one AEC adviser reckoned, the United States "had a stockpile capable of somewhat more than reproducing World War II in a single day."

Thus, less than a year after American and Soviet soldiers had jubilantly met at the Elbe River to celebrate Hitler's defeat, the Cold War had begun. It would be waged by economic pressure, nuclear intimidation, propaganda, subversion, and proxy wars (fought by governments and peoples allied to the principals rather than a direct military clash of the principals). Many Americans would view it as an ideological conflict pitting democracy against dictatorship, freedom against totalitarianism, religion against atheism, and capitalism against socialism. It would affect American life as decisively as any military engagement that the nation had fought.

Containing Communism

On February 21, 1947, the British informed the United States that they could no longer afford to assist Greece and Turkey in their struggles against communist-supported insurgents and Soviet pressure for access to the Mediterranean. A stricken Britain asked the United States to bear the costs of thwarting communism in the eastern Mediterranean. The harsh European winter, the most severe in memory, intensified the sense of urgency in Washington. The economies of Western Europe had come to a near-halt. Famine and tuberculosis plagued the Continent. European colonies in Africa and Asia had risen in revolt. Cigarettes and candy bars circulated as currency in Germany, and the communist parties in France and Italy appeared ready to topple democratic coalition governments. Truman decided to meet the challenge.

He first had to mobilize support for a radical departure from the American tradition of avoiding entangling alliances. In a tense White House on February 27, the new secretary of state, former army chief of staff George C. Marshall, presented the case for

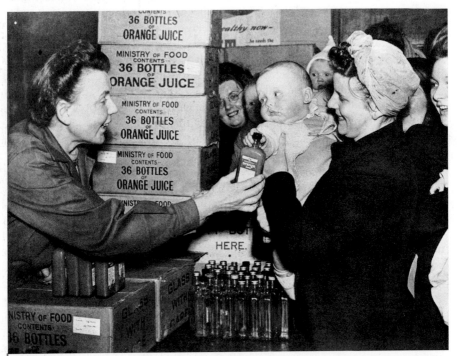

American Food for a Hungry Europe *Grateful English mothers line up for orange juice sent by the United States to assist Europeans devastated by the Second World War.*

aid to Greece and Turkey. Congressional leaders balked, more concerned about inflation at home than civil war in Greece. But Dean Acheson, the newly appointed undersecretary of state, seized the moment. The issue, he said, was not one of assisting the repressive Greek oligarchy and Turkey's military dictatorship, but rather a universal struggle of freedom against tyranny. "Like apples in a barrel infected by the corruption of one rotten one," he warned, the fall of Greece or Turkey would open Asia, Western Europe, and the oil fields of the Middle East to the Red menace. "The Soviet Union [is] playing one of the greatest gambles in history," Acheson declaimed. "We and we alone are in a position to break up this play." Shaken, the congressional leaders agreed to support the administration's request if Truman could "scare hell out of the country."

Truman could and did. On March 12, 1947, addressing a joint session of Congress and a national radio audience, he asked for $400 million in military assistance to Greece and Turkey. Going far beyond the immediate issues in the two countries, the **Truman Doctrine** pictured the matter as part of a global struggle "between alternative ways of life." One way promised "freedom" and "liberty," the other "oppression" and "terror." In a world endangered by evil communism, therefore, the United States must support free peoples everywhere "resisting attempted subjugation by armed minorities or by outside pressures." His rhetorical defense of freedom—using the words "free" or "freedom" twenty-four times in an eighteen-minute speech—worked. Congress appropriated funds that helped the Greek monarchy defeat the rebel movement and helped Turkey stay out of the Soviet orbit.

The Truman Doctrine of active U.S. engagement to contain communism persisted long after the crisis in the Mediterranean. It proclaimed the nation's intention to be a global policeman, everywhere on guard against advances by the Soviet Union and its allies, and it became as comprehensive as the Monroe Doctrine's "Keep Out" sign posted on the Western Hemisphere. Most Americans accepted its notion of America defending freedom against the forces of darkness as the essence of the Cold War, and the doctrine guided American foreign policy for much of the next four decades.

To back up the new international initiative, Congress passed the **National Security Act of 1947,** unifying the armed forces under a single Department of Defense, creating the National Security Council (NSC) to provide foreign-policy information to the White House and advise the president on strategic matters, and establishing the Central Intelligence Agency (CIA) to gather information abroad and engage in covert activities in support of the nation's security. Congress also approved the administration's proposal for massive U.S. assistance for European recovery in 1947. Advocated by the secretary of state, and thus called the **Marshall Plan,** the European Recovery Plan (ERP) was to be another weapon in the arsenal against the spread of communism. With Europe, in Churchill's words, "a rubble heap . . . a breeding ground of pestilence and hate," Truman wanted to end the economic devastation believed to spawn communism. Truman correctly guessed that the Soviet Union and its satellites would refuse to take part in the plan, because of the controls linked to it, and accurately foresaw that Western European economic recovery would expand sales of American goods abroad and promote prosperity in the United States.

Although denounced by the Left as a "Martial Plan" and by isolationist voices on the Right as a "Share-the-American-Wealth Plan," the Marshall Plan more than fulfilled its sponsors' hopes. By 1952, industrial production had risen 200 percent in Western Europe, and the economic and social chaos that communists had exploited had been overcome in the sixteen nations that shared the $17 billion in aid provided by the ERP. Its slogan, "Prosperity Makes You Free," had been vindicated, and, not incidentally, Western Europe had become a major center of American trade and investment.

Confrontation in Germany The Soviet Union reacted to the Truman Doctrine and the Marshall Plan by tightening its grip on Eastern Europe. Communist takeovers added Hungary and Czechoslovakia to the Soviet bloc in 1947 and 1948, and Stalin set his sights on Germany. The 1945 Potsdam Agreement had divided Germany into four separate zones (administered by France, Great Britain, the Soviet Union, and the United States) and created a joint four-power administration for Germany's capital, Berlin, lying 110 miles within the Soviet-occupied eastern zone. As the Cold War intensified, the Western powers moved toward uniting their zones into an anti-Soviet West German state to help contain communism. Stalin responded in June 1948 by blocking all rail and highway routes through the Soviet zone into Berlin. He calculated that the Western powers would be unable to provision the 2 million Berliners under their control and would either have to abandon plans to create a West German nation or accept a communist Berlin.

Truman resolved neither to abandon Berlin nor to shoot his way into the city and possibly trigger World War III. Instead he ordered a massive airlift to provide Berliners with the food and fuel necessary for survival. American cargo planes landed in West Berlin every three minutes around the clock, bringing a mountain of supplies. To prevent the Soviets from shooting down the U.S. planes, Truman hinted that he would use "the bomb" if necessary and ordered a fleet of B-29s, the only planes capable of delivering atomic bombs, to English bases in July 1948. Tensions rose. The president confided to his diary "we are very close to war." Meanwhile, the **Berlin airlift** continued to provide the blockaded city with a precarious lifeline.

In May 1949 the Soviets ended the blockade. Stalin's gambit had failed. The airlift highlighted American determination and technological prowess, revealed Stalin's readiness to use innocent people as pawns, and dramatically heightened anti-Soviet feeling in the West. U.S. public-opinion polls in late 1948 revealed an overwhelming demand for "firmness and increased 'toughness' in relations with Russia."

Continuing fears of a Soviet attack on Western Europe fostered support for a rearmed West German state and for an Atlantic collective security alliance. In May 1949 the United States, Britain, and France ended their occupation of Germany and approved the creation of the Federal Republic of Germany (West Germany). A month earlier, ten nations of Western Europe had signed the North Atlantic Treaty, establishing a mutual defense pact with the United States and Canada in which "an armed attack against one or more of them . . . shall be considered an attack against them all." For the first time in its history, the United States entered into a peacetime military alliance. In effect, Western Europe now lay under the American "nuclear umbrella," protected from Soviet invasion by the U.S. threat of nuclear retaliation. Senator Robert Taft of Ohio, speaking for a small band of Republican senators, warned that this agreement would provoke the Soviets to respond in kind, stimulate a massive arms race, and open the floodgates of American military aid to Europe. But the Senate overwhelmingly approved the treaty, and in July the United States officially joined the **North Atlantic Treaty Organization (NATO),** marking the formal end of U.S. isolationism.

Truman ranked the Marshall Plan and NATO as his proudest achievements, convinced that if the latter had been in existence in 1914 and 1939, the world would have been spared two disastrous wars. Accordingly, he spurred Congress to authorize $1.3 billion for military assistance to NATO nations, persuaded General Dwight D. Eisenhower to become supreme commander of NATO forces, and authorized the stationing of four American army divisions in Europe as the nucleus of the NATO armed force. As Taft had predicted, the Soviet Union responded in kind. It created the German Democratic Republic (East Germany) in 1949, exploded its own atomic bomb that same year, and, in 1955, set up a rival Eastern bloc military alliance, the Warsaw Pact. The United States and Soviet Union had divided Europe into two armed camps.

The Cold War in Asia   Moscow-Washington hostility also carved Asia into contending camps. The Russians created a sphere of influence in Manchuria; the Americans denied Moscow a role in postwar Japan; and both partitioned a helpless Korea.

As head of the U.S. occupation forces in Japan, General Douglas MacArthur oversaw that nation's transformation from an empire in ruins into a prosperous democracy. In 1952, the occupation ended, but a military security treaty allowed the U.S. to retain its Japanese bases on the Soviet-Asian perimeter and brought Japan under the American "nuclear umbrella." In further pursuit of containment, the United States helped crush a procommunist insurgency in the Philippines and aided French efforts to reestablish colonial rule in Indochina (Vietnam, Laos, and Cambodia), despite American declarations in favor of national self-determination and against imperialism.

In China, however, U.S. efforts to block communism failed. The Truman administration first tried to mediate the civil war between the Nationalist government of Jiang Jieshi and the communist forces of **Mao Zedong,** hoping to arrange a coalition government that would end the bloody conflict raging since the 1930s. It also sent nearly $3 billion in aid to the Nationalists between 1945 and 1949. But American dollars could not force Jiang's corrupt and unpopular government to reform itself and win the support of the Chinese people. As Mao's well-disciplined and motivated troops marched south, Jiang's soldiers mutinied or surrendered without a fight. Unable to stem revolutionary sentiment or to hold the countryside, where 85 percent of the population lived and where the communists, in Mao's words, "swam like fishes in the peasant sea," Jiang's regime collapsed and withdrew to the island of Taiwan.

Mao's establishment of the communist People's Republic of China (PRC) shocked Americans. The most populous nation in the world, seen by Washington as a counterforce to Asian communism and a market for American exports, had become "Red China." Although the Truman administration insisted that it could have done nothing to alter the outcome and placed the blame for Jiang's defeat on his failure to reform China, most Americans were unconvinced. China's "fall" especially embittered conservatives who believed that America's interests lay in Asia, not Europe. "China asked for a sword," proclaimed one Republican senator, "and we gave her a dull paring knife." The pressure from conservatives influenced the administration's refusal to recognize the PRC, block its admission to the United Nations, and proclaim Jiang's Nationalist regime in Taiwan as the legitimate government of China.

In September 1949, as the "Who lost China" debate raged, the president announced that the Soviet Union had exploded an atomic bomb. The loss of the nuclear monopoly

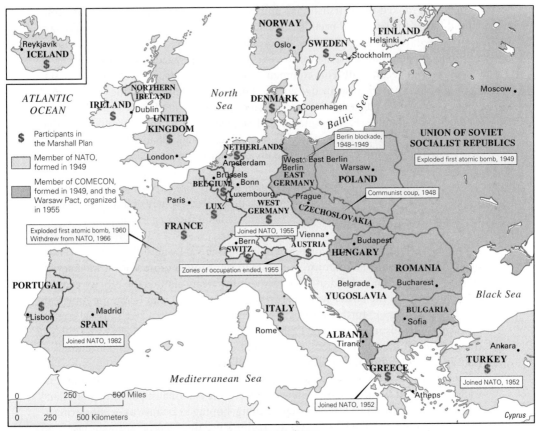

MAP 26.1 The Postwar Division of Europe, 1945–1989

The wartime dispute between the Soviet Union and the Western Allies over Poland's future hardened after World War II into a Cold War that split Europe into competing American and Russian spheres of influence. Across an "iron curtain," NATO countries faced the Warsaw Pact nations.

shattered illusions of American invincibility. Ordinary Americans sought safety in civil defense. Public schools held air-raid drills. "We took the drills seriously," recalled novelist Annie Dillard; "surely Pittsburgh, which had the nation's steel, coke, and aluminum, would be the enemy's first target." Four million Americans volunteered to be Sky Watchers, looking for Soviet planes. More than a million purchased or constructed their own family bomb shelters. Those who could not afford a bomb shelter were advised by the Federal Civil Defense Administration to "jump in any handy ditch or gutter . . . bury your face in your arms . . . never lose your head."

In January 1950, stung by charges that he was "soft on communism," Truman ordered a crash program to build a fusion-based hydrogen bomb (H-bomb). In November 1952, the United States exploded its first thermonuclear bomb, nicknamed Mike, 500 times more powerful than an atomic bomb. The blast completely vaporized one of the Marshall Islands in the Pacific, carved a mile-long crater in the ocean floor, and

FIGURE **26.2**
National Defense Spending, 1941–1960

In 1950, the defense budget was $13 billion, less than a third of the total federal outlay. In 1961, defense spending reached $47 billion, fully half of the federal budget and almost 10 percent of the gross national product. *Source:* From *American Promise, Vol. 2, 4th ed.,* by James A. Henretta et al. Reprinted with permission of Bedford/St. Martin's.

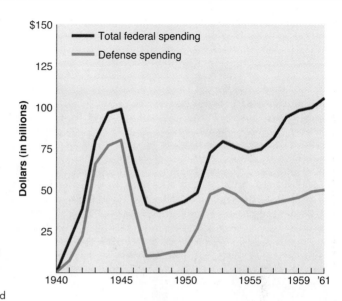

spilled radioactive dust over thousands of square miles. "You would swear the whole world was on fire," a sailor wrote home. Nine months later the Soviets detonated their own H-bomb. The balance of terror escalated.

Truman also called for a top-secret review of defense policy by the National Security Council in early 1950. Completed in April, its secret report, **NSC-68,** emphasized the Soviet Union's military strength and aggressive intentions. To counter the USSR's "design for world domination"—the mortal challenge posed by the Soviet Union "not only to this Republic but to civilization itself"—NSC-68 urged massive increases in America's nuclear arsenal, a large standing army, vigorous covert actions by the CIA, and a quadrupling of the defense budget to wage a global struggle against communism. Truman hesitated to swallow the NSC's expensive medicine. An aide to Secretary of State Acheson recalled, "We were sweating over it, and then, with regard to NSC-68, thank God Korea came along." By the end of 1950 NSC-68 had become official U.S. policy.

The Korean War, 1950–1953
After World War II the United States and Soviet Union temporarily divided Korea, which had been controlled by Japan since the Russo-Japanese War of 1904, at the thirty-eighth parallel. This line then solidified into a *de facto* border between the American-supported Republic of Korea, or South Korea, and the Soviet-backed Democratic People's Republic of Korea in the north, each claiming the sole right to rule all of Korea, and each seeking to undermine the other with economic pressure and military raids.

On June 24, 1950, North Korean troops, aided by Soviet arms and Chinese training, swept across the thirty-eighth parallel to attack South Korea. Truman decided to fight back, viewing the assault not as an intensification of a simmering Korean civil war but rather as a communist test of U.S. will and its containment policy. "Korea is the Greece

A Racially Integrated Unit in the Korean War *The Korean War was the first war in U.S. history in which most soldiers fought in racially integrated units. President Truman had ordered the integration of the armed forces in 1948, despite the oppositon of many military officers, and the successful performance of African-Americans in Korea accelerated acceptance of military integration.*

of the Far East," Truman maintained. "If we are tough enough now, if we stand up to them like we did in Greece . . . they won't take any next steps." Mindful of the failure of appeasement at Munich in 1938, he believed that the communists were doing in Korea exactly what Hitler and the Japanese had done in the 1930s: "Nobody had stood up to them. And that is what led to the Second World War." Having been accused of "selling out" Eastern Europe and "losing" China, Truman needed to prove he could stand up to "the Reds."

Without consulting Congress, Truman ordered air and naval forces to Korea from their bases in Japan on June 27. That same day he asked the United Nations to authorize action to repel the invasion. The Soviet delegate was boycotting the Security Council to protest the UN's unwillingness to seat a representative from Mao's China, and Truman gained approval for a UN "police action" to restore South Korea's border. He appointed General Douglas MacArthur to command the UN effort and ordered American ground troops into what now became the **Korean War.** The Cold War had turned hot.

North Korean forces initially routed the disorganized American and South Korean troops. "All day and night we ran like antelopes," recalled Sergeant Raymond Remp. "We didn't know our officers. They didn't know us. We lost everything we had." Then, in mid-September, with UN forces cornered on the tip of the peninsula around Pusan, struggling to avoid being pushed into the sea, MacArthur's troops landed at Inchon in a brilliant amphibious maneuver. Within two weeks, U.S. and South Korean forces

MAP 26.2 The Korean War, 1950–1953

The experience of fighting an undeclared war for the limited objective of containing communism confused the generation of Americans who had just fought an all-out war for the total defeat of the Axis. General MacArthur spoke for the many who were frustrated by the Korean conflict's mounting costs in blood and dollars: "There is no substitute for victory."

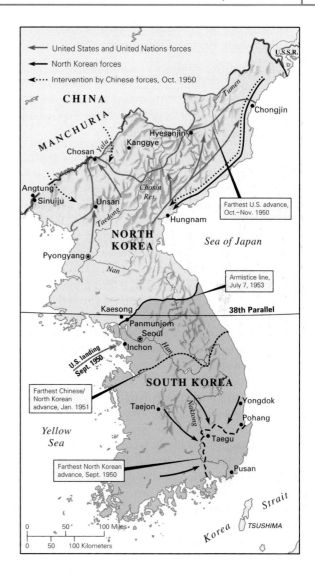

United States and United Nations forces

North Korean forces

Intervention by Chinese forces, Oct. 1950

CHINA

MANCHURIA

U.S.S.R.

Tumen

Chongjin

Hyesanjin

Kanggye

Chosan   Yalu

Angtung

Sinuiju   Unsan

Taedong

Chosin Res.

Farthest U.S. advance, Oct.–Nov. 1950

Hungnam

NORTH KOREA

Sea of Japan

Pyongyang

Nan

Armistice line, July 7, 1953

Kaesong

Panmunjom

Seoul

Inchon

Han

38th Parallel

U.S. landing Sept. 1950

Farthest Chinese/ North Korean advance, Jan. 1951

SOUTH KOREA

Taejon

Naktong

Yongdok

Pohang

Yellow Sea

Taegu

Farthest North Korean advance, Sept. 1950

Pusan

Korea   Strait   TSUSHIMA

0   50   100 Miles

0   50   100 Kilometers

drove the North Koreans back across the thirty-eighth parallel. Basking in victory, MacArthur persuaded Truman to let him go beyond the UN mandate to repel aggression and to cross the border to liberate all of Korea from communism.

As UN troops approached the Yalu River—the boundary between Korea and China—the Chinese warned that they would not "sit back with folded hands and let the Americans come to the border." Dismissing the threat as "hot air," MacArthur deployed his forces in a thin line below the river. On November 25, thirty-three Chinese divisions (about three hundred thousand men) counterattacked, driving stunned marines and soldiers below the thirty-eighth parallel in what *Time* magazine called "the worst military setback the United States has ever suffered." By March 1951, the fighting was deadlocked at roughly the original dividing line between the two Koreas.

"We were eyeball to eyeball," recalled Bev Scott, one of the first black lieutenants to head a racially integrated infantry squad.

> Just 20 meters of no man's land between us. We couldn't move at all in the daytime without getting shot at. . . . It was like World War I. We lived in a maze of bunkers and deep trenches. . . . There were bodies strewn all over the place. Hundreds of bodies frozen in the snow. We could see the arms and legs sticking up. Nobody could get their dead out of there.

Stalemated, Truman reversed course and sought a negotiated peace based on the original objective of restoring the integrity of South Korea. MacArthur rocked the boat, however, calling for an escalation of the war. Chafing at civilian control of the military, the general wanted authority to blockade and bomb Mao's China and to "unleash" Jiang Jieshi's forces to invade the mainland. But Truman, fearing such actions would bring the Soviet Union into the conflict and perhaps trigger a nuclear war, would have none of it. "We are trying to prevent a world war—not start one."

When MacArthur bluntly and repeatedly criticized Truman's limited war—the "appeasement of Communism"—the president fired the general for insubordination on April 10, 1951, replacing him with General Matthew Ridgway. The Joint Chiefs endorsed Truman's decision, but public opinion backed the general. He returned to the United States a genuine folk hero. The very idea of limited war, of containing rather than defeating the enemy, baffled many Americans; and the mounting toll of American casualties in pursuit of a stalemate angered them. It seemed senseless. Despite the warning by General Omar Bradley, chairman of the Joint Chiefs of Staff, that MacArthur's proposals "would involve us in the wrong war at the wrong place in the wrong time and with the wrong enemy," a growing number of Americans listened sympathetically to Republican charges that communist agents controlled American policy.

Truman, meanwhile, found himself bogged down in Korea, unable to win the war or craft a peace. After two more years of fighting, the two sides reached an armistice in July 1953 that left Korea as divided as it had been at the start of the war. The "limited" conflict cost the United States 54,246 lives (about 33,700 of them direct battlefield deaths), another 103,284 wounded, and some $54 billion. The Chinese lost about 900,000 men, and the two Korean armies lost some 800,000. Following the pattern of World War II, massive U.S. "carpet bombing" killed over 2 million civilians, and left North Korea looking like a moonscape.

The Korean War had significant consequences. It accelerated implementation of NSC-68 and the expansion of the containment doctrine into a global commitment. Between 1950 and 1953, defense spending zoomed from $13 billion to $60 billion—from one-third to two-thirds of the entire federal budget—the U.S. army grew from about half a million men to 3.6 million, and the American atomic stockpile mushroomed from 150 to 750 nuclear warheads. The United States acquired new bases around the world, committed itself to rearm West Germany, and joined a mutual-defense pact with Australia and New Zealand. Increased military aid flowed to Jiang Jieshi on Taiwan, and American dollars supported the French army fighting the communist Ho Chi Minh in Indochina. By 1954, the United States was paying three-quarters of French war costs in Vietnam.

Truman's intervention in Korea preserved a precarious balance of power in Asia, and stepped up the administration's commitment to the anticommunist struggle. Containment, originally advanced to justify U.S. aid to Greece and Turkey, had become the ideological foundation for a major war in Korea and, ominously, for a deepening U.S. involvement in Vietnam, intensifying public fears of communist aggression and subversion. Truman's actions enhanced the powers of an already powerful presidency and set the precedent for later undeclared wars. They also helped spark an economic boom, added fuel to a second Red Scare, and fostered Cold War attitudes that lasted long after the war ended.

THE TRUMAN ADMINISTRATION AT HOME, 1945–1952

Since 1929 many Americans had known little but the sufferings and shortages of depression and war. They now wanted to enjoy life. The Cold War both hindered that desire and helped create a postwar affluence that changed dreams into reality. Americans flocked to the suburbs, launched a huge baby boom, and rushed to buy refrigerators and new cars. Sales of TV sets soared from fewer than seven thousand in 1946 to more than 7 million by 1949; by 1953 half of all U.S. homes had at least one television. However, not all Americans shared these good times. Poverty remained a stark fact of life for millions. Minorities experienced the grim reality of racism. Yet a major movement by African-Americans for equality gradually emerged from these Cold War years.

But it did not triumph. Family and career, not public issues, interested most Americans. An increasingly conservative temper trumped liberalism. Some second- and third-generation white Americans, whose recent prosperity had dimmed memories of the Great Depression, and who no longer felt the pull of the New Deal, began to reject liberals at the polls. They worried about high taxes, not unemployment, and they favored a fiscally responsible administration more than one committed to social justice. These former Democratic voters cared more about the growing crime rate and the decline in family authority than about the civil rights of African-Americans. They feared communist subversives, not the loss of civil liberties. Fervently patriotic, they championed a muscular anticommunism, demanding victory, not stalemate, in the Cold War. Although Truman occasionally sought liberal measures, the stirrings of conservative sentiments in places like southern California undercut efforts for progressive change.

The Eightieth Congress, 1947–1948   Many Republicans in the Eightieth Congress interpreted the 1946 elections as a mandate to reverse the New Deal. As "Mr. Republican," Senator Robert A. Taft of Ohio, declared, "We have got to break with the corrupting idea that we can legislate prosperity, legislate equality, legislate opportunity." Congress defeated Democratic bills to raise the minimum wage and to provide federal funds for education and housing.

Truman and the conservatives waged their major battle over the pro-union Wagner Act of 1935 (see Chapter 24). Massive postwar strikes had created a national consensus for curbing union power. In 1947, more than twenty states passed laws to restrict union activities, and Congress passed the **Taft-Hartley Act** (officially the Labor-Management Relations Act), which barred the closed shop—a workplace where only union members could be hired—outlawed secondary boycotts, required union officials to sign loyalty oaths, and permitted the president to call a cooling-off period to delay any strike that might endanger national safety or health. The act weakened organizing drives in the nonunion South and West, hastening the relocation of labor-intensive industries, such as textiles, from the Northeast and Midwest to the Sunbelt. It also helped drive leftists out of CIO leadership positions, weakening organized labor as a force for social justice.

Eager for labor's support in the 1948 presidential election, Truman vetoed the bill. Congress overrode the veto. But Truman had taken a major step in regaining organized labor's support and reforging FDR's New Deal coalition. Truman now played the role of a staunch New Dealer to the hilt, urging Congress to repeal Taft-Hartley; raise the minimum wage, social-security benefits, and price supports for farmers; enact federal aid to education and housing; and adopt a federal health-insurance program. To woo ethnic voters of Eastern European descent, Truman stressed his opposition to the Iron Curtain. To court Jewish-American voters as well as express his deep sympathy toward Holocaust survivors, he overrode the objections of the State Department, which feared alienating the oil-rich Arab world, and extended diplomatic recognition to the new state of Israel immediately after it proclaimed independence on May 14, 1948.

The Politics of Civil Rights and the Election of 1948   As the head of the NAACP noted in 1945, "World War II has immeasurably magnified the Negro's awareness of the disparity between the American profession and practice of democracy." The war heightened African-American expectations for racial equality, and numerous blacks demanded a permanent Fair Employment Practices Commission (FEPC), the outlawing of lynching, and the right to vote. Voter-registration drives raised the percentage of southern blacks registered to vote from 2 percent in 1940 to 12 percent in 1947.

Fearful of the increasing assertiveness of African-Americans to, in the words of Harlem congressman Adam Clayton Powell, Jr., "make the dream of America become flesh and blood, bread and butter, freedom and equality," some southern whites reacted brutally. In 1946, whites killed several black war veterans who had voted that year in rural Georgia, flogged to death an "uppity" black tenant farmer in Mississippi, blow-torched a young black in Louisiana for daring to enter a white woman's house, and blinded a black soldier for failing to sit in the rear of a bus in South Carolina. In Columbia, Tennessee, in 1946 whites rioted against blacks who insisted on their rights. Police arrested seventy blacks and looked the other way as a white mob broke into the jail to murder two black prisoners.

President Truman, responding to the pressure brought by local black protest movements and knowing the political importance of the growing black vote, particularly in northern cities, vowed to act. He understood that white racism damaged U.S. relations with much of the world. The USSR highlighted the mistreatment of African-Americans, both to undercut U.S. appeals to the nonwhites of Africa, Asia, and Latin America, and to counter criticism of its own repression behind the Iron Curtain. Accordingly, Truman established the first **President's Committee on Civil Rights.** Its 1947 report, *To Secure These Rights*, dramatized the inequities of life in Jim Crow America and emphasized all the compelling moral, economic, and international reasons for the government to enact federal legislation outlawing lynching and the poll tax, establishing a permanent FEPC, desegregating the armed forces, and supporting a legal assault on segregation in education, housing, and interstate transportation.

Southern segregationists accused Truman of "stabbing the South in the back" and warned of a boycott of the national Democratic ticket. Truman backtracked. Fearful of

Jackie Robinson, 1947 *Before he became the first African-American to play major-league baseball, Robinson had excelled at track as well as baseball at UCLA and had been an army officer in World War II. Even his brilliant play for the Brookyn Dodgers did not save him from racial taunts of fans and players or exclusion from restaurants and hotels that catered to his white teammates.*

losing the Solid South, he dropped plans to submit civil-rights bills to Congress and endorsed a weak civil-rights plank for the Democratic platform. But liberals and urban politicians who needed the votes of African-Americans rejected the president's feeble civil-rights plank at the Democratic convention in July 1948 and committed the party to act on Truman's original proposals. Thirty-five delegates from Alabama and Mississippi stalked out, joining other segregationists to form the States' Rights Democratic Party, which nominated Governor Strom Thurmond of South Carolina for the presidency. The "Dixiecrats" hoped to restore their dominance in the Democratic Party, and preserve the segregationist "southern way of life." The Dixiecrats would be an important step toward future Republican conservatism in the South; in 1948, placing their electors on the ballot as the regular Democratic ticket in several states, they posed a major roadblock to Truman's chances of victory.

Truman's 1948 electoral hopes faded further when left-wing Democrats joined with communists to launch a new Progressive Party and nominated Henry A. Wallace for president. The Wallace candidacy threatened Truman's chances in northern states, where many urban Democrats saw Wallace as the true heir of New Deal liberalism. To capitalize on Democratic divisions, Republicans played it safe, nominating the moderate governor of New York, Thomas E. Dewey. Confident of victory, Dewey ran a complacent campaign designed to offend the fewest people. Truman, in contrast, campaigned vigorously, blasting the "no-good, do-nothing" Republican-controlled Eightieth Congress. To shouts of "Give 'em hell, Harry," the president hammered away at the GOP as the party of "privilege, pride, and plunder." Pollsters applauded Truman's spunk but predicted a Dewey victory.

Yet the president won the biggest electoral upset in U.S. history. Ironically, the Progressives and Dixiecrats had helped Truman. Their radicalism had kept moderate Democrats safely in the fold. The Berlin crisis, a coup in Czechoslovakia, and Wallace's failure to repudiate communist support forced most liberals away from the Progressives. Although the support for Thurmond signaled the first cracks in the Solid South, few southern Democrats felt sufficiently threatened by Truman's civil-rights stand to desert the party in 1948. "The only sane and constructive course to follow is to remain in the house of our fathers—even though the roof leaks, and there be bats in the belfry, rats in the pantry, a cockroach in the kitchen and skunks in the parlor," explained a southern officeholder. Moreover, Dixiecrat defections had freed Truman to campaign as a champion of civil rights. In July 1948, responding to a protest campaign led by A. Philip Randolph, Truman issued executive orders barring discrimination in federal employment and ending racial segregation in the armed services. Truman also benefited from Supreme Court decisions declaring segregation in interstate bus transportation unconstitutional (*Morgan* v. *Virginia,* 1946) and outlawing restrictive housing covenants that forbade the sale or rental of property to minorities (*Shelley* v. *Kraemer,* 1948).

The Fair Deal   Despite his narrow victory margin, Truman proposed a **Fair Deal** agenda that included civil rights, national health-care legislation, and federal aid to education. Unlike the New Deal, the Fair Deal was based on the belief in continual economic growth: the constantly expanding economic pie would mean a progressively bigger piece for most Americans (so they would not resent helping those left behind) and for the government (so it would have the revenue to pay for social-welfare programs).

The Eighty-first Congress extended existing programs but rejected new Fair Deal measures. It raised the hourly minimum wage from forty to seventy-five cents; increased social-security benefits and coverage; expanded appropriations for public power, conservation, and slum clearance; and authorized the construction of nearly a million low-income housing units. It also enacted the Displaced Persons Act of 1948, which allowed entry to the United States to 205,000 persons, primarily non-Jews, who had survived the concentration camps, fled the Axis forces, or refused repatriation to the Eastern zone. Another act, in 1950, eliminated the anti-Jewish provisions of the 1948 measure and allowed entry to an additional 200,000 persons. But Congress rejected federal aid to education, national health insurance, civil-rights legislation, and repeal of the Taft-Hartley Act.

Congress's rejection of most Fair Deal proposals stemmed from Truman's own lessening commitment to domestic reform in favor of foreign and military affairs, as well as from the strengthening of the congressional coalition of Republicans and conservative Democrats. The postwar congresses mirrored the public lack of enthusiasm for liberal reform caused by increasing prosperity and by fears of communism.

THE POLITICS OF ANTICOMMUNISM

As the Cold War worsened, some Americans concluded that the roots of the nation's difficulties abroad lay in domestic treason and subversion. How else could the communists have defeated Jiang in China and built an atomic bomb? Millions of fearful Americans enlisted in a crusade that equated dissent with disloyalty and blamed scapegoats for the nation's problems.

Similar intolerance had prevailed in the Red Scare of 1919–1920 (see Chapter 22). Since its establishment in 1938, the House Committee on Un-American Activities (later called the House Un-American Activities Committee, or HUAC) had served as a platform for right-wing denunciations of the New Deal as a communist plot. Only the extreme Right initially took such charges seriously. But after World War II mounting numbers of Democrats and Republicans climbed aboard the anti-Red bandwagon.

The **Second Red Scare** influenced both governmental and personal actions. Millions of Americans were subjected to security investigations and loyalty oaths. Anticommunist extremism destroyed the Left, undermined labor militancy, and discredited liberalism. It spawned a "silent generation" of college students, and ensured anticommunist foreign-policy rigidity.

Loyalty and Security The Cold War raised legitimate concerns about American security. The Communist Party had claimed eighty thousand members in the United States during the Second World War, and far more sympathizers. Just how many party members or secret communists occupied sensitive government and military positions no one knew. In mid-1945 a raid on the offices of a procommunist magazine revealed that classified documents had been given to the periodical by State Department employees and a naval intelligence officer. Then the Canadian government exposed a major spy network that had passed American atomic secrets to the Soviets during the war. Republicans accused the Democratic administration of being "soft on communism."

A week after his Truman Doctrine speech of March 1947, the president issued Executive Order 9835, establishing the Federal Employee Loyalty Program to root out subversives in the government. The first such peacetime program, it barred members of the Communist Party and anyone guilty of "sympathetic association" with it from federal employment. "Reasonable grounds for belief that the person is disloyal," which was defined to include being homosexual, led to dismissal. Those suspected were allowed neither to face their accusers nor to require investigators to reveal sources. Instead of focusing on potential subversives in high-risk areas, review boards extended the probe to the associations and beliefs of every government worker.

Mere criticism of American foreign policy could result in an accusation of disloyalty. Clouds of suspicion hovered over those who liked foreign films or who favored the unionization of federal workers. "Of course the fact that a person believes in racial equality doesn't prove he's a communist," mused an Interior Department Loyalty Board chairman, "but it certainly makes you look twice, doesn't it?" Some people lost jobs because they associated with radical friends or had once belonged to organizations now declared disloyal.

Of the 4.7 million jobholders and applicants who underwent loyalty checks by 1952, 560 were fired or denied jobs on security grounds, several thousand resigned or withdrew their applications, and countless more were intimidated. Although Loyalty Board probes uncovered no evidence of espionage or subversion, they heightened fears of what Truman called "the enemy within," adding credibility to the Red Scare. "If communists like apple pie and I do," claimed one federal worker, "I see no reason why I should stop eating it. But I would."

The Anticommunist Crusade   The very existence of a federal loyalty probe fed mounting anticommunist hysteria. It promoted fears of communist infiltrators and legitimated a witch-hunt for subversives. At Yale, the FBI, with the consent of the college administration, spied on students and faculty, screening candidates for jobs and fellowships. Many universities banned controversial speakers, and popular magazines featured articles like "Reds Are After Your Child." Comics joined the fray: "Beware, commies, spies, traitors, and foreign agents! Captain America, with all loyal, free men behind him, is looking for you, ready to fight until the last one of you is exposed for the yellow scum you are." Truman's Office of Education introduced a "Zeal for Democracy" campaign, providing local school boards with curriculum materials to combat "communist subversion."

By the end of Truman's term, thirty-nine states had created loyalty programs. Few had any procedural safeguards. Schoolteachers, college professors, and state and city employees throughout the nation had to sign loyalty oaths or lose their jobs. No one knows for sure how many were dismissed, denied tenure, or drifted away, leaving behind colleagues too frightened to speak out.

In 1947, the **House Un-American Activities Committee** began hearings to expose communist influence in American life. HUAC's probes blurred distinctions between dissent and disloyalty, between radicalism and subversion. Those called to testify were in a bind. When asked whether they had ever been members of the Communist Party, witnesses could say yes and be forced to reveal the names of others; say no and be vulnerable to charges of perjury; or refuse to answer, pleading the First or Fifth Amendment, and risk being viewed by the public as a communist. To gain publicity for itself and to influence the content of movies, HUAC investigated Hollywood. They saw as proof of communist activity wartime films about the Soviet Union showing Russians smiling, or movies featuring the line "share and share alike, that's democracy." In 1947, HUAC cited for contempt of Congress a group of film directors and screenwriters who, claiming the freedom of speech and assembly guaranteed by the First Amendment, refused to say whether they had been members of the Communist Party. The so-called Hollywood Ten—some of them communists, all of them leftists—were convicted of contempt and sent to prison. The threat of further investigations prompted the movie colony, financially dependent on favorable press and public opinion, to deny work to other "unfriendly witnesses." Soon the studios established a blacklist barring the employment of anyone suspected of having been a communist.

HUAC also frightened the labor movement into expelling communists and avoiding progressive causes. Fearful of appearing "red," or even "pink," most unions focused on securing better pay and benefits for their members.

The 1948 presidential election campaign also fed national anxieties. Truman lambasted Henry Wallace as a Stalinist dupe and accused the Republicans of being "unwittingly the ally of the communists." In turn, the GOP dubbed the Democrats "the party of treason." To blunt such accusations, Truman's Justice Department prosecuted eleven top leaders of the American Communist Party under the Smith Act of 1940, which outlawed any conspiracy advocating the overthrow of the government. The Supreme Court upheld the Smith Act's constitutionality (*Dennis* v. *United States*, 1951), declaring that Congress could curtail freedom of speech if national security required such restriction, and affirmed the conviction and jailing of the communists, despite the absence of any acts of violence or espionage.

Ironically, the Communist Party was fading into obscurity at the very time when politicians magnified its threat. By 1950 its membership had shrunk to fewer than thirty thousand. Yet Truman's attorney general warned that American Reds "are everywhere—in factories, offices, butcher stores, on street corners, in private businesses—and each carries in himself the germ of death for society."

Alger Hiss and the Rosenbergs

Nothing set off more alarms of a diabolic Red conspiracy in Washington than the matter of **Alger Hiss and Whittaker Chambers.** During the 1948 political campaign, HUAC had conducted a hearing in which Chambers, a *Time* editor and former Soviet agent who had broken with the communists in 1938, identified Hiss as an underground communist in the 1930s.

A rumpled, repentant, former communist and college dropout, Chambers seemed a tortured soul crusading to save the West from the Red peril. The elegant Hiss, in contrast, symbolized the liberal establishment: a Harvard-trained lawyer who had clerked for Supreme Court Justice Oliver Wendell Holmes, he had served FDR in the New Deal and later as a State Department official, presiding over the inaugural meeting of the United Nations. For conservative Republicans, a better villain could not have been invented. Hiss denied any communist affiliation and claimed not to know Chambers. Most liberals believed him. They saw him as a victim of conservatives bent on tarnishing New Deal liberalism. Truman denounced Chambers's allegation as a "red herring" to deflect attention from the failures of the Eightieth Congress.

To those suspicious of the Roosevelt liberal tradition, Chambers's persistence and Hiss's fumbling retreat intensified fears that the Democratic administration teemed with communists. Under relentless questioning by Congressman (and later president) Richard Nixon, Hiss finally admitted that he had known Chambers and had even let Chambers have his car and live in his apartment. But he denied ever having been a communist. Chambers then broadened his accusation, claiming that Hiss had committed espionage in the 1930s by giving him secret State Department documents to be sent to the Soviet Union. To prove his charge, Chambers led federal agents to his farm in Maryland, where, in a hollowed-out pumpkin, he had microfilm copies of confidential government papers that had been copied on a typewriter traced to Hiss. A grand jury indicted Hiss for perjury, or lying under oath. (The statute of limitations for espionage prevented a charge of treason.) In January 1950 Hiss was convicted and given a five-year prison sentence. Republican conservatives were emboldened. Who knew how many other bright young New Dealers had betrayed the country?

Hard on the heels of the Hiss conviction, another spy case shocked Americans. In February 1950, the British arrested Klaus Fuchs, a German-born scientist involved in the Manhattan Project, for passing atomic secrets to the Soviets during the Second World War. Fuchs's confession led to the arrest of his American accomplice and a machinist who had worked at Los Alamos, who then named his brother-in-law and sister,

Julius and Ethel Rosenberg, as co-conspirators in the wartime spy network. The Rosenbergs insisted they were victims of anti-Semitism and were being prosecuted for their leftist beliefs. In March 1951, a jury found them both guilty of conspiring to commit espionage. Declaring their crime "worse than murder," the trial judge sentenced them to die in the electric chair. Offered clemency if they named other spies, neither Rosenberg would confess. On June 19, 1953, they were executed—the first American civilians to lose their lives for espionage.

Both the Rosenbergs and Alger Hiss protested their innocence to their end, and their defenders continued to do so for decades. Soviet secret documents released by the National Security Agency in the 1990s—called the Venona Intercepts—lent weight to Chambers's charges against Hiss and confirmed Julius Rosenberg's guilt. (Ethel's role in her husband's spying remained uncertain.)

McCarthyism

At this point, when few Americans could separate fact from fantasy, the Hiss and Rosenberg cases tarnished liberalism and fueled other loyalty investigations. Only a conspiracy, it seemed, could explain U.S. weakness and Soviet might. Frustrated by their unexpected failure to win the White House in 1948, Republicans eagerly exploited the fearful mood and accused the "Commiecrats" of selling out America.

No individual would inflict so many wounds on the Democrats as Republican senator **Joseph R. McCarthy** of Wisconsin. Falsely claiming to be a wounded war hero, "Tail-Gunner Joe" won a Senate seat in the 1946 Republican landslide, and promptly gained a reputation for lying and heavy drinking. His political future in jeopardy, McCarthy decided to imitate Republicans like Richard Nixon who had gained popularity by accusing Democrats of being "soft on communism." In February 1950 McCarthy told an audience in Wheeling, West Virginia, that the United States found itself in a "position of impotency" because of "the traitorous actions" of high officials in the Truman administration. "I have here in my hands a list of 205," McCarthy boldly claimed as he waved a laundry ticket, "a list of names known to the Secretary of State as being members of the Communist party and who nevertheless are still working and shaping policy." Although McCarthy offered no evidence to support his accusations, the newspapers printed his charges, giving him a national forum. McCarthy soon repeated his accusations, reducing his numbers first to 81, then to 57, and finally to "a lot," and reducing his indictment from "card-carrying communists" to "subversives" to "bad risks." A Senate committee found McCarthy's charges "a fraud and a hoax," but he persisted.

Buoyed by the partisan usefulness of Senator McCarthy's onslaught, Republicans encouraged even more accusations. Even the normally fair-minded Robert Taft, who privately dismissed McCarthy's charges as "nonsense," urged him "to keep talking, and if one case doesn't work, try another." He did, and "McCarthyism" became a synonym for personal attacks on individuals by means of indiscriminate allegations and unsubstantiated charges.

As the Korean War dragged on, McCarthy's efforts to "root out the skunks" escalated. He ridiculed Secretary of State Dean Acheson as the "Red Dean," termed Truman's dismissal of MacArthur "the greatest victory the communists have ever won," and charged George Marshall with having "aided and abetted a communist conspiracy so immense as to dwarf any previous such venture in the history of man."

McCarthyism especially appealed to midwestern Republicans indignant about the Europe-first emphasis of Truman's foreign policy and eager to turn the public's fears into votes for the GOP. For many in the American Legion and the Chambers of Commerce, anticommunism was a weapon of revenge against liberals and internationalists, as well as a means to regain the controlling position that conservative forces had once held. McCarthy also won a devoted following among blue-collar workers who identified with his charge that a person was either a true American who detested "communists and queers" or an "egg sucking phony liberal." Laborers praised his demand that the war against communism be fought with brass knuckles, not kid gloves, while both small and big businessmen sniffed an opportunity to destroy the power of organized labor. McCarthy's flag-waving appeals held a special attraction for traditionally Democratic Catholic ethnics, who sought to gain acceptance as "100 percent Americans" through a show of anticommunist zeal. Countless Americans also shared McCarthy's scorn for the privileged, for the "bright young men who are born with silver spoons in their mouths," for the "striped-pants boys in the State Department." His conspiracy theory, moreover, offered a simple answer to the perplexing questions of the Cold War.

McCarthy's political power rested on the support of the Republican establishment and Democrats fearful of antagonizing him. McCarthy appeared invincible after he helped GOP candidates in the 1950 congressional elections unseat Democrats who had denounced him. "Look out for McCarthy," warned the new majority leader, Democrat Lyndon B. Johnson of Texas; "Joe will go that extra mile to destroy you." Few dared incur McCarthy's wrath.

Over Truman's veto, Congress in 1950 adopted the **McCarran Internal Security Act,** which required organizations deemed communist by the attorney general to register with the Department of Justice. It also authorized the arrest and detention during a national emergency of "any person as to whom there is reason to believe might engage in acts of espionage or sabotage." As part of this effort, a Senate committee sought to root out homosexuals holding government jobs. The linking of disloyalty with homosexuality in turn legitimated the armed forces' effort to dismiss "queers" and the raiding of gay bars by city police. The McCarran-Walter Immigration and Nationality Act of 1952, also adopted over Truman's veto, maintained the quota system that severely restricted immigration from southern and eastern Europe and from Asia, but did end the ban on Japanese immigration and made Issei eligible for naturalized citizenship. In the name of national security, moreover, the law increased the attorney general's authority to exclude or deport "undesirable" aliens, particularly those suspected of homosexuality or supporting communism.

The Election of 1952

In 1952 public apprehension about the loyalty of government employees combined with frustration over the Korean stalemate to sink Democratic hopes to their lowest level since the 1920s. Both business and labor also resented Truman's freeze on wages and prices during the Korean conflict. Revelations of bribery and influence peddling by some of Truman's old political associates gave Republicans ammunition for charging the Democrats with "plunder at home, and blunder abroad."

With Truman too unpopular to run for reelection, dispirited Democrats drafted Governor Adlai Stevenson of Illinois. But Stevenson could not separate himself politically from Truman, and his lofty speeches failed to stir most voters. An intellectual out of touch with the common people, he was jokingly referred to as an "egghead," someone with more brains than hair. Above all, Stevenson could not overcome the widespread sentiment that twenty years of Democratic rule was enough.

Compounding Democratic woes, the GOP nominated the hugely popular war hero Dwight D. Eisenhower. Essentially apolitical, Eisenhower had once insisted that "lifelong professional soldiers should abstain from seeking higher political office." But in 1952 he answered the call of the moderate wing of the Republican Party and accepted the nomination. As a concession to the hard-line anticommunists in the party, "Ike" chose as his running mate Richard Nixon, who had won a seat in the Senate in 1950 by red-baiting his opponent, Helen Gahagan Douglas, as "pink right down to her underwear."

Eisenhower and Nixon proved unbeatable. With a captivating grin and unimpeachable record of public service, Eisenhower projected both personal warmth and the vigorous authority associated with military command. His smile, wrote one commentator, was one "of infinite reassurance." At the same time, Nixon kept public apprehensions at the boiling point. Accusing the Democrats of treason, he charged that the election of "Adlai the appeaser . . . who got a Ph.D. from Dean Acheson's College of Cowardly Communist Containment" would bring "more Alger Hisses, more atomic spies."

The GOP ticket stumbled when newspapers revealed the existence of a "slush fund" that California businessmen created to keep Nixon in "financial comfort." But Nixon saved himself with a heart-tugging television defense. Less than two weeks before the election, Eisenhower dramatically pledged to "go to Korea" to end the stalemated war. It worked, and 62.7 percent of those eligible to vote (compared to just 51.5 percent in 1948) turned out in 1952 and gave the Republican ticket 55 percent of the ballots. Ike cracked the Solid South, carrying thirty-nine states (and 442 electoral votes). Enough Republicans rode his coattails to give the GOP narrow control of both houses of Congress.

CONCLUSION

After nearly two decades of depression and war, the end of World War II meant the beginning of a better life and a new era of hope for most Americans. Millions of returning veterans took advantage of the GI Bill to go to college and to receive low-interest loans to start businesses and purchase homes. Although temporarily disadvantaging women in securing employment or a college degree, the GI Bill, in the long run, democratized higher education, helped fuel a baby boom and suburbanization, and played a major role in the postwar economic boom that for the first time provided a middle-class standard of living for a majority of Americans.

At the same time, an assertive United States, eager to protect and expand its influence and power in the world, sought to contain a Soviet Union obsessed with its own security and self-interest. Stalin's aggressive posture toward Eastern Europe and the Persian Gulf was met by an American policy of containment, in whose name the United States aided Greece and Turkey, established the Marshall Plan, airlifted supplies into Berlin for a year, approved the creation of the Federal Republic of Germany (West Germany), established NATO, implemented NSC-68, financed France's war in Vietnam, and went to war in Korea. The resulting stalemate would last for four decades, define American politics and society, transform its economy, and condition the thinking of a generation.

The Cold War obsession with communism, as well as postwar prosperity, weakened the appeal of liberal reform. In a political climate far more conservative than that of the

1930s, New Deal measures remained in place, but Truman's Fair Deal to assist the disadvantaged with new initiatives in education, health insurance, and civil rights failed. Anticommunist hysteria squashed the left and narrowed the range of politically acceptable ideas. Bold proposals to end racism and discrimination—often labeled "communistic" by segregationists—had little chance in Congress; but the need of the United States to appeal to the nonwhites of the world during the Cold War brought racial issues to the fore in American politics and forced President Truman to take executive actions. Most immediately, and of paramount consequence, Truman's actions at home and abroad fed America's fear of communism. The president's responses to the Soviet detonation of an atomic bomb, the fall of China to the communists, and the invasion of South Korea, in addition to his own loyalty probe to root out subversive government workers, spawned anxieties. In an atmosphere of paranoia, caused by witch-hunts for communism in American life and the discovery of a Soviet atomic spy ring, Truman's actions encouraged others to seek scapegoats for American failures abroad and legitimated conservative accusations that equated dissent with disloyalty. The Republicans would ride "McCarthyism" back to the seat of power in Washington; it would be up to President Eisenhower to restore unity and renew hopefulness.

27

America at Midcentury, 1952–1960

THE EISENHOWER PRESIDENCY

Rarely in U.S. history has a president better fit the national mood than did **Dwight David Eisenhower.** Exhausted by a quarter-century of upheaval—the depression, World War II, the Cold War—Americans craved peace and stability. Eisenhower delivered. He gave a nation weary of partisanship a sense of unity; he inspired confidence; and his moderate politics, steering a middle course between Democratic liberalism and traditional Republican conservatism, pleased most Americans. So did his largely hands-off approach to McCarthyism and the desegregation of public schools.

"Dynamic Conservatism"   The most lauded American general of the Second World War, Eisenhower projected the image of a plain but good man. He expressed complicated issues in simple terms, yet governed a complex, urban, technological society. A grandfatherly figure, a hero who had vanquished Hitler, Ike comforted an anxious people.

Born in Denison, Texas, on October 14, 1890, Dwight Eisenhower grew up in Abilene, Kansas, in a poor, strongly religious family. More athletic than studious, he graduated from the U.S. Military Academy at West Point in 1915. A brilliant war planner, respected for his managerial ability and skill at conciliation, Eisenhower's approach to the presidency reflected his wartime leadership style. He concentrated on "the big picture," delegating authority while reconciling contending factions. His restrained view of presidential powers stemmed from his respect for the constitutional balance of power as well as his sense of the dignity of the Oval Office. He rarely intervened publicly in the legislative process. He shunned using his office as a "bully pulpit." He promised his cabinet that he would "stay out of its hair." This low-key style led Democrats to scoff at Eisenhower as a bumbler who preferred golf to government, who "reigned but did not rule."

Chronology , 1952–1960

1946 • ENIAC, the first electronic computer, begins operation.

1947 • Levittown, New York, development started.

1948 • Bell Labs develops the transistor.

1950 • *Asosiación Nacional México-Americana* established.

1952 • Dwight D. Eisenhower elected president.

1953 • Korean War truce signed.
Earl Warren appointed chief justice.
Operation Wetback begins.

1954 • Army-McCarthy hearings.
Brown v. *Board of Education of Topeka.*
Fall of Dienbienphu; Geneva Conference.
Father Knows Best begins on TV.

1955 • Salk polio vaccine developed.
AFL-CIO merger.
First postwar U.S.-Soviet summit meeting.
James Dean stars in *Rebel Without a Cause.*
Montgomery bus boycott begins.

1956 • Interstate Highway Act.
Suez crisis.
Soviet intervention in Poland and Hungary.

1957 • Eisenhower Doctrine announced.
Civil Rights Act (first since Reconstruction).
Little Rock school-desegregation crisis.
Soviet Union launches *Sputnik.*
Peak of baby boom (4.3 million births).
Southern Christian Leadership Conference founded.

1958 • National Defense Education Act.
United States and Soviet Union halt atomic tests.
National Aeronautics and Space Administration (NASA) founded.

1959 • Fidel Castro comes to power in Cuba.
Khrushchev and Eisenhower meet at Camp David.

1960 • U-2 incident.
Second Civil Rights Act.
Suburban population almost equals that of central city.

The image of passivity actually masked an active and occasionally ruthless politician. Determined to govern the nation on business principles, Eisenhower staffed his administration with corporate executives. "Eight millionaires and a plumber," jested one journalist about the cabinet. (The "plumber" was union leader Martin Durkin, who headed the Labor Department, and soon resigned.) The president initially worked with the Republican-controlled Congress to reduce the size of government and to slash the federal budget. He promoted the private development of hydroelectric and nuclear power, and persuaded Congress to turn over to coastal states the oil-rich "tidelands" that the Supreme Court had awarded to the federal government.

For the most part, however, the Eisenhower administration followed a centrist course, which the president labeled "dynamic conservatism" and "modern Republicanism." More pragmatic than ideological, he wished to reduce taxes, contain inflation, and govern efficiently without surrendering the fundamentals of the New Deal. When recessions struck in 1953 and 1957, Eisenhower abandoned his balanced budgets and increased spending to restore prosperity. As Milton Eisenhower summed up his brother's views: "We should keep what we have, catch our breath for a while, and improve administration; it does not mean moving backward."

Ike supported extending social-security benefits, raising the minimum wage, adding 4 million more workers to those eligible for unemployment benefits, and providing federally financed public housing for low-income families. He also approved establishing a Department of Health, Education and Welfare; constructing the St. Lawrence Seaway, linking the Great Lakes and the Atlantic Ocean; and building freeways (see Technology and Culture: The Interstate Highway System). With the Republicans crowing "Everything's booming but the guns," Ike won reelection in 1956 by a landslide over Democrat Adlai Stevenson. Despite having suffered a major heart attack in 1955, Eisenhower carried all but seven states.

The Downfall of Joseph McCarthy Although he despised McCarthy—and called him a "pimple on the path to progress," Eisenhower considered it beneath his dignity to "get into the gutter with that guy." Fearing a direct confrontation with the senator, he first tightened security requirements for government employees, to steal McCarthy's thunder, and then allowed McCarthy to grab plenty of rope in hopes that the demagogue would hang himself. He did. Angry that one of his aides had not received a draft deferment, the senator accused the army in 1954 of harboring communist spies. The army countered that McCarthy had tried to get preferential treatment for the aide who had been drafted.

The resulting nationally televised Senate investigation, begun in April 1954, brought McCarthy down. A national audience witnessed McCarthy's boorish behavior firsthand on television. His dark scowl, raspy voice, endless interruptions ("point of order, Mr. Chairman, point of order"), and disregard for the rights of others repelled many viewers. He behaved like the bad guy in a TV western, observed novelist John Steinbeck: "He had a stubble of a beard, he leered, he sneered, he had a nasty laugh. He bullied and shouted. He looked evil." In June McCarthy slurred the reputation of a young lawyer assisting Joseph Welch, the army counsel. Suddenly the mild-mannered Welch turned his wrath on McCarthy, "Until this moment, Senator, I think I really never gauged your cruelty or your recklessness. . . . Have you no sense of decency?" The gallery burst into applause.

The Interstate Highway System

As a young captain after World War I, Dwight Eisenhower had been given the task of accompanying a convoy of army trucks across the country. The woefully inadequate state of the roads for military transport dismayed him then as much as he would later be impressed by the German autobahns that allowed Hitler to deploy troops around Germany with incredible speed. Not surprisingly, when he became president he sought a transportation system that would facilitate the rapid movement of the military, as well as increase road safety and aid commerce. The arms race with the Soviet Union, moreover, necessitated a network of highways for evacuating cities in case of a nuclear attack—a change, according to the *Bulletin of the Atomic Scientists,* from "Duck and Cover" to "Run Like Hell."

In 1954 Eisenhower set up a high-powered commission to recommend a highway program that would cost as much as a war. He appointed an army general to head it to emphasize the connection between highways, national defense, and the concerns Americans had about their security. The next year, with the entire federal budget at $71 billion, Eisenhower asked Congress for a $40 billion, forty-one-thousand-mile construction project, to be financed by government bonds. Conservative Republicans, fearful of increasing the federal debt, balked. So Ike switched to a financing plan based on new gasoline, tire, bus, and trucking taxes. The federal government would use the taxes to pay 90 percent of the construction costs in any state willing to come up with the other 10 percent.

Millions of suburbanites commuting to central cities loved the idea of new multilane highways. So did motorists dreaming of summer travel; the powerful coalition of automobile manufacturers, oil companies, asphalt firms, and truckers, who stood to benefit financially the most; and the many special interests in virtually every congressional district, including real-estate developers, shopping mall entrepreneurs, engineers, and construction industries. Indeed, the interstate highway bill promised something to almost everybody except the inner-city poor. It sailed through Congress in 1956, winning by voice vote in the House and by an 89 to 1 margin in the Senate.

The largest and most expensive public-works scheme in American history, the interstate highway system was designed and built as a single project for the entire country, unlike the haphazard development of the canal and railroad networks. It required taking more land by eminent domain than had been taken in the entire history of road building in the United States. Expected increases in highway use, speed of travel, and weight of loads necessitated drastic changes in road engineering and materials. Utilizing the technological advances that had produced high-quality concrete and asphalt, diesel-powered roadbed graders, reinforced steel, and safely controlled explosives, construction crews built superhighways with standardized twelve-foot-wide lanes, ten-foot shoulders, and median strips of at least thirty-six feet in rural areas. Terrain in which a dirt trail was difficult to blaze was laced with cloverleaf intersections and some sixteen thousand exits and entrances. More than fifty thousand bridges, tunnels, and overpasses traversed swamps, rivers, and mountains. Road curves were banked for speeds of seventy miles per hour, with grades no greater than 3 percent and minimum sight distances of six hundred feet. The massive amounts of concrete poured, Ike later boasted, could have made "six sidewalks to the moon" or sixty Panama Canals.

The network of four-to-eight-lane roads linking cities and suburbs made it possible to drive from New York to San Francisco without encountering a stoplight. It more than fulfilled the initial hopes of most of its backers, enormously speeding the movement of goods and people across the country, invigorating the tourist industry, providing steady work for construction firms, enriching those who lived near the interstates and sold their lands to developers, and hastening suburban development.

The freeways that helped unify Americans by increasing the accessibility of once-distant regions also helped homogenize the nation with interchangeable shopping malls, motels, and fast-food chains. In 1955, Ray Kroc, who supplied the Multimixers for milk shakes to the original McDonald's drive-in in San Bernardino, California, began to franchise similar family restaurants beside highways, each serving the same standardized foods under the instantly rec-

ognizable logo of the golden arches. By century's end, McDonald's would be the world's largest private real-estate enterprise, as well as the largest food provider, serving more than 40 million meals daily in some hundred countries.

Moreover, the expressways boosted the interstate trucking business and hastened the decline of the nation's railroad lines and urban mass-transportation systems. The highways built to speed commuters into the central cities— "white men's roads through black men's bedrooms," said the National Urban League—often bulldozed minority neighborhoods out of existence or served as barriers between black and white neighborhoods. The beltways that lured increasingly more residents and businesses to suburbia eroded city tax bases, which, in turn, accelerated urban decay, triggering the urban crisis that then furthered suburban sprawl. The interstates had locked the United States into an ever-increasing reliance on cars and trucks, drastically increasing air pollution and American dependence on a constant supply of cheap and plentiful gasoline.

Questions for Analysis

- Why did Congress authorize the construction of an interstate highway system?

- Describe some of the unintended consequences of the new highway system.

McCarthy's popularity ratings plummeted. With the GOP no longer needing him to drive the "Commiecrats" from power, and the Democrats eager to be rid of their scourge, the Senate, with Eisenhower applying pressure behind the scenes, voted in December 1954 to censure McCarthy for contemptuous behavior. This powerful rebuke—only the third in the Senate's history—demolished McCarthy as a political force. McCarthyism, Ike gloated, had become "McCarthywasism."

In 1957 McCarthy died from alcoholism. But the fears he exploited lingered. Congress continued to fund the House Un-American Activities Committee's search for suspected radicals. State and local governments continued to require teachers to take loyalty oaths.

McCarthyism also remained a rallying call of conservatives disenchanted with the postwar consensus. Young conservatives like William F. Buckley, Jr. (a recent Yale graduate who founded the *National Review* in 1955), and the Christian Anti-Communist Crusade continued to claim that domestic communism was a major subversive threat. None did so more than the John Birch Society, which denounced Eisenhower as a conscious agent of the communist conspiracy, and equated liberalism with treason. Its grass-roots network of as many as a hundred thousand activists promoted like-minded political candidates, while waging local struggles against taxes, gun control, and sex education in the schools. Although few saw all the dangers lurking in every shadow that the John Birch Society did, Barry Goldwater and Ronald Reagan, among others, used its anticommunist, antigovernment rhetoric to advantage. Stressing victory over communism, rather than its containment, the self-proclaimed "new conservatives" (or radical right, as their opponents called them) criticized the "creeping socialism" of Eisenhower, advocated a return to traditional moral standards, and condemned the liberal rulings of the Supreme Court.

Jim Crow in Court   Led by a new chief justice, **Earl Warren** (1953), the Supreme Court incurred conservatives' wrath for defending the rights of persons accused of subversive beliefs. In *Jencks* v. *United States* (1957) the Court held that the accused had the right to inspect government files used by the prosecution. In *Yates* v. *United States* (1957) the justices overturned the convictions of Communist Party officials under the Smith Act (see Chapter 26), emphasizing the distinction between unlawful concrete acts and the teaching of revolutionary ideology. *Yates* essentially ended further prosecutions of communists, and right-wing opponents of the decision demanded limitations on the Court's powers and plastered "Impeach Earl Warren" posters on highway billboards.

These condemnations paled beside those of segregationists following ***Brown v. Board of Education of Topeka*** (May 17, 1954). Following a series of cases brought by the NAACP in the 1930s and 1940s, which did not attack segregation head-on but rather called for greater equality within "separate but equal," the NAACP's Thurgood Marshall combined lawsuits from four states and the District of Columbia, reflecting the growing determination of black Americans to demand their rights, in which black plaintiffs claimed that segregated public education *per se* was unconstitutional. *Brown* built on an earlier federal court ruling that had prohibited the segregation of Mexican-American children in California schools, as well as on decisions in 1950 in which the Supreme Court had significantly narrowed the possibility of separate law school and graduate education being in fact equal education, and thus constitutional. Chief Justice Warren, speaking for a unanimous Court, reversed *Plessy* v. *Ferguson* (see Chapter 20). Largely citing psychological studies, the high court held that separating schoolchildren "solely because of their race generates a feeling of inferiority as to their status in the community that may affect their hearts and minds in a way unlikely ever to be undone," thereby violating the equal protection clause of the Fourteenth Amendment. "In the field of public education," the Court concluded, "the doctrine of 'separate but equal' has no place. Separate educational facilities are inherently unequal." A year later, the Court ordered federal district judges to monitor compliance with *Brown*, vaguely requiring that desegregation proceed "with all deliberate speed"—an oxymoron that implied gradualism—the price Warren paid to gain a unanimous decision.

In the border states, African-American and white students sat side by side for the first time in history. But in the South, where segregation was deeply entrenched in law and custom, politicians vowed resistance, and Eisenhower refused to press them to comply: "I don't believe you can change the hearts of men with laws or decisions." Although not personally a racist, Ike never publicly endorsed the *Brown* decision and privately called his appointment of Earl Warren "the biggest damn fool mistake I ever made."

Public-opinion polls in 1954 indicated that some 80 percent of white southerners opposed the *Brown* decision. Encouraged by the president's silence, white resistance stiffened. White Citizens Councils sprang up, and the Ku Klux Klan revived. Declaring *Brown* "null, void, and of no effect," southern legislatures claimed the right to "interpose" themselves against the federal government and adopted a strategy of "massive resistance" to thwart compliance with the law. They closed down or denied state aid to school systems that desegregated, and enacted pupil-placement laws that permitted school boards to assign black and white children to different schools.

In 1956, more than a hundred members of Congress signed the **Southern Manifesto,** denouncing *Brown* as "a clear abuse of judicial power." White southern politicians competed in their opposition to desegregation. When a gubernatorial candidate in Alabama promised to go to jail to defend segregation, his opponent swore that he would die for it. Segregationists also resorted to violence and economic reprisals against blacks to maintain all-white schools. At the end of 1956, not a single African-American attended school with whites in the Deep South, and few did so in the Upper South.

| The Laws of the Land | Southern resistance reached a climax in September 1957. Although the Little Rock school board had accepted a federal court order to desegregate Central High School, Arkansas governor Orval E. Faubus mobilized the state's National Guard to bar nine African-American students from entering the school. After another court order forced Faubus to withdraw the guardsmen, an angry mob of whites blocked the black students' entry. |

Although Eisenhower sought to avoid the divisive issue of civil rights, he believed he had to uphold federal law. He worried that the Soviets were "gloating over this incident and using it everywhere to misrepresent our whole nation." The Cold War had made segregation in the United States a national security liability. Understanding that racism at home hampered American efforts to gain the support of nonwhite Third World nations, the president federalized the Arkansas National Guard and, for the first time since Reconstruction, dispatched federal troops to protect blacks' rights. To ensure the safety of the black students, soldiers patrolled Central High for the rest of the year. Rather than accept integration, however, Faubus shut down Little Rock's public high schools for two years. At the end of the decade, fewer than 1 percent of African-American students in the Deep South attended desegregated schools.

Nevertheless, Little Rock strengthened the determination of African-Americans to end Jim Crow. The crisis foreshadowed television's vital role in the demise of Jim Crow.

Little Rock, 1957   *Elizabeth Eckford, age fifteen, one of the nine black students to desegregate Central High School, endures abuse on her way to school, September 4, 1957. Such scenes of angry whites jeering, screaming, and threatening African-American students were televised to the nation, showing the human suffering caused by racist hatred in the South. By so doing, television made Americans aware of the stark consequences of racism. Forty years later, the young white woman in this picture shouting insults asked for forgiveness.*

The contrast between the images of howling white racists and those of resolute black students projected on the TV screen immensely aided the civil-rights cause. According to a 1957 public-opinion poll, fully 90 percent of whites outside the South approved the use of federal troops in Little Rock.

Most northern whites also favored legislation to enfranchise southern blacks, and during the 1956 campaign Eisenhower proposed a voting rights bill. The Civil Rights Act of 1957, the first since Reconstruction, established a permanent commission on civil rights with broad investigatory powers, but did little to guarantee the ballot to blacks. The Civil Rights Act of 1960 only slightly strengthened the first measure's enforcement provisions. Neither act empowered federal officials to register African-Americans to vote. Like the *Brown* decision, however, these laws implied a changing view of race relations by the federal government, and that further encouraged blacks to fight for their rights.

THE COLD WAR CONTINUES

Eisenhower continued Truman's containment policy. Stalin's death in 1953 and Eisenhower's resolve to reduce the risk of nuclear war brought a thaw in the Cold War, but the United States and the USSR remained deadlocked. Neither the Cold War nor American determination to check communism ceased. Global fear of a nuclear holocaust mounted in step with both countries' increasingly destructive weapons.

Honoring his campaign pledge, Eisenhower visited South Korea in December 1952, but the fate of thousands of prisoners of war (POWs) who did not want to return to communist rule remained the sticking point preventing a settlement. Then the uncertainty in the communist world after Stalin's death and Eisenhower's veiled threat to use nuclear weapons broke the stalemate. The armistice signed in July 1953 established a panel from neutral nations to oversee the return of POWs and set the boundary between North and South Korea once again at the thirty-eighth parallel. Some Americans claimed that communist aggression had been thwarted and containment vindicated; others condemned the truce as peace without honor.

Ike and Dulles   Eager to ease Cold War tensions, Eisenhower first had to quiet the GOP right-wing's clamor to roll back the Red tide. To do so he chose as his secretary of state, **John Foster Dulles.** A rigid Presbyterian whose humorlessness led some to dub him "Dull, Duller, Dulles," the secretary of state talked of a holy war against "atheistic communism," rejected containment as a "negative, futile and immoral policy," and advocated "liberating" the captive peoples of Eastern Europe and unleashing Jiang Jieshi against communist China. He threatened "instant, massive retaliation" with nuclear weapons in response to Soviet aggression, and insisted on the necessity of "brinksmanship," the art of never backing down in a crisis, even if it meant risking war.

Such saber-rattling pleased the Right, but Eisenhower preferred conciliation. Partly because he feared a nuclear war with the Soviet Union, which had tested its own H-bomb in 1953, Eisenhower refused to translate Dulles's rhetoric into action. Aware of the limits of American power, the United States did nothing to check the Soviet interventions that crushed uprisings in East Germany (1953) and Hungary (1956).

As multimegaton thermonuclear weapons replaced atom bombs in the U.S. and Soviet arsenals, Eisenhower worked to reduce the probability of mutual annihilation. He proposed an "atoms for peace" plan, whereby both superpowers would contribute fissionable materials to a new UN agency for use in industrial projects. In the absence of a positive Soviet response, the government began construction of an electronic air defense system to provide warning of a missile attack.

Work also began on commercial nuclear plants in the mid-1950s, promising electricity "too cheap to meter." However, most money for nuclear research continued to be military-related, like that going to naval captain Hyman Rickover's development of nuclear-powered submarines. Mounting fears over radioactive fallout from atmospheric atomic tests, especially the 1954 U.S. test series in the Pacific that spread strontium 90 over a wide area, heightened world concern about the nuclear-arms race.

In 1955 Eisenhower and Soviet leaders met in Geneva for their first summit conference since World War II. Mutual talk of "peaceful coexistence" led reporters to hail the "spirit of Geneva." The two nations could not agree on a plan for arms control, but

Moscow suspended further atmospheric tests of nuclear weapons in March 1958, and the United States followed suit.

Still, the Cold War continued. Dulles negotiated mutual-defense pacts with any nation that would join the United States in opposing communism. His "pactomania" committed the United States to the defense of forty-three nations. The administration relied primarily on the U.S. nuclear arsenal to deter the Soviets. Tailored to suit fiscally conservative Republicans, the "New Look" defense program promised "more bang for the buck" by emphasizing nuclear weapons over conventional forces. It spurred the Soviets to seek "more rubble for the ruble" by enlarging their nuclear stockpile. In anticipation of nuclear war, Congress built a 112,000-square-foot bunker for itself 700 feet below the grounds of the elegant Greenbrier resort in West Virginia. It featured dormitories, a restaurant, an operating clinic, decontamination showers, and chambers in which the legislators would meet.

As the decade wore on, the focus of the Cold War shifted from Europe to the Third World, the nonwhite developing nations. In 1959, Alaska and Hawaii became, respectively, the forty-ninth and fiftieth states in the Union. The first states not contiguous to the continental forty-eight, they were geographically important because of Hawaii's strategic location in the Pacific Ocean and Alaska's closeness to the Soviet Union and Asia. Both were racially and culturally diverse, moreover, and their diversity was seen as an aid to the United States in its relations with nonwhite nations.

CIA Covert Actions To command the Central Intelligence Agency, Eisenhower chose **Allen Dulles,** a veteran of wartime OSS cloak-and-dagger operations and the brother of the secretary of state. Established in 1947 to conduct foreign intelligence gathering, the CIA became increasingly involved in secret operations to topple regimes friendly to communism. By 1957 half its personnel and 80 percent of its budget were devoted to "covert action"—assassinations, political coups, financially supporting foreign political parties and leaders, and subsidizing foreign newspapers and labor unions that hewed a pro-American line.

To woo influential foreigners away from communism, the CIA also sponsored intellectual conferences and jazz concerts. It bankrolled exhibitions of abstract expressionist paintings to counter Soviet socialist realism art. It purchased the film rights to George Orwell's *Animal Farm* and *1984* to make their messages more overtly anticommunist. It subsidized magazines to publish articles supporting Washington's foreign policy. And it recruited businessmen and college students traveling abroad as "fronts" in clandestine CIA activities.

In 1953, the CIA orchestrated a coup to overthrow the government of Iran. Fearing that the prime minister, who had nationalized oil fields, might open oil-rich Iran to the Soviets, the CIA replaced him with pro-American Shah Reza Pahlavi. The United States thus gained a loyal ally on the Soviet border, and American oil companies prospered when the shah made low-priced oil available to them. But Iranian hatred of America took root—an enmity that would haunt the United States a quarter-century later.

Also in 1953, the CIA intervened in Philippine elections to ensure a pro-American government. The next year, a CIA-trained and -financed band of mercenaries overthrew the leftist elected government in Guatemala, which had nationalized and redistributed tracts of land owned by the United Fruit Company. The new pro-American military dictatorship returned the expropriated lands to United Fruit and trampled political opposition.

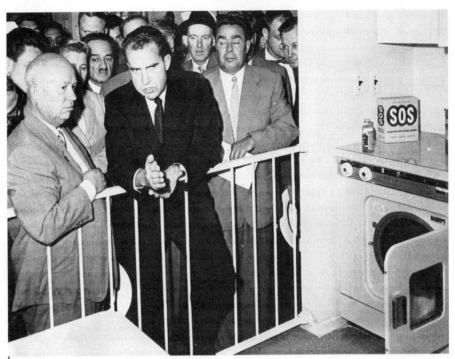

The Great Debate, July 24, 1959 *At the opening of the American National Exhibit in Moscow, Vice President Richard Nixon and Soviet premier Nikita Khrushchev engaged in a "kitchen debate," arguing not about the strength of their rockets or bombs but about the relative merits of American and Soviet washing machines and television sets.*

The Vietnam Domino

The most extensive CIA covert operations during the 1950s took place in Indochina. As a result of Mao Zedong's victory in China and the outbreak of war in Korea, the United States viewed Indochina as a key battleground in the Cold War. The Truman administration provided France with large-scale military assistance to fight the Vietminh, a broad-based Vietnamese nationalist coalition led by the communist Ho Chi Minh (see Chapter 26). By 1954 American aid accounted for three-quarters of French expenditures. Nevertheless, France tottered near defeat. In early 1954, the Vietminh besieged twelve thousand French troops in the northern valley of Dienbienphu.

France appealed for U.S. intervention, and some American officials toyed with the idea of a nuclear strike. "You boys must be crazy," the president replied. "We can't use those awful things against Asians for the second time in ten years." With the Korean War just recently ended, Ike also refused to involve the United States in another land war in Asia. In May, the French surrendered at Dienbienphu. An international conference in Geneva arranged a cease-fire and temporarily divided Vietnam at the seventeenth parallel, pending elections in 1956 to choose the government of a unified nation.

Although unwilling to go to war, Eisenhower would not accept a communist takeover of Vietnam. In what became known as the **domino theory,** Eisenhower warned that if Vietnam went communist, then Thailand, Burma, Indonesia, and ultimately all of Asia would fall like dominos. The United States refused to sign the Geneva Peace Accords, and in late 1954 created the Southeast Asia Treaty Organization (SEATO), a military alliance patterned on NATO.

The United States installed Ngo Dinh Diem, a fiercely anticommunist Catholic, as premier and then president of an independent South Vietnam. CIA agents helped Diem train his armed forces and secret police, eliminate political opposition, and block the 1956 election to reunify Vietnam specified by the Geneva agreement. As Eisenhower admitted, "possibly 80 percent of the population would have voted for the communist Ho Chi Minh as their leader." Washington pinned its hopes on Diem, and Vietnam became a test of its ability to defeat communism in Asia with American dollars rather than American lives.

The autocratic Diem's Catholicism alienated the predominantly Buddhist population, and his refusal to institute land reform and to end corruption spurred opposition. In December 1960, Diem's opponents coalesced in the **National Liberation Front** (NLF). Backed by North Vietnam, the insurgency attracted broad support and soon controlled half of South Vietnam. The administration's commitment to "sink or swim with Ngo Dinh Diem" had cost over $1 billion, and Diem was sinking.

Troubles in the Third World
In 1956, Eisenhower faced his greatest challenge in the Middle East, the **Suez crisis.** In 1954, Gamal Abdel Nasser came to power in Egypt, determined to modernize his nation. To woo him, the United States offered to finance a dam at Aswan to harness the Nile River. When Nasser purchased arms from Czechoslovakia and officially recognized the People's Republic of China, Dulles canceled the loan. Nasser then nationalized the British-owned Suez Canal.

Viewing the canal as the lifeline of its empire, Britain planned to take it back by force. The British were supported by France, which feared Arab nationalism in their Algerian colony, and by Israel, which feared the Egyptian arms buildup. The three countries, America's closest allies, attacked Egypt in October 1956 without consulting Eisenhower. Ike fumed that the military action would drive the Arab world and its precious oil to the Russians. When Moscow threatened to intervene, Eisenhower forced his allies to withdraw their troops.

The Suez crisis had major consequences. It swelled antiwestern sentiment in the Third World, and the United States replaced Britain and France as the protector of Western interests in the Middle East. Determined to guarantee the flow of oil to the West, the president announced the **Eisenhower Doctrine** in 1957, proclaiming that the United States would send military aid and, if necessary, troops to any Middle Eastern nation threatened by "Communist aggression." To show he meant it, Eisenhower ordered fourteen thousand marines into Lebanon in July 1958 to quell a threatened Muslim revolt against its prowestern regime.

Such interventions intensified anti-American feelings in the Third World. Shouting "yanqui imperialism," angry crowds in Peru and Venezuela spat at Vice President Nixon and stoned his car in 1958. In 1959, Fidel Castro overturned a dictatorial regime in Cuba. He confiscated without compensation American properties constituting 90 percent of Cuban mining operations, 80 percent of its utilities, and nearly half its sugar operations. In 1960 anti-American riots in Japan forced Eisenhower to cancel a trip there.

An even tougher blow struck on May 1, 1960. Two weeks before a scheduled summit conference with Soviet premier Nikita Khrushchev, the Soviets shot down a U.S. spy plane far inside their border. Khrushchev displayed the captured CIA pilot and the photos he had taken of Soviet missile sites. Eisenhower refused to apologize and the summit to limit nuclear testing collapsed.

The Eisenhower Legacy   Just before leaving office, Eisenhower offered Americans a farewell and warning. The demands of national security, he stated, had produced the "conjunction of an immense military establishment and a large arms industry that is new in the American experience." Swollen defense budgets had yoked American economic well-being to military expenditures. Military contracts had become the staff of life for research scholars, politicians, and the nation's largest corporations. This combination of interests, Eisenhower believed, exerted enormous leverage and threatened the traditional subordination of the military in American life. "We must guard against the acquisition of unwarranted influence . . . by the **military-industrial complex.** The potential for the disastrous rise of misplaced power exists and will persist."

The president concluded that he had avoided war but that lasting peace was not in sight. Most scholars agreed. Eisenhower ended the Korean War, avoided direct intervention in Vietnam, began relaxing tensions with the Soviet Union, and suspended atmospheric nuclear testing. At the same time, he presided over an accelerating nuclear-arms race and a widening Cold War. He encouraged the CIA to intervene in local conflicts around the globe, which, in Vietnam, would soon lead to the most disastrous military conflict in American history.

The moderate Eisenhower pleased neither Left nor Right. His acceptance of New Deal social-welfare measures angered conservative Republicans, while liberal Democrats faulted his passivity toward McCarthyism and racism. Yet Ike had given most Americans what they most wanted—prosperity, reassurance, and a breathing spell in which to relish the comforts of life.

THE AFFLUENT SOCIETY

In 1958, the economist John Kenneth Galbraith published *The Affluent Society,* a study of postwar America whose title reflected the broad-based prosperity that made the 1950s seem the fulfillment of the American Dream. By the end of the decade, about 60 percent of American families owned homes; 75 percent, cars; and 87 percent, at least one TV. Government spending, a huge upsurge in productivity, and steadily increasing consumer demand pushed the gross national product (GNP) up 50 percent.

Three brief recessions and a national debt of almost $290 billion by 1961 evoked concern but did little to stifle economic growth or optimism. The United States had achieved the world's highest living standard ever. By 1960 the average worker's income, adjusted for inflation, was 35 percent higher than in 1945. With just 6 percent of the world's population, the United States produced and consumed nearly half of everything made and sold on Earth.

The New Industrial Society Federal spending constituted a major source of economic growth. It nearly doubled in the 1950s to $180 billion, and the outlays of state and local governments kept pace. Federal expenditures (accounting for 17 percent of the GNP in the mid-1950s, compared to just 1 percent in 1929) built roads and airports, financed home mortgages, supported farm prices, and provided stipends for education. More than half the federal budget—10 percent of the GNP—went to defense spending. Continued superpower rivalry in atomic munitions, missile-delivery systems, and the space race kept the federal government the nation's main financier of scientific and technological research and development (R&D).

For the West, especially, it was as if World War II never ended, as the new Air Force Academy in Colorado Springs signified. Politicians from both parties labored to keep defense spending flowing westward. Liberal and conservative members of Congress from California sought contracts for Lockheed. So did those from Texas for General Dynamics and those from Washington State for Boeing. By the late 1950s California alone received half the space budget and a quarter of all major military contracts. By then, Denver had the largest number of federal employees outside Washington, D.C.; Albuquerque boasted more Ph.D. degrees per capita than any other U.S. city; and over a third of workers in Los Angeles depended on defense industries. Utah, once the Mormon dream of an agricultural utopia, received the nation's highest per capita expenditures on space and defense research. Government spending transformed the mythic West of individualistic cowboys, miners, and farmers into a West of bureaucrats, manufacturers, and scientists dependent on federal funds.

Science became a ward of the state, with government funding and control transforming both the U.S. military and industry. Financed by the Atomic Energy Commission (AEC) and utilizing navy scientists, the Duquesne Light Company began construction in Shippingport, Pennsylvania, of the nation's first nuclear-power plant in 1954. Chemicals surged from the fiftieth-largest industry before the war to the nation's fourth-largest in the 1960s. As chemical fertilizers and pesticides contaminated groundwater supplies, and as the use of plastics for consumer products reduced landfill space, Americans—unaware of the hidden perils—marveled at fruits and vegetables covered with Saran Wrap and delighted in their Dacron suits, Orlon shirts, Acrilan socks, and Teflon-coated pots and pans.

Electronics became the fifth-largest American industry, providing industrial equipment and consumer appliances. Electricity consumption tripled in the 1950s as industry automated and consumers, "to live better electrically," as commercials urged, purchased electric washers and dryers, freezers, blenders, television sets, and stereos. Essential to the expansion of both the chemical and the electronics industries was inexpensive petroleum. With domestic crude-oil production increasing close to 50 percent and petroleum imports rising from 74 million to 371 million barrels between 1945 and 1960, oil replaced coal as the nation's main energy source. Hardly anyone paid attention when a physicist warned in 1953 that "adding 6 billion tons of carbon dioxide to the atmosphere each year is warming up the Earth."

Plentiful, cheap gasoline fed the growth of the automobile and aircraft industries. The nation's third-largest industry in the 1950s, aerospace depended heavily on defense spending and on federally funded research. In Washington State, the manufacturers of jet aircraft, ballistic missiles, and space equipment employed more people than did logging and timbering firms. Seattle, Dallas–Fort Worth, San Diego, and Los Angeles accounted for nearly all of the nation's aircraft production. The automobile industry, still the titan of the American economy, also utilized technological R&D. Where machines had earlier replaced some human workers, automation now controlled the machines. Between 1945 and 1960 the industry halved the number of hours and of workers required to produce a car. Other industries followed, investing $10 billion a year throughout the fifties on laborsaving machinery.

The Age of Computers

The computer was a major key to the technological revolution. In 1944, International Business Machines (IBM), cooperating with Harvard scientists, had produced the Mark I calculator to decipher secret Axis codes. It was a slow, cumbersome device with five hundred miles of wiring. In late 1945, to improve artillery accuracy, the military devised ENIAC, the first electronic computer. Still unwieldly, with eighteen thousand vacuum tubes, ENIAC could perform five thousand calculations per second. Next came the development of operating instructions, or programs, that could be stored inside the computer's memory; the substitution of printed circuits for wired ones; and in 1948, at Bell Labs, the invention of tiny solid-state transistors that ended reliance on radio tubes.

The computer changed the American economy and society as fundamentally as the steam engine in the First Industrial Revolution and the electric motor and internal combustion engine in the Second. Sales of electronic computers to industry rose from twenty in 1954 to more than a thousand in 1957 and more than two thousand in 1960. Major manufacturers used them to monitor production lines, track inventory, and ensure quality control. The government, which used three machines in computing the 1950 census returns, employed several hundred on the 1960 census. They became as indispensable to Pentagon strategists playing war games as to the Internal Revenue Service, as integral to meteorologists as to scientists "flying" rockets on the drawing board. By the mid-1960s more than thirty thousand mainframe computers were used by banks, hospitals, and universities. Further developments led to the first integrated circuits and to what would ultimately become the Internet, fundamentally changing the nature of work as well as its landscape.

The development of the high-technology complex known as Silicon Valley began with the opening of the Stanford Industrial Park in 1951. Seeking to develop its landholdings around Palo Alto and to attract financial aid from business and the military, Stanford University utilized its science and engineering faculties to design and produce products for the Fairchild Semiconductor and Hewlett-Packard companies. This relationship became a model followed by other high-tech firms. Soon apricot and cherry orchards throughout the Santa Clara valley gave way to industrial parks filled with computer firms and pharmaceutical laboratories. Initially a far cry from dirty eastern factories, these campus-like facilities would eventually choke the valley with traffic congestion, housing developments, and smog. Similar developments would follow the military-fueled research complexes along Boston's Route 128, near Austin, Texas, and in North Carolina's Research Triangle.

The Costs of Bigness

Rapid technological advances accelerated the growth and power of big business. In 1950, twenty-two U.S. firms had assets of more than $1 billion; ten years later more than fifty did.

By 1960 one-half of 1 percent of all companies earned more than half the total corporate income in the United States. The wealthiest, which could afford huge R&D outlays, became oligopolies, swallowing up weak competitors. Three television networks monopolized the nation's airwaves; three automobile and three aluminum companies produced more than 90 percent of America's cars and aluminum; and a handful of firms controlled the lion's share of assets and sales in steel, petroleum, chemicals, and electrical machinery. Corporations acquired overseas facilities to become "multinational" enterprises, and formed "conglomerates" by merging companies in unrelated industries: International Telephone and Telegraph (ITT) branched out from communications into car rental, home building, motel chains, insurance, and more. Despite talk of "people's capitalism," the oil-rich Rockefeller family alone owned more corporate stock than all the nation's wage earners combined.

Growth and consolidation meant greater bureaucratization. "Executives" replaced "capitalists." Success required conformity not creativity, teamwork not individuality. According to sociologist David Riesman's *The Lonely Crowd* (1950), the new "company people" were "other-directed," eager to follow the cues from their peers and not think innovatively or act independently. In the old nursery rhyme "This Little Pig Went to Market," Riesman noted, each pig went his own way. "Today, however, all little pigs go to market; none stay home; all have roast beef, if any do; and all say 'we-we.'"

Changes in American agriculture paralleled those in industry. Farming grew increasingly scientific and mechanized. Technology cut the work hours necessary to grow crops by half between 1945 and 1960, causing many farm families to migrate to cities. In 1956 alone, one-eleventh of the farm population left the land. Meanwhile, heavily capitalized farm businesses, running "factories in the field," prospered by using more machines, more chemicals, and more migrant laborers.

Until the publication of Rachel Carson's *Silent Spring* in 1962, few Americans understood the extent to which fertilizers, herbicides, and pesticides poisoned the environment. Carson, a former researcher for the Fish and Wildlife Service, dramatized the problems caused by the use of the insecticide DDT and its spread through the food chain. Her depiction of a "silent spring" caused by the death of songbirds from DDT toxicity led many states to ban its use. The federal government followed suit. But the incentives for cultivating more land, and more marginal land, led to further ravages. The Army Corps of Engineers and the Bureau of Reclamation dammed the waters of the West, turning the Columbia and Missouri Rivers into rows of slack-water reservoirs, killing fish and wildlife as well as immersing hundreds of square miles of Indian tribal lands.

Blue-Collar Blues Consolidation also transformed the labor movement. In 1955, the merger of the AFL and CIO brought 85 percent of union members into a single federation. Although labor leadership promised aggressive unionism, organized labor fell victim to its success at the bargaining table. Higher wages, shorter workweeks, paid vacations, health-care coverage, and automatic wage hikes tied to the cost of living led most workers to view themselves as middle class rather than the proletariat. The 1950s saw far fewer strikes than the 1930s.

A decrease in the number of blue-collar workers further sapped labor militancy. Most of the new jobs in the 1950s were in the service sector and in public employment, which banned collective bargaining by labor unions. Automation cut membership in the once-mighty coal, auto, and steelworkers' unions by more than half; and unions' very success in raising wages led employers to mechanize more aspects of manufacturing. In 1956, for the first time in U.S. history, white-collar workers outnumbered blue-collar workers. Some proclaimed the United States a "postindustrial" society. This notion minimized the fact that more service jobs involved manual labor than intellect. Most office work was as routinized as any factory job. Yet few unions sought to woo white-collar workers. The percentage of the unionized labor force dropped from a high of 36 percent in 1953 to 31 percent in 1960, and kept falling.

Prosperity and the Suburbs

As real income (adjusted for inflation) rose, Americans spent less of their income on necessities and more on powered lawnmowers and air conditioners. They heaped their shopping carts with frozen, dehydrated, and fortified foods. When they lacked cash, they borrowed. In 1950 Diner's Club issued the first credit card; American Express followed in 1958. Installment buying, home mortgages, and auto loans tripled Americans' total private indebtedness in the 1950s. Advertising expenditures also tripled. Appealing to the desire for status and glamour in its effort to convince people to buy what they did not need, business spent more on advertising than the nation did on public schools. "Our ability to consume is endless," gloated the head of the Macy's department store. "The luxuries of today are the necessities of tomorrow."

Responding to the slogan "You auto buy now," Americans purchased 58 million new cars during the 1950s. Manufacturers enticed people to trade in and up by offering flashier models, two-tone color, tail fins, and extra-powerful engines—like Pontiac's 1955 "Sensational Strato-Streak V-8," which could go more than twice as fast as any speed limit. Seat belts remained an unadvertised extra-cost option. The consequences were increases in highway deaths, air pollution, oil consumption, and "autosclerosis"—clogged urban arteries.

Government policy as well as "auto mania" spurred white Americans' exodus to the suburbs. Federal spending on highways skyrocketed from $79 million in 1946 to $2.6 billion in 1960, putting once-remote areas within "commuting distance" for city workers (see Technology and Culture: The Interstate Highway System). The income tax code stimulated home sales by allowing deductions for home-mortgage interest payments and for property taxes. Both the Federal Housing Administration (FHA) and Veterans Administration (VA) offered low-interest loans; and both continued to deny loans to blacks who sought to buy homes in white neighborhoods. New homeowners frequently had to sign a contract pledging never to sell or rent to "members of other than the Caucasian race," despite the Supreme Court's 1948 ruling that state courts could not enforce restrictive covenants (see Chapter 26). In 1960 suburbia was 98 percent white.

Eighty-five percent of the 13 million new homes built in the 1950s were in the suburbs. While social critics lampooned the "ticky-tacky" houses in "disturbia," many families considered them the embodiment of the American Dream. They longed for single-family homes of their own, good schools, a safe environment for the children, fresh air, and friendly neighbors just like themselves.

Park Forest, Illinois, was carefully planned to be a "complete community for middle-income families with children." While wives stayed home to raise the kids and shop at the Plaza, husbands commuted the thirty miles to Chicago on the Illinois Central Rail-

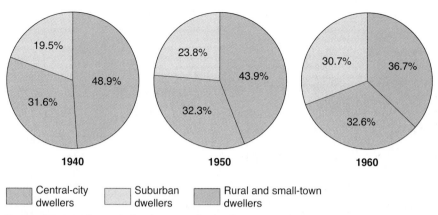

1940   **1950**   **1960**

Central-city dwellers   Suburban dwellers   Rural and small-town dwellers

FIGURE 27.1 **Urban, Suburban, and Rural Americans, 1940–1960**

In the fifteen years following World War II, more than 40 million Americans migrated to the suburbs, where, as one father put it, "a kid could grow up with grass stains on his pants." Over the same period, fourteen of the fifteen largest U.S. cities lost population. *Source:* Adapted from U.S. Bureau of the Census, *Current Censuses,* 1930–1970 (Washington, D.C.: U.S. Government Printing Office).

road or drove into the city on Western Avenue. On Long Island, some thirty miles from midtown Manhattan, Alfred and William Levitt used the mass-production construction techniques they perfected during the war to construct thousands of standardized 720-square-foot houses as quickly as possible. All looked alike. Deeds to the property required door chimes, not buzzers, prohibited picket fences, mandated regular lawn mowing, and even specified when the wash could be hung to dry in the backyard. All the town streets curved at the same angle. A tree was planted every twenty-eight feet. The Levitts then built a second, larger Levittown in Bucks County, Pennsylvania, and a third in Willingboro, New Jersey.

In the greatest internal migration in its history, some 20 million Americans moved to the suburbs in the 1950s—doubling the numbers and making the suburban population equal to that of the central cities. Contractors built 2 million new homes a year, 85 percent of them in the suburbs. By 1960 over 60 percent of American families owned their homes—the symbol of the affluent society.

Many former servicemen who had first glimpsed the Sunbelt in military camps returned to take up residence, as did others lured by job opportunities, the climate, and the pace of life. California's population went from 9 to 19 million between 1945 and 1964, supplanting New York as the most populous state. Los Angeles epitomized the enormous expansion of the suburbs as well as the rapid growth of the Sunbelt. It boasted the highest per capita ownership of private homes and automobiles of any city, as well as 250 miles of freeways by 1960. Initially designed to lure shoppers downtown, the highway system instead had become the road to a home in the suburbs. Orange County, bordering Los Angeles, doubled its population in the 1940s and then tripled it in the 1950s.

Industry also headed south and west, drawn by low taxes, low energy costs, and anti-union right-to-work laws. Senior citizens, attracted to places like Sun City, Arizona,

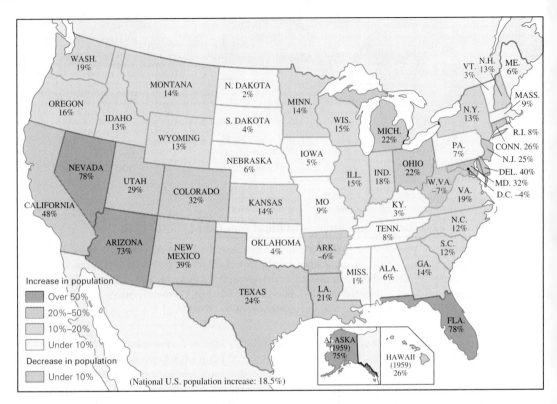

MAP 27.1 Rise of the Sunbelt, 1950–1960

The years after the Second World War saw a continuation of the migration of Americans to the Sunbelt states of the Southwest and the West Coast.

"a complete community geared to older Americans," also brought a more conservative outlook to the Southwest. By 1980 the population of the **Sunbelt,** which stretched from the old Confederacy across Texas to southern California, exceeded that of the North and East. The political power of the Republican Party rose accordingly.

CONSENSUS AND CONSERVATISM

Not everyone embraced the conformity of 1950s consumer culture. Intellectuals found an audience for their attack on "an America of mass housing, mass markets, massive corporations, massive government, mass media, and massive boredom." David Riesman, in *The Lonely Crowd* (1950), described modern Americans as "other-directed" conformists, shaped by the opinions of their peers rather than by their own consciences, and lacking the inner resources to dare be different. Other critics targeted "organization men" incapable of independent thought and "status seekers" pursuing external rewards to compensate for inner insecurities. Some took aim at the consumerist middle class: "all items in a national supermarket—categorized, processed, labeled, priced, and readied for merchandising."

This social criticism oversimplified reality. It ignored ethnic and class diversity. It overlooked the acquisitiveness and conformity of earlier generations—the peer-group pressures in small-town America. It failed to gauge the currents of dissent swirling beneath the surface. It caricatured rather than characterized American society. But the critique rightly spotlighted the elevation of comfort over challenge, and of private pleasures over public affairs. It was, in the main, a time of political passivity and preoccupation with personal gain.

Togetherness and the Baby Boom	In 1954, *McCall's* magazine coined the term *togetherness* to celebrate the "ideal" couple: the man and woman who centered their lives on home and children. Confident in contin-

ued economic prosperity and influenced by popular culture, Americans in the 1950s wed at an earlier age than had their parents (one woman in three married by age nineteen), and had more babies sooner. The fertility rate (the number of births per thousand women) was 80 in 1940, and peaked at 123 in 1957, when an American baby was born every seven seconds.

New antibiotics subdued diphtheria and whooping cough, and the Salk and Sabin vaccines ended the dread of polio. The decline in childhood mortality helped raise American life expectancy from 65.9 years in 1945 to 70.9 years in 1970. Coupled with the "baby boom," it led to a 19 percent increase in the U.S. population during the 1950s—a larger jump than in any previous decade. By 1960 children under fourteen constituted one-third of the population.

The immense size of the **baby-boom** generation (the 76 million Americans born between 1946 and 1964) ensured its impact and historical importance. Its needs and expectations at each stage of life would be as contorting as the digestion of a pig by a boa constrictor. First came the bulge in baby carriages; in the 1950s school construction boomed; and in the 1960s college enrollments soared. Then in the 1970s—as the baby boomers had their own families—home construction peaked. The 1980s and 1990s brought a surge in retirement investments, and the twenty-first century a preoccupation with health matters. In the 1950s, the baby boom also made child rearing a huge concern, reinforcing the idea that women's place was in the home. With Americans convinced of the psychological importance of early childhood experiences, motherhood became an increasingly vital, demanding calling.

No one did more to emphasize children's need for the love and care of full-time mothers than **Dr. Benjamin Spock.** Only the Bible outsold his *Common Sense Book of Baby and Child Care* (1946) in the 1950s. Spock urged mothers not to work outside the home, in order to create the atmosphere of warmth and intimacy necessary for their children to mature into well-adjusted adults. Crying babies were to be comforted so that they would not feel rejected. Breast-feeding came back into vogue. Spock's advice also led to less scolding and spanking and to more "democratic" family discussions. In some homes his "permissive" approach produced a "filiarchy" in which kids ruled the roost; in many it unduly burdened mothers.

Domesticity	Popular culture in the 1950s glorified marriage and parenthood, emphasizing a woman's role as a helpmate to her hus-

band and a full-time mother to her children. As Hollywood actress Debbie Reynolds declared in *The Tender Trap* (1955), "A woman isn't a woman until she's been married and had children."

Television mostly pictured women as at-home mothers. Women's magazines featured articles with titles like "Cooking to Me Is Poetry." *Life* lauded Marjorie Sutton for marrying at sixteen, cooking and sewing for the family, raising four children, being a pillar of the PTA and Campfire Girls, and working out on a trampoline "to keep her size 12 figure." *Housekeeping Monthly* published "The Good Wife's Guide" in 1955 to remind women:

- Catering to his comfort will provide you with immense personal satisfaction.
- Don't complain if he's home late for dinner or stays out all night.
- Don't ask him questions about his actions or question his judgement.
- A good wife always knows her place.

Education reinforced these notions. While girls learned typing and cooking, boys were channeled into carpentry and courses leading to professional careers. Guidance counselors cautioned young women not to "miss the boat" of marriage by pursuing higher education. "Men are not interested in college degrees but in the warmth and humanness of the girls they marry," stressed a textbook on the family. More men than women went to college, and only one-third of college women completed a degree. They dropped out, women joked, to get their M.R.S. degree or a Ph.T.—"Putting Hubbie Through." The laughter sometimes hid dissatisfaction: cooking the perfect dinner could still leave a woman starved for fulfillment.

Profound changes, however, were under way. Despite domesticity's holding sway, increasing numbers of women entered the work force. By 1952, 2 million more women worked outside the home than had during the war; and by 1960, twice as many did as in 1940. In 1960 one-third of the labor force was female, and one out of three married women worked outside the home. Of all women workers that year, 60 percent were married, while 40 percent had school-age children. Their median wage, however, was less than half that for men.

Forced back into low-paying, gender-segregated jobs, most women worked to add to the family income, not to fulfill personal aspirations or challenge stereotypes. White women mostly filled clerical positions, while African-Americans held service jobs in private households and restaurants. Some women, as during World War II, developed a heightened sense of expectations and empowerment as a result of employment. Transmitted to their daughters, their experience would lead to a feminist resurgence in the late 1960s.

Religion and Education

"Today in the U.S.," *Time* claimed in 1954, "the Christian faith is back in the center of things." Domestic anxieties and Cold War fears catalyzed a surge of religious activity. Evangelist **Billy Graham,** Roman Catholic Bishop Fulton J. Sheen, and Protestant minister Norman Vincent Peale all had syndicated newspaper columns, best-selling books, and radio and television programs. None was more influential than Graham. Backed to the hilt by the Hearst press and Luce publications, Graham peddled a potent mixture of religious salvation and aggressive anticommunism. In what he pictured as a duel to the death against the atheistic Kremlin, Graham supported McCarthyism and backed GOP demands to "unleash" Jiang's troops against mainland China. He termed communism "a great sinister anti-Christian movement masterminded by Satan" and echoed Billy Sunday's emphasis on the traditional morality of the nineteenth-century American village, lashing out at homosexuals and working wives.

The turn to religion found expression in Hollywood religious extravaganzas, such as *Ben Hur* and *The Ten Commandments,* and in popular songs like "I Believe" and "The Man Upstairs." Sales of Bibles reached an all-time high. Television proclaimed that "the family that prays together stays together." Dial-a-Prayer offered telephone solutions for spiritual problems. Congress added "under God" to the Pledge of Allegiance and required "IN GOD WE TRUST" to be put on all U.S. currency.

"Everybody should have a religious faith," President Eisenhower declared, "and I don't care what it is." Buffalo Bob agreed: kids watching *The Howdy Doody Show* were regularly exhorted to worship "at the church or synagogue of your choice." Church attendance swelled, and the percentage of people who said they belonged to a church or synagogue increased from 49 percent in 1940 to 55 percent in 1950, and to a historic-high 69 percent in 1959. It had become "un-American to be unreligious," noted *The Christian Century.*

While increasing numbers of Americans identified with some denomination, the intensity of religious faith diminished for many. Religious belief was intermixed with patriotism, family togetherness, and Thursday night bingo. Mainstream Protestant churches downplayed sin and evil and emphasized fellowship, offering a sense of belonging in a rapidly changing society. Many Jews spurned the orthodoxy of their parents for the easier-to-follow practices of Reform or Conservative Judaism. Catholicism broadened its appeal as a new pope, John XXIII, charmed the world with ecumenical reforms.

Similarly, education swelled in the 1950s yet seemed less rigorous than in earlier decades. Primary school enrollment rose by 10 million in the 1950s (compared with 1 million in the 1940s). California opened a new school every week throughout the decade and still faced a classroom shortage. The proportion of college-age Americans in higher education climbed from 15 percent in 1940 to more than 40 percent by the early 1960s. "Progressive" educators promoted sociability and self-expression over science, math, and history. The "well-rounded" student became more prized than the highly skilled or intelligent student. Surveys of college students found them conservative, conformist, and careerist, a "silent generation" seeking security and comfort.

While administrators ran universities like businesses, few faculty challenged the economic structure or ideology of the United States, or addressed the problems of minorities and the poor. Historians downplayed past class conflicts, and highlighted the pragmatic ideas and values held by most Americans. Consensus—the widely shared agreement on most matters of importance, especially respect for private property, individualism, and equal opportunity—was frequently depicted as an integral part of America's history and the key to its greatness.

The Culture of the Fifties American culture reflected the expansive spirit of prosperity as well as Cold War anxieties. With increasing leisure time and fatter paychecks, Americans spent one-seventh of their GNP on entertainment. Yellowstone National Park lured four times as many people through its gates each summer as lived in Wyoming; Glacier National Park attracted more visitors than lived in Montana. Spectator sports boomed; new symphony halls opened; and book sales doubled.

With the opening of a major exhibit of abstract expressionists by the Museum of Modern Art in 1951, New York replaced Paris as the capital of the art world. Like the immense canvases of Jackson Pollock and the cool jazz of trumpeter Miles Davis, introspection and improvisation characterized the major novels of the era. Their personal yearnings sharply contrasted with the political engagement and social realism of literature in the 1930s. Novels like John Updike's *Rabbit Run* (1960) presented characters dissatisfied with jobs and home, longing for a more vital and authentic existence, yet incapable of decisive action.

Southern, African-American, and Jewish-American writers turned out the decade's most vital fiction. William Faulkner continued his dense saga of Yoknapatawpha County, Mississippi, while Eudora Welty evoked southern small-town life in *The Ponder Heart* (1954). The black experience found memorable expression in James Baldwin's *Go Tell It on the Mountain* (1953) and Ralph Ellison's *Invisible Man* (1951). Bernard Malamud's *The Assistant* (1957) explored the Jewish immigrant world of New York's Lower East Side, and Philip Roth's *Goodbye Columbus* (1959) dissected the very different world of upwardly mobile Jews.

The many westerns, musicals, and costume spectacles churned out by Hollywood reflected the diminished interest in political issues. Most films about contemporary life portrayed Americans as one happy white, middle-class family. Minorities and the poor remained invisible, and the independent career women of films of the 1940s were replaced by "dumb blondes" and cute helpmates. But as TV viewing soared, movie attendance dropped 50 percent. A fifth of the nation's theaters became bowling alleys and supermarkets by 1960. Hollywood tried to recoup by developing three-dimensionality and wide-screen processes that accentuated the difference from television's small black-and-white image. No technological wizardry, however—not even Smell-O-Vision and its rival Aroma-Rama—could stem TV's astounding growth.

The Television Culture

No cultural medium ever became as popular and as powerful as quickly, or so reinforced the public mood, as television. Ownership of a TV set soared from one of every eighteen thousand households in 1946 to nine of ten American homes by 1960. By then, more Americans had televisions than had bathrooms.

Business capitalized on the phenomenon. The three main radio networks—ABC, CBS, and NBC—gobbled up virtually every TV station in the country, and, just as in radio, they profited by selling time to advertisers who wanted to reach the largest possible audiences. By the mid-fifties, the three networks each had larger advertising revenues than any other communications medium in the world. By 1959, their advertising income would top $1.5 billion.

Introduced in 1952, *TV Guide* outsold every other periodical and was being published in fifty-three separate regional editions by 1960. The TV dinner, first marketed in 1954, altered the nation's eating habits. When Walt Disney produced a show on Davy Crockett in 1955, stores could not keep up with the massive demand for "King of the Wild Frontier" coonskin caps. Corporations spent fortunes on TV ads, convincing middle-class suburban viewers that the good life was based on endless consumption. "The message of the media," a critic noted, "is the commercial."

Geared to its initial small audiences, TV showcased talent and creativity. Opera performances appeared in prime time, as did sophisticated comedies and political dramas, and documentaries like Edward R. Murrow's *See It Now*. Early situation comedies such as *The Life of Riley* and *The Goldbergs* featured ethnic working-class families. As the price of TV sets came down and program producers felt the chill of McCarthyism, the networks' appetite for a mass audience transformed TV into a cautious celebration of conformity and consumerism. Controversy went off the air. Only a few situation comedies, like Jackie Gleason's *The Honeymooners,* set in Brooklyn, did not feature suburban, consumer-oriented, upper-middle-class families. Most, like *Father Knows Best* and *The Adventures of Ozzie and Harriet,* portrayed perfectly coiffed moms who loved to vacuum in high heels, frisky yet ultimately obedient kids, and all-knowing dads who never lost their tempers.

Decrying TV's mediocrity in 1961, the head of the Federal Communications Commission dared broadcasters to watch their own shows for a day: "I can assure you that you will observe a vast wasteland." A steady parade of soaps, unsophisticated comedies, and violent westerns led others to call TV the "idiot box."

Measuring television's impact is difficult. Depending on the many factors that differentiate individuals, people read the "texts" of TV (or of movies or books) their own way and so receive their own messages or signals from the media. While TV bound some to the status quo, it brought others glimpses of possibilities that raised expectations. It functioned simultaneously as conservator and spur to change. In the main, television reflected existing values and institutions. It stimulated the desire to be included in American society, not to transform it. It spawned mass fads for Barbie dolls and hula hoops, spread the message of consumerism, and made Americans ever more name-brand conscious. It reinforced gender and racial stereotypes. TV rarely showed African-Americans and Latinos—except in servile roles or prison scenes. It extolled male violence in fighting evil; and it portrayed women as either zany madcaps (*My Friend*

Figure 27.2 The Television Revolution, 1950–1994

As televisions became commonplace in the 1950s, TV viewing altered the nature of American culture and politics. *Source:* Statistical Abstracts of the United States.

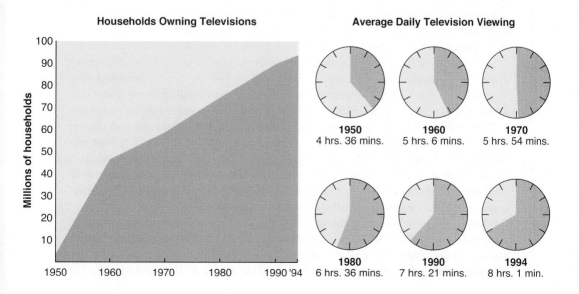

Households Owning Televisions

Millions of households

1950   1960   1970   1980   1990 '94

Average Daily Television Viewing

1950
4 hrs. 36 mins.

1960
5 hrs. 6 mins.

1970
5 hrs. 54 mins.

1980
6 hrs. 36 mins.

1990
7 hrs. 21 mins.

1994
8 hrs. 1 min.

Motorala TV Family Ad *The television set itself, so grandly advertised and dis-played, was a symbol of postwar affluence, and both advertising and program-ming, which featured largely middle-class, consumption-oriented suburban familes, stimulated the consumer culture. Overall, TV powerfully reinforced the conservative, celebratory values of everyday American life in the 1950s.*

Irma) or self-effacing moms (*The Donna Reed Show*). It virtually ended network radio, returning local stations to a music-based format, especially "Top-40" programs geared to youth. While promoting professional baseball and football into truly national phe-nomena, TV decreased the audience of motion picture theaters and of general interest magazines such as *Look* and *Life*.

Television also changed the political life of the nation. Politicians could effectively appeal to the voters over the heads of party leaders, and appearance mattered more than content. The millions watching Senator Estes Kefauver grill mobsters about their ties to city governments instantly made him a serious contender for the presidency. The 20 million observing the combative Senator Joseph McCarthy bully and demean witnesses during his crusade against the army doomed his career. The 58 million who witnessed Richard Nixon's appeal for support in the "Checkers" speech saved his place on the GOP ticket. And Eisenhower's pioneering use of brief "spot advertisements" clinched Ike's smashing presidential victories. In 1960, John F. Kennedy's "telegenic" image would play a major role in his winning the presidency.

Television vastly increased the cost of political campaigning while decreasing the content level of political discussion. It helped produce a more national culture, dimin-ishing provincialism and regional differences. Its overwhelming portrayal of a con-tented citizenry reinforced complacency and hid the reality of "the other America."

THE OTHER AMERICA

"I am an invisible man," declared the African-American narrator of Ralph Ellison's *Invisible Man;* "I am invisible, understand, simply because people refuse to see me." Indeed, few middle-class white Americans perceived the extent of social injustice in the United States. "White flight" from cities to suburbs produced physical separation of the races and classes. New expressways walled off ghettos and rural poverty from middle-class motorists speeding by. Popular culture focused on affluent Americans enjoying the "good life." In the consensus of the Eisenhower era, deprivation had supposedly disappeared. In reality, poverty and racial discrimination were rife and dire, and the struggles for social justice intensified.

Poverty and Urban Blight   Although the percentage of poor families (defined as a family of four with a yearly income of less than three thousand dollars) declined from 34 percent in 1947 to 22 percent in 1960, 35 million Americans remained below the "poverty line." Eight million senior citizens existed on annual incomes below one thousand dollars. A third of the poor lived in depressed rural areas, where 2 million migrant farm workers experienced the most abject poverty. Observing a Texas migratory-labor camp in 1955, a journalist reported that 96 percent of the children had consumed no milk in the previous six months; eight out of ten adults had eaten no meat; and most slept "on the ground, in a cave, under a tree, or in a chicken house." In California's Imperial Valley, the infant death rate among migrant workers was more than seven times the statewide average.

The bulk of the poor huddled in decaying inner-city slums. Displaced southern blacks and Appalachian whites, Native Americans forced off reservations, and newly arrived Hispanics strained cities' inadequate facilities. Nearly two hundred thousand Mexican-Americans were herded into San Antonio's Westside barrio. A local newspaper described them as living like cattle in a stockyard, "with roofed-over corrals for homes and chutes for streets." A visitor to New York City's slums in 1950 found "25 human beings living in a dark and airless coal cellar ten feet below the street level. . . . No animal could live there long, yet here were 17 children, the youngest having been born here two weeks before." The "'promised land' that Mammy had been singing about in the cotton fields for many years," observed Claude Brown, had become a slum, "a dirty, stinky, uncared-for closet-size section of a great city."

As described by Michael Harrington in *The Other America: Poverty in the United States* (1962), the poor were trapped in a vicious cycle of want and a culture of deprivation. Because they could not afford good housing, a nutritious diet, and doctors, the poor got sick more often and for longer than more affluent Americans. Losing wages and finding it hard to hold steady jobs, they could not pay for the decent housing, good food, or doctors that would keep them from getting and staying sick. The children of the poor started school disadvantaged, quickly fell behind, and, lacking encouragement and expectation of success, dropped out. Living with neither hope nor the necessary skills to enter the mainstream of American life, the poor bequeathed a similar legacy to their children.

The pressing need for low-cost housing went unanswered. In 1955 fewer than 200,000 of the 810,000 public-housing units called for in the Housing Act of 1949 had been built. A decade later only 320,000 had been constructed. "Slum clearance" generally meant "Negro clearance," and "urban renewal" meant "poor removal," as developers razed low-income neighborhoods to put up parking garages and expensive housing. The Los Angeles barrio of Chavez Ravine was bulldozed to construct Dodger Stadium.

At the same time, landlords, realtors, and bankers deliberately excluded nonwhites from decent housing. Half of the housing in New York's Harlem predated 1900. A dozen people might share a tiny apartment with broken windows, faulty plumbing, and gaping holes in the walls. Harlem's rates of illegitimate births, infant deaths, narcotics use, and crime soared above the averages for the city and the nation. "Where flies and maggots breed, where the plumbing is stopped up and not repaired, where rats bite helpless infants," black social psychologist Kenneth Clark observed, "the conditions of life are brutal and inhuman."

Blacks' Struggle for Justice   The collision between the hopes raised by the 1954 *Brown* decision and the indignities of persistent discrimination and segregation sparked a new phase in the civil-rights movement. To sweep away the separate but rarely equal Jim Crow facilities in the South, African-Americans turned to new tactics, organizations, and leaders. They utilized nonviolent direct-action protest to engage large numbers of blacks in their own freedom struggle and to arouse white America's conscience.

In the 1950s racism still touched even the smallest details of daily life. In Montgomery, Alabama, black bus riders had to surrender their seats so that no white rider would stand. Although they were more than three-quarters of all passengers, the African-Americans had to pay their fares at the front of the bus, leave, and reenter through the back door, sit only in the rear, and then give up their seats to any standing white passengers.

On December 1, 1955, **Rosa Parks,** for many years an officer of the Montgomery NAACP and a veteran of civil-rights protests in the 1930s and 1940s, refused to get up so that a white man could sit. "I was not tired physically," she later wrote. "No, the only tired I was, was tired of giving in." Her arrest sparked Jo Ann Robinson of the Women's Political Council, and other blacks who had been engaged in the freedom struggle in Montgomery, to propose a boycott of the buses—the beginning of the mass phase of the civil-rights movement. They founded the Montgomery Improvement Association (MIA) to organize the protest, and elected **Martin Luther King, Jr.,** a twenty-seven-year-old African-American minister, to lead the boycott. "There comes a time when people get tired," declared King, articulating the anger of Montgomery blacks, "tired of being segregated and humiliated; tired of being kicked about by the brutal feet of oppression." The time had come, he continued, to cease being patient "with anything less than freedom and justice." In King, Montgomery blacks found a spokesman who repeatedly stirred their souls and encouraged them to boycott the buses for a year, organize carpools or walk miles to work, brave legal harassment and violence. "My soul has been tired for a long time," an old woman told a minister who had stopped his car to offer her a ride; "now my feet are tired, and my soul is resting." When the city leaders would not budge, the blacks challenged the constitutionality of bus segregation. In November 1956, the U.S. Supreme Court affirmed a lower-court decision outlawing segregation on the buses.

The Montgomery bus boycott demonstrated African-American strength and determination. It shattered the myth that African-Americans approved of segregation and that only outside agitators opposed Jim Crow. It affirmed the possibility of social change and inspired protests elsewhere in the South. It vaulted Dr. King, whose oratory simultaneously inspired black activism and touched white consciences, into the national spotlight. As no one before, King presented the case for black rights in a vocabulary that echoed both the Bible and the freedom values of the Founding Fathers.

King's philosophy of civil disobedience fused the spirit of Christianity with the strategy of achieving racial justice by nonviolent resistance. His emphasis on direct action gave every African-American an opportunity to demonstrate the moral evil of racial discrimination; and his insistence on nonviolence diminished the likelihood of bloodshed. Preaching that blacks must lay their bodies on the line to provoke crises that would force whites to confront their racism, King urged his followers to love their enemies. By so doing, he believed, blacks would convert their oppressors and bring "redemption and reconciliation." In 1957 King and a group of black ministers formed the Southern Christian Leadership Conference (SCLC) "to carry on nonviolent crusades against the evils of second-class citizenship." Yet more than on leaders, the movement's triumphs would depend on the domestic servants who walked instead of riding the buses, the children on the front lines of the battle for school desegregation, and the tens of thousands of ordinary people who marched, rallied, and demonstrated extraordinarily.

Latinos and Latinas Hispanic Americans initially made less headway in ending discrimination. High unemployment on the Caribbean island and the advent of direct air service to New York in 1945 brought a steady stream of Puerto Ricans, who as U.S. citizens could enter the mainland without restriction. From seventy thousand in 1940 to a quarter of a million in 1950 and then nearly a million in 1960, El Barrio in New York City's East Harlem had a larger Puerto Rican population and more bodegas than San Juan by the late 1960s.

In New York they suffered from inadequate schools and police harassment, and were denied decent jobs and political recognition. More than half lived in inadequate housing. Like countless earlier immigrants, Puerto Ricans gained greater personal freedom in the United States while losing the security of a strong cultural tradition. Family frictions flared in the transition to unaccustomed ways. Parents felt upstaged by children who learned English and obtained jobs that were closed to them. The relationship between husbands and wives changed as women found readier access to jobs than did men. One migrant explained, "Whether I have a husband or not I work . . . and if my husband dare to complain, I throw him out. That is the difference; in Puerto Rico Ishould have to stand for anything a man asks me to do because he pays the rent. Here I belong to myself." Others hoped to earn money in the United States and then return home. Most stayed. Yet however much they tried to embrace American ways, many could not enjoy the promise of the American Dream because of their skin color, culture, and language. Increasingly they turned to organizations like Antonia Pantoja's Puerto Rican Association for Community Affairs (PRACA), which sought to end discrimination against Puerto Ricans and *Nuyoricans*—those born in New York City.

Mexican-Americans suffered the same indignities. Most were underpaid, overcharged, and segregated from mainstream American life. The presence of countless "undocumented aliens" compounded their woes.

After World War II, new irrigation systems added 7.5 million acres to the agricultural lands of the Southwest, stimulating farm owners' desire for cheap Mexican labor. In 1951, to stem the resulting tide of illegal Mexican immigrants, Congress reintroduced

Mexican Wetbacks Being Pulled Back into Mexico by Mexican Police
Following World War II, the U.S goverment continued to use the bracero program *when it needed inexpensive laborers to do the arduous work in the hot agricutural fields of the Sunbelt, and then deported millions of Mexicans when it no longer needed them, as in this photo taken during "Operation Wetback" in the recession of 1953–1955.*

the ***bracero* program,** a wartime "temporary worker" measure that brought in seasonal farm laborers. The *braceros* were supposed to return to Mexico at the end of their labor contract, but many stayed without authorization, joining a growing number of Latinos who entered the country illegally.

During the 1953–1955 recession, the Eisenhower administration's "Operation Wetback" (*wetback* was a term of derision for illegal Mexican immigrants who supposedly swam across the Rio Grande to enter the United States) deported some 3 million allegedly undocumented entrants. Periodic roundups, however, did not substitute for a sound labor policy or an effective enforcement strategy, and millions of Mexicans continued to cross the poorly guarded two-thousand-mile border. The *bracero* program itself peaked in 1959, admitting 450,000 workers. Neither the *Asociación Nacional México-Americana* (founded in 1950) nor the older League of United Latin American Citizens (LULAC) could stop their exploitation or the widespread violations of the rights of Mexican-American citizens.

The Mexican-American population of Los Angeles County doubled to more than six hundred thousand, and the *colonias* of Denver, El Paso, Phoenix, and San Antonio grew proportionately as large. The most rural of all major ethnic groups in 1940, the percentage of Mexican-Americans living in urban areas rose to 65 percent in 1950 and to 85 percent by 1970. As service in World War II gave Hispanics an increased sense of their own American identity and a claim on the rights supposedly available to all American citizens, urbanization gave them better educational and employment opportunities. Unions like the United Cannery, Agricultural, Packing and Allied Workers of America sought higher wages and better working conditions for their Mexican-American members, and such middle-class organizations as LULAC, the GI Forum, and the Unity League campaigned to end discrimination and segregation, and won important court decisions that declared school segregation of Mexican-Americans unconstitutional (*Mendez*, 1947, and *Delgado*, 1948) and ended their exclusion from Texas jury lists (*Hernandez*, 1954).

The mobilization of Hispanic voters led to the election of the first Mexican-American mayor, in El Paso in 1958. Latinos also took pride in baseball star Roberto Clemente and their growing numbers in the major leagues, in Nobel Prize winners like biologist Severo Ochoa, and in such Hollywood stars as Ricardo Montalban and Anthony Quinn. But the existence of millions of undocumented aliens and the continuation of the *bracero* program stigmatized all people of Spanish descent and depressed their wages. The median income of Hispanics was less than two-thirds that of Anglos. At least a third lived in poverty.

Native Americans   Native Americans remained the poorest minority, with a death rate three times the national average. Unemployment rates on reservations during the 1950s reached 70 percent for the Blackfeet of Montana and the Hopi of New Mexico, and a staggering 86 percent for the Choctaw of Mississippi. After World War II Congress veered away from John Collier's efforts to reassert Indian sovereignty and cultural autonomy and had moved toward the goal of assimilation. This meant terminating treaty relationships with tribes, ending the federal trusteeship of Indians. Some favored it as a move toward Indian self-sufficiency; others desired an end to the communal culture of Indians; and still others wanted access to Indian lands and mineral resources. Between 1954 and 1962 Congress passed a dozen termination bills, withdrawing financial support from sixty-one reservations.

First applied to Menominees of Wisconsin and Klamaths of Oregon, who owned valuable timberlands, the termination policy proved disastrous. Further impoverishing the Indians whom it affected, the law transferred more than five hundred thousand acres of Native American lands to non-Indians. To lure Indians off the reservations and into urban areas, and to speed the sale of Indian lands to developers, the government established the Voluntary Relocation Program. It provided Native Americans with moving costs, assistance in finding housing and jobs, and living expenses until they obtained work. "We're like wheat," said one Hopi woman who went to the city. "The wind blows, we bend over. . . . You can't stand up when there's wind."

By the end of the decade about sixty thousand reservation Indians had been relocated to cities. Some became assimilated into middle-class America, marrying whites and losing their tribal identity. Others could not find work and ended up on state welfare rolls living in rundown shantytowns, addicted to alcohol. A third returned to the reservations. Not surprisingly, the National Congress of American Indians vigorously opposed termination, and most tribal politicians advocated Indian sovereignty, treaty rights, federal trusteeship, and the special status of Indians.

SEEDS OF DISQUIET

Late in the 1950s, apprehension ruffled the calm surface of American life. Questions about the nation's values and goals, periodic recessions, rising unemployment, and the growing national debt made Khrushchev's 1959 warning that the Soviet Union would bury the United States economically and his boast that "your grandchildren will live under communism" ring in American ears. Third World anticolonialism, especially in Cuba, diminished Americans' sense of national pride. So did the growing alienation of American youth and a technological breakthrough by the Soviet Union.

Sputnik   On October 4, 1957, the Soviet Union launched the first artificial satellite, *Sputnik* ("Little Traveler"). Weighing 184 pounds and a mere twenty-two inches in diameter, *Sputnik* dashed the American myth of unquestioned technological superiority. When *Sputnik II*, carrying a dog, went into a more distant orbit on November 3, Democrats charged that Eisenhower had allowed a "technological Pearl Harbor."

The Eisenhower administration publicly disparaged the Soviet achievement. Behind the scenes it hurried to have the American Vanguard missile launch a satellite. On December 6, with millions watching on TV, the Vanguard rose six feet in the air and exploded. Newspapers ridiculed America's "Flopnik."

Eisenhower did not laugh. He doubled the funds for missile development to $4.3 billion in 1958 and then raised the amount to $5.3 billion in 1959. He also established the Science Advisory Committee, whose recommendations led to the creation of the National Aeronautics and Space Administration (NASA) in July 1958. By decade's end, the United States had launched several space probes and successfully tested the Atlas intercontinental ballistic missile (ICBM).

Spurred by *Sputnik,* Americans embarked on a crash program to improve American education. The National Defense Education Act (1958) for the first time provided direct federal funding to higher education, especially to improve the teaching of the sciences, mathematics, and foreign languages. Far more funds went to university research to ensure national security. By 1960, nearly a third of scientists and engineers on university faculties worked full-time on government research, primarily defense projects. Some observers dubbed it the "military-industrial-educational complex."

The number of college students skyrocketed from 2.5 million in 1955 to 3.6 million in 1960. That year the U.S. government funneled $1.5 billion to universities, a hundredfold increase over 1940. Linked directly to the Cold War, this hike in federal aid to education raised unsettling questions.

A Different Beat   Few adults considered the social implications of their affluence on the young, or the consequences of having a teenage generation stay in school instead of working. Few pondered growing up in an age when traditional values like thrift and self-denial had declining relevance, or of maturing when young people had the leisure and money to shape their own subculture. Little attention was paid to the decline in the age of menarche (first menstruation), or the ways that the relatively new institution of the junior high school affected the behavior of youth. Despite talk of family togetherness, busy fathers paid little attention to their children, and mothers sometimes spent more time chauffeuring their young than listening to them. Indeed, much of what adults knew about teenagers (a noun that first appeared in the 1940s and was not commonly used until the 1950s) they learned from the mass media, which focused on the sensational and the superficial.

Accounts of juvenile delinquency abounded, portraying high schools as war zones, city streets as jungles, and teenagers as zip-gun-armed hoodlums. A cover story in *Time* blared "Teenagers on the Rampage." Highly publicized hearings by a Senate subcommittee on juvenile delinquency stoked the fears. Teenage crime, in fact, had barely increased. Male teenagers aroused alarm by sporting leather jackets and slicking their hair in a "ducktail."

As dismaying to parents, young Americans embraced rock-and-roll. In 1951, Alan Freed, the host of a classical music program on Cleveland radio, had observed white teenagers dancing to rhythm-and-blues records by such black performers as Chuck Berry, Bo Diddley, and Little Richard. In 1952, Freed started a new radio program to play "race music," and in 1954 he took the program to New York, creating a national craze for "rock-and-roll," the very term that had been used in blues songs for sexual intercourse.

Just as white musicians in the 1920s and 1930s had adapted black jazz for white audiences, white performers in the 1950s transformed rock-and-roll. In 1954, Bill Haley and the Comets dropped the sexual allusions from Joe Turner's "Shake, Rattle, and Roll," added country-and-western guitar riffs, and had the first major white rock-and-roll hit. When Haley performed "Rock Around the Clock" in *The Blackboard Jungle,* a 1955 film about juvenile delinquency, many parents linked rock-and-roll with disobedience and crime. Red-hunters saw it as a communist plot to corrupt youth. Segregationists claimed it was a ploy "to mix the races." Psychiatrists feared it was "a communicable disease." Some churches condemned it as the "devil's music."

Nothing confirmed their dismay as much as raucous, swaggering **Elvis Presley.** Born in Tupelo, Mississippi, Elvis was a nineteen-year-old truck driver in 1954 when he paid four dollars to record two songs at a Memphis studio. He melded the Pentecostal music of his boyhood with the powerful beat and sexual energy of the rhythm-and-blues music he heard on Memphis's Beale Street, and his songs like "Hound Dog" and "All Shook Up" transformed the cloying pop music that youth found wanting into a proclamation of teenage "separateness." Presley's gyrating pelvis and bucking hips—exuding sexuality—shocked middle-class adults. The more adults condemned rock-and-roll, the more teenagers loved it. Record sales tripled between 1954 and 1960, and Dick Clark's *American Bandstand* became the decade's biggest TV hit. As teens listened to 45-rpm records in their own rooms and to radios in their own cars, the music directed to them by such "outsiders" as Buddy Holly from West Texas, Richie Valens (Valenzuela) from East Los Angeles, and Frankie Lymon from Spanish Harlem nourished the roots of the coming youth revolt.

Portents of Change Teens cherished rock-and-roll for its frankness and exuberance. They elevated characters played by Marlon Brando in *The Wild One* (1954) and James Dean in *Rebel Without a Cause* (1955) to cult status for rejecting society's mores. They delighted in *Mad* magazine's ridiculing of the phony and pretentious in middle-class America. They customized their cars to reject Detroit's standards. All were signs of their variance from the adult world, of their distinct community.

Nonconformist writers known as the **Beats** expressed a more fundamental revolt against middle-class society. In Allen Ginsberg's *Howl* (1956) and Jack Kerouac's *On the Road* (1957), the Beats scorned conformity, religion, family values, and materialism as much as they did conventional punctuation. They scoffed at the "square" America described by Kerouac as "rows of well-to-do houses with lawns and television sets in each living room with everybody looking at the same thing and thinking the same thing at the same time." They romanticized society's outcasts—the mad ones, wrote Kerouac, "the ones who never yawn or say a commonplace thing, but burn, burn, burn like fabulous yellow roman candles exploding like spiders across the stars." Outraging respectability, they glorified uninhibited sexuality and spontaneity in the search for "It," the ultimate authentic experience, foreshadowing the counterculture to come.

The mass media scorned the Beats, as they did all dissenters. *Look* magazine derided them as Americans "turned inside out. The goals of the Beats are *not* watching TV, *not* wearing gray flannel, *not* owning a home in the suburbs, and especially—*not* working." But some college youth admired their rejection of conformity and celebration of sexual experimentation. They read poetry and listened to jazz, and some students even protested capital punishment and demonstrated against the continuing investigations of the House Un-American Activities Committee. Others decried the nuclear-arms race. In 1958 and 1959, thousands participated in Youth Marches for Integrated Schools in Washington. Together with the Beats and rock music, this vocal minority of the "silent generation" heralded a youth movement that would explode in the 1960s.

CONCLUSION

A far more complex era than that implied in the stereotype of the "nifty fifties," the decade encompassed contradictions. Although mightier than any nation in history and basking in prosperity, many Americans felt uneasiness as the Cold War continued and boom times brought unsettling changes. Most were pleased that continuity rather than change characterized the switch from a Democratic to a Republican administration. Differing from Truman's policies more in degree than in kind, Eisenhower pursued a centrist course in domestic affairs. While tilting to the right in favoring private corporations, the Eisenhower administration left New Deal reforms in place, expanded existing social-welfare benefits, employed Keynesian deficit spending to curtail economic recessions, made no effort to hamper labor unionization, and proposed construction of a vast interstate highway system—the largest domestic spending program in the nation's history. The size and scope of the federal government expanded.

So did its involvement throughout the world. The Eisenhower administration followed that of Truman's in its determination to contain communism while putting new emphasis on the need to avoid nuclear war and to fight communism in the Third World. Eisenhower and Dulles gained short-term victories in local conflicts by clandestine means, ignoring the nationalistic yearnings and socioeconomic deprivations of the local peoples, and increasingly allying the United States with reactionary, repressive regimes.

The postwar era was one of unparalleled material prosperity for most Americans. Building on the accumulated savings and pent-up demand for consumerism from the

Second World War, high levels of government spending and new technologies that increased productivity spurred an economic boom that further enriched the rich, transformed the working class into the middle class, and left the poor isolated on a remote island of deprivation and powerlessness.

Overall, the United States in the 1950s seemed the very model of a contented, complacent society. There was, indeed, much conservatism and conformity. But there were also cracks in the picture of a placid people. Unrest coexisted with consensus. Along with bland TV programs, Americans saw a renaissance of creativity in the arts and literature. Racism remained omnipresent in American society, yet the African-American struggle to end white supremacy quickened its pace. In the courts, the NAACP ceased requesting that separate facilities really be equal and instead insisted that true equality required desegregation. In the streets, Martin Luther King, Jr., and the Southern Christian Leadership Conference employed the techniques of nonviolent civil disobedience to mobilize the black masses to attack Jim Crow. The passage of the first civil-rights acts since Reconstruction and Supreme Court decisions that nullified the legal foundations of segregation brought some gains. More vitally, they stimulated the hopefulness that spurred further protest by blacks, as well as by Hispanics and Native Americans.

The Beats and many intellectuals criticized the hypocrisies of postwar America; and some young people, unwilling to accept their parents' embrace of the status quo, became alienated and rebellious. But most middle-class whites ignored the inequities in American society and the voices of discontent. Enjoying their private pleasures, they rejected radicalism, extolled religion, and idealized traditional gender roles, domesticity, and togetherness. Busy working and consuming, they left for a future decade the festering problems of poverty, urban decay, and racial injustice, and the explosive consequences of a younger generation rejecting their parents' conformity and conservatism.

28

The Liberal Era, 1960–1968

THE KENNEDY PRESIDENCY, 1961–1963

Projecting an image of youthful vigor, **John F. Kennedy** personified the self-confident liberal who believed that an activist state could improve life at home and confront the communist challenge abroad. His wealthy father, Joseph P. Kennedy, seethed with ambition and instilled in his sons a passion to excel and to rule. Despite a severe back injury, John Kennedy served in the navy in World War II, and the elder Kennedy persuaded a popular novelist to write articles lauding John's heroism in rescuing his crew after their PT boat had been sunk in the South Pacific.

Esteemed as a war hero, John Kennedy used his charm and his father's connections to win election to the House of Representatives in 1946 from a Boston district where he had never lived. Although Kennedy earned little distinction in Congress, Massachusetts voters sent him to the Senate in 1952 and overwhelmingly reelected him in 1958. By then he had a beautiful wife, Jacqueline, and a Pulitzer Prize for *Profiles in Courage* (1956), written largely by a staff member.

Despite the obstacle of his Roman Catholic faith, the popular Kennedy won a first-ballot victory at the 1960 Democratic convention. Just forty-three years old, he sounded the theme of a "New Frontier" to "get America moving again."

A New Beginning   "All at once you had something exciting," recalled a University of Nebraska student. "You had a guy who had little kids and who liked to play football on his front lawn. Kennedy was talking about pumping new life into the nation and steering it in new directions." But most voters, middle aged and middle class, wanted the stability and security of Eisenhower's "middle way" promised by the Republican candidate, Vice President Richard M. Nixon. Although scorned by

CHRONOLOGY , 1960–1968

1960 • Sit-ins to protest segregation begin.

1961 • John F. Kennedy elected president
Peace Corps and Alliance for Progress created.
Bay of Pigs invasion.
Freedom rides.
Berlin Wall erected.

1962 • Cuban missile crisis.

1963 • Civil-rights demonstrations in Birmingham.
March on Washington.
Test-Ban Treaty between the Soviet Union and the United States.
Kennedy assassinated; Lyndon B. Johnson becomes president.
Betty Friedan, *The Feminine Mystique.*

1964 • Freedom Summer in Mississippi.
California becomes most populous state.
Civil Rights Act.
Gulf of Tonkin incident and resolution.
Economic Opportunity Act initiates War on Poverty.
Johnson elected president.

1965 • Bombing of North Vietnam and Americanization of the war begin.
Assassination of Malcolm X.
Civil-rights march from Selma to Montgomery.
César Chávez's United Farm Workers strike in California.
Teach-ins to question U.S. involvement in war in Vietnam begin.
Voting Rights Act.
Watts riot in Los Angeles.

1966 • Stokely Carmichael calls for Black Power.
Black Panthers formed.
National Organization for Women (NOW) founded.

1967 • Massive antiwar demonstrations.
Race riots in Newark, Detroit, and other cities.

liberals for his McCarthyism, Nixon was better known and more experienced than Kennedy, identified with the still-popular Ike, and a Protestant.

Nixon fumbled his opportunity, agreeing to meet his challenger in televised debates. More than 70 million tuned in to the first televised debate between presidential candidates, a broadcast that secured the dominance of television in American politics. Nixon, sweating visibly, appeared haggard and insecure; in striking contrast, the tanned, telegenic Kennedy radiated confidence. Radio listeners judged the debate a draw, but the

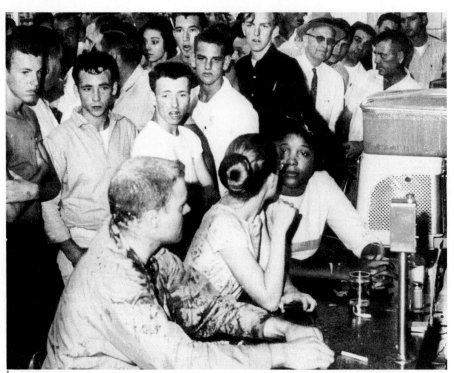

The Sit-Ins   *The sit-ins of 1960 initiated the student phase of the civil-rights movement. Across the South, young black activists challenged segregation by staging nonviolent demonstrations to demand access to public facilities. Their courage and commitment reinvigorated the movement, leading to still greater grass-roots activism.*

far more numerous television viewers declared Kennedy the victor. He shot up in the polls, and Nixon never regained the lead.

Kennedy also benefited from an economic recession in 1960, and from his choice of a southern Protestant, Senate Majority Leader Lyndon B. Johnson, as his running mate. Still, the election was the closest since 1884. Only 120,000 votes separated the two candidates. Kennedy's religion cost him millions of popular votes, but his capture of 80 percent of the Catholic vote in the closely contested midwestern and northeastern states delivered crucial Electoral College votes, enabling him to squeak to victory.

Kennedy's inauguration set the tone of a new era: "the torch has been passed to a new generation of Americans." In sharp contrast to Eisenhower's reliance on businessmen (see Chapter 27), Kennedy surrounded himself with liberal intellectuals. For attorney general, he selected his younger brother Robert Kennedy, joking "I see nothing wrong with giving Robert some legal experience before he goes out to practice law."

"America's leading man," novelist Norman Mailer called him. Kennedy seemed more a celebrity than a politician, and his dash played well on TV. Aided by his wife, he adorned his presidency with the trappings of culture and excellence, inviting distinguished artists to perform at the White House and studding his speeches with quotations from Emerson. Awed by his grace and taste, as well as by his wit and wealth, the media extolled him as a vibrant leader and adoring husband. The public knew nothing of his fragile health, frequent use of mood-altering drugs to alleviate pain, and extra-marital affairs.

Kennedy's Domestic Record
Media images obscured Kennedy's lackluster domestic record. The conservative coalition of Republicans and southern Democrats that had stifled Truman's Fair Deal also doomed the New Frontier. Lacking the votes, JFK rarely pressed Congress for social legislation, maintaining that "there is no sense in raising hell, and then not being successful."

JFK made stimulating economic growth his domestic priority. To that end he combined higher defense expenditures with investment incentives for private enterprise. In 1961 he persuaded Congress to boost the defense budget by 20 percent. He vastly increased America's nuclear stockpile, strengthened the military's conventional forces, and established the Special Forces ("Green Berets") to engage in guerrilla warfare. By 1963 the defense budget reached its highest level as a percentage of total federal expenditures in the entire Cold War era. Kennedy also persuaded Congress to finance a "race to the moon," which Americans would win in 1969 at a cost of more than $25 billion. Most importantly, Kennedy took his liberal advisers' Keynesian advice to call for a huge cut in corporate taxes, which would greatly increase the deficit but would presumably provide capital for business to invest. This would stimulate the economy, increase tax revenues, and thus create a better life for all Americans. When the Kennedy presidency ended in November 1963, the proposed tax cut was bottled up in Congress. Military spending, continued technological innovation, heightened productivity, and low-cost energy, however, had already doubled the 1960 rate of economic growth, decreased unemployment, and held increases in inflation to 1.3 percent a year. The United States was in the midst of its longest uninterrupted economic expansion.

The boom would both cause further ecological damage and provide the affluence that enabled Americans to care about the environment. It would build on an older conservation movement, emphasizing the efficient use of resources, a preservation movement (focusing on preserving "wilderness"), and the fallout scare of the 1950s, which raised questions about the biological well-being of the planet. The publication in 1962 of Rachel Carson's *Silent Spring* (see Chapter 27), documenting the hazards of pesticides, intensified concern. Additionally, postwar prosperity made many Americans less concerned with increased production and more concerned with the quality of life. In response, Kennedy appointed an advisory committee that warned against widespread pesticide use. In 1963, Congress passed a Clean Air Act, regulating automotive and industrial emissions. After decades of heedless pollution, Washington hesitatingly began to address environmental problems.

Cold War Activism
In his inaugural address Kennedy proclaimed, "we shall pay any price, bear any burden, meet any hardship, support any friend, oppose any foe to assure the survival and success of liberty." He launched a major military buildup and surrounded himself with Cold Warriors who shared his belief that American security depended on superior force and the willingness to use it. At the same time, he gained congressional backing for economic assistance to Third World countries to counter the appeal of communism. The Peace Corps, created in 1961, exemplified the New Frontier's liberal anticommunism. By 1963, five thousand Peace Corps volunteers were serving two-year stints as teachers, sanitation engineers, crop specialists, and health workers in more than forty Third World nations. They were,

according to liberal historian and Kennedy aide Arthur Schlesinger, Jr., "reform-minded missionaries of democracy."

In early 1961 a crisis flared in Laos, a tiny, landlocked nation created by the Geneva agreement in 1954. There a civil war between American-supported forces and Pathet Lao rebels seemed headed toward a communist triumph. In July 1962 Kennedy agreed to a face-saving compromise that restored a neutralist government but left communist forces dominant in the countryside. The accord stiffened Kennedy's resolve not to allow further communist gains in Asia, which resulted in his deepening of the American commitment to support a noncommunist South Vietnam.

Spring 1961 brought Kennedy's first major foreign-policy crisis. To eliminate a communist outpost on America's doorstep, he approved a CIA plan, drawn up in the Eisenhower administration, to invade Cuba. In April, fifteen hundred anti-Castro exiles, "La Brigada," stormed Cuba's Bay of Pigs, expecting their arrival to trigger a general uprising to overthrow Fidel Castro. It was a fiasco. Deprived of air cover by Kennedy's desire to conceal U.S. involvement, the invaders had no chance against Castro's superior forces. Although Kennedy accepted blame for the failure, he neither apologized nor ceased attempting to topple Castro.

In July 1961, Kennedy met Soviet premier Nikita Khrushchev in Vienna to try to resolve a peace treaty with Germany (see Chapter 26). Comparing American troops in the divided city of Berlin to "a bone stuck in the throat," Khrushchev threatened war unless the West retreated. A shaken Kennedy returned to the United States and declared the defense of West Berlin essential to the Free World. He doubled draft calls, mobilized 150,000 reservists, and called for increased defense spending. The threat of nuclear war escalated until mid-August, when the Soviets constructed a wall to seal off East Berlin and end the exodus of brains and talent to the West. The Berlin Wall became a concrete symbol of communism's denial of personal freedom until it fell in 1989.

To the Brink of Nuclear War

In mid-October 1962, aerial photographs revealed that the Soviet Union had built bases for intermediate-range ballistic missiles (IRBMs) in Cuba, capable of striking U.S. soil. Smarting from the Bay of Pigs disaster, fearing unchecked Soviet interference in the Western Hemisphere, and believing that his credibility was at stake, Kennedy responded forcefully. In a somber televised address, he denounced the "provocative threat to world peace" and announced that the United States would "quarantine" Cuba—impose a naval blockade—to prevent delivery of more missiles and would dismantle by force the missiles already in Cuba if the Soviets did not do so.

The world held its breath during the **Cuban missile crisis.** The two superpowers appeared on a collision course toward nuclear war. Soviet technicians worked feverishly to complete missile launch pads, and Soviet missile-carrying ships steamed toward the blockade. American B-52s armed with nuclear bombs took to the air, and nearly a quarter-million troops assembled in Florida to invade Cuba. Secretary of State Dean Rusk gulped, "We're eyeball to eyeball."

"I think the other fellow just blinked," a relieved Rusk announced on October 25. Kennedy received a message from Khrushchev promising to remove the missiles if the U.S. pledged never to invade Cuba. As Kennedy prepared to respond positively, a second, more belligerent message arrived from Khrushchev insisting that American missiles be withdrawn from Turkey as part of the deal. Hours later an American U-2 reconnaissance plane was shot down over Cuba. It was "the blackest hour of the crisis," recalled a Kennedy aide. Some advisers urged an immediate invasion, but the president, heeding Robert Kennedy's advice, decided to accept the first message and ignore the second one. The next morning Khrushchev pledged to remove the missiles in return for Kennedy's noninvasion promise. Less publicly, Kennedy subsequently removed U.S. missiles from Turkey.

The full extent of the crisis became known only after the end of the Cold War, when the Russians disclosed that Soviet forces in Cuba had possessed thirty-six nuclear warheads as well as nine tactical nuclear weapons for battlefield use. Soviet field commanders had independent authority to use these weapons. Worst of all, Kennedy had not known that the Soviets already had the capability to launch a nuclear strike from Cuba. Speaking in 1992, former secretary of defense Robert McNamara recalled the pressure on Kennedy to invade and the likely consequence: "No one should believe that U.S. troops could have been attacked by tactical nuclear warheads without the U.S.'s responding with nuclear warheads. . . . And where would it have ended? In utter disaster."

Chastened by coming to the brink of nuclear war, Kennedy and Khrushchev installed a telephone "hot line" so that the two sides could communicate instantly in future crises, and then agreed to a treaty outlawing atmospheric and undersea nuclear testing. These efforts signaled a new phase of the Cold War, later called détente, in which the superpowers moved from confrontation to negotiation. Concurrently, the Cuban missile crisis escalated the arms race by convincing both sides of the need for nuclear superiority.

| The Thousand-Day Presidency | On November 22, 1963, during a trip to Texas to shore up his reelection chances, John and Jackie Kennedy rode in an open car along Dallas streets lined with cheering crowds. Shots rang |

out. The president slumped, dying, his skull and throat shattered. Soon after, aboard Air Force One, Lyndon B. Johnson was sworn in as president.

Grief and disbelief numbed the nation. Millions of Americans spent the next four days in front of their TV sets staring at replays of the murder of accused assassin Lee Harvey Oswald in the Dallas city jail by a nightclub owner; at the somber state funeral, with the small boy saluting his father's casket; at the grieving family lighting an eternal flame at Arlington National Cemetery. Few who watched would forget. Kennedy had helped make television central to American politics; now, in death, it made him the fallen hero-king of Camelot.

The assassination made a martyr of JFK. More admired in death than in life, the public ranked him as one of the very few "great" presidents, associating him with a spirit of energy and innovation. While Kennedy loyalists continued to stress his intelligence and his ability to change and grow, most historians pointed to his lack of achievements and the discrepancy between his public image and his private philandering. Some also deplored his aggressive Cold War tactics, his raising unrealistic expectations, and his vast expansion of presidential powers.

Kennedy's rhetoric expressed the new liberalism, but he rarely translated ideals into deeds. He frequently compromised with conservatives and segregationists in Congress; economic expansion came from spending on missiles and the space race, not on social welfare and human needs. Partly because his own personal behavior made him beholden to FBI director J. Edgar Hoover, JFK allowed the agency to infringe on civil liberties, even as the CIA plotted with the Mafia to assassinate Fidel Castro. (Scholars are still trying to untangle the plots and policies that enmeshed the Kennedy brothers, Hoover, organized crime, and the national security agencies.)

Internationally, Kennedy left a mixed record. He signed the world's first nuclear-test-ban treaty, yet initiated a massive arms buildup. He compromised on Laos but deepened U.S. involvement in Vietnam. He came to question the need for confronting the Soviet Union yet insisted on U.S. global superiority and aggressively prosecuted the Cold War. He did so, moreover, by increasing the powers of the White House staff. As never before, a small group of aides, personally loyal to the president, secretly dominated policy making.

Yet, JFK inspired Americans to expect greatness, aroused the poor and the powerless, and stimulated the young to activism. Dying during the calm before the storm, he left his successor soaring expectations at home and a deteriorating entanglement in Vietnam. His legacy and assassination would shatter illusions and optimism, leading millions of Americans to doubt their government and their future.

THE STRUGGLE FOR BLACK EQUALITY, 1961–1968

Following the lunch-counter sit-ins, civil-rights activists tried to convince Kennedy to act on their behalf. He would not do so, fearing it would split the Democratic Party, immobilize Congress in filibusters, and jeopardize his reelection. He viewed civil rights as a thorny thicket to avoid, not a moral issue. He balanced his appointment of a record number of African-Americans to federal jobs with the nomination of white segregationists to judgeships. He stalled for two years on his promise to outlaw discrimination in federally funded housing by executive order, and then issued a weak order that barely made a dent in segregation. Only action by civil-rights groups that secured public favor held out the possibility of forcing Kennedy's hand.

Nonviolence and Violence   In spring 1961, the Congress of Racial Equality (CORE) organized a "freedom ride" through the Deep South to dramatize the flouting of a 1960 Supreme Court edict banning segregation in interstate transportation facilities. It aroused white wrath. Mobs beat the freedom riders in Anniston, Alabama, burned a bus, and mauled the protestors in Birmingham, making the freedom rides front-page news. Yet only after further assaults on the freedom riders in Montgomery did Kennedy, fearful that the violence would undermine American prestige abroad, deploy federal marshals to restore peace. And only after scores more freedom rides and the arrests of hundreds of protesters did the president prod the Interstate Commerce Commission to enforce the law. Only crisis, not moral suasion, forced Kennedy to act.

Many of the freedom riders were members of the **Student Nonviolent Coordinating Committee (SNCC),** formed in April 1960 by participants in the sit-ins. SNCC stressed both the nonviolent civil disobedience strategy of Martin Luther King, Jr., and the need to stimulate local, grass-roots activism and leadership. In fall 1961, it chose Albany, Georgia, as the site of a campaign to desegregate public facilities. Despite King's involvement, wily local authorities avoided the overt violence that had won the freedom riders national sympathy. Without the national indignation that brought a White

House response, the Albany movement collapsed. But the lesson had been learned by civil-rights leaders.

It had not been learned by southern whites. An angry mob rioted in fall 1962 when a federal court ordered the University of Mississippi to enroll James Meredith, a black air force veteran. Rallying behind Confederate flags, troublemakers laid siege to the campus, attacking the federal marshals who escorted Meredith to "Ole Miss." The clash left two dead and scores injured before thousands of troops quelled the violence and protected Meredith's right to attend the university of his home state.

The African-American Revolution

As television coverage of the struggle for racial equality brought mounting numbers of African-Americans into the movement, civil-rights leaders applied increasing pressure on Kennedy to intervene. They realized that it would take decades to dismantle segregation piecemeal; the only practical remedy would be comprehensive national legislation, backed by the power of the federal government, guaranteeing full citizenship for African-Americans. To get such legislation from the Kennedy administration, they would need to induce an outrage by segregationists that would cause millions of Americans to demand that the president act.

Determined to expose the violent extremism of southern racism, **Martin Luther King, Jr.,** launched nonviolent marches, sit-ins, and pray-ins in Birmingham, Alabama. The most rigidly segregated big city in America, Birmingham's officials had even removed a book from the library that featured white and black rabbits. Past violence by whites against civil-rights protestors had earned the city the nickname "Bombingham," and the black neighborhood, "Dynamite Hill." Few doubted Police Commissioner Eugene "Bull" Connor's pledge that "blood would run in the streets of Birmingham before it would be integrated."

When jailed for instigating a march that a local court had prohibited, King penned the "Letter from Birmingham Jail." It detailed the humiliations of racial discrimination and segregation. It vindicated the nonviolent struggle against Jim Crow. And it justified civil disobedience to protest unjust laws, such as segregation statutes.

> We know through painful experience that freedom is never voluntarily given by the oppressor; it must be demanded by the oppressed. Frankly, I have yet to engage in a direct-action campaign that was "well-timed" in the view of those who have not suffered unduly from the disease of segregation. For years now I have heard the word "Wait!" It rings in the ear of every Negro with piercing familiarity. This "Wait" has almost always meant "Never." We must come to see, with one of our distinguished jurists, that "justice too long delayed is justice denied."

In May, thousands of schoolchildren, some only six years old, joined King's crusade. The bigoted Connor lost his temper. He unleashed his men—armed with electric cattle prods, high-pressure water hoses, and snarling attack dogs—on the nonviolent demonstrators. The ferocity of Connor's attacks, caught on camera and television, horrified the world.

"The civil-rights movement should thank God for Bull Connor," JFK remarked. "He's helped it as much as Abraham Lincoln." Indeed, Connor's vicious tactics seared the nation's conscience and pushed Kennedy to help negotiate a settlement that ended the demonstrations in return for an agreement by the city's department stores to desegregate their facilities and to hire black workers. By mid-1963, the rallying cry "Freedom

Now!" reverberated through the land as all the civil-rights groups became more militant, competing with each other in assisting ad hoc, local protests. The number of protests soared. Most were spontaneous initiatives led by black women who put their bodies on the line to compel changes at the community level. Concerned about America's image abroad as well as the "fires of frustration and discord" raging at home, Kennedy could no longer temporize. The government must propose changes in race relations, he reasoned; otherwise blacks would turn to violent leaders and methods. When Governor George Wallace refused to allow two black students to enter the University of Alabama in June 1963, Kennedy forced Wallace—who had pledged "Segregation now! Segregation tomorrow! Segregation forever!"—to capitulate to a court desegregation order.

On June 11, the president went on television to define civil rights as "a moral issue" and to declare that "race has no place in American life or law." A week later, Kennedy proposed a bill outlawing segregation in public facilities and authorizing the federal government to withhold funds from programs that discriminated. As the bill bogged down in Congress, civil-rights adherents planned to march on Washington to muster support for the legislation.

The March on Washington, 1963
The idea for a March on Washington had originally been proposed by A. Philip Randolph in 1941 to protest discrimination against blacks in the defense mobilization (see Chapter 25). Twenty-two years later, Randolph revived the idea and convinced the major civil-rights leaders to support a March on Washington for Jobs and Freedom.

A quarter of a million people, including some fifty thousand whites, converged on Washington, D.C., on August 28, 1963. It was the largest political assembly to date. After a long, sweltering day of speeches and songs, Martin Luther King, Jr., took the podium to remind Americans that the hopes generated by the Emancipation Proclamation had still not been fulfilled.

Summoning images of shackled, hobbled black slaves, he maintained, "The life of the Negro is still sadly crippled by the manacles of segregation and the chains of discrimination. . . . One hundred years later, the Negro is still not free." He described the promises of the Declaration of Independence as "a sacred obligation," which has proved to be, for African-Americans, a bad check. But, he roared, we have come to collect on the promise, to cash the check "that will give us upon demand the riches of freedom and the security of justice." Blacks would not brook delay or gradualism: "This sweltering summer of the Negro's legitimate discontent will not pass until there is an invigorating autumn of freedom and equality." He warned: "There will be neither rest nor tranquility in America until the Negro is granted his citizenship rights. The whirlwinds of revolt will continue to shake the foundations of our nation until the bright day of justice emerges." As the multitude cheered, King concluded by reiterating his dream of true brotherhood in America.

King's eloquence did not speed passage of the civil-rights bill. It did not end racism or erase poverty and despair. It did not quell the rage of white racists. In September, the Ku Klux Klan bombing of a black church in Birmingham killed four girls attending Sunday school. (Not until 2002 was the last of the four main suspects brought to justice.) It did not prevent the ghetto riots that lay ahead, or the white backlash that would ultimately smother the civil-rights movement. Yet King had turned a political rally into a historic event, recalling America to the ideals of justice and equality, to the fundamental notion that the color of one's skin ought never be a burden in American life.

The Civil Rights and Voting Rights Acts Kennedy's assassination brought to the White House a southerner, Lyndon Johnson, who knew he had to prove himself on the race issue or the liberals "would get me. They'd throw up my background against me. . . . I had to produce a civil rights bill," he later wrote, "that was even stronger than the one they'd have gotten if Kennedy had lived." Johnson succeeded in doing just that, employing his vast skills to toughen the bill and break a southern filibuster in the Senate.

The **Civil Rights Act** of 1964, the most significant civil-rights law in U.S. history, banned racial discrimination and segregation in public accommodations. It outlawed bias in federally funded programs; granted the federal government new powers to fight school segregation; and created the Equal Employment Opportunity Commission (EEOC) to enforce the ban on job discrimination.

The Civil Rights Act did not address the right to vote. So CORE and SNCC activists, believing that the ballot held the key to power for southern blacks, mounted a major campaign to register black voters. They organized the Mississippi Freedom Summer Project of 1964 to focus on the state most hostile to black rights. Although 42 percent of Mississippi's population, blacks were only 5 percent of the registered voters. A thousand students, from nearly two hundred colleges and universities, volunteered to help register black voters and to teach the practices of democracy and black history in "Freedom Schools" that emphasized African-American self-worth. Harassed by Mississippi law-enforcement officials and Ku Klux Klansmen, the activists endured the firebombing of black churches and civil-rights headquarters, as well as arrests and even murders.

Although they registered only twelve hundred blacks to vote, the civil-rights workers enrolled nearly sixty thousand disfranchised blacks in the Mississippi Freedom Democratic Party (MFDP). In August 1964, they took their case to the national Democratic convention. "I was beaten till I was exhausted," Fannie Lou Hamer, the twentieth child of poor sharecroppers, told the convention. "All of this on account we wanted to register, to become first class citizens. If the Freedom Democratic party is not seated now, I question America." The MFDP was not seated. To stop a threatened walkout by southern white delegates, Johnson forged a compromise that offered two at-large seats to the MFDP and barred delegations from states that disfranchised blacks from all future conventions. The compromise pleased no one. The MFDP rejected it as a "token" gesture and left the convention in a huff. Within SNCC, the failure of the Democrats to support seating the MFDP delegates proved to be a turning point in their disillusionment with liberalism.

In 1964, most blacks still shared the optimism of Martin Luther King, Jr., and over 90 percent of African-American voters cast their ballots for the Democrats, leaving Johnson and the liberals in firm control. King now set his sights on opening the voting booths to blacks. Determined to win a strong voting-rights law, the SCLC organized mass protests in Selma, Alabama, in March 1965. Blacks were half the population of Dallas County, where Selma was located, but only 1 percent were registered to vote.

King knew he again had to create a crisis to pressure Congress to act. He masterfully provoked Selma's county sheriff, Jim Clark, every bit as violence-prone as Birmingham's "Bull" Connor, to reveal his brutality, arresting and beating thousands. When civil-rights activists sought to march from Selma to Montgomery, to petition Governor George Wallace, they were clubbed, shocked with cattle prods, and tear-gassed by lawmen. Showcased on TV, the spectacle provoked national outrage. Johnson grasped the mood of the country and delivered a televised address urging Congress to pass a

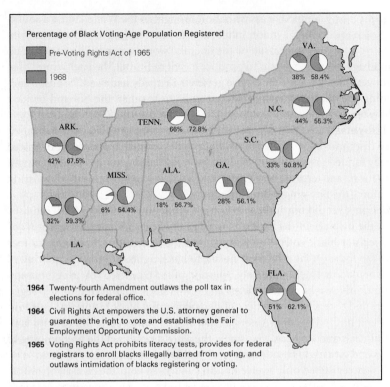

Percentage of Black Voting-Age Population Registered

▓ Pre-Voting Rights Act of 1965

▓ 1968

VA. 38% 58.4%

N.C. 44% 55.3%

TENN. 66% 72.8%

S.C. 33% 50.8%

ARK. 42% 67.5%

MISS. 6% 54.4%

ALA. 18% 56.7%

GA. 28% 56.1%

LA. 32% 59.3%

FLA. 51% 62.1%

1964 Twenty-fourth Amendment outlaws the poll tax in elections for federal office.

1964 Civil Rights Act empowers the U.S. attorney general to guarantee the right to vote and establishes the Fair Employment Opportunity Commission.

1965 Voting Rights Act prohibits literacy tests, provides for federal registrars to enroll blacks illegally barred from voting, and outlaws intimidation of blacks registering or voting.

MAP 28.1 Voter Registration of African-Americans in the South, 1960–1968

As blacks overwhelmingly registered to vote as Democrats, some former segregationist politicians, among them George Wallace, started to court the black vote, and many southern whites began to cast their ballots for Republicans, inaugurating an era of real two-party competition in the South.

voting-rights bill, beseeching all Americans, "Their cause must be our cause, too." Because "it's not just Negroes, really, it's all of us who must overcome the crippling legacy of bigotry and injustice. And," invoking the movement's anthem, "we *shall* overcome."

Signed by the president in August 1965, the **Voting Rights Act** invalidated the use of any test or device to deny the vote and authorized federal examiners to register voters in states that had disfranchised blacks. The law dramatically expanded black suffrage, boosting the number of registered black voters in the South from 1 million in 1964 to 3.1 million in 1968, and transformed southern politics.

The number of blacks holding office in the South swelled from fewer than two dozen in 1964 to nearly twelve hundred in 1972, including half the seats on Selma's city council and the first two African-Americans elected to Congress from the former Confederacy since the nineteenth century. Electoral success brought jobs for African-Americans, contracts for black businesses, and improvements in facilities and services in black neighborhoods. Most importantly, as Fannie Lou Hamer recalled, when African-Americans could not vote, "white folks would drive past your house in a pickup truck with guns hanging up on the back and give you hate stares. . . . Those same people now call me Mrs. Hamer."

Fire in the Streets   The civil-rights movement changed, but did not revolutionize, race relations. It ended legal segregation, broke the monopoly on political power in the South held by whites, and galvanized a new black sense of self-esteem. The movement raised hopes for the possibility of greater change and legitimated protest. But its inability to transform equality of opportunity into equality of results underscored the limitations of liberal change, especially in the urban ghetto. The movement did not bring African-Americans economic equality or material well-being, and the anger bubbling below the surface soon boiled over.

On August 11, 1965, five days after the signing of the Voting Rights Act, a scuffle between white police and blacks in Watts, the largest African-American district in Los Angeles, ignited the most destructive race riot in decades. For six days thousands of blacks looted shops, firebombed white-owned businesses, and sniped at police officers and firefighters. When the riot ended, thirty-four people were dead, nine hundred injured, and four thousand arrested. Blacks in Chicago and Springfield, Massachusetts, then took to the streets, looting, burning, and battling police.

The violence in 1965 proved to be just a prelude to a succession of "long hot summers." In the summer of 1966, more than a score of ghetto outbreaks erupted in northern cities. Blacks rioted to force whites to pay heed to the squalor of the slums and to the brutal behavior of police in the ghetto—problems that the southern civil-rights movement had ignored. Extensive poverty and the unequal distribution of income and wealth in the nation, moreover, had exacerbated all the racial problems of the inner cities. Frustrated by the allure of America's wealth portrayed on TV and by what seemed the empty promise of civil-rights laws, black mobs stoned passing motorists, ransacked stores, torched white-owned buildings, and hurled bricks at the troops sent to quell the disorder.

The following summer, black rage at oppressive conditions and impatience with liberal change erupted in 150 racial skirmishes and 40 riots—the most intense and destructive period of racial violence in U.S. history. In Newark, New Jersey, twenty-seven people died and more than eleven hundred were injured. The following week, Detroit went up in smoke in the decade's worst riot. As the fires spread, so did the looting. Children joined adults in racing from store to store to fill their arms with liquor and jewelry; cars pulled up to businesses so they could be stocked with appliances. By the time the Michigan National Guard and U.S. army paratroopers quelled the riot, forty-three people had died, two thousand were injured, and seven thousand had been arrested Then in 1968, following the assassination of Martin Luther King, Jr. (see Chapter 29), black uprisings flared in the ghettos of a hundred cities. The 1964–1968 riot toll would include some two hundred dead, seven thousand injured, forty thousand arrested, and at least $500 million in property destroyed—mostly white-owned stores and tenements that exemplified exploitation in the ghetto.

A frightened, bewildered nation asked why such rioting occurred just when blacks achieved many of their goals. Militant blacks saw the uprisings as revolutionary violence to overthrow a racist, reactionary society; poet Imamu Amiri Baraka (formerly LeRoi Jones) termed them spontaneous rebellions against authority. The Far Right saw them as evidence of a communist plot. Many conservatives described them as senseless outbursts by troublemakers. The administration's National Advisory Commission on

Bobby Seale and Huey Newton *Founded by Bobby Seale and Huey Newton in Oakland, California, in response to police brutality against African-Americans, the Black Panther Party was organized along semimilitary lines and advocated fighting for black justice, in Newton's words, "through the barrel of a gun."*

Civil Disorders (known as the Kerner Commission) blamed them on an "explosive mixture" of poverty, slum housing, poor education, and police brutality caused by "white racism." Warning that "our nation is moving toward two societies, one black, one white—separate and unequal," the commission recommended increased federal spending to create new jobs for urban blacks, construct additional public housing, and end de facto school segregation in the North. Johnson and Congress, aware of the backlash against the War on Poverty as well as the cost of the war in Vietnam, ignored the warning. "Each war feeds on the other," observed Senator William Fulbright, "and, although the President assures us that we have the resources to win both wars, in fact we are not winning either of them."

"Black Power"　For many young African-Americans, liberalism's response to racial inequality proved "too little, too late." The demand for **Black Power** sounded in 1966 paralleled the fury of the urban riots; it expressed the eagerness of militant activists for militant self-defense and rapid social change. The slogan encapsulated both their bitterness toward a white society that blocked their aspirations and their rejection of King's commitment to nonviolence, racial integration, and alliances with white liberals.

Derived from a long tradition of black nationalism, Black Power owed much to the militant rhetoric and vision of Malcolm X. Born in Omaha, Nebraska, in 1925, the son of a preacher active in the Marcus Garvey movement, Malcolm Little pimped and sold drugs before being jailed in 1946. In prison, he converted to the Nation of Islam (NOI), the Black Muslim group founded by Wallace Fard and led by Elijah Muhammad (Elijah Poole). Released in 1952 and renamed Malcolm X, as a symbolic repudiation of his "slavemaster" name, he quickly became the Black Muslims' most dynamic street orator and charismatic leader, bringing black nationalism to public attention.

Building on separatist and nationalist impulses with deep roots in the black community—racial solidarity and uplift, self-sufficiency, and self-help—Malcolm X called on blacks to "wake up, clean up, and stand up" to achieve true independence. "I don't see any American dream," he declared. "I see an American nightmare." He urged blacks "to recapture our heritage and identity." He wanted them to see themselves with their "own eyes not the white man's," and to separate themselves from the "white devil." Ridiculing civil-rights leaders like King—"just a twentieth-century Uncle Tom"—for emphasizing desegregation instead of the social and economic problems that beset most African-Americans, he insisted that blacks seize their freedom "by any means necessary." "If ballots won't work, bullets will," he said. "If someone puts a hand on you, send him to the cemetery." In February 1965, after he broke with the Nation of Islam to find a more effective approach to solving the problems of blacks, Malcolm X was murdered by three Black Muslim gunmen. He was not silenced. He became a martyr, and his account of his life and beliefs, *The Autobiography of Malcolm X* (1965), became the main text of the rising Black Power movement and its celebration of a new black consciousness.

Two days after winning the world heavyweight championship in 1964, boxer Cassius Clay shocked the sports world by announcing his conversion to the Nation of Islam and his new name, Muhammad Ali. Refusing induction into the armed services on religious grounds, Ali was found guilty of draft evasion, stripped of his title, and exiled from boxing for three and a half years during his athletic prime. Inspired by the examples of Ali and Malcolm X, and bitter at the failure of the established civil-rights organizations to achieve a fundamental distribution of wealth and power, young, urban African-Americans abandoned civil disobedience and reformist strategies. They embraced the word *black* and a new agenda based on racial identity. In 1966 CORE and SNCC changed from interracial organizations committed to achieving integration nonviolently to all-black groups advocating racial separatism and Black Power "by any means necessary." To SNCC chairman Stokely Carmichael, racial integration was "a subterfuge for the maintenance of white supremacy" that implied the superiority of white institutions and values.

The boldest champion of self-determination for African-American communities was the Black Panther Party for Self-Defense. Founded in Oakland, California, in 1966 by Huey P. Newton and Bobby Seale, it urged black men to become "panthers—smiling, cunning, scientific, striking by night and sparing no one." Although the Panthers also sponsored community centers and school breakfast programs, they attained national notoriety from their fearsome paramilitary style and shootouts with the police. Expressing contempt for the nonviolent, church-based civil-rights movement, Newton claimed that the "heirs of Malcolm X have picked up the gun." Violent confrontations with police and the FBI left many of its members dead or in prison, effectively destroying the organization and, together with the riots, splintering the black-white civil-rights alliance and contributing to the rightward turn in politics.

Although the concept remained imprecise, ranging from notions of black capitalism to local control of schools to revolutionary schemes to overthrow the American system, Black Power exerted a significant influence. Its origins lay in the racial pride and spirit of resistance bred by generations of white oppression; and most African-Americans took it to mean gaining the power to make the decisions that governed their day-to-day lives and destinies, to define their own goals, and to lead their own organizations. Empowerment was the key to its meaning. Scores of new community self-help groups and self-reliant black institutions exemplified it, as did the establishment of black studies programs at colleges, the mobilization of black voters to elect black candidates, and the encouragement of racial pride and self-esteem—"black is beautiful." The "Godfather of Soul," James Brown sang, "Say it loud—I'm black and I'm proud," and as never before African-Americans rejected skin bleaches and hair straighteners, gave their children Islamic names and Kwanzaa gifts instead of Christmas presents, and gloried in soul music. Artists and writers produced work rooted in the black experience that resonated with a black audience. "I may have lost hope," SCLC leader Jesse Jackson had students repeating with him, "but I am . . . somebody. . . . I am . . . black . . . beautiful . . . proud. . . . I must be respected." This message reverberated with other marginalized groups as well, and helped shape their protest movements.

LIBERALISM ASCENDANT, 1963–1968

Although a firm New Dealer in the 1930s, **Lyndon Baines Johnson** came to be distrusted by liberals as "a Machiavelli in a Stetson" and regarded as a usurper by Kennedy partisans. He had achieved his highest ambition as a result of the assassination of a

The LBJ Treatment   *Not content unless he could wholly dominate friend as well as foe, Lyndon Johnson used his body as well as his voice to bend others to his will and gain his objectives.*

popular president in Johnson's home state of Texas. Though just nine years older than JFK, he seemed a relic of the past, a back-room wheeler-dealer, as crude as Kennedy was smooth, as insecure as his predecessor was self-confident.

Yet Johnson had substantial political assets. He had served in Washington almost continuously since 1932, accruing enormous experience and a close association with the Capitol Hill power brokers who controlled the legislative process. He excelled at wooing allies, neutralizing opponents, building coalitions, and achieving results. He loved the political maneuvering and legislative detail that Kennedy loathed.

Johnson's first three years as president demonstrated his determination to prove himself to liberals. He deftly handled the transition of power, won a landslide victory in 1964, and guided through Congress the greatest array of liberal legislation in U.S. history, surpassing the New Deal agenda. But LBJ's swollen yet fragile ego could not abide the sniping of Kennedy loyalists, and he frequently complained that the media did not give him "a fair shake." Wondering aloud, "Why don't people like me?" Johnson labored to ensure that everyone shared in the promise of the American Dream, and to vanquish all foes at home and abroad. Ironically, in seeking consensus and adoration, Johnson would divide the nation and leave office repudiated.

Johnson Takes Over   Calling for quick passage of the tax-cut and civil-rights bills as a memorial to JFK, Johnson used his skills to win passage of the Civil Rights Act of 1964 (see pp. 895) and a $10 billion tax-reduction bill, which produced a surge in capital investment and personal consumption that spurred economic growth and shrank the budget deficit. More boldly, Johnson declared "unconditional war on poverty in America."

Largely invisible in an affluent America, according to Michael Harrington's *The Other America* (1962), some 40 million people dwelled in substandard housing and subsisted on inadequate diets. Living with little hope in a "culture of poverty," they lacked the education, medical care, and employment opportunities that most Americans took for granted. To be poor, Harrington asserted, "is to be an internal alien, to grow up in a culture that is radically different from the one that dominates the society."

LBJ championed a campaign to bring these "internal exiles" into the mainstream. Designed to promote greater opportunity, to offer a "hand up, not a handout," the Economic Opportunity Act (1964) established the Office of Economic Opportunity to wage "unconditional **war on poverty.**" Its programs included a Job Corps to train young people in marketable skills; VISTA (Volunteers in Service to America), a domestic peace corps; Project Head Start, to provide free compensatory education for preschoolers from disadvantaged families; a Community Action Program to encourage the "maximum feasible participation" of the poor in decisions that affected them; and public-works and training programs.

Summing up his goals in 1964, Johnson offered his vision of the **Great Society.** First must come "an end to poverty and racial injustice." In addition, the Great Society would be a place where all children could enrich their minds and enlarge their talents, where people could renew their contact with nature, and where all would be "more concerned with the quality of their goals than the quantity of their goods."

The 1964 Election   Johnson's Great Society horrified the "new conservatives," such as William F. Buckley and the college students who belonged to the Young Americans for Freedom (YAF). The most persuasive criticism came from Arizona senator **Barry Goldwater,** who had voted against the Civil Rights Act. A product of the twentieth-century West, Goldwater was an outsider fighting the power of Washington, a fervent anticommunist, a proponent of individual freedom. He railed against liberalism's reliance on deficit spending and on a powerful federal government to cure social ills. He advocated as little federal governmental intervention in the economy as possible, and opposed government efforts to expand and protect civil rights and liberties. And he proposed that the U.S. roll back communism in the world rather than just contain it.

Johnson's advocacy of civil rights frightened southern segregationists and blue-collar workers in northern cities who dreaded the integration of their neighborhoods, schools, and workplaces. Their support of Alabama's segregationist governor George Wallace in the spring 1964 presidential primaries heralded a "white backlash" against the civil-rights movement.

Buoyed by this backlash, conservatives took control of the GOP in 1964. They nominated Barry Goldwater for the presidency and adopted a platform totally opposed to liberalism. Determined to offer the nation "a choice not an echo," Goldwater lauded his opposition to civil-rights legislation and his vote against the censure of McCarthy. In Appalachia, he denounced the War on Poverty, in Tennessee he called for the sale of the TVA to private interests, in the Midwest he opposed high price supports for farmers, and in the retirement community of St. Petersburg, Florida, he advocated scrapping social security. "We have gotten where we are," he declared, "not because of government, but in spite of government." Goldwater also accused the Democrats of a "no-win" strategy in the Cold War, hinting that he might use nuclear weapons against Cuba and North Vietnam. His candidacy appealed most to those angered by the Cold War stalemate, by the erosion of traditional moral values, and by the increasing militancy of African-Americans. His campaign slogan, "In your heart you know he's right," allowed his liberal opponents to quip, "In your guts you know he's nuts."

LBJ and his running mate, Senator Hubert Humphrey of Minnesota, depicted Goldwater as an extremist not to be trusted with the nuclear trigger. When the Arizonan charged that the Democrats had not pursued total victory in Vietnam, Johnson appeared the apostle of restraint: "We are not going to send American boys nine or ten thousand miles from home to do what Asian boys ought to be doing for themselves."

LBJ won a landslide victory, 43 million votes to Goldwater's 27 million. Goldwater carried only Arizona and five southern states. The GOP lost thirty-eight seats in the House of Representatives, two in the Senate, and five hundred in state legislatures. Many proclaimed the death of conservatism. Rather, it heralded a grass-roots revival of antigovernment westerners, economic and religious conservatives, and anti-integrationist whites that presaged the Right's future triumph. It transformed the Republicans from a moderate, eastern-dominated party to one decidedly conservative, southern, and western. It built a national base of financial support for conservative candidates; catalyzed the creation of new conservative publications and think-tanks; energized volunteers like Phyllis Schlafly to campaign for Goldwater and stay involved in politics; mobilized future leaders of the party, like Ronald Reagan; and led to Richard Nixon's "southern strategy" (see Chapter 29). But in the short run, the liberals controlled all three branches of government.

"Hurry, boys, hurry," LBJ urged his aides. "Get that legislation up to the hill and out. Eighteen months from now ol' Land-slide Lyndon will be Lame-Duck Lyndon." Johnson flooded Congress with liberal proposals—sixty-three of them in 1965 alone. He got most of what he requested.

The Eighty-ninth Congress—"the Congress of Fulfillment" to LBJ, and Johnson's "hip-pocket Congress" to his opponents—enlarged the War on Poverty and passed a milestone voting-rights act. It enacted **Medicare** to provide health insurance for the aged under social security, and a **Medicaid** health plan for the poor. By 1975 the two programs would be serving 47 million people, and account for a quarter of the nation's total health-care expenditures. The legislators appropriated funds for public education and housing, for aid to Appalachia, and for revitalizing inner-city neighborhoods. They also created new cabinet departments of transportation and of housing and urban development (the latter headed by Robert Weaver, the first African-American cabinet member), and the National Endowments for the Arts and the Humanities.

Of enormous future significance, Congress enacted the **Immigration Act of 1965,** abolishing the national-origins quotas of the 1920s and transforming America's racial and ethnic kaleidoscope. Annual legal immigration would increase from about 250,000 to well over a million, and the vast majority of new immigrants would come from Asia and Latin America. Less than 1 percent of the U.S. population in 1960, Asian-Americans would be more than 4 percent in 2000; and the Hispanic population would increase from 4.5 percent in 1970 to nearly 12 percent in 2000. This increasing population diversity vastly expanded the nation's culinary, linguistic, musical, and religious spectrum.

The Great Society also battled what LBJ described as the problem "of vanishing beauty, of increasing ugliness, of shrinking open space, and of an overall environment that is diminished daily by pollution and noise and blight." In 1964 Congress passed the National Wilderness Preservation Act, setting aside 9.1 million acres of wilderness. It established Redwood National Park and defeated efforts to dam the Colorado River and flood the lower Grand Canyon; strengthened the Clean Water and Clean Air Acts; protected endangered species; preserved scenic rivers; and lessened the number of junkyards and billboards. Responding to the uproar caused by Ralph Nader's revelations about unsafe cars, Congress set the first federal safety standards for automobiles and required states to establish highway safety programs.

The Great Society increased opportunity and improved the lives of millions. The proportion of the poor in the population dropped from 22 percent in 1960 to 13 percent in 1969; infant mortality declined by a third; Head Start reached more than 2 million poor children; and African-American family income rose from 54 percent to 61 percent of white family income. The percentage of blacks living below the poverty line plummeted from 40 percent to 20 percent. But in part because Johnson oversold the Great Society and Congress underfunded it, liberal aspirations outdistanced results.

Despite its many successes, the Great Society remained more a dream than a reality for some. The war against poverty, Martin Luther King, Jr., asserted, was "shot down on the battlefields of Vietnam." In 1966, Johnson spent twenty times more to wage war in Vietnam than to fight poverty in the United States. Yet the perceived liberality of federal spending and the "ungratefulness" of rioting blacks alienated many middle- and working-class whites. Others resented liberal regulation of business and the growing intrusiveness of government. The Democrats' loss of forty-seven House seats in 1966 ended the dominance of liberalism in Congress.

The Warren Court in the Sixties   The Supreme Court, led by Chief Justice Earl Warren, did much to promote the liberal agenda. Kennedy's appointment of two liberals to the Court, and Johnson of two more, including Thurgood Marshall, the Court's first black justice, resulted in a solid liberal majority that expanded individual rights to a greater extent than ever before in American history.

In a series of landmark cases, the Court prohibited Bible reading and prayer in public schools, limited local power to censor books and films, and overturned state bans on contraceptives. It ordered states to apportion legislatures on the principle of "one person, one vote," increasing the representation of urban minorities.

The Court's upholding of the rights of the accused in criminal cases, at a time of soaring crime rates, particularly incensed many Americans.

Criticism of the Supreme Court reached a climax in 1966 when it ruled in **Miranda v. Arizona** that police must advise suspects of their right to remain silent and to have counsel during questioning. In 1968, both Richard Nixon and George Wallace would win favor by promising to appoint judges who emphasized "law and order" over individual liberties.

VOICES OF PROTEST

The aura of liberalism in the 1960s markedly affected Native Americans Hispanic-Americans, Asian-Americans, and women. They, too, were inspired by Kennedy's rhetoric, by Johnson's actions, and by the assertive outlook of Black Power. Each followed the black lead in challenging the status quo, demanding full and equal citizenship rights, emphasizing group identity and pride, and seeing its younger members push for ever more radical action.

Native American Activism   In 1961 representatives of sixty-seven tribes drew up a Declaration of Purposes criticizing the termination policy of the 1950s as a subterfuge for neglect (see Chapter 27). In 1964 hundreds of Indians lobbied in Washington for the inclusion of Native Americans in the War on Poverty. Indians suffered the worst poverty, the most inadequate housing, the highest disease and death rates, and the least access to education of any group in the United States. Native American life expectancy, just 44 years, was a third less than that of other Americans. President Johnson responded by establishing the National Council on Indian Opportunity in 1965. It funneled more federal funds onto reservations than any previous program. Johnson also appointed the first Native American to head the Bureau of Indian Affairs (BIA) since 1870, and promised to erase "old attitudes of paternalism." Advocating Indian self-determination, Johnson insisted in a special message to Congress in 1968 on "the right of the First Americans to remain Indians while exercising their rights as Americans."

Militant Native Americans, meanwhile, began to organize. The National Indian Youth Council, organized in 1961, sponsored demonstrations and marches, and Native Americans in the San Francisco Bay Area established the Indian Historical Society in 1964 to present history from the Indian point of view. By 1968 younger Indian activists, calling themselves "Native Americans," demanded "Red Power." They voiced dissatisfaction with the accommodationist approach of their elders, the lack of protection for Indian land and water rights, the desecration of Indian graves and sacred sites, and legal prohibitions against certain Indian religious practices. They mocked Columbus Day and staged sit-ins against museums that housed Indian bones. They established reservation cultural programs to reawaken spiritual beliefs and teach Native languages. The Wampanoag in Massachusetts named Thanksgiving a National Day of Mourning. The Navajo and Hopi protested strip-mining in the Southwest, and the Taos Pueblo organized to reclaim the Blue Lake sacred site in northern New Mexico. The Puyallup held "fish-ins" to assert old treaty rights to fish in the Columbia River and Puget Sound, and in 1968 the Supreme Court declared that states could not invalidate fishing and hunting rights that Native Americans had acquired in treaties.

The most militant group, the **American Indian Movement** (AIM), was founded in 1968 by Chippewas, Sioux, and Ojibwa living in and around Minneapolis. Its goals were to promote the traditional ways of Native Americans, prevent police brutality and harassment of Indians in urban "red ghettos," and establish "survival schools" to teach Indian history and values. It established a "powwow circuit" to publicize Indian protest activities across the country, and in November 1969 AIM occupied Alcatraz Island in San Francisco Bay. Citing a Sioux Indian treaty that unused federal lands would revert to Indian control, an armed AIM contingent held the island for nineteen months before being dispersed. They made Alcatraz a symbol of the conditions on reservations: "It has no running water; it has inadequate sanitation facilities; there is no industry, and so unemployment is very great; there are no health care facilities; the soil is rocky and unproductive." The occupation helped foster a new sense of identity among American Indians. As one participant glowed, "we got back our worth, our pride, our dignity, our humanity."

AIM's militancy aroused other Native-Americans to be proud of their heritage. Their members "had a new look about them, not that hangdog reservation look I was used to," Mary Crow Dog remembered, and they "loosened a sort of earthquake inside me." Many of the eight hundred thousand who identified themselves as Indians in the 1970 census did so for the first time.

Hispanic-Americans Organize

The fastest-growing minority, Latinos, or Hispanic-Americans, also grew impatient with their establishment organizations. The Mexican American Political Association and other organizations had been able to do little to ameliorate the dismal existence of most of the 5 million Hispanic-Americans. With a median annual wage half the poverty level, with 40 percent of Mexican-American adults functionally illiterate, and with de facto segregation common throughout the Southwest, Latinos like **César Estrada Chávez** turned to the more militant tactics and strategies of the civil-rights movement.

Born on an Arizona farm first cultivated in the 1880s by his grandfather, Chávez grew up a migrant farm worker, joined the U.S. navy in World War II, and then devoted himself to gaining union recognition and improved working conditions for the mostly Mexican-American farm laborers in California—suffering from extremely high rates of illiteracy, unemployment, and poverty. A charismatic leader who, like Martin Luther King, Jr., blended religion with nonviolent resistance to fight for social change, Chávez led his followers in the Delano vineyards of the San Joaquin valley to strike in 1965. Similar efforts had been smashed in the past. But Chávez and United Farm Worker (UFW) cofounder Dolores Huerta organized consumer boycotts of table grapes to dramatize the farm workers' struggle. They made *La Causa,* as the farm workers' movement became known, part of the common struggle of the entire Mexican-American community and part of the larger national movement for civil rights and social justice. For the first time, farm workers gained the right to unionize to secure better wages; and by mid-1970, two-thirds of California grapes were grown under UFW contracts. Just as the UFW flag featured an Aztec eagle and the Virgin of Guadalupe, Chávez combined religion, labor militancy, and Mexican heritage to stimulate ethnic pride and politicization.

Also in the mid-1960s young Hispanic activists began using the formerly pejorative terms **Chicano** and **Chicana** to express a militant sense of collective identity and solidarity for all those of Mexican descent. They saw themselves as a people whose heritage had been rejected and whose culture had been taken from them. They insisted on their self-selected name to highlight pride in Mexico's culture and revolutionary tradition, and their insistence on self-determination: "Our main goal is to orient the Chicano to *think* Chicano so as to achieve equal status with other groups, not to emulate the Anglo."

Rejecting assimilation, Chicano student organizations came together in *El Movimiento Estudiantil Chicano de Aztlan* (MEChA) in 1967. They led Chicano high-school students in Los Angeles, Denver, and San Antonio in boycotts of classes (called "blowouts") in 1968 to protest poor educational conditions in their schools and to demand bilingual education. Congress responded by enacting legislation that encouraged school districts to adopt bilingual education programs to instruct non-English speakers in both English and their native language. Chicanos demonstrated at colleges to obtain courses that emphasized the history, art, language, and literature of Mexican-Americans. At the inaugural Chicano Youth Liberation Conference in 1969, they adopted *El Plan Espiritual de Aztlan,* a manifesto of cultural and political nationalism, and, on September 16, Mexican Independence Day, they led high-school students carrying placards emblazoned with "Viva la Raza!" in the First National Chicano Boycott of schools throughout the Southwest.

Similar zeal led poet Rodolfo "Corky" Gonzales to found the Crusade for Justice in Colorado in 1965 to fight police brutality, foster Chicano culture, and improve job opportunities for Mexican-Americans. It led Reies Lopez Tijerina to form the *Alianza Federal de Mercedes* in New Mexico to reclaim land usurped by whites in the 1848 Treaty of Guadalupe Hidalgo. It also led Jose Angel Gutierrez and others in Texas to create an alternative political party in 1967, *La Raza Unida,* to elect Latinos and instill cultural pride. Four Mexican-Americans would win seats in Congress in the 1960s, including Senator Joseph Montoya of New Mexico. Chicano activism also led to the expansion of the one person, one vote concept in much of the Southwest. It pushed many more Hispanics to go to college and to get involved in local politics; it helped create the first major English-speaking-and-writing intellectual community in the history of Latinos in the United States; and it ushered in a "brown is beautiful" vogue and the paramilitary Brown Berets.

Puerto Ricans in New York City founded the Young Lords, which they too modeled on the Black Panthers. They published *Palante* ("forward in the struggle"), which, like the newspapers *La Raza* in Los Angeles and *El Papel* in Albuquerque, popularized movement strategies and aims. The Young Lords started drug treatment programs, and hijacked ambulances and occupied a hospital to demand better medical services in the South Bronx. They also blockaded the streets of East Harlem with trash to force the city to provide improved sanitation services for the six hundred thousand Puerto Ricans living there.

Asian-American Activism

Like their counterparts, young activists with roots in East Asia rejected the term *Oriental* in favor of *Asian-American,* to signify their new ethnic consciousness. Formed at the University of California in 1968, the **Asian American Political Alliance** brought together Chinese-, Filipino-, and Japanese-American students. It encouraged Asian-Americans to claim their own cultural identity and, in racial solidarity with their "Asian brothers and sisters," to protest against the U.S. war in Vietnam. Many Asian-American students condemned the war as a racist attack upon the peoples of Southeast Asia and as a violation of the sovereignty of a small Asian nation.

As did other ethnic groups, Asian-American students marched, sat in, and went on strike to promote causes emphasizing their unique identity. Mainly in California, Hawaii, and New York, they campaigned for courses on Asian-American studies, and some universities, like the City College of New York, set up interdisciplinary departments. Students from the Philippines and South Korea organized protests against the repressive dictatorships in their homeland, while those from Samoa denounced the damage caused by nuclear testing in the Pacific islands.

Many Asian-American activists focused on improving the lives of their compatriots in need. In 1968, they organized demonstrations and marches in San Francisco to protest the poor housing and medical facilities in Chinatown, and led a struggle to save a low-income residential facility for Chinese and Filipino men. Others worked with trade union organizers to upgrade the pay and working conditions of Asians in garment manufacturing and in hotel and restaurant jobs. The Redress and Reparations Movement, initiated by third-generation Japanese Americans, agitated to force the government to make restitution for the wartime internment.

None of these movements for ethnic pride and power could sustain the fervent activism and media attention that they attracted in the late sixties. But by elevating the consciousness and nurturing the confidence of the younger generation, each contributed to the cultural pride of its respective group, and to the politics of identity that would continue to grow in importance.

A Second
Feminist Wave

The rising tempo of activism in the 1960s also stirred a new spirit of self-awareness and dissatisfaction among educated women. A revived feminist movement emerged, profoundly altering women's view of themselves and their role in American life.

Several events fanned the embers of discontent into flames. The 1963 report of John Kennedy's Presidential Commission on the Status of Women documented occupational inequities that were similar to those endured by minorities. Women received less pay than men for comparable work; and they made up only 7 percent of the nation's doctors and less than 4 percent of its lawyers. The women who served on the presidential commission successfully urged that the Civil Rights Act of 1964 prohibit gender-based as well as racial discrimination in employment.

Dismayed by the Equal Employment Opportunity Commission's reluctance to enforce the ban on sex discrimination in employment, these women formed the **National Organization for Women (NOW)** in 1966. A civil-rights group for women, NOW labored "to bring women into full participation in the mainstream of American society." It lobbied for equal opportunity, filed lawsuits against gender discrimination, and mobilized public opinion against sexism.

NOW's prominence owed much to the publication of Betty Friedan's critique of domesticity, *The Feminine Mystique* (1963). Friedan's account of unfulfilled housewives deplored the notion that women should seek fulfillment solely as wives and mothers. Suburban domesticity—the "velvet ghetto"—left many women with feelings of emptiness, silently wondering, "Is this all?" Friedan urged women to return to school and to pursue careers that would establish their own, independent identity. What she called "the problem that has no name"—the deep but unexpressed feeling that home-making was not enough—resonated with many educated middle-class women. It informed them that they were not alone, and gave them a vocabulary with which to express their dissatisfaction.

Still another catalyst for feminism came from the involvement of younger women in the civil-rights and anti–Vietnam War movements. These activists had gained confidence in their own potential, an ideology to understand oppression, and experience in the strategy and tactics of organized protest. They also became conscious of their own second-class status, as they were sexually exploited and relegated to menial jobs by male activists. In the words of two women deeply involved in the civil-rights movement:

> Assumptions of male superiority are as widespread and deep-rooted and every much as crippling to the woman as the assumptions of white supremacy are to the Negro. . . . [We need to] stop the discrimination and start the slow process of changing values and ideas so that all of us gradually come to understand that this is no more a man's world than it is a white world.

The young women who shared such thoughts would soon create a women's liberation movement more critical of sexual inequality than NOW.

Women's Liberation   In 1968 militant feminists adopted "consciousness-raising" as a recruitment device and a means of transforming women's perceptions of themselves and society. Tens of thousands of women assembled in small groups to share experiences and air grievances. They learned that others felt dissatisfaction similar to their own. "When I saw that what I always felt were my own personal hangups was as true for every other woman in that room as it was for me! Well, that's when my consciousness was raised," a participant recalled. Women came to understand that their personal, individual problems were in fact shared problems with social causes and collective solutions—"the personal is political." They saw the power dynamics in marriage, the family, and the workplace. Consciousness-raising opened eyes and minds, and begot a sense that "sisterhood is powerful."

Women's liberation groups employed a variety of publicity-generating and confrontational tactics. In 1968 radical feminists crowned a sheep Miss America to dramatize their belief that such contests degraded women, and set up "freedom trash cans" in which women could discard high-heeled shoes, girdles, and other symbols of subjugation. They demanded inclusion in the Boston Marathon, no longer accepting the excuse that "it is unhealthy for women to run long distances." Overcoming male condescension and ridicule, they established health collectives and shelters for abused women, created day-care centers and rape crisis centers, founded abortion-counseling services and women's studies programs. They demanded equality in education and the workplace, and protested the negative portrayals of women in the media and advertising. Terms like *male chauvinist pig* entered the vocabulary and those like *chicks* exited. Some feminists claimed patriarchy, the power of men, to be the main cause of all oppressions and exploitations. Most rejected the notion that women were naturally passive and emotional, or that they suffered from "penis envy."

Despite a gulf between female radicals and liberals, they set aside their differences in August 1970 to join in the largest women's rights demonstration ever. Commemorating the fiftieth anniversary of woman suffrage, the Women's Strike for Equality brought out tens of thousands of women to parade for the right to equal employment and safe, legal abortions. By then the women's movement had already pressured many financial institutions to issue credit to single women and to married women in their own names. It had filed suit against numerous colleges and universities to secure salary raises for women faculty members victimized by discrimination, and ended newspapers' practice of listing employment opportunities under separate "Male" and "Female" headings. Guidelines that required corporations receiving federal funds to adopt nondiscriminatory hiring practices and equal pay scales had been established; and by 1970 more than 40 percent of all women held full-time jobs outside the home.

The right to control their own sexuality and decisions whether to have children also became a feminist rallying cry. In 1960 "the Pill" came on the market, giving women greater freedom to be sexually active without the risk of pregnancy (see Technology and Culture: The Pill). Many women, aware of the dangers of illegal abortions, pushed for their legalization. Some challenged demeaning obstetrical practices. Others explored alternatives to hospital births and popularized alternatives to radical mastectomy for breast cancer. Although antifeminism persisted, many women had become aware, in historian Gerda Lerner's words,

> that they belong to a subordinate group; that they have suffered wrongs as a group;
> that their condition of subordination is not natural, but societally determined; that
> they must join with other women to remedy these wrongs; and finally, that they
> must and can provide an alternative vision of societal organization in which
> women as well as men will enjoy autonomy and self-determination.

THE LIBERAL CRUSADE IN VIETNAM, 1961–1968

The activist liberals who boldly tried to uplift the downtrodden also went to war to contain communism and export democracy. Kennedy escalated Eisenhower's efforts in Vietnam in order to hold "the cornerstone of the Free World in Southeast Asia, the keystone in the arch, the finger in the dike." Johnson resolved, "I am not going to lose Vietnam, I am not going to be the president who saw Southeast Asia go the way China went." They would make a stand. The war in Vietnam pursued by liberals ended the era of liberalism. The nation's longest, most controversial, and only losing war ended the liberal consensus and divided the United States as had nothing since the Civil War.

Kennedy and Vietnam Following the compromise settlement in Laos, President Kennedy resolved, as had President Eisenhower, not to give further ground in Southeast Asia. He feared the likely success of the nationalist guerrilla movement led by Ho Chi Minh, which sought to overthrow the American puppet government in Saigon and unify the country under communist rule, unless the United States acted. Accordingly, JFK ordered massive shipments of weaponry to South Vietnam, stepped up clandestine operations against the North, and increased the number of American forces stationed in Vietnam from less than seven hundred in 1960 to more than sixteen thousand by the end of 1963. Although he never instituted the massive troop buildup advocated by some in the Pentagon, JFK refused

The Pill

The pill to prevent conception had many fathers and at least two mothers. Most of them were initially concerned with world overpopulation, not women's sexual freedom. In Margaret Sanger (see Chapter 21) and Katharine McCormick, heir to the International Harvester Company fortune, the goals of the movements for birth control and for population control meshed. The two women wanted a safe, inexpensive contraceptive that would be easy to use in the poverty-stricken slums of the world. In the postwar climate that favored technological solutions to social problems, they recruited Gregory Pincus, a pharmaceutical scientist working in a small Massachusetts laboratory grandly called the Worcester Foundation for Experimental Biology. Pincus desperately needed money to keep his lab afloat. Assured of McCormick's support to the tune of $2 million, he went to work in 1950 on Sanger's request for an oral contraceptive that would be as simple to use and as plentiful as aspirin.

Like most scientists, Pincus drew heavily on the earlier work of others. Chemists in the 1930s had synthesized estrogen, the female hormone that prevents ovulation (stopping the female body from forming and releasing an egg). Others had worked on progestin, the hormone in the ovaries that keeps sperm from fertilizing an egg. Pincus utilized their experiments with rabbits, as well as Carl Djerassi's synthesis of steroids and the work of gynecologist Dr. John Rock. None of these scientists had birth control on their minds. Indeed, Rock, a Catholic, was seeking an effective hormonal pill to help women get pregnant.

After years of experimenting with hundreds of combinations of substances, Pincus and his collaborator, Dr. M. C. Chiang, synthesized a mixture of estrogen and progestin that they believed safe and effective in suppressing ovulation in most women. In dubiously ethical practices, Pincus set up field trials with psychiatric patients and male prisoners (thinking it might work on men). Puerto Rico was the site for his first large-scale clinical trial of the oral contraceptive—because he could "attempt in Puerto Rico certain experiments which would be very difficult in this country." He followed that with tests in Haiti. Called Enovid, and produced by the G. D. Searle drug company, the pills were approved by the Food and Drug Administration (FDA) in 1957, but for gynecological disorders—not as a contraceptive.

At the time, thirty states still had laws banning or restricting contraceptive use, and most drug companies feared the controversy such a pill would arouse. The other drug companies left it to G. D. Searle to ask the FDA to approve the drug as a contraceptive. In May 1960 the FDA approved Enovid for contraceptive use. It did so, in large part, because of widespread concern about overpopulation and the threat of communism. Many feared that a teeming nonwhite underclass was tailor-made for a communist takeover, and thought the likelihood of that threat could be minimized by controlling population and thus reducing hunger, poverty, and disease in the world.

Many American women embraced the new technology with enthusiasm, and Enovid unexpectedly helped to foster a sexual revolution in the United States. By

1965, despite being condemned as immoral by the Catholic Church and denounced as a technology of genocide by African-American militants, "the Pill" (as it was commonly called) had become the most popular form of birth control in the United States, used by 6.5 million married women (unmarried women were not counted in official reports). In 1968 Americans spent as much on the Pill as on all other contraceptive methods combined. By 1970 more than 10 million American women were "on the Pill."

Pincus was deluged with fan letters. A grateful user in St. Paul kissed his picture in the newspaper, "for this is the first year in her eight years of marriage that she has not been pregnant." And in a song named "The Pill," Loretta Lynn sang, "All these years I've stayed at home while you had all your fun/ And ev'ry year that's gone by another baby's come/ There's gonna be some changes made right here on Nurs'ry Hill/ You've set this chicken your last time, 'cause now I've got the Pill."

Although widespread use of the Pill and the sexual revolution occurred together, the former did not cause the latter. Primarily married women consumed the Pill in the 1960s. It would take larger social changes in the United States before doctors would readily prescribe it for unmarried women, before the young would claim sexual pleasure as a right, and before a woman's liberation movement would be strong enough to insist on a woman's right to control her own sexuality. Permissiveness resulted more from affluence and mobility, from changed attitudes and laws, than from the Pill. Still, the Pill disconnected fears of pregnancy from the pursuit of sexual pleasure, and breaking reproductive shackles made sexual freedom more likely. The greater degree of autonomy and

choice in women's sexual-reproductive lives changed the experience and meaning of sex, in and out of marriage.

The Pill has not been a universal panacea. One woman's medical miracle became another's social concern and a third woman's health problem. High amounts of estrogen in the early pills caused blood clots and strokes, disabling many women. Because the Pill was available only with a doctor's prescription, the oral contraceptive increased doctors' control over the sexual lives of women. While conservatives sought to stem the tide of promiscuity and pornography they blamed on the Pill, feminists charged that women bore the costs of contraception because men controlled the medical profession and pharmaceutical industry. At the same time, liberalized sexual behavior proved less emancipating and more exploitative than feminists first expected, and the disagreement about such issues as birth control, abortion, premarital sex, and obscenity hastened the demise of the liberal consensus.

To date, the Pill has neither significantly limited population growth in the Third World nor ended the scourge of unwanted pregnancies in the United States. It has changed the dynamics of women's health care and altered gender relations. The first medicine produced for a social, rather than therapeutic, purpose, it remains the pharmaceutical swallowed as a daily routine by more humans than any other prescribed medication in the world.

Questions for Analysis

- To what extent is the Pill the cause of the sexual revolution?

- What have been the chief negative and positive consequences of the development of the Pill?

to accept a unified, communist Vietnam. He feared it would lead to a Republican-led, anticommunist backlash, damaging him politically. Like Eisenhower, he believed that letting "aggression" go unchecked would lead to wider wars (the Munich analogy), and that the communist takeover of one nation would lead to others going communist (the domino theory). Kennedy viewed international communism as a monolithic force, a global enemy controlled by Moscow and Beijing. Seeing Third World conflicts as tests of America's, and his own, will, he determined to show the world that the United States was not the "paper tiger" that Mao Zedong (Mao Tse-tung) mocked.

To counter Vietcong, or National Liberation Front (NLF), gains in the countryside, the United States dropped both chemical defoliants to destroy vegetation and deprive the Vietcong of natural cover, and napalm bombs—whose petroleum jelly burned at 1,000 degrees and clung to whatever it touched, including human flesh. It also forcibly uprooted Vietnamese peasants and moved them into fortified villages, or "strategic hamlets," to prevent infiltration by the Vietcong. But South Vietnamese president Diem rejected American pressure to gain popular support through reform measures, instead crushing demonstrations by students and Buddhists. By mid-1963, Buddhist monks were setting themselves on fire to protest Diem's repression, and Diem's own generals were plotting a coup.

Frustrated American policy makers concluded that only a new government could prevent a Vietcong victory and secretly encouraged a coup by Vietnamese army officers to overthrow Diem. On November 1, the military leaders struck, captured Diem and his brother, and shot them. Although the United States promptly recognized the new government (the first of nine South Vietnamese regimes in the next five years), it too made little headway against the Vietcong. JFK now faced two unpalatable alternatives: increase the combat involvement of American forces or withdraw and seek a negotiated settlement.

What Kennedy would have done remains unknown. Less than a month after Diem's death, John Kennedy himself fell to an assassin's bullet. His admirers contend that by late 1963 he favored the withdrawal of American forces after the 1964 election. "It is their war," he said publicly; ". . . it is their people and their government who have to win or lose the struggle." Yet the president followed this comment with a ringing restatement of his belief in the domino theory and a promise that America would not withdraw from the conflict. He had already transformed Eisenhower's "limited-risk gamble" into a major American military commitment, and he and his advisers continued to hold that an American victory in Vietnam was essential to check communism in Asia. National Security Adviser McGeorge Bundy, Secretary of Defense Robert McNamara, and Secretary of State Dean Rusk would counsel Kennedy's successor accordingly.

Escalation of the War

Now it was Johnson who had to choose between intervening decisively or withdrawing from an inherited conflict that three previous presidents had insisted the communists must not win. Privately describing Vietnam as "a raggedy-ass fourth-rate country" undeserving of American blood and dollars, LBJ feared that an all-out American military effort might lead to World War III. He foresaw that full-scale engagement in "that bitch of a war" would destroy "the woman I really loved—the Great Society." Yet Johnson also accepted the domino theory and Munich analogy, and thought that only American resolve would prevent a wider war. He, too, feared being thought "a coward, an unmanly man," and worried that a pullout would leave him vulnerable to conservative

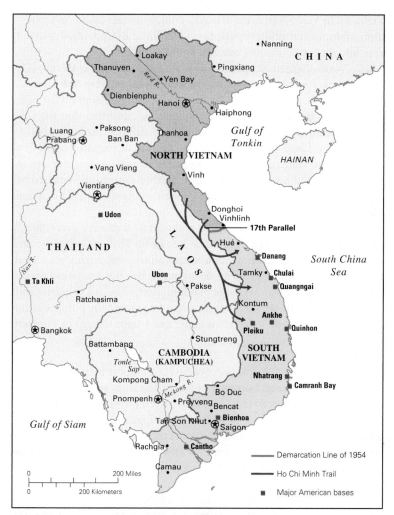

MAP 28.2 The Vietnam War, to 1968

Wishing to guarantee an independent, noncommunist government in South Vietnam, Lyndon Johnson remarked in 1965, "We fight because we must fight if we are to live in a world where every country can shape its own destiny. To withdraw from one battlefield means only to prepare for the next."

accusations that he was "soft" on communism and to the destruction of his liberal programs.

Trapped between unacceptable alternatives, Johnson expanded the war, hoping that U.S. firepower would force Ho Chi Minh to the bargaining table. But the North Vietnamese and NLF calculated that they could gain more by outlasting the United States than by negotiating. So the war ground on.

In 1964 Johnson took bold steps to impress North Vietnam with American resolve and to block his opponent, Barry Goldwater, from capitalizing on Vietnam in the presidential campaign. In February he ordered the Pentagon to prepare for air strikes against North Vietnam. In May his advisers drafted a congressional resolution authorizing an escalation of American military action, and in July LBJ appointed General Maxwell Taylor, an advocate of escalation, as ambassador to Saigon.

In early August, North Vietnamese patrol boats allegedly clashed with two U.S. destroyers in the Gulf of Tonkin. Evidence of the attack was unclear, yet Johnson announced that Americans had been victims of Hanoi's "open aggression on the high seas." Johnson condemned the attacks as unprovoked, never admitting that the U.S. ships took part in covert raids against North Vietnam. He ordered air strikes on North Vietnamese naval bases and asked Congress to pass the previously prepared resolution giving him the authority to "take all necessary measures to repel any armed attack against the forces of the United States and to prevent further aggression." Assured by the president that this meant no "extension of the present conflict," the Senate passed the **Gulf of Tonkin Resolution** 88 to 2, and the House 416 to 0.

Privately, LBJ called the resolution "grandma's nightshirt—it covered everything." He considered it a mandate to commit U.S. forces as he saw fit. The blank check to determine the level of force made massive intervention more likely; and having once used force against North Vietnam made it easier to do so again. But the resolution would eventually allow opponents of the war to charge that Johnson had misled Congress and lied to the American people, as he would do again when he assured the public during the 1964 campaign that he would neither deploy American troops to fight in Vietnam nor extend the war by bombing North Vietnam.

The Endless War   Early in 1965, Johnson ordered "Operation Rolling Thunder," the sustained bombing of North Vietnam. It aimed to "break the will of North Vietnam" and force Hanoi to negotiate, to boost the morale of the Saigon government, and to stop the flow of soldiers and supplies coming from North Vietnam via the so-called Ho Chi Minh Trail. But despite the dropping of eight hundred tons of bombs a day on North Vietnam between 1965 and 1968, three times the tonnage dropped by all the combatants in World War II, it failed to achieve its objectives.

Unable to turn the tide by bombing, Johnson committed U.S. combat troops. Adopting a "meat-grinder" or attrition strategy, Johnson sought to inflict unacceptable casualties on the communists to force them to the peace table. Johnson sent 485,000 troops (a greater military force than the U.S. had deployed in Korea) to Vietnam by the end of 1967. But superiority in numbers and weaponry did not defeat an enemy that could choose when and where to attack and then melt back into the jungle. Determined to battle until the United States lost the will to fight, Hanoi matched each American troop increase with its own. No end was in sight.

Doves Versus   First among pacifists and socialists, then on college campuses,
Hawks   and lastly in the wider society, a growing number of Americans opposed the war. In March 1965, students and faculty at the University of Michigan staged the first teach-in to raise questions about U.S. intervention. All-night discussions of the war followed at universities from Maine to Oregon. Some twenty-five thousand people, mainly students, rallied in Washington that spring to protest the escalation, giving the antiwar movement crucial television coverage. In 1966, large-scale campus antiwar protests erupted. Students demonstrated against the draft and university research for the Pentagon. They proved to be only a prelude to 1967's massive Spring Mobilization to End the War in Vietnam protests in

LBJ's Vietnam Nightmare *The Vietnam War spelled Johnson's undoing. Young peace demonstrators made known their feelings about the president's role in the war during a massive antiwar protest at the Pentagon in October 1967.*

New York and San Francisco, which drew half a million participants, and the October demonstrations at the Pentagon by another hundred thousand.

Intellectuals penning essays against the war, clergy holding peace vigils, and women lobbying Congress for "a peaceful solution" joined the chorus of opposition to the war. Some decried the massive bombing of an underdeveloped nation; some doubted that the United States could win at any reasonable cost; some feared the demise of the Great Society and liberalism. In 1967, prominent critics of the war, including Democratic senators William Fulbright, Robert Kennedy, and George McGovern, pediatrician Dr. Benjamin Spock, and Martin Luther King, Jr., spurred hundreds of thousands to participate in antiwar protests.

Critics also noted that the war's toll fell most heavily on the poor. Owing to college deferments, the use of influence, and a military-assignment system that shunted the better-educated to desk jobs, lower-class youths were twice as likely to be drafted and, when drafted, twice as likely to see combat duty as middle-class youths. About 80 percent of the enlisted men who fought in Vietnam came from poor and working-class families.

TV coverage of the war further eroded support. Scenes of children maimed by U.S. bombs and of dying Americans, replayed nightly, laid bare the horror of war and undercut the optimistic reports of government officials. Americans shuddered as they watched U.S. troops, supposedly winning the hearts and minds of the Vietnamese, burn villages and desecrate burial grounds.

Yet for every protestor shouting "Hell No, We Won't Go!" many more war supporters affixed bumper stickers reading "America, Love It or Leave It!" Until 1968, most Americans either supported the war or remained undecided. "I want to get out, but I don't want to give up" expressed a widespread view. They were not prepared to accept a communist victory over the United States.

Equally disturbing was how polarized the nation had grown. **"Hawks"** would accept little short of total victory, whereas **"doves"** insisted on negotiating, not fighting. Civility vanished. As Johnson lashed out at his critics as "nervous Nellies" and refused to de-escalate the conflict, demonstrators paraded past the White House chanting, "Hey, hey, LBJ, how many kids did you kill today?" By 1968, the president had become a virtual prisoner in the White House, unable to speak in public without being shouted down. So ended an era of hope and liberalism. Few Americans now believed in Kennedy's assurance that the nation could "pay any price, bear any burden, meet any hardship, support any friend, oppose any foe."

CONCLUSION

The Kennedy style of "can-do" vigor and liberal rhetoric captivated the media and obscured a so-so domestic record. Stymied by the conservative coalition in Congress, Kennedy did more to stimulate hope than to achieve change. Others would force changes from the bottom up, and the next president, Lyndon Johnson, would persuade Congress to make a reality of the liberal ideal of an activist government promoting a fairer life for all Americans. Fed up with the more legalistic, cautious strategy of the civil-rights movement in the past, young African-Americans initiated a new direct action phase in black America's struggle for equal rights. Their activism, bubbling up from the local level, led to the landmark Civil Rights and Voting Rights Acts, which ended the legality of racial discrimination and black disfranchisement, provided greater equality of opportunity for African-Americans, and nurtured the self-esteem of blacks. However, the laws left untouched the maladies of the urban black ghetto. There, unfulfilled expectations and frustrated hopes exploded into rioting, which, in turn, triggered a white backlash that undermined support for the liberal agenda.

That agenda had prompted Johnson to secure the Civil Rights Act and a tax cut in 1964. Then came the Great Society legislation promoting health, education, voting rights, urban renewal, immigration reform, federal support for the arts and humanities, protection of the environment, and a war against poverty—the most sweeping liberal measures since the New Deal, and a significant enlargement in the role of the federal government in the lives of most Americans.

This outpouring of liberal measures, along with the model of the African-American struggle for justice, inspired other minorities and women to fight for equality and dignity. Native Americans, Hispanic-Americans, Asian-Americans, and women took to the streets to demand their fair due. Subsequently, their younger, more militant activists, like their black counterparts, also parted ways with liberals over means and ends.

Most of all, the Vietnam War destroyed the liberal consensus. To prevent South Vietnam from being taken over by the communists, Kennedy significantly increased the number and fighting role of American advisers in Vietnam and gave the green light for a coup to overthrow Diem, the unpopular head of the government in Saigon. Inheriting a deteriorating limited war from Kennedy, LBJ also chose to escalate America's involvement, hoping to force North Vietnam to negotiate a compromise. Three years later, a half-million American troops were stationed in Vietnam, and the United States was dropping more bombs on Vietnam than had been dropped in World War II. Still, the United States was no closer to achieving its objective; and the nation was now polarized. While the administration claimed to see the light at the end of the tunnel, critics saw the light as a speeding train about to crash into American society.

29

A Time of Upheaval, 1968–1974

THE YOUTH MOVEMENT

In the 1950s, the number of American students pursuing higher education rose from 1 million to 4 million, and the number doubled to 8 million in the 1960s. By then, more than half the U.S. population was under thirty years of age. Breaking with its forty-year tradition, *Time* magazine in 1967 selected the entire baby-boom generation as its "Man of the Year." Their sheer numbers gave the young a collective identity and guaranteed that their actions would have impact. And not just in the United States. Major student demonstrations shook the governments of Japan, Korea, Turkey, and Venezuela in 1960 alone.

Most baby boomers followed conventional paths. They sought a secure place in the system, not its overthrow. They preferred beer to drugs, and football to political demonstrations. They joined fraternities and sororities and majored in subjects that would equip them for the job market. Whether or not they went to college—and fewer than half did—the vast majority had their eyes fixed on a good salary, a new car, and a traditional family. Many disdained long-haired protesters and displayed "My Country—Right or Wrong" bumper stickers.

Some politically engaged young people mobilized on the right, joining organizations like Young Americans for Freedom (YAF), which by 1970 boasted fifty thousand members—far more than any other student group. These youths idolized Barry Goldwater, not John Kennedy. They demanded a rollback of big government at home and called for victory in Vietnam. While many adhered to traditional values, other young conservatives embraced libertarian notions. Although a part of a conservative movement that would grow increasingly more powerful in the future, YAF was overshadowed in the 1960s by young activists in the New Left.

Toward a New Left Although a tiny minority of youth, an insurgent band of liberal arts majors and graduate students got the lion's share of attention. This liberal-minded minority welcomed the idealism of the civil-rights movement and the rousing call of President Kennedy for service to the nation. They admired the mavericks and outsiders of the fifties: iconoclastic comedian Mort Sahl; Beat poet Allen Ginsberg; and pop-culture rebel James Dean.

In June 1962, some sixty students adopted the Port Huron Statement. Determined not to be a "silent generation," they issued a broad critique of American society and a call for more genuine human relationships. Proclaiming themselves "a new left," they gave birth to the **Students for a Democratic Society (SDS).** Inspired by the sit-ins and freedom rides, SDS envisioned a nonviolent youth movement transforming the United States into a "participatory democracy" in which individuals would participate in making the decisions that affected their lives. SDS assumed that people who controlled their own lives would value love and creativity, and would end materialism, militarism, and racism.

The generation of activists who found their agenda in the Port Huron Statement had their eyes opened by the police dogs and fire hoses in Birmingham, the assassination of President Kennedy, and the destruction of Vietnam brought so graphically into their homes by television. Most never joined SDS, instead associating with what they vaguely called "the Movement" or "the New Left." Unlike the Leftists of the 1930s, they rejected Marxist ideology and emulated SNCC's rhetoric and style. Many became radicalized by the rigidity of campus administrators and mainstream liberalism's inability to achieve fundamental change. Only a radical rejection of compromise and consensus, they presumed, could restructure society along humane and democratic lines.

From Protest to Resistance Returning from the Mississippi Freedom Summer to the Berkeley campus of the University of California in fall 1964, Mario Savio and other student activists ventured to solicit funds and recruit volunteers near the campus gate, a spot traditionally open to political activities. Prodded by local conservatives, the university suddenly banned such practices. That led Savio to found the **Berkeley Free Speech Movement (FSM),** a coalition of student groups insisting on the right to campus political activity. Likening the university to a giant machine, and its students to interchangeable machine parts, Savio insisted, "There is a time when the operation of the machine becomes so odious, makes you so sick to heart, that you've got to put your bodies upon the gears and upon the wheels . . . and you've got to make it stop." More than a thousand students joined Savio in a sit-in on the administrative "gears." Their arrests led to more demonstrations and a strike by nearly 70 percent of the student body.

By 1965 Mario Savio's call for students to throw their bodies upon "the machine" until it ground to a halt had reverberated on campuses nationwide. The FSM catalyzed a wave of campus protests. Students sat in to halt compulsory ROTC (Reserve Officers' Training Corps) programs, rallied to protest dress codes and parietal rules, and marched to demand changes in the grading system. They demanded fewer required courses, smaller classes, and teaching-oriented rather than research-oriented professors. They threatened to close down universities unless they admitted more minority students and stopped doing research for the military-industrial complex.

The escalation of the war in Vietnam, and the abolition of automatic student deferments from the draft in January 1966, turned the Movement into a *mass* movement.

CHRONOLOGY, 1964–1974

1964 • Berkeley Free Speech Movement (FSM).
The Beatles arrive in the United States.

1965 • Ken Kesey and Merry Pranksters stage first "acid test."

1966 • Abolition of automatic student deferments from the draft.

1967 • March on the Pentagon.
Israeli-Arab Six-Day War.

1968 • Tet offensive.
Martin Luther King, Jr., assassinated; race riots sweep nation.
Students take over buildings at Columbia University.
Robert F. Kennedy assassinated.
Violence mars Democratic convention in Chicago.
Vietnam peace talks open in Paris.
Richard Nixon elected president.

1969 • Apollo 11 lands first Americans on the moon.
Nixon begins withdrawal of U.S. troops from Vietnam.
Woodstock festival.

1970 • United States invades Cambodia.
Students killed at Kent State and Jackson State Universities.
Beatles disband.
Earth Day first celebrated.

1971 • United States invades Laos.
Swann v. *Charlotte-Mecklenburg Board of Education.*
New York Times publishes Pentagon Papers.
Nixon institutes wage-and-price freeze.
South Vietnam invades Laos with the help of U.S. air support.

1972 • Nixon visits China and the Soviet Union.
SALT I agreement approved.
Break-in at Democratic National Committee headquarters in
Watergate complex.
Nixon reelected president.

1973 • Vietnam cease-fire agreement signed.
Senate establishes special committee to investigate Watergate.
President Salvador Allende ousted and murdered in Chile.
Vice President Spiro Agnew resigns; Gerald Ford appointed vice president.
Roe v. *Wade.*
Yom Kippur War; OPEC begins embargo of oil to the West.
Saturday Night Massacre.

1974 • House Judiciary Committee votes to impeach Nixon.
Nixon resigns; Ford becomes president.

Popularizing the slogan "Make Love—Not War," SDS organized teach-ins, sponsored antiwar marches and rallies, and harassed campus recruiters for the military and the Dow Chemical Company, the chief producer of flesh-burning napalm and Agent Orange, the chemical used to defoliate Vietnam forests. In 1967 SDS leaders encouraged even more provocative protests. With the rallying cry "From Protest to Resistance," they supported draft resistance and civil disobedience in selective service centers, and clashed with federal marshals during the "siege of the Pentagon" in October's "Stop the Draft Week." At the Spring Mobilization to End the War in Vietnam, which attracted a half-million antiwar protesters, SDS members led the chants of "Burn cards, not people" and "Hell, no, we won't go!" By 1968 SDS claimed one hundred thousand members on three hundred campus chapters.

Spring 1968 saw at least forty thousand students on a hundred campuses demonstrate against war and racism. Most, but not all, stayed peaceful. In April militant Columbia University students shouting "Gym Crow must go" took over the administration building and held a dean captive to denounce the university's proposed expansion into Harlem to construct a gymnasium. The protest then expanded into a demonstration against the war and university military research. A thousand students barricaded themselves inside campus buildings, declaring them "revolutionary communes." Outraged by the harshness of the police who retook the buildings by storm and sent more than a hundred demonstrators to the hospital, the moderate majority of Columbia students joined a boycott of classes that shut down the university. Elsewhere, students in France, Germany, Ireland, Italy, Japan, and Mexico rose up to demand reform that year. In Prague, Czechoslovakian students singing Beatles songs battled Soviet tanks.

1969 saw the high point of the Movement with the New Mobilization, a series of huge antiwar demonstrations culminating in mid-November with a March Against Death. Three hundred thousand protestors came to Washington, D.C., to march through a cold rain carrying candles and signs with the names of soldiers killed or villages destroyed in Vietnam. By then, antiwar sentiment pervaded national institutions, and by 1972 it would be dominant. In sharp contrast to the apolitical students of the 1950s, youth in the 1960s proved themselves able to influence what affected their own lives.

Kent State and Jackson State

A storm of violence in spring of 1970 marked the effective end of the student movement as a political force. On April 30, 1970, Richard M. Nixon, LBJ's successor, jolted a war-weary nation by announcing that he had ordered U.S. troops to invade Cambodia, a neutral Indochinese nation that had become a staging area for North Vietnamese forces. Nixon had decided to extricate the United States from Vietnam by "Vietnamizing" the ground fighting (that is, using South Vietnamese troops instead of Americans) and intensifying bombing. Students, lulled by periodic announcements of troop withdrawals from Vietnam, now felt betrayed.

At Kent State University in Ohio, as elsewhere, student frustrations unleashed new turmoil. Radicals broke windows and torched the ROTC building. Nixon branded the protesters "bums," his vice president compared them to Nazi storm troopers, and the Ohio governor slapped martial law on the university. Three thousand National Guardsmen in full battle gear rolled onto the campus in armored personnel carriers.

"My God, They're Killing Us" *Following President Nixon's announcement of the military incursion into Cambodia, a formally neutral nation, many colleges exploded in anger. To quell the protests at Kent State University, where more than a thousand students clashed with local police, Ohio National Guardsmen fired on students, killing four. News of the shootings outraged many students nationwide, touching off yet another round of campus protests, which led hundreds of colleges to cancel final exams and shut down for the semester.*

The day after the guard's arrival, six hundred Kent State students demonstrated against the Cambodian invasion. Suddenly a campus policeman boomed through a bullhorn, "This assembly is unlawful! This is an order—disperse immediately!" Students shouted back, "Pigs off campus!" Some threw stones. With bayonets fixed, the guardsmen moved toward the rally and laid down a blanket of tear gas. Hundreds of demonstrators and onlookers, choking and weeping, ran from the advancing troops. Guardsmen in Troop G, poorly trained in crowd control, raked the retreating students with M-1 rifle fire. When the shooting stopped, four students lay dead and eleven wounded. None was a campus radical.

Ten days later, Mississippi state patrolmen responding to a campus protest fired into a women's dormitory at historically black **Jackson State College,** killing two students and wounding a dozen others. Nationwide, students exploded in protest against the violence, the war, and the president. Student strikes closed down four hundred colleges, many of which had seen no previous unrest. The war had come home.

The nation was polarized. Although many students blamed Nixon for widening the war and applauded the demonstrators' goals, most Americans blamed the victims for the violence and criticized students for undermining U.S. foreign policy. They had enough of sit-ins at local draft boards, antiwar demonstrations, and draft-card burnings. Patriotism, class resentment of privileged college students, and a fear of social chaos animated America's condemnation of protesters. Many Kent townspeople shared the view of a local merchant who asserted that the guard had "made only one mistake—they should have fired sooner and longer." A local ditty promised, "The score is four, and next time more."

Legacy of Student Frenzy   The campus disorders after the invasion of Cambodia were the final spasm of a tumultuous movement. When a bomb planted by three antiwar radicals destroyed a science building at the University of Wisconsin in summer 1970, killing a graduate student, most young people condemned the tactic. With the resumption of classes in the fall, the fad of "streaking"—racing across campus in the nude—more reminiscent of the 1920s than the 1960s, signaled a change in the student mood. By then, Nixon had significantly reduced the number of young men being drafted, and the entire conscription system was soon to be ended, decreasing student opposition to the war. In addition, antiwar activists turned to other causes, or to communes, careers, and parenthood. A handful of radicals went underground, committing terrorist acts that justified the government's repression of the remnants of the antiwar movement. The New Left fell victim to government harassment, to its own internal contradictions, and to Nixon's winding down the Vietnam War.

The consequences of campus upheavals outlived the New Left. Student radicalism spurred the resentment of millions of Americans, helping shatter the liberal consensus. It gave religious evangelicals, southern segregationists, and blue-collar workers yet another reason to vote conservative, and propelled Republicans like Ronald Reagan to prominence. In 1966 he won California's governorship by denouncing Berkeley demonstrators and Watts rioters. The actor-turned-politician then won a resounding reelection victory by condemning young radicals. "If it takes a bloodbath, let's get it over with," he declared. "No more appeasement!" Nationwide, Republicans gained office with similar promises, heralding a vital change in American politics from liberalism to conservatism.

The New Left had, however, helped mobilize public opposition to the Vietnam War. It energized campuses into a force that the government could not ignore, and it made continued U.S. involvement in Vietnam difficult. The Movement also liberalized many facets of campus life and made university governance less authoritarian. Dress codes and curfews virtually vanished; ROTC disappeared entirely from some campuses, and went from a requirement to an elective at others; minority recruitment increased, and Black Studies programs proliferated; and students gained a larger role in decision making on campus.

Some New Left veterans remained active in 1970s causes, especially environmentalism, consumer advocacy, and the antinuclear movement. Female students in the Movement formed the backbone of a women's liberation movement. These involvements, however, fell short of the New Left vision of remaking the social and political order. While masses of students could be mobilized in the short run for a particular cause, only a few made long-term commitments to Movement activism. The generation that the New Left had hoped would be the vanguard of radical change preferred pot to politics, and rock to revolution.

THE COUNTERCULTURE

The alienation and hunger for change that drew some youths into radical politics led others to cultural rebellion, to focusing on personal rather than political change, to discarding middle-class values, attitudes, and practices. Rejecting the repressed authority of the established order, hardcore **hippies** disdained employment and consumerism, preferring to make what they needed, share it with others, and not want what they did not have. Love, cooperation, community, and immediate gratification became their mantra. In the second half of the 1960s they joined communes and tribes that glorified liberation from monogamy and private property. In urban areas such as San Francisco's Haight-Ashbury district and Atlanta's Fourteenth Street—"places where you could take a trip without a ticket"—they experimented with drugs, mysticism, and uninhibited sexuality. Some embarked on an almost religious quest for "authenticity" and "personal fulfillment." Historian Theodore Roszack called them "a **'counter culture'** . . . a culture so radically disaffiliated from the mainstream assumptions of our society that it scarcely looks to many as a culture at all, but takes on the alarming appearance of a barbarian intrusion."

Hippies and Drugs   Illustrative of the gap between the two cultures, one saw marijuana as a "killer weed," a menace to health and life, and the other thought it a harmless social relaxant. In the absence of scientific evidence proving the drug dangerous, at least half the college students in the late sixties tried marijuana. A minority used hallucinogenic or mind-altering drugs, particularly LSD. The high priest of LSD was Timothy Leary, a former Harvard psychologist fired in 1963 for encouraging students to experiment with drugs—to "tune in, turn on, drop out." On the West Coast, writer Ken Kesey and his followers, the Merry Pranksters, conducted "acid tests" (distributing free tablets of LSD in orange juice), and created the "psychedelic" craze of Day-Glo-painted bodies gyrating to electrified rock music under flashing strobe lights.

The counterculture sought a world in which magic and mysticism replaced science and reason, and where competitive individuals became caring and loving. Some youths distanced themselves from middle-class respectability, flaunted outrageous personal styles ("do your own thing"), and expressed contempt for consumerism by wearing surplus military clothing, torn jeans, and tie-dyed T-shirts. Especially galling to adults, many young men sported shaggy beards and long hair. Typical of the generation that had been schooled in the deprivation and duty of the 1930s and 1940s, Governor Ronald Reagan of California defined a hippie as one "who looked like Tarzan, walked like Jane, and smelled like Cheetah."

Musical Revolution   Popular music both echoed and developed a separate generational identity, a distinct youth culture. In the early 1960s folk songs protesting war and racism mirrored the early decade's optimistic idealism. Bob Dylan sang hopefully of changes "blowin' in the wind" and indignantly of changes that would "shake your windows and rattle your walls."

"Beatlemania" swept the country in 1964. They would soon be joined by the Rolling Stones, the Motown rhythm-and-blues black performers, and eardrum-shattering acid rockers—each extolling "sex, drugs, and rock-and-roll" for a generation at war.

In August 1969, four hundred thousand young people gathered for the **Woodstock festival** in New York's Catskill Mountains to celebrate their vision of freedom and harmony. For three days and nights, they reveled in rock music and openly shared drugs, sexual partners, and contempt for the Establishment. The counterculture heralded Woodstock as the dawning of an era of love, peace, and sharing—the Age of Aquarius.

In fact, the counterculture's luster had already dimmed. Prominent rock performers died of drug overdoses. The pilgrimage of "flower children" to the Haight-Ashbury district of San Francisco and to New York's East Village in 1967 brought a train of rapists and dope peddlers. In December 1969, hippie Charles Manson and his "family" of runaways ritually murdered a pregnant movie actress and four of her friends, and the Rolling Stones hired the Hell's Angels motorcycle gang to guard them at the rock concert at the Altamont Raceway near San Francisco. While the Stones performed, the Hell's Angels terrorized spectators and stabbed and stomped a young black man to death. In 1970, the Beatles disbanded. On his own, John Lennon sang, "The dream is over. What can I say?"

Advertisers awoke to the economic potential of the youth culture, using "rebellion" and "revolution" to sell cars and jeans. Most youths found conventional jobs and adopted traditional lifestyles. Although cynics concluded that counterculture values were not deeply held, its rosy view of human nature and skeptical attitude toward authority continued to influence American education and society long after the 1960s. Self-fulfillment remained a popular goal, and the repressive sexual standards of the 1950s did not return.

The Sexual Revolution

The counterculture's "if it feels good, do it" approach to sex fit the hedonistic and permissive ethic of the 1960s. This shift in attitude and behavior accelerated the sexual revolution. Although the AIDS epidemic and the graying of the baby boomers in the late 1980s chilled the ardor of heedless promiscuity, liberalized sexual mores were more publicly accepted than ever before, making full gender equality a realizable goal.

Many commentators linked the increase in sexual permissiveness to waning fears of unwanted pregnancy. In 1960 oral contraceptives reached the market, and by 1970 ten million women were taking the Pill. Still other women used the intrauterine device (IUD, later banned as unsafe) or the diaphragm. Some states legalized abortion. In New York in 1970 one fetus was legally aborted for every two babies born. The Supreme Court's *Roe v. Wade* (1973) struck down all remaining state laws infringing on a woman's right to abortion during the first trimester (three months) of pregnancy. Further fueling the sexual revolution, many universities ended their rules on dormitory visits and living off campus, and the counterculture emphasized casual sex, public nudity, and a four-letter word as a revolutionary challenge to bourgeois "uptight Amerika."

By the end of the 1960s, the Supreme Court had ruled unconstitutional any laws restricting "sexually explicit" art with "redeeming social importance." Mass culture exploited the new permissiveness. *Playboy* featured ever-more-explicit erotica, and women's periodicals encouraged their readers to enjoy recreational sex. The commercial success of films given "R" or "X" ratings led Broadway producers to present plays featuring full-frontal nudity and mock orgies. Even television began to allow sexual jokes and frank discussions of once forbidden subjects. Identifying pornography and obscenity as "a matter of national concern," Congress established a special commission to suggest a plan of attack. Instead, the commission in 1970 recommended the repeal of all obscenity and pornography laws. By then, most barriers to expressions of sexuality had fallen in literature, Broadway plays, and Hollywood films.

Attitudinal changes brought behavioral changes, and vice versa. Cohabitation—living together without marriage—became thinkable to average middle-class Americans. Some marital counselors even touted "open marriage" (in which spouses are free to have sex with other partners) and "swinging" (sexual sharing with other couples) as cures for stale relationships. The use of contraceptives (and to some extent, even of abortion) spread to women of all religious backgrounds—including Roman Catholics, despite the Catholic Church's stand against "artificial" birth control.

Gay Liberation   Stimulated by the other protest movements in the sixties, **gay liberation** emerged publicly in late June 1969. During a routine raid by New York City police, the homosexual patrons of the Stonewall Inn, a gay bar in Greenwich Village, unexpectedly fought back. The furor triggered a surge of "gay pride," a new sense of identity and self-acceptance, and widespread activism. The gay liberation movement that emerged built on the reform-minded Mattachine Society and the Daughters of Bilitis, as well as other "homophile" groups that focused on equal rights and assimilation. But the new liberation movement went far beyond the "rights-based" organizations in brazenly asserting its sexual orientation, "We are going to be who we are."

Supporters of the Gay Liberation Front came primarily from the gay subcultures found in the largest cities. By 1973 some eight hundred openly gay groups were fighting for equal rights for homosexuals, for incorporating lesbianism into the women's movement, and for removing the stigma of immorality and depravity attached to being gay. That year, they succeeded in getting the American Psychiatric Association to rescind its official view of homosexuality as a mental disorder, and to reclassify it as a normal sexual orientation.

Simultaneously, several cities and states began to broaden their civil-rights statutes to include "sexual orientation" as a protected status, and in 1975 the U.S. Civil Service Commission officially ended its ban on the employment of homosexuals. Millions of gays had "come out," demanding public acceptance of their sexual identity.

The baby boomers transformed sexual relations as much as gender and racial relations. The institutions of marriage and family were fundamentally altered. Women could have access to birth control, abortion, and an active sex life with or without a male partner. But what some hailed as liberation others bemoaned as moral decay. Offended by openly gay men and lesbians, and by "topless" bars, X-rated theaters, and "adult" bookstores, many Americans applauded politicians who promised a war on immorality. The public association of the counterculture, the sexual revolution, and gay liberation with student radicalism and ghetto riots swelled the tide of conservatism as the decade ended.

1968: THE POLITICS OF UPHEAVAL

The social and cultural upheavals of the late sixties unfolded against a backdrop of frustration with the war in Vietnam and disillusionment with liberalism. The stormy events of 1968 would culminate in a tempest of a political campaign and a turbulent realignment in American politics, the first since the New Deal.

The Tet Offensive in Vietnam In January 1968 liberal Democratic senator **Eugene McCarthy** of Minnesota, a Vietnam War critic, announced that he would challenge LBJ for the presidential nomination. Experts scoffed that McCarthy had no chance of unseating Johnson, who had won the presidency in 1964 by the largest margin in U.S. history. The last time such an insurgency had been attempted, in 1912, even the wildly popular Teddy Roosevelt had failed. Yet McCarthy persisted, determined that at least one Democrat enter the primaries on an antiwar platform.

Suddenly, on January 31—the first day of Tet, the Vietnamese New Year—America's hopes for victory in Vietnam exploded, and with them LBJ's political fortunes. National Liberation Front (NLF) and North Vietnamese forces mounted a huge **Tet offensive,** attacking more than a hundred South Vietnamese cities and towns, and even the U.S. embassy in Saigon for a few hours. U.S. and South Vietnamese troops eventually repulsed the offensive, inflicting a major military defeat on the communists, who failed to unleash a general uprising against the government in Saigon or to hold any South Vietnamese city.

Victory, however, came at an enormous psychological cost. The dramatic initial reports of the media, highlighting the number of American casualties and the grand scope of the Tet offensive, undercut Johnson's and General Westmoreland's claims of imminent victory, of "light at the end of the tunnel." However much supporters of the war blamed the media for ignoring the heavy losses to the NLF and the North Vietnamese, thereby turning "victory" into "defeat," the Tet offensive deepened the growing mood of gloom about the war and intensified doubts that the United States could win at an acceptable cost. Public approval of the president's conduct of the war fell to just 26 percent in the immediate aftermath of Tet.

After Tet, McCarthy's criticism of the war won many new sympathizers. *Time, Newsweek,* and influential newspapers published editorials urging a negotiated settlement. NBC's news anchorman concluded that "the grand objective—the building of a free nation—is not nearer, but further, from realization." The nation's premier newscaster, Walter Cronkite of CBS, observed, "It seems more certain than ever that the bloody experience of Vietnam is to end in a stalemate." "If I've lost Walter," LBJ sighed, "then it's over. I've lost Mr. Average Citizen." The number of Americans who described themselves as prowar "hawks" slipped from 62 percent in January to 41 percent in March, while the antiwar "doves" jumped from 22 percent to 42 percent.

A Shaken President Beleaguered, Johnson pondered a change in American policy. When the Joint Chiefs of Staff sought 206,000 more men for Vietnam, he turned to old friends for advice. Former secretary of state and venerable Cold Warrior Dean Acheson told him, "the Joint Chiefs of Staff don't know what they're talking about." Clark Clifford, once a hawk and now secretary of defense, concluded "that the military course we were pursuing was not only endless but hopeless."

Meanwhile, nearly five thousand college students had swarmed to New Hampshire to stuff envelopes and ring doorbells for Eugene McCarthy in the nation's first primary contest. "Clean for Gene," they cut their long hair and dressed conservatively so as not to alienate potential supporters. McCarthy astonished the experts by winning nearly half the popular vote in a state usually regarded as conservative.

After this upset, twice as many students converged on Wisconsin to canvass its more liberal voters. Expecting Johnson to lose, Senator **Robert Kennedy,** also promising to end the war, entered the Democratic contest. Projecting the familiar Kennedy glamour and magnetism, Robert Kennedy was the one candidate whom Johnson feared could deny him renomination. Indeed, millions viewed Kennedy as the rightful heir to the White House. Appealing to minorities, the poor, and working-class ethnic whites, Kennedy became, according to a columnist, "our first politician for the pariahs, our great national outsider."

On March 31, exactly three years after the marines had splashed ashore at Danang, Johnson surprised a television audience by announcing a halt to the bombing in North Vietnam. Adding that he wanted to devote all his efforts to the search for peace, LBJ startlingly announced, "I shall not seek, and I will not accept, the nomination of my party for another term as your president." Embittered by the personal abuse he had endured and reluctant to polarize the nation further, LBJ called it quits. "I tried to make it possible for every child of every color to grow up in a nice house, eat a solid breakfast, to attend a decent school and to get a good and lasting job," he grumbled privately. "But look at what I got instead. Riots in 175 cities. Looting. Burning. Shooting. . . . Young people by the thousands leaving the university, marching in the streets." Both physically and emotionally spent, LBJ lamented, "The only difference between the [John F.] Kennedy assassination and mine is that I am alive and it has been more torturous." Two days later, pounding the final nail into Johnson's political coffin, McCarthy trounced the president in the Wisconsin primary.

Ignored and often forgotten in retirement, Johnson died of a heart attack in January 1973—ironically, on the same day that the Paris Peace Accords ended America's direct combat role in Vietnam. In many ways a tragic figure, he had carried out Vietnam policies shaped by his predecessors and received little acclaim for his enduring domestic achievements, especially in civil rights and reducing poverty. Although he often displayed high idealism and generosity of spirit, the enduring image of LBJ remained that of a crude, overbearing politician with an outsized ego that masked deep insecurities.

Assassinations and Turmoil

Three days after the Wisconsin primary, a high-powered bullet from a sniper's rifle killed Martin Luther King, Jr., as he stood on a motel balcony in Memphis, Tennessee. Because of his increasing concern about poverty in America, and his plans for an upcoming Poor People's Campaign, King had gone there to support striking black sanitation workers. The assassin, James Earl Ray, an escaped convict and white racist, would confess, be found guilty, and then recant, leaving aspects of the killing unclear. As in the assassination of John Kennedy, it seemed too insignificant that one misfit was alone responsible. What was clear in 1968 was that the national symbol of nonviolent protest and progressive social change had been murdered. As the news spread, black ghettos in 125 cities burst into violence. Twenty blocks of Chicago's West Side went up in flames, and Mayor Richard Daley ordered police to shoot to kill arsonists. In Washington, D.C., under night skies illuminated by seven hundred fires, army units in combat gear set up machine-gun nests outside the Capitol and White House. The rioting left 46 dead, 3,000 injured, and nearly 27,000 in jail.

Entering the race as the favorite of the party bosses and labor chieftains, LBJ's vice president, **Hubert Humphrey,** turned the contest for the nomination into a three-cornered scramble. McCarthy remained the candidate of the "new politics"—a moral crusade against war and injustice directed to affluent, educated liberals. Kennedy campaigned as the tribune of the less privileged, the sole candidate who appealed to both the white ethnic working class and the minority poor. In early June, after his victory in the California primary, the brother of the murdered president was himself assassinated by a deranged Palestinian refugee, Sirhan Sirhan, who loathed Kennedy's pro-Israeli views.

The deaths of King and Kennedy further estranged young activists, convinced others of the futility of nonviolence, and devastated the already beleaguered forces of liberalism. The dream of peace and justice turned to despair. "I won't vote," a youth said. "Every good man we get they kill." "We shall not overcome," concluded a Kennedy speechwriter. "From this time forward things would get worse, not better. Our best political leaders were part of memory now, not hope."

While Kennedy's death cleared the way for Humphrey's nomination, increasing numbers of Democrats turned to third-party candidate George Wallace's thinly veiled appeal for white supremacy or to the GOP nominee Richard M. Nixon. The Republican appealed to those disgusted with inner-city riots and antiwar demonstrations. He claimed to have a "secret plan" to end the war, lambasted the liberal decisions of the Warren Court, and derided hippies and protestors. Nixon also said he would heed "the voice of the great majority of Americans, the forgotten Americans, the non-shouters, the non-demonstrators, those who do not break the law, people who pay their taxes and go to work, who send their children to school, who go to their churches, . . . who love this country." Tapping the same wellsprings of anger and frustration, but without Nixon's restraint, Wallace pitched a fiery message to southern segregationists and working-class northerners, denouncing welfare mothers, antiwar demonstrators, and black militants. If elected, Wallace vowed to throw "over-educated, ivory-tower" federal bureaucrats "into the Potomac," and to crack down on "long-hair, pot-smoking, draft-card-burning youth."

In August 1968, violence outside the Democratic National Convention in Chicago reinforced the appeal of both Wallace and Nixon. Thousands descended on the city to protest peacefully against the war. Some radicals, however, wanted to provoke a confrontation to discredit the Democrats, and a handful of anarchistic **"Yippies"** (the Youth International Party, led by counterculture guru Abbie Hoffman) sought to ridicule the political system by threatening to dump LSD in Chicago's water system and to release greased pigs in the city's crowded Loop area.

Determined to avoid the rioting that had wracked Chicago after King's assassination, Mayor Richard Daley denied demonstrators permits to march or engage in meaningful protest, and gave police a green light to attack "the hippies, the Yippies, and the flippies." The savagery of the Chicago police fulfilled the radicals' desire for mass disorder. On August 28, as a huge national television audience looked on and protesters chanted "The whole world is watching," Daley's bluecoats took off their badges and clubbed demonstrators, tossed tear gas at bystanders, and bloodied reporters and photographers. The brutality on the streets overshadowed Humphrey's nomination, tore the Democrats farther apart, and created an enduring image of them as the party of dissent and disorder. Although an investigative panel later described the melee as a "police riot," 70 percent of Americans supported the police violence against the protestors. The real victor in Chicago was conservatism.

Conservative Resurgence

Nixon capitalized on the televised turmoil to attract the support of voters desperate for "law and order." His TV campaign commercials flashed images of campus and ghetto upheavals. He portrayed himself as the candidate of the Silent Majority, "the working Americans who have become forgotten Americans." He criticized the Supreme Court for safeguarding criminals and radicals, vowed to get people off welfare rolls and on payrolls, and asserted that "our schools are for education—not integration."

Also appealing to the reaction against liberalism, George Wallace stoked the fury of the working class against "bearded anarchists, smart-aleck editorial writers, and pointy-headed professors looking down their noses at us." Promising to keep peace in the streets, he vowed that "if any demonstrator ever lays down in front of my car, it'll be the last car he'll ever lie down in front of." In September Wallace climbed to 21 percent in voter-preference polls. Although many shared his views, few believed he had any chance of winning, and either did not vote or switched to his opponents. Still, 14 percent of the electorate—primarily young, lower-middle-class, small-town workers—cast their votes for Wallace.

MAP 29.1 The Election of 1968

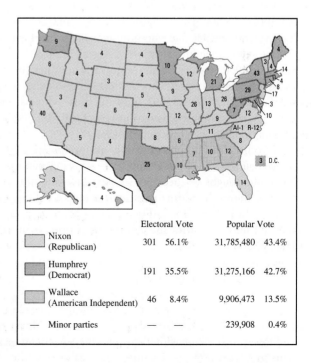

		Electoral Vote		Popular Vote	
Nixon (Republican)		301	56.1%	31,785,480	43.4%
Humphrey (Democrat)		191	35.5%	31,275,166	42.7%
Wallace (American Independent)		46	8.4%	9,906,473	13.5%
— Minor parties		—	—	239,908	0.4%

Nixon and Humphrey split the rest of the vote almost evenly. Nixon's 301 votes in the Electoral College was the narrowest triumph since Woodrow Wilson's in 1916. But, with Humphrey receiving just 38 percent of the white vote and not even close to half the labor vote, the long-dominant New Deal coalition was shattered and the liberal era ended.

The 57 percent of the electorate who chose Nixon or Wallace would dominate American politics for the rest of the century. While the Democratic Party fractured into a welter of contending groups, the Republicans attracted a new majority, many of whom lived in the Sunbelt—the metropolitan South, the sun country of Florida, the desert Southwest and Texas, and populous southern California. Kevin Phillips, whose advice to Nixon to focus on Sunbelt voters was published in 1969 as *The Emerging Republican Majority*, described its residents as "the pleasure-seekers, the bored, the ambitious, the space-age technicians and the retired—a super-slice of the rootless, socially mobile group known as the American middle class." Phillips also recognized the attraction of Sunbelt attitudes—on government spending, defense, race, and taxes—to residents in the suburbs and ethnic working-class neighborhoods of the North. So did the authors of *The Real Majority*, who deeply impressed Nixon with their assertion that the new key to a winning coalition was the "47 year old Catholic housewife in Dayton, Ohio whose husband is a machinist." Although she and her blue-collar husband had always voted Democratic, they would defect to the Republicans because of the couple's conservative views on black rioters, antiwar protesters, pornography, and drugs. Wooing these voters—who he named the Silent Majority in a 1969 speech—became the centerpiece of Nixon's political strategy.

NIXON AND WORLD POLITICS

A Californian of Quaker origins, Richard Milhous Nixon was elected to Congress as a navy veteran in 1946. He won prominence for his role in the House Un-American Activities Committee investigation of Alger Hiss (see Chapter 26) and advanced to the Senate in 1950 by accusing his Democratic opponent of disloyalty. He served two terms as Eisenhower's vice president, but lost the presidency to Kennedy in 1960 and the California governorship in 1962. Ignoring those who proclaimed the end of his political career, Nixon campaigned vigorously for GOP candidates in 1966, and won his party's nomination and the presidency in 1968.

In office, Nixon focused mainly on foreign affairs. Considering himself a master of *realpolitik*—a pragmatic approach stressing national interest rather than ethical goals—he sought to check Soviet expansionism and to reduce superpower conflict, to limit the nuclear-arms race, and to enhance America's economic well-being. He planned to get the United States out of Vietnam and into a new era of détente—reduced tensions—with the communist world. To manage diplomacy, Nixon chose **Henry Kissinger,** a refugee from Hitler's Germany and professor of international relations, who shared Nixon's penchant for secrecy and for the concentration of decision-making power in the White House.

Vietnamization

Nixon's grand design hinged on ending the Vietnam War. It was sapping American military strength, worsening inflation, and thwarting détente with China and the Soviet Union. Announcing the Nixon Doctrine in August 1969, he redefined America's role in the Third World as that of a help-

The My Lai Massacre   *Under the command of First Lieutenant William Calley, the men of Charlie Company entered the small village of My Lai in March 1968 to attack the Vietcong believed to be there. Instead, they found unarmed civilians, mostly women and children, and massacred them. The military kept the incident secret for a year, but when news of the incident surfaced late in 1969 it became symbolic of the war's brutality and the futility of the U.S. effort in the Vietnam War.*

ful partner rather than a military protector. Nations facing communist subversion could count on U.S. support, but they would have to defend themselves.

The Nixon Doctrine reflected the president's recognition of war weariness by both the electorate and troops in Vietnam. Johnson's decision to negotiate rather than escalate had left American troops with the sense that little mattered except survival. Morale plummeted. Discipline collapsed. Army desertions rocketed from twenty-seven thousand in 1967 to seventy-six thousand in 1970, and absent-without-leave (AWOL) rates rose even higher. Racial conflict became commonplace. Drug use soared; the Pentagon estimated that two out of three soldiers in Vietnam smoked marijuana and that one in three tried heroin. The army reported hundreds of cases of "fragging"—enlisted men killing officers and noncommissioned officers.

The toll of atrocities against the Vietnamese also mounted. Increasing instances of Americans' dismembering enemy bodies, torturing captives, and murdering civilians came to light. In March 1968 an army unit led by Lieutenant William Calley massacred several hundred South Vietnamese in the hamlet of **My Lai.** The soldiers gang-raped girls, lined up women and children in ditches and shot them, and then burned the village. Revelations of such incidents, and the increasing number of returned soldiers who joined Vietnam Veterans Against the War, undercut the already-diminished support for the war.

Despite pressure to end the war, Nixon would not sacrifice U.S. prestige. Seeking "peace with honor," he acted on three fronts. First was "Vietnamization," replacing American troops with South Vietnamese. It was hardly a new idea; the French had tried *jaunissement* or "yellowing" in 1951, and it had not worked. By 1972, the U.S. forces had dropped from half a million to thirty thousand. Second, bypassing South Vietnamese leaders, Nixon sent Kissinger to negotiate secretly with North Vietnam's foreign minister, Le Duc Tho. Third, to force the communists to compromise despite the U.S. troop withdrawal, Nixon escalated the bombing of North Vietnam and secretly ordered air strikes on Cambodia and Laos. He told an aide,

> I want the North Vietnamese to believe I've reached the point where I might do anything to stop the war. We'll just slip the word to them that "for God's sake, you know Nixon is obsessed about communism. We can't restrain him when he's angry—and he has his hand on the nuclear button"—and Ho Chi Minh himself will be in Paris in two days begging for peace.

LBJ's War Becomes Nixon's War   The secret B-52 raids against Cambodia neither made Hanoi beg for peace nor disrupted communist supply bases. They did, however, undermine the stability of that tiny republic. In early 1970, North Vietnam increased its infiltration of troops into Cambodia both to aid the Khmer Rouge (Cambodian communists) and to escalate its war in South Vietnam. Nixon ordered a joint U.S.–South Vietnamese incursion into Cambodia at the end of April 1970. They seized large caches of arms and bought time for Vietnamization. But the costs were high. The invasion ended Cambodia's neutrality, widened the war throughout Indochina, and provoked massive American protests against the war, culminating in the student deaths at Kent State University and Jackson State College.

In February 1971, Nixon had South Vietnamese troops invade Laos to destroy communist bases there and to restrict the flow of supplies southward from North Vietnam. The South Vietnamese were routed. Emboldened, North Vietnam mounted a major campaign in April 1972—the Easter Offensive—their largest since 1968. Nixon retaliated by mining North Vietnam's harbors and unleashing B-52s on its major cities. He vowed: "The bastards have never been bombed like they are going to be bombed this time."

America's Longest War Ends   The 1972 bombing helped break the impasse in the Paris peace talks, stalemated since 1968. In late October, just days before the 1972 presidential election, Kissinger announced that "peace is at hand." The cease-fire agreement he had secretly negotiated with Le Duc Tho required the withdrawal of all U.S. troops, provided for the return of American prisoners of war, and allowed North Vietnamese troops to remain in South Vietnam.

Kissinger's negotiation sealed Nixon's reelection, but South Vietnam's President Thieu refused to sign a cease-fire permitting North Vietnamese troops to remain in the South. An angry Le Duc Tho then pressed Kissinger for additional concessions. Nixon again resorted to massive B-52 raids. The 1972 Christmas bombing of Hanoi and Haiphong, the most destructive of the war, roused fierce opposition domestically and globally but broke the deadlock. Nixon's secret reassurance to Thieu that the United States would "respond with full force should the settlement be violated by North Vietnam" ended Saigon's recalcitrance.

The Paris Accords, signed in late January 1973, essentially restated the terms of the October truce. The agreement ended hostilities between the United States and North Vietnam, but left unresolved the differences between North and South Vietnam, guaranteeing that Vietnam's future would yet be settled on the battlefield.

The war in Vietnam would continue despite fifty-eight thousand American dead, three hundred thousand wounded, and an expenditure of at least $150 billion. Twenty percent of the Americans who served in Vietnam, nearly five hundred thousand, received less-than-honorable discharges—a measure of the desertion rate, drug usage, antiwar sentiment in the military, and immaturity of the troops (the average U.S. soldier in Vietnam was just nineteen years old, seven years younger than the average GI in World War II).

Virtually all who survived, wrote one marine, returned "as immigrants to a new world. For the culture we had known dissolved while we were in Vietnam, and the culture of combat we lived in so intensely . . . made us aliens when we returned." Beyond media attention on the psychological difficulties of readjusting to civilian life, which principally fostered an image of them as disturbed and dangerous, the nation paid little heed to its Vietnam veterans—reminders of a war that Americans wished to forget.

Relieved that the long nightmare had ended, most Americans wanted "to put Vietnam behind us." The bitterness of many veterans, and of hawks and doves, moderated with time. Few gave much thought to the 2 million Vietnamese casualties, or to the suffering in Laos, or the price paid by Cambodia. In 1975, the fanatical Khmer Rouge (Cambodian communists), led by Pol Pot, took power and turned Cambodia into a genocidal "killing field," murdering some 2 million, an estimated third of the population.

"We've adjusted too well," complained Tim O'Brien, a veteran and novelist of the war. "Too many of us have lost touch with the horror of war. . . . It would seem that the memories of soldiers should serve, at least in a modest way, as a restraint on national bellicosity. But time and distance erode memory. We adjust, we lose the intensity. I fear that we are back where we started. I wish we were more troubled."

Détente

Disengagement from Vietnam helped Nixon achieve **détente** with the communist superpowers. These developments, the most significant shift in U.S. foreign policy since the start of the Cold War, created a new relationship among the United States, the Soviet Union, and China.

Presidents from Truman to Johnson had refused to recognize the People's Republic of China, to allow its admission to the United Nations, and to permit American allies to trade with it. But by 1969 a widening Sino-Soviet split made the prospect of improved relations attractive to both Mao Zedong and Nixon. China wanted to end its isolation; the United States wanted to play one communist power off against the other; and both wanted to thwart USSR expansionism in Asia.

In June 1971, Kissinger began secret negotiations with Beijing, laying the groundwork for Nixon's historic February 1972 trip to China "to seek the normalization of relations." The first visit ever by a sitting American president to the largest nation in the world, it ended more than twenty years of Chinese-American hostility. Full diplomatic recognition followed in 1979.

Equally significant, Nixon went to Moscow in May 1972 to sign agreements with the Soviets on trade, technological cooperation, and the limitation of nuclear weapons. Fear of a Sino-American alliance and a desire to slow the incredibly expensive arms race made the Soviet Union eager for better relations with the U.S. The Strategic Arms Limitation Treaty (SALT I) froze each side's offensive nuclear missiles for five years, and committed both countries to strategic equality rather than nuclear superiority; and the Anti-Ballistic Missile (ABM) Treaty restricted the deployment by both sides of nation-wide missile-defense systems. Although they did not end the arms race, the treaties symbolized a first step toward that goal, reduced Soviet-American tensions and, in an election year, enhanced Nixon's stature.

Shuttle Diplomacy   Not even better relations with China and the Soviet Union ensured global stability. In the Middle East, Israel, fearing an imminent Arab attack, launched a preemptive strike on its neighbors in 1967, routing them in six days, and seizing Sinai and the Gaza Strip from Egypt, the West Bank and East Jerusalem from Jordan, and Syria's Golan Heights. Israel promised to give up the occupied lands in exchange for a negotiated peace, but the Arab states refused to negotiate with Israel or to recognize its right to exist. Palestinians, many of them refugees since the creation of Israel in 1948, turned to the Palestine Liberation Organization (PLO), which demanded Israel's destruction.

War exploded again in 1973 when Egypt and Syria attacked Israel on the Jewish high holy day of Yom Kippur. Only massive shipments of military supplies from the United States enabled a reeling Israel to stop the assault. In retaliation, the Arab states embargoed shipments of crude oil to the United States and its allies. The five-month embargo dramatized U.S. dependence on foreign energy sources, and then the spike in the price of crude oil from three dollars to more than twelve dollars a barrel sharply intensified inflation and spurred the use of nuclear power.

The dual shocks of the energy crisis at home and rising Soviet influence in the Arab world spurred Kissinger to engage in "shuttle diplomacy." Flying from one Middle East capital to another for two years, he negotiated a cease-fire, pressed Israel to cede some captured territory, and persuaded the Arabs to end the oil embargo. Although Kissinger's diplomacy left the Palestinian issue festering, it successfully excluded the Soviets from a major role in Middle Eastern affairs.

To counter Soviet influence, the Nixon administration also supplied arms and assistance to the shah of Iran, the white supremacist regime of South Africa, and President Ferdinand Marcos in the Philippines. Nixon-Kissinger *realpolitik* based American aid on a nation's willingness to oppose the Soviet Union, not on the nature of its government. The administration gave aid to antidemocratic regimes in Argentina, Brazil, and South Korea, as well as to Portuguese colonial authorities in Angola.

When Chileans elected a Marxist, Salvador Allende, president in 1970, Nixon secretly funded the CIA to support opponents of the leftist regime. The United States also cut off economic aid to Chile and blocked banks from granting it loans. In 1973 a military junta overthrew the Chilean government and killed Allende. Nixon quickly recognized the dictatorship, and economic aid and investment again flowed to Chile.

Although committed to containing communist influence, Nixon understood the limits of U.S. power and the changed realities of world affairs. Discarding the model of a bipolar conflict that had shaped American foreign policy since 1945, Nixon took advantage of the Sino-Soviet rift to improve relations with both nations. His administration also improved the U.S. position in the Middle East and ended American involvement in Vietnam. The politician who had built his reputation as a staunch Cold Warrior had initiated a new era of détente.

DOMESTIC PROBLEMS AND DIVISIONS

Richard Nixon yearned to be remembered as an international statesman, but domestic affairs kept intruding. He tried to reform the welfare system and solve complex economic problems. But the underside of Nixon's personality appealed to the darker recesses of the nation and intensified the fears and divisions among Americans.

The Nixon Presidency

Close observers of Nixon noted the multiple levels of his character. Beneath the calculated public persona hid a shadowy man who rarely revealed himself. Largely hidden was the insecure Nixon, suspicious and filled with anger. Seething with resentments, he believed enemies lurked everywhere, waiting to destroy him. Accordingly, he sought to annihilate his partisan enemies, particularly the "eastern liberal establishment."

The classic outsider, reared in pinched surroundings, physically awkward, unable to relate easily to others, Nixon remained fearful, even at the height of national power, that he would never be accepted. At the beginning of his administration, however, his strengths stood out. He spoke of national reconciliation, took bold initiatives internationally, and dealt with domestic problems responsibly.

Symbolic of his positive start, the nation celebrated the first successful manned mission to the moon. On July 21, 1969, the Apollo 11 lunar module, named *Eagle,* descended to the Sea of Tranquility. As millions watched on television, astronaut **Neil Armstrong** walked on the moon's surface and proclaimed, "That's one small step for man, one giant leap for mankind." Five more lunar expeditions followed, and in 1975 the space race essentially ended with the United States and the Soviet Union engaging in cooperative efforts to explore the rest of the universe.

The first newly elected president since 1849 whose party controlled neither house of Congress, Nixon cooperated with the Democrats to increase social-security benefits, build subsidized housing, expand the Job Corps, and grant the vote to eighteen-year-olds. Responding to the growing environmental awareness and energized environmental movement, which brought out 20 million Americans for the first Earth Day in 1970, the president approved new laws limiting pesticide use, protecting endangered species and marine mammals, safeguarding coastal lands, and controlling strip-mining. Nixon also signed bills creating the Occupational Safety and Health Administration (OSHA), to enforce health and safety standards in the workplace, and the Environmental Protection Agency (EPA), requiring federal agencies to prepare an environmental-impact analysis of all proposed projects.

Conservatives grumbled as government grew larger and more intrusive and as race-conscious employment policies, including quotas, were mandated for all federal contractors. Conservatives grew still angrier when Nixon unveiled the Family Assistance Plan (FAP) in 1969. A bold effort to overhaul the welfare system, FAP proposed a guaranteed minimum annual income for all Americans. Caught between liberals who thought the income inadequate and conservatives who disliked it on principle, FAP died in the Senate.

A Troubled Economy

Nixon inherited the fiscal consequences of President Johnson's effort to wage the Vietnam War and finance the Great Society by deficit financing—to have both "guns and butter." Facing a "whopping" budget deficit of $25 billion in 1969 and an inflation rate of 5 percent, Nixon cut government spending and encouraged the Federal Reserve Board to

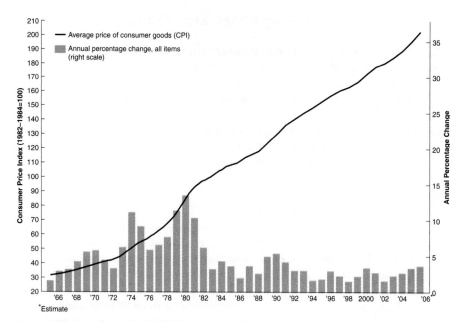

FIGURE 29.1 Inflation, 1965–2006

Inflation, which had been moderate during the two decades following the Second World War, began to soar with the escalation of the war in Vietnam in the mid-1960s. In 1979 and 1980 the nation experienced double-digit inflation in two consecutive years for the first time since World War I.

raise interest rates. The result was a combination of inflation and recession that economists called "stagflation" and Democrats termed "Nixonomics."

Accelerating inflation lowered the standard of living of many families and sparked a wave of strikes as workers sought wage hikes to keep up with the cost of living. It encouraged the wealthy to invest in art and real estate rather than technology and factories. Hence, more plants shut down, industrial jobs dwindled, and many displaced workers lost their savings, their health and pension benefits, and their homes.

Throughout 1971 Nixon lurched from policy to policy. Declaring "I am now a Keynesian," he increased deficit spending to stimulate the private sector. It resulted in the largest budget deficit since World War II. Then Nixon devalued the dollar to correct the balance-of-payment deficit. Finally, he imposed a freeze on wages, prices, and rents, a short-term fix that gave the economy a shot in the arm until after the 1972 election. Then Nixon again reversed course, replacing controls with voluntary—and ineffective—guidelines. Inflation zoomed as the Organization of Petroleum Exporting Countries (OPEC) boycott raised the price of crude oil, and sluggish growth dogged the economy throughout the decade.

Law and Order   Despite his public appeals for unity, Nixon hoped to divide the American people in ways that would bring about a realignment in politics and create a new Republican majority coalition. His "southern strategy" sought to attract Dixie's white Democrats into the GOP fold, while his stands on crime, drugs, antiwar protestors, and black militants wooed blue-collar laborers and suburbanites—voters whom political strategist Kevin Phillips described as "in motion between a Democratic past and a Republican future." To outflank George Wallace, Nixon opposed court-ordered busing and took a tough stand against campus unrest and black radicalism.

To combat the militants he despised, Nixon had the IRS audit their tax returns; the Small Business Administration deny them loans; and the National Security Agency illegally wiretap them. The FBI worked with local law officials to disrupt and immobilize the Black Panthers, the CIA illegally investigated and compiled dossiers on thousands of American citizens, and the Justice Department prosecuted antiwar activists and black radicals in highly publicized trials. Nixon himself drew up an "enemies list" of adversaries to be harassed by the government.

In 1970, Nixon widened his offensive against the antiwar movement. The Huston Plan called for extensive wiretapping and infiltrating of radical organizations, as well as break-ins to gather or plant evidence. But FBI chief J. Edgar Hoover opposed the plan as a threat to the bureau's power. Blocked, Nixon secretly created his own White House unit to discredit his opposition and ensure executive secrecy. Nicknamed **"the plumbers"** because of their assignment to plug government leaks, the team was headed by former FBI agent G. Gordon Liddy and former CIA operative E. Howard Hunt.

The plumbers first targeted Daniel Ellsberg, a former Defense Department analyst who had given the press the **Pentagon Papers,** a secret documentary history of U.S. involvement in Vietnam. On June 13 the *New York Times* began publishing the Pentagon Papers, revealing a long history of White House lies to Congress, foreign leaders, and the American people. Although the papers contained nothing about his administration, Nixon, fearing that they would undermine trust in government and establish a precedent for publishing classified material, sought to bar their publication. The Supreme Court, however, ruled that their publication was protected by the First Amendment. Livid, Nixon directed the Justice Department to indict Ellsberg for theft and ordered the plumbers to break into the office of Ellsberg's psychiatrist in search of information to discredit the man who had become a hero to the antiwar movement.

| The Southern Strategy | Nixon especially courted whites upset by the drive for racial equality. The administration opposed extension of the Voting Rights Act of 1965, sought to cripple enforcement of the Fair |

Housing Act of 1968, pleaded for the postponement of desegregation in Mississippi's schools, and filed suits to prohibit the busing of children to desegregate public schools. In 1971, when the Supreme Court upheld busing as a constitutional and necessary tactic in *Swann* v. *Charlotte-Mecklenburg Board of Education,* Nixon condemned the ruling and asked Congress to enact a moratorium on busing. The strategy of wooing white southerners also dictated Nixon's Supreme Court nominations. To reverse the Warren court's liberalism, he sought strict constructionists, judges who would not "meddle" in social issues or be "soft" on criminals. In 1969 he appointed Warren Burger as chief justice. Although the Senate then twice rejected southern conservatives nominated by Nixon, the president succeeded in appointing Harry Blackmun of Minnesota, Lewis Powell of Virginia, and William Rehnquist of Arizona. Along with Burger, they steered the Court in a centrist direction, ruling liberally in cases involving abortion, desegregation, and the death penalty, while shifting to the right on civil liberties, community censorship, and police power.

As the 1970 congressional elections neared, Nixon encouraged his vice president, Spiro T. Agnew, to step up attacks on "hooligans, hippies, and radical liberals." Agnew assailed the Democrats as "sniveling hand-wringers," intellectuals as "an effete corps of impudent snobs," and the news media as "nattering nabobs of negativism." Liberals deplored Agnew's alarming alliterative allegations, but many others found them on target. The 1970 elections were a draw, with the GOP losing nine House seats and winning two Senate seats.

THE CRISIS OF THE PRESIDENCY

In his second inaugural, Nixon pledged "to make the next four years the best four years in America's history." Ironically, they would rank among its sorriest. His vice president would resign in disgrace; his closest aides would go to jail; and he would serve barely a year and a half of his second term before resigning to avoid impeachment.

The Election of 1972
Nixon's reelection appeared certain. He faced a deeply divided Democratic Party and counted on his diplomatic successes and the winding down of the Vietnam War to win over moderate voters. He expected his southern strategy and law-and-order posture to attract Wallace voters. Nixon's only possible worry, another third-party candidacy by Wallace, vanished on May 15, 1972, when Wallace was shot during a campaign stop and paralyzed from the waist down. He withdrew from the race, leaving Nixon a monopoly on the white backlash.

The Senate's most outspoken dove, **George McGovern** of South Dakota, capitalizing on antiwar sentiment, blitzed the Democratic primaries. He gained additional support from new party rules requiring state delegations to include minority, female, and youthful delegates in approximate proportion to their numbers. Actress Shirley MacLaine approvingly described California's delegation as "looking like a couple of high schools, a grape boycott, a Black Panther rally, and four or five politicians who walked in the wrong door." McGovern won the nomination on the first ballot.

Perceptions of McGovern as inept and radical drove away all but the most committed supporters. After pledging to stand behind his vice-presidential running mate Thomas Eagleton "1,000 percent" when it became known that Eagleton had received electric-shock therapy for depression, McGovern dumped him and suffered the embarrassment of having several prominent Democrats publicly decline to run with him. McGovern's endorsement of decriminalization of marijuana, immediate withdrawal from Vietnam, and pardons for those who had fled the United States to avoid the draft exposed him to GOP ridicule as the candidate of the radical fringe.

Remembering his narrow loss to Kennedy in 1960 and too-slim victory in 1968, Nixon left no stone unturned. To do whatever was necessary to win, he appointed his attorney general, John Mitchell, to head the Committee to Re-Elect the President (CREEP). Millions of dollars in campaign contributions financed "dirty tricks" to create dissension in Democratic ranks and paid for an espionage unit to spy on the opposition. Led by Liddy and Hunt, the "White House plumbers" had been created to plug the leaks concerning the secret bombing of Cambodia, which Nixon feared would increase congressional and public opposition to the war. In 1972 it received Mitchell's approval to wiretap telephones at the Democratic National Committee headquarters in the Watergate apartment and office complex in Washington. Early one morning in June 1972, a security guard foiled the break-in to install bugs. Arrested were James McCord, the security coordinator of CREEP, and several other Liddy and Hunt associates.

Earth Day, May 4, 1970 *Designed to alert people about the threats to the air, land, and water, the first Earth Day signaled the emergence of the modern environmental movement. It would put pressure on the federal government to take major steps in cleaning up the nation's environment and educate a generation of Americans to understand the ecology of the planet as a delicate, interconnected series of elements, in which damage to any single element damages many others.*

A White House cover-up began immediately. Nixon announced that "no one in the White House staff, no one in this administration, presently employed, was involved in this bizarre incident." He then ordered staff members to expunge Hunt's name from the White House telephone directory, to buy the silence of those arrested with $400,000 in hush money and hints of a presidential pardon, and to direct the CIA to halt the FBI's investigation of the Watergate break-in on the pretext that the investigation would damage national security.

With the McGovern campaign a shambles and Watergate seemingly contained, Nixon amassed nearly 61 percent of the popular vote and an overwhelming 520 electoral votes. Supported primarily by minorities and low-income voters, McGovern carried only Massachusetts and the District of Columbia. The election solidified the 1968 realignment. Nevertheless, the GOP gained only twelve seats in the House and lost two in the Senate, demonstrating the growing difficulty of unseating incumbents, the rise in ticket-splitting, and the decline of both party loyalty and voter turnout. Only 55.7 percent of eligible voters went to the polls (down from 63.8 percent in 1960).

The Watergate Upheaval The scheme to conceal links between the White House and the accused Watergate burglars had succeeded during the 1972 campaign. But after the election, federal judge "Maximum John" Sirica, known for his tough treatment of criminals, refused to accept the defendants' claim that they had acted on their own. Threatening severe prison sentences,

Driving Southward and Backward *To outflank George Wallace and win the votes of both southern whites and urban blue-collar workers in the North, Nixon's "southern strategy" included delaying school desegregation plans and strong opposition to busing children to achieve racial balance in the schools.*

Sirica coerced James McCord of CREEP into confessing that White House aides had known in advance of the break-in and that the defendants had committed perjury during the trial. Two *Washington Post* reporters, Carl Bernstein and Bob Woodward, wrote a succession of front-page stories tying the break-in to illegal contributions and "dirty tricks" by CREEP. They had followed clues furnished by a secret informant named **"Deep Throat."** (Only in 2005 did W. Mark Felt, the former No. 2 man in the FBI, step forward at age 91 to unmask himself as the mysterious source.)

In February 1973 the Senate established the Special Committee on Presidential Campaign Activities to investigate. As the trail of revelations led closer to the Oval Office, Nixon fired his special counsel, John Dean, who refused to be a scapegoat, and announced the resignations of his principal aides, H. R. Haldeman and John Ehrlichman. Pledging to get to the bottom of the scandal, he appointed Secretary of Defense Elliot Richardson, a Boston patrician of unassailable integrity, as his new attorney general, and instructed him to appoint a special Watergate prosecutor with broad powers of investigation and subpoena. Richardson selected Archibald Cox, a Harvard law professor and a Democrat.

In May the special Senate committee began a televised investigation. Chaired by Sam Ervin of North Carolina, the hearings revealed the existence of a White House "enemies list," the president's use of government agencies to harass opponents, and administration favoritism in return for illegal campaign donations. Most damaging to Nixon, the hearings exposed the White House's active involvement in the Watergate cover-up. But the Senate still lacked concrete evidence of the president's criminality, the "smoking gun" that would prove Nixon's guilt. Because it was his word against that of John Dean, who testified that the president directed the cover-up, Nixon expected to survive the crisis.

Then another presidential aide dropped a bombshell by revealing that Nixon had installed a secret taping system that recorded all conversations in the Oval Office. The Ervin committee and Cox insisted on access to the tapes, but Nixon refused, claiming executive privilege. In October 1973, when Cox sought a court order to obtain the tapes, Nixon ordered Richardson to fire him. Richardson instead resigned in protest, as did the deputy attorney general, leaving it to the third-ranking official in the Department of Justice, Solicitor General Robert Bork, to dump Cox. The furor stirred by this "Saturday Night Massacre" sent Nixon's public-approval rating rapidly downward. Even as Nixon named a new special prosecutor, Leon Jaworski, the House Judiciary Committee began impeachment proceedings.

A President
Disgraced

Adding to Nixon's woes that October, Vice President Agnew, charged with income-tax evasion and accepting bribes, pleaded no contest—"the full equivalent to a plea of guilty," according to the trial judge. Dishonored, Agnew left office with a three-year suspended sentence and a $10,000 fine. House Minority Leader Gerald R. Ford of Michigan replaced Agnew.

In March 1974, Jaworski and the House Judiciary Committee subpoenaed the president for the tape recordings of Oval Office conversations after the Watergate break-in. Nixon released edited transcripts of the tapes, filled with gaps and the phrase "expletive deleted." Despite the excisions, the president sounded petty and vindictive.

Nixon's sanitized version of the tapes satisfied neither Jaworski nor the House Judiciary Committee. Both pressed for unedited tapes. In late July the Supreme Court rebuffed the president's claim to executive privilege. Citing the president's obligation to provide evidence necessary for the due process of law, Chief Justice Burger ordered Nixon to release the unexpurgated tapes.

In late July, the House Judiciary Committee adopted three articles of impeachment, accusing President Nixon of obstruction of justice for impeding the Watergate investigation, abuse of power for his partisan use of the FBI and IRS, and contempt of Congress for refusing to obey a congressional subpoena for the tapes. Checkmated, Nixon conceded in a televised address on August 5 that he had withheld relevant evidence. He then surrendered the subpoenaed tapes, which contained the "smoking gun" proving that the president had ordered the cover-up, obstructed justice, subverted one government agency to prevent another from investigating a crime, and lied about his role for more than two years. Certain that the Senate would vote to convict him if impeached, Richard Nixon, on August 9, 1974, became the first president to resign, and Gerald Ford took office as the nation's first chief executive who had not been elected either president or vice president.

CONCLUSION

Baby boomers took material comfort and their own importance for granted. Longing for meaning in their lives, as well as personal liberty, they sought a more humane democracy, a less racist and materialist society, and an end to the war in Vietnam. Failing to force a quick end to the war, the New Left became increasingly radical and violent. Most of the young, however, were more interested in "sex, drugs, and rock-and-roll." Ultimately, the student movement and counterculture helped prod the United States into becoming a more tolerant, diverse, and permissive society. They helped pave the way for the environmental movement and other causes in the 1970s, and spurred an end to America's longest war—which had cost the nation dearly in lives and dollars, in turning Americans against one another, and in diverting society from pressing needs.

The youth rebellion, racial rioting, and the Tet offensive in Vietnam brought politics to a boil in 1968. The year of assassinations and turmoil cost Democrats the White House, made Richard Nixon president, and triggered a conservative resurgence and major political realignment. Pursuing the national interest by *realpolitik,* Nixon and Kissinger adopted a strategy of "Vietnamization" while extending the American air war to Cambodia and Laos, and simultaneously holding secret negotiations with North Vietnam to end hostilities. At the same time, they opened the way for reduced tensions with China and the Soviet Union, enhancing the world outlook for peace, while also giving economic and military assistance to anticommunist dictatorships.

Equally vital to his political success, Nixon wooed whites upset by civil strife and the counterculture, and emphasized law and order to attract the silent majority concerned with the upsurge of criminality and breakdown of traditional values. Following a "southern strategy," he nominated conservatives for the Supreme Court, opposed extension of the Voting Rights Act and school busing for racial integration, and cracked down on peace advocates, militant blacks, and young radicals.

In 1972 the secret schemes Nixon had put in place to spy upon and destroy those who opposed his Vietnam policies began to unravel. His obsession for secrecy and his paranoia about those who opposed him brought his downfall. The arrest of the Watergate burglars and the subsequent attempted cover-up of White House involvement led to revelations of a host of "dirty tricks" and criminal acts, the indictment of nearly fifty Nixon administration officials and the jailing of a score of his associates, and a House Judiciary Committee vote to impeach the president. To avoid certain conviction, a disgraced Nixon resigned.

When his successor, Gerald Ford, took the oath of office, many Americans took pride in the smooth continuity of the political system and in its ability to curb excesses and abuses. Others worried that so many Americans had for so long just shrugged off Watergate as politics as usual, and that the Nixon scandals might never have come to light if not for coercion by a federal judge and the president's desire to tape and preserve his conversations. The deepening public disenchantment with politicians and disillusionment with government would last into the next century.

30

Conservative Resurgence, Economic Woes, Foreign Challenges, 1974–1989

CHAPTER OUTLINE

Cultural Trends • Economic and Social Changes in Post-1960s America • Years of Malaise: Post-Watergate Politics and Diplomacy, 1974–1981 • The Reagan Revolution, 1981–1984 • Reagan's Second Term, 1985–1989

CULTURAL TRENDS

As personal pursuits and leisure diversions shaped 1970s' American culture, women in large numbers entered the work force. The sexual revolution continued, but the shadow of AIDS introduced a sobering note. While antiwar and black-power protests faded, some activist causes rooted in the 1960s gained momentum, notably environmentalism, the women's movement, and gay rights. A conservative turn; a revival of evangelical religion; and sharp divisions over abortion, homosexuality, and other issues also shaped 1970s' culture.

Personal Pursuits and Diversions The Vietnam War shattered the early-1960s' liberal consensus, and the radical New Left movement soon fragmented as well, creating political turmoil on the Left. The Watergate crisis, in turn, temporarily disoriented conservatives. With politics in disarray, personal preoccupations beckoned.

Some young people practiced Transcendental Meditation or joined the Reverend Sun Myung Moon's Unification Church. Others embraced the International Society for Krishna Consciousness, whose shaved-head, saffron-robed followers added an exotic note in airports, city streets, and college campuses. Several thousand rural communes arose as some counterculture veterans sought to escape the urban-corporate world, practice organic farming, revive old technologies, and live in harmony with nature. Most of these ventures proved short-lived.

By the early 1980s, journalists discovered the "Yuppie" (young urban professional), preoccupied with physical fitness and consumer goods. The stereotype had some basis in fact. Physical well-being became a middle-class obsession. Yuppies jogged and exercised, ate pesticide-free natural foods, and stopped smoking when medical evidence linked cigarettes to lung cancer and heart disease. The actress Jane Fonda, earlier an antiwar and antinuclear-power activist, promoted a series of exercise videos beginning in 1982. In a process known as gentrification, yuppies purchased and restored run-down inner-city apartments, often displacing poor and elderly residents in the process.

Self-improvement could easily turn selfish. Novelist Tom Wolfe satirized the "Me Generation." *Newsweek* magazine, proclaiming "the Year of the Yuppie" in 1984, commented, "[T]hey're making lots of money, spending it conspicuously, and switching political candidates like they test cuisines."

In the cultural arena, the politically engaged songs of the 1960s gave way to disco, suitable for dancing but carrying little cultural weight. Blockbuster movies like *Jaws* (1975), *Rocky* (1976), *Star Wars* (1977), and *E.T.* (1982) offered escapist fare. *Happy Days*, the top TV show of 1976–1977, evoked nostalgia for the 1950s. The TV series *Dallas*, chronicling the steamy affairs of a Texas oil family, captivated millions in the early 1980s. Walt Disney World, the Disney Corporation's sprawling Florida theme park, opened in 1971 and proved enormously popular. Football's Super Bowl and other sports extravaganzas attracted vast TV audiences.

Cable TV, introduced in the early 1970s, broadened viewers' options. By 1988, over half of U.S. homes had cable. Innovations in consumer electronics also shaped the era. By the early 1990s, 70 percent of U.S. households had VCRs (videocassette recorders), enabling users to tape TV shows for later viewing and to rent movies on cassette. In the music field, the compact disc (CD), introduced in 1983, offered high-quality sound. In a development of great future significance, the late 1970s also saw the advent of the personal computer.

American culture in these years was not all escapism and technological novelties, however. Bruce Springsteen's songs such as "Darkness at the Edge of Town" (1978) evoked the stresses of working-class life and bleakly described widening class divisions in America. Springsteen's "Born in the USA" (1984) told of a young man "sent . . . to a foreign land to go and kill the yellow man" who now finds himself "in the shadow of the penitentiary" with "[n]owhere to run . . . , nowhere to go." Bob Dylan's "Blood on the Tracks" (1974) expressed distrust of authority while celebrating defiant outsiders.

The 1970s also saw the rise of punk rock, an aggressively anti-establishment genre promoted by such groups as the Sex Pistols, the Ramones, and the Clash; of Tejano (Spanish for "Texan") music, which spread from Texas to win national popularity thanks to performers such as Selena Quintanilla, before her murder by a deranged fan in 1995; and of rap or hip-hop, with roots in Jamaican reggae music and West African storytelling traditions. Rap, beginning in the 1970s in poor black New York City neighborhoods, and involving free-form improvised recitations, gained a broad following in the 1980s and beyond.

Along with escapist movie fare, directors also produced brilliant films exploring the darker side of American life. Robert Altman's *Nashville* (1975) offered a disturbing vision of cynical mass-culture producers, manipulative politicians, and alienated drifters. Roman Polanski's *Chinatown* (1974) probed the corruption beneath the sunny surface of southern California life. *Network* (1976) explored the mass media's potentially

CHRONOLOGY, 1974–1989

1974 • Richard Nixon resigns presidency; Gerald Ford sworn in.
Indian Self-Determination Act.

1975 • South Vietnamese government falls.
Mayagüez incident.

1976 • Jimmy Carter elected president.

1977 • Panama Canal treaties ratified.
Introduction of Apple II computer.
Gay Pride parades in New York and San Francisco.

1978 • Carter authorizes federal funds to relocate Love Canal residents.

1979 • Menachem Begin and Anwar el-Sadat sign peace treaty at White House.
Second round of OPEC price increases.
Accident at Three Mile Island nuclear plant.
Carter restores full diplomatic relations with the People's Republic
of China.

1980 • Alaska Lands Act.
Soviet invasion of Afghanistan.
Iran hostage crisis.
Ronald Reagan elected president.

1981 • Major cuts in taxes and domestic spending, coupled with large increases
in military budget.
AIDS first diagnosed.

1982 • Equal Rights Amendment dies.
CIA funds contra war against Nicaragua's Sandinistas.
Central Park rally for nuclear-weapons freeze.

1983 • 239 U.S. marines die in Beirut terrorist attack.
U.S. deploys Pershing II and cruise missiles in Europe.
Reagan proposes Strategic Defense Initiative (Star Wars).
U.S. invasion of Grenada.

1984 • Reagan defeats Walter Mondale to win second term.

1984–1986 • Congress bars military aid to contras.

1985 • Rash of airline hijackings and other terrorist acts.

1986 • Congress passes South African sanctions.
Immigration Reform and Control Act.

1987 • Congressional hearings on Iran-contra scandal.
Stock-market crash.

1988 • Reagan trip to Moscow.

Breaking the Gender Barrier   *Martha Fransson, the sole female member of the Class of 1970 at the Tuck School of Business at Dartmouth College, poses with her classmates.*

destructive power. *The Deer Hunter* (1978) dramatized the Vietnam War's psychological aftermath. Such work, too, is part of the cultural legacy of the decade.

Changing Gender Roles and Sexual Behavior

Many women's lives changed dramatically in these years. Spurred by a resurgent women's movement as well as by inflation pressures (see below), the number of women working outside the home leaped from under 20 million in 1960 to nearly 60 million by 1990.

Women's wages still lagged behind those of men, however, and the workplace remained gender-segregated. Women were concentrated in such fields as nursing, teaching, retail sales, and secretarial work, while men dominated management positions and the professions. But even this changed as women entered the ranks of management. (Top management remained a male preserve, however, a phenomenon known as the "glass ceiling.") By the early 1990s the legal and medical professions were nearly 20 percent female, while growing numbers of women in professional schools of all kinds promised more changes ahead.

As women pursued higher education or careers, their median age at first marriage rose from twenty in 1960 to twenty-four in 1990. The birthrate fell as well, and by 1980 the statistically average U.S. family had 1.6 children, far below earlier levels. In the wake of the landmark *Roe* v. *Wade* decision of 1973 (see Chapter 29), the number of abortions rose from about 750,000 in 1973 to more than 1.5 million in 1980 and then leveled off.

The challenge to prevailing sexual codes and taboos posed by the 1960s' counterculture had long-lasting effects. In 1960 about 30 percent of unwed nineteen-year-old U.S. women reported having had sexual experience. By 1980 more than half did, and the figure rose higher by 2000. The number of unmarried couples living together jumped from 523,000 in 1970 to 3.5 million by 1993.

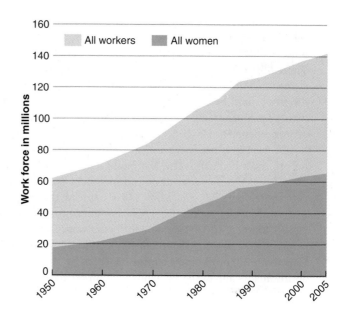

FIGURE 30.1 Women in the Work Force, 1950–2005

After 1960 the numbers of American women who were wage earners surged upward. Both the women's movement and economic pressures encouraged this trend. *Source:* U.S. Department of Labor, Bureau of Labor Statistics (www.bls.gov).

The freer attitude toward sex received a setback with the spread of the deadly viral infection **AIDS** (acquired immune deficiency syndrome), first diagnosed in 1981. AIDS spread mainly among sexually active homosexuals and bisexuals, intravenous drug users sharing needles, and persons having sexual intercourse with these high-risk individuals. (Early in the epidemic some persons, including tennis star Arthur Ashe, contracted AIDS through blood transfusions.) Though the worst lay ahead, more than thirty-one thousand Americans had died of AIDS by the end of the 1980s.

Medical authorities warned against unprotected sex. The message was driven home when film star Rock Hudson died of AIDS in 1985, and basketball superstar Earvin ("Magic") Johnson and Olympic diver Greg Louganis announced that they carried the HIV virus, a precursor of AIDS. While the epidemic emboldened some Americans to express their hatred of homosexuality (see below), it also stimulated medical research and an outpouring of concern. A large AIDS quilt honoring victims toured the nation. Under the shadow of AIDS, many Americans grew more cautious in their sexual behavior. The exuberant 1960s slogan "Make Love, Not War" gave way to a more somber message: "Safer Sex."

The Persistence of Social Activism

The environmental-protection movement, a legacy of the 1960s, grew stronger in the 1970s. Older organizations such as the Sierra Club and the Wilderness Society, as well as new ones such as Greenpeace, won fresh recruits. Greenpeace was founded in 1971 when Canadian activists protested a planned U.S. nuclear test on an island in the Bering Sea. The U.S. branch, established soon after, worked to preserve old-growth forests and protect the world's oceans. By 2000, Greenpeace had 250,000 U.S. members. The Save the Whales campaign, launched by the Animal Welfare Institute in 1971, opposed the slaughter of the world's largest mammals by fleets of floating processing factories to provide dog-and-cat food.

Environmentalists also targeted the nuclear-power industry. Adopting techniques from the civil-rights and antiwar campaigns, activists protested at planned nuclear-power plants. The movement crested in 1979 when a partial meltdown crippled the **Three Mile Island** nuclear-power plant in Pennsylvania. A Jane Fonda movie released at the same time, *China Syndrome*, portrayed a fictitious but plausible nuclear-power disaster caused by a California earthquake. The Three Mile Island accident, coupled with a far more serious one at the Chernobyl nuclear-power plant in the Ukraine in 1986, deepened public concerns about nuclear power.

Of the 1960s' many legacies, the revitalized women's movement (see Chapter 28) proved most enduring. The National Organization for Women (NOW), founded in 1966, boasted nearly fifty thousand members by 1975. Feminist support groups and Gloria Steinem's *Ms.* magazine (1972) spread the message. While NOW remained mainly white and middle class, African-American, Latina, and Asian women organized as well. Women workers agitated for better wages and working conditions (see below).

With the movement's growth came political clout. The National Women's Political Caucus (1971) promoted a feminist agenda. By 1972, many states had liberalized their abortion laws and outlawed gender bias in hiring. That same year Congress passed an

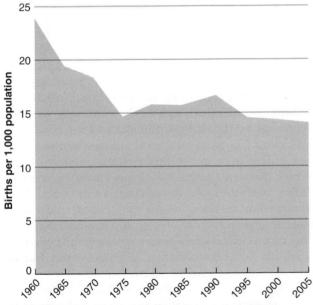

FIGURE 30.2 **The American Birthrate, 1960–2005**

Families of five or six children or more were once common in the United States, and the birthrate remained high in the baby-boom years of the later 1940s and the 1950s. (The nearly 80 million children of the baby boomers, born between 1982 and 1995, were dubbed "echo boomers.") The U.S. birthrate fell dramatically from 1960 to the mid-1970s, rose slightly, and then resumed its downward trend after 1990. *Source:* National Center for Health Statistics, U.S. Dept. of Health and Human Services.

equal rights amendment (ERA) to the Constitution barring discrimination on the basis of sex. Twenty-eight states quickly ratified it, and ultimate adoption seemed likely. Other feminist organizations defended women's reproductive rights in the face of a conservative backlash against *Roe* v. *Wade* (see below).

The women's movement splintered in the late 1970s, as Betty Friedan and other moderates opposed the lesbians who were becoming more assertive (see below). The moderates also deplored the strident rhetoric of some radical feminists and criticized their downgrading of motherhood and homemaking. In *The Second Stage* (1981), Friedan added family-protection issues to the feminist agenda.

Conservatives worried that women's changing roles would weaken the family. Women themselves conceded the stresses of balancing career and family, but few pined for the era when child care, housework, and volunteerism had defined "women's sphere." As the 1980s ended, many American women enjoyed unprecedented opportunities, but barriers persisted and complex issues remained.

As we saw in Chapter 29, many gay men and lesbians "came out of the closet" in the 1970s, openly avowing their sexual preference and protesting job discrimination and harassment. In 1977, "Gay Pride" parades drew seventy-five thousand marchers in New York City and three hundred thousand in San Francisco, a center of gay activism. Two years later, a national gay and lesbian civil-rights parade attracted one hundred thousand marchers to Washington, D.C. More taboos fell as Elaine Noble, an avowed lesbian, won a seat in the Massachusetts legislature in 1974 and Harvey Milk, an openly gay candidate, was elected to the San Francisco board of supervisors in 1977. In 1987 Massachusetts congressman Barney Frank acknowledged his homosexuality.

Organizations like the National Gay Task Force, founded in 1973 (and later renamed the National Gay and Lesbian Task Force), and a militant New York group called ACT-UP (1987) demanded the repeal of anti-gay laws and passage of legislation protecting homosexuals' civil rights. Responding to the pressure, many states and cities repealed laws against same-sex relations between consenting adults and barring job discrimination on the basis of sexual orientation.

Grass-Roots Conservatism	But a backlash was building, rooted in the 1960s and earlier. The sixties was a polarizing decade. While the counterculture

and antiwar protests drew media attention, many Americans deplored what they viewed as the decade's radical excesses. As blue-collar and white ethnic Democrats reacted against what they saw as the party's takeover by hippies and radical leftists, their traditional party loyalty eroded. As we saw in Chapter 29, Richard Nixon exploited this disaffection to win the White House in 1968.

The conservative resurgence had even deeper roots. **William F. Buckley** had launched the conservative *National Review* magazine in 1955; founded Young Americans for Freedom in 1960; and started a conservative TV talk show, *Firing Line*, in 1966. Barry Goldwater's 1964 presidential campaign alerted conservatives both to their potential power within the Republican Party and to the importance of broadening their appeal beyond the hard-core conservative loyalists who had rallied to the far-right John Birch Society, founded in 1958.

The career of Phyllis Schlafly, devout Roman Catholic, law-school graduate, mother of six, and tireless activist, illustrates the movement's post-1960 evolution. Schlafly's *A Choice Not an Echo* (1964) championed Goldwater and denounced the Republican

Party's liberal, East Coast wing. Her *Phyllis Schlafly Report,* begun in 1967, attacked the New Left and the counterculture. In the 1970s, Schlafly and her organization, The Eagle Forum, focused on hot-button cultural issues such as abortion; gay rights; and the Equal Rights Amendment, which she fiercely opposed.

In local communities, especially in the fast-growing South and West, conservatives found each other, shared their concerns, and mobilized politically. This process was especially evident in southern California's Orange County, a region recently transformed from ranches and citrus groves to suburban developments. Orange County conservatives—mostly upwardly mobile white evangelical Protestants, often newcomers from the East—were intensely anticommunist, dismayed by 1960s' radicals, and suspicious of the "liberal intellectuals" dominating the media and national politics. Political scientist Lisa McGirr describes their political mobilization:

> At living room bridge clubs, at backyard barbecues, and at kitchen coffee klatches, the middle-class men and women of Orange County "awakened" to what they perceived as the threats of communism and liberalism. Sensing an urgent need for action, they forged study groups, multiplied chapters of national right-wing organizations, and worked within the Republican party to make their voices heard. In so doing, they became the cutting edge of the conservative movement in the 1960s.

Foreshadowing changes ahead nationally, Orange County helped elect **Ronald Reagan** governor of California in 1966 and in 1978 helped pass Proposition 13, a state referendum calling for deep cuts in property taxes. Conservative think tanks like the Heritage Foundation, founded by the Colorado beer baron Joseph Coors in 1973, instructed local conservatives as they solidified their ideology.

As Schlafly's campaigns illustrate, 1970s' conservatives mobilized around specific issues, especially abortion. In the wake of *Roe* v. *Wade,* a "Right to Life" movement led by Roman Catholic and conservative Protestant activists pressed for a constitutional amendment outlawing abortion. The "murder of the unborn," they charged, eroded respect for human life. "Pro-life" advocates rallied, signed petitions, and picketed abortion clinics and pregnancy-counseling centers.

Responding to the pressure, Congress in 1976 ended Medicaid funding for most abortions, in effect denying this procedure to the poor. Most feminists, by contrast, adopted a "pro-choice" stance, arguing that women and their physicians, not the government, should make reproductive decisions. Opinion polls reflected deep divisions, although a majority favored the "pro-choice" position. Handing conservatives another victory, President Nixon in 1972 had vetoed a bill setting up a national network of daycare centers, criticizing its "communal approach to child-rearing." The Equal Rights Amendment, denounced by Schlafly and other conservatives, died in 1982, three states short of the three-fourths required for ratification.

Gay and lesbian activism particularly inflamed conservatives, who saw it as evidence of society's moral collapse. TV evangelist Jerry Falwell thundered, "God . . . destroyed the cities of Sodom and Gomorrah because of this terrible sin." In 1977, singer Anita Bryant led a campaign against a Miami ordinance protecting homosexuals' civil rights. "God created Adam and Eve, not Adam and Bruce," she pointed out. Thanks in part to Bryant's efforts, voters repealed the ordinance. Soon after, readers of *Good Housekeeping* magazine voted Bryant "the most admired woman in America." Other cities, too, reversed earlier measures favoring gay rights.

In 1978, as the backlash intensified, a member of the San Francisco board of supervisors fatally shot gay board-member Harvey Milk and Milk's ally, Mayor George Moscone. "[T]he city weeps" headlined the *San Francisco Examiner*. When the killer received a light sentence (after claiming that eating sugary junk foods had impaired his judgment), riots erupted in the city. In 1980 disco singer Donna Summer, popular in the gay community, announced her religious conversion and speculated that God had sent AIDS "to punish homosexuals."

Evangelical Protestants Mobilize   The conservative movement also found expression in the rapid growth of evangelical Protestantism, with its emphasis on strict morality, biblical inerrancy, and a personal "born again" conversion experience. Evangelical denominations such as the Assemblies of God and the Southern Baptist Convention grew explosively in the 1970s and 1980s, as did independent suburban megachurches such as Chuck Smith's Calvary Chapel in Orange County, typically conservative theologically and culturally. Meanwhile, liberal denominations such as the Methodists, Congregationalists, and Unitarians, whose ministers had rallied behind the civil-rights and antiwar movements, lost members.

Many evangelicals plunged into politics. As one observed in 1985, "I always thought that churches should stay out of politics. Now it seems almost a sin not to get involved." Evangelicals had pursued social reform before the Civil War, including the abolition of slavery, and their modern-day successors also preached reform, but of a conservative variety. Jerry Falwell's Moral Majority, founded in 1979 as a "pro-life, pro-family, pro-moral, and pro-America" crusade, actively supported conservative candidates.

Pat Robertson, head of the Christian Broadcasting Network and host of its popular *700 Club,* mounted an unsuccessful presidential bid in 1988. Another leading evangelical, the Reverend Tim LaHaye of San Diego, was active in Christian Voice, a group that encouraged grassroots organizing to promote conservative causes. In 1981 LaHaye founded the Council for National Policy, a secretive conservative lobbying organization.

While battling abortion, homosexuality, and pornography, often in alliance with conservative Catholics, evangelicals also attacked the Supreme Court's 1962 **Engel v. Vitale** decision banning organized prayer in public schools as a violation of the First Amendment. While pushing to reverse this ruling, evangelicals also advocated home schooling and private Christian schools, to shield children from what they saw as the secularist (nonreligious) values and lax morals pervading the public schools. Most evangelicals also embraced militant anticommunism.

Not all evangelicals were political conservatives. Most African-American evangelicals, in particular, remained loyal to the Democratic Party. In general, however, resurgent evangelicalism went hand in hand with the larger conservative movement of the 1970s.

For many evangelicals, Bible prophecy reinforced their political mobilization. Hal Lindsey's *The Late Great Planet Earth* (1970), a popularization of one system of prophetic interpretation, was *the* nonfiction best seller of the 1970s. Lindsey found the Soviet Union, communist China, the Arab-Israeli conflict, the United Nations, the European Union, and growing domestic wickedness all foretold in the Bible. He urged true believers to rally on the side of righteousness as the End approached.

Christian bookstores, radio stations, and TV evangelists fueled the revival. Along with Falwell's *Old Time Gospel Hour* and Robertson's *700 Club,* popular broadcasts included Jim and Tammy Bakker's *PTL* (Praise the Lord) program and Jimmy Swaggart's telecasts from Louisiana. The so-called electronic church suffered after 1987 amid sexual and financial scandals, but the evangelical resurgence continued. In a world of change, evangelicals found certitude, reassurance, and a sense of community in their shared faith. In the process, they profoundly influenced late-twentieth-century American life.

ECONOMIC AND SOCIAL CHANGES IN POST-1960s AMERICA

Inflation, industrial decline, and other economic problems offered a troubling counterpoint to the cultural and political developments of these years. Many white-collar professionals and people involved with the emerging information-based economy prospered. Others, however, including displaced factory workers, did not. Although many African-Americans enjoyed upward mobility as the civil-rights revolution expanded opportunities, others remained in poverty. While Native Americans faced adversities, the 1970s also brought brighter prospects and a new assertiveness in pursuing treaty rights. Shifting patterns of immigration, meanwhile, changed the nation's ethnic and demographic profile, with major implications for the future.

A Changing Economy

Disturbing economic developments influenced U.S. politics and shadowed the lives of millions of Americans in the 1970s. Largely owing to surging oil prices (see below), the inflation rate spiked to around 11 percent in 1973, dipped a bit, and then soared to almost 14 percent by 1980. Overall, consumer prices more than doubled from 1970 to 1980. This grinding rate of inflation battered American families, drove many wives into the work force out of necessity, and turned hard-pressed taxpayers against the welfare programs adopted during past Democratic administrations.

The ranks of family farmers, once revered as the backbone of America, thinned in these years. In 1960 about 6 percent of the U.S. labor force worked on farms; by 1994 the figure was 2.5 percent. As farm youth migrated to the cities, the dwindling ranks of small-farm operators often took second jobs to make ends meet. Overall farm production increased, however. As big operators bought and consolidated failing farms, average farm size grew from 375 to 430 acres between 1970 and 1990, and farms of several thousand acres were not unusual. Large-scale wheat, corn, and soybean production involved major capital investment and heavy-duty equipment, and factory farms dominated poultry and hog production. Federal subsidy programs encouraged the rise of giant agribusinesses. As Secretary of Agriculture Earl Butz put it: "Adapt or die." In the 1985 film *The Trip to Bountiful,* an aging Texas woman, movingly played by Geraldine Page in an Oscar-winning role, pays a nostalgic visit to her girlhood farm home, only to find it falling to ruin.

Industrial stagnation, or **deindustrialization,** worsened the era's economic woes. In a process that would intensify in the future (see Chapter 32), the steel and automobile industries were especially hard hit. As soaring gasoline prices boosted sales of more fuel-efficient foreign imports, U.S. car makers suffered. U.S. purchases of foreign cars, mainly from Japan, grew from 2 million in 1970 to 4 million in 1989. Facing severe production cutbacks, GM, Ford, and Chrysler laid off more than 225,000 workers.

Longer-term sources of industrial decline included aging machinery, inefficient production methods, and fierce competition from foreign companies using state-of-the-art equipment, paying lower wages, and unburdened by the pension plans and other benefits enjoyed by U.S. workers. As auto plants, steel mills, and other midwestern industries laid off workers, the unemployment rate reached 8.5 percent in 1975. In one five-year period, 1979–1983, 11.5 million U.S. workers lost jobs because of plant closings and production cutbacks. Statistics cannot convey the anxiety and disruption experienced by workers, their families, and entire communities as once-secure jobs vanished. Service-sector employment grew by 55 percent in the 1970s, partially counterbalancing the losses, but for laid-off factory workers, this was cold comfort.

As imports increased, the United States in 1971, for the first time in the twentieth century, ran a trade deficit. (That is, the total value of imports exceeded the total value of exports.) Trade deficits became the rule from 1976 on, and, as we shall see, their size mushroomed in the 1980s and beyond. As U.S. dollars flowed abroad to cover this trade imbalance, the domestic economy suffered.

As industrial workers lost jobs, the union movement weakened. In 1960, 31 percent of U.S. workers belonged to unions; in 1985, the figure stood at 18 percent, with further declines ahead. Some workers did join unions in these years, mainly teachers, public employees, flight attendants, and service workers, many of whom were female. The Coalition of Labor Union Women, founded in Chicago in 1974, encouraged unionization by women workers. Declared one delegate: "You can . . . tell [George Meany, head of the ALF-CIO] there are three thousand women in Chicago, and they didn't come to swap recipes." Female-dominated labor unions focused not only on wages but also on such issues as maternity leaves. While important in labor history and women's history, however, service-sector unionization only slowed, but did not reverse, the overall decline of union membership.

The Two Worlds of Black America Millions of blacks experienced significant upward mobility in these years, thanks to the civil-rights movement. In 1965, black students accounted for under 5 percent of total college enrollment; by 1990 the figure had risen to 12 percent, close to their proportion in the general population. By 1990 some 46 percent of black workers held white-collar jobs. TV's *Cosby Show,* a late-1980s comedy in which Bill Cosby played a doctor married to a lawyer, portrayed this upwardly mobile world.

Outside this world lay the inner-city slums, inhabited by perhaps a third of the black population. Here, up to half the young people never finished high school, and the jobless rate soared as high as 60 percent. As jobs disappeared owing to suburbanization, deindustrialization, and urban decline, inner-city black communities were hard hit. In 1980, the poverty rate among African-Americans stood at 32 percent, three times the rate for non-Hispanic whites.

Cocaine and other drugs pervaded the inner cities. Some black children recruited as lookouts for drug dealers eventually became dealers themselves. With drugs also came violence. In the 1980s, a young black male was six times as likely to be murdered as a young white male. In Los Angeles, two rival gangs, the Bloods and the Crips, accounted for more than four hundred killings in 1987. Warned the psychologist Jewelle Taylor Gibbs: "Young black males in America's inner cities are an endangered species . . . , [the] rejects of our affluent society."

In truth, despite the tough **Comprehensive Drug Abuse Act** of 1970, drug abuse affected all social levels, including yuppies, show-business celebrities, and young corporate executives. It was even glorified in movies, songs, and rock concerts. But drug use and drug trafficking particularly devastated the inner cities.

Unmarried women—mostly young and poor—accounted for nearly 60 percent of all black births in 1980. Scarcely beyond childhood themselves, these single mothers often survived on welfare payments. Buffeted by complex social and economic forces, and at risk of becoming a permanent underclass, the mainly nonwhite inner-city populations posed a major social challenge. Both significant upward mobility and educational advances by African-Americans, and serious social problems among those left behind in the inner cities, would continue into the twenty-first century (see Chapter 32).

To compensate for past racial discrimination, some cities set aside a percentage of building contracts for minority businesses. Some educational institutions reserved slots for minority applicants. These so-called **affirmative-action** programs faced court challenges, however. In *Bakke* v. *United States* (1978), a pivotal case brought by a rejected white medical-school applicant, the Supreme Court overthrew the quota system by which a California medical school had tried to increase its minority enrollment. In 1989, the Supreme Court invalidated a Richmond, Virginia requirement that 30 percent of building contracts go to minority businesses. The courts, did, however, uphold programs to encourage minority businesses or minority-student enrollment in higher education, so long as they did not involve specific quotas.

Brightening
Prospects for
Native Americans

Building on their occupation of Alcatraz Island in San Francisco Bay (see Chapter 28), members of the militant American Indian Movement briefly occupied the Bureau of Indian Affairs in Washington in 1972, and in 1973 took over a trading post at Wounded Knee, South Dakota, site of an 1890 Indian massacre by the U.S. army (see Chapter 17). In response to spreading protests, the **Indian Self-Determination Act** of 1974 granted tribes control of federal aid programs on the reservations and oversight of their own schools.

The 1990 census recorded more than 1.7 million persons as American Indians, in contrast to some eight hundred thousand in 1970. This upsurge reflected not only natural increase and ethnic pride, but also economic advantages associated with tribal membership. Under a 1961 law permitting them to buy or develop land for commercial and industrial projects, tribes launched business ventures ranging from resorts to mining and logging operations. They licensed food-processing plants, electronics firms, manufacturing enterprises, and gambling casinos on tribal lands, providing jobs and income.

Indian tribes also reasserted long-ignored treaty rights through the Indian Claims Commission, a federal agency set up in 1946. In 1971, the Native peoples of Alaska won 40 million acres and nearly $1 billion in settlement of treaty claims. In 1980, the Sioux were awarded $107 million for South Dakota lands taken from them illegally. The Penobscot Indians in Maine won claims based on a 1790 federal law. In 1988, after years of protests, the Puyallup tribe of Washington State received $162 million in settlement of their claim that the city of Tacoma occupied land granted them in the 1850s. Among other projects, the Puyallups laid plans to restore salmon runs on the Puyallup River.

Sid Gutierrez, Astronaut
Hispanics entered all arenas of American life in the late twentieth century. Gutierrez, a native of Albuquerque, New Mexico, piloted space shuttle Columbia *on a 1991 NASA mission.*

High rates of joblessness, alcoholism, and disease persisted among Indians. But renewed pride, economic ventures, and progress in asserting treaty rights offered hope. In the popular culture, movies such as *Little Big Man* (1970) and *Dances with Wolves* (1990), while idealizing Indians, represented an improvement over the negative stereotypes of earlier films.

New Patterns of
Immigration

These years saw a steady influx of immigrants, both legal and illegal. Whereas most immigrants once arrived from Europe, some 45 percent now came from the Western Hemisphere and 30 percent from Asia. As in the past, economic need drew these newcomers. In oil-rich Mexico, for example, falling oil prices in the 1980s worsened the nation's chronic poverty, spurring many to seek jobs in the north. But life in the United States was often harsh. In 1980, some 26 percent of persons of Hispanic origin in the United States lived in poverty, twice the national rate. Despite adversity, Hispanic newcomers preserved their language and traditions, influencing U.S. culture in the process. Many neighborhoods of Los Angeles, Miami, and other major cities were wholly Hispanic.

Millions of Hispanic immigrants lacked official documentation. Working long hours with few legal protections, these migrants, mostly Mexicans and Haitians (as well as Puerto Ricans, who are U.S. citizens), sweated in the garment trades, cleaned houses, held low-paying service-sector jobs, and labored in agricultural fields. The **Immigration Reform and Control Act** of 1986, an update of the 1965 Immigration Act (see Chapter 28), outlawed the hiring of undocumented immigrants, but offered legal status to aliens who had lived in the United States for five years. Debates over immigration policy persisted, however, as did efforts to tighten U.S. border controls (see Chapter 32).

Immigration from Asia climbed as newcomers arrived from South Korea, Vietnam, and the Philippines. The motive, again, was primarily economic, though many Hmong (pronounced "mong"), the indigenous people of Indochina who had supported the United States in the Vietnam War, came for political reasons. Valuing education, many Asian immigrants advanced academically and economically. The younger generation, torn between new and old, sought to balance family and group loyalties with the appeal of the larger society beyond.

YEARS OF MALAISE: POST-WATERGATE POLITICS AND DIPLOMACY, 1974–1981

In the aftermath of the Vietnam failure and Richard Nixon's disgrace, Presidents **Gerald Ford** and Jimmy Carter grappled with domestic and foreign problems. Amid inflation, recession, and industrial stagnation, unease gripped the nation. Globally, the later 1970s brought mostly humiliations, from the final Vietnam withdrawal to a maddening hostage crisis. The familiar polarities of the Cold War blurred as problems in the Middle East and elsewhere highlighted issues the United States would face in the future.

The confident 1950s and early 1960s, when prosperous America had savored its role as the Free World's leader, equal to any challenge, now seemed remote. A nation long convinced that it was immune to the historical forces that constrained other societies seemed prey to forces beyond its control. But while the Vietnam experience encouraged isolationist tendencies, events made clear that America could not evade global involvement.

The Caretaker Presidency of Gerald Ford, 1974–1977   Gerald Ford took the presidential oath on August 9, 1974, following Richard Nixon's forced resignation. A Michigan congressman who had been House minority leader before becoming vice president, Ford conveyed a likable decency as he urged Americans to move beyond the "long national nightmare" of Watergate. The honeymoon soon ended, however, when Ford pardoned Richard Nixon for "any and all crimes" committed while in office. Ford said he wanted to help heal the body politic, but many Americans reacted with outrage.

On domestic issues, Ford proved more conservative than Nixon, vetoing a series of environmental, social-welfare, and public-interest measures, among them a 1974 freedom of information bill granting citizens greater access to government records. The Democratic Congress overrode most of these vetoes.

Economic problems dogged Ford's presidency. In 1973, oil prices had shot up as a result of an Arab oil embargo and price hikes by the **Organization of Petroleum Exporting Countries** (OPEC), a marketing consortium formed in 1960. The United States, heavily dependent on imported oil, felt the shock as surging prices of gasoline, heating oil, and other petroleum-based products worsened the inflationary spiral and produced long lines of angry drivers at gas stations. In October 1974, Ford unveiled a program of voluntary price restraint dubbed "Whip Inflation Now" (WIN), but prices continued to zoom. When the Federal Reserve Board tried to cool the economy by raising interest rates, a severe recession resulted. Unemployment approached 11 percent by 1975. As oil and gas prices soared, Americans for the first time since World War II struggled to curb energy consumption. Congress set fuel-efficiency standards for automobiles in 1975 and imposed a national speed limit of fifty-five miles per hour.

National morale sank further in April 1975 when the South Vietnamese government fell, ending two decades of U.S. effort in Vietnam. The TV networks chronicled desperate helicopter evacuations from the U.S. embassy in Saigon (soon renamed Ho Chi Minh City) as North Vietnamese troops closed in. A few weeks later, Cambodia seized a U.S. merchant ship, the *Mayagüez*. A military rescue ordered by Ford freed the thirty-nine *Mayagüez* crew members but cost the lives of forty-one U.S. servicemen. As the nation entered the election year 1976—also the bicentennial of the Declaration of Independence—Americans found little reason for optimism.

The Outsider as Insider: President Jimmy Carter, 1977–1981	Gerald Ford won the 1976 Republican nomination despite a challenge from former California governor Ronald Reagan. **Jimmy Carter,** a Georgia peanut grower and former governor, swept the Democratic primaries by stressing themes that appealed to post-Watergate America: his honesty, his status as a

Washington outsider, his evangelical Christian faith. As his running mate, Carter chose a northern liberal, Minnesota senator Walter Mondale.

Carter's early lead eroded as voters sensed vagueness in his program, but he won by a narrow margin. The vote broke along class lines: the well-to-do went for Ford; the poor, overwhelmingly for Carter. The Georgian swept the South and received 90 percent of the black vote. Despite the rising conservative tide, popular revulsion against Nixon and Watergate temporarily interrupted the Republican advance, and Carter won.

Underscoring his outsider image, Carter rejected the trappings of what some had called Nixon's "imperial presidency." On inauguration day, with his wife and daughter, he walked from the Capitol to the White House. In an echo of Franklin Roosevelt's radio chats, he delivered some TV speeches wearing a sweater and seated by a fireplace. To broad public approval, he appointed a number of women and members of minority groups to federal judgeships.

Despite the populist symbolism and gestures of inclusiveness, Carter never framed a clear political philosophy. Liberals and conservatives both claimed him. Relying on young staff members from Georgia, he avoided socializing with politicians. A graduate of the U.S. Naval Academy and former nuclear-submarine engineer, Carter did best when focused on specific problems. He and Congress fought the recession with a tax cut and a modest public-works program, and the jobless rate fell to around 5 percent by late 1978. But with public opinion turning against "big government," he offered few proposals to deal with inner-city poverty, industrial decline, the trade imbalance, and other major problems.

Environmental issues loomed large for Carter, however, as they did for many Americans. In 1980, in a major victory for the administration, Congress passed the **Alaska Lands Act,** which set aside more than 100 million acres of public land in Alaska for parks, wildlife refuges, and national forests, and added twenty-six rivers to the nation's Wild and Scenic River System. Energy companies hoping to tap Alaska's oil fields protested, and laid plans to carry on the battle.

Carter confronted an environmental crisis in Niagara Falls, New York, where for years the Hooker Chemical and Plastics Corporation had dumped tons of waste in a district known as the Love Canal. In 1953, Hooker had covered the landfill with earth and sold it to the city. Schools, homes, and apartments soon sprang up, but residents complained of odors and strange substances oozing from the soil. In the later 1970s, tests confirmed that toxic chemicals, including deadly dioxin, were seeping into basements, polluting the air, and discharging into the Niagara River. Medical researchers found elevated levels of cancer, miscarriages, and birth defects among Love Canal residents. The Love Canal Homeowners' Association, founded by Lois Marie Gibbs, demanded action.

In 1978 President Carter authorized federal funds to relocate Love Canal families. In 1980, he declared the Love Canal situation a national emergency, freeing more federal money for relocation and clean-up. In late 1980, as his term ended, Carter signed legislation creating a federal "Superfund" to clean up the nation's most polluted industrial sites. The Alaska Lands Act, involving long-term wilderness preservation, and the Love Canal crisis, involving hazardous poisons, underscored the diversity of the environmental challenges facing the nation.

Overall, Carter's domestic record proved thin. Congress ignored his proposals for administrative reforms in the civil service and in the executive branch of government. His calls for a national health-insurance program, overhaul of the welfare system, and reform of the income-tax laws fell flat. "Carter couldn't get the Pledge of Allegiance through Congress," groused one legislator. His problems arose from his own ineptness, but also from the sharp conservative turn in the political climate.

Carter's foreign-policy record proved similarly mixed. As a candidate he had urged more emphasis on protecting human rights worldwide, in contrast to Henry Kissinger's single-minded focus on U.S. national interests. His secretary of state, Cyrus Vance, worked to combat abuses in Chile, Argentina, South Africa, and elsewhere. (Abuses by U.S. allies such as South Korea and the Philippines received less attention.)

In Latin America, Carter sought improved relations with Panama. Since 1964, when anti-American riots had rocked Panama, U.S. diplomats had been working on a new Panama Canal treaty that would address Panama's grievances. The Carter administration completed negotiations on treaties transferring the Canal Zone to Panama by 1999. Although these agreements protected U.S. security interests, conservatives attacked them as proof of America's post-Vietnam loss of nerve, and recalled Teddy Roosevelt's boldness in bringing the canal into existence. But in a rare success for Carter, the Senate ratified the treaties.

In dealing with America's Cold War adversaries China and the Soviet Union, Carter pursued the Nixon-Kissinger strategy of seeking better relations. After China's long-time leader Mao Zedong died in 1976, his successor, Deng Xiaoping, expressed interest in closer ties. Carter responded by restoring full diplomatic relations with Beijing in 1979, thus opening the door to scientific, cultural, and commercial exchanges. Relations remained rocky because of China's human-rights abuses, but the era of total hostility and diplomatic isolation had ended.

Toward the Soviet Union, Carter first showed conciliation, but toughness ultimately won out. In 1979, Carter and the Soviet leader Leonid Brezhnev signed the

SALT II treaty, limiting each side's nuclear arsenals. Senate ratification stalled, however, when advocates of a strong military attacked the treaty for allegedly favoring the Soviets. Support dissolved entirely in January 1980 when Russia invaded Afghanistan. The reasons were complex, but many Americans saw the invasion as proof of Moscow's expansionist designs. As U.S.-Soviet relations soured, Carter withdrew SALT II from the Senate and adopted a series of anti-Soviet measures. These included a boycott of the 1980 Summer Olympics in Moscow, which frustrated U.S. athletes, and an embargo on grain shipments to Russia, which angered midwestern farmers. This hard-line policy reflected the growing influence of Carter's national security adviser, Polish-born Zbigniew Brzezinski, who advocated a tough stance toward Moscow.

The Middle East: Peace Accords and Hostages Carter's best and worst moments came in the Middle East. Despite Henry Kissinger's efforts, Israel and Egypt remained in a state of war. When Egyptian leader Anwar el-Sadat unexpectedly flew to Israel in 1977 to negotiate with Israeli prime minister Menachem Begin, Carter saw an opening. In September 1978, he hosted Sadat and Begin at Camp David, the presidential retreat in Maryland. The resulting **Camp David Accords** set a timetable for giving more autonomy to the Palestinians in the West Bank and Gaza, occupied by Israel since the 1967 war. In March 1979, the two leaders signed a formal peace treaty at the White House.

Carter's efforts for a broader Middle Eastern peace failed, however. Israel continued to build Jewish settlements in the occupied territories, and the other Arab states rejected the Camp David Accords. Islamic fundamentalists assassinated Sadat in 1981, and peace remained as elusive as ever.

A new Middle Eastern crisis erupted in 1979. For years, Iran had been ruled by Shah Mohammed Reza Pahlavi, who had come to power in 1953 with CIA help (see Chapter 27) and imposed a harshly repressive but pro-U.S. regime. For Washington, Iran under the shah represented a bulwark against Soviet expansion. Iran's Shiite Muslims, however, inspired by their exiled spiritual head, Ayatollah Ruhollah Khomeini, hated the shah and his ties to the West. In January 1979, amid rising Shiite unrest, the shah fled Iran. Khomeini returned in triumph, imposed strict Islamic rule, and denounced America.

In November, after Carter admitted the shah to the United States for cancer treatment, Khomeini supporters stormed the U.S. embassy in Tehran and seized more than fifty American hostages. Thus began a 444-day ordeal that nearly paralyzed the Carter administration. TV images of blindfolded hostages, anti-American mobs, and U.S. flags being used as garbage bags rubbed American nerves raw. A botched rescue attempt in April 1980 left eight GIs dead. Secretary of State Vance, who had opposed the rescue effort, resigned. Not until January 20, 1981, the day Carter left office, did the Iranian authorities release the hostages.

Troubles and Frustration as Carter's Term Ends The decade's second oil crisis hit in 1979. When OPEC again boosted oil prices, U.S. gasoline prices edged toward the then-unheard-of level of $1 a gallon. The national mood soured as inflation surged and as lines of fuming motorists again surrounded gas stations. As the Federal Reserve Board battled inflation by raising interest rates, mortgages and business loans became prohibitively expensive. Economic activity stalled, worsening so-called **stagflation,** the combination of business stagnation and price inflation that characterized the U.S. economy through much of the 1970s.

For Carter, the lesson of the crisis was clear: the cheap, unlimited energy that for decades had fueled U.S. economic growth could no longer be counted on, and energy conservation demanded high priority. As early as 1977 Carter had created a new Department of Energy and proposed higher oil and gasoline taxes, tax credits for conservation measures, and research on alternative energy sources. Congress had passed a watered-down version of this energy bill in 1978, but Carter now decided that tougher measures were needed. However, he failed to resolve either the hostage crisis abroad or the energy crisis at home.

As with Herbert Hoover in the early 1930s, Americans turned against the remote figure in the White House. When Carter's approval rating sagged to 26 percent in mid-1979 (lower than Nixon's at the depths of Watergate), he retreated to Camp David and emerged to deliver a TV address that seemed to blame the American people for their collective "malaise" and "crisis of confidence." A cabinet reshuffle followed, but suspicions deepened that Carter himself was the problem. The 1980 Democratic convention glumly renominated Carter, but defeat in November loomed.

Carter's sudden emergence in 1976 illustrated how, in the TV era, a relative unknown could bypass party power brokers and win a national following. Voters longing to see integrity restored to the presidency had embraced him. Keenly analytical, Carter identified many emerging issues, including environmental protection; energy conservation; and reform of the nation's tax, welfare, and health-care systems. But in contrast to Franklin Roosevelt and Lyndon Johnson, he lacked the political skills to build a consensus around his proposed solutions. A post-presidential career of public service restored Carter's reputation, and brought him the Nobel Peace Prize in 2002. But when he left office in January 1981, few expressed regrets.

THE REAGAN REVOLUTION, 1981–1984

In 1980, with Carter's popularity abysmally low, Ronald Reagan, a Republican who promised a break with the past, won the presidency. The Reagan era saw mixed economic developments. It began with a recession, and ended with a stock-market crash. In between, however, inflation eased, business activity picked up, and the stock market surged. Nevertheless, continued industrial decline and inner-city problems created stubborn unemployment and pockets of real suffering. While Reagan's program of tax cuts, military spending, and business deregulation provided some economic stimulus, these policies also gave rise to mounting federal deficits and other problems.

An avid Cold Warrior, Reagan in his first term blasted the Soviets rhetorically, pursued a costly military build-up, and financed guerrillas seeking to overthrow leftist regimes in Latin America. Like other presidents before and since, he also grappled with crises in the Middle East.

Roots of the
Reagan Revolution
Ronald Reagan grew up in Dixon, Illinois, the son of an alcoholic father and a churchgoing evangelical mother. In 1937, after college and a stint as a radio sports announcer in Des Moines, he went to Hollywood for a screen test. His fifty-four films proved forgettable, but he gained political experience as president of the Screen Actors' Guild. A New

Dealer in the 1930s, Reagan had moved to the right in the 1950s, and in 1954 had become the General Electric Company's corporate spokesperson. In a 1964 TV speech for Barry Goldwater, he lauded American individualism and the free-enterprise system. As governor of California (1967–1975), he popularized conservative ideas and denounced campus demonstrators, but also proved open to compromise.

In the 1980 Republican primaries, Reagan easily bested his principal opponent, George H. W. Bush (father of the later President George W. Bush), whom he then chose as his running mate. Belying his sixty-nine years, he campaigned with youthful vigor. Posing the question "Are you better off now than you were four years ago?" Reagan garnered 51 percent of the vote in the general election to 41 percent for the Carter-Mondale Democratic ticket. (An independent candidate, liberal Republican John Anderson, collected most of the balance.)

Republicans gained eleven Senate seats, giving them a majority for the first time since 1955, and trimmed thirty-five seats from the Democrats' majority in the House of Representatives. The Republican successes revealed the power of conservative political action committees (PACs), which used computerized mass mailings focusing on emotional issues like abortion and gun control. (Liberal PACs used the same techniques, of course.)

Benefiting from the erosion of Democratic strength in the South fostered by George Wallace and by Richard Nixon's southern strategy, Reagan carried every southern state except Carter's own Georgia. He also swept every state west of the Mississippi except Minnesota and Hawaii. Over half of white blue-collar workers, once solidly Democratic, voted Republican. Of FDR's New Deal coalition, only black voters remained firmly Democratic.

Jerry Falwell and other politicized evangelicals helped Reagan's cause. Falwell's pro-Reagan Moral Majority registered an estimated 2 million new voters in 1980 and 1984. The organization disbanded after 1984, but Pat Robertson's Christian Coalition took its place, mobilizing conservative Christians to elect candidates to town councils and school boards as a prelude to expanded national influence.

Population changes also contributed to Reagan's success. While New York City, Chicago, Detroit, and other Democratic strongholds in the Northeast and Midwest had lost population in the 1970s, Texas, California, Florida, and other more conservative Sunbelt states had grown rapidly.

What underlay Reagan's appeal? First, voters frightened by stagflation welcomed his seemingly painless panacea: a big tax cut that would stimulate the economy. Moreover, Reagan's praise of self-help and private initiative struck many voters as preferable to the liberal ideology of "government handouts." His antigovernment rhetoric and dismissal of social-welfare programs like Lyndon Johnson's War on Poverty resonated with white middle-class and blue-collar Americans. Like his one-time political hero Franklin Roosevelt, Reagan promised voters a new deal. But unlike FDR, Reagan's new deal meant individualism, smaller government, lower taxes, and untrammeled free enterprise.

Reagan also embraced the cultural values of the emerging conservative movement. Many Americans at all socioeconomic levels found deeply disturbing the New Left politics, social turmoil, and sexual revolution of the 1960s, as well as legalized abortion, radical feminism, the gay-rights movement, sex and violence in the media, godless school textbooks, and the ban on school prayer. They longed for a return to a partially imagined time when life was simpler and traditional values prevailed.

Reagan, a seasoned actor and public speaker, wove these essentially negative themes into an appealing positive message of moral affirmation and support for "traditional values." At a time of national malaise, he seemed confident and assured. His unabashed patriotism, calls for military strength, and praise of America's greatness soothed the battered psyche of a nation traumatized by Vietnam, Watergate, and the multiple problems of the Ford and Carter years. Some thought Reagan glib and superficial, and his ideology fundamentally mean-spirited. But in 1980, a majority of voters found his hopeful and upbeat message persuasive and even inspiring.

Reaganomics

Reagan's economic program, called Reaganomics by the media, boiled down to the belief that U.S. capitalism, if freed from heavy taxes and government regulation, would achieve wonders of productivity. Reagan's first budget message proposed a 30 percent cut in federal income taxes over three years. Trimming this proposal slightly, Congress voted a 25 percent cut: 5 percent in 1981, 10 percent in 1982 and 1983.

To counterbalance the lost revenues, Reagan proposed cuts in such programs as school lunches, student loans, job training, and urban mass transit. Congress cut less than Reagan wanted, but it did slash more than $40 billion from domestic spending. Conservative southern Democrats joined Republicans in voting for these reductions. Not since FDR's Hundred Days of 1933 had government shifted gears so dramatically. Economists warned that the tax cut would produce huge federal deficits, but Reagan insisted that lower tax rates would stimulate business growth, pushing up tax revenues. In the Republican primary campaign, George Bush had ridiculed Reagan's rosy predictions as "voodoo economics," but once in the administration he tactfully remained silent.

Reaganomics also involved less government regulation of business. Deregulation had begun under Carter, but Reagan extended it into new areas such as banking, the savings-and-loan industry, transportation, and communications. The Federal Communications Commission cut federal rules governing the broadcast industry. The secretary of transportation cut regulations aimed at reducing air pollution and improving vehicle efficiency and safety.

The Rev. Pat Robertson *Head of the Christian Broadcasting Network (CBN) and founder of the Christian Coalition, Robertson helped mobilize evangelical Christians politically in the 1980s and beyond.*

Secretary of the Interior James Watt of Wyoming opened federal wilderness areas, forest lands, and coastal waters to oil, gas, and timber companies, and cut back on environmental-protection and endangered-species laws. Before coming to Washington, Watt had headed the Mountain States Legal Foundation, which spearheaded the so-called Sagebrush Rebellion, a movement of ranchers, farmers, and mineowners aimed at shifting federal lands in the West to state and county control. The Sierra Club and other environmental organizations protested Watt's privatizing approach, and petitions demanding his ouster garnered more than a million signatures. After a series of public-relations gaffes, Watt resigned in 1983.

Strongly pro-business, Reagan took a tough line against organized labor. In 1981, when the Professional Air Traffic Controllers Organization (PATCO) went on strike, Reagan invoked the 1948 Taft-Hartley law against strikes by federal employees, and ordered them back to work. When more than 11,000 PATCO members defied the order, Reagan fired them and barred them permanently from federal employment. (President Bill Clinton would reverse this order in 1993.) Reagan acted within the law, but other federal workers had struck in the past without such dire punishment.

Although Reagan's campaign against "big government" affected tax policy, corporate regulation, the environment, and other areas, it had little overall impact. The century-long growth of the federal budget and bureaucracy continued in the 1980s.

While implementing Reaganomics, the administration also faced the immediate problem of inflation. The Federal Reserve Board led the charge, pushing interest rates ever higher. This harsh medicine, coupled with a drop in oil prices, did its job. Inflation fell to around 4 percent in 1983 and held steady thereafter.

The Fed's high interest rates soon brought on a recession, however. By late 1982, unemployment stood at 10 percent. Reagan's cuts in social programs worsened the plight of the poor, including inner-city blacks and Hispanics. The Fed's policy also hurt U.S. exports. As foreign investors bought dollars to earn high U.S. interest rates, the dollar rose in value vis-à-vis foreign currencies, making U.S. goods more expensive abroad. With exports declining and U.S. consumers buying cars, TVs, and stereo systems made in Japan and elsewhere, the U.S. annual trade deficit shot up, reaching a whopping $111 billion in 1984.

Soaring federal deficits added to the economic muddle. Reagan's tax cuts reduced federal revenues without immediately producing the predicted business boom, while increased military appropriations far exceeded domestic spending cuts. With the budget and trade deficits mounting, the industrial sector struggling, and critics denouncing him as callous toward the poor, Reagan in 1982–1983 accepted a reduced rate of military spending, less drastic cuts in social programs, emergency job programs, and various tax increases disguised as "revenue-enhancement measures."

The economy remained worrisome through 1982. Like other recent presidents, Reagan appeared headed for failure. In the 1982 midterm elections, the Democrats regained twenty-six House seats. But 1983 brought an economic rebound. Encouraged by tax cuts, falling interest rates, better job statistics, and evidence that inflation had been tamed at last, consumers went on a buying binge and a booming stock market evoked memories of the 1920s. The five-year bull market actually began in August 1982. Money managers like Ivan Boesky, an apparent genius at stock transactions, became celebrities. E. F. Hutton and other brokerage firms advertised heavily to lure new investors. Corporate mergers proliferated. Chevron bought Gulf for $13 billion; GE acquired RCA (and its NBC subsidiary) for $6.3 billion. Banks and savings-and-loan companies, newly deregulated and flush with the deposits of eager investors, ladled out billions to developers planning shopping malls, luxury apartments, condominiums, and retirement villages. Through it all, the stock market roared on.

The Wall Street frenzy had an unsavory underside. In 1985, E. F. Hutton officials pled guilty to illegal fund manipulation. Ivan Boesky went to prison after a 1986 conviction for insider trading (profiting through advance knowledge of corporate actions). On October 19, 1987, the stock market crashed, reducing the paper value of the nation's stocks by 20 percent overnight. Thanks to prompt government action to ease credit, the market soon recovered, but the collapse had a sobering effect on giddy investors.

Even during the great bull market, economic problems persisted. The trade gap widened; the deficit passed $200 billion in 1986; and many farmers, inner-city poor, recent immigrants, and displaced industrial workers suffered through the boom times. But by 1988—just in time for another election campaign—the overall economic picture looked brighter than it had in years.

The "Evil Empire" and Crises in the Middle East
The anti-Soviet rhetoric of the late 1970s intensified during Reagan's first term. Addressing a convention of Protestant evangelicals, the president demonized the Soviet Union as "the focus of evil in the modern world." Anti-Soviet fury exploded in September 1983 when the Russians shot down a Korean passenger plane that had strayed into their airspace, killing all 269 aboard.

The administration's anti-Soviet obsession influenced its policy toward El Salvador and Nicaragua, two impoverished Central American nations caught up in revolutionary turmoil. The Reagan White House backed the Salvadoran military junta in its brutal suppression of a leftist insurgency supported by Fidel Castro's Cuba. A U.S.-backed moderate won El Salvador's 1984 presidential election, but the killing of the regime's opponents went on.

In Nicaragua, the Carter administration had initially granted aid to the Sandinista revolutionaries who overthrew dictator Anastasio Somoza in 1979. Reagan reversed this policy, claiming that the Sandinistas were turning Nicaragua into a procommunist state like Cuba. In 1982, the CIA organized and financed an anti-Sandinista guerrilla army, called the contras, based in neighboring Honduras and Costa Rica. The contras, with links to the hated Somoza regime, conducted raids, planted mines, and carried out sabotage inside Nicaragua that took a heavy toll of civilian lives.

For Reagan, the campaign to overthrow the Sandinistas and to control events in Latin America became an obsession. "The national security of all the Americas is at stake," he somberly told a joint session of Congress in May 1983. "[I]f we cannot defend ourselves there . . . the safety of our homeland would be put at jeopardy."

Fearing another Vietnam, Americans grew alarmed as details of this U.S.-run war leaked out. Congress voted a yearlong halt in U.S. military aid to the contras in December 1982 and imposed a two-year ban in 1984. Despite these prohibitions, the White House continued to funnel money contributed by foreign governments and right-wing groups in the United States to the contras. Reagan grudgingly backed a 1988 truce between the Sandinistas and the contras arranged by Central American leaders, but he still hoped for a contra victory.

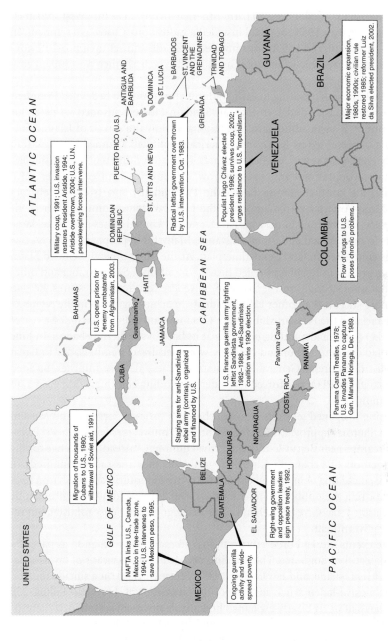

MAP 30.1 The United States in Central America and the Caribbean, 1978–2006

Plagued by poverty, population pressures, repressive regimes, and drug trafficking, this region has experienced turmoil and conflict—but also some hopeful developments—in recent decades.

UNITED STATES

ATLANTIC OCEAN

GULF OF MEXICO

Migration of thousands of Cubans to U.S., 1980; withdrawal of Soviet aid, 1991.

NAFTA links U.S., Canada, Mexico in free-trade zone, 1994; U.S. intervenes to save Mexican peso, 1995.

MEXICO

BAHAMAS

CUBA

Guantánamo

U.S. opens prison for "enemy combatants" from Afghanistan, 2003.

JAMAICA

HAITI

Military coup, 1991; U.S. invasion restores President Aristide, 1994; Aristide overthrown, 2004; U.S., U.N., peacekeeping forces intervene.

DOMINICAN REPUBLIC

PUERTO RICO (U.S.)

ST. KITTS AND NEVIS

ANTIGUA AND BARBUDA

DOMINICA

ST. LUCIA

BARBADOS

ST. VINCENT AND THE GRENADINES

TRINIDAD AND TOBAGO

GRENADA

Radical leftist government overthrown by U.S. intervention, Oct. 1983.

CARIBBEAN SEA

Staging area for anti-Sandinista rebel army (contras), organized and financed by U.S.

BELIZE

GUATEMALA

Ongoing guerrilla activity and wide-spread poverty.

EL SALVADOR

Right-wing government and opposition leaders sign peace treaty, 1992.

HONDURAS

NICARAGUA

U.S. finances guerrilla army fighting leftist Sandinista government, 1982–1988. Anti-Sandinista coalition wins 1990 election.

COSTA RICA

PANAMA

Panama Canal

Panama Canal Treaties, 1978; U.S. invades Panama to capture Gen. Manuel Noriega, Dec. 1989.

Populist Hugo Chávez elected president, 1998; survives coup, 2002; urges resistance to U.S. "imperialism."

VENEZUELA

COLOMBIA

Flow of drugs to U.S. poses chronic problems.

GUYANA

BRAZIL

Major economic expansion, 1980s, 1990s; civilian rule restored 1985; reformer Luiz da Silva elected president, 2002.

PACIFIC OCEAN

Reagan's one unqualified success in Latin America involved the tiny West Indian island of Grenada, where a 1983 coup had installed a radical pro-Castro government. In October 1983, two thousand U.S. troops invaded Grenada and set up a pro-U.S. government. Democrats grumbled, but most Grenadians, as well as other West Indian governments, approved.

The Middle East, so frustrating to earlier administrations, also bedeviled President Reagan. Late in 1980, Iraq under strongman Saddam Hussein invaded its neighbor Iran. The incoming Reagan administration, hoping to slow the spread of Islamic fundamentalism as represented by Iran's anti-American Ayatollah Khomeini, backed Iraq in this bloody eight-year war. (Two decades later, under very different circumstances, the United States would invade Iraq to overthrow Saddam Hussein [see Chapter 32].)

Meanwhile, the conflict among Israel, the Palestinians, and Israel's Arab foes dragged on. Many Americans, remembering the Holocaust and admiring Israel's vibrant democracy, felt a strong bond with Israel, and the United States gave Israel large annual grants in military aid and other assistance. Many Bible-prophecy believers saw Israel's fate as connected to God's end-time plan. At the same time, the United States also gave extensive aid to Egypt and relied heavily on oil from Saudi Arabia and other Arab states that were strongly anti-Israel. Whipsawed by conflicting pressures, Reagan enjoyed no more success than other U.S. presidents in achieving peace in the region.

In 1981 Israel and the Palestine Liberation Organization (PLO) concluded a ceasefire. But the PLO continued building up forces at its base in southern Lebanon. In June 1982, when PLO extremists shot and critically wounded Israel's ambassador to Great Britain, Israeli troops under General Ariel Sharon, Israel's defense minister, invaded Lebanon, defeated the PLO, and forced its leaders, including chairman Yasir Arafat, to evacuate Lebanon.

This invasion deepened tensions among Lebanon's various Christian and Muslim factions. With Sharon's approval, a Lebanese Christian militia force entered two Palestinian refugee camps near Beirut to root out armed gunmen. Instead, in revenge for the earlier assassination of Lebanon's Christian president, they massacred hundreds of camp residents, including women and children. An Israeli inquiry judged Sharon negligent for permitting the militiamen to enter the camp, but found no evidence that he knew of the planned massacre beforehand. Sharon resigned as defense minister, but remained in the government.

After these events, Reagan ordered two thousand marines to Lebanon as part of a multinational peacekeeping force. The Muslims accused the Americans of favoring Israel and the Christian side, and in October 1983 a Shiite Muslim on a suicide mission crashed an explosive-laden truck into a poorly guarded U.S. barracks, killing 239 marines. Reagan had never clearly explained how the deployment served U.S. interests, and the disaster further discredited his policy. In early 1984 he withdrew the surviving marines. Reagan's efforts to promote a wider Middle East peace settlement proved equally ineffective. In September 1982, he tried to restart Arab-Israeli peace talks based on the 1978 Camp David Accords, but the effort failed.

Military Buildup and Antinuclear Protest

Insisting that post-Vietnam America had grown dangerously weak, Reagan launched a massive military expansion. The Pentagon's budget nearly doubled, reaching more than $300 billion by 1985. The buildup included nuclear weapons. Secretary of State Alexander Haig spoke of using "nuclear warning shots" in a conventional war, and other administration officials mused about the "winnability" of nuclear war. Despite popular protests across Europe, the administration deployed 572 nuclear-armed missiles in Western Europe in 1983, fulfilling a NATO decision to match Soviet missiles in Eastern Europe. The Federal Emergency Management Agency issued a nuclear-war defense plan whereby city-dwellers would flee to nearby small towns. A Defense Department official proposed backyard shelters as adequate protection in a nuclear war. "With enough shovels," he asserted, "everybody's going to make it."

Such talk, coupled with the military buildup and Reagan's anti-Soviet rhetoric, alarmed many Americans. A campaign for a verifiable multinational freeze on the manufacture and deployment of nuclear weapons won strong support. Antinuclear protesters packed New York's Central Park in June 1982. That November, voters in nine states, including California and Wisconsin, approved nuclear-freeze resolutions.

To counter the freeze campaign, Reagan in March 1983 proposed the **Strategic Defense Initiative** (SDI), a computerized anti-missile system involving space-based lasers and other high-tech components. Critics quickly dubbed the scheme "Star Wars," and experts warned of its monumental technical hurdles and the danger that it would further escalate the nuclear-arms race. Nevertheless, Reagan prevailed, and a costly SDI research program began.

Reagan Reelected   The 1984 Republican convention enthusiastically renominated Reagan and Bush. The convention, staged for TV, accented themes of patriotism, prosperity, and Reagan's personal charm. To his admirers, the president had fulfilled his promise to revitalize the free-enterprise system, rebuild U.S. military might, and make America again "stand tall" in the world. They applauded his tax cuts, his attacks on big government, and his tough stance toward the Soviets. The booming economy further strengthened his popularity.

Reagan's 1981 selection of Sandra Day O'Connor as the first woman justice on the U.S. Supreme Court had won widespread praise. So had his jaunty response in March 1981 when a ricocheting bullet fired by a deranged young man struck him in the chest. Rushed to the hospital, Reagan had insisted on walking in. "Please tell me you're all Republicans," he had quipped to physicians. (The attack disabled Reagan's press secretary, James Brady, who with his wife Sarah later joined the campaign for stricter gun control.)

The field of Democratic hopefuls included **Jesse Jackson,** an African-American civil-rights leader and former aide to Martin Luther King, Jr., who proposed a "rainbow coalition" of African-Americans, Hispanics, displaced workers, and other outsiders. In a surprisingly strong showing in the Democratic primaries, Jackson garnered 3.5 million votes and won in five southern states. But former vice president Walter Mondale came in first overall, and won the nomination with backing from labor unions, party leaders, and various interest groups. His vice-presidential choice, New York congresswoman Geraldine Ferraro, became the first woman to run on a major-party presidential ticket. Democratic campaigners criticized Reagan for runaway military spending, Cold War belligerence, massive budget deficits, cuts in social programs, and assaults on the government's regulatory powers.

Reagan and Bush won 59 percent of the popular vote and carried every state but Mondale's Minnesota plus the District of Columbia. Many white working-class voters again defected to Reagan. Despite Ferraro's presence on the Democratic ticket, a higher percentage of women voted Republican in 1984 than in 1980. Reagan's ideological appeal and his mastery of TV, combined with prosperity, had carried the day. The

Democrats still controlled the House of Representatives and many state and local offices, but the Republicans' post-1968 dominance of the White House—interrupted only by Jimmy Carter's single term—continued.

Some frustrated Democrats sought to reverse their image as a "big government" and "tax-and-spend" party dominated by special interests. In 1985 Arkansas governor Bill Clinton, Senator Al Gore of Tennessee, and other moderates formed the **Democratic Leadership Council** (DLC) to stake out a more centrist party position. In the early 1990s Clinton would use the DLC as a springboard for a presidential bid.

REAGAN'S SECOND TERM, 1985–1989

Economic problems persisted in Reagan's second term, and the president made two Supreme Court appointments. But events abroad—and a major scandal related to the administration's foreign policy—dominated these years. A dramatic and unexpected easing of Cold War tensions signaled the approaching end of that long conflict. Continued tensions in the Middle East and a wave of terrorist attacks made clear, however, that even a post–Cold War world would remain dangerous.

Supreme Court Appointments, Budget Deficits, the Iran-Contra Scandal

Reagan's second term brought some legislative achievements, including the Immigration Reform and Control Act, discussed earlier, and a tax-reform law that made the system fairer and spared some 6 million low-income Americans from paying any income taxes. Reagan reshaped the Supreme Court in 1986 by elevating William Rehnquist, a Nixon appointee, to the chief justiceship upon the retirement of Warren Burger, and appointing Antonin Scalia to replace him. Scalia would prove one of the Court's most outspokenly conservative members and a champion of the view that the "original intent" of the authors of the Constitution must prevail over later interpretations.

When another vacancy opened in 1987, Reagan nominated Robert Bork, a judge and legal scholar whose abrasive personality and inflexible views led the Senate to reject him. Reagan's next nominee withdrew after admitting that he had smoked marijuana as an adult. Reagan's third choice, Anthony Kennedy, a conservative California jurist, won quick confirmation.

Federal budget deficits—a byproduct of Reagan's tax cuts and military spending increases—surpassed $200 billion in 1985 and 1986, and hovered at about $150 billion for the next two years. This, coupled with the yawning trade gap and a savings-and-loan industry scandal related to deregulation (see Chapter 31), were Reagan's principal economic legacies.

The worst crisis of Reagan's presidency, the so-called **Iran-contra scandal,** began obscurely late in 1986 when a Beirut newspaper reported that in 1985 the United States had shipped, via Israel, 508 antitank missiles to Iran, America's avowed enemy. Admitting the sale, Reagan claimed that the goal had been to encourage "moderate elements" in Tehran and to gain the release of U.S. hostages held in Lebanon by pro-Iranian groups. In February 1987 a presidentially appointed investigative panel blamed Reagan's chief of staff, Donald Regan, who resigned.

More details soon emerged, including the revelation that Lieutenant Colonel Oliver North, a National Security Council aide in the White House, had secretly diverted prof-

President Reagan at the Berlin Wall, June 1987 *Celebrating the city's 750th anniversary, Reagan speaks before the Brandenburg Gate, with a part of the wall visible behind him. Erected in 1961, the Berlin Wall came to symbolize Europe's Cold War division. With his flair for the dramatic, Reagan directly challenged the leader of the Soviet Union: "Mr. Gorbachev, tear down this wall."*

its from the Iran arms sales to the Nicaraguan contras at a time when Congress had forbidden such aid. To hide this crime, North and his secretary had altered and deleted sensitive computer files and destroyed incriminating documents. North implicated CIA director William Casey in illegalities, but Casey's death thwarted this line of investigation.

In May 1987 a joint House-Senate investigative committee opened hearings on the scandal. The nation watched in fascination as North, resplendent in his marine uniform, boasted of his patriotism, and as National Security Adviser John Poindexter testified that he had deliberately concealed the fund-diversion scheme from Reagan. The committee found no positive proof of Reagan's knowledge of illegalities, but roundly criticized the lax management style and contempt for the law that had pervaded the Reagan White House. In 1989, North was convicted of obstructing a congressional inquiry and destroying and falsifying official documents. (The conviction was later reversed on the technicality that some testimony used against North had been given under a promise of immunity.) Although ultimately less damaging to the presidency than the Watergate scandal, the Iran-contra affair dogged the Reagan administration's final years as a serious abuse of executive power.

Other scandals plagued Reagan's second term, including allegations of bribery in military-procurement contracts. Attorney General Edwin Meese resigned in 1988 amid charges that he had used his influence to promote ventures in which he had a financial interest. In 1989 came revelations that former interior secretary James Watt and other prominent Republicans had been paid hundreds of thousands of dollars for using their influence on behalf of housing developers seeking federal subsidies.

Reagan's popularity seemed unaffected by all this dirty linen. The veteran actor possessed an uncanny ability to convey warmth and sincerity and to shrug off damaging revelations with a disarming joke. Some dubbed him the Teflon president—nothing seemed to stick to him. Moreover, a surprising turn of events in Russia would end his presidency on a high note.

Reagan's Mission to Moscow   A dramatic warming in Soviet-American relations began early in Reagan's second term. At meetings in Europe in 1985 and 1986, Reagan and the new Soviet leader, Mikhail Gorbachev, revived the stalled arms-control process. Beset by profound economic and political problems in Russia and by spreading unrest in Poland, East Germany, and elsewhere in the Soviet sphere, Gorbachev worked to reduce superpower tensions to gain breathing space as he struggled with mounting crises at home. His ambitious program involved nothing less than restructuring and democratizing the Russian government and economy, ending the Communist Party's absolute power, and loosening Moscow's grip on the sprawling Soviet Union and the satellite nations of Eastern Europe.

In June 1987, speaking near the Berlin Wall, President Reagan dramatically declared: "Mr. Gorbachev, tear down this wall!" That December, in Washington, the two leaders signed the **Intermediate-range Nuclear Forces (INF) Treaty,** eliminating 2,500 U.S. and Soviet missiles from Europe. This treaty, in turn, led to Reagan's historic visit to Moscow in May 1988, where the two leaders strolled and chatted in Red Square.

Some Reaganites protested as their hero, having earlier denounced the Soviet Union as an "evil empire," cozied up to the world's top communist. One conservative paper called Reagan's trip "a sad week for the free world." Reagan himself, with his usual confidence, pointed to Gorbachev's reforms and argued that "the evil empire" was becoming more benign. Most Americans welcomed improved relations with the Cold War enemy.

The INF treaty and Reagan's trip to Moscow marked the beginning of the end of the Cold War. Historians still debate the relative importance of Reagan's military buildup versus the Soviet Union's own internal weaknesses in bringing about this outcome. Whatever history's judgment on that point, the fact that one of America's most dedicated Cold Warriors presided over the early stages of its demise remains one of the ironies of recent American history.

The Middle East: Tensions and Terrorism   As relations with Moscow improved, conditions in the Middle East worsened. In 1987, Palestinians in Gaza and the West Bank rose up against Israeli occupation. In response, Secretary of State George Shultz (who had replaced Alexander Haig in 1982) proposed talks among Israel, the Palestinians, and Jordan on a plan for Palestinian autonomy. Israel refused to negotiate until the uprising ended, and the Palestinians rejected Shultz's proposals as not going far enough toward creating a Palestinian state. Over U.S. objections, Israel continued to build settlements in the disputed West Bank.

A deadly byproduct of the Middle East conflict was a series of bombings, assassinations, hijackings, and hostage-takings by anti-Israel and anti-American terrorists. At the 1972 Summer Olympics in Munich, Palestinian gunmen killed two Israeli athletes and took nine more hostage. In the ensuing gun battle with German police, all nine hostages died, along with five of the terrorists and a policeman.

In 1985, terrorists set off bombs in the Vienna and Rome airports and hijacked a TWA flight en route from Athens to Rome, holding the crew and 145 passengers hostage for seventeen days and killing one passenger, a U.S. sailor. That same year, four heavily armed men demanding the release of Palestinians held by Israel hijacked an Italian cruise ship, the *Achille Lauro,* dumping a wheelchair-bound Jewish-American tourist into the sea.

In 1986, the bombing of a Berlin disco club popular with U.S. troops killed two GIs and injured others. Accusing Libyan strongman Muammar al-Qadaffi of masterminding this and other attacks, Reagan ordered the bombing of Libyan military sites. But the terrorist attacks intensified in frequency. In December 1988, a concealed bomb detonated aboard Pan Am flight 103, en route from London to New York. It crashed near Lockerbie, Scotland, killing all 259 aboard, including many Americans. In 1991, the United States and Great Britain formally charged two Libyan officials in the attack. In 2001, after years of stalling by Qaddafi, a special Scottish court sitting in the Netherlands acquitted one of the men but convicted the other of murder and imposed a life sentence.

This cycle of terrorism reflected profound religious and political divisions in the Middle East. Hatred of Israel, and even denial of the Jewish state's right to exist, gripped parts of the Arab world, particularly among a growing Islamic fundamentalist movement. This movement appealed especially to poor, ill-educated young Muslims attracted by clerical calls for *jihad* (holy war in defense of Islam) against a secular West that seemed increasingly dominant militarily, economically, and culturally. The Palestinian leader Yasir Arafat bore responsibility as well, for leadership failures and missed opportunities. The stationing of U.S. troops in Saudi Arabia, as well as expanding Jewish settlements in the Palestinian territories, also fed the anger that fueled terrorist attacks.

Assessing the Reagan Years   After Nixon's disgrace, Ford's caretaker presidency, and Carter's rocky tenure, Ronald Reagan's two terms restored a sense of stability and continuity to U.S. politics. Domestically, Reagan compiled a mixed record. Inflation eased, and the economy improved after 1982. But the federal deficit soared, and the administration largely ignored festering social issues, environmental concerns, and long-term economic problems.

Reaganism offered little to the poor beyond the hope that free-enterprise capitalism, stimulated by tax cuts and deregulation, would generate enough jobs that everyone could improve their lot. Building on Richard Nixon's strategy (see Chapter 29), Reagan exploited the anxieties and resentments of middle-class white voters. He criticized affirmative-action programs and ridiculed the welfare system by passing along mythic stories about Cadillac-driving black "welfare queens" and poor people who used food stamps to buy lemons for their gin-and-tonics.

Reagan's critics dismissed his presidency as a time when self-interest trumped the public good, or, at best, as an interlude marked by nostalgia and drift rather than positive achievement. They noted how readily Reagan's celebration of individual free-dom could morph into self-centered materialism. Apart from anticommunism and flag-waving patriotism, they contended, Reagan offered few goals around which all Americans could rally.

In 1988, former chief of staff Donald Regan, still smarting over his forced resigna-tion, published a memoir that portrayed Reagan as little more than an automaton: "Every moment of every public appearance was scheduled, every word was scripted, every place where Reagan was expected to stand was chalked with toe marks." He also reported the central White House role of Nancy Reagan, and her reliance on a San Francisco astrologer in planning her husband's schedule. Others noted that Reagan's benign public image masked less appealing traits. One former aide called him "the most warmly ruthless man I've ever seen."

To his admirers, such criticism was itself mean-spirited, and beside the point. They credited Reagan for reasserting traditional values of self-reliance and free enterprise; criticizing governmental excesses; and restoring national pride with his infectious op-timism and patriotism.

Reagan's militant anticommunism spawned the Iran-contra scandal, but also, his admirers believed, contributed mightily to America's victory in the Cold War—a vic-tory whose full dimensions would become apparent after he left office.

Alzheimer's disease darkened Reagan's post-presidential years. He died in 2004, at ninety-three. But ideas underlying "the Reagan revolution" lived on, and still influence American politics.

Conclusion

After the turbulent 1960s, an escapist tone dominated popular culture in the 1970s, and many young people pursued personal and careerist goals. Activist energies sur-vived, however, in a revitalized women's movement, a gay-rights campaign, and support for environmental causes. A grass-roots conservative movement gained mo-mentum as well, however, reinforced by an evangelical religious revival. Opposing abortion, gay rights, costly social-welfare programs, and secular cultural trends, con-servatives mobilized politically, laying the groundwork for Ronald Reagan's electoral victories.

Industrial decline, oil-price hikes, and runaway inflation caused serious economic problems through most of the 1970s. The 1980s, though bracketed by a recession and a stock-market crash, saw a five-year boom that brought prosperity to many. However, a persistent trade gap, massive federal deficits linked to President Reagan's tax cuts, and a continued erosion of factory jobs posed warning flags for the future.

Displaced industrial workers and inner-city minorities struggled in a high-tech economy that increasingly demanded advanced education and specialized skills. Many African-Americans enjoyed upward mobility, but others remained in poverty. Native Americans faced continuing deprivation but also new economic opportunities and benefits from long-ignored treaty rights. Immigration from Latin America and Asia, meanwhile, reshaped the nation's ethnic profile.

During his brief presidency, Gerald Ford proposed voluntarist strategies for bat-tling inflation. President Jimmy Carter crafted strategies to address the energy crisis, environmental hazards, and other emerging issues. But as Americans reacted to successive oil shocks and setbacks abroad, neither president seemed up to the challenges confronting the nation. Carter brokered a peace settlement between Egypt and Israel, but the Iranian hostage crisis bedeviled his final fourteen months in office.

Ronald Reagan entered the White House in 1981 as a champion of conservative cultural values that many Americans saw as threatened, and a proponent of a political ideology stressing free enterprise, lower taxes, and a smaller government bureaucracy, coupled with military might and aggressive anticommunism. After a series of failed and frustrating presidencies, millions of Americans welcomed Reagan's optimism, uncomplicated patriotism, and firmly held political beliefs.

The so-called Iran-contra scandal, arising from the Reagan administration's secret military aid to Iran and from its determined effort to overthrow Nicaragua's leftist regime, preoccupied the nation in 1987. Reagan's reputation survived largely unscathed, however. U.S.-Soviet relations, after deteriorating in the late 1970s and early 1980s, improved dramatically in Reagan's second term. Mikhail Gorbachev, contending with grave economic and political problems in Russia and throughout the Soviet sphere, intensified by the need to match Reagan's defense buildup, took conciliatory steps that signaled the Cold War's end.

As the Cold War faded, however, worsening conditions in the Middle East and an upsurge of terrorism, which announced itself with assassinations, exploding bombs, and crashing airplanes, signaled the onset of an era no less hazardous in its way than the darkest days of the Cold War.

31

Beyond the Cold War: Charting a New Course, 1988–2000

THE BUSH YEARS: GLOBAL RESOLVE, DOMESTIC DRIFT, 1988–1993

Ronald Reagan's vice president, **George Bush,** elected president in 1988, was a patrician in politics. Son of a Connecticut senator, Yale graduate, and World War II veteran, he had entered the Texas oil business, served in Congress, lost a Senate race, and been U.N. ambassador and CIA director before becoming Reagan's running mate in 1980.

As president, Bush compiled an uneven record. Internationally, he reacted decisively when Iraq invaded Kuwait, and he worked to ease Israeli-Palestinian tensions. His domestic record was thin, however, as he typically substituted platitudes for policy.

The Election of 1988

Vice President Bush easily won the 1988 Republican presidential nomination. In his acceptance speech, he called for a "kinder, gentler America" and pledged, "Read my lips: no new taxes." As his running mate he selected Senator Dan Quayle of Indiana, son of a newspaper publisher.

The field of Democratic contenders eventually narrowed to the black leader Jesse Jackson and Massachusetts governor Michael Dukakis. Jackson, urging concern for the poor and a war on drugs, ran well in the primaries. But Dukakis's primary victories in

1988 • George Bush elected president.

1989 • Massive Alaskan oil spill by *Exxon Valdez*.
Supreme Court, in several 5-to-4 decisions, restricts civil-rights laws.
U.S. invasion of Panama; Manuel Noriega overthrown.
China's rulers crush prodemocracy movement.
Berlin Wall is opened.

1990 • Federal Clean Air Act strengthened.
Americans with Disabilities Act passed.
Iraq invades Kuwait.
Recession (1990–1993).
Germany reunified; Soviet troops start withdrawal from Eastern Europe.

1991 • Persian Gulf War (Operation Desert Storm).
Hearings on Clarence Thomas's Supreme Court nomination.
Collapse of Soviet Union.

1992 • Supreme Court in *Planned Parenthood* v. *Casey* approves abortion restrictions but upholds *Roe* v. *Wade*.
President Bush commits U.S. troops in Somalia.
Bill Clinton elected president.

1993 • Congress approves NAFTA treaty.
Economy expands, stock market surges (1993–2000).
Clinton health-care reform plan fails (1993–1994).
Some eighty Branch Davidians die in fire as federal agents raid compound in Waco, Texas.
World Trade Center bombing kills six.

1994 • Christian Coalition gains control of Republican Party in several states.
Yasir Arafat and Yitzhak Rabin sign Oslo Accords at White House.
Clinton withdraws U.S. forces from Somalia.
United States joins the World Trade Organization (WTO).
Republicans proclaim "Contract with America"; win control of House and Senate; Newt Gingrich becomes Speaker.

1995 • Oklahoma City federal building bombed.
Dayton Accords achieve cease-fire in Bosnia; Clinton commits U.S. troops to enforce agreement.

1996 • Welfare Reform Act.
Clinton defeats Bob Dole to win second term.

1997 • Congressional battle over tobacco-industry regulation.

1998 • Clinton impeached by House of Representatives in sex scandal.

1999 • Senate dismisses impeachment charges.
Columbine High School shootings.
U.S. and NATO forces intervene in Kosovo.

2000 • George W. Bush wins presidency when Supreme Court ends Florida election dispute.

New York and California proved decisive. As his running mate, Dukakis chose Texas senator Lloyd Bentsen.

In the campaign Bush stressed Reagan's achievements while distancing himself from the Iran-contra scandal. Emphasizing peace and prosperity, he pointed to better Soviet relations, low inflation, and the 14 million new jobs created during the 1980s. A TV commercial aired by Bush supporters, playing on racist stereotypes, featured a black convict who committed rape and murder after his release under a Massachusetts prisoner-furlough program.

Dukakis emphasized his managerial skills. "This election is not about ideology, it's about competence," he insisted. He hammered at the failures of the "Swiss-cheese" Reagan economy (that is, full of holes) and urged "Reagan Democrats" to return to the fold. But Dukakis seemed wooden, and his dismissal of ideology made it difficult for him to define his political vision. Both candidates relied on TV-oriented "photo opportunities," vague slogans, and sound bites. Bush visited flag factories and military plants. Dukakis proved his toughness on defense by posing in a tank. Editorial writers deplored the "junk-food" campaign.

Bush won, carrying forty states and garnering 54 percent of the vote. Dukakis prevailed in only ten states plus the District of Columbia. The Democrats, however, retained control of Congress and most state legislatures.

The Cold War Ends   As the Bush administration took power in Washington, the Soviet collapse symbolized by the opening of the Berlin Wall proceeded with breathtaking rapidity. Germany was reunited for the first time since 1945. Estonia, Latvia, and Lithuania, the Baltic republics annexed by Moscow in 1940, declared independence. The other Soviet republics moved toward autonomy as well.

In August 1991 President Bush and Mikhail Gorbachev signed a treaty in Moscow reducing their strategic nuclear arsenals by 25 percent. Secretary of Defense Dick Cheney proposed a 25 percent reduction in U.S. military forces over five years. NATO announced major troop reductions.

As the Russian Communist Party's centralized control collapsed and the economy sank into crisis, reformers called for a Western-style market economy. In August 1991, hard-line communists tried to overthrow Gorbachev. But thousands of Muscovites, rallied by Boris Yeltsin, president of the Russian Republic, protectively surrounded Moscow's parliament building, and the coup failed.

Exuberant crowds toppled statues of Lenin and Stalin. Leningrad resumed its pre-Soviet name, St. Petersburg. Late in 1991 most of the Soviet republics proclaimed the end of the USSR. Gorbachev, overwhelmed by forces he himself had unleashed, resigned. In Moscow, Boris Yeltsin filled the power vacuum.

Secretary of State James Baker, a longtime Bush ally, proceeded cautiously as these events unfolded. U.S. influence was limited, in any event, as long-suppressed forces of nationalism and ethnicity burst forth in Eastern Europe and in the former Soviet Union. Baker did work to ensure the security of the twenty-seven thousand nuclear weapons based in Russia and in newly independent Ukraine, Belarus, and Kazakhstan, and to prevent rogue states or terrorist groups from acquiring nuclear materials or know-how from these countries. As negotiations with Yeltsin and other leaders went forward, Bush announced further reductions in the U.S. nuclear arsenal.

For decades, the superpowers had backed their client states and rebel insurgencies in the Third World. As the Cold War faded, prospects brightened for resolving some local disputes. In Nicaragua, for example, Bush abandoned the U.S.-funded contra war against the leftist Sandinista government. Instead, Bush and Congress crafted a program aimed at reintegrating the contras into Nicaraguan life and politics. A multiparty anti-Sandinista coalition won the 1990 Nicaraguan elections.

Poverty and economic exploitation still plagued Latin America, however, and the flow of cocaine and heroin to U.S. cities from the region continued. In 1989, Bush ordered a U.S. invasion of Panama to capture the nation's ruler, General Manuel Noriega. Formerly on the CIA payroll, Noriega had accepted bribes to permit drugs to pass through Panama on their way north. Convicted of drug trafficking, he received a life prison term.

U.S. relations with the Philippines, a former colony and longtime ally, shifted as well. In 1991 the Philippines legislature ended an agreement permitting two U.S. naval bases in the islands. With the Cold War over, the Bush administration closed the bases.

Meanwhile, South Africa's policy of racial segregation, called apartheid, provoked growing protests by U.S. black leaders and campus activists. In 1986, over a Reagan veto, Congress had imposed economic sanctions against white-ruled South Africa, including a ban on U.S. corporate investment. Economic pressure by America and other nations strengthened a powerful anti-apartheid campaign in South Africa itself, led by Anglican bishop Desmond Tutu. The South African government in 1990 released black leader Nelson Mandela after years in prison and opened negotiations with Mandela's African National Congress. When South Africa scrapped its apartheid policy in 1991, President Bush lifted the sanctions. In 1994, underscoring the new political order in South Africa, Mandela was elected president.

In 1989, Chinese troops brutally crushed a pro-democracy demonstration in Beijing's Tiananmen Square, killing several hundred unarmed students and workers. A wave of arrests and public executions followed. The Bush administration curtailed diplomatic contacts and urged banks to postpone loans to China. But Bush, committed to U.S. trade expansion, did not break diplomatic relations or cancel trade agreements with Beijing.

As the Cold War faded, trade issues loomed large. America's trade deficit with Japan stirred special concern. Early in 1992, facing a recession and rising unemployment in an election year, President Bush turned an Asian trip into a trade mission. Joined by U.S. business leaders, he urged the Japanese to buy more U.S. products. The trade gap continued, however.

The Persian Gulf War, 1991　One foreign crisis brought a forceful response. On August 2, 1990, Iraq invaded its neighbor Kuwait. Iraq's dictator, Saddam Hussein, viewed Kuwait's ruling sheiks as Western puppets and asserted Iraq's historic claims to Kuwait's vast oil fields.

Under Saddam, Iraq had pursued chemical- and nuclear-weapons programs and threatened not only Kuwait but also other Arab nations and Israel. During the Iran-Iraq War, however, the United States had favored Iraq, and even assisted Saddam's military buildup (see Chapter 30). Now, however, confronted by Iraq's invasion of Kuwait, Washington protested vigorously.

Avoiding Lyndon Johnson's mistakes in Vietnam, Bush built a consensus in Congress, at the United Nations, and among the American people for a clear objective: Iraq's withdrawal from Kuwait. Deploying more than 500,000 U.S. troops to achieve that goal, Bush also built a coalition of thirty-four nations, including five in the Persian Gulf, which contributed an additional 160,000 troops.

MAP 31.1 The Mideast Crisis, 1980–2000

With terrorist attacks, the Iran-Iraq War, the Persian Gulf War, and the ongoing struggle between Israel and the Palestinians, the Middle East was the site of almost unending violence, conflict, and tension in these years.

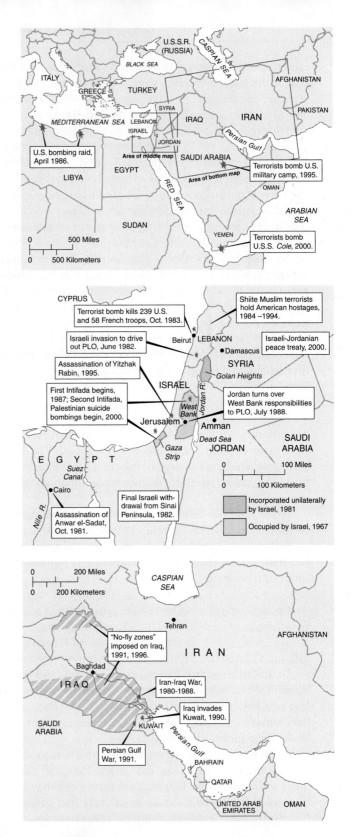

U.S. bombing raid, April 1986.

Area of middle map

Area of bottom map

Terrorists bomb U.S. military camp, 1995.

Terrorists bomb U.S.S. *Cole*, 2000.

Terrorist bomb kills 239 U.S. and 58 French troops, Oct. 1983.

Israeli invasion to drive out PLO, June 1982.

Assassination of Yitzhak Rabin, 1995.

First Intifada begins, 1987; Second Intifada, Palestinian suicide bombings begin, 2000.

Shiite Muslim terrorists hold American hostages, 1984–1994.

Israeli-Jordanian peace treaty, 2000.

Jordan turns over West Bank responsibilities to PLO, July 1988.

Final Israeli withdrawal from Sinai Peninsula, 1982.

Assassination of Anwar el-Sadat, Oct. 1981.

Incorporated unilaterally by Israel, 1981

Occupied by Israel, 1967

"No-fly zones" imposed on Iraq, 1991, 1996.

Iran-Iraq War, 1980-1988.

Iraq invades Kuwait, 1990.

Persian Gulf War, 1991.

Kuwait, 1991 *Burning oil fields, set ablaze by retreating Iraqis, provide an eerie backdrop to motorized U.S. troops participating in Operation Desert Storm, the high point of the Bush presidency.*

The UN imposed economic sanctions against Iraq and insisted that Saddam withdraw by January 15, 1991. On January 12, the Senate and the House endorsed military action. Most Democrats voted against war, favoring continued economic sanctions. The shadow of Vietnam hovered in the background as Americans debated another war.

The air war began on January 16. For six weeks B-52 and F-16 bombers pounded Iraqi troops, supply depots, and command centers in Iraq's capital, Baghdad. The air forces of other nations participated as well. In retaliation, Saddam fired Soviet-made Scud missiles against Tel Aviv and other Israeli cities, as well as against the Saudi capital, Riyadh. As TV news programs showed distant targets through aircraft bombsights and U.S. Patriot missiles intercepting incoming Scuds, the war resembled a glorified video game.

On February 23 two hundred thousand U.S. troops under General H. Norman Schwarzkopf moved across the desert toward Kuwait. Although rain turned the sand to soup, the army pushed on. Iraqi soldiers fled or surrendered en masse. U.S. forces destroyed thirty-seven hundred Iraqi tanks while losing only three. With Iraqi resistance crushed, President Bush declared a cease-fire, and Kuwait's ruling family returned to power. U.S. casualties numbered 148 dead—including 35 killed inadvertently by U.S. firepower—and 467 wounded. Iraqi military casualties, estimated at 25,000 to 65,000, included as many as 12,000 killed in the bombing campaign. The Iraqi government claimed that U.S. bombs also killed 2,300 civilians.

For President Bush, the **Persian Gulf War** proved that Americans were again ready to use military might to pursue national interests. "By God, we've kicked the Vietnam syndrome once and for all," he declared.

Some had urged President Bush to invade Iraq and overthrow Saddam Hussein. Bush and National Security Adviser Brent Scowcroft rejected this course, however. Invading Iraq, they feared, could involve an extended occupation and unleash sectarian conflict. Somewhat chastened, Saddam granted UN inspectors access to his weapons-production facilities. The UN also imposed "no-fly zones" on Iraqi aircraft, but Saddam's army brutally suppressed uprisings by Shiite Muslims in the south and ethnic Kurds in the north.

Home-Front Problems and Domestic Policies   In the early 1990s the impact of Reagan-era tax cuts and deregulation began to hit home. First came the collapse of the savings-and-loan (S&L) industry, provider of home loans and a modest but secure return to depositors. As interest rates had risen in the late 1970s because of inflation, the S&Ls had offered higher interest to attract deposits, even though their assets were mostly in fixed-rate mortgages. Money freed up by the Reagan tax cuts flowed into S&Ls with their high rates of return. Meanwhile, in the deregulation fervor, Congress eased the rules governing S&Ls, enabling them to make loans on risky real-estate ventures. As recession hit, many of these investments went bad. In 1988–1990, nearly six hundred S&Ls failed, especially in the Southwest, wiping out many depositors' savings.

Because the government insures S&L deposits, the Bush administration in 1989 set up a program to repay depositors and sell hundreds of foreclosed office towers and apartment buildings in a depressed real-estate market. Estimates of the bailout's cost topped $400 billion. "'Savings and loan,'" wrote a journalist, "has become synonymous with 'bottomless pit.'"

The federal deficit, a byproduct of Reagan's tax cuts and military spending, continued to mount. In 1990, Congress and Bush agreed on a deficit-reduction plan involving spending cuts and tax increases. Bush's retreat from his 1988 "no new taxes" pledge angered many voters. Despite the agreement, the deficit reached $290 billion in 1992. The Gulf War, the S&L bailout, and soaring welfare and Medicare/Medicaid payments sank the budget-balancing effort.

Making matters worse, recession struck in 1990. Retail sales slumped; housing starts fell. The auto industry, battered by Japanese imports, fared disastrously. GM cut its work force by more than seventy thousand. By 1992 the jobless rate exceeded 7 percent and the number of Americans living in poverty had risen by 2.1 million, to about 34 million. If 1984 was "morning in America," wrote a columnist, quoting a Reagan campaign slogan, this was "the morning after."

The recession worsened inner-city joblessness and despair. In April 1992, an outbreak of arson and looting erupted in a poor black district of Los Angeles. The immediate cause was black outrage (shared by many others) over a jury's acquittal of four white police officers whose beating of a black motorist had been captured on videotape. The riots left some forty persons dead and millions in property damage, underscoring the desperate conditions in the inner cities. When Bush came to Atlanta in 1992 to observe Martin Luther King Day, Dr. King's daughter, a minister, declared, "How dare we celebrate in . . . a recession, when nobody is sure whether their jobs are secure?"

Proclaiming himself the "education president," Bush called for national testing of schoolchildren and supported a voucher system to enable children to attend private schools at public expense. In the view of many educators, such proposals bore little relationship to the plight of many crowded and underfunded public schools.

The **Americans with Disabilities Act** of 1990, supported by Bush, barred discrimination against disabled persons in hiring or education. In an echo of the earlier African-American civil-rights campaign, Congress passed this law following demonstrations and lobbying by the disabled and organizations representing them. Thanks to this law, job opportunities for handicapped persons increased and the number of physically or cognitively impaired children attending public schools rose significantly.

Environmental concerns surged in 1989 when a giant oil tanker, the *Exxon Valdez,* ran aground in Alaska's Prince William Sound, spilling more than 10 million gallons of oil. The accident fouled coastal habitats, killed thousands of sea otters and shore birds, and jeopardized Alaska's herring and salmon industries. That summer, air pollution in more than one hundred U.S. cities exceeded federal standards. A 1991 Environmental Protection Agency study found that pollutants were seriously depleting the atmosphere's ozone layer, which reduces cancer-causing solar radiation.

Squeezed between public worries and corporate resistance to regulation, Bush compiled a mixed environmental record. In a bipartisan effort, the White House and the Democratic Congress agreed on a toughened Clean Air Act in 1990. (California and other states adopted even tighter auto-emission standards.) The government also began the costly task of disposing of radioactive wastes and cleaning up the contamination around nuclear facilities. On the other hand, the administration scuttled treaties on global warming, backed oil exploration in Alaskan wilderness preserves, and proposed to open protected wetlands to developers. Bush's self-serving speech to a UN environmental conference in Rio de Janeiro in 1992 further alienated environmentalists.

President Bush made two Supreme Court nominations. David Souter, a New Hampshire judge of moderate views, won easy confirmation in 1990. With **Clarence Thomas,** however, Bush continued Reagan's effort to shift the court sharply to the right. Bush nominated Thomas in 1991 to replace Thurgood Marshall, a black who had fought segregation as an NAACP lawyer. Thomas, also an African-American, supported right-wing causes and opposed affirmative-action programs. Having risen from poverty to attend Yale Law School and to head the Equal Employment Opportunity Commission (EEOC) under Reagan, Thomas viewed individual effort, not government programs, as the avenue of upward mobility for the disadvantaged. Noting his weak qualifications, critics charged Bush with playing racial politics.

In the Senate Judiciary Committee hearings, a former Thomas associate at EEOC, **Anita Hill,** accused him of sexual harassment. Thomas narrowly won confirmation, but Republican efforts to discredit Hill's testimony alienated many women. When women candidates did very well in the 1992 elections (see below), many observers concluded that resentment over the Thomas hearings had played a role.

On the Court, Thomas allied with Justice Antonin Scalia in upholding executive power, interpreting the Constitution narrowly, and championing conservative social issues. Overall, the Reagan/Bush appointments blunted the Supreme Court's liberal thrust that began in the 1930s and continued under Chief Justice Earl Warren and others. In 1990–1991, the Court narrowed the rights of arrested persons and upheld regulations barring physicians in federally funded clinics from discussing abortion with their patients. In *Planned Parenthood* v. *Casey,* a five-to-four decision in 1992, the Court affirmed *Roe* v. *Wade* but upheld a Pennsylvania law restricting abortion rights by imposing a twenty-four-hour waiting period and other requirements. Conservative activism was replacing liberal activism on the high court.

1992: Clinton Versus Bush, and a Third-Party Challenge

George Bush's approval ratings soared after the Persian Gulf War, only to fall below 50 percent as the recession hit. A 1991 *New York Times* editorial commented: "[Bush is] shrewd and energetic in foreign policy . . . , clumsy and irresolute at home. . . . The domestic Bush flops like a fish, leaving the impression that he doesn't know what he thinks or doesn't much care, apart from the political gains to be extracted from an issue."

Intimidated by Bush's post–Gulf War popularity, top Democrats stayed out of the 1992 presidential race. But Governor Bill Clinton of Arkansas took the plunge. Fending off reports of marital infidelity, Clinton defeated other hopefuls in the primaries and won the nomination. As his running mate, he chose Senator **Albert Gore, Jr.,** of Tennessee. In his acceptance speech, Clinton pledged action on environmental, health-care, and economic issues.

President Bush quashed a primary challenge by conservative columnist Pat Buchanan, but at the Republican Party convention Buchanan and evangelist Pat Robertson gave divisive speeches staking out deeply conservative positions on contested cultural issues. Delegates from Robertson's Christian Coalition cheered, but moderate Republicans deplored the party's rightward turn.

Political outsider **H. Ross Perot,** founder of a Texas data-processing firm, also entered the race. The nation's economic problems were simple, Perot insisted on TV talk shows; only party politics stood in the way of solving them. He proposed electronic "town meetings" by which the public would govern directly. At his peak of popularity, nearly 40 percent of the voters supported Perot. His eccentricities and thin-skinned response to critics cost him support, but he remained a wild card in the election.

Bush attacked Clinton's character and charged that he had evaded the Vietnam-era draft. As for the recession, Bush promised to put James A. Baker in charge of domestic affairs in a second term. Clinton, meanwhile, focused on the economy and the problems of the middle class. He pledged to work for a national health-care system, welfare reform, and programs to promote economic growth and new technologies.

Clinton won 43 percent of the vote to Bush's 38 percent. Perot amassed 19 percent—the best showing for a third-party candidate since Teddy Roosevelt in 1912. Clinton carried such key states as California, Ohio, and New Jersey; lured back many blue-collar and suburban "Reagan Democrats"; and did well in the South. Clinton's move to the center (see below), coupled with Bush's indecisiveness and the divisive Perot campaign, had brought him victory.

In the congressional races, thirty-eight African-Americans and seventeen Hispanics won seats. A California congressional district sent the first Korean-American to Washington. California also became the first state to elect two women senators, Barbara Boxer and Dianne Feinstein. Illinois elected the first African-American woman senator, Carol Moseley Braun. Overall, the new Congress included fifty-three women: six in the Senate and forty-seven in the House. Magazines hailed "The Year of the Woman." With Democrats in control of Congress and the executive branch, an end to the much-deplored Washington "gridlock" seemed possible.

THE CLINTON ERA BEGINS: DEBATING DOMESTIC POLICY, 1993–1996

In contrast to George Bush, a member of the World War II generation, **William Jefferson (Bill) Clinton** was the first president from the baby-boom generation that came of age in the era of JFK, Vietnam, and the Beatles. Born in Arkansas in 1946, he admired Elvis Presley, played the saxophone, and once considered becoming a pop musician. His early interest in politics led him to attend Georgetown University in Washington, D.C., Oxford University (as a Rhodes scholar), and Yale Law School, where he met his future wife, Hillary Rodham. He returned to Arkansas after graduation, ran unsuccessfully for Congress, but won the governorship in 1979, at age thirty-two.

Clinton's presidency soon encountered setbacks, and the 1994 midterm election produced a Republican landslide. The newly energized congressional Republicans pursued their conservative agenda, including—with Clinton's cooperation—sweeping welfare reform.

Shaping a Domestic Agenda   In contrast to Republican predecessors like Nixon and Bush, Clinton preferred domestic issues to foreign policy. Of course, like all presidents, Clinton confronted serious diplomatic challenges. (See "Clinton's Foreign Policy: Defining America's Role in a Post–Cold War World" below.) For the most part, however, domestic policy dominated his attention.

Secretary of State Madeleine Albright Meets with Japanese Defense Minister Fumio Kyuka, February 1997   *Appointed secretary of state by President Bill Clinton in 1996, the first woman to hold that post, Albright grappled with the complexities of a post–Cold War world.*

Clinton and Vice President Al Gore were leaders of the New Democratic Coalition, a group of moderates unhappy with the party's ultra-liberal, "tax and spend" reputation. To win back middle-class and blue-collar voters, Clinton's campaign stressed Middle America's concerns: jobs, health care, soaring welfare costs. As he steered the party toward the middle and muted its concern with the poor, traditional liberals and black leaders expressed uneasiness. Seeking middle ground on abortion, he said it should be "safe, legal, and rare." Clinton firmly endorsed environmental protection, a popular cause with voters. Indeed, Al Gore in 1992 had published an environmental manifesto, *Earth in the Balance.*

Lending symbolic support to the women's movement, Clinton named women to head the Departments of Justice, Energy, and Health and Human Services; the Council of Economic Advisers; the Environmental Protection Agency; the United Nations delegation; and the Bureau of the Budget. To fill a Supreme Court vacancy in 1993, he nominated Judge Ruth Bader Ginsberg. (When a second vacancy arose in 1994, Clinton chose moderate liberal Stephen G. Breyer, a federal judge in Boston.) In 1997 he named **Madeleine K. Albright** as secretary of state—the highest U.S. government office ever held by a woman.

Clinton's early effort to fulfill a campaign pledge to end homosexuals' exclusion from military service proved extremely contentious. A study commission eventually crafted a compromise summed up in the phrase "Don't ask, don't tell." According to this policy, so long as homosexual or bisexual soldiers do not openly reveal their sexual orientation, commanders may not investigate it.

On the economic front, Clinton proposed military-spending cuts and tax increases to ease the budget deficit. To combat the recession, he recommended programs to stimulate job creation and economic growth. In August 1993, Congress adopted Clinton's spending cuts and tax increases. But with the economy improving, the economic-stimulus package fell by the wayside.

Clinton also urged ratification of the **North American Free Trade Agreement** (NAFTA) negotiated by the Bush administration. This pact admitted Mexico to the free-trade zone that the United States and Canada had created earlier. While critics warned that U.S. jobs would flee to Mexico, NAFTA backers, including most economists, predicted a net gain in jobs as Mexican markets opened to U.S. products. Congress approved NAFTA in 1993, handing Clinton a welcome victory.

With Medicare and Medicaid costs exploding, health-care reform stood high on Clinton's "to do" list. From 1980 to 1992, government payments for these programs ballooned from 8 percent to 14 percent of the federal budget. Liberal critics also noted the uneven distribution of health care and the millions of citizens who lacked health insurance.

Clinton appointed his wife Hillary to head a health-care task force. This body, working mainly in secret, devised a sweeping plan for universal health insurance, with employers paying 80 percent of workers' costs. To cover start-up expenses, the plan proposed new tobacco taxes. The task force's cost-containment plan included health-care purchasing cooperatives, a national board to monitor costs, and caps on health-insurance premiums and on Medicare/Medicaid payments.

Lobbyists for doctors, the insurance industry, tobacco companies, and other groups ganged up to oppose the plan. Critics attacked the secretive way it had been formulated. By fall 1994, health-care reform was stalled. Clinton had misread public complaints about medical costs and bureaucratic red tape as support for radical change. But soaring costs, gaps in coverage, and other health-care problems guaranteed that this issue would remain on the political agenda.

Crime and welfare reform also ranked high among voter concerns. In 1994, Clinton proposed an anticrime bill including a ban on assault weapons and funds for more prisons and police officers. After much partisan maneuvering, Congress enacted a crime bill similar to Clinton's proposal.

In 1994, Clinton offered a welfare-reform bill. It required able-bodied recipients of payments from the government's major welfare program, Aid to Families with Dependent Children (AFDC), to go to work after two years, in a public-service job if necessary. The bill included job training and child-care provisions, as well as measures to force absent fathers ("deadbeat dads") to support their offspring. It also permitted states to deny additional payments to welfare mothers who had more children. Congress delayed welfare reform until 1995, however, when Republican majorities in both houses shaped their own bill.

By 1994, Clinton's popularity was sagging. Exploiting the "character issue," critics publicized the Clintons' earlier involvement in a shady Arkansas real-estate speculation, the Whitewater Development Company. The 1993 suicide of assistant White House counsel Vincent Foster, the Clintons' close friend, attracted conspiracy theorists. In 1994, Paula Jones, an Arkansas state employee, filed a lawsuit claiming that Clinton when governor had solicited sexual favors.

Favorable economic news helped Clinton weather the setbacks. By 1994, the unemployment rate had fallen to the lowest level in four years, and inflation remained well under control. The federal deficit dropped each year from 1993 to 1997. Nevertheless, by mid-1994 Clinton's approval ratings had sunk to 42 percent.

Sensing Clinton's vulnerability, the opposition grew bolder. Radio commentator Rush Limbaugh won fans for his jeering attacks on liberals. By 1994, Pat Robertson's **Christian Coalition,** with some nine hundred chapters nationwide, controlled several state Republican parties. With its passion and organizational energy, the religious Right represented an increasingly potent political force.

A Sharp Right Turn: 1994–1996   Bill Clinton had run in 1992 as a "new Democrat," but by 1994 many voters saw him as an old Democrat of the big-government, "tax-and-spend" variety, beholden to gays, feminists, and other "special interests." To critics, Clinton's failed health-care plan embodied all the flaws of the New Deal/Great Society style of top-down reform.

Meanwhile, a network of organizations, from the Christian Coalition to the National Rifle Association, built on the conservative movement dating to the 1970s (see Chapter 30, "Grass–Roots Conservatism") to orchestrate a sharp rightward swing in the body politic. Heavily endowed conservative think tanks such as the Heritage Foundation and the American Enterprise Institute issued books and position papers promoting movements to downsize government, reduce welfare, slash taxes, deregulate business, and shift power from Washington to the states. A torrent of mass mailings and an endless drumbeat of conservative radio commentary denounced the "liberal elite" and inflamed differences over such hot-button issues as obscenity, abortion, gun control, gay rights, school prayer, "radical feminism," sex education, and an alleged erosion of "family values."

Normally, prosperity helps the party in power, but the recovery did little for ordinary Americans (see "An Uneven Prosperity"). In October 1994, an ominous 58 percent of Americans told pollsters that they felt no better off despite the economic upturn.

Republican congressman **Newt Gingrich** of Georgia mobilized the discontent. In a September 1994 ceremony on the Capitol steps, some three hundred Republican congressional candidates signed Gingrich's "Contract with America" pledging to propose tax cuts, congressional term limits, tougher crime laws, antipornography measures, a balanced-budget amendment, and other reforms. The Contract nationalized the midterm election, normally fought on local issues.

In November, voters gave the GOP control of both houses of Congress for the first time since 1954; increased the number of Republican governors; and cut down such Democratic giants as New York governor Mario Cuomo and Texas governor Ann Richards. Although only 38 percent of eligible voters went to the polls, the outcome signaled a significant rightward shift. Evangelical Christians, energized by politicized preachers like Falwell and Robertson, turned out in large numbers, mostly to vote Republican.

Republicans hailed the election as a further step in a conservative resurgence launched by Barry Goldwater in 1964. In the Senate, the reactionary Jesse Helms of North Carolina became chairman of the Foreign Relations Committee, and ninety-two-year-old Strom Thurmond of South Carolina, presidential candidate of the States' Rights (Dixiecrat) Party in 1948, headed the Armed Services Committee.

In the House of Representatives, a jubilant horde of 230 Republicans, 73 of them newly elected, chose Newt Gingrich as Speaker, made Rush Limbaugh an "honorary member," and set about enacting the Contract with America. A constitutional amendment requiring a balanced federal budget passed the House but narrowly failed in the Senate. House Republicans also targeted the Public Broadcasting System, accused of liberal bias, and the National Endowment for the Arts for funding projects some found offensive. Fulfilling pledges to combat pornography, Congress passed a Communications Decency Act strengthening the government's censorship powers. (In 1997, the Supreme Court ruled the law unconstitutional.)

The torrent of bills, hearings, and press releases recalled the heady days of the early New Deal and Lyndon Johnson's Great Society. Now, however, the activist energy came from the conservative side of the political spectrum.

The architect of this revolution, Newt Gingrich, stumbled in 1995 when he first accepted, and then turned down, a $4.5 million advance from a publishing house owned by Rupert Murdoch, a media tycoon with interests in federal legislation. Journalists also focused on Gingrich's network of political action groups, dubbed "Newt, Inc.," funded by corporate money and conservative foundations. The 1994 election also signaled a go-it-alone view of America's world role. The Contract with America largely ignored foreign policy, and key Republican legislators pushed isolationist views. Jesse Helms denounced the United Nations, criticized environmental treaties, and belittled UN peacekeeping efforts and America's foreign-aid program. Congressional Republicans refused to pay $1 billion in past UN dues. Bending to the shifting political winds (and to Pentagon objections), the Clinton administration rejected a multinational treaty banning land mines.

Savoring their electoral triumph, conservatives renewed the battle for welfare reform. They offered two arguments. The first was economic. AFDC, with 14.2 million women and children on its rolls, cost about $125 billion in 1994, including direct payments, food stamps, and Medicaid benefits, a sharp jump since 1989. Though dwarfed by the benefits enjoyed by the middle class through social security, Medicare, farm subsidies, and various tax loopholes, this was still a heavy budgetary drain. The second argument was ideological: the belief that welfare had become a "lifelong entitlement" that encouraged indolence and irresponsible behavior and trapped recipients in a multigenerational cycle of dependence. Many observers linked the soaring rate of out-of-wedlock births to AFDC policies that paid mothers higher benefits for each child. Though partially based on stereotypes rather than empirical data, such views were widely held.

As a broad consensus gradually emerged that the existing welfare system had serious flaws, the debate focused not on whether to change it, but how. While Clinton favored federally funded child care and job-training programs to ease the transition from welfare to work, Republicans argued that businesses, the states, and private agencies could best provide these services. Clinton vetoed two welfare bills that lacked the safeguards he thought essential.

At last, in August, as another presidential campaign unfolded, Clinton signed the landmark **Welfare Reform Act of 1996.** Reversing sixty years of welfare policy, the law ended the largest federal program, AFDC. Instead, states would now receive block grants to develop their own programs within strict funding limits and guidelines limiting most recipients to two years of continuous coverage, with a five-year lifetime total.

Supporters argued that ending welfare as a lifetime entitlement would encourage personal responsibility. Critics warned of the effects on inner-city welfare mothers lacking education or job skills. Traditional Democratic liberals such as Massachusetts senator Edward Kennedy, as well as advocates for children, the poor, and minority groups, argued that Clinton had not fought strongly enough to protect welfare recipients in negotiating with congressional Republicans.

The direst predictions did not materialize. From 1996 to 2005 the number of families on welfare fell by 57 percent, and the birthrate among unmarried women leveled off. The percentage of unmarried mothers in the work force rose from around 48 percent in 1996 to around 65 percent in 2000, although many held low-paying, unskilled jobs, and changed jobs frequently. On balance, however, most observers rated welfare reform at least a qualified success.

THE ECONOMIC BOOM OF THE 1990S

The 1990s saw one of the longest periods of sustained economic growth in U.S. history. Productivity increased, unemployment fell, and inflation remained low. Prosperity helped cut crime rates and reduce welfare rolls. Federal deficits dropped as tax revenues increased. In 1998, for the first time since 1969, the federal budget actually showed a surplus.

For some, the surging stock market stimulated the urge to get rich quick, acquire more possessions, and enjoy the good times. But real wages lagged behind the stock market, and workers who lacked the skills required by the emerging knowledge-based economy faced difficulties. America's participation in an increasingly global economy fueled economic growth, but when foreign economies faltered, the U.S. economy stumbled as well.

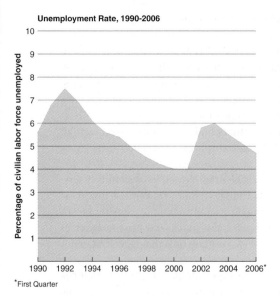

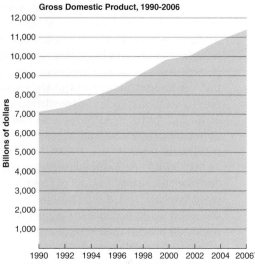

*First Quarter

*Annual estimate based on First Quarter statistics.

FIGURE 31.1 The U.S. Economy, 1990-2006

The unemployment rate fell, and the gross domestic product rose during the boom years of the 1990s. As recession hit in 2001, however, the jobless rate increased and the GDP flattened (see Chapter 32). *Source:* Unemployment Rate Chart: Bureau of Labor Statistics, U.S. Department of Labor; GDP: U.S. Department of Commerce. http://www.bea.gov/bea/dn/gdplev.xls

An Uneven Prosperity

The economic boom of the 1990s had various sources, but the new products, efficiencies, and business opportunities associated with the personal computer and the information revolution were certainly crucial (see Chapter 32). Rising international trade, a low inflation rate, and the Federal Reserve Board's low interest rates all helped sustain the boom. Unemployment, which stood at 7.5 percent in 1992, fell to 4 percent by 2000. Corporate earnings soared. The gross domestic product, a key economic indicator, rose nearly 80 percent in the decade.

Wall Street boomed as stock prices far outran many companies' actual value or earnings prospects. From under 3,000 in 1991, the Dow Jones Industrial Average edged toward 12,000 by early 2001. New investors flocked into the market. By 1998, nearly 50 percent of U.S. families owned stock directly or through their pension plans. The rising stock market stimulated a quest for luxury goods and leisure pursuits (see below). In 2000, Americans spent $105 billion on new cars; $107 billion on video, audio, and computer equipment; and $81 billion on foreign travel. As in 1929, a few economists warned that the market's inevitable downturn could have severe consequences. As early as 1996 Federal Reserve Board chairman Alan Greenspan warned of "irrational exuberance" in the stock market, but with little effect.

Information-technology (IT) stocks proved especially popular. The NASDAQ composite index, loaded with technology stocks, soared from under 500 in 1991 to over 5,000 by early 2000. Some stock offerings by IT start-up companies hit fantastic levels, turning young entrepreneurs into paper millionaires. Brokers who managed these offerings (and profited as the stock prices rose) hyped them with glowing assessments of new companies' prospects.

Corporate mergers multiplied as companies sought to improve their profitability. In 2000, the communications giant Viacom swallowed CBS for $41 billion, and the pharmaceutical company Pfizer acquired rival Warner-Lambert for $90 billion. In the biggest merger of all, the Internet company America Online (AOL) acquired Time-Warner (itself the product of earlier mergers) for $182 billion.

The prosperity was very unevenly distributed, however. From 1979 to 1996 the portion of total income going to the wealthiest 20 percent of Americans increased by 13 percent, while the share going to the poorest 20 percent *dropped* by 22 percent. Commented economist Richard Freeman in 1998, "The U.S. has the most unequal distribution of income among advanced countries—and the degree of inequality has increased more here than in any comparable country." Adjusted for inflation, the buying power of the average worker's paycheck fell or remained flat through much of the period from 1986 to 2000. As corporations maintained profits by "downsizing" and cost cutting, job worries gnawed at many Americans. The growing service sector included not only high-income white-collar positions and IT work, but also low-paying jobs in fast-food outlets, custodial work, car washes, telemarketing, and so forth.

While many service workers, teachers, and other white-collar groups belonged to unions, only 13.5 percent of the total labor force was unionized in 2000, weakening this means by which workers had historically bettered their wages and job conditions. Unions' political clout diminished as well. Congress ratified the 1993 NAFTA treaty, for example, despite protests from organized labor.

Job-market success increasingly required special training and skills, posing problems for high-school graduates, displaced industrial workers, and welfare recipients entering the labor force. Overall employment statistics also obscured racial and ethnic variables. In 2000, the jobless rate for blacks and Hispanics, despite having dropped, remained significantly higher than the rate for whites. In short, while the economic boom benefited many, a wide gap separated those who prospered and those who experienced minimal gains or none at all.

America and the Global Economy   As the NAFTA agreement made plain, foreign trade ranked high on Clinton's agenda. When the U.S. trade deficit hit $133 billion in 1993, including a $59 billion trade gap with Japan, Clinton, like his predecessor, pressured the Japanese to buy more U.S. goods.

Clinton also preserved trading ties with China despite Beijing's human-rights abuses and one-party rule. Clinton welcomed Chinese president Jiang Zemin for a state visit in 1997 and visited China in 1998. This reflected economic realities. China had become America's fourth largest trading partner, after Canada, Mexico, and Japan. In 2000, when U.S. imports from China surpassed $100 billion, Congress granted China the same status as America's other trading partners, rather than making trade with China dependent on year-by-year agreements.

Economic **globalization** increasingly shaped U.S. policy. When the Mexican peso collapsed in 1995, jeopardizing U.S.-Mexican trade and threatening to increase illegal migration northward, Clinton quickly granted Mexico $40 billion in loan guarantees.

In 1997–1998, when political corruption and other factors weakened the economies of Thailand, South Korea, Indonesia, and other Asian nations, the Clinton administration worked to promote stability in the region. Chaos especially threatened Indonesia, the world's fourth most populous nation, ruled until 1998 by an aging autocrat. Working through the International Monetary Fund, the administration sought to reduce the regime's corruption and strengthen Indonesia's faltering economy.

As the Asian economic crisis spread, Japan's banks faltered, the Tokyo stock market fell, and the yen lost value. This, in turn, unsettled the U.S. stock market and jeopardized U.S. exports and investments in Asia. Recognizing the threat, the administration pressed Japan to undertake needed economic reforms. As Brazil and Argentina also sank into recession, analysts questioned how long the U.S. boom could continue. All these developments underscored how deeply the United States had become enmeshed in a complex global economy (see Beyond America—Global Interactions: The Challenge of Globalization).

CLINTON'S FOREIGN POLICY: DEFINING AMERICA'S ROLE IN A POST–COLD WAR WORLD

Bill Clinton preferred domestic issues to foreign policy. Yet America could not withdraw from the world. When Clinton's attention turned abroad, he faced four key challenges: protecting U.S. trade and investment interests (see "America and the Global Economy"); using American power wisely as Russia, Eastern Europe, and the Balkans emerged from the Soviet era; promoting peace between Israel and the Palestinians; and responding to security threats, including nuclear proliferation and terrorism by Muslim extremists.

The Balkans, Russia, and Eastern Europe in the Post-Soviet Era
The aftershocks of the Soviet collapse unsettled the region of southeastern Europe known as the Balkans. In Yugoslavia, an unstable nation comprised of Serbia, Bosnia, Croatia, and other enclaves and administrative divisions, the ruling communist party gave up power in 1990. In 1991–1992, as Yugoslavia broke apart, Serbian forces launched a campaign of "ethnic cleansing" in neighboring Bosnia. This meant supporting Bosnia's ethnic Serbs while killing or driving out Muslims and Croats. Incited by Serbia's president Slobodan Milosevic, Serbian troops overran UN-designated "safe havens" and slaughtered Muslims. When a UN peacekeeping force failed to stop the killing, a joint U.S. and NATO operation launched air strikes against Bosnian Serb targets in August 1995.

Later in 1995, the Clinton administration flew the leaders of Bosnia's warring factions to Dayton, Ohio, for talks. The resulting Dayton Accords imposed a cease-fire and created a framework for governing the region. Clinton committed twenty thousand U.S. troops to a NATO force in Bosnia to enforce the cease-fire.

In 1998, Serbian forces attacked Muslims in Serbia's southern province, **Kosovo.** Early in 1999, as the bloodshed continued, NATO, under U.S. leadership, bombed Serbian facilities in Kosovo and in Serbia itself, including Belgrade, the capital. This reliance on air power, with minimal risk of U.S. casualties, became Clinton's preferred form of military engagement. Haunted by Vietnam, American public opinion wavered as well, appalled by the suffering and refugee crisis in the Balkans as well as in Rwanda (see below), but wary of expanding U.S. involvement. In June 1999, however, U.S. troops joined a NATO occupying force in Kosovo. With the Serbian army restrained, the refugees trickled back. Slobodan Milosevic was overthrown in 2001, and the new

Serbian government, eager for Western aid, delivered him to a war-crimes tribunal at the Hague. The trial ended inconclusively with Milosevic's death in 2006.

Although Russia generally backed Serbia, a traditional ally, Russian forces joined in NATO's occupation of Kosovo. Facing unrest among its own Muslim population, Russia in 1995–1996 invaded the breakaway Islamic republic of Chechnya. Some called this unpopular conflict Russia's Vietnam. Amid these troubles, Russia's hasty conversion to a free-market economy triggered an economic crisis and massive corruption that threatened the survival of President Boris Yeltsin. Having given Russia billions in loans, the Clinton administration watched anxiously as chaos threatened.

U.S. diplomacy also continued to focus on the safe disposal of nuclear weapons in the former Soviet Union. In the 1993 **Strategic Arms Reduction Treaty** (START II), the United States and Russia agreed to cut their long-range nuclear arsenals by half. This left many deactivated nuclear weapons in Russia, Ukraine, Kazakhstan, and Belarus. Both the Bush and Clinton administrations used diplomacy, economic aid, and technical assistance to assure the secure destruction of these weapons.

Despite U.S. disapproval of the Chechnya war and concern over Boris Yeltsin's alcoholism and increasingly erratic behavior, Clinton continued to support the Russian president. In 1999, the administration backed Russia's admission to the Group of Seven (G-7), the world's leading industrial nations. In the same year, however, over Russia's protests, NATO with U.S. support admitted three new members from the former Soviet bloc—Hungary, Poland, and the Czech Republic. With Yeltsin's resignation in December 1999, Prime Minister Vladimir Putin, a former agent of the KGB, the Soviet secret police, succeeded him as president.

The Middle East: Seeking an Elusive Peace, Combating a Wily Foe

After hopeful beginnings, Clinton's pursuit of peace in the Middle East failed. The 1987 Palestinian uprising, or Intifada, against Israel's military occupation of the West Bank and Gaza (see Chapter 30) continued into the 1990s. Prospects for peace brightened in 1993, after Israeli and Palestinian negotiators meeting in Norway agreed on a six-year timetable for peace. The so-called Oslo Accords provided for a Palestinian state, the return of most Israeli-held land in the West Bank and Gaza to the Palestinians, and further talks on the claims of Palestinian refugees and the final status of Jerusalem. In 1994, President Clinton presided as Israeli prime minister Yitzhak Rabin and Yasir Arafat, head of the Palestine Liberation Organization, signed the agreement at the White House.

The bloodshed continued, however, and in 1995 a young Israeli opposed to the Oslo Accords assassinated Rabin. Israel's next election brought Benjamin Netanyahu of the hard-line Likud Party to power. Suicide bombings by Palestinian extremists in 1996–1997 killed some eighty Israelis, triggering retaliatory attacks. Under U.S. pressure, Netanyahu in 1998 agreed to withdraw Israeli forces from some West Bank areas in return for security guarantees. But as attacks continued, Netanyahu halted the withdrawal. Jewish settlements, with accompanying highways, checkpoints, and infrastructure, spread across Palestinian territory. By 2000, the West Bank and Gaza had an estimated two hundred thousand Israeli settlers. Secretary of State Madeleine K. Albright struggled to persuade the two sides to resume negotiations.

Ehud Barak of Israel's more moderate Labour Party became prime minister in 1999. In July 2000, Clinton invited Barak and Arafat to Camp David. In these talks, Barak made major concessions, reportedly including Israel's withdrawal from 95

The Challenge of Globalization

A Chicago advertising copywriter, dressed casually in a top sewn in Bangladesh, jeans made in India, and shoes manufactured in South Korea, finishes a day spent working on the Toyota account. Coming home, she goes jogging (wearing her Nikes made in Brazil), orders Vietnamese take-out, and turns on her television (imported from Japan) to watch a CNN report, relayed live via satellite, of a deadly earthquake in Java. At her computer (assembled in Mexico), she clicks the website of a London-based humanitarian organization and makes a credit-card contribution to aid the victims. After checking the Nikkei stock index in Tokyo, she settles down to enjoy a book of Italian Renaissance art, printed in Hong Kong.

This is globalization. By a convergence of economic, technological, and cultural trends, humanity is becoming increasingly interconnected and interdependent.

A surge in world trade is globalization's most obvious manifestation (see "America and the Global Economy"). Total world exports of goods and services in 2004 neared $11 trillion. American consumer products—from computers, TVs, microwaves, and cell phones to sneakers, clothing, and toys—mostly come from abroad. So does information. Americans seeking help with computer problems typically talk to technicians in Dublin, Manila, New Delhi, or Bangalore.

The first effort to regulate world trade, in 1947, was the General Agreement on Tariffs and Trade, or GATT (see Chapter 26), which in 1995 became the World Trade Organization (WTO).

With 149 member nations, the WTO works to reduce trade barriers and resolve trade disputes. The European Union (EU) and the North American Free Trade Association (NAFTA) set trading policies and arbitrate trade disputes within their regions.

Despite such agencies, international trade remains contentious. U.S. and European aircraft builders battle for market share. American media companies protest China's failure to prosecute black marketeers who pirate their CDs and DVDs. Exporters of agricultural commodities to America denounce Washington's farm subsidies as a hidden tariff. When Canadian cattle ranchers and timber companies secured a WTO ruling against discriminatory U.S. trading practices, the United States simply ignored the ruling.

Economic globalization can be painful as well as turbulent. As Japanese and other foreign automakers increased their U.S. market share, American automakers fired thousands of workers (see Chapter 32). In response, Toyota and other foreign automakers point to the U.S. jobs created by their manufacturing, marketing, and advertising.

Globalization pervades the corporate world. The world's largest corporations, whatever their home base, are global in scope. GM, Ford, Caterpillar, and other U.S. businesses operate worldwide. Seattle-based Starbucks sells coffee in thirty-seven countries.

European and Asian conglomerates are major players in the United States. In 2005, foreign investment in U.S. companies totaled $1.5 trillion. The U.S. holdings of the German-based Bertelsmann Group include the book publishers Doubleday, Random House, and Knopf; the magazines *Family Circle, Parents,* and *McCall's;* and the Arista and RCA record labels.

Economic globalization stirs opposition, often with good reason. American labor leaders and activists charge that multinational corporations, working through local contractors, operate factories where the workers, often young women, live in prison-like barracks away from their families, laboring long hours at repetitive tasks for a pittance in wages with no benefits. Environmentalists deplore these factories' dismal environmental record. Activists pressure Wal-Mart and other mass marketers to monitor their foreign suppliers' labor policies more strictly. The annual WTO meetings, from Seattle in 1999 to Hong Kong in 2005, regularly attract protesters who charge the United States and other rich nations with contributing to environmental degradation through their trading policies and exploiting workers in poor countries.

Most economists argue that, on balance, globalization benefits America. U.S. popular-culture products and some information-technology innovations, for example, are highly sought after abroad. But globalization has also meant major disruptions for U.S. workers and raised troubling ethical and public-policy issues.

Some fear that globalization compromises national sovereignty. A political firestorm erupted in 2006 when a company based in Dubai, an Arab emirate in the Persian Gulf, acquired a British firm that manages America's East Coast ports. Politicians angrily complained that even port security was being outsourced (that is, shifted abroad). The Dubai company backed off, seeking a U.S. buyer for this portion of its operations.

Globalization is more than trade, jobs, and finance. In today's world, issues of life and death transcend national borders. Environmental hazards such as global warming require a global response (see Chapter 32, "Technology and Culture: Developing New Tools for Measuring Global Warming"). Public-health dangers—from malaria, tuberculosis, and AIDS to impure water and a threatened avian flu pandemic—preoccupy international health organizations.

As the Beatles and the Rolling Stones first demonstrated in the 1960s, globalization is also a cultural phenomenon. Celebrity musicians and orchestra conductors jet around the world. U.S. movies, TV series, and popular music attract a global following. For millions, Coca Cola and McDonald's symbolize American culture. American televangelists spread their beliefs globally via communications satellites. Americans, in turn, listen to West African popular music; savor Thai, Ethiopian, and Cuban food; practice Yoga and T'ai Chi; buy CDs by Scandinavian rock groups; play Japanese video games; and enjoy British comedy or Puerto Rican jazz festivals on public television.

Satellite TV and the Internet have created a global communication grid. In December 2004, when a tsunami triggered by an Indian Ocean earthquake killed thousands of people in Indonesia and other countries, magazines, TV, and Internet websites carried heart-rending images of the devastation, producing a world-wide outpouring of contributions, volunteer relief efforts, and fundraising concerts.

But cultural globalization also stirs protests, with the United States a frequent target. Cultural nationalists in France and other countries try to erect barriers against the inroads of American movies, TV, and fast food. Islamist fundamentalists denounce the popular culture of the West, with its global saturation, as a threat to Islamic values and practices.

More than forty years ago, in *Understanding Media* (1964), the Canadian scholar Marshall McLuhan foresaw an emerging "global village." Wrote McLuhan: "[A]fter more than a century of electronic technology, we have extended our central nervous system itself in a global embrace, abolishing both space and time." The intervening decades amply confirmed McLuhan's insight. For better or worse, globalization—and the reactions against it—have become driving forces in our comtemporary world.

Questions for Analysis

- What economic, technological, and cultural developments underlie globalization?

- In what specific ways does globalization affect your everyday life?

percent of the West Bank and all of Gaza; the creation of a Palestinian state; Palestinian control of East Jerusalem; and the transfer of Jerusalem's Temple Mount, sacred to both Muslims and Jews, to a vaguely defined "religious authority." In return, the PLO would end hostilities and give up further claims on Israel.

Arafat rejected Barak's offer, however, and the summit failed. In September, the Likud leader Ariel Sharon—with nearly one thousand Israeli soldiers and police—made a provocative foray onto Temple Mount, symbolically asserting Israel's control of the site. Soon after, Palestinians launched a new Intifada against Israel. In 2001, Israelis elected Sharon prime minister. As Clinton left office, the Israeli-Palestinian conflict raged on (see Chapter 32).

Iraq also demanded Clinton's attention. After the Persian Gulf War, the United Nations had imposed strict sanctions on Iraqi oil exports and set up an inspection system to prevent Iraq from building chemical or nuclear weapons. In 1997, when Saddam Hussein barred UN inspectors from certain sites, Clinton dispatched ships, bombers, and thirty thousand troops to the Persian Gulf. He sought to rally support for a military strike, as George Bush had done in 1991, but France, Russia, and various Arab states resisted. Clinton drew back after the UN secretary general, Kofi Annan, secured Saddam's agreement to open inspections. Saddam soon reneged, however, and the crisis continued (see Chapter 32).

Nuclear Proliferation, Terrorism, and Peacekeeping Challenges	Nations that signed the 1968 Nuclear Nonproliferation Treaty pledged not to develop nuclear weapons. India and Pakistan, long at odds over Kashmir, did not sign, however, and in 1988 India tested a nuclear bomb. Despite urgent pleas from the United States and other powers, Pakistan followed suit. Both the Bush and Clinton administrations imposed sanctions on the two countries, but

the spread of nuclear weapons in this region deepened proliferation fears.

Communist North Korea also roused concern. Despite having signed the Nonproliferation Treaty, North Korea began a program of nuclear-weapons development and missile testing. In 1994, facing UN economic sanctions and the loss of $9 billion in international assistance, North Korea pledged to halt its nuclear-weapons program. In 1999, confronting famine and economic crisis, North Korea suspended long-range missile testing in return for an easing of U.S. trade and travel restrictions. The country's nuclear intentions remained worrisome.

Attacks by anti-American Islamic extremists continued. In February 1993, a powerful bomb exploded in a parking garage beneath one of the towers of New York's World Trade Center. Six persons died in the blast and hundreds were injured as fifty thousand workers hastily evacuated. Five Islamic militants, including a blind Egyptian sheik, Omar Abdel Rhaman, the alleged mastermind, were arrested. Three, including Sheik Omar, were convicted of murder and given life sentences.

In 1992, President Bush had committed some twenty-six thousand U.S. troops to a UN humanitarian mission to Somalia, an East African nation afflicted by civil war and famine. As the warring factions battled, forty-four Americans were killed, including eighteen murdered in Mogadishu, Somalia's capital. President Clinton withdrew the U.S. force in 1994, and the UN mission ended a year later. Later evidence implicated anti-American Islamic extremists loyal to **Osama bin Laden** in the Mogadishu killings. A wealthy Saudi Arabian and Islamic fundamentalist militant, bin Laden had been expelled from Saudi Arabia in 1991 and taken refuge in Sudan, where he financed large-scale construction and agricultural projects but also planned anti-Western terrorist activities.

Two bombings at U.S. military installations in Saudi Arabia in 1995–1996 killed twenty-four Americans. On August 7, 1998, simultaneous bomb blasts at the U.S. embassies in Nairobi, Kenya, and Dar-es-Salaam, Tanzania, killed 220, including Americans and many local people. U.S. intelligence again pinpointed Osama bin Laden as the mastermind of the attacks. Expelled from Sudan in 1996, bin Laden had shifted his base of operations to Afghanistan, where he organized terrorist training camps. Clinton ordered cruise missile strikes on one of bin Laden's Afghan camps as well as on a suspected chemical-weapons factory in Sudan allegedly financed by bin Laden. A U.S. grand jury indicted bin Laden on charges of planning the embassy attacks and also of inciting the earlier killing of GIs in Somalia.

In 1999, Clinton called for redoubled efforts against rogue states and terrorist groups in danger of acquiring nuclear, chemical, or biological weapons. "[W]e are involved here in a long-term struggle . . . ," declared Secretary of State Albright. "This is, unfortunately, the war of the future." Underscoring Albright's grim assessment, on October 12, 2000, a bomb aboard a small boat in the harbor of Aden, Yemen, ripped a gaping hole in the U.S. destroyer *Cole*, killing seventeen sailors.

Closer home, in Haiti, a Caribbean island-nation wracked by poverty and disease, a military junta overthrew President Jean-Bertrand Aristide in September 1991 and terrorized his supporters. In 1991–1993, thousands of Haitians set out for Florida in leaky boats, only to be intercepted by the U.S. Coast Guard and returned to an uncertain fate in Haiti. Pressured by Haitian-Americans and U.S. black leaders, the Clinton administration supported a 1994 UN resolution authorizing military action against the junta. With a U.S.-led invasion flotilla anchored offshore, the junta's leaders went into exile, and Aristide, backed by a U.S. occupation force, resumed the presidency. (Ten years later, facing another uprising, Aristide again went into exile, and a UN peacekeeping force arrived to maintain order.)

A New World Order Painfully Emerges The peaceful post–Cold War era that many had anticipated seemed an ever-receding mirage as Americans of the 1990s confronted international issues of maddening complexity.

The USS *Cole* After a Suicide Bombing During a Refueling Stop in the Port of Aden, October 2000 *The bomb, concealed in a small boat that came alongside the Cole, killed seventeen U.S. sailors and injured many more. These years saw a rising level of terrorist attacks by anti-American militants based in the Middle East and in North Africa.*

The Soviet adversary had collapsed, and the threat of global thermonuclear war receded, but crises still flared around the world. Like firefighters battling many small blazes rather than a single conflagration, policy makers now wrestled with a baffling tangle of issues. Somalia, Bosnia, Iraq, Kosovo, North Korea, Pakistan, Afghanistan, Israel, the Palestinians, shadowy terrorist cells—all demanded attention.

Confronting such complexities, some citizens simply gave up. In a 1997 poll, only 20 percent of Americans said that they followed foreign news, down sharply from the 1980s, with the biggest drop among young people. TV coverage of events abroad fell by more than 50 percent from 1989 to 1995. Seeking to clarify the confusing world situation, analysts noted at least four large-scale trends in the post–Cold War era:

- First, economic considerations played an ever-greater role in international affairs. Multinational networks of trade, communications, and finance increasingly shaped America's foreign-policy interests. (See Beyond America—Global Interactions: The Challenge of Globalization.)

- Second, a growing chasm divided the prosperous, comparatively stable industrialized world from societies marked by poverty, disease, illiteracy, and explosive population growth. This vast gulf helped spawn resentment, hatred, and even terrorism.

- Third, despite and partially because of a globalizing economy and mass culture, ethnic divisions and religious fundamentalisms intensified. The lethal ethno-religious conflict in the former Yugoslavia was far from unique. Similar clashes erupted in many other regions. In the tiny Central African Republic of Rwanda, as many as a million people perished in genocidal violence in 1994, as militias of the ruling Hutu ethnic group systematically massacred members of the once-dominant Tutsi group. Thousands more fled in panic, creating a massive refugee crisis. (The 2004 film *Hotel Rwanda*, about a courageous Rwandan hotel manager who sheltered over a thousand Tutsi refugees, conveys the horror of the genocide.) Traumatized by the Somalia fiasco, President Clinton failed to intervene.

  As Muslim fundamentalists denounced Western liberalism and secularism, a small but lethal minority embraced violence as a religious duty. Some Israeli Jews (supported by U.S. Christian fundamentalists) claimed a God-given right to Palestinian lands. In India, violence erupted in 1992 when Hindu militants destroyed an ancient Muslim mosque they claimed had been built on an even more ancient Hindu shrine. Tensions increased when a fundamentalist Hindu party gained power in India in 1998.

- Finally, the United Nations worked to define its role in the new era. With the Cold War's end, many Americans pulled back from engaging with the world community. Some even demanded U.S. withdrawal from the United Nations. Others, however, found reason to hope that the United Nations, long a pawn of the superpowers' conflict, might at last function as its supporters had hoped in 1945. Indeed, by 2000 more than forty thousand UN peacekeeping forces and civilian personnel were serving in fifteen world trouble spots. UN agencies addressed global environmental, nutritional, public-health, and human-rights issues. UN-sponsored judicial bodies brought to justice perpetrators of terrible deeds in Bosnia, Rwanda, and elsewhere.

Despite the countertrends, opinion polls indicated that most Americans supported internationalist approaches to world problems and viewed the UN favorably, despite its flaws and shortcomings. While attention to foreign affairs sometimes flagged, Americans could become engaged when they understood an issue in human terms. With the Cold War over, America's position as simply one player—albeit a major player—in a truly global order became inescapably clear.

THE CLINTON ERA ENDS: DOMESTIC POLITICS, IMPEACHMENT, DISPUTED ELECTION, 1996–2000

Straddling the political center, Bill Clinton won reelection in 1996. His second term saw a battle over tobacco-industry regulation, a commitment of U.S. forces in Kosovo, and a final effort to resolve the Israeli-Palestinian dispute. It is mainly remembered, however, for a sex scandal that led to Clinton's impeachment—a crisis that further poisoned a contentious political climate. A disputed presidential election in 2000 did little to heal the nation's divisions.

Campaign 1996 and After: Battling Big Tobacco; Balancing the Budget

Bill Clinton had won the nickname "the Comeback Kid" after a long-shot victory in the 1992 New Hampshire primary, and after the 1994 Republican landslide he again hit the comeback trail. The Republicans suffered a black eye in 1995 when House Speaker Newt Gingrich, battling Clinton over the budget, twice allowed a partial government shutdown.

Clinton got another lucky break: a weak Republican opponent. When General Colin Powell, the popular former chairman of the Joint Chiefs of Staff, declined to run, Kansas senator Bob Dole, a partially disabled World War II hero, won the nomination. The seventy-three-year-old Dole ran a lackluster campaign, and Clinton won with 49 percent of the vote, to Dole's 41 percent. (The Texas maverick H. Ross Perot garnered 8 percent.) The Republicans held control of Congress, though GOP legislators proved less combative than after their 1994 triumph.

Fundraising scandals marked the 1996 contest as TV advertising continued to drive up campaign expenses. A Democratic fundraiser with links to Indonesian and possibly Chinese businesses raised $3.4 million. After an event at a Los Angeles Buddhist temple attended by Vice President Al Gore, priests and nuns sworn to poverty contributed over a hundred thousand dollars to the Democratic cause. The money apparently came from Asian businessmen seeking favor with the administration.

Tobacco regulation, a major public-health issue, loomed large in Clinton's second term. In 1997, facing lawsuits by former smokers and by states saddled with medical costs linked to smoking-related diseases, the tobacco industry agreed to pay some $368 billion in settlement. The agreement limited tobacco advertising, especially when directed at young people.

Since the agreement required government approval, the debate now shifted to Washington. Southern legislators close to the tobacco companies defended the industry, but the Clinton administration backed a bill imposing tougher penalties, higher cigarette taxes, and stronger antismoking measures. Supporters of this bill documented the industry's manipulation of nicotine levels and targeting of children. The industry struck back with a $40 million lobbying campaign and heavy contributions to key legislators, killing the bill. The Republican Party, commented John McCain, Arizona's maverick Republican senator, appeared to be "in the pocket of the tobacco companies."

In 1998, the tobacco industry reached a new settlement, scaled back to $206 billion, with forty-six states. In 1999, Clinton ordered the Justice Department to sue the tobacco industry for $280 billion to cover Medicare costs for treating smoking-related illnesses. (In 2005 a federal judge threw out this lawsuit, and the Supreme Court rejected the government's appeal.)

Following his strategy of offering modest proposals that appealed to progressives without alienating moderates, Clinton in his January 1998 State of the Union address offered some initiatives to help the poor, such as enrolling the nation's 3 million uninsured children in Medicaid. But he also introduced proposals attractive to the middle class (college-tuition tax credits; extending Medicare to early retirees) and to fiscal conservatives (reducing the national debt; shoring up social security). Some liberals dismissed the speech as "Progressivism Lite," but it had political appeal, and under normal conditions would have certified Clinton's political comeback.

Scandal Grips the White House But conditions were not normal. Even as Clinton spoke, scandal swirled around the White House. Adultery charges had long clung to Clinton, and now he faced the Paula Jones sexual-harassment suit, dating from his days as Arkansas governor. The Supreme Court had helped Jones's case by permitting lawsuits against sitting presidents.

Seeking to show a pattern of sexual harassment, Jones's lawyers subpoenaed Clinton and quizzed him about reports linking him to a young White House intern, **Monica Lewinsky.** The president denied everything, as did Lewinsky. As the rumors became public (via an Internet website devoted to political gossip), Clinton denounced them as false. Hillary Clinton blamed "a vast right-wing conspiracy." In fact, political conservatives *were* digging for damaging information on Clinton, and he helpfully provided them with ample material. Clinton settled Paula Jones's suit by paying her $850,000, but more problems awaited. In telephone conversations illegally taped by her "friend" Linda Tripp, Monica Lewinsky had described an affair with Clinton from 1995, when she was twenty-one, through early 1997. In January 1998, Tripp passed the tapes to Kenneth Starr, an independent counsel appointed to investigate the Clintons' murky real-estate dealings in Arkansas. At Starr's request, FBI agents fitted Tripp with a recording device and secured further Lewinsky evidence.

Starr's investigation now shifted to whether Clinton had committed perjury in his Paula Jones testimony and if he had persuaded Lewinsky to lie. In August, after jail threats and a promise of immunity, Lewinsky admitted the affair before Starr's grand jury. Soon after, in videotaped testimony, Clinton admitted "conduct that was wrong" with Lewinsky but denied a "sexual relationship" under his narrow definition of the term. In a brief TV address, Clinton conceded "inappropriate" behavior with Lewinsky, but called his testimony in the Jones lawsuit "legally accurate" and attacked Starr as politically motivated.

Other presidents had pursued extramarital affairs, but by the 1990s changing standards, sexual-harassment laws, and the glare of media publicity had made such behavior more objectionable and harder to conceal. Unsurprisingly, the scandal unfolded in tabloid headlines, late-night television jokes, Internet humor, and conservative radio talk shows.

In a September 1998 report to the House Judiciary Committee, Kenneth Starr narrated the Clinton-Lewinsky affair in lurid detail. He recommended impeachment on the grounds that Clinton had committed perjury, influenced others to do so, and obstructed justice by retrieving gifts he had given Lewinsky and coaching his secretary on his version of events.

The Judiciary Committee, on a party-line vote, forwarded four articles of impeachment to the House of Representatives. In a similarly partisan vote, the House approved and sent to the Senate two articles of impeachment: perjury and obstruction of justice. Clinton thus became the first president since Andrew Johnson to be impeached (though Nixon came close).

Opinion polls sent the Republicans an ominous message: most Americans opposed impeachment. In the 1998 midterm elections, as the impeachment process unfolded, the Democrats gained five House seats.

Since removing a president requires a two-thirds Senate vote and the Republicans held only fifty-five Senate seats, the impeachment process seemed foredoomed. Nevertheless, in January 1999 the trial began. As Chief Justice William Rehnquist presided, House Republicans presented their case. White House lawyers challenged what one called a "witches' brew of speculation."

Through it all, Clinton's approval ratings soared. While people deplored his behavior, few believed that it met the Constitution's "high crimes and misdemeanors" standard for removal from office. With the economy booming and Clinton's political positions generally popular, the public appeared willing to tolerate his personal flaws. Further, many saw him as the target of Republican zealots.

On February 12, the Senate rejected the impeachment charges and ended the trial. While some Republicans spoke darkly of a double standard of justice, most Americans simply felt relief. In January 2001, as he left office, Clinton admitted to perjury, paid a $25,000 fine, and lost his law license for five years.

While escaping the worst, Clinton had suffered grievous damage, mostly self-inflicted. He remained active in his final two years in office, committing U.S. forces to Kosovo and working to resolve the Israeli-Palestinian dispute, for example, but the scandal unquestionably eroded his leadership and tarnished his presidency.

The Republican Party suffered as well, as some of its most partisan members took center stage, rubbing raw the divisions roiling the nation. In 1999 Newt Gingrich, closely identified with the impeachment effort, and embroiled in ethical controversies and issues involving his marital life, resigned as Speaker and left Congress.

Election 2000: Bush Versus Gore

As the 2000 campaign got under way, the Democrats, bouncing back from the impeachment crisis, confidently nominated Vice President Al Gore for the top job. As his running mate, Gore chose Connecticut senator Joseph Lieberman, making him the first Jewish-American candidate on a major party ticket. (Barry Goldwater, the Republican presidential candidate in 1964, was of Jewish ancestry, but his father had converted to the Episcopal faith.) The fact that Lieberman had denounced the Lewinsky affair and Clinton's attempted cover-up helped insulate Gore from the "sleaze factor" in the Clinton legacy.

The Republican contest narrowed to Arizona senator John McCain, a former prisoner of war in Vietnam, and Texas governor **George W. Bush,** son of the former president. McCain, a champion of campaign-finance reform and a critic of corporate influences in his party, made a strong bid. Bush, however, with powerful backers and a folksy manner, won the nomination. His running mate Dick Cheney, defense secretary in the first Bush administration, had more recently headed the Halliburton Corporation, a Texas energy company. The Green Party nominated consumer advocate Ralph Nader.

Both Gore and Bush courted the center while trying to hold their bases. For Bush, this meant corporate interests, religious conservatives, and the so-called Reagan Democrats in the middle and working classes. Gore's base included liberals, academics and professionals, union members, African-Americans, and many Hispanics.

Gore pointed to the nation's prosperity (downplaying signs of weakness) and pledged to extend health-care coverage and protect social security. In televised debates Gore was far more articulate and displayed greater mastery of detail than Bush. But the vice president, tainted by fund-raising scandals in the 1996 campaign, had image problems. Many voters found him pompous. The factual mastery he displayed in the debates struck some as arrogant. Eager to prove his political independence, Gore distanced himself from Clinton, despite the president's popularity.

Bush, with an easygoing manner but little national or foreign-policy experience, was widely seen as a lightweight wholly dependent on family influence. As one Texas Democrat quipped, "George was born on third base and thought he had hit a home run." Calling himself a "compassionate conservative," Bush subtly reminded voters of Clinton's misdeeds by promising to restore dignity to the White House. Polls showed that most voters agreed with Gore on the issues, approved the Democrats' economic policies, and conceded Gore's intellectual edge. Ominously for Gore, however, they preferred Bush as a person. The election seemed a toss-up.

The resulting disputed election worsened the partisan rancor of these years, so evident in the impeachment crisis. Gore won the popular vote by more than 500,000, but the Electoral College remained up for grabs. The struggle narrowed to Florida, whose twenty-five electoral votes would determine the outcome.

Flaws in Florida's electoral process quickly became apparent. In Palm Beach County, a poorly designed ballot led several thousand Gore supporters to vote for Pat Buchanan, running on Ross Perot's Reform Party ticket. In other counties with many poor and African-American voters, antiquated voting machines rejected thousands of ballots in which the paper tabs, called "chads," were not fully punched out. When Gore supporters demanded a hand count of these rejected ballots, Bush's lawyers sued to stop the recounts. Florida's secretary of state, Katherine Harris (the co-chair of Bush's Florida campaign and an ally of Florida governor Jeb Bush, the candidate's brother), refused to extend the deadline for certifying the vote, making a recount more difficult.

On November 21 the Florida Supreme Court, with a preponderance of Democrats, unanimously ruled that a hand recount should constitute the official result. Bush's lawyers appealed to the U.S. Supreme Court. Despite a well-established precedent of letting state courts decide electoral disputes, the justices accepted the case. Overturning the Florida ruling, the Supreme Court on December 4 sent the case back to Tallahassee for clarification.

Meanwhile, on November 26, Katherine Harris had certified the Florida vote, awarding Bush the state. But on December 8, ten days before the scheduled Electoral College vote, the Florida Supreme Court ordered an immediate recount of all suspect ballots. "At this rate," mused a radio commentator, "the Inaugural Ball will be a surprise party."

The U.S. Supreme Court again heard an appeal, and on December 12, by a 5-to-4 vote, halted the recount. Gore conceded the next day. Five Supreme Court justices (all Republican appointees) had made George W. Bush president. Ralph Nader also helped Bush's cause. Had the 97,488 Floridians who voted for Nader not had that option, Gore would probably have won the state and the presidency.

The election produced an evenly divided Senate. Each party had fifty senators, giving Vice President Cheney the deciding vote. (The Republicans narrowly held the House of Representatives.) **Hillary Rodham Clinton** won election as senator from New York, becoming the first presidential wife to pursue an independent political career. Overall, the new Senate included thirteen women, a record number.

As he left office, Bill Clinton issued presidential pardons to 167 people, including his half-brother, in trouble on drug charges; persons caught up in Clinton-related scandals; and white-collar offenders who had White House influence or were big Democratic contributors, including a commodities trader holed up in Switzerland to avoid trial for tax evasion and other crimes. Despite Clinton's political skills and good intentions, few expressed regret as he left Washington.

Would George W. Bush heal the nation's divisions and pursue a wise foreign-policy course? Americans waited hopefully.

CULTURAL TRENDS AT CENTURY'S END

American life in the 1990s reflected both the decade's prosperity and its cultural conflicts. While the newly rich flaunted their wealth and Americans pursued leisure diversions, undercurrents of violence also marked the decade. As cultural disagreements deepened, the values of openness and tolerance for diversity seemed under threat.

Affluence and a Search for Heroes   The economic boom of the 1990s produced instant fortunes for some and an orgy of consumption that set the decade's tone. Wall Street and Silicon Valley spawned thousands of youthful millionaires. In 1997, surveying the lifestyles of the newly rich, *Vanity Fair* magazine described New York as "the champagne city, making the brash consumption of the 1980s look like the depression." Elegant restaurants offered absurdly expensive cigars and rare wines, and exclusive shops sold $13,000 handbags. In 1999, the nation's top one hundred advertisers spent $43 billion promoting their goods.

The boom also encouraged a hard-edged "winner take all" mentality like that of the Gilded Age, when the rich had turned their backs on the larger society. In *Bowling Alone: The Collapse and Revival of American Community* (2000), political scientist Robert Putnam found diminished civic engagement and weakened interest in public issues, as evidenced by declines in voting, political activism, and civic participation. He even claimed to find less informal socializing, from dinners with friends to card parties and bowling leagues. While some saw the Internet as a new form of community, Putnam viewed it as further evidence of a diminished public sphere.

Anecdotal evidence supported Putnam's conclusions. A 1997 survey of college students found that 77 percent expected to become millionaires. *The Prayer of Jabez* (2000), a best-selling motivational book, cited a shepherd's prayer recorded in the Bible ("Bless me indeed, and enlarge my territory") as a key to success. "If Jabez had worked on Wall Street," wrote the author, "he might have prayed 'Lord, increase the value of my investment portfolio.'"

With the stock market surging, the Cold War over, and new threats only coming into focus, many Americans set out to enjoy themselves. Attendance at the Disney theme parks in Florida and California neared 30 million in 2000. The sales of bulky sport-utility vehicles (SUVs) soared. When a White House press secretary was asked in 2001 if people should reduce consumption to conserve energy, he replied, "[I]t should be the goal of policy makers to protect the American way of life—the American way of life is a blessèd one."

As in the 1980s, the mass culture offered escapist fare. Popular movies included historical extravaganzas like *Braveheart* (1995) and *Gladiator* (2000). The 1997 blockbuster *Titanic*, with spectacular special effects, grossed $600 million. The top-rated TV show of 1999–2000, *Who Wants to Be a Millionaire?*, celebrated raw greed. So-called reality shows like *Survivor* offered viewers a risk-free taste of the hazards that American life itself (at least for the privileged) conspicuously lacked.

Millions avidly followed TV coverage of the 1995 trial of O. J. Simpson, a former football star accused of killing his former wife and her friend. The 1996 murder of a six-year-old Colorado girl whose parents had pushed her into child beauty pageants similarly mesmerized the public. The Clinton sex scandals often seemed little more than another media diversion in a sensation-hungry decade.

However, as in the 1980s, popular-culture evidence can also suggest a more complex picture. For example, some critics interpreted *Titanic,* which sided with its working-class hero in steerage against the rich snobs in first class, as a comment on America's widening class differences. One even called the movie "an exercise in class hatred." The 1992 Clint Eastwood western *Unforgiven,* winner of the Academy Award for best picture, expressed nostalgia for an era when life presented rugged challenges and hard moral choices. The same longings, some suggested, underlay the tide of admiring biographies of past heroes, such as Stephen Ambrose's *Eisenhower* (1991) and David McCullough's *Truman* (1993).

Americans of the 1990s also relived the heroic era of World War II in TV specials, books such as Tom Brokaw's *The Greatest Generation* (1998), and movies like *Saving Private Ryan* (1998) and *Pearl Harbor* (2001). The *New York Times* columnist Frank Rich saw *Pearl Harbor* as "more about the present than the past," reflecting longing "for what is missing in our national life: some cause larger than ourselves." Concluded Rich: "Even those Americans who are . . . foggy about World War II . . . know intuitively that it was fought over something more blessed than the right to guzzle gas."

Outbursts of Violence Stir Concern	A popular 1999 film, *American Beauty*, and TV's *The Sopranos,* an HBO series about a mobster and his family, which debuted in 1999, explored dark impulses and violent undercurrents in American life. The violence was not limited to

pop-culture fantasy. True, the overall crime rate fell nearly 20 percent between 1992 and 2000—a decline experts attributed to prosperity, stricter gun-control laws, a drop in the young male population, the waning crack-cocaine epidemic, and tougher sentencing rules. (The U.S. prison population approached 2 million by 2000.)

But bursts of violence punctuated the decade. The annual toll of gun deaths exceeded twenty-eight thousand in 2000. Multiple shootings drew special attention. In 1999 an Atlanta man distraught by investment losses shot and killed nine employees at a financial firm. Also in 1999, two students at Columbine High School near Denver fatally shot twelve students and a teacher before committing suicide. These episodes produced anxious discussions of America's obsession with firearms, the alleged breakdown of parental authority, and the influence of mass-media violence. After the Columbine massacre President Clinton again called for stricter gun-control laws, but the firearms lobby, led by the National Rifle Association, fought such efforts.

The violence sometimes reflected the intensity of the nation's culture wars. In 1998, two youths tortured and murdered a gay student at the University of Wyoming, Matthew Shepard, because of his sexual orientation. As the abortion controversy raged, some "pro-life" advocates turned violent. In 1995 an anti-abortion activist fatally shot a physician and his bodyguard outside a Florida abortion clinic, and an unstable youth murdered two people and wounded five others at a clinic near Boston. In 1997 bombers struck abortion clinics in Tulsa and Atlanta. The following year, a Buffalo physician who performed abortions was shot dead.

Criticizing the NRA *Amid a wave of school shootings, a political cartoonist offered a sardonic comment on the National Rifle Association's enthusiastic defense of the right to gun ownership.*

On April 19, 1995, in the decade's most horrifying burst of mass violence, five thousand pounds of explosives concealed in a rental truck demolished the nine-story Murrah Federal Building in Oklahoma City, Oklahoma. The blast killed 168 people, including 19 children in the building's day-care center. Police soon arrested Timothy McVeigh, a Gulf War veteran with vague links to secretive antigovernment militia groups obsessed with conspiracy theories. McVeigh, convicted of murder, was executed in 2001. A coconspirator, Terry Nichols, received a life sentence.

The **Oklahoma City bombing** came precisely two years after a government raid on the Waco, Texas, compound of the Branch Davidians, an apocalyptic religious sect led by David Koresh, charged with firearms violations. An earlier raid in February 1993 had left four government agents and six Davidians dead. The April raid ended tragically when fires probably set by Koresh and others erupted inside the compound as federal tanks moved in, leaving some eighty Branch Davidians dead. Timothy McVeigh claimed that his Oklahoma City attack was in retaliation for the deaths at Waco.

Culture Wars: A Broader View   Fortunately, the decade's culture wars typically involved words and symbolic gestures, not bullets and bombs. For example, the Smithsonian Institution canceled a 1995 exhibit marking the fiftieth anniversary of the atomic bombing of Japan when politicians and veterans' organizations attacked it for documenting the bombs' human toll and for presenting differing views of President Truman's decision.

But if the culture wars, whose origins lay in the 1960s, did not often descend into violence, they did involve fierce contests that some viewed as nothing less than a struggle for the nation's soul. The Christian Coalition's attempted takeover of the Republican Party was part of a larger campaign to reverse what conservatives saw as America's moral decay. In the nineteenth century, cultural conflicts had pitted native-born Protestants against Catholic and Jewish immigrants. During the Cold War, the ideological menace had been external: atheistic communism, centered in Moscow. Now many Americans applied the same black-and-white world view to the home front, and searched for the enemy within.

The struggle unfolded on many fronts, from televangelists' programs, bookstore shelves, and radio talk shows to school-board protests, shouting matches at family-planning clinics, and boycotts of TV shows deemed immoral. Religious conservatives proposed a constitutional amendment permitting prayer in classrooms and called for a renewal of traditional morality and "family values." Other groups criticized history textbooks for being insufficiently patriotic or excessively multicultural.

As gays and lesbians grew more vocal politically (and more visible in the media), conservative politicians at the state and local level continued to mobilize against their demands for equality. The Southern Baptist Convention, America's largest Protestant denomination, urged a boycott of Disney World because it had unofficially sponsored "Gay Pride" days.

The fast-growing evangelical and charismatic churches, including suburban megachurches with thousands of members, denounced society's wickedness and the government's complicity in the moral decline. In 1997 some seven hundred thousand men representing a conservative Protestant movement called Promise Keepers rallied in Washington, D.C., for a day of prayer, hymn singing, and pledges to reclaim moral leadership of their households. President Clinton's sexual misdeeds underscored for conservatives the moral rot they saw eating away at America.

Pat Robertson's *The New World Order* (1991) saw much of world history as a vast conspiracy that will soon end in the rule of the Antichrist. The best-selling *Left Behind* series of novels (1995–2004), coauthored by the conservative activist Tim LaHaye (see Chapter 30) and loosely based on certain biblical prophecies, described an End Time apocalypse in which Jesus Christ and an army of true believers will destroy the sinister forces of evil increasingly dominating the modern world.

The culture warriors experienced frustration as well as successes. The Christian Coalition and other religious conservative groups complained bitterly about Republican politicians who courted their votes but ignored their agenda once in power.

In *One Nation After All* (1998), sociologist Alan Wolfe reported on his interviews with middle-class Americans, whom he found accepting of diversity and suspicious of extremist positions. The virtues of tolerance and live-and-let-live, Wolfe suggested, still prevailed in Middle America. As one of Wolfe's interviewees reflected, "[W]e can't just stand back and whine about the ways things are. . . . We've got to move forward and trust that we can . . . get to a solution eventually." In its optimism and moderate tone, such a perspective captured a deep-seated pragmatic approach to cultural differences, and struck a cautiously encouraging note amid the clash of contending viewpoints as the twentieth century ended.

Conclusion

As the Soviet Union's collapse transformed the international order, President Reagan's successor, George Bush, confronted new challenges. Bush successfully handled the major foreign crisis he faced, rallying home-front support and mobilizing a multinational coalition to repel Iraq's invasion of Kuwait. Domestically, however, Bush faltered in dealing with a recession, racial violence, and environmental hazards, and in 1992 he lost to the Democrat Bill Clinton.

The failure of Clinton's sweeping health-care reform plan, coupled with other missteps, laid the groundwork for a Republican landslide in the 1994 midterm elections. Adapting to a more conservative political climate, Clinton signed a welfare-reform bill sponsored by Republicans. A rebounding economy that stimulated a stock-market boom helped Clinton's political standing. While the good times benefited some, including white-collar service workers and those involved with computer-based information technologies, most inner-city residents and displaced industrial workers did not share in the general prosperity.

Internationally, the Clinton administration worked to combat nuclear proliferation and joined in multinational efforts to halt ethnic violence in the Balkans. Clinton stood aside as genocidal slaughter overwhelmed Rwanda, however, and despite his determined peacemaking efforts, the Israeli-Palestinian conflict raged on.

The political and cultural conflicts of the later 1990s were intensified by the political mobilization of conservative Christian evangelicals; by differences over such emotion-laden issues as abortion and homosexuality; and by Clinton's own indiscretions. Caught in lies as he tried to conceal an embarrassing sex scandal, Clinton was impeached by a highly partisan House of Representatives. Though he escaped removal from office, his reputation suffered. In the disputed 2000 presidential election, finally resolved by the Supreme Court, George W. Bush, son of the former president Bush, defeated Vice President Al Gore.

Newly affluent Americans flaunting their wealth helped set the cultural tone of the 1990s. However, outbursts of violence, from school shootings to a catastrophic bombing in Oklahoma City, coupled with profound cultural divisions and a poisonous political climate, left many citizens feeling deeply apprehensive as the nation entered a new century.

32

Global Dangers, Global Challenges, 2001 to the Present

AMERICA UNDER ATTACK: SEPTEMBER 11, 2001, AND ITS AFTERMATH

Although George W. Bush had campaigned as a centrist, his early appointments and proposals suggested a hard-line conservative approach. On September 11, 2001, a horrific attack by airplane hijackers on U.S. buildings and citizens riveted the nation's attention. Targeting the mastermind of the attack, Bush mobilized a multinational coalition to invade Osama bin Laden's stronghold in Afghanistan. He also secured new laws and reorganized federal agencies to tighten homeland security. Insisting that Iraq's dictator Saddam Hussein had conspired in the 9/11 attacks and possessed weapons of mass destruction, Bush launched an invasion of Iraq as well.

The Bush Administration Begins
George W. Bush, who turned fifty-five in 2001, was a president's son and a senator's grandson. After graduating from Yale, serving in the Texas Air National Guard during the Vietnam War, and earning an MBA at Harvard, Bush entered the oil business in Texas. He was known for partying and drinking, but a religious conversion and marriage to Laura Welch stabilized his life. Bush's business ventures failed, but in 1989 he joined a group that bought the Texas Rangers baseball team. This visibility, plus family connections, helped him win the Texas governorship in 1994 and the Republican presidential nomination in 2000. **Richard (Dick) Cheney** became his running mate (see Chapter 31).

Bush named **Colin Powell,** former head of the Joint Chiefs of Staff, as secretary of state, making him the highest-ranking African-American to serve in a presidential administration. **Condoleezza Rice** of Stanford University, also African-American, became national security adviser even though her academic specialization, Soviet affairs, had become less relevant with the end of the Cold War.

Other Bush appointees were, like Vice President Cheney, veterans of earlier Republican administrations with corporate ties. Secretary of Defense **Donald Rumsfeld** had held the same post under President Ford and later headed a pharmaceutical company. Treasury Secretary Paul O'Neill had been CEO of Alcoa Corporation. Army Secretary Thomas E. White came from Houston's Enron Corporation. The Republican right wing welcomed ultra-conservative John Ashcroft as attorney general.

As we shall see, on issues from taxes and energy to education and medical research, Bush proposed measures that reflected the interests of the wealthy; corporate America; and the religious right, whose alienation had helped defeat his father in 1992. Bush's conservative appointments and domestic policies troubled many moderate Republicans, including Vermont senator James Jeffords, who in May 2001 left the Republican Party to become an independent. (With Jeffords's vote Senate Democrats briefly regained the majority, only to lose it in the 2002 elections.) By the summer of 2001, Bush's approval rating had fallen to about 50 percent. But all this faded as the administration and the nation faced an awesome crisis.

Day of Horror: September 11, 2001   On the morning of **September 11, 2001,** three commercial airplanes hijacked by terrorists slammed into the Pentagon outside Washington, D.C., and the twin towers of New York's World Trade Center. As Americans watched in horror, the blazing towers collapsed, carrying more than 2,800 men and women to their deaths. The Pentagon attack left 245 dead on the ground. A fourth plane crashed in Pennsylvania when heroic passengers prevented terrorists from hitting another target, possibly the White House. At the World Trade Center, nearly 350 firefighters and 23 police officers perished. Along with the dead on the ground, 246 passengers and crew, plus 19 hijackers, died in the four planes.

The hijackers deliberately targeted symbols of U.S. economic and military power. The destruction of the World Trade Center that terrorists had attempted in 1993 (see Chapter 31) had now tragically been achieved. The government soon identified the hijackers, all Muslims from the Middle East, and traced their movements before September 11, including enrollment in flight-training schools in Florida, Oklahoma, and Minnesota.

Terrorism—whether assassinations or the bombing of buildings, buses, ships, and planes—was familiar elsewhere, and had taken many American lives, civilian and military, in the 1980s and 1990s. But not since the War of 1812 had foreign enemies attacked major cities on the U.S. mainland. As the nation mourned, political divisions faded. Flags appeared everywhere. The World War II anthem "God Bless America" enjoyed renewed popularity. Editorial writers evoked memories of the 1941 Japanese surprise attack at Pearl Harbor. "United We Stand" proclaimed banners, billboards, and bumper stickers. President Bush urged Americans to distinguish between a few Islamic terrorists and the world's 1.2 billion Muslims, including some 6 million in America. Nevertheless, U.S. Muslims faced hostility and even violence.

CHRONOLOGY, 2001–2006

2001 • Bush administration repudiates Kyoto protocol on emission standards.
Congress passes $1.35 trillion tax cut bill.
Stockmarket falls; Enron Corporation collapses; wave of corporate bankruptcies and scandals.
Congress passes No Child Left Behind Act.
U.S. withdraws from ABM (Anti-Ballistic Missile) Treaty and begins missile defense system.
Terrorist attacks on World Trade Center, Pentagon (September 11).
U.S. and allied forces defeat Taliban regime in Afghanistan.
Captured Taliban fighters and others imprisoned at Guantánamo Bay, Cuba.
USA-Patriot Act passed.

2002 • Bipartisan Campaign Reform Act (McCain-Feingold law).
Department of Homeland Security created.
Sarbanes-Oxley Act tightens business accounting regulations.
Bush secretly authorizes National Security Administration to spy without warrants.
Republicans gain in midterm elections.

2003 • U.S. and coalition forces invade Iraq (March 21).
North Korea withdraws from Nuclear Non-Proliferation Treaty.
Prescription-drug benefits added to Medicare.

2004 • Revelation of abuses at Baghdad's Abu Ghraib prison.
George W. Bush wins second term, defeating John Kerry.

2005 • Congress passes Energy Act.
Bush signs bill barring "cruel, inhuman, and degrading" treatment of prisoners.
Trade deficit and budget deficit hit record levels.
Bush names John Roberts and Samuel Alito to Supreme Court.
Hurricane Katrina devastates New Orleans.
Lobbyist Jack Abramoff indicted on multiple criminal charges.

2006 • Tom Delay resigns House seat.
Congressional report documents government failures in Hurricane Katrina response.
Radical Hamas organization wins Palestinian elections.
Iran resumes nuclear enrichment program.
U.S. sells India nuclear fuel and reactor parts.
GM and Ford announce major layoffs.
Congress debates immigration-law changes; Hispanic immigrants march in major cities.
Democrats gain control of both houses in midterm elections
Resignation of Defense Secretary Donald Rumsfeld.

When the damaged New York Stock Exchange reopened after six days, stock prices plunged. They soon recovered, but consumer confidence remained fragile. The airline and travel industries reeled as jittery travelers canceled trips. "Vacant Rooms, Empty Tables, and Scared Tourists," headlined a New York newspaper.

In October, an editor at the *National Enquirer,* a tabloid that had attacked Osama bin Laden, died of anthrax, a rare bacterial disease, contracted from spores mailed in a letter. Letters containing anthrax spores next appeared in the offices of NBC news and two senators. Police closed the Senate Office Building for decontamination. Four other persons, including two postal workers, died from anthrax-tainted mail. As panic spread, scientists traced the spores to a U.S. research laboratory, and investigators focused on finding a domestic perpetrator rather than a foreign terrorist.

Confronting the Enemy in Afghanistan President Bush on September 12 declared the attacks an "act of war." On September 14, the Senate unanimously authorized Bush to use "all necessary and appropriate force" to retaliate and to prevent future acts of terrorism. On September 20, addressing a joint session of Congress, a somber Bush blamed the attack on a terrorist network called **al Qaeda** ("the base") headed by Osama bin Laden in Afghanistan. Bin Laden, the renegade son of a wealthy Saudi Arabian contractor, was already under indictment for the 1998 attack on U.S. embassies in Africa (see Chapter 31). He had long denounced America for supporting Israel and for stationing "infidel" troops on Saudi soil. (Ironically, the United States had backed bin Laden in the 1980s, when he was

America Under Attack *Rescuers remove a flag-draped body from the ruins of the World Trade Center.*

fighting Russian forces in Afghanistan.) A videotape in which bin Laden boasted of the attack and laughed about the massive damage, discovered by U.S. forces in Afghanistan, confirmed his responsibility. Though bin Laden claimed to be defending Islam, most Islamic leaders repudiated him. Among the poor in some Arab cities and Palestinian refugee camps, however, the attacks produced celebratory demonstrations.

Bush announced his determination to uproot al Qaeda. He also targeted al Qaeda's protectors, the Taliban, a Pakistan-based movement of strict and militant Muslims, which had controlled Afghanistan since 1996. This phase of America's antiterrorist effort enjoyed broad international backing. Despite the pro-Taliban sympathies of Muslim fundamentalists in Pakistan, that country's military government endorsed Bush's campaign. British prime minister Tony Blair offered strong support. On October 7, U.S., British, Canadian, Pakistani, and other forces launched the attack. For the first time, NATO forces fought in defense of a member nation. Anti-Taliban groups within Afghanistan, gathered in a loose coalition called the Northern Alliance, assisted in the campaign as well.

The Taliban soon surrendered Kabul, the Afghan capital, and other strongholds. By mid-December, despite sporadic resistance, the United States and its allies claimed victory. Hundreds of captured al Qaeda fighters were sent to the U.S. base in **Guantánamo Bay,** Cuba. In June 2002, with U.S. support, Afghan tribal leaders established a new government and named an interim prime minister, Hamid Karzai. Afghanistan's eighty-nine-year-old former king, back in Kabul after years in exile, endorsed the effort. Osama bin Laden remained at large, however, and many al Qaeda loyalists retreated to mountainous eastern Afghanistan and prepared to fight on. The top Taliban leader, Mullah Omar, went into hiding as well.

Tightening Home-Front Security

Bush's September 20 speech also signaled a broader response to the attacks. America would target not only al Qaeda, he said, but "every terrorist group of global reach," and employ not only military strikes but "covert operations, secret even in success." Americans would experience "the delays and inconveniences that may accompany tighter security," he warned, and they must "give law enforcement the additional tools it needs to track down terror here at home."

In one step to shore up domestic security, Congress late in 2001 required that the nation's 28,000 airport security personnel be U.S. citizens and meet performance standards set by a newly created Transportation Security Administration. But other aspects of the open-ended antiterrorism campaign hinted at by Bush proved more controversial. The Justice Department detained hundreds of Middle Easterners living in the United States, some for minor visa violations, and held them without filing charges or even revealing their names. Some local police officials, troubled by civil-liberties issues, resisted this wholesale roundup of persons simply on the basis of their ethnicity or national origin.

The **USA-Patriot Act,** the administration's sweeping antiterrorist bill passed by Congress in October 2001, extended the government's powers to monitor telephone and e-mail communications and library patrons' Internet searches. Civil-liberties organizations protested. Even some conservatives, traditionally suspicious of big government, questioned this expansion of federal power. (Despite growing reservations, Congress renewed the Patriot Act in 2005, though with some modifications.) In November 2001, Bush signed an executive order empowering the government to try

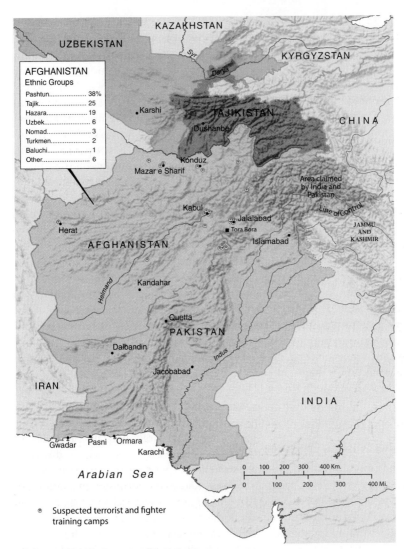

AFGHANISTAN
Ethnic Groups

Pashtun	38%
Tajik	25
Hazara	19
Uzbek	6
Nomad	3
Turkmen	2
Baluchi	1
Other	6

⊕ Suspected terrorist and fighter training camps

MAP 32.1 Afghanistan and Pakistan

After the attacks of September 11, 2001, U.S. and NATO forces attacked the terrorist organization al Qaeda, based in Afghanistan. Afghanistan's radical Islamist Taliban regime was overthrown, but many fighters retreated to the mountains along the Afghan-Pakistan border. As of late 2006, Afghanistan remained violent and unsettled, and al Qaeda leader Osama bin Laden was still at large.

noncitizens accused of fomenting terrorism in secret military tribunals rather than in civil courts. While precedent existed for such tribunals in wartime, this order, issued without consulting Congress, roused widespread criticism. In 2002, news media reported disturbing evidence of missed clues before the 9/11 attack. In August 2001, for example, a Minnesota flight school had warned the FBI that a suspicious person named Zacarias Moussaoui had tried to enroll. Moussaoui had been arrested on immigration charges, but the Justice Department had denied an FBI request for permission to check his computer. (After September 11 Moussaoui's link to bin Laden was documented, and in 2006 he was tried in Virginia and sentenced to life in prison.) Administration officials also acknowledged that through the summer of 2001, President Bush's daily security briefings had included warnings of an al Qaeda plot to hijack a U.S. airliner.

To coordinate antiterrorism efforts, Congress created a new cabinet-level **Department of Homeland Security** in November 2002. The new department absorbed the Coast Guard, the Customs Service, the Federal Emergency Management Agency (FEMA), the Immigration and Naturalization Service, and other agencies. The FBI and the CIA remained independent. The department's first head, former Pennsylvania governor Tom Ridge, announced a color-coded system to alert citizens to the level of national-security danger. Skeptics doubted whether such warnings, and a reshuffling of existing agencies, actually increased security.

In 2003 Bush named a blue-ribbon commission, headed by Republican Thomas Kean, a former New Jersey governor, and Democrat Lee Hamilton, a former congressman, to examine pre-9/11 intelligence failures. The commission's 2004 report pinpointed a lack of communication between the FBI, the CIA, and other agencies, and called for a restructuring of U.S. intelligence operations. In 2005 Bush named John Negroponte, a career diplomat, as Director of National Intelligence, to coordinate fifteen civilian and military intelligence agencies, including the CIA. Nevertheless, when Thomas Kean was asked about homeland security in 2006, he replied: "It's not a priority for the government right now. . . . [A] lot of the things we need to do . . . to prevent another 9/11 just simply aren't being done." Critics noted that most incoming shipping containers went unchecked, and U.S. chemical plants remained vulnerable.

The Campaign in Iraq, 2003–2004   Although Afghanistan remained unstable and Osama bin Laden uncaptured, the administration's attention shifted elsewhere. In his January 2002 State of the Union address, President Bush identified Iran, Iraq, and North Korea as an "axis of evil." Of the three, Iraq loomed largest. Iraq's ruler, Saddam Hussein, had been a thorn in America's flesh since the Persian Gulf War, which had left him weakened but still in power. In a barrage of speeches, Bush, Vice President Cheney, Defense Secretary Rumsfeld, and National Security Adviser Rice accused Saddam of complicity in the 9/11 attacks and of stockpiling or developing nuclear, chemical, and biological weapons.

This shift of focus to Iraq was orchestrated by a close-knit group of Republican **neoconservatives.** (The term, meaning "new conservatives," originally applied to one-time Democrats who favored a militant anti-Soviet foreign policy in the Cold War and who turned to the Republican Party when the Democratic Party shifted leftward in the 1960s.)

This group advocated an aggressive foreign policy dedicated to spreading democracy in the Arab world and beyond. Skeptical of multilateral approaches, neoconservatives believed that the United States, as the world's superpower, should act alone to pursue its goals. Such a policy, they believed, would advance freedom and create a safer environment for Israel, America's ally in the Middle East. Prominent neoconservatives included Paul Wolfowitz, Douglas Feith, and Richard Perle, who all held positions in Rumsfeld's Pentagon; Gary Adelman, a former Reagan administration official; and William Kristol, editor of *The Weekly Standard,* a political journal. For neoconservatives, democratizing Iraq was a first step in their ambitious agenda.

The call for invading Iraq proved controversial from the start. Critics challenged the administration to prove its claims. A preemptive war would not only violate U.S.

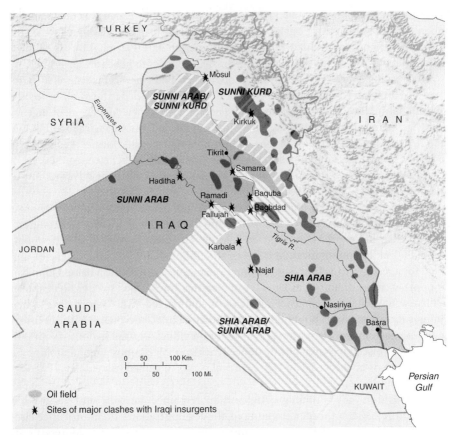

MAP 32.2 Iraq

With Saddam Hussein's overthrow by U.S.-led forces in 2003, violence erupted among Iraq's ethnic and religious groups, including the majority Shia Muslims concentrated in the southeast and the minority Sunni Muslims, who had ruled the country under Saddam and earlier.

principles, they charged, but could also drag on for years, unleash anger across the Arab world, and undermine the larger antiterrorist campaign. Great Britain's Tony Blair backed the administration, but other NATO allies, as well as Russia and most Arab leaders, objected. To counter the rush to war, they called for a UN resolution demanding that Iraq readmit UN weapons inspectors, who had departed in 1998 when Iraq blocked their access to some sites.

In October 2002, Congress passed a resolution sponsored by the administration authorizing President Bush to "defend the national security of the United States against the continuing threat posed by Iraq." While Republicans overwhelmingly supported the resolution, Democrats were divided, fearful of opposing Bush on an issue he called vital to American security. As Lyndon Johnson had cited the Gulf of Tonkin Resolution to justify escalating the Vietnam War (see Chapter 28), President Bush would later use this resolution as the legal basis for invading Iraq. Bush also presented the case against Saddam in a UN address.

As the November 2002 midterm elections approached, President Bush, enjoying post-9/11 approval ratings close to 70 percent, campaigned tirelessly, stressing his leadership in the war on terror. Democrats hammered at the recession, corporate scandals, and Bush's environmental record. With 9/11 memories still raw, Bush's talk of terrorism hit home. As a Colorado voter commented: "[W]e need protection and I don't want to see President Bush get stalemated . . . [in] protecting our country." The outcome strengthened Bush's hand, as Republicans regained control of the Senate and increased their House majority. In the wake of the defeat, the House minority leader, Missouri's Richard Gephardt, resigned. Nancy Pelosi of California replaced him, the first woman of either party to hold this position.

Bolstered by the election, the administration pushed its Iraq invasion plans. In November 2002 the UN Security Council imposed tough new weapons-inspection requirements on Iraq. Baghdad agreed, and UN inspectors returned. They soon withdrew, however, as U.S. and British forces assembled in the Persian Gulf. In a February 2003 UN speech, Secretary of State Colin Powell, relying on evidence supplied by the CIA, insisted that Saddam Hussein was developing weapons of mass destruction (WMDs).

The war began on March 19, 2003, as U.S. cruise missiles rained down on Baghdad. The land invasion commenced on March 21. U.S. and British troops moved first into southern Iraq, populated by Shiite Muslims who had been brutally oppressed by Saddam. Securing the oil fields around Basra, the invaders moved north. Field commanders, encountering unexpected guerrilla resistance, raised caution flags, but the top commander, General Tommy Franks, dismissed their warnings. In early April, U.S. troops occupied Baghdad and toppled a large statue of Saddam. As the regime fell and Saddam fled, basic services in the city collapsed and widespread looting erupted.

On May 1, after a navy jet had brought him to the aircraft carrier *Abraham Lincoln* off San Diego, President Bush declared major combat operations over. A banner behind him proclaimed "Mission Accomplished." Bush named L. Paul Bremer, a career Foreign Service officer, to administer civil affairs in Iraq. Two of Saddam's sons died resisting arrest in July. Saddam himself was captured in December, and later put on trial.

Iraq's Sunni Muslims, though a minority, had long dominated Iraqi politics. Resisting their loss of power, they mobilized to expel the invaders. Bremer's decision to disband the Iraqi army and dismiss all government officials who had served under Saddam created a power vacuum, encouraging sectarian violence. Radical Muslim fighters from outside Iraq, led by a Jordanian, Abu Musab al-Zarqawi, added to the unrest. So did a fiery young Shiite cleric, Moqtada al-Sadr, popular among Baghdad's poor. Anti-American and anti-Sunni, al-Sadr also feuded with senior Shiite religious leaders.

Conditions worsened through 2004 as bombings, kidnappings, and deadly highway blasts caused by improvised explosive devices (IEDs) occurred daily. In March, insurgents ambushed and killed four U.S. employees of a security company, and burned their bodies. In June, Paul Bremer transferred power to a provisional Iraqi government headed by Iyad Allawi. A physician who had led a London-based anti-Saddam movement, Allawi had close ties to Western intelligence agencies. But little changed. In September, the toll of U.S. dead in Iraq passed 1,000. As the year ended, the war that the Bush team had launched so confidently seemed mired in bloodshed and violence. Vice President Cheney had predicted that the Iraqis would welcome the Americans as liberators. The head of the CIA had assured Bush that victory would be a "slam dunk." Now reality blasted such wishful thinking.

POLITICS AND THE ECONOMY IN BUSH'S FIRST TERM, 2001–2005

Although the 9/11 attacks and their aftermath dominated Bush's first term, the administration also proposed a series of economic and social initiatives. Debate over these measures unfolded amid a sharp recession and a cascade of corporate bankruptcies and scandals.

Economic Reverses and Corporate Scandals   The prosperity and stock-market boom of the 1990s (see Chapter 31) barely outlasted the decade. As Asian and Latin American economies faltered, the U.S. economy suffered as well. In March 2001, the stock market recorded its worst week since 1989, falling by 6 percent. The high-flying Silicon Valley information-technology companies, which had led the boom of the later 1990s, were especially hard hit. An estimated 250 such businesses collapsed in a few months' time. As the market value of the surviving companies plummeted, instant millionaires watched their portfolios shrivel.

Few shed tears when luxury boutiques and pricey restaurants suffered reverses. But the recession that began in Silicon Valley and Wall Street soon spread. Industrial production dropped, and every state lost jobs. Service-sector employment fell faster in the last quarter of 2001 than in any comparable period since the 1940s. Unskilled workers and former welfare recipients seeking entry-level jobs struggled. By June 2003, with the unemployment rate at 6.4 percent, 2.6 million workers had lost their jobs.

The longest economic boom in American history had ended with a thud. The Bush administration, having inherited a budget surplus, now projected years of deficits. To stimulate the economy, the Federal Reserve Board cut interest rates eleven times in 2001, to a forty-year low. A wave of corporate bankruptcies and scandals, particularly in the energy and telecommunications fields, further eroded investor confidence. Business deregulation, a culture of greed, and the emergence of new information-based enterprises and complex corporate structures that investors did not understand well had created a situation that invited fraudulent corporate practices.

Houston's Enron Corporation, with close ties to the administration, was an early casualty. A marketer of electric power, Enron flourished in the 1990s and moved into utilities and telecommunications. In 2000, claiming revenues of $101 billion, Enron ranked seventh in *Fortune* magazine's list of America's top corporations. The end came abruptly. Late in 2001 Enron filed for bankruptcy and admitted to falsifying profit reports. More than five thousand Enron workers lost both their jobs and their retirement funds, which consisted mostly of Enron stock. Shortly before the collapse, Enron founder Kenneth Lay and other top officials had sold their Enron stock, profiting handsomely. The Chicago accounting firm that had certified Enron's financial reports collapsed as well. Enron's chief financial officer pled guilty to criminal charges and cooperated with the prosecution. In 2006, a Houston jury convicted Lay and former Enron CEO Jeffry Skilling on multiple counts of fraud and conspiracy. The company's logo, a crooked "E," seemed all too appropriate. Lay died of a heart attack in July 2006.

The overextended fiber-optics industry, having laid 100 million miles of optical fiber worldwide in 1999–2001, stumbled badly as recession hit. Lucent Technologies, a telecommunications giant, cut nearly one hundred thousand jobs in 2001. In 2002 WorldCom, America's second-largest telecommunications company, admitting that it had overstated profits by billions, filed for bankruptcy and fired seventeen thousand employees. CEO Bernard Ebbers, convicted of securities fraud in 2005, received a twenty-five-year prison sentence.

The parade continued. John T. Rigas, head of Adelphia Corporation, the nation's sixth-largest cable company, was arrested in July 2002 with his two sons for a fraud that cost stockholders $2.5 billion. He received a fifteen-year prison term. In September, Dennis Kozlowski, the CEO of Tyco, an industrial products and service company, was indicted along with Tyco's chief financial officer for looting the company of $600 million. Kozlowski's trial included testimony about a $6,000 shower curtain for his New York apartment and a $2 million Mediterranean birthday party for his wife. Kozlowski received a long prison sentence, was fined $70 million, and was ordered to repay Tyco $134 million.

Top mutual-fund managers faced charges of increasing their bonuses by advising investors to buy stocks at inflated prices while privately disparaging the same stocks. "Let's put lipstick on this pig," one analyst joked to another, discussing a stock he was pushing. Under investigation by New York attorney general Eliot Spitzer, the Wall Street investment firm Merrill Lynch paid $200 million in fines.

Despite some positive economic news, the stock market fell through much of 2002 and early 2003, as traumatized investors remained wary. Executives who had been celebrities in the 1990s now faced public hostility if not criminal investigation. The University of Maryland business school took students on field trips to penitentiaries where white-collar inmates warned them to be honest. Declared the chairman of Goldman Sachs, a Wall Street investment bank, "I cannot think of a time when business . . . has been held in less repute."

Politicians responded to mounting public anger. President Bush delivered a stern speech upholding business morality. In July 2002 Congress passed the Sarbanes-Oxley Act, named for its sponsors, which imposed stricter accounting and financial reporting rules and toughened criminal penalties for business fraud.

Stimulated by low interest rates, the U.S. economy grew by 4.2 percent in 2004 and 3.5 percent in 2005. But this growth was unevenly distributed geographically, being heavily concentrated west of the Mississippi. Also, while the real income of the nation's richest 1 percent increased by more than 12 percent in 2004, the average real income of the remaining 99 percent grew by only 1.5 percent. Job growth remained weak. Discussing these data, the economist Paul Krugman wrote: "[I]t's a great economy if you're a high-level corporate executive or someone who owns a lot of stock. For most other Americans, economic growth is a spectator sport." By mid-2006, even this uneven recovery faltered. As oil prices soared, world conditions deteriorated, and the Federal Reserve Board raised interest rates to combat inflation, job growth slowed, and the jittery stock market again sank.

The Republican Domestic Agenda   In February 2001, fulfilling a campaign promise, President Bush proposed a $1.6 trillion cut in income taxes over a ten-year period. Though the measure reduced all rates, wealthy taxpayers received the highest percentage reduction. As the recession began, Bush argued that the cuts would stimulate investment and speed recovery. Democrats attacked the bill for favoring the rich, and warned that slashing taxes, as President Reagan had in 1981, would produce huge federal deficits.

In May Congress passed a $1.35 trillion tax cut—lower than Bush's proposal and somewhat less slanted toward the rich. Mounting budget deficits predictably followed, erasing the surplus Clinton had achieved. Economists, estimating lost federal revenue over a twenty-year period at $4 trillion, warned of a mountainous national debt. Nevertheless, the Republican-led Congress added another $320 billion in tax cuts in 2003 and $95 billion in 2005.

The administration's 2001 energy bill emerged from secret meetings of oil and gas executives with Vice President Cheney, himself a former head of Halliburton, an energy company. Kenneth Lay, a major GOP contributor, played a key role before Enron's collapse. The bill proposed more nuclear power plants; eased environmental regulations on energy companies; and included incentives to expand coal, oil, and natural-gas production, including drilling in Alaska's **Arctic National Wildlife Refuge** (ANWR). President Bush defended the bill as a way to reduce U.S. dependence on foreign oil.

The 9/11 attacks and all that followed intervened, but in August 2005 Congress passed an energy bill. It granted $14.5 billion in tax breaks to oil, natural gas, coal, and nuclear-power companies; exempted them from some environmental laws; and eased the process of securing permits to drill or mine on public lands. The law offered a one-year tax credit for purchasers of hybrid vehicles and energy-efficient appliances and included incentives for research on renewable and cleaner energy sources, including ethanol, made from corn, which won supporters in the corn belt. The law did not approve drilling in ANWR, but Alaska's powerful senator, Ted Stevens, vowed to continue that fight. Despite lobbying by environmental groups, it did not tighten vehicle fuel-efficiency requirements, even on gas-guzzling trucks and SUVs. Overall, said one critic, the measure was "Christmas in August" for the energy companies.

On education, Bush pushed a program he labeled **"No Child Left Behind."** As governor of Texas, Bush had addressed education issues, and the subject interested his wife Laura, a former school librarian. Embracing education reform also enhanced his image as a "compassionate conservative." Bush's plan called for standardized national tests in grades four and eight to measure reading and math skills, with penalties for schools that fell short. In 2001, Congress mandated annual testing. Fourth-grade reading scores improved somewhat by 2003, but eighth-grade reading and math scores showed little change. Some schools, focusing on raising test scores, cut back art, music, history, and other subjects. Poorly performing schools, often in disadvantaged neighborhoods, protested the threatened penalties. The massive federal intrusion in public education, historically a local matter, troubled some conservatives.

Christian conservatives ranked among Bush's strongest supporters in 2000. Moving quickly to reward them, Bush in 2001 created an Office of Faith-Based and Community Initiatives to funnel federal grants to churches for social programs. Under this initiative, grants went to anti-abortion groups, organizations promoting teenage sexual abstinence, and prison ministries run by evangelicals. Operation Blessing, a charity operated by televangelist Pat Robertson, received $22 million in direct grants and food surpluses. A black church in Milwaukee led by a prominent Republican received $1.4 million.

Bush's education plan also included a voucher system by which children could attend private or religious schools at taxpayers' expense. Congress rejected this proposal, but some states introduced their own voucher plans. By 2006 some 4,000 private and church-sponsored schools were partially supported by student vouchers. Some did well; others showed no better results than the public schools; and some 400 had closed for various reasons.

President Bush also sought favor with Christian conservatives, who overwhelmingly oppose abortion, by restricting stem-cell research. Stem cells are produced during an early stage of human embryo development, and fertility clinics often have "surplus" fertilized embryos. Since stem cells can develop into more specialized human cells, they are valuable for medical research. Some anti-abortion groups oppose research using fertilized embryos, however. In a 2001 presidential directive, Bush permitted federal funding of research on a handful of existing stem-cell lines, but barred funding for research on stem cells harvested from human embryos in the future. Medical researchers warned that this restriction could inhibit their work.

Campaign Finance Reform and the Election of 2004 As political campaign costs soared, reformers worked to curb the endless fundraising the system required. They especially targeted so-called soft money contributions to political parties that then flowed on to specific candidates. Big soft-money contributors ranged from (mostly Republican) business lobbies, anti-abortion groups, and the National Rifle Association to (mostly Democratic) labor unions, trial lawyers, and teachers. In the 2000 election, soft-money contributions reached $400 million.

In 2002 President Bush signed a reform bill co-sponsored by Arizona Republican John McCain and Wisconsin Democrat Russell Feingold. It banned soft-money contributions; barred fake TV "issue ads" designed to influence elections; and included other provisions to reduce the power of money in politics. As lobbying organizations sought loopholes and challenged the law on free-speech grounds, its ultimate impact remained unclear.

As the 2004 election approached, Howard Dean, a physician and former Vermont governor, emerged as the early frontrunner for the Democratic presidential nomination. Dean criticized the Iraq War and Democrats who had supported it. Like Jimmy Carter in 1976, he bypassed party leaders and appealed directly to voters. He built a following via the Internet, especially on college campuses. But while Dean's candor energized the Democratic base, it also alienated many voters. In the Iowa primary kicking off the campaign, he finished a weak third behind Senators **John Kerry** of Massachusetts and John Edwards of North Carolina. When he again lost to Kerry in the New Hampshire primary a week later, his campaign faded. Nevertheless, Dean had bluntly criticized the Iraq War while other leading Democrats hung back. He also demonstrated the Internet's potential for fundraising and rallying support.

John Kerry won the nomination. Democratic strategists hoped that his military record as a decorated Vietnam War veteran would neutralize charges that Democrats were weak on defense. He named Senator Edwards, a successful trial lawyer, as his running mate. George W. Bush and Dick Cheney again headed the Republican ticket. Bush began the campaign with a massive war chest of some $150 million from corporate sources and wealthy donors called "Pioneers." Bypassing the McCain-Feingold restrictions on organizational contributions, the Pioneers raised money from friends and colleagues. Of 246 "Pioneers," 104 later received appointments in the Bush administration.

In the campaign, Kerry criticized the administration's response to 9/11. Although he had voted for the Patriot Act and supported a Senate resolution approving the use of force in Iraq as a last resort, Kerry now accused Bush of misleading the nation about Saddam Hussein, and criticized parts of the Patriot Act as threats to civil liberties. President Bush defended both the Iraq conflict and the Patriot Act as crucial to the war on terrorism. Citing Kerry's changing positions, Republicans accused him of "flip-flopping" indecisiveness.

Attacking Bush's environmental record, Kerry called for vigorous enforcement of environmental laws, tougher fuel-efficiency standards, and more support for renewable energy. Highlighting Bush's less than distinguished military record, Kerry played up his tour in Vietnam. At the Democratic convention he opened his acceptance speech with a salute and the line: "I'm John Kerry, and I'm reporting for duty." (Anti-Kerry TV commercials questioned his Vietnam record and emphasized his 1971 antiwar testimony before the Senate Foreign Relations Committee on behalf of Vietnam Veterans Against the War.) Kerry, a Catholic, sought to counter Bush's edge with evangelical Christians. "I don't wear my religion on my sleeve," he said in his acceptance speech. "But faith has given me values and hope to live by, from Vietnam to this day."

The candidates' positions on cultural issues reflected national divisions. Kerry opposed the death penalty; Bush supported it. Kerry supported *Roe* v. *Wade;* Bush favored a ban on all abortions except in rare circumstances. Kerry backed stricter gun control; Bush opposed it.

The divisive issue of same-sex marriage loomed large during the campaign. In 2004, San Francisco's mayor challenged California law by allowing same-sex couples to marry, and the Massachusetts Supreme Court ruled that banning same-sex marriage violated the state constitution's equal-rights guarantee. As gay and lesbian couples in San Francisco and Massachusetts applied for marriage licenses, opinion polls found 63 percent of Americans opposed to same-sex marriage. (By 2006 that figure had dropped to 51 percent.) While Kerry favored leaving this issue to the states, Bush endorsed a constitutional amendment banning gay marriage. As eleven states added referenda banning same-sex marriage to the fall ballot, the issue energized religious conservatives. The referenda passed by lopsided margins in all eleven states, and Bush won in nine of the eleven, including closely contested Ohio.

On election day, Bush garnered 51 percent of the popular vote to Kerry's 48 percent. Kerry won New England, New York, and Pennsylvania. In the Upper Midwest he carried Michigan, Illinois, Wisconsin, and Minnesota. California, Oregon, and Washington also fell his way. In the rest of the nation, the majority went for Bush. Bush narrowly won the Electoral College vote, with Ohio the pivotal state. Republicans gained a net of four Senate seats and four House seats. In South Dakota, a Republican defeated Tom Daschle, the Senate Democratic leader. Voters most worried about terrorism, as well as evangelical Christians and other cultural conservatives, overwhelmingly voted Republican.

Kerry had won the two largest states, California and New York, and 55 percent of voters under thirty—an age group that increased its strength at the polls by 9 percent between 2000 and 2004—voted Democratic. In Illinois, a charismatic young Democrat, Barak Obama, won election to the Senate. Overall, however, a tax-cutting president seen as a leader in the "war on terror" and a defender of embattled conservative cultural values had eked out a narrow victory.

The election highlighted the political role of new technologies. MoveOn.org and democracyforamerica.com, two Internet-based Democratic initiatives that emerged from the campaign, continued to raise funds and to generate e-mail and telephone campaigns in support of liberal candidates and causes. Hundreds of bloggers (independent website operators) sustained a freewheeling flow of political commentary. While conservative organizations had long mobilized their supporters via magazines, direct mail, radio, and TV, liberals appeared to have the edge in the new arena of Internet-based activism, especially among young people.

Indeed, the popular culture offered many challenges to conservative ideology. Michael Moore's 2004 documentary *Fahrenheit 9/11* mounted a sharp and witty critique of the administration's response to 9/11. *Democracy Now,* a left-oriented news program, was available on radio, the Internet, and some public TV stations. Singers Bruce Springsteen and Neil Young and the Dixie Chicks country trio stirred controversy for their outspoken criticism of Bush. Even on talk radio, a conservative bastion, individuals such as Bill Maher and Al Franken voiced opposing views.

The 2004 election again underscored the political role of organized groups. Conservative organizations and those on the religious right, some dating to the 1970s (see Chapters 30 and 31), remained active. Highlighting such volatile issues as gay marriage and school prayer, Pat Robertson's Christian Coalition, Donald E. Wildmon's American Family Association, James Dobson's Focus on the Family, and other groups mobilized Bush's base of religious and cultural conservatives. These groups, too, used the Internet to promote their cause.

But organizations opposed to the conservative agenda were active as well. People for the American Way, the American Civil Liberties Union, Planned Parenthood, the Sierra Club, Amnesty International, the Union of Concerned Scientists, Emily's List (which supported women candidates who endorsed liberal and feminist goals), and many other groups advocated for liberal candidates or rallied opposition to administration policies they opposed. Even among evangelical Christians, support for Bush was not unanimous. Jim Wallis, founder of the evangelical Sojourners movement based in Washington, D.C., sharply criticized the religious right in his *Sojourners* magazine and his book *God's Politics: Why the Right Gets It Wrong and the Left Doesn't Get It* (2005). Ronald Sider, founder of Evangelicals for Social Action, called on evangelicals to embrace such issues as peacemaking, concern for the poor, and environmental protection. In full-page newspaper ads in 2006, leading evangelicals challenged the administration's environmental and energy policies.

FOREIGN POLICY IN A THREATENING ERA

By 2005, two years into the Iraq War, insurgent violence and sectarian conflict raged unabated. Home-front support eroded amid accusations of prisoner abuse, illegal spying in the name of security, and deceptions in the administration's case for invading Iraq. The continuing Israeli-Palestinian struggle, threats of nuclear proliferation, and rising international concern about environmental hazards further challenged U.S. policy makers.

The Continuing Struggle in Iraq; Sagging Home-Front Support   In his second inaugural address in January 2005, Bush described the Iraq War as part of a global campaign to spread democracy, "with the ultimate goal of ending tyranny in our world." The speech echoed Woodrow Wilson's 1917 war message proclaiming America's mission to make the world "safe for democracy" (see Chapter 22). But Secretary of State Colin Powell, who had privately opposed the war, had resigned in November 2004; Bush named National Security Adviser Condoleezza Rice to replace him.

Chaos in Iraq: Aftermath of the Destruction of the Imam Ali Mosque in Najaf, August 29, 2003 *As Shiite Muslims crowded into the mosque for Friday prayers, a massive car bomb killed at least 125 people, including a top Shiite religious leader, and destroyed the mosque, one of Shia Islam's holiest shrines. The bombing was part of a pattern of worsening sectarian violence in Iraq following the U.S.-led invasion.*

In Iraq the conflict dragged on, with daily news of roadside IEDs, suicide bombings, kidnappings, and assassinations. A Sunni-led insurgency centered in Baghdad and a region north of the city called the "Sunni triangle." Determined to prevent a government of Shiites allied with the Kurds of northern Iraq, Sunnis organized a campaign of disruption, targeting police, soldiers, and government officials. A February 2005 bombing at a police recruiting station near Baghdad killed 127 and wounded many more. U.S. troops periodically raided Sunni strongholds. A November 2004 operation in Fallujah, involving more than 10,000 U.S. and Iraqi forces, left 38 Americans dead and 275 wounded. Typically, however, the insurgents returned once the troops withdrew. Suicide attacks by outside fighters, including al Qaeda loyalists, added to the unrest.

Amid the turmoil, U.S. attempts to train an Iraqi army faltered, as did the reconstruction effort. In Baghdad and other cities, electricity and other basic services remained unpredictable. A subsidiary of the Halliburton Company, once headed by Vice President Cheney, with $3.6 billion in reconstruction contracts awarded with no bidding competition, faced accusations of fraud and overcharging. Company officials denied wrongdoing and noted the difficulty of working in a war zone. Oil exports, Iraq's major income source, remained below prewar levels. Amid widespread corruption, some funds from oil sales were diverted through shadowy channels to the insurgents.

Bringing democracy to Iraq proved equally difficult. Sunnis boycotted a January 2005 election to choose a National Assembly. Dominated by Shiites, the Assembly chose as prime minister Ibrahim al-Jaafari, a Shiite religious party leader with links to the radical cleric Moqtada al-Sadr, whose private militias attacked Sunnis, U.S. soldiers, journalists, and foreign contractors. Sectarian hatred worsened when U.S. troops found a secret prison and torture center run by the Interior Ministry of the Shiite-dominated government. Sunnis accused Shiite militias and even rogue Interior Ministry "death squads" of targeting Sunni leaders for kidnapping and killing and detonating car bombs in Sunni neighborhoods and commercial districts.

Sunnis participated in a second round of parliamentary voting in December 2005, but the vote followed sectarian lines, and the violence continued. In one day in January 2006, suicide bombers killed more than sixty Shiite pilgrims in Karbala and more than fifty applicants for police jobs in Ramadi. In February, suicide bombers destroyed a revered Shiite shrine, the golden-domed Al-Askariya Mosque in Samarrah, triggering anti-Sunni reprisal attacks. (The Kurds in northern Iraq, hoping for an eventual independent Kurdish state, mostly remained aloof from the carnage.)

Nearly four thousand Iraqi security forces and civilians died in sectarian violence in the first four months of 2006. Thousands of fearful refugees found shelter in makeshift camps. As the estimated Iraqi death toll since March 2003 topped 50,000, former prime minister Allawi observed: "If this is not civil war, then God knows what civil war is." In April 2006, another Shiite politician, Nouri al-Maliki, replaced al-Jaafari as prime minister. Maliki announced plans for tightened security and a program of "national reconciliation," but the sectarian and insurgent killings, kidnappings, and bombings only intensified.

Historically a patchwork of ethnic and religious groups ruled by successive Persian, Greek, and Arab invaders, Iraq was governed by British colonial administrators after World War I and became an independent nation only in 1932. Whether it could avoid fragmenting into separate Sunni, Shiite, and Kurdish enclaves amid the chaos that followed Saddam's overthrow remained deeply problematic.

The 133,000 U.S. troops fought few open battles, but casualties continued. By October 2006 more than 2,700 GIs had been killed in Iraq and more than 20,000 wounded, nearly half of them severely. Casualties among journalists, contractors, and other U.S. civilians in Iraq pushed the grim total still higher. Combined with operations in Afghanistan, the war's cost stood at around $440 billion, with billions more in prospect. As other nations in the coalition withdrew their forces, the burden fell more heavily on the United States.

In November 2005, Pennsylvania congressman Jack Murtha urged immediate withdrawal from Iraq. A decorated Vietnam veteran with a hawkish record on military matters, Murtha had initially supported the war but now labeled it "a flawed policy, wrapped in an illusion." Similar calls came from across the political spectrum. "[T]he American objective in Iraq has failed," the conservative leader William Buckley bluntly declared. Observed the liberal *New York Times:* "Iraq is becoming a country that America should be ashamed to support, let alone occupy." Amid spreading sectarian violence, journalist Tom Friedman reflected: "The fate of the entire U.S. enterprise now hangs in the balance . . . ; once this kind of venom gets unleashed, it poisons everything." By May 2006, according to the Harris poll, Bush's approval ratings had fallen below 30 percent.

As the war lost support, criticism of the administration's decision for war intensified. In *Against All Enemies: Inside America's War on Terrorism* (2004), President Bush's former counterterrorism coordinator, Richard Clarke, reported that the day after 9/11, Bush had repeatedly pressured him to focus on Saddam Hussein. Under scrutiny, the key arguments in the administration's case for invading Iraq, Saddam's alleged WMD program and his connections to 9/11, both crumbled. After the invasion, CIA investigators found no WMDs in Iraq. President Bush's claim in his 2003 State of the Union address that Iraq had imported uranium from Africa proved false, and no credible evidence linked Saddam to the 9/11 attacks.

Were these distortions deliberate? The Senate Intelligence Committee and a presidential commission looking into prewar intelligence failures concluded that the CIA had supplied faulty or incomplete information on Iraq's alleged WMD program. But the Senate inquiry also found "significant pressure" by administration officials on the CIA to link Saddam to al Qaeda. Much evidence suggested that Cheney and other officials "cherry picked" intelligence that strengthened the case against Iraq, and downplayed contradictory data.

Critics also questioned Secretary of Defense Rumsfeld's prewar assurances that a small U.S. ground force equipped with high-tech weaponry could achieve victory, and that Iraq's army would switch sides once Saddam fell. When army chief of staff General Eric Shineski told Congress in March 2003 that success in Iraq would require several hundred thousand troops, Rumsfeld had derided this estimate as "far from the mark."

The Pentagon's lack of planning for post-invasion pacification and reconstruction faced intense criticism. In *Cobra II: The Inside Story of the Invasion and Occupation of Iraq* (2006), retired general Bernard Trainor and a co-author identified these lapses as crucial errors that underlay Iraq's descent into sectarian violence. In April 2006 Bush rejected a call by six retired generals for Rumsfeld's dismissal. "I am the decider," he declared, "and I decide what is best. And what's best is for Don Rumsfeld to remain as secretary of defense."

Evidence of prisoner mistreatment deepened home-front uneasiness. In April 2004, revolting photographs surfaced showing the abuse and sexual humiliation of Iraqis held by U.S. forces at Baghdad's Abu Ghraib prison. The army transferred Lieutenant General Ricardo Sanchez, commander of ground forces in Iraq, to Germany; demoted the general in command of the Abu Ghraib prison; and court-martialed some participants. One ringleader received a ten-year prison sentence and a dishonorable discharge. However, despite evidence that the army's interrogation guidelines encouraged abuses, the repercussions initially went no higher.

Further allegations soon surfaced charging prisoner abuse in Afghanistan, in Iraq, and at Guantánamo Bay, where more than 500 men seized in Afghanistan were held. In a secret 2002 memo, Justice Department lawyer John Yoo argued that the Geneva Conventions protecting prisoners of war did not apply to persons the president designated as "enemy combatants." The only interrogations that constituted torture, Yoo wrote, were those causing "death, organ failure, or serious impairment of bodily functions." All else was permissible. Yoo's "torture memo," approved by White House counsel (and future attorney general) Alberto Gonzales, became public in 2004, unleashing more controversy.

In 2004, the International Committee of the Red Cross described interrogation methods at Guantánamo as "tantamount to torture." A 2005 report by Amnesty International, a prisoner-rights organization, similarly alleged human-rights violations at

U.S. military prisons. One technique singled out for criticism was "water boarding," in which the victim is nearly drowned.

The Bush administration claimed the right to hold these prisoners without trial as "enemy combatants" as long as the "war on terrorism" continued. The army asserted that its interrogation techniques were "safe, secure, and humane." As of early 2006, only ten of the detainees had been formally charged. Evidence also surfaced that the CIA had secretly transported detainees to an uncertain fate in Egyptian and Eastern European prisons. UN agencies and officials in Great Britain, Spain, and other countries called upon the United States to close the Guantánamo facility.

In 2005, defying the White House, Congress passed an amendment proposed by Senator John McCain to a military appropriations bill. McCain's amendment outlawed "cruel, inhuman, and degrading" treatment of prisoners. McCain, who had been tortured as a POW in Vietnam, argued that information secured through torture is unreliable. For the United States to condone torture, he cautioned, placed captured American soldiers in greater jeopardy. Bush signed the bill, but in an increasingly common practice he issued a "signing statement" asserting, in effect, that he was not bound to obey the McCain amendment.

Deepening civil-liberties concerns, Americans learned in 2005 that President Bush in 2002 had secretly authorized the National Security Agency (NSA) to tap U.S. citizens' overseas phone calls and e-mails without securing a warrant from a special court created in 1978 to review requests for such clandestine surveillance. (The NSA, so secret that it has been jokingly called "No Such Agency," was created by President Truman in 1952.) John Yoo, author of the so-called "torture memo," also crafted the Justice Department memo justifying this action.

Defending this spying as vital to catching terrorists, Bush and Attorney General Gonzales argued that the September 2001 congressional resolution authorizing the president to use "all necessary and appropriate force" to prevent future attacks covered the NSA's monitoring of U.S. citizens' phone records without a warrant. Evidence that the NSA had electronically monitored domestic as well as foreign phone calls and e-mails, and that the FBI had targeted peace groups and journalists for surveillance, deepened the sense of uneasiness.

Bush's "signing statement" asserting his right to ignore the McCain antitorture amendment was one of many such pronouncements by which the president "interpreted" bills he was signing. Such "signing statements" have no constitutional standing. The Constitution empowers presidents to veto bills and grants Congress the power to override vetoes by a two-thirds vote. Bush's actions bypassed this constitutional procedure. The *New York Times,* criticizing Bush's "out-of-control sense of his powers in combating terrorism," editorialized in May 2006: "This president seems determined not to play by any rules other than the ones of his own making."

Early in 2006 Wisconsin senator Russell Feingold proposed a resolution censuring Bush for unconstitutional actions. A CBS News opinion poll found that most Americans thought that Bush had exceeded his authority in approving warrantless NSA spying on U.S. citizens. Even many Republicans, traditionally suspicious of governmental excesses, found Bush's actions disturbing. Congress took no action on Feingold's proposal, however.

In June 2006, the U.S. Supreme Court rejected the administration's claims that it could set up special military tribunals, not bound by the usual rules of courtroom procedure, to try the Guantánamo prisoners. Such tribunals, the Court held, violated both federal law and the Geneva Conventions governing the treatment of prisoners of war. In a broader sense, the Court rejected the Bush administration's claim that it could pursue the war on terrorism with little regard for Congress, the Constitution, or international law.

Adding to the accumulation of disturbing developments, *Time* magazine in March 2006 reported that in November 2005, U.S. marines had killed twenty-four unarmed Iraqi men, women, and children in the town of Haditha in Iraq's Anbar Province after a roadside IED had killed a member of their unit. In July 2006, four GIs and one recently discharged GI were charged with raping and murdering a fifteen-year-old Iraqi girl and killing three members of her family in a village near Baghdad. As military criminal-justice teams investigated these alleged incidents, and subsequent cover-ups, memories of the Vietnam era massacre at My Lai stirred uneasily.

Central to America's relationships with the Muslim world was U.S. support for Israel and for a "two state" solution recognizing Palestinian interests. On this front, prospects seemed bleak. When Palestinian leader Yasir Arafat rejected the Camp David peace plan and a second Palestinian Intifada began in 2000 (see Chapter 31), violence in the region escalated. Ariel Sharon of the hard-line Likud Party, elected Israel's prime minister in February 2001, demanded an end to violence before talks could resume. In response, Arafat insisted that protests would continue so long as Israel fostered Jewish settlements in Palestinian territory. In June 2002, Israel began building a security barrier, partially extending into the West Bank, to control access and prevent suicide attacks.

A U.S.-sponsored "road map to peace," proposed in 2003, called on the Palestinians to renounce violence and on Israel to withdraw from the West Bank and support a Palestinian state. Peace prospects briefly brightened in November 2004 when Arafat died and Mahmoud Abbas, a moderate, replaced him. In August 2005 Israel withdrew all Jewish settlements from Gaza.

But in this conflict, one step forward always seems to be followed by two steps back. In January 2006, Palestinian elections gave victory to the radical Hamas organization, which had perpetrated many attacks on Israeli civilians and even denied Israel's right to exist. The United States, the European Union, Russia, and the UN, collectively called the Quartet, called on Hamas to renounce violence and recognize Israel. When Hamas refused, the Quartet halted its regular grants to the Palestinian Authority.

After Sharon suffered a stroke in January 2006, his deputy Ehud Olmert succeeded him. While pursuing plans to withdraw from parts of the West Bank, Olmert announced that three large Jewish settlements would remain. He also asserted Israel's unilateral right to set its borders with the West Bank; extend the intrusive security barrier; and determine the future of Jerusalem, a highly sensitive issue. All Palestinian groups rejected any settlement that left West Bank territory under Israeli control; denied full sovereignty to a Palestinian state; and left Jerusalem's future status up to Israel.

Violence exploded in June 2006 as Palestinian militants in Gaza killed two Israeli soldiers on the border and kidnapped a third. Israel retaliated with heavy bombing in Gaza. Tensions escalated as Hezbollah, a militant organization supported by Iran and Syria and based in southern Lebanon, killed three Israeli soldiers, kidnapped two more, and lobbed scores of rockets into northern Israel, including the major city of Haifa. Denouncing this "act of war," Israel bombed not only Hezbollah bases but also the Beirut airport and bridges and highways throughout Lebanon, resulting in heavy property damage and loss of life. As in Iraq, America's influence in mediating this deepening conflict seemed steadily to diminish.

Nuclear Proliferation Threats   Although the end of the Cold War had reduced fears of the ultimate nightmare, global thermonuclear war, nuclear-related issues remained. President Reagan's antimissile "Star Wars" initiative (see Chapter 30), downgraded by President Clinton, was revived by George W. Bush. A modest, ground-based missile-defense system was technically feasible, supporters argued, and could protect America against a missile attack from North Korea or other "rogue states." Bush's proposed system violated the 1972 Anti-Ballistic Missile (ABM) Treaty between the United States and Russia. But Russian president Vladimir Putin, eager for U.S. investment and NATO membership, agreed to abandon the ABM Treaty if both sides further reduced their nuclear arsenals. The Bush administration agreed, and in 2002 the ABM Treaty officially lapsed. Soon after, Bush and Putin signed a treaty pledging to reduce their nuclear weapons by two-thirds within ten years, and NATO granted Russia a consultative relationship, though not full membership. In 2002 work began at Fort Greely, Alaska, on a ground-based missile-defense system. Despite test failures, eight interceptor missiles were in place by 2006.

Meanwhile, the administration joined with other nations to address the specter of nuclear proliferation, especially in North Korea and Iran. Isolated and impoverished North Korea, ruled by an eccentric dictator, Kim Jong Il, displayed an almost paranoid suspicion of outsiders. (The presence of more than 30,000 U.S. troops in South Korea, combined with President Bush's inclusion of North Korea in the "axis of evil" in his 2002 State of the Union address, doubtless contributed to North Korea's edginess.)

Claiming to fear a U.S. attack, North Korea boasted of its nuclear-weapons program (see Chapter 31), and in 2003 withdrew from the Nuclear Non-Proliferation Treaty. Six-nation negotiations led by China got nowhere, as North Korea demanded economic aid, one-on-one talks with the United States, a U.S. pledge not to attack, and assistance with its nuclear-power program. A North Korean long-range missile test in July 2006, although unsuccessful, deepened tensions. North Korea appeared to be using nuclear bluster to achieve other goals, but the proliferation risk could not be ignored.

Dissidents in Iran, meanwhile, revealed in 2002 the existence of uranium-enrichment laboratories needed for nuclear-power development, but also essential for building nuclear weapons. Many suspected that Iran had secured vital information from Abdul Khan, a Pakistani nuclear scientist who had confessed to passing nuclear know-how to other nations. Iran suspended its nuclear program in 2004 but resumed it early in 2006 after Mahmoud Ahmadinejad's election as president. A fiery nationalist, and Islamic fundamentalist, Ahmadinejad taunted America, called the Holocaust a myth, and said Israel "should be wiped off the map." He denied that Iran sought nuclear weapons, but insisted on its sovereign right to develop nuclear power.

In February 2006, the International Atomic Energy Agency (IAEA), backed by the United States, the European Union, and Russia, reported Iran to the UN Security Council for violating IAEA inspection guidelines. Amid talk of possible U.S. military action, Secretary of State Rice pursued the diplomatic path, working with European allies to offer Iran incentives to comply with UN guidelines.

On another front, in March 2006 President Bush agreed to sell India fuel and parts for its nuclear-power reactors even though India had secretly developed nuclear weapons and refused to sign the 1970 Nuclear Non-Proliferation Treaty. Bush said the agreement would help a democratic ally meet its energy needs and reduce fossil-fuel emissions. Critics said the agreement weakened the nonproliferation cause and undermined efforts to prevent North Korea and Iran from going nuclear.

A Widening Trade Gap and China's Growing Power
As the pace of globalization increased (see "Beyond America—Global Interactions: The Challenge of Globalization," Chapter 31), the most immediate impact for the United States was a surging trade deficit, which hit a record $726 billion in 2005. This massive imbalance mainly reflected rising prices on imported oil; surging foreign car sales, particularly from Japan (see below); and a yawning trade gap with China. With China's admission to the **World Trade Organization** in 2001, its exports boomed. Low-paid Chinese workers now produced many of the export goods formerly made in South Korea, Taiwan, and other Asian nations. In 2005, as American consumers snapped up Chinese-made clothing, sneakers, housewares, toys, electronics, and appliances, the U.S. trade deficit with China neared $202 billion. In 2006, even the U.S. State Department purchased 15,000 computers from a Chinese-owned company.

As imports grew, so did protectionist pressures. In 2002, Bush slapped tariffs on steel imports from China, the EU, and other nations, even though this violated WTO rules. He lifted the tariffs in 2003 as the EU threatened to retaliate against Florida citrus and other U.S. exports.

U.S. manufacturers complained that China artificially manipulated its currency, the yuan, to make Chinese exports cheaper. In 2005, as Congress threatened tariffs on Chinese imports, China partially eased controls on the yuan and promised eventually to let market forces determine its value. This would raise the price of Chinese imports, benefiting U.S. manufacturers.

The situation was complex, however. Cheap Chinese imports helped U.S. retailers keep their prices low. When U.S. textile manufacturers pressured Bush to impose quotas on clothing imported from China, Wal-Mart and other discount chains fought the effort. Also, many Chinese imports were produced for U.S. companies that reaped the profits when these goods were sold. As one economist noted: "While China gets the wage benefits of globalization, it does not get . . . the profits of globalization." Finally, many products labeled "Made in China" were manufactured elsewhere, with only the final assembly in China.

With a GDP approaching $2 trillion in 2004, China was the world's fourth-largest economy, behind the United States, Japan, and Germany. Some economists predicted it would be first in twenty years. On a 2005 visit to Beijing, President Bush acknowledged China's centrality in the global marketplace and in the U.S. economy while criticizing the regime's repressiveness and its restraints on religious freedom. Others attacked China's poor environmental record, including massive greenhouse-gas emissions. A U.S. visit by Chinese leader Hu Jintao in 2006 revealed a similar combination of wariness and recognition of the two nations' interdependence. With 40 percent of its 1.3 billion people living at the subsistence level, China urgently needs continued economic development, and for this, the U.S. market is crucial. As a Chinese diplomat wrote in *Foreign Affairs* in 2005: "[China] must maintain a close relationship with the United States if its modernization efforts are to succeed. . . . [A] cooperative partnership with Washington is of primary importance to Beijing."

Environmental
Hazards Become
a Global Concern

Three Mile Island, Love Canal, and the *Exxon Valdez* disaster (see Chapters 30 and 31) all underscored modern technology's environmental risks. A 1986 nuclear-power plant explosion at Chernobyl in the Ukraine and a 1984 disaster in Bhopal, India, in which deadly gases from a U.S.-owned chemical plant killed seventeen hundred people, highlighted the global scope of these risks. Environmental issues remained central in the early twenty-first century.

With the Cold War over, the United States helped Russia, Ukraine, and Kazakhstan dispose of their nuclear-weapons materials (see Chapter 31). America also faced the task of disposing of its own radioactive waste from nuclear-weapons facilities, uranium and plutonium from dismantled nuclear weapons, and spent fuel rods from aging nuclear-power plants. Since these materials will remain deadly for thousands of years, the issue proved highly contentious. In 2002, over protests by local politicians, President Bush designated Yucca Mountain in the Nevada desert as the nation's nuclear-waste disposal site. Scientists warned of seismic activity and corrosive water seepage in the area, but planning proceeded, with the facility scheduled to open by 2010.

Other environmental hazards threatened as well. Acid rain carrying sulfur dioxide and other pollutants from U.S. factories and vehicle exhaust damaged Appalachian forests and Canadian lakes. As fluorocarbons from aerosol cans, refrigeration equipment, and other sources depleted the atmosphere's ozone layer, more solar radiation reached the earth's surface, increasing skin-cancer risks. Air and water pollution posed global health hazards, from respiratory ailments to deadly intestinal diseases. Above all, **global warming** posed a long-range hazard. (See Technology and Culture: Developing New Tools for Measuring Global Warming).

The United States, with other industrialized and developing nations, was deeply implicated in these global environmental trends. With under 5 percent of the world's population, America accounts for 25 percent of global energy consumption. And this energy comes heavily from the fossil fuels that figure prominently in global-warming discussions. To be sure, environmental laws had some effect. With stricter emission standards, U.S. vehicles and factories produced one-third less carbon monoxide from 1970 to 2003. Air quality in some cities, notably Los Angeles, improved. But other key indicators of environmental pollution worsened. A 2005 EPA study found that U.S. motor vehicles were, on average, significantly less fuel efficient than they had been in the late 1980s.

The Bush administration's environmental record was mixed at best. On taking office, Bush halted the EPA's implementation of measures to reduce carbon dioxide emissions from power plants. Government scientists who questioned administration policies were marginalized. In 2002, when the EPA cited scientific data confirming global warming, Bush dismissed it as "a report put out by the bureaucracy." The administration's energy program (see above) downplayed the environmental impact of fossil-fuel consumption. Conservation might be a "sign of personal virtue," said Vice President Cheney, but had no place in energy-policy discussions. Rejecting calls for stricter emission laws and fuel-efficiency standards, the administration instead touted distant and uncertain alternative energy sources, such as hydrogen-powered fuel cells.

A UN-sponsored conference on global warming, held in Kyoto, Japan, in 1997, drafted a protocol setting strict emission targets for industrialized nations. President Clinton had signed it but did not submit it for Senate ratification, fearing defeat. President Bush repudiated the protocol entirely, charging that it would jeopardize

America's standard of living. He criticized the document for exempting developing nations such as China and India, which are, indeed, major polluters.

At a follow-up conference in Bonn, Germany, in 2001, delegates from 178 nations crafted a new plan for cutting fossil-fuel emissions designed to meet U.S. objections. Again, the administration rejected it. The Bonn treaty was "not in [America's] interests," declared National Security Adviser Condoleezza Rice. The revised **Kyoto Accords** went into effect in 2005, with only the United States, Australia, India, and China refusing to cooperate. Reviewing this record, the head of the EPA under President Richard Nixon commented: "[T]his administration is not a conservative administration. . . . [I]t's a radical administration. It represents a radical rollback of environmental policy going back . . . many, many years."

Social and Cultural Trends in Contemporary America

In the late twentieth and early twenty-first centuries the long-term migration from the Northeast, Midwest, and Plains states to the South and West continued, as did the flow of immigrants from Asia and Latin America. Fundamental economic changes affected millions of Americans, benefiting some but creating difficulties for others, including displaced industrial workers and inner-city residents.

An Increasingly Diverse People   The rapid growth, geographic mobility, and ethnic diversity long characteristic of U.S. society continued in these years, as did the historic shift to the South and West, reflecting both internal migration and immigration patterns. The West added 10.4 million residents in the 1990s, with California alone increasing by more than 4 million. Maricopa County, Arizona (which includes Phoenix), grew by nearly 1 million. The South expanded by nearly 15 million in the decade.

Household arrangements continue to evolve. The proportion of "traditional" families headed by a married heterosexual couple fell from 74 percent in 1960 to 50 percent in 2004. People living alone made up 26 percent of households in 2004, while 4.2 percent of households were maintained by unmarried partners. Commenting on these statistics, the *New York Times* observed, "[T]he nuclear family is not the only kind of family or even the only healthy kind of family. In modern America no type of family can really be recognized to the exclusion of all others."

The graying of the baby-boom generation (those born between 1946 and 1964) pushed the median age from around 33 in 1990 to 36 in 2004, the highest in American history. On the public-health front, average life expectancy at birth rose from seventy-four to seventy-seven between 1980 and 2002. (Life expectancy differs by gender, race, and other variables, however.) The decline in cigarette smoking by Americans continues, falling to under 25 percent of the population in 2004. Ominously, however, nearly 40 percent of 18- to 25-year-olds are smokers.

America is becoming increasingly diverse and multicultural. Growing immigration from Asia and Latin America in recent decades reversed a long decline in the proportion of foreign-born persons in the population. From a low of about 5 percent in 1970, this figure reached nearly 12 percent in 2004.

The population of 299 million (as of mid-2006) is about 13 percent Hispanic, 12 percent black, 4 percent Asian, and 1 percent American Indian. The Asian category includes persons who trace their ancestry to India, China, the Philippines, Vietnam, Laos, India, Korea, and elsewhere. The number of persons with ancestral roots in Haiti (where the languages are Creole and French) reached 385,000 by 2000. Some 6 million Muslims, mainly from the Middle East and North Africa, add to the ethno-religious mix.

The nation's Hispanics (who may be of any race but share a common language, Spanish) are nearly 60 percent of Mexican origin, with Puerto Ricans, Cubans, and Salvadorans comprising most of the balance. With their high birthrate, Hispanics are predicted to comprise 25 percent of the population by 2050. (The name most frequently given male babies in California and Texas in 1999 was José.) Many Mexicans working in the United States bypassed immigration checkpoints, making dangerous treks across the desert led by guides called "coyotes." As border controls tightened, they took more perilous routes, and in 2003–2005 over 800 died making the attempt. (See "Debating Immigration" below.)

Upward Mobility and Social Problems in a Multiethnic Society While these groups faced problems, opportunity beckoned. For African-Americans, median family income in 2003 approached $30,000. While well below the median for non-Hispanic white families ($47,777), this was 14 percent higher, in constant dollars, than the 1990 figure. College-educated blacks enjoyed significantly higher earnings, while the number of black-owned businesses reached 1.2 million in 2002. Of black high-school graduates in 2005, 57 percent went on to college. Reversing a long trend, many blacks moved from the North to the South after 1990, strengthening the thriving black middle-class and professional communities in Atlanta and other cities. The substantial black middle and professional classes, in short, are growing and thriving.

But blacks in the inner cities, where the unskilled have few job prospects, school dropout rates soar, and drug trafficking is pervasive, face a different reality. The black unemployment rate of 11 percent in 2005 (already twice the national rate) zoomed to 50 percent among men aged 22–30 lacking a college education, and 72 percent among high-school dropouts. By age thirty-five, nearly a third of black males lacking a college education have served prison time.

Inner-city black women face risks as well, particularly drug use, HIV/AIDS infection, and out-of-wedlock pregnancy. In 1970, unmarried women accounted for 37 percent of black births; in 2002, the figure stood at 68 percent. Many of these births were to teenage girls, reducing their prospects for education and employment. (Out-of-wedlock births to white women rose as well, but at a far lower rate.)

But the inner cities present hopeful trends as well, as church leaders, dedicated community activists, and private agencies such as Baltimore's Center for Fathers, Families, and Workforce Development work to provide opportunities and break the cycle of self-destructive behavior. Battling urban violence, several cities sued gun manufacturers for injuries or deaths caused by unregistered firearms. The manufacturers deliberately overproduced guns, the suits alleged, knowing that many would be sold illegally. In April 2006 the mayors of New York, Boston, Milwaukee, and other cities held a summit conference to address the plague of illegal guns.

Developing New Tools for Measuring Global Warming

Since the time of the Industrial Revolution, technology has brought great benefits to humanity, but at a cost. The technologies we rely on for light, heat, transportation, and countless other benefits consume enormous amounts of energy. The resulting emissions are having major environmental effects, including, most scientists argue, an impact on global warming, with profound future implications.

The fact of global warming is beyond dispute. The Earth's average temperature rose by one degree Fahrenheit in the twentieth century, and the rate of increase shot up after 1970. The century's ten hottest years came after 1985, and 2005 was the hottest year ever recorded. Global warming is real, reported the National Science Foundation in 2001, and likely to intensify.

Nearly all scientists also agree that carbon dioxide, methane, and other gases from fossil-fuel combustion in factories, homes, and motor vehicles contribute significantly to global warming. Just as the glass of a greenhouse traps the sun's heat, so the carbon dioxide, methane, and other "greenhouse gases" blanketing the Earth prevent solar heat from escaping. In 2005, a report issued by the leading scientific bodies of the United States, Canada, France, Italy, Germany, Great Britain, Japan, China, India, Russia, and Brazil concluded that "most of the warming in recent decades can be attributed to human activities."

From 1980 to 2003, U.S. carbon dioxide emissions from fossil fuels grew from 4.7 to 5.8 million metric tons. The output from India and China increased enormously in these same years.

Naturally occurring greenhouse gases are essential. Without their warming effect, the Earth would be a frozen waste. But in recent decades, these gases have increased to dangerous levels. Throughout Earth's known history, carbon dioxide levels remained within a range of 180 to 300 parts per million. However, beginning around 1950 the level crept up. In 2005 it reached 380 parts per million, trapping more solar heat and driving up temperatures. As polar ice melted, sea levels rose 6 to 8 inches.

Projecting current trends, scientists predict a 40 percent increase in carbon dioxide emissions by 2020, with a corresponding surge in global warming. If this happens, scientists foresee not only hotter temperatures, but also still higher sea levels from melting polar ice, disrupted climatic conditions affecting crops and plant and animal habitats, and ferocious tropical storms caused by the rise in ocean temperatures.

The impact of global warming can already be seen. Storm surges are destroying homes in Shishmaref, an Inupiat village on an island in northwestern Alaska, as a protective ice barrier melts. In 2002, the residents voted to move farther inland to preserve their community. As one said: "[P]eople here in Alaska are like everyone else. We want to keep our culture alive."

The mountain pine beetle, a pest that arrived with rising temperatures, has devastated millions of acres of spruce forest in Alaska and western Canada. As the permafrost melts, Alaskan highways are buckling, houses in Fairbanks are developing cracks, and the stability of Alaska's oil pipeline from Prudhoe Bay to Valdez is threatened.

Technology not only contributes to global warming, but also enables scientists to document the phenomenon. Hundreds of weather stations track temperature changes worldwide. Botanists and entomologists record shifts in plant and insect distribution as temperatures rise. In 2005, amphibian-disease experts reported a massive decline in rare Latin American frog species because of a spreading fungus they attributed to global warming. Australian researchers report dying coral reefs as ocean temperatures rise.

Two satellites, nicknamed Tom and Jerry, launched from a former Russian ICBM site in 2002, are measuring the polar icecaps. Using these data, scientists reported in 2006 that Antarctica's icecap is melting at a rate of thirty-six cubic miles per year—180 times the annual water consumption of Los Angeles. Satellite data show a similar melt-off in the Greenland and Arctic Ocean icecaps.

Using ice-core sampling, scientists are tracing carbon dioxide levels over vast periods of time. In the 1990s, a team of U.S., Russian, and French scientists extracted a two-mile-long ice core in Antarctica and examined trapped air bubbles to measure carbon dioxide levels over a 440,000-year span. In 2005, European researchers reported on ice cores extending back 650,000 years. Both teams concluded that current carbon dioxide levels far exceed any levels found in that incredibly long time span. As one scientist observed: "There's no natural condition that we know about in a really long time where the greenhouse gas levels were anywhere near what they are now."

Using computer simulations, climatologists predict greater temperature increases by 2100. The resulting polar melting could increase sea levels up to five feet, endangering coastal cities from Boston to San Francisco. In low-lying Bangladesh, flooding could displace 6 million people.

Mass-culture technologies heighten public awareness. Hundreds of Internet websites discuss global warming. In 2006 alone, the PBS science program *Nova* aired a global-warming episode; Al Gore's film *An Inconvenient Truth* documented the dangers; and an HBO special, *Too Hot Not to Handle,* urged grass-roots action to reduce greenhouse gases.

Hollywood has used lurid plots and awesome special effects to dramatize global warming. In *Waterworld* (1995), melting polar ice inundates the whole world. Isolated floating communities shelter the only survivors except for Kevin Costner, a mutant who has developed gills. In *Day After Tomorrow* (2004), freaky weather triggered by global warming floods Manhattan, pounds Tokyo with giant hailstones, and finishes off Los Angeles with killer tornadoes. In the 2006 animated film *Ice Age: The Meltdown,* lovable creatures including Manny the Mammoth and Syd the Sloth flee to safety as melting ice threatens their habitat.

Fanciful as they are, such mass-culture productions translate sober scientific warnings into mass-culture fare. As a reviewer of *Day After Tomorrow* noted: "It's . . . a depressing comment on our crippled political culture . . . that it takes [a movie] to do what environmental groups have been trying to do for decades: get the message out about global warming."

The technologies underlying our fossil-fuel-based economy now threaten human well-being. But other technologies enable us to document the danger; alert the public; and research solar, wind, thermal, and other power alternatives. The Kyoto Accords represent a major multinational commitment to reducing greenhouse gases. The U.S. government has set emissions standards for factories and some vehicles, but California and other states have enacted even stricter standards. Research on hybrid vehicles that are far more fuel efficient is going forward.

How each society responds to the crisis is a matter not only of science or technology, but of political will. Whether that response will match the magnitude of the challenge remains an urgent question as the global community, including the United States, confronts its future.

Questions for Analysis

- What technologies help scientists document global warming?

- What strategies are being used to reduce greenhouse gases?

Among Native Americans, renewed tribal pride and activism continued. Citing Article VI of the Constitution, which describes all U.S. treaties as "the supreme law of the land," tribes sued to enforce the 331 Indian treaties ratified between 1778 and 1871. Indian gambling casinos, approved by Congress in 1988, proliferated. Connecticut's giant Foxwoods Casino, run by the Mashantucket Pequots, earned $6 billion annually. As they competed for casino licenses, Indian tribes became major political contributors (see below). Many citizens deplored the spread of gambling, and some Indians lamented the tribal conflicts and social disruption the casinos brought in their wake. But casino income did enable tribes to support schools, museums, community centers, job training, and substance-abuse programs.

The Hispanic population, too, resisted sweeping generalizations. While Mexican-Americans concentrated in the Southwest and West Coast, many lived in other regions as well. Cubans, Puerto Ricans, and other Hispanic groups, as well as Haitians, resided mainly in Florida, New York, New Jersey, and Illinois. Many Hispanics were well educated, prosperous, and upwardly mobile. Hispanic households' median income rose to $33,000 by 2003, and unemployment among Hispanics dropped from 9 percent in 1995 to 5.5 percent in early 2006. The 1.6 million Hispanic-owned businesses in 2002 represented a 31 percent increase in five years.

In 2004, 22 percent of Hispanics were living in poverty, many in inner-city neighborhoods plagued by gangs, alcohol and drug addiction, teen pregnancy, and erratic school attendance. Religion and family loom large in Hispanic culture, but stressful social conditions took their toll. Many unskilled Hispanic newcomers took poorly paid jobs as gardeners, maids, day laborers, and migrant farm workers. As the British journal *The Economist* wrote in 1998, "Wherever the booming [U.S.] economy cries out for workers . . . the ever-arriving and ever-progressing Latinos will move in. Nothing daunts them."

Americanization, Twenty-first-Century Style *Recent immigrants from Afghanistan join a fitness class in Fremont, California, in 2001.*

Hispanics, like other immigrant groups, mobilized to promote their interests. In 2005, more than five thousand Hispanics held elective public office, including Los Angeles mayor Antonio Villaraigosa, the city's first Hispanic mayor since 1872. Though Hispanics have tended to vote at lower rates than non-Hispanic whites, 7.6 million cast ballots in 2004, making them an increasingly important constituency.

Of the nation's 13 million Asian-Americans in 2004, 75 percent had arrived since 1980. This group, too, presents a variegated picture, though with certain commonalities. Prizing education and supported by family networks, many followed a trajectory of academic achievement and upward mobility. In 2004 nearly 50 percent of adult Asian-Americans held college degrees. Among Asian-American high-school graduates in 2005, the college-enrollment rate neared 90 percent.

After passage of the Immigration Reform Act of 1965, many Indian doctors, engineers, and academics emigrated to America, often joined later by parents and other family members. In Fremont, California, the Asian population grew from 19 percent in 1990 to 40 percent in 2000, with many of the newcomers working in nearby Silicon Valley. The Hmong comprise was yet another distinct Asian immigrant group contributing a new strand to American life.

By 2050, demographers calculate, no single ethno-racial group will be a majority in America. Non-Hispanic whites, in other words, while still a plurality, will simply be another minority. Many Americans of mixed origins, like the golfer Tiger Woods, of Thai, Chinese, African-American, and American Indian ancestry, resist being pigeonholed. From 1960 to 2000, the number of interracial married couples in the United States rose

FIGURE 32.1 U.S. Population by Race and Hispanic Origin, 2000 and 2050 (Projected)

By 2050, the Census Bureau projects, with some 40 million Asian-Americans, 90 million Hispanics, and 60 million African-Americans, non-Hispanic whites will constitute less than half the total U.S. population. *Source:* U.S. Census Bureau, 2000.

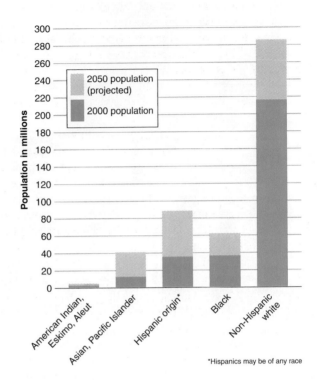

*Hispanics may be of any race

from 149,000 to 1.5 million. Recognizing these realities, in 2000 the Census Bureau permitted citizens to check more than one racial category, or none at all.

Not everyone welcomed the new diversity, and the phenomenon of "white flight" continued. Between 1990 and 1995 both Los Angeles and New York lost more than 1 million native-born inhabitants, approximately equal to the new arrivals from Asia and Latin America. Language became a major battleground. While some campaigned to make English America's "official language," others called for school instruction in children's native tongue, or at least bilingual classes. Interestingly, a 1998 study found that immigrant children themselves overwhelmingly wished to learn and speak English in school.

In an increasingly diverse nation, some observers foresaw a society divided psychologically if not physically along lines of race, ethnicity, religion, or national origin. In a 2005 Los Angeles poll, 70 percent of blacks and 64 percent of Hispanics rated race relations as "poor" or "not so good." The 2005 movie *Crash,* winner of the Academy Award for best picture, portrayed a society seething with racial and ethnic hostility. Whether through a shared awareness of prejudice or economic inequity, or in reaction to the anonymity of mass society, many people clearly seek the reassurance of a clear-cut group identity. Others retreat into enclaves defined by wealth, profession, or social status. The persistence of the culture wars and abusive political rhetoric (see Chapter 31) deepens the divisions.

In such a situation, what does it mean to be "American"? In his 1908 play *The Melting Pot,* Israel Zangwill, a Jewish immigrant from England, foresaw the blending of immigrants into a common national identity. A century later, Zangwill's metaphor has faded, in part because its advocates usually assumed that entering the "melting pot" meant abandoning one's ethnic roots and cultural traditions and conforming to an Anglo or northwestern European model. If the "melting pot" model doesn't work, what will unite this diverse society? Americans share a common identity as consumers of goods and mass-culture entertainment. Is this enough? Can the nation's civic culture match its commercial and leisure culture? The answer remains unclear.

The "New Economy" and the Old Economy

In *The Coming of Post-Industrial Society: A Venture in Social Forecasting* (1973), sociologist Daniel Bell offered a remarkably accurate prediction of changes in the U.S. economy. In the late nineteenth and early twentieth centuries, America's mainly farm economy gave way to one driven by industrial production. As the twentieth century ended, an equally profound transformation occurred: the decline of industry and the rise of a professional and service-based economy. Farming and manufacturing continued, of course, but not as major sources of employment.

A snapshot of the U.S. labor force in 2004 tells the story. In a work force of 140 million, 62 percent held white-collar jobs, ranging from business and financial management and professions such as medicine, the law, teaching, engineering, telecommunications, and computer programming to sales, office work, and careers in the entertainment and leisure fields. Lower-paid service-sector workers in health care, personal services, custodial work, and food-related occupations comprised another 16 percent. A mere 23 percent worked in fields that as recently as 1960 had dominated the labor market: manufacturing, farming, construction, and transportation. Daniel Bell's "post-industrial society" has become a reality.

The rewards of the new economy were unevenly distributed. Some young people with the necessary education, skills, and contacts found exciting challenges and good salaries in the new electronics, programming, and telecommunications fields. For less-privileged youths, supermarkets, car washes, fast-food outlets, and discount superstores provided entry-level jobs, but few long-term career prospects. For displaced industrial workers, the impact could be devastating.

Globalization contributed to the transformation of the U.S. economy. The availability of cheap imported products hastened the decline of U.S. manufacturing, from toys and textiles to steel and automobiles. As VW, Toyota, Honda, Subaru, and other foreign automakers grabbed more U.S. sales, America's automakers, in trouble since the 1970s (see Chapter 30), faced a crisis. Ford's market share fell from 25 percent in 2000 to 17 percent in 2005. Early in 2006, Ford announced plans to eliminate up to 30,000 jobs and close 14 factories. Chrysler (now Daimler-Chrysler through merger with a German firm) faced problems as well. As gas prices hit $3 a gallon in 2006, sales of SUVs and light trucks, moneymakers for U.S. automakers in the 1990s, plummeted, worsening the crisis.

General Motors, another icon of America's industrial might, having lost $10.6 billion in 2005 and watched its stock price tumble by 50 percent, announced plans to lay off 30,000 of its 113,000 factory workers and thousands of white-collar employees, and close or scale back a dozen plants. Workers willing to quit were offered buyouts of up to $140,000. Said one GM engineer: "This once was the premier company . . . to work for. You were at the top of the heap, the major leagues. . . . Today, you know this company is crumbling around you." Delphi, GM's parts supplier, went bankrupt in 2006 and prepared to close most of its twenty-nine U.S. plants. GM's pension and medical costs for 1.1 million retirees and their families, written into union contracts in better times, added to the crushing burden. One wit described GM as a health-care company that also makes cars. In other countries with national health-insurance plans paid for by taxes, governments rather than individual companies cover these costs.

Altogether, in 2000–2006 the big three automakers announced plans to cut some 140,000 jobs. In these circumstances, the long decline in union membership continued, sinking to only 12 percent of the work force in 2004. As unions grew weaker, workers had less bargaining power to resist wage cuts and other concessions demanded by management. As if to rub salt in the wound, Toyota, poised to overtake GM as the world's largest carmaker, set an all-time monthly U.S. sales record of 220,000 vehicles in March 2006. The big foreign automakers took pains to emphasize that they are also major U.S. employers. Toyota boasts of supporting 386,000 U.S. jobs through its nine manufacturing plants in seven states plus its dealerships, parts suppliers, R&D centers, and advertising agencies. Toyota's Camry plant in Georgetown, Kentucky, alone employs 7,000 workers. In auto making, as throughout the U.S. economy, globalization's effects are complicated. One thing is clear, however: the economic order familiar to the parents and grandparents of today's youth is gone forever.

DOMESTIC POLICY SINCE 2004

President Bush called for social-security reform and expanded prescription-drug benefits for seniors, but his domestic policies did little to lift his approval ratings. The administration's slow response to the devastation of Hurricane Katrina in 2005 brought new charges of incompetence. Bush sought to preserve his conservative legacy through two Supreme Court appointments, but a mushrooming federal deficit, lobbying scandals, blatant congressional spending on pet projects, and soaring gasoline prices as oil companies reported record profits further soured the public mood as the 2006 midterm elections approached.

Funding Social Security and Health Care as the Federal Deficit Soars Since social-security was introduced in 1935, conservative Republicans have argued for its abolition or privatization. Launching his second term, Bush called for a partial privatization of social-security, enabling workers to shift some of their social-security funds to private investment accounts. Bush pushed this proposal heavily, but the public remained cool. Most citizens preferred a government-run program to the uncertainties of the market. Democrats dismissed the idea as simply another expression of the administration's ideological commitment to privatization and to reducing the government's role in the economy.

In 2003, the Republican Congress expanded the 1965 Medicare program (see Chapter 28) to cover part of seniors' prescription-drug expenses beginning in 2006. Drug costs worried older Americans, but the plan proved extremely complicated, and many seniors felt more aggravation than gratitude as they battled the red tape. "I have a Ph.D., and it's too complicated to suit me," said one. Democrats criticized the plan as designed to benefit drug firms and insurance companies more than retirees. Since retirees vote in large numbers, their frustration worried GOP strategists.

The prescription-drug benefit further burdened an already costly program. In 2004, Medicare and Medicaid, the government's health-insurance systems for the elderly and the poor, cost $600 billion, more than double the 1990 figure. These costs, along with social-security benefits, will soar even higher as baby boomers retire. These entitlement programs, plus Iraq War costs and interest payments on the $9 trillion national debt, produced explosive federal deficits. The deficit, $319 billion in 2005 was projected to surpass $420 billion in 2006.

Despite such numbers, Bush insisted that his tax cuts be made permanent. This action, budget experts predicted, would drive the deficit over $500 billion by 2015. As Washington issued bonds to cover the growing debt, China and other foreign governments awash in dollars because of the U.S. trade deficit snapped them up. But economists warned that this method of funding the debt would eventually dry up, leaving future generations of Americans to pay off the massive debt racked up during the Bush years.

Worsening the deficit crisis, Congress members continued the long-standing practice of quietly inserting into spending bills special provisions known as "earmarks" that benefited their districts. A 2005 highway bill included 6,000 earmarks promoting pet projects, including two "bridges to nowhere" proposed by Alaska senator Ted Stevens. In a 2006 spending bill covering Iraq War and Hurricane Katrina costs, legislators added $14 billion for unrelated pet projects.

Hurricane Katrina Tests the Bush Administration   In August 2005, **Hurricane Katrina** struck the Gulf Coast, taking as many as 1,400 lives. Coastal areas of Alabama, Mississippi, and Louisiana suffered massive damage. Disrupted shipping on the Mississippi River hurt corn and soybean growers far to the north. Katrina and a subsequent hurricane smashed oil refineries and offshore oil rigs.

The most catastrophic damage hit New Orleans, the legendary "Big Easy" at the mouth of the Mississippi. Much of the city lies below sea level, protected by levees from the Gulf of Mexico and Lake Pontchartrain. Over the years, developers had drained thousands of acres around New Orleans. This had not only done severe ecological damage but also increased the flood hazard by eliminating the sponge-like marshlands that could absorb the water when Lake Pontchartrain overflowed. Inadequate levees and poor levee maintenance, revealed in post-storm investigations, had heightened the danger.

As levees burst under Katrina's storm surge, rampaging water flooded New Orleans's lower sections, populated mainly by poor blacks. Many residents drowned or died awaiting rescue. Others escaped with their lives as houses and possessions disappeared. Thousands poured into New Orleans's Superdome, which soon became a squalid disaster zone. Buses transported others to cities as far away as Houston. Some died of heat prostration as they waited along highways for rescue. The toll among the elderly and residents of nursing homes and hospitals was especially high. The longer-term impact was equally devastating, as public schools, churches, and hospitals closed their doors. Tulane University and the city's other institutions of higher education experienced major disruptions. In May 2006, New Orleans's population was only about 40 percent of its pre-storm level.

As New Orleans endured the worst natural disaster in recent U.S. history, the government response at all levels was appallingly inadequate. While many New Orleans police officers performed well, others disappeared, either caring for their own families or overwhelmed by the crisis. State and federal officials did little better. FEMA head Michael Brown, a political appointee with no disaster experience, proved hopelessly ineffectual. Though initially praised by Bush ("Heck of a job, Brownie"), he soon resigned. President Bush made token visits and delivered a TV speech in the city's historic district, but the administration's performance did not match the president's rhetoric.

A 2006 congressional report documented the scope of the failure. A FEMA official who observed a major levee break on Monday, August 29, had urgently notified Michael Brown, who immediately alerted the Department of Homeland Security and the White House. Yet the next day Homeland Security director Michael Chertoff flew to a meeting in Atlanta unrelated to Katrina, and President Bush, vacationing in Texas, expressed pleasure that New Orleans had "dodged the bullet." The distribution of emergency relief funds involved massive fraud. FEMA spent $900 million on 26,000 mobile homes, many of which sat empty and unused. Despite the post-9/11 reorganization of the security bureaucracy, Hurricane Katrina revealed the same pattern of slow response and failed communication among responsible officials.

By summer 2006 no coherent plan had emerged for reconstructing New Orleans's destroyed districts or bringing back the city's scattered residents. The levees were hastily repaired, yet no one knew how they would withstand future hurricanes. Recovery in the hardest-hit parts of the city remained stalled. As streets stood silent and empty, with no electricity and rows of shattered and abandoned houses, sections of New Orleans resembled a ghost town.

Extending Republican Influence: From the Supreme Court to K Street

When Supreme Court justice Sandra Day O'Connor, a Reagan appointee who had emerged as a key swing vote in many 5–4 decisions, announced her retirement in July 2005, Bush nominated as her replacement federal appeals-court judge John G. Roberts, Jr., who had held posts in the Reagan Justice Department and White House. When Chief Justice William Rehnquist died in September, Bush nominated Roberts as chief justice. He won easy Senate confirmation while revealing little about his judicial philosophy.

To fill the second vacancy, Bush chose White House counsel Harriet Miers, a longtime Texas friend and adviser. While conservatives criticized Miers on ideological grounds, others questioned her qualifications. When Miers withdrew, Bush nominated Samuel Alito, Jr., a federal appeals-court judge enthusiastically supported by conservatives. As a Justice Department lawyer in the Reagan administration, and later as a judge, Alito had espoused a very broad view of the powers of the executive branch—a view embraced by the Bush administration to justify its actions at home and abroad after 9/11.

At his confirmation hearings Alito recalled his humble Italian-American origins, but proved equally unwilling to discuss his judicial philosophy. This frustrated Democrats who feared that he might vote to overturn *Roe* v. *Wade* and join Antonin Scalia and Clarence Thomas (President Bush's two favorite justices) in upholding White House claims to vast powers. Critics also worried that he would interpret the Constitution so narrowly as to restrict the court's engagement with social-justice and civil-rights issues. Alito, too, won confirmation, though on a much closer vote than Roberts.

The Court now had five Roman Catholic justices, something unthinkable in earlier eras of anti-Catholic prejudice.

In a challenge to *Roe* v. *Wade*, the South Dakota legislature in 2006 passed an extreme abortion ban with no exceptions even for rape or the mother's health. This law was sure to face legal challenge, perhaps reaching the Supreme Court. Public opinion on abortion remained remarkably consistent, with most leading polls showing about 55 percent of Americans supporting legal abortions with certain restrictions, 24 percent favoring no restrictions at all, and 20 percent believing that all abortion should be banned.

As Supreme Court politics drew the nation's attention, so did the growing influence of Washington lobbyists. Lobbying has been a part of American politics from the beginning. (The term comes from the fact that individuals seeking to influence legislation gathered in the lobbies of the Capitol or state legislatures to buttonhole politicians, because they were barred from the actual legislative chambers.) Today, many Washington lobbyists, often ex-legislators or legislative aides, have offices on K Street, near the White House.

Lobbyists' influence grew enormously during the ascendancy of Congressman Tom DeLay of Texas, nicknamed "the Hammer," the Republican majority whip (1995–2003) and majority leader (2003–2005). The ranks of registered lobbyists expanded from around 15,000 in 2000 to nearly 33,000 in 2005, with many more unregistered ones. Implementing a plan dubbed "the K Street project," DeLay pressured lobbying organizations to hire Republicans, and he extracted campaign contributions from lobbyists seeking to influence legislation. In 2003 DeLay engineered a Texas congressional redistricting under which Republicans gained five seats, a step toward the larger goal of creating a permanent Republican majority.

A series of high-visibility cases in 2005 focused attention on lobbyists and the role of money in politics. In September, DeLay resigned as majority leader after his indictment by a Texas grand jury for violating state election laws. In November, a San Diego Republican congressman admitted accepting more than $2 million in bribes and unreported campaign contributions from defense contractors. In December, a federal grand jury indicted Jack Abramoff, a high-flying Washington lobbyist with close ties to DeLay, who soon resigned from Congress. The indictments of Abramoff and a top aide alleged that they had obtained millions of dollars from corporations interested in influencing legislation, including $82 million from Indian tribes promoting their casino interests. Laundered though dummy organizations such as the "Capital Athletic Foundation," much of this money went as bribes or campaign donations to Congress members—mostly Republicans but also some prominent Democrats—while Abramoff himself allegedly siphoned off millions. Pleading guilty at his hearing early in 2006, Abramoff admitted "a multitude of mistakes." Both DeLay and Abramoff had close connections with President Bush, but the White House denied any wrongdoing.

DeLay and Abramoff emerged as symbols of a corrupt system by which lobbyists influenced legislation through contributions, gifts, lavish dinners, expensive golf junkets, and hiring politicians' relatives. Republican congressman Bob Ney of Ohio, chair of the powerful Committee on House Administration, came under Justice Department scrutiny for a golf vacation in Scotland funded by Abramoff and for involvement in a 2002 Abramoff scheme by which a Texas Indian tribe seeking a casino permit gave Ney's campaign committee $32,000. As public disgust mounted, politicians scrambled to return Abramoff's contributions, distance themselves from lobbyists, and regulate lobbyists' behavior more strictly. Said Democratic senator Christopher Dodd of Connecticut: "There's a sign that's now up in front of the Capitol. It says 'Not for Sale.'" Whether the flurry of reform would reduce the power of money in government in the long run remained unclear.

Debating Immigration   The thorny issue of immigration reform surged to prominence in 2006. Attention focused on the estimated 11 million illegal immigrants, 78 percent of them from Mexico or elsewhere in Latin America, up from 3.9 million in 1992. Many worked for low wages in a "shadow economy" as migrant agricultural laborers, motel cleaners, janitors, gardeners, fast-food employees, and nursing-home attendants, or in food-processing plants such as Cargill, or Tyson, the poultry company.

In 2001, President Bush had proposed a "guest worker" program by which short-term immigrants would receive temporary work visas requiring them to return to their own country when the permit expired. The 9/11 attacks and the Iraq War temporarily eclipsed the issue, but when the administration introduced an immigration-reform bill late in 2005, it again seized public attention.

The debate was complex, and emotions ran high. Some invoked America's tradition of welcoming newcomers, symbolized by the Statue of Liberty, and argued that the

Antonio Villaraigosa, Mayor-Elect of Los Angeles, May 2005   *The first Hispanic mayor of Los Angeles since the 1870s, Villaraigosa speaks on the phone beneath a photo of John and Robert Kennedy, his political heroes. His election symbolized the growing political power of the nation's rapidly expanding Hispanic population.*

undocumented immigrants did the hard but necessary work that few others would do. Others argued that if undocumented immigrants working for low wages were excluded, the law of supply-and-demand would push up the wages for these jobs and U.S. citizens would take them, increasing opportunities for the unemployed.

As the debate went on, private citizens in the Southwest organized the Minuteman Project in 2005 to monitor the U.S.-Mexican border and report illegal entries to the Border Patrol. Late in 2005, the House of Representatives passed a tough immigration bill introduced by Wisconsin's James Sensenbrenner. This bill criminalized illegal aliens and required their deportation. It also called for the construction of a 700-mile barrier along the U.S.-Mexican border and made it a felony for anyone, including ministers, priests, and health-care providers, to help undocumented immigrants.

Reaction to the Sensenbrenner bill was swift. Catholic bishops denounced the criminalizing of aid to illegal immigrants, and advised priests to disobey such a law. In March and April 2006, immigrant advocates organized protest demonstrations in Los Angeles, Phoenix, Chicago, and other cities. Over half a million marched in Los Angeles; 100,000 in Chicago. Said Jessica Aranda, an organizer of the Chicago rally: "Our community is coming into our own, and realizing our own power." Spanish-language radio stations and TV channels—an increasingly important segment of the mass media—supported the demonstrations.

A backlash quickly erupted. "My first thought is anger, folks," declared right-wing radio pundit Rush Limbaugh. When Hispanic stations broadcast "Nuestro Himno," a Spanish version of "The Star-Spangled Banner," some citizens angrily protested.

In the Senate, meanwhile, a bipartisan bill provided for beefed-up border control, but also established procedures by which undocumented immigrants could eventually secure citizenship. Opponents denounced this as a covert form of "amnesty" for illegal immigrants.

With the Hispanic vote up for grabs (some called it "the sleeping giant of American politics"), and with many native-born citizens angry about illegal immigration, both parties proceeded cautiously. The final legislative outcome remained uncertain.

The Election of 2006

Mid-term elections often focus on local issues. In 2006, however, the voters rendered a stinging judgment on the Iraq War, the Republican Congress, and the Bush administration. Even President Bush admitted that his party had taken a "thumping." In the House of Representatives, the Democrats won at least 29 seats, to regain the majority. They also won control of the Senate, by the barest of margins, 51-49. The number of women in the Senate inched upward, from 14 to 16, a record high. Also, for the first time since 1994, a majority of governorships—28—fell into Democratic hands. In Massachusetts, Deval Patrick became only the second African American elected governor since Reconstruction.

The results made clear voters' discontent over the nation's direction, and especially over the Iraq War, from the deceptions with which it was launched to the disastrous way it was conducted. Facing this reality, President Bush the day after the election announced the resignation of Defense Secretary Donald Rumsfeld, the chief architect of the war.

Other issues influencing the outcome were massive federal budget deficits and a constant stream of corruption and personal scandals that dominated the news in the months before the election. Facing all these negatives, the Republicans could not capitalize on favorable economic news, such as a rising stock market, lower gas prices, and falling unemployment.

New technologies loomed large in the campaign, including computerized phone banks, video cameras and blogs that publicized candidates' embarrassing gaffes, and even the personal websites on YouTube. Millions of voters used sophisticated (but sometimes problem-prone) touch screen and optical scanner machinery for the first time.

The Democratic victories meant new Congressional leadership in 2007: Harry Reid of Nevada as Senate Majority Leader, and Nancy Pelosi of San Francisco as Speaker of the House of Representatives, the first woman to hold that post. At a victory party in Washington, D.C., Pelosi told her fellow Democrats: "Today we have made history. Now let us make progress." Despite the euphoria of victory for the Democrats and the sting of defeat for Republicans, politicians in both parties recognized that America faced grave problems at home and abroad, and that leaders of all political persuasions, backed by an informed and engaged citizenry, would have to work together to put the nation back on course.

CONCLUSION

George W. Bush's presidency had scarcely begun when the attacks of September 11, 2001, shocked the nation. Americans supported Bush as he mobilized an attack on al Qaeda terrorists in Afghanistan, and Congress overwhelmingly passed the administration's antiterrorism legislation, the USA-Patriot Act. The invasion of Iraq, promoted as an antiterrorism measure, won broad initial support.

As the stock market fell sharply and scandal rocked corporate America, Bush called for tax cuts that favored the wealthy and measures to increase domestic fossil-fuel production. Bush's education program involved universal testing in reading and math, plus public funding of private charter schools.

Domestic support for the war eroded amid worsening sectarian violence in Iraq, revelations of abuses by the U.S. military and domestic spying in the name of security, and skepticism about the administration's case for invading Iraq. Other troubling world developments included worsening Israeli-Palestinian relations; nuclear programs in North Korea and Iran; and China's growing economic and military power. As global warming and other environmental hazards roused concern, the Bush administration downplayed the threat, advocated voluntarist responses, and rejected international efforts to address the crisis.

Major social trends in these years included continuing migration to the South and West, chronic inner-city problems, and increasing ethnic diversity as the Hispanic and Asian populations grew. On the economic front, the long-term shift from industrial production to an information-based and service economy proceeded, and a massive tide of foreign imports stirred uneasiness, especially in the troubled domestic auto industry.

Several developments heightened public frustration after 2004, as Bush's second term began, including a growing federal deficit and pressures on Medicare and social security as the baby boomers retired. Washington's flawed response to the devastation of Hurricane Katrina; influence-peddling scandals; and legislators' lavish spending on pet projects deepened many citizens' skepticism about the integrity and competence of government. As job worries focused attention on illegal immigrants, various strategies emerged for dealing with the problem.

In 2001, accepting the Nobel Peace Prize a few weeks after 9/11, UN Secretary General Kofi Annan said: "We have entered the third millennium through a gate of fire." But Annan went on to evoke the vision that had inspired the UN's founders in 1945. Despite the hatred and inequalities dividing nations and peoples, he insisted, the fate of all Earth's inhabitants is interconnected. The task of the twenty-first century, he said, is to achieve "a new, more profound awareness of the sanctity and dignity of every human life, regardless of race or religion. . . . Humanity is indivisible."

As we conclude this history of America and its people, what is the "enduring vision" of our title? There is, of course, no single vision, but many. That is part of America's meaning. Nor is this a vision of a foreordained national destiny unfolding effortlessly, but rather of successive generations' laborious, often frustrating struggle to define what their common life as a people should be. For all the failures, setbacks, and wrong turns, the shared visions, at their best, are rooted in hope, not fear. In 1980, Jesse de la Cruz, a Mexican-American woman who fought for years to improve conditions for California's migrant workers, summed up the philosophy that kept her going: "Is America progressing toward the better? . . . We're the ones that are gonna do it. We have to keep on struggling. . . . With us, there's a saying: *La esperanza muere al ultimo.* Hope dies last. You can't lose hope. If you lose hope, that's losing everything."

Credits

Photo Credits

CHAPTER 1 *p. 6:* Richard Alexander Cooke III. *p. 10:* Richard Alexander Cooke III. *p. 13:* Courtesy of the Illinois Transportation Archaeological Research Program, University of Illinois.

CHAPTER 2 *p. 22:* Courtesy of Entwistle Gallery, London / Werner Forman Archives / Art Resource, New York. *p. 42:* George H.H. Huey. *p. 46:* Manuscripts Division, Department of Rare Books and Special Collections / Princeton University Library.

CHAPTER 3 *p. 61:* The Granger Collection, New York. *p. 70:* drawing from John Underhill's *News from America*, 1638. *p. 73:* This item is reproduced by permission of the *Huntington Library, San Marino, California.*

CHAPTER 4 *p. 94:* Library Company of Philadelphia. *p. 101:* Library of Congress. *p. 108:* Mackinac State Historic Parks Collection. *p. 119:* © Copyright the Trustees of The British Museum.

CHAPTER 5 *p. 124:* courtesy of the John Carter Brown Library. *p. 136:* The Metropolitan Museum of Art, Bequest of Charles Allen Munn, 1924. Photograph © The Metropolitan Museum of Art, New York. *p. 152:* Library of Congress. *p. 159:* Art Gallery, Williams Center, Lafayette College, Easton, Pennsylvania.

CHAPTER 6 *p. 162:* The Metropolitan Museum of Art, Bequest of Charles Allen Munn, 1929. Photograph © 1989 The Metropolitan Museum of Art, New York. *p. 168:* Library of Congress. *p. 174:* Fenimore Art Museum, Cooperstown, New York. *p. 193:* Colonial Williamsburg Foundation, Gift of Mrs. George S. Robbins.

CHAPTER 7 *p. 204:* Courtesy of Credit Suisse. *p. 212:* Chicago History Museum, P&S-1932.0018. *p. 225:* Library Company of Philadelphia. *p. 229:* Courtesy Bureau of American Ethnology Collection, Smithsonian Institution, Washington, D.C., negative 1169A.

CHAPTER 8 *p. 236:* Library of Congress. *p. 247:* Cincinnati Museum Center. *p. 252:* The Granger Collection, New York. *p. 255:* Washington and Lee University, Lexington, Virginia.

CHAPTER 9 *p. 264:* Library of Congress. *p. 277:* Jack Naylor Collection / Picture Research Consultants and Archives. *p. 281:* The Granger Collection, New York.

CHAPTER 10 *p. 296:* Memphis Brooks Museum of Art, Memphis, Tennessee; Memphis Park Commission Purchase 46.2. *p. 301:* Collection of The New-York Historical Society, image

42459. *p. 313:* Boston Athenaeum. *p. 318:* Elizabeth Cady Stanton Trust / Picture Research Consultants and Archives.

Chapter 11 *p. 326:* Library of Congress. *p. 333:* Stereo daguerreotype by Antoine Claudet, Courtesy George Eastman House, #GEH22760. *p. 348:* National Museum of American Art / Art Resource, New York.

Chapter 12 *p. 358:* Missouri Historical Society. *p. 370:* John Verelst / Library and Archives of Canada / C-092414 / National Archives of Canada. *p. 375:* Valentine Richmond History Center.

Chapter 13 *p. 394:* Daughters of the Republic of Texas Library. Gift of the Tanaguana Society. *p. 405:* Henry Groskinsky. *p. 409:* Library of Congress.

Chapter 14 *p. 419:* Warshaw-Moving Pictures, Archives Center, National Museum of American History / Smithsonian Institution, Washington, D.C. *p. 425:* Miriam and Ira D. Wallach Division of Art, Prints and Photographs, The New York Public Library, Astor, Lenox and Tilden Foundations. *p. 427:* Library of Congress. *p. 433:* Library of Congress.

Chapter 15 *p. 455:* Antietam National Battlefield, Sharpsburg, Maryland. *p. 463:* Chicago History Museum, ICHi-22051. *p. 472:* Library of Congress.

Chapter 16 *p. 482:* Courtesy of Special Collections, LSU Libraries, Louisiana State University. *p. 492:* Schlesinger Library, Radcliffe Institute / Harvard University. *p. 494:* The Museum of the Confederacy, Richmond, Virginia. *p. 502:* Collection of The New-York Historical Society, image 50819.

Chapter 17 *p. 523:* (left) National Anthropological Archives / Smithsonian Institution, Washington, D.C. *p. 523:* (right) National Anthropological Archives, neg. 07-0222 / Smithsonian Institution, Washington, D.C. *p. 527:* Kansas Collection, University of Kansas Libraries. *p. 520:* Alaska and Polar Regions Archives, Elmer E. Rasmunson Library, University of Alaska.

Chapter 18 *p. 551:* Frank and Marie-Therese Wood Print Collections, Alexandria, Virginia. *p. 564: Harper's Weekly,* March 26, 1877. *p. 568:* Library of Congress. *p. 573:* Museum of American Political Life, University of Hartford, West Hartford, Connecticut.

Chapter 19 *p. 582:* Lewis W. Hine photo, 1909, Courtesy George Eastman House. *p. 594:* from the Sophia Smith Collection, Smith College. *p. 603:* from the Collection of The Henry Ford Museum and Greenfield Village. *p. 612:* © Bettmann / Corbis.

Chapter 20 *p. 621:* The Granger Collection, New York. *p. 628:* Library of Congress. *p. 637:* Collection of David J. and Janice L. Frent. *p. 644:* National Archives.

Chapter 21 *p. 650:* Brown Brothers. *p. 660:* Courtesy Philadelphia City Archives. *p. 670:* Library of Congress. *p. 678:* © Bettmann / Corbis.

Chapter 22 *p. 690:* The Granger Collection, New York. *p. 701:* U.S. Military History Institute. *p. 715:* Collection of David J. and Janice L. Frent.

CHAPTER 23 *p. 723:* Walter P. Reuther Library / Wayne State University. *p. 731:* Courtesy of the Arizona Historical Society, Tucson, AHS #62669. *p. 738:* Frank Driggs Collection / Getty Images. *p. 742:* Library of Congress.

CHAPTER 24 *p. 755:* © Bettmann / Corbis. *p. 767:* Library of Congress. *p. 770:* Library of Congress. *p. 777:* Library of Congress.

CHAPTER 25 *p. 784:* Thomas McAvoy / TIMEPIX / Getty Images. *p. 795:* Myron H. Davis. *p. 804:* National Archives. *p. 818:* U.S. Army / Franklin D. Roosevelt Library, Hyde Park, New York.

CHAPTER 26 *p. 826:* Courtesy Indiana University Archives. *p. 832:* National Archives. *p. 838:* © Bettmann / Corbis. *p. 843:* Hy Peskin / TIMEPIX / Getty Images.

CHAPTER 27 *p. 859:* © Bettmann / Corbis. *p. 862:* AP Images. *p. 876:* Courtesy of Motorola Museum © 1955 Motorola, Inc. / Picture Research Consultants and Archives. *p. 882:* © Bettmann / Corbis.

CHAPTER 28 *p. 888:* © Bettmann-Corbis. *p. 898:* AP Images. *p. 900:* Lyndon B. Johnson Presidential Library, Austin, Texas. *p. 915:* © Bettmann / Corbis.

CHAPTER 29 *p. 921:* John Filo / Getty Images. *p. 931:* Ron Haeberle / TIMEPIX / Getty Images. *p. 939:* Flip Schulkel / Black Star / Stock Photo. *p. 940:* Cartoon News International.

CHAPTER 30 *p. 946:* Courtesy Tuck School of Business Archives, Dartmouth College, Hanover, New Hampshire. *p. 955:* NASA / Johnson Space Center. *p. 962:* © Wally McNamee / Bettmann / Corbis. *p. 969:* AP Images.

CHAPTER 31 *p. 979:* Bruno Barbey / Magnum Photos. *p. 983:* Yoshikazu Tsuno / Getty Images. *p. 996:* AP Images. *p. 998:* Cartoon Stock, Ltd.

CHAPTER 32 *p. 1010:* Dan Tellock / Gamma / Zuma Press. *p. 1022:* AP Images. *p. 1035:* Monica Almeida / The New York Times. *p. 1042:* David Hume Kennerly / Getty Images.

Text Credits

CHAPTER 12 *p. 352:* Reprinted with permission of the McGraw-Hill Companies from *Ordeal By Fire: The Civil War And Reconstruction*, Second Edition, by James M. McPherson. Copyright © 1992 by The McGraw-Hill Companies.

CHAPTER 26 *p. 837:* From *American Promise*, Vol. 2, 4th ed., by James A. Henretta et al. Reprinted with permission of Bedford/St. Martin's.

Index